PRO FOOTBALL GUIDE

1982 EDITION

Editors/Pro Football Guide
HOWARD BALZER
CARL CLARK
DAVE SLOAN

President-Chief Executive Officer
RICHARD WATERS

Editor
DICK KAEGEL

Director of Books and Periodicals
RON SMITH

Published by

The Sporting News

1212 North Lindbergh Boulevard
P.O. Box 56 — St. Louis, Mo. 63166

Copyright © 1982
The Sporting News Publishing Company
a Times Mirror company

ISSN 0732-1902   51   ISBN 0-89204-093-9

TABLE OF CONTENTS

ON THE COVER: Cincinnati quarterback Ken Anderson was THE SPORTING NEWS' NFL Player of the Year in 1981.

Photograph by Richard Pilling

THE NATIONAL FOOTBALL LEAGUE

GEORGE HALAS
President
National Football
Conference

PETE ROZELLE
Commissioner
National Football
League

LAMAR HUNT
President
American Football
Conference

COMMISSIONER'S OFFICE

PETE ROZELLE, Commissioner
DON WEISS, Executive Director
BILL RAY, Treasurer
JIM HEFFERNAN, Director of Public Relations
JOE BROWNE, Director of Information
JAY MOYER, Counsel to Commissioner
VAL PINCHBECK, Director of Broadcasting
JAN VAN DUSER, Director of Operations
JOEL BUSSERT, Director of Player Personnel
PETER HADHAZY, Administrative Coordinator
ART McNALLY, Supervisor of Officials
JACK READER, Assistant Supervisor of Officials
NICK SKORICH, Assistant Supervisor of Officials
BILL GRANHOLM, Special Projects Manager
BUDDY YOUNG, Director of Player Relations
JIM STEEG, Director of Special Events
MAXINE ISENBERG, Assistant Dir. of Special Events
WARREN WELSH, Director of Security.
CHARLES JACKSON, Assistant Director of Security
STU KIRKPATRICK, Officiating Assistant

AMERICAN FOOTBALL CONFERENCE

LAMAR HUNT, President
AL WARD, Assistant to the President
FRAN CONNORS, Director of Information

NATIONAL FOOTBALL CONFERENCE

GEORGE HALAS, President
JOE RHEIN, Assistant to the President
DICK MAXWELL, Director of Information

LEAGUE OFFICES
410 Park Avenue
New York, New York 10022

TELEPHONE (Area Code 212)
Commissioner's Office: 758-1500

NATIONAL FOOTBALL LEAGUE—1981

FINAL STANDINGS OF THE TEAMS

AMERICAN FOOTBALL CONF.

Eastern Division

	W.	L.	T.	Pct.	Pts.	Opp.
*Miami	11	4	1	.719	345	275
†N.Y. Jets	10	5	1	.656	355	287
†Buffalo	10	6	0	.625	311	276
Baltimore	2	14	0	.125	259	533
New England	2	14	0	.125	322	370

Central Division

	W.	L.	T.	Pct.	Pts.	Opp.
*Cincinnati	12	4	0	.750	421	304
Pittsburgh	8	8	0	.500	356	297
Houston	7	9	0	.438	281	355
Cleveland	5	11	0	.313	276	375

Western Division

	W.	L.	T.	Pct.	Pts.	Opp.
*San Diego	10	6	0	.625	478	390
Denver	10	6	0	.625	321	289
Kansas City	9	7	0	.563	343	290
Oakland	7	9	0	.438	273	343
Seattle	6	10	0	.375	322	388

NATIONAL FOOTBALL CONF.

Eastern Division

	W.	L.	T.	Pct.	Pts.	Opp.
*Dallas	12	4	0	.750	367	277
†Philadelphia	10	6	0	.625	368	221
†N.Y. Giants	9	7	0	.563	295	257
Washington	8	8	0	.500	347	349
St. Louis	7	9	0	.438	315	408

Central Division

	W.	L.	T.	Pct.	Pts.	Opp.
*Tampa Bay	9	7	0	.563	315	268
Detroit	8	8	0	.500	397	322
Green Bay	8	8	0	.500	324	361
Minnesota	7	9	0	.438	325	369
Chicago	6	10	0	.375	253	324

Western Division

	W.	L.	T.	Pct.	Pts.	Opp.
*San Francisco	13	3	0	.813	357	250
Atlanta	7	9	0	.438	426	355
Los Angeles	6	10	0	.375	303	351
New Orleans	4	12	0	.250	207	.378

*Division Champion.   †Wild Card for playoffs.

NOTE: San Diego won AFC Western title on the basis of a better conference record than Denver (8-4 to 7-5).

AFC PLAYOFFS

FIRST ROUND
Buffalo 31, N.Y. Jets 27

DIVISIONAL PLAYOFFS
San Diego 41, Miami 38 (OT)
Cincinnati 28, Buffalo 21

NFC PLAYOFFS

FIRST ROUND
N.Y. Giants 27, Philadelphia 21

DIVISIONAL PLAYOFFS
Dallas 38, Tampa Bay 0
San Francisco 38, N.Y. Giants 24

AFC CHAMPIONSHIP
Cincinnati 27, San Diego 7

NFC CHAMPIONSHIP
San Francisco 28, Dallas 27

NFL CHAMPIONSHIP
San Francisco 26, Cincinnati 21

AFC-NFC PRO BOWL
AFC 16, NFC 13

NATIONAL FOOTBALL LEAGUE CHAMPIONS

Year—Team	Coach
1921—Decatur Staleys†	George Halas
1922—Canton Bulldogs	Guy Chamberlain
1923—Canton Bulldogs	Guy Chamberlain
1924—Cleveland Bulldogs‡	Guy Chamberlain
1925—Chicago Cardinals	Norman Barry
1926—Frankford Yellowjackets	Guy Chamberlain
1927—New York Giants	Earl Potteiger
1928—Providence Steamrollers	Jim Conzelman
1929—Green Bay Packers	Curly Lambeau
1930—Green Bay Packers	Curly Lambeau
1931—Green Bay Packers	Curly Lambeau
1932—Chicago Bears	Ralph Jones
1933—Chicago Bears	George Halas
1934—New York Giants	Steve Owen
1935—Detroit Lions	Potsy Clark
1936—Green Bay Packers	Curly Lambeau
1937—Washington Redskins	Ray Flaherty
1938—New York Giants	Steve Owen
1939—Green Bay Packers	Curly Lambeau
1940—Chicago Bears	George Halas
1941—Chicago Bears	George Halas
1942—Washington Redskins	Ray Flaherty
1943—Chicago Bears	Luke Johnsos & Hunk Anderson
1944—Green Bay Packers	Curly Lambeau
1945—Cleveland Rams	Adam Walsh
1946—Chicago Bears	George Halas
1947—Chicago Cardinals	Jim Conzelman
1948—Philadelphia Eagles	Greasy Neale
1949—Philadelphia Eagles	Greasy Neale
1950—Cleveland Browns	Paul Brown
1951—Los Angeles Rams	Joe Stydahar
1952—Detroit Lions	Buddy Parker
1953—Detroit Lions	Buddy Parker
1954—Cleveland Browns	Paul Brown
1955—Cleveland Browns	Paul Brown
1956—New York Giants	Jim Lee Howell
1957—Detroit Lions	George Wilson
1958—Baltimore Colts	Weeb Ewbank
1959—Baltimore Colts	Weeb Ewbank
1960—Philadelphia Eagles	Buck Shaw
1961—Green Bay Packers	Vince Lombardi
1962—Green Bay Packers	Vince Lombardi
1963—Chicago Bears	George Halas
1964—Cleveland Browns	Blanton Collier
1965—Green Bay Packers	Vince Lombardi
1966—Green Bay Packers*	Vince Lombardi
1967—Green Bay Packers*	Vince Lombardi
1968—Baltimore Colts	Don Shula
1969—Minnesota Vikings	Bud Grant
1970—Baltimore Colts	Don McCafferty
1971—Dallas Cowboys	Tom Landry
1972—Miami Dolphins	Don Shula
1973—Miami Dolphins	Don Shula
1974—Pittsburgh Steelers	Chuck Noll
1975—Pittsburgh Steelers	Chuck Noll
1976—Oakland Raiders	John Madden
1977—Dallas Cowboys	Tom Landry
1978—Pittsburgh Steelers	Chuck Noll
1979—Pittsburgh Steelers	Chuck Noll
1980—Oakland Raiders	Tom Flores
1981—San Francisco 49ers	Bill Walsh

†Later called the Chicago Staleys and then the Chicago Bears.
‡Franchise moved from Canton.
*Won AFL-NFL Championship Game.

AMERICAN FOOTBALL LEAGUE CHAMPIONS

Year—Team	Coach
1960—Houston Oilers	Lou Rymkus
1961—Houston Oilers	Wally Lemm
1962—Dallas Texans	Hank Stram
1963—San Diego Chargers	Sid Gillman
1964—Buffalo Bills	Lou Saban
1965—Buffalo Bills	Lou Saban
1966—Kansas City Chiefs	Hank Stram
1967—Oakland Raiders	John Rauch
1968—New York Jets*	Weeb Ewbank
1969—Kansas City Chiefs*	Hank Stram

*Won AFL-NFL Championship Game.

ATLANTA FALCONS
(Western Division, National Conference)

Leeman Bennett

Chairman of the Board—Rankin M. Smith, Sr.
President—Rankin M. Smith, Jr.
Executive Vice-President—Eddie LeBaron
General Manager—Tom Braatz
Pro Personnel—Bill Jobko
Head Coach—Leeman Bennett (5 years: 41-37-0)
Assistant Coaches:
    Defensive Coordinator and Defensive Backs—Jerry Glanville
    Administrative Assistant—Mike McDonnell
    Special Teams—Wayne McDuffie
    Offensive Backs—John North
    Receivers—Jimmy Raye
    Linebackers—Doug Shively
    Defensive Line—Jim Stanley
    Offensive Line—Bill Walsh
    Quarterbacks—Dick Wood
Public Relations Director—Charlie Dayton
    (Office Phone: 588-1111—Area Code 404)
Offices—I-85 & Suwanee Rd., Suwanee, Ga. 30174
Stadium—Atlanta-Fulton County Stadium (Capacity: 60,748)
Team Colors—Red, Black, White and Silver
Training Site—Atlanta Falcon Complex, Suwanee, Ga.

1982 SCHEDULE
(All times local.
All games Sunday unless noted otherwise.)

Sept. 12	at New York Giants	1:00
Sept. 19	OAKLAND	1:00
Sept. 23	at Kansas City (Thurs.)	7:30
Oct. 3	SAN DIEGO	1:00
Oct. 10	at Los Angeles	1:00
Oct. 17	at Detroit	1:00
Oct. 24	SAN FRANCISCO	1:00
Oct. 31	at New Orleans	12:00
Nov. 7	at Chicago	12:00
Nov. 15	PHILADELPHIA (Mon.)	9:00
Nov. 21	LOS ANGELES	1:00
Nov. 28	ST. LOUIS	1:00
Dec. 5	at Denver	2:00
Dec. 12	NEW ORLEANS	4:00
Dec. 19	at San Francisco	6:00
Dec. 26	GREEN BAY	1:00

1981 RESULTS—(Won 7, Lost 9)

Falcons		Opp.		Att.
27	New Orleans	0	(H)	57,406
31	Green Bay	17	(A)	55,382
34	San Francisco	17	(H)	56,653
17	Cleveland	28	(A)	78,283
13	Philadelphia	16	(A)	71,488
35	Los Angeles	37	(H)	57,841
41	St. Louis	20	(H)	51,428
24	New York Giants (OT)	27	(H)	48,410
41	New Orleans	10	(A)	63,637
14	San Francisco	17	(A)	59,127
20	Pittsburgh	34	(H)	57,485
31	Minnesota	30	(H)	54,086
31	Houston	27	(A)	40,201
23	Tampa Bay	24	(A)	69,221
16	Los Angeles	21	(A)	57,054
28	Cincinnati	30	(H)	35,972

1981 GAMES STARTED

16 games: William Andrews, Steve Bartkowski, Bobby Butler, Lynn Cain, Buddy Curry, Wallace Francis, Bob Glazebrook, Alfred Jenkins, Kenny Johnson, Mike Kenn, Fulton Kuykendall, Junior Miller, Tom Pridemore, Al Richardson, Don Smith, R.C. Thielemann, Jeff Van Note, Jeff Yeates.

14 games: Dave Scott.

10 games: Warren Bryant, Jeff Merrow.

Less than 10 games: Wilson Faumuina (6), Pat Howell (2), Jim Laughlin (7), Eric Sanders (6), Lyman White (1), Joel Williams (8).

ATLANTA FALCONS 1982 VETERAN ROSTER

No.	Name	Pos.	Ht.	Wt.	NFL Exp.	Birth-date	College	Games in '81	How Acquired
31	Andrews, William	RB	6-0	200	4	12-25-55	Auburn	16	D3b, '79
10	Bartkowski, Steve	QB	6-4	213	8	11-12-52	California	16	D1, '75
	Beeson, Terry	LB	6-3	235	6	9-19-55	Kansas	15	T-Sea, 82
	Blount, Tony	DB	6-1	195	2	11-5-58	Virginia	*0	FA, '82
66	Bryant, Warren	T	6-6	270	6	11-11-55	Kentucky	11	D1a, '77
23	Butler, Bobby	CB	5-11	170	2	5-28-59	Florida State	16	D1, '81
21	Cain, Lynn	RB	6-1	205	4	10-16-55	Southern California	16	D4a, '79
50	Curry, Buddy	LB	6-3	221	3	6- 4-58	North Carolina	16	D2, '80
59	Davis, Paul	LB	6-1	215	2	7-10-58	North Carolina	13	FA, '81
55	Daykin, Tony	LB	6-1	215	6	5-13-55	Georgia Tech	16	FA, '79
74	Faumuina, Wilson	DE	6-5	275	6	8-11-54	San Jose State	16	D1b, '77
89	Francis, Wallace	WR	5-11	190	10	11- 7-51	Arkansas-Pine Bluff	16	T-Buf, '75
34	Gaison, Blane	S	6-0	185	2	5-13-58	Hawaii	14	OFA, '81
36	Glazebrook, Bob	S	6-1	200	5	3- 7-56	Fresno State	16	FA, '78
64	Howell, Pat	G	6-5	253	4	3-12-57	Southern California	16	D2, '79
85	Jackson, Alfred	WR	5-11	176	5	8- 3-55	Texas	16	D7a, '78
6	James, John	P	6-3	200	11	1-21-49	Florida	16	OFA, '72
84	†Jenkins, Alfred	WR	5-10	172	8	1-25-52	Morris Brown	16	FA, '75
37	Johnson, Kenny	CB	5-10	176	3	1- 7-58	Mississippi State	16	D5b, '80
20	Jones, Earl	CB	6-0	178	3	7-19-57	Norfolk State	16	D3, '80
78	Kenn, Mike	T	6-6	257	5	2- 9-56	Michigan	16	D1, '78
54	Kuykendall, Fulton	LB	6-5	225	8	6-10-53	UCLA	16	D6, '75
51	Laughlin, Jim	LB	6-0	212	3	7- 5-58	Ohio State	14	D4a, '80
22	Lawrence, Rolland	CB	5-10	179	9	3-24-51	Tabor	*0	OFA, '73
18	Luckhurst, Mick	K	6-0	180	2	3-31-58	California	16	OFA, '81
39	Mayberry, James	RB	5-11	210	4	11- 5-57	Colorado	16	D3a, '79
75	Merrow, Jeff	DE	6-4	255	8	7-11-53	West Virginia	11	D11, '75
87	Mikeska, Russ	TE	6-3	225	4	9-10-55	Texas A&M	16	OFA, '79
80	Miller, Junior	TE	6-4	235	3	11-26-57	Nebraska	16	D1, '80
15	Moroski, Mike	QB	6-4	200	4	9- 4-57	California-Davis	3	D6, '79
96	Musser, Neal	LB	6-2	218	2	3-20-57	North Carolina State	7	OFA, '81
27	Pridemore, Tom	S	5-10	186	5	4-29-56	West Virginia	16	D9, '78
56	Richardson, Al	LB	6-2	206	3	9-23-57	Georgia Tech	16	D8, '80
33	Robinson, Bo	RB	6-2	225	4	5-27-56	West Texas State	15	FA, '81
67	Sanders, Eric	T	6-6	255	2	10-22-58	Nevada-Reno	16	D5, '81
70	Scott, Dave	G	6-4	265	7	12-26-53	Kansas	14	D3, '76
61	Scully, John	C	6-5	255	2	8- 2-58	Notre Dame	16	D4, '81
65	Smith, Don	DT	6-5	248	4	5- 9-57	Miami	16	D1, '79
25	Strong, Ray	RB	5-9	184	5	5- 7-56	Nevada-Las Vegas	16	D10b, '78
72	Teague, Matthew	DE	6-5	240	2	10-22-58	Prairie View	11	SupD, '80
68	Thielemann, R. C.	G	6-4	247	6	8-12-55	Arkansas	16	D2, '77
57	Van Note, Jeff	C	6-2	247	14	2- 7-46	Kentucky	16	D11, '69
52	White, Lyman	LB	6-0	217	2	1- 3-59	Louisiana State	16	D2, '81
58	Williams, Joel	LB	6-0	215	4	12-13-56	Wisconsin-LaCrosse	10	W-Mia, '79
30	Woerner, Scott	S	6-0	195	2	12-18-58	Georgia	16	D3, '81
79	Yeates, Jeff	DE	6-3	248	11	8- 3-51	Boston College	16	FA, '76
63	Zele, Mike	DT	6-3	236	4	7- 3-56	Kent State	14	D5, '79

*Blount last active with New York Giants in 1980; Lawrence missed 1981 season due to injury.
†Option playout; subject to developments.

D—Draft; T—Trade; W—Waivers; FA—Free Agent; OFA—Original Free Agent; VFA—Veteran Free Agent; VA—Veteran Allocation; SupD—Supplemental Draft.

Also played with Falcons in 1981—FB Mickey Fitzgerald (1 game), QB June Jones (4), S Tom Moriarty (9), WR Reggie Smith (15).

ATLANTA FALCONS
1982 DRAFT CHOICES

(Number following name designates order of selection among 334 players drafted.)

Round and Player		Position	College
1. RIGGS, Gerald	9	RB	Arizona State
2. ROGERS, Doug	36	DE	Stanford
3. BAILEY, Stacey	63	WR	San Jose State
4. BROWN, Reggie	95	RB	Oregon
5. MANSFIELD, Von	122	DB	Wisconsin
6. KELLEY, Mike	149	QB	Georgia Tech
7. TOLOUMU, David	176	RB	Hawaii
8. EBERHARDT, Ricky	203	DB	Morris Brown
9. HORAN, Mike	235	P	Cal St.-Long B
10. STOWERS, Curtis	262	LB	Mississippi St.
11. KELLER, Jeff	288	WR	Washington St.
12. LEVENICK, Dave	315	LB	Wisconsin

ATLANTA FALCONS
1982 ROOKIE AND FIRST-YEAR ROSTER

(1) Indicates player in previous NFL camp.
All others classified as rookies.

Name	Pos.	Hgt.	Wgt.	Birth-date	College	How Acquired
Bailey, Stacey	WR	6-0	162	2-10-60	San Jose St.	D3
Boeke, Greg	C	6-5	258	1-10-59	Illinois	FA
Bond, David	G	6-4	254	6-20-59	Kentucky	FA
Bradley, Nate	CB	5-10	194	7- 5-60	Washington St.	FA
Brown, Reggie	RB	5-11	211	3-12-60	Oregon	D4
Christian, William	DT	6-5	253	5-20-58	Tennessee	FA
Colbert, Stacy (1)	CB	5-7	160	4-23-59	Utah St.	FA
Cole, Mel	LB	6-1	232	12-10-59	Iowa	FA
Cowell, Vince (1)	G	6-3	254	11-14-58	Alabama	FA
Curran, William	WR	5-10	175	12-30-59	UCLA	FA
Davis, Darren	C	6-2	248	6-28-60	Southern Illinois	FA
Duvick, Rolf	G	6-3	250	....	Illinois St.	FA
Eberhart, Ricky	DB	6-2	185	9-16-59	Morris Brown	D8
Harris, Morris	RB	5-10	206	10-22-58	Tennessee St.	FA
Henninger, Dwight	DT	6-3	265	11-25-57	West Chester St.	FA
Hodge, Floyd (1)	WR	6-0	195	7-18-59	Utah	*FA ('81)
Horan, Mike	P	5-10	185	2- 1-59	Long Beach St.	D9
Keller, Jeff	WR	5-11	178	11-16-58	Washington St.	D11
Kelley, Mike	QB	6-4	181	12-31-59	Georgia Tech	D6
Kennedy, Mike	S	6-0	198	2-26-59	Toledo	FA
Koehne, Christopher	T	6-5	266	5-23-60	North Carolina State	FA
LeGrande, Donnie	CB	5-9	178	8-28-59	North Carolina State	FA
Levenick, Dave	LB	6-2	222	5-28-59	Wisconsin	D12
Little, Donnie	QB	6-1	202	10-14-59	Texas	FA
Mansfield, Von	DB	5-11	185	7-12-60	Wisconsin	D5
Mason, Darryl	TE	6-1	220	10-27-60	Arkansas	FA
McCloney, Maurice	WR	6-0	190	9- 8-58	Texas	FA
McNeely, Tony	DB	6-1	200	5-25-60	Kansas	FA
Millwood, Mark	WR	6-0	172	6-17-60	Arkansas Tech	FA
Norwood, Scott	K	5-11	204	7-17-60	James Madison	FA
Phillips, Anthony (1)	WR	5-11	178	2-20-57	Morris Brown	FA
Riggs, Gerald	RB	6-1	230	11- 6-60	Arizona State	D1
Rogers, Doug	DE	6-5	255	6-23-60	Stanford	D2
Simonsen, Tod	LB	6-3	235	12-10-59	Iowa	FA
Stanback, Harry (1)	DE	6-5	255	8- 2-58	North Carolina	*D6 ('81)
Steverson, Ron	DB	5-11	195	10- 9-60	Wisconsin	FA
Stover, Bernard	CB	5-11	174	12-31-58	Georgia Tech	FA
Stowers, Curtis	LB	6-3	215	7- 3-60	Mississippi St.	D10
Thomas, Wallace	DB	5-9	181	9-25-60	Pittsburgh	FA
Toloumu, David	RB	5-11	190	3- 3-60	Hawaii	D7
White, Bill	RB	5-9	205	1- 3-59	Missouri	FA

*Hodge and Stanback missed 1981 season due to injuries.

BALTIMORE COLTS
(Eastern Division, American Conference)

Frank Kush

President and Treasurer—Robert Irsay
General Manager—Ernie Accorsi
Player Personnel Director—Fred Schubach
Pro Personel Director—Bob Terpening
Head Coach—Frank Kush (First Year)
Assistant Coaches:
 Offensive Coordinator and Quarterbacks—Zeke Bratkowski
 Defensive Coordinator and Defensive Backs—Bud Carson
 Defensive Line—Gunther Cunningham
 Offensive Line—Hal Hunter
 Wide Receivers—Richard Mann
 Running Backs—Roger Theder
 Special Teams, Linebackers and Defensive Backs—
  Bob Valesente
 Linebackers—Rick Venturi
 Weight Training Coordinator and Assistant Offensive Line—
  Mike Westhoff
Public Relations Director—Walter Gutowski
 (Office Phone: 356-9600—Area Code 301)
Mailing Address—P. O. Box 2000, Owings Mills, Md. 21117
Stadium—Memorial Stadium (Capacity: 60,763)
Team Colors—Royal Blue and White
Training Site—Goucher College, Towson, Md.

1982 SCHEDULE
(All times local.
All games Sunday unless noted otherwise.)

Sept. 12	NEW ENGLAND	2:00
Sept. 19	at Miami	4:00
Sept. 26	NEW YORK JETS	4:00
Oct. 3	at Detroit	1:00
Oct. 10	BUFFALO	2:00
Oct. 17	at Cleveland	1:00
Oct. 24	MIAMI	2:00
Oct. 31	TAMPA BAY	2:00
Nov. 7	at New England	1:00
Nov. 14	OAKLAND	2:00
Nov. 21	at New York Jets	1:00
Nov. 28	at Buffalo	1:00
Dec. 5	CINCINNATI	2:00
Dec. 12	at Minnesota	12:00
Dec. 19	GREEN BAY	2:00
Dec. 26	at San Diego	1:00

1981 RESULTS—(Won 2, Lost 14)

Colts		Opp.		Att.
29	New England	28	(A)	49,572
3	Buffalo	35	(H)	44,950
10	Denver	28	(A)	74,802
28	Miami	31	(H)	41,630
17	Buffalo	23	(A)	77,811
19	Cincinnati	41	(H)	33,060
14	San Diego	43	(H)	41,921
28	Cleveland	42	(A)	78,986
10	Miami	27	(A)	46,061
14	New York Jets	41	(H)	31,521
13	Philadelphia	38	(A)	68,618
24	St. Louis	35	(H)	24,784
0	New York Jets	25	(A)	53,595
13	Dallas	37	(H)	54,871
14	Washington	38	(A)	46,706
23	New England	21	(H)	17,073

1981 GAMES STARTED

16 games: Larry Braziel, Ray Butler, Ray Donaldson, Jeff Hart, Ken Huff, Randy McMillan, Herb Orvis.

15 games: Roger Carr, Curtis Dickey, Wade Griffin, Bert Jones, Robert Pratt.

14 games: Bruce Laird, Reese McCall.

13 games: Nesby Glasgow, Derrick Hatchett, Barry Krauss.

12 games: Mike Ozdowski, Donnell Thompson.

11 games: Sanders Shiver.

10 games: Joe Federspiel, Bubba Green.

Less than 10 games: Kim Anderson (5), Mike Barnes (2), Randy Burke (1), Zachary Dixon (1), Mike Fultz (5), David Humm (1), Jimmy Moore (1), Reggie Pinkney (3), Tim Sherwin (2), Ed Simonini (1), Ed Smith (8), Hosea Taylor (6), Mike Woods (7).

BALTIMORE COLTS 1982 VETERAN ROSTER

No.	Name	Pos.	Ht.	Wt.	NFL Exp.	Birth-date	College	Games in '81	How Acquired
26	Anderson, Kim	CB	5-11	182	3	7-19-57	Arizona State	14	D3, '79
47	Braziel, Larry	CB	6-0	184	4	9-25-54	Southern California	16	D5, '79
84	Burke, Randy	WR	6-2	198	5	5-26-55	Kentucky	16	D1, '77
80	Butler, Ray	WR	6-3	197	3	6-28-56	Southern California	16	D4, '80
81	Carr, Roger	WR	6-2	195	9	7- 1-52	Louisiana Tech	15	D16, '74
	Delaney, Jeff	S	6-1	197	3	12-28-56	Pittsburgh	*7	FA, '82
87	DeRoo, Brian	WR	6-3	200	4	4-25-56	Redlands	16	W-NYG, '79
27	Dickey, Curtis	RB	6-1	205	3	11-27-56	Texas A&M	15	D1a, '80
31	Dixon, Zachary	RB	6-1	204	4	3- 5-56	Temple	16	FA, '80
53	Donaldson, Ray	C	6-3	263	3	5-18-58	Georgia	16	D2a, '80
78	Foley, Tim	OT	6-6	275	2	5-30-58	Notre Dame	6	D2b, '80
66	Foote, Chris	C	6-3	247	3	12- 2-56	Southern California	16	D6, '80
28	Franklin, Cleveland	FB	6-2	220	5	4-24-55	Baylor	9	FA, '80
72	Fultz, Mike	DT	6-5	278	6	1-28-54	Nebraska	*9	FA, '81
25	Glasgow, Nesby	DB	5-11	185	4	4-15-57	Washington	14	D8b, '79
91	Green, Bubba	DT	6-4	278	2	9-30-57	North Carolina State	15	D6, '81
69	Griffin, Wade	OT	6-5	278	6	8- 7-54	Mississippi	15	FA, '77
68	Hart, Jeff	OT	6-5	272	6	9-10-53	Oregon State	16	FA, '79
42	Hatchett, Derrick	CB	6-0	186	3	8-14-58	Texas	16	D1b, '80
58	Heimkreiter, Steve	LB	6-2	226	2	6- 9-57	Notre Dame	*0	D8a, '79
44	Henry, Steve	DB	6-2	190	3	3- 5-57	Emporia State	2	FA, '81
62	Huff, Ken	G	6-5	253	8	2-21-53	North Carolina	16	D1, '75
10	Humm, David	QB	6-2	190	8	4- 2-52	Nebraska	1	FA, '81
51	Jones, Ricky	LB	6-2	222	6	3- 9-55	Tuskegee	16	FA, '80
	Justin, Sid	CB	5-10	170	2	8-14-54	Long Beach State	*0	FA, '82
55	Krauss, Barry	LB	6-4	238	4	3-17-57	Alabama	16	D1, '79
11	Landry, Greg	QB	6-4	210	15	12-18-46	Massachusetts	11	T-Det, '79
86	McCall, Reese	TE	6-6	243	5	6-16-56	Auburn	16	D1, '78
23	†McCauley, Don	RB	6-1	211	12	5-12-49	North Carolina	16	D1a, '71
32	McMillan, Randy	FB	6-1	226	2	12-17-58	Pittsburgh	16	D1a, '81
65	Moore, Jimmy	OG	6-5	268	2	1-28-57	Ohio State	4	D6, '79
88	Orvis, Herb	DT	6-5	255	11	10-17-46	Colorado	16	T-Det, '78
71	Ozdowski, Mike	DE	6-5	243	5	9-24-55	Virginia	12	D2, '77
	Partridge, Rick	P	6-1	175	3	8-26-57	Utah	*0	FA, '82
37	†Pinkney, Reggie	SS	6-0	187	6	5-27-55	East Carolina	16	FA, '79
61	Pratt, Robert	G	6-4	250	9	5-25-51	North Carolina	15	D3b, '74
83	Sherwin, Tim	TE	6-5	239	2	5- 4-58	Boston College	16	D4, '81
54	Shiver, Sanders	LB	6-2	230	7	2-14-55	Carson-Newman	14	D5a, '76
85	Shula, Dave	WR	5-11	182	2	3-12-59	Dartmouth	16	OFA, '81
	Simmons, Dave	LB	6-4	220	2	1-19-57	North Carolina	*0	FA, '82
56	Simonini, Ed	LB	6-0	206	7	2- 2-54	Texas A&M	1	D3a, '76
39	Sims, Marvin	FB	6-4	234	3	6-18-57	Clemson	16	D12, '80
52	Smith, Ed	LB	6-3	216	3	5-18-57	Vanderbilt	16	FA, '80
90	Taylor, Hosea	DE	6-5	250	2	12- 3-58	Houston	16	D8b, '81
99	Thompson, Donnell	DE	6-5	252	2	10-27-58	North Carolina	13	D1b, '81
79	Van Divier, Randy	OT	6-5	282	2	6- 5-58	Washington	16	D3, '81
21	Williams, Kevin	RB	5-8	168	2	1- 7-58	Southern California	11	FA, '81
16	Wood, Mike	PK	5-11	199	4	9- 3-54	SE Missouri State	16	T-SD, '81

*Delaney played 5 games with Detroit, 2 with Tampa Bay in 1981; Fultz played 5 games with Baltimore, 4 with Miami in '81; Heimkreiter missed 1981 season due to injury; Justin last active with Los Angeles in 1979; Partridge last active with San Diego in 1980; Simmons last active with Detroit in 1980.

†Option playout; subject to developments.

D—Draft; T—Trade; W—Waivers; FA—Free Agent; OFA—Original Free Agent; VFA—Veteran Free Agent; VA—Veteran Allocation; SupD—Supplemental Draft.

Also played with Colts in 1981—DT Mike Barnes (6 games), LB Joe Federspiel (11), P Mike Garrett (16), DE Dallas Hickman (5), QB Bert Jones (15), S Bruce Laird (15), DT Daryl Wilkerson (5), LB Mike Woods (7).

BALTIMORE COLTS
1982 DRAFT CHOICES

(Number following name designates order of selection among 334 players drafted.)

Round and Player		Position	College
1. COOKS, Johnie	2	LB	Mississippi St.
SCHLICHTER, Art from Los Angeles (a)	4	QB	Ohio State
2. WISNIEWSKI, Leo	28	DT	Penn State
STARK, Rohn from Los Angeles (a)	34	P	Florida State
3. BURROUGHS, James	57	DB	Michigan State
4. PAGEL, Mike	84	QB	Arizona State
5. CROUCH, Terry	113	G	Oklahoma
6. BEACH, Pat	140	TE	Washington St.
7. JENKINS, Fletcher	169	DT	Washington
8. LOIA, Tony	196	G	Arizona State
9. BERRYHILL, Tony	225	C	Clemson
10. DEERY, Tom	252	DB	Widener
11. MEACHAM, Lamont	280	DB	W'ern Kentucky
12. WRIGHT, Johnnie	307	RB	South Carolina

(a) Acquired picks for quarterback Bert Jones, April 27, 1982.

BALTIMORE COLTS
1982 ROOKIE AND FIRST-YEAR ROSTER

(1) Indicates player in previous NFL camp.
All others classified as rookies.

Name	Pos.	Hgt.	Wgt.	Birth-date	College	How Acquired
Allen, Thomas (1)	DE	6-4	255	7-26-58	Arizona State	FA
Beach, Pat	TE	6-4	245	12-28-59	Washington State	D6
Benjamin, Bill (1)	LB	6-2	228	9-14-58	San Jose State	FA
Berryhill, Tony	OT	6-5	240	4-18-59	Clemson	D9
Bouza, Matt (1)	WR	6-3	205	4- 8-58	California	FA
Bowens, Bill (1)	LB	6-3	230	6-10-58	Northern Alabama	FA
Boyd, Willie	WR	6-1	200	1-27-59	Illinois State	FA
Burroughs, Jim	CB	6-1	190	1-21-58	Michigan State	D3
Carnell, Mike	RB	6-0	194	4-20-60	Ohlone J C	FA
Cooks, Johnie	LB	6-4	240	11-23-58	Mississippi State	D1a
Crosby, Cleveland (1)	DE	6-4	250	4- 3-56	Arizona	FA
Crouch, Terry	G	6-1	275	7- 6-59	Oklahoma	D5
Danenhauer, Bill (1)	T-G	6-3	275	12- 1-57	Nebraska-Omaha	FA
Deery, Tom	S	6-2	190	2- 4-60	Widener College	D10
Detzie, Jeff	C	6-1	251	9-11-56	East Stroudsburg State	FA
Dunek, Ken (1)	TE	6-6	240	6-20-57	Memphis State	FA
Guthrie, Zachary (1)	G	6-5	280	9-16-56	Texas A&M	FA
Harman, Vaughn	G	6-3	253	4- 8-59	Towson State	FA
Henry, Bernard	WR	6-1	180	4- 9-60	Arizona State	FA
Hunter, James (1)	DE	6-4	245	9-13-57	Southern California	FA
Jenkins, Fletcher	DT	6-2	247	11- 4-59	Washington	D7
Jernigan, Hugh (1)	CB	6-0	175	8-28-59	Arkansas	FA
Levasa, Roger	C	6-2	240	5-18-59	Oregon State	FA
Loia, Tony	T	6-3	346	2- 1-60	Arizona State	D8
Meacham, Lamont	CB	6-0	170	1-20-61	Western Kentucky	D11
Meehan, Ron (1)	QB	6-4	210	3-10-59	Towson State	FA
Noel, Dana (1)	CB	5-10	185	8-27-58	Minnesota	FA
Padjen, Gary (1)	LB	6-2	240	7- 2-58	Arizona State	FA
Pagel, Mike	QB	6-2	200	9-13-60	Arizona State	D4
Peters, Joel (1)	DE	6-6	245	3-12-57	Arizona State	FA
Postell, Jeffrey (1)	WR	6-4	209	11-12-58	Morehouse College	FA
Reeves, Morgan (1)	FB	5-11	190	11-23-58	Michigan State	FA
Robinson, Kenneth (1)	WR	5-10	185	3- 5-59	Louisville	FA
Schlichter, Art	QB	6-3	208	4-25-60	Ohio State	D1b
Schoepflin, Bill (1)	DB	5-10	175	5-12-59	Brigham Young	*FA ('81)
Seidel, William	LB	6-1	219	7-22-58	Cal State (Pa.)	FA
Shupryt, Robert (1)	LB	6-2	210	9-29-58	New Mexico	FA
Sitton, Ken (1)	S	6-3	200	8-24-58	Oklahoma	*D8 ('81)
Smigelsky, Dave (1)	P	5-11	180	7- 3-59	Virginia Tech	Waiv.
Stark, Rohn	P	6-3	195	6- 4-59	Florida State	D2b
Sullivan, Brian (1)	PK-P	6-1	175	3-26-59	Santa Clara	*FA ('81)
Tongue, Marco	S	5-9	174	4- 6-60	Bowie State	FA
Upshaw, Bob	LB	6-2	226	2-27-60	Western Maryland	FA
Utt, Ben (1)	G	6-4	255	6-13-59	Georgia Tech	FA
Vitiello, Sandro (1)	K	6-3	200	2-21-58	Massachusetts	FA
Wisniewski, Leo	DT	6-1	251	11- 6-59	Penn State	D2a
Wright, Johnnie	RB	6-1	205	9-13-58	South Carolina	D12

*Schoepflin, Sitton and Sullivan missed 1981 season due to injuries.

BUFFALO BILLS
(Eastern Division, American Conference)

Chuck Knox

President—Ralph C. Wilson, Jr.

Vice-President, Administration—Stew Barber

Vice-President in Charge of Football Operations & Head Coach
—Chuck Knox (9 years: 87-46-1)

Director of College Scouting—Norm Pollom

Vice-President, Public Relations—Budd Thalman
(Office Phone: 648-1800—Area Code 716)

Assistant Coaches:
Assistant Head Coach-Defensive Coordinator and Line-
backers—Tom Catlin
Receivers—Jack Donaldson
Defensive Line—George Dyer
Offensive Backfield—Chick Harris
Defensive Backfield—Ralph Hawkins
Special Assignments—Miller McCalmon
Offensive Assistant-Special Teams—Steve Moore
Offensive Coordinator-Line—Ray Prochaska
Quarterbacks—Kay Stephenson

Offices—One Bills Drive, Orchard Park, N. Y. 14127

Stadium—Rich Stadium (Capacity: 80,020)

Team Colors—Royal Blue, White and Scarlet

Training Site—Fredonia State University, Fredonia, N. Y.

1982 SCHEDULE
(All times local.
All games Sunday unless noted otherwise.)

Sept. 12	KANSAS CITY	1:00
Sept. 16	MINNESOTA (Thurs.)	8:30
Sept. 26	at Houston	12:00
Oct. 3	NEW ENGLAND	1:00
Oct. 10	at Baltimore	2:00
Oct. 18	at New York Jets (Mon.)	9:00
Oct. 24	DETROIT	1:00
Oct. 31	at Denver	2:00
Nov. 7	NEW YORK JETS	4:00
Nov. 14	at New England	1:00
Nov. 21	MIAMI	1:00
Nov. 28	BALTIMORE	1:00
Dec. 5	vs. Green Bay (Milw.)	12:00
Dec. 12	PITTSBURGH	1:00
Dec. 19	at Tampa Bay	1:00
Dec. 27	at Miami (Mon.)	9:00

1981 RESULTS—(Won 11, Lost 7)

Bills		Opp.		Att.
31	New York Jets	0	(H)	79,754
35	Baltimore	3	(A)	44,950
14	Philadelphia	20	(H)	80,020
24	Cincinnati (OT)	27	(A)	46,418
23	Baltimore	17	(H)	77,811
31	Miami	21	(H)	80,020
14	New York Jets	33	(A)	54,607
9	Denver	7	(H)	80,020
22	Cleveland	13	(H)	80,020
14	Dallas	27	(A)	62,583
0	St. Louis	24	(A)	46,214
20	New England	17	(H)	76,374
21	Washington	14	(H)	61,452
28	San Diego	27	(A)	51,488
19	New England	10	(A)	42,549
6	Miami	16	(A)	72,956
PLAYOFF GAME				
31	New York Jets	27	(A)	57,050
PLAYOFF GAME				
21	Cincinnati	28	(A)	55,420

1981 GAMES STARTED

16 games: Mark Brammer, Jerry Butler, Mario Clark, Joe Devlin, Joe Ferguson, Steve Freeman, Will Grant, Jim Haslett, Frank Lewis, Isiah Robertson, Charles Romes, Lucious Sanford, Bill Simpson, Fred Smerlas, Sherman White, Ben Williams.

15 games: Joe Cribbs, Ken Jones.

13 games: Conrad Dobler.

10 games: Shane Nelson.

Less than 10 games: Jon Borchardt (9), Curtis Brown (8), Roland Hooks (1), Chris Keating (2), Roosevelt Leaks (5), Tom Lynch (2), Lawrence McCutcheon (3), Reggie McKenzie (6), Jim Ritcher (3), Phil Villapiano (4).

BUFFALO BILLS 1982 VETERAN ROSTER

No.	Name	Pos.	Ht.	Wt.	NFL Exp.	Birth-date	College	Games in '81	How Acquired
87	Alvers, Steve	TE	6-4	240	2	4- 4-58	Miami (Fla.)	16	FA, '81
	Barnes, Mike	DT	6-6	251	10	12-24-50	Miami	*6	FA, '82
84	Barnett, Buster	TE	6-5	225	2	11-24-58	Jackson State	16	D11, '81
28	Bess, Rufus	CB	5-9	180	4	9-13-56	South Carolina State	16	W-Oak, '80
73	Borchardt, Jon	T	6-5	255	4	8-13-57	Montana State	16	D3, '79
86	Brammer, Mark	TE	6-3	235	3	5- 3-58	Michigan State	16	D3a, '80
47	Brown, Curtis	FB	5-10	203	6	12- 7-54	Missouri	14	D3a, '77
80	Butler, Jerry	WR	6-0	178	4	10-12-57	Clemson	16	D1b, 79
7	Cater, Greg	P	6-0	191	3	4-17-57	Tennessee-Chattanooga	16	D10, '80
29	Clark, Mario	CB	6-2	195	7	3-29-54	Oregon	16	D1, '76
	Crews, Ron	DT	6-3	256	2	10- 9-56	Nevada-Las Vegas	*0	FA, '82
20	Cribbs, Joe	RB	5-11	190	3	1- 5-58	Auburn	15	D2a, '80
70	Devlin, Joe	T	6-5	250	7	2-23-54	Iowa	16	D2b, '76
12	Ferguson, Joe	QB	6-1	195	10	4-23-50	Arkansas	16	D3a, '73
85	Franklin, Byron	WR	6-1	179	2	9- 3-58	Auburn	13	D2b, '81
22	Freeman, Steve	SS	5-11	185	8	5- 8-53	Mississippi State	16	W-NE, '75
53	Grant, Will	C	6-4	248	5	3- 7-54	Kentucky	16	D10, '78
55	Haslett, Jim	LB	6-3	232	4	12- 9-55	Indiana, Pa.	16	D2b, '79
25	†Hooks, Roland	RB	6-0	195	7	1- 2-53	North Carolina State	16	D10, '75
50	Humiston, Mike	LB	6-3	238	2	1- 8-59	Weber State	16	OFA, '81
97	Irvin, Darrell	DE	6-4	255	3	1-21-51	Oklahoma	13	OFA, '80
91	Johnson, Ken	DE	6-5	253	4	3-25-55	Knoxville	16	D4a, '79
72	Jones, Ken	T	6-5	250	7	12- 1-52	Arkansas State	15	D2a, '76
71	†Kadish, Mike	NT	6-5	250	10	5-27-50	Notre Dame	16	T-Mia, '73
	Keating, Chris	LB	6-2	223	4	10-12-57	Maine	2	OFA, '79
42	Kush, Rod	SS	6-0	188	3	12-29-56	Nebraska-Omaha	16	D5a, '79
48	†Leaks, Roosevelt	RB	5-10	225	8	1-31-53	Texas	16	W-Bal, '80
82	Lewis, Frank	WR	6-1	196	12	7- 4-47	Grambling	16	T-Pit, '78
61	Lynch, Tom	G	6-5	250	6	5-24-55	Boston College	5	T-Sea, '81
30	McCutcheon, Lawrence	FB	6-1	205	11	6- 2-50	Colorado State	6	FA, '81
67	McKenzie, Reggie	G	6-5	242	11	7-27-50	Michigan	6	D2, '72
5	†Mike-Mayer, Nick	PK	5-9	185	10	3- 1-50	Temple	16	FA, '79
59	Nelson, Shane	LB	6-1	225	6	5-25-55	Baylor	10	OFA, '77
38	Nixon, Jeff	FS	6-3	190	4	10-13-56	Richmond	13	D4b, '79
62	Parker, Ervin	LB	6-5	240	3	8-20-58	South Carolina State	16	D4, '80
	Parrish, Lemar	CB	5-10	170	13	12-13-47	Lincoln	12	T-Was, '82
89	†Piccone, Lou	WR	5-9	175	9	7-17-49	West Liberty State	14	T-NYJ, '77
40	Riddick, Robb	RB	6-0	195	2	4-26-57	Millersville State, Pa.	10	D9, '81
51	Ritcher, Jim	G-C	6-3	251	3	5-21-58	North Carolina State	14	D1, '80
58	†Robertson, Isiah	LB	6-3	225	12	8-17-49	Southern	16	T-LA, '79
17	Robinson, Matt	QB	6-2	196	6	6-28-55	Georgia	15	W-Den, '81
26	Romes, Charles	CB	6-1	190	6	12-16-53	North Carolina Central	16	D12, '77
57	Sanford, Lucius	LB	6-2	216	5	2-13-56	Georgia Tech	16	D4, '78
45	†Simpson, Bill	FS	6-1	191	8	12- 5-51	Michigan State	16	T-LA, '80
76	Smerlas, Fred	NT	6-3	270	4	4- 8-57	Boston College	16	D2a, '79
41	Villapiano, Phil	LB	6-2	225	12	2-26-49	Bowling Green	16	T-Oak, '80
65	Vogler, Tim	C	6-3	245	4	10-20-56	Ohio State	14	OFA, '79
83	White, Sherman	DE	6-5	250	11	10- 6-48	California	16	T-Cin, '76
	Wilkerson, Daryl	DT	6-4	260	2	9-25-58	Houston	*5	FA, '82
77	Williams, Ben	DE	6-3	245	7	9- 1-54	Mississippi	16	D3, '76

*Barnes played 6 games with Baltimore in 1981; Crews last active with Cleveland in 1980; Wilkerson played 5 games with Baltimore in 1981.

†Option playout; subject to developments.

D—Draft; T—Trade; W—Waivers; FA—Free Agent; OFA—Original Free Agent; VFA—Veteran Free Agent; VA—Veteran Allocation; SupD—Supplemental Draft.

Also played with Bills in 1981—WR Ron Jessie (15) games. Retired: G Conrad Dobler (14).

BUFFALO BILLS
1982 DRAFT CHOICES

(Number following name designates order of selection among 334 players drafted.)

Round and Player		Position	College
1. TUTTLE, Perry	19	WR	Clemson
from Denver (a)			
Choice to Denver (a)			
2. KOFLER, Matt	48	QB	San Diego St.
3. MARVE, Eugene	59	LB	Saginaw Valley
from Cleveland (b)			
Choice to Seattle (c)			
4. WILLIAMS, Van	93	RB	Car-Newman
from St. Louis (d)			
Choice to Denver (a)			
5. Choice to Washington (e)			
6. CHIVERS, DeWayne	160	TE	South Carolina
7. ANDERSON, Gary	171	K	Syracuse
from Cleveland (f)			
Choice to Detroit through Los Angeles (g)			
8. TOUSIGNANT, Luc	218	QB	Fairmont State
9. EDWARDS, Dennis	245	DT	Southern Cal.
10. JAMES, Vic	272	DB	Colorado
11. KALIL, Frank	298	G	Arizona
12. SUBER, Tony	329	DT	Gardner-Webb

(a) Switched first-round positions and traded fourth-round pick, April 27, 1982.
(b) Acquired pick and second-round pick in 1981 for guard Joe DeLamielleure, September 1, 1980.
(c) Traded pick for guard Tom Lynch, October 13, 1981.
(d) Acquired pick for third-round pick in 1983, April 27, 1982.
(e) Traded pick for cornerback Lemar Parrish, April 27, 1982.
(f) Acquired pick for running back Terry Miller, May 5, 1981.
(g) Traded pick to Los Angeles for wide receiver Ron Jessie, July 31, 1980; Los Angeles traded pick and ninth-round pick to Detroit for seventh-round pick, April 28, 1982.

BUFFALO BILLS
1982 ROOKIE AND FIRST-YEAR ROSTER

(1) Indicates player in previous NFL camp.
(2) Indicates player with CFL experience.
    All others classified as rookies.

Name	Pos.	Hgt.	Wgt.	Birth-date	College	How Acquired
Anderson, Brad	WR	6-0	167	11- 4-58	USC	FA
Anderson, Gary	K	5-9	156	7-16-59	Syracuse	D7

Name	Pos.	Hgt.	Wgt.	Birth-date	College	How Acquired
Ariri, Obed (1)	K	5-8	165	4- 7-56	Clemson	FA
Asmus, Jim (1)	P/K	6-1	195	12- 2-58	Hawaii	FA
Baldwin, Brian	TE	6-4	239	6-25-57	Dayton	FA
Bayle, David (1)	TE	6-4	230	2-16-59	Washington	FA
Bradley, Gene (1)	QB	6-4	214	11-26-57	Arkansas State	*D2 ('80)
Bubniak, Tony	C	6-4	253	6- 6-58	Colgate	FA
Budness, James	LB	6-2	234	2-24-60	Boston College	FA
Charles, Stacy (1)	WR	5-10	167	8-15-58	Bethune-Cookman	FA
Chivers, Dewayne	TE	6-4	226	6-26-59	South Carolina	D6
Clark, Keith (1)	LB	6-5	224	7-27-58	Memphis State	*D12 ('81)
Cook, Arthur (1)	LB	6-3	219	8-24-58	Morgan State	FA
Cross, Justin (1)	T	6-6	257	4-29-59	Western State, Colo.	*D10 ('81)
Crump, Richard (2)	RB	5-10	208	2-28-55	N.E. Oklahoma A&M	D12 ('78)
D'Amico, Joseph	WR	5-10	185	5-18-58	Buffalo	FA
Danenhauer, Robert (1)	LB	6-3	230	10- 9-59	Nebraska-Omaha	FA
Dennison, Rick (1)	LB	6-3	230	6-22-58	Colorado State	FA
Donald, George (1)	RB	6-1	200	7-12-59	Elmhurst	FA
Duncan, James	WR	6-0	160	2- 7-60	Ithaca	FA
Edwards, Dennis	DT	6-3	253	10- 6-59	USC	D9
Finch, Aaron	C	6-4	255	2-13-59	Colorado State	FA
Franz, Nolan	WR	6-2	183	9-11-59	Tulane	FA
Garcia, Danny (1)	WR	6-2	185	1-20-58	USC	*FA ('81)
Geathers, Robert (1)	DE/NT	6-6	286	7-30-57	South Carolina State	*D3a ('81)
Gompf, William	LB	6-2	225	4- 2-60	Utah	FA
Graham, Pat (1)	DE	6-4	269	4-21-59	California	FA
Grimes, Greg (1)	DB	6-0	192	11-18-57	Washington	FA
Guess, Michael (1)	DE	5-11	188	4-21-58	Ohio State	FA
Guthrie, Edgar	RB	6-0	210	11-27-57	Georgia	FA
Harbison, Charles	DB	6-1	182	10-27-59	Gardner-Webb	FA
Holt, Robert (1)	WR	6-1	182	10- 4-59	Baylor	*D6 ('81)
Jackson, Gregory	S	6-1	200	6- 6-59	Puget Sound	FA
James, Timothy (1)	C/G	6-3	250	11-25-56	Elon	FA
James, Victor	CB	5-11	196	2- 6-61	Colorado	D10
Kaifes, Eric	P	6-3	210	7-16-60	Southern Methodist	FA
Kalil, Frank	G	6-3	255	9- 1-59	Arizona	D11
Klena, Richard	LB	6-0	220	12- 7-59	Cal-Poly-Pomona	FA
Kofler, Matt	QB	6-3	192	8-30-59	San Diego State	D2
Lee, Roderick	WR	6-1	181	4- 5-59	Hillsdale	FA
Lewis, Alvin (1)	DB	6-0	193	8-25-59	Colorado State	FA
Love, Terry (1)	SS	6-2	200	8-25-58	Murray State	FA
Lumpkin, Joey	LB	6-2	230	2-19-60	Arizona State	FA
Marve, Eugene	LB	6-2	230	8-14-60	Saginaw Valley State	D3
Menhardt, Herb (1)	K	5-11	185	3- 8-58	Penn State	FA
Mitchell, Lee	DB	5-10	170	1- 7-60	Wyoming	FA
Moeller, Michael (1)	T	6-5	275	2- 2-59	Drake	FA
Moore, Booker (1)	FB	5-11	224	6-23-59	Penn State	*D1 ('81)
Mosley, Mike (1)	WR	6-2	192	6- 6-58	Texas A&M	*D3 ('81)
Najarian, Mal (1)	RB	5-11	188	4-28-58	Boston U.	FA
Pierce, Kurt (1)	G	6-2	255	1-24-59	Virginia	FA
Rikard, Robert	WR	6-0	170	9-11-58	Boston College	FA
Roopenian, Mark (1)	NT	6-5	254	7-10-58	Boston College	*FA ('81)
Sampson, Kenneth (!)	RB	6-0	196	4-18-59	Grambling	FA
Schmeding, John (1)	G	6-4	265	12-27-55	Boston College	*D3a ('80)
Schroeder, John	T	6-5	255	12- 1-59	Missouri Valley	FA
Shaver, Don (1)	FB	6-1	235	5- 6-59	Kutztown State	FA
Simpson, Michael (1)	DB	6-0	192	2-17-59	Central Michigan	FA
Skillings, Vincent (1)	DB	5-11	177	5- 3-59	Ohio State	FA
Smith, Steve (1)	RB	5-9	184	9-15-59	Michigan State	FA
Suber, Tony	DE/NT	6-3	276	9-23-59	Gardner-Webb	D12
Torosian, Ted	FB	6-0	225	4- 8-59	Cal State-Fresno	FA
Tuttle, Perry	WR	6-0	178	8- 2-59	Clemson	D1
Verrilli, Ronald	K	5-8	180	5- 6-58	Missouri	FA
White, Garry (1)	FB	5-11	207	11- 5-58	Minnesota	FA
Williams, Chris (1)	CB	6-0	197	1-12-59	Louisiana State	*D2 ('81)
Williams, Van	RB	6-0	208	3-15-59	Carson-Newman	D4

*Bradley, Clark, Cross, Garcia, Geathers, Holt, Moore, Mosley and Roopenian missed 1981 season due to injuries; Schmeding retired prior to 1981 season; C. Williams played 1 game with Bills in 1981.
NOTE: 8th-round draft choice Luc Tousignant signed with Montreal of the CFL.

CHICAGO BEARS
(Central Division, National Conference)

Mike Ditka

Chairman of the Board—George S. Halas
Executive Vice-President & General Manager—Jim Finks
Assistant to General Manager—Bill McGrane
Collegiate Scouting Director—Jim Parmer
Pro Scouting Director—Bill Tobin
Head Coach—Mike Ditka (First Year)
Assistant Coaches:
  Research and Quality Control—Jim Dooley
  Defensive Line—Dale Haupt
  Offensive Coordinator—Ed Hughes
  Special Teams—Steve Kazor
  Backs-Special Teams—Hank Kuhlmann
  Defensive Backs—Jim LaRue
  Receivers—Ted Plumb
  Defensive Coordinator—Buddy Ryan
  Offensive Line—Dick Stanfel
Public Relations Director—Patrick McCaskey
  (Office Phone 663-5100—Area Code 312)
Offices—55 East Jackson (Suite 1200), Chicago, Ill. 60604
Stadium—Soldier Field (Capacity: 64,410)
Team Colors—Orange, Navy Blue and White
Training Site—Halas Hall, Lake Forest College, Lake Forest, Ill.

1982 SCHEDULE
(All times local.
All games Sunday unless noted otherwise.)

Sept. 12	at Detroit	1:00
Sept. 19	NEW ORLEANS	12:00
Sept. 26	at San Francisco	1:00
Oct. 3	MINNESOTA	12:00
Oct. 10	GREEN BAY	12:00
Oct. 17	at St. Louis	12:00
Oct. 24	TAMPA BAY	12:00
Oct. 31	at Green Bay	12:00
Nov. 7	ATLANTA	12:00
Nov. 14	at Tampa Bay	1:00
Nov. 21	DETROIT	12:00
Nov. 28	at Minnesota	12:00
Dec. 5	NEW ENGLAND	12:00
Dec. 12	at Seattle	1:00
Dec. 19	ST. LOUIS	12:00
Dec. 26	at Los Angeles	1:00

1981 RESULTS—(Won 6, Lost 10)

Bears		Opp.		Att.
9	Green Bay	16	(H)	62,411
17	San Francisco	28	(A)	49,520
28	Tampa Bay	17	(H)	60,130
7	Los Angeles	24	(H)	62,461
21	Minnesota	24	(A)	43,827
7	Washington	24	(H)	57,683
17	Detroit	48	(A)	71,274
20	San Diego (OT)	17	(H)	52,906
10	Tampa Bay	20	(A)	63,688
16	Kansas City (OT)	13	(A)	60,605
17	Green Bay	21	(A)	55,338
7	Detroit	23	(H)	50,820
9	Dallas	10	(A)	63,499
10	Minnesota	9	(H)	50,766
23	Oakland	6	(A)	40,834
35	Denver	24	(H)	40,125

1981 GAMES STARTED

16 games: Ted Albrecht, Gary Campbell, Vince Evans, Gary Fencik, Dan Hampton, Reuben Henderson, Noah Jackson, Dan Neal, Jim Osborne, Alan Page, Walter Payton, Terry Schmidt.

15 games: Brian Baschnagel, Robin Earl.

14 games: Matt Suhey.

12 games: Doug Plank, Keith Van Horne, Otis Wilson, Emanuel Zanders.

11 games: Al Harris.

Less than 10 games: Marcus Anderson (1), Brian Cabral (4), Mike Cobb (1), Bob Fisher (1), Roland Harper (2), Mike Hartenstine (5), Dan Jiggetts (1), Lee Kunz (7), Dennis Lick (3), Ken Margerum (6), Mike Singletary (9), Revie Sorey (4), Lenny Walterscheid (4), Rickey Watts (9).

CHICAGO BEARS 1982 VETERAN ROSTER

No.	Name	Pos.	Ht.	Wt.	NFL Exp.	Birth-date	College	Games in '81	How Acquired
64	Albrecht, Ted	T-G	6-4	250	6	10- 8-54	California	16	D1, '77
88	Anderson, Marcus	WR	5-11	168	2	6-12-59	Tulane	12	FA, '81
7	Avellini, Bob	QB	6-2	210	8	8-28-53	Maryland	9	D6a, '75
84	†Baschnagel, Brian	WR	6-0	184	7	1- 8-54	Ohio State	16	D3, '76
25	Bell, Todd	S	6-0	207	2	11-28-58	Ohio State	16	D4, '81
54	Cabral, Brian	LB	6-1	224	4	6-23-56	Colorado	16	FA, '81
59	Campbell, Gary	LB	6-1	220	6	3- 4-52	Colorado	16	FA, '77
87	Cobb, Mike	TE	6-5	243	5	12-10-55	Michigan State	16	T-Cin, '78
81	Earl, Robin	TE-P	6-5	240	6	3-18-55	Washington	16	D3, '77
8	†Evans, Vince	QB	6-2	212	6	6-14-55	Southern California	16	D6, '77
67	Fairchild, Greg	G	6-4	254	3	3-10-55	Tulsa	*0	FA, '82
45	Fencik, Gary	S	6-1	197	7	6-11-54	Yale	16	FA, '76
	Fergerson, Duke	WR	6-1	185	5	4-21-54	San Diego State	*0	FA, '82
85	Fisher, Bob	TE	6-3	240	3	3-17-58	Southern Methodist	6	D12, '80
24	Fisher, Jeff	CB	5-10	188	2	2-25-58	Southern California	16	D7, '81
21	Frazier, Leslie	DB	6-0	189	2	4- 3-59	Alcorn State	13	OFA, '81
83	Haines, Kris	WR	5-11	180	3	7-23-57	Notre Dame	1	FA, '79
99	Hampton, Dan	DL	6-5	255	4	9-19-57	Arkansas	16	D1a, '79
35	†Harper, Roland	RB	5-11	210	7	2-28-53	Louisiana Tech	15	D17, '75
90	Harris, Al	DE	6-5	240	4	12-21-56	Arizona State	16	D1b, '79
73	Hartenstine, Mike	DE	6-3	243	8	7-27-53	Penn State	16	D2, '75
20	Henderson, Reuben	CB	6-1	200	2	10- 3-58	San Diego State	16	D6, '81
51	Herron, Bruce	LB	6-2	220	5	4-14-54	New Mexico	16	FA, '78
63	Hilgenberg, Jay	C	6-3	250	2	3-21-59	Iowa	16	OFA, '81
65	Jackson, Noah	G	6-2	265	8	4-14-51	Tampa	16	T-Bal, '75
62	Jiggetts, Dan	T	6-5	270	7	3-10-54	Harvard	16	D6, '76
57	†Kunz, Lee	LB	6-2	225	4	4-21-57	Nebraska	16	D7, '79
	Lawless, Burton	G	6-4	256	8	11- 1-53	Florida	*0	FA, '82
	Lee, John	DE	6-2	260	7	2-17-53	Nebraska	4	T-NE, '82
70	Lick, Dennis	T	6-3	265	7	4-26-54	Wisconsin	3	D1, '76
89	Margerum, Ken	WR	5-10	170	2	10- 5-58	Stanford	16	D3, '81
37	McClendon, Willie	RB	6-1	205	4	9-13-57	Georgia	16	D3, '79
76	McMichael, Steve	DL	6-1	245	3	10-17-57	Texas	10	FA, '81
43	†Moorehead, Emery	WR	6-2	210	6	3-22-54	Colorado	9	W-Den, '81
58	†Muckensturm, Jerry	LB	6-4	220	6	10-13-53	Arkansas State	*0	D7, '76
52	Neal, Dan	C	6-4	255	10	8-30-49	Kentucky	16	FA, '75
68	†Osborne, Jim	DT	6-3	245	11	9- 7-49	Southern	16	D7b, '72
86	Parsons, Bob	P	6-5	225	11	6-29-50	Penn State	16	D5, '72
34	Payton, Walter	RB	5-10	202	8	7-25-54	Jackson State	16	D1, '75
46	Plank, Doug	S	5-11	202	8	3- 4-53	Ohio State	16	D12, '75
9	Roveto, John	K	6-0	180	2	2-20-58	Southwestern Louisiana	11	FA, '81
44	Schmidt, Terry	CB	6-0	177	9	5-28-52	Ball State	16	W-NO, '76
89	Scott, James	WR	6-1	190	6	3-28-52	Henderson, J.C.	*0	FA, '76
72	Shearer, Brad	DT	6-3	247	4	8-10-55	Texas	6	D3, '78
	Shoate, Rod	LB	6-1	215	7	4-26-53	Oklahoma	16	T-NE, '82
50	Singletary, Mike	LB	5-11	230	2	10- 9-58	Baylor	16	D2, '81
30	Skibinski, John	RB	6-0	222	4	4-27-55	Purdue	11	D6a, '78
69	Sorey, Revie	G	6-2	260	8	9-10-53	Illinois	16	D5, '75
26	Suhey, Matt	RB	5-11	217	3	7- 7-58	Penn State	15	D2, '80
53	Tabor, Paul	C	6-4	241	2	11-30-56	Oklahoma	*0	D5, '80
16	Thomas, Bob	K	5-10	175	7	8- 7-52	Notre Dame	2	W-LA, '75
78	Van Horne, Keith	T	6-6	265	2	11- 6-57	Southern California	14	D1, '81
	Vincent, Ted	DT	6-4	265	4	8-10-56	Wichita State	*0	FA, '82
23	Walterscheid, Lenny	S	5-11	190	6	9-13-54	Southern Utah State	6	OFA, '74
80	Watts, Rickey	WR	6-1	203	4	5-16-57	Tulsa	12	D2, '79
83	Williams, Brooks	TE	6-4	226	5	12- 7-54	North Carolina	*12	FA, '81
22	†Williams, David	RB	6-2	207	6	3-10-54	Colorado	8	FA, '79
55	Wilson, Otis	LB	6-2	222	3	9-15-57	Louisville	15	D1, '80
79	†Zanders, Emanuel	G	6-1	248	9	7-31-51	Jackson State	12	FA, '81

*Muckensturm and Tabor missed 1981 due to injuries; Fairchild last active with Cleveland in 1978; Fergerson last active with Buffalo in 1980; Lawless active for 4 games with Miami in 1981, did not play; Scott last active with Chicago in 1980, played with Montreal-CFL in 1981; Vincent last active with San Francisco in 1980; B. Williams played 7 games with New Orleans, 5 with Chicago in 1981.

†Option playout; subject to developments.

D—Draft; T—Trade; W—Waivers; FA—Free Agent; OFA—Original Free Agent; VFA—Veteran Free Agent; VA—Veteran Allocation; SupD—Supplemental Draft.

Also played with Bears in 1981—K Hans Nielsen (3 games), QB Mike Phipps (3). Retired: DT Alan Page (16).

CHICAGO BEARS
1982 DRAFT CHOICES

(Number following name designates order of selection among 334 players drafted.)

Round and Player		Position	College
1. McMAHON, Jim	5	QB	Brigham Young
2. Choice to Tampa Bay (a)			
3. WRIGHTMAN, Tim	62	TE	UCLA
4. GENTRY, Dennis	89	RB	Baylor
5. HARTNETT, Perry	116	G	SMU
TABRON, Dennis from San Diego (b)	134	DB	Duke
6. BECKER, Kurt	146	G	Michigan
7. WAECHTER, Henry	173	DT	Nebraska
8. DOERGER, Jerry	200	T	Wisconsin
9. HATCHETT, Mike	230	DB	Texas
10. TURNER, Joe	257	DB	USC
11. BOLIAUX, Guy	283	LB	Wisconsin
12. YOUNG, Ricky	313	LB	Oklahoma State

(a) Traded pick for first-round pick in 1983, April 27, 1982.

(b) Acquired pick for past considerations involving cornerback Allan Ellis, October 7, 1981.

CHICAGO BEARS
1982 ROOKIE AND FIRST-YEAR ROSTER

(1) Indicates player in previous NFL camp.
(2) Indicates player with minor league experience.
   All others classified as rookies.

Name	Pos.	Hgt.	Wgt.	Birth-date	College	How Acquired
Becker, Kurt	G	6-5	251	12-22-58	Michigan	D6
Boliaux, Guy	LB	6-1	214	9-21-59	Wisconsin	D11
Bornholdt, Mark	RB	6-0	215	12- 4-59	Ball State	FA
Brockington, Fred	WR	6-3	200	8-15-58	Michigan	FA
Carsello, Brett (2)	C-G	6-3	258	2-26-58	Wisconsin-Eau Claire	FA
Clark, Tim	WR	5-10	186	11-20-58	Alabama	FA
Clifford, Tim (1)	QB	6-1	207	11-28-58	Indiana	*D10 ('81)
Davenport, Clinton (2)	G-T	6-3	280	12-15-57	Eastern Illinois	FA
Dean, Pat	DT	6-2	260	4-20-59	Iowa	FA
DiClementi, Pete	S	5-10	194	2-24-60	Oklahoma State	FA
Doerger, Jerry	T	6-5	270	7-18-60	Wisconsin	D8
Dry, Mike	LB	6-3	218	12- 6-58	Texas Christian	FA
Ehlebracht, T.K. (1)	WR	6-1	174	2-10-58	North Central, Ill.	*FA ('81)
Gentry, Dennis	RB	5-8	173	2-10-59	Baylor	D4
Harris, Jim Bob	S	6-2	195	12-19-59	Alabama	FA
Hartnett, Perry	G	6-5	275	4-28-60	Southern Methodist	D5a
Hatchett, Mike	DB	5-10	176	1- 9-60	Texas	D9
Huskisson, Bill	DT	6-2	267	4-22-57	Western Illinois	FA
Hyble, Bret	LB	6-2	220	7-13-60	Central Michigan	FA
Jensen, Bill (1)	T	6-4	260	2-17-58	Arizona	Waiv.
Marshall, Dupre (1)	DT	6-3	250	12- 2-58	California	Waiv.
Masztak, Dean	TE	6-4	243	1-27-60	Notre Dame	FA
McMahon, Jim	QB	6-0	187	8-21-59	Brigham Young	D1
Meyer, Bob	RB	5-9	187	2- 5-60	Missouri	FA
Orlando, Jeff	DE	5-9	180	11-16-58	Cal-Lutheran	FA
Porter, Terry	WR	5-10	175	10-21-59	Montclair State	FA
Rains, Dan (1)	LB	6-1	220	4-26-56	Cincinnati	FA
Rouse, Eric (1)	WR	6-0	194	10-26-57	Illinois	FA
Runck, Dennis	RB	5-10	194	8-15-59	Dartmouth	FA
Scharnus, Mike	CB-S	6-3	200	1-14-58	Virginia Tech	FA
Schletzer, Jim (1)	P	6-2	202	7-17-57	Lees-McRae JC	FA
Sheets, Todd (1)	WR	6-0	183	7-22-57	Northwestern	*FA ('81)
Stevenson, Mark (1)	C-G	6-3	266	2-24-56	Western Illinois	FA
Tabron, Dennis	CB-S	5-9	182	3-19-60	Duke	D5b
Thomas, Calvin	RB	5-11	220	1- 7-60	Illinois	FA
Turner, Joe	DE	6-0	204	12-31-59	Southern California	D10
Veith, Steve	K	6-1	202	4- 2-57	Wisconsin	FA
Waechter, Henry	DT	6-5	270	2-13-59	Nebraska	D7
Wrightman, Tim	TE	6-2	237	3-27-60	UCLA	D3
Young, Ricky	LB	5-11	218	9- 1-60	Oklahoma State	D12

*Clifford, Ehlebracht and Sheets missed 1981 season due to injuries.

CINCINNATI BENGALS
(Central Division, American Conference)

Forrest Gregg

Chairman of the Board—Austin E. Knowlton
President—John Sawyer
Vice-President, General Manager—Paul Brown
Assistant General Manager—Michael Brown
Director of Player Personnel—Pete Brown
Head Coach—Forrest Gregg (5 years: 36-37-0)
Assistant Coaches:
    Defensive Coordinator-Linebackers—Hank Bullough
    Special Teams-Tight Ends—Bruce Coslet
    Offensive Coordinator—Lindy Infante
    Defensive Backfield—Dick LeBeau
    Offensive Line—Jim McNally
    Defensive Line—Dick Modzelewski
    Offensive Backfield—George Sefcik
    Strength—Kim Wood
Director of Public Relations—Allan Heim
    (Office Phone: 621-3550—Area Code 513)
Offices—200 Riverfront Stadium, Cincinnati, O. 45202
Stadium—Riverfront Stadium (Capacity: 59,754)
Team Colors—Orange, Black and White
Training Site—Wilmington College, Wilmington, O.

1982 SCHEDULE
(All times local.
All games Sunday unless noted otherwise.)

Sept. 12	HOUSTON	1:00
Sept. 19	at Pittsburgh	1:00
Sept. 27	at Cleveland (Mon.)	9:00
Oct. 3	MIAMI	1:00
Oct. 10	at New England	1:00
Oct. 17	at New York Giants	1:00
Oct. 24	DALLAS	9:00
Oct. 31	PITTSBURGH	1:00
Nov. 7	WASHINGTON	1:00
Nov. 14	at Houston	12:00
Nov. 21	at Philadelphia	1:00
Nov. 28	OAKLAND	1:00
Dec. 5	at Baltimore	2:00
Dec. 12	CLEVELAND	1:00
Dec. 20	at San Diego (Mon.)	6:00
Dec. 26	SEATTLE	1:00

1981 RESULTS—(Won 14, Lost 5)

Bengals		Opp.		Att.
27	Seattle	21	(H)	41,177
31	New York Jets	30	(A)	49,454
17	Cleveland	20	(H)	52,170
27	Buffalo (OT)	24	(H)	46,418
10	Houston	17	(A)	44,350
41	Baltimore	19	(A)	33,060
34	Pittsburgh	7	(H)	57,090
7	New Orleans	17	(A)	46,336
34	Houston	21	(H)	54,736
40	San Diego	17	(A)	51,209
24	Los Angeles	10	(H)	56,836
38	Denver	21	(H)	57,207
41	Cleveland	21	(A)	75,186
3	San Francisco	21	(H)	56,796
17	Pittsburgh	10	(A)	50,623
30	Atlanta	28	(A)	35,972

PLAYOFF GAME

28	Buffalo	21	(H)	55,420

AFC CHAMPIONSHIP GAME

27	San Diego	7	(H)	46,302

NFL CHAMPIONSHIP GAME

21	San Francisco	26	(*)	81,270

*—Silverdome, Pontiac, Mich.

1981 GAMES STARTED

16 games: Ken Anderson, Louis Breeden, Ross Browner, Blair Bush, Glenn Cameron, Cris Collinsworth, Bo Harris, Pete Johnson, Max Montoya, Anthony Munoz, Ken Riley, Dan Ross, Reggie Williams, Mike Wilson.

14 games: Charles Alexander, Isaac Curtis, Jim LeClair.

13 games: Eddie Edwards.

12 games: Bryan Hicks, Wilson Whitley.

10 games: Bobby Kemp, Dave Lapham.

Less than 10 games: Greg Bright (2), Glenn Bujnoch (5), Gary Burley (3), Mike Fuller (6), Archie Griffin (2), Ray Griffin (2), Rod Horn (4), Steve Kreider (1), Pat McInally (1), Mike Obrovac (1), Rick Razzano (2).

CINCINNATI BENGALS 1982 VETERAN ROSTER

No.	Name	Pos.	Ht.	Wt.	NFL Exp.	Birth-date	College	Games in '81	How Acquired
40	Alexander, Charles	RB	6-1	221	4	7-28-57	Louisiana State	15	D1b, '79
14	Anderson, Ken	QB	6-3	212	12	2-15-49	Augustana, Ill.	16	D3, '71
84	Bass, Don	WR	6-2	220	5	3-11-56	Houston	6	D3b, '78
10	Breech, Jim	PK	5-6	161	4	4-11-56	California	16	FA, '80
34	Breeden, Louis	CB	5-11	185	5	10-26-53	North Carolina Central	16	D7a, '77
79	Browner, Ross	DE	6-3	261	5	3-22-54	Notre Dame	16	D1a, '78
74	Bujnoch, Glenn	G	6-6	265	7	12-20-53	Texas A&M	6	D2a, '76
67	Burley, Gary	DE	6-3	274	7	12- 8-52	Pittsburgh	16	D3a, '75
58	Bush, Blair	C	6-3	252	5	11-25-56	Washington	16	D1b, '78
50	Cameron, Glenn	LB	6-2	228	8	2-21-53	Florida	16	D1, '75
80	Collinsworth, Cris	WR	6-5	192	2	1-27-59	Florida	16	D2, '81
85	Curtis, Isaac	WR	6-1	192	10	10-20-50	San Diego State	15	D1, '73
21	Davis, Oliver	S	6-1	205	6	8-29-54	Tennessee	10	W-Cle, '81
52	Dinkel, Tom	LB	6-3	237	5	7-25-56	Kansas	16	D5a, '78
73	Edwards, Eddie	DE	6-5	256	6	4-25-54	Miami	14	D1a, '77
49	Frazier, Guy	LB	6-2	215	2	7-20-59	Wyoming	16	D4, '81
42	Fuller, Mike	S	5-10	182	8	4- 7-53	Auburn	15	W-SD, '81
45	Griffin, Archie	RB	5-9	184	7	8-21-54	Ohio State	16	D1b, '76
44	Griffin, Ray	CB	5-10	186	5	6-29-56	Ohio State	8	D2a, '78
36	Hargrove, Jim	RB	6-2	228	2	11-13-57	Wake Forest	15	OFA, '81
53	Harris, Bo	LB	6-3	226	8	1-16-53	Louisiana State	16	D3c, '75
83	Harris, M.L.	TE	6-5	238	3	1-16-54	Kansas State	15	FA, '80
27	Hicks, Bryan	S	6-0	192	3	1-24-57	McNeese	16	D5, '80
30	Jauron, Dick	S	6-0	190	9	10- 7-50	Yale	*0	FA, '78
46	Johnson, Pete	RB	6-0	249	6	3- 2-54	Ohio State	16	D2, '77
26	Kemp, Bobby	S	6-0	186	2	5-29-59	Cal-State Fullerton	16	D8, '81
86	Kreider, Steve	WR	6-3	192	4	5-12-58	Lehigh	16	D6, '79
62	Lapham, Dave	G	6-4	262	9	6-24-52	Syracuse	13	D3a, '74
55	LeClair, Jim	LB	6-3	234	11	10-30-50	North Dakota	14	D3, '72
87	McInally, Pat	P-WR	6-6	212	7	5- 7-53	Harvard	16	D5a, '75
65	Montoya, Max	G	6-5	275	4	5-12-56	UCLA	16	D7, '79
60	Moore, Blake	C	6-5	267	3	5- 8-58	Wooster	14	OFA, '80
78	Munoz, Anthony	T	6-6	278	3	8-19-58	Southern California	16	D1, '80
68	Obrovac, Mike	T	6-6	275	2	10-11-55	Bowling Green	6	FA, '81
51	Razzano, Rick	LB	5-11	227	3	11-15-55	Virginia Tech	16	FA, '80
13	Riley, Ken	CB	6-0	183	14	8- 6-47	Florida A&M	16	D6, '69
89	Ross, Dan	TE	6-4	235	4	2- 9-57	Northeastern	16	D2, '79
72	St. Clair, Mike	DE	6-5	254	7	9- 2-53	Grambling	16	FA, '80
15	Schonert, Turk	QB	6-1	185	3	1-15-57	Stanford	4	W-Chi, '80
59	Schuh, Jeff	LB	6-2	228	2	5-22-58	Minnesota	16	D7, '81
25	Simmons, John	CB	5-11	192	2	12- 1-58	Southern Methodist	11	D3, '81
56	Simpkins, Ron	LB	6-1	235	2	4- 2-58	Michigan	*0	D7a, '80
12	Thompson, Jack	QB	6-3	217	4	5-18-56	Washington State	8	D1a, '79
81	Verser, David	WR	6-1	200	2	3- 1-58	Kansas	16	D1, '81
75	Whitley, Wilson	NT	6-3	265	6	4-28-55	Houston	14	D1b, '77
57	Williams, Reggie	LB	6-0	228	7	9-19-54	Dartmouth	16	D3b, '76
77	Wilson, Mike	T	6-5	271	5	5-28-55	Georgia	16	D4b, '77

*Jauron and Simpkins missed the 1981 season due to injuries.

D—Draft; T—Trade; W—Waivers; FA—Free Agent; OFA—Original Free Agent; VFA—Veteran Free Agent; VA—Veteran Allocation; SupD—Supplemental Draft.

Also played with Bengals in 1981—S Greg Bright (4 games), CB Clarence Chapman (5), T Brad Oates (5), RB Elvis Peacock (3), T Bobby Whitten (1). Retired: DT Rod Horn (16).

CINCINNATI BENGALS
1982 DRAFT CHOICES

(Number following name designates order of selection among 334 players drafted.)

Round and Player		Position	College
1. COLLINS, Glen	26	DE	Mississippi St.
2. WEAVER, Emanuel	54	DT	South Carolina
3. HOLMAN, Rodney	82	TE	Tulane
4. TATE, Rodney	110	RB	Texas
5. SORENSEN, Paul	138	DB	Washington St.
6. KING, Arthur	166	DT	Grambling
7. NEEDHAM, Ben	194	LB	Michigan
8. YLI-RENKO, Kari	222	T	Cincinnati
9. BENNETT, James	250	WR	N.W. Louisiana
10. HOGUE, Larry	278	DB	Utah State
11. DAVIS, Russell	305	RB	Idaho
12. FERADAY, Dan	333	QB	Toronto

CINCINNATI BENGALS
1982 ROOKIE AND FIRST-YEAR ROSTER

(1) Indicates player in previous NFL camp.
All others classified as rookies.

Name	Pos.	Hgt.	Wgt.	Birth-date	College	How Acquired
Bedard, Kipp	WR	6-0	181	9-22-59	Boise State	FA
Bennett, James	WR	6-1	190	7-17-59	Northwest Louisiana	D9
Bettis, James	RB	5-9	175	2-20-59	Cincinnati	FA
Burrell, Bart (1)	WR	6-1	185	3- 4-59	Purdue	FA
Collins, Glen	DE	6-6	260	7-10-59	Mississippi State	D1
Cotton, Brian	S	6-1	195	2- 6-58	Eastern Michigan	FA
Davis, Russell	RB	5-10	187	3- 5-60	Idaho	D11
Durden, Gwaine	RB	5-10	186	9- 9-59	Tennessee-Chattanooga	FA
Evans, Anthony	CB-S	5-9	182	8-31-59	Georgetown, Ky.	FA
Feraday, Dan	QB	6-1	205	6-30-56	Toronto	D12
Ferranti, Jim (1)	WR	5-9	165	10-30-57	Youngstown State	FA
Fowler, Reggie	LB	6-0	220	2- 4-59	Wyoming	FA
Hannula, Jim (1)	OT-P	6-6	251	7- 2-59	Northern Illinois	*D9 ('81)
Hausauer, Ron	G	6-3	280	8-16-59	Jamestown College, N.D.	FA
Hogue, Larry	CB	5-10	175	9-26-60	Utah State	D10
Holman, Rodney	TE	6-3	230	4-20-60	Tulane	D3
Jackson, Robert (1)	S	5-10	184	10-10-58	Central Michigan	*D11 ('81)
King, Arthur	NT	6-4	260	6-20-60	Grambling	D6
Lee, Oudious (1)	NT	6-2	257	6-14-56	Nebraska	FA
Leone, Fred	LB	6-2	210	6-12-60	Yale	FA
Needham, Ben	LB	6-4	220	11-19-58	Michigan	D7
Samoa, Samoa (1)	RB	6-2	207	9-23-56	Washington State	*D9 ('81)
Simon, Victor	LB	6-0	220	10- 9-59	Southern Methodist	FA
Sorensen, Paul	CB-S	6-0	195	7-15-59	Washington State	D5
Sydney, Harry (1)	RB	6-0	218	6-26-59	Kansas	FA
Tate, Rodney	RB	5-11	190	2-14-59	Texas	D4
Wagner, Ray	T	6-3	290	11-15-57	Kent State	FA
Walker, Patrick (1)	RB	6-2	185	3-13-59	Miami, Fla.	FA
Weaver, Emanuel	NT	6-4	260	6-28-60	South Carolina	D2
Yli-Renko, Kari	T	6-5	280	11-17-59	Cincinnati	D8

*Hannula, Jackson and Samoa missed 1981 season due to injuries.

CLEVELAND BROWNS
(Central Division, American Conference)

Sam Rutigliano

President—Arthur B. Modell
Vice-President and General Counsel—James Baily
Assistant to President—Paul Warfield
Director of Personnel—Bill Davis
Director of Pro Personnel—Allen Webb
Director of Research and Development—Jim Garrett
Director of Publicity—Kevin Byrne
Vice-President and Director of Public Relations—Nate Wallack
  (Office Phone: 696-5555—Area Code 216)
Head Coach—Sam Rutigliano (4 years: 33-31-0)
Assistant Coaches:
  Linebackers—Dave Adolph
  Defensive Secondary—Len Fontes
  Quarterbacks—Paul Hackett
  Offensive Line—Rod Humenuik
  Receivers—Rich Kotite
  Special Teams—John Petercuskie
  Defensive Line—Tom Pratt
  Strength—Dave Redding
  Running Backs—Joe Scannella
  Defensive Coordinator—Marty Schottenheimer
Offices—Cleveland Stadium, Cleveland, O. 44114
Stadium—Cleveland Municipal Stadium (Capacity: 80,322)
Team Colors—Brown, Orange and White
Training Site—Lakeland Community College, Mentor, O.

1982 SCHEDULE
(All times local.
All games Sunday unless noted otherwise.)

Sept. 12	at Seattle	1:00
Sept. 19	PHILADELPHIA	1:00
Sept. 27	CINCINNATI (Mon.)	9:00
Oct. 3	at Washington	1:00
Oct. 10	at Oakland	1:00
Oct. 17	BALTIMORE	1:00
Oct. 24	at Pittsburgh	1:00
Oct. 31	HOUSTON	1:00
Nov. 7	NEW YORK GIANTS	1:00
Nov. 14	at Miami	4:00
Nov. 21	NEW ENGLAND	1:00
Nov. 25	at Dallas (Thanksgiving)	3:00
Dec. 5	SAN DIEGO	1:00
Dec. 12	at Cincinnati	1:00
Dec. 19	PITTSBURGH	1:00
Dec. 26	at Houston	12:00

1981 RESULTS—(Won 5, Lost 11)

Browns		Opp.		Att.
14	San Diego	44	(H)	78,904
3	Houston	9	(H)	79,483
20	Cincinnati	17	(A)	52,170
28	Atlanta	17	(H)	78,283
16	Los Angeles	27	(A)	63,924
7	Pittsburgh	13	(A)	53,255
20	New Orleans	17	(H)	76,059
42	Baltimore	28	(H)	78,986
13	Buffalo	22	(A)	80,020
20	Denver (OT)	23	(A)	74,859
15	San Francisco	12	(A)	52,445
10	Pittsburgh	32	(H)	77,958
21	Cincinnati	41	(H)	75,186
13	Houston	17	(A)	44,502
13	New York Jets	14	(H)	56,866
21	Seattle	42	(A)	51,435

1981 GAMES STARTED

16 games: Dick Ambrose, Ron Bolton, Henry Bradley, Joe DeLamielleure, Doug Dieken, Don Goode, Clay Matthews, Ozzie Newsome, Cody Risien, Clarence Scott, Brian Sipe.

15 games: Lyle Alzado, Mike Pruitt.

14 games: Hanford Dixon, Robert L. Jackson, Dave Logan.

13 games: Robert E. Jackson

12 games: Marshall Harris.

11 games: Reggie Rucker.

10 games: Thom Darden.

Less than 10 games: Autry Beamon (4), Thomas Brown (4), Clinton Burrell (2), Tom DeLeone (8), Ricky Feacher (7), Elvis Franks (1), Bruce Huther (2), Lawrence Johnson (2), Cleo Miller (3), Greg Pruitt (5), Henry Sheppard (3), Gerry Sullivan (8), Charles White (9).

CLEVELAND BROWNS 1982 VETERAN ROSTER

No.	Name	Pos.	Ht.	Wt.	NFL Exp.	Birth-date	College	Games in '81	How Acquired
80	Adams, Willis	WR	6-2	194	4	8-22-56	Houston	7	D1, '79
52	Ambrose, Dick	LB	6-0	228	8	1-17-53	Virginia	16	D12, '75
9	Bahr, Matt	PK	5-10	165	4	7- 6-56	Penn State	*15	T-SF, '81
28	Bolton, Ron	CB	6-2	170	11	4-16-50	Norfolk State	16	T-NE, '76
91	Bradley, Henry	DT	6-2	260	4	9- 4-53	Alcorn State	16	FA, '79
97	Brown, Thomas	DE	6-4	240	3	7- 8-57	Baylor	16	T-Phi, '81
	Bullard, Louis	G	6-6	265	4	5- 6-56	Jackson State	*0	FA, '82
49	Burrell, Clinton	S	6-1	192	3	9- 4-56	Louisiana State	2	D6a, '79
53	Cowher, Bill	LB	6-3	225	2	5- 8-57	North Carolina State	*0	FA, '80
15	Cox, Steve	K	6-4	195	2	5-11-58	Arkansas	16	D5, '81
21	Davis, Gary	RB	5-10	210	7	9- 7-54	Cal Poly-SLO	*7	FA, '81
64	DeLamielleure, Joe	G	6-3	245	10	3-16-51	Michigan State	16	T-Buf, '80
54	DeLeone, Tom	C	6-2	248	11	8-13-50	Ohio State	8	FA, '74
73	Dieken, Doug	T	6-5	252	12	2-12-49	Illinois	16	D6a, '71
29	Dixon, Hanford	CB	5-11	182	2	12-25-58	Southern Mississippi	16	D1, '81
83	Feacher, Ricky	WR	5-10	174	7	2-11-54	Mississippi Valley	16	FA, '76
20	Flint, Judson	CB	6-0	201	3	1-26-57	Memphis State	16	FA, '80
94	Franks, Elvis	DE	6-4	238	3	7- 9-59	Morgan State	16	D5, '80
86	Fulton, Dan	WR	6-2	186	3	9- 2-56	Nebraska-Omaha	5	FA, '81
26	Hall, Dino	RB	5-7	165	4	12- 6-55	Glassboro State	12	OFA, '79
90	Harris, Marshall	DE	6-6	261	3	12- 6-55	Texas Christian	15	T-NYJ, '80
58	Huther, Bruce	LB	6-1	220	6	7-23-54	New Hampshire	16	T-Dal, '81
68	Jackson, Robert	G	6-5	260	8	4- 1-53	Duke	16	OFA, '75
51	Johnson, Eddie	LB	6-1	210	2	2- 3-59	Louisville	16	D7, '81
48	Johnson, Lawrence	CB	5-11	204	3	9-11-57	Wisconsin	16	D2a, '79
85	Logan, Dave	WR	6-4	216	7	2- 2-54	Colorado	14	D3, '76
57	Matthews, Clay	LB	6-2	230	5	3-15-56	Southern California	16	D1a, '78
16	McDonald, Paul	QB	6-2	185	3	2-23-58	Southern California	12	D4b, '80
30	Miller, Cleo	RB	5-11	214	9	9- 5-52	Arkansas-Pine Bluff	12	FA, '75
71	Miller, Matt	T	6-6	270	3	7-30-56	Colorado	16	D4, '79
82	Newsome, Ozzie	TE	6-2	232	5	3-15-56	Alabama	16	D1b, '78
84	Oden, McDonald	TE	6-4	215	3	3-28-58	Tennessee State	16	OFA, '80
	Parker, Steve	DT	6-6	265	2	12- 8-56	Idaho	*0	FA, '82
69	Patten, Joel	T	6-6	240	2	2- 7-58	Duke	*0	OFA, '80
43	Pruitt, Mike	RB	6-0	225	7	4- 3-54	Purdue	16	D1, '76
63	Risien, Cody	T	6-7	255	4	3-22-57	Texas A&M	16	D7, '79
92	Robinson, Mike	DE	6-4	260	2	8-19-56	Arizona	10	D4, '81
33	Rucker, Reggie	WR	6-2	190	13	9-21-47	Boston University	14	T-NE, '75
22	Scott, Clarence	S	6-0	190	12	4- 9-49	Kansas State	16	D1, '71
65	Sheppard, Henry	G	6-6	263	7	11-12-52	Southern Methodist	9	D5, '76
17	Sipe, Brian	QB	6-1	195	9	8- 8-49	San Diego State	16	D13, '72
79	Sullivan, Gerry	C-T	6-4	250	9	1-15-52	Illinois	16	D7b, '74
12	Trocano, Rick	QB	6-0	188	2	4- 4-59	Pittsburgh	6	W-Pit, '81
55	Weathers, Curtis	LB	6-5	220	4	9-16-56	Mississippi	13	D9b, '79
25	White, Charles	RB	5-10	198	3	1-22-58	Southern California	16	D1, '80

*Cowher, Patten, and Wright missed 1981 season due to injuries; Bahr played 4 games with San Francisco, 11 with Cleveland in 1981; Bullard last active with Seattle in 1980; Davis played 7 games with Tampa Bay and was active for 2 with Cleveland in 1981; Parker last active with New Orleans in 1980.

D—Draft; T—Trade; W—Waivers; FA—Free Agent; OFA—Original Free Agent; VFA—Veteran Free Agent; VA—Veteran Allocation; SupD—Supplemental Draft.

Also played with Browns in 1981—DE Lyle Alzado (15 games), S Thom Darden (13), LB Don Goode (16), LB Robert L. Jackson (14), K Dave Jacobs (5), KR Cleotha Montgomery (4), RB Greg Pruitt (15). Retired: RB Calvin Hill (14), DT Jerry Sherk (15), WR Keith Wright (*0).

CLEVELAND BROWNS
1982 DRAFT CHOICES

(Number following name designates order of selection among 334 players drafted.)

Round and Player		Position	College
1. BANKS, Chip	3	LB	USC
2. BALDWIN, Keith	31	DE	Texas A & M
3. Choice to Buffalo (a)			
4. WALKER, Dwight	87	WR	Nicholls State
5. BAAB, Mike	115	C	Texas
6. Choice to Dallas (b)			
WHITWELL, Mike from Denver (c)	162	WR	Texas A & M
7. Choice to Buffalo (d)			
8. KAFENTZIS, Mark	199	DB	Hawaii
HEFLIN, Van from Oakland (e)	204	TE	Vanderbilt
JACKSON, Bill from Washington (f)	211	DB	North Carolina
9. BAKER, Milton	227	TE	West Texas St.
10. FLOYD, Ricky	255	RB	Southern Miss.
11. MICHUTA, Steve	282	QB	Grand Valley St.
12. NICOLAS, Scott	310	LB	Miami

(a) Traded pick and second-round pick in 1981 for guard Joe DeLamielleure, September 1, 1980.   •

(b) Traded pick for linebacker Bruce Huther, August 24, 1981.

(c) Acquired pick for linebacker Robert Jackson, April 27, 1982.

(d) Traded pick for running back Terry Miller, May 5, 1981.

(e) Acquired pick for defensive end Lyle Alzado, April 28, 1982.

(f) Acquired pick for two 10th-round picks in 1981, April 29, 1981.

CLEVELAND BROWNS
1982 ROOKIE AND FIRST-YEAR ROSTER

(1) Indicates player in previous NFL camp.
(2) Indicates player with CFL experience.
All others classified as rookies.

Name	Pos.	Hgt.	Wgt.	Birth-date	College	How Acquired
Axson, Mozell	LB	5-11	229	7- 6-59	Miami	FA
Baab, Mike	C	6-4	270	12- 6-59	Texas	D5
Baker, Milton	TE	6-3	217	5- 8-60	West Texas State	D9
Baldwin, Keith	DE	6-4	245	10-13-60	Texas A&M	D2
Banks, Chip	LB	6-4	233	9-18-59	Southern California	D1
Blatcher, Phil	RB	5-9	188	7- 9-58	Iowa	FA
Bloch, Ray (1)	T	6-7	255	2- 6-59	Ohio University	*FA ('81)
Byrd, Eugene (1)	WR	6-0	180	6- 7-57	Michigan State	FA
Chaney, Chris	CB-S	6-3	190	12- 5-58	Dayton	FA
Chrest, Craig (1)	WR	6-1	180	12-20-55	Wisconsin-LaCrosse	FA
Cousineau, Tom (2)	LB	6-3	232	5- 6-57	Ohio State	T-Buf, '82
Davis, Kent (1)	CB	5-11	172	4-22-57	Southeast Missouri	FA
Floyd, Ricky	RB	5-9	178	2-10-60	Southern Mississippi	D10
Friday, Larry (1)	S	6-4	205	1-23-58	Mississippi	*D11 ('81)
Gerdon, Steve	CB-S	5-11	185	10- 7-59	Richmond	FA
Heflin, Van	TE	6-2	230	4- 4-59	Vanderbilt	D8b
Hill, Aaron	CB-S	5-9	172	6- 6-60	Lamar	FA
Jackson, Bill	CB-S	6-1	202	7- 1-60	North Carolina	D8c
Jacquemain, Joe	G	6-4	230	3-15-59	Michigan State	FA
Jenkins, Joe (1)	TE	6-5	228	11- 5-57	Alcorn State	FA
Johnson, Daryl	S-DB	5-10	180	2-19-60	Wabash	FA
Kafentzis, Mark	S-DB	5-10	185	6-30-58	Hawaii	D8a
Kirkland, Fred (1)	WR-KR	5-9	166	9- 4-57	Ferris State	FA
Lantz, Doug (1)	C	6-3	248	3-17-57	Miami, Ohio	FA
McCall, Ron (1)	WR	6-2	197	8-16-58	Arkansas-Pine Bluff	FA
McCarroll, John	CB	6-2	192	9-12-59	Kansas	FA
McGill, Kevin (1)	T	6-7	262	3-17-58	Oregon	*D12 ('81)
McKinnie, Marcus	CB	6-0	189	8-16-60	Purdue	FA
Michuta, Steve	QB	6-3	201	9- 3-60	Grand Valley State	D11
Murray, Lind	CB	6-2	200	3-18-59	West Virginia	FA
Nicolas, Scott	LB	6-3	226	8- 7-60	Miami	D12
Oliver, Harry	K	5-11	181	6- 5-60	Notre Dame	FA
Paulsen, Mark	TE	6-4	250	6-29-59	Kansas	FA
Steinke, Stephen (1)	P-K	5-8	180	6-28-59	Utah State	FA
Stump, Don	K	6-1	205	2-11-60	McNeese State	FA
Tate, Ronald (1)	RB	6-1	210	7-12-58	North Carolina Central	FA
Thomas, Rodney	FB	5-10	200	9-20-58	Western Illinois	FA
Treadwell, Don	WR	5-9	165	6-10-60	Miami, Ohio	FA
Walker, Dwight	RB	5-9	185	1-10-59	Nicholls State	D4
Webb, Ray (1)	NT	6-3	250	6-29-59	Texas-Arlington	FA
Wheeler, Ron (1)	TE	6-5	230	9- 5-58	Washington	Waiv.
Whitwell, Mike	WR	6-0	175	11-14-58	Texas A&M	D6
Woodland, Thomas	NT	6-1	255	1- 7-59	Missouri	FA
Yoho, Todd	RB	5-11	195	11-24-59	Ohio University	FA

*Bloch active for 1 game with Browns in 1981, did not play; Friday and McGill missed 1981 season due to injuries.

DALLAS COWBOYS
(Eastern Division, National Conference)

Tom Landry

Chairman of the Board—Clint W. Murchison, Jr.
President and General Manager—Texas E. Schramm
Vice-President, Personnel Development—Gil Brandt
Vice-President, Administration—Joe Bailey
Vice-President, Treasurer—Don Wilson
Head Coach—Tom Landry (22 years: 196-112-6)
Assistant Coaches:
  Research and Development—Ermal Allen
  Quality Control—Neill Armstrong
  Running Backs—Al Lavan
  Special Teams—Al Lowry
  Quarterbacks—John Mackovic
  Assistant Head Coach-Offensive Line—Jim Myers
  Receivers—Dick Nolan
  Defensive Backs—Gene Stalings
  Defensive Coordinator-Defensive Line—Ernie Stautner
  Linebackers—Jerry Tubbs
  Conditioning—Bob Ward
Public Relations Director—Doug Todd
  (Office Phone: 369-8000—Area Code 214)
Offices—6116 North Central Expressway, Dallas, Tex. 75206
Stadium—Texas Stadium (Capacity: 65,101)
Team Colors—Royal Blue, Metallic Blue and White
Training Site—California Lutheran College, Thousand Oaks, Calif.

1982 SCHEDULE
(All times local.
All games Sunday unless noted otherwise.)

Sept. 13	PITTSBURGH (Mon.)	8:00
Sept. 19	at St. Louis	12:00
Sept. 26	at Minnesota	12:00
Oct. 3	NEW YORK GIANTS	3:00
Oct. 10	WASHINGTON	12:00
Oct. 17	at Philadelphia	4:00
Oct. 24	at Cincinnati	9:00
Oct. 31	at New York Giants	4:00
Nov. 7	ST. LOUIS	12:00
Nov. 14	at San Francisco	1:00
Nov. 21	TAMPA BAY	12:00
Nov. 25	CLEVELAND (Thanksgiving)	3:00
Dec. 5	at Washington	4:00
Dec. 13	at Houston (Mon.)	8:00
Dec. 19	NEW ORLEANS	3:00
Dec. 26	PHILADELPHIA	3:00

1981 RESULTS—(Won 13, Lost 5)

Cowboys		Opp.		Att.
26	Washington	10	(A)	55,045
30	St. Louis	17	(H)	63,602
35	New England	21	(A)	61,297
18	New York Giants	10	(H)	63,449
17	St. Louis	20	(A)	49,477
14	San Francisco	45	(A)	57,574
29	Los Angeles	17	(H)	64,649
28	Miami	27	(H)	64,221
17	Philadelphia	14	(A)	72,111
27	Buffalo	14	(H)	62,583
24	Detroit	27	(A)	79,694
24	Washington	10	(H)	64,583
10	Chicago	9	(H)	63,499
37	Baltimore	13	(A)	54,871
21	Philadelphia	10	(H)	64,955
10	New York Giants (OT)	13	(A)	73,009

PLAYOFF GAME

38	Tampa Bay	0	(H)	64,848

NFC CHAMPIONSHIP GAME

27	San Francisco	28	(A)	60,525

1981 GAMES STARTED

16 games: Bob Breunig, Jim Cooper, Pat Donovan, Tony Dorsett, John Dutton, Ed Jones, D.D. Lewis, Harvey Martin, Herbert Scott, Dennis Thurman, Charlie Waters, Randy White.

15 games: Michael Downs, Billy Joe DuPree, Drew Pearson, Tom Rafferty, Danny White.

14 games: Kurt Peterson.

13 games: Ron Springs.

12 games: Everson Walls.

10 games: Mike Hegman.

Less than 10 games: Benny Barnes (1), Guy Brown (6), Glenn Carano (1), Tony Hill (9), Butch Johnson (7), Jay Saldi (5), Robert Shaw (3), Steve Wilson (4).

DALLAS COWBOYS 1982 VETERAN ROSTER

No.	Name	Pos.	Ht.	Wt.	NFL Exp.	Birth-date	College	Games in '81	How Acquired
31	Barnes, Benny	CB	6-1	203	11	3- 3-51	Stanford	16	OFA, '72
76	Bethea, Larry	DT	6-5	249	5	7-21-56	Michigan State	16	D1, '78
53	Breunig, Bob	LB	6-2	223	8	7- 4-53	Arizona State	16	D3, '75
59	Brown, Guy	LB	6-4	228	6	6- 1-55	Houston	16	D4, '77
18	Carano, Glenn	QB	6-3	198	6	11-18-55	Nevada-Las Vegas	5	D2, '77
47	Clinkscale, Dextor	S	5-11	189	2	4-13-58	South Carolina	*0	OFA, '80
61	Cooper, Jim	T	6-5	263	6	9-28-55	Temple	16	D6, '77
84	Cosbie, Doug	TE	6-6	226	4	2-27-56	Santa Clara	16	D3, '79
51	Dickerson, Anthony	LB	6-2	222	3	6- 9-57	Southern Methodist	16	FA, '80
83	Donley, Doug	WR	6-0	175	2	2- 6-59	Ohio State	11	D2, '81
67	Donovan, Pat	T	6-4	259	8	7- 1-53	Stanford	16	D4a, '75
33	Dorsett, Tony	RB	5-11	185	6	4- 7-54	Pittsburgh	16	D1, '77
26	Downs, Michael	S	6-3	198	2	6- 9-59	Rice	15	OFA, '81
89	DuPree, Billy Joe	TE	6-4	228	10	3- 7-50	Michigan State	16	D1, '73
78	Dutton, John	DT	6-7	263	9	2- 6-51	Nebraska	16	T-Bal, '79
27	Fellows, Ron	CB	6-0	170	2	11- 7-58	Missouri	16	D7a, '81
71	Frederick, Andy	T	6-6	265	6	7-25-54	New Mexico	16	D5, '77
58	Hegman, Mike	LB	6-1	225	7	1-17-53	Tennessee State	11	D7, '75
80	Hill, Tony	WR	6-2	206	6	6-23-56	Stanford	16	D3a, '77
14	Hogeboom, Gary	QB	6-4	200	3	8-21-58	Central Michigan	1	D5, '80
42	Hughes, Randy	S	6-4	207	7	4- 3-53	Oklahoma	*0	D4b, '75
86	Johnson, Butch	WR	6-1	180	7	5-28-54	Cal-Riverside	16	D3c, '76
72	†Jones, Ed	DE	6-9	272	7	2-23-51	Tennessee State	16	D1a, '74
23	Jones, James	RB	5-10	196	3	12- 6-58	Mississippi State	16	D3b, '80
57	King, Angelo	LB	6-1	220	2	2-10-58	South Carolina State	15	OFA, '81
79	Martin, Harvey	DE	6-5	252	10	11-16-50	East Texas State	16	D3, '73
44	†Newhouse, Robert	RB	5-10	220	11	1- 9-50	Houston	16	D2a, '72
30	Newsome, Timmy	RB	6-1	232	3	5-17-58	Winston-Salem State	15	D6, '80
88	Pearson, Drew	WR	6-0	190	10	1-12-51	Tulsa	16	OFA, '73
65	Petersen, Kurt	G	6-4	266	3	6-17-57	Missouri	16	D4, '80
64	Rafferty, Tom	G	6-3	258	7	8- 2-54	Penn State	16	D4, '76
70	Richards, Howard	T	6-6	248	2	8- 7-59	Missouri	16	D1, '81
56	Roe, Bill	LB	6-3	230	2	2- 6-58	Colorado	*0	D3a, '80
87	Saldi, Jay	TE	6-3	223	7	10- 8-54	South Carolina	16	OFA, '76
68	Scott, Herbert	G	6-2	258	8	1-18-53	Virginia Union	16	D13, '75
1	Septien, Rafael	PK	5-9	174	6	12-12-53	Southwest Louisiana	16	FA, '78
52	Shaw, Robert	C	6-4	260	4	10-15-56	Tennessee	3	D1, '79
55	Spradlin, Danny	LB	6-1	221	2	3- 3-59	Tennessee	16	D5, '81
20	Springs, Ron	RB	6-1	216	4	11- 1-56	Ohio State	16	D5c, '79
77	Thornton, Bruce	DE	6-5	262	4	2-14-58	Illinois	12	D8, '79
32	Thurman, Dennis	CB	5-11	178	5	4-13-58	Southern California	16	D11, '78
63	Titensor, Glen	G	6-4	257	2	2-21-58	Brigham Young	16	D3, '81
24	Walls, Everson	CB	6-1	189	2	12-28-59	Grambling	16	OFA, '81
66	Wells, Norm	G	6-5	261	2	9- 8-57	Northwestern	*0	D12, '80
11	White, Danny	QB	6-2	196	7	2- 9-52	Arizona State	16	D3a, '74
54	White, Randy	DT	6-4	250	8	1-15-53	Maryland	16	D1a, '75
45	Wilson, Steve	CB	5-10	193	4	8-24-57	Howard	16	OFA, '79
73	Wright, Steve	T	6-5	250	2	4- 8-59	Northern Iowa	16	OFA, '81

*Clinkscale, Hughes, Roe and Wells missed the 1981 season due to injuries.

†Option playout; subject to developments.

D—Draft; T—Trade; W—Waivers; FA—Free Agent; OFA—Original Free Agent; VFA—Veteran Free Agent; VA—Veteran Allocation; SupD—Supplemental Draft.

Retired: LB D.D. Lewis (16 games played in 1981), S Charlie Waters (16), C John Fitzgerald (0).

DALLAS COWBOYS
1982 DRAFT CHOICES

(Number following name designates order of selection among 334 players drafted.)

Round and Player		Position	College
1. HILL, Rod	25	DB	Kentucky State
2. ROHRER, Jeff	53	LB	Yale
3. ELIOPULOS, Jim	81	LB	Wyoming
4. CARPENTER, Brian	101	DB	Michigan
from Tampa Bay (a)			
HUNTER, Monty	109	DB	Salem, W. Va.
5. POZDERAC, Phil	137	T	Notre Dame
6. HAMMOND, Ken	143	G	Vanderbilt
from Cleveland (b)			
DAUM, Charles	165	DT	Cal Poly-SLO
7. PURIFOY, Bill	193	DE	Tulsa
8. PEOPLES, George	216	RB	Auburn
from Denver through Buffalo (c)			
SULLIVAN, Dwight	221	RB	No. Carolina St.
9. GARY, Joe	249	DT	UCLA
10. ECKERSON, Todd	277	T	No. Carolina St.
11. THOMPSON, George	295	WR	Albany St., Ga.
from Tampa Bay (d)			
WHITING, Mike	304	RB	Florida State
12. BURTNESS, Rich	332	G	Montana

(a) Acquired pick and seventh-round pick in 1981 for defensive end Dave Stalls, August 6, 1980.

(b) Acquired pick for linebacker Bruce Huther, August 24, 1981.

(c) Acquired pick from Buffalo for wide receiver Wade Manning, August 18, 1981; Buffalo had acquired pick from Denver for Manning, August 24, 1981.

(d) Acquired pick for safety Aaron Mitchell, August 31, 1981.

DALLAS COWBOYS
1982 ROOKIE AND FIRST-YEAR ROSTER

(1) Indicates player in previous NFL camp.
  All others classified as rookies.

Name	Pos.	Hgt.	Wgt.	Birth-date	College	How Acquired
Abrams, Willie	FB	5-11	210	6-29-58	Bethune-Cookman	FA
Baldinger, Brian	G	6-4	255	1- 7-59	Duke	FA
Barker, Mike (1)	DT	6-3	266	12- 3-59	Grambling	FA
Baumgardner, Wayne	WR	6-1	190	11- 6-59	Wake Forest	FA
Beane, Don	K	6-3	261	1-25-59	None	FA
Benefield, Greg	C	6-2	266	2-10-60	Texas-El Paso	FA
Benson, Allen	LB	6-1	228	3-24-59	Oklahoma State	FA
Berry, James	RB	5-10	191	12- 2-59	Tennessee	FA
Biale, Stephen	G	6-2	259	2-17-59	Lafayette (Pa.)	FA
Blackwell, Louis	LB	6-1	228	1-17-58	Oklahoma State	FA
Burnett, Harris	C	6-3	266	11-10-59	California-Fullerton	FA
Burtness, Richard	G	6-4	257	6-25-60	Montana	D12
Carpenter, Brian	DB	5-10	166	11-27-60	Michigan	D4a
Corp, Chris	WR	6-4	187	4-23-60	Idaho State	FA
Culver, Ed	T	6-3	277	12-16-57	Oklahoma	FA

Name	Pos.	Hgt.	Wgt.	Birth-date	College	How Acquired
Cypert, Zac	LB	6-1	210	5-17-58	North Texas State	FA
Daum, Charles	DL	6-6	241	11- 3-59	Cal. Poly. SLO	D6b
Deveaux, Matt	WR	6-2	182	1-31-59	Newberry	FA
Durham, Steve (1)	DE	6-5	260	10-11-58	Clemson	FA
Dykstra, Jim	T	6-5	287	12- 7-58	Stanford	FA
Eckerson, Todd	T	6-4	263	1-24-60	North Carolina State	D10
Eliopulos, Jim	LB	6-3	229	4-18-59	Wyoming	D3
Evans, Greg	DB	5-11	198	8-25-59	Murray State	FA
Ferrill, Glen	DE	6-3	252	2-25-60	S.E. Louisiana	FA
Finzer, David	P-K	6-0	199	2- 3-59	DePauw	FA
Gary, Joe	DT	6-5	273	5-13-59	UCLA	D9
Gill, Yancy	T	6-5	249	5-25-59	Evansville (Indiana)	FA
Graham, David	DT	6-5	246	4- 6-59	Morehouse (Ga.)	FA
Hall, Leamon	QB	6-6	215	11- 8-55	Army	FA
Hall, Tracy	WR	6-1	167	6-20-59	Temple	FA
Hammond, Ken	G	6-4	270	12- 7-59	Vanderbilt	D6a
Haney, Kevin	FB	6-2	218	5- 1-60	Texas Christian	FA
Harvey, Pete	WR	5-10	175	12-22-59	North Texas State	FA
Hill, Alan	DB	6-0	171	5-14-58	DePauw	FA
Hill, Rod	DB	6-0	185	3-14-59	Kentucky State	D1
Hunter, Monty	DB	6-0	201	1-21-59	Salem (West Virginia)	D4b
Johnson, Bobby	DB	5-11	189	9- 1-60	Texas	FA
Jones, Greg	RB	5-8	182	6-10-59	Miami (Ohio)	FA
Jones, Havan	DB	6-1	195	2- 9-60	Eastern (Oregon)	FA
Jones, Max	DB	6-3	222	10-22-60	Massachusetts	FA
Klinkhammer, Joseph	DT	6-4	242	2-26-60	St. Thomas	FA
Lecy, Todd	LB	6-3	227	7- 4-60	North Dakota State	FA
Lee, Keith	LB	6-4	226	5-11-60	Virginia	FA
Lyons, Anthony	T	6-4	248	1- 5-59	Cameron	FA
McClure, Guy	P	6-1	196	12- 5-57	Utah State	FA
McLean, Scott	LB	6-4	231	12-16-60	Florida State	FA
Mason, Mike	T	6-6	257	12-30-58	UCLA	FA
Matthies, Thomas	DT	6-6	251	11- 8-57	Kearney State	FA
May, Marc	TE	6-4	226	1- 1-57	Purdue	FA
Menefee, David	G	6-3	238	2-14-61	Toledo	FA
Miller, Dan	RB	5-8	178	5- 4-59	Citadel	FA
Morze, David	LB	6-4	229	9-12-60	Stanford	FA
Office, Tony	LB	6-1	234	2-24-60	Illinois State	FA
Opatz, Craig	T	6-2	261	3-17-60	Montana Tech	FA
Pace, John	LB	5-11	217	10-25-60	Arizona	FA
Peoples, George	FB	6-0	211	8-25-60	Auburn	D8a
Peru, Reynaldo	DE	6-5	252	1- 1-59	Arizona State	FA
Pierce, Jeff	P	6-2	200	2-19-60	Georgia Tech	FA
Porter, Greg	K	5-9	160	7-28-60	TCU	FA
Pozderac, Phil	T	6-9	260	12-19-59	Notre Dame	D5
Purifoy, Bill	DE	6-7	249	11-15-59	Tulsa	D7
Robinson, Kelly	LB	6-3	224	2-12-60	Colgate	FA
Rohrer, Jeff	LB	6-3	224	12-25-58	Yale	D2
Sanford, Mark	FB	6-1	213	11-12-58	Virginia	FA
Setterlund, Scott (1)	DT	6-5	249	12-18-58	Oregon	FA
Spears, Ron (1)	DE	6-6	252	11-23-59	San Diego State	*FA ('81)
Skelton, Lance	LB	6-0	197	9-22-60	Georgia Tech	FA
Smerek, Don (1)	DT	6-7	256	12-20-57	Nevada-Reno	*FA ('81)
Smith, Gilbert	WR	5-10	173	1- 3-60	Texas-Arlington	FA
Strandberg, Al	DB	6-2	208	11-30-57	Moorhead (Minnesota)	FA
Striegel, Tom	P	6-0	191	11-16-59	Southern Illinois	FA
Sullivan, Dwight	FB	6-0	205	4-24-59	North Carolina State	D8b
Sweitzer, Ken	QB	6-2	190	6-13-60	Connecticut	FA
Thompson, George	TE	6-3	209	3-12-59	Albany State (Georgia)	D11a
Tucker, Darryl	RB	5-9	175	1-20-60	Central Michigan	FA
Vann, Roger	RB	6-0	187	5- 9-59	Wisconsin-Eau Claire	FA
Vega, Sergio	P	5-8	168	2-19-59	Arizona	FA
Whiting, Mike	FB	6-1	210	1-11-60	Florida State	D11b
Wilkerson, Lewis	DB	6-1	188	10-30-60	Florida A&M	FA
Williams, Donnie	RB	5-10	198	9-27-59	Southwest Texas	FA
Williams, Kendall	DB	5-9	186	2- 7-59	Arizona State	FA
Woods, Rodney	TE	6-4	230	5-15-59	Wichita State	FA
Wright, Brad (1)	QB	6-2	209	5-15-59	New Mexico	FA
Wright, Eddie	RB	6-0	196	1-15-58	Houston	FA
Wysocki, Charlie	RB	5-10	212	12- 7-59	Maryland	FA

*Smerek played 2 games with Cowboys in 1981; Spears missed 1981 season due to injury.

DENVER BRONCOS
(Western Division, American Conference)

Dan Reeves

Chairman, Board of Directors—Edgar F. Kaiser, Jr.

General Manager—Grady Alderman

Director of Player Personnel—John Beake

Head Coach—Dan Reeves (1 year: 10-6)

Assistant Coaches:
Special Assistant—Marvin Bass
Assistant Head Coach-Defense—Joe Collier
Receivers—Rod Dowhower
Offensive Line—Jerry Frei
Defensive Line—Stan Jones
Defensive Backs—Richie McCabe
Running Backs—Nick Nicolau
Tight Ends and Special Teams—Fran Polsfoot
Linebackers—Bob Zeman

Director of Public Relations—Charlie Lee
(Office Phone: 623-8778—Area Code 303)

Offices—5700 Logan St., Denver, Colo. 80216

Stadium—Mile High Stadium (Capacity: 75,123)

Team Colors—Orange, Blue and White

Training Site—University of Northern Colorado, Greeley, Colo.

1982 SCHEDULE
(All times local. All games Sunday unless noted otherwise.)

Sept. 12	SAN DIEGO	2:00
Sept. 19	SAN FRANCISCO	2:00
Sept. 26	at New Orleans	12:00
Oct. 3	PITTSBURGH	2:00
Oct. 10	at New York Jets	4:00
Oct. 17	at Houston	12:00
Oct. 24	OAKLAND	2:00
Oct. 31	BUFFALO	2:00
Nov. 7	at Seattle	1:00
Nov. 14	at Kansas City	12:00
Nov. 21	SEATTLE	2:00
Nov. 28	at San Diego	1:00
Dec. 5	ATLANTA	2:00
Dec. 12	at Los Angeles	1:00
Dec. 19	KANSAS CITY	2:00
Dec. 26	at Oakland	1:00

1981 RESULTS—(Won 10, Lost 6)

Broncos		Opp.		Att.
9	Oakland	7	(H)	74,796
10	Seattle	13	(A)	58,513
28	Baltimore	10	(H)	74,802
42	San Diego	24	(H)	74,844
17	Oakland	0	(A)	51,035
27	Detroit	21	(H)	74,816
14	Kansas City	28	(A)	74,672
7	Buffalo	9	(A)	80,020
19	Minnesota	17	(H)	78,834
23	Cleveland (OT)	20	(H)	74,859
24	Tampa Bay	7	(A)	64,518
21	Cincinnati	38	(A)	57,207
17	San Diego	34	(A)	51,533
16	Kansas City	13	(H)	74,744
23	Seattle	13	(H)	74,527
24	Chicago	35	(A)	40,125

1981 GAMES STARTED

16 games: Rubin Carter, Barney Chavous, Larry Evans, Tom Glassic, Randy Gradishar, Tom Jackson, Rulon Jones, Aaron Kyle, Rick Parros, Dave Studdard, Bob Swenson, Bill Thompson.

15 games: Paul Howard, Craig Morton, Riley Odoms.

14 games: Bill Bryan, Dave Preston.

13 games: Steve Foley, Claudie Minor, Steve Watson.

10 games: Rick Upchurch.

Less than 10 games: Kelvin Clark (4), Steve DeBerg (1), Ron Egloff (6), Mike Harden (3), Glenn Hyde (2), Ken Lanier (1), Haven Moses (6), Dennis Smith (4), Perry Smith (4), Louis Wright (8).

DENVER BRONCOS 1982 VETERAN ROSTER

No.	Name	Pos.	Ht.	Wt.	NFL Exp.	Birth-date	College	Games in '81	How Acquired
54	†Bishop, Keith	C-G	6-3	260	2	3-10-57	Baylor	*0	D6, '80
77	Boyd, Greg	DE	6-6	280	5	9-15-53	San Diego State	15	FA, '80
64	Bryan, Bill	C	6-2	244	6	6-21-55	Duke	14	D4, '77
58	Busick, Steve	LB	6-4	227	2	12-10-58	Southern California	16	D7, '81
35	Canada, Larry	RB	6-2	226	4	12-16-54	Wisconsin	16	OFA, '77
68	†Carter, Rubin	DT	6-0	253	8	12-12-52	Miami	16	D5b, '75
79	†Chavous, Barney	DE	6-3	245	10	3-22-51	South Carolina State	16	D2, '73
73	Clark, Kelvin	T	6-3	245	4	1-30-56	Nebraska	16	D1, '79
17	DeBerg, Steve	QB	6-2	205	6	1-19-54	San Jose State	14	T-SF, '81
85	Egloff, Ron	TE	6-5	227	6	10- 3-55	Wisconsin	16	OFA, '77
56	†Evans, Larry	LB	6-2	220	7	7-11-53	Mississippi College	16	D14, '76
43	Foley, Steve	S	6-2	190	7	11-11-53	Tulane	16	D8, '75
62	Glassic, Tom	G	6-3	250	7	4-17-54	Virginia	16	D1, '76
53	Gradishar, Randy	LB	6-2	231	9	3- 3-52	Ohio State	16	D1, '74
31	Harden, Mike	S	6-1	190	3	2-16-58	Michigan	16	D5a, '80
10	Herrmann, Mark	QB	6-4	184	2	1- 8-59	Purdue	*0	D4, '81
60	†Howard, Paul	G	6-3	260	9	9-12-50	Brigham Young	16	D3a, '73
65	Hyde, Glenn	C-G	6-3	252	7	3-14-51	Pittsburgh	16	FA, '76
	Jackson, Robert	LB	6-1	230	5	8- 7-54	Texas A&M	14	T-Cle, '82
57	†Jackson, Tom	LB	5-11	228	10	4- 4-51	Louisville	16	D4, '73
75	Jones, Rulon	DE	6-6	260	3	3-25-58	Utah State	16	D2, '80
22	†Kyle, Aaron	CB	5-11	185	7	4- 6-54	Wyoming	16	FA, '80
76	Lanier, Ken	T	6-3	269	2	7- 8-59	Florida State	8	D5, '81
72	Latimer, Don	DT	6-2	253	5	3- 1-55	Miami	16	D1, '78
41	Lytle, Rob	RB	5-11	195	6	11-12-54	Michigan	16	D2, '77
83	Manning, Wade	WR	5-11	190	3	7-25-55	Ohio State	16	T-Buf, '81
66	Manor, Brison	DE	6-4	248	6	8-10-52	Arkansas	16	FA, '76
59	Merrill, Mark	LB	6-4	240	4	5- 5-55	Minnesota	15	FA, '81
71	Minor, Claudie	T	6-4	275	9	4-21-51	San Diego State	13	D3, '74
	Mitchell, Mack	DE	6-8	245	6	8-16-52	Houston	*0	FA, '82
7	Morton, Craig	QB	6-4	211	18	2- 5-43	California	15	T-NYG, '77
88	Odoms, Riley	TE	6-4	235	11	3- 1-50	Houston	15	D1, '72
24	Parros, Rick	RB	5-11	200	2	6-14-58	Utah State	16	D4, '80
	Poole, Nathan	RB	5-8	205	3	12-17-56	Louisville	*0	FA, '82
46	Preston, Dave	RB	5-10	195	5	5-29-55	Bowling Green	16	FA, '78
11	Prestridge, Luke	P	6-4	235	4	9-17-56	Baylor	16	D7, '79
32	Reed, Tony	RB	5-10	197	6	3-30-55	Colorado	15	T-KC, '81
	Robinson, Jimmy	WR	5-9	170	6	1- 3-53	Georgia Tech	*0	FA, '81
50	Ryan, Jim	LB	6-1	212	4	5-18-57	William & Mary	16	OFA, '79
49	Smith, Dennis	S	6-3	200	2	2 -3-59	Southern California	16	D1, '81
45	Smith, Perry	CB	6-1	190	10	3-29-52	Colorado State	12	T-St.L, '80
39	Solomon, Roland	CB	6-0	189	3	2- 6-56	Utah	4	FA, '81
19	†Steinfort, Fred	PK	5-11	180	7	11- 3-52	Boston College	16	FA, '79
70	Studdard, Dave	T	6-4	255	4	11-22-55	Texas	16	FA, '79
51	†Swenson, Bob	LB	6-3	225	7	7- 1-53	California	16	OFA, '75
36	†Thompson, Billy	S	6-1	197	14	10-10-46	Maryland State	16	D3, '69
37	Trimble, Steve	CB	5-10	181	2	5-11-58	Maryland	3	OFA, '81
80	Upchurch, Rick	WR	5-10	176	8	5-20-52	Minnesota	13	D4b, '75
81	Watson, Steve	WR	6-4	192	4	5-28-57	Temple	16	OFA, '79
87	Wright, Jim	TE	6-3	240	4	9- 1-56	Texas Christian	16	FA, '80
20	†Wright, Louis	CB	6-2	200	8	1-31-53	San Jose State	8	D1, '75

* Bishop and Robinson missed '81 season due to injury; Herrmann active for 16 games but did not play; Mitchell last active with Cincinnati in 1979; Poole last active in NFL with Cincinnati in 1980, played 1 game with Toronto-CFL in 1981.

†Option playout; subject to developments.

D—Draft; T—Trade; W—Waivers; FA—Free Agent; OFA—Original Free Agent; VFA—Veteran Free Agent; VA—Veteran Allocation; SupD—Supplemental Draft.

Retired: WR Haven Moses (16 games played in 1981).

1982 DRAFT CHOICES

(Number following name designates order of selection among 334 players drafted.)

Round and Player	Position		College
1. Choice to Buffalo (a)			
WILLHITE, Gerald from Buffalo (a)	21	RB	San Jose State

2. McDANIEL, Orlando	50	WR	Louisiana State	
3. Choice to Houston through Los Angeles (b)				
4. Choice to Kansas City (c)				
PLATER, Dan from Buffalo (a)	106	WR	Brigham Young	
5. WINDER, Sammy	131	RB	Southern Miss.	
6. Choice to Cleveland (d)				
7. RUBEN, Alvin	189	DE	Houston	
8. Choice to Dallas through Buffalo (e)				
9. UECKER, Keith	243	T	Auburn	
10. WOODARD, Ken	274	LB	Tuskegee	
11. YATSKO, Stuart	300	G	Oregon	
12. CLARK, Brian	327	G	Clemson	

(a) Switched first-round positions and acquired fourth-round pick, April 27, 1982.

(b) Traded pick to Los Angeles for running back Lawrence McCutcheon, April 15, 1980; Los Angeles traded pick, second-round pick and tight end Lewis Gilbert to Houston for tight end Mike Barber and third- and eighth-round picks, April 27, 1982.

(c) Traded pick and third-round pick in 1981 for running back Tony Reed, April 28, 1981.

(d) Traded pick for linebacker Robert Jackson, April 27, 1982.

(e) Traded pick to Buffalo for wide receiver Wade Manning, August 24, 1981; Buffalo traded pick to Dallas for Manning, August 18, 1981.

1982 ROOKIE AND FIRST-YEAR ROSTER

(1) Indicates player in previous NFL camp. (2) Indicates player with CFL experience. All others classified as rookies.

Name	Pos.	Hgt.	Wgt.	Birth-date	College	How Acquired
Allen, Chuck (1)	DE	6-3	265	5-27-59	South Carolina	FA
Armbrust, Ken	T	6-5	260	12-23-58	Arkansas State	FA
Arnold, Anthony (1)	WR	5-11	176	12-18-58	Georgia	*FA ('81)
Barbour, David	TE	6-4	215	1-27-59	Hawaii	FA
Blackburn, Ed	TE	6-5	217	11-10-59	Wayne State	FA
Blanshan, Alan (1)	T	6-5	270	11- 3-57	Minnesota	FA
Boucher, Scott	T-G	6-3	250	9-15-58	Northeast Louisiana	FA
Brady, Mark	S	6-0	185	3-26-59	Brigham Young	FA
Brady, Steve	CB-S	6-0	185	3-26-59	Brigham Young	FA
Brannon, Tom	G	6-3	245	5-22-59	Florida State	FA
Braswell, Matt (1)	C-G	6-2	255	6- 6-58	Georgia	*FA ('81)
Bresolin, Andy	G	6-2	260	12-18-59	Washington	FA
Brown, Clay (1)	TE	6-2	223	9-20-58	Brigham Young	*D2 ('81)
Brown, Kelby	C-G	6-4	257	7-27-60	Northwestern	FA
Byrom, Bruce (1)	C-G	6-4	250	6-21-59	Maryland	FA
Clark, Brian	G	6-6	260	9-22-60	Clemson	D12
Clark, Terry	TE	6-4	235	5-27-60	Furman	FA
Coleman, Drew	LB	6-1	226	1-30-60	Vanderbilt	FA
Comeaux, Darren	LB	6-1	227	4-15-60	Arizona State	FA
Compton, Jerry (2)	WR	6-0	185	5-31-58	E. Central Oklahoma State	FA
Cotton, Ricky	WR	6-1	182	6-28-57	Alabama State	FA
Coursey, Jarvis	LB	6-4	225	11- 1-59	Florida State	FA
Davis, Mike	S	6-0	205	12-18-59	Wyoming	FA
Davis, Tom (1)	C-G	6-2	245	7-31-55	Nebraska	*FA ('80)
Delegato, Mike	C	6-4	260	4- 9-59	Oregon	FA
Duncan, Alan (1)	K	5-11	190	11-13-58	Tennessee	FA
Eliasara, Matt	NT	6-3	250	9-25-59	Washington State	FA
Elston, Terry (1)	WR	6-4	208	6- 5-58	Houston	FA
Ferguson, Eric	LB	6-2	238	8-17-60	Southern Methodist	FA
Ferraro, Joe	NT	6-4	250	5-23-60	Boston College	FA
Foster, Carl	WR	6-2	202	2-28-60	New Mexico	FA
Garza, Rich (1)	G	6-1	260	3-27-58	Temple	FA

Name	Pos.	Hgt.	Wgt.	Birth-date	College	How Acquired
Geathers, Eddie (1)	CB	6-1	182	12- 9-58	Clemson	FA
Gerken, Greg (1)	LB	6-5	228	4-30-59	Northern Arizona	FA
Gilbow, Paul	T	6-4	260	10-30-58	Arkansas State	FA
Gooden, Bennie	RB	6-1	190	11- 7-59	Cal Poly-Pomona	FA
Gortz, Steve (1)	P	6-2	205	5-23-56	Nevada-Las Vegas	FA
Hale, Ron (1)	T	6-6	300	12-20-57	Vanderbilt	FA
Hall, Tom	LB	6-4	215	3-22-59	Stanford	FA
Harris, Larry (1)	WR	6-2	195	5- 8-59	Stanford	FA
Harris, Steve (1)	DB	6-2	200	8- 6-58	North Alabama	FA
Hobbs, Chris	RB	5-10	191	6-27-60	Miami	FA
Hooper, Max	T	6-4	265	5-18-59	San Jose State	FA
Jackson, Roger	CB	6-0	186	2-28-59	Macon	FA
Jones, Arrington (1)	RB	6-1	225	2-16-59	Richmond	*FA
Karlis, Rick (1)	K	6-0	180	5-23-59	Salem, Ohio	FA
Keller, Elvin	NT	6-2	255	11- 8-59	West Texas State	FA
Koegel, Tim	QB	6-4	205	10-28-58	Notre Dame	FA
Krout, Bart	TE	6-3	235	10-20-59	Alabama	FA
Lane, Bill	DT-G	6-2	250	2- 5-57	South Carolina	FA
Lindblad, Rick	RB	5-9	226	6- 6-59	Puget Sound	FA
Lisowski, Bob (1)	TE	6-3	235	8-21-58	St. Bonaventure	FA
Lopes, Merv	WR	6-0	175	10- 1-58	Hawaii	FA
Lundy, Nate (1)	WR	6-1	175	10-15-58	Indiana	FA
Marsh, Ron	G	6-1	245	9-14-60	Minot State	FA
McAndrews, Jim	T	6-5	260	1-28-59	Syracuse	FA
McDaniel, Orlando	WR	6-0	180	12- 1-60	Louisiana State	D2
McKay, Mark	G	6-3	250	2-15-59	Washington State	FA
McMillin, Troy	G	6-3	255	1-19-59	Illinois	FA
Mihaly, Serge	NT	6-4	250	3-30-60	Yale	FA
Miller, Jim	C	6-3	255	11-30-59	Louisville	FA
Miller, Kelly	S	6-2	190	12-10-58	Idaho	FA
Noonan, John (1)	WR	6-1	192	12-11-58	Nebraska	FA
Overly, Bobby	LB	6-0	220	7- 9-59	San Jose State	FA
Plater, Dan	WR	6-1	182	7-22-60	Brigham Young	D4
Pressley, Keith	DE-DT	6-4	260	6- 9-60	Texas-Arlington	FA
Price, Rick	T	6-6	270	4-15-59	Oregon	FA
Quinn, John	QB	6-0	185	2-10-59	Iowa State	FA
Ramsey, Guy	S	6-2	185	7-22-58	Delaware	FA
Ray, Al	RB	6-0	190	3-22-60	Rutgers	FA
Robertson, Adrian	NT	6-4	255	3-21-59	Elon	FA
Robinson, Rex (1)	K	5-11	210	3-17-59	Georgia	FA
Ruben, Alvin	DE	6-4	245	9-20-58	Houston	D7
Sax, Scott	T	6-8	260	6-17-59	Montana State	FA
Sellers, Davy	QB	6-3	205	12-28-58	Southern Mississippi	FA
Skutack, Dan	LB	6-2	210	8-13-59	Auburn	FA
Smith, Bill	LB	6-4	230	9-28-59	Clemson	FA
Smith, Mike (1)	P	5-11	195	12-22-57	Wyoming	FA
Stamp, Steve	QB	6-0	200	11- 4-59	Texas Christian	FA
Stanton, Stan	DL	6-4	270	5- 7-60	Newberry College	FA
Stephenson, Bob	TE	6-3	235	9-20-59	Indiana	FA
Stewart, David	T	6-6	240	7-30-59	Miami	FA
Suydam, Ryck	NT	6-3	265	7- 2-60	Maine	FA
Tarver, Marcus	LB	6-0	220	4-23-60	Hawaii	FA
Thomas, Anthony	CB	5-9	175	2- 2-60	New Mexico State	FA
Thompson, Emmuel	S	5-11	180	11-15-59	Texas A&I	FA
Trusty, Ron	T-G	6-4	250	7-13-59	Arkansas	FA
Turner, Calvin	NT	6-4	263	4-10-60	West Virginia	FA
Uecker, Keith	G	6-5	260	6-20-60	Auburn	D9
Vernon, Skip (1)	K	5-10	175	10-12-56	New Mexico State	FA
Walden, Rod	NT	6-6	270	4- 8-54	Indiana	FA
White, Vic	G	6-4	260	8-25-60	Texas Tech	FA
Whitlock, Ormando	S	5-11	190	2-14-60	Southeast Louisiana	FA
Whittingham, Kyle	LB	6-0	232	11-21-59	Brigham Young	FA
Willhite, Gerald	RB	5-10	200	5-30-59	San Jose State	D1
Wilson, Steve	T	6-4	252	8- 9-60	Texas Christian	FA
Winder, Sammy	RB	5-11	203	7-15-59	Southern Mississippi	D5
Woodard, Ken	LB	6-1	218	1-22-60	Tuskegee Institute	D10
Yatsko, Stu	G	6-4	250	3-30-59	Oregon	D11
Young, Emanuel	S	5-10	180	2-28-60	No. Alabama	FA

*Arnold, Braswell and C. Brown missed 1981 season due to injury; T. Davis missed 1980 and '81 seasons due to injury; Jones played 1 game with San Francisco in 1981.

DETROIT LIONS
(Central Division, National Conference)

Monte Clark

Owner & President—William Clay Ford

Executive Vice-President and General Manager—J. Russell Thomas

Director of Player Personnel—Tim Rooney

Head Coach and Director of Football Operations—Monte Clark (5 years: 34-44-0)

Assistant Coaches:
Defensive Coordinator-Linebackers—Maxie Baughan
Offensive Backfield—John Brunner
Special Assignments—Don Doll
Offensive Line—Fred Hoaglin
Defensive Line—Ed Khayat
Special Teams—Joe Madden
Offensive Coordinator-Quarterbacks—Ted Marchibroda
Defensive Backfield—Mel Phillips
Receivers—Larry Seiple
Strength and Conditioning—Gary Wade

Public Relations Director—Don Kremer
(Office Phone: 335-4131—Area Code 313)

Offices—1200 Featherstone Road, Box 4200, Pontiac, Mich. 48057

Stadium—Pontiac Silverdome (Capacity: 80,638)

Team Colors—Honolulu Blue and Silver

Training Site—Oakland University, Rochester, Mich.

1982 SCHEDULE
(All times local.
All games Sunday unless noted otherwise.)

Sept. 12	CHICAGO	1:00
Sept. 19	at Los Angeles	1:00
Sept. 26	TAMPA BAY	1:00
Oct. 3	BALTIMORE	1:00
Oct. 10	at Miami	4:00
Oct. 17	ATLANTA	1:00
Oct. 24	at Buffalo	1:00
Nov. 1	at Minnesota (Mon.)	8:00
Nov. 7	at Philadelphia	1:00
Nov. 14	GREEN BAY	1:00
Nov. 21	at Chicago	12:00
Nov. 25	N.Y. GIANTS (Thanksgiving)	12:30
Dec. 6	NEW YORK JETS (Mon.)	9:00
Dec. 12	at Green Bay	12:00
Dec. 19	MINNESOTA	1:00
Dec. 26	at Tampa Bay	1:00

1981 RESULTS—(Won 8, Lost 8)

Lions		Opp.		Att.
24	San Francisco	17	(H)	62,123
23	San Diego	28	(A)	51,624
24	Minnesota	26	(A)	45,350
16	Oakland	0	(H)	77,919
10	Tampa Bay	28	(A)	71,733
21	Denver	27	(A)	74,816
48	Chicago	17	(H)	71,274
31	Green Bay	27	(H)	76,063
13	Los Angeles	20	(A)	61,814
31	Washington	33	(A)	52,096
27	Dallas	24	(H)	79,694
23	Chicago	7	(A)	50,820
27	Kansas City	10	(H)	76,735
17	Green Bay	31	(A)	54,481
45	Minnesota	7	(H)	79,428
17	Tampa Bay	20	(H)	80,444

1981 GAMES STARTED

16 games: Karl Baldischwiler, Russ Bolinger, Garry Cobb, Keith Dorney, Homer Elias, Doug English, Ken Fantetti, Amos Fowler, Ray Oldham, Wayne Smith, Leonard Thompson, Stan White.

15 games: Jimmy Allen, Dexter Bussey, David Hill, Dave Pureifory, Freddie Scott.

14 games: William Gay, Billy Sims.

12 games: James Hunter.

11 games: Al Baker.

10 games: Eric Hipple.

Less than 10 games: Gary Danielson (4), Joe Ehrmann (2), Steve Furness (2), Hector Gray (4), Curtis Green (4), Rick Kane (2), Jeff Komlo (2), Ulysses Norris (2), Vince Thompson (1).

DETROIT LIONS 1982 VETERAN ROSTER

No.	Name	Pos.	Ht.	Wt.	NFL Exp.	Birth-date	College	Games in '81	How Acquired
40	Allen, Jimmy	S	6-2	194	9	3- 6-52	UCLA	15	T-Pit, '78
60	Baker, Al	DE	6-6	250	5	12- 9-56	Colorado State	11	D2, '78
76	Baldischwiler, Karl	T	6-5	265	5	1-19-56	Oklahoma	16	T-Mia, '78
73	Bolinger, Russ	G	6-5	255	6	9-10-54	Long Beach State	16	D3a, '76
24	Bussey, Dexter	FB	6-1	210	9	3-11-52	Texas-Arlington	16	D3, '74
31	Callicutt, Ken	RB	6-0	190	5	8-20-55	Clemson	16	OFA, '78
53	Cobb, Garry	LB	6-2	220	4	3-16-57	Southern California	16	FA, '79
77	Culp, Curley	DT	6-1	265	14	10-10-46	Arizona State	2	FA, '80
16	†Danielson, Gary	QB	6-2	195	6	9-10-51	Purdue	6	FA, '76
72	Dieterich, Chris	T	6-3	269	3	7-27-58	North Carolina State	7	D6, '80
70	Dorney, Keith	T	6-5	265	4	12- 3-57	Penn State	16	D1, '79
74	†Ehrmann, Joe	DT	6-3	250	10	3-29-49	Syracuse	4	FA, '81
61	Elias, Homer	G	6-3	255	5	5- 1-55	Tennessee State	16	D4b, '78
78	English, Doug	DT	6-5	255	6	8-25-53	Texas	16	D2, '75
57	Fantetti, Ken	LB	6-2	230	4	4- 7-57	Wyoming	16	D2, '79
65	Fowler, Amos	C	6-3	250	5	2-11-56	Southern Mississippi	16	D5a, '78
71	†Furness, Steve	DT	6-4	248	11	12- 5-50	Rhode Island	9	FA, '81
79	Gay, William	DL	6-3	250	5	5-28-58	Southern California	16	T-Den, '78
66	Ginn, Tommie	G	6-3	255	3	1-25-58	Arkansas	12	D5b, '80
26	Gray, Hector	CB	6-1	197	2	1- 2-57	Florida State	16	FA, '81
62	Green, Curtis	DL	6-3	256	2	6- 3-57	Alabama State	14	D2, '81
35	Hall, Alvin	CB	5-10	193	2	8-12-58	Miami, Ohio	16	FA, '81
51	Harrell, James	LB	6-2	215	4	7-19-57	Florida	16	W-Den, '79
81	Hill, David	TE	6-2	230	7	1- 1-54	Texas A&I	15	D2b, '76
17	Hipple, Eric	QB	6-1	196	3	9-16-57	Utah State	16	D4, '80
28	Hunter, James	CB	6-2	195	7	3- 8-54	Grambling	12	D1a, '76
32	Kane, Rick	RB	6-0	200	6	11-12-54	San Jose State	16	D3, '77
25	King, Horace	FB	5-10	210	8	3- 5-53	Georgia	16	D6b, '75
19	Komlo, Jeff	QB	6-2	200	4	7-30-56	Delaware	3	D9, '79
64	Lee, Larry	G-C	6-2	274	2	9-10-59	UCLA	16	D5, '81
83	Martin, Robbie	WR	5-8	179	2	12- 3-58	Cal Poly-SLO	16	W-Pit, '81
3	Murray, Ed	PK	5-9	164	3	8-29-56	Tulane	16	D7, '80
86	Nichols, Mark	WR	6-2	213	2	10-29-59	San Jose State	12	D1, '81
80	Norris, Ulysses	TE	6-4	230	4	1-15-57	Georgia	12	D4a, '79
23	Oldham, Ray	S	5-11	192	10	2-23-51	Middle Tennessee	16	W-NYG, '80
89	Porter, Tracy	WR	6-1	196	2	6- 1-59	Louisiana State	12	D4, '81
75	Pureifory, Dave	DE	6-1	255	11	7-12-49	Eastern Michigan	15	FA, '78
87	Scott, Fred	WR	6-2	175	9	8- 5-52	Amherst	16	T-Bal, '78
20	Sims, Billy	RB	6-0	212	3	9-18-55	Oklahoma	14	D1, '80
1	Skladany, Tom	P	6-0	195	4	6-29-55	Ohio State	16	T-Cle, '78
44	Smith, Wayne	CB	6-0	170	3	5- 9-57	Purdue	16	D11, '80
50	Tautolo, Terry	LB	6-2	235	7	8-30-54	UCLA	*16	FA, '81
84	Thompson, Jesse	WR	6-1	185	3	3-12-56	California	*0	D6c, '78
39	†Thompson, Leonard	WR	5-11	190	8	7-28-52	Oklahoma State	16	D8, '75
38	Thompson, Vince	FB	6-0	230	2	2-21-57	Villanova	13	FA, '81
54	†Towle, Steve	LB	6-2	233	7	10-23-53	Kansas	*0	T-Mia, '81
55	Turnure, Tom	C	6-3	243	3	7- 9-57	Washington	16	D3a, '80
52	White, Stan	LB	6-1	223	11	10-24-49	Ohio State	16	T-Bal, '80
30	Williams, Ray	KR	5-9	173	2	9-22-58	Washington State	*0	D12, '80

* J. Thompson, Towle and Williams missed '81 season due to injury; Tautolo played 5 games with San Francisco, 11 with Detroit in 1981.

†Option playout; subject to developments.

D—Draft; T—Trade; W—Waivers; FA—Free Agent; OFA—Original Free Agent; VFA—Veteran Free Agent; VA—Veteran Allocation; SupD—Supplemental Draft.

Also played with Lions in 1981—S Luther Bradley (16 games), S Jeff Delaney (5), DT Edgar Fields (2), TE Bob Niziolek (4), LB Charlie Weaver (7).

DETROIT LIONS
1982 DRAFT CHOICES

(Number following name designates order of selection among 334 players drafted.)

Round and Player		Position	College
1. WILLIAMS, Jimmy	15	LB	Nebraska
2. WATKINS, Bobby	42	DB	S.W. Texas St.
3. DOIG, Steve	69	LB	New Hampshire
4. McNORTON, Bruce	96	DB	Georgetown, Ky.
5. GRAHAM, William	127	DB	Texas
6. MACHUREK, Mike	154	QB	Idaho State
7. BATES, Phil from Houston (a)	175	RB	Nebraska
Choice to Los Angeles (b)			
SIMMONS, Victor from Buffalo through Los Angeles (c)	187	WR	Oregon State
8. MOSS, Martin	208	DE	UCLA
9. WAGONER, Danny from Oakland through Los Angeles (d)	231	DB	Kansas
Choice to Miami (e)			
10. BARNES, Roosevelt	266	LB	Purdue
11. LEE, Edward	292	WR	So. Carolina St.
12. PORTER, Ricky	319	RB	Slippery Rock
RUBICK, Rob from San Diego (f)	326	TE	Grand Valley St.

(a) Acquired pick for safety Luther Bradley, April 28, 1982.

(b) Traded pick for seventh- and ninth-round picks, April 28, 1982.

(c) Buffalo traded pick to Los Angeles for wide receiver Ron Jessie, July 31, 1980; Los Angeles traded pick to Detroit (See b).

(d) Oakland traded pick to Los Angeles for cornerback Dwayne O'Steen, September 1, 1980; Los Angeles traded pick to Detroit (See b).

(e) Traded pick for linebacker Steve Towle, July 14, 1981.

(f) Acquired pick for defensive tackle John Woodcock, September 15, 1981.

DETROIT LIONS
1982 ROOKIE AND FIRST-YEAR ROSTER

(1) Indicates player in previous NFL camp.
All others classified as rookies.

Name	Pos.	Hgt.	Wgt.	Birth-date	College	How Acquired
Auten, Todd	K	6-0	173	2-26-60	North Carolina State	FA
Barnes, Roosevelt	LB	6-2	215	8- 3-58	Purdue	D10
Bates, Phil	FB	6-1	230	9- 4-58	Nebraska	D7a
Bryson, Mercer	DB	5-11	185	6- 1-58	Northern Michigan	FA
Burney, Jacob	DT	6-0	250	1-24-59	Tennessee-Chattanooga	FA
Doig, Steve	LB	6-3	240	3-28-60	New Hampshire	D3
Essery, Scott	P	6-2	200	6-24-58	Windsor	FA
Grabowski, Mark	DT	6-1	250	5-13-59	Wayne State	FA
Graham, William	S	5-11	188	9-27-59	Texas	D5
Greco, Don (1)	G	6-3	260	4- 1-59	Western Illinois	*D3 ('81)
Hartman, Dennis (1)	RB	6-0	228	2-14-59	Syracuse	*FA ('81)
Hayes, Jay	DE	6-5	231	3- 3-60	Idaho	FA
Houston, Steve	T	6-3	246	3-25-60	Fresno State	FA
Jackson, Willie (1)	CB	5-10	194	10- 9-57	Mississippi State	*D11 ('81)
Jett, DeWayne (1)	WR	6-2	194	2-24-58	Hawaii	*D9 ('80)
Lee, Edward	WR	5-11	185	12- 8-59	South Carolina State	D11
Machurek, Mike	QB	6-0	202	7-22-60	Idaho State	D6
McNorton, Bruce	CB	5-11	172	2-28-59	Georgetown, Ky.	D4
Mitchell, Reggie	RB	5-7	174	9-16-60	Central Michigan	FA
Mitchell, William	RB	6-0	191	11- 9-59	Mars Hill	FA
Moore, Frank	TE	6-3	225	5-30-59	East Texas State	FA
Moss, Martin	DT	6-4	250	12-16-58	UCLA	D8
Olivieri, Gino (1)	RB	6-0	205	5-18-59	Delaware	*FA ('81)
Porter, Rick	RB	5-10	190	1-14-60	Slippery Rock State	D12a
Repko, Jay (1)	TE	6-3	240	6-12-58	Ursinus	FA
Riley, Michael	LB	6-2	220	3- 8-59	Kuztown State	FA
Rubick, Rob	TE	6-2	225	9-27-60	Grand Valley State	D12b
Searcey, Bill (1)	G-T	6-2	265	3- 3-58	Alabama	FA
Simmons, Victor	WR	6-1	198	11- 5-60	Oregon State	D7b
Stinger, Chris	G	6-2	260	6- 7-58	Temple	FA
Szczepaniuk, Jim	LB	6-1	228	1-21-60	Northern Michigan	FA
Wagoner, Dan	DB	5-10	175	12-12-59	Kansas	D9
Wangler, John (1)	QB	6-1	191	6-10-58	Michigan	FA
Watkins, Bobby	DB	5-11	184	5-31-60	Southwest Texas State	D2
Weston, Michael	G	6-1	256	6-16-59	Adrian	FA
White, Darnell (1)	DB	5-11	199	1- 1-59	Angelo State	FA
Williams, Jimmy	LB	6-3	221	11-16-60	Nebraska	D1

Greco, Hartman, Jackson and Olivieri missed 1981 season due to injuries; Jett missed 1980 and '81 seasons due to injury.

GREEN BAY PACKERS
(Central Division, National Conference)

Bart Starr

President—Dominic Olejniczak

Head Coach—Bart Starr (7 years: 39-65-2)

Player Personnel Director—Dick Corrick

Pro Personnel Director—Burt Gustafson

Assistant Coaches:
 Receivers—Lew Carpenter
 Secondary—Ross Fichtner
 Quarterbacks-Offensive Backs—Pete Kettela
 Linebackers—John Marshall
 Offensive Line—Ernie McMillan
 Defensive Coordinator—John Meyer
 Offensive Line—Bill Meyers
 Special Teams—Dick Rehbein
 Offensive Coordinator—Bob Schnelker
 Defensive Line—Richard Urich

Public Relations Director—Lee Remmel
 (Office Phone: 494-2351—Area Code 414)

Offices—1265 Lombardi Ave., Green Bay, Wisc. 54303

Stadium—Lambeau Field, Green Bay (Capacity: 56,267); County Stadium, Milwaukee (Capacity: 55,958)

Team Colors—Green and Gold

Training Site—St. Norbert College, De Pere, Wisc. (food and lodging only; workouts at Lambeau Field, Green Bay)

1982 SCHEDULE
(All times local.
All games Sunday unless noted otherwise.)

Sept. 12	LOS ANGELES (Milw.)	12:00
Sept. 20	at New York Giants (Mon.)	9:00
Sept. 26	MIAMI	12:00
Oct. 3	PHILADELPHIA (Milw.)	12:00
Oct. 10	at Chicago	12:00
Oct. 17	TAMPA BAY	12:00
Oct. 24	at Minnesota	12:00
Oct. 31	CHICAGO	12:00
Nov. 7	at Tampa Bay	1:00
Nov. 14	at Detroit	1:00
Nov. 21	MINNESOTA (Milw.)	12:00
Nov. 28	at New York Jets	1:00
Dec. 5	BUFFALO (Milw.)	12:00
Dec. 12	DETROIT	12:00
Dec. 19	at Baltimore	2:00
Dec. 26	at Atlanta	1:00

1981 RESULTS—(Won 8, Lost 8)

Packers		Opp.		Att.
16	Chicago	9	(A)	62,411
17	Atlanta	31	(H)	55,382
23	Los Angeles	35	(A)	61,286
13	Minnesota	30	(H)	55,012
27	New York Giants	14	(A)	73,684
10	Tampa Bay	21	(H)	55,264
3	San Francisco	13	(H)	50,171
27	Detroit	31	(A)	76,063
34	Seattle	24	(H)	49,467
26	New York Giants	24	(H)	54,138
21	Chicago	17	(H)	55,338
3	Tampa Bay	37	(A)	63,251
35	Minnesota	23	(A)	46,025
31	Detroit	17	(H)	54,481
35	New Orleans	7	(A)	45,518
3	New York Jets	28	(A)	56,340

1981 GAMES STARTED

16 games: John Anderson, Mike Butler, Paul Coffman, George Cumby, Mike Douglass, Leotis Harris, Maurice Harvey, Terry Jones, Greg Koch, Mark Lee, James Lofton, Larry McCarren, Mike McCoy, Rich Wingo.

15 games: Gerry Ellis, Derrell Gofourth, Casey Merrill.

13 games: Lynn Dickey, John Jefferson.

12 games: Harlan Huckleby, Mark Koncar.

Less than 10 games: Johnnie Gray (9), Tim Huffman (1), Eddie Lee Ivery (1), Jim Jensen (1), Ezra Johnson (1), Gary Lewis (2), Terdell Middleton (2), Mark Murphy (7), Fred Nixon (1), Tim Stokes (3), Arland Thompson (1), Aundra Thompson (2), David Whitehurst (3).

GREEN BAY PACKERS 1982 VETERAN ROSTER

No.	Name	Pos.	Ht.	Wt.	NFL Exp.	Birth-date	College	Games in '81	How Acquired
60	Allerman, Kurt	LB	6-2	222	6	8-30-55	Penn State	16	FA, '80
59	Anderson, John	LB	6-3	221	5	2-14-56	Michigan	16	D1b, '78
61	Ane, Charlie	C	6-1	237	8	8-12-52	Michigan State	16	FA, '81
62	Aydelette, Buddy	T	6-4	250	2	8-19-56	Alabama	*0	D7, '80
73	Braggs, Byron	DT	6-4	290	2	10-10-59	Alabama	16	D5, '81
77	Butler, Mike	DE	6-5	265	6	4- 4-54	Kansas	16	D1a, '77
19	Campbell, Rich	QB	6-4	224	2	12-22-58	California	2	D1, '81
88	Cassidy, Ron	WR	6-0	185	4	7-23-57	Utah State	11	D8a, '79
	Chapman, Clarence	DB	5-10	185	7	12-10-53	Eastern Michigan	*5	FA, '82
82	Coffman, Paul	TE	6-3	218	5	3-29-56	Kansas State	16	OFA, '78
52	Cumby, George	LB	6-0	215	3	7- 5-56	Oklahoma	16	D1b, '80
12	Dickey, Lynn	QB	6-4	220	12	10-19-49	Kansas State	13	T-Hou, '76
53	Douglass, Mike	LB	6-0	224	5	3-15-55	San Diego State	16	D5a, '78
31	Ellis, Gerry	FB	5-11	216	3	11-12-57	Missouri	15	FA, '80
98	Godfrey, Chris	G	6-3	250	2	5-17-58	Michigan	*0	W-NYJ, '81
57	Gofourth, Derrel	G	6-3	260	6	3-20-55	Oklahoma State	15	D7a, '77
24	Gray, Johnnie	S	5-11	185	7	12-18-53	Cal State-Fullerton	9	OFA, '75
69	Harris, Leotis	G	6-1	267	5	6-28-55	Arkansas	16	D6, '78
23	Harvey, Maurice	S	5-10	190	4	1-14-56	Ball State	16	W-Den, '81
38	Hood, Estus	CB	5-11	180	3	11-14-55	Illinois State	16	D3, '78
25	Huckleby, Harlan	RB	6-1	199	3	12-30-57	Michigan	16	FA, '80
74	Huffman, Tim	T	6-5	277	2	8-31-59	Notre Dame	6	D9, '81
	Hunt, Mike	LB	6-2	240	4	10-6-56	Minnesota	*0	D2, '78
40	Ivery, Eddie Lee	RB	6-0	210	3	7-30-57	Georgia Tech	1	D1, '79
83	Jefferson, John	WR	6-1	198	5	2- 3-56	Arizona State	13	T-SD, '81
33	Jensen, Jim	RB	6-3	235	6	11-28-53	Iowa	15	FA, '81
90	Johnson, Ezra	DE	6-4	240	6	10- 2-55	Morris Brown	16	D1b, '77
21	Jolly, Mike	S	6-3	185	2	3-19-58	Michigan	*0	W-NO, '80
63	Jones, Terry	DT	6-2	259	5	11- 8-56	Alabama	16	D11, '78
64	Kitson, Syd	G	6-4	252	2	9-27-58	Wake Forest	11	D3, '80
68	Koch, Greg	T	6-4	265	6	6-14-55	Arkansas	16	D2, '77
79	Koncar, Mark	T	6-5	268	6	5- 5-53	Colorado	14	D1,'76
22	Lee, Mark	CB	5-11	187	3	3-20-58	Washington	16	D2, '80
56	Lewis, Cliff	LB	6-1	226	2	11- 9-59	Southern Mississippi	16	D12, '81
81	Lewis, Gary	TE	6-5	234	2	12-30-58	Texas Arlington	16	D2, '81
	Livers, Virgil	CB	5-8	183	7	3-26-52	Western Kentucky	*0	FA, '81
80	Lofton, James	WR	6-3	187	5	7- 5-56	Stanford	16	D1a, '78
	Manucci, Dan	QB	6-2	194	3	9- 3-57	Kansas State	*0	FA, '82
	Matthews, Ira	RB	5-8	175	4	8-23-57	Wisconsin	*5	FA, '82
54	McCarren, Larry	C	6-3	238	10	11- 9-51	Illinois	16	D12, '73
29	McCoy, Mike	CB	5-11	183	7	8-16-53	Colorado	16	D3, '76
78	Merrill, Casey	DE	6-4	255	4	7-16-57	California-Davis	16	FA, '79
34	Middleton, Terdell	RB	6-0	195	6	4- 8-55	Memphis State	12	D3, '77
37	Murphy, Mark	S	6-2	199	2	4-22-58	West Liberty State	16	OFA, '80
84	Nixon, Fred	WR	5-11	191	3	9-22-58	Oklahoma	8	D4, '80
72	Oates, Brad	T	6-6	275	4	9-30-53	Brigham Young	*5	FA, '81
51	Prather, Guy	LB	6-2	230	2	3-28-58	Grambling	16	FA, '81
58	Rudzinski, Paul	LB	6-1	220	4	7-28-56	Michigan State	*0	OFA, '78
55	Scott, Randy	LB	6-1	220	2	1-31-59	Alabama	16	OFA, '81
16	Stachowicz, Ray	P	5-11	185	2	3- 6-59	Michigan State	16	D3, '81
10	Stenerud, Jan	PK	6-2	190	16	11-26-43	Montana State	16	FA, '80
76	Stokes, Tim	T	6-5	252	9	3-16-50	Oregon	*10	T-Was, '78
67	Swanke, Karl	T-C	6-6	251	3	12-29-57	Boston College	4	D6, '80
71	Thompson, Arland	G	6-4	265	2	9-19-57	Baylor	10	FA, '81
87	Thompson, John	TE	6-3	228	3	1-18-57	Utah State	2	D9, '79
26	Torkelson, Eric	RB	6-2	210	9	3- 3-52	Connecticut	9	D11, '74
75	Turner, Rich	DT	6-2	260	2	2-14-59	Oklahoma	16	D4, '81
30	Whitaker, Bill	S	6-0	182	2	11-18-59	Missouri	16	D7, '81
17	Whitehurst, David	QB	6-2	204	6	4-27-55	Furman	8	D8, '77
60	Wingo, Rich	LB	6-1	230	4	7-16-56	Alabama	16	D7b, '79

*Chapman played 5 games with Cincinnati in 1981; Livers last active with Chicago in 1979; Aydelette, Godfrey, Jolly and Rudzinski missed the '81 season due to injuries; Hunt retired prior to 1981 season due to injury; Manucci last active in NFL with Buffalo in 1980, played six games with Toronto-CFL in 1981; Matthews played 5 games with Oakland in 1981; Oates played 5 games with Cincinnati and was active for 1 game with Green Bay in 1981; Stokes played 3 games with N.Y. Giants, 7 with Green Bay in 1981.

†Option playout; subject to developments.

D—Draft; T—Trade; W—Waivers; FA—Free Agent; OFA—Original Free Agent; VFA—Veteran

Free Agent; VA—Veteran Allocation; SupD—Supplemental Draft.
    Also played with Packers in 1981—RB Steve Atkins (3 games), S David Petway (5), WR Aundra Thompson (3), RB Delvin Williams (1).

GREEN BAY PACKERS
1982 DRAFT CHOICES

(Number following name designates order of selection among 334 players drafted.)

Round and Player		Position	College
1. Choice to New Orleans through San Diego (a)			
HALLSTROM, Ron	22	G	Iowa
from San Diego (b)			
2. Choice to New England through San Diego (c)			
3. RODGERS, Del	71	RB	Utah
4. BROWN, Robert	98	LB	Virginia Tech
5. MEADE, Mike	126	RB	Penn State
6. PARLAVECCHIO, Chet	152	LB	Penn State
7. WHITLEY, Joey	183	DB	Texas-El Paso
8. BOYD, Thomas	210	LB	Alabama
9. RIGGINS, Charles	237	DE	Bethune-Cook.
10. GARCIA, Eddie	264	K	SMU
11. MACAULAY, John	294	C	Stanford
12. EPPS, Phillip	321	WR	Texas Christian

(a) Traded pick to San Diego in first-round switch along with second-round picks in 1982 and 1984, first-round pick in 1983 and wide receiver Aundra Thompson for wide receiver John Jefferson, September 17, 1981; San Diego traded pick, third-round pick and Thompson to New Orleans for wide receiver Wes Chandler, September 29, 1981.

(b) See (a).

(c) Green Bay traded pick to San Diego (See a); San Diego traded pick and third-round pick in 1983 to New England for safety Tim Fox, April 27, 1982.

GREEN BAY PACKERS
1982 ROOKIE AND FIRST-YEAR ROSTER

(1) Indicates player in previous NFL camp.
(2) Indicates player with CFL experience.
All others classified as rookies.

Name	Pos.	Hgt.	Wgt.	Birth-date	College	How Acquired
Boyd, Thomas......................	LB	6-2	210	11-24-59	Alabama	D8
Brown, Robert......................	LB	6-2	238	5-21-60	Virginia Tech	D4
Buggs, Wamon	WR	6-2	200	2- 4-60	Vanderbilt	FA
Cathey, James (1)	T	6-4	260	12-31-58	Tulane	FA
Christian, Marvin (1)........	FB	6-0	222	1-18-58	Tulane	FA
Davidson, James (1)	LB	6-4	247	4-20-57	Kansas State	FA
DeLoach, Ralph (1)	DE	6-5	255	1-13-57	California	FA
Driscoll, Phillip (1)	DE	6-4	250	8-21-57	Mankato State	FA
Epps, Phillip	WR	5-10	165	11-11-58	Texas Christian	D12
Frageorgia, David (1).......	WR-KR	6-0	192	12-19-57	Rhode Island	FA
Freeman, Britt.....................	WR	5-11	192	1- 8-59	Montana State	FA
Garcia, Eddie	K	5-8	188	4-15-59	Southern Methodist	D10
Hafner, Kerry......................	TE	6-1	228	10-11-58	Wisconsin-Stout	FA
Hall, Nickie (1)...................	QB	6-4	205	8- 1-59	Tulane	*D10 ('81)
Hallstrom, Ron....................	G	6-6	286	6-11-59	Iowa	D1
Macaulay, John...................	C	6-3	254	4-27-59	Stanford	D11
Meade, Mike	FB	5-10	228	2-12-60	Penn State	D5
Parlavecchio, Chet	LB	6-2	225	2-14-60	Penn State	D6
Pfohl, Lawrence (2)..........	G	6-3	270	6- 2-58	Miami	FA
Pittard, Robert (1)	P	6-3	195	12-20-56	McMurray	FA
Reaves, Willard (1)...........	RB	5-11	198	8-17-59	Northern Arizona	*FA ('81)
Riggins, Charlie.................	DE	6-3	245	11- 9-59	Bethune-Cookman	D9
Rodgers, Del	RB	5-10	197	6-22-60	Utah	D3
Rubens, Larry	C	6-1	253	1-25-59	Montana State	FA
Sible, Scott..........................	WR	5-10	184	10-25-58	North Michigan State	FA
Speelman, Brian (1)..........	K	5-11	185	3-18-57	Capital University	FA
Vitale, Tony	G	6-3	262	9- 2-59	Central Michigan	FA
Valley, George...................	DT	6-2	261	8- 7-60	VMI	FA
Ware, Reggie (1)................	S	6-1	195	6-21-58	Arizona	FA

*Hall and Reaves missed 1981 season due to injuries.
NOTE: 7th-round pick Joey Whitley failed mini-camp physical and was released.

HOUSTON OILERS
(Central Division, American Conference)

Ed Biles

Owner-President—K. S. (Bud) Adams, Jr.

Executive Vice-President and General Manager—
Ladd K. Herzeg

Assistant General Manager—Mike Holovack

Head Coach—Ed Biles (1 year: 7-9)

Assistant Coaches:
Receivers—Andy Bourgeois
Offensive Line—Ray Callahan
Defensive Backfield—Bob Gambold
Defensive Assistant—Ken Houston
Offensive Backfield—Elijah Pitts
Linebackers—Dick Selcer
Offensive Coordinator—Jim Shofner
Defensive Line—Ralph Staub

Director of Marketing—Rick Nichols

Media Relations Director—Bob Hyde
(Office Phone: 797-1272—Area Code 713)

Office—6910 Fannin, Houston, Tex. 77030

Mailing Address—P. O. Box 1516, Houston, Tex. 77001

Stadium—Astrodome (Capacity: 50,000)

Team Colors—Scarlet, Columbia Blue and White

Training Site—Angelo State University, San Angelo, Tex.

1982 SCHEDULE
(All times local.
All games Sunday unless noted otherwise.)

Sept. 12	at Cincinnati		1:00
Sept. 19	SEATTLE		3:00
Sept. 26	BUFFALO		12:00
Oct. 3	at New York Jets		1:00
Oct. 10	at Kansas City		12:00
Oct. 17	DENVER		12:00
Oct. 24	WASHINGTON		12:00
Oct. 31	at Cleveland		1:00
Nov. 7	at Pittsburgh		1:00
Nov. 14	CINCINNATI		12:00
Nov. 21	PITTSBURGH		12:00
Nov. 28	at New England		1:00
Dec. 5	at New York Giants		1:00
Dec. 13	DALLAS (Mon.)		8:00
Dec. 19	at Philadelphia		1:00
Dec. 26	CLEVELAND		12:00

1981 RESULTS—(Won 7, Lost 9)

Oilers		Opp.		Att.
27	Los Angeles	20	(A)	63,198
9	Cleveland	3	(A)	79,483
10	Miami	16	(H)	47,379
17	New York Jets	33	(A)	50,309
17	Cincinnati	10	(H)	44,350
35	Seattle	17	(H)	42,671
10	New England	38	(A)	60,474
13	Pittsburgh	26	(A)	52,732
21	Cincinnati	34	(A)	54,736
17	Oakland	16	(H)	45,519
10	Kansas City	23	(A)	73,984
24	New Orleans	27	(H)	49,581
27	Atlanta	31	(H)	40,201
17	Cleveland	13	(H)	44,502
6	San Francisco	28	(A)	55,707
21	Pittsburgh	20	(H)	41,056

1981 GAMES STARTED

16 games: Gregg Bingham, Robert Brazile, Ken Burrough, Earl Campbell, Ed Fisher, Leon Gray, Ken Kennard, Vernon Perry, Mike Reinfeldt, Morris Towns, Ted Washington.

15 games: Andy Dorris, John Schuhmacher, Greg Stemrick.

14 games: Elvin Bethea, J.C. Wilson.

13 games: David Carter, Daryl Hunt.

12 games: Mike Renfro, Ken Stabler.

11 games: Dave Casper.

Less than 10 games: Adger Armstrong (2), Jesse Baker (2), Mike Barber (5), Rob Carpenter (4), Carter Hartwig (1), Michael Holston (4), Bill Kay (2), Carl Mauck (4), Gifford Nielsen (2), John Reaves (2), Tim Smith (1), Mike Stensrud (1), Art Stringer (1), Ted Thompson (2), Tim Wilson (9).

HOUSTON OILERS 1982 VETERAN ROSTER

No.	Name	Pos.	Ht.	Wt.	NFL Exp.	Birth-date	College	Games in '81	How Acquired
39	Armstrong, Adger	RB	6-0	222	3	6-21-57	Texas A&M	16	FA, '80
11	Bailey, Harold	WR	6-2	197	2	4- 2-57	Oklahoma State	11	D8, '80
75	Baker, Jesse	DE	6-5	266	4	7-10-57	Jacksonville State	16	D2b, '79
65	Bethea, Elvin	DE	6-2	254	15	3- 1-46	North Carolina A&T	15	D3, '68
54	Bingham, Gregg	LB	6-1	229	10	3-13-51	Purdue	16	D4, '73
	Bradley, Luther	S	6-2	195	5	5- 7-55	Notre Dame	16	T-Det, '82
52	Brazile, Robert	LB	6-4	237	8	2- 7-53	Jackson State	16	D1a, '75
88	Brooks, Billy	WR	6-3	196	6	8-22-53	Oklahoma	*10	W-SD, '81
00	Burrough, Ken	WR	6-3	215	12	7-14-48	Texas Southern	16	T-NO, '71
34	Campbell, Earl	RB	5-11	237	5	3-29-55	Texas	16	D1, '78
58	†Carter, David	G-C	6-2	258	6	11-27-53	Western Kentucky	16	D6b, '77
87	†Casper, Dave	TE	6-4	249	9	2- 2-52	Notre Dame	16	T-Oak, '80
47	Coleman, Ronnie	RB	5-11	203	9	7- 9-51	Alabama A&M	16	OFA, '74
57	Corker, John	LB	6-5	240	3	12-29-58	Oklahoma State	11	D5, '80
66	Davidson, Greg	C	6-2	249	3	4-24-58	North Texas State	16	OFA, '80
69	Dorris, Andy	DE	6-4	262	10	8-11-51	New Mexico State	15	FA, '77
	Evans, Johnny	QB-P	6-2	197	4	2-18-56	North Carolina State	*0	FA, '82
78	Eyre, Nick	T	6-5	276	2	6-16-59	Brigham Young	4	D4, '81
77	Fields, Angelo	T	6-6	319	3	9-14-57	Michigan State	14	D2a, '80
60	Fisher, Ed	G	6-3	260	9	5-31-49	Arizona State	16	W-KC, '74
	Floyd, John	WR	6-1	195	4	9-10-56	Northeast Louisiana	*4	FA, '82
16	Fritsch, Toni	PK	5-7	201	11	7-10-45	No College	16	FA, '77
	Gant, Earl	RB	6-0	207	3	7- 6-57	Missouri	*0	FA, '82
	Gilbert, Lewis	TE	6-4	227	4	5-24-56	Florida	6	T-LA, '82
	Goodspeed, Mark	G	6-5	270	2	12- 1-56	Nebraska	*0	FA, '82
74	†Gray, Leon	T	6-3	258	10	11-15-51	Jackson State	16	T-NE, '79
36	†Hartwig, Carter	CB-S	6-0	205	4	2- 2-56	Southern California	16	D8, '79
84	Holston, Mike	WR	6-3	184	2	1- 8-58	Morgan State	16	D3, '81
50	Hunt, Daryl	LB	6-3	234	4	11- 3-56	Oklahoma	16	D6a, '79
22	Kay, Bill	DB	6-1	190	2	1-10-60	Purdue	16	D6, '81
71	Kennard, Ken	MG	6-2	258	6	10- 4-54	Angelo State	16	OFA, '77
	McGee, Carl	LB	6-3	228	2	7-15-56	Duke	*0	FA, '82
14	Nielsen, Gifford	QB	6-4	210	5	10-25-54	Brigham Young	5	D3, '78
18	Parsley, Cliff	P	6-1	223	6	12-26-54	Oklahoma State	16	T-NO, '77
32	Perry, Vernon	S	6-2	210	4	9-22-53	Jackson State	16	FA, '79
	Phillips, Wes	OT	6-5	265	2	8- 1-53	Georgia State	*0	FA, '82
	Reihner, George	G	6-4	263	4	4-27-55	Penn State	*0	D2, '77
37	†Reinfeldt, Mike	S	6-2	196	8	5- 6-53	Wisconsin-Milwaukee	16	W-Oak, '76
72	Renfro, Mike	WR	6-0	184	5	6-19-55	Texas Christian	12	D4, '78
53	Riley, Avon	LB	6-3	211	2	2-10-59	UCLA	16	D9, '81
85	Roaches, Carl	WR	5-8	165	3	10- 2-53	Texas A&M	16	FA, '80
	Roberts, Wesley	DT	6-6	253	2	8- 1-57	Texas Christian	*0	FA, '82
62	†Schuhmacher, John	G	6-3	266	4	9-23-55	Southern California	16	D12, '78
90	Skaugstad, Daryle	MG	6-5	254	2	4- 8-57	California	16	D2b, '80
83	Smith, Tim	WR	6-2	192	3	3-20-57	Nebraska	4	D3, '80
12	Stabler, Ken	QB	6-3	210	13	12-25-45	Alabama	13	T-Oak, '80
27	Stemrick, Greg	CB	5-11	185	8	10-25-51	Colorado State	16	FA, '75
67	Stensrud, Mike	DE	6-5	280	4	2-19-56	Iowa State	16	D2a, '79
56	Stringer, Art	LB	6-2	223	5	1-30-54	Ball State	5	D9, '76
28	Thomaselli, Rich	RB	6-1	196	2	2-26-57	West Virginia Wesleyan	12	OFA, '81
51	†Thompson, Ted	LB	6-1	229	8	1-17-53	Southern Methodist	16	OFA, '75
76	Towns, Morris	T-G	6-5	251	6	1-10-54	Missouri	16	D1, '77
20	Tullis, Willie	DB	6-0	190	2	4- 5-58	Troy State	16	D8, '81
59	Washington, Ted	LB	6-2	248	10	2-16-48	Mississippi Valley	16	T-NYJ, '74
33	Wilson, J.C.	CB	6-0	178	5	3-11-56	Pittsburgh	16	D8, '78
45	Wilson, Tim	RB	6-3	230	6	1-14-55	Maryland	16	D3a, '77

*Brooks played 7 games with San Diego, 3 with Houston in 1981; Evans last active with Cleveland in 1980; Floyd played 4 games with St. Louis in 1981; Gant last active with Kansas City in 1980; Goodspeed last active with St. Louis in 1980; McGee last active with San Diego in 1980; Phillips last active with Houston in 1979; Reihner missed 1980 season due to injury and retired prior to 1981; Roberts last active with New York Jets in 1980.

†Option playout; subject to developments.

D—Draft; T—Trade; W—Waivers; FA—Free Agent; OFA—Original Free Agent; VFA—Veteran Free Agent; VA—Veteran Allocation; SupD—Supplemental Draft.

Also played with Oilers in 1981—TE Mike Barber (16 games), RB Rob Carpenter (4), C Carl Mauck (14), QB John Reaves (5).

HOUSTON OILERS
1982 DRAFT CHOICES

(Number following name designates order of selection among 334 players drafted.)

Round and Player		Position	College
1. MUNCHAK, Mike	8	G	Penn State
2. Choice to Oakland (a)			
LUCK, Oliver	44	QB	West Virginia
from Tampa Bay through Miami and Los Angeles (b)			
3. Choice to Los Angeles (c)			
EDWARDS, Stanley	72	RB	Michigan
from New York Giants (d)			
ABRAHAM, Robert	77	LB	N.C. State
from Denver through Los Angeles (e)			
4. BRYANT, Steve	94	WR	Purdue
5. TAYLOR, Malcolm	121	DE	Tennessee St.
6. ALLEN, Gary	148	RB	Hawaii
7. Choice to Detroit (f)			
8. Choice to Los Angeles (g)			
9. BRADLEY, Matt	234	DB	Penn State
10. REEVES, Ron	261	QB	Texas Tech
11. CAMPBELL, Jim	287	TE	Kentucky
12. CRAFT, Donnie	314	RB	Louisville

(a) Traded pick and first- and second-round picks in 1981 for tight end Dave Casper, October 14, 1980.

(b) Tampa Bay traded pick and running back Jimmy DuBose to Miami for cornerback Norris Thomas and running back Gary Davis, August 25, 1980; Miami traded pick and second- and third-round picks in 1981 to Los Angeles for linebacker Bob Brudzinski and second-round pick in 1981, April 28, 1981; Los Angeles traded pick, third-round pick and tight end Lewis Gilbert to Houston for tight end Mike Barber and third- and eighth-round picks, April 27, 1982.

(c) See last part of (b).

(d) Acquired pick for running back Rob Carpenter, September 29, 1981.

(e) Denver traded pick to Los Angeles for running back Lawrence McCutcheon, April 15, 1980; Los Angeles traded pick to Houston (See c).

(f) Traded pick for safety Luther Bradley, April 28, 1982.

(g) See (c).

HOUSTON OILERS
1982 ROOKIE AND FIRST-YEAR ROSTER

(1) Indicates player in previous NFL camp.
All others classified as rookies.

Name	Pos.	Hgt.	Wgt.	Birth-date	College	How Acquired
Abraham, Robert	LB	6-1	212	7-13-60	North Carolina State	D3b
Allen, Gary	RB	5-10	175	4-23-60	Hawaii	D6
Baker, Renie	WR	6-0	181	12-15-59	Texas Tech	FA
Banks, Norris (1)	RB	6-2	215	1-21-55	Kansas	FA
Bradley, Matt	S	6-1	220	5-20-60	Penn State	D9
Brown, Greg	LB	6-3	233	2-27-59	Indiana	FA
Bryant, Steve	WR	6-2	185	10-10-59	Purdue	D4
Campbell, Jim	TE	6-2	230	11- 9-59	Kentucky	D11
Craft, Donnie	RB	6-0	195	11-19-59	Louisville	D12
Cole, Dennis	S	6-2	195	10-23-58	Cal State-Long Beach	FA
Davis, Eric	CB-S	6-2	200	5-31-60	Houston	FA
Edwards, Stanley	FB	6-0	208	5-20-60	Michigan	D3a
Feasel, Gregory (1)	T	6-7	285	11- 7-57	Abilene-Christian	FA
Fortune, Hosea	WR	6-0	175	3- 4-59	Rice	FA
Fowler, Delbert (1)	LB	6-2	214	5- 4-58	West Virginia	*D5 ('81)
Grigsby, James	DT	6-5	273	4- 6-59	Texas Christian	FA
Harris, James	CB	6-0	185	7-11-60	Florida State	FA
Harrison, Broderick	DB	5-11	180	10-15-56	Bishop	FA
Hubert, Wes (1)	C	6-3	255	11- 7-57	Texas	FA
Jackson, Ken	RB	5-11	205	10- 1-59	Grambling	FA
James, Arlis (1)	DT	6-3	255	9- 5-58	Texas A & M	FA
Jones, Larry (1)	RB	5-10	184	9-16-59	Colorado State	*D10 ('81)
Kempf, Florian (1)	K	5-9	160	5-25-56	Pennsylvania	FA
Kirchbaum, Kelly (1)	LB	6-2	225	6-14-57	Kentucky	FA
Krueger, Todd (1)	QB	6-4	202	9-10-57	Northern Michigan	FA
Love, Donnie	S	6-1	185	10-19-58	Houston	FA
Luck, Oliver	QB	6-2	190	4- 5-60	West Virginia	FA
Mathews, Claude (1)	MG	6-2	254	1-15-58	Auburn	*D11 ('81)
McCall, Ben (1)	RB	6-0	200	7-31-59	Purdue	FA
Minor, Ed	S	6-3	198	7-21-60	Wilmington	FA
Mueske, Daryl	G	6-2	243	1-25-60	Arizona State	FA
Munchak, Mike	G	6-3	257	5- 3-60	Penn State	D1
O'Connell, Mark (1)	QB	6-2	210	3-14-58	Ball State	FA
Pederson, Lance (1)	C	6-2	245	11-28-58	Southern Methodist	FA
Pheonix, Kurt (1)	LB	6-1	220	8-22-58	Lamar	FA
Reeves, Ron	QB	6-2	215	3- 4-60	Texas Tech	D10
Smith, Gregory	WR	6-0	190	12-21-55	Ellsworth	FA
Tanner, Ed	RB	5-10	180	1- 4-57	Los Angeles City College	FA
Taylor, Malcolm	DT	6-6	250	6-20-60	Tennessee State	D5
Watts, Ben	DT	6-2	256	3-18-60	Stephen F. Austin	FA
Williams, Ralph (1)	OT	6-3	270	3-27-58	Southern	*FA ('81)
Williams, Reginald	LB	6-1	225	11- 5-60	Nevada-Las Vegas	FA
Wright, Felix	CB-S	6-2	186	6-22-59	Drake	FA

*Fowler, Jones, Mathews and Ralph Williams missed 1981 season due to injuries.

KANSAS CITY CHIEFS
(Western Division, American Conference)

Marv Levy

Owner—Lamar Hunt
President—Jack W. Steadman
General Manager—Jim Schaaf
Director of Pro Personnel—Ron Waller
Director of Player Personnel—Les Miller
Assistant Director of Player Personnel—J. D. Helm
Head Coach—Marv Levy (4 years: 28-36-0)
Assistant Coaches:
    Strength and Conditioning—Rick Abernethy
    Offensive Line—Tom Bresnahan
    Defensive Backs—Walt Cory
    Linebackers—Ted Cottrell
    Receivers-Quarterbacks—Kav Dalton
    Kicking Teams-Tight Ends—Frank Gansz
    Offensive Backs—J.D. Helm
    Defensive Line—Don Lawrence
    Defensive Coordinator—Rod Rust
Public Relations Director—Bob Sprenger
    (Office Phone: 924-9300—Area Code 816)
Offices—One Arrowhead Drive, Kansas City, Mo. 64129
Stadium—Arrowhead Stadium (Capacity: 78,198)
Team Colors—Red and Gold
Training Site—William Jewell College, Liberty, Mo.

1982 SCHEDULE
(All times local.
All games Sunday unless noted otherwise.)

Sept. 12	at Buffalo	1:00
Sept. 19	SAN DIEGO	12:00
Sept. 23	ATLANTA (Thurs.)	7:30
Oct. 3	at Seattle	1:00
Oct. 10	HOUSTON	12:00
Oct. 17	at San Diego	1:00
Oct. 24	NEW YORK JETS	12:00
Oct. 31	SEATTLE	12:00
Nov. 7	at Oakland	1:00
Nov. 14	DENVER	12:00
Nov. 21	at New Orleans	12:00
Nov. 28	at Los Angeles	1:00
Dec. 5	at Pittsburgh	1:00
Dec. 12	OAKLAND	3:00
Dec. 19	at Denver	2:00
Dec. 26	SAN FRANCISCO	12:00

1981 RESULTS—(Won 9, Lost 7)

Chiefs		Opp.		Att.
37	Pittsburgh	33	(A)	53,305
19	Tampa Bay	10	(H)	50,555
31	San Diego	42	(H)	63,866
20	Seattle	14	(A)	59,255
17	New England	33	(A)	55,931
27	Oakland	0	(H)	76,543
28	Denver	14	(H)	74,672
28	Oakland	17	(A)	38,500
20	San Diego	22	(A)	51,307
13	Chicago (OT)	16	(H)	60,605
23	Houston	10	(H)	73,984
40	Seattle	13	(H)	49,002
10	Detroit	27	(A)	76,735
13	Denver	16	(A)	74,744
7	Miami	17	(H)	57,407
10	Minnesota	6	(A)	41,110

1981 GAMES STARTED

16 games: Gary Barbaro, Mike Bell, Brad Budde, Tom Condon, Charles Getty, Gary Green, Eric Harris, Matt Herkenhoff, Jack Rudnay, Gary Spani.

15 games: James Hadnot, J.T. Smith.

14 games: Lloyd Burruss, Al Dixon.

13 games: Bill Kenney.

12 games: Henry Marshall.

11 games: Charles Jackson, Art Still.

10 games: Joe Delaney.

Less than 10 games: Jerry Blanton (9), Phil Cancik (1), Carlos Carson (1), Herb Christopher (2), Steve Fuller (3), Thomas Howard (7), Billy Jackson (1), Ken Kremer (8), Dave Lindstrom (5), Frank Manumaleuga (4), Ted McKnight (5), Don Parrish (8), Whitney Paul (9), Cal Peterson (7), Stan Rome (4), Willie Scott (3).

KANSAS CITY CHIEFS 1982 VETERAN ROSTER

No.	Name	Pos.	Ht.	Wt.	NFL Exp.	Birth-date	College	Games in '81	How Acquired
	Acker, Bill	NT	6-2	255	3	11- 7-56	Texas	*8	FA, '82
26	Barbaro, Gary	S	6-4	204	7	2-11-54	Nicholls State	16	D3b, '76
85	Beckman, Ed	TE	6-4	237	6	1- 2-55	Florida State	15	OFA, '77
99	Bell, Mike	DE	6-4	255	3	8-30-57	Colorado State	16	D1a, '79
35	Belton, Horace	RB	5-8	200	4	7-16-55	Southeastern Louisiana	*0	FA, '78
57	Blanton, Jerry	LB	6-1	236	4	12-20-56	Kentucky	9	FA, '78
30	Bledsoe, Curtis	RB	5-11	215	2	3-19-57	San Diego State	13	FA, '81
	Bryant, Trent	CB	5-9	180	2	8-14-59	Arkansas	*4	FA, '82
66	Budde, Brad	G	6-4	264	3	5- 9-58	Southern California	16	D1, '80
34	Burruss, Lloyd	S	6-0	201	2	10-31-57	Maryland	16	D3c, '81
56	Cancik, Phil	LB	6-1	230	3	4-19-57	Northern Arizona	15	FA, '81
88	Carson, Carlos	WR-KR	5-10	172	3	12-28-58	Louisiana State	5	D5a, '80
42	Carter, M.L.	CB	5-9	173	4	12- 9-55	Cal State-Fullerton	10	FA, '79
95	Case, Frank	DE	6-4	242	2	8-14-58	Penn State	6	D11, '81
20	Cherry, Deron	S	5-11	185	2	9-12-59	Rutgers	13	OFA, '81
41	Christopher, Herb	S	5-10	202	4	4- 7-54	Morris Brown	16	FA, '79
65	Condon, Tom	G	6-3	272	9	10-26-52	Boston College	16	D10, '74
37	Delaney, Joe	RB	5-10	184	2	10-30-58	Northwest Louisiana	15	D2, '81
84	Dixon, Al	TE	6-5	235	6	4- 5-54	Iowa State	16	FA, '79
4	Fuller, Steve	QB	6-4	198	4	1- 5-57	Clemson	13	D1b, '79
11	Gagliano, Bob	QB	6-3	193	2	9- 5-58	Utah State	*0	D12, '81
21	Gaines, Clark	RB	6-1	212	6	2- 1-54	Wake Forest	1	W-NYJ, '81
77	Getty, Charlie	T	6-4	269	9	7-24-52	Penn State	16	D2, '74
7	Gossett, Jeff	P	6-2	195	2	1-25-57	Eastern Illinois	7	FA, '81
24	Green, Gary	CB	5-11	184	6	10- 2-55	Baylor	16	D1, '77
1	Grupp, Bob	P	5-11	204	4	5- 8-55	Duke	9	FA, '79
48	Hadnot, James	RB	6-2	244	3	7-11-57	Texas Tech	16	D3, '80
44	Harris, Eric	CB	6-3	191	3	8-11-55	Memphis State	16	D4d, '77
83	Harvey, Marvin	TE	6-3	220	2	10-17-59	Southern Mississippi	7	D3a, '81
60	Herkenhoff, Matt	T	6-4	270	7	4- 2-51	Minnesota	16	D4, '74
75	Hicks, Sylvester	DE	6-4	252	5	4- 2-55	Tennessee State	2	D2, '78
	Hoke, Jon	S	5-11	175	2	1-24-57	Ball State	*0	FA, '82
62	Howard, Thomas	LB	6-2	215	6	8-18-54	Texas Tech	9	D3, '77
43	Jackson, Billy	RB	5-10	223	2	9-13-59	Alabama	16	D7, '81
51	†Jackson, Charles	LB	6-2	220	5	3-22-55	Washington	14	FA, '81
9	Kenney, Bill	QB	6-4	210	4	1-20-55	Northern Colorado	13	FA, '79
55	Klug, Dave	LB	6-4	230	2	5-17-58	Concordia, Minn.	15	D4, '80
91	Kremer, Ken	NT	6-4	250	4	7-16-57	Ball State	16	D7, '79
31	Lewis, Will	CB	5-10	195	3	11-16-58	Millersville State	*10	FA, '81
71	Lindstrom, Dave	DE	6-6	257	5	11-16-54	Boston University	16	W-SD, '78
8	Lowery, Nick	K	6-4	190	3	5-27-56	Dartmouth	16	FA, '80
74	†Mangiero, Dino	NT	6-2	265	3	12-19-58	Rutgers	9	OFA, '80
54	Manumaleuga, Frank	LB	6-2	245	4	5- 9-56	San Jose State	5	D4, '79
89	Marshall, Henry	WR	6-2	214	7	8- 9-54	Missouri	12	D3c, '76
22	McKnight, Ted	RB	6-1	216	6	2-26-54	Minnesota-Duluth	5	W-Oak, '77
82	Murphy, James	WR	5-10	177	2	10-10-59	Utah State	*10	FA, '81
61	Parrish, Don	NT	6-2	264	5	4- 6-55	Pittsburgh	16	FA, '78
53	Paul, Whitney	LB	6-3	220	7	10- 8-55	Colorado	15	D10, '76
50	Peterson, Cal	LB	6-4	230	7	10- 6-52	UCLA	11	FA, '79
87	Rome, Stan	WR	6-5	218	4	6- 4-56	Clemson	16	D11, '79
70	Rourke, Jim	G-T	6-5	265	3	2-10-57	Boston College	12	FA, '80
58	Rudnay, Jack	C	6-2	242	13	11-20-47	Northwestern	16	D4, '69
81	Scott, Willie	TE	6-4	245	2	2-13-59	South Carolina	16	D1, '81
73	Simmons, Bob	G	6-4	260	6	7- 7-54	Texas	4	FA, '77
86	Smith, J.T.	KR-WR	6-2	185	5	10-29-55	North Texas State	16	FA, '78
59	Spani, Gary	LB	6-2	230	5	1- 9-56	Kansas State	16	D3, '78
67	Still, Art	DE	6-8	252	5	12- 5-55	Kentucky	11	D1, '78
76	Taylor, Roger	T	6-6	271	2	1- 5-58	Oklahoma State	13	D3b, '81
62	Thomas, Todd	C	6-5	262	2	12- 2-59	North Dakota	15	D5, '81
40	Williams, Mike	RB	6-3	222	4	10-14-57	New Mexico	3	D8a, '79

*Belton missed 1981 season due to injury; Acker played 8 games with St. Louis in 1981; Bryant played 4 games with Washington in 1981; Gagliano active for 16 games in 1981, but did not play; Hoke last active with Chicago in 1980; Lewis played 10 games with Seattle and active for 1 with Kansas City, but did not play; Murphy active for 1 game with Atlanta, but did not play, played 10 games with Kansas City in 1981.

†Option playout; subject to developments.

D—Draft; T—Trade; W—Waivers; FA—Free Agent; OFA—Original Free Agent; VFA—Veteran Free Agent; VA—Veteran Allocation; SupD—Supplemental Draft.

Also played with Chiefs in 1981—RB Rick Moser (1 game).

KANSAS CITY CHIEFS
1982 DRAFT CHOICES

(Number following name designates order of selection among 334 players drafted.)

Round and Player		Position	College
1. HANCOCK, Anthony from St. Louis (a)	11	WR	Tennessee
Choice to St. Louis (a)			
2. DANIELS, Calvin	46	LB	North Carolina
3. Choice to St. Louis (a)			
4. HAYNES, Louis	100	LB	North Texas St.
ANDERSON, Stuart from Denver (b)	104	DT	Virginia
5. THOMPSON, Delbert	130	RB	Texas-El Paso
6. ROQUEMORE, Durwood	157	DB	Texas A & I
7. SMITH, Greg	184	DT	Kansas
8. DE BRUIJN, Case	214	P-K	Idaho State
9. BYFORD, Lyndle	241	T	Oklahoma
10. BRODSKY, Larry	268	WR	Miami
11. CARTER, Bob	297	WR	Arizona
12. MILLER, Mike	324	DB	S.W. Texas St.

(a) Switched first-round positions and traded third-round pick, April 27, 1982.

(b) Acquired pick and third-round pick in 1981 for running back Tony Reed, April 28, 1981.

KANSAS CITY CHIEFS
1982 ROOKIE AND FIRST-YEAR ROSTER

(1) Indicates player in previous NFL camp.
All others classified as rookies.

Name	Pos.	Hgt.	Wgt.	Birth-date	College	How Acquired
Anderson, Stuart	LB-NT	6-1	247	12-25-59	Virginia	D4b
Banks, Douglas (1)	RB	5-11	205	10-26-57	East Carolina	FA
Barnes, Robert (1)	C	6-4	255	4-20-58	Southern Methodist	FA
Bearden, Jerome	S	6-1	189	2-26-59	San Jose State	FA
Bennett, Thomas (1)	RB	5-11	190	7-23-58	C.W. Post	FA
Birdsey, Don (1)	P	6-0	175	8-16-58	Kansas State	FA
Blakley, Robert	WR	6-0	190	9-20-59	North Dakota State	FA
Brodsky, Larry	WR	5-11	188	1-19-60	Miami (Fla.)	D10
Bungartz, John (1)	LB	6-3	220	9-16-58	Cal. State-Fullerton	FA
Byford, Lyndle	T	6-5	270	12-27-58	Oklahoma	D9
Carter, Bob	CB	6-0	173	2-28-60	Arizona	D11
Clark, Danny	WR	6-0	189	10-16-59	West Texas State	FA
Crouse, Ray	RB	5-10	200	3-16-59	Nevada-Las Vegas	FA
Daniels, Calvin	LB	6-3	236	12-26-58	North Carolina	D2
deBruijn, Case	P-K	6-0	176	4-11-60	Idaho State	D8
Ditchfield, Mike (1)	K	5-10	183	6-22-57	Penn State	FA
Flanagan, Tim	LB	6-2	220	2-14-60	Miami (Fla.)	FA
Hancock, Anthony	WR	6-0	187	6-10-60	Tennessee	D1
Haynes, Louis	LB	6-0	227	1-17-60	North Texas State	D4a
Hogensen, Greg	TE	6-4	238	7-13-59	Oregon	FA
Jones, Lyndell (1)	CB	5-9	170	3-18-59	Hawaii	FA
Jones, Ronnie	CB	6-0	195	7-27-58	Tuskegee Institute	FA
Kildahl, James	QB	6-2	200	10- 6-59	Wisconsin-LaCrosse	FA
Kuhlman, Garry	T	6-3	265	5-27-59	Delaware	FA
Lane, Eric	LB	6-1	220	7-27-59	San Jose State	FA
Lavitt, Dan	WR	5-11	185	5-25-58	Missouri-Kansas City	FA
Martin, David (1)	S	5-9	180	3-15-59	Villanova	FA
McNorton, Kyle	LB	6-1	220	5-20-60	Kansas	FA
Miller, Mike	S	6-1	198	11- 9-59	Southwest Texas State	D12
Mobley, James	CB	5-11	185	4- 6-59	Southern Methodist	FA
Olive, Rick (1)	DE	6-5	251	10- 8-58	Georgia Tech	FA
O'Neil, Chris	T	6-2	263	5-21-60	Massachusetts	FA
Perry, Pete	DE	6-5	250	8-13-58	Colorado	FA
Phillips, Mike	TE	6-4	241	2- 5-59	William Jewell	FA
Prater, Dean (1)	DE	6-5	245	9-29-58	Oklahoma State	FA
Purdham, Robert	TE	6-1	230	9-24-59	Virginia Tech	FA
Rogers, Steve	T	6-4	265	1- 9-59	Brigham Young	FA
Roquemore, Durwood	S	6-1	180	1-19-80	Texas A&I	D6
Smith, Greg	NT	6-2	275	10-22-59	Kansas	D7
Spengler, John (1)	PK	5-10	167	1- 5-59	Bowling Green	FA
Steinfeld, Al (1)	T	6-4	256	10-28-58	C.W. Post	FA
Stenslokken, Jeff	DE	6-4	245	8-20-60	Kearney State	FA
Stewart, George (1)	G	6-3	260	12-29-58	Arkansas	*FA ('81)
Studdard, Les (1)	G	6-4	255	12-14-58	Texas	*D10 ('81)
Thompson, Del	RB	6-0	203	2-21-58	Texas-El Paso	D5
Washington, Ron (1)	WR	5-11	190	1- 6-58	Arizona State	*D4 ('81)
Wayenberg, Gene	WR	6-2	185	4-24-59	Pittsburgh State	FA
Weeks, Sean (1)	RB	6-1	225	11- 5-59	Boston University	FA
Yocavitch, Joe	LB	6-2	225	8-21-58	Chowan J.C.	FA

*Stewart, Studdard and Washington missed 1981 season due to injuries.

LOS ANGELES RAMS
(Western Division, National Conference)

Ray Malavasi

President—Georgia Frontiere
Vice-President and General Manager—Don Klosterman
Director of Player Personnel—John Math
Head Coach—Ray Malavasi (5 years: 42-34-0)
Assistant Coaches:
    Conditioning—Clyde Evans
    Offensive Coordinator—John Hadl
    Quarterbacks—Paul Lanham
    Linebackers—Herb Paterra
    Offensive Line—Jim Ringo
    Defensive Line—Fritz Shurmer
    Receivers—Jack Snow
    Special Teams—Fred Whittingham
Director of Public Relations—Jerry Wilcox
(Office Phones: 535-7267—Area Code 714; 585-5400—Area Code 213)
Offices—2327 W. Lincoln Ave., Anaheim, Calif. 92801
Stadium—Anaheim Stadium (Capacity: 69,000)
Team Colors—Royal Blue, Gold and White
Training Site—California St. University, Fullerton, Calif.

1982 SCHEDULE
(All times local.
All games Sunday unless noted otherwise.)

Sept. 12	vs. Green Bay (Milw.)	12:00
Sept. 19	DETROIT	1:00
Sept. 26	at Philadelphia	1:00
Oct. 3	at St. Louis	12:00
Oct. 10	ATLANTA	1:00
Oct. 17	at San Francisco	1:00
Oct. 24	NEW ORLEANS	1:00
Oct. 31	at San Diego	1:00
Nov. 7	at New Orleans	12:00
Nov. 14	NEW YORK GIANTS	1:00
Nov. 21	at Atlanta	1:00
Nov. 28	KANSAS CITY	1:00
Dec. 2	SAN FRANCISCO (Thurs.)	6:00
Dec. 12	DENVER	1:00
Dec. 18	at Oakland (Sat.)	1:00
Dec. 26	CHICAGO	1:00

1981 RESULTS—(Won 6, Lost 10)

Rams		Opp.		Att.
20	Houston	27	(H)	63,198
17	New Orleans	23	(A)	62,063
35	Green Bay	23	(H)	61,286
24	Chicago	7	(A)	62,461
27	Cleveland	16	(H)	63,924
37	Atlanta	35	(A)	57,841
17	Dallas	29	(A)	64,649
17	San Francisco	20	(A)	59,190
20	Detroit	13	(H)	61,814
13	New Orleans	21	(H)	61,068
10	Cincinnati	24	(A)	56,836
31	San Francisco	33	(H)	63,456
0	Pittsburgh	24	(A)	51,854
7	New York Giants	10	(A)	59,659
21	Atlanta	16	(H)	57,054
7	Washington	30	(H)	52,224

1981 GAMES STARTED

16 games: Nolan Cromwell, Carl Ekern, Mike Fanning, Johnnie Johnson, Cody Jones, Rod Perry, Rich Saul, Jack Youngblood, Jim Youngblood.

15 games: George Andrews, Wendell Tyler, Preston Dennard.

14 games: Billy Waddy.

13 games: Dennis Harrah, Doug Smith.

12 games: Cullen Bryant, Irv Pankey.

11 games: Pat Haden, Kent Hill, Jackie Slater.

Less than 10 games: Walt Arnold (9), Bill Bain (3), Larry Brooks (8), Henry Childs (7), Reggie Doss (8), Doug France (1), Mike Guman (4), Joe Harris (1), Drew Hill (2), Leroy Irvin (7), Willie Miller (1), Dan Pastorini (5), Jewerl Thomas (1), Pat Thomas (9).

LOS ANGELES RAMS 1982 VETERAN ROSTER

No.	Name	Pos.	Ht.	Wt.	NFL Exp.	Birth-date	College	Games in '81	How Acquired
52	Andrews, George	LB	6-3	221	4	11-28-55	Nebraska	15	D1a, '79
84	Arnold, Walt	TE	6-3	230	3	8-31-58	New Mexico	16	OFA, '80
62	Bain, Bill	G	6-4	285	7	8- 9-52	Southern California	16	FA, '79
	Barber, Mike	TE	6-3	233	6	6- 4-53	Louisiana Tech	16	T-Hou, '82
81	Battle, Ron	TE	6-3	225	2	3-27-59	North Texas State	4	D7a, '81
90	Brooks, Larry	DT	6-3	255	11	6-10-50	Va. State-Petersburg	8	D14, '72
32	Bryant, Cullen	FB	6-1	235	10	5-20-51	Colorado	13	D2a, '73
54	Carson, Howard	LB	6-2	230	2	2-11-57	Howard Payne	10	OFA, '80
57	Celotto, Mario	LB	6-3	228	4	8-23-56	Southern California	*10	FA, '81
83	Childs, Henry	TE	6-2	226	9	4-16-51	Kansas State	7	T-Was, '81
97	Cobb, Bob	DE	6-4	250	2	10-12-57	Arizona	6	D3b, '81
50	Collins, Jim	LB	6-2	230	2	6-11-58	Syracuse	7	D2, '81
42	Collins, Kirk	CB	5-11	183	2	7-18-58	Baylor	16	D7a, '80
3	Corral, Frank	K	6-2	233	5	6-16-55	UCLA	16	D3a, '78
21	Cromwell, Nolan	S	6-1	200	6	1-30-55	Kansas	16	D2a, '77
88	Dennard, Preston	WR	6-1	183	5	11-28-55	New Mexico	15	OFA, '78
71	Doss, Reggie	DE	6-4	263	5	12- 7-56	Hampton Institute	16	D7, '78
55	Ekern, Carl	LB	6-3	222	6	5-27-54	San Jose State	16	D5a, '76
79	Fanning, Mike	DT	6-6	255	8	2- 2-53	Notre Dame	16	D1a, '75
77	France, Doug	T	6-5	270	8	4-26-53	Ohio State	8	D1c, '75
44	Guman, Mike	RB	6-2	218	3	4-21-58	Penn State	16	D6, '80
60	Harrah, Dennis	G	6-5	255	8	3- 9-53	Miami	15	D1b, '75
51	Harris, Joe	LB	6-1	230	7	12- 6-52	Georgia Tech	16	FA, '79
87	Hill, Drew	WR	5-9	170	4	10- 5-56	Georgia Tech	16	D12, '79
72	Hill, Kent	G	6-5	260	4	3- 7-57	Georgia Tech	16	D1b, '79
47	Irvin, LeRoy	CB	5-11	184	3	9-15-57	Kansas	16	D3b, '80
20	Johnson, Johnnie	S	6-1	183	3	10- 8-56	Texas	16	D1, '80
	†Jones, Bert	QB	6-3	218	10	9- 7-51	Louisiana State	15	T-Bal, '82
76	Jones, Cody	DT	6-5	255	8	5- 3-51	San Jose State	16	D5b, '73
9	Kemp, Jeff	QB	6-0	201	2	7-11-59	Dartmouth	1	OFA, '81
69	Meisner, Greg	DE	6-3	253	2	4-23-59	Pittsburgh	9	D3a, '81
82	Miller, Willie	WR	5-9	173	7	4-26-48	Colorado State	13	FA, '77
86	Moore, Jeff	WR	6-1	188	3	3- 2-57	Tennessee	10	D3a, '79
95	Murphy, Phil	DT	6-5	300	3	9-26-57	South Carolina State	16	D3c, '80
58	Owens, Mel	LB	6-2	224	2	12- 7-58	Michigan	16	D1, '81
75	Pankey, Irv	T	6-4	267	3	2-15-58	Penn State	13	D2, '80
22	Penaranda, Jairo	FB	5-11	215	2	6-15-58	UCLA	16	D12, '81
49	Perry, Rod	CB	5-9	185	8	9-11-53	Colorado	16	D4, '75
8	Rutledge, Jeff	QB	6-2	187	4	1-22-57	Alabama	4	D9, '79
78	Slater, Jackie	T	6-4	271	7	5-27-54	Jackson State	11	D3, '76
56	Smith, Doug	C-G	6-3	253	5	11-25-56	Bowling Green	16	OFA, '78
23	Smith, Lucious	CB	5-10	190	3	1-17-57	Cal State-Fullerton	16	OFA, '80
37	Sully, Ivory	S	6-0	201	4	6-20-57	Delaware	16	OFA, '79
33	Thomas, Jewerl	FB	5-10	228	3	9-10-57	San Jose State	15	D3a, '80
27	Thomas, Pat	CB	5-9	190	7	9- 1-54	Texas A&M	12	D2a, '76
26	Tyler, Wendell	RB	5-10	198	5	5-20-55	UCLA	15	D3b, '77
80	Waddy, Billy	WR	5-11	190	6	2-19-54	Colorado	15	D2b, '77
85	Youngblood, Jack	DE	6-4	242	12	1-26-50	Florida	16	D1b, '71
53	Youngblood, Jim	LB	6-3	231	10	2-23-50	Tennessee Tech	16	D2c, '73

*Celotto played 7 games with Oakland, active for one with Baltimore and played 3 with Los Angeles in 1981.

†Option playout; subject to developments.

D—Draft; T—Trade; W—Waivers; FA—Free Agent; OFA—Original Free Agent; VFA—Veteran Free Agent; VA—Veteran Allocation; SupD—Supplemental Draft.

Also played with Rams in 1981—DE Fred Dryer (2 games), TE Lewis Gilbert (6), OT Phil McKinnely (7), QB Dan Pastorini (7). Retired: QB Pat Haden (13), C Rich Saul (16).

LOS ANGELES RAMS
1982 DRAFT CHOICES

(Number following name designates order of selection among 334 players drafted.)

Round and Player		Position	College
1. Choice to Baltimore (a)			
REDDEN, Barry from Washington (b)	14	RB	Richmond
2. Choice to Baltimore (a)			
3. Choice to Washington (c)			
BECHTOLD, Bill from Houston (d)	67	C	Oklahoma
4. GAYLORD, Jeff	88	LB	Missouri
5. KERSTEN, Wally from Seattle (e)	117	T	Minnesota
BARNETT, Doug	118	DE	Azusa Pacific
6. LOCKLIN, Kerry	145	TE	New Mexico St.
7. Choice to Pittsburgh through Washington (f)			
SHEARIN, Joe from Detroit (g)	181	G	Texas
8. JONES, Jam	202	RB	Texas
REILLY, Mike from Houston (d)	207	DE	Oklahoma
9. SPEIGHT, Bob	229	T	Boston U.
10. McPHERSON, Miles	256	DB	New Haven
11. COFFMAN, Ricky	285	WR	UCLA
12. COLEY, Raymond	312	DT	Alabama A&M

(a) Traded picks for quarterback Bert Jones, April 27, 1982.

(b) Acquired pick for second-round pick, third-round pick in 1981 and two fifth-round picks in 1981, April 28, 1981.

(c) See (b).

(d) Acquired picks and tight end Mike Barber for tight end Lewis Gilbert and second- and third-round picks, April 27, 1982.

(e) Acquired pick for running back Jim Jodat, August 26, 1980.

(f) Los Angeles traded pick and third-round pick to Washington for tight end Henry Childs, May 6, 1981; Washington traded pick and third-round pick in 1983 to Pittsburgh for quarterback Mike Kruczek, July 28, 1980.

(g) Acquired pick for seventh- and ninth-round picks, April 28, 1982.

LOS ANGELES RAMS
1982 ROOKIE AND FIRST-YEAR ROSTER

(1) Indicates player in previous NFL camp.
All others classified as rookies.

Name	Pos.	Hgt.	Wgt.	Birth-date	College	How Acquired
Alexander, Robert (1)	RB	6-0	185	4-21-58	West Virginia	*D10 ('81)
Andersen, Robin	TE	6-3	240	10-25-57	Brigham Young	FA
Barnett, Doug	DE	6-3	250	4-12-60	Azusa Pacific	D5b
Bechtold, Bill	C	6-4	255	4- 7-59	Oklahoma	D3
Carr, Gary (1)	FB	5-10	215	9-15-58	Fresno State	FA
Coffman, Ricky	WR	5-11	190	11- 5-58	UCLA	D11
Coley, Ray	DE	6-3	250	9-29-59	Alabama A&M	D12
DeAnda, Alejandro	K	6-2	210	11- 6-56	Mexico Polytechnic	FA
Dorvall, Bill	WR	6-0	170	8-22-58	Cal. State-Irvine	FA
Douglas, Brian	DT	6-1	245	1- 9-60	Tulane	FA
Farmer, George (1)	WR	5-10	175	12- 5-58	Southern	*D9 ('80)
Filiaga, Pulusila	DT	6-1	258	11- 7-59	Brigham Young	FA
Gary, Greg	LB	6-0	208	11-30-58	Cal. State—Fullerton	FA
Gaylord, Jeff	LB	6-3	230	10-15-58	Missouri	D4
Gillberg, Carl	C	6-3	235	3-23-59	Cal. Poly-SLO	FA
Griffin, Darrel (1)	WR	5-11	180	9-29-58	Tulane	FA
Gomeztrejo, Fred	S	5-10	187	9-21-60	La Verne	FA
Hernandez, Tony (1)	S	5-11	190	7- 6-56	Brigham Young	FA
Jones, Jam	RB	6-1	202	5-30-59	Texas	D8a
Kersten, Wally	T	6-5	270	12- 8-59	Minnesota	D5a
Knight, Tom (1)	CB	5-10	180	2-14-58	Hawaii	FA
Leidelmeyer, Lewis	WR	5-11	175	9-29-59	Cal. State-Long Beach	FA
Lilja, George (1)	C	6-4	250	3- 3-58	Michigan	*D4 ('81)
Locklin, Kerry	TE	6-3	217	9- 9-59	New Mexico State	D6
Majette, Lloyd	RB	5-10	170	11-14-57	No College	FA
McCray, John	DT	6-3	285	11-27-58	Kansas	FA
McPherson, Miles	S	6-0	175	3-30-60	New Haven College	D10
Misko, John (1)	P	6-5	207	10- 1-54	Oregon State	FA
Parma, Rick (1)	WR	5-11	180	12- 4-57	San Jose State	FA
Pitcock, Charles (1)	T	6-4	265	2-20-58	Tulane	FA
Ponek, Martin	C	6-1	240	8- 7-58	Cal. Poly—SLO	FA
Redden, Barry	FB	5-10	205	7-21-60	Richmond	D1
Reilly, Mike	LB	6-4	217	2-14-59	Oklahoma	D8b
Scudday, Brian	C	6-3	253	4- 6-59	San Diego State	FA
Shearin, Joe	G	6-4	250	4-16-60	Texas	D7
Speight, Bob	T	6-4	260	11- 4-58	Boston University	D9
Stablein, Jerry	T	6-5	264	3-21-59	San Diego State	FA
Williams, Henry (1)	WR	5-11	183	5-16-58	Cal. State-Long Beach	FA
Wilson, Lee	CB	5-9	174	7-19-59	Compton College	FA

*Alexander and Lilja missed 1981 season due to injuries; Farmer missed 1980 and '81 seasons due to injuries.

MIAMI DOLPHINS
(Eastern Division, American Conference)

Don Shula

President—Joseph Robbie

Executive Vice-President and General Manager—J. Michael Robbie

Vice President—Joe Thomas

Director, Pro Scouting—Charlie Winner

Director, Player Personnel—Chuck Connor

Vice-President and Head Coach—Don Shula (19 years: 194-74-6)

Assistant Coaches:
 Assistant Head Coach-Defense—Bill Arnsparger
 Special Teams—Steve Crosby
 Quarterbacks—Wally English
 Defensive Backfield-Punters—Tom Keane
 Offensive Line-Running Game—John Sandusky
 Defensive Line-Run Defense—Mike Scarry
 Offensive Backfield-Special Teams—Carl Taseff

Public Relations Director—Bob Kearney
 (Office Phone: 576-1000—Area Code 305)

Offices—3550 Biscayne Blvd., Miami, Fla. 33137

Stadium—Orange Bowl (Capacity: 75,459)

Team Colors—Aqua and Orange

Training Site—Biscayne College, Miami, Fla.

1982 SCHEDULE
(All times local.
All games Sunday unless noted otherwise.)

Sept. 12	at New York Jets	4:00
Sept. 19	BALTIMORE	4:00
Sept. 26	at Green Bay	12:00
Oct. 3	at Cincinnati	1:00
Oct. 10	DETROIT	4:00
Oct. 17	NEW ENGLAND	1:00
Oct. 24	at Baltimore	2:00
Oct. 31	at Oakland	1:00
Nov. 8	SAN DIEGO (Mon.)	9:00
Nov. 14	CLEVELAND	4:00
Nov. 21	at Buffalo	1:00
Nov. 29	at Tampa Bay (Mon.)	9:00
Dec. 5	MINNESOTA	1:00
Dec. 12	at New England	1:00
Dec. 18	NEW YORK JETS (Sat.)	12:30
Dec. 27	BUFFALO (Mon.)	9:00

1981 RESULTS—(Won 11, Lost 5, Tied 1)

Dolphins	Opp.		Att.
20 St. Louis	7	(A)	50,351
30 Pittsburgh	10	(H)	74,190
16 Houston	10	(A)	47,379
31 Baltimore	28	(A)	41,630
28 New York Jets (OT)	28	(H)	69,631
21 Buffalo	31	(A)	80,020
13 Washington	10	(H)	47,367
27 Dallas	28	(A)	64,221
27 Baltimore	10	(H)	46,061
30 New England (OT)	27	(A)	61,297
17 Oakland	33	(H)	61,777
15 New York Jets	16	(A)	59,962
13 Philadelphia	10	(H)	67,797
24 New England	14	(H)	50,421
17 Kansas City	7	(A)	57,407
16 Buffalo	6	(H)	72,956

PLAYOFF GAME
38 San Diego	41	(H)	73,735

1981 GAMES STARTED

16 games: Bob Baumhower, Glenn Blackwood, Bob Brudzinski, A. J. Duhe, Jon Giesler, Larry Gordon, Eric Laakso, Ronnie Lee, Ed Newman, Earnest Rhone, Gerald Small.

15 games: Doug Betters, David Woodley.

14 games: Vern Den Herder.

12 games: Andra Franklin, Don McNeal.

11 games: Mark Dennard, Nat Moore, Tony Nathan.

10 games: Lyle Blackwood, Duriel Harris.

Less than 10 games: Bill Barnett (2), Woody Bennett (3), Don Bessillieu (6), Kim Bokamper (1), Jimmy Cefalo (5), Bruce Hardy (6), Eddie Hill (2), Steve Howell (2), Bob Kuchenberg (9), Dwight Stephenson (5), Don Strock (1), Ed Taylor (2), Jeff Toews (7), Tommy Vigorito (1), Fulton Walker (2).

MIAMI DOLPHINS 1982 VETERAN ROSTER

No.	Name	Pos.	Ht.	Wt.	NFL Exp.	Birth-date	College	Games in '81	How Acquired
88	Bailey, Elmer	WR	6-0	195	3	12-13-57	Minnesota	16	D4, '80
70	Barnett, Bill	DE	6-4	260	3	5-10-56	Nebraska	9	D3, '80
73	Baumhower, Bob	DT	6-5	260	6	8- 4-55	Alabama	16	D2, '77
34	Bennett, Woody	RB	6-2	222	4	3-24-55	Miami	3	W-NYJ, '80
46	Bessillieu, Don	S	6-1	200	4	5- 4-56	Georgia Tech	16	D5, '79
75	Betters, Doug	DE	6-7	260	5	6-11-56	Nevada-Reno	15	D6, '78
47	Blackwood, Glenn	S	6-0	186	4	2-23-57	Texas	16	D8b, '79
42	†Blackwood, Lyle	S	6-1	188	10	5- 2-51	Texas Christian	12	FA, '81
58	Bokamper, Kim	DE	6-6	250	6	9-25-54	San Jose State	16	D1b, '76
59	Brudzinski, Bob	LB	6-4	230	6	1- 1-55	Ohio State	16	T-LA, '81
81	Cefalo, Jimmy	WR	5-11	188	5	10- 5-56	Penn State	16	D3b, '78
	Cunningham, Eric	G	6-3	257	3	3-16-57	Penn State	*0	FA, '82
	Darby, Paul	WR	5-10	192	3	10-22-56	Southwest Texas State	*0	FA, '82
63	Dennard, Mark	C	6-1	252	4	11- 2-55	Texas A&M	11	D10, '78
77	Duhe, A. J.	LB	6-4	248	6	11-27-55	Louisiana State	16	D1, '77
37	Franklin, Andra	FB	5-10	225	2	8-22-59	Nebraska	16	D2, '81
79	Giesler, Jon	T	6-4	260	4	12-23-56	Michigan	16	D1, '79
50	Gordon, Larry	LB	6-4	230	7	7- 8-54	Arizona State	16	D1a, '76
74	Green, Cleveland	T	6-3	262	4	9-11-57	Southern	6	OFA, '79
84	Hardy, Bruce	TE	6-4	230	5	6- 1-56	Arizona State	16	D9, '78
82	Harris, Duriel	WR	5-11	176	7	11-27-54	New Mexico State	15	D3, '76
31	Hill, Eddie	RB	6-2	210	4	5-13-57	Memphis State	11	T-LA, '81
36	Howell, Steve	RB	6-2	230	4	12-20-56	Baylor	10	D4, '79
11	Jensen, Jim	QB	6-4	212	2	11-14-58	Boston University	16	D11, '81
40	Kozlowski, Mike	S	6-0	198	3	2-24-56	Colorado	14	D10b, '79
67	Kuechenberg, Bob	G	6-2	255	13	10-14-47	Notre Dame	16	FA, '70
68	†Laakso, Eric	T	6-4	265	5	11-29-56	Tulane	16	D4b, '78
86	Lee, Ronnie	TE	6-3	236	4	12-24-56	Baylor	16	D3c, '79
28	McNeal, Don	CB	5-11	192	3	5- 6-58	Alabama	12	D1, '80
89	Moore, Nat	WR	5-9	188	9	9-19-51	Florida	13	D3, '74
22	Nathan, Tony	RB	6-0	206	4	12-14-56	Alabama	13	D3a, '79
64	Newman, Ed	G	6-2	255	10	6- 4-51	Duke	16	D6, '73
3	Orosz, Tom	P	6-1	204	2	9-26-59	Ohio State	16	OFA, '81
78	Poole, Ken	DE	6-3	251	2	10-20-58	Northeast Louisiana	16	D5a, '81
54	Potter, Steve	LB	6-3	235	2	11- 6-57	Virginia	16	FA, '81
55	Rhone, Earnie	LB	6-2	224	7	8-20-53	Henderson, Ark.	16	OFA, '75
80	Rose, Joe	TE	6-3	230	3	6-24-57	California	16	D7, '80
52	Shull, Steve	LB	6-1	220	3	3-27-58	William & Mary	16	OFA, '80
48	Small, Gerald	CB	5-11	192	5	8-10-56	San Jose State	16	D4a, '78
57	Stephenson, Dwight	C	6-2	255	3	11-20-57	Alabama	16	D2, '80
10	Strock, Don	QB	6-5	220	9	11-27-50	Virginia Tech	16	D5a, '73
	Suggs, Shafer	S	6-1	204	6	4-28-53	Ball State	*0	FA, '82
45	Taylor, Ed	CB	6-0	175	8	5-13-53	Memphis State	6	FA, '79
60	Toews, Jeff	G	6-3	255	4	11- 4-57	Washington	9	D2, '79
32	Vigorito, Tom	RB	5-10	197	2	10-23-59	Virginia	16	D5b, '81
5	von Schamann, Uwe	PK	6-0	188	4	4-23-56	Oklahoma	16	D7, '79
41	Walker, Fulton	CB	5-10	193	2	4-30-58	West Virginia	16	D6b, '81
16	Woodley, David	QB	6-2	204	3	10-25-58	Louisiana State	15	D8b, '80

*Cunningham and Darby last active with New York Jets in 1980; Suggs last active in NFL with Cincinnati in 1980, played 2 games with Montreal-CFL in 1981.

†Option playout; subject to developments.

D—Draft; T—Trade; W—Waivers; FA—Free Agent; OFA—Original Free Agent; VFA—Veteran Free Agent; VA—Veteran Allocation; SupD—Supplemental Draft.

Also played with Dolphins in 1981—DT Mike Fultz (4 games), RB Nick Giaquinto (8), RB Bo Matthews (3), CB Ricky Ray (8), FB Terry Robiskie (1), LB Rodell Thomas (3). Retired: DE Vern Den Herder (16).

MIAMI DOLPHINS
1982 DRAFT CHOICES

(Number following name designates order of selection among 334 players drafted.)

Round and Player		Position	College
1. FOSTER, Roy	24	G	Southern Cal.
2. DUPER, Mark	52	WR	N.W. Louisiana
3. LANKFORD, Paul	80	DB	Penn State
4. BOWSER, Charles	108	LB	Duke
5. NELSON, Bob from Minnesota (a)	120	DT	Miami
DIANA, Rich	136	RB	Yale
6. TUTSON, Tom from San Diego (b)	161	DB	So. Carolina St.
HESTER, Ron	164	LB	Florida State
7. JOHNSON, Dan from New Orleans (c)	170	TE	Iowa State
COWAN, Larry	192	RB	Jackson State
8. RANDLE, Tate	220	DB	Texas Tech
9. CLARK, Steve from Detroit (d)	239	DE	Utah
BOATNER, Mack	248	RB	S.E. Louisiana
10. FISHER, Robin from Philadelphia (e)	271	LB	Florida
JONES, Wayne	276	T	Utah
11. CRUM, Gary	303	T	Wyoming
12. RODRIGUE, Mike	331	WR	Miami

(a) Acquired pick and sixth-round pick in 1981 for center Jim Langer, September 24, 1980.
(b) Acquired pick for punter George Roberts, August 31, 1981.
(c) Acquired pick and fourth-round pick in 1981 for quarterback Guy Benjamin, September 1, 1980.
(d) Acquired pick for linebacker Steve Towle, July 14, 1981.
(e) Acquired pick for running back Steve Howell, August 18, 1981.

MIAMI DOLPHINS
1982 ROOKIE AND FIRST-YEAR ROSTER

(1) Indicates player in previous NFL camp.
All others classified as rookies.

Name	Pos.	Hgt.	Wgt.	Birth-date	College	How Acquired
Allen, Carl (1)	C	6-2	237	4-26-58	Long Beach State	FA
Baker, Herb (1)	QB	6-0	193	8-27-57	Stephen F. Austin	FA
Boatner, Mack	FB	6-0	222	10- 4-58	Southeastern Louisiana	D9b
Bowser, Charles	LB	6-3	222	10- 2-59	Duke	D4
Burton, Ron	LB	5-11	211	....	South Carolina State	FA
Clark, Steve	DE	6-4	255	8- 2-60	Utah	D9a
Cowan, Larry	RB	5-11	190	7-11-60	Jackson State	D7b
Crenshaw, Keith	S	5-9	171	12-27-59	Duke	FA
Crum, Gary	T	6-5	285	8-12-59	Wyoming	D11
Diana, Rich	RB	5-9	220	9- 6-60	Yale	D5b
Doss, James	RB	5-11	214	10- 3-58	Mississippi State	FA
Duper, Mark	WR	5-9	185	1-25-59	Northwestern Louisiana	D2
Fisher, Robin	LB	6-0	231	12-13-59	Florida	D10a
Foster, Roy	G-T	6-4	275	5-24-60	Southern California	D1
Gruber, Bob (1)	T	6-5	263	6- 7-58	Pittsburgh	FA
Hester, Ron	LB	6-1	218	5-26-59	Florida State	D6b
Ingram, Lee	DE	6-1	254	12-31-58	Fort Valley State	FA
Johnson, Billy (1)	FB	6-0	262	3-29-57	North Carolina	FA
Johnson, Dan	TE	6-3	240	5-17-60	Iowa State	D7a
Jones, Wayne	C	6-4	273	2-10-60	Utah	D10b
Judson, William (1)	CB	6-1	181	3-26-59	South Carolina State	*D8 ('81)
Lankford, Paul	CB	6-1	178	6-15-58	Penn State	D3
Lockett, Frank (1)	WR	5-11	202	6- 1-57	Nebraska	FA
Nelson, Bob	DT	6-3	257	3- 3-59	Miami	D5a
Randle, Tate	S	6-0	197	8-15-59	Texas Tech	D8
Robinson, Joe (1)	T	6-4	285	10-10-56	Ohio State	FA
Rodrigue, Mike	WR	6-0	184	1-17-60	Miami	D12
Rollins, Kevin	FB	6-0	223	2- 5-59	Concord, W. Va.	FA
Rozier, Wendell	DE	6-2	268	5-18-59	Albany State	FA
Simon, Matt	RB	5-11	206	9- 5-59	Georgia	FA
Thomas, Cedric (1)	WR	6-0	188	9- 1-57	West Virginia	FA
Thompson, Frank	DE	6-6	247	12-23-58	Jackson State	FA
Tutson, Thomas	CB	6-1	178	8-27-58	South Carolina State	D6a
Verria, Joe (1)	DT	6-2	254	11- 4-57	Bridgewater State	FA
Weaver, Ed	DT	5-11	266	4-25-60	Georgia	FA

*Judson missed 1981 season due to injury.

MINNESOTA VIKINGS
(Central Division, National Conference)

Bud Grant

President—Max Winter
Vice-President & General Manager—Mike Lynn
Director of Football Operations—Jerry Reichow
Player Personnel Director—Frank Gilliam
Head Coach—Harry P. (Bud) Grant (15 years: 138-75-5)
Assistant Coaches:
  Offense—Jerry Burns
  Defensive Line—Tom Cecchini
  Defense—Bob Hollway
  Defensive Backfield—Jed Hughes
  Offensive Backfield—Bus Mertes
  Offensive Line—John Michaels
  Linebackers—Floyd Reese
  Receivers—Les Steckel
Public Relations Director—Merrill Swanson
  (Office Phone: 828-6500—Area Code 612)
Offices—9520 Viking Drive, Eden Prairie, Minn. 55344
Stadium—Metrodome, Minneapolis, Minn. (Capacity: 63,000)
Team Colors—Purple, Gold and White
Training Site—Mankato State University, Mankato, Minn.

1982 SCHEDULE
(All times local.
All games Sunday unless noted otherwise.)

Sept. 12	TAMPA BAY	12:00
Sept. 16	at Buffalo (Thurs.)	8:30
Sept. 26	DALLAS	12:00
Oct. 3	at Chicago	12:00
Oct. 10	at Tampa Bay	1:00
Oct. 17	NEW ORLEANS	12:00
Oct. 24	GREEN BAY	12:00
Nov. 1	DETROIT (Mon.)	8:00
Nov. 7	at San Francisco	1:00
Nov. 14	at Washington	1:00
Nov. 21	vs. Green Bay (Milw.)	12:00
Nov. 28	CHICAGO	12:00
Dec. 5	at Miami	1:00
Dec. 12	BALTIMORE	12:00
Dec. 19	at Detroit	1:00
Dec. 26	NEW YORK JETS	12:00

1981 RESULTS—(Won 7, Lost 9)

Vikings	Opp.		Att.
13 Tampa Bay	21	(A)	66,287
10 Oakland	36	(H)	47,186
26 Detroit	24	(H)	45,350
30 Green Bay	13	(A)	55,012
24 Chicago	21	(H)	43,827
33 San Diego	31	(A)	50,708
35 Philadelphia	23	(H)	45,459
17 St. Louis	30	(A)	48,039
17 Denver	19	(A)	78,834
25 Tampa Bay	10	(H)	47,038
20 New Orleans	10	(A)	45,215
30 Atlanta	31	(A)	54,086
23 Green Bay	35	(H)	46,025
9 Chicago	10	(A)	50,766
7 Detroit	45	(A)	79,428
6 Kansas City	10	(H)	41,110

1981 GAMES STARTED

16 games: Matt Blair, Ted Brown, Wes Hamilton, Tom Hannon, Kurt Knoff, Fred McNeill, Steve Riley, Joe Senser, Scott Studwell, Willie Teal, James White, Sammy White, Ron Yary.

15 games: Mark Mullaney, Ahmad Rashad, Jeff Siemon, Dennis Swilley.

14 games: Tommy Kramer.

13 games: Jim Hough, Rickey Young.

10 games: John Turner.

Less than 10 games: Brent Boyd (3), Steve Dils (2), Tony Galbreath (1), Randy Holloway (8), Dennis Johnson (1), Jim Langer (1), Terry LeCount (2), Leo Lewis (1), Doug Martin (9), John Swain (1), Walt Williams (5).

MINNESOTA VIKINGS 1982 VETERAN ROSTER

No.	Name	Pos.	Ht.	Wt.	NFL Exp.	Birth-date	College	Games in '81	How Acquired
59	Blair, Matt	LB	6-5	229	9	9-20-51	Iowa State	16	D2b, '74
62	Boyd, Brent	G	6-3	260	3	3-23-57	UCLA	3	D3, '80
23	Brown, Ted	RB	5-10	198	4	2- 2-57	North Carolina State	16	D1, '79
82	†Bruer, Bob	TE	6-5	235	4	5- 2-53	Mankato State	15	FA, '80
8	Coleman, Greg	P	6-0	178	6	9- 9-54	Florida A&M	15	FA, '78
7	Danmeier, Rick	K	6-0	183	5	4- 8-52	Sioux Falls	16	FA, '77
12	†Dils, Steve	QB	6-1	190	4	12- 8-55	Stanford	2	D4, '79
65	Elshire, Neil	DE	6-6	250	2	3- 8-58	Oregon	4	W-Was, '81
32	Galbreath, Tony	RB	6-0	230	7	1-29-54	Missouri	14	T-NO, '81
61	Hamilton, Wes	G	6-3	255	7	4-24-53	Tulsa	16	D3, '76
45	Hannon, Tom	S	5-11	193	6	3- 5-55	Michigan State	16	D3, '77
36	Harrell, Sam	RB	6-2	213	2	2- 7-57	East Carolina	4	D11, '80
75	Holloway, Randy	DE	6-5	245	5	8-26-55	Pittsburgh	16	D1, '78
51	Hough, Jim	C	6-2	267	5	8- 4-56	Utah State	16	D4, '78
56	Huffman, Dave	C	6-6	255	4	4- 4-57	Notre Dame	13	D2, '79
76	Irwin, Tim	T	6-6	275	2	12-13-56	Tennessee	7	D3, '81
52	Johnson, Dennis	LB	6-3	230	3	6-19-58	Southern California	16	D4, '80
53	Johnson, Henry	LB	6-2	235	3	3-20-58	Georgia Tech	16	D7, '80
25	Knoff, Kurt	S	6-2	188	7	4- 6-54	Kansas	16	W-Hou, '79
9	Kramer, Tommy	QB	6-1	199	6	3- 7-55	Rice	14	D1, '77
58	†Langer, Jim	C	6-2	253	13	5-16-48	South Dakota State	9	T-Mia, '80
80	LeCount, Terry	WR	5-10	172	5	7- 9-56	Florida	16	W-SF, '79
87	Lewis, Leo	WR	5-8	170	2	8-17-56	Missouri	4	FA, '81
79	Martin, Doug	DE	6-3	258	3	5-22-57	Washington	16	D1, '80
88	McDole, Mardye	WR	5-11	195	2	5- 1-59	Mississippi State	9	D2a, '81
54	McNeill, Fred	LB	6-2	229	9	5- 6-52	UCLA	16	D1a, '74
77	Mullaney, Mark	DE	6-6	242	8	4-30-53	Colorado State	15	D1, '75
49	Nord, Keith	S	6-0	197	4	3-13-57	St. Cloud State	16	OFA, '79
40	Paschal, Doug	RB	6-2	219	2	3- 5-58	North Carolina	*0	D5a, '80
36	Payton, Eddie	KR	5-6	179	6	8- 3-51	Jackson State	16	FA, '80
28	Rashad, Ahmad	WR	6-2	200	10	11-19-49	Oregon	16	T-Sea, '76
22	Redwine, Jarvis	RB	5-10	198	2	5-16-57	Nebraska	3	D2c, '81
78	Riley, Steve	T	6-6	253	9	11-23-52	Southern California	16	D1b, '74
57	Sendlein, Robin	LB	6-3	224	2	12- 1-58	Texas	16	D2b, '81
81	Senser, Joe	TE	6-4	238	3	8-18-56	West Chester State	16	D6, '79
55	Studwell, Scott	LB	6-2	224	6	8-27-54	Illinois	16	D9, '77
29	Swain, John	CB	6-1	195	2	8- 4-59	Miami	12	D4, '81
67	Swilley, Dennis	C	6-3	241	6	6-28-55	Texas A&M	16	D2, '77
37	Teal, Willie	CB	5-10	195	3	12-20-57	Louisiana State	16	D2, '80
27	Turner, John	CB	6-0	199	5	9-22-56	Miami	13	D2, '78
72	White, James	DT	6-3	263	7	10-26-53	Oklahoma State	16	D1, '76
85	White, Sammy	WR	5-11	189	7	3-16-54	Grambling	16	D2, '76
44	†Williams, Walt	CB	6-1	185	6	7-10-54	New Mexico State	16	FA, '81
11	Wilson, Wade	QB	6-3	212	2	2- 1-59	East Texas State	3	D8, '81
91	Yakavonis, Ray	DE	6-4	243	2	1-20-57	East Stroudsburg State	15	D6, '80
73	Yary, Ron	T	6-6	255	15	8-16-46	Southern California	16	D1, '68
34	Young, Rickey	RB	6-2	195	8	12-12-53	Jackson State	16	T-SD, '78

*Paschal missed 1981 season due to injury.

†Option playout; subject to developments.

D—Draft; T—Trade; W—Waivers; FA—Free Agent; OFA—Original Free Agent; VFA—Veteran Free Agent; VA—Veteran Allocation; SupD—Supplemental Draft.

Also played with Vikings in 1981—LB Jeff Siemon (16 games).

MINNESOTA VIKINGS
1982 DRAFT CHOICES

(Number following name designates order of selection among 334 players drafted.)

Round and Player		Position	College
1. NELSON, Darrin	7	RB	Stanford
2. TAUSCH, Terry	39	T	Texas
3. Choice to New Orleans (a)			
4. FAHNHORST, Jim	92	LB	Minnesota
5. Choice to Miami (b)			
6. STORR, Greg	147	LB	Boston College
7. JORDAN, Steve	179	TE	Brown
8. HARMON, Kirk	206	LB	Pacific
9. HOWARD, Bryan	233	DB	Tennessee St.
10. LUCEAR, Gerald	260	WR	Temple
11. ROUSE, Curtis	286	G	Tenn.-Chatt
12. MILNER, Hobson	318	RB	Cincinnati

(a) Traded pick for running back Tony Galbreath, August 31, 1981.

(b) Traded pick and sixth-round pick in 1981 for center Jim Langer, September 24, 1980.

MINNESOTA VIKINGS
1982 ROOKIE AND FIRST-YEAR ROSTER

(1) Indicates player in previous NFL camp.
All others classified as rookies.

Name	Pos.	Hgt.	Wgt.	Birth-date	College	How Acquired
Bergdale, John	WR	6-0	190	10-27-59	Augustana	FA
Bodin, Amory (1)	P	5-11	190	12-26-57	Minnesota-Duluth	FA
Bush, Michael (1)	WR	6-1	185	4-14-58	California Poly-SLO	FA
D'Andrea, Michael	LB	6-2	222	11-17-59	Ohio State	FA
Fahnhorst, Jim	LB	6-3	232	11- 8-58	Minnesota	D4
Gabbidon, Earl (1)	TE	6-3	223	1-15-58	Arizona State	FA
Harmon, Kirk	LB	6-2	235	10-22-58	Pacific	D8
Harvey, Ken	WR	6-0	175	5-16-58	Northern Iowa	FA
Howard, Bryan	S	6-1	200	3- 6-59	Tennessee State	D9
Jordan, Steve	TE	6-3	228	1-10-61	Brown University	D7
Lawrence, Tom	DB	6-0	182	10-11-58	Minnesota-Duluth	FA
Lucear, Gerald	WR	5-11	179	10-24-59	Temple	D10
McGill, Michael	KR	5-11	185	1-17-59	William Jewell, Mo.	FA
Milner, Hobson	RB	6-1	218	3-13-59	Cincinnati	D12
Murtha, Greg (1)	T	6-6	268	4-23-57	Minnesota	*FA ('81)
Neilson, Steve	S	6-0	205	7-15-60	St. Thomas	FA
Nelson, Darrin	RB	5-8	181	1- 2-59	Stanford	D1
Ray, Wendell (1)	DE	6-4	233	10-19-56	Missouri	*D5 ('81)
Rouse, Curtis	G	6-2	304	7-13-60	Chattanooga	D11
Schluchter, Wayne	S	6-3	202	10-14-59	North Dakota State	FA
Stephanos, Bill (1)	T	6-4	262	3-24-57	Boston College	*D11 ('81)
Storr, Greg	LB	6-2	224	10-16-60	Boston College	D6
Tausch, Terry	T	6-4	278	2- 5-59	Texas	D2
Wilson, Jeffrey	P	6-2	190	3-15-60	Bethel College	FA

*Murtha, Ray and Stephanos missed 1981 season due to injuries.

NEW ENGLAND PATRIOTS
(Eastern Division, American Conference)

Ron Meyer

President—William H. Sullivan, Jr.
General Manager—Francis (Bucko) Kilroy
Assistant General Manager—Patrick Sullivan
Director of Player Development—Dick Steinberg
Director of Pro Scouting—Bill McPeak
Head Coach—Ron Meyer (First Year)
Assistant Coaches:
    Defensive Line—Tommy Brasher
    Running Backs—Cleve Bryant
    Strength and Conditioning—LeBaron Caruthers
    Receivers—Steve Endicott
    Offensive Coordinator-Quarterbacks—Lew Erber
    Defensive Coordinator—Jim Mora
    Offensive Line—Bill Muir
    Special Teams-Tight Ends—Dante Scarnecchia
    Linebackers—Steve Sidwell
    Secondary—Steve Walters
Director of Media Relations—Tom Hoffman
    (Office Phone: 543-7911—Area Code 617)
Offices—Schaefer Stadium, Route 1, Foxboro, Mass. 02035
Stadium—Schaefer Stadium, Foxboro, Mass. (Capacity: 61,297)
Team Colors—Red, White and Blue
Training Site—Bryant College, Smithfield, R. I.

1982 SCHEDULE
(All times local.
All games Sunday unless noted otherwise.)

Sept. 12	at Baltimore	2:00
Sept. 19	NEW YORK JETS	1:00
Sept. 26	SEATTLE	1:00
Oct. 3	at Buffalo	1:00
Oct. 10	CINCINNATI	1:00
Oct. 17	at Miami	1:00
Oct. 24	ST. LOUIS	1:00
Oct. 31	at New York Jets	1:00
Nov. 7	BALTIMORE	1:00
Nov. 14	BUFFALO	1:00
Nov. 21	at Cleveland	1:00
Nov. 28	HOUSTON	1:00
Dec. 5	at Chicago	12:00
Dec. 12	MIAMI	1:00
Dec. 19	at Seattle	1:00
Dec. 26	at Pittsburgh	1:00

1981 RESULTS—(Won 2, Lost 14)

Patriots		Opp.		Att.
28	Baltimore	29	(H)	49,572
3	Philadelphia	13	(A)	71,089
21	Dallas	35	(H)	61,297
21	Pittsburgh (OT)	27	(A)	53,344
33	Kansas City	17	(H)	55,931
24	New York Jets	28	(A)	55,093
38	Houston	10	(H)	60,474
22	Washington	24	(A)	50,394
17	Oakland	27	(A)	44,246
27	Miami (OT)	30	(H)	61,297
6	New York Jets	17	(H)	45,342
17	Buffalo	20	(A)	76,374
20	St. Louis	27	(H)	39,946
14	Miami	24	(A)	50,421
10	Buffalo	19	(H)	42,549
21	Baltimore	23	(A)	17,073

1981 GAMES STARTED

16 games: Julius Adams, Richard Bishop, Pete Brock, Ray Clayborn, Tim Fox, John Hannah, Shelby Jordan, Rod Shoate.

15 games: Bob Cryder, Mike Hawkins, Harold Jackson.

14 games: Don Hasselbeck, Rick Sanford.

13 games: Stanley Morgan.

12 games: Steve Nelson.

11 games: Anthony Collins, Dwight Wheeler.

Less than 10 games: Mark Buben (4), Don Calhoun (7), Matt Cavanaugh (8), Sam Cunningham (8), Lin Dawson (3), Vagas Ferguson (5), Bob Golic (9), Steve Grogan (7), Mike Haynes (6), Brian Holloway (5), Roland James (6), Steve King (1), John Lee (4), Keith Lee (6), Bill Matthews (9), Tony McGee (9), Tom Owen (1), Carlos Pennywell (2), Garry Puetz (1), Mosi Tatupu (1), Don Westbrook (1), John Zamberlin (1).

NEW ENGLAND PATRIOTS 1982 VETERAN ROSTER

No.	Name	Pos.	Ht.	Wt.	NFL Exp.	Birth-date	College	Games in '81	How Acquired
85	Adams, Julius	DE	6-4	263	11	4-26-48	Texas Southern	16	D2, '71
64	Bishop, Richard	NT	6-1	260	7	3-23-50	Louisville	16	FA, '76
55	Blackmon, Don	LB	6-3	235	2	3-14-58	Tulsa	16	D4, '81
58	Brock, Pete	C	6-5	260	7	7-14-54	Colorado	16	D1b, '76
37	Brown, Preston	WR	5-10	184	2	3- 2-58	Vanderbilt	*0	D6, '80
63	Buben, Mark	DE	6-3	260	3	3-23-57	Tufts	16	OFA, '79
44	Calhoun, Don	RB	6-0	212	9	4-29-52	Kansas State	14	FA, '75
3	Camarillo, Rich	P	5-11	189	2	11-29-59	Washington	9	OFA, '81
12	Cavanaugh, Matt	QB	6-1	210	5	10-27-56	Pittsburgh	16	D2, '78
35	Clark, Allan	RB	5-10	186	3	6- 8-57	Northern Arizona	*0	D10b, 79
65	Clark, Steve	DE	6-5	260	2	10-29-59	Kansas State	7	D5, '81
26	Clayborn, Ray	CB	6-1	190	6	1- 2-55	Texas	16	D1a, '77
33	Collins, Tony	RB	5-11	202	2	5-27-59	East Carolina	16	D2, '81
75	Cryder, Bob	G	6-4	265	5	9- 7-56	Alabama	15	D1, '78
39	Cunningham, Sam	RB	6-3	230	9	8-15-50	Southern California	11	D1b, '73
87	Dawson, Lin	TE	6-3	235	2	6-24-59	North Carolina State	15	D8b, '81
47	*Dombroski, Paul	CB	6-0	185	3	8- 8-56	Linfield	*11	W-KC, '81
43	Ferguson, Vagas	RB	6-1	194	3	3- 6-57	Notre Dame	13	D1b, '80
51	Golic, Bob	LB	6-2	240	3	10-26-57	Notre Dame	16	D2, '79
14	Grogan, Steve	QB	6-4	208	8	7-24-53	Kansas State	8	D5a, '75
71	Hamilton, Ray	NT	6-1	245	10	1-20-51	Oklahoma	15	D14, '73
73	Hannah, John	G	6-2	265	10	4- 4-51	Alabama	16	D1a, '73
80	Hasselbeck, Don	TE	6-7	245	6	4- 1-55	Colorado	14	D2b, '77
59	Hawkins, Mike	LB	6-2	232	5	11-29-55	Texas A&I	15	D7, '78
40	Haynes, Mike	CB	6-2	195	7	7- 1-53	Arizona State	8	D1a, '76
76	Holloway, Brian	T	6-7	273	2	7-25-59	Stanford	16	D1, '81
38	James, Roland	DB	6-2	189	3	2-18-58	Tennessee	16	D1a, '80
32	Johnson, Andy	RB	6-0	204	8	10-18-52	Georgia	16	D5a, '74
74	Jordan, Shelby	T	6-7	260	7	1-23-52	Washington, Mo.	16	FA, '74
52	King, Steve	LB	6-4	230	10	6-10-51	Tulsa	16	OFA, '73
22	Lee, Keith	DB	5-11	192	2	12-22-57	Colorado State	15	FA, '81
53	Matthews, Bill	LB	6-2	235	4	3-12-56	South Dakota State	16	D5, '78
78	McGee, Tony	DE	6-4	250	12	1-18-49	Bishop	16	T-Chi, '74
50	McGrew, Larry	LB	6-4	231	2	7-23-57	Southern California	*0	D2, '80
86	Morgan, Stanley	WR	5-11	180	6	2-17-55	Tennessee	13	D1b, '77
57	Nelson, Steve	LB	6-2	230	9	4-26-51	North Dakota State	12	D2b, '74
17	†Owen, John	QB	6-1	194	9	9- 1-52	Wichita State	2	T-SF, '76
83	†Pennywell, Carlos	WR	6-2	180	5	3-18-56	Grambling	5	D3, '78
25	Sanford, Rick	DB	6-1	192	4	1- 9-57	South Carolina	16	D1, '79
1	Smith, John	PK	6-0	185	9	12-30-48	Southampton, Eng.	16	FA, '74
30	Tatupu, Mosi	RB	6-0	229	5	4-26-55	Southern California	16	D8b, '78
82	Toler, Ken	WR	6-2	195	2	5- 9-59	Mississippi	16	D7, '81
83	Westbrook, Don	WR	5-10	185	6	11- 1-53	Nebraska	12	FA, '76
62	Wheeler, Dwight	T	6-3	255	4	1-13-55	Tennessee State	16	D4, '78
54	Zamberlin, John	LB	6-2	239	4	2-13-56	Pacific Lutheran	16	D5, '79

*Brown, A. Clark and McGrew missed 1981 season due to injuries; Dombroski played 5 games with Kansas City, 6 with New England in 1981.

†Option playout; subject to developments.

D—Draft; T—Trade; W—Waivers; FA—Free Agent; OFA—Original Free Agent; VFA—Veteran Free Agent; VA—Veteran Allocation; SupD—Supplemental Draft.

Also played with Patriots in 1981—S Tim Fox (16 games), P Ken Hartley (2), P Mike Hubach (5), RB Horace Ivory (1), WR Harold Jackson (16), DE John Lee (4), OT Garry Puetz (15), LB Rod Shoate (16), CB Darrell Wilson (1). Retired: C Bill Lenkaitis (12).

NEW ENGLAND PATRIOTS
1982 DRAFT CHOICES

(Number following name designates order of selection among 334 players drafted.)

Round and Player		Position	College
1. SIMS, Ken	1	DE	Texas
WILLIAMS, Lester from San Francisco (a)	27	DT	Miami
2. Choice to San Francisco (b)			
WEATHERS, Robert from Green Bay through San Diego (c)	40	RB	Arizona State
TIPPETT, Andre from Washington through San Francisco (d)	41	LB	Iowa
HALEY, Darryl from San Francisco (a)	55	T	Utah
3. JONES, Cedric	56	WR	Duke
WEISHUHN, Clayton from Seattle (e)	60	LB	Angelo State
4. CRUMP, George	85	DE	East Carolina
INGRAM, Brian from San Francisco (a)	111	LB	Tennessee
5. MARION, Fred	112	DB	Miami
6. SMITH, Ricky	141	DB	Alabama State
7. ROBERTS, Jeff	168	LB	Tulane
8. COLLINS, Ken	197	LB	Washington St.
9. MURDOCK, Kelvin	224	WR	Troy State
10. CLARK, Brian	253	K	Florida
11. Choice exercised in 1981 Supplemental Draft (f)			
12. SANDON, Steve from New York Giants (g)	296	QB	Northern Iowa
TAYLOR, Greg	308	KR	Virginia

(a) Acquired first-, fourth- and two second-round picks for tight end Russ Francis and second-round pick, April 27, 1982.

(b) See (a).

(c) Green Bay traded pick, first-round pick in 1983, second-round pick in 1984, wide receiver Aundra Thompson and switched first-round positions with San Diego for wide receiver John Jefferson, September 17, 1981; San Diego traded pick and third-round pick in 1983 to New England for safety Tim Fox, April 27, 1982.

(d) Washington traded pick and second-round pick in 1981 to San Francisco for running back Wilbur Jackson, August 21, 1980; San Francisco traded pick to New England (See a).

(e) Acquired pick for running back Horace Ivory, September 25, 1981.

(f) Selected wide receiver Chy Davidson.

(g) Acquired pick for safety Bill Currier, August 31, 1981.

NEW ENGLAND PATRIOTS
1982 ROOKIE AND FIRST-YEAR ROSTER

(1) Indicates player in previous NFL camp.
(2) Indicates player with minor league experience.
   All others classified as rookies.

Name	Pos.	Hgt.	Wgt.	Birth-date	College	How Acquired
Adell, Bernie	RB	5-10	205	5-10-59	Notre Dame	FA
Arnold, Ray	WR	6-0	188	1-13-60	Cal. State-Hayward	FA
Brown, Richard	WR	5-11	178	12-22-57	Fitchburg State	FA
Bynum, Ricky	DB	6-0	195	2- 6-59	Colorado	FA
Clark, Brian	PK	6-2	198	6-28-58	Florida	D10
Coash, Beau	TE	6-2	220	6-12-60	Middlebury	FA
Collins, Ken	LB	6-3	236	7-27-60	Washington State	D8
Conran, Pat	CB	6-1	185	10-29-60	Yale	FA
Cook, Charles (1)	DE	6-3	255	5-13-59	Miami (Fla.)	*FA ('81)
Cruise, Mark (1)	DB	6-1	195	3-10-59	Rhode Island	FA
Crump, George	DE	6-4	260	7-22-59	East Carolina	D4a
Dean, Roy	WR	6-0	185	5-23-57	Alabama A&M	FA
Dickert, Mark	P	5-11	165	7-18-58	Florida	FA
DiRenzo, Jim	PK	5-10	185	5-20-59	Acadia (Canada)	FA
Donnalley, Kevin	S	6-0	178	1-17-58	N. Dakota State	*FA ('81)
Donnelly, Jim	TE	6-4	250	8-29-59	Long Beach State	FA
Ellis, John	T-G	6-3	270	12- 9-59	Rhode Island	FA
Franklin, Jerrell	G-C	6-3	260	5- 4-59	Southern	FA
Golden, Tim (1)	LB	6-2	220	11-15-59	Florida	FA
Green, Tony	NT	6-4	275	8- 1-58	Springfield	FA
Haley, Darryl	T	6-4	279	2-16-61	Utah	D2c
Henson, Luther (1)	DT-DE	6-0	275	3-25-59	Ohio State	Waiv.
Hersey, Richard (1)	RB	6-2	200	3-24-59	Arizona	FA
Ingram, Brian	LB	6-4	230	10-31-59	Tennessee	D4b
Jones, Cedric	WR-KR	5-11	184	6- 1-60	Duke	D3a
Jordan, Roosevelt	RB	5-10	185	8- 6-58	Tuskegee	FA
Kerrigan, Mike	QB	6-3	190	4-27-60	Northwestern	FA
Lahay, Bruce	P-K	6-1	225	2-24-59	Arkansas	FA
Marion, Fred	S	6-2	196	8- 2-59	Miami (Fla.)	D5
Monroe, Terry	NT	6-3	270	1- 7-58	Houston	FA
Murdock, Kelvin	WR	6-0	166	4- 7-60	Troy State	D9
Musselman, Brian (1)	C	6-2	255	5- 9-59	Virginia	FA
Owens, Dennis	DT	6-1	252	2-24-60	North Carolina State	FA
Pagley, Lou (2)	QB	6-3	210	6-15-58	Notre Dame	FA
Roberts, Jeff	LB	6-2	234	12-23-60	Tulane	D7
Rose, Anthony	S	5-9	180	12-18-59	Clemson	FA
Sandon, Steve	QB	6-3	206	11-11-59	Northern Iowa	D11
Sims, Ken	DE	6-5	279	10-31-59	Texas	D1a
Smith, Ricky	CB	6-0	174	7-20-60	Alabama State	D6
Smith, Terry	DB	5-11	192	1-29-59	Furman	FA
Tautolo, John (1)	G	6-3	260	5-29-59	UCLA	*FA ('81)
Taylor, Greg	WR-KR	5-8	175	10-23-58	Virginia	D12
Tippett, Andre	LB	6-3	231	12-27-59	Iowa	D2b
Villella, Rich (1)	RB	5-11	197	1-18-59	Brown	*FA ('81)
Weathers, Robert	RB	6-2	217	9-13-60	Arizona	D2a
Weishuhn, Clayton	LB	6-2	218	10- 9-59	Angelo State	D3b
Williams, Brian (1)	TE	6-5	230	10-14-57	Southern	FA
Williams, Lester	NT	6-3	272	1-19-59	Miami	D1b
Wooten, Ron (1)	G	6-4	257	6-28-59	North Carolina	*D6 ('81)
Wright, Gary (1)	TE	6-3	235	4- 8-57	American Int'l.	*FA ('81)

*Cook, Tautolo, Villella, Wooten and Wright missed 1981 season due to injuries; Donnalley played 1 game with Patriots in 1981.

NEW ORLEANS SAINTS
(Western Division, National Conference)

Bum Phillips

Owner—John W. Mecom, Jr.
President—Eddie Jones
Vice President-Administration—Fred Williams
Director of Operations—Harry Hulmes
Director of Player Negotiations—Pat Peppler
Director of Pro Personnel—Ernie Hefferle
Director of Player Personnel—Bob Whitman
Head Coach and General Manager—O. A. (Bum) Phillips (7 years: 59-47-0)
Assistant Coaches:
   Tight Ends—Andy Everest
   Offensive Coordinator—King Hill
   Offensive Backfield—John Levra
   Assistant Offensive Line—Carl Mauck
   Receivers—Lamar McHan
   Strength—Russell Paternostro
   Defensive Coordinator—Wade Phillips
   Special Teams—Harold Richardson
   Offensive Line—Joe Spencer
   Defensive Backs—Lance Van Zandt
   Linebackers—John Paul Young
   Defensive Line—Willie Zapalac
Director of Public Relations—Greg Suit
   (Office Phone: 587-3034—Area Code 504)
Offices—1500 Poydras St., New Orleans, La. 70112
Stadium—Louisiana Superdome (Capacity: 71,330)
Team Colors—Old Gold, Black and White
Training Site—Dodgertown, Vero Beach, Fla.

1982 SCHEDULE
(All times local.
All games Sunday unless noted otherwise.)

Sept. 12	ST. LOUIS	12:00
Sept. 19	at Chicago	12:00
Sept. 26	DENVER	12:00
Oct. 3	at Oakland	1:00
Oct. 10	SAN FRANCISCO	12:00
Oct. 17	at Minnesota	12:00
Oct. 24	at Los Angeles	1:00
Oct. 31	ATLANTA	12:00
Nov. 7	LOS ANGELES	12:00
Nov. 14	at San Diego	1:00
Nov. 21	KANSAS CITY	12:00
Nov. 28	at San Francisco	1:00
Dec. 5	TAMPA BAY	12:00
Dec. 12	at Atlanta	4:00
Dec. 19	at Dallas	3:00
Dec. 26	WASHINGTON	12:00

1981 RESULTS—(Won 4, Lost 12)

Saints	Opp.		Att.
0 Atlanta	27	(A)	57,406
23 Los Angeles	17	(H)	62,063
7 New York Giants	20	(A)	69,814
14 San Francisco	21	(A)	44,433
6 Pittsburgh	20	(H)	64,578
14 Philadelphia	31	(H)	52,728
17 Cleveland	20	(A)	76,059
17 Cincinnati	7	(H)	46,336
10 Atlanta	41	(H)	63,637
21 Los Angeles	13	(A)	61,068
10 Minnesota	20	(A)	45,215
27 Houston	24	(A)	49,581
14 Tampa Bay	31	(H)	62,209
3 St. Louis	30	(A)	46,923
7 Green Bay	35	(H)	45,518
17 San Francisco	21	(H)	43,639

1981 GAMES STARTED

16 games: Sam Adams, Stan Brock, Elois Grooms, Larry Hardy, Rickey Jackson, Derland Moore, Glenn Redd, George Rogers, Fred Sturt.

15 games: Jack Holmes, Jim Kovach, Tommy Myers, Johnnie Poe.

14 games: Russell Gary.

13 games: Jeff Groth, Rob Nairne, Dave Waymer.

12 games: James Taylor.

11 games: John Hill, Archie Manning, Guido Merkens.

Less than 10 games: Gordon Banks (1), Barry Bennett (3), Monte Bennett (6), Ken Bordelon (3), Jerry Boyarsky (7), Hoby Brenner (1), Wes Chandler (4), Chuck Evans (1), Ike Harris (3), Dave Lafary (4), Jim Pietrzak (5), Ricky Ray (4), Bobby Scott (1), Frank Wattelet (3), Dave Wilson (4).

NEW ORLEANS SAINTS 1982 VETERAN ROSTER

No.	Name	Pos.	Ht.	Wt.	NFL Exp.	Birth-date	College	Games in '81	How Acquired
61	Adams, Sam	G	6-3	260	11	9-20-48	Prairie View A&M	16	T-NE, '81
63	Bennett, Barry	DT	6-4	257	5	12-10-56	Concordia, Minn.	3	D3, '78
91	Bennett, Monte	DT	6-3	260	2	4-27-59	Kansas State	16	OFA, '81
50	Bordelon, Ken	LB	6-4	226	6	8-26-54	Louisiana State	15	T-LA, '76
77	Boyarsky, Jerry	DT	6-3	290	2	5-15-59	Pittsburgh	11	D5b, '81
	Bradshaw, Craig	QB	6-5	215	2	8-14-57	Utah State	*0	FA, '82
85	Brenner, Hoby	TE	6-4	240	2	6- 2-59	Southern California	9	D3b, '81
67	Brock, Stan	T	6-6	275	3	6- 8-58	Colorado	16	D1, '80
14	Erxleben, Russell	P	6-4	219	3	1-13-57	Texas	16	D1, '79
59	Evans, Chuck	LB	6-3	235	3	12-19-56	Stanford	16	D8, '80
20	Gary, Russell	S	5-11	195	2	7-31-59	Nebraska	14	D2a, '81
78	Grooms, Elois	DE	6-4	250	8	5-20-53	Tennessee Tech	16	D3b, '75
48	Groth, Jeff	WR	5-10	172	4	7- 2-57	Bowling Green	15	FA, '81
87	Hardy, Larry	TE	6-3	230	5	7- 9-56	Jackson State	16	D12, '78
82	Harris, Ike	WR	6-3	210	8	11-27-52	Iowa State	3	T-St.L, '78
62	Hill, John	C	6-2	246	11	4-16-50	Lehigh	13	W-NYG, '75
45	Holmes, Jack	RB	6-0	210	5	6-20-53	Texas Southern	16	FA, '78
69	Hudson, Nat	G	6-3	270	2	10-11-57	Georgia	16	D6a, '81
57	Jackson, Rickey	LB	6-2	230	2	3-20-58	Pittsburgh	16	D2b, '81
52	Kovach, Jim	LB	6-2	225	4	5- 1-56	Kentucky	15	D4, '79
64	Lafary, Dave	T	6-7	280	6	1-13-55	Purdue	16	D5a, '77
8	Manning, Archie	QB	6-3	200	12	5-19-49	Mississippi	12	D1, '71
86	†Martini, Rich	WR	6-2	185	4	11-19-55	California-Davis	12	FA, '81
56	Mathis, Reggie	LB	6-2	220	3	3-18-56	Oklahoma	*0	D2, '79
84	Mauti, Rich	WR	6-0	190	5	5-25-54	Penn State	*0	OFA, '77
19	Merkens, Guido	WR	6-1	195	5	8-14-55	Sam Houston State	16	FA, '80
74	Moore, Derland	DT	6-4	253	10	10- 7-51	Oklahoma	16	D2a, '73
37	Myers, Tommy	S	6-0	180	11	10-24-50	Syracuse	16	D3b, '72
55	†Nairne, Rob	LB	6-4	227	6	3-24-54	Oregon State	16	T-Den, '81
83	Owens, Tinker	WR	5-11	170	6	10- 3-54	Oklahoma	*0	D4, '76
53	Pelluer, Scott	LB	6-2	215	2	4-28-59	Washington State	16	W-Dal, '81
76	†Pietrzak, Jim	C	6-5	260	8	2-21-53	Eastern Michigan	16	FA, '79
25	Poe, Johnnie	CB	6-1	182	2	8-29-59	Missouri	15	D6b, '81
58	Redd, Glen	LB	6-1	225	2	6-17-58	Brigham Young	16	D6c, '81
1	Ricardo, Benny	K	5-10	170	6	1- 4-54	San Diego State	16	FA, '80
38	Rogers, George	RB	6-1	224	2	12- 8-58	South Carolina	16	D1, '81
41	Rogers, Jimmy	RB	5-10	190	3	6-29-55	Oklahoma	15	FA, '80
54	†Ryczek, Paul	C	6-2	245	8	6-25-52	Virginia	8	W-Atl, '81
12	Scott, Bobby	QB	6-1	197	11	4- 2-49	Tennessee	4	D14, '71
47	Spivey, Mike	CB	6-0	198	6	3-10-54	Colorado	12	FA, '80
32	Stauch, Scott	RB	5-11	204	2	1- 3-59	UCLA	10	W-SF, '81
68	†Sturt, Fred	G	6-4	235	8	1- 6-51	Bowling Green	16	FA, '78
71	Taylor, James	T	6-4	265	5	8-12-56	Missouri	12	D2, '78
89	Thompson, Aundra	WR	6-1	186	6	1- 2-53	East Texas State	*14	T-SD, '81
42	Tyler, Toussaint	RB	6-2	220	2	3-19-59	Washington	15	D9, '81
73	Warren, Frank	DE	6-4	275	2	9-14-59	Auburn	16	D3a, '81
49	Wattelet, Frank	FS	6-0	185	2	10-25-58	Kansas	16	OFA, '81
44	Waymer, Dave	CB	6-1	195	3	7- 1-58	Notre Dame	16	D2, '80
94	Wilks, Jim	DT	6-4	252	2	3-12-58	San Diego State	16	D12, '81
18	Wilson, Dave	QB	6-3	195	2	4-27-59	Illinois	11	SupD, '81
30	Wilson, Wayne	RB	6-3	208	4	9- 4-57	Shepherd	16	FA, '79
	Winston, Dennis	LB	6-0	228	6	10-25-55	Arkansas	14	T-Pit, '82

*Bradshaw last active with Houston in 1980; Mathis, Mauti and Owens missed 1981 season due to injuries; Thompson played 1 game with San Diego, 3 with Green Bay and 10 with New Orleans in 1981.

†Option playout; subject to developments.

D—Draft; T—Trade; W—Waivers; FA—Free Agent; OFA—Original Free Agent; VFA—Veteran Free Agent; VA—Veteran Allocation; SupD—Supplemental Draft.

Also played with Saints in 1981—WR Gordon Banks (6 games), TE Rich Caster (4), WR Wes Chandler (4), CB Ricky Ray (4), TE Brooks Williams (7), G Bob Young (2).

NEW ORLEANS SAINTS
1982 DRAFT CHOICES

(Number following name designates order of selection among 334 players drafted.)

Round and Player		Position	College
1. Choice exercised in 1981 Supplemental Draft (a)			
SCOTT, Lindsay from Green Bay through San Diego (b)	13	WR	Georgia
2. EDELMAN, Brad	30	C	Missouri
3. LEWIS, Rodney	58	DB	Nebraska
GOODLOW, Eugene from Minnesota (c)	66	WR	Kansas State
DUCKETT, Ken from Washington (d)	68	WR	Wake Forest
KRIMM, John from San Diego (e)	76	DB	Notre Dame
4. ANDERSEN, Morten	86	K	Michigan State
5. ELLIOTT, Tony	114	DE	N. Texas State
6. LEWIS, Marvin	142	RB	Tulane
7. Choice to Miami (f)			
8. SLAUGHTER, Chuck	198	T	South Carolina
9. Choice to Washington (g)			
10. Choice to Washington (g)			
11. Choice to Washington (g)			
12. Choice to Washington (g)			

(a) Selected quarterback Dave Wilson.

(b) Green Bay traded pick, first-round pick in 1983, second-round pick in 1984, wide receiver Aundra Thompson and switched first-round positions with San Diego for wide receiver John Jefferson, September 17, 1981; San Diego traded pick, third-round pick and Thompson to New Orleans for wide receiver Wes Chandler, September 29, 1981.

(c) Acquired pick for running back Tony Galbreath, August 31, 1981.

(d) Acquired pick for tight end Henry Childs, April 30, 1981.

(e) See second part of (b).

(f) Traded pick and fourth-round pick in 1981 for quarterback Guy Benjamin, September 1, 1980.

(g) Traded picks and eighth-round pick for fourth-round pick in 1983, April 28, 1982.

NEW ORLEANS SAINTS
1982 ROOKIE AND FIRST-YEAR ROSTER

(1) Indicates player in previous NFL camp.
(2) Indicates player with CFL experience.
    All others classified as rookies.

Name	Pos.	Hgt.	Wgt.	Birth-date	College	How Acquired
Andersen, Morten	K	6-2	190	8-19-60	Michigan State	D4
Berry, Raymond (1)	DB	5-9	175	6- 5-58	Texas Christian	FA
Bolden, Willie (1)	TE	6-3	223	12- 2-56	Bishop, Tex.	FA
Close, Calvin	G	6-3	254	11- 6-57	Brigham Young	FA
Dixon, David	FB	6-3	220	7-31-58	Hampton Institute	FA
Duckett, Kenny	WR	6-0	187	10- 1-59	Wake Forest	D3c
Echols, Donnie (1)	TE	6-4	235	12-16-57	Oklahoma State	*FA ('81)
Edelman, Brad	C	6-6	255	9- 3-60	Missouri	D2
Elliott, Tony	DE	6-2	247	4-23-59	North Texas State	D5
Freeney, Vindell (1)	CB	5-10	177	11- 6-58	Sam Houston State	FA
Gajan, Hokie (1)	FB	5-11	214	9- 6-59	Louisiana State	*D10 ('81)
Gladys, Gene (1)	LB	6-0	216	11-13-57	Penn State	*D8b ('81)
Gray, Kevin	DB	5-11	179	9-11-57	Eastern Illinois	FA
Greene, Lonnie (1)	DT	6-4	265	2-16-58	Mississippi State	FA
Harper, Jeff (1)	C	6-3	237	10-27-57	Georgia	*FA ('81)
Hill, Alfondia	WR	6-3	202	7-17-59	Arizona	FA
Hurley, Bill (1)	DB	6-2	205	6-16-57	Syracuse	*Waiv. ('81)
Jackson, Kenneth	FB	5-11	212	8- 8-59	Cal State-Fullerton	FA
Kearns, Tom (1)	G	6-4	265	5- 6-58	Kentucky	*FA ('81)
Knafelc, Greg (1)	T	6-4	220	2-20-59	Notre Dame	FA
Krimm, John	S	6-2	190	5-30-60	Notre Dame	D3d
Lewis, Marvin	RB	6-3	208	1-15-60	Tulane	D6
Lewis, Reggie (1)	DE	6-1	220	1-20-54	San Diego State	FA
Lewis, Rodney	CB	5-11	190	4- 2-59	Nebraska	D3a
Mahfouz, Bobby	QB	6-1	195	10-30-59	Southeastern La.	FA
Megna, Gerald (1)	DB	5-11	192	11-23-58	East Tennessee State	FA
Mickens, Lester (1)	WR	5-11	173	9- 9-58	Kansas	*D12 ('81)
Morris, Teddy	LB	6-0	225	1-24-59	Arkansas	FA
Morrison, Tim (1)	G	6-3	265	12-10-58	Georgia	FA
Oubre, Louis (1)	G	6-4	262	5-15-58	Oklahoma	*D5a ('81)
Parham, Robert (1)	FB	6-1	220	1-17-58	Grambling	FA
Penn-White, Al	RB	6-0	191	12-30-58	Southeast Oklahoma	FA
Pittman, Perry	CB	6-1	190	12- 6-55	Langston, Okla.	FA
Quinn, Marcus (2)	CB	6-1	200	6-27-59	Louisiana State	FA
Ruyle, Clay	DE	6-5	256	10-11-58	Stephen F. Austin	FA
Sally, Jerome	DT	6-3	253	2-24-59	Missouri	FA
Salter, Robert (1)	DB	6-0	183	2-26-58	Grambling	FA
Scott, Lindsay	WR	6-1	190	12- 6-60	Georgia	D1
Sella, Chris (1)	DB	6-2	203	9-22-55	Southwest Missouri	FA
Slaughter, Chuck	T	6-5	260	11-21-58	South Carolina	D8
Stamm, Carter	TE	6-2	225	8- 3-58	Millsaps	FA
Stewart, Bobby	WR	5-11	170	11-27-57	Texas Christian	FA
Stewart, Ronnie	FB	5-10	206	5-18-59	Georgia	FA
Talley, Stan (1)	P	6-5	220	9- 5-58	Texas Christian	FA
Tolliver, Arthur	LB	6-0	243	3-29-59	Nicholls State	FA
Wells, Joe (1)	LB	6-2	230	4-26-59	Southern Utah	FA
Whitten, Bobby (1)	G-T	6-3	265	5- 7-59	Kansas	*FA

*Echols, Gajan, Gladys, Harper, Hurley, Kearns, Mickens and Oubre missed 1981 season due to injuries; Whitten played 1 game with Cincinnati in 1981.

NOTE: 3rd-round draft choice Eugene Goodlow is playing with Winnipeg of the CFL.

NEW YORK GIANTS
(Eastern Division, National Conference)

Ray Perkins

President—Wellington T. Mara
Vice-President and Treasurer—Timothy J. Mara
Vice-President, Secretary—Raymond J. Walsh
General Manager—George Young
Assistant General Manager—Terry Bledsoe
Director of Player Personnel—Tom Boisture
Director of Pro Personnel—Ernie Adams
Head Coach—Ray Perkins (3 years: 19-29-0)
Assistant Coaches:
   Offensive Line—Bill Austin
   Special Teams-Linebackers—Bill Belichick
   Special Assignments, Special Teams and Defense—Romeo
     Crennel
   Assistant Offensive Coordinator—Ron Erhardt
   Defensive Backs—Fred Glick
   Receivers—Pat Hodgson
   Defensive Line—Lamar Leachman
   Offensive Backfield—Bob Lord
   Defensive Coordinator-Linebackers—Bill Parcells
   Conditioning—Jim Williams
Director of Media Services—Ed Croke
   (Office Phone: 935-8111—Area Code 201)
Offices—Giants Stadium, East Rutherford, N. J. 07073
Stadium—Giants Stadium (Capacity: 76,891)
Team Colors—Royal Blue, Red and White
Training Site—Pace University, Pleasantville, N. Y.

1982 SCHEDULE
(All times local.
All games Sunday unless noted otherwise.)

Sept. 12	ATLANTA	1:00
Sept. 20	GREEN BAY (Mon.)	9:00
Sept. 26	at Pittsburgh	1:00
Oct. 3	at Dallas	3:00
Oct. 10	ST. LOUIS	1:00
Oct. 17	CINCINNATI	1:00
Oct. 25	at Philadelphia (Mon.)	9:00
Oct. 31	DALLAS	4:00
Nov. 7	at Cleveland	1:00
Nov. 14	at Los Angeles	1:00
Nov. 21	WASHINGTON	4:00
Nov. 25	at Detroit (Thanksgiving)	12:30
Dec. 5	HOUSTON	1:00
Dec. 11	PHILADELPHIA (Sat.)	12:30
Dec. 19	at Washington	1:00
Dec. 26	at St. Louis	12:00

1981 RESULTS—(Won 10, Lost 8)

Giants	Opp.		Att.
10 Philadelphia	24	(H)	71,459
17 Washington	7	(A)	53,343
20 New Orleans	7	(H)	69,814
10 Dallas	18	(A)	63,449
14 Green Bay	27	(H)	73,684
34 St. Louis	14	(H)	67,128
32 Seattle	0	(A)	56,134
27 Atlanta (OT)	24	(A)	48,410
7 New York Jets	26	(H)	74,740
24 Green Bay	26	(A)	54,138
27 Washington (OT)	30	(H)	63,133
20 Philadelphia	10	(A)	66,827
10 San Francisco	17	(A)	57,186
10 Los Angeles	7	(H)	59,659
20 St. Louis	10	(A)	47,358
13 Dallas (OT)	10	(H)	73,009
PLAYOFF GAME			
27 Philadelphia	21	(A)	71,611
PLAYOFF GAME			
24 San Francisco	38	(A)	58,360

1981 GAMES STARTED

16 games: Harry Carson, Mark Haynes, Terry Jackson, Brian Kelley, Gordon King, Bill Neill, Beasley Reece, Lawrence Taylor, J.T. Turner.

15 games: Mike Friede.

14 games: Bill Currier, Curtis McGriff, Johnny Perkins, Gary Shirk.

13 games: Brad Van Pelt.

11 games: Gary Jeter.

10 games: Brad Benson, Ernie Hughes, Roy Simmons, Phil Simms.

Less than 10 games: Billy Ard (6), Leon Bright (1), Scott Brunner (6), Rob Carpenter (8), Jim Clack (6), Larry Flowers (2), Ike Forte (3), Earnest Gray (3), Byron Hunt (3), Louis Jackson (3), Doug Kotar (4), George Martin (6), Bo Matthews (1), Tom Mullady (3), Leon Perry (8), Tim Stokes (1), Phil Tabor (1), Billy Taylor (3), Jeff Weston (5).

NEW YORK GIANTS 1982 VETERAN ROSTER

No.	Name	Pos.	Ht.	Wt.	NFL Exp.	Birth-date	College	Games in '81	How Acquired
	Anderson, Anthony	RB	6-0	200	3	9-27-56	Temple	*0	FA, '82
67	Ard, Billy	G	6-3	250	2	3-12-59	Wake Forest	13	D8c, '81
60	Benson, Brad	T	6-3	258	5	11-25-55	Penn State	11	FA, '77
45	Bright, Leon	RB	5-9	192	2	5-19-55	Florida State	15	FA, '81
12	Brunner, Scott	QB	6-5	200	3	3-24-57	Delaware	16	D6, '80
64	Burt, Jim	DT	6-1	255	2	6- 7-59	Miami	13	OFA, '81
26	†Carpenter, Rob	RB	6-1	230	6	4-20-55	Miami, Ohio	*14	T-Hou, '81
53	Carson, Harry	LB	6-2	235	7	11-26-53	South Carolina State	16	D4b, '76
	Correal, Chuck	C	6-3	247	3	6-16-55	Penn State	*0	FA, '82
29	†Currier, Bill	S	6-0	195	6	1- 5-55	South Carolina	16	T-NE, '81
18	Danelo, Joe	PK	5-9	166	8	9- 2-53	Washington State	16	T-GB, '76
46	Dennis, Mike	CB	5-10	190	3	6- 7-58	Wyoming	16	OFA, '80
37	Flowers, Larry	S	6-1	190	2	4-19-58	Texas Tech	16	W-TB, '80
35	†Forte, Ike	RB	6-0	210	7	3- 8-54	Arkansas	5	FA, '81
88	Friede, Mike	WR	6-3	205	3	9-22-57	Indiana	16	FA, '80
83	Gray, Earnest	WR	6-3	195	4	3- 2-57	Memphis State	16	D2, '79
79	Hardison, Dee	DE	6-4	269	5	5- 2-56	North Carolina	*0	FA, '81
36	Haynes, Mark	CB	5-11	185	3	11- 6-58	Colorado	16	D1, '80
27	Heater, Larry	RB	5-11	205	3	1- 9-58	Arizona	*0	W-KC, '80
61	Hughes, Ernie	C	6-3	265	4	1-24-55	Notre Dame	10	FA, '81
57	Hunt, Byron	LB	6-4	230	2	12-17-58	Southern Methodist	16	D9, '81
21	Jackson, Louis	RB	5-11	195	2	1-27-58	Cal Poly-SLO	11	D7, '81
24	Jackson, Terry	CB	5-11	197	5	12- 9-55	San Diego State	16	D5a, '78
13	Jennings, Dave	P	6-4	205	9	6- 8-52	St. Lawrence	16	FA, '74
70	Jeter, Gary	DE	6-4	260	6	3-24-55	Southern California	12	D1, '77
	Johnson, Dennis	RB	6-3	220	4	2-26-56	Mississippi State	*0	FA, '80
55	Kelley, Brian	LB	6-3	222	10	9- 1-51	California Lutheran	16	D14, '73
72	King, Gordon	T	6-6	275	5	2- 3-56	Stanford	16	D1, '78
44	Kotar, Doug	RB	5-11	205	9	6-11-51	Kentucky	7	T-Pit, 74
71	Lapka, Myron	DT	6-4	260	3	5-10-56	Southern California	*0	D3, '80
	Lloyd, Dan	LB	6-2	225	5	11- 9-53	Washington	*0	D6, '76
51	Marion, Frank	LB	6-3	228	6	3-16-51	Florida A&M	16	FA, '76
75	Martin, George	DE	6-4	245	8	2-16-53	Oregon	16	D11, '75
59	McGlasson, Ed	C	6-4	248	4	7-11-56	Youngstown State	16	W-LA, '81
76	McGriff, Curtis	DE	6-5	265	3	5-17-58	Alabama	14	OFA, '80
52	McLaughlin, Joe	LB	6-1	235	4	7- 1-57	Massachusetts	16	FA, '80
85	Mistler, John	WR	6-2	186	2	10-28-58	Arizona State	16	D3, '81
81	Mullady, Tom	TE	6-3	232	4	1-30-57	Southwestern	16	FA, '79
77	Neill, Bill	DT	6-4	255	2	3-15-59	Pittsburgh	16	D5, '81
	Niziolek, Bob	TE	6-4	220	2	6-30-58	Colorado	*4	FA, '82
86	Perkins, Johnny	WR	6-2	205	6	4-21-53	Abilene Christian	16	D2, '77
30	Perry, Leon	RB	5-11	224	3	8-14-57	Mississippi	16	OFA, '80
82	Pittman, Danny	WR	6-2	205	3	4- 3-58	Wyoming	8	D4, '80
28	Reece, Beasley	S	6-1	195	7	3-18-54	North Texas State	16	W-Dal, '77
87	Shirk, Gary	TE	6-1	220	7	2-23-50	Morehead State	16	FA, '76
69	Simmons, Roy	G	6-3	264	4	11- 8-56	Georgia Tech	16	D8b, '79
11	Simms, Phil	QB	6-3	216	4	11- 3-56	Morehead State	10	D1, '79
65	Sinnott, John	T	6-4	275	2	4-18-58	Brown	*0	FA, '80
80	Tabor, Phil	DE	6-4	255	4	11-30-56	Oklahoma	16	D4, '79
56	Taylor, Lawrence	LB	6-3	237	2	2- 4-59	North Carolina	16	D1, '81
68	Turner, J.T.	G	6-3	250	6	4-17-53	Duke	16	FA, '77
10	Van Pelt, Brad	LB	6-5	235	10	4- 5-51	Michigan State	14	D2, '73
73	Weston, Jeff	T	6-5	280	4	4-10-56	Notre Dame	14	W-Mia, '79
62	Whittington, Mike	LB	6-2	220	3	8- 9-58	Notre Dame	6	OFA, '80
	Wyatt, Kervin	LB	6-1	235	2	10-17-57	Maryland	*0	OFA, '80
89	Young, Dave	TE	6-6	242	2	2- 9-59	Purdue	11	D2, '81

†Option playout; subject to developments.

*Anderson last active with Atlanta in 1980; Carpenter played 4 games with Houston, 10 with Giants in 1981; Correal active for 2 games with Cleveland in 1981, did not play; Hardison active for 2 games in 1981, but did not play; Heater, Johnson, Lapka, Sinnott and Wyatt missed 1981 season due to injuries; Lloyd missed 1980 and 1981 seasons because of cancer treatments; Niziolek played 4 games with Detroit in 1981.

D—Draft; T—Trade; W—Waivers; FA—Free Agent; OFA—Original Free Agent; VFA—Veteran Free Agent; VA—Veteran Allocation; SupD—Supplemental Draft.

Also played with Giants in 1981—DT Carl Barasich (2 games), WR Alvin Garrett (9), RB Bo Matthews (5), T Tim Stokes (3), RB Billy Taylor (5). Retired: C Jim Clack (6).

NEW YORK GIANTS
1982 DRAFT CHOICES

(Number following name designates order of selection among 334 players drafted.)

Round and Player		Position	College
1. WOOLFOLK, Butch	18	RB	Michigan
2. MORRIS, Joe	45	RB	Syracuse
3. Choice to Houston (a)			
4. RAYMOND, Gerry	102	G	Boston College
5. UMPHREY, Rich	129	C	Colorado
6. NICHOLSON, Darrell	156	LB	North Carolina
7. WISKA, Jeff	186	G	Michigan State
8. HUBBLE, Robert	213	TE	Rice
9. HIGGINS, John	240	DB	Nev.-Las Vegas
10. BALDINGER, Rich	270	T	Wake Forest
11. Choice to New England (b)			
12. SEALE, Mike	323	DT	Richmond

(a) Traded pick for running back Rob Carpenter, September 29, 1981.
(b) Traded pick for safety Bill Currier, August 31, 1981.

NEW YORK GIANTS
1982 ROOKIE AND FIRST-YEAR ROSTER

(1) Indicates player in previous NFL camp.
(2) Indicates player with CFL experience.
(3) Indicates player with minor league experience.
All others classified as rookies.

Name	Pos.	Hgt.	Wgt.	Birth-date	College	How Acquired
Anderson, Gregory	WR	5-10	156	5-20-59	Alabama State	FA
Baldinger, Richard	T	6-4	272	12-31-59	Wake Forest	D10
Bednarek, Jeffrey (1)	DT	6-4	265	6-12-58	Pacific	FA
Blackwell, Ted (1)	RB	5-11	203	10-25-58	Rutgers	FA
Brownlee, Cedric (1)	RB	5-10	210	9- 7-58	Jacksonville State	FA
Carino, Andrew	LB	6-2	225	7-31-60	Rutgers	FA
Carolina, Willis...................	LB	6-1	209	1-14-60	Tulsa	FA
Chatman, Cliff (1)..............	RB	6-2	225	3-13-59	Central State	*D4 ('81)
Clemmens, Maurice..........	LB	6-1	227	8-10-60	Kent State	FA
Coffey, Larry (1).................	RB	5-10	205	6- 7-59	W. Va. Wesleyan	FA
Dawson, Scott	T	6-1	260	2-15-59	Oklahoma	FA
Eddings, Floyd	WR	5-11	177	12-15-58	California	FA
Evans, Kevin (1).................	DB	6-1	194	4- 5-58	Arkansas	FA
Fitzgerald, Mickey (1)	RB	6-2	235	4-10-58	Virginia Tech	*FA
Gray, Calvin (3)	DB	5-11	180	6-25-57	Virginia Union	FA
Grayson, Bobby	WR	5-9	178	4- 8-60	Oklahoma	FA
Gyetvay, Michael	LB	6-3	238	8- 1-59	Syracuse	FA
Haynes, Mike......................	DB	5-11	167	3-16-59	Grambling State	FA
Hemsley, Robert.................	WR	6-1	204	10-23-59	Missouri	FA
Higgins, John	DB	6-2	205	1-26-59	Nevada-Las Vegas	D9
Hubble, Robert...................	TE	6-7	250	9-20-58	Rice	D8
Hurley, Dan........................	G	6-3	270	4-16-59	Nebraska	FA
Hutchins, Reno...................	S	6-0	199	1-23-60	Tulsa	FA
Johnson, Homes.................	RB	5-8	179	2- 1-58	Florida State	FA
Kimball, Bruce (1)	G	6-2	260	8-19-59	Massachusetts	*FA ('81)
Kirchner, Bruce (1)	C-G	6-2	255	8- 7-56	Colorado	*FA ('81)
Kurdyla, Kevin (1)..............	T	6-3	260	6-14-59	Rutgers	*FA ('81)
Lafraniere, William	WR	5-11	183	1- 9-59	Northeastern	FA
Leopard, Edward	K	6-1	193	8-26-59	South Carolina	FA
Lewis, Johnny.....................	LB	6-1	240	5-17-60	Oklahoma	FA
Lush, Michael (1)	S	6-1	194	4-18-58	East Stroudsburg St.	FA
Mayock, Michael (1).........	S	6-2	195	8-14-58	Boston College	FA
McCants, Mark (1).............	DB	6-0	190	2-17-58	Temple	FA
McGrew, Sly	LB	6-3	233	2-27-60	Tulane	FA
Miller, Kenneth...................	TE	6-4	246	4-10-60	Connecticut	FA
Mitchell, Mike (2)..............	DE	6-2	239	12-19-58	Ferrum Jr. College	FA
Morris, Joe	RB	5-7	190	9-15-60	Syracuse	D2
Murphy, Bob (1).................	S	6-2	200	3- 8-82	Ohio State	FA
Nicholson, Darrell.............	LB	6-2	235	8-23-59	North Carolina	D6
Oliver, Reggie	LB	6-1	226	4-15-60	No. Michigan	FA
Osbun, Tony	T	6-5	260	5- 1-58	Michigan	FA
Phillips, Scott (1)	WR	6-2	185	11-11-58	Brigham Young	FA
Raeford, Peter	DB	5-9	175	12-13-59	No. Michigan	FA
Raymond, Gerry.................	G	6-3	260	6- 6-59	Boston College	D4
Reed, Mark (1)...................	QB	6-3	195	2-21-59	Moorhead St.	*D8 ('81)
Roncarati, Robert	T	6-2	255	5-28-59	Holy Cross	FA
Seale, Mark	DE	6-3	250	3-10-60	Richmond	D12
Slawson, Mark (1)	WR	6-2	184	6-11-59	The Citadel	*FA ('81)
Sopp, Sam	DB	5-11	171	2-16-60	Kent State	FA
Spencer, Herbie (1)...........	LB	6-3	225	9-23-59	Newberry	FA
Trent, Boo	RB	5-9	212	8-22-58	Ferrum Jr. College	FA
Umphrey, Richard.............	C	6-3	255	12-13-58	Colorado	D5
Walton, Teddy (1)	DB	5-11	195	8-11-57	Connecticut	FA
White, Kenneth...................	WR	6-2	172	10-28-59	Alabama A & M	FA
Williams, Michael (1)........	DB	5-11	188	12-21-55	Texas A & M	FA
Wiska, Jeff..........................	G	6-4	260	10-17-59	Michigan State	D7
Woolfolk, Butch..................	RB	6-1	207	3- 1-60	Michigan	D1

*Chatman, Kimball, Kirchner, Kurdyla, Reed and Slawson missed 1981 season due to injuries; Fitzgerald played 1 game with Atlanta and Philadelphia in 1981.

NEW YORK JETS

(Eastern Division, American Conference)

Walt Michaels

Chairman of the Board—Leon Hess
President—Jim Kensil
Director of Player Personnel—Mike Hickey
Director of Pro Personnel—Jim Royer
Head Coach—Walt Michaels (5 years: 33-44-1)
Assistant Coaches:
  Defensive Backs—Billy Baird
  Linebackers—Ralph Baker
  Offensive Line—Bob Fry
  Defensive Coordinator—Joe Gardi
  Running Backs—Bob Ledbetter
  Receivers—Pete McCulley
  Special Teams—Larry Pasquale
  Defensive Line—Dan Sekanovich
  Offensive Coordinator-Quarterbacks—Joe Walton
Director of Public Relations—Frank Ramos
  (Office Phone: 421-6600—Area Code 212)
Offices—598 Madison Ave., New York, N.Y. 10022
Stadium—Shea Stadium (Capacity: 60,372)
Team Colors—Kelly Green and White
Training Site—Hofstra University, Hempstead, N.Y.

1982 SCHEDULE

(All times local.
All games Sunday unless noted otherwise.)

Sept. 12	MIAMI	4:00
Sept. 19	at New England	1:00
Sept. 26	at Baltimore	4:00
Oct. 3	HOUSTON	1:00
Oct. 10	DENVER	4:00
Oct. 18	BUFFALO (Mon.)	9:00
Oct. 24	at Kansas City	12:00
Oct. 31	NEW ENGLAND	1:00
Nov. 7	at Buffalo	4:00
Nov. 14	at Pittsburgh	1:00
Nov. 21	BALTIMORE	1:00
Nov. 28	GREEN BAY	1:00
Dec. 6	at Detroit (Mon.)	9:00
Dec. 12	TAMPA BAY	1:00
Dec. 18	at Miami (Sat.)	12:30
Dec. 26	at Minnesota	12:00

1981 RESULTS—(Won 10, Lost 6, Tied 1)

Jets		Opp.		Att.
0	Buffalo	31	(A)	79,754
30	Cincinnati	31	(H)	49,454
10	Pittsburgh	38	(A)	52,934
33	Houston	17	(H)	50,309
28	Miami (OT)	28	(A)	69,631
28	New England	24	(H)	55,093
33	Buffalo	14	(H)	54,607
3	Seattle	19	(A)	49,678
26	New York Giants	7	(A)	74,740
41	Baltimore	14	(A)	31,521
17	New England	6	(A)	45,342
16	Miami	15	(H)	59,962
25	Baltimore	0	(H)	53,595
23	Seattle	27	(A)	53,105
14	Cleveland	13	(A)	56,866
28	Green Bay	3	(H)	56,340
	PLAYOFF GAME			
27	Buffalo	31	(H)	57,050

1981 GAMES STARTED

16 games: Jerome Barkum, Stan Blinka, Joe Fields, Mark Gastineau, Joe Klecko, Darrol Ray, Abdul Salaam, Ken Schroy, Richard Todd, Chris Ward.

15 games: Dan Alexander, Lance Mehl, Randy Rasmussen.

14 games: Greg Buttle, Marvin Powell.

13 games: Derrick Gaffney, Jerry Holmes, Wesley Walker.

12 games: Marty Lyons.

Less than 10 games: Mike Augustyniak (8), Ron Crosby (3), Scott Dierking (4), Donald Dykes (9), Bruce Harper (7), Bobby Jackson (6), Jesse Johnson (4), Bobby Jones (3), Johnny Jones (3), Freeman McNeil (6), Tom Newton (7), John Roman (2), Ben Rudolph (4), Stan Waldemore (2).

NEW YORK JETS 1982 VETERAN ROSTER

No.	Name	Pos.	Ht.	Wt.	NFL Exp.	Birth-date	College	Games in '81	How Acquired
60	Alexander, Dan	G	6-4	260	6	6-17-55	Louisiana State	16	D8a, '77
35	Augustyniak, Mike	RB	5-11	220	2	7-17-56	Purdue	10	FA, '81
83	Barkum, Jerome	TE	6-4	227	11	7-18-50	Jackson State	16	D1a, '72
64	Bingham, Guy	OL	6-3	255	3	2-25-58	Montana	16	D10, '80
54	Blinka, Stan	LB	6-2	234	4	4-29-57	Sam Houston State	16	D5b, '79
51	Buttle, Greg	LB	6-3	232	7	6-20-54	Penn State	15	D3, '76
55	Crosby, Ron	LB	6-3	227	5	3- 2-55	Penn State	16	FA, '79
25	Dierking, Scott	RB	5-10	220	6	5-24-55	Purdue	16	D4, '77
26	Dykes, Donald	CB	5-11	188	4	8-24-55	Southeast Louisiana	14	D3, '79
65	Fields, Joe	C	6-2	253	8	11-14-53	Widener	16	D14, '75
81	Gaffney, Derrick	WR	6-1	182	5	5-24-55	Florida	16	D8a, '78
	Garrett, Mike	P	6-1	184	2	6-13-57	Georgia	16	W-Bal, '82
99	Gastineau, Mark	DE	6-5	276	4	11-20-56	East Central Oklahoma	16	D2, '79
42	Harper, Bruce	RB	5-8	177	6	6-20-55	Kutztown State	16	OFA, '77
47	Holmes, Jerry	DB	6-2	175	3	12-22-57	West Virginia	16	OFA, '80
40	Jackson, Bobby	CB	5-10	180	5	12-23-56	Florida State	9	D6a, '78
27	Johnson, Jesse	DB	6-3	188	3	8-23-57	Colorado	16	D4, '80
89	Jones, Bobby	WR	5-11	185	5	7-12-55	No College	16	OFA, '78
80	Jones, Lam	WR	5-11	180	3	4- 4-58	Texas	15	D1, '80
73	Klecko, Joe	DE	6-3	272	6	10-15-53	Temple	16	D6, '77
5	Leahy, Pat	K	6-0	189	9	3-19-51	St. Louis	16	FA, '74
20	Lewis, Kenny	RB	6-0	196	3	10- 2-57	Virginia Tech	5	FA, '80
33	Long, Kevin	RB	6-1	218	6	1-20-55	South Carolina	16	D7c, '77
29	Lynn, Johnny	CB	6-0	195	3	12-19-56	UCLA	13	D4b, '79
93	Lyons, Marty	DT	6-5	269	4	1-15-57	Alabama	12	D1, '79
53	McKibben, Mike	LB	6-3	224	3	9- 3-56	Kent State	*0	OFA, '79
24	McNeil, Freeman	RB	5-11	225	2	4-22-59	UCLA	11	D1, '81
56	Mehl, Lance	LB	6-3	235	3	2-14-58	Penn State	15	D3, '80
77	Neil, Kenny	DL	6-4	244	2	1- 8-59	Iowa State	16	D7, '81
44	Newton, Tom	RB	6-0	220	6	3- 8-54	California	16	OFA, '77
79	Powell, Marvin	T	6-5	271	6	8-30-55	Southern California	14	D1, '77
	Powell, Steve	RB	5-11	186	3	1- 2-56	Northeast Missouri	*0	FA, '82
15	Ramsey, Chuck	P	6-2	189	6	2-24-52	Wake Forest	16	FA, '77
66	Rasmussen, Randy	G	6-2	260	16	5-10-45	Kearney State	15	D12, '67
28	Ray, Darrol	S	6-1	206	3	6-25-58	Oklahoma	16	D2a, '80
61	Roman, John	T	6-4	270	7	8-31-52	Idaho State	16	FA, '76
76	Rudolph, Ben	DL	6-5	271	2	8-29-57	Long Beach State	15	D3, '81
10	Ryan, Pat	QB	6-3	205	5	9-16-55	Tennessee	15	D11, '78
74	Salaam, Abdul	DT	6-3	269	7	2-12-53	Kent State	16	D7a, '76
48	Schroy, Ken	S	6-2	198	6	9-22-52	Maryland	16	FA, '76
82	Shuler, Mickey	TE	6-3	236	5	8-21-56	Penn State	6	D3, '78
87	Sohn, Kurt	WR	5-11	176	2	6-26-57	Fordham	16	FA, '81
45	Springs, Kirk	DB	6-0	192	2	8-10-58	Miami, Ohio	10	FA, '81
86	Stephens, Steve	TE	6-3	227	2	3- 4-57	Oklahoma State	16	FA, '81
14	Todd, Richard	QB	6-2	206	7	11-19-53	Alabama	16	D1, '76
70	Waldemore, Stan	OL	6-4	269	5	2-20-55	Nebraska	16	FA, '78
85	Walker, Wesley	WR	6-0	179	6	5-26-55	California	13	D2, '77
72	Ward, Chris	T	6-3	267	5	12-16-55	Ohio State	16	D1, '78
52	Washington, Al	LB	6-3	235	2	9-25-58	Ohio State	16	D4, '81
57	Woodring, John	LB	6-2	230	2	4- 4-59	Brown	12	D6, '81

*McKibben missed '81 season due to injury; S. Powell last active with Buffalo in 1979.

D—Draft; T—Trade; W—Waivers; FA—Free Agent; OFA—Original Free Agent; VFA—Veteran Free Agent; VA—Veteran Allocation; SupD—Supplemental Draft.

Also played with Jets in 1981—RB Billy Taylor (3 games), LB Marty Wetzel (5).

NEW YORK JETS
1982 DRAFT CHOICES

(Number following name designates order of selection among 334 players drafted.)

Round and Player		Position	College
1. CRABLE, Bob	23	LB	Notre Dame
2. MC ELROY, Reggie	51	T	West Texas St.
3. CRUTCHFIELD, Dwayne	79	RB	Iowa State
4. FLOYD, George	107	DB	E. Kentucky
5. JERUE, Mark	135	LB	Washington
6. PHEA, Lonell	163	WR	Houston
7. COOMBS, Tom	191	TE	Idaho
8. TEXADA, Lawrence	219	RB	Henderson, Ark.
9. KLEVER, Rocky	247	RB	Montana
10. HEMPHILL, Darryl	275	DB	West Texas St.
11. PARMELEE, Perry	302	WR	Santa Clara
12. CARLSTROM, Tom	330	G	Nebraska

NEW YORK JETS
1982 ROOKIE AND FIRST-YEAR ROSTER

(1) Indicates player in previous NFL camp.
(2) Indicates player with minor league experience.
   All others classified as rookies.

Name	Pos.	Hgt.	Wgt.	Birth-date	College	How Acquired
Alston, Doug (1)	CB	5-11	187	8-27-58	Boston	FA
Augustine, Andre	DT	6-2	250	1-25-58	Colorado State	FA

NEW YORK JETS ROOKIE ROSTER—Continued

Name	Pos.	Hgt.	Wgt.	Birth-date	College	How Acquired
Barber, Marion (1)............	RB	6-3	224	12- 6-59	Minnesota	*D2 ('81)
Bennek, Bill (1).................	T	6-4	255	5- 5-58	Florida	FA
Brockhaus, Jeff (1)............	K	6-2	200	4-15-59	Missouri	FA
Bruton, Charles (1)	CB	5-11	191	10-19-58	Southern Methodist	FA
Capone, Tom	TE	6-3	235	7-26-59	C.W. Post	FA
Carlstrom, Tom	G	6-6	263	12- 2-58	Nebraska	D12
Clausen, Kent (1)..............	LB	6-4	233	12- 6-57	Montana	*FA ('81)
Columbia, Paul (1)	TE	6-5	227	12- 3-57	Villanova	FA
Cook, Chuck (1).................	S	5-11	193	11-29-58	Southern Mississippi	FA
Coombs, Tom......................	TE	6-3	230	5-31-59	Idaho	D7
Cotton, Tim (1)...................	WR	6-0	190	11-29-54	Xavier	*Waiv. ('81)
Crable, Bob	LB	6-3	228	9-22-59	Notre Dame	D1
Crutchfield, Dwayne.........	RB	6-0	235	9-30-59	Iowa State	D3
Darns, Phil	DT	6-3	245	7-27-59	Mississippi Valley	FA
DeGasperi, Mark...............	DT	6-2	245	10- 9-59	Nassau CC	FA
DeLia, Dan.........................	S	5-10	175	2-26-58	Boston University	FA
Elion, Kolas (1)..................	WR	5-11	197	1-10-58	Middle Tennessee	FA
Faulkner, Mike (1)............	DE	6-2	240	5-21-57	Virginia Tech	*FA ('81)
Feil, Henry	G	6-3	270	2- 9-59	Purdue	FA
Ferrari, Phil	LB	6-3	208	9-29-60	Maine	FA
Floyd, George.....................	S-KR	5-11	190	12-21-60	Eastern Kentucky	D4
Goddard, Derrick (1)........	DB	6-1	207	10- 7-57	Drake	FA
Grate, Zack	LB	6-2	217	4- 6-59	South Carolina State	FA
Greenhalgh, Dave (1)	TE	6-4	225	7-27-57	Southwestern Oklahoma	FA
Happel, Brian	K	6-0	185	11-27-60	Texas-Arlington	FA
Hemphill, Darryl	CB	6-0	195	3-29-60	West Texas State	D10
Hitt, Paul	LB	6-1	223	7-30-56	Rhode Island	FA
Hoskins, Tim......................	WR-KR	5-9	170	7-25-60	Mississippi Western	FA
Hyland, Vince (1)	DB	6-1	195	4- 9-58	Delaware	FA
Jerue, Mark	LB	6-3	225	1-15-60	Washington	D5
Jones, Craig (1).................	K	5-11	174	7-22-58	VMI	FA
Jones, LeRoid (1)	RB	6-0	215	8-17-58	Louisiana State	*Waiv. ('81)
Kahn, Jeff (1).....................	P	6-2	189	3- 7-58	Cal. State-Fullerton	FA
Kestner, Jeff (1)..................	T	6-3	251	6-14-58	Tennessee-Chattanooga	FA
Klever, Rocky	RB	6-3	225	7-10-59	Montana	D9
Kumerow, Craig	LB	6-3	225	8-26-60	Indiana	FA
Luscinski, Jim (1)	T-G	6-5	275	12-16-58	Norwich	FA
McConnaughey, Tom (1)..	WR	6-3	187	8- 1-57	Central Arkansas	FA
McElroy, Reggie.................	T-G	6-6	270	3- 4-60	West Texas State	D2
Moccia, Randy (2).............	G	6-2	265	4-21-58	Delaware	FA
Monello, Frank	CB-KR	5-8	195	4-17-59	Springfield	FA
Moorer, Kevin (1)	LB	6-2	220	12- 2-56	New Haven University	FA
Mordaga, John	DE	6-6	260	7-14-59	Trenton State	FA
Newhall, Mike (1)..............	TE	6-2	220	4- 9-58	Virginia	FA
Nitti, John (1)	RB	6-1	215	12-22-58	Yale	*FA ('81)
Owens, Reginald (1)	S	6-2	190	11-17-56	Bethune-Cookman	FA
Parmelee, Perry.................	WR	6-3	180	5- 3-60	Santa Clara	D11
Pellegrini, Joe (1)..............	C	6-4	252	4- 8-57	Harvard	*FA ('81)
Phea, Lonell......................	WR-KR	5-10	175	9-29-58	Houston	D6
Piurowski, Paul (1)	LB	6-2	220	3-16-59	Florida State	FA
Rich, Phil (1)	G	6-4	266	11- 7-57	Western Kentucky	FA
Riley, Darron (2)................	T	6-5	260	11- 2-58	New York Tech	FA
Rogan, John	QB	6-2	188	1-30-60	Yale	FA
Sadler, Kevin (1)................	G	6-3	259	3-18-59	Missouri	FA
Singleton, John (1)	DE	6-5	266	12-22-56	Texas-El Paso	FA
Sisco, Lance (1)..................	TE	6-2	224	4- 7-57	William Paterson, N.J.	*FA ('81)
Sturdevant, John...............	DE	6-4	245	5-25-58	Ohio State	FA
Suttora, Tony	G	6-2	248	7-19-60	C.W. Post	FA
Texada, Lawrence.............	RB	5-11	200	1-14-60	Henderson, Ark.	D8
Thumm, Steve	TE	6-3	232	1-18-60	Brooklyn	FA
Townsend, Jeff (1).............	DB	6-1	184	8-13-59	Wichita State	FA
Truvillion, Eric	WR	6-3	199	6-18-59	Florida A&M	FA
Venuto, Jay (1)...................	QB	6-1	193	2- 5-59	Wake Forest	*Waiv.

*Barber, Clausen, Faulkner, L. Jones, Nitti, Pellegrini and Sisco missed 1981 season due to injuries; Venuto active for 2 games with Baltimore in 1981; did not play.

OAKLAND RAIDERS
(Western Division, American Conference)

Tom Flores

General Partners—Al Davis, E. W. McGah
Managing General Partner—Al Davis
Executive Assistant—Al LoCasale
Personnel and Operations—Ron Wolf
Player Personnel—Tom Grimes
Head Coach—Tom Flores (3 years: 27-21-0)
Assistant Coaches:
Offensive Line—Sam Boghosian
Special Assistant—Willie Brown
Defensive Backfield—Chet Franklin
Research and Development—Larry Kennan
Defensive Line—Earl Leggett
Strength and Conditioning—Bob Mischak
Special Teams-Football Operations—Steve Ortmayer
Linebackers—Charlie Sumner
Offensive Assistant—Tom Walsh
Offensive Backfield—Ray Willsey
Publications and Speakers Bureau—Bill Glazier
(Office Phone: 562-5900—Area Code 415)
Offices—7850 Edgewater Drive, Oakland, Calif. 94621
Stadium—Oakland-Alameda County Coliseum (Capacity: 54,616)
Team Colors—Silver and Black
Training Site—El Rancho Motel, Santa Rosa, Calif.

1982 SCHEDULE
(All times local.
All games Sunday unless noted otherwise.)

Sept. 12	at San Francisco	1:00
Sept. 19	at Atlanta	1:00
Sept. 26	at San Diego	1:00
Oct. 3	NEW ORLEANS	1:00
Oct. 10	CLEVELAND	1:00
Oct. 17	at Seattle	1:00
Oct. 24	at Denver	2:00
Oct. 31	MIAMI	1:00
Nov. 7	KANSAS CITY	1:00
Nov. 14	at Baltimore	2:00
Nov. 22	SAN DIEGO (Mon.)	6:00
Nov. 28	at Cincinnati	1:00
Dec. 5	SEATTLE	1:00
Dec. 12	at Kansas City	3:00
Dec. 18	LOS ANGELES (Sat.)	1:00
Dec. 26	DENVER	1:00

1981 RESULTS—(Won 7, Lost 9)

Raiders		Opp.		Att.
7	Denver	9	(A)	74,796
36	Minnesota	10	(A)	47,186
20	Seattle	10	(H)	45,725
0	Detroit	16	(A)	77,919
0	Denver	17	(H)	51,035
0	Kansas City	27	(A)	76,543
18	Tampa Bay	16	(H)	42,288
17	Kansas City	28	(H)	38,500
27	New England	17	(H)	44,246
16	Houston	17	(A)	45,519
33	Miami	17	(A)	61,777
21	San Diego	55	(H)	50,199
32	Seattle	31	(A)	57,147
30	Pittsburgh	27	(H)	51,769
6	Chicago	23	(H)	40,834
10	San Diego	23	(A)	52,696

· 1981 GAMES STARTED

16 games: Dave Browning, Lester Hayes, Ted Hendricks, Henry Lawrence, Rod Martin, Mickey Marvin, John Matuszak, Randy McClanahan, Matt Millen, Burgess Owens, Johnny Robinson.

15 games: Cliff Branch.

14 games: Kenny King, Odis McKinney.

13 games: Derrick Jensen, Art Shell.

12 games: Derrick Ramsey.

11 games: Curt Marsh.

10 games: Monte Jackson.

Less than 10 games: Malcolm Barnwell (1), Morris Bradshaw (8), Bob Chandler (7), Raymond Chester (5), Dave Dalby (7), Mike Davis (2), Lindsey Mason (3), Dwayne O'Steen (6), Jim Plunkett (7), Steve Sylvester (9), Gene Upshaw (5), Mark van Eeghen (3), Arthur Whittington (2), Marc Wilson (9).

OAKLAND RAIDERS 1982 VETERAN ROSTER

No.	Name	Pos.	Ht.	Wt.	NFL Exp.	Birth-date	College	Games in '81	How Acquired
	Alzado, Lyle	DE	6-3	250	12	4- 3-49	Yankton	15	T-Cle, '82
10	Bahr, Chris	K	5-10	175	7	2- 3-53	Penn State	16	FA, '80
	Bailey, Mark	RB	6-3	235	3	12-13-54	Long Beach State	*0	FA, '82
56	Barnes, Jeff	LB	6-2	225	6	3- 1-55	California	15	D5b, '77
80	Barnwell, Malcolm	WR	5-11	185	2	6-28-58	Virginia Union	16	D7, '80
	Berns, Rick	RB	6-2	205	3	2- 5-56	Nebraska	*0	FA, '82
54	Bracelin, Greg	LB	6-1	215	3	4-16-57	California	15	FA, '81
81	†Bradshaw, Morris	WR	6-1	195	9	10-19-52	Ohio State	15	D4, '74
21	Branch, Cliff	WR	5-11	170	11	8- 1-48	Colorado	16	D4a, '72
	Bright, Greg	S	6-0	205	3	8- 2-57	Morehead State	*4	FA, '82
73	Browning, Dave	DE	6-5	245	5	8-18-56	Washington	16	D2, '78
85	Chandler, Bob	WR	6-1	180	11	4-24-49	Southern California	11	T-Buf, '80
88	Chester, Raymond	TE	6-4	235	13	6-28-48	Morgan State	16	T-Bal, '78
46	Christensen, Todd	TE-RB	6-3	230	4	8- 3-56	Brigham Young	16	FA, '79
50	Dalby, Dave	C	6-3	250	11	8-19-50	UCLA	16	D4b, '72
79	Davis, Bruce	T	6-6	280	4	6-21-56	UCLA	16	D11, '79
36	Davis, Mike	S	6-3	205	5	4-15-56	Colorado	7	D2a, '77
	Fisher, Mike	WR	5-11	172	2	4-22-58	Baylor	*2	FA, '82
	Goode, Don	LB	6-2	240	9	6-21-51	Kansas	16	T-Cle, '82
	Grossart, Kyle	QB	6-4	210	2	1-19-55	Oregon State	*0	FA, '82
8	Guy, Ray	P	6-3	195	10	12-22-49	Southern Mississippi	16	D1, '73
86	Hardman, Cedrick	DE	6-4	245	13	10- 4-48	North Texas State	16	T-SF, '80
27	Hawkins, Frank	RB	5-9	210	2	7- 3-59	Nevada-Reno	13	D10, '81
37	Hayes, Lester	CB	6-0	200	6	1-22-55	Texas A&M	16	D5a, '77
83	†Hendricks, Ted	LB	6-7	230	14	11- 1-47	Miami	16	VFA, '75
48	Hill, Kenny	S	6-0	195	2	7-25-58	Yale	9	D8, '80
42	†Jackson, Monte	CB	5-11	195	8	7-14-53	San Diego State	16	T-LA, '78
31	Jensen, Derrick	RB	6-1	220	4	4-27-56	Texas-Arlington	16	D3a, '78
90	Jones, Willie	DE	6-4	250	4	11-22-57	Florida State	8	D2, '79
33	King, Kenny	RB	5-11	205	4	3- 7-57	Oklahoma	14	T-Hou, '80
62	Kinlaw, Reggie	DT	6-2	245	3	1- 9-57	Oklahoma	1	D12b, '79
70	†Lawrence, Henry	T	6-4	270	9	9-26-51	Florida A&M	16	D1, '74
75	Long, Howie	DE	6-5	265	2	1-12-60	Villanova	16	D2, '81
60	Marsh, Curt	G	6-5	270	2	8-25-59	Washington	11	D1b, '81
53	Martin, Rod	LB	6-2	215	6	4- 7-54	Southern California	16	FA, '77
65	Marvin, Mickey	G	6-4	275	6	10- 5-55	Tennessee	16	D4, '77
71	Mason, Lindsey	T	6-5	275	4	8- 1-55	Kansas	11	D3b, '78
72	Matuszak, John	DE	6-8	285	10	10-25-50	Tampa	16	FA, '76
57	McClanahan, Randy	LB	6-5	235	5	12-12-54	Southwestern Louisiana	16	FA, '80
23	McKinney, Odis	S	6-2	190	5	5-19-57	Colorado	16	T-NYG, '80
55	Millen, Matt	LB	6-2	255	2	3-12-58	Penn State	16	D2, '80
	Miller, Mark	QB	6-2	185	3	8-13-56	Bowling Green	*0	FA, '82
28	Montgomery, Cleotha	RB	5-8	185	2	7- 1-56	Abilene Christian	*5	FA, '81
51	Nelson, Bob	LB	6-4	235	6	6-30-53	Nebraska	*0	FA, '80
	Odom, Cliff	LB	6-2	225	2	8-15-58	Texas-Arlington	*0	FA, '82
35	O'Steen, Dwayne	CB	6-1	195	5	12-20-54	San Jose State	16	T-LA, '80
44	Owens, Burgess	S	6-2	200	10	8- 2-51	Miami	16	T-NYJ, '80
16	Plunkett, Jim	QB	6-2	215	12	12- 5-47	Stanford	9	FA, '78
	Pruitt, Greg	RB	5-10	190	10	8-18-51	Oklahoma	15	T-Cle, '82
84	Ramsey, Derrick	TE	6-5	235	5	12-23-56	Kentucky	16	D5, '78
68	Robinson, Johnny	DT	6-2	260	2	2-14-58	Louisiana Tech	16	D4, '81
78	Shell, Art	T	6-5	285	15	11-26-46	Maryland State	16	D3, '68
66	Sylvester, Steve	C-G	6-4	260	8	3- 4-53	Notre Dame	15	D10, '75
	Taylor, Billy	RB	6-0	215	5	7- 6-56	Texas Tech	*7	FA, '82
63	Upshaw, Gene	G	6-5	255	16	8-15-45	Texas A&I	15	D1, '67
30	van Eeghen, Mark	RB	6-2	220	9	4-19-52	Colgate	8	D3, '74
	Vaughan, Ruben	DT	6-2	263	2	8-6-56	Colorado	*0	FA, '82
41	Watts, Ted	CB	6-0	190	2	5-29-59	Texas Tech	16	D1a, '81
52	Westbrooks, Greg	LB	6-3	230	8	2-24-53	Colorado	4	FA, '81
22	Whittington, Arthur	RB	5-11	185	5	9- 4-55	Southern Methodist	16	D7a, '78
	Wilkinson, Jerry	DE	6-9	290	3	2-27-56	Oregon State	*0	FA, '82
38	Willis, Chester	RB	5-11	195	2	5- 2-58	Auburn	15	D11, '81
6	Wilson, Marc	QB	6-6	205	3	2-15-57	Brigham Young	13	D1, '80

*Bailey last active with Kansas City in 1978; Berns last active with Tampa Bay in 1980; Bright played 4 games with Cincinnati in 1981; Fisher played 2 games with St. Louis in 1981; Miller last active with Green Bay in 1980; Grossart active for 3 games with New York Jets in 1981 but did not play; Montgomery played 4 games with Cleveland, 1 with Oakland in 1981; Nelson missed 1981 season due to injuries; Odom last active with Cleveland in 1980; Taylor played 5 games with New York Giants, 2 with

New York Jets in 1981; Vaughan last active with San Francisco in 1979; Wilkinson last active with San Francisco in 1980.

†Option playout; subject to developments.

D—Draft; T—Trade; W—Waivers; FA—Free Agent; OFA—Original Free Agent; VFA—Veteran Free Agent; VA—Veteran Allocation; SupD—Supplemental Draft.

Also played with Raiders in 1981—DE Joe Campbell (3 games), LB Mario Celotto (7), WR-KR Ira Matthews (5).

OAKLAND RAIDERS
1982 DRAFT CHOICES

(Number following name designates order of selection among 334 players drafted.)

Round and Player		Position	College
1. ALLEN, Marcus	10	RB	USC
2. SQUIREK, Jack from Houston (a)	35	LB	Illinois
ROMANO, Jim	37	C	Penn State
3. MC ELROY, Vann	64	DB	Baylor
4. MURANSKY, Ed	91	T	Michigan
5. JACKSON, Ed	123	LB	Louisiana Tech
6. Choice to San Francisco (b)			
7. JACKSON, Jeff	177	DE	Toledo
8. Choice to Cleveland (c)			
9. Choice to Detroit through Los Angeles (d)			
10. D'AMICO, Rich	263	LB	Penn State
11. TURNER, Willie	289	WR	Louisiana State
12. SMITH, Randy	316	WR	East Texas St.

(a) Acquired pick and first- and second-round picks in 1981 for tight end Dave Casper, October 14, 1980.

(b) Traded pick and fifth-round pick in 1983 for defensive end Cedrick Hardman, May 30, 1980.

(c) Traded pick for defensive end Lyle Alzado, April 28, 1982.

(d) Traded pick to Los Angeles for cornerback Dwayne O'Steen, September 1, 1980; Los Angeles traded pick and ninth-round pick to Detroit for seventh-round pick, April 28, 1982.

OAKLAND RAIDERS
1982 ROOKIE AND FIRST-YEAR ROSTER

(1) Indicates player in previous NFL camp.
(2) Indicates player with CFL experience.
(3) Indicates player with minor league experience.
    All others classified as rookies.

Name	Pos.	Hgt.	Wgt.	Birth-date	College	How Acquired
Adams, Stan	LB	6-2	220	5-22-60	Memphis State	FA
Allen, Marcus	RB	6-2	210	3-26-60	Southern California	D1
Bybee, Royce	QB	6-2	185	6-2-56	Brigham Young	FA
Carter, James	G	6-3	255	3-17-59	Washington	FA
Collins, Dan (3)	TE	6-5	230	6-17-58	Chico State	FA
D'Amico, Rich	LB	6-2	230	5-20-60	Penn State	D10
Davis, James (1)	CB	6-0	205	6-12-57	Southern	*D5 ('81)
Drake, Don (1)	LB	6-3	245	9-20-59	Cal Poly-Pomona	FA
Durrette, Mike	G	6-3	265	8-11-57	West Virginia	FA
Escalara, Paul	WR	6-2	195	4-29-59	Washington State	FA
Fields, Mike	G	6-3	255	3-31-59	Jackson State	FA
Gabriel, Robin	QB	6-4	215	10-30-60	New Mexico	FA
Geishauser, George	S	6-1	180	7-11-59	Tulane	FA
Goularte, Rich	QB	6-2	210	12-10-58	Chico State	FA
Green, Sherrod	S	5-11	190	6- 2-59	Alcorn State	FA
Henderson, Curtis (1)	WR	5-10	195	8- 4-58	Morgan State	FA
Hill, Jerry (1)	WR	6-1	175	2-17-59	North Alabama	FA
Holland, Ron	TE	6-3	250	7-20-59	Tennessee State	FA
Irving, Reggie (1)	G	6-2	260	12-22-57	Grambling	FA
Jackson, Ed	LB	6-3	220	2- 5-59	Louisiana Tech	D5
Jackson, Jeff	DE	6-7	265	8-21-59	Toledo	D7
Jackson, Keith	DE	6-3	245	10- 6-59	Mississippi State	FA
Kahianui, Rob (3)	RB	5-10	185	1- 9-58	Brigham Young	FA
King, Court	DT	6-7	275	12- 8-58	Chico State	FA
Land, Doug	RB	6-0	225	10-14-59	Cal State-Long Beach	FA
McCaughey, John	C	6-1	250	6- 8-60	Arkansas State	FA
McClaran, Glen	S	5-9	190	8- 2-59	San Jose State	FA
McElroy, Vann	S	6-2	190	1-13-60	Baylor	D3
Mitchell, Ron (1)	TE	6-3	230	10-25-59	Northern Arizona	FA
Muhammad, Calvin (1)	WR	5-11	185	12-10-58	Texas Southern	*D12 ('80)
Muransky, Ed	T	6-7	280	1-20-60	Michigan	D4
Palumbo, Paul	RB	5-9	205	2- 6-59	San Diego State	FA
Pringle, Greg	CB	6-1	175	11- 2-59	South Carolina State	FA
Rogers, Tom	WR	6-4	210	6-25-60	Colgate	FA
Romano, Jim	C	6-3	260	9- 7-59	Penn State	D2b
Sample, Ted	RB	5-11	225	8-22-58	East Texas State	FA
Scoggins, Eric (1)	LB	6-2	235	1-23-59	Southern California	FA
Smith, Kenny	CB	6-0	190	8-16-57	Southern Mississippi	FA
Smith, Randy	WR	6-1	170	4- 3-60	East Texas State	D12
Spivey, Lee (1)	T	6-2	275	12- 7-57	Southern Methodist	FA
Squirek, Jack	LB	6-4	225	2-16-59	Illinois	D2a
Taylor, Ken (1)	CB	6-1	190	4-10-58	Georgia Tech	FA
Tillman, Leveren	DE	6-4	265	8-29-57	Arkansas State	FA
Trupovnicks, Jani	T	6-7	285	6-18-59	Tennessee	FA
Turner, Willie (2)	WR	5-11	195	1-16-59	Louisiana State	D11
Whitley, Rhett	LB	6-1	210	12-29-58	Southern Mississippi	FA
Whitmire, Brian	QB	6-3	200	2- 7-60	Davidson	FA

*Davis and Muhammad missed 1981 season due to injuries.

PHILADELPHIA EAGLES
(Eastern Division, National Conference)

Dick Vermeil

Owner & President—Leonard H. Tose
General Manager—Jim Murray
Director of Player Personnel—Carl Peterson
Head Coach—Dick Vermeil (6 years: 51-41-0)
Assistant Coaches:
  Running Backs—John Becker
  Secondary—Fred Bruney
  Defensive Coordinator—Marion Campbell
  Defensive Line—Chuck Clausen
  Receivers—Dick Coury
  Quarterbacks—Sid Gillman
  Linebackers—George Hill
  Offensive Line-Special Teams—Ken Iman
  Administrative Assistant, Tight Ends, Special Teams—
    Lynn Stiles
  Offensive Line-Running Game—Jerry Wampfler
  Honorary Coach—Chuck Bednarik
Director of Public Relations—Jim Gallagher
  (Office Phone: 463-2500—Area Code 215)
Offices—Veterans Stadium, Philadelphia, Pa. 19148
Stadium—Veterans Stadium (Capacity: 71,529)
Team Colors—Kelly Green, White and Silver
Training Site—West Chester State College, West Chester, Pa.

1982 SCHEDULE
(All times local.
All games Sunday unless noted otherwise.)

Sept. 12	WASHINGTON	1:00
Sept. 19	at Cleveland	1:00
Sept. 26	LOS ANGELES	1:00
Oct. 3	vs. Green Bay (Milw.)	12:00
Oct. 11	at Pittsburgh (Mon.)	9:00
Oct. 17	DALLAS	4:00
Oct. 25	NEW YORK GIANTS (Mon.)	9:00
Oct. 31	at St. Louis	12:00
Nov. 7	DETROIT	1:00
Nov. 15	at Atlanta (Mon.)	9:00
Nov. 21	CINCINNATI	1:00
Nov. 28	at Washington	1:00
Dec. 5	ST. LOUIS	1:00
Dec. 11	at New York Giants (Sat.)	12:30
Dec. 19	HOUSTON	1:00
Dec. 26	at Dallas	3:00

1981 RESULTS—(Won 10, Lost 7)

Eagles		Opp.		Att.
24	New York Giants	10	(A)	71,459
13	New England	3	(H)	71,089
20	Buffalo	14	(A)	80,020
36	Washington	13	(H)	70,664
16	Atlanta	13	(H)	71,488
31	New Orleans	14	(A)	52,728
23	Minnesota	35	(A)	45,459
20	Tampa Bay	10	(H)	70,714
14	Dallas	17	(H)	72,111
52	St. Louis	10	(A)	48,421
38	Baltimore	13	(H)	68,618
10	New York Giants	20	(H)	66,827
10	Miami	13	(A)	67,797
10	Washington	15	(A)	52,206
10	Dallas	21	(A)	64,955
38	St. Louis	0	(H)	56,656
	PLAYOFF GAME			
21	New York Giants	27	(H)	71,611

1981 GAMES STARTED

16 games: Ron Baker, Harold Carmichael, Al Chesley, Herman Edwards, Carl Hairston, Ron Jaworski, Charlie Johnson, Keith Krepfle, Frank LeMaster, Randy Logan, Guy Morriss, Jerry Sisemore, Stan Walters.

15 games: Wilbert Montgomery, Jerry Robinson, Brenard Wilson.

14 games: Charles Smith.

13 games: Roynell Young.

12 games: Dennis Harrison.

11 games: Steve Kenney.

10 games: Hubert Oliver.

Less than 10 games: Richard Blackmore (3), John Bunting (8), Louie Giammona (1), Perry Harrington (4), Claude Humphrey (4), Petey Perot (5), Ray Phillips (1), Booker Russell (1), John Sciarra (1), John Spagnola (3), Reggie Wilkes (8).

PHILADELPHIA EAGLES 1982 VETERAN ROSTER

No.	Name	Pos.	Ht.	Wt.	NFL Exp.	Birth-date	College	Games in '81	How Acquired
38	Atkins, Steve	RB	6-0	219	4	6-22-56	Maryland	*4	FA, '81
63	Baker, Ron	G	6-4	250	5	11-19-54	Oklahoma State	16	T-Bal, '80
27	Blackmore, Richard	CB	5-10	174	4	8-14-56	Mississippi State	16	OFA, '79
	Brown, Aaron	LB	6-2	235	4	1-15-56	Ohio State	*0	FA, '82
98	Brown, Gregory	DE	6-5	240	2	1- 5-57	Kansas State	16	OFA, '81
95	Bunting, John	LB	6-1	220	11	7-15-50	North Carolina	9	D10, '72
37	Campfield, Billy	RB	6-0	205	5	8-20-56	Kansas	16	D11, '78
17	Carmichael, Harold	WR	6-8	225	12	9-22-49	Southern	16	D7, '71
59	Chesley, Al	LB	6-3	240	4	8-23-57	Pittsburgh	16	D11, '79
71	Clarke, Ken	MG	6-2	255	5	8-28-56	Syracuse	16	OFA, '78
57	Curcio, Mike	LB	6-1	237	2	1-24-57	Temple	16	D8, '80
46	Edwards, Herm	CB	6-0	190	6	4-27-54	San Diego State	16	OFA, '77
24	Ellis, Ray	DB	6-1	192	2	4-27-59	Ohio State	16	D12, '81
86	Folsom, Steve	TE	6-4	230	2	3-21-58	Utah	3	FA, '81
1	Franklin, Tony	PK	5-8	182	4	11-18-56	Texas A&M	16	D3, '79
33	Giammona, Louie	RB-KR	5-9	180	6	3- 3-53	Utah State	8	FA, '78
79	Giddens, Frank	T	6-7	300	2	1-20-59	New Mexico	16	OFA, '81
78	Hairston, Carl	DE	6-3	260	7	12-15-52	Maryland-East. Shore	16	D7, '76
35	Harrington, Perry	RB	5-11	210	3	3-13-58	Jackson State	4	D2, '80
20	Harris, Leroy	RB	5-9	230	4	7- 3-54	Arkansas State	*0	T-Mia, '79
68	Harrison, Dennis	DE	6-8	275	5	7-31-56	Vanderbilt	13	D4, '78
89	Henry, Wally	WR-PR	5-8	180	6	10-30-54	UCLA	16	OFA, '77
	Hines, Andre	T	6-6	275	2	2-28-58	Stanford	*0	FA, '82
80	Hooks, Alvin	WR	5-11	170	2	5- 7-57	Cal State-Northridge	3	OFA, '81
87	Humphrey, Claude	DE	6-5	258	15	6-29-44	Tennessee A&I State	12	T-Atl, '79
	Jacobs, David	PK	5-7	151	3	7-15-57	Syracuse	*5	FA, '82
7	Jaworski, Ron	QB	6-2	196	8	3-23-51	Youngstown State	16	T-LA, '77
65	Johnson, Charlie	MG	6-3	262	6	1-17-52	Colorado	16	D7, '77
	Johnson, Charles	MG	6-1	262	4	6-29-57	Maryland	*0	FA, '82
73	Kenney, Steve	G	6-4	262	3	12-26-55	Clemson	13	OFA, '79
	King, Jerome	DB	5-10	175	2	1- 4-55	Purdue	*0	FA, '82
55	LeMaster, Frank	LB	6-2	238	9	3-12-52	Kentucky	16	D4, '74
41	Logan, Randy	S	6-1	195	10	5- 1-51	Michigan	16	D3, '73
99	Mitchell, Leonard	DE	6-7	272	2	10-12-58	Houston	16	D1, '81
31	Montgomery, Wilbert	RB	5-10	195	6	9-16-54	Abilene Christian	15	D6b, '77
50	Morriss, Guy	C	6-4	255	10	5-13-51	Texas Christian	16	D2, '73
42	Murray, Calvin	RB	5-11	185	2	10-18-58	Ohio State	7	D4, '81
34	Oliver, Hubert	FB	5-10	212	2	11-12-57	Arizona	13	D10, '81
83	Parker, Rodney	WR	6-1	190	3	7-18-53	Tennessee State	11	FA, '80
62	Perot, Pete	G	6-2	261	4	4-18-57	Northwest Louisiana	16	D2, '79
52	Phillips, Ray	LB	6-4	230	6	3-18-54	Nebraska	16	FA, '78
9	Pisarcik, Joe	QB	6-4	220	6	7- 2-52	New Mexico State	7	T-NYG, '80
56	Robinson, Jerry	LB	6-2	218	4	12-18-56	UCLA	15	D1, '79
4	Runager, Max	P	6-1	189	4	3-24-56	South Carolina	15	D8b, '79
32	Russell, Booker	RB	6-2	235	5	2-28-56	Southwest Texas State	12	FA, '81
21	Sciarra, John	S	5-11	185	5	3- 2-54	UCLA	10	T-TB, '78
76	Sisemore, Jerry	T	6-4	265	10	7-16-51	Texas	16	D1a, '73
61	Slater, Mark	C	6-2	257	5	2- 1-55	Minnesota	16	FA, '79
81	Smith, Ron	WR	6-0	185	5	11-20-56	San Diego State	*12	FA, '81
88	Spagnola, John	TE	6-4	240	4	8- 1-57	Yale	11	FA, '79
	Steptoe, Jack	WR	6-1	175	2	1-25-56	Utah	*0	FA, '82
	Turner, David	RB	5-11	210	4	1- 2-55	San Diego State	*0	FA, '82
42	Wagner, Steve	LB	6-2	208	6	4-18-54	Wisconsin	*0	W-GB, '80
75	Walters, Stan	T	6-6	275	11	5-27-48	Syracuse	16	T-Cin, '75
51	Wilkes, Reggie	LB	6-4	230	5	5-27-56	Georgia Tech	14	D3, '78
22	Wilson, Brenard	S	6-0	175	4	8-15-55	Vanderbilt	15	OFA, '78
43	Young, Roynell	CB	6-1	181	3	12- 1-57	Alcorn State	13	D1, '80

*Atkins played 3 games with Green Bay, 1 with Philadelphia in 1981; Bergey, Harris, and Wagner missed '81 season due to injuries; A. Brown last active with Tampa Bay in '80; Hines last active with Seattle in '80; Jacobs played 5 games with Cleveland in 1981; Charles Johnson last active with Green Bay in '80; King last active with N.Y. Giants in '80; R. Smith played 9 games with San Diego, 3 with Philadelphia in 1981; Steptoe last active with San Francisco in '78, Turner last active with Cincinnati in 1980.

†Option playout; subject to developments.

D—Draft; T—Trade; W—Waivers; FA—Free Agent; OFA—Original Free Agent; VFA—Veteran Free Agent; VA—Veteran Allocation; SupD—Supplemental Draft.

Also played with Eagles in 1981—RB Mickey Fitzgerald (1 game), DB Jo Jo Heath (15), TE Keith Krepfle (16), WR Charles Smith (16). Retired: LB Bill Bergey (*0).

PHILADELPHIA EAGLES
1982 DRAFT CHOICES

(Number following name designates order of selection among 334 players drafted.)

Round and Player		Position	College
1. QUICK, Mike	20	WR	No. Carolina St.
2. SAMPLETON, Lawrence	47	TE	Texas
3. KAB, Vyto	78	TE	Penn State
4. GRIGGS, Anthony	105	LB	Ohio State
5. DeVAUGHAN, Dennis	132	DB	Bishop
6. GRIEVE, Curt	159	WR	Yale
7. ARMSTRONG, Harvey	190	DT	SMU
8. FRITZSCHE, Jim	217	T	Purdue
9. WOODRUFF, Tony	244	WR	Fresno State
10. Choice to Miami (a)			
11. INGRAM, Ron	301	WR	Oklahoma State
12. TAYLOR, Rob	328	T	Northwestern

(a) Traded pick to Miami for running back Steve Howell, August 18, 1981.

PHILADELPHIA EAGLES
1982 ROOKIE AND FIRST-YEAR ROSTER

(1) Indicates player in previous NFL camp.   (2) Indicates player with CFL experience.

Name	Pos.	Hgt.	Wgt.	Birth-date	College	How Acquired
Anae, Brad	DE	6-5	250	10- 3-57	Brigham Young	FA
Anderson, John (1)	DE	6-6	250	9-16-58	Central Florida	FA
Armstrong, Harvey	DT	6-2	255	12-29-59	Southern Methodist	D7
Askew, Mike	HB	5-9	175	4- 4-59	Kean College	FA
Beauvais, Rick	FB	5-11	215	7-13-59	Pennsylvania	FA
Blair, Ken (1)	WR	6-2	195	5- 9-58	Missouri	*FA ('81)
Brown, Wiley	TE	6-8	240	10-19-60	Louisville	FA
Burkhardt, Fred	G	6-4	250	8-17-60	Western Michigan	FA
Burris, Scott	G	6-3	263	5- 7-58	Ohio State	FA
Cannavino, Andy (1)	LB	6-1	228	4-20-59	Michigan	FA
Carroll, Terry	LB	6-1	225	8-29-60	Indiana, Pa.	FA
Carter, Richard (1)	DB	5-11	180	11-19-59	North Carolina State	FA
Commiskey, Chuck (1)	C	6-4	280	3- 2-58	Mississippi	*FA ('81)
Davis, Gail (1)	DT	6-4	270	6- 1-59	Virginia Union	*D11 ('81)
DeVaughn, Dennis	DB	5-10	175	10-28-60	Bishop	D5
Dindak, Rob	LB	6-1	212	1-10-60	California State, Pa.	FA
Dudak, Scott	RB	5-10	215	4-27-60	Gettysburg	FA
Franco, Brian	K	5-9	170	12- 3-59	Penn State	FA
Fritzsche, Jim	T	6-8	265	10-11-60	Purdue	D8
General, Ernie	DB	6-2	205	1- 6-60	New York Tech	FA
Gilbert, George	DT	6-3	260	3-11-59	Tulsa	FA
Grieve, Curtis	WR	6-4	195	8-23-59	Yale	D6
Griggs, Anthony	LB	6-3	220	2-12-60	Ohio State	D4
Grube, Rich	T	6-7	285	3-20-58	North Carolina State	FA
Hamilton, James	DE	6-2	265	7-11-59	Elizabeth City State	FA
Happe, Joe	C	6-2	245	8-23-58	Georgia	FA
Hines, Steve (2)	DB	5-11	180	9-26-57	San Jose State	FA
Hipp, I. M. (1)	HB	6-0	203	2-15-56	Nebraska	FA
Hoover, Melvin (1)	WR	6-0	185	8-21-59	Arizona State	FA
Ingram, Ron	WR	5-10	173	10-27-59	Oklahoma State	D11
Jenkins, Ken	HB	5-9	183	5- 8-59	Bucknell	FA
Jones, Homer (1)	RB	5-10	195	8- 1-59	Brigham Young	FA
Kab, Vyto	TE	6-5	255	12-23-59	Penn State	D3
Keeler, K. C.	DB	6-0	192	7-26-59	Delaware	FA
Krejci, Jeff	DB	6-0	180	10-10-58	Nebraska	FA
Krohn, Jim (2)	QB	6-3	195	7-27-57	Arizona	FA
Kyger, Jeff	P	6-0	195	3-27-59	Slippery Rock	FA
Link, Ron	DT	6-3	240	10-13-59	Edinboro State	FA ('81)
Miraldi, Dean (1)	G	6-5	254	4- 8-58	Utah	*D2 ('81)
Moor, Buddy (1)	DT	6-5	252	12- 1-58	Eastern Kennedy	*FA ('81)
Murphy, Casey (1)	P	6-2	185	4- 4-58	Temple	FA
Nicolopulos, Craig	LB	6-1	215	12-28-59	Fresno State	FA
Payne, Dean	LB	6-4	220	4- 2-59	Northwestern	FA
Plemmons, Brad	LB	6-4	210	6-24-59	UCLA	FA
Quick, Mike	WR	6-2	190	5-14-59	North Carolina State	D1
Rodenberger, Jeff	FB	6-3	238	11- 3-59	Maryland	FA
Ryan, Dan	WR	6-1	185	6-20-60	Lehigh	FA
Sampleton, Lawrence	TE	6-5	233	9-25-59	Texas	D2
Scicli, Chuck	DB	5-10	192	11- 5-60	Cal Poly-Pomona	FA
Shankle, Doug	LB	6-0	230	2-24-60	Texas	FA
Smith, Dale	G	6-3	256	10-17-55	East Tennessee	FA
Smith, Johnny	WR	6-0	182	8- 1-58	Florida	FA
Steels, Anthony	WR	5-9	190	1- 8-59	Nebraska	FA
Stromberg, Bill	WR	6-2	190	3-10-60	Johns Hopkins	FA
Sydnor, Ray (1)	TE	6-8	225	4- 9-58	Wisconsin	*Waiv.('80)
Taylor, Rob	T	6-6	281	4-14-60	Northwestern	D12
Thomas, Lowell	LB	6-3	228	8-30-59	College of Alameda	FA
Tolbert, Willie	HB-WR	6-3	211	8- 1-59	Cheyney State	FA
Tumpich, Joe (1)	DB	5-11	185	8-30-58	Kansas	FA
Warner, Dave	QB	6-2	205	5-10-60	Syracuse	FA
Williams, Charles	DB	5-11	180	1- 6-60	Dartmouth	FA
Woodruff, Tony	WR	6-0	175	11-12-58	Fresno State	D9
Zielinski, David	DB	5-11	185	7-21-59	Lock Haven State	FA
Zupancic, John	LB	6-0	222	10-20-60	Miami (O.)	FA

*Blair, Commiskey, Davis, Miraldi and Moor missed 1981 season due to injuries; Sydnor missed 1980 and '81 seasons due to injuries.

PITTSBURGH STEELERS

(Central Division, American Conference)

Chuck Noll

Chairman of the Board—Arthur J. Rooney
President—Daniel M. Rooney
Vice-President—John R. McGinley
Vice-President—Arthur J. Rooney, Jr.
Director of Player Personnel—Dick Haley
Head Coach—Chuck Noll (13 years: 117-72-1)
Assistant Coaches:
  Offensive Line—Rollie Dotsch
  Defensive Backfield—Tony Dungy
  Offensive Backfield—Dick Hoak
  Conditioning—Jon Kolb
  Receivers—Tom Moore
  Assistant Head Coach—George Perles
  Defensive Coordinator—Robert (Woody) Widenhofer
Publicity Director—Joe Gordon (323-1200—Area Code 412)
Offices—Three Rivers Stadium, 300 Stadium Circle, Pittsburgh, Pa. 15212
Stadium—Three Rivers Stadium (Capacity: 54,000)
Colors—Black and Gold
Training Site—St. Vincent's College, Latrobe, Pa.

1982 SCHEDULE

(All times local.
All games Sunday unless noted otherwise.)

Sept. 13	at Dallas (Mon.)	8:00
Sept. 19	CINCINNATI	1:00
Sept. 26	NEW YORK GIANTS	1:00
Oct. 3	at Denver	2:00
Oct. 11	PHILADELPHIA (Mon.)	9:00
Oct. 17	at Washington	1:00
Oct. 24	CLEVELAND	1:00
Oct. 31	at Cincinnati	1:00
Nov. 7	HOUSTON	1:00
Nov. 14	NEW YORK JETS	1:00
Nov. 21	at Houston	12:00
Nov. 28	at Seattle	1:00
Dec. 5	KANSAS CITY	1:00
Dec. 12	at Buffalo	1:00
Dec. 19	at Cleveland	1:00
Dec. 26	NEW ENGLAND	1:00

1981 RESULTS—(Won 8, Lost 8)

Steelers		Opp.		Att.
33	Kansas City	37	(H)	53,305
10	Miami	30	(A)	74,190
38	New York Jets	10	(H)	52,934
27	New England (OT)	21	(H)	53,344
20	New Orleans	6	(A)	64,578
13	Cleveland	7	(H)	53,255
7	Cincinnati	34	(A)	57,090
26	Houston	13	(H)	52,732
14	San Francisco	17	(H)	52,878
21	Seattle	24	(A)	59,058
34	Atlanta	20	(A)	57,485
32	Cleveland	10	(A)	77,958
24	Los Angeles	0	(H)	51,854
27	Oakland	30	(A)	51,769
10	Cincinnati	17	(H)	50,623
20	Houston	21	(A)	41,056

1981 GAMES STARTED

16 games: Mel Blount, Steve Courson, Franco Harris, Jack Lambert, John Stallworth, J.T. Thomas, Mike Webster, Craig Wolfley.

15 games: Bennie Cunningham, Gary Dunn.

14 games: Terry Bradshaw, Larry Brown, Donnie Shell, Dwayne Woodruff.

13 games: Robin Cole.

12 games: John Banaszak, Lynn Swann.

11 games: Jack Ham, Ray Pinney.

10 games: John Goodman, Frank Pollard.

Less than 10 games: Tom Beasley (9), Joe Greene (7), L.C. Greenwood (5), Randy Grossman (1), Tunch Ilkin (1), Ron Johnson (3), Bob Kohrs (6), Jon Kolb (6), Mark Malone (3), Jim Smith (3), Sidney Thornton (6), Loren Toews (4), Anthony Washington (1), Dennis Winston (4).

PITTSBURGH STEELERS 1982 VETERAN ROSTER

No.	Name	Pos.	Ht.	Wt.	NFL Exp.	Birth-date	College	Games in '81	How Acquired
30	Anderson, Larry	CB-KR	5-11	188	5	9-25-56	Louisiana Tech	16	D4, '78
76	Banaszak, John	DE-DT	6-3	250	8	8-24-50	Eastern Michigan	12	OFA, '75
65	Beasley, Tom	DT	6-5	248	5	8-11-54	Virginia Tech	13	D3a, '77
47	Blount, Mel	CB	6-3	205	13	4-10-48	Southern	16	D3, '70
12	Bradshaw, Terry	QB	6-3	210	13	9- 2-48	Louisiana Tech	14	D1, '70
79	Brown, Larry	T	6-4	270	12	6-16-49	Kansas	14	D5a, '71
56	Cole, Robin	LB	6-2	220	6	9-11-55	New Mexico	14	D1, '77
5	Colquitt, Craig	P	6-1	182	5	6- 9-54	Tennessee	16	D3, '78
77	Courson, Steve	G	6-1	260	5	10- 1-55	South Carolina	16	D5b, '77
89	Cunningham, Bennie	TE	6-5	260	7	12-23-54	Clemson	15	D1, '76
45	Davis, Russell	RB	6-1	231	3	9-15-56	Michigan	16	D4a, '79
	Dornbrook, Thom	G-C	6-2	256	3	12-1-56	Kentucky	*0	FA, '82
67	Dunn, Gary	DT	6-3	260	6	8-24-53	Miami	16	D6a, '76
95	Goodman, John	DE-DT	6-6	250	2	11-21-58	Oklahoma	15	D2b, '80
68	Greenwood, L.C.	DE	6-6	250	14	9- 8-46	Arkansas AM&N	14	D10, '69
84	Grossman, Randy	TE	6-1	225	9	9-20-52	Temple	16	OFA, '74
59	Ham, Jack	LB	6-1	225	12	12-23-48	Penn State	12	D2, '71
32	Harris, Franco	RB	6-2	225	11	3- 7-50	Penn State	16	D1, '72
27	Hawthorne, Greg	RB	6-2	225	4	9- 5-56	Baylor	10	D1, '79
62	Ilkin, Tunch	T	6-3	253	3	9-23-57	Indiana State	16	D6, '80
29	Johnson, Ron	CB-S	5-10	200	5	6- 8-56	Eastern Michigan	12	D1, '78
90	Kohrs, Bob	DE	6-3	245	2	11- 8-58	Arizona State	16	D2a, '80
58	Lambert, Jack	LB	6-4	220	9	7- 8-52	Kent State	16	D2, '74
50	Little, David	LB	6-1	220	2	1- 3-59	Florida	16	D7, '81
16	Malone, Mark	QB	6-4	223	3	11-22-58	Arizona State	8	D1, '80
61	McGriff, Tyrone	G	6-0	267	3	1-13-58	Florida A&M	12	D12b, '80
39	Moser, Rick	RB	6-0	210	5	12-18-56	Rhode Island	*7	FA, '81
66	Petersen, Ted	T	6-5	244	6	2- 7-55	Eastern Illinois	2	D4a, '77
74	Pinney, Ray	T-C	6-4	256	6	6-29-54	Washington	16	D2a, '76
44	Pollard, Frank	RB	5-10	210	3	6-15-57	Baylor	14	D11, '80
31	Shell, Donnie	S	5-11	190	9	8-26-52	South Carolina State	14	OFA, '74
86	Smith, Jim	WR-KR	6-2	205	6	7-20-55	Michigan	15	D3b, '77
82	Stallworth, John	WR	6-2	191	9	7-15-52	Alabama A&M	16	D4a, '74
18	Stoudt, Cliff	QB	6-4	218	6	3-27-55	Youngstown State	2	D5a, '77
88	Swann, Lynn	WR	6-0	180	9	3- 7-52	Southern California	13	D1, '74
85	Sweeney, Calvin	WR	6-2	190	3	1-12-55	Southern California	14	D4b, '79
24	Thomas, J.T.	S	6-2	196	6	4-22-51	Florida State	16	D1, '73
38	Thornton, Sidney	RB	5-11	230	6	9- 2-54	Northwestern Louisiana	16	D2, '77
51	Toews, Loren	LB	6-3	220	10	11- 3-51	California	16	D8a, '73
1	Trout, David	K	5-6	165	2	11-12-57	Pittsburgh	16	OFA, '81
54	Valentine, Zack	LB	6-2	220	4	5-29-57	East Carolina	16	D2, '79
42	Washington, Anthony	CB	6-1	204	2	2- 4-58	Fresno State	16	D2, '81
52	Webster, Mike	C	6-1	255	9	3-18-52	Wisconsin	16	D5, '74
73	Wolfley, Craig	G	6-1	265	3	5-19-58	Syracuse	16	D5, '80
49	Woodruff, Dwayne	CB-S	5-11	198	4	2-18-57	Louisville	16	D6b, '79

*Dornbrook last active with Miami in 1980; Moser played 1 game with Kansas City, 6 with Pittsburgh in 1981.

D—Draft; T—Trade; W—Waivers; FA—Free Agent; OFA—Original Free Agent; VFA—Veteran Free Agent; VA—Veteran Allocation; SupD—Supplemental Draft.

Also played with Steelers in 1981—WR Johnnie Dirden (6 games), LB Dennis Winston (14). Retired: G Sam Davis (0), DT Joe Greene (14), T Jon Kolb (15).

PITTSBURGH STEELERS
1982 DRAFT CHOICES

(Number following name designates order of selection among 334 players drafted.)

Round and Player		Position	College
1. ABERCROMBIE, Walter	12	RB	Baylor
2. MEYER, John	43	T	Arizona State
3. MERRIWEATHER, Mike	70	LB	Pacific
4. WOODS, Rick	97	DB	Boise State
5. DALLAFIOR, Ken	124	T	Minnesota
6. PERKO, Mike	155	DT	Utah State
BINGHAM, Craig	167	LB	Syracuse
from San Francisco through New Orleans (a)			
7. NELSON, Ed	172	DT	Auburn
from Los Angeles through Washington (b)			
BOURES, Emil	182	C	Pittsburgh
8. GOODSON, John	209	P	Texas
9. HIRN, Mike	236	TE	Central Mich.
10. SUNSERI, Sal	267	LB	Pittsburgh
11. ABDUL-SABOOR, Mikal	293	G	Morgan State
12. HUGHES, Al	320	DE	Western Mich.

(a) San Francisco traded pick to New Orleans for quarterback Guy Benjamin, July 13, 1981; New Orleans traded pick to Pittsburgh for linebacker Dennis Winston, April 27, 1982.

(b) Los Angeles traded pick and third-round pick to Washington for tight end Henry Childs, May 6, 1981; Washington traded pick and fifth-round pick in 1983 to Pittsburgh for quarterback Mike Kruczek, July 28, 1980.

PITTSBURGH STEELERS
1982 ROOKIE AND FIRST-YEAR ROSTER

(1) Indicates player in previous NFL camp.
(2) Indicates player with CFL experience.
(3) Indicates player with minor league experience.
All others classified as rookies.

Name	Pos.	Hgt.	Wgt.	Birth-date	College	How Acquired
Abdul-Saboor, Mikal	G	6-2	261	2-28-60	Morgan State	D11
Abercrombie, Walter	RB	5-11	201	9-26-59	Baylor	D1
Bingham, Craig	LB	6-2	211	9-26-59	Syracuse	D6b
Boures, Emil	C	6-1	262	1-29-60	Pittsburgh	D7b
Collins, Frank (1)	RB-WR	5-9	180	7-31-54	Utah	FA
Cooper, George	LB	6-2	210	12-24-58	Michigan State	FA
Costello, Owen	LB	6-1	220	6-19-59	William & Mary	FA
Cugliari, Joe (1)	DT	6-3	270	12- 4-58	Indiana, Pa.	*FA ('81)
Dallafior, Ken	T	6-3	268	8-26-59	Minnesota	D5
DeCicco, Dominic	TE	6-4	235	4- 9-59	Waynesburg	FA
DeGruttola, John	RB	5-10	215	3-12-60	Westminster	FA
Donnalley, Rick (1)	C-G	6-2	247	12-11-58	North Carolina	*D3 ('81)
Evans, Billy	WR	6-3	185	7-20-59	West Virginia	FA
Fedell, Steve (1)	LB	6-2	238	12-19-57	Pittsburgh	*FA ('81)
Fielder, Don	DE	6-3	240	10-29-59	Kentucky	FA
French, Ernest	S	5-11	188	9- 5-59	Alabama A&M	FA
Goodson, John	P	6-3	204	3-18-60	Texas	D8
Harris, Pete	S	6-1	203	4- 7-57	Penn State	FA
Himic, Jim (1)	T	6-5	237	10- 5-57	West Virginia	FA
Hinkle, Bryan (1)	LB	6-1	214	6- 4-59	Oregon	*D6 ('81)
Hirn, Mike	TE	6-3	225	5-20-60	Central Michigan	D9
Hughes, Al	DE	6-3	238	9- 8-59	Western Michigan	D12
Longo, Paul	RB	5-9	175	12- 3-58	Wayne State (Mich.)	FA
Martin, Ricky (1)	WR	6-2	201	10-26-58	New Mexico	*D5 ('81)
McCauley, Gary	TE	6-4	230	3-11-59	Clarion State	FA
McCoy, Karl (2)	CB-S	5-11	175	7-29-57	Penn State	FA
McCulloch, Ken (1)	P-K	6-3	210	5- 8-55	Arkansas	FA
Melontree, Lester	DE	6-6	210	6- 2-59	Stephen F. Austin	FA
Merriweather, Mike	LB	6-2	215	11-26-60	Pacific	D3
Meyer, John	T	6-6	257	5-28-59	Arizona State	D2
Mungin, Ben	WR	6-0	185	2-15-58	South Carolina State	FA
Nelson, Edmund	DT	6-3	247	4-30-60	Auburn	D7a
Perko, Mike	DT	6-2	241	3-30-57	Utah State	D6a
Powers, John (1)	G	6-3	270	4- 6-58	Michigan	FA
Purifoy, Don	DE	6-3	240	10-29-57	Tulsa	FA
Quinn, Jeff (1)	QB	6-3	206	2-16-58	Nebraska	FA
Rademacher, Philip	DE	6-6	245	3-15-58	Niagara	FA
Redenius, Eric	WR	6-0	195	3- 3-59	Arizona State	FA
Rodgers, John	TE	6-2	220	2- 7-60	Louisiana Tech	FA
Ruff, Guy	LB	6-1	215	8-18-60	Syracuse	FA
Sams, Eric (3)	RB	5-10	200	2-17-59	Wisconsin-Superior	FA
Seguin, Marc	LB	6-4	225	2-16-59	Rice	FA
Smith, Gary	G	6-1	253	1-27-60	Virginia Tech	FA
Snow, Patrick	WR-KR	6-1	180	1-29-60	Akron	FA
Stoneburner, Ted	RB	5-10	205	7-14-59	Central Connecticut State	FA
Sunseri, Sal	LB	6-0	224	8- 1-59	Pittsburgh	D10
Sydnor, Willie	WR-KR	5-11	170	3-21-59	Syracuse	FA
Tabor, Tom	DT	6-3	260	4-18-60	Baylor	FA
Walls, Craig	LB	6-1	210	12-24-58	Indiana	FA
Washington, Sam	CB	5-8	180	3- 7-60	Mississippi Valley State	FA
Willis, Keith	DT	6-1	251	7-29-59	Northeastern	FA
Wilson, Frank (1)	TE-RB	6-2	233	10-11-58	Rice	*D8 ('81)
Wilson, Woodrow (2)	CB	5-9	183	10- 9-56	North Carolina State	D10 ('80)
Woods, Rick	S	6-0	196	11-16-59	Boise State	D4

*Cugliari, Donnalley, Fedell, Hinkle, Martin and F. Wilson missed 1981 season due to injuries.

ST. LOUIS CARDINALS
(Eastern Division, National Conference)

Jim Hanifan

Chairman of the Board—William V. Bidwill
President, Chief Operating Officer—Bing Devine
Director of Pro Personnel—Larry Wilson
Director of Player Personnel—George Boone
Head Coach—Jim Hanifan (2 years: 12-20-0)
Assistant Coaches:
  Special Teams—Chuck Banker
  Defensive Coordinator—Tom Bettis
  Flexibility-Strength—Don Brown
  Linebackers—Rudy Feldman
  Quarterbacks—Harry Gilmer
  Offensive Backfield—Dick Jamieson
  Offensive Line—Tom Lovat
  Special Assistant to Head Coach—Leon McLaughlin
  Assistant Head Coach—Floyd Peters
  Receivers—Emmitt Thomas
Media Coordinator—Marty Igel
  (Office Phone: 421-0777—Area Code 314)
Offices—200 Stadium Plaza, St. Louis, Mo. 63102
Stadium—Busch Memorial Stadium (Capacity: 51,392)
Team Colors—Cardinal Red, White and Black
Training Site—Eastern Illinois University, Charleston, Ill.

1982 SCHEDULE
(All times local. All games Sunday unless noted otherwise.)

Sept. 12	at New Orleans	12:00
Sept. 19	DALLAS	12:00
Sept. 26	at Washington	1:00
Oct. 3	LOS ANGELES	12:00
Oct. 10	at New York Giants	1:00
Oct. 17	CHICAGO	12:00
Oct. 24	at New England	1:00
Oct. 31	PHILADELPHIA	12:00
Nov. 7	at Dallas	12:00
Nov. 14	SEATTLE	12:00
Nov. 21	SAN FRANCISCO	3:00
Nov. 28	at Atlanta	1:00
Dec. 5	at Philadelphia	1:00
Dec. 12	WASHINGTON	12:00
Dec. 19	at Chicago	12:00
Dec. 26	NEW YORK GIANTS	12:00

1981 RESULTS—(Won 7, Lost 9)

Cardinals	Opp.		Att.
7 Miami	20	(H)	50,351
17 Dallas	30	(A)	63,602
40 Washington	30	(H)	47,592
10 Tampa Bay	20	(A)	65,850
20 Dallas	17	(H)	49,477
14 New York Giants	34	(A)	67,128
20 Atlanta	41	(A)	51,428
30 Minnesota	17	(H)	48,039
21 Washington	42	(A)	50,643
10 Philadelphia	52	(H)	48,421
24 Buffalo	0	(H)	46,214
35 Baltimore	24	(A)	24,784
27 New England	20	(A)	39,946
30 New Orleans	3	(H)	46,923
10 New York Giants	20	(H)	47,358
0 Philadelphia	38	(A)	56,656

1981 GAMES STARTED

16 games: Ottis Anderson, Tom Brahaney, Mike Dawson, Dan Dierdorf, Terry Stieve, Pat Tilley.

15 games: Ken Greene, Lee Nelson, Bob Pollard.

14 games: Joe Bostic.

13 games: Rush Brown, George Collins, E.J. Junior, Wayne Morris.

12 games: Mel Gray, Curtis Greer.

11 games: Greg LaFleur, Eric Williams.

10 games: Dave Ahrens.

Less than 10 games: Carl Allen (8), Charles Baker (8), Mark Bell (1), Theotis Brown (3), Tim Collier (6), Chris Combs (2), Barney Cotton (2), Calvin Favron (7), John Floyd (1), Roy Green (2), Jeff Griffin (9), Jim Hart (9), Tim Kearney (6), Rusty Lisch (1), Neil Lomax (7), Doug Marsh (3), Bruce Radford (1), Don Schwartz (1), Roger Wehrli (9), Keith Wortman (3).

ST. LOUIS CARDINALS 1982 VETERAN ROSTER

No.	Name	Pos.	Ht.	Wt.	NFL Exp.	Birth-date	College	Games in '81	How Acquired
58	Ahrens, Dave	LB	6-3	230	2	12- 5-58	Wisconsin	16	D6, '81
27	Allen, Carl	CB	6-0	188	6	12-21-55	Southern Mississippi	10	T-Cin, '77
32	Anderson, Ottis	RB	6-2	220	4	1-19-57	Miami	16	D1, '79
52	Baker, Charlie	LB	6-2	218	3	9-26-57	New Mexico	14	D3b, '80
18	Birdsong, Carl	P	6-0	192	2	1- 1-59	Southwest Oklahoma St.	16	W-Buf, '81
71	Bostic, Joe	G	6-3	268	4	4-20-57	Clemson	14	D3, '79
51	Brahaney, Tom	C	6-2	247	10	10-23-51	Oklahoma	16	D5, '73
69	Brown, Rush	DT	6-2	257	3	6-27-54	Ball State	16	D10, '80
43	Carpenter, Steve	DB	6-2	205	2	6- 7-59	Western Illinois	1	FA, '81
64	Clark, Randy	C-G	6-3	254	3	7-27-57	Northern Illinois	16	FA, '80
86	Clayton, Ralph	WR	6-3	222	2	9-29-58	Michigan	7	FA, '81
61	Coder, Ron	G	6-4	260	5	5-24-54	Penn St.	*0	FA, '80
44	Collier, Tim	CB	6-0	176	7	5-31-54	East Texas State	14	T-KC, '80
66	Collins, George	T	6-2	265	5	12- 9-55	Georgia	16	D4a, '78
80	Combs, Chris	TE	6-4	249	3	3-17-58	New Mexico	16	FA, '80
60	Cotton, Barney	G	6-5	265	4	9-30-56	Nebraska	2	FA, '80
73	Dawson, Mike	DT	6-4	275	7	10-16-53	Arizona	16	D1, '76
72	Dierdorf, Dan	T	6-3	288	11	6-29-49	Michigan	16	D2, '71
59	Favron, Calvin	LB	6-1	227	4	7- 3-57	Southeastern La. State	14	D2b, '79
50	Field, Doak	LB	6-2	227	2	10- 8-58	Baylor	7	FA, '81
57	Gillen, John	LB	6-3	228	2	11- 5-58	Illinois	16	D5, '81
85	Gray, Mel	WR	5-9	175	12	9-28-48	Missouri	12	D6, '71
25	Green, Roy	WR	6-0	195	4	6-30-57	Henderson State	16	D4, '79
37	†Greene, Ken	S	6-3	205	5	5- 8-56	Washington State	15	D1b, '78
75	Greer, Curtis	DE	6-4	258	3	11-10-57	Michigan	16	D1, '80
35	Griffin, Jeff	CB	6-0	185	2	7-19-58	Utah	16	D3, '81
39	Harrell, Willard	RB	5-8	182	8	9-16-52	Pacific	16	FA, '78
17	Hart, Jim	QB	6-1	210	17	4-29-44	Southern Illinois	10	OFA, '66
46	Johnson, Charles	CB	5-10	180	4	5- 5-56	Grambling	5	FA, '81
	Johnson, Ken	RB	6-2	220	2	11-27-56	Miami	*0	FA, '82
54	Junior, E.J.	LB	6-3	235	2	12- 8-59	Alabama	16	D1, '81
89	LaFleur, Greg	TE	6-4	236	2	9-16-58	Louisiana State	16	W-Phi, '81
16	Lisch, Rusty	QB	6-3	215	3	12-21-56	Notre Dame	9	D4, '80
15	Lomax, Neil	QB	6-3	214	2	2-17-59	Portland State	14	D2, '81
40	Love, Randy	RB	6-1	205	4	9-30-56	Houston	16	FA, '79
62	Markham, Dale	T	6-8	280	2	7-24-57	North Dakota	2	FA, '81
87	Marsh, Doug	TE	6-3	238	3	6-18-58	Michigan	4	D2, '80
76	Mays, Stafford	DE	6-2	250	3	3-13-58	Washington	16	D9, '80
30	Mitchell, Stump	RB	5-9	188	2	3-15-59	Citadel	16	D9, '81
24	Morris, Wayne	RB	6-0	208	7	5- 3-54	Southern Methodist	16	D5, '76
38	Nelson, Lee	S	5-10	185	7	1-30-54	Florida State	15	D15, '76
11	O'Donoghue, Neil	PK	6-6	210	6	6-18-53	Auburn	16	FA, '80
70	Plunkett, Art	T	6-7	262	2	3- 8-59	Nevada-Las Vegas	8	W-LA, '81
79	Radford, Bruce	DE	6-5	260	4	9- 5-55	Grambling	9	FA, '81
48	Schwartz, Don	S	6-1	194	5	2-24-56	Washington State	5	FA, '81
21	Stief, Dave	DB	6-3	195	5	1-29-56	Portland State	12	D7, '78
68	Stieve, Terry	G	6-2	265	6	3-10-54	Wisconsin	16	T-NO, '78
83	Tilley, Pat	WR	5-10	175	7	2-15-53	Louisiana Tech	16	D4, '76
74	Times, Ken	DT	6-2	248	2	1- 1-56	Southern	2	FA, '81
	Waddy, Ray	DB	5-11	175	3	8-21-56	Texas A&I	*0	FA, '82
22	Wehrli, Roger	CB	6-0	194	14	11-26-47	Missouri	16	D1, '69
55	Williams, Eric	LB	6-2	235	6	6-17-55	Southern California	15	D8, '77
42	Williams, Herb	DB	6-0	200	3	8-30-58	Southern	3	FA, '81

*Coder missed 1981 season due to injury; K. Johnson last active with N. Y. Giants in 1979; Waddy last active with Washington in '80.

†Option playout; subject to developments.

D—Draft; T—Trade; W—Waivers; FA—Free Agent; OFA—Original Free Agent; VFA—Veteran Free Agent; VA—Veteran Allocation; SupD—Supplemental Draft.

Also played with Cardinals in 1981—DT Bill Acker (8 games), WR Mark Bell (1), RB Theotis Brown (4), DE Kirby Criswell (2), WR Mike Fisher (2), WR John Floyd (4), LB Tim Kearney (6), DE Bob Pollard (15), T Keith Wortman (4).

ST. LOUIS CARDINALS
1982 DRAFT CHOICES

(Number following name designates order of selection among 334 players drafted.)

Round and Player		Position	College
1. Choice to Kansas City (a)			
SHARPE, Luis from Kansas City (a)	16	T	UCLA
2. GALLOWAY, David	38	DT	Florida
3. PERRIN, Benny	65	DB	Alabama
GUILBEAU, Rusty from Kansas City (a)	73	DE	McNeese State
4. ROBBINS, Tootie from Seattle (b)	90	T	East Carolina
5. BEDFORD, Vance	119	DB	Texas
FERRELL, Earl from Washington (c)	125	RB	East Tenn. St.
6. SHAFFER, Craig	150	LB	Indiana State
7. SEBRO, Bob	178	C	Colorado
8. LINDSTROM, Chris	205	DT	Boston U.
9. DAILEY, Darnell	232	LB	Maryland
10. McGILL, Eddie	259	TE	West. Carolina
11. WILLIAMS, James	290	DE	No. Car. A&T
12. ATHA, Bob	317	K	Ohio State

(a) Switched first-round positions and acquired third-round pick, April 27, 1982.
(b) Acquired pick and 1983 pick for running back Theotis Brown, October 13, 1981.
(c) Acquired pick for running back Terry Metcalf, May 8, 1981.

ST. LOUIS CARDINALS
1982 ROOKIE AND FIRST-YEAR ROSTER

(1) Indicates player in previous NFL camp.
All others classified as rookies.

Name	Pos.	Hgt.	Wgt.	Birth-date	College	How Acquired
Adams, Joe (1)	G	6-5	255	11- 2-57	Nebraska	*D12 ('81)
Adams, John	C	6-3	250	2-19-59	Brigham Young	FA
Anton, Scott	LB	6-1	215	7-11-58	Wayne State	FA
Atha, Bob	K-RB	5-11	180	9-22-60	Ohio State	D12
Bedford, Vance	DB	6-0	170	8-20-58	Texas	D5a
Bolton, Dave	WR	6-3	190	8-28-60	Washington U., Mo.	FA
Chancey, Keith	WR	5-11	190	8-22-57	Ouachita Baptist	FA
Dailey, Darnell	LB	6-2	223	9- 8-59	Maryland	D9
Davis, Dave	DE	6-5	250	1-30-59	Wichita State	FA
Ferrell, Earl	RB	6-0	215	3-27-58	East Tennessee State	D5b
Galloway, David	DE	6-3	277	2-16-59	Florida	D2
Guilbeau, Rusty	DE	6-4	250	11-20-58	McNeese State	D3b
Joiner, Jim (1)	WR	6-2	195	6-25-59	Miami	D10 ('81)
Kehr, Rick (1)	T	6-4	265	6-18-59	Carthage College	FA
Lindstrom, Chris	DT	6-7	245	8- 3-60	Boston University	D8
Mallard, James	WR	6-2	185	11-29-57	Alabama	*D10 ('81)
Marshall, Mike	CB-S	5-11	182	7-19-59	Michigan	FA
McCord, Prince	RB	5-11	188	7-21-59	Alabama A&M	FA
McGill, Eddie	TE	6-6	225	7- 5-60	Western Carolina	D10
Perrin, Benny	CB-S	6-2	175	10-20-59	Alabama	D3a
Poole, Walter	RB	5-11	190	3-27-60	Southern Illinois	FA
Reid, Lawrence (1)	RB	6-1	212	1-22-59	Michigan	FA
Reliford, Ron	LB	6-3	230	12-12-56	Northeast Louisiana	FA
Robbins, Tootie	T	6-5	278	6- 2-58	East Carolina	D4
Sebro, Bob	G-T	6-4	255	3- 9-59	Colorado	D7
Sharpe, Luis	T	6-4	260	6-16-60	UCLA	D1
Shaffer, Craig	LB	6-0	230	3-31-59	Indiana State	D6
Thompson, Ken (1)	WR	6-2	170	12- 6-58	Utah State	FA
Vereen, Tony (1)	S	5-10	202	9- 4-58	Southeast Louisiana	FA
Whitley, Eddy (1)	TE	6-3	228	2-12-58	Kansas State	FA
Williams, James	DE	6-7	258	12-31-57	North Carolina A&T	D11
Williams, Marcus	S	6-0	190	3- 2-60	Vanderbilt	FA
Young, Joe	QB	6-1	200	12-20-58	Southeast Missouri	FA

*Adams missed 1981 season due to injury; Mallard suffered heart ailment in 1981 prior to signing.

SAN DIEGO CHARGERS
(Western Division, American Conference)

Don Coryell

President—Eugene V. Klein
General Manager—John R. Sanders
Assistant General Manager—Paul (Tank) Younger
Assistant to President—Jack Teele
Head Coach—Don Coryell (9 years: 83-46-1)
Assistant Coaches:
  Defensive Coordinator—Tom Bass
  Special Assistant—Marv Braden
  Offensive Backs—Earnel Durden
  Offensive Line—Dave Levy
  Defensive Line—Jerry Smith
  Defensive Backs—Jim Wagstaff
  Offensive Coordinator—Larrye Weaver
  Linebackers—Chuck Weber
Public Relations Director—Rick Smith.
  (Office Phone: 280-2111—Area Code 714)
Offices—San Diego Stadium, P. O. Box 20666, San Diego, Calif.
  92120
Stadium—San Diego Stadium (Capacity: 52,596)
Team Colors—Blue and Gold
Training Site—University of California, San Diego

1982 SCHEDULE
(All times local.
All games Sunday unless noted otherwise.)

Sept. 12	at Denver	2:00
Sept. 19	at Kansas City	12:00
Sept. 26	OAKLAND	1:00
Oct. 3	at Atlanta	1:00
Oct. 10	SEATTLE	1:00
Oct. 17	KANSAS CITY	1:00
Oct. 24	at Seattle	1:00
Oct. 31	LOS ANGELES	1:00
Nov. 8	at Miami (Mon.)	9:00
Nov. 14	NEW ORLEANS	1:00
Nov. 22	at Oakland (Mon.)	6:00
Nov. 28	DENVER	1:00
Dec. 5	at Cleveland	1:00
Dec. 11	at San Francisco (Sat.)	1:00
Dec. 20	CINCINNATI (Mon.)	6:00
Dec. 26	BALTIMORE	1:00

1981 RESULTS—(Won 11, Lost 7)

Chargers		Opp.		Att.
44 Cleveland	14	(A)		78,904
28 Detroit	23	(H)		51,624
42 Kansas City	31	(A)		63,866
24 Denver	42	(A)		74,844
24 Seattle	10	(H)		51,463
31 Minnesota	33	(H)		50,708
43 Baltimore	14	(A)		41,921
17 Chicago (OT)	20	(A)		52,906
22 Kansas City	20	(H)		51,307
17 Cincinnati	40	(H)		51,209
23 Seattle	44	(A)		58,628
55 Oakland	21	(A)		50,199
34 Denver	17	(H)		51,533
27 Buffalo	28	(H)		51,488
24 Tampa Bay	23	(A)		67,388
23 Oakland	10	(H)		52,696

PLAYOFF GAME
41 Miami	38	(A)	73,735

AFC CHAMPIONSHIP GAME
7 Cincinnati	27	(A)	46,302

1981 GAMES STARTED

16 games: Willie Buchanon, Dan Fouts, Gary Johnson, Charlie Joiner, Linden King, Woodrow Lowe, Billy Shields, Ed White, Doug Wilkerson, Kellen Winslow.

15 games: Don Macek.

14 games: Leroy Jones, Louie Kelcher, Chuck Muncie.

13 games: Russ Washington.

12 games: Pete Shaw, Mike Williams, John Woodcock.

11 games: Wes Chandler, Bob Horn.

10 games: Eric Sievers.

Less than 10 games: James Brooks (2), John Cappelletti (5), Fred Dean (2), Frank Duncan (4), Glen Edwards (8), Allan Ellis (6), Keith Ferguson (1), Bob Gregor (6), Chuck Loewen (3), Don Reese (2), Bob Rush (1), Dwight Scales (4), Ron Smith (1), Clifford Thrift (5), Jimmy Webb (1), Clarence Williams (1), Wilbur Young (2).

SAN DIEGO CHARGERS 1982 VETERAN ROSTER

No.	Name	Pos.	Ht.	Wt.	NFL Exp.	Birth-date	College	Games in '81	How Acquired
	Allen, Jeff	CB	5-11	185	2	7-18-58	California-Davis	*0	FA, '82
37	Bauer, Hank	RB	5-11	204	6	7-15-54	California Lutheran	16	FA, '77
45	†Beaudoin, Doug	S	6-0	190	7	5-15-54	Minnesota	4	W-Mia, '81
42	Bell, Ricky	RB	6-2	220	5	4- 8-55	Southern California	7	T-TB, '82
6	Benirschke, Rolf	PK	6-1	178	6	2- 7-55	California-Davis	16	W-Oak, '77
50	Bradley, Carlos	LB	6-0	221	2	4-27-60	Wake Forest	8	D11b, '81
21	Brooks, James	RB	5-9	180	2	12-28-58	Auburn	14	D1, '81
28	Buchanon, Willie	CB	6-0	185	11	11-14-50	San Diego State	16	T-GB, '78
25	Cappelletti, John	FB	6-1	224	8	8- 9-52	Penn State	16	T-LA, '80
89	Chandler, Wes	WR	5-11	186	5	8-22-56	Florida	*16	T-NO, '81
77	Claphan, Sam	T	6-6	267	2	10-10-56	Oklahoma	16	FA, '81
	Cook, Fred	DE	6-4	252	8	4-15-52	Southern Mississippi	*0	FA, '82
73	DeJurnett, Charles	DT	6-4	260	6	6-17-52	San Jose State	*0	FA, '76
47	Duncan, Frank	S	6-1	188	4	11- 6-56	San Francisco State	7	D12, '79
27	†Edwards, Glen	FS	6-0	183	12	7-31-47	Florida A&M	8	T-Pit, '78
76	Ferguson, Keith	DE	6-5	240	2	4- 3-59	Ohio State	16	D5, '81
81	Fitzkee, Scott	WR	6-0	187	4	8- 4-57	Penn State	5	W-Phi, '81
14	Fouts, Dan	QB	6-3	204	10	6-10-51	Oregon	16	D3, '73
	Fox, Tim	S	5-11	190	7	11- 1-53	Ohio	16	T-NE, '82
43	Gregor, Bob	S	6-2	187	2	2-10-57	Washington State	14	D4b, '80
12	†Harris, James	QB	6-3	221	13	7-20-47	Grambling	1	T-LA, '77
32	Henderson, Wyatt	CB	5-10	180	2	11-10-56	Fresno State	15	FA, '81
89	Holohan, Pete	TE	6-4	226	2	7-25-59	Notre Dame	7	D7, '81
79	Johnson, Gary	DT	6-3	252	8	8-31-53	Grambling	16	D1a, '75
18	†Joiner, Charlie	WR	5-11	183	14	10-14-47	Grambling	16	T-Cin, '76
68	Jones, Leroy	DE	6-8	271	7	9-29-50	Norfolk State	16	T-LA, '76
74	Kelcher, Louie	DT	6-5	282	8	8-23-53	Southern Methodist	14	D2a, '75
57	King, Linden	LB	6-4	237	5	6-28-55	Colorado State	16	D3, '77
	Laird, Bruce	S	6-1	194	11	5-23-50	American International	15	T-Bal, '82
54	†Laslavic, Jim	LB	6-2	229	9	10-24-51	Penn State	16	T-Det, '78
58	Lewis, David	LB	6-4	240	6	10-15-54	Southern California	13	T-TB, '82
64	Loewen, Chuck	G-T	6-3	259	3	1-23-57	South Dakota State	9	D7a, '80
51	Lowe, Woodrow	LB	6-0	227	7	6- 9-54	Alabama	16	D5, '76
11	Luther, Ed	QB	6-2	211	3	1- 2-57	San Jose State	16	D4a, '80
62	Macek, Don	C	6-2	253	7	7- 2-54	Boston College	15	D2, '76
	Monroe, Henry	CB	5-11	180	2	12-30-56	Mississippi State	*0	FA, '82
46	Muncie, Chuck	RB	6-3	218	8	3-17-53	California	15	T-NO, '80
23	Phillips, Irvin	CB	6-1	192	2	1-23-60	Arkansas Tech	15	D3, '81
52	Preston, Ray	LB	6-0	218	7	1-25-54	Syracuse	16	D11, '76
4	Roberts, George	K	6-0	186	5	6-10-54	Virginia Tech	16	T-Mia, '81
56	Rush, Bob	C-T	6-5	264	6	2-27-55	Memphis State	16	D1, '77
87	Scales, Dwight	WR	6-2	185	6	5-30-53	Grambling	16	FA, '81
	Selmon, Dewey	LB	6-1	240	6	11-19-53	Oklahoma	*0	T-TB, '82
44	Shaw, Pete	S	5-10	183	6	8-25-54	Northwestern	16	D6c, '77
66	Shields, Billy	T	6-8	275	8	8-23-53	Georgia Tech	16	D6b, '75
	Siemon, Jeff	LB	6-3	237	11	6- 2-50	Stanford	16	T-Min, '82
85	Sievers, Eric	TE	6-4	234	2	11-19-57	Maryland	16	D4b, '81
59	Thrift, Cliff	LB	6-2	232	4	5- 3-56	East Central Oklahoma	7	D3, '79
70	Washington, Russ	T	6-7	288	15	12-17-46	Missouri	13	D1a, '68
61	Webb, Jimmy	DT	6-5	252	8	4-13-52	Mississippi State	16	FA, '81
67	White, Ed	G	6-2	271	14	4- 4-47	California	16	T-Min, '78
63	Wilkerson, Doug	G	6-3	254	13	3-27-47	North Carolina Central	16	T-Hou, '70
40	Williams, Clarence	FB	5-10	185	6	1-25-55	South Carolina	14	D5a, '77
72	Williams, Jeff	G-T	6-4	260	5	4-15-55	Rhode Island	12	T-Was, '81
29	Williams, Mike	CB	5-10	176	8	11-22-53	Louisiana State	14	D1b, '75
80	Winslow, Kellen	TE	6-5	242	4	11- 5-57	Missouri	16	D1, '79
90	Woodcock, John	DE	6-3	255	6	3-19-54	Hawaii	12	T-Det, '81
99	Young, Wilbur	DT	6-6	290	12	4-20-49	William Penn, Iowa	*12	W-Was, '81

*DeJurnett and Selmon missed 1981 season due to injuries; Allen last active in NFL with Miami in 1980, played 1 game with Toronto-CFL in 1981; Cook last active with Baltimore in 1980; Chandler played 4 games with New Orleans, 12 with San Diego in 1981; Monroe last active with Philadelphia in 1979; Young played 7 games with Washington, 5 with San Diego in 1981.

†Option playout; subject to developments.

D—Draft; T—Trade; W—Waivers; FA—Free Agent; OFA—Original Free Agent; VFA—Veteran Free Agent; VA—Veteran Allocation; SupD—Supplemental Draft.

Also played with Chargers in 1981—WR Billy Brooks (7 games), DE Fred Dean (3), CB Allan Ellis (11), LB Bob Horn (16), DE Don Reese (5), WR Ron Smith (9), WR Aundra Thompson (1).

SAN DIEGO CHARGERS
1982 DRAFT CHOICES

(Number following name designates order of selection among 334 players drafted.)

Round and Player		Position	College
1. Choice to Green Bay (a)			
2. Choice to Washington through Los Angeles (b)			
3. Choice to New Orleans (c)			
4. Choice to Tampa Bay (d)			
5. Choice to Chicago (e)			
6. Choice to Miami (f)			
7. HALL, Hollis	188	DB	Clemson
8. BUFORD, Maury	215	P	Texas Tech
9. LYLES, Warren	246	DT	Alabama
10. YOUNG, Andre	273	DB	Louisiana Tech
11. WATSON, Anthony	299	DB	New Mexico St.
12. Choice to Detroit (g)			

(a) Traded pick and wide receiver John Jefferson for first-round picks in 1982 and 1983, second-round picks in 1982 and 1984 and wide receiver Aundra Thompson, September 17, 1981.

(b) San Diego traded pick to Los Angeles for running back John Cappelletti, March 21, 1980; Los Angeles traded pick, third-round pick in 1981 and two fifth-round picks in 1981 to Washington for first-round pick in 1982.

(c) Traded pick, first-round pick and wide receiver Aundra Thompson for wide receiver Wes Chandler, September 29, 1981.

(d) Traded pick for running back Ricky Bell, March 9, 1982.

(e) Traded pick for past considerations involving cornerback Allan Ellis, October 7, 1981.

(f) Traded pick for punter George Roberts, August 31, 1981.

(g) Traded pick for defensive tackle John Woodcock, September 15, 1981.

SAN DIEGO CHARGERS
1982 ROOKIE AND FIRST-YEAR ROSTER

(1) Indicates player in previous NFL camp.
(2) Indicates player with CFL experience.
(3) Indicates player with minor league experience.
   All others classified as rookies.

Name	Pos.	Hgt.	Wgt.	Birth-date	College	How Acquired
Ackerman, Richard (1).....	DT	6-4	255	6-16-59	Memphis State	*FA ('81)
Armour, Ned........................	WR	6-1	185	3- 6-58	San Diego State	FA
Bledsoe, Morris...................	QB	6-1	195	9-21-58	Weber State	FA
Bolar, Terry (1)	LB	6-4	245	2-14-58	Long Beach State	FA
Browne, Michael (1)..........	K	6-3	205	3-18-57	Idaho	FA
Buford, Maury.....................	P	6-1	180	2-18-60	Texas Tech	D8
Byers, Norman....................	FS	5-11	180	7- 3-58	Long Beach State	FA
Doolittle, Steve (1)	LB	6-3	225	1- 5-59	Colorado	FA
Duckworth, Bobby (1).......	WR	6-3	198	11-27-58	Arkansas	*D6a ('81)
Ellis, Russell (1).................	RB	5-11	192	12-13-56	Nevada-Las Vegas	FA
Finister, Carlton	FB	5-11	195	1-20-59	Northwestern (La.) State	FA
Foppe, Rod (3)	WR	5-11	170	2-26-56	Louisiana Tech	FA
Gissinger, Drew (1)	T	6-4	280	7- 4-59	Syracuse	*D6 ('81)
Goedeker, Mike	LB	5-11	217	8-25-59	Miami (Fla.)	FA
Hall, Hollis...........................	CB	5-9	173	5-19-60	Clemson	D7
Hendrix, Brad (1)...............	G	6-4	245	3-17-57	North Alabama	*FA ('80)
Justin, Tyrone (2)...............	DB	5-10	174	1-17-58	Fullerton State	FA
Lyles, Warren.......................	DT	6-1	261	7- 2-59	Alabama	D9
Martin, Derrick (1)...........	CB	5-11	185	5-31-57	San Jose State	FA
McKnight, Dennis (1)........	C-G	6-2	260	9-12-59	Drake	FA
Miller, Curt........................	WR	6-2	200	2- 9-60	Weber State	FA
Nelson, Derrie (1)	LB	6-2	225	2- 8-58	Nebraska	FA
Patterson, Byron	DB	5-9	183	6-13-59	Ferris State, Mich.	FA
Phillips, Henry	WR	6-1	170	3-24-57	Long Beach State	FA
Spadafore, Tom (1)	P-K	6-2	205	5- 3-58	Boise State	FA
Tolbert, Mark (1)................	WR	5-9	170	2-15-59	Cal-Poly Pomona	FA
Tucker, Jimmy Lee (1).....	RB-WR	5-11	188	12-14-57	Nevada-Las Vegas	FA
Watson, Anthony	S	6-0	205	11- 9-59	New Mexico State	D11
Whitman, Steve (1)	LB	6-3	231	6-27-57	Alabama	*D9 ('80)
Young, Andre	S	5-11	196	11-22-60	Louisiana Tech	D10

*Ackerman, Duckworth, Gissinger, Hendrix and Whitman missed 1981 season due to injuries.

SAN FRANCISCO 49ers
(Western Division, National Conference)

Bill Walsh

President—Edward J. DeBartolo Jr.

General Manager & Head Coach—Bill Walsh (3 years: 21-27-0)

Vice President, Administration—John McVay

Director of College Scouting—Tony Razzano

Assistant Coaches:
Linebackers—Norb Hecker
Special Teams-Receivers—Milt Jackson
Running Backs—Billie Matthews
Offensive Line—Bobb McKittrick
Defensive Line—Bill McPherson
Secondary—George Seifert
Defensive Coordinator—Chuck Studley
Strength-Conditioning—Al Vermeil
Quarterbacks—Sam Wyche

Public Relations Director—George Heddleston
(Office Phone: 365-3420—Area Code 415)

Offices—711 Nevada Street, Redwood City, Calif. 94061

Stadium—Candlestick Park (Capacity: 61,185)

Team Colors—49er Gold and Scarlet

Training Site—Sierra Community College, Rocklin, Calif.

1982 SCHEDULE
(All times local.
All games Sunday unless noted otherwise.)

Sept. 12	OAKLAND	1:00
Sept. 19	at Denver	2:00
Sept. 26	CHICAGO	1:00
Oct. 4	at Tampa Bay (Mon.)	9:00
Oct. 10	at New Orleans	12:00
Oct. 17	LOS ANGELES	1:00
Oct. 24	at Atlanta	1:00
Oct. 31	at Washington	1:00
Nov. 7	MINNESOTA	1:00
Nov. 14	DALLAS	1:00
Nov. 21	at St. Louis	3:00
Nov. 28	NEW ORLEANS	1:00
Dec. 2	at Los Angeles (Thurs.)	6:00
Dec. 11	SAN DIEGO (Sat.)	1:00
Dec. 19	ATLANTA	6:00
Dec. 26	at Kansas City	12:00

1981 RESULTS—(Won 16, Lost 3)

49ers		Opp.		Att.
17	Detroit	24	(A)	62,125
28	Chicago	17	(H)	49,520
17	Atlanta	34	(A)	56,653
21	New Orleans	14	(H)	44,433
30	Washington	17	(A)	51,843
45	Dallas	14	(H)	57,574
13	Green Bay	3	(A)	50,171
20	Los Angeles	17	(H)	59,190
17	Pittsburgh	14	(A)	52,878
17	Atlanta	14	(H)	59,127
12	Cleveland	15	(H)	52,445
33	Los Angeles	31	(A)	63,456
17	New York Giants	10	(H)	57,186
21	Cincinnati	3	(A)	56,796
28	Houston	6	(H)	55,707
21	New Orleans	17	(A)	43,639

PLAYOFF GAME

38	New York Giants	24	(H)	58,360

NFC CHAMPIONSHIP GAME

28	Dallas	27	(H)	60,525

NFL CHAMPIONSHIP GAME

26	Cincinnati	21	(*)	81,270

*—Silverdome, Pontiac, Mich.

1981 GAMES STARTED

16 games: Dan Audick, John Ayers, Dwight Clark, Randy Cross, Keith Fahnhorst, Willie Harper, Dwight Hicks, Ronnie Lott, Joe Montana, Fred Quillan, Archie Reese, Jack Reynolds, Carlton Williamson, Eric Wright, Charle Young.

15 games: Ricky Patton, Freddie Solomon, Jim Stuckey.

14 games: Keena Turner.

11 games: Dwaine Board, Earl Cooper.

Less than 10 games: Dan Bunz (8), Johnny Davis (5), Fred Dean (2), Walt Easley (1), Bobby Leopold (2), Lawrence Pillers (6), Craig Puki (6), Mike Shumann (1).

SAN FRANCISCO 49ers 1982 VETERAN ROSTER

No.	Name	Pos.	Ht.	Wt.	NFL Exp.	Birth-date	College	Games in '81	How Acquired
61	Audick, Dan	T-G	6-3	253	5	11-15-54	Hawaii	16	T-SD, '81
68	Ayers, John	G	6-5	260	6	4-14-53	West Texas State	16	D8, '76
7	Benjamin, Guy	QB	6-3	210	5	6-27-55	Stanford	4	T-NO, '81
76	Board, Dwaine	DE	6-5	250	4	11-29-56	North Carolina A&T	16	W-Pit, '79
72	Bungarda, Ken	T	6-6	270	2	1-25-57	Missouri	*0	FA, '80
57	Bunz, Dan	LB	6-4	225	5	10- 7-55	Cal State-Long Beach	14	D1b, '78
60	Choma, John	G-C	6-6	261	2	2- 9-55	Virginia	14	FA, '81
33	Churchman, Ricky	S	6-1	193	3	3-14-58	Texas	3	D4a, '80
87	Clark, Dwight	WR	6-4	210	4	1- 8-57	Clemson	16	D10a, '79
49	Cooper, Earl	RB	6-2	227	3	9-17-57	Rice	16	D1a, '80
	Crawford, Rufus	RB	5-10	180	2	5-21-55	Virginia State	*0	FA, '82
51	Cross, Randy	G	6-3	250	7	4-25-54	UCLA	16	D2a, '76
38	Davis, Johnny	RB	6-1	235	5	7-17-56	Alabama	16	T-TB, '81
74	Dean, Fred	DE	6-2	230	8	2-28-52	Louisiana Tech	*14	T-SD, '81
62	Downing, Walt	C-G	6-3	254	5	6-11-56	Michigan	16	D2, '78
31	Easley, Walt	RB	6-1	226	2	9- 8-57	West Virginia	12	OFA, '81
71	Fahnhorst, Keith	T	6-6	263	9	2- 6-52	Minnesota	16	D2a, '74
	Francis, Russ	TE	6-6	235	6	4- 3-53	Oregon	*0	T-NE, '82
24	Gervais, Rick	S	5-11	190	2	11- 4-59	Stanford	8	OFA, '81
59	Harper, Willie	LB	6-2	215	9	7-30-50	Nebraska	16	D2, '73
75	Harty, John	DT	6-4	253	2	12-17-58	Iowa	14	D2a, '81
22	Hicks, Dwight	S	6-1	189	4	4- 5-56	Michigan	16	FA, '79
	Horn, Bob	LB	6-4	230	7	2- 6-54	Oregon State	16	T-SD, '81
66	Kennedy, Allan	T	6-7	275	2	1- 8-58	Washington State	3	FA, '81
77	Kugler, Pete	DT	6-4	255	2	8- 9-59	Penn State	13	D6, '81
20	Lawrence, Amos	RB	5-10	179	2	1- 9-58	North Carolina	13	T-SD, '81
52	Leopold, Bobby	LB	6-1	215	3	10-18-57	Notre Dame	16	D8, '80
42	Lott, Ronnie	CB	6-0	199	2	5- 8-59	Southern California	16	D1, '81
29	Martin, Saladin	CB	6-1	180	3	1-17-56	San Diego State	15	FA, '81
53	McColl, Milt	LB	6-6	220	2	8-28-59	Stanford	16	OFA, '81
3	Miller, Jim	P	5-11	183	3	7- 5-57	Mississippi	16	D3a, '80
16	Montana, Joe	QB	6-2	200	3	6-11-56	Notre Dame	16	D3, '79
	Moore, Jeff	RB	6-0	195	3	8-20-56	Jackson State	*2	FA, '82
32	Patton, Ricky	RB	5-11	192	5	4- 6-54	Jackson State	16	FA, '80
65	Pillers, Lawrence	DE	6-4	260	7	11- 4-52	Alcorn State	14	W-NYJ, '80
54	Puki, Craig	LB	6-1	231	3	1-18-57	Tennessee	16	D3b, '80
56	Quillan, Fred	C	6-5	260	5	1-27-56	Oregon	16	D7, '78
80	Ramson, Eason	TE	6-2	234	4	4-30-56	Washington State	11	FA, '79
78	Reese, Archie	DT	6-3	262	5	2- 4-56	Clemson	16	D5a, '78
64	Reynolds, Jack	LB	6-1	232	13	11-22-47	Tennessee	16	FA, '81
30	Ring, Bill	RB	5-10	215	2	12-13-56	Brigham Young	12	FA, '81
84	Shumann, Mike	WR	6-0	175	5	10-13-55	Florida State	13	FA, '81
88	Solomon, Freddie	WR	5-11	185	8	1-11-53	Tampa	15	T-Mia, '78
79	Stuckey, Jim	DE	6-4	251	3	6-21-58	Clemson	15	D1b, '80
28	Thomas, Lynn	CB	5-11	181	2	7- 9-59	Pittsburgh	15	D5a, '81
58	Turner, Keena	LB	6-2	219	3	10-22-58	Purdue	16	D2, '80
90	†Visger, George	DT	6-4	250	2	9-26-58	Colorado	*0	FA, '80
14	Wersching, Ray	PK	5-11	210	10	8-21-50	California	12	FA, '77
27	Williamson, Carlton	S	6-0	204	2	6-12-58	Pittsburgh	16	D3, '81
85	Wilson, Mike	WR	6-3	210	2	12-19-58	Washington State	16	FA, '81
21	Wright, Eric	CB	6-1	180	2	4-18-59	Missouri	16	D2b, '81
86	†Young, Charle	TE	6-4	234	10	2- 5-51	Southern California	16	T-LA, '80

*Crawford last active in NFL with Seattle in 1978, played 13 games with Hamilton-CFL in 1981; Dean played 3 games with San Diego, 11 with San Francisco in 1981; Moore played 2 games with Seattle in 1981; Bungarda and Visger missed 1981 season due to injuries; Francis last active with New England in 1980.

†Option playout; subject to developments.

D—Draft; T—Trade; W—Waivers; FA—Free Agent; OFA—Original Free Agent; VFA—Veteran Free Agent; VA—Veteran Allocation; SupD—Supplemental Draft.

Also played with 49ers in 1981—K Matt Bahr (4 games), WR Matt Bouza (1), RB Arrington Jones (1), LB Jim Looney (1), TE Brian Peets (5), LB Terry Tautolo (5). Retired: RB Lenvil Elliott (4), RB Paul Hofer (12).

SAN FRANCISCO 49ers
1982 DRAFT CHOICES

(Number following name designates order of selection among 334 players drafted.)

Round and Player		Position	College
1. Choice to New England (a)			
2. PARIS, Bubba from New England (b)	29	T	Michigan
3. Choice to Tampa Bay through San Diego (c)			
4. Choice to New England (a)			
5. WILLIAMS, Newton	139	RB	Arizona St.
6. WILLIAMS, Vince from Oakland (d)	151	RB	Oregon
Choice to Pittsburgh through New Orleans (e)			
7. FERRARI, Ron	195	LB	Illinois
8. Choice to Washington through New Orleans (f)			
9. CLARK, Bryan	251	QB	Michigan State
10. Mc LEMORE, Dana from Tampa Bay (g)	269	KR	Hawaii
BARBIAN, Tim	279	DT	Western Illinois
11. GIBSON, Gary	306	LB	Arizona
12. WASHINGTON, Tim	334	DB	Fresno State

(a) Traded picks and two second-round picks for tight end Russ Francis and second-round pick, April 27, 1982.

(b) See (a).

(c) San Francisco traded pick to San Diego for offensive lineman Dan Audick, August 17, 1981; San Diego traded pick and fourth-round pick in 1984 to Tampa Bay for linebacker David Lewis, February 1, 1982.

(d) Acquired pick and fifth-round pick in 1983 for defensive end Cedrick Hardman, May 30, 1980.

(e) San Francisco traded pick to New Orleans for quarterback Guy Benjamin, July 13, 1981; New Orleans traded pick to Pittsburgh for linebacker Dennis Winston, April 27, 1982.

(f) San Francisco traded pick to New Orleans for wide receiver Artie Owens, July 21, 1981; New Orleans traded pick, ninth-, 10th-, 11th- and 12th-round picks to Washington for fourth-round pick in 1983, April 28, 1982.

(g) Acquired pick for defensive tackle Ted Vincent, May 1, 1981.

SAN FRANCISCO 49ers
1982 ROOKIE AND FIRST-YEAR ROSTER

(1) Indicates player in previous NFL camp.
(2) Indicates player with minor league experience.
   All others classified as rookies.

Name	Pos.	Hgt.	Wgt.	Birth-date	College	How Acquired
Abbott, Vince (1)	K	5-10	180	5-31-58	Cal. State-Fullerton	FA
Barbian, Tim	DT	6-3	230	4-16-59	Western	D10b
Bell, Myron	RB	5-11	202	6-10-59	Southern	FA
Brown, Delrick (1)	WR	5-10	190	1-22-57	Houston	FA
Castellanos, Rudy	QB	6-2	205	11-29-55	San Diego State	FA
Clark, Bryan	QB	6-2	196	7-27-60	Michigan State	D9
Collins, Mickey (1)	RB	5-10	190	5-14-59	Wichita State	FA
Crawford, Rufus (1)	RB	5-10	180	5-21-55	Virginia State	FA
Ellis, Craig	WR	6-0	180	1-26-61	San Diego State	FA
Ferrari, Ron	LB	6-0	212	7-30-59	Illinois	D7
Frazier, Frank	T-G	6-3	275	10-15-60	Miami	FA
Gibson, Gary	LB	6-1	215	1-31-59	Arizona	D11
Glass, John (1)	LB	6-2	240	7- 2-57	University of Pacific	FA
Hall, Darryl	DB	5-10	185	10-23-59	San Diego State	FA
Herring, Eric (1)	WR	6-1	180	9-19-58	Houston	*FA ('81)
Hout, Kurt	C	6-4	260	7- 6-60	University of Pacific	FA
Jonker, Kurtis (1)	T-G	6-5	265	1-21-57	Augustana College	FA
Judie, Ed (1)	LB	6-2	231	7- 6-59	Northern Arizona	*FA ('81)
Kundsen, Chris	G-T	6-4	255	11-26-59	Arizona	FA
Lopez, John	WR	6-2	190	5-27-60	Illinois	FA
McKale, Bill	TE	6-4	235	2-22-59	Hawaii	FA
McLemore, Dana	KR-S	5-10	183	7- 1-60	Hawaii	D10a
Nehemiah, Renaldo	WR	6-1	177	3-24-59	Maryland	FA
Otey, Dave	C	6-3	265	5-25-58	UCLA	FA
Parham, Gus (1)	DT	6-6	260	9-19-56	San Jose State	*FA ('81)
Paris, Bubba	T	6-6	293	10- 6-60	Michigan	D2
Pryor, Benjie (1)	TE	6-3	235	9-11-59	Pittsburgh	FA
Ramona, Dave	LB	6-1	228	5- 7-59	Santa Clara	FA
Rayford, John (1)	RB	5-10	188	12-21-58	Cal. State-Fullerton	FA
Remington, Mark	LB	6-3	225	6-26-59	Colorado	FA
Redd, Verlon	DB	6-0	190	2-28-60	Hawaii	FA
Stover, Jeff	DT	6-5	275	5-22-58	Oregon	FA
Summers, Jay	LB	6-5	220	10-19-60	Stanford	FA
Thompson, Gary	DB	6-0	180	2-23-59	College of the Redwoods	FA
Ussery, Charles	DL	6-3	250	9- 7-60	Southern California	FA
Vassar, Brad (1)	LB	6-2	225	4-24-57	University of Pacific	FA
Ware, John	T-G	6-3	265	5-26-59	Drake	FA
Washington, Tim	CB	5-9	184	11- 7-59	Fresno State	D12
Weinlein, Gary (1)	S-KR	5-10	183	6-22-54	Hudson Valley C.C.	FA
Westering, Scott (1)	TE	6-4	235	9- 2-58	Pacific Lutheran	FA
Whatley, Jimbo (1)	WR	6-1	190	5- 7-59	Washington State	FA
Williams, Milt (1)	RB	6-1	195	6-18-59	Norwich University	FA
Williams, Newton	RB	5-10	204	5-10-59	Arizona State	D5
Williams, Vince	FB	6-0	231	10-24-59	Oregon	D6
Worman, Larry (2)	QB	6-2	195	10-11-57	Nevada-Reno	FA

*Herring, Judie and Parham missed 1981 season due to injuries.

SEATTLE SEAHAWKS
(Western Division, American Conference)

Jack Patera

Managing General Partner—Elmer Nordstrom
General Manager—John Thompson
Assistant General Manager—Mark Duncan
Director of Player Personnel—Dick Mansperger
Director of Pro Scouting—Chuck Allen
Director of Football Operations—Mike McCormack
Head Coach—Jack Patera (6 years: 35-57-0)
Assistant Coaches:
   Defensive Backfield—Jack Christiansen
   Defensive Line—Frank Lauterbur
   Running Backs—Andy McDonald
   Offensive Line—Howard Mudd
   Offensive Coordinator—Jerry Rhome
   Defensive Coordinator—Jackie Simpson
   Special Teams—Rusty Tillman
Director of Public Relations—Don Andersen
Director of Publicity—Gary Wright
   (Office Phone: 827-9777—Area Code 206)
Offices—5305 Lake Washington Blvd., Kirkland, Wash. 98033
Stadium—The Kingdome (Capacity: 64,752)
Team Colors—Blue, Green and Silver
Training Site—Eastern Washington State College, Cheney, Wash.

1982 SCHEDULE
(All times local.
All games Sunday unless noted otherwise.)

Sept. 12	CLEVELAND	1:00
Sept. 19	at Houston	3:00
Sept. 26	at New England	1:00
Oct. 3	KANSAS CITY	1:00
Oct. 10	at San Diego	1:00
Oct. 17	OAKLAND	1:00
Oct. 24	SAN DIEGO	1:00
Oct. 31	at Kansas City	12:00
Nov. 7	DENVER	1:00
Nov. 14	at St. Louis	12:00
Nov. 21	at Denver	2:00
Nov. 28	PITTSBURGH	1:00
Dec. 5	at Oakland	1:00
Dec. 12	CHICAGO	1:00
Dec. 19	NEW ENGLAND	1:00
Dec. 26	at Cincinnati	1:00

1981 RESULTS—(Won 6, Lost 10)

Seahawks	Opp.		Att.
21 Cincinnati	27	(A)	41,177
13 Denver	10	(H)	58,513
10 Oakland	20	(A)	45,725
14 Kansas City	20	(H)	59,255
10 San Diego	24	(A)	51,463
17 Houston	35	(A)	42,671
0 New York Giants	32	(H)	56,134
19 New York Jets	3	(A)	49,678
24 Green Bay	34	(A)	49,467
24 Pittsburgh	21	(H)	59,058
44 San Diego	23	(H)	58,628
13 Kansas City	40	(A)	49,002
31 Oakland	32	(H)	57,147
27 New York Jets	23	(H)	53,105
13 Denver	23	(A)	74,527
42 Cleveland	21	(H)	51,435

1981 GAMES STARTED

16 games: Steve August, Keith Butler, Ron Essink, Jacob Green, John Harris, Michael Jackson, Steve Largent, John Sawyer, Manu Tuiasosopo.

15 games: Edwin Bailey, Bob Newton.

14 games: Kenny Easley, Sam McCullum.

13 games: Robert Hardy, Jim Zorn.

12 games: Keith Simpson.

10 games: Dave Brown.

Less than 10 games: Fred Anderson (5), Terry Beeson (6), Theotis Brown (7), Dan Doornink (9), Bill Dugan (2), Greg Gaines (1), David Hughes (2), Jim Jodat (5), Greggory Johnson (3), Kerry Justin (9), Dave Krieg (3), Art Kuehn (7), Joe Norman (7), Sherman Smith (8), Doug Sutherland (6), Rodell Thomas (2), Mike Tice (3), Mike White (8), John Yarno (9).

SEATTLE SEAHAWKS 1982 VETERAN ROSTER

No.	Name	Pos.	Ht.	Wt.	NFL Exp.	Birth-date	College	Games in '81	How Acquired
12	Adkins, Sam	QB	6-2	214	6	5-21-55	Wichita State	3	D10, '77
2	Alvarez, Wilson	PK	6-0	165	2	3-22-57	Southeast Louisiana	4	OFA, '81
63	†Anderson, Fred	DE	6-4	245	4	10-30-54	Prairie View	14	W-Cin, '80
76	August, Steve	T	6-5	254	6	9- 4-54	Tulsa	16	D1, '77
65	Bailey, Edwin	G	6-4	265	2	5-15-59	South Carolina State	16	D5, '81
82	Bell, Mark	DE	6-4	240	3	8-30-57	Colorado State	*0	D4, '79
68	Boyd, Dennis	T	6-6	255	5	11- 5-55	Oregon State	16	D3, '77
36	Brinson, Larry	RB	6-0	214	5	6- 6-54	Florida	*0	W-Dal, '80
22	Brown, Dave	CB	6-2	190	8	1-16-53	Michigan	10	VA, '76
30	Brown, Theotis	RB	6-3	225	4	4-20-57	UCLA	*13	T-St.L, '81
53	Butler, Keith	LB	6-4	225	5	5-16-56	Memphis State	16	D2, '78
33	Doornink, Dan	RB	6-3	210	5	2- 1-56	Washington State	15	T-NYG, '79
25	Dufek, Don	S	6-0	195	6	4-28-54	Michigan	15	D5a, '76
66	Dugan, Bill	G	6-4	271	2	6- 5-59	Penn State	16	D3, '81
45	Easley, Kenny	S	6-3	206	2	1-15-59	UCLA	14	D1, '81
64	Essink, Ron	T	6-6	254	3	7-30-58	Grand Valley State	16	D10a, '80
50	Flones, Brian	LB	6-1	228	2	9- 1-59	Washington State	4	OFA, '81
56	Gaines, Greg	LB	6-3	220	2	10-16-58	Tennessee	8	OFA, '81
79	Green, Jacob	DE	6-3	247	3	1-21-57	Texas A&M	16	D1, '80
75	Hardy, Robert	DT	6-2	250	4	7- 3-56	Jackson State	14	D10, '79
44	†Harris, John	S	6-2	200	5	6-13-56	Arizona State	16	D7, '78
1	†Herrera, Efren	PK	5-9	190	8	7-30-51	UCLA	12	T-Dal, '78
46	Hughes, David	RB	6-0	220	2	6- 1-59	Boise State	16	D2, '81
32	Ivory, Horace	RB	6-0	198	6	8- 8-54	Oklahoma	*7	T-NE, '81
55	Jackson, Michael	LB	6-1	220	4	7-15-57	Washington	16	D3, '79
43	Jodat, Jim	FB	5-11	213	6	3- 3-54	Carthage	12	T-LA, '80
85	Johns, Paul	WR	5-11	170	2	11-14-58	Tulsa	16	OFA, '81
27	Johnson, Greggory	CB	6-1	188	2	10-20-58	Oklahoma State	16	OFA, '81
26	Justin, Kerry	CB	5-11	175	5	5- 3-55	Oregon State	15	OFA, '78
17	Krieg, Dave	QB	6-1	185	3	10-20-58	Milton	7	OFA, '80
54	Kuehn, Art	C	6-3	255	7	2-12-53	UCLA	16	VA, '76
37	Lane, Eric	RB	6-0	195	2	1- 6-59	Brigham Young	14	D8, '81
80	Largent, Steve	WR	5-11	184	7	9-28-54	Tulsa	16	T-Hou, '76
84	McCullum, Sam	WR	6-2	190	9	11-30-52	Montana State	16	VA, '76
89	McGrath, Mark	WR	5-11	175	2	12-17-57	Montana State	6	OFA, '80
21	Minor, Vic	S	6-0	198	3	11-28-58	Northeast Louisiana	4	D8a, '80
78	†Newton, Bob	G	6-5	260	12	8-16-49	Nebraska	15	W-Chi, '76
52	Norman, Joe	LB	6-1	220	4	10-15-56	Indiana	8	D2, '79
83	Raible, Steve	WR	6-2	195	7	6- 2-54	Georgia Tech	9	D2c, '76
81	Sawyer, John	TE	6-2	230	7	7-26-53	Southern Mississippi	16	W-Hou, '77
42	Simpson, Keith	CB	6-1	195	5	3- 9-56	Memphis State	12	D1, '78
47	Smith, Sherman	RB	6-4	225	7	11- 1-54	Miami, Ohio	16	D2b, '76
69	Sutherland, Doug	DT	6-3	250	13	4- 1-48	Wisconsin-Superior	16	W-Min, '81
59	Thomas, Rodell	LB	6-2	225	2	8- 2-58	Alabama State	*14	FA, '81
86	Tice, Mike	TE	6-7	250	2	2- 2-59	Maryland	16	OFA, '81
74	Tuiasosopo, Manu	DE	6-3	252	4	8-30-57	UCLA	16	D1, '79
60	Turner, Kevin	LB	6-2	225	3	2- 5-58	Pacific	*12	FA, '81
8	West, Jeff	P	6-2	220	7	4- 6-53	Cincinnati	15	FA, '81
70	†White, Mike	DT	6-5	266	4	8-11-57	Albany State	15	FA, '81
51	Yarno, John	C	6-5	251	6	12-17-54	Idaho	11	D4a, '77
10	Zorn, Jim	QB	6-2	200	7	5-10-53	Cal Poly-Pomona	13	FA, '76

*Bell and Brinson missed 1981 season due to injuries; T. Brown played 4 games with St. Louis, 9 with Seattle in 1981; Ivory played 1 game with New England, 6 with Seattle in 1981; Thomas played 3 games with Miami, 11 with Seattle in 1981; Turner played 4 games with Washington, 8 with Seattle in 1981.

†Option playout; subject to development.

D—Draft; T—Trade; W—Waivers; FA—Free Agent; OFA—Original Free Agent; VFA—Veteran Free Agent; VA—Veteran Allocation; SupD—Supplemental Draft.

Also played with Seahawks in 1981—LB Terry Beeson (15 games), LB Pete Cronan (5), CB Will Lewis (10), RB Terry Miller (1), RB Jeff Moore (2).

SEATTLE SEAHAWKS
1982 DRAFT CHOICES

(Number following name designates order of selection among 334 players drafted.)

Round and Player		Position	College
1. BRYANT, Jeff	6	DE	Clemson
2. SCHOLTZ, Bruce	33	LB	Texas
3. Choice to New England (a)			
METZELAARS, Pete from Buffalo (b)	75	TE	Wabash
4. Choice to St. Louis (c)			
5. Choice to Los Angeles (d)			
6. CAMPBELL, Jack	144	T	Utah
7. WILLIAMS, Eugene	174	LB	Tulsa
8. COOPER, Chester	201	WR	Minnesota
9. JEFFERSON, David	228	LB	Miami
10. AUSTIN, Craig	258	LB	South Dakota
11. CLANCY, Sam	284	DL	Pittsburgh
12. NAYLOR, Frank	311	C	Rutgers

(a) Traded pick for running back Horace Ivory, September 25, 1981.
(b) Acquired pick for guard Tom Lynch, October 13, 1981.
(c) Traded pick and 1983 pick for running back Theotis Brown, October 13, 1981.
(d) Traded pick for running back Jim Jodat, August 26, 1980.

SEATTLE SEAHAWKS
1982 ROOKIE AND FIRST-YEAR ROSTER

(1) Indicates player in previous NFL camp.
All others classified as rookies.

Name	Pos.	Hgt.	Wgt.	Birth-date	College	How Acquired
Agee, Ken	RB	5-10	180	4-25-59	Findlay	FA
Alexander, Robert	S	6-2	190	1-20-59	Prairie View	FA
Anderson, Jim	DT	6-4	255	10-10-57	Huron	FA
Austin, Craig	LB	6-3	220	11-14-59	South Dakota	D10
Bell, Bernard	S	6-1	183	3- 5-58	McNeese State	FA
Bolstad, Jon	S	6-1	180	4-13-60	Valley City State	FA
Brown, Alex	G	6-3	269	3-22-59	Wake Forest	FA
Brown, Marion	WR	6-0	175	6- 6-59	South Carolina State	FA
Bryant, Jeff	DE	6-5	260	5-22-60	Clemson	D1
Campbell, Jack	T	6-5	277	12-16-58	Utah	D6

Name	Pos.	Hgt.	Wgt.	Birth-date	College	How Acquired
Castro, Dale (1)	P	6-1	190	11-26-59	Maryland	FA
Clancy, Sam	TE	6-7	250	5-29-58	Pittsburgh	D11
Collier, Cleo	WR	5-10	170	8-29-60	Ark.-Pine Bluff	FA
Cooper, Chester	WR	6-2	200	8-13-59	Minnesota	D8
Cordle, Steve	S	5-9	180	3-25-59	Fresno State	FA
Curry, Pat	DE	6-6	255	9-23-60	Montana	FA
Demski, Brian	QB	6-2	190	12-10-59	Wisconsin-Stevens Point	FA
DeSanto, Mike	K	5-8	160	12- 6-57	Washington State	FA
Dewart, Al (1)	P	6-1	200	6- 1-59	San Francisco State	FA
Evans, Donnie	DT	6-4	250	8- 1-58	Western Kentucky	FA
Ewing, Charles	WR	6-2	182	9-24-60	Idaho State	FA
Fenstermaker, Paul	WR	6-1	185	3- 2-58	Eastern New Mexico	FA
Fletcher, Lawson	RB	6-0	179	5- 9-58	North Alabama	FA
Ford, Mark	TE	6-3	207	5-19-60	Houston	FA
Gaillard, Jerry	WR	6-0	175	2- 5-60	Clemson	FA
Gall, Ed (1)	G	6-4	262	4-25-58	Maryland	FA
Garl, Kurt	LB	6-1	220	10-13-58	Humboldt State	FA
Green, Mark	WR	6-1	188	9-16-59	Ohio	FA
Hagen, Mike	FB	6-0	215	6-30-59	Montana	FA
Hardcastle, Kevin	LB	6-2	221	2- 6-59	Arizona	FA
Hebron, Chuck	WR	5-9	160	3-27-59	Salisbury State	FA
Herring, Don	G	6-4	255	12- 9-59	Norfolk State	FA
Hilbert, Jay	T	6-6	255	11-30-59	North Dakota	FA
Jackson, Tony	S	5-10	174	10-25-59	Michigan	FA
Jefferson, David	LB	6-2	220	11-24-59	Miami	D9
Johnson, Norm	K	6-2	193	5-31-60	UCLA	FA
Kauahi, Kani	G	6-2	260	9- 6-59	Hawaii	FA
Kilgore, Al	WR	6-0	190	7- 4-59	Southwestern Oklahoma	FA
Kingdom, Roy	RB	6-1	210	6-26-59	Albany State	FA
Knapton, Bob	LB	6-1	215	5-22-60	Northern Colorado	FA
Krainock, Steve	QB	6-3	185	12-21-59	Richmond	FA
Mallett, Ronnie	WR	6-0	175	1-20-60	Central Arkansas	FA
McAlister, Ken	LB	6-5	210	4-15-60	San Francisco	FA
Metzelaars, Pete	TE	6-7	240	5-24-60	Wabash	D3
Nash, Joe	DT	6-3	250	10-11-60	Boston College	FA
Naylor, Frank	C	6-2	245	1-25-59	Rutgers	D12
Noiel, Cary	RB	5-10	215	10-10-60	East Texas State	FA
Nowotarski, Bernie	CB	5-11	185	2-22-60	Kutztown State	FA
Ponder, Charles	WR	5-10	175	10-17-60	Murray State	FA
Reeves, Jeff	S	6-1	192	7- 3-60	Michigan	FA
Ridge, Bill	T	6-3	270	12-18-58	Frostburg State	FA
Robinson, Shelton	LB	6-2	233	9-14-60	North Carolina	FA
Rogers, Grayson	QB	6-4	212	11- 7-58	Pacific	FA
Rustemeyer, Mike	DT	6-3	275	3-22-60	Rutgers	FA
Sage, Larry	WR	6-3	190	12-15-58	Northern Colorado	FA
Scholtz, Bruce	LB	6-6	240	9-26-58	Texas	D2
Seawell, Ron (1)	LB	6-1	240	2-17-59	Portland State	FA
Sewell, Don (1)	G	6-5	252	12-17-56	Georgia Tech	FA
Shumway, Andy	FB	6-1	205	7-22-59	Wisconsin-Stevens Point	FA
Sims, Sammy	S	6-0	193	3-22-58	Nebraska	FA
Smallwood, Reggie	S	6-4	185	1-17-59	Norfolk State	FA
Smith, Darren	S	6-1	175	2- 5-60	East Texas State	FA
Smith, Horace	WR	5-10	185	11-28-60	South Carolina	FA
Smith, Jeff	LB	6-1	212	11-18-59	Alcorn State	FA
Solomon, Michael	RB	6-0	205	12-13-59	Florida A&M	FA
Thomas, Charles	RB	6-1	200	11-19-60	Auburn	FA
Tiesing, Scot	TE	6-4	218	2-27-59	UCLA	FA
Todd, Willie	RB	6-0	230	12-12-59	Central Michigan	FA
Tolbert, James	RB	6-0	202	12- 2-59	Arkansas	FA
Toney, Jeff	S	5-9	194	2- 8-60	Alabama A&M	FA
Vernoy, Scott	P	6-5	205	5-12-60	Cal State-Fullerton	FA
Voltapetti, Barry	T	6-7	260	8-30-59	Florida State	FA
Wagner, Vince (1)	K	6-0	180	7-15-59	Northwestern, Minn.	*FA ('81)
Walker, Byron	WR	6-4	190	7-28-60	Citadel	FA
West, Mike	OT	6-4	275	11- 9-59	No. Carolina A&T	FA
Williams, Eugene	LB	6-1	220	6-15-60	Tulsa	D7
Willis, John	CB	5-10	170	10- 9-57	Central Washington	FA
Worsowicz, Greg	S	6-0	185	6-14-60	University of South	FA
Zelinsky, Steve	G	6-3	250	2-15-60	Wayne State, Neb.	FA

*Wagner active for 1 game with Seahawks in 1981.

TAMPA BAY BUCCANEERS
(Central Division, National Conference)

John McKay

President—Hugh F. Culverhouse
Vice President and Head Coach—John McKay (6 years: 31-60-1)
Vice President—Joey Culverhouse
Assistant to the President—Phil Krueger
Director of Player Personnel—Ken Herock
Pro Personnel Scout—Jack Bushofsky
Assistant Coaches:
  Receivers—Boyd Dowler
  Special Teams—Frank Emanuel
  Defensive Coordinator and Secondary—Wayne Fontes
  Defensive Linemen—Abe Gibron
  Running Backs—Jim Gruden
  Offensive Linemen—Bill Johnson
  Quarterbacks—Bill Nelsen
  Linebackers—Howard Tippett
Director of Public Relations—Bob Best
  (Office Phone: 870-2700—Area Code 813)
Offices—One Buccaneer Place, Tampa, Fla. 33607
Stadium—Tampa Stadium (Capacity: 72,128)
Team Colors—Florida Orange, White and Red
Training Site—Tampa, Fla.

1982 SCHEDULE
(All times local.)
All games Sunday unless noted otherwise.

Sept. 12	at Minnesota	12:00
Sept. 19	WASHINGTON	4:00
Sept. 26	at Detroit	1:00
Oct. 4	SAN FRANCISCO (Mon.)	9:00
Oct. 10	MINNESOTA	1:00
Oct. 17	at Green Bay	12:00
Oct. 24	at Chicago	12:00
Oct. 31	at Baltimore	2:00
Nov. 7	GREEN BAY	1:00
Nov. 14	CHICAGO	1:00
Nov. 21	at Dallas	12:00
Nov. 29	MIAMI (Mon.)	9:00
Dec. 5	at New Orleans	12:00
Dec. 12	at New York Jets	1:00
Dec. 19	BUFFALO	1:00
Dec. 26	DETROIT	1:00

1981 RESULTS—(Won 9, Lost 8)

Buccaneers		Opp.		Att.
21	Minnesota	13	(H)	66,287
10	Kansas City	19	(A)	50,555
17	Chicago	28	(A)	60,130
20	St. Louis	10	(H)	65,850
28	Detroit	10	(H)	71,733
21	Green Bay	10	(A)	55,264
16	Oakland	18	(A)	42,288
10	Philadelphia	20	(A)	70,714
20	Chicago	10	(H)	63,688
10	Minnesota	25	(A)	47,038
7	Denver	24	(H)	64,518
37	Green Bay	3	(H)	63,251
31	New Orleans	14	(A)	62,209
24	Atlanta	23	(H)	69,221
23	San Diego	24	(H)	67,388
20	Detroit	17	(A)	80,444

PLAYOFF GAME

0	Dallas	38	(A)	64,848

1981 GAMES STARTED

16 games: Neal Colzie, Jimmie Giles, Hugh Green, Kevin House, Cecil Johnson, David Logan, James Wilder, Doug Williams, Richard Wood.

15 games: Cedric Brown, Norris Thomas, Steve Wilson.

14 games: Greg Roberts, Gene Sanders.

13 games: Lee Roy Selmon.

12 games: Jerry Eckwood, Charlie Hannah, Andy Hawkins, Bill Kollar, Ray Snell, Mike Washington.

Less than 10 games: Ricky Bell (3), Theo Bell (9), John Holt (6), Gordon Jones (4), Jim Leonard (3), David Lewis (4), Jim Obradovich (3), James Owens (1), Dave Reavis (5), Dave Stalls (7), George Yarno (5).

TAMPA BAY BUCCANEERS 1982 VETERAN ROSTER

No.	Name	Pos.	Ht.	Wt.	NFL Exp.	Birth-date	College	Games in '81	How Acquired
83	Bell, Theo	WR	5-11	180	6	12-21-53	Arizona	16	FA, '81
52	Brantley, Scot	LB	6-1	230	3	2-24-58	Florida	16	D3, '80
34	Brown, Cedric	S	6-2	205	6	5- 6-54	Kent State	16	FA, '77
79	Campbell, Joe	DE	6-6	250	6	5- 8-55	Maryland	*10	FA, '81
3	Capece, Bill	PK	5-7	170	2	4- 1-59	Florida State	13	FA, '81
87	Carter, Gerald	WR	6-1	185	3	6-19-57	Texas A&M	16	FA, '80
44	Cesare, Billy	S	5-11	190	4	6- 2-55	Miami	16	FA, '81
20	Colzie, Neal	S	6-2	200	8	2-28-53	Ohio State	16	FA, '80
33	Cotney, Mark	S	6-0	205	7	6-25-52	Cameron State	*0	VA, '76
71	Crowder, Randy	NT	6-3	250	6	7-30-52	Penn State	*0	FA, '78
27	Davis, Tony	RB	5-11	210	7	1-21-53	Nebraska	16	T-Cin, '79
43	Eckwood, Jerry	RB	6-0	200	4	12-26-54	Arkansas	16	D3a, '79
10	Ford, Mike	QB	6-3	220	2	1-30-59	Southern Methodist	*0	D9, '81
14	†Fusina, Chuck	QB	6-1	195	4	5-31-57	Penn State	4	D5, '79
88	Giles, Jimmie	TE	6-3	245	6	11- 8-54	Alcorn State	16	T-Hou, '78
	Golsteyn, Jerry	QB	6-4	210	4	8- 6-54	Northern Illinois	*0	FA, '82
53	Green, Hugh	LB	6-2	225	2	7-27-59	Pittsburgh	16	D1, '81
73	Hannah, Charley	T	6-6	265	6	7-26-55	Alabama	15	D3, '77
59	Hawkins, Andy	LB	6-2	230	3	3-31-58	Texas A&I	16	D10a, '80
21	Holt, John	CB	5-11	180	2	5-14-59	West Texas State	16	D4, '81
89	House, Kevin	WR	6-1	175	3	12-20-57	Southern Illinois	16	D2, '80
70	Hutchinson, Scott	DE	6-3	245	5	5-27-56	Florida	16	W-Buf, '81
56	Johnson, Cecil	LB	6-2	235	6	8-19-55	Pittsburgh	16	OFA, '77
84	Jones, Gordon	WR	6-0	190	4	7-25-57	Pittsburgh	13	D2b, '79
77	Kollar, Bill	DE	6-4	250	9	11-12-52	Montana State	12	W-Cin, '77
62	†Leonard, Jim	C-G	6-3	250	3	10-19-57	Santa Clara	16	D7, '80
76	Logan, David	NT	6-2	250	4	10-25-56	Pittsburgh	16	D12, '79
55	Melontree, Andrew	LB	6-3	225	2	12- 1-57	Baylor	*0	FA, '82
45	Mitchell, Aaron	S	6-1	195	4	12-15-56	Nevada-Las Vegas	13	T-Dal, '81
51	Nafziger, Dana	LB	6-1	225	5	10-26-53	Cal Poly-SLO	16	OFA, '77
86	Obradovich, Jim	TE	6-2	230	8	4- 2-53	Southern California	16	T-SF, '78
26	Owens, James	RB	5-11	190	4	7- 5-55	UCLA	16	T-SF, '81
75	Reavis, Dave	T	6-5	265	8	6-19-50	Arkansas	12	VA, '76
61	Roberts, Greg	G	6-3	260	4	11-19-56	Oklahoma	16	D2a, '79
80	Samuels, Tony	TE	6-4	235	5	12-30-54	Bethune-Cookman	*0	FA, '80
74	Sanders, Gene	T	6-3	270	4	11-10-56	Texas A&M	16	D8, '79
63	Selmon, Lee Roy	DE	6-3	250	7	10-20-54	Oklahoma	14	D1, '76
64	Short, Laval	NT	6-3	250	3	9-29-58	Colorado	4	FA, '81
72	Snell, Ray	G	6-3	260	3	2-24-58	Wisconsin	16	D1, '80
65	Stalls, Dave	DE	6-4	250	6	9-19-55	Northern Colorado	16	T-Dal, '80
9	Swider, Larry	P	6-2	195	4	2- 1-55	Pittsburgh	13	FA, '81
41	Thomas, Norris	CB	5-11	185	6	5- 1-54	Southern Mississippi	16	T-Mia, '81
40	Washington, Mike	CB	6-2	200	7	7- 1-53	Alabama	14	T-Bal, '76
90	White, Brad	NT	6-2	250	2	10-18-58	Tennessee	16	D12, '81
32	Wilder, James	RB	6-2	220	2	5-12-58	Missouri	16	D2, '81
12	Williams, Doug	QB	6-4	215	5	8- 9-55	Grambling	16	D1, '78
50	Wilson, Steve	C	6-3	265	7	5-19-54	Georgia	15	D5b, '76
54	Wood, Richard	LB	6-2	230	8	5-31-53	Southern California	16	T-NYJ, '76
68	Yarno, George	G	6-2	255	4	8-12-57	Washington State	16	OFA, '79

*Austin, Cotney, Crowder, Samuels and D. Selmon missed '81 season due to injuries; Campbell played 3 games with Oakland, 7 with Tampa Bay in 1981; Ford active for 16 games but did not play; Golsteyn last active with Baltimore in 1979; Melontree last active with Cincinnati in '80.

†Option playout; subject to developments.

D—Draft; T—Trade; W—Waivers; FA—Free Agent; OFA—Original Free Agent; VFA—Veteran Free Agent; VA—Veteran Allocation; SupD—Supplemental Draft.

Also played with Buccaneers in 1981—OL Darrell Austin (*0), RB Ricky Bell (7 games), P Tom Blanchard (3), RB Gary Davis (7), S Jeff Delaney (2), LB David Lewis (13), K Garo Yepremian (3).

TAMPA BAY BUCCANEERS
1982 DRAFT CHOICES

(Number following name designates order of selection among 334 players drafted.)

Round and Player		Position	College
1. FARRELL, Sean	17	G	Penn State
2. REESE, Booker	32	DE	Bethune-Cookman
from Chicago (a)			
Choice to Houston through Miami and Los Angeles (b)			
3. BELL, Jerry	74	TE	Arizona State
CANNON, John	83	DE	William & Mary
from San Francisco through San Diego (c)			
4. Choice to Dallas (d)			
BARRETT, Dave	103	RB	Houston
from San Diego (e)			
5. DAVIS, Jeff	128	LB	Clemson
6. TYLER, Andre	158	WR	Stanford
7. MORRIS, Tom	185	DB	Michigan State
8. ATKINS, Kelvin	212	LB	Illinois
9. LANE, Bob	242	QB	N.E. Louisiana
10. Choice to San Francisco (f)			
11. Choice to Dallas (g)			
12. MORTON, Michael	325	KR	Nev.-Las Vegas

(a) Acquired pick for first-round pick in 1983, April 27, 1982.

(b) Tampa Bay traded pick and running back Jimmy DuBose to Miami for cornerback Norris Thomas and running back Gary Davis, August 25, 1980; Miami traded pick and second- and third-round picks in 1981 to Los Angeles for linebacker Bob Brudzinski and second-round pick in 1981, April 28, 1981; Los Angeles traded pick, third-round pick and tight end Lewis Gilbert to Houston for tight end Mike Barber and third- and eighth-round picks, April 27, 1982.

(c) San Francisco traded pick to San Diego for offensive lineman Dan Audick, August 17, 1981; San Diego traded pick and fourth-round pick in 1984 to Tampa Bay for linebacker David Lewis, February 1, 1982.

(d) Traded pick and seventh-round pick in 1981 for defensive end Dave Stalls, August 6, 1980.

(e) Acquired pick for running back Ricky Bell, March 9, 1982.

(f) Traded pick for defensive tackle Ted Vincent, May 1, 1981.

(g) Traded pick for safety Aaron Mitchell, August 31, 1981.

TAMPA BAY BUCCANEERS
1982 ROOKIE AND FIRST-YEAR ROSTER

(1) Indicates player in previous NFL camp.
(2) Indicates player with minor league experience.
   All others classified as rookies.

Name	Pos.	Hgt.	Wgt.	Birth-date	College	How Acquired
Alford, John (1)	DT	6-2	270	1-30-58	South Carolina State	FA
Atkins, Kal	LB	6-4	225	7- 3-60	Illinois	D8
Barrett, Dave	RB	6-0	230	9- 9-59	Houston	D4
Bell, Jerry	TE	6-5	230	3- 7-59	Arizona State	D3
Brown, Norman	WR	6-0	180	2-17-60	Cal State-Fullerton	FA
Cade, Al	LB	6-1	220	7-15-60	Northwest Missouri	FA
Cannon, John	DE	6-5	250	7-30-60	William & Mary	D3
Carion, Curt (1)	P	5-11	180	8-11-59	West Virginia	FA
Carver, Melvin	RB	5-11	210	7-14-59	Nevada-Las Vegas	FA
Clark, David (1)	DL	6-3	250	7- 2-58	Nebraska	*FA ('81)
Davis, Jeff	LB	6-0	225	1-26-60	Clemson	D5
DeBose, Ron (1)	TE	6-5	230	10- 3-58	UCLA	Waiv.
Farrell, Sean	G	6-3	260	5-25-60	Penn State	D1
Frederick, Ron	WR	5-10	180	12-23-58	Duke	FA
Gettel, Steve (1)	G	6-1	255	5-20-59	South Carolina	*FA ('81)
Gordon, Jerry	WR	5-10	175	9-10-59	Grambling	FA
Hotz, Ed	K	5-9	165	2-13-60	Southeast Missouri	FA
Jarrell, Arlie (2)	DT-DE	6-2	270	7-28-58	Austin Peay	FA
Johnson, Lonnie (1)	RB	6-1	210	6- 7-59	Indiana	FA
Jones, Keith	T	6-5	275	8- 3-57	West Virginia	FA
LaBeaux, Sandy	CB-S	6-3	205	8-22-61	Cal State-Hayward	FA
Lane, Bob	QB	6-3	200	4-12-59	Northeast Louisiana	D9
Larry, Admiral Dewey (1)	CB	5-11	185	9- 1-58	Nevada-Las Vegas	FA
McCune, Ken (1)	DE	6-6	250	2-12-59	Texas	*D10 ('81)
McNeel, Dave	LB	6-3	220	12- 4-59	Missouri	FA
Morris, Thomas	S	5-11	175	4- 2-60	Michigan State	D7
Morton, Mike	RB-KR	5-8	180	2- 6-60	Nevada-Las Vegas	D12
Moy, Sylvester	WR	6-0	180	7- 1-59	Grambling	FA
Petrzelka, Matt (1)	T	6-6	270	12-31-58	Iowa	FA
Reese, Booker	DE	6-6	260	9-20-59	Bethune-Cookman	D2
Sherrod, Mike (1)	TE	6-6	240	1-17-58	Illinois	FA
Smith, Johnny Ray (1)	S	5-9	180	9- 7-57	Lamar	*D11 ('81)
Smith, Tim (1)	CB	6-1	195	8-17-57	Oregon State	FA
Stone, Jim (1)	RB	6-1	205	11-18-58	Notre Dame	FA ('81)
Tyler, Andre	WR	6-0	185	7-17-59	Stanford	D6
Washington, Don (1)	CB-S	6-1	190	1-28-58	Texas A & I	FA

*Clark, Gettel and McCune spent 1981 season on left-camp retired list; J. Smith missed 1981 season due to injury.

WASHINGTON REDSKINS
(Eastern Division, National Conference)

Joe Gibbs

President—Edward Bennett Williams
Chairman, Chief Operating Executive—Jack Kent Cooke
Senior Vice-President—Gerard T. Gabrys
General Manager—Bobby Beathard
Director of Player Personnel—Mike Allman
Director of Pro Scouting—Kirk Mee
Director of College Scouting—Dick Daniels
Head Coach—Joe Gibbs (1 year: 8-8-0)
Assistant Coaches:
  Offensive Backfield—Don Breaux
  Offensive Backfield—Joe Bugel
  Assistant Head Coach—Danny Henning
  Administrative Assistant—Bill Hickman
  Linebackers—Larry Peccatiello
  Defensive Coordinator—Richie Petitbon
  Special Teams—Wayne Sevier
  Strength and Conditioning—Dan Riley
  Tight Ends—Warren Simmons
  Receivers—Charley Taylor
  Defensive Line—LaVern Torgeson
Public Relations—Charlie Taylor, Joe Blair
  (Office Phone: 471-9100—Area Code 703)
Offices—Redskin Park, 13832 Redskin Drive, Herndon, Va.; P. O. Box 17247, Dulles International Airport, Washington, D. C. 20041
Stadium—Robert F. Kennedy Memorial Stadium (Capacity: 55,045)
Team Colors—Burgundy and Gold
Training Site—Dickinson College, Carlisle, Pa.

1982 SCHEDULE
(All times local.
All games Sunday unless noted otherwise.)

Sept. 12	at Philadelphia	1:00
Sept. 19	at Tampa Bay	4:00
Sept. 26	ST. LOUIS	1:00
Oct. 3	CLEVELAND	1:00
Oct. 10	at Dallas	12:00
Oct. 17	PITTSBURGH	1:00
Oct. 24	at Houston	12:00
Oct. 31	SAN FRANCISCO	1:00
Nov. 7	at Cincinnati	1:00
Nov. 14	MINNESOTA	1:00
Nov. 21	at New York Giants	4:00
Nov. 28	PHILADELPHIA	1:00
Dec. 5	DALLAS	4:00
Dec. 12	at St. Louis	12:00
Dec. 19	NEW YORK GIANTS	1:00
Dec. 26	at New Orleans	12:00

1981 RESULTS—(Won 8, Lost 8)

Redskins		Opp.		Att.
10	Dallas	26	(H)	55,045
7	New York Giants	17	(H)	53,343
30	St. Louis	40	(A)	47,592
13	Philadelphia	36	(A)	70,664
17	San Francisco	30	(H)	51,843
24	Chicago	7	(A)	57,683
10	Miami	13	(A)	47,367
24	New England	22	(H)	50,394
42	St. Louis	21	(H)	50,643
33	Detroit	31	(H)	52,096
30	New York Giants (OT)	27	(A)	63,133
10	Dallas	24	(A)	64,583
14	Buffalo	21	(A)	61,452
15	Philadelphia	13	(H)	52,206
38	Baltimore	14	(H)	46,706
30	Los Angeles	7	(A)	52,224

1981 GAMES STARTED

16 games: Jeff Bostic, Dave Butz, Joe Lavender, Art Monk, Mark Murphy, Tony Peters, Joe Theismann, Don Warren.

14 games: Neal Olkewicz.

13 games: Russell Grimm, Joe Jacoby, John Riggins, George Starke, Joe Washington.

12 games: Perry Brooks.

11 games: Monte Coleman, Dexter Manley.

10 games: Melvin Jones, Karl Lorch.

Less than 10 games: Coy Bacon (3), Peter Cronan (2), Brad Dusek (9), Wilbur Jackson (2), Mel Kaufman (6), Mark May (8), Mat Mendenhall (9), Terry Metcalf (5), Rich Milot (6), Lemar Parrish (9), Ron Saul (7), Virgil Seay (6), Ricky Thompson (6), Rick Walker (3), Jeris White (7), Wilbur Young (3).

WASHINGTON REDSKINS 1982 VETERAN ROSTER

No.	Name	Pos.	Ht.	Wt.	NFL Exp.	Birth-date	College	Games in '81	How Acquired
	Batton, Bobby	RB	6-0	190	2	3-17-57	Nevada-Las Vegas	*0	FA, '82
53	Bostic, Jeff	C	6-2	246	2	9-18-58	Clemson	16	FA, '80
69	Brooks, Perry	DT	6-3	260	5	12- 4-54	Southern	15	FA, '77
65	Butz, Dave	DT	6-7	295	10	6-23-50	Purdue	16	VFA, '75
82	†Caster, Rich	TE	6-5	230	13	11-16-48	Jackson State	*7	FA, '81
35	Claitt, Rickey	RB	5-10	206	3	4-12-57	Bethune-Cookman	13	OFA, '80
75	Clark, Mike	DE	6-4	240	2	3-30-59	Florida	5	FA, '81
51	Coleman, Monte	LB	6-2	230	4	11- 4-57	Central Arkansas	12	D11a, '79
10	†Connell, Mike	P	6-1	200	4	3-15-56	Cincinnati	16	FA, '80
28	Crissy, Cris	CB-WR	5-11	195	2	2- 3-59	Princeton	1	FA, '81
65	†Cronan, Peter	LB	6-2	238	5	1-13-55	Boston College	*15	FA, '81
63	Dean, Fred	G	6-3	253	5	3-30-55	Texas Southern	*0	FA, '78
59	†Dusek, Brad	LB	6-2	223	9	12-13-50	Texas A&M	10	T-NE, '73
12	Flick, Tom	QB	6-1	190	2	8-30-58	Washington	6	D4, '81
89	Garrett, Alvin	WR	5-7	178	3	10- 1-56	Angelo State	*13	W-NYG, '81
30	Giaquinto, Nick	RB	5-11	204	3	4- 4-55	Connecticut	*14	W-Mia, '81
77	Grant, Darryl	G	6-1	230	2	11-22-59	Rice	15	D9, '81
68	Grimm, Russ	G	6-3	250	2	5- 2-59	Pittsburgh	14	D3, '81
38	Harmon, Clarence	RB	5-11	209	6	11-30-55	Mississippi State	5	OFA, '77
78	Hickman, Dallas	DE-LB	6-6	242	7	12-16-52	California	*15	D9, '75
	Jackson, Cleveland	TE	6-4	240	2	10- 1-56	Nevada-Las Vegas	*0	FA, '82
40	Jackson, Wilbur	RB	6-1	219	8	11-19-51	Alabama	6	T-SF, '80
66	Jacoby, Joe	T	6-7	290	2	7- 6-59	Louisville	14	OFA, '81
61	Jones, Melvin	G	6-2	260	2	9-27-56	Houston	11	D7, '80
22	Jordan, Curtis	DB	6-2	205	6	1-25-54	Texas Tech	2	W-TB, '81
55	Kaufman, Mel	LB	6-2	214	2	2-24-58	Cal Poly-SLO	11	OFA, '81
20	Lavender, Joe	CB	6-4	185	10	2-10-49	San Diego State	16	T-Phi, '76
56	Lowry, Quentin	LB	6-2	225	2	11-11-57	Youngstown State	9	FA, '81
72	Manley, Dexter	DE	6-3	240	2	7- 2-59	Oklahoma State	16	D5a, '81
73	May, Mark	T	6-6	270	2	11- 2-59	Pittsburgh	16	D1, '81
45	McDaniel, LeCharls	CB	5-9	169	2	10-15-58	Cal Poly-SLO	6	OFA, '81
76	Mendenhall, Matt	DE	6-6	253	2	5-14-57	Brigham Young	14	D2, '80
26	Metcalf, Terry	RB	5-10	183	7	9-24-51	Long Beach State	16	VFA, '81
57	Milot, Rich	LB	6-4	230	3	5-28-57	Penn State	11	D7, '79
81	Monk, Art	WR	6-3	209	3	12- 5-57	Syracuse	16	D1, '80
3	Moseley, Mark	K	6-0	205	11	3-12-48	Stephen F. Austin	16	FA, '74
29	Murphy, Mark	FS	6-4	210	6	7-13-55	Colgate	16	OFA, '77
21	Nelms, Mike	FS	6-1	185	3	4- 8-55	Baylor	16	FA, '80
79	Ogrin, Pat	DT	6-5	265	2	2-10-58	Wyoming	5	OFA, '80
52	Olkewicz, Neal	LB	6-0	227	4	1-30-57	Maryland	14	OFA, '79
23	Peters, Tony	SS	6-1	177	8	4-28-53	Oklahoma	16	T-Cle, '79
86	Raba, Bob	TE	6-4	235	5	4-23-55	Maryland	8	FA, '81
44	Riggins, John	RB	6-2	230	11	8- 4-49	Kansas	15	VFA, '76
64	Saul, Ron	G	6-3	254	13	2- 5-48	Michigan State	10	T-Hou, '76
80	Seay, Virgil	WR	5-8	170	2	1- 1-58	Troy State	16	FA, '81
74	Starke, George	T	6-5	250	10	7-18-48	Columbia	14	W-Dal, '72
7	Theismann, Joe	QB	6-0	195	9	9- 9-49	Notre Dame	16	T-Mia, '74
83	Thompson, Ricky	WR	6-0	177	7	5-15-54	Baylor	16	T-Bal, '78
88	Walker, Rick	TE	6-4	235	6	5-26-55	UCLA	16	FA, '80
85	Warren, Don	TE	6-4	236	4	5- 5-56	San Diego State	16	D4, '79
25	Washington, Joe	RB	5-10	179	6	9-24-53	Oklahoma	14	T-Bal, '81
58	Weaver, Charlie	LB	6-2	225	12	7-12-49	Southern California	*12	W-Det, '81
45	White, Jeris	CB	5-10	188	9	9- 3-52	Hawaii	16	T-TB, '80
39	Wonsley, Otis	RB	5-10	214	2	8-13-57	Alcorn State	15	FA, '81

*Batton last active with N.Y. Jets in 1980; Caster played 4 games with Houston, 3 with Washington in 1981; Cronan played 5 games with Seattle, 10 with Washington in 1981; Dean missed 1981 season due to injury; Garrett played 9 games with N.Y. Giants, 4 with Washington in 1981; Giaquinto played 8 games with Miami, 6 with Washington in 1981; Hickman played 5 games with Baltimore, 10 with Washington in 1981; C. Jackson last active with N.Y. Giants in 1979; Weaver played 7 games with Detroit, 5 with Washington in 1981.

†Option playout; subject to developments.

D—Draft; T—Trade; W—Waivers; FA—Free Agent; OFA—Original Free Agent; VFA—Veteran Free Agent; VA—Veteran Allocation; SupD—Supplemental Draft.

Also played with Redskins in 1981—DE Coy Bacon (3 games), CB Trent Bryant (4), LB Dave Graf (6), DE Karl Lorch (16), TE Gregg McCrary (5), CB Lemar Parrish (12), T Jerry Scanlan (3), LB Kevin Turner (4), DE Wilbur Young (7).

WASHINGTON REDSKINS
1982 DRAFT CHOICES

(Number following name designates order of selection among 334 players drafted.)

Round and Player		Position	College
1. Choice to Baltimore through Los Angeles (a)			
2. Choice to New England through San Francisco (b)			
DEAN, Vernon from San Diego through Los Angeles (c)	49	DB	San Diego St.
3. POWELL, Carl from Los Angeles (d)	61	WR	Jackson State
Choice to New Orleans (e)			
4. LIEBENSTEIN, Todd	99	DE	Nev.-Las Vegas
5. Choice to St. Louis (f)			
WILLIAMS, Michael from Buffalo (g)	133	TE	Alabama A & M
6. JEFFERS, Lemont	153	LB	Tennessee
7. SCHACHTNER, John	180	LB	N. Arizona
8. Choice to Cleveland (h)			
WARTHEN, Ralph from San Francisco through New Orleans (i)	223	DT	Gardner-Webb
9. COFFEY, Ken from New Orleans (j)	226	DB	S.W. Texas St.
TRAUTMAN, Randy	238	DT	Boise State
10. SMITH, Harold from New Orleans (j)	254	DE	Kentucky State
DANIELS, Terry	265	DB	Tennessee
11. MILLER, Dan from New Orleans (j)	281	K	Miami
HOLLY, Bob	291	QB	Princeton
12. LASTER, Don from New Orleans (j)	309	T	Tennessee St.
GOFF, Jeff	322	LB	Arkansas

(a) Washington traded pick to Los Angeles for second-round pick, third-round pick in 1981 and two fifth-round picks in 1981, April 28, 1981; Los Angeles traded pick and second-round pick to Baltimore for quarterback Bert Jones, April 27, 1982.

(b) Washington traded pick and second-round pick in 1981 to San Francisco for running back Wilbur Jackson, August 21, 1980; San Francisco traded pick, another second-round pick, first-round pick and fourth-round pick to New England for tight end Russ Francis and second-round pick, April 27, 1982.

(c) Los Angeles acquired pick from San Diego for running back John Cappelletti, March 21, 1980; Washington acquired pick from Los Angeles. See (a).

(d) Acquired pick and seventh-round pick for tight end Henry Childs, May 6, 1981.

(e) Traded pick for tight end Henry Childs, April 30, 1981.

(f) Traded pick for running back Terry Metcalf, May 8, 1981.

(g) Acquired pick for cornerback Lemar Parrish, April 27, 1982.

(h) Traded pick for two 10th-round picks in 1981, April 29, 1981.

(i) New Orleans acquired pick from San Francisco for wide receiver Artie Owens, July 21, 1981; Washington acquired pick, ninth-, 10th- 11th- and 12th-round picks from New Orleans for fourth-round pick in 1983, April 28, 1982.

(j) See second part of (i).

WASHINGTON REDSKINS
1982 ROOKIE AND FIRST-YEAR ROSTER

(1) Indicates player in previous NFL camp.
(2) Indicates player with CFL experience.
(3) Indicates player with minor league experience.
   All others classified as rookies.

Name	Pos.	Hgt.	Wgt.	Birth-date	College	How Acquired
Andreoli, John	LB	6-3	236	3-30-60	Holy Cross	FA
Barry, Tim	P	6-2	205	11- 9-60	Holy Cross	FA
Bollinger, Alan	P	6-1	190	9-16-59	Auburn	FA
Brown, Charlie (1)	WR	5-10	179	10-29-57	South Carolina State	*D8 ('81)
Caldwell, Greg	P	6-1	215	1-12-60	James Madison	FA
Carr, Frank (1)	WR	6-0	198	7-29-59	North Carolina A&T	FA
Chisley, Charles	WR	6-0	173	3- 2-58	Univ. of District of Columbia	FA
Clark, Calvin (1)	DE	6-4	260	3- 8-59	Purdue	*FA ('81)
Coffey, Ken	CB	6-0	185	7-11-60	Southwest Texas State	D9
Daniels, Kenny	CB-S	5-10	179	6- 1-60	San Jose State	FA
Daniels, Terry	S	5-11	177	12-30-60	Tennessee	D10
Daum, Mike (1)	T	6-6	260	10-25-58	Cal Poly-SLO	*FA ('81)
Davidson, Chy (1)	WR	5-11	170	5- 9-59	Rhode Island	FA
Dean, Vernon	CB-S	5-11	178	5- 5-59	San Diego State	D2
Didier, Clint (1)	TE	6-5	240	4- 4-59	Portland State	*D12 ('81)
Dloughy, Duane	TE	6-4	224	7-25-60	Boise State	FA
Evans, Reggie	WR	5-11	190	1- 5-59	Richmond	FA
Foley, Richard	S	5-10	175	4-29-60	Southeast Louisiana	FA
Garrity, Chris	QB	6-1	190	9-29-60	William & Mary	FA
Goff, Jeff	LB	6-1	215	12-27-59	Arkansas	D12
Goosby, Rodney (2)	WR	6-2	185	5-20-58	Nevada-Las Vegas	FA
Hayes, Jeff	P	5-11	175	8-19-59	North Carolina	FA
Holley, Willie (3)	S	5-10	180	1-28-57	East Carolina	FA
Holly, Bob	QB	6-2	205	6- 1-60	Princeton	D11
Howard, Antonio	WR	5-9	179	2-23-58	Winston Salem State	FA
Jackson, Ed (1)	DE	6-4	280	1- 9-58	Maryland-Eastern Shore	FA
Jeffers, Lemont	DE	6-3	210	4- 5-60	Tennessee	D6
Jezulin, Mike	P	6-0	184	1- 8-60	San Diego State	FA
Jones, Rick	G-C	6-3	240	8- 5-59	Cal Poly-SLO	FA
Kessel, Phil (1)	QB	6-2	190	4-28-58	Northern Michigan	*D10 ('81)
Kittle, Bruce	G-T	6-4	260	1-20-59	Iowa	FA
Kubin, Larry (1)	LB	6-2	234	2-26-59	Penn State	*D6 ('81)
Laster, Donald	T	6-5	285	12-13-58	Tennessee State	D12
Lewis, George	LB	6-2	210	12-17-59	Massachusetts	FA
Liebenstein, Todd	DE	6-6	245	1- 9-60	Nevada-Las Vegas	D4
Miller, Dan	K	5-10	172	12-30-60	Miami	D11
Minor, Darryl	RB	5-10	165	12-24-58	Oregon State	FA
Montana, Scott (2)	DB	5-10	175	8- 3-57	Trinity, Tex.	FA
McCollum, John	G	6-3	252	4-13-60	Syracuse	FA
Norman, Tim	T	6-6	265	7-10-59	Illinois	FA
North, Lee	C	6-2	258	2-27-60	Tennessee	FA
Powell, Carl	WR	6-0	182	4- 6-58	Jackson State	D3
Rogusky, Vince	TE	6-2	205	3- 2-58	Lehigh	FA
Salata, Rod	P	6-3	210	11-17-55	Illinois State	FA
Sayre, Gary (1)	G	6-5	270	9-26-57	Cameron State	*D5 ('81)
Schachtner, John	LB	6-3	220	4- 9-59	Northern Arizona	D7
Smith, Bennie	DT	6-3	248	1- 5-60	Missouri	FA
Smith, Harold	DE	6-3	240	9-22-59	Kentucky State	D10
Taylor, Juan	G	6-2	265	6-30-60	Lamar	FA
Trautman, Randy	DT	6-3	255	5-27-60	Boise State	D9
Warthen, Ralph	DT	6-4	265	7-30-58	Gardner-Webb	D8
Williams, Greg	S	5-11	185	8- 1-59	Mississippi State	FA
Williams, Leon	S	5-9	180	3-23-59	Louisville	FA
Williams, Michael	TE	6-4	245	8-27-59	Alabama A&M	D5
Wilson, Kirk	WR	5-11	180	8-12-59	Indiana State	FA

*Clark and Daum active for 1 game with Redskins in 1981, did not play; Brown, Didier, Kessel and Kubin missed 1981 season due to injuries; Sayre spent 1981 season on left-camp retired list.

The Year of the Rookie

By **LARRY FELSER**

By the Columbus Day weekend (October 11), those who follow the National Football League were getting the idea that this would not be your standard season.

That was the weekend on which the defending Super Bowl champions, the Oakland Raiders, were shut out, 27-0, by the Kansas City Chiefs. Since the Raiders had been shut out, 17-0, by Denver the week before; and by Detroit, 16-0, the week before that, the idea of 1981 being a routine NFL season was evaporating fast.

No team since the woeful 1943 Brooklyn Dodgers ever had been shut out in three consecutive games.

And there was more.

Out in San Francisco, the Dallas Cowboys came to town eager to atone for a 20-17 upset loss they had suffered to St. Louis the week before, which broke their four-game winning streak. Instead of atonement, there was mortification.

The young, feisty 49ers not only won—they blasted the Cowboys, 45-14.

Meanwhile, in Baltimore, the Cincinnati Bengals were putting it on the Colts, 41-19, to force a three-way tie among Pittsburgh, Houston and themselves for first place.

What was going on here?

What was going on was a mini-revolution, a football version of agrarian reform. The last were going to be first, or at least a wild-card team.

As it turned out, the Super Bowl was a match of teams which had identical 6-10 records in 1980. But there were many other uprisings besides those in San Francisco and Cincinnati.

Six of the 10 playoff teams were new. The only repeaters were Buffalo and San Diego in the American Conference, although the Bills lost their Eastern Division title to Miami; and Philadelphia and Dallas in the National Conference, with the Eagles losing their NFC East title to the Cowboys.

The Jets made the playoffs for the first time in a decade. The Giants made it for the first time since 1963, and it took a longshot daily double to make it happen on the final weekend of the season.

All the Giants needed to do was beat Dallas in Giants Stadium on Saturday and then wait for the Jets to beat Green Bay in Shea Stadium on Sunday. But beating the Cowboys, even at home, is no easy task.

Joe Danelo, the Giants' placekicker, saw his entire life flash before him several times during the Dallas game. Danelo missed three makeable field goals, one of them in overtime. Any of the three would have clinched the victory.

Then, six minutes and 19 seconds into overtime, Danelo hit from 35 yards away and the Giants had their victory.

The wait for the Jets' game was, for the Giants, a nail-biting affair.

But something called "The New York Sack Exchange" took all the drama out of it. The Jets' pass rush, led by ends Joe Klecko and Mark Gastineau, mugged Green Bay quarterback Lynn Dickey nine times for 57 yards in losses as the Jets waltzed, 28-3.

That famous bumper sticker of the '70s, "Let's bring back pro football to New York," was now inoperative. Both New York teams were in the playoffs.

The Jets experienced one of the year's oddest turnabouts. Pumped up by their own front office as having the talent of a Super Bowl contender, they opened with a 31-0 loss to Buffalo. The next week they lost to Cincinnati, 31-30, which seemed worse than it was, since the Bengals had not established their own winning reputation yet.

In their third game, they were almost totally embarrassed when the Pittsburgh Steelers ran up 566 yards in total offense in winning, 38-10. Those in New York who weren't calling for Coach Walt Michaels to be fired were expecting him to resign.

Michaels wasn't fired, he didn't resign, and neither did the Jets. They lost only two of their next 13 games. Strangely, both losses were to the Seattle Seahawks, who won only six times all season.

The key to the "Sack Exchange" was Klecko, who had 20½ sacks by himself, setting a team record.

The season's most explosive team was, not surprisingly, the San Diego Chargers. The Chargers led the NFL in scoring with 478 points, 52 ahead of runner-up Atlanta. But the Chargers also gave up 390 points, which was 86 points higher than any other team that made the playoffs.

Oakland never did regain its balance after the string of three shutouts. Jim Plunkett, the star of the Raiders' 1981 Super Bowl team, lost his quarterbacking job to young Marc Wilson. The Raiders had their first losing season since 1964.

Something else also changed for the first time in years. After a decade of being dominated by its younger, brasher, more aggressive rival, the National Football Conference finally won the season series against the AFC, 28-24.

Tex Schramm, president of the Dallas Cowboys and one of the most partisan of NFC executives, attributed the turnabout to the natural cycle of sports and "the fact that the NFC has most of the top young quarterbacks."

In only his first year, outside linebacker Lawrence Taylor made a good New York Giants defense a great one.

But just as important is defense; and it was played more tightly in the NFC. The four teams allowing the fewest points during the season—Philadelphia, San Francisco, the New York Giants and Tampa Bay—all are NFC teams.

The 49ers, fueled by their genius coach, Bill Walsh, were the most innovative NFL team. They won with a third-year quarterback and a secondary which featured three rookies.

San Francisco didn't have an outstanding ball carrier, and then lost the best it had in Paul Hofer. But they controlled the ball with intricate short and medium passing, relying on the timing and movement of their receivers.

When the Niners defeated Dallas, 28-27, in the NFC title game at Candlestick Park, it was with an 89-yard drive in the final five minutes.

In the game-winning drive, that same broken-down running game surprised the Cowboys four times. At the Dallas 35, the 49ers caught the Cowboys flatfooted and ran a reverse, with Freddie Solomon gaining 14 yards.

On third down at the Dallas 6, quarterback Joe Montana, with linebacker D.D. Lewis and defensive end Ed "Too Tall" Jones coming after him, calmly threw a pass which seemed way too high to catch.

But Dwight Clark, the 49ers' rangy and strong wide receiver, leaped higher than anyone thought he could to catch the touchdown pass that put the 49ers in the Super Bowl.

The 49ers' victory over Dallas almost made the Super Bowl anti-climatic, but there were other memorable playoff games as well.

Buffalo ran up a 24-0 lead on the New York Jets before the Jets knew what happened, but the young New Yorkers came storming back. It took a last-minute interception by Bill Simpson, deep in Buffalo territory, to preserve the Bills' victory.

Buffalo nearly made a similar comeback against Cincinnati in their game the following week but a key first-down pass from quarterback Joe Ferguson to Lou Piccone was wiped out by the Bills' failure to get the play off before the 30-second clock expired. The Bengals won, 28-21.

The playoff game to end all playoff games was held in Miami, between the Dolphins and Chargers.

It began as a San Diego blowout. Wes Chandler of the Chargers scored on a 56-yard punt return and it seemed to unleash a San Diego flood. Dan Fouts passed effortlessly against the Dolphins and, by the end of the first quarter, the Chargers had a 24-0 lead.

The Dolphins appeared to be in shock, but that appearance was deceiving.

Miami came back in thunderous fashion. Just before halftime, the Dolphins pulled off a play never to be forgotten. Don Strock, who had relieved starting quarterback David Woodley, threw a 15-yard pass to Duriel Harris.

Harris caught the ball after coming in for it, his body squarely facing Strock. The Charger defenders surrounded him in anticipation of his faking to one direction, then running in the other.

Harris did neither.

Almost as soon as he caught the ball, he tossed a lateral to Tony Nathan, who was streaking down the sideline. Nathan ran the last 25 yards to score.

This time it was the Chargers who were shocked.

The second half was no less exciting. Fouts threw a 25-yard touchdown pass to Kellen Winslow. Strock countered with a 50-yard touchdown pass to Bruce Hardy. Miami finally took the lead on Nathan's 12-yard run. But with 58 seconds to play in the fourth quarter, Fouts threw to rookie halfback James Brooks, deep in the end zone, to tie the game.

The exhausted players labored back and forth in the extra period. Two field goals were missed by Uwe von Schamann of Miami and one by Rolf Benirschke of San Diego. Benirschke finally ended the game with a 29-yarder just one minute and eight seconds from the end of the first overtime period.

Winslow became a young legend in the game. Not only did he catch 13 passes for 166 yards—repeatedly bulling for vital first downs—but he starred on the special teams, blocking one field goal and obstructing von Schamann's view on another. Twice Winslow had to leave the field because of injury and exhaustion, but he returned each time.

"I feel like I've been to the top of the mountain," he said, "but I'm not sure I looked over."

There were also some memorable games during the regular season.

Miami was leading Dallas, 27-14, with less than four minutes to play. Then Danny White delivered a perfect impersonation of former Cowboy quarterback Roger Staubach. White threw a touchdown pass to Doug Cosbie with 3:48 to play and then, 31 seconds later, threw another to Ron Springs. Rafael Septien kicked both extra points and the Cowboys had a victory just like the kind Staubach used to pull off.

The day Detroit upset Dallas, 27-24, Billy Sims outdueled Tony Dorsett by running for 119 yards and then catching an 81-yard touchdown pass. But that wasn't the story of the game. The story was the 47-yard field goal which was kicked by Eddie Murray to break a 24-24 tie as time expired.

The Cowboys almost expired, too, when they saw that the Lions had 12 men on the field. The officials never noticed the extra player and let the field goal stand.

Films of the play documented Dallas' complaint the next day, but Commissioner Pete Rozelle pointed out that, "the NFL has no provisions for replaying the game. It stands."

The New England Patriots, favored to win

Three of the year's top rookies were, left to right, the Chiefs' Joe Delaney, the Bengals' Cris Collinsworth and the 49ers' Ronnie Lott.

the AFC East, finished tied for the worst record in the NFL (2-14).

On November 22, the Patriots held a 17-13 lead over Buffalo in Rich Stadium with five seconds to play. The Bills were on the New England 36. And then it came: The Hail Mary.

The Patriots knew it. The fans in the stands knew it. The television audience knew it. All the Pats had to do was bat away the pass.

They did. Linebacker Mike Hawkins leaped high and batted it away from wide receiver Frank Lewis. Unfortunately for New England, the deflection ended up in the hands of Buffalo running back Roland Hooks and Buffalo won, 20-17.

The only team with a chance to surpass, if that is the proper word, New England for the worst record was Baltimore. The teams met on the final day of the season, as they had on the first day. The Colts won again 23-21.

There were great individual performances in 1981.

Cincinnati quarterback Ken Anderson made a fine comeback to win most of the acclaim as the AFC's top player. Joe Montana of the 49ers won similar honors in the NFC.

Sims and Dorsett waged a personal battle for rushing supremacy in the NFC. Earl Campbell led the AFC in rushing again.

Dan Fouts threw for an eye-boggling 4,802 yards and 33 touchdowns. Craig Morton's career as a quarterback in Denver was resurrected by a new coach, his former Dallas teammate Dan Reeves.

But, more than anything else, it was the year of the rookie.

George Rogers, the Heisman Trophy winner from South Carolina, led the entire NFL in rushing with 1,674 yards and scored 13 touchdowns, giving New Orleans' long-suffering fans some hope for the future.

Unheralded Joe Delaney of Northwest Louisiana gave the Kansas City offense some needed excitement, gaining 1,121 yards and scaring the opposition with his blazing speed.

Cincinnati made Kansas' David Verser their first-round draft choice and the first wide receiver picked in the '81 draft, but it was their second-round selection, Cris Collinsworth of Florida, who caught 67 passes, eight of them for touchdowns.

The Giants already had a good defense, but the man who took them beyond good to great was Lawrence Taylor, the North Carolina linebacker who was drafted second overall behind Rogers.

St. Louis went on a four-game victory streak, making an unexpected pass at the playoffs, when rookie Neil Lomax replaced veteran Jim Hart at quarterback.

Dallas had a major problem in its pass defense in 1980, and alleviated it by using two rookies in the secondary—safety Michael Downs and cornerback Everson Walls. Walls, signed as a free agent out of Grambling, led the NFL with 11 interceptions.

But no one got more mileage out of their rookies than the 49ers. Coach Bill Walsh used three of them—first-round draftee Ronnie Lott of USC, Eric Wright (Missouri) and Carlton Williamson (Pittsburgh)—in the defensive backfield. A fourth, Lynn Thomas, came in during special situations.

Lott was the most potent defensive back in the NFL, returning four interceptions for touchdowns during the regular season and playoffs.

Wright made the game-saving tackle on Dallas' Drew Pearson in the NFC championship game. That came after the 49ers scored the go-ahead points in the final minute. Danny White passed down the middle for 31 yards to Pearson as soon as the Cowboys regained the ball. Pearson was in the clear and only Wright's strength saved it. He reached out from behind and pulled down the Dallas star with one hand on Pearson's shoulder.

Six rookies—Rogers, Taylor, Lott, Delaney, Walls and Collinsworth—were named to the Pro Bowl squads.

A couple of promising rookies never made it to the NFL. Oklahoma halfback David Overstreet, Miami's first-round choice, and Oklahoma defensive end Keith Gary, the No. 1 pick of the Pittsburgh Steelers, both signed with Montreal of the Canadian Football League.

The CFL also raided the Los Angeles Rams for quarterback Vince Ferragamo and the Chicago Bears for wide receiver James Scott. As it turned out, Ferragamo had a miserable year and was offered back to the Rams by the financially-trouble Alouettes after the season. Scott was released and re-signed with Chicago.

Linebacker Tom Cousineau, whom Buffalo made the first pick overall in the 1979 draft, also will come down to the NFL for 1982. He played three years with Montreal. Another top defender, lineman Bruce Clark, also will return after two years in Toronto.

There were only four new coaches in the NFL in 1981 and they had varying results.

Denver, under Reeves, led the AFC West for a while, just missing out on the playoffs with a 10-6 record. Ed Biles, who succeeded Bum Phillips in Houston, started out well but then lost six of seven games.

Phillips, inheriting the team with the worst record in '80, the Saints, improved them to 4-12. The record included two victories over the slumping Los Angeles Rams.

Joe Gibbs lost his first five games in Washington, then won seven of his last nine on the way to an 8-8 record.

After the season there were just three head coaching changes.

Chicago Bears patriarch George Halas took control of the team again at the age of 87 and fired Neill Armstrong, replacing him with ex-Bear star tight end Mike Ditka. New England

fired Ron Erhardt and hired Southern Methodist University's head coach, Ron Meyer. Baltimore replaced Mike McCormack with controversial Frank Kush, who coached Hamilton of the CFL after resigning from Arizona State University under pressure.

There also were some significant transactions in the NFL.

The 49ers might not have made it to the Super Bowl except for two excellent deals made by Walsh. One was the signing of inside linebacker Jack Reynolds, from right under the noses of the Buffalo Bills. Buffalo had him in their offices and had called a press conference to announce his signing.

The other was the trade which brought them San Diego defensive end Fred Dean.

"You just can't find guys who can rush the passer like Dean," said Atlanta's Pro Bowl tackle, Mike Kenn, after he had been beaten for three sacks by Dean.

Bob Brudzinski had trouble adjusting to the 3-4 defense in Miami, but when he did, the ex-Los Angeles linebacker played a prominent role in the Dolphins' winning the AFC Eastern Division championship.

When John Jefferson, San Diego's outstanding wide receiver, held out far into the season, the Chargers traded him to Green Bay, giving the Packers two of the best pass catchers in football—Jefferson and James Lofton. San Diego then traded for another top wide receiver, Wes Chandler of New Orleans.

When Buffalo broke Miami's unbeaten streak at five games, 31-21, its joy was tempered by the loss of star offensive guard Reggie McKenzie with a knee injury. Buffalo later made a deal with Seattle for holdout guard Tom Lynch. Lynch contributed heavily to the Bills' stretch run to the playoffs.

Seattle started miserably, but the Seahawks went 5-4 after they traded with St. Louis for running back Theotis Brown.

The biggest football news off the field was the long running battle between the league, the Oakland Raiders and the Los Angeles Coliseum Commission; and the collective bargaining negotiations between the Players Association and the NFL Management Council.

The Raiders-LA vs. the NFL finally went to court in Los Angeles, but the long, acrimonious trial ended with a hung jury. The battle continues.

The players' union was insisting on a percentage of the profits, with 55 percent the figure most often mentioned, as the principal clause in the new contract. The Management Council, the negotiating arm of the owners, insisted that it wouldn't agree to any set percentage.

The NFL already scheduled one of its latest openings in history for 1982—September 12. And it appeared possible that the schedule may be delayed even longer if the two sides don't reach an agreement.

1981 REGULAR SEASON GAMES

FIRST WEEK

BUCCANEERS 21, VIKINGS 13

TAMPA—The Minnesota Vikings' gamble turned out to be costly and exactly what Tampa Bay needed to assure a victory in their opener.

The Vikings were trailing, 14-13, with 35 seconds to play, third down and four yards to go on the Tampa 26. Rick Danmeier already had booted two field goals for Minnesota, from 45 and 25 yards.

But the Vikings elected to let young reserve quarterback Steve Dils pass. Playing in place of injured Tommy Kramer, Dils tried a sideline pass to Terry LeCount. Cornerback Neal Colzie picked off the pass and raced 82 yards for the Buccaneers' clinching TD. Said Colzie: "I took a big gamble, but smart defensive players know what the other team is going to do and I'd watched them throw that dinky down and out all night."

"There was no pressure on the interception," said Dils. "I guess I hung the pass a little too much. I saw Colzie but I thought I could get it in."

Said Vikings Coach Bud Grant: "We had one timeout left and we were saving that for the field goal. That's why we were passing and not running. Colzie just made a tremendous play."

Tampa had forged its lead with quarterback Doug Williams, who connected with Kevin House on a 55-yard TD pass play and ran 10 yards for a touchdown.

Dils completed 37 of 62 passes for 361 yards and just one interception, but that one did hurt. The 62 attempts tied Joe Namath for second place in NFL history, behind George Blanda's 68. The 37 completions tied Blanda for third, behind Richard Todd of the New York Jets (42) and Kramer (38).

SATURDAY, SEPTEMBER 5
SCORE BY PERIODS

Minnesota	0	0	6	7—13
Tampa Bay	7	0	0	14—21

SCORING

Tampa Bay—House 55 pass from Williams (Yepremian kick).
Minnesota—Field goal Danmeier 45.
Minnesota—Field goal Danmeier 25.
Tampa Bay—Williams 10 run (Yepremian kick).
Minnesota—Senser 4 pass from Dils (Danmeier kick).
Tampa Bay—Colzie 82 interception return (Yepremian kick).

TEAM STATISTICS

	Minnesota	Tampa Bay
First downs	27	10
Rushes-Yards	27-100	28-111
Passing yards	343	108
Sacks by-Yards	0-0	2-18
Return yards	151	149
Passes	37-63-2	8-22-0
Punts	5-39.8	9-47.6
Fumbles-Lost	4-2	3-0
Penalties-Yards	4-30	6-50
Time of possession	37:13	22:47

Attendance—66,287.

INDIVIDUAL STATISTICS

Rushing—Minnesota, Young 2-7, Brown 20-79, Redwine 1-0, Dils 4-14; Tampa Bay, Wilder 8-14, Eckwood 6-36, R. Bell 11-35, Williams 3-26.

Passing—Minnesota, Dils 37-62-1—361, Brown 0-1-1—0; Tampa Bay, Williams 8-22-0—108.

Receiving—Minnesota, Young 7-47, Brown 12-77, S. White 8-92, Rashad 2-30, Senser 5-60, LeCount 2-38, Harrell 1-17; Tampa Bay, Giles 1-20, House 3-74, R. Bell 1-11, Wilder 2-minus 3, Jones 1-6.

Kickoff Returns—Minnesota, Payton 3-70, Nord 1-22; Tampa Bay, G. Davis 2-38, Obradovich 1-14, Brantley 1-0.

Punt Returns—Minnesota, Payton 6-59; Tampa Bay, T. Bell 1-8.

Interceptions—Tampa Bay, Colzie 2-89.

Punting—Minnesota, Coleman 5-39.8; Tampa Bay, Blanchard 9-47.6.

Field Goals—Minnesota, Danmeier 2-2; Tampa Bay, Yepremian 0-1.

CHIEFS 37, STEELERS 33

PITTSBURGH—Steelers Coach Chuck Noll was left wearing a long face and facing the prospect of a long season.

His Pittsburgh team had just been clipped by the young Kansas City Chiefs in its National Football League opener. Seven turnovers, including six in the second half, helped the Chiefs to score 20 of their 37 points.

"I really don't know what it is," Noll said. "I guess it was a combination of things—concentration, mechanics, Kansas City hits. Correcting it will be very important, or it will be a long, long year."

Despite an afternoon filled with mistakes, the Steelers looked like survivors when Terry Bradshaw's 41-yard touchdown pass to Jim Smith gave them a 33-30 lead with just over seven minutes left.

Five minutes later, Bradshaw had a first down at the K.C. 28-yard line with fine prospects of getting a clinching touchdown or at least running out the clock. Then Chiefs linebacker Frank Manumaleuga jarred the quarterback before he could complete a handoff to Franco Harris. The football popped loose and along came another K.C. linebacker, Thomas Howard.

Howard snatched the ball and, winning a foot race with Harris, went 65 yards for the game-winning TD.

The Steelers lost five of their eight fumbles and Bradshaw was intercepted twice—the second time by cornerback Gary Barbaro, a turn-

First Week—Continued

over that enabled the Chiefs to run out the final moments of the game.

Kansas City committed two turnovers, both in the first half. And both led to Pittsburgh TDs.

Chiefs quarterback Bill Kenney launched scoring passes of 48 yards to Henry Marshall and 53 yards to Carlos Carson. Kenney was starting because Steve Fuller was out with a knee injury.

It had been a decade since the Chiefs' last victory over the Steelers. Pittsburgh had won the previous seven games between the teams.

SEPTEMBER 6
SCORE BY PERIODS

Kansas City	10	3	10	14—37
Pittsburgh	6	13	7	7—33

SCORING

Pittsburgh—Swann 18 pass from Bradshaw (kick failed).
Kansas City—Marshall 48 pass from Kenney (Lowery kick).
Kansas City—Field goal Lowery 35.
Pittsburgh—Harris 7 run (kick failed).
Pittsburgh—Harris 1 run (Trout kick).
Kansas City—Field goal Lowery 40.
Kansas City—Carson 53 pass from Kenney (Lowery kick).
Pittsburgh—Hawthorne 1 run (Trout kick).
Kansas City—Field goal Lowery 42.
Kansas City—McKnight 3 run (Lowery kick).
Pittsburgh—Smith 41 pass from Bradshaw (Trout kick).
Kansas City—Howard 65 fumble recovery (Lowery kick).

TEAM STATISTICS

	Kansas City	Pittsburgh
First downs	17	29
Rushes-Yards	40-139	33-96
Passing yards	214	312
Sacks by-Yards	1-7	3-28
Return yards	114	112
Passes	14-26-1	21-36-2
Punts	5-39.8	3-38.7
Fumbles-Lost	1-1	8-5
Penalties-Yards	11-89	2-15
Time of possession	30:04	29:56
Attendance—53,305.		

INDIVIDUAL STATISTICS

Rushing—Kansas City, Hadnot 8-42, McKnight 17-59, B. Jackson 2-2, Delaney 9-43, Williams 1-minus 3, Marshall 1-4, Kenney 2-minus 8; Pittsburgh, Harris 19-70, Thornton 6-6, Hawthorne 7-20, Bradshaw 1-0.

Passing—Kansas City, Kenney 14-26-1—242; Pittsburgh, Bradshaw 21-36-2—319.

Receiving—Kansas City, McKnight 1-10, Williams 1-3, Marshall 4-89, Delaney 2-10, Smith 3-53, Carson 1-53, Hadnot 2-24; Pittsburgh, Thornton 1-1, Harris 3-28, Stallworth 6-107, Swann 2-35, Cunningham 4-52, Smith 4-84, Hawthorne 1-12.

Kickoff Returns—Kansas City, Carson 2-54, Williams 1-7; Pittsburgh, Anderson 3-66, Dirden 1-9.

Punt Returns—Kansas City, Smith 1-5; Pittsburgh, Smith 3-20.

Interceptions—Kansas City, Harris 1-24, Barbaro 1-24; Pittsburgh, Woodruff 1-17.

Punting—Kansas City, Grupp 5-39.8; Pittsburgh, Colquitt 3-38.7.

Field Goals—Kansas City, Lowery 3-4; Pittsburgh, None attempted.

BILLS 31, JETS O

ORCHARD PARK—The New York Jets did a fine job at stopping the Buffalo ground game. "But when you do that," noted Bills running back Joe Cribbs, "you leave yourself open for the pass."

And so it was. The Bills' Joe Ferguson threw for 254 yards, including touchdown passes to Cribbs and Jerry Butler. Butler gathered in six passes for 123 yards.

In addition to his 28-yard scoring catch, Cribbs ran for a 14-yard TD in the Bills' 21-point third quarter.

The Jets' passing and rushing yardage totaled just 231 and they had just eight first downs.

"Evidently, we weren't as ready to play as we thought we were. As a result, we got a good whipping," said Jets Coach Walt Michaels. "But it's not the end of the world—we've got 15 games left."

The shutout was the first dealt to the Jets since December 18, 1977, when they lost to the Philadelphia Eagles, 27-0.

SEPTEMBER 6
SCORE BY PERIODS

New York Jets	0	0	0	0— 0
Buffalo	3	7	21	0—31

SCORING

Buffalo—Field goal Mike-Mayer 21.
Buffalo—Cribbs 28 pass from Ferguson (Mike-Mayer kick).
Buffalo—Butler 19 pass from Ferguson (Mike-Mayer kick).
Buffalo—Cribbs 14 run (Mike-Mayer kick).
Buffalo—Leaks 1 run (Mike-Mayer kick).

TEAM STATISTICS

	New York	Buffalo
First downs	8	25
Rushes-Yards	25-102	44-182
Passing yards	129	236
Sacks by-Yards	2-18	1-9
Return yards	173	119
Passes	16-25-2	15-24-1
Punts	8-39.1	5-47.6
Fumbles-Lost	3-0	1-0
Penalties-Yards	9-100	10-84
Time of possession	20:31	39:29
Attendance—79,754.		

INDIVIDUAL STATISTICS

Rushing—New York, Dierking 3-13, Todd 6-32, Long 3-12, McNeil 3-16, Newton 3-7, Harper 2-3, Augustyniak 4-12, Lewis 1-7; Buffalo, Cribbs 15-61, Brown 7-19, Leaks 12-36, Brammer 1-6, Hooks 7-40, McCutcheon 2-20.

Passing—New York, Todd 16-25-2—138; Buffalo, Ferguson 15-24-1—254.

Receiving—New York, Gaffney 2-33, Walker 3-40, Dierking 2-12, Barkum 3-25, Harper 3-11, Long 3-17; Buffalo, Lewis 5-87, Butler 6-123, Jessie 1-0, Cribbs 1-28, Brammer 1-10.

Kickoff Returns—New York, Sohn 4-73, Lewis 1-30, Stephens 1-7. Buffalo, none.

Punt Returns—New York, Harper 3-29, Sohn 1-10; Buffalo, Piccone 2-19, Hooks 2-20.

Interceptions—New York, Ray 1-24; Buffalo, Romes 1-35, Clark 1-45.

Punting—New York, Ramsey 8-39.1; Buffalo, Cater 5-47.6.

Field Goals—New York, None attempted; Buffalo, Mike-Mayer 1-2.

Buffalo's two Joes, Ferguson and Cribbs, ganged up on the New York Jets as the Bills trounced the Jets, 34-0, in the first week of the 1981 season.

First Week—Continued

EAGLES 24, GIANTS 10

EAST RUTHERFORD—The Philadelphia Eagles proved they had more than one gun in their arsenal while defeating the New York Giants for the 12th straight time.

The Giants went all out to defuse Harold Carmichael, the NFC champions' big-catch receiver. That strategy worked well enough in the first period when the Giants took a 3-0 lead.

Then the Eagles turned to Wilbert Montgomery, their brilliant running back. Montgomery proceeded to rush for 84 yards in 16 carries and he caught six passes for another 33 yards.

Quarterback Ron Jaworski also delivered for Philadelphia, hitting on 16 of 26 passes for 158 yards, including a 55-yard TD toss to Rodney Parker in the third quarter. The pass to Parker gave the Eagles a 17-3 lead.

The Eagles' defense sacked Giants quarterback Phil Simms six times and held New York to three yards rushing in the second half. Simms still managed to complete 20 of 37 passes for 241 yards.

Montgomery predicted that Philadelphia's 27-10 loss to Oakland in Super Bowl XV will motivate the Eagles this year.

"We weren't as good as we thought we were," said Montgomery. "This year we have something to prove. Let's face it. Getting to the Super Bowl just isn't enough."

SEPTEMBER 6
SCORE BY PERIODS

Philadelphia	0	10	7	7—24
New York Giants	3	0	0	7—10

SCORING

New York—Field goal Danelo 27.
Philadelphia—Harrington 1 run (Franklin kick).
Philadelphia—Field goal Franklin 47.
Philadelphia—Parker 55 pass from Jaworski (Franklin kick).
Philadelphia—Montgomery 1 run (Franklin kick).
New York—Perry 19 pass from Simms (Danelo kick).

TEAM STATISTICS

	Philadelphia	New York
First downs	21	14
Rushes-Yards	43-178	23-55
Passing yards	147	175
Sacks by-Yards	6-66	1-11
Return yards	64	149
Passes	16-26-1	20-37-0
Punts	6-40.2	6-42.5
Fumbles-Lost	1-1	3-1
Penalties-Yards	8-49	8-60
Time of possession	32:30	27:30

Attendance—71,459.

INDIVIDUAL STATISTICS

Rushing—Philadelphia, Montgomery 16-84, Harrington 10-51, Jaworski 1-3, Oliver 7-9, Giammona 9-31; New York, Matthews 3-12, Taylor 7-12, Simms 5-8, Perry 5-13, Kotar 2-8, Garrett 1-2.

Passing—Philadelphia, Jaworski 16-26-1—158; New York, Simms 20-37-0—241.

Receiving—Philadelphia, Harrington 4-4, Montgomery 6-33, Campfield 2-31, Krepfle 1-10, Spagnola 1-6, Parker 1-55, Carmichael 1-19; New York, Matthews 2-13, Taylor 6-62, Perry 4-49, Perkins 2-39, Mullady 2-33, Gray 3-26, Shirk 1-19.

Kickoff Returns—Philadelphia, Campfield 1-16, Henry 1-7; New York, Garrett 4-93.

Punt Returns—Philadelphia, Henry 6-41; New York, Garrett 2-31.

Interceptions—New York, T. Jackson 1-25.

Punting—Philadelphia, Runager 6-40.2; New York, Jennings 6-42.5.

Field Goals—Philadelphia, Franklin 1-1; New York, Danelo 1-3.

COLTS 29, PATRIOTS 28

FOXBORO—Baltimore Colts Coach Mike McCormack had promised that fullback Randy McMillan, the team's No. 1 draft choice from Pitt, would be "explosive." The New England Patriots were the first to hear the boom.

McMillan, a Baltimore native, rushed 16 times for 146 yards and two fourth-quarter touchdowns in his NFL debut. He scored on a 35-yard run to finish off a 78-yard drive and bulled over from the 2 at the end of an 88-yard march.

McMillan said he was nervous but optimistic as the game began.

"I can break tackles because of my size (6-1, 228 pounds) and I do have speed," McMillan said. "A lot of times the defense didn't expect me to keep going, but I did."

McMillan gained 94 yards in the fourth quarter alone.

"He played the way we wanted him to play," McCormack said. "He's a tough kid. I was scared right until the end but then Randy took charge."

Patriots cornerback Mike Haynes talked as if he couldn't believe his eyes.

"We saw McMillan in the films," he said, "but he didn't do the things he did today."

McMillan's clinching TD, which gave the Colts a 29-21 lead, was set up when Patriots cornerback Raymond Clayborn was nailed for pass interference on Ray Butler. That call gave the Colts a 39-yard gain and McMillan plunged for his two-yard score.

The Patriots got within a point on Steve Grogan's four-yard toss to Don Hasselbeck with 2:31 left. But New England never got the ball back.

SEPTEMBER 6
SCORE BY PERIODS

Baltimore	10	3	3	13—29
New England	0	14	0	14—28

SCORING

Baltimore—Field goal Wood 48.
Baltimore—Dickey 19 run (Wood kick).
New England—Tatupu 8 pass from Johnson (Smith kick).
Baltimore—Field goal Wood 19.
New England—Pennywell 22 pass from Grogan (Smith kick).
Baltimore—Field goal Wood 35.
Baltimore—McMillan 35 run (kick failed).
New England—Calhoun 1 run (Smith kick).

Baltimore—McMillan 2 run (Wood kick).
New England—Hasselbeck 4 pass from Grogan (Smith kick).

TEAM STATISTICS

	Baltimore	New England
First downs	21	22
Rushes-Yards	43-249	28-114
Passing yards	97	274
Sacks by-Yards	3-11	2-16
Return yards	144	106
Passes	12-20-0	16-29-2
Punts	4-44.3	3-37.0
Fumbles-Lost	1-1	2-1
Penalties-Yards	10-75	8-84
Time of possession	32:24	27:36

Attendance—49,572.

INDIVIDUAL STATISTICS

Rushing—Baltimore, McMillan 16-146, Dickey 22-80, McCauley 2-11, Dixon 1-9, Jones 2-3; New England, Collins 15-81, Tatupu 5-20, Calhoun 8-13.

Passing—Baltimore, Jones 12-20-0—113; New England, Grogan 14-27-2—261, Johnson 2-2-0—24.

Receiving—Baltimore, Dickey 3-31, McMillan 3-13, Carr 2-34, McCauley 1-12, Butler 1-9, Sherwin 1-8, Dixon 1-6; New England, Hasselbeck 6-111, Collins 3-48, Pennywell 2-37, Tatupu 2-30, Westbrook 1-32, Grogan 1-16, Johnson 1-11.

Kickoff Returns—Baltimore, Dixon 4-92, Anderson 1-11; New England, Collins 3-65, Lee 1-16.

Punt Returns—New England, James 2-25.

Interceptions—Baltimore, Glasgow 1-31, Krauss 1-10.

Punting—Baltimore, Garrett 4-44.3; New England, Hubach 3-37.0.

Field Goals—Baltimore, Wood 3-3; New England, Smith 0-2.

PACKERS 16, BEARS 9

CHICAGO—Green Bay Coach Bart Starr said he was hoping for a miracle, and that's what he got with 23 seconds to play.

It came in the form of a fumble recovery by Packers safety Johnnie Gray on the Packers' 1-yard line. That thwarted the Chicago Bears' longest drive of the day and preserved the Packers' triumph.

Matt Suhey, subbing for the injured Roland Harper, apparently crossed the goal line after the Bears had traveled from their own 46 to the Packers' 3. But officials ruled that Suhey fumbled before crossing the goal when hit by Mike McCoy, and Gray pounced on the ball.

Said Starr: "Both teams played poorly. There were a lot of fundamental mistakes you wouldn't even see in high school. I was hoping some miracle would happen, like the one that did."

Said Bears Coach Neill Armstrong: "I want to make one thing perfectly clear. We had no excuses. We got whipped at the line, made too many mistakes."

It was the second successive year the Packers opened the season with a win over the Bears. In 1980, Chester Marcol's TD run in overtime after his field goal try had been blocked gave Green Bay a 12-6 victory.

This time the Bears fumbled six times and lost four of them. Chicago's offense finally started to roll in the third period, with Walter Payton scoring on an 11-yard run. Payton had what amounted to a so-so day for him, 81 yards in 19 rushes.

The Packers used the running of Eddie Lee Ivery and Gerry Ellis, plus the passing of Lynn Dickey, to take a 13-0 halftime lead. Ivery scored from the 2 and gained 72 yards before he reinjured his knee in the third quarter. Ellis tallied from the 4 and led all rushers with 94 yards. Dickey hit on 10 of 23 passes for 165 yards.

Jan Stenerud connected on a 30-yard field goal for Green Bay, moving into third place on the all-time NFL field goal list.

SEPTEMBER 6
SCORE BY PERIODS

Green Bay	7	6	0	3	16
Chicago	0	0	6	3	9

SCORING

Green Bay—Ivery 2 run (Wingo pass from Stachowicz).
Green Bay—Ellis 4 run (kick failed).
Chicago—Payton 11 run (kick failed).
Green Bay—Field goal Stenerud 30.
Chicago—Field goal Thomas 25.

TEAM STATISTICS

	Green Bay	Chicago
First downs	20	20
Rushes-Yards	46-193	30-145
Passing yards	153	161
Sacks by-Yards	3-24	2-12
Return yards	74	166
Passes	10-23-1	17-35-0
Punts	6-42.0	6-44.0
Fumbles-Lost	2-2	6-4
Penalties-Yards	6-52	10-72
Time of possession	32:36	27:24

Attendance—62,411.

INDIVIDUAL STATISTICS

Rushing—Green Bay, Ellis 17-94, Ivery 14-72, Middleton 6-26, Atkins 5-minus 3, Dickey 3-2, A. Thompson 1-2; Chicago, Payton 19-81, Suhey 5-47, Harper 3-9, Evans 2-4, Williams 1-4.

Passing—Green Bay, Dickey 10-23-1—165; Chicago, Evans 17-35-0—185.

Receiving—Green Bay, Lofton 5-84, Ivery 2-10, Coffman 1-27, A. Thompson 1-25, Nixon 1-19; Chicago, Baschnagel 4-67, Payton 4-29, Suhey 4-19, Watts 2-35, Williams 2-19, Margerum 1-16.

Kickoff Returns—Green Bay, Nixon 2-40; Chicago, Williams 3-75, B. Fisher 1-9.

Punt Returns—Green Bay, Nixon 4-34; Chicago, J. Fisher 4-60.

Interceptions—Chicago, Henderson 1-22.

Punting—Green Bay, Stachowicz 6-42.0; Chicago, Parsons 6-44.0.

Field Goals—Green Bay, Stenerud 1-1; Chicago, Thomas 1-1.

DOLPHINS 20, CARDS 7

ST. LOUIS—David Woodley could afford to go heavy on sympathy, and that's what the Miami quarterback did. After leading the Dolphins to an easy victory over the St. Louis Cardinals, Woodley commented on the plight of Neil Lomax, the Cardinals' rookie quarterback.

First Week—Continued

Lomax had to replace Jim Hart, who twisted his knee while being sacked in the first period, and the first pass the rookie threw was intercepted, triggering Miami's first score. Recalled Woodley, now in his second NFL season:

"The same thing happened to me last year. He played a lot better than I did in my first game. We lost, 34-0, and only crossed midfield once. It was a total disaster. It's tough to be thrown into a situation like that."

Hart's absence enabled Miami's defense to control the situation, with four sacks for 34 yards in St. Louis losses. The Dolphins also held running back Ottis Anderson to 52 yards in 20 carries.

Lomax hit on 14 of 30 passes for 151 yards. Woodley was 14 of 24 for 178 yards, including TD tosses of 22 and 47 yards to Jimmy Cefalo.

Miami safety Glenn Blackwood picked off Lomax' first pass and returned it 34 yards to the St. Louis 39. That set up a 27-yard field goal by Uwe von Schamann for a 3-0 Miami lead early in the second period.

On the Dolphins' next possession, Woodley capped a 73-yard march with his 22-yard TD toss to Cefalo. Von Schamann contributed a second field goal before the half and Woodley put Miami ahead 20-0, with his other TD pass to Cefalo, in the third quarter.

The Cardinal touchdown came in the last period after Lee Nelson sacked Woodley, whose fumble was recovered by Stafford Mays at the Miami 23. Anderson went over from the one. Cardinals Coach Jim Hanifan praised Lomax, declaring: "He was a real bright spot. He certainly didn't expect to be called on that soon. He kept his cool and did well."

SEPTEMBER 6
SCORE BY PERIODS

Miami	0	13	7	0—	20
St. Louis	0	0	0	7—	7

SCORING

Miami—Field goal von Schamann 27.
Miami—Cefalo 22 pass from Woodley (von Schamann kick).
Miami—Field goal von Schamann 30.
Miami—Cefalo 47 pass from Woodley (von Schamann kick).
St. Louis—Anderson 1 run (O'Donoghue kick).

TEAM STATISTICS

	Miami	St. Louis
First downs	14	14
Rushes-Yards	33-144	29-61
Passing yards	141	142
Sacks by-Yards	4-34	4-37
Return yards	97	154
Passes	14-24-1	17-35-1
Punts	6-42.2	7-43.6
Fumbles-Lost	3-2	1-1
Penalties-Yards	3-20	5-50
Time of possession	27:42	32:18

Attendance—50,351.

Rushing—Miami, Bennett 13-40, Nathan 7-50, Woodley 6-12, Vigorito 3-9, Hill 4-33; St. Louis, Anderson 20-52, Brown 5-2, Morris 4-7.

Passing—Miami, Woodley 14-24-1—178; St. Louis, Hart 3-5-0—25, Lomax 14-30-1—151.

Receiving—Miami, Nathan 2-18, Moore 3-17, Harris 2-31, Bennett 1-4, Hill 1-4, Lee 1-5, Cefalo 3-90, Vigorito 1-9; St. Louis, Tilley 4-62, Stief 2-19, Anderson 6-40, Floyd 2-27, Morris 1-9, Harrell 1-6, Combs 1-13.

Kickoff Returns—Miami, Walker 2-28; St. Louis, Harrell 1-10, Green 3-58, Mitchell 1-36.

Punt Returns—Miami, Kozlowski 1-9, Vigorito 2-20, Blackwood 1-6; St. Louis, Mitchell 5-33.

Interceptions—Miami, Blackwood 1-34; St. Louis, Collier 1-17.

Punting—Miami, Orosz 6-42.2; St. Louis, Birdsong 7-43.6.

Field Goals—Miami, von Schamann 2-2; St. Louis, None attempted.

BENGALS 27, SEAHAWKS 21

CINCINNATI—Cincinnati Coach Forrest Gregg knew his Bengals needed help. That was obvious. They trailed the Seattle Seahawks, 21-0, in the first quarter and quarterback Ken Anderson was playing miserably.

Anderson's first-quarter log showed five completions in 15 passes, and two interceptions. But his backup, Jack Thompson, couldn't play because of a twisted ankle. That left third-stringer Turk Schonert, who had never played a down in a regular-season NFL game.

"I've always felt Turk could play if he got the opportunity," Gregg said.

Schonert, second-year pro from Stanford, trotted in to play the second quarter. And he promptly fumbled away his first NFL snap from center.

"I was cool when I went into the game," Schonert declared afterward. "When I fumbled, all I wanted to do was get back in there."

He did, and directed the Bengals in five scoring drives. The game-winning score came with 5:04 left as fullback Pete Johnson rammed over for his second TD. Johnson carried 20 times for 84 yards.

The Seahawks scored first on John Harris' 29-yard interception return. Then Jim Zorn and receiver Steve Largent combined on a 36-yard TD play. Then Kerry Justin's 43-yard fumble return set up a Jim Jodat TD.

The Cincinnati crowd indicated its extreme displeasure.

"I deserved to be booed the way I played," Anderson said.

After his fumbling start, Schonert directed second-quarter drives that netted a field goal by Jim Breech and a three-yard TD run by Johnson.

In the third quarter, Breech hit a 40-yarder and Archie Griffin ran three yards for his first rushing touchdown in five years to cut Seattle's lead to 21-20. Schonert was at his best in the fourth period, moving the Bengals 84 yards in 15 plays with Johnson scoring from the 2.

Schonert hit 9-of-18 passes for 130 yards and scrambled seven times for 41 yards.

It was the sixth straight opening-day loss for the Seahawks and their 10th consecutive regular-season defeat.

The 21 points were the most ever allowed by the Bengals in a first quarter in their 14-year history.

SEPTEMBER 6
SCORE BY PERIODS

Seattle	21	0	0	0—21
Cincinnati	0	10	10	7—27

SCORING

Seattle—Harris 29 pass interception (Herrera kick).
Seattle—Largent 36 pass from Zorn (Herrera kick).
Seattle—Jodat 1 run (Herrera kick).
Cincinnati—Field goal Breech 25.
Cincinnati—Johnson 3 run (Breech kick).
Cincinnati—Field goal Breech 40.
Cincinnati—A. Griffin 3 run (Breech kick).
Cincinnati—Johnson 2 run (Breech kick).

TEAM STATISTICS

	Seattle	Cincinnati
First downs	17	24
Rushes-Yards	23-60	45-210
Passing yards	230	165
Sacks by-Yards	3-4	1-0
Return yards	159	125
Passes	21-41-1	14-33-2
Punts	6-39.7	4-46.0
Fumbles-Lost	4-3	4-2
Penalties-Yards	6-52	5-40
Time of possession	19:38	40:22
Attendance—41,177.		

INDIVIDUAL STATISTICS

Rushing—Seattle, Smith 8-9, Jodat 8-21, Zorn 1-7, Doornink 5-8, Moore 1-15; Cincinnati, Alexander 10-41, Johnson 20-84, Schonert 7-41, A. Griffin 8-44.

Passing—Seattle, Zorn 21-41-1—230; Cincinnati, Anderson 5-15-2—39, Schonert 9-18-0—130.

Receiving—Seattle, Largent 8-114, Smith 3-25, McCullum 4-35, Sawyer 3-22, Doornink 2-24, Moore 1-10; Cincinnati, Collinsworth 4-65, Johnson 1-6, Kreider 3-32, Alexander 2-18, Ross 3-33, Curtis 1-15.

Kickoff Returns—Seattle, Lewis, 4-71, Johnson 1-12; Cincinnati, Chapman 2-36, R. Griffin 2-31.

Punt Returns—Seattle, Lewis 4-34; Cincinnati, Fuller 3-15.

Interceptions—Seattle, Harris 1-29, Simpson 1-13; Cincinnati, B. Harris 1-43.

Punting—Seattle, West 6-39.7; Cincinnati, McInally 4-46.0.

Field Goals—Seattle, Herrera 0-1; Cincinnati, Breech 2-3.

COWBOYS 26, REDSKINS 10

WASHINGTON—It's just about as certain as death and taxes. When Tony Dorsett gains 100 yards, the Dallas Cowboys win. Actually, that Dorsett formula hasn't held true 100 percent of the time, just 95 percent.

It certainly held true in the Cowboys' season opener. Dorsett rolled up 132 yards in 21 carries and the Cowboys romped over the Washington Redskins.

While Dorsett was doing his thing, the Dallas defense was superb, as usual. The Cowboys held the Redskins to 44 yards on the ground, intercepted four of Joe Theismann's 48 passes and recovered two of five Washington fumbles.

One of Theismann's passes went for a 15-yard TD to Joe Washington, and Mark Moseley kicked a 42-yard field goal. That was all the offense Washington could muster.

Meantime, Danny White fired a 33-yard touchdown pass to Billy Joe DuPree and a 42-yarder to Drew Pearson in the second quarter. In the second half, Rafael Septien kicked four Dallas field goals from 29, 42, 23 and 18 yards.

The key interception for the Cowboys was the one by cornerback Dennis Thurman on the Dallas goal line with five minutes to play and the score 23-10. He returned it 96 yards to the Washington 4. And all day long, the Dallas front four of Harvey Martin, John Dutton, Randy White and Ed Jones was giving Theismann a very hard time.

"We had chances to make big plays, but Dallas made the big plays instead," said Joe Gibbs, making his bow as an NFL head coach.

Dallas lost rookie defensive back Michael Downs, who had an interception, with a hamstring pull and linebacker Mike Hegman with a broken right arm.

SEPTEMBER 6
SCORE BY PERIODS

Dallas	0	14	6	6—26
Washington	0	7	3	0—10

SCORING

Dallas—DuPree 33 pass from D. White (Septien kick).
Washington—Washington 15 pass from Theismann (Moseley kick).
Dallas—Pearson 42 pass from D. White (Septien kick).
Dallas—Field goal Septien 29.
Washington—Field goal Moseley 42.
Dallas—Field goal Septien 42.
Dallas—Field goal Septien 23.
Dallas—Field goal Septien 18.

TEAM STATISTICS

	Dallas	Washington
First downs	20	20
Rushes-Yards	44-206	18-44
Passing yards	140	280
Sacks by-Yards	3-33	1-5
Return yards	212	178
Passes	12-24-0	23-49-4
Punts	6-44.2	5-41.0
Fumbles-Lost	2-1	5-2
Penalties-Yards	10-87	7-89
Time of possession	30:51	29:09
Attendance—55,045.		

INDIVIDUAL STATISTICS

Rushing—Dallas, Dorsett 21-132, Springs 15-58, Newhouse 2-2, J. Jones 5-14, D. White 1-0; Washington, Riggins 8-25, Washington 6-17, Metcalf 1-0, Jackson 1-7, Theismann 1-0, Monk 1-minus 5.

Passing—Dallas, D. White 12-24-0—145; Washington, Theismann 22-48-4—281, Washington 1-1-0—32.

Receiving—Dallas, Johnson 1-7, Cosbie 1-4, Pearson 3-70, DuPree 1-33, Dorsett 3-26, Springs 2-3, J. Jones 1-2; Washington, Monk 3-38, Warren 1-32, Riggins 1-22, Washington 10-124, Harmon 3-24, Seay 2-30, Metcalf 2-38, McCrary 1-5.

Kickoff Returns—Dallas, J. Jones 1-17, Fellows 2-55; Washington, Nelms 2-62, Metcalf 3-85, Wonsley 1-18.

First Week—Continued

OILERS 27, RAMS 20

ANAHEIM—Usually, it's the retired employee who gets the watch. The Houston Oilers reversed the procedure after their season opener, against the Rams. They gave a watch to rookie Willie Tullis.

All Willie did in his first pro game was race 95 yards with a kickoff for a touchdown with 57 seconds to play. It gave Houston a 27-20 victory, just seconds after the Rams had tied the score on Frank Corral's 36-yard field goal.

Said Tullis, looking at the expensive wristwatch his teammates gave him as the game's most valuable player:

"I'll never forget this moment. It's a very emotional moment for me. I'll never trade this watch, not for anything. It's my first NFL game and I get voted most valuable player. This is just unbelievable.

"I was just trying to follow my blockers and get us in a good position for a field goal," said the 6-foot, 190-pound speedster from Troy State.

Tullis had some help in the hero department from Ken Stabler, the 36-year-old Houston quarterback who came out of a brief retirement for his 13th NFL season. Stabler tossed two third-quarter touchdown passes to erase Houston's 17-6 halftime deficit and give the Oilers a 20-17 lead.

Stabler's first TD strike was for 33 yards to Rob Carpenter and the second was good for 20 yards to Ken Burrough. Stabler had played just two series of downs in the Oilers' final warmup game when he returned to the club after he learned that Gifford Nielsen, his replacement, had been injured.

The veteran quarterback had other obstacles, too. The state of California had threatened to order his arrest on a charge of missing alimony payments. And there had been reports linking him with a New Jersey gambling figure, Nicholas Dudich. But Stabler completed 13 of 20 passes for 192 yards.

"All I can do is play as well as I can," said Stabler. "I've had to put up with a lot of baloney, but I just have to forget that stuff. The only thing I care about is the other 44 guys on this team."

Among the other 44 was Earl Campbell, who did his part against the Rams by rushing for 122 yards in 27 carries. Campbell left the game with four minutes to play after suffering a shoulder injury.

Rams quarterback Pat Haden completed 11 of 20 passes for 168 yards but threw three interceptions. He was replaced in the fourth period by Jeff Rutledge, who was 5-for-8 for 97 yards and one interception. Haden was the target of booing by Anaheim fans.

SEPTEMBER 6
SCORE BY PERIODS

Houston	3	3	14	7—27
Los Angeles	7	10	0	3—20

SCORING

Los Angeles—Tyler 67 pass from Haden (Corral kick).
Houston—Field goal Fritsch 50.
Houston—Field goal Fritsch 41.
Los Angeles—Field goal Corral 35.
Los Angeles—Arnold 19 pass from Haden (Corral kick).
Houston—Carpenter 33 pass from Stabler (Fritsch kick).
Houston—Burrough 20 pass from Stabler (Fritsch kick).
Los Angeles—Field goal Corral 36.
Houston—Tullis 95 kickoff return (Fritsch kick).

TEAM STATISTICS

	Houston	Los Angeles
First downs	14	17
Rushes-Yards	37-140	32-137
Passing yards	192	248
Sacks by-Yards	2-17	1-12
Return yards	289	129
Passes	14-21-0	16-28-4
Punts	3-37.3	4-37.3
Fumbles-Lost	3-3	1-0
Penalties-Yards	4-35	7-50
Time of possession	30:13	29:47

Attendance—63,198.

INDIVIDUAL STATISTICS

Rushing—Houston, Campbell 27-122, Carpenter 6-12, Armstrong 2-7, T. Wilson 1-1, Stabler 1-minus 2; Los Angeles, Tyler 20-90, Bryant 9-57, Childs 1-0, J. Thomas 2-minus 10.

Passing—Houston, Stabler 13-20-0—192, Parsley 1-1-0—12; Los Angeles, Haden 11-20-3—168, Rutledge 5-8-1—97.

Receiving—Houston, Renfro 4-54, Carpenter 3-36, Burrough 2-43, Campbell 2-34, Coleman 1-13, Armstrong 1-12, Casper 1-12; Los Angeles, Tyler 4-90, Waddy 3-48, Childs 2-46, Dennard 2-29, D. Hill 2-18, Bryant 2-15, Arnold 1-19.

Kickoff Returns—Houston, Roaches 2-49, Tullis 3-134; Los Angeles, D. Hill 3-70, Sully 1-12.

Punt Returns—Houston, Roaches 2-16; Los Angeles, Irvin 2-47.

Interceptions—Houston, Perry 1-34, Stemrick 1-38, Bingham 1-17, J.C. Wilson 1-1.

Punting—Houston, Parsley 3-37.3; Los Angeles, Corral 4-37.3.

Field Goals—Houston, Fritsch 2-3; Los Angeles, Corral 2-3.

LIONS 24, 49ers 17

PONTIAC—Detroit fans couldn't seem to decide whether to love the Lions or hate them. The fans booed every mistake the Lions made, and they made plenty of them, but the crowd was cheering at the end because Detroit finished on top of the San Francisco 49ers.

"We were the favorites and then we were the jerks," noted Lions Coach Monte Clark. "But the important thing was that they were behind us at the end."

What finally won over the Silverdome crowd of 62,123 was the running of Billy Sims. He carried the ball on the last five plays of Detroit's final possession and scored the winning touchdown with 18 seconds to play on a one-yard plunge.

"It wasn't pretty, but we won," said Sims. "Everybody had the jitters."

Sims had scored the first Detroit TD on a 39-yard pass from quarterback Gary Danielson. After Joe Montana fired a 21-yard TD toss to Freddie Solomon to bring the 49ers up to a 17-17 tie in the last period, the Lions left it to Sims, who had been checked for most of the contest. He finished with just 59 yards in 21 rushes.

Said 49ers Coach Bill Walsh: "Our kickoffs killed us. Ray Wersching pulled a muscle in his leg in pregame warmups and we had problems the whole game. The kicking game allowed the Lions good field position. I knew we were in trouble, even on extra points."

SEPTEMBER 6
SCORE BY PERIODS

San Francisco	0	3	0	14	17
Detroit	0	10	0	14	24

SCORING

San Francisco—Field goal Wersching 25.
Detroit—Sims 39 pass from Danielson (Murray kick).
Detroit—Field goal Murray 29.
San Francisco—Patton 1 run (Wersching kick).
Detroit—King 17 pass from Danielson (Murray kick).
San Francisco—Solomon 21 pass from Montana (Wersching kick).
Detroit—Sims 1 run (Murray kick).

TEAM STATISTICS

	San Francisco	Detroit
First downs	19	21
Rushes-Yards	32-127	30-127
Passing yards	170	168
Sacks by-Yards	4-28	5-25
Return yards	105	47
Passes	18-28-1	16-27-1
Punts	3-33.7	4-46.3
Fumbles-Lost	2-2	1-1
Penalties-Yards	8-54	7-65
Time of possession	31:56	28:04
Attendance—62,123.		

INDIVIDUAL STATISTICS

Rushing—San Francisco, Patton 15-72, Easley 7-23, Cooper 9-22, Montana 1-10; Detroit, Sims 21-59, Bussey 4-23, L. Thompson 1-17, King 2-10, V. Thompson 1-12, Danielson 1-6.

Passing—San Francisco, Montana 18-28-1—195; Detroit, Danielson 16-27-1—196.

Receiving—San Francisco, Solomon 8-94, Clark 5-57, Cooper 3-11, Young 2-33; Detroit, Sims 5-66, L. Thompson 3-63, King 3-24, Scott 2-23, Norris 2-15, Kane 1-5.

Kickoff Returns—San Francisco, Jones 3-43, Patton 1-0; Detroit, Hall 2-17, King 2-19.

Punt Returns—San Francisco, Solomon 2-16, Hicks 2-46; Detroit, Martin 1-11.

Interceptions—San Francisco, Reynolds 1-0; Detroit, Allen 1-0.

Punting—San Francisco, Miller 3-33.7; Detroit, Skladany 4-46.3.

Field Goals—San Francisco, Wersching 1-2; Detroit, Murray 1-2.

FALCONS 27, SAINTS 0

ATLANTA—Steve Bartkowski said he was weak from a bout with the flu, but the Atlanta quarterback was strong enough to fire three touchdown passes as the Falcons routed the New Orleans Saints.

"I had some kind of virus I caught yesterday," said Bartkowski afterward. "I had nothing to eat yesterday and nothing but a couple of rolls at breakfast. I woke up about 3:00 a.m. in a full sweat, but then I felt better and knew I'd be able to play."

Bartkowski made TD tosses of 10 and 19 yards to Wallace Francis in the first half. Then he connected on a 25-yard scoring pass to Alfred Jenkins in the fourth period. The Falcons also tallied in the third quarter when cornerback Kenny Johnson grabbed a fumble by Saints tight end Rich Caster and returned it 35 yards to the end zone.

Heisman Trophy winner George Rogers of South Carolina gained 61 yards on 13 carries for New Orleans in his debut. Of those, 25 came on his last carry. Said new Saints Coach Bum Phillips: "He looked good under the circumstances, but he really couldn't get started against Atlanta's defense."

"When we got behind, we had to turn to the pass" said Rogers. "I never felt intimidated by the Falcons, although they are a good, hard-hitting football team."

New Orleans quarterback Archie Manning completed 15 of 28 for 122 yards.

SEPTEMBER 6
SCORE BY PERIODS

New Orleans	0	0	0	0	0
Atlanta	7	7	7	6	27

SCORING

Atlanta—Francis 10 pass from Bartkowski (Luckhurst kick).
Atlanta—Francis 19 pass from Bartkowski (Luckhurst kick).
Atlanta—Johnson 35 fumble return (Luckhurst kick).
Atlanta—Jenkins 25 pass from Bartkowski (pass failed).

TEAM STATISTICS

	New Orleans	Atlanta
First downs	14	21
Rushes-Yards	20-76	38-164
Passing yards	173	135
Sacks by-Yards	2-19	3-20
Return yards	80	46
Passes	23-41-1	16-26-2
Punts	5-40.4	3-37.7
Fumbles-Lost	4-3	3-2
Penalties-Yards	4-30	6-54
Time of possession	30:53	29:07
Attendance—57,406.		

INDIVIDUAL STATISTICS

Rushing—New Orleans, Rogers 13-61, Holmes 4-10, Tyler 2-2, W. Wilson 1-3; Atlanta, Andrews 18-86, Cain 11-53, Mayberry 6-19, Strong 3-6.

Passing—New Orleans, Manning 15-28-0—122, Scott 8-12-1—71, Merkens 0-1-0—0; Atlanta, Bartkowski 16-25-1—154, Moroski 0-1-1—0.

Receiving—New Orleans, Chandler 8-117, Holmes 3-22, W. Wilson 3-11, Hardy 2-15, Caster 2-12, Banks 1-6, Lafary 1-5, Merkens 1-4, Rogers 1-1, Tyler 1-0; Atlanta,

Cain 5-47, Jenkins 3-41, Francis 3-32, Andrews 2-14, Miller 2-10, Jackson 1-10.

Kickoff Returns—New Orleans, Merkens 2-38, Banks 1-9; Atlanta, R. Smith 1-22.

Punt Returns—New Orleans, Banks 2-0; Atlanta, R. Smith 2-4, Woerner 2-20.

Interceptions—New Orleans, Poe 1-0, Ray 1-33; Atlanta, Musser 1-0.

Punting—New Orleans, Erxleben 5-40.4; Atlanta, James 3-37.7.

Field Goals—New Orleans, Ricardo 0-1; Atlanta, Luckhurst 0-1.

BRONCOS 9, RAIDERS 7

DENVER—The Oakland Raiders, defending NFL champions, went to the Mile High City and took a nasty tumble. The Denver defense sacked Raiders quarterback Jim Plunkett five times for a total loss of 41 yards. And the Broncos neutralized any plans Plunkett and the Raiders had for long bombing sorties.

"We didn't have time," Plunkett said. "They were fired up. Once they got tired, we thought we could go deep more, later on."

But the Denver defensive unit never seemed to tire, mainly because the Broncos' offense dominated time of possession (nearly 36 minutes to Oakland's 24). The defense was able to stay fresh.

"Except for one drive, Oakland never really threatened to score," noted Dan Reeves, a winner in his first game as Denver coach.

Reeves, former offensive coordinator for the Dallas Cowboys, had installed a multiple offense and it was anticipated the Broncos would need time to get the new system clicking. Even though the Denver attack was balanced (182 yards passing and 176 running), Reeves was disappointed by the inability to get into the end zone more often.

The Raiders' Burgess Owens grumbled that the Broncos' only TD was tainted. He said wide receiver Rick Upchurch was out of bounds when he caught Craig Morton's pitch for a 44-yard score.

Fred Steinfort's 29-yard field goal in the second quarter gave Denver its winning margin. But Steinfort had a rough afternoon. He missed on five other field-goal tries, four in the fourth quarter.

SEPTEMBER 6
SCORE BY PERIODS

Oakland	7	0	0	0—7
Denver	6	3	0	0—9

SCORING

Oakland—Chester 9 pass from Plunkett (Bahr kick).
Denver—Upchurch 44 pass from Morton (kick failed).
Denver—Field goal Steinfort 29.

TEAM STATISTICS

	Oakland	Denver
First downs	12	21
Rushes-Yards	24-81	45-176
Passing yards	84	182
Sacks by-Yards	2-12	5-41
Return yards	97	87
Passes	14-24-2	12-25-0
Punts	6-53.3	4-35.3
Fumbles-Lost	1-1	1-1
Penalties-Yards	9-73	7-54
Time of possession	24:20	35:40
Attendance—74,796.		

INDIVIDUAL STATISTICS

Rushing—Oakland, van Eeghen 8-30, Whittington 8-24, King 7-22, Plunkett 1-5; Denver, Preston 19-87, Parros 15-47, Reed 7-29, Morton 2-6, Watson 1-6, Canada 1-1.

Passing—Oakland, Plunkett 14-24-2—125; Denver, Morton 12-25-0—194.

Receiving—Oakland, Chester 5-33, King 4-30, Whittington 2-11, Branch 1-38, van Eeghen 1-8, Chandler 1-5; Denver, Moses 2-29, Odoms 2-38, Upchurch 2-64, Preston 3-21, Watson 1-28, Egloff 1-8, Reed 1-6.

Kickoff Returns—Oakland, Barnwell 3-71; Denver, Manning 2-33.

Punt Returns—Oakland, Matthews 1-26; Denver, Upchurch 2-24, Manning 3-31.

Interceptions—Denver, Evans 1-1, Thompson 1-0.

Punting—Oakland, Guy 5-57.6, Bahr 1-32.0; Denver, Prestridge 4-35.3.

Field Goals—Oakland, Bahr 0-1; Denver, Steinfort, 1-6.

CHARGERS 44, BROWNS 14

CLEVELAND—It was no contest. The game was even more lopsided than the score indicates. The Chargers completely had their way with the Browns.

"Everything fell into place," said Chargers Coach Don Coryell. "I can't recall another game where just about everything we did worked."

Everything ran from stomps around end by fullback Chuck Muncie to seemingly uncontested slant-ins to Charlie Joiner.

The pulverization began immediately. After the opening kickoff, the Chargers stopped the Browns on downs, then scored on their first possession, with James Brooks going over from the 4.

At one point, Dan Fouts completed 15 consecutive passes, breaking the Chargers record of 13 set by John Hadl in 1964. He finished the night 19-for-25 for 330 yards and three touchdowns.

Six of those passes went to Joiner, who said that it was a case of taking what the defense offered. "I told the coaches upstairs that their cornerbacks were playing extremely wide, so we decided to use a lot of inside slants," said Joiner.

Mixing that pattern with jaunts by Muncie, who ran for 161 yards and one TD on 24 carries, the Chargers marched 80 yards in seven plays after the second-half kickoff. A 13-yard toss to Brooks made the score 27-7.

The Browns narrowed the gap on a four-yard scoring toss from Brian Sipe to Mike Pruitt, but Fouts threw for two more TDs and Rolf Benirschke kicked his third field goal.

Sipe set Browns records for completions (31)

and attempts (57) and totaled 375 yards, but penalties and poor performance in the scoring zone kept Cleveland from challenging.

Said Browns Coach Sam Rutigliano: "We were never able to get into a game plan. We were immediately put into an urgency situation, both on offense and defense. We expected a shootout, but we didn't expect it to be so one-sided."

MONDAY, SEPTEMBER 7
SCORE BY PERIODS

San Diego	10	10	14	10—44
Cleveland	0	7	7	0—14

SCORING

San Diego—J. Brooks 4 run (Benirschke kick).
San Diego—Field goal Benirschke 50.
Cleveland—Feacher 18 pass from Sipe (Jacobs kick).
San Diego—Muncie 9 run (Benirschke kick).
San Diego—Field goal Benirschke 43.
San Diego—J. Brooks 13 pass from Fouts (Benirschke kick).
Cleveland—G. Pruitt 4 pass from Sipe (Jacobs kick).
San Diego—Bauer 4 pass from Fouts (Benirschke kick).
San Diego—Field goal Benirschke 32.
San Diego—Smith 38 pass from Fouts (Benirschke kick).

TEAM STATISTICS

	San Diego	Cleveland
First downs	28	27
Rushes-Yards	41-205	14-53
Passing yards	330	366
Sacks by-Yards	2-9	0-0
Return yards	51	149
Passes	19-25-0	31-57-2
Punts	2-42.0	5-38.6
Fumbles-Lost	1-0	3-0
Penalties-Yards	8-45	6-55
Time of possession	31:27	28:33

Attendance—78,904.

INDIVIDUAL STATISTICS

Rushing—San Diego, Munice 24-161, J. Brooks 8-28, Fouts 2-9, Cappelletti 5-14, Luther 2-minus 7; Cleveland, M. Pruitt 8-30, G. Pruitt 1-11, Sipe 4-10, Hill 1-2.

Passing—San Diego, Fouts 19-25-0—330; Cleveland, Sipe 31-57-2—375.

Receiving—San Diego, Joiner 6-191, Muncie 4-23, Winslow 2-23, J. Brooks 2-9, Smith 1-38, B. Brooks 1-21, Scales 1-16, Sievers 1-5, Bauer 1-4; Cleveland, G. Pruitt 7-86, Newsome 6-87, M. Pruitt 6-30, Rucker 5-68, Logan 4-71, Hill 2-15, Feacher 1-18.

Kickoff Returns—San Diego, J. Brooks 1-29; Cleveland, White 4-90, Hall 1-16, C. Miller 3-35.

Punt Returns—San Diego, J. Brooks 2-22; Cleveland, Hall 1-8.

Interceptions—San Diego, M. Williams 1-0, Gregor 1-0.

Punting—San Diego, Roberts 2-42.0; Cleveland, Cox 5-38.6.

Field Goals—San Diego, Benirschke 3-3; Cleveland, Jacobs 0-1.

SECOND WEEK

DOLPHINS 3O, STEELERS 1O

MIAMI—Things were looking up for Miami, but the same couldn't be said for Pittsburgh. The Dolphins picked on the Steelers in a Thursday night nationally televised game.

The Dolphins did it with style, too, serving up some big gainers to their fans instead of the old grind-it-out technique they used so successfully in the 1970s.

Second-year quarterback David Woodley scored one touchdown himself on a sneak and passed 13 yards to running back Tony Nathan for another. Nathan rushed for 77 yards and caught Woodley passes for another 84. Said Miami Coach Don Shula:

"Nathan just did it all. He ran, he blocked and he caught."

Meanwhile, the Steelers were offering further evidence of a sharp decline after their four Super Bowl crowns. This was the first time since 1970 that they had opened the season with two defeats.

"We've got to win a game to realize we can win," said Terry Bradshaw, the Steelers' 33-year-old quarterback. "I think we need to relax, quit thinking about mistakes and have some fun."

One who had fun against the Steelers was Miami safety Glenn Blackwood, who racked up his second and third interceptions of the season. His first set up Woodley's sneak and the other set up Uwe von Schamann's 32-yard field goal.

One of the Dolphins' TDs came on an 87-yard punt return by rookie running back Tommy Vigorito in the third quarter.

THURSDAY, SEPTEMBER 10
SCORE BY PERIODS

Pittsburgh	3	7	0	0—10
Miami	0	13	14	3—30

SCORING

Pittsburgh—Field goal Trout 23.
Miami—Woodley 1 run (bad snap).
Miami—Franklin 1 run (von Schamann kick).
Pittsburgh—Smith 33 pass from Bradshaw (Trout kick).
Miami—Nathan 13 pass from Woodley (von Schamann kick).
Miami—Vigorito 87 punt return (von Schamann kick).
Miami—Field goal von Schamann 32.

TEAM STATISTICS

	Pittsburgh	Miami
First downs	15	25
Rushes-Yards	26-117	36-185
Passing yards	183	161
Sacks by-Yards	0-0	4-39
Return yards	155	205
Passes	15-33-2	14-34-1
Punts	6-37.2	3-40.0
Fumbles-Lost	1-0	1-0
Penalties-Yards	10-84	5-43
Time of possession	30:14	29:46

Attendance—74,190.

INDIVIDUAL STATISTICS

Rushing—Pittsburgh, Harris 13-38, Pollard 11-63, Bradshaw 2-16; Miami, Nathan 10-77, Bennett 10-42, Woodley 4-26, Franklin 10-37, Hill 1-1, Vigorito 1-2.

Passing—Pittsburgh, Bradshaw 15-33-2—222; Miami, Woodley 14-34-1—161.

Receiving—Pittsburgh, Stallworth 4-63, Cunningham 4-62, Smith 4-78, Harris 1-9, Pollard 2-10; Miami, Harris 2-55, Nathan 8-84, Vigorito 2-1, Bennett 1-10, Cefalo 1-11.

Kickoff Returns—Pittsburgh, Anderson 4-105, Dirden 1-14; Miami, Walker 2-55.

Punt Returns—Pittsburgh, Anderson 1-6, Smith 1-5; Miami, Vigorito 1-87, Bessillieu 1-12.

Interceptions—Pittsburgh, Lambert 1-25; Miami, Blackwood 2-51.

Punting—Pittsburgh, Colquitt 6-37.2; Miami, Orosz 3-40.0.

Field Goals—Pittsburgh, Trout 1-2; Miami, von Schamann 1-3.

SAINTS 23, RAMS 17

NEW ORLEANS—With a fired-up defense that sacked Los Angeles quarterback Pat Haden three times and picked up four turnovers, the Saints equaled their victory total for 1980, producing a cheerful locker room scene in the Superdome for the first time in two years.

Archie Manning, the veteran quarterback who suffered through the Saints' 1-15 season in 1980, cautioned that one win does not a season make. But it sure helps, said Manning, who was sidelined with a pulled hamstring in his first series against the Rams.

The Saints had opened the season with a 27-0 loss to Atlanta, reminding New Orleans fans of the dreadful 1980 campaign. Said Manning, "Certainly, a win is the best remedy. This season is a whole different deal. A win just makes the whole thing better."

The most obvious difference in this edition of the Saints was the presence of a running attack. Their No. 1 draft choice, Heisman Trophy winner George Rogers of South Carolina, set two club records as he carried the ball 29 times and gained 162 yards.

"After the loss to Atlanta, a lot of us were kind of down," Rogers said. "We wanted to come back and prove that we did have a good team and that we could play under pressure."

The Saints got inside the Los Angeles 20-yard line five times in the first half and took a 16-3 lead, on three field goals by Benny Ricardo and a five-yard touchdown run by Rogers.

Although Haden threw second-half TD passes of nine yards and 15 yards to Preston Dennard, the Rams never could get closer than six points. New Orleans clinched its victory on a 23-yard scoring pass from Bobby Scott to Wes Chandler midway through the fourth quarter. That gave the Saints a 23-10 lead and it redeemed Scott for having thrown interceptions on his previous three passes.

Scott, subbing for Manning, was only 4-for-14 and the New Orleans fans chanted "We want Wilson!" after Scott's three straight interceptions. David Wilson, the Saints' rookie quarterback, had been impressive in preseason play.

Coach Bum Phillips said he never considered using Wilson, and Scott ignored the boos. "If you win the game, they're going to be hollering for you," said the quarterback. "Heck, they don't bother me."

Rogers came through with some key yardage as the Saints kept possession of the ball and ran down the clock in the final minutes.

"No, I didn't draft him for the last three minutes of the game," said Phillips. "I drafted him for the first 57."

As for Rogers' rushing total, Phillips said, "I thought it was a team effort. Although George made 162 yards, I don't think he made 'em by himself."

Coach Ray Malavasi, his Rams off to an 0-2 start, said, "We didn't play well in the first half, and that's what did it to us. We had bad field position most of the time."

SEPTEMBER 13
SCORE BY PERIODS

Los Angeles	0	3	7	7—17
New Orleans	6	10	0	7—23

SCORING

New Orleans—Field goal Ricardo 45.
New Orleans—Field goal Ricardo 46.
New Orleans—G. Rogers 5 run (Ricardo kick).
New Orleans—Field goal Ricardo 34.
Los Angeles—Field goal Corral 40.
Los Angeles—Dennard 9 pass from Haden (Corral kick).
New Orleans—Chandler 23 pass from Scott (Ricardo kick).
Los Angeles—Dennard 15 pass from Haden (Corral kick).

TEAM STATISTICS

	Los Angeles	New Orleans
First downs	17	19
Rushes-Yards	24-88	50-226
Passing yards	167	78
Sacks by-Yards	1-12	3-34
Return yards	162	142
Passes	20-34-2	4-17-3
Punts	5-39.6	2-32.0
Fumbles-Lost	3-2	3-0
Penalties-Yards	8-50	9-70
Time of possession	25:22	34:38
Attendance—62,063.		

INDIVIDUAL STATISTICS

Rushing—Los Angeles, Tyler 16-59, Bryant 5-18, Haden 3-11; New Orleans, G. Rogers 29-162, W. Wilson 11-37, Holmes 5-21, Manning 1-13, Caster 1-minus 3, Scott 3-minus 4.

Passing—Los Angeles, Haden 20-34-2—201, New Orleans, Scott 4-14-3—90, Manning 0-2-0—0, Myers 0-1-0—0.

Receiving—Los Angeles, Bryant 6-19, Dennard 3-37, D. Hill 2-36, Moore 2-27, Tyler 2-25, Waddy 2-25, Childs 2-20, Guman 1-12; New Orleans, Caster 1-31, Chandler 1-23, Harris 1-20, Hardy 1-16.

Kickoff Returns—Los Angeles, D. Hill 6-116; New Orleans, J. Rogers 3-64, Groth 1-12.

Punt Returns—New Orleans, Groth 4-32.

Interceptions—Los Angeles, P. Thomas 1-26, Jack Youngblood 1-20, Perry 1-0; New Orleans, Wattelet 1-16, Nairne 1-18.

Punting—Los Angeles, Corral 5-39.6; New Orleans, Erxleben 2-32.0.

Field Goals—Los Angeles, Corral 1-1; New Orleans, Ricardo 3-3.

FALCONS 31, PACKERS 17

GREEN BAY—The Green Bay Packers found out in a hurry why the Atlanta Falcons had been picked by many experts to win the

New Orleans' George Rogers showed why he was the Heisman Trophy winner and No. 1 choice in the NFL draft when he carried the ball 29 times for 162 yards—both club records—as the Saints beat the Rams, 23-17.

Second Week—Continued

NFL championship. Green Bay had a 17-0 lead over the Falcons after three quarters only to wind up losing, 31-17. Atlanta produced 24 points in a span of 4 minutes, 24 seconds and 14 of those points came within 48 seconds.

"The tide is going to turn against you every once in a while," said Packers quarterback Lynn Dickey. "We had a tidal wave today."

"An avalanche" corrected Packers Coach Bart Starr. "It's one thing having points scored against you, and quite another to have them scored all at once."

Dickey threw two touchdown passes and Jan Stenerud kicked a 44-yard field goal as Green Bay built its lead. The 55,382 fans in Lambeau Field stood and applauded the Packers as the third quarter ended.

And then the wheels came off for the Packers. Mick Luckhurst kicked a field goal for Atlanta's first points. After the Pack failed to move, Reggie Smith fielded a line-drive punt from Ray Stachowicz, slipped between four Packer defenders and returned 53 yards to the Green Bay 2. William Andrews scored on the next play and it was 17-10.

The next Atlanta possession consisted of two plays. Steve Bartkowski passed for 22 yards to Alfred Jenkins and then went back to Jenkins for a 30-yard TD play. That tied the score.

Atlanta kicked off, and Dickey attempted a pass. Linebacker Fulton Kuykendall intercepted and returned 20 yards for the TD that put Atlanta ahead, 24-17, with eight minutes left.

The Falcons' final TD came with 1:34 left, when linebacker Joel Williams snapped up a fumble by Terdell Middleton and scampered 57 yards into the end zone.

Leeman Bennett, the Atlanta coach, said of the comeback, "The way I look at it, we were three plays behind (when it was 17-0). We had the big plays. We sure did."

The Falcons overcame injuries to both their quarterbacks. Bartkowski went out with a rib injury when he was hit by defensive end Mike Butler in the first half. Mike Moroski stepped in and suffered a broken collarbone, necessitating Bartkowski's return.

The Packers stopped the Falcons twice at the goal line in the first half, once on a fourth-down tackle of Andrews by Rich Wingo and Johnnie Gray and once by George Cumby's interception.

SEPTEMBER 13
SCORE BY PERIODS

Atlanta	0	0	0	31	31
Green Bay	7	7	3	0	17

SCORING

Green Bay—Swanke 2 pass from Dickey (Stenerud kick).
Green Bay—Ellis 11 pass from Dickey (Stenerud kick).
Green Bay—Field goal Stenerud 44.
Atlanta—Field goal Luckhurst 32.
Atlanta—Andrews 2 run (Luckhurst kick).

Atlanta—Jenkins 30 pass from Bartkowski (Luckhurst kick).
Atlanta—Kuykendall 20 pass interception (Luckhurst kick).
Atlanta—Williams 57 fumble return (Luckhurst kick).

TEAM STATISTICS

	Atlanta	Green Bay
First downs	19	22
Rushes-Yards	31-116	23-96
Passing yards	219	300
Sacks by-Yards	5-42	3-16
Return yards	190	63
Passes	17-32-4	30-44-3
Punts	4-40.5	6-39.2
Fumbles-Lost	1-0	3-2
Penalties-Yards	4-68	3-10
Time of possession	30:01	29:59
Attendance—55,382.		

INDIVIDUAL STATISTICS

Rushing—Atlanta, Andrews 19-87, Cain 9-15, Moroski 1-14, Bartkowski 2-0; Green Bay, Middleton 12-39, Ellis 9-59, Dickey 1-minus 4, Atkins 1-2.

Passing—Atlanta, Bartkowski 16-30-4—233, Moroski 1-2-0—2; Green Bay, Dickey 30-44-3—342.

Receiving—Atlanta, Miller 2-26, Francis 4-69, Cain 4-15, Andrews 1-9, Jenkins 6-116; Green Bay, Middleton 5-33, Lofton 8-179, Swanke 1-2, Ellis 8-47, Coffman 6-68, A. Thompson 1-5, Nixon 1-8.

Kickoff Returns—Atlanta, R. Smith 3-74, Mayberry 1-15; Green Bay, none.

Punt Returns—Atlanta, R. Smith 2-61; Green Bay, Nixon 2-17.

Interceptions—Atlanta, Kuykendall 1-20, Pridemore 1-2, Glazebrook 1-18; Green Bay, Cumby 1-17, Harvey 1-13, McCoy 1-16, Lee 1-0.

Punting—Atlanta, James 4-40.5; Green Bay, Stachowicz 6-39.2.

Field Goals—Atlanta, Luckhurst 1-2; Green Bay, Stenerud 1-1.

COWBOYS 30, CARDINALS 17

IRVING—Dallas raced out of the starting blocks to score on its first five possessions and fought off gambling St Louis, which went for the big play at almost every opportunity.

"Sure," said Cardinals Coach Jim Hanifan, "we were gambling. We tried some things. We thought they might have a chance to work."

Neil Lomax, making his debut as a starting quarterback, brought about by the knee injury to Jim Hart in the season opener, had his moments. Lomax completed only 14 of 41 passes, but he picked up 295 yards. And if St. Louis had not been plagued by several dropped passes, it might have been closer.

"I am very high on the young man," Hanifan said of Lomax. "He might have been a little nervous, but he got himself out of trouble and showed a lot of poise. And that came against a team that can give a quarterback a lot of problems."

The Cardinals tried the bomb early and often, ran a handoff on the opening kickoff and tried an onside kickoff after their first TD.

"We thought they would have to try to win on big plays," said Dallas Coach Tom Landry. "They had to do that to stay in the game, the way we were scoring. They couldn't just go with their regular running game."

Dallas drove 73, 55, 88, 41 and 65 yards in the first half to score three touchdowns—all by fullback Ron Springs—and a pair of field goals by Rafael Septien.

St. Louis countered with a touchdown pass of 62 yards from Lomax to running back Willard Harrell and an 11-yard scoring run by Theotis Brown that followed a 60-yard pass from Lomax to Roy Green, who previously was playing defensive back.

Dallas quarterback Danny White completed 21 of 29 passes for 240 yards while Tony Dorsett ran for 129 yards on 16 carries. The Cardinals' Ottis Anderson, who had averaged 122 yards against Dallas in his previous four games, carried 16 times for 80 yards.

Temperatures on the artificial turf were in excess of 100 degrees, causing many players to stop and try to catch their breath from time to time. Landry wore his coat and tie throughout the game, but said afterward, "I'll probably have to throw the coat in the waste paper basket. I think it's about used up."

SEPTEMBER 13
SCORE BY PERIODS

St. Louis	7	7	0	3	—17
Dallas	14	13	3	0	—30

SCORING

Dallas—Springs 1 run (Septien kick).
St. Louis—Harrell 62 pass from Lomax (O'Donoghue kick).
Dallas—Springs 4 run (Septien kick).
Dallas—Field goal Septien 47.
Dallas—Springs 1 run (Septien kick).
St. Louis—T. Brown 11 run (O'Donoghue kick).
Dallas—Field goal Septien 32.
Dallas—Field goal Septien 25.
St. Louis—Field goal O'Donoghue 24.

TEAM STATISTICS

	St. Louis	Dallas
First downs	18	24
Rushes-Yards	27-142	35-181
Passing yards	262	210
Sacks by-Yards	3-30	4-33
Return yards	156	72
Passes	14-41-2	21-29-1
Punts	4-36.0	4-43.3
Fumbles-Lost	0-0	2-1
Penalties-Yards	11-84	6-35
Time of possession	28:12	31:48
Attendance—63,602.		

INDIVIDUAL STATISTICS

Rushing—St. Louis, Anderson 16-80, T. Brown 4-31, Lomax 2-18, Mitchell 4-10, Morris 1-3; Dallas, Dorsett 16-129, Springs 15-45, J. Jones 3-7, D. White 1-0.

Passing—St. Louis, Lomax 14-41-2—295; Dallas, D. White 21-29-1—240.

Receiving—St. Louis, Anderson 4-60, Tilley 3-46, Harrell 1-62, Green 1-60, T. Brown 1-28, Mitchell 1-16, Combs 1-12, Floyd 1-5, LaFleur 1-6; Dallas, Dorsett 5-45, Johnson 4-80, Springs 4-23, Hill 2-30, Pearson 2-27, Cosbie 2-23, DuPree 1-7, Saldi 1-5.

Kickoff Returns—St. Louis, Mitchell 1-57, Green 5-81; Dallas, Fellows 2-37, Cosbie 1-0.

Punt Returns—St. Louis, Mitchell 1-18; Dallas, Fellows 3-14.

Interceptions—St. Louis, Greene 1-0; Dallas, Waters 2-21.

Punting—St. Louis, Birdsong 4-36.0; Dallas, D. White 4-43.3.

Field Goals—St. Louis, O'Donoghue 1-2; Dallas, Septien 3-3.

CHIEFS 19, BUCCANEERS 10

KANSAS CITY—With the help of their special teams, the Chiefs scored their second victory, downing Tampa Bay, whose special teams' performance was less than overpowering.

The Chiefs' offense and defense were miserable in the first half. But Nick Lowery kicked four field goals, J. T. Smith returned five Tampa Bay punts for 107 yards and Bob Grupp averaged 43.3 yards per kick.

Meanwhile, the Tampa Bay punting unit handed Kansas City its only touchdown before the game was three minutes old. The Bucs were on their 20 when the snap from center rolled back to punter Tom Blanchard, who was tackled on the 14. Two plays later, Ted McKnight scored for the Chiefs from the 8.

Blanchard later fumbled a snap and got off a 19-yard punt.

"We played horrible special teams," said Tampa Bay Coach John McKay. "The problem just popped up today. I thought coming in here there was a chance we would lose, but I never thought it would be because of the special teams."

Lowery kicked field goals of 20, 20, 42 and 41 yards. Since replacing Jan Stenerud in 1980, Lowery had kicked 27 field goals in 34 tries. His second field goal against Tampa gave the Chiefs the lead for good in the third period.

"I believe that any time we get the ball to the 35, we can come away with at least a field goal," said Chiefs quarterback Bill Kenney. "I see Nick in practice and I hold for him occasionally. He's safe from 50 yards in. It's a tremendous feeling for the offense having him on the sidelines."

Smith, the NFL's top punt returner in 1980 with a 14.5 average, ran one back against Tampa Bay for 62 yards to set up a Lowery field goal that tied the score.

Doug Williams completed 20 of 43 passes for 294 yards, but Kansas City held the Bucs' ground attack to 12 yards on 23 carries.

With the victory, the Chiefs were 2-0 for the first time since 1969, when they went on to win Super Bowl IV.

SEPTEMBER 13
SCORE BY PERIODS

Tampa Bay	7	3	0	0	—10
Kansas City	7	3	3	6	—19

SCORING

Kansas City—McKnight 8 run (Lowery kick).
Tampa Bay—Wilder 2 run (Yepremian kick).
Tampa Bay—Field goal Yepremian 44.
Kansas City—Field goal Lowery 20.

Second Week—Continued

Kansas City—Field goal Lowery 20.
Kansas City—Field goal Lowery 42.
Kansas City—Field goal Lowery 41.

TEAM STATISTICS

	Tampa Bay	Kansas City
First downs	17	13
Rushes-Yards	23-12	41-157
Passing yards	286	99
Sacks by-Yards	0-0	1-8
Return yards	115	171
Passes	20-43-0	12-25-0
Punts	8-36.3	7-43.3
Fumbles-Lost	3-0	1-0
Penalties-Yards	3-27	7-62
Time of possession	26:17	33:43

Attendance—50,555.

INDIVIDUAL STATISTICS

Rushing—Tampa Bay, R. Bell 8-9, Wilder 5-5, Williams 1-3, Blanchard 1-0, Eckwood 8-minus 5; Kansas City, Delaney 13-57, Hadnot 9-36, McKnight 12-33, Kenney 5-24, B. Jackson 1-8, Carson 1-minus 1.

Passing—Tampa Bay, Williams 20-43-0—294; Kansas City, Kenney 12-25-0—99.

Receiving—Tampa Bay, R. Bell 6-70, House 5-87, Jones 5-58, Eckwood 2-45, Giles 1-24, T. Bell 1-10; Kansas City, Carson 2-35, Rome 2-26, Dixon 2-18, Smith 2-9, McKnight 2-6, Hadnot 1-10, Delaney 1-minus 5.

Kickoff Returns—Tampa Bay, Owens 4-62, G. Davis 1-21; Kansas City, Carson 2-42, B. Jackson 1-22.

Punt Returns—Tampa Bay, T. Bell 6-32; Kansas City, Smith 5-107.

Interceptions—None.

Punting—Tampa Bay, Blanchard 8-36.3; Kansas City, Grupp 7-43.3.

Field Goals—Tampa Bay, Yepremian 1-1; Kansas City, Lowery 4-4.

49ers 28, BEARS 17

SAN FRANCISCO—Walter Payton, the Chicago running back, fumbled twice at critical times and the Bears went down to a second straight defeat.

One of Payton's fumbles, recovered by Dan Bunz at the Chicago 33 with the Bears leading 17-14 in the third quarter, set up the 49ers' go-ahead touchdown, a five-yard pass from Joe Montana to tight end Charle Young.

Then, in the final period, with Chicago driving for a winning TD, Payton fumbled on first down at the San Francisco two-yard line and Craig Puki recovered for the 49ers. In the closing minutes, running back Ricky Patton upstaged his famous cousin—Payton—by scooting 12 yards for the clinching score.

"We saw ourselves self-destruct," said Bears Coach Neill Armstrong. "Amazing, isn't it? How many times is Walter going to fumble the ball like that? He can go half a year without fumbling once."

Montana threw TD passes of 31 yards to Patton and 46 yards to Freddie Solomon to give the Niners a 14-0 lead. He finished the day 20-for-32 for 287 yards, with no interceptions.

Then Payton learned about the rebuilt 49ers defense—linebackers Bunz, Puki, Jack Reyn-

olds and Milt McColl and the secondary of rookies Ronnie Lott, Eric Wright and Carlton Williamson, plus third-year safety Dwight Hicks.

"The 49er defensive backs played a good game and their linebackers never let us break into the open," said Payton, who was limited to 97 yards in 27 carries.

SEPTEMBER 13
SCORE BY PERIODS

Chicago	0	10	7	0—	17
San Francisco	7	7	7	7—	28

SCORING

San Francisco—Patton 31 pass from Montana (Bahr kick).
San Francisco—Solomon 46 pass from Montana (Bahr kick).
Chicago—Payton 2 run (Thomas kick).
Chicago—Field goal Thomas 37.
Chicago—Earl 12 pass from Evans (Thomas kick).
San Francisco—Young 5 pass from Montana (Bahr kick).
San Francisco—Patton 12 run (Bahr kick).

TEAM STATISTICS

	Chicago	San Francisco
First downs	18	20
Rushes-Yards	36-123	32-125
Passing yards	216	287
Sacks by-Yards	0-0	1-0
Return yards	106	110
Passes	19-33-1	20-32-0
Punts	6-41.5	5-38.0
Fumbles-Lost	2-2	2-2
Penalties-Yards	4-16	3-25
Time of possession	25:16	34:44

Attendance—49,520.

INDIVIDUAL STATISTICS

Rushing—Chicago, Payton 27-97, Suhey 6-25, Evans 2-7, Neal 1-minus 6; San Francisco, Patton 14-67, Cooper 14-56, Easley 3-5, Solomon 1-minus 3.

Passing—Chicago, Evans 19-33-1—216; San Francisco, Montana 20-32-0—287.

Receiving—Chicago, Watts 5-74, Earl 4-48, Williams 4-25, Payton 3-11, Baschnagel 2-41, Margerum 1-17; San Francisco, Clark 6-81, Solomon 5-113, Cooper 4-28, Patton 2-34, Young 2-19, Elliott 1-12.

Kickoff Returns—Chicago, Williams 3-59, Baschnagel 1-23; San Francisco, Lott 3-55, Davis 1-0.

Punt Returns—Chicago, J. Fisher 2-24; San Francisco, Solomon 4-40, Hicks 1-7.

Interceptions—San Francisco, Hicks 1-8.

Punting—Chicago, Parsons 6-41.5; San Francisco, Miller 5-38.0.

Field Goals—Chicago, Thomas 1-2; San Francisco, Bahr 0-2.

SEAHAWKS 13, BRONCOS 10

SEATTLE—Victory-starved Seattle fans finally were rewarded and 58,513 of them showed their appreciation with a standing ovation after the Seahawks' victory over Denver.

It was Seattle's first home victory since 1979. Efren Herrera's second field goal of the game gave Seattle its winning margin in the third period.

Herrera's fake field goal try led to his winning effort. He appeared about to attempt a

51-yarder, but instead quarterback Jim Zorn took the snap and fired a 21-yard pass to rookie David Hughes. Then Herrera booted one from 22 yards.

Seattle grabbed a 10-3 edge on Zorn's three-yard TD pass to tight end Dennis Boyd and Herrera's 43-yard field goal. Denver tied it when Craig Morton led an 85-yard drive, capped by the 38-year-old quarterback's 11-yard TD toss to Riley Odoms.

The Seahawks dominated the second half, leading Denver Coach Dan Reeves to comment: "Everything we accomplished by beating Oakland last week we lost by losing to Seattle. We didn't execute at all, especially in the third quarter."

Seahawks Coach Jack Patera praised his defensive unit, his special teams and the running of Sherman Smith, Seattle's leading rusher in 1979 who sat out 1980 with injuries. Smith ran 11 times for 58 yards.

"I can't tell you how much we needed this victory," said Manu Tuiasosopo, the Seahawks' defensive co-captain. "Denver is not a team to be taken lightly. They beat the world champs last week. This is really going to help us."

SEPTEMBER 13
SCORE BY PERIODS

Denver	3	7	0	0—10
Seattle	7	3	3	0—13

SCORING

Denver—Field goal Steinfort 30.
Seattle—Boyd 3 pass from Zorn (Herrera kick).
Seattle—Field goal Herrera 43.
Denver—Odoms 11 pass from Morton (Steinfort kick).
Seattle—Field goal Herrera 22.

TEAM STATISTICS

	Denver	Seattle
First downs	16	18
Rushes-Yards	24-110	29-111
Passing yards	142	156
Sacks by-Yards	5-43	3-19
Return yards	91	92
Passes	14-25-1	24-34-2
Punts	6-42.5	5-37.0
Fumbles-Lost	1-1	2-0
Penalties-Yards	6-60	4-40
Time of possession	25:31	34:29
Attendance—58,513.		

INDIVIDUAL STATISTICS

Rushing—Denver, Parros 13-69, Reed 5-23, Preston 6-18; Seattle, Smith 11-58, Jodat 7-23, Hughes 8-21, Lane 1-5, Zorn 2-4.

Passing—Denver, Morton 14-25-1—161; Seattle, Zorn 24-34-2—199.

Receiving—Denver, Preston 4-27, Odoms 3-35, Watson 2-36, Reed 2-22, Parros 2-16, Moses 1-25; Seattle, Hughes 6-59, Largent 5-45, McCullum 4-38, Sawyer 2-23, Smith 2-17, Moore 2-8, Boyd 1-3, Lane 1-3, Jodat 1-3.

Kickoff Returns—Denver, Manning 4-58; Seattle, Johnson 2-45, Lane 1-17.

Punt Returns—Denver, Manning 3-3; Seattle, Lewis 3-30.

Interceptions—Denver, Manor 1-16, Thompson 1-14; Seattle, Butler 1-0.

Punting—Denver, Prestridge 6-42.5; Seattle, West 5-37.0.

Field Goals—Denver, Steinfort 1-1; Seattle, Herrera 2-2.

CHARGERS 28, LIONS 23

SAN DIEGO—It took some last-seconds heroics by both the offense and defense for San Diego to subdue Detroit.

It appeared the Chargers had wrapped up their second victory on John Cappelletti's two-yard touchdown dash with 56 seconds left. That gave San Diego a 28-23 edge after Ed Murray's third field goal had pushed Detroit in front, 23-21, with less than five minutes to play.

But Gary Danielson then connected on three passes to spark the fired-up Lions to the San Diego 8-yard line. With seven seconds to play, Danielson fired another pass toward David Hill in the end zone. Safety Frank Duncan intercepted it on the 1-yard line to save San Diego's victory.

The Lions, the NFL's No. 1 team in defense against the rush in 1980, limited the Chargers to 57 yards on the ground, 36 of them by Chuck Muncie, who scored two Charger TDs.

"Detroit came out here with upset on their minds and played a hell of a game," said Chargers quarterback Dan Fouts, who completed 18 of 25 passes for 316 yards. Fouts became the seventh active quarterback to rack up 20,000 yards passing for a career.

Billy Sims led Detroit's rushing attack with 98 yards in 23 carries, including a TD on a 12-yard run in the fourth period.

The Lions took a 10-7 edge in the third quarter when Danielson scrambled for an 11-yard TD. Murray's 37-yard field goal boosted the edge to 13-7 before San Diego regained the lead, 14-13, on Kellen Winslow's seven-yard TD reception from Fouts.

Sims and Muncie each tallied a touchdown before Murray's 30-yard field goal put Detroit ahead, 23-21.

SEPTEMBER 13
SCORE BY PERIODS

Detroit	3	0	10	10—23
San Diego	7	0	7	14—28

SCORING

San Diego—Muncie 1 run (Benirschke kick).
Detroit—Field goal Murray 18.
Detroit—Danielson 11 run (Murray kick).
Detroit—Field goal Murray 37.
San Diego—Winslow 7 pass from Fouts (Benirschke kick).
Detroit—Sims 12 run (Murray kick).
San Diego—Muncie 1 run (Benirschke kick).
Detroit—Field goal Murray 30.
San Diego—Cappelletti 2 run (Benirschke kick).

TEAM STATISTICS

	Detroit	San Diego
First downs	26	17
Rushes-Yards	41-178	24-57
Passing yards	207	310
Sacks by-Yards	1-6	3-22
Return yards	149	118
Passes	19-27-1	18-25-1
Punts	3-36.7	3-41.7
Fumbles-Lost	1-1	3-1
Penalties-Yards	4-35	4-59
Time of possession	38:19	21:41
Attendance—51,624.		

Second Week—Continued

Rushing—Detroit, Sims 23-98, Bussey 9-40, Danielson 4-14, L. Thompson 1-14, King 2-7, Kane 2-5; San Diego, Muncie 15-36, Fouts 6-17, Cappelletti 3-4.

Passing—Detroit, Danielson 18-26-1—213, Skladany 1-1-0—16; San Diego, Fouts 18-25-1—316.

Receiving—Detroit, Scott 6-84, Kane 5-38, Bussey 3-31, Sims 2-53, Callicutt 1-16, L. Thompson 1-5, Norris 1-2; San Diego, Joiner 7-166, Winslow 3-35, Sievers 3-26, Scales 2-57, Muncie 2-23, J. Brooks 1-9.

Kickoff Returns—Detroit, Martin 2-41, Hall 2-49, King 1-14; San Diego, J. Brooks, 3-88, Shaw 1-15, C. Williams 1-15.

Punt Returns—Detroit, Martin 2-23.

Interceptions—Detroit, Allen 1-22; San Diego, Duncan 1-0.

Punting—Detroit, Skladany 3-36.7; San Diego, Roberts 3-41.7.

Field Goals—Detroit, Murray 3-3; San Diego, None attempted.

GIANTS 17, REDSKINS 7

WASHINGTON—Defensive end George Martin led the cheers as New York celebrated its first victory of the season. Martin had been a ringleader, scooping up a fumble by Joe Theismann and rambling eight yards to score the clinching touchdown with 2:43 left.

"I always enjoyed scoring a touchdown, but the excitement just isn't the same after the first one because I've had four, you know," Martin said, tongue-in-cheek.

In 1977, Martin scored on a 30-yard interception return against Theismann. In '78, against Atlanta, he took a lateral after a blocked field goal attempt and went 11 yards for a TD. In 1980, lining up as a tight end, he caught a four-yard TD pass that helped upend Dallas.

Martin always seems to have a good day against the Redskins. In 1978, he sacked Theismann four times in a 17-6 Giants victory. This time, he had one sack—for a nine-yard loss.

"It's nothing personal against Theismann," said Martin, explaining his touchdown play. "In fact, Phil Tabor deserves the credit for this one. I really hammered Joe and caused the fumble."

Theismann was back to pass, trying to overcome the Giants' 10-7 lead, when Tabor came in untouched from right defensive end. Martin, the left end, picked up the loose ball and scored.

Theismann hit on 27 of 48 passes for 318 yards, all career highs, but produced only a six-yard TD pass to Ricky Thompson. Billy Taylor's five-yard TD run for New York tied the score.

The Redskins lost three fumbles and an interception, were penalized 97 yards and their running game accounted for only 65 yards.

Running back Joe Washington, the Redskins' top receiver, went out with a torn Achilles tendon on the game's first play. Later,

the 'Skins lost guard Russ Grimm (torn cartilage in his left knee), linebacker Monte Coleman (shoulder fracture) and fullback John Riggins (bruised right thigh).

SEPTEMBER 13
SCORE BY PERIODS

New York Giants	0	0	7	10—17
Washington	0	0	7	0— 7

SCORING

Washington—Thompson 6 pass from Theismann (Moseley kick).
New York—Taylor 5 run (Danelo kick).
New York—Field goal Danelo 25.
New York—Martin 8 fumble return (Danelo kick).

TEAM STATISTICS

	New York	Washington
First downs	10	19
Rushes-Yards	34-76	22-65
Passing yards	81	284
Sacks by-Yards	3-34	2-12
Return yards	102	98
Passes	8-27-1	27-48-1
Punts	11-46.5	10-39.6
Fumbles-Lost	2-1	3-3
Penalties-Yards	10-80	11-97
Time of possession	28:53	31:07
Attendance—53,343.		

INDIVIDUAL STATISTICS

Rushing—New York, Taylor 10-36, Perry 8-23, Kotar 13-38, Bright 2-minus 10, Perkins 1-minus 11; Washington, Riggins 6-28, Washington 1-2, Metcalf 7-23, Jackson 6-8, Harmon 1-4, Wonsley 1-0.

Passing—New York, Simms 8-27-1-93; Washington, Theismann 27-48-1—318.

Receiving—New York, Friede 2-33, Perkins 1-11, Perry 1-8, Shirk 4-41; Washington, Monk 7-74, Thompson 3-80, Warren 1-23, Harmon 5-34, Seay 1-28, Metcalf 5-36, Jackson 4-38, Wonsley 1-5.

Kickoff Returns—New York, Bright 2-65; Washington, Metcalf 3-58.

Punt Returns—New York, Bright 8-37; Washington, Metcalf 1-2, Nelms 5-38.

Interceptions—New York, Currier 1-0; Washington, Peters 1-0.

Punting—New York, Jennings 11-46.5; Washington, Connell 10-39.6.

Field Goals—New York, Danelo 1-1; Washington, Moseley 0-1.

OILERS 9, BROWNS 3

CLEVELAND—Houston Coach Ed Biles glanced at the Central Division standings and said, "It's a long year and two games don't make a season. A lot of people are going to write off Pittsburgh and Cleveland, but it's too early for that."

After two weeks, Biles' Oilers were tied with Cincinnati at 2-0 and Pittsburgh and Cleveland, the division favorites, shared last place at 0-2. Cleveland lost its first two games in 1980, too, before roaring back to take the division title.

The Browns' Brian Sipe threw 53 times, completing 25, against the Oilers. Although he gained 234 yards, only four of Sipe's completions were to wide receivers and the Oilers' defense pounded him repeatedly.

"We were in a 3-8 defense most of the time, keeping our defensive backs deep," said Houston safety Mike Reinfeldt. "Our goal was to take away all the deep passes and make Sipe dump it off to his running backs. That way, they have to work to sustain a 70-yard drive, and a lot of things can happen."

The Oilers sacked Sipe four times, for 31 yards lost. Two sacks came in succession when the Browns were close to scoring in the third quarter.

Houston's points came on field goals of 42, 27 and 36 yards by Toni Fritsch. David Jacobs booted a 29-yarder for Cleveland. He also was wide on a field goal attempt and defensive end Elvin Bethea blocked two other kicks.

"Never in my life had I blocked two field goals," said Bethea. "It's not too often you do that at my age (35)."

Fritsch criticized Jacobs' technique, saying, "He is too slow. He has to learn to speed up his approach and get under the ball. It's tough to get kicks up on that field (Municipal Stadium) anyway."

Cleveland held Earl Campbell to 42 yards before he left the game in the fourth quarter with a sore neck. But even that was little consolation to Browns Coach Sam Rutigliano. "It was no surprise containing Campbell," Rutigliano said. "I didn't do any back flips."

SEPTEMBER 13
SCORE BY PERIODS

Houston	3	0	3	3—9
Cleveland	0	3	0	0—3

SCORING

Houston—Field goal Fritsch 42.
Cleveland—Field goal Jacobs 29.
Houston—Field goal Fritsch 27.
Houston—Field goal Fritsch 36.

TEAM STATISTICS

	Houston	Cleveland
First downs	8	20
Rushes-Yards	30-91	24-99
Passing yards	118	203
Sacks by-Yards	4-31	2-13
Return yards	129	142
Passes	10-18-1	25-53-1
Punts	6-39.8	6-46.0
Fumbles-Lost	5-3	1-1
Penalties-Yards	5-36	7-65
Time of possession	26:08	33:52

Attendance—79,483.

INDIVIDUAL STATISTICS

Rushing—Houston, Campbell 17-42, Carpenter 7-40, Armstrong 4-10, Stabler 2-minus 1; Cleveland, White 9-40, M. Pruitt 5-30, C. Miller 6-16, G. Pruitt 4-13.

Passing—Houston, Stabler 10-18-1—131; Cleveland, Sipe 25-53-1—234.

Receiving—Houston, Carpenter 5-13, Burrough 3-57, Armstrong 1-48, Renfro 1-13; Cleveland, G. Pruitt 9-65, Newsome 6-57, C. Miller 4-28, Logan 2-20, Feacher 1-41, Adams 1-24, M. Pruitt 1-7, White 1-minus 8.

Kickoff Returns—Houston, Roaches 1-88, T. Wilson 1-16; Cleveland, Montgomery 4-77.

Punt Returns—Houston, Roaches 3-18; Cleveland, Montgomery 6-43.

Interceptions—Houston, Brazile 1-7; Cleveland, Darden 1-22.

Punting—Houston, Parsley 6-39.8; Cleveland, Cox 6-46.0.

Field Goals—Houston, Fritsch 3-3; Cleveland, Jacobs 1-4.

BENGALS 31, JETS 30

NEW YORK—After erasing a 21-0 deficit to beat Seattle in their opener, the Cincinnati Bengals were trailing the New York Jets, 17-3, in New York.

Then Ken Anderson fired a couple of touchdown passes and the Jets committed numerous errors, enabling Cincinnati to escape with a 31-30 triumph. After two weeks, the Bengals were one of six unbeaten AFC teams and the Jets were 0-2.

Penalties were a key factor for the Jets. They were assessed 111 yards on 14 penalties, four of which were charged to cornerback Bobby Jackson. Said Jets Coach Walt Michaels: "It was a comedy of errors. When you have as many penalties as we had, you can't win. We've talked and talked about mistakes. Believe it or not, we are trying to teach them to stay onsides."

Quarterback Richard Todd threw three touchdown passes, two of which gave the Jets a 14-0 lead. But Todd also fumbled on the New York 12 late in the game. Defensive end Mike St. Clair scooped up the ball and ran into the end zone to give Cincinnati a 31-23 lead.

Said Bengals Coach Forrest Gregg: "Our defense rose up and we came from behind again. We just kept working and struggling and things happened to our benefit."

The first of Pat Leahy's three field goals boosted New York's lead to 17-3. Then Anderson led a drive from midfield that culminated in his seven-yard TD toss to Steve Kreider. In the third period, following Leahy's second field goal, Anderson drove the Bengals 56 yards, capped by Archie Griffin's one-yard TD run that cut New York's lead to 20-17.

Leahy stretched that to 23-17 with his third field goal early in the fourth period. But Anderson again took charge, marching the Bengals 67 yards, ending with his three-yard TD pass to Griffin that put Cincinnati ahead, 24-23.

Just 31 seconds later, the Bengals padded their lead to eight points on Todd's fumble. Jim Breech, who had booted a 44-yard field goal in the second period, kicked the decisive extra point. Todd narrowed the gap to one point in the closing seconds when he hit Jerome Barkum with an eight-yard scoring pass, but the Bengals then ran out the clock.

SEPTEMBER 13
SCORE BY PERIODS

Cincinnati	0	10	7	14—31
New York Jets	0	17	3	10—30

SCORING

New York—Barkum 40 pass from Todd (Leahy kick).
New York—Walker 14 pass from Todd (Leahy kick).

Second Week—Continued

Cincinnati—Field goal Breech 44.
New York—Field goal Leahy 49.
Cincinnati—Kreider 7 pass from Anderson (Breech kick).
New York—Field goal Leahy 23.
Cincinnati—A. Griffin 1 run (Breech kick).
New York—Field goal Leahy 27.
Cincinnati—A. Griffin 3 pass from Anderson (Breech kick).
Cincinnati—St. Clair 12 fumble return (Breech kick).
New York—Barkum 8 pass from Todd (Leahy kick).

TEAM STATISTICS

	Cincinnati	New York
First downs	22	19
Rushes-Yards	29-77	30-164
Passing yards	227	224
Sacks by-Yards	4-27	4-19
Return yards	139	162
Passes	21-33-1	18-29-0
Punts	5-44.8	6-38.8
Fumbles-Lost	0-0	2-1
Penalties-Yards	6-61	14-111
Time of possession	29:36	30:24
Attendance—49,454.		

INDIVIDUAL STATISTICS

Rushing—Cincinnati, A. Griffin 15-49, Johnson 9-19, Anderson 5-9; New York, McNeil 13-78, Newton 7-28, Harper 3-23, Dierking 2-18, Long 2-13, Todd 2-9, Jones 1-minus 5.

Passing—Cincinnati, Anderson 21-33-1—246; New York, Todd 18-29-0—251.

Receiving—Cincinnati, A. Griffin 9-48, Curtis 5-108, Johnson 3-42, Collinsworth 2-33, Ross 1-8, Kreider 1-7; New York, Barkum 7-82, Newton 4-37, Gaffney 2-60, McNeil 2-23, Long 1-3, J. Jones 1-32, Walker 1-14.

Kickoff Returns—Cincinnati, Chapman 1-15, Verser 4-115; New York, Sohn 5-99, Rudolph 1-8.

Punt Returns—Cincinnati, Fuller 1-9; New York, Sohn 4-39.

Interceptions—New York, Ray 1-16.

Punting—Cincinnati, McInally 5-44.8; New York, Ramsey 6-38.8.

Field Goals—Cincinnati, Breech 1-2; New York, Leahy 3-3.

EAGLES 13, PATRIOTS 3

PHILADELPHIA—The Eagles' offensive line, a question mark in the preseason, jelled against New England, clearing the way for Wilbert Montgomery and Perry Harrington as Philadelphia rolled up 220 yards rushing. The Eagles went to 2-0 and the Patriots dropped to 0-2.

Montgomery zoomed for 137 yards in 18 carries and Harrington added 60 yards and had a six-yard touchdown run in the third quarter.

The Eagles were working in some new offensive linemen. Ron Baker was at right guard in place of the retired Woody Peoples; at left guard, in place of injured Petey Perot, was converted tackle Steve Kenney.

All-Pro tackle Stan Walter said, "Right now, we're developing confidence. The pressure in preseason was just a matter of getting back to the proficiency the coaches expect from us."

Harrington and placekicker Tony Franklin, both roasted by Coach Dick Vermeil in the off-season for attitude problems, provided all the Eagles' points. Franklin kicked field goals of 46 and 22 yards and booted an extra point.

Franklin's 22-yard field goal broke a 3-3 tie in the third quarter. An interception by linebacker Frank LeMaster—one of five pass thefts by the Eagles—set up Harrington's touchdown.

"I thought Perry played a good game," Vermeil said of his second-year fullback who became a starter after a disabling injury to Leroy Harris. "It's a matter of Perry gaining confidence in himself to the point where he's a mean S.O.B."

Although New England's rushing defense was shredded for the second consecutive week —Baltimore had run for 249 yards in the season opener—Coach Ron Erhardt seemed more disappointed over the opportunities squandered by the Patriots' offense.

"When we didn't capitalize on some of the long drives we had, that really hurt," Erhardt said.

The Pats' starting quarterback, Steve Grogan, was intercepted three times. Matt Cavanaugh came on in the third period and had two passes picked off.

SEPTEMBER 13
SCORE BY PERIODS

New England	3	0	0	0— 3
Philadelphia	0	3	10	0—13

SCORING

New England—Field goal Smith 22.
Philadelphia—Field goal Franklin 46.
Philadelphia—Field goal Franklin 22.
Philadelphia—Harrington 6 run (Franklin kick).

TEAM STATISTICS

	New England	Philadelphia
First downs	14	18
Rushes-Yards	32-146	40-220
Passing yards	137	142
Sacks by-Yards	1-10	1-9
Return yards	20	104
Passes	11-31-5	11-25-0
Punts	6-41.7	6-46.5
Fumbles-Lost	1-0	4-2
Penalties-Yards	5-40	8-55
Time of possession	28:08	31:52
Attendance—71,089.		

INDIVIDUAL STATISTICS

Rushing—New England, Collins 18-71, Calhoun 7-60, Cavanaugh 2-16, Tatupu 1-3, Grogan 2-2, Jackson 1-minus 9, Pennywell 1-3; Philadelphia, Montgomery 18-137, Harrington 14-60, Giammona 4-10, Jaworksi 3-6, Oliver 1-7.

Passing—New England, Grogan 7-19-3—105, Cavanaugh 4-12-2—41; Philadelphia, Jaworksi 11-25-0—152.

Receiving—New England, Johnson 3-32, Collins 3-32, Calhoun 2-15, Jackson 1-34, Westbrook 1-21, Hasselbeck 1-12; Philadelphia, Carmichael 5-70, Montgomery 2-57, Campfield 2-6, Harrington 1-12, Giammona 1-7.

Kickoff Returns—New England, Ivory 1-19; Philadelphia, Campfield 2-52.

Punt Returns—New England, James 2-1; Philadelphia, Henry 4-27.

Interceptions—Philadelphia, Edwards 1-0, Wilson 1-1, LeMaster 1-22, Johnson 1-0, Young 1-2.

Punting—New England, Hubach 6-41.7; Philadelphia, Runager 6-46.5.

Field Goals—New England, Smith 1-1; Philadelphia, Franklin 2-3.

BILLS 35, COLTS 3

BALTIMORE—If defense can carry a team to the Super Bowl, the Bills were in good shape. They followed their season-opening shutout of the New York Jets by shutting down the Colts.

Baltimore gained just 73 yards on the ground and passed for 74 against the ferocious Bills. Nose tackle Fred Smerlas led the Buffalo charge and his first-quarter sacking of Bert Jones resulted in a stiff elbow that kept the injury-prone Colts quarterback out for the second half.

"It wasn't just one play that got us the win," said Smerlas. "It was 11 guys hustling as hard as they could and keeping after their offense. When you've got that many people coming after you for that long, you're in trouble."

Bills quarterback Joe Ferguson riddled Baltimore's secondary, completing 16 of 28 passes for 261 yards and four touchdowns. Buffalo rolled up 430 yards in total offense.

Ferguson's scoring tosses went for 33 yards to running back Joe Cribbs, 54 yards to wide receiver Jerry Butler, five yards to tight end Mark Brammer and three yards to Buster Barnett, backup to Brammer. Roland Hooks ran five yards for the final TD.

Mike Wood's 22-yard field goal in the second period accounted for the Colts' points. Rookie fullback Randy McMillan, who had bolted for 146 yards in Baltimore's season opener, was held to 29 by the Bills.

SEPTEMBER 13
SCORE BY PERIODS

Buffalo	7	14	7	7—35
Baltimore	0	3	0	0— 3

SCORING

Buffalo—Cribbs 33 pass from Ferguson (Mike-Mayer kick).
Baltimore—Field goal Wood 22.
Buffalo—Butler 54 pass from Ferguson (Mike-Mayer kick).
Buffalo—Brammer 5 pass from Ferguson (Mike-Mayer kick).
Buffalo—Barnett 3 pass from Ferguson (Mike-Mayer kick).
Buffalo—Hooks 5 run (Mike-Mayer kick).

TEAM STATISTICS

	Buffalo	Baltimore
First downs	26	11
Rushes-Yards	39-169	26-73
Passing yards	261	74
Sacks by-Yards	5-46	0-0
Return yards	94	117
Passes	16-28-1	12-28-2
Punts	3-47.7	6-43.3
Fumbles-Lost	2-2	3-1
Penalties-Yards	9-65	1-5
Time of possession	34:51	25:09
Attendance—44,950.		

INDIVIDUAL STATISTICS

Rushing—Buffalo, Cribbs 17-66, Brown 9-47, McCutcheon 2-8, Hooks 6-30, Leaks 3-11, Robinson 1-minus 2, Ferguson 1-9; Baltimore, McMillan 10-29, Dickey 14-35, Dixon 1-minus 2, Landry 1-11.

Passing—Buffalo, Ferguson 16-28-1—261; Baltimore, Jones 5-11-1—30, Landry 7-17-1—90.

Receiving—Buffalo, J. Butler 3-74, Lewis 4-82, Cribbs 3-46, Brammer 4-55, McCutcheon 1-1, Barnett 1-3; Baltimore, Dickey 3-30, R. Butler 1-11, McMillan 3-25, Carr 4-50, McCauley 1-4.

Kickoff Returns—Buffalo, Brown 1-21, Piccone 1-16; Baltimore, Dixon 3-58, Anderson 1-24, Shula 1-10, Sims 1-22.

Punt Returns—Buffalo, Piccone 4-15, Hooks 1-7; Baltimore, Shula 1-0.

Interceptions—Buffalo, Williams 1-0, Romes 1-35; Baltimore, Smith 1-3.

Punting—Buffalo, Cater 3-47.7; Baltimore, Garrett 6-43.3.

Field Goals—Buffalo, Mike-Mayer 0-1; Baltimore, Wood 1-1.

RAIDERS 36, VIKINGS 10

BLOOMINGTON—Outstanding defensive play helped the Raiders rack up their 13th consecutive Monday night victory. The defending Super Bowl champions, defeated in their season opener at Denver, turned back the Vikings despite 124 yards in penalties.

After a lackluster first quarter, the Raiders began to get things under control in the second period when Burgess Owens picked off a pass in the left flat and raced 30 yards for a touchdown. Later in the quarter, Jim Plunkett gave the Raiders a 16-0 lead with the first of his two TD passes, a 21-yard strike to Todd Christensen. It was the fourth-year running back's first NFL reception.

Eddie Payton took the ensuing kickoff at the 1-yard line and scampered all the way to the Raiders' end zone to make the score 16-7 at halftime.

The Raiders dominated the second half. After the Vikings drew to within six points on a 37-yard field goal by Rick Danmeier, Oakland posted three unanswered touchdowns. Plunkett fired another scoring pass, 12 yards to Morris Bradshaw. Then, midway through the final quarter, defensive lineman Cedrick Hardman scooped up a fumble and motored 52 yards for the score.

"For a time there," said Plunkett, "I wasn't sure whether our defense might not outscore our offense."

Minutes later, Marc Wilson, Plunkett's backup, lofted a 61-yard TD pass to Malcolm Barnwell.

Steve Dils and rookie Wade Wilson, filling in for injured Vikings quarterback Tommy Kramer, did well to complete 23 of 50 passes for 294 yards. They were sacked eight times for 67 yards in losses, and the Vikings' running game netted just 42 yards—27 of those in their final possession.

MONDAY, SEPTEMBER 14
SCORE BY PERIODS

Oakland	3	13	7	13—36
Minnesota	0	7	3	0—10

SCORING

Oakland—Field goal Bahr 21.
Oakland—Owens 30 interception return (Bahr kick).

Second Week—Continued

Oakland—Christensen 21 pass from Plunkett (kick blocked).
Minnesota—Payton 99 kickoff return (Danmeier kick).
Minnesota—Field goal Danmeier 37.
Oakland—Bradshaw 12 pass from Plunkett (Bahr kick).
Oakland—Hardman 62 fumble recovery (Bahr kick).
Oakland—Barnwell 61 pass from Wilson (kick blocked).

TEAM STATISTICS

	Oakland	Minnesota
First downs	14	19
Rushes-Yards	33-149	19-42
Passing yards	161	227
Sacks by-Yards	8-67	1-9
Return yards	134	198
Passes	12-25-1	23-50-1
Punts	8-44.5	7-39.1
Fumbles-Lost	1-0	4-2
Penalties-Yards	11-124	10-71
Time of possession	27:58	32:02
Attendance—47,186.		

INDIVIDUAL STATISTICS

Rushing—Oakland, King 14-79, van Eeghen 9-43, Whittington 9-27, Plunkett 1-0; Minnesota, Redwine 4-20, Brown 10-11, Harrell 1-7, Young 3-2, Galbreath 1-2.

Passing—Oakland, Plunkett 11-24-1—109, Wilson 1-1-0—61; Minnesota, Dils 17-40-1—246, Wilson 6-10-0—48.

Receiving—Oakland, Barnwell 1-61, Branch 2-27, Bradshaw 3-27, Chester 2-11, King 2-10, van Eeghen 1-13, Christensen 1-21; Minnesota, S. White 7-140, Young 5-48, Senser 4-27, Galbreath 3-19, Brown 1-9, Bruer 1-8, Harrell 1-6, Rashad 1-37.

Kickoff Returns—Oakland, Matthews 3-78; Minnesota, Payton 4-171, McDole 1-0.

Punt Returns—Oakland, Matthews 3-26; Minnesota, Payton 2-19.

Interceptions—Oakland, Owens 1-30; Minnesota, Teal 1-8.

Punting—Oakland, Guy 8-44.5; Minnesota, Coleman 7-39.1.

Field Goals—Oakland, Bahr 1-1; Minnesota, Danmeier 1-1.

THIRD WEEK

EAGLES 20, BILLS 14

ORCHARD PARK—Although Ron Jaworski grew up in nearby Lackawanna, a suburb of Buffalo, and rooted for the Bills, the Philadelphia quarterback didn't show his old favorites any mercy, throwing touchdown passes to tight end Keith Krepfle and wide receiver Harold Carmichael in the Eagles' victory.

"I'm a Bills fan. I held a season ticket in the Rock Pile (old War Memorial Stadium) for years," said Jaworski. "I hope they win their next 13 games."

"I don't know what his statistics were, but he played super," said Eagles Coach Dick Vermeil, whose team won its third straight game.

The Eagles' running attack gained 160 yards against a Bills defense that had allowed a total of 175 yards on the ground and three points in Buffalo's first two games. Halfback Wilbert Montgomery rushed for 125 yards on 27 carries.

Jaworski's one-yard touchdown toss to Krep-

fle capped a 76-yard drive which gave the Eagles a 7-0 first-quarter lead and silenced a sellout crowd of 78,991 at Rich Stadium. The Bills came right back, however, when halfback Joe Cribbs ran off right tackle for four yards to tie the game at 7-7 early in the second quarter.

The Eagles countered with a 29-yard field goal by Tony Franklin, but the Bills gained a 14-10 halftime lead when quarterback Joe Ferguson found wide receiver Frank Lewis for a 20-yard scoring pass.

Philadelphia marched 66 yards on its first possession of the second half, with Jaworski throwing a 15-yard pass to Carmichael to put the Eagles ahead, 17-14. Carmichael's scoring catch was his 67th as an Eagle, breaking the old team mark of 66 he shared with Tommy McDonald.

After the Bills drove to the Philadelphia 2, Nick Mike-Mayer missed a 20-yard field goal attempt, which would have tied the score, on the first play of the fourth quarter. The Eagles' Franklin then hit a 46-yarder to conclude the scoring.

"We played the second half without two starters (wide receiver Jerry Butler had been poked in the eye and linebacker Shane Nelson had a strained left knee), but that's not the reason we lost," said Bills Coach Chuck Knox. "Philadelphia just did a heck of a job. We had our chances and didn't capitalize."

THURSDAY, SEPTEMBER 17
SCORE BY PERIODS

Philadelphia	0	10	7	3—20
Buffalo	0	14	0	0—14

SCORING

Philadelphia—Krepfle 1 pass from Jaworski (Franklin kick).
Buffalo—Cribbs 4 run (Mike-Mayer kick).
Philadelphia—Field goal Franklin 29.
Buffalo—Lewis 20 pass from Ferguson (Mike-Mayer kick).
Philadelphia—Carmichael 15 pass from Jaworski (Franklin kick).
Philadelphia—Field goal Franklin 46.

TEAM STATISTICS

	Philadelphia	Buffalo
First downs	24	17
Rushes-Yards	38-160	31-90
Passing yards	236	187
Sacks by-Yards	0-0	1-4
Return yards	100	127
Passes	20-32-1	14-30-2
Punts	3-38.7	4-41.0
Fumbles-Lost	3-2	1-1
Penalties-Yards	10-65	4-35
Time of possession	33:59	26:01
Attendance—80,020.		

INDIVIDUAL STATISTICS

Rushing—Philadelphia, Harrington 9-25, Montgomery 27-125, Giammona 1-3, LeMaster 1-7; Buffalo, Cribbs 22-63, Brown 2-6, Leaks 1-4, Ferguson 1-minus 1, McCutcheon 5-18.

Passing—Philadelphia, Jaworski 20-32-1—240; Buffalo, Ferguson 14-30-2—187.

Receiving—Philadelphia, Montgomery 3-54, Harrington 4-11, Parker 2-24, Krepfle 2-26, Carmichael 4-61, Smith 5-64; Buffalo, Butler 3-28, Brown 1-7, Lewis 7-108, Jessie 1-6, Cribbs 1-26, Brammer 1-12.

Kickoff Returns—Philadelphia, Henry 3-70; Buffalo, Brown 2-52, Franklin 3-40.

Punt Returns—Philadelphia, Henry 3-3; Buffalo, Hooks 2-23.

Interceptions—Philadelphia, Wilson 2-27; Buffalo, Bess 1-12.

Punting—Philadelphia, Runager 3-38.7; Buffalo, Cater 4-41.0.

Field Goals—Philadelphia, Franklin 2-3; Buffalo, Mike-Mayer 0-1.

VIKINGS 26, LIONS 24

BLOOMINGTON—Tommy Kramer, making his first appearance since suffering a preseason knee injury, guided Minnesota 81 yards to set up Rick Danmeier's game-winning 20-yard field goal with four seconds to go against Detroit.

"Kramer made the difference," Vikings Coach Bud Grant said.

It was as simple as that. Kramer had been pressed back into duty when backup quarterback Steve Dils suffered a shoulder separation in the Vikes' Monday night loss to Oakland the previous week. The third-year starter completed 25 of 42 passes for 333 yards.

Kramer paid the price for his return to action. He was hit hard in the fourth period and was shaken up, replaced by rookie Wade Wilson. But he didn't stay on the sideline for long. When Wilson's only pass was incomplete, Kramer charged onto the field, complaining that an official had blown an interference call.

The official penalized Kramer for unsportsmanlike conduct. "That showed me Tommy had all his faculties back," Grant said.

Billy Sims ran for 112 yards and two TDs and Eddie Murray booted a 25-yard field goal with 10:21 left as Detroit took a 24-23 lead. Minnesota got the ball at its 18 with 1:56 left. Kramer hit on five of seven passes for 65 yards as the Vikes moved to the Detroit 1-yard line before Danmeier's winning kick.

At the end of the first half, Kramer had hit on four passes to take the Vikings 58 yards to the Detroit 21. Danmeier kicked a 39-yard field goal for a 17-14 lead with one second left.

"You've got to have a quarterback who can get you out of certain situations and make something out of them," said Vikings receiver Sammy White. "Tommy can do it because of his experience."

SEPTEMBER 20
SCORE BY PERIODS

Detroit	0	14	7	3—24
Minnesota	7	10	6	3—26

SCORING

Minnesota—Brown 1 run (Danmeier kick).
Minnesota—Senser 4 pass from Kramer (Danmeier kick).
Detroit—Sims 2 run (Murray kick).
Detroit—Sims 3 run (Murray kick).
Minnesota—Field goal Danmeier 39.

Minnesota—Brown 59 pass from Kramer (kick blocked).
Detroit—Danielson 1 run (Murray kick).
Detroit—Field goal Murray 25.
Minnesota—Field goal Danmeier 20.

TEAM STATISTICS

	Detroit	Minnesota
First downs	19	18
Rushes-Yards	42-172	21-94
Passing yards	232	312
Sacks by-Yards	2-21	0-0
Return yards	114	80
Passes	14-26-1	25-43-2
Punts	7-48.0	7-50.3
Fumbles-Lost	3-1	3-1
Penalties-Yards	6-47	9-66
Time of possession	33:54	26:06

Attendance—45,350.

INDIVIDUAL STATISTICS

Rushing—Detroit, Sims 27-112, Bussey 11-40, L. Thompson 1-15, Danielson 3-5; Minnesota, Brown 18-77, Young 3-17.

Passing—Detroit, Danielson 14-26-1—232; Minnesota, Kramer 25-42-2—333, Wilson 0-1-0—0.

Receiving—Detroit, Scott 5-113, Nichols 1-45, Sims 3-21, L. Thompson 2-20, Hill 1-18, King 2-15; Minnesota, Brown 9-115, Rashad 5-70, LeCount 1-43, Senser 3-40, S. White 2-31, Young 4-23, Galbreath 1-11.

Kickoff Returns—Detroit, Hall 2-43, Martin 2-39, Callicutt 1-11; Minnesota, Payton 1-16, Nord 2-18, McDole 1-21.

Punt Returns—Detroit, Martin 3-1; Minnesota, Payton 4-25.

Interceptions—Detroit, Allen 1-5, White 1-5, Oldham 0-10; Minnesota, Hannon 1-0.

Punting—Detroit, Skladany 7-48.0; Minnesota, Coleman 7-50.3.

Field Goals—Detroit, Murray 1-2; Minnesota, Danmeier 2-2.

BROWNS 20, BENGALS 17

CINCINNATI—Cleveland fullback Mike Pruitt concedes his coaches "are a little smarter than me."

Pruitt thought the Browns' coaches "must be crazy" when they called for a second successive draw play late in the game with Cleveland leading Cincinnati, 13-10.

The ball was on the Cincinnati 12-yard line. Pruitt sped into the end zone for a 20-10 lead with 4:20 to play and the Browns wound up with their first victory of the season after two losses.

On the previous play, the Browns had faced a first-and-20 situation on the Cincinnati 24 because of a penalty. A draw play that time resulted in Pruitt gaining 12 yards to the 12.

"When I got back to the huddle," said Pruitt. "I was surprised that the coaches sent in another draw play. I figured Cincinnati had to be waiting for it. I was wrong."

The Bengals almost pulled off a game-winning rally for the third successive week. They had overcome deficits to whip both Seattle and the New York Jets. This time, they cut their disadvantage to 20-17 on Pete Johnson's one-yard TD run with 1:57 to play. But they failed to regain the ball in the last two minutes.

Third Week—Continued

Brian Sipe passed for 259 yards for the Browns, but he called Charles White, the 1979 Heisman Trophy winner from USC and Cleveland's top draft pick in 1980, the key to victory.

"Charles White was the difference," said the quarterback. "His blocking, running and pass receiving gave us a whole new dimension."

White was particularly effective as a receiver, grabbing seven passes for 73 yards.

SEPTEMBER 20
SCORE BY PERIODS

Cleveland	3	10	0	7—20
Cincinnati	0	0	3	14—17

SCORING
Cleveland—Field goal Jacobs 28.
Cleveland—Field goal Jacobs 30.
Cleveland—Newsome 4 pass from Sipe (Jacobs kick).
Cincinnati—Field goal Breech 21.
Cincinnati—Collinsworth 41 pass from Anderson (Breech kick).
Cleveland—M. Pruitt 12 run (Jacobs kick).
Cincinnati—Johnson 1 run (Breech kick).

TEAM STATISTICS

	Cleveland	Cincinnati
First downs	31	15
Rushes-Yards	44-186	14-48
Passing yards	237	233
Sacks by-Yards	1-5	2-22
Return yards	95	161
Passes	24-35-0	16-25-0
Punts	3-43.3	4-52.3
Fumbles-Lost	0-0	0-0
Penalties-Yards	6-83	6-46
Time of possession	41:59	18:01
Attendance—52,170.		

INDIVIDUAL STATISTICS

Rushing—Cleveland, C. Miller 21-97, G. Pruitt 2-2, Sipe 2-5, White 6-12, M. Pruitt 13-70; Cincinnati, Johnson 8-21, A. Griffin 4-minus 1, Anderson 2-28.

Passing—Cleveland, Sipe 24-35-0—259; Cincinnati, Anderson 16-25-0—238.

Receiving—Cleveland, G. Pruitt 2-7, White 7-73, Newsome 5-42, Feacher 2-30, C. Miller 3-24, M. Pruitt 3-20, Rucker 2-63; Cincinnati, Curtis 4-79, Collinsworth 3-66, Ross 3-35, McInally 2-19, A. Griffin 1-17, Johnson 1-minus 3, Kreider 2-25.

Kickoff Returns—Cleveland, Montgomery 3-59; Cincinnati, Verser 2-95, Chapman 1-25.

Punt Returns—Cleveland, Montgomery 3-36; Cincinnati, Fuller 2-41.

Interceptions—None.

Punting—Cleveland, Cox 3-43.3; Cincinnati, McInally 4-52.3.

Field Goals—Cleveland, Jacobs 2-3; Cincinnati, Breech 1-3.

BRONCOS 28, COLTS 10

DENVER—A little adversity never has bothered Craig Morton, Denver's 38-year-old quarterback. For instance, on the Broncos' first three possessions against Baltimore, Morton threw interceptions each time. Before the first half ended, he'd tossed another interception.

But when it was all over, Morton had also thrown for 291 yards and four touchdowns,

enough to give Denver its second win in three games. Baltimore went home 1-2.

It was a milestone game for Morton, who topped 25,000 yards gained by passing for his career. He lifted his total to 25,166, or 14th on the list, exceeding retired Bob Griese's figure of 25,092.

Morton has taken a great deal of abuse during his 17-year career. "I've been called all sorts of things," he recalled, "but this (25,000 yards) is something very few guys have done. I've really worked to accomplish this. It's important to me."

Three of Morton's TD passes against Baltimore went to third-year pro Steve Watson, a wide receiver who'd never before caught a scoring pass in the NFL. Now he has TD receptions of seven, 18 and 48 yards.

Said Colts Coach Mike McCormack: "Our strengths have all of a sudden become our weaknesses. At the start of the second half, we began to make a game of it, and then we couldn't play defense. We had no zone, no man-to-man."

SEPTEMBER 20
SCORE BY PERIODS

Baltimore	0	0	10	0—10
Denver	0	14	14	0—28

SCORING
Denver—Egloff 7 pass from Morton (Steinfort kick).
Denver—Watson 29 pass from Morton (Steinfort kick).
Baltimore—Field goal Wood 21.
Baltimore—Dickey 63 run (Wood kick).
Denver—Watson 18 pass from Morton (Steinfort kick).
Denver—Watson 48 pass from Morton (Steinfort kick).

TEAM STATISTICS

	Baltimore	Denver
First downs	10	27
Rushes-Yards	26-161	35-127
Passing yards	48	315
Sacks by-Yards	3-26	2-17
Return yards	165	110
Passes	7-19-1	24-33-4
Punts	6-50.0	2-49.0
Fumbles-Lost	2-2	1-0
Penalties-Yards	8-63	9-65
Time of possession	21:56	38:04
Attendance—74,802.		

INDIVIDUAL STATISTICS

Rushing—Baltimore, McMillan 8-17, Dickey 12-115, Dixon 5-28, B. Jones 1-1; Denver, Preston 12-47, Parros 14-65, Canada 6-13, Reed 1-2, Lytle 1-0, Watson 1-0.

Passing—Baltimore, B. Jones 7-19-1—65; Denver, Morton 20-28-4—291, DeBerg 4-5-0—50.

Receiving—Baltimore, Carr 1-19, McMillan 4-29, Dixon 1-4, Dickey 1-13; Denver, Preston 6-46, Watson 7-143, Reed 3-40, Odoms 3-33, Egloff 1-7, Moses 1-30, Manning 1-8, Wright 1-14, Canada 1-20.

Kickoff Returns—Baltimore, Dixon 1-46, Anderson 2-41.

Punt Returns—Baltimore, Shula 2-14; Denver, Manning 5-97.

Interceptions—Baltimore, Green 1-3, Braziel 2-27, Laird 1-24; Denver, Gradishar 1-13.

Punting—Baltimore, Garrett 6-50.0; Denver, Prestridge 2-49.0.

Field Goals—Baltimore, Wood 1-1; Denver, Steinfort 0-1.

Denver's Craig Morton, a 17-year NFL veteran, went over the 25,000-yard mark in career passing yardage as the Broncos whipped the Colts, 28-10. Morton also had four touchdown passes in the victory.

Third Week—Continued

CARDINALS 40, REDSKINS 30

ST. LOUIS—Roy Green said he hadn't seen so much action since he was Mr. Everything for his high school team, the Mighty Panthers of Magnolia, Ark.

"I even kicked off in high school," said Green, who led the Panthers to the state championship his senior year before going on to Henderson State and then being drafted by the St. Louis Cardinals as a defensive back in 1979.

Green returned to his Mr. Everything role for the Cardinals in their triumph over the Washington Redskins. Starting at wide receiver in an emergency role, he caught four passes for 115 yards and one touchdown (on a 58-yard bomb from Jim Hart). He returned a kickoff 17 yards as part of his duty on special teams and he played as the "nickel" defensive back, intercepting a pass to stop the Redskins' last drive.

"I loved it," said Green. "It kind of reminded me of high school when I never came off the field."

St. Louis won for the first time in three games and the Redskins fell to 0-3 despite a 388-yard passing performance by Joe Theismann and a 104-yard rushing effort by Wilbur Jackson.

Green had caught one pass for 15 yards in his rookie season, 1979, and he tied the National Football League record that year with a 106-yard kickoff return against Dallas. But his role had been defensive back-special teams until the Cardinals lost wide receiver Mel Gray with a preseason knee injury.

The second week of the season, Green had been used at wide receiver against Dallas and caught a 60-yard pass from Neil Lomax. That earned him a start against Washington.

"Playing defense has helped a lot because I can walk up to the line as a wide receiver and see what kind of defense they're in," he said. "The Redskins had single coverage on me. They knew I didn't have any experience and they weren't gonna waste two men on me."

Hart, returning from a knee injury that had kept him out of the Dallas game, was 12-for-22 passing for 226 yards and three TDs. His other scoring passes went to tight end Greg LaFleur and wide receiver Dave Stief.

St. Louis took the lead for good at 12-10 on Neil O'Donoghue's 47-yard field goal in the second quarter. Then rookie Stump Mitchell raced 50 yards to score on a punt return.

"They hit us with some big things and turned the game around," said Washington Coach Joe Gibbs. "It seems every time we get a chance to win a game, we find a way to mess it up."

Theismann threw four TD passes and his 388 yards marked his career high. Ricky Thompson took two scoring throws and Art Monk grabbed one for a 79-yard play.

Cardinals Coach Jim Hanifan, praising the play of Green, said, "That guy is an unusual individual. He has unbelievable stamina. He can probably go out and dance tonight."

SEPTEMBER 20
SCORE BY PERIODS

Washington	10	7	0	13—30
St. Louis	9	17	0	14—40

SCORING

St. Louis—Field goal O'Donoghue 24.
Washington—Field goal Moseley 21.
Washington—Thompson 34 pass from Theismann (Moseley kick).
St. Louis—Green 58 pass from Hart (kick blocked).
St. Louis—Field goal O'Donoghue 47.
St. Louis—Mitchell 50 punt return (O'Donoghue kick).
Washington—Monk 79 pass from Theismann (Moseley kick).
St. Louis—LaFleur 27 pass from Hart (O'Donoghue kick).
St. Louis—Stief 6 pass from Hart (O'Donoghue kick).
St. Louis—Anderson 7 run (O'Donoghue kick).
Washington—Walker 20 pass from Theismann (kick failed).
Washington—Thompson 10 pass from Theismann (Moseley kick).

TEAM STATISTICS

	Washington	St. Louis
First downs	24	18
Rushes-Yards	27-133	37-107
Passing yards	388	208
Sacks by-Yards	2-18	0-0
Return yards	140	178
Passes	25-37-1	12-22-0
Punts	4-42.8	5-40.2
Fumbles-Lost	4-1	1-0
Penalties-Yards	8-67	8-60
Time of possession	29:23	30:37
Attendance—47,592.		

INDIVIDUAL STATISTICS

Rushing—Washington, Jackson 22-104, Metcalf 3-18, Theismann 1-11, Connell 1-0; St. Louis, Morris 13-60, Anderson 20-48, Harrell 3-1, Lomax 1-minus 2.

Passing—Washington, Theismann 25-37-1—388; St. Louis, Hart 12-22-0—226.

Receiving—Washington, Thompson 7-106, Monk 4-128, Metcalf 4-69, Walker 3-41, Jackson 3-13, Warren 2-12, Harmon 1-23, McCrary 1-minus 4; St. Louis, Green 4-115, Anderson 3-29, Stief 2-35, Harrell 2-20, LaFleur 1-27.

Kickoff Returns—Washington, Metcalf 8-140; St. Louis, Mitchell 3-69, Green 1-17.

Punt Returns—St. Louis, Mitchell 3-69, Harrell 1-8.

Interceptions—St. Louis, Green 1-15.

Punting—Washington, Connell 4-42.8; St. Louis, Birdsong 5-40.2.

Field Goals—Washington, Moseley 1-1; St. Louis, O'Donoghue 2-2.

DOLPHINS 16, OILERS 10

HOUSTON—Coach Don Shula is a bold strategist, and that's one reason the Miami Dolphins were 3-0 in the National Football League.

Shula's Dolphins were leading the Houston Oilers, 9-7, at halftime in a match of unbeaten AFC teams at the Astrodome. At this point, Shula benched regular quarterback David Woodley. Into the game went Don Strock, who hadn't played since the preseason, when he completed 24 of 26 passes.

This time Strock completed seven of 10

passes, including the game winner, a three-yard touchdown toss to fullback Andra Franklin with 6:40 to play. That gave Miami a 16-10 victory, to which Uwe von Schamann also contributed mightily with three first-half field goals. It was Houston's first loss in three games.

Shula made no explanation for the quarterback switch except to say: "The Oilers gave us a lot of different coverages and Strock had more experience."

Woodley had overthrown several open receivers and had 11 completions in 22 tries, with no interceptions. Said Woodley: "All he said to me was, 'I'm gonna go with Don in the second half.' He's got a right to do what's best for the team."

The Miami defense, led by middle guard Bob Baumhower, did a tremendous job. Baumhower ran over Houston center Carl Mauch to account for four of the eight sacks registered against quarterback Ken Stabler. Miami has logged 16 sacks in three games.

The Dolphins also bottled up star running back Earl Campbell, who gained just 78 yards in 19 carries. Miami's only defensive lapse came when wide receiver Ken Burrough ran past cornerback Gerald Small and caught Stabler's 71-yard TD bomb in the first quarter. Stabler passed for 178 yards and was absolved of all blame by Houston Coach Ed Biles. "Kenny didn't have any protection. We were totally outmuscled up front," said the coach. "I was very disappointed in the intensity of the line."

Miami's two running backs both were injured. Fullback Woody Bennett suffered a twisted knee and Tony Nathan had bruised ribs.

SEPTEMBER 20
SCORE BY PERIODS

Miami	6	3	0	7—16
Houston	7	0	3	0—10

SCORING

Miami—Field goal von Schamann 42.
Houston—Burrough 71 pass from Stabler (Fritsch kick).
Miami—Field goal von Schamann 37.
Miami—Field goal von Schamann 27.
Houston—Field goal Fritsch 40.
Miami—Franklin 3 pass from Strock (von Schamann kick).

TEAM STATISTICS

	Miami	Houston
First downs	16	9
Rushes-Yards	33-124	21-85
Passing yards	133	117
Sacks by-Yards	8-61	1-11
Return yards	106	150
Passes	18-32-1	16-26-1
Punts	7-40.4	8-42.0
Fumbles-Lost	0-0	0-0
Penalties-Yards	6-50	8-74
Time of possession	33:10	26:50
Attendance—47,379.		

INDIVIDUAL STATISTICS

Rushing—Miami, Franklin 11-56, Nathan 4-40, Bennett 5-22, Vigorito 8-6, Giaquinto 1-5, Woodley 1-1, Strock 3-minus 6; Houston, Campbell 19-78, Stabler 1-4, Carpenter 1-3.

Passing—Miami, Woodley 11-22-0—82, Strock 7-10-1—62; Houston, Stabler 16-26-1—178.

Receiving—Miami, Harris 4-37, Vigorito 4-28, Rose 1-22, Giaquinto 2-18, Nathan 2-16, Hardy 1-9, Bennett 2-8, Lee 1-3, Franklin 1-3; Houston, Burrough 3-76, Renfro 5-51, Carpenter 5-31, Barber 2-15, Campbell 1-5.

Kickoff Returns—Miami, Walker 2-44, Rose 1-5; Houston, Roaches 5-128.

Punt Returns—Miami, Vigorito 4-49; Houston, Roaches 3-3.

Interceptions—Miami, Kozlowski 1-8; Houston, Washington 1-19.

Punting—Miami, Orosz 7-40.4; Houston, Parsley 8-42.0.

Field Goals—Miami, von Schamann 3-4; Houston, Fritsch 1-1.

CHARGERS 42, CHIEFS 31

KANSAS CITY—One thing is clear: San Diego can do very well despite the loss of ace wide receiver John Jefferson, whose contract dispute finally culminated in his trade to Green Bay.

Charger players had expressed sympathy for Jefferson's financial cause, but that didn't slow them on the field. They made Kansas City their third victim in three starts, handing the Chiefs their first loss.

"It was important for us to get on with it," said San Diego quarterback Dan Fouts, who threw for 284 yards and three touchdowns against the Chiefs. "We've got goals and we have to pursue them, with or without J. J."

One big reason the Chargers haven't missed Jefferson is Kellen Winslow, the tight end who led NFL receivers in 1980 with 89 catches. Winslow enjoyed his biggest day of the season, grabbing six passes for 96 yards and a touchdown.

Chuck Muncie sparked San Diego's ground game, as usual, gaining 93 yards. Muncie was a key part of the air attack, too, catching nine passes for 85 yards.

Fouts failed in his bid for a record fifth successive game with 300 yards gained passing. He got off shakily with four incompletions and an interception in his first five tries. He rallied, however, to throw three TD passes in the first half and give San Diego a 28-14 lead.

Kansas City quarterback Bill Kenney threw for 303 yards and led a rally that cut the Chargers' lead to 35-31 with 10 minutes to play. With 1:53 left, Chargers linebacker Linden King deflected a Kenney pass that was intercepted by defensive end Leroy Jones at the Kansas City 10. Jones ran a few yards and then lateraled to defensive tackle Gary Johnson, who stepped the final five yards to score.

"Gary was yelling at me to throw it to him," Jones cracked. "I hated to give it up. It was a big sacrifice to make, but I gave it up."

San Diego wound up with three interceptions, three sacks and seven turnovers. Cornerback Willie Buchanon had two interceptions and a fumble recovery.

Third Week—Continued

SCORE BY PERIODS

San Diego	14	14	7	7—42
Kansas City	7	7	14	3—31

SCORING

Kansas City—McKnight 1 run (Lowery kick).
San Diego—Winslow 13 pass from Fouts (Benirschke kick).
San Diego—J. Brooks 29 pass from Fouts (Benirschke kick).
San Diego—Muncie 1 run (Benirschke kick).
San Diego—Sievers 12 pass from Fouts (Benirschke kick).
Kansas City—Dixon 7 pass from Kenney (Lowery kick).
Kansas City—McKnight 3 run (Lowery kick).
San Diego—Muncie 3 run (Benirschke kick).
Kansas City—B. Jackson 4 run (Lowery kick).
Kansas City—Field goal Lowery 37.
San Diego—G. Johnson 5 run with lateral (Benirschke kick).

TEAM STATISTICS

	San Diego	Kansas City
First downs	23	29
Rushes-Yards	24-114	37-148
Passing yards	284	278
Sacks by-Yards	3-25	0-0
Return yards	213	169
Passes	22-43-3	22-41-5
Punts	5-40.2	3-39.3
Fumbles-Lost	2-0	4-3
Penalties-Yards	9-50	11-104
Time of possession	25:41	34:19
Attendance—63,866.		

INDIVIDUAL STATISTICS

Rushing—San Diego, Muncie 17-93, Fouts 3-8, J. Brooks 2-7, Cappelletti 1-4, Roberts 1-2; Kansas City, Delaney 9-66, McKnight 14-40, Hadnot 11-33, B. Jackson 2-6, Williams 1-3.

Passing—San Diego, Fouts 22-43-3—284; Kansas City, Kenney 22-41-5—303.

Receiving—San Diego, Muncie 9-85, Winslow 6-96, Sievers 2-43, J. Brooks 2-30, Carson 2-23, Smith 1-7; Kansas City, Smith 9-140, Marshall 5-53, Dixon 3-44, Delaney 2-37, Hadnot 2-16, Carson 1-13.

Kickoff Returns—San Diego, J. Brooks 5-119; Kansas City, Carson 5-110, Delaney 1-11.

Punt Returns—San Diego, J. Brooks 1-23, Shaw 1-1; Kansas City, Smith 4-20.

Interceptions—San Diego, Buchanon 2-20, King 1-28, Gregor 1-11, Jones 1-6, G. Johnson 0-5; Kansas City, Manumaleuga 2-17, Barbaro 1-11.

Punting—San Diego, Roberts 5-40.2; Kansas City, Grupp 3-39.3.

Field Goals—San Diego, Benirschke 0-2; Kansas City, Lowery 1-2.

RAMS 35, PACKERS 23

ANAHEIM—Jeff Rutledge is no stranger to success. He was a four-year starter for Alabama and broke Joe Namath's school record by firing 30 touchdown passes.

In his first two years with Los Angeles, however, he had been a seldom-used player. He threw 32 passes in 1979 and only four in 1980.

But when Pat Haden suffered the umpteenth injury of his career—this time, bruised ribs—Rutledge came on to lead the Rams over Green Bay for their first victory of the year. Rutledge completed five of 10 passes for 70 yards and one TD, which started a 21-point splurge in a span of 7 minutes, 47 seconds.

Whether Rutledge had won a starting berth for any length of time was questionable. The Rams were on the verge of signing free agent Dan Pastorini, who had been working out with the team for nearly a week.

Rutledge's touchdown pass, a 30-yarder to Drew Hill, wiped out a 16-14 Packer lead late in the third period. The Rams then boosted their lead to 28-16 on a two-yard TD run by Cullen Bryant. On Green Bay's next possession, Pat Thomas intercepted a Lynn Dickey pass and returned 64 yards to the Packer 11, setting up a TD plunge by Wendell Tyler.

"I had a rough start, but I wasn't nervous," said Rutledge. "The first couple of times I went back to pass, I got sacked and that sure doesn't help. But it was good to get a win under our belts."

The Packers' Dickey, just the opposite of Rutledge, had a fast start and a rough finish. He was 10-for-13 in the first half, but only 5-for-16 for 21 yards after intermission. He was sacked five times and had to leave the game when he was shaken up with 2:53 left.

Haden went out when he was smacked by defensive end Mike Butler early in the second quarter.

SCORE BY PERIODS

Green Bay	0	10	6	7—23
Los Angeles	0	14	7	14—35

SCORING

Green Bay—Ellis 3 run (Stenerud kick).
Los Angeles—Harris 21 fumble return (Corral kick).
Los Angeles—Tyler 2 run (Corral kick).
Green Bay—Field goal Stenerud 18.
Green Bay—Field goal Stenerud 23.
Green Bay—Field goal Stenerud 44.
Los Angeles—D. Hill 30 pass from Rutledge (Corral kick).
Los Angeles—Bryant 2 run (Corral kick).
Los Angeles—Tyler 1 run (Corral kick).
Green Bay—Lofton 19 pass from Dickey (Stenerud kick).

TEAM STATISTICS

	Green Bay	Los Angeles
First downs	19	19
Rushes-Yards	33-122	43-177
Passing yards	78	26
Sacks by-Yards	5-50	6-47
Return yards	192	173
Passes	15-34-1	6-12-1
Punts	6-45.5	7-39.7
Fumbles-Lost	4-3	2-2
Penalties-Yards	11-95	14-120
Time of possession	32:31	27:29
Attendance—61,286.		

INDIVIDUAL STATISTICS

Rushing—Green Bay, Middleton 11-45, Jensen 9-27, Atkins 5-13, Ellis 4-9, Whitehurst 2-15, Dickey 2-13; Los Angeles, Tyler 25-108, Bryant 8-38, Guman 5-21, J. Thomas 4-12, Rutledge 1-minus 2.

Passing—Green Bay, Dickey 15-29-1—125, Whitehurst 0-5-0—0; Los Angeles, Haden 1-2-0—6, Rutledge 5-10-1—70.

Receiving—Green Bay, Lofton 5-73, Coffman 3-16, G. Lewis 2-24, Ellis 1-6, Jensen 1-5, Huckleby 1-3, Atkins

1-2, Middleton 1-minus 4; Los Angeles, Waddy 2-24, D. Hill 1-30, Childs 1-9, Dennard 1-9, Tyler 1-4.

Kickoff Returns—Green Bay, Nixon 3-50, Huckleby 2-52; Los Angeles, D. Hill 5-88, Pankey 1-0.

Punt Returns—Green Bay, Nixon 5-47; Los Angeles, Irvin 4-21.

Interceptions—Green Bay, Harvey 1-43; Los Angeles, P. Thomas 1-64.

Punting—Green Bay, Stachowicz 6-45.5; Los Angeles, Corral 7-39.7.

Field Goals—Green Bay, Stenerud 3-3; Los Angeles, None attempted.

FALCONS 34, 49ers 17

ATLANTA—Steve Bartkowski, a self-described "old crippled horse," performed well in harness as Atlanta ran its record to 3-0 at the expense of San Francisco.

Bartkowski, wearing a flak jacket to protect a cracked rib and a brace on his right knee, threw three touchdown passes as he completed 13 of 22 throws for 208 yards.

"I am excited about the potential of this team, but I don't think it's time to make reservations for the Super Bowl," Bartkowski said. "If we do that, we're going to get our rear ends beat."

The Falcons took advantage of early turnovers to jump to a 17-0 lead in the first quarter. Bartkowski threw TD passes of 29 yards to Alfred Jackson and 18 yards to Lynn Cain, and Mick Luckhurst boomed a 47-yard field goal. After San Francisco pulled within 17-10, Bartkowski rifled a 15-yard scoring pass to Alfred Jenkins to make it 24-10 at the half.

The 49ers drove from their 27 to the Atlanta 6 early in the third quarter before Falcon safety Tom Pridemore made the play of the game. He picked off a Joe Montana pass and returned 101 yards for a clinching TD.

"The ball was underthrown," said Pridemore. "Buddy Curry made a good block on Young (49ers tight end Charle Young, the intended receiver) and once I made it to the sideline, it was wide open."

Atlanta Coach Leeman Bennett said Pridemore's return was a 14-point swing. "They kept the ball for 5½ minutes, but we ended up getting the points," he said.

Montana finished the game 24-for-34 for 274 yards and two TDs.

SEPTEMBER 20
SCORE BY PERIODS

San Francisco	0	10	0	7—17
Atlanta	17	7	10	0—34

SCORING

Atlanta—Jackson 29 pass from Bartkowski (Luckhurst kick).
Atlanta—Field goal Luckhurst 47.
Atlanta—Cain 18 pass from Bartkowski (Luckhurst kick).
San Francisco—Young 11 pass from Montana (Bahr kick).
San Francisco—Field goal Bahr 47.
Atlanta—Jenkins 15 pass from Bartkowski (Luckhurst kick).

Atlanta—Pridemore 101 interception return (Luckhurst kick).
Atlanta—Field goal Luckhurst 18.
San Francisco—Solomon 12 pass from Montana (Bahr kick)

TEAM STATISTICS

	San Francisco	Atlanta
First downs	23	18
Rushes-Yards	30-113	34-163
Passing yards	273	200
Sacks by-Yards	2-22	1-1
Return yards	110	199
Passes	24-34-2	14-23-0
Punts	3-53.3	3-36.7
Fumbles-Lost	1-1	2-0
Penalties-Yards	3-25	4-50
Time of possession	32:08	27:52
Attendance—56,653.		

INDIVIDUAL STATISTICS

Rushing—San Francisco, Cooper 9-40, Patton 12-30, Easley 4-18, Elliott 4-17, Solomon 1-8; Atlanta, Andrews 12-85, Cain 12-48, Robinson 6-19, Mayberry 3-12, Jones 1-minus 1.

Passing—San Francisco, Montana 24-34-2—274; Atlanta, Bartkowski 13-22-0—208, Jones 1-1-0—14.

Receiving—San Francisco, Clark 9-77, Young 3-55, Solomon 3-36, Cooper 3-29, Wilson 2-34, Patton 2-16, Hofer 1-22, Peets 1-5; Atlanta, Andrews 4-37, Cain 3-28, Jenkins 2-82, Jackson 2-42, Miller 2-22, Francis 1-11.

Kickoff Returns—San Francisco, Lott 3-56, Ring 1-23, Wilson 1-22; Atlanta, R. Smith 2-55.

Punt Returns—San Francisco, Solomon 2-9; Atlanta, R. Smith 1-9, Woerner 1-9.

Interceptions—Atlanta, Williams 1-25, Pridemore 1-101.

Punting—San Francisco, Miller 3-53.3; Atlanta, James 3-36.7.

Field Goals—San Francisco, Bahr 1-2; Atlanta, Luckhurst 2-3.

STEELERS 38, JETS 10

PITTSBURGH—Coach Chuck Noll claimed his Pittsburgh Steelers entered the game wanting to do more passing than they had while losing their first two games.

The Steelers did the exact opposite—and it suited Noll just fine. They exploded for 343 yards on the ground in overwhelming the New York Jets. The Jets fell to 0-3 and were getting plenty of flak from a New York press that was demanding Coach Walt Michaels' scalp.

"We've definitely got it on track!" said Ray Pinney, a member of an offensive line that helped Pittsburgh pile up 566 yards total offense.

Steelers quarterback Terry Bradshaw played a bit more than three quarters before yielding to backup Cliff Stoudt.

The Steelers' running attack featured two youngsters rarely used before this season—Russell Davis and Frank Pollard. Davis carried 13 times for 100 yards and one touchdown. Pollard gained 79 yards and scored twice in 12 carries while old reliable Franco Harris contributed 68 yards in 13 carries.

All five Pittsburgh touchdowns came on runs. It was the first time since 1976 that the Steelers had scored that many on the ground.

The Jets' scoring was confined to a 47-yard field goal by Pat Leahy and a 17-yard pass from backup QB Pat Ryan to Freeman McNeil.

"Pittsburgh was ready to play and we weren't," said Michaels. "They beat us offensively and defensively. It was a complete Pittsburgh effort."

SEPTEMBER 20
SCORE BY PERIODS

New York Jets	0	3	0	7—10
Pittsburgh	7	10	14	7—38

SCORING

Pittsburgh—Davis 9 run (Trout kick).
Pittsburgh—Field goal Trout 25.
Pittsburgh—Pollard 23 run (Trout kick).
New York—Field goal Leahy 47.
Pittsburgh—Bradshaw 1 run (Trout kick).
Pittsburgh—Pollard 1 run (Trout kick).
Pittsburgh—Thornton 1 run (Trout kick).
New York—McNeil 17 pass from Ryan (Leahy kick).

TEAM STATISTICS

	New York	Pittsburgh
First downs	16	33
Rushes-Yards	21-84	56-343
Passing yards	174	223
Sacks by-Yards	2-19	2-19
Return yards	127	52
Passes	14-33-2	15-30-0
Punts	5-43.4	2-37.0
Fumbles-Lost	0-0	2-1
Penalties-Yards	6-45	8-75
Time of possession	19:51	40:09

Attendance—52,934.

INDIVIDUAL STATISTICS

Rushing—New York, Newton 7-16, McNeil 7-43, Todd 2-5, Harper 1-1, Dierking 2-4, Lewis 1-4, Augustyniak 1-11; Pittsburgh, Harris 13-68, Pollard 12-79, Davis 13-100, Bradshaw 7-41, Stallworth 1-17, Thornton 7-29, Colquitt 1-8, Stoudt 2-1.

Passing—New York, Todd 11-28-2—149, Ryan 3-5-0—44; Pittsburgh, Bradshaw 14-28-0—225, Stoudt 1-2-0—17.

Receiving—New York, McNeil 4-59, Walker 1-12, Harper 2-25, Newton 2-16, Dierking 2-12, B. Jones 1-21, Gaffney 1-39, Augustyniak 1-9; Pittsburgh, Smith 1-36, Cunningham 2-24, Swann 2-34, Stallworth 8-134, Pollard 2-14.

Kickoff Returns—New York, Sohn 3-87, Lewis 2-40; Pittsburgh, Anderson 1-19, Dirden 1-22.

Punt Returns—New York, Sohn 1-0; Pittsburgh, Smith 3-8.

Interceptions—Pittsburgh, Thomas 1-1, Lambert 1-2.

Punting—New York, Ramsey 5-43.4; Pittsburgh, Colquitt 2-37.0.

Field Goals—New York, Leahy 1-2; Pittsburgh, Trout 1-1.

RAIDERS 20, SEAHAWKS 10

OAKLAND—Just about everybody in the NFL knows you can't afford to give Jim Plunkett time to throw the ball. Seattle learned it the hard way.

Plunkett ran all over the place looking for receivers. If his first and second choices were covered, he usually found a third one open. It all added up to Oakland's second victory in

three starts and Seattle's second defeat against one victory.

Plunkett threw for 262 yards, including a 29-yard scoring pass to Morris Bradshaw. He also ran 13 yards for a TD against a shaken Seahawks defense.

Sharing the spotlight with Plunkett was sub running back Derrick Jensen, who filled a gap created by an injury to Mark van Eeghen. The first time he carried the ball, van Eeghen suffered a pulled hamstring in his left leg.

Jensen carried 19 times for 84 yards, including a one-yard plunge for Oakland's last touchdown.

Plunkett wasn't especially pleased with his effort, which included two interceptions. "We've got to get better inside the 20 and put more points on the board when we get there," he said.

Kenny Easley, Seattle's top draft pick from UCLA, was burned by Plunkett on the TD toss. "Plunkett did an excellent job picking up his receivers," said the rookie. "We made the mistake of letting him have the short game and I gave up the bomb."

SEPTEMBER 20
SCORE BY PERIODS

Seattle	0	3	7	0—10
Oakland	7	6	0	7—20

SCORING

Oakland—Plunkett 13 run (Bahr kick).
Seattle—Field goal Herrera 26.
Oakland—Bradshaw 29 pass from Plunkett (kick failed).
Seattle—McCullum 36 pass from Zorn (Herrera kick).
Oakland—Jensen 1 run (Bahr kick).

TEAM STATISTICS

	Seattle	Oakland
First downs	18	26
Rushes-Yards	16-82	41-190
Passing yards	308	242
Sacks by-Yards	4-20	2-19
Return yards	116	74
Passes	24-43-1	20-30-2
Punts	6-37.2	4-46.3
Fumbles-Lost	2-1	3-1
Penalties-Yards	6-40	5-45
Time of possession	22:45	37:15

Attendance—45,725.

INDIVIDUAL STATISTICS

Rushing—Seattle, S. Smith 4-25, Jodat 5-22, Hughes 4-17, Miller 2-4, Zorn 1-14; Oakland, Jensen 19-84, King 14-74, Whittington 4-17, Plunkett 3-10, van Eeghen 1-5.

Passing—Seattle, Zorn 24-43-1—327; Oakland, Plunkett 20-30-2—262.

Receiving—Seattle, McCullum 6-122, Largent 6-92, S. Smith 6-38, Jodat 2-47, Hughes 2-12, Sawyer 2-16; Oakland, Jensen 7-74, Branch 4-64, Bradshaw 3-74, Christensen 2-22, Whittington 2-10, King 1-12, Chester 1-6.

Kickoff Returns—Seattle, Johnson 2-41, Cronan 1-21; Oakland, Matthews 2-28, Barnwell 1-22.

Punt Returns—Seattle, Lewis 2-24; Oakland, Matthews 3-12.

Interceptions—Seattle, Harris 2-30; Oakland, Watts 1-12.

Punting—Seattle, West 6-37.2; Oakland, Guy 4-46.3.

Field Goals—Seattle, Herrera 1-2; Oakland, Bahr 0-1.

BEARS 28, BUCCANEERS 17

CHICAGO—The Bears' first victory of the year could be traced to a team meeting, called by veteran players one day after Chicago had lost to San Francisco in the second week of the season.

The meeting had to do with the Bears' attitude problems. After guiding the Bears past Tampa Bay, quarterback Vince Evans said, "I'd say the meeting had a lot to do with it (the victory). Despite our slow start, everyone kept plugging."

Coach Neill Armstrong, who got a game ball, echoed Evans. "They played like they practiced after the meeting," he said. "The team leaders did an outstanding job and everyone played together."

Mike Washington's 29-yard interception return gave the Bucs a quick 7-0 lead before the Bears, who had been looking for some big plays, finally got a couple.

Safety Gary Fencik intercepted a pass and returned it to the Bucs' 20. With 3:24 left in the half, Matt Suhey plunged in for a TD that tied the score.

Tampa Bay was forced to punt and rookie Jeff Fisher returned the kick 88 yards for a touchdown, which put the Bears ahead 38 seconds before halftime. The entire Bears team, which has been accused of lacking emotion, rushed onto the field to congratulate Fisher.

Although the Bucs came back to tie the score at 14-14 on Doug Williams' 11-yard pass to Kevin House in the third quarter, Evans put the game away with an eight-yard TD run and an 18-yard scoring pass to Dave Willians.

Walter Payton was held to 64 yards rushing, but that was enough to give him fourth place on the NFL career ground-gaining list. His total of 8,628 yards sent him past Jim Taylor, who had 8,597 yards.

Tampa Bay Coach John McKay, bitter as usual after a defeat, was particularly upset by Fisher's long punt return.

"Our special teams should have stayed home," McKay said. "We're asking too much from our highly paid athletes."

The Bucs' bright spot was the running of Jerry Eckwood, who gained 114 yards in 23 carries.

SEPTEMBER 20
SCORE BY PERIODS

Tampa Bay	7	0	7	3	—17
Chicago	0	14	7	7	—28

SCORING

Tampa Bay—Washington 29 interception return (Yepremian kick).

Chicago—Suhey 1 run (Nielsen kick).

Chicago—J. Fisher 88 punt return (Nielsen kick).

Tampa Bay—House 11 pass from Williams (Yepremian kick).

Chicago—Evans 7 run (Nielsen kick).

Tampa Bay—Field goal Yepremian 32.

Chicago—Williams 18 pass from Evans (Nielsen kick).

TEAM STATISTICS

	Tampa Bay	Chicago
First downs	22	15
Rushes-Yards	29-141	38-121
Passing yards	309	126
Sacks by-Yards	0-0	1-15
Return yards	91	179
Passes	17-40-2	13-24-1
Punts	5-36.2	7-42.9
Fumbles-Lost	1-1	0-0
Penalties-Yards	14-101	3-40
Time of possession	31:38	28:22
Attendance—60,130.		

INDIVIDUAL STATISTICS

Rushing—Tampa Bay, Eckwood 23-114, Williams 3-18, Wilder 1-4, R. Bell 1-3, T. Davis 1-2; Chicago, Payton 21-64, Suhey 14-48, Evans 3-9.

Passing—Tampa Bay, Williams 17-40-2—324; Chicago, Evans 13-23-1—126, Payton 0-1-0—0.

Receiving—Tampa Bay, House 6-91, Giles 5-109, Jones 4-68, T. Bell 1-47, Wilder 1-9; Chicago, Suhey 4-19, Willians 2-29, Earl 2-18, Watts 2-35, Margerum 1-15, Baschnagel 1-6, Payton 1-4.

Kickoff Returns—Tampa Bay, Owens 2-45, G. Davis 1-12; Chicago, Williams 4-66.

Punt Returns—Tampa Bay, T. Bell 5-5; Chicago, J. Fisher 2-93.

Interceptions—Tampa Bay, Washington 1-29; Chicago, Fencik 1-20, Walterscheid 1-0.

Punting—Tampa Bay, Blanchard 5-36.2; Chicago, Parsons 7-42.9.

Field Goals—Tampa Bay, Yepremian 1-2; Chicago, Nielsen 0-1.

GIANTS 20, SAINTS 7

EAST RUTHERFORD—New York quarterback Phil Simms is just three years into his NFL education, but he's not too green to teach an inexperienced New Orleans defense some lessons the hard way.

Simms gave the Saints' young secondary a year's worth of schooling, hitting 28 of 41 passes for 324 yards in the Giants' triumph. But he singled out his much-maligned offensive line for giving him the time to probe a defense featuring four rookie starters, including defensive backs Johnnie Poe and Frank Wattelet.

"The key to the game was the guys up front," said Simms, who hit tight end Gary Shirk with a 12-yard touchdown pass early in the second quarter to give New York a 7-0 lead. "I had the time to go to three different receivers if I wanted to."

But Simms primarily kept coming back to just two—Shirk and Johnny Perkins. Shirk tied a club record with 11 receptions and Perkins, making his first start of the year in place of Earnest Gray, caught eight passes for 118 yards.

Joe Danelo kicked a pair of field goals—including a club-record 55-yarder—and running back Billy Taylor scored on a one-yard plunge. The Giants were 2-1 after three games for only the second time since 1972.

"This was Phil's best game as a pro," New York Coach Ray Perkins said of Simms. "We could have scored twice the amount of points we did. Phil took what they gave him and our defense was simply outstanding."

The Giants' defense limited Saints running back George Rogers to 75 yards in 20 carries and stifled starting quarterback Bobby Scott, who was 5-for-15 passing. Archie Manning (hamstring pull) missed the game.

The Saints didn't advance past the Giants' 36 until rookie quarterback David Wilson directed a 62-yard drive midway through the fourth quarter. Wayne Wilson's two-yard scoring run capped the drive.

"We didn't do anything well in the first half. I think we were in another time zone," said Saints Coach Bum Phillips.

The Giants lost defensive end George Martin on the third play from scrimmage when he suffered a fractured elbow.

SEPTEMBER 20
SCORE BY PERIODS

New Orleans	0	0	0	7— 7
New York Giants	0	13	7	0—20

SCORING

New York—Shirk 12 pass from Simms (Danelo kick).
New York—Field goal Danelo 20.
New York—Field goal Danelo 55.
New York—B. Taylor 1 run (Danelo kick).
New Orleans—W. Wilson 2 run (Ricardo kick).

TEAM STATISTICS

	New Orleans	New York
First downs	18	26
Rushes-Yards	28-109	33-106
Passing yards	190	315
Sacks by-Yards	2-9	2-25
Return yards	119	67
Passes	16-38-2	28-42-0
Punts	5-43.2	3-45.3
Fumbles-Lost	3-1	4-2
Penalties-Yards	7-65	10-75
Time of possession	26:26	33:34

Attendance—69,814.

INDIVIDUAL STATISTICS

Rushing—New Orleans, G. Rogers 20-75, Holmes 7-32, W. Wilson 1-2; New York, Kotar 8-46, Bright 6-33, Perry 8-22, Simms 4-0, B. Taylor 7-5.

Passing—New Orleans, Scott 5-15-1—61, D. Wilson 11-23-1—154; New York, Simms 28-41-0—324, Brunner 0-1-0—0.

Receiving—New Orleans, Holmes 1-0, Hardy 1-12, Caster 3-52, Harris 1-13, Chandler 4-73, Tyler 1-10, W. Wilson 4-37, Groth 1-18; New York, Shirk 11-101, Perkins 8-118, Kotar 2-14, Bright 2-42, Friede 1-11, Gray 2-28, B. Taylor 1-5, Perry 1-5.

Kickoff Returns—New Orleans, J. Rogers 2-41, W. Wilson 2-49; New York, Bright 1-20.

Punt Returns—New Orleans, Groth 2-29; New York, Bright 2-16.

Interceptions—New York, Currier 1-0, Reece 1-31.

Punting—New Orleans, Erxleben 5-43.2; New York, Jennings 3-45.3.

Field Goals—New Orleans, None attempted; New York, Danelo 2-5.

COWBOYS 35, PATRIOTS 21

FOXBORO—Bad calls by officials are something that happen in all kinds of sporting events. But seldom do bad calls actually decide the outcome of a game; usually, they cause the tide of momentum to shift from one side to the other.

Such was the case when the New England Patriots fell to the Dallas Cowboys, 35-21, on the third Monday night game of the season.

The disputed play was an 18-yard TD pass from Pats quarterback Matt Cavanaugh to running back Andy Johnson early in the second quarter. The touchdown, if it were allowed, would have put the Patriots ahead, 14-10. But it wasn't allowed. The officials claimed that defensive end Harvey Martin of the Cowboys had sacked Cavanaugh before the pass. Actually, Martin had an arm on Cavanaugh's shoulder and had hardly slowed the quarterback—let alone stop him. The momentum quickly shifted to the Cowboys and they scored on a 75-yard scamper by Tony Dorsett to go up 17-7.

"Some of the calls were brutal," said New England Coach Ron Erhardt.

Although the negated touchdown hurt the Patriots, that alone was not why they lost. Dorsett rambled for 162 yards on 19 carries and Danny White riddled the New England secondary for another 218 yards with 24-for-34 passing.

Their own mistakes also doomed the Patriots. The normally sure-handed Johnson fumbled on the Dallas 3 to kill one drive and Roland James, a second-year player out of Tennessee, made an ill-advised attempt to field a towering Danny White punt and fumbled the ball. The Cowboys recovered and, seven plays later, scored the touchdown that put them in the lead for good.

MONDAY, SEPTEMBER 21
SCORE BY PERIODS

Dallas	7	10	7	11—35
New England	7	7	7	0—21

SCORING

Dallas—Johnson 28 pass from D. White (Septien kick).
New England—Calhoun 4 run (Smith kick).
Dallas—Field goal Septien 26.
Dallas—Dorsett 75 run (Septien kick).
New England—Collins 3 run (Smith kick).
New England—Tatupu 38 run (Smith kick).
Dallas—DuPree 1 pass from D. White (Septien kick).
Dallas—Field goal Septien 26.
Dallas—Safety, intentional grounding in end zone.
Dallas—Field goal Septien 27.
Dallas—Field goal Septien 25.

TEAM STATISTICS

	Dallas	New England
First downs	22	16
Rushes-Yards	46-237	22-108
Passing yards	218	225
Sacks by-Yards	2-10	0-0
Return yards	151	148
Passes	24-34-0	14-27-4
Punts	4-36.3	2-34.0
Fumbles-Lost	4-1	3-3
Penalties-Yards	7-75	5-38
Time of possession	38:34	21:26

Attendance—61,297.

Rushing—Dallas, Dorsett 19-162, Springs 14-62, J. Jones 6-14, Cosbie 1-7, Newhouse 1-0, D. White 5-minus 8; New England, Tatupu 6-63, Calhoun 8-26, Collins 8-19.

Passing—Dallas, D. White 24-34-0—218; New England, Cavanaugh 14-26-4—235, Jackson 0-1-0—0.

Receiving—Dallas, Springs 11-72, Dorsett 4-22, Hill 3-49, Johnson 3-47, DuPree 2-9, Pearson 1-19; New England, Morgan 4-68, Hasselbeck 3-93, Jackson 3-48, Collins 3-12, Johnson 1-14.

Kickoff Returns—Dallas, J. Jones 3-39, Newsome 1-11; New England, Collins 7-142, Hasselbeck 1-7.

Punt Returns—Dallas, J. Jones 2-3; New England, James 1-minus 1.

Interceptions—Dallas, Walls 2-55, Brown 1-28, Thurman 1-15.

Punting—Dallas, D. White 4-36.3; New England, Hubach 2-34.0.

Field Goals—Dallas, Septien 4-5; New England, Smith 0-1.

FOURTH WEEK

COWBOYS 18, GIANTS 10

IRVING—Coming off a Monday night game, Dallas was in a vulnerable position, staggering like a boxer who had chosen the wrong afternoon to step into the ring.

But New York could never apply the knockout punch, and the Cowboys managed to do what good teams are supposed to do—win when they shouldn't.

"We didn't recover from the Monday night game and the loss of sleep," said Coach Tom Landry, referring to the Cowboys' 35-21 victory the previous week over New England. "We had no zip all week in practice."

There was just enough zip, however, to hand the Giants (2-2) their 13th loss in the last 14 meetings with the Cowboys, who boosted their record to 4-0. The heat was also a factor as the temperature rose above 100 degrees on the Texas Stadium turf before kickoff.

The Cowboys used two big plays—one by receiver Butch Johnson and the other by defensive end Ed (Too Tall) Jones.

A lightning-quick 86-yard march that ended with a 41-yard touchdown throw from quarterback Danny White to Johnson 69 seconds before halftime provided the Cowboys with a 10-3 lead.

During the first half, the Giants drove to the Dallas 17, 39, 20 and 39, but came up with only three points—on a 42-yard field goal by Joe Danelo.

"Our offense couldn't take advantage of the opportunities that presented themselves in the first half," said New York Coach Ray Perkins. "In the second half we couldn't get anything going."

But neither could the Cowboys. Despite numerous chances, the Cowboys could manage only two Rafael Septien field goals during the second half, plus a critical safety that came when Jones stripped the ball from Giants quar-terback Phil Simms. The ball bounced back into the end zone, where Giants guard Roy Simmons recovered it to prevent a Dallas touchdown. The Giants' touchdown came with 56 seconds to play on a 20-yard throw from Simms to Johnny Perkins.

"Our offense has an allergy. We must be allergic to the end zone," said White. "We had a lot of chances to put the game away and we didn't."

Dallas intercepted three of Simms' passes, two in the second half, and Simms found himself constantly harassed by the Cowboys' pass rush.

"It was a day for the defense," said Landry. "There was a lot of pressure on Simms, particularly by Randy White. That was the story of the game."

Simms was sacked four times for 27 yards in losses, but he still passed for 285 yards. White, meanwhile, threw for 204 yards. Tony Dorsett, who entered the game as the NFL's leading rusher, picked up only 70 yards in 22 carries.

"If we play this way for 60 minutes every game this season, we are going to win a few games," said Ray Perkins. "Overall, I think we had as good a game as we could expect."

Johnson summed up the game from the Cowboys' standpoint.

"I think we are always flat against the Giants," said the Dallas receiver. "We just can't get motivated because we think we can beat them and that's no knock against the Giants. We feel that we have a better coaching staff and better athletes."

SEPTEMBER 27
SCORE BY PERIODS

New York Giants	0	3	0	7—10
Dallas	3	7	0	8—18

SCORING

Dallas—Field goal Septien 36.
New York—Field goal Danelo 42.
Dallas—Johnson 41 pass from D. White (Septien kick).
Dallas—Field goal Septien 20.
Dallas—Safety, Simms fumbled into end zone.
Dallas—Field goal Septien 21.
New York—Perkins 20 pass from Simms (Danelo kick).

TEAM STATISTICS

	New York	Dallas
First downs	16	16
Rushes-Yards	24-85	41-124
Passing yards	258	193
Sacks by-Yards	2-11	4-27
Return yards	114	104
Passes	18-35-3	14-27-0
Punts	5-45.4	7-43.3
Fumbles-Lost	3-0	1-0
Penalties-Yards	7-52	3-25
Time of possession	26:31	33:29

Attendance—63,449.

INDIVIDUAL STATISTICS

Rushing—New York, B. Taylor 13-52, Bright 5-16, Perry 5-15, Matthews 1-2; Dallas, Dorsett 22-70, Springs 10-17, D. White 2-14, Pearson 1-11, J. Jones 4-10, Newhouse 2-2.

Passing—New York, Simms 18-35-3—285; Dallas, D. White 14-27-0—204.

Fourth Week—Continued

Receiving—New York, Perkins 5-129, Shirk 4-78, Gray 3-38, Mullady 2-17, Friede 1-7, Perry 2-12, B. Taylor 1-4; Dallas, Pearson 4-76, Dorsett 3-33, Johnson 2-59, Springs 2-2, Cosbie 1-22, DuPree 1-6, Donley 1-6.

Kickoff Returns—New York, Garrett 1-24, Bright 4-68; Dallas, J. Jones 1-26, Wilson 1-17.

Punt Returns—New York, Bright 3-22; Dallas, J. Jones 3-21.

Interceptions—Dallas, Thurman 1-27, Walls 1-13, Downs 1-0.

Punting—New York, Jennings 5-45.4; Dallas, D. White 7-43.3.

Field Goals—New York, Danelo 1-3; Dallas, Septien 3-3.

EAGLES 36, REDSKINS 13

PHILADELPHIA—At halftime, the statistics showed Washington with a bulge of 265 yards to 55 in total offense, an edge of 45-17 in offensive plays and a spread of 21 minutes to nine in time of possession. Yet, Philadelphia held a 7-6 lead.

With 10:29 left in the game, the Redskins trailed by only 14-13. Then they self-destructed for the fourth consecutive week, and the Eagles soared to their fourth consecutive victory.

The Redskins entered Philadelphia territory four times in the first half, but came up with only two field goals by Mark Moseley, who was nursing a pulled groin muscle and missed two other attempts. An apparent seven-yard touchdown pass from Joe Theismann to Art Monk was wiped out by a delay-of-game penalty.

"We're talking about a killer-half there," said Eagles noseguard Charlie Johnson. "We're a comeback team, but if we had to come back from 28 points down, that would have been tough. They were inside the 10 three times, but they didn't get any touchdowns."

The Philadelphia defense forced three turnovers, which led to 13 points, and picked up a safety as the Eagles scored 22 points in a span of 6:13 in the fourth period to put the game away.

As a result, the Eagles were off to a 4-0 start for the first time since 1954 and the Redskins were 0-4 for the first time since 1965.

The roof fell in for Washington as follows:

After John Riggins' three-yard touchdown run made the score 14-13, the Redskins allowed Wally Henry to get loose for a 43-yard kickoff return. Five plays later, Ron Jaworski threw a 29-yard TD pass to Charlie Smith.

On Washington's next play from scrimmage, a Theismann pass was tipped and intercepted by Reggie Wilkes, setting up a 28-yard field goal by Tony Franklin.

On the next Redskin play, Theismann was trapped in the end zone by noseguard Ken Clarke for the Eagles' first safety since 1972.

On Washington's next possession, Terry Metcalf fumbled and linebacker Frank LeMaster

recovered. This set up a 36-yard field goal by Franklin.

Tom Flick replaced Theismann at quarterback for the Redskins, and he fumbled as he was sacked. Rookie defensive end Greg Brown recovered for the Eagles and ran seven yards to score.

"We played toe-to-toe with them and beat them in the stats, but we didn't score. And when you don't do that, you don't win," said Theismann.

The Eagles were without star running back Wilbert Montgomery, nursing a hamstring pull, and then they lost starting fullback Perry Harrington, who suffered a broken leg and may be out for the season. Louis Giammona, subbing for Montgomery, scored two touchdowns.

SEPTEMBER 27
SCORE BY PERIODS

Washington	0	6	0	7—13
Philadelphia	0	7	7	22—36

SCORING

Philadelphia—Giammona 13 pass from Jaworski (Franklin kick).
Washington—Field goal Moseley 19.
Washington—Field goal Moseley 22.
Philadelphia—Giammona 1 run (Franklin kick).
Washington—Riggins 3 run (Moseley kick).
Philadelphia—Smith 29 pass from Jaworski (Franklin kick).
Philadelphia—Field goal Franklin 28.
Philadelphia—Safety, Theismann sacked in end zone.
Philadelphia—Field goal Franklin 36.
Philadelphia—Brown 7 fumble recovery (Franklin kick).

TEAM STATISTICS

	Washington	Philadelphia
First downs	23	15
Rushes-Yards	33-109	25-70
Passing yards	228	151
Sacks by-Yards	2-16	4-37
Return yards	110	148
Passes	22-34-1	15-27-1
Punts	3-51.0	4-46.0
Fumbles-Lost	3-2	0-0
Penalties-Yards	8-98	10-77
Time of possession	32:53	27:07
Attendance—70,664.		

INDIVIDUAL STATISTICS

Rushing—Washington, Jackson 17-64, Riggins 9-22, Metcalf 5-14, Walker 1-5, Theismann 1-4; Philadelphia, Giammona 18-49, Campfield 5-19, Harrington 1-4, Pisarcik 1-minus 2.

Passing—Washington, Theismann 22-32-1—265, Flick 0-2-0—0; Philadelphia, Jaworski 14-26-1—150, Pisarcik 1-1-0—17.

Receiving—Washington, Metcalf 8-123, Thompson 4-52, Monk 4-33, Warren 2-33, Riggins 2-18, Harmon 1-6, Walker 1-0; Philadelphia, Giammona 5-47, Campfield 4-27, Carmichael 3-49, Smith 3-44.

Kickoff Returns—Washington, Nelms 2-50, Wonsley 1-22; Philadelphia, Henry 4-115.

Punt Returns—Washington, Nelms 4-8; Philadelphia, Henry 2-22.

Interceptions—Washington, Lavender 1-30; Philadelphia, Wilkes 1-11.

Punting—Washington, Connell 3-51.0; Philadelphia, Runager 4-46.0.

Field Goals—Washington, Moseley 2-4; Philadelphia, Franklin 2-2.

LIONS 16, RAIDERS O

PONTIAC—The Detroit Lions went into their game against the Oakland Raiders with the worst pass defense record in the National Football Conference. So guess what happened?

The Lions not only held Oakland to 102 yards through the air and sacked quarterback Jim Plunkett six times, but they hung the first shutout on the Raiders in 15 years with a 16-0 triumph.

Until the fired-up Lions stopped them in the Silverdome, the Raiders had scored in 219 consecutive regular-season games since September 10, 1966, when the Houston Oilers beat them, 31-0.

The Lions limited the defending Super Bowl champions to 131 yards total offense. Billy Sims rushed for 133 yards and Dexter Bussey ran for 48, moving past Altie Taylor as Detroit's all-time leading rusher. Bussey has a career total of 4,334 yards.

Lions quarterback Gary Danielson was injured on the next-to-last series of the first half. Backup quarterback Jeff Komlo took over and directed the Lions to all 16 points. Eddie Murray kicked field goals of 36, 39, and 39 yards and Sims scored on a three-yard run on first play after Oakland's Malcolm Barnwell fumbled on a kickoff return and the loose ball was recovered by Detroit safety Luther Bradley.

"This was a very important game to us," said Komlo. "The whole team looked at it as a must game. Going into the season, we all decided we needed to be at least 2-2 in our first four games."

"There was no way we could come out of this game with a loss or a tie," said Bussey. "The justification for losing this game was about zilch."

Oakland's scoring chances were about zilch. The only time the Raiders got close was early in the fourth period, when Plunkett directed a drive from the Oakland 6 to the Detroit 18. Chris Bahr's attempt for 36-yard field goal, which would have tied the score at 3-3, sailed wide to the right.

The Lions then marched to Murray's second field goal, with the key play an eight-yard pass from punt formation by Tom Skladany to Ken Callicutt.

On the ensuing kickoff, Barnwell fumbled and Sims raced around left end for the game's only touchdown—his sixth of the season. The Lions had 10 points in a span of 21 seconds and Oakland was beaten.

"We just didn't get the job done," said Raiders Coach Tom Flores. "The Lions pass-rushed well and our missed field goal hurt. Defensively, we gave them too many opportunities. You can't leave your defense on the field that long, especially against great players like Billy Sims."

SEPTEMBER 27

SCORE BY PERIODS

Oakland	0	0	0	0— 0
Detroit	0	3	0	13—16

SCORING

Detroit—Field goal Murray 36.
Detroit—Field goal Murray 39.
Detroit—Sims 3 run (Murray kick).
Detroit—Field goal Murray 39.

TEAM STATISTICS

	Oakland	Detroit
First downs	14	20
Rushes-Yards	32-86	35-181
Passing yards	45	79
Sacks by-Yards	4-30	6-57
Return yards	82	136
Passes	11-21-1	12-27-2
Punts	8-50.0	5-42.2
Fumbles-Lost	3-1	3-1
Penalties-Yards	7-42	10-100
Time of possession	29:21	30:39

Attendance—77,919.

INDIVIDUAL STATISTICS

Rushing—Oakland, Jensen 19-65, King 10-15, Whittington 2-5, Plunkett 1-1; Detroit, Sims 21-133, Bussey 12-48, Scott 1-3, L. Thompson 1-minus 3.

Passing—Oakland, Plunkett 11-21-1—102; Detroit, Danielson 3-10-2—36, Komlo 8-16-0—65, Skladany 1-1-0—8.

Receiving—Oakland, Bradshaw 4-49, Chester 3-27, Jensen 2-12, Ramsey 1-10, Upshaw 1-4; Detroit, Hill 4-34, L. Thompson 2-27, Scott 2-24, King 1-9, Callicutt 1-8, Sims 1-7, Bussey 1-0.

Kickoff Returns—Oakland, Matthews 2-38, Barnwell 2-13, Christensen 1-19; Detroit, Hall 1-30.

Punt Returns—Oakland, Matthews 2-8; Detroit, Martin 6-76.

Interceptions—Oakland, Hayes 1-0, McKinney 1-4; Detroit, Allen 1-30.

Punting—Oakland, Guy 7-55.6, Bahr 1-11.0; Detroit, Skladany 5-42.2.

Field Goals—Oakland, Bahr 0-1; Detroit, Murray 3-3.

49ers 21, SAINTS 14

SAN FRANCISCO—Freddie Solomon is neither the biggest nor the best wide receiver in the NFL, but he's gifted in the art of catching the football in traffic and knowing what to do once he's caught it.

Solomon grabbed a pass from San Francisco quarterback Joe Montana in the third quarter and then avoided three tacklers en route to a 60-yard touchdown that enabled the 49ers to beat New Orleans.

With the score tied 7-7, Montana hit Solomon with a 25-yard strike to the Saints 35, and he outmaneuvered the defense to put the 49ers ahead for good.

"I got hit, but I kept my balance," said Solomon.

The 49ers later got a 26-yard touchdown run from rookie defensive back Ronnie Lott on an interception return, which put the game out of reach for the Saints.

Four fumbles, three interceptions and 19 penalties for 185 yards marred the contest. Naturally, 49ers coach Bill Walsh was pleased

Fourth Week—Continued

with the outcome since his team evened its record at 2-2.

"Our team showed good character, especially defensively," said Walsh. "We didn't move the ball as we normally do, but you have to give credit to the Saints for that."

Montana completed 16 of 22 passes for 175 yards, but the 49ers could hardly muster a ground attack, with Johnny Davis gaining 48 yards in 11 carries and Ricky Patton 42 in 14. George Rogers led the Saints with 115 yards in 25 carries.

Rookie Dave Wilson, making his first NFL start in place of the ailing Archie Manning, hit on 11 of 22 for 180 yards. His 24-yard toss to Jeff Groth gave the Saints a 7-0 first-quarter lead.

The 49ers tied the game five minutes into the second quarter on a six-yard run by Davis, capping a 15-play, 69-yard drive. Manning entered the game early in the fourth quarter and directed the Saints to their second touchdown, the final play a nine-yard pass to fullback Wayne Wilson.

"I hate getting close and getting nothing," said New Orleans Coach Bum Phillips, whose team dropped to 1-3. "But I can't do nothing about it. I thought we did pretty well. What the hell do you expect from a football team?"

SEPTEMBER 27
SCORE BY PERIODS

New Orleans	7	0	0	7—14
San Francisco	0	7	7	7—21

SCORING

New Orleans—Groth 24 pass from D. Wilson (Ricardo kick).
San Francisco—Davis 6 run (Bahr kick).
San Francisco—Solomon 60 pass from Montana (Bahr kick).
San Francisco—Lott 26 pass interception (Bahr kick).
New Orleans—W. Wilson 9 pass from Manning (Ricardo kick).

TEAM STATISTICS

	New Orleans	San Fran.
First downs	18	15
Rushes-Yards	37-163	39-146
Passing yards	250	168
Sacks by-Yards	1-7	0-0
Return yards	192	102
Passes	21-38-2	16-22-1
Punts	6-40.2	9-45.1
Fumbles-Lost	3-2	1-1
Penalties-Yards	11-106	8-79
Time of possession	30:44	29:16

Attendance—44,433.

INDIVIDUAL STATISTICS

Rushing—New Orleans, G. Rogers 25-115, W. Wilson 5-27, Tyler 2-13, D. Wilson 1-9, Holmes 3-8, Myers 1-minus 9; San Francisco, Davis 11-48, Patton 14-42, Hofer 4-19, Montana 3-17, Cooper 5-10, Solomon 1-5, Easley 1-5.

Passing—New Orleans, D. Wilson 11-22-1—180, Manning 10-16-1—70; San Francisco, Montana 16-22-1-175.

Receiving—New Orleans, Chandler 4-72, Tyler 4-30, Holmes 3-11, Groth 2-56, W. Wilson 2-27, Williams 2-17, G. Rogers 2-16, Caster 1-13, Hardy 1-8; San Francisco, Young 3-41, Clark 3-30, Cooper 3-6, Solomon 2-80, Patton 2-8, Hofer 2-7, Lawrence 1-3.

Kickoff Returns—New Orleans, Groth 1-21, J. Rogers 1-16, Brock 1-12, W. Wilson 1-21; San Francisco, Lott 1-0, Lawrence 1-26.

Punt Returns—New Orleans, Groth 6-91; San Francisco, Solomon 3-14, Hicks 1-10.

Interceptions—New Orleans, Waymer 1-31; San Francisco, Lott 1-26, Wright 1-26.

Punting—New Orleans, Erxleben 6-40.2; San Francisco, Miller 9-45.1.

Field Goals—New Orleans, None attempted; San Francisco, None attempted.

VIKINGS 30, PACKERS 13

MILWAUKEE—The euphoria created by John Jefferson's prance onto the field at the start of the game didn't last long for Green Bay as the Minnesota defense took control and decked the Packers.

Jefferson, the All-Pro wide receiver obtained from San Diego, made his debut with the Packers. He contributed a 15-yard run on a reverse play as Green Bay marched 76 yards for a first-quarter touchdown. Then, after Lynn Dickey's six-yard scoring pass to James Lofton, Jefferson greeted the Packers' other All-Pro receiver with a leaping "high five" on the sideline.

On the ensuing kickoff, the Pack's Mark Murphy recovered a fumble by Keith Nord to set up a field goal by Jan Stenerud. Green Bay was off to a 10-0 lead and things looked rosy.

Then the Vikings' defense fattened up at the expense of Green Bay's injury-riddled offensive line. Minnesota recorded eight quarterback sacks, recovered two fumbles and blocked a punt.

Defensive end Doug Martin contributed sacks on consecutive plays in the second quarter. The first knocked Dickey out of the game. The second forced a fumble by David Whitehurst, which was returned 45 yards for a touchdown by defensive tackle Randy Holloway. That tied the score at 10-10.

Next, the Vikes' Robin Sendlein blocked a punt and recovered on the Green Bay 11, setting up a field goal by Rick Danmeier that put Minnesota ahead. Just before halftime, Tommy Kramer threw a 54-yard TD pass to Bob Bruer to make the score 20-10. And then, Green Bay's Fred Nixon fumbled the second-half kickoff, Minnesota recovered and Kramer threw a seven-yard TD pass to Ahmad Rashad, making it 27-10 just 24 seconds into the third quarter.

Jefferson had seven receptions for 121 yards and Lofton caught eight balls for 101 yards. Including Jefferson's 15-yard run, the two receivers combined for 237 of Green Bay's 316 net yards.

Starr said he was pleased with Jefferson's debut, but not with the team. "There were a lot of areas where we have to go back to square one," he said. "We'll correct them."

Newly acquired wide receiver John Jefferson of Green Bay catches his first pass as a member of the Packers. The former San Diego All-Pro caught six other passes in the game but the Packers lost anyway, 30-13, to Minnesota.

Fourth Week—Continued

SEPTEMBER 27

SCORE BY PERIODS

Minnesota	0	20	10	0—30
Green Bay	10	0	3	0—13

SCORING

Green Bay—Lofton 6 pass from Dickey (Stenerud kick).
Green Bay—Field goal Stenerud 24.
Minnesota—Field goal Danmeier 34.
Minnesota—Holloway 45 fumble recovery (Danmeier kick).
Minnesota—Field goal Danmeier 30.
Minnesota—Bruer 1 pass from Kramer (Danmeier kick).
Minnesota—Rashad 7 pass from Kramer (Danmeier kick).
Green Bay—Field goal Stenerud 27.
Minnesota—Field goal Danmeier 25.

TEAM STATISTICS

	Minnesota	Green Bay
First downs	27	22
Rushes-Yards	32-157	19-71
Passing yards	253	245
Sacks by-Yards	8-58	0-0
Return yards	79	120
Passes	19-34-0	22-40-0
Punts	0-0.0	3-42.7
Fumbles-Lost	4-3	3-2
Penalties-Yards	8-88	9-79
Time of possession	30:15	29:45
Attendance—55,012.		

INDIVIDUAL STATISTICS

Rushing—Minnesota, Brown 21-109, Galbreath 5-39, Young 6-9; Green Bay, Jensen 7-35, Middleton 5-5, Jefferson 1-15, Huckleby 4-13, Dickey 1-0, Whitehurst 1-3.

Passing—Minnesota, Kramer 19-34-0—253; Green Bay, Dickey 19-33-0—251, Whitehurst 3-7-0—52.

Receiving—Minnesota, S. White 3-57, Rashad 5-66, Senser 4-66, LeCount 1-21, Young 3-19, Bruer 1-1, Brown 2-23; Green Bay, Lofton 8-101, Coffman 5-67, Middleton 1-7, Jefferson 7-121, Jensen 1-7.

Kickoff Returns—Minnesota, Payton 1-13, Nord 2-22, McDole 1-15; Green Bay, Nixon 5-95, Huckleby 1-25.

Punt Returns—Minnesota, Payton 2-19.

Interceptions—None.

Punting—Minnesota, None; Green Bay, Stachowicz 3-42.7.

Field Goals—Minnesota, Danmeier 3-4; Green Bay, Stenerud 2-3.

CHIEFS 20, SEAHAWKS 14

SEATTLE—A porous defense almost wrecked the Kansas City Chiefs, but they stopped Seattle's final charge on the 1-yard line to preserve their third victory in four games.

The Chiefs scored four of the first five times they had the ball to take a 20-0 lead. The scores came on short TD runs by Ted McKnight and quarterback Bill Kenney and 38-yard and 30-yard field goals by Nick Lowery.

That proved enough to enable Kansas City to share the AFC West lead with San Diego and Denver. But Jim Zorn, Seattle's scrambling quarterback, got hot in the second half, completing 14 straight passes.

The Seahawks were trailing, 20-14, in the fourth quarter and had the ball inside the Kansas City 1 on fourth down. Then cornerback

Gary Green made a game-saving tackle that stopped running back Sherman Smith short of the goal line.

"Smith broke off tackle and Gary came up and made a super in-your-face tackle," said Don Parrish, the Chiefs' defensive tackle.

"I don't really know what happened," said Smith. "Gary Green came in and submarined my legs and stopped my progress. They just made a good play."

Zorn was Seattle's leading rusher with 48 yards on four carries.

SEPTEMBER 27

SCORE BY PERIODS

Kansas City	7	13	0	0—20
Seattle	0	7	7	0—14

SCORING

Kansas City—McKnight 2 run (Lowery kick).
Kansas City—Kenney 1 run (Lowery kick).
Kansas City—Field goal Lowery 30.
Kansas City—Field goal Lowery 38.
Seattle—McCullum 11 pass from Zorn (Herrera kick).
Seattle—Smith 2 run (Herrera kick).

TEAM STATISTICS

	Kansas City	Seattle
First downs	26	23
Rushes-Yards	42-154	19-82
Passing yards	227	277
Sacks by-Yards	3-31	1-12
Return yards	71	97
Passes	16-25-0	31-47-0
Punts	2-42.5	3-39.3
Fumbles-Lost	3-2	3-1
Penalties-Yards	4-40	7-50
Time of possession	32:01	27:59
Attendance—59,255.		

INDIVIDUAL STATISTICS

Rushing—Kansas City, Delaney 15-45, B. Jackson 5-40, McKnight 10-37, Hadnot 9-34, Kenney 2-3, Dixon 1-minus 5; Seattle, Zorn 4-48, Smith 11-23, Hughes 2-6, Jodat 2-5.

Passing—Kansas City, Kenney 16-25-0—239; Seattle, Zorn 31-47-0—308.

Receiving—Kansas City, Smith 5-81, McKnight 5-61, Marshall 2-31, Delaney 2-26, Dixon 1-31, Hadnot 1-9; Seattle, Hughes 12-103, McCullum 5-46, Smith 5-35, Johns 4-62, Largent 4-52, McGrath 1-10.

Kickoff Returns—Kansas City, B. Jackson 2-38, Burruss 1-22; Seattle, Lewis 4-80, Johnson 1-11.

Punt Returns—Kansas City, Smith 3-11; Seattle, Lewis 2-6.

Interceptions—None.

Punting—Kansas City, Grupp 2-42.5; Seattle, West 3-39.3.

Field Goals—Kansas City, Lowery 2-3; Seattle, None attempted.

BRONCOS 42, CHARGERS 24

DENVER—Craig Morton fired four touchdown passes for the second consecutive week and the Denver Broncos raced to a 28-0 halftime lead to shock the San Diego Chargers, 42-24, at Mile High Stadium.

The victory left Denver, San Diego and the Kansas City Chiefs tied at 3-1 atop the American Football Conference Western Division.

Morton completed 17 of 18 passes for 308

yards. He got the Broncos off to a 21-0 lead in the first quarter, and San Diego never recovered. Meanwhile, the Broncos' pass rush was able to swarm over Charger quarterback Dan Fouts, producing five sacks and three interceptions.

Two of Morton's touchdown passes went to Steve Wilson, the fourth-year wide receiver who never had caught a scoring pass until this season. He grabbed three against Baltimore in the Broncos' third game, and had scoring plays of 93 and 22 yards against San Diego.

The 93-yarder was a fluke. Denver had a 7-0 lead (on a Morton-to-Riley Odoms pass) late in the first quarter and was backed up on its 7-yard line. Morton threw to Watson at the 20 and Chargers safety Frank Duncan moved in to make the tackle. Instead, Duncan bumped the receiver into the clear. Watson staggered to regain his balance and then went untouched to score.

"Somebody hit me from inside, and they all fell off," Watson said. "I guess they ran into each other and there was nobody to chase me. It was a long way. I was thinking about the 110s we run in practice, so I was prepared to go 93."

The Broncos got a break following the long TD. Clarence Williams fumbled the kickoff and Denver's Mike Harden recovered on the 3, setting up a two-yard pass from Morton to tight end Jim Wright that made the score 21-0.

An interception by Steve Foley stopped a San Diego drive in the second quarter, and Morton marched the Broncos 78 yards. The payoff was Watson's 22-yard TD catch.

That made it 28-0 at the half and, noted San Diego Coach Don Coryell, "What can you say (in the locker room) when you're 28 down?"

Denver went ahead, 35-0, in the third quarter when Dave Preston got the Broncos' first rushing TD this season. Coach Dan Reeves then replaced Morton with Steve DeBerg, but after the Chargers roared back with 24 points, Morton went back into the game. The Broncos got their final TD on a 34-yard drive following a fumble recovery.

"I thought we did an excellent job, but in the second half we had about three turnovers, and all of a sudden you look up and they are back in the game," said Reeves. "It was kind of scary."

San Diego lost two key running backs. Chuck Muncie, who went into the game as the AFC's leading rusher, suffered a broken hand in the first half. In the fourth quarter, rookie James Brooks suffered a pulled hamstring.

SEPTEMBER 27
SCORE BY PERIODS

San Diego	0	0	10	14—24
Denver	21	7	7	7—42

SCORING
Denver—Odoms 19 pass from Morton (Steinfort kick).
Denver—Watson 93 pass from Morton (Steinfort kick).
Denver—J. Wright 2 pass from Morton (Steinfort kick).
Denver—Watson 22 pass from Morton (Steinfort kick).
Denver—Preston 2 run (Steinfort kick).
San Diego—Smith 39 pass from Fouts (Benirschke kick).
San Diego—Field goal Benirschke 52.
San Diego—Cappelletti 1 run (Benirschke kick).
San Diego—Winslow 1 pass from Fouts (Benirschke kick).
Denver—Lytle 3 run (Steinfort kick).

TEAM STATISTICS

	San Diego	Denver
First downs	23	20
Rushes-Yards	22-84	37-103
Passing yards	265	350
Sacks by-Yards	2-17	5-33
Return yards	100	95
Passes	26-47-3	21-24-0
Punts	3-40.0	3-42.7
Fumbles-Lost	2-2	3-3
Penalties-Yards	6-40	6-55
Time of possession	27:06	32:54
Attendance—74,844.		

INDIVIDUAL STATISTICS
Rushing—San Diego, Muncie 7-16, J. Brooks 7-41, Cappelletti 7-26, C. Williams 1-1; Denver, Parros 6-15, Preston 14-32, Reed 4-minus 2, Canada 8-43, Morton 2-6, Lytle 3-9.

Passing—San Diego, Fouts 26-47-3—298; Denver, Morton 17-18-0—308, DeBerg 4-6-0—59.

Receiving—San Diego, Muncie 3-35, Sievers 3-26, Winslow 10-106, Cappelletti 2-26, Joiner 3-32, J. Brooks 2-6, Smith 1-39, C. Williams 1-12, Scales 1-16; Denver, Watson 8-178, Manning 2-41, Odoms 4-71, J. Wright 1-2, Preston 2-25, Reed 2-7, Moses 2-43.

Kickoff Returns—San Diego, Shaw 1-24, Thompson 2-44, C. Williams 3-32; Denver, Manning 2-42, Preston 1-1.

Punt Returns—Denver, Manning 2-10.

Interceptions—Denver, Foley 3-42.

Punting—San Diego, Roberts 3-40.0; Denver, Prestridge 3-42.7.

Field Goals—San Diego, Benirschke 1-1; Denver, Steinfort 0-1.

BUCCANEERS 20, CARDINALS 10

TAMPA—The scrambling ability of quarterback Doug Williams and an unusual tripping penalty that nullified a St. Louis field goal made the difference as Tampa Bay rallied in the fourth period to pull out its second victory of the season.

The Cardinals had a 10-6 lead and had been moving the ball at will most of the second half. With a little over 11 minutes remaining, Neil O'Donoghue boomed a 47-yard field goal that apparently increased St. Louis' lead to 13-6.

But wait! Linebacker Calvin Favron, in the backfield blocking for the kicker, was called for tripping the Bucs' John Holt as the rookie cornerback charged in, attempting to block the kick. The 15-yard penalty moved the ball out of field goal range and Tampa Bay took over on its 20 after the Cardinals punted into the end zone.

"I thought that was turning point of the game," said St. Louis Coach Jim Hanifan. "We had the momentum. We were running the ball up and down the field on them. Neil goes in and kicks it straight between the uprights and we've got a 13-6 lead. We're feeling safe be-

Fourth Week—Continued

cause it's the start of the fourth quarter and that lead might be sufficient."

Given the reprieve, Williams moved the Bucs 80 yards for the go-ahead score. He kept the drive alive with two fourth-down gambles. On fourth and five at the St. Louis 32, Williams took the snap in the shotgun formation and scrambled 13 yards for a first down. Moments later, on fourth and seven at the 16, he fired a 14-yard pass to tight end Jimmie Giles to the St. Louis 2.

James Owens, on his first carry as a member of the Bucs, scored from one yard out to give Tampa the lead with 2:41 left. The former Olympic trials sprinter had been used only on kick returns since being obtained from San Francisco.

On the Cardinals' next possession, linebacker Cecil Johnson intercepted a Jim Hart pass and returned it to the St. Louis 39. On third down, Jerry Eckwood sprinted 31 yards for the clinching score, with 1:51 to play.

The Cardinals' Favron admitted that he was guilty on the penalty that nullified the field goal.

"I tripped him, just a little bit, to throw him off," Favron said. "But I have done that before, and it's never been called. You can either use that technique or double-bump him. I chose to trip him. It was a bad call."

In the Bucs' go-ahead drive, which required 16 plays and ate up 8:25 on the clock, Williams ran twice for 23 yards and completed six passes for 51 yards.

Rookie running back James Wilder was the Bucs' workhorse. He ran 15 times for 76 yards and caught nine passes for 72 yards.

SEPTEMBER 27
SCORE BY PERIODS

St. Louis	0	3	7	0—10
Tampa Bay	6	0	0	14—20

SCORING

Tampa Bay—Field goal Capece 29.
Tampa Bay—Field goal Capece 23.
St. Louis—Field goal O'Donoghue 20.
St. Louis—Harrell 1 run (O'Donoghue kick).
Tampa Bay—Owens 1 run (Capece kick).
Tampa Bay—Eckwood 31 run (Capece kick).

TEAM STATISTICS

	St. Louis	Tampa Bay
First downs	18	18
Rushes-Yards	38-176	34-167
Passing yards	79	154
Sacks by-Yards	1-8	2-20
Return yards	101	29
Passes	12-19-1	17-30-0
Punts	4-41.8	5-46.2
Fumbles-Lost	2-1	1-1
Penalties-Yards	6-60	7-97
Time of possession	29:37	30:23
Attendance—65,850.		

INDIVIDUAL STATISTICS

Rushing—St. Louis, Anderson 20-97, Mitchell 5-18, Morris 12-60, Harrell 1-1; Tampa Bay, Eckwood 13-71, Wilder 15-76, Williams 5-19, Owens 1-1.

Passing—St. Louis, Hart 11-18-1—91, Lomax 1-1-0—8; Tampa Bay, Williams 17-30-0—162.

Receiving—St. Louis, Tilley 1-11, Anderson 3-8, Green 2-24, Harrell 2-13, Stief 1-23, Mitchell 1-5, Morris 1-11, LaFleur 1-4; Tampa Bay, Wilder 9-72, Giles 3-36, T. Bell 2-24, Obradovich 1-13, House 2-17.

Kickoff Returns—St. Louis, Mitchell 3-64, Love 1-5; Tampa Bay, T. Davis 1-21.

Punt Returns—St. Louis, Mitchell 3-32; Tampa Bay, T. Bell 1-5.

Interceptions—Tampa Bay, Johnson 1-3.

Punting—St. Louis, Birdsong 4-41.8; Tampa Bay, Swider 5-46.2.

Field Goals—St. Louis, O'Donoghue 1-2; Tampa Bay, Capece 2-2.

BROWNS 28, FALCONS 17

CLEVELAND—There's something different about the Browns this year, despite their 2-2 record that merely matched their pace after four games last season.

The difference is in the defense, which linebacker Clay Matthews thinks is superior to what the Browns had a year ago when they won the AFC Central title. Said Matthews after the Browns had handed Atlanta its first loss in four games:

"In the past, we had a tendency to let the opposition move the ball, and that led to our 'Kardiac Kids' finishes. We want to choke them off when we get ahead."

That's what the Browns did to the Falcons, who did manage to take a 10-0 lead on Steve Bartkowski's 18-yard TD pass to Alfred Jenkins and a 35-yard field goal by Mick Luckhurst. But the Browns were ahead for good, 21-10, at the half after Brian Sipe scored on a one-yard run. He also tossed scoring passes to Mike Pruitt and Ozzie Newsome.

A fumbled punt by Reggie Smith and Jenkins' fumble after catching a pass led to two Cleveland scores.

"I'd like to think we could have won without those two quick touchdowns," said Sipe. "Still, it was quite a psychological boost to take into the locker room at halftime."

"I think we were fortunate that Steve Bartkowski wasn't 100 percent healthy," said Browns Coach Sam Rutigliano, referring to cracked ribs the Falcons quarterback suffered two weeks earlier. "But we beat an excellent football team. It's a compliment to our team that we beat a club that I think might go to the Super Bowl."

SEPTEMBER 27
SCORE BY PERIODS

Atlanta	3	7	0	7—17
Cleveland	0	21	7	0—28

SCORING

Atlanta—Field goal Luckhurst 35.
Atlanta—Jenkins 18 pass from Bartkowski (Luckhurst kick).
Cleveland—M. Pruitt 13 pass from Sipe (Jacobs kick).

Cleveland—Newsome 23 pass from Sipe (Jacobs kick).
Cleveland—Sipe 1 run (Jacobs kick).
Cleveland—M. Pruitt 1 run (Jacobs kick).
Atlanta—Jenkins 5 pass from Bartkowski (Luckhurst kick).

TEAM STATISTICS

	Atlanta	Cleveland
First downs	14	26
Rushes-Yards	23-112	44-178
Passing yards	150	207
Sacks by-Yards	1-8	3-26
Return yards	84	97
Passes	12-30-2	21-34-2
Punts	7-45.0	4-43.8
Fumbles-Lost	2-2	5-3
Penalties-Yards	9-100	6-53
Time of possession	23:05	36:55
Attendance—78,283.		

INDIVIDUAL STATISTICS

Rushing—Atlanta, Andrews 16-97, Cain 6-13, Daykin 1-2; Cleveland, M. Pruitt 20-99, White 17-72, C. Miller 3-9, Sipe 4-minus 2.

Passing—Atlanta, Bartkowski 12-30-2—176; Cleveland, Sipe 21-34-2—215.

Receiving—Atlanta, Jenkins 6-136, Cain 3-20, Andrews 2-9, Miller 1-11; Cleveland, Newsome 6-78, M. Pruitt 4-33, White 4-32, G. Pruitt 3-26, Logan 2-32, Rucker 1-8, C. Miller 1-6.

Kickoff Returns—Atlanta, R. Smith 2-44, Mayberry 1-8; Cleveland, Montgomery 2-64, E. Johnson 1-7.

Punt Returns—Atlanta, R. Smith 2-2; Cleveland, Montgomery 6-26.

Interceptions—Atlanta, Butler 1-0, Pridemore 1-30; Cleveland, Flint 1-0, Logan 1-0.

Punting—Atlanta, James 7-45.0; Cleveland, Cox 4-43.8.

Field Goals—Atlanta, Luckhurst 1-1; Cleveland, Jacobs 0-2.

BENGALS 27, BILLS 24
(Overtime)

CINCINNATI—The Bengals are growling again. Their scratch-and-claw overtime victory against Buffalo was their third triumph in four games, the team's best start in five years.

"I'm happy to be 3-1 because it's a big step in the right direction," said Coach Forrest Gregg, who was hired to put some bite back into the Bengals.

The Bengals sent the Bills (2-2) back to Buffalo wondering what happened to their vaunted defense. Buffalo entered the game with the best defense against scoring in the NFL, allowing an average of eight points a game. But Cincinnati pushed the Bills all over the field, mounting scoring drives of 97, 91, 84, 70 and 58 yards.

"We just couldn't stop them," said Bills safety Steve Freeman. "I don't know why."

Quarterback Ken Anderson pierced the Bills' defense, completing 28 of 40 passes for 328 yards and three touchdowns.

"I don't know how anyone can play a better football game than Anderson did," said Gregg. The previous week, Anderson had been booed by hometown fans in a 20-17 loss to Cleveland.

Jim Breech provided the game-winning margin on a 28-yard field goal 9 minutes and 33 seconds into overtime. Buffalo sent the game

into overtime on a 40-yard field goal by Nick Mike-Mayer with only one second remaining in regulation time.

The Bengals opened the scoring two minutes into the second quarter with Anderson firing a 13-yard touchdown pass to Cris Collinsworth. Buffalo used a fake punt on fourth and one from midfield to continue a drive which Joe Ferguson finished with an eight-yard scoring pass to Frank Lewis.

A fumbled punt led to the Bills' second touchdown, a four-yard pass to tight end Mark Brammer, but the Bengals cut the lead to 14-10 on Breech's 23-yard field goal on the final play of the second half.

Ferguson fired his third TD pass at the start of the fourth quarter, connecting with Lewis for a 21-10 Buffalo lead, but Anderson threw a pair of 16-yard scoring passes to Steve Kreider for a 24-21 edge.

"Our defense just had a tough time out there," said Ferguson, who passed for 287 yards and three touchdowns. "Now, we're going to find out just what kind of team we have. We're going to see if we can bounce back."

SEPTEMBER 27
SCORE BY PERIODS

Buffalo	0	14	0	10	0—24
Cincinnati	0	10	0	14	3—27

SCORING

Cincinnati—Collinsworth 13 pass from Anderson (Breech kick).
Buffalo—Lewis 9 pass from Ferguson (Mike-Mayer kick).
Buffalo—Brammer 4 pass from Ferguson (Mike-Mayer kick).
Cincinnati—Field goal Breech 23.
Buffalo—Lewis 5 pass from Ferguson (Mike-Mayer kick).
Cincinnati—Kreider 16 pass from Anderson (Breech kick).
Cincinnati—Kreider 16 pass from Anderson (Breech kick).
Buffalo—Field goal Mike-Mayer 40.
Cincinnati—Field goal Breech 28.

TEAM STATISTICS

	Buffalo	Cincinnati
First downs	25	30
Rushes-Yards	30-102	31-113
Passing yards	287	316
Sacks by-Yards	3-12	0-0
Return yards	95	50
Passes	25-46-0	28-40-0
Punts	4-43.8	3-55.7
Fumbles-Lost	2-1	3-2
Penalties-Yards	9-55	6-49
Time of possession	35:06	34:27
Attendance—46,418.		

INDIVIDUAL STATISTICS

Rushing—Buffalo, McCutcheon 3-7, Cribbs 18-48, Leaks 7-37, Hooks 2-10; Cincinnati, Johnson 22-85, Alexander 5-1, Anderson 2-21, Griffin 2-6.

Passing—Buffalo, Ferguson 25-45-0—287, Mike-Mayer 0-1-0—0; Cincinnati, Anderson 28-40-0—328.

Receiving—Buffalo, Lewis 8-132, Jessie 4-37, Butler 1-26, Cribbs 7-54, Brammer 3-26, McCutcheon 2-12; Cincinnati, Collinsworth 10-111, Ross 1-17, Alexander 1-13, Griffin 3-21, Kreider 4-75, Johnson 3-29, Hargrove 1-0, Curtis 2-18, McInally 2-21, Verser 1-23.

Kickoff Returns—Buffalo, Hooks 3-68, Bess 1-6; Cincinnati, Verser 1-21, Chapman 1-29.

— 163 —

Fourth Week—Continued

JETS 33, OILERS 17

NEW YORK—Richard Todd has had his fill of the news media. Blasted in the press and booed by fans after the New York Jets lost their first three games, the quarterback refused to speak to reporters following his superb effort which helped flatten Houston.

"I ain't saying nothing to nobody," Todd announced after throwing three touchdown passes. "I'm not talking to a damned soul."

Todd's actions on the field spoke volumes, however. He fired two TD tosses to Wesley Walker within 95 seconds in the second period. That put the Jets in the lead to stay.

The key play came with the Jets ahead, 14-7, after Johnny Lynn intercepted Stabler's pass at the Houston 38. On the Jets' first play, Todd handed off to fullback Mike Augustyniak, who stopped at the line of scrimmage, then tossed the ball back to Todd. The QB then fired a 38-yard TD toss to Walker.

"That was the play that broke their backs," Jets Coach Walt Michaels said of the flea-flicker.

The much-maligned Jets defense did its job, too. After giving up a league-leading 100 points in three games, Jets defenders logged eight sacks, seven of them at the expense of Ken Stabler.

The Jets also held Earl Campbell, Houston's great runner, to 88 yards. Houston permitted eight sacks for the second consecutive week and committed six turnovers in falling to 2-2.

Todd hit on 25 of 39 passs for 312 yards and Walker caught eight tosses for 128 yards.

Ken Burrough cut the Oilers' deficit to six points with a 70-yard TD run after catching Stabler's short pass in the third quarter. The Jets canceled that on Kevin Long's two-yard touchdown plunge early in the fourth period.

Stabler has been sacked 15 times in the two games and the frustration was showing.

Said Stabler, referring to the Houston coaching staff: "I'm trying to please this guy. I'm trying to please that guy. All I know is I'm up to my elbows in alligators."

SEPTEMBER 27
SCORE BY PERIODS

Houston	7	3	7	0—17	
New York Jets	7	14	5	7—33	

SCORING

New York—Long 1 pass from Todd (Leahy kick).
Houston—Campbell 3 run (Fritsch kick).

New York—Walker 28 pass from Todd (Leahy kick).
New York—Walker 39 pass from Todd (Leahy kick).
Houston—Field goal Fritsch 38.
New York—Safety, Carter tackled in end zone.
Houston—Burrough 70 pass from Stabler (Fritsch kick).
New York—Field goal Leahy 41.
New York—Long 2 run (Leahy kick).

TEAM STATISTICS

	Houston	New York
First downs	16	25
Rushes-Yards	23-116	46-171
Passing yards	105	307
Sacks by-Yards	2-5	8-78
Return yards	138	121
Passes	15-30-3	25-39-0
Punts	4-42.8	6-45.8
Fumbles-Lost	4-3	2-2
Penalties-Yards	5-30	15-116
Time of possession	23:22	36:38

Attendance—50,309.

INDIVIDUAL STATISTICS

Rushing—Houston, Campbell 16-88, Carpenter 4-19, T. Wilson 1-7, Armstrong 1-2, Stabler 1-0; New York, McNeil 17-70, Augustyniak 9-35, Harper 2-20, Long 6-8, Todd 3-11, Newton 3-16, Dierking 2-4, Lewis 4-7.

Passing—Houston, Stabler 10-20-2—138, Reaves 5-10-1—45; New York, Todd 25-39-0—312.

Receiving—Houston, Burrough 3-86, Renfro 3-40, Holston 1-15, Campbell 4-14, Barber 2-7, Armstrong 1-11, T. Wilson 1-10; New York, Walker 8-128, Barkum 3-54, Harper 2-32, Augustyniak 4-48, Lewis 2-14, B. Jones 2-21, Newton 1-4, Long 1-1, McNeil 2-10.

Kickoff Returns—Houston, Roaches 3-61, Tullis 1-69; New York, Sohn 3-62, Lewis 1-30, Harper 1-13.

Punt Returns—Houston, Roaches 1-8; New York, Sohn 1-minus, Harper 3-10.

Interceptions—New York, Lynn 1-0, Ray 1-2, Mehl 1-7.

Punting—Houston, Parsley 4-42.8; New York, Ramsey 6-45.8.

Field Goals—Houston, Fritsch 1-1; New York, Leahy 1-1.

STEELERS 27, PATRIOTS 21 (Overtime)

PITTSBURGH—The Steelers blew numerous chances to win in regulation time, but cashed in on their first opportunity to defeat New England in sudden-death overtime.

"It was a great effort by our team," said Pittsburgh Coach Chuck Noll, "but I felt fortunate to get into the overtime because we didn't captialize on some things we had going for us."

The Steelers evened their record at 2-2 at 3:19 of the overtime on Terry Bradshaw's 24-yard touchdown pass to Lynn Swann. The winning TD came after the Pats had won the toss and elected to receive, but were forced to punt.

Pittsburgh salvaged the victory after Matt Cavanaugh had rallied the winless Patriots to two fourth-period TDs that tied the score, 21-21. The Pats launched their tying drive with only 1:45 left in regulation time. With 23 seconds to go, Cavanaugh hit Stanley Morgan with a 12-yard TD pass.

The Steelers held a 14-7 lead when they had a first down on the New England 1-yard line with seven seconds remaining before the half. Bradshaw failed to spot Frank Pollard, wide open in the end zone, and handed off to Franco Harris, who was stopped at the line of scrimmage. Then Bradshaw failed when he tried to score himself as the half ended.

Steelers rookie Dave Trout missed two second-half field goals, from 39 and 48 yards. And just before the Pats scored the tying TD, the Steelers tried for a first down on fourth and two from the Pats' 33. The play gained only one yard and the Pats took over.

Pittsburgh rolled up 498 yards, 251 rushing and 247 passing, and committed no turnovers. The Pats were effective on offense, too, with 438 yards, 325 of them coming on Cavanaugh's 22 completions in 42 tries.

SEPTEMBER 27
SCORE BY PERIODS

New England	0	7	0	14	0—21
Pittsburgh	7	7	7	0	6—27

SCORING

Pittsburgh—Harris 1 run (Trout kick).
Pittsburgh—Cunningham 1 pass from Bradshaw (Trout kick).
New England—Cavanaugh 1 run (Smith kick).
Pittsburgh—Harris 1 run (Trout kick).
New England—Collins 10 run (Smith kick).
New England—Morgan 12 pass from Cavanaugh (Smith kick).
Pittsburgh—Swann 24 pass from Bradshaw.

TEAM STATISTICS

	New England	Pittsburgh
First downs	24	27
Rushes-Yards	32-115	45-251
Passing yards	323	247
Sacks by-Yards	0-0	2-11
Return yards	22	189
Passes	23-43-1	15-30-0
Punts	7-39.4	5-37.0
Fumbles-Lost	0-0	0-0
Penalties-Yards	11-105	6-55
Time of possession	32:20	30:59
Attendance—53,344.		

INDIVIDUAL STATISTICS

Rushing—New England, Collins 16-55, Tatupu 3-4, Calhoun 3-10, Cavanaugh 3-17, Cunningham 6-24, Johnson 1-5; Pittsburgh, Harris 17-63, Pollard 13-75, Bradshaw 5-49, Davis 10-64.

Passing—New England, Cavanaugh 22-42-1—325, Johnson 1-1-0—9; Pittsburgh, Bradshaw 15-30-0—247.

Receiving—New England, Calhoun 2-28, Morgan 5-87, Collins 4-38, Tatupu 1-1, Jackson 5-126, Johnson 4-36, Hasselbeck 1-9, Cavanaugh 1-9; Pittsburgh, Cunningham 8-94, Stallworth 3-63, Smith 1-22, Swann 3-68.

Kickoff Returns—New England, Collins 1-22; Pittsburgh, Anderson 4-89.

Punt Returns—Pittsburgh, Smith 6-65.

Interceptions—Pittsburgh, Washington 1-35.

Punting—New England, Hubach 7-39.4; Pittsburgh, Colquitt 5-37.0.

Field Goals—New England, None attempted; Pittsburgh, Trout 0-2.

DOLPHINS 31, COLTS 28

BALTIMORE—Miami's victory over Baltimore was no surprise to Dolphins wide receiver Duriel Harris, who caught three passes for 73 yards.

"All week long we were looking forward to that single-man coverage," said Harris. "We feel we can get open when there's just one man on us."

Miami receivers did get open consistently as the Dolphins retained their lead in the AFC East with a 4-0 record. They were the conference's only unbeaten team.

Harris made a diving catch good for 45 yards late in the fourth quarter. That set up Uwe von Schamann's 28-yard field goal that won the game.

David Woodley, the 22-year-old quarterback who sat out the crucial moments of Miami's victory over Houston the previous week, was right on target against the Colts. He passed for 309 yards and two TDs in sending Baltimore to its third loss in four games.

Baltimore quarterback Bert Jones, who hadn't thrown a touchdown pass this season, fired three of them against Miami and passed for 357 yards. He completed 10 of 12 passes in the second half and led a 69-yard drive that enabled the Colts to tie the score, 28-28, on Curtis Dickey's one-yard plunge with 4:35 to go.

The Colts entered the game averaging just 234 yards on offense, but produced 514 against Miami. The Dolphins penetrated Baltimore's defense for 428 yards.

Dolphins Coach Don Shula received an additional thrill when he saw his 22-year-old son Dave play for Baltimore. A son playing against a team coached by his father was a first in the National Football League.

Young Shula stopped Dolphins kick returner Fulton Walker after a 14-yard return. Said the elder Shula:

"It certainly was a big deal for me. I'm very proud of him. I think he showed he's a heady football player who will do all he can to win a game."

SEPTEMBER 27
SCORE BY PERIODS

Miami	7	7	7	10—31
Baltimore	0	7	14	7—28

SCORING

Miami—Vigorito 31 pass from Woodley (von Schamann kick).
Miami—Franklin 10 run (von Schamann kick).
Baltimore—Dickey 32 pass from B. Jones (Wood kick).
Baltimore—Butler 19 pass from B. Jones (Wood kick).
Miami—Giaquinto 14 pass from Woodley (von Schamann kick).
Baltimore—Butler 68 pass from B. Jones (Wood kick).
Miami—Franklin 1 run (von Schamann kick).
Baltimore—Dickey 1 run (Wood kick).
Miami—Field goal von Schamann 28.

TEAM STATISTICS

	Miami	Baltimore
First downs	22	20
Rushes-Yards	33-119	32-166
Passing yards	309	348
Sacks by-Yards	1-9	0-0
Return yards	147	128
Passes	19-30-0	20-27-1
Punts	4-41.8	2-40.0

Fourth Week—Continued

	Miami	Baltimore
Fumbles-Lost	0-0	1-0
Penalties-Yards	4-35	6-52
Time of possession	32:57	27:03
Attendance—41,630.		

INDIVIDUAL STATISTICS

Rushing—Miami, Franklin 20-76, Vigorito 7-19, Woodley 4-9, Howell 1-9, Giaquinto 1-6; Baltimore, Dickey 13-77, McMillan 17-73, B. Jones 1-16, Anderson 1-0.

Passing—Miami, Woodley 19-30-0—309; Baltimore—B. Jones 20-27-1—357.

Receiving—Miami, Howell 1-4, Vigorito 6-60, Cefalo 4-64, Moore 2-69, Hardy 1-11, Rose 1-14; Giaquinto 1-14, Harris 3-73; Baltimore, McCall 1-4, McCauley 2-23, Carr 3-42, Butler 4-145, McMillan 4-61, Dickey 5-65, Burke 1-17.

Kickoff Returns—Miami, Walker 4-99, Harris 1-20; Baltimore, Anderson 4-87, Dixon 1-41, Foote 1-0.

Punt Returns—Miami, Blackwood 1-2, Walker 1-10.

Interceptions—Miami, Rhone 1-16.

Punting—Miami, Orosz 4-41.8; Baltimore, Garrett 2-40.0.

Field Goals—Miami, von Schamann 1-1; Baltimore, None attempted.

RAMS 24, BEARS 7

CHICAGO—It had been 20 years since a member of the Los Angeles Rams returned a punt for a touchdown in an NFL game. It wasn't an unknown statistic to Leroy Irvin, who runs back kicks for the Rams.

"The coaches drilled it into me in every practice that it had been 20 years without a return for a TD," said Irvin.

The second-year pro out of the University of Kansas put an end to that 20-year dry spell when he streaked 55 yards with a third-quarter Chicago punt to increase the Rams' lead over the Bears to 16-0.

"The blocks were in the right places. The only thing I wanted to do after I crossed the goal line was make sure there were no penalties," said the fleet-footed Irvin.

Dick Bass, in a 1961 game against the Green Bay Packers, was the last Rams player to run a punt back for a touchdown. Bass' return covered 90 yards.

While Irvin's runback was the most spectacular play of the game, it wasn't the only one that crushed the Bears. Wendell Tyler scored two touchdowns—on runs of 1 and 2 yards—and Pat Haden completed 13 of 29 passes for 210 yards.

The Rams defense, which had allowed 73 points in its first three games, was outstanding. It held All-Pro running back Walter Payton to only 45 yards in 17 carries, recorded six quarterback sacks and forced three turnovers. The Chicago ground attack was able to muster only 88 yards all night and the Bears passing game—directed at various times by Vince Evans, Bob Avellini and Mike Phipps—was good for only 135 yards.

Los Angeles	7	3	7	7—24
Chicago	0	0	0	7— 7

SCORING

Los Angeles—Tyler 2 run (Corral kick).
Los Angeles—Field goal Corral 24.
Los Angeles—Irvin 55 punt return (Corral kick).
Los Angeles—Tyler 1 run (Corral kick).
Chicago—Williams 14 pass from Phipps (Nielsen kick).

TEAM STATISTICS

	Los Angeles	Chicago
First downs	20	17
Rushes-Yards	35-134	30-88
Passing yards	195	135
Sacks by-Yards	6-40	1-15
Return yards	123	115
Passes	13-29-0	16-34-1
Punts	6-46.5	9-39.4
Fumbles-Lost	2-2	2-2
Penalties-Yards	9-81	9-93
Time of possession	28:07	31:53
Attendance—62,461.		

INDIVIDUAL STATISTICS

Rushing—Los Angeles, Tyler 17-68, Bryant 10-42, Guman 3-13, Haden 3-5, J. Thomas 1-3, Dennard 1-3; Chicago, Payton 17-45, Suhey 10-40, Avellini 2-3, Harper 1-0.

Passing—Los Angeles, Haden 13-29-0—210; Chicago, Evans 1-8-0—3, Avellini 8-14-1—64, Phipps 7-12-0—108.

Receiving—Los Angeles, Tyler 4-43, Dennard 3-47, Waddy 2-56, Miller 2-37, Childs 1-19, Bryant 1-8; Chicago, Payton 7-111, Suhey 4-38, Williams 3-15, Harper 1-8, Baschnagel 1-3.

Kickoff Returns—Los Angeles, D. Hill 1-22, J. Thomas 1-15; Chicago, Williams 4-86.

Punt Returns—Los Angeles, Irvin 3-69, D. Hill 1-10; Chicago, J. Fisher 3-26, Plank 1-3.

Interceptions—Los Angeles, Harris 1-7.

Punting—Los Angeles, Corral 6-46.5; Chicago, Parsons 9-39.4.

Field Goals—Los Angeles, Corral 1-1; Chicago, None attempted.

FIFTH WEEK

49ers 30, REDSKINS 17

WASHINGTON—At age 25, Dwight Hicks is the old man in the San Francisco secondary. He and three rookies—Ronnie Lott, Eric Wright and Carlton Williamson—make up the 49ers' defensive backfield, but opponents have been unable to take advantage of their inexperience.

Hicks turned a fumble recovery and one of his two interceptions into touchdowns as the 49ers coasted to victory over Washington.

Hicks went 80 yards with a fumble recovery for a first-quarter touchdown and returned an interception 32 yards in the third quarter for another score. Ricky Patton ran 16 yards and Johnny Davis went one yard for the 49ers' other TDs and Matt Bahr added a 43-yard field goal.

Hicks also had a 72-yard interception return in the third quarter that did not produce a score. He totaled 184 yards on his three run-backs, and his 104 yards on the two interception returns set a club record.

Hicks' two interceptions and one each by Lott and rookie linebacker Milt McColl stymied the Redskins' passing attack, which had gained 1,180 yards in four games. The 49ers held Washington quarterback Joe Theismann and his replacement, Tom Flick, to 241 yards on 22 completions in 46 attempts, intercepting each passer twice.

"There was absolutely nothing special about what I did and nothing different about our defense to create plays like that," said Hicks of his heroics. "On the fumble touchdown, the ball just happened to fall into my hands after Ronnie made a great hit on (Terry) Metcalf. All I had to do was run down the sideline."

Metcalf was headed around right end on a reverse when he tried to leap over Lott. Lott upended Metcalf and the ball popped into the air and into Hicks' arms.

The Redskins got fourth-quarter touchdowns on Mike Nelms' 58-yard punt return and Joe Washington's five-yard run to go with Mark Moseley's 34-yard field goal in the second quarter.

The last time the Redskins started 0-5 was in 1965.

OCTOBER 4

SCORE BY PERIODS

San Francisco	14	10	6	0	30
Washington	0	3	0	14	17

SCORING

San Francisco—Patton 16 run (Bahr kick).
San Francisco—Hicks 80 fumble return (Bahr kick).
San Francisco—Field goal Bahr 43.
Washington—Field goal Moseley 34.
San Francisco—Davis 1 run (Bahr kick).
San Francisco—Hicks 32 interception return (bad snap).
Washington—Nelms 58 punt return (Moseley kick).
Washington—Washington 5 run (Moseley kick).

TEAM STATISTICS

	San Francisco	Washington
First downs	16	19
Rushes-Yards	35-128	23-83
Passing yards	168	221
Sacks by-Yards	2-20	2-25
Return yards	176	224
Passes	15-28-1	22-46-4
Punts	5-40.0	5-40.4
Fumbles-Lost	1-1	4-2
Penalties-Yards	3-27	7-50
Time of possession	29:17	30:43
Attendance—51,843.		

INDIVIDUAL STATISTICS

Rushing—San Francisco, Patton 9-43, Cooper 6-21, Easley 2-1, Elliott 3-12, Davis 13-37, Lawrence 2-14; Washington, Riggins 13-47, Washington 7-30, Metcalf 2-5, Theismann 1-1.

Passing—San Francisco, Montana 15-28-1—193; Washington, Theismann 10-24-2—123, Flick 12-22-2—118.

Receiving—San Francisco, Clark 1-21, Solomon 5-77, Cooper 1-2, Young 2-24, Elliott 6-69; Washington, Monk 4-42, Thompson 2-42, Warren 1-12, Washington 8-49, Harmon 1-11, Metcalf 3-44, McCrary 1-12, Walker 2-29.

Kickoff Returns—San Francisco, Lawrence 2-41;

Washington, Nelms 4-123, Seay 1-19, Wonsley 1-20.

Punt Returns—San Francisco, Solomon 2-9; Washington, Nelms 2-59.

Interceptions—San Francisco, Hicks 2-104, Lott 1-0, McColl 1-22; Washington, Nelms 1-3.

Punting—San Francisco, Miller 5-40.0; Washington, Connell 5-40.4.

Field Goals—San Francisco, Bahr 1-2; Washington, Moseley 1-1.

DOLPHINS 28, JETS 28 (Overtime)

MIAMI—No, the Miami Dolphins didn't beat the New York Jets. But Coach Don Shula must have seen some encouraging signs after the 28-28 overtime tie in the Orange Bowl at Miami.

The Jets had beaten the Dolphins six straight times and they barely missed making it seven when Pat Leahy's 47-yard field goal attempt missed on the final play of overtime.

"Anyway, it's a big step in the right direction against the Jets," a grim Shula said afterward. "The way we were hanging on in the overtime, I'm happy with the tie. It's certainly better than a loss."

The deadlock was the first blemish on Miami's record (4-0-1) this season.

Jets quarterback Richard Todd threw four touchdown passes, connecting on 28 of 39 tosses for 310 yards—his best performance in four years.

Todd threw touchdown passes of 15 yards to Jerome Barkum, nine and 14 yards to Wesley Walker, and 36 yards to backup wide receiver Bobby Jones. The throw to Jones came with one minute, nine seconds left in regulation time and tied the score at 28-28. Jones was covered by two Miami defenders, but maintained his concentration to make the catch and then brake away into the end zone.

Todd's performance nearly overshadowed the play of Miami wide receiver Nat Moore and the Dolphins' veteran backup quarterback, Don Strock, the man Shula calls "the Goose Gossage of pro football."

Strock relieved starter David Woodley, who went down with a sprained back in the first quarter. The eight-year veteran hit on 19 of 29 passes for 279 yards, without an interception.

Moore caught seven passes for 210 yards, including touchdown receptions of six and 23 yards, as he became the first receiver in Dolphins history to top 200 yards for a game and 5,000 yards for his career.

"I can't say enough about Nat, the way he was getting open and making fantastic catches," said Shula. Moore had made a diving grab for his 23-yard TD, which gave Miami a 28-21 lead late in the fourth quarter.

In overtime, the Dolphins got no farther than their own 37. New York drove to the Miami 30 before Leahy's field-goal try sailed wide to the right.

Fifth Week—Continued

OCTOBER 4

SCORE BY PERIODS

New York Jets	14	0	0	14	0—28
Miami	7	7	7	7	0—28

SCORING

New York—Barkum 15 pass from Todd (Leahy kick).
Miami—Franklin 2 run (von Schamann kick).
New York—Walker 9 pass from Todd (Leahy kick).
Miami—Moore 6 pass from Strock (von Schamann kick).
Miami—Franklin 1 run (von Schamann kick).
New York—Walker 14 pass from Todd (Leahy kick).
Miami—Moore 23 pass from Strock (von Schamann kick).
New York—B. Jones 36 pass from Todd (Leahy kick).

TEAM STATISTICS

	New York	Miami
First downs	32	17
Rushes-Yards	51-242	29-98
Passing yards	304	301
Sacks by-Yards	1-5	2-6
Return yards	87	179
Passes	28-39-1	21-34-0
Punts	6-44.8	8-41.9
Fumbles-Lost	3-2	2-0
Penalties-Yards	5-45	9-65
Time of possession	46:29	28:31

Attendance—69,631.

INDIVIDUAL STATISTICS

Rushing—New York, McNeil 12-79, Augustyniak 7-33, Harper 15-61, Todd 3-6, Newton 5-25, Dierking 1-7, Long 8-31; Miami, Giaquinto 1-20, Franklin 16-37, Vigorito 7-15, Woodley 1-25, Howell 2-5, Strock 2-minus 4.

Passing—New York, Todd 28-39-1—310; Miami, Woodley 3-5-0—27, Strock 18-29-0-279.

Receiving—New York, B. Jones 1-36, Gaffney 2-20, Barkum 2-25, Augustyniak 1-11, Walker 8-112, L. Jones 1-35, Todd 1-1, Newton 3-13, Harper 5-38, Long 4-19; Miami, Hardy 2-21, Vigorito 7-30, Harris 3-37, Moore 7-210, Giaquinto 1-minus 1, Rose 1-9.

Kickoff Returns—New York, Sohn 3-54, Lewis 1-8; Miami, Walker 2-60, Kozlowski 1-40.

Punt Returns—New York, Harper 3-20, Sohn 1-0, Schroy 1-5; Miami, Walker 4-40.

Interceptions—Miami, G. Blackwood 1-39.

Punting—New York, Ramsey 6-44.8; Miami, Orosz 8-41.9.

Field Goals—New York, Leahy 0-2; Miami, von Schamann 0-2.

CARDINALS 20, COWBOYS 17

ST. LOUIS—The way quarterback Jim Hart sliced it, the St. Louis Cardinals' 20-17 victory over the previously unbeaten Dallas Cowboys had three equal parts.

"Each third of the team had its back to the wall and had to respond," said Hart. As he explained, it was "the offense getting the ball into position for the field goal, the special teams kicking it, and the defense holding them."

The Cardinals' winning points came on a 37-yard field goal by Neil O'Donoghue with 23 seconds remaining at Busch Stadium. That kick booted the Cowboys out of a share of the National Football Conference East lead.

Every member of the Cardinals got a game ball—the first time that had happened since St.

Louis won at Dallas, 24-17, in a Monday night game in 1977. That was the last time the Cardinals had beaten the Cowboys, although they had come close each year at home. They lost by 24-21 in 1978, by 22-21 in '79 and by 27-24 last year.

"There was some kind of myth that Dallas always comes up with the big play," said St. Louis defensive end Curtis Greer. "We disposed of that today. We've always been in the game; there's just been some obstacle in our way."

If each Cardinal got a game ball, perhaps Roy Green deserved three. Besides playing on the special teams and batting away two passes as an extra defensive back, Green caught five passes as a wide receiver. Included was a leaping, one-handed grab of a Hart pass for a 30-yard touchdown in the third quarter. Green reached out and clutched the ball, then pulled it to his chest before his knee hit the turf and he went over the back line in the end zone.

"It was one of the greatest all-time catches I've ever seen in my life," Coach Jim Hanifan said of the reception that put the Cardinals ahead, 17-10.

Green's last catch was a 19-yarder to the Dallas 48 on the drive to the winning field goal. The Cardinals advanced to the Dallas 20 before O'Donoghue came on.

"You can't be too hyped up about it," O'Donoghue said of his last-minute heroics. "You've gotta control your emotions. It's like a golf swing. I didn't try to rush it (the kick). Everything was under control as far as I was concerned."

O'Donoghue did in the Cowboys from start to finish. On the opening kickoff, James Jones fumbled and O'Donoghue recovered on the Dallas 9. Wayne Morris bolted into the end zone on the Cardinals' first play and O'Donoghue converted for a 7-0 lead with the game 18 seconds old.

Tony Dorsett ran for 99 yards and scored both Dallas touchdowns—on a seven-yard run and an 11-yard screen pass from Danny White. The Cowboys reached the St. Louis 8 in the second quarter, but had to settle for a field goal by Rafael Septien. That was the 11th time this season Dallas had failed to score a touchdown when it was inside the opponent's 10.

OCTOBER 4

SCORE BY PERIODS

Dallas	7	3	7	0—17
St. Louis	10	0	7	3—20

SCORING

St. Louis—Morris 9 run (O'Donoghue kick).
Dallas—Dorsett 7 run (Septien kick).
St. Louis—Field goal O'Donoghue 19.
Dallas—Field goal Septien 26.
St. Louis—Green 30 pass from Hart (O'Donoghue kick).
Dallas—Dorsett 11 pass from D. White (Septien kick).
St. Louis—Field goal O'Donoghue 37.

St. Louis' Roy Green brought back memories of the two-way performers of yesteryear when the Cardinals upset the Dallas Cowboys, 20-17. In addition to playing on special teams, Green caught five passes as a wide receiver —one for a TD—and batted away two passes as an extra defensive back.

Fifth Week—Continued

	Dallas	St. Louis
First downs	17	18
Rushes-Yards	33-140	29-115
Passing yards	166	184
Sacks by-Yards	3-15	3-16
Return yards	102	113
Passes	15-28-1	16-29-1
Punts	7-37.7	6-45.2
Fumbles-Lost	3-1	3-2
Penalties-Yards	5-45	5-41
Time of possession	29:17	30:43

Attendance—49,477.

INDIVIDUAL STATISTICS

Rushing—Dallas, Dorsett 21-99, Springs 10-39, D. White 2-2; St. Louis, Anderson 20-72, Morris 5-24, Mitchell 3-11, Stief 1-8.

Passing—Dallas, D. White 15-28-1—182; St. Louis, Hart 16-29-1—199.

Receiving—Dallas, Johnson 5-101, Pearson 1-25, Hill 2-21, J. Jones 1-16, Dorsett 4-13, Springs 1-6, DuPree 1-0; St. Louis, Green 5-89, Tilley 5-73, Marsh 1-20, Gray 3-16, Harrell 2-1.

Kickoff Returns—Dallas, J. Jones 4-70; St. Louis, Mitchell 3-73, Griffin 1-26.

Punt Returns—Dallas, J. Jones 2-9; St. Louis, Mitchell 2-10.

Interceptions—Dallas, Downs 1-23; St. Louis, Griffin 1-4.

Punting—Dallas, D. White 7-37.7; St. Louis, Birdsong 6-45.2.

Field Goals—Dallas, Septien 1-1; St. Louis, O'Donoghue 2-2.

BILLS 23, COLTS 18

ORCHARD PARK—Saddled with a mediocre 3.3-yard rushing average and a longest gain of just 14 yards in the first four games, second-year running back Joe Cribbs broke loose for 159 yards on 17 carries to lead Buffalo past Baltimore at Rich Stadium.

Cribbs took off on jaunts of 28, 30, 35 and 19 yards—with each of the long gains keying a Buffalo scoring drive.

"On the first one, I felt so strange that for a while I didn't know what I was doing," Cribbs said. "I made some mistakes, but I'd have to say it was one of my better games."

Cribbs rushed for 1,185 yards last year, with his top game a 128-yard effort.

Against Baltimore, Cribbs' runs set up a Joe Ferguson-to-Jerry Butler TD pass, a one-yard scoring plunge by Roosevelt Leaks and two of Nick Mike-Mayer's three field goals.

Baltimore's Bert Jones completed 22 of 36 passes for 275 yards and two TDs. The final score came with nine seconds left, and the Colts then failed to recover an onside kickoff.

Watching Cribbs' footwork was a disappointment to Colts Coach Mike McCormack, who lost his top two running backs during the game. Halfback Curtis Dickey went out with an arch injury and fullback Randy McMillan was lost with a hip-pointer.

There were 17 penalties, including several personal fouls and face-mask infractions. Buffalo guard Conrad Dobler and Baltimore defensive tackle Mike Barnes were observed elbowing, slapping and kicking each other on a number of plays.

OCTOBER 4
SCORE BY PERIODS

Baltimore	0	3	0	14—17
Buffalo	14	0	3	6—23

SCORING

Buffalo—Butler 16 pass from Ferguson (Mike-Mayer kick).
Buffalo—Leaks 1 run (Mike-Mayer kick).
Baltimore—Field goal Wood 32.
Buffalo—Field goal Mike-Mayer 34.
Baltimore—Carr 6 pass from B. Jones (Wood kick).
Buffalo—Field goal Mike-Mayer 44.
Buffalo—Field goal Mike-Mayer 45.
Baltimore—Butler 14 pass from B. Jones (Wood kick).

TEAM STATISTICS

	Baltimore	Buffalo
First downs	23	22
Rushes-Yards	31-133	36-229
Passing yards	245	137
Sacks by-Yards	1-11	4-30
Return yards	104	67
Passes	22-36-1	14-29-1
Punts	5-31.2	3-42.3
Fumbles-Lost	2-1	3-0
Penalties-Yards	10-55	7-49
Time of possession	29:00	31:00

Attendance—77,811.

INDIVIDUAL STATISTICS

Rushing—Baltimore, B. Jones 2-minus 2, Dickey 10-78, McMillan 1-1, Franklin 12-36, Dixon 6-20; Buffalo, Cribbs 17-159, McCutcheon 15-64, Leaks 3-7, Ferguson 1-minus 1.

Passing—Baltimore, B. Jones 22-36-1—275; Buffalo, Ferguson 14-29-1—148.

Receiving—Baltimore, Dickey 3-80, Burke 1-11, McCall 1-6, Dixon 2-24, McCauley 5-21, Franklin 3-14, Butler 3-75, Carr 4-44; Buffalo, Lewis 2-16, Butler 4-73, McCutcheon 2-27, Cribbs 3-20, Brammer 3-12.

Kickoff Returns—Baltimore, Anderson 1-30, Dixon 2-35, Shula 1-16; Buffalo, Franklin 2-65, Freeman 1-0.

Punt Returns—Baltimore, Shula 1-0; Buffalo, Hooks 1-2.

Interceptions—Baltimore, Laird 1-23; Buffalo, Simpson 1-0.

Punting—Baltimore, Garrett 5-31.2; Buffalo, Cater 3-42.3.

Field Goals—Baltimore, Wood 1-1; Buffalo, Mike-Mayer 3-4.

PACKERS 27, GIANTS 14

EAST RUTHERFORD—Green Bay finally learned that the best way to hold a lead is to hold on to the ball.

The Packers had lost three straight games on crucial fumbles and interceptions prior to the game in Giants Stadium, so Bart Starr, the Packers' coach, decided to stick to a ball-control offense. The strategy worked, with a couple of unlikely heroes emerging.

"When you have quality receivers like John Jefferson and James Lofton, it opens things up for the tight end and gives the running backs more of a chance," said Starr of his All-Pro wide receivers, who served as effective decoys when they weren't catching passes.

With the Giants overly concerned with stopping Jefferson and Lofton, quarterback Lynn Dickey exploited the soft middle of the New York defense with key passes to tight end Paul Coffman, who caught six for 92 yards. And Harlan Huckleby, in his first NFL start, rushed for 88 yards on 30 carries as the Packers controlled the ball for 41 minutes and 25 seconds.

Dickey received plenty of time to pass behind an offensive line that had allowed 21 sacks in four games. He completed 17 of 22 passes for 208 yards. The Packers converted nine of 14 third-down situations.

Green Bay scored 20 points before the Giants put a point on the scoreboard. The Packers, who have outscored opponents 27-0 in first quarters this season, scored on Jan Stenerud's 50-yard field goal for a 3-0 first-quarter lead. A one-yard touchdown pass to Coffman and a 35-yard field goal by Stenerud gave the Packers 13-0 halftime lead.

Huckleby's one-yard touchdown run increased Green Bay's lead to 20-0 after Mike Douglass intercepted a Phil Simms pass. A 26-yard strike to Jefferson iced the game for the Packers in the fourth quarter, completing a 19-play, 80-yard drive, kept alive by three New York penalties.

The Giants, 2-3, didn't cross midfield until the third quarter against a Green Bay defense that had yielded an average of 33 points per game in the previous three weeks. The Giants were shut out until Doug Kotar's one-yard touchdown run late in the third period. Earnest Gray caught a two-yard touchdown pass from Simms to close out the scoring.

OCTOBER 4
SCORE BY PERIODS

Green Bay	3	10	7	7—27
New York Giants	0	0	7	7—14

SCORING

Green Bay—Field goal Stenerud 50.
Green Bay—Coffman 1 pass from Dickey (Stenerud kick).
Green Bay—Field goal Stenerud 35.
Green Bay—Huckleby 1 run (Stenerud kick).
New York—Kotar 1 run (Danelo kick).
Green Bay—Jefferson 26 pass from Dickey (Stenerud kick).
New York—Gray 2 pass from Simms (Danelo kick).

TEAM STATISTICS

	Green Bay	New York
First downs	27	17
Rushes-Yards	49-148	16-41
Passing yards	215	221
Sacks by-Yards	1-9	2-16
Return yards	41	89
Passes	18-23-1	20-32-2
Punts	2-50.5	4-42.8
Fumbles-Lost	1-0	1-0
Penalties-Yards	12-90	9-70
Time of possession	41:25	18:35

Attendance—73,684.

INDIVIDUAL STATISTICS

Rushing—Green Bay, Ellis 18-56, Huckleby 30-88, Torkelson 1-4; New York, Kotar 9-31, Perry 3-7, Bright 2-2, Simms 2-1.

Passing—Green Bay, Dickey 17-22-1—208, Ellis 1-1-0—23; New York, Simms 20-32-2—230.

Receiving—Green Bay, Ellis 3-16, Coffman 6-92, Lofton 5-75, Jefferson 2-31, Huckleby 2-17; New York, Kotar 4-10, Friede 5-73, Shirk 1-5, Perkins 4-69, Gray 2-27, Mistler 1-14, Bright 3-32.

Kickoff Returns—Green Bay, Jefferson 1-3, Lee 1-11; New York, Garrett 1-13, Bright 3-43, McLaughlin 1-5.

Punt Returns—Green Bay, Lee 3-8; New York, Garrett 1-7, Bright 1-14.

Interceptions—Green Bay, Douglass 1-6, Lee 1-13; New York, Reece 1-7.

Punting—Green Bay, Stachowicz 2-50.5; New York, Jennings 4-42.8.

Field Goals—Green Bay, Stenerud 2-2; New York, None attempted.

BRONCOS 17, RAIDERS O

OAKLAND—Denver, playing letter-perfect defense and taking advantage of Oakland mistakes, handed the defending Super Bowl champion Raiders their second consecutive shutout.

In the season opener, the Broncos had held Oakland to 165 yards in a 9-7 victory at Denver. This time, they limited the Raiders to 168 yards. While the Broncos' record stood at 4-1, the Raiders were 2-3 and sinking.

Before the 1981 season, the Raiders had been shut out only four times in their history—twice in 1961, once in '63 and once in '66. A 16-0 whitewash by the Detroit Lions preceded Denver's shutout.

Dan Reeves, Denver's rookie head coach, was delighted that his club won on a day the Broncos generated little offense. Craig Morton passed for only 90 yards.

"Our game plan didn't exactly shake up the Raiders, because they adjusted very well," said Reeves. "When you can win while gaining only 252 yards against the world champions, that's a pretty good day."

The Oakland offense wasn't as bad as the numbers indicated. But the Raiders suffered two interceptions and lost four fumbles. The Broncos converted two of the mistakes into 10 points to put the game away in the third quarter.

Dave Preston ran four yards for a first-half touchdown. In the third quarter, Fred Steinfort booted a 31-yard field goal after a fumble recovery and an interception set up a 20-yard TD run by Rick Parros.

Jim Plunkett was 13-for-20 passing for Oakland, and Coach Tom Flores replaced him with Marc Wilson in the fourth period. Wilson was only 1-for-8 and threw one interception.

The Raiders' only scoring chance came on the last play of the first half, when Chris Bahr was a yard short on a 54-yard field goal attempt.

OCTOBER 4
SCORE BY PERIODS

Denver	0	7	10	0—17
Oakland	0	0	0	0— 0

Fifth Week—Continued

SCORING

Denver—Preston 4 run (Steinfort kick).
Denver—Field goal Steinfort 31.
Denver—Parros 20 run (Steinfort kick).

TEAM STATISTICS

	Denver	Oakland
First downs	17	12
Rushes-Yards	45-162	21-78
Passing yards	90	90
Sacks by-Yards	7-33	3-51
Return yards	32	101
Passes	10-17-0	14-28-2
Punts	9-35.1	6-46.3
Fumbles-Lost	2-0	7-4
Penalties-Yards	5-55	4-30
Time of possession	37:13	22:47

Attendance—51,035.

INDIVIDUAL STATISTICS

Rushing—Denver, Parros 18-73, Preston 21-70, Reed 5-17, Canada 1-2; Oakland, King 15-53, Jensen 4-12, Plunkett 2-13.

Passing—Denver, Morton 9-16-0—117, DeBerg 1-1-0 —24; Oakland, Plunkett 13-20-1—115, Wilson 1-8-1—8.

Receiving—Denver, Odoms 3-33, Reed 2-23, Parros 1-24, Moses 1-19, Preston 1-17, Egloff 1-14, Watson 1-11; Oakland, King 6-34, Jensen 3-41, Ramsey 3-19, Bradshaw 1-15, Branch 1-14.

Kickoff Returns—Oakland, Willis 4-81.

Punt Returns—Denver, Manning 4-29; Oakland, Matthews 6-20.

Interceptions—Denver, Thompson 1-0, Swenson 1-3.

Punting—Denver, Prestridge 9-35.1; Oakland, Guy 6-46.3.

Field Goals—Denver, Steinfort 1-1; Oakland, Bahr 0-1.

RAMS 27, BROWNS 16

ANAHEIM—The Los Angeles Rams, given up for dead three weeks earlier, proved that their obituary was premature. They were right back in the NFC Western Division race after subduing the Cleveland Browns.

As they did in 1980, the Rams opened this season with two successive losses. In 1980, they rebounded with five straight victories. After soundly defeating the Browns, the Rams have won three straight.

"You can't figure us out, can you?" defensive tackle Larry Brooks asked reporters. "We like to keep you in suspense. Hey, we don't practice playing with our backs to the wall, but maybe it takes criticism to get us going."

Rams quarterback Pat Haden, off to a slow start, found the groove by engineering several long drives against the Browns.

"We did a good job of controlling the ball and that was the key," Haden said. "Our offensive line did a super job. They allowed me to stand back there with all day to throw."

Wendell Tyler ran for one touchdown and caught a TD pass and Frank Corral kicked a pair of field goals to lead the Rams.

The Browns took a 3-0 lead on Dave Jacobs' 35-yard field goal, but the Rams charged back and took the lead for good, with Tyler going in from the two. Tyler was removed from the

game with a groin injury late in the third quarter. He gained just 29 yards in 12 carries.

The Rams increased their lead to 14-3 on Tyler's catch of a one-yard TD toss after safety Johnnie Johnson blocked a Cleveland field goal attempt.

Cleveland cut its deficit to 14-10 in the third period on Mike Pruitt's one-yard scoring run, but the Rams retaliated on Mike Guman's four-yard touchdown run following Leroy Irvin's interception of a Brian Sipe pass.

Corral then kicked field goals of 38 and 41 yards before Cleveland scored the final points with 3½ minutes left on Sipe's 38-yard touchdown pass to Ozzie Newsome.

Haden completed 21 of 31 passes for 205 yards while Sipe connected on 14 of 28 for 250 yards. Rams fullback Cullen Bryant led all rushers with 93 yards in 19 carries while teammate Preston Dennard led receivers with seven catches for 90 yards.

OCTOBER 4
SCORE BY PERIODS

Cleveland	3	0	7	6—16
Los Angeles	7	7	0	13—27

SCORING

Cleveland—Field goal Jacobs 35.
Los Angeles—Tyler 2 run (Corral kick).
Los Angeles—Tyler 1 pass from Haden (Corral kick).
Cleveland—M. Pruitt 1 run (Jacobs kick).
Los Angeles—Guman 4 run (Corral kick).
Los Angeles—Field goal Corral 38.
Los Angeles—Field goal Corral 41.
Cleveland—Newsome 38 pass from Sipe (kick failed).

TEAM STATISTICS

	Cleveland	Los Angeles
First downs	16	29
Rushes-Yards	26-78	46-213
Passing yards	240	197
Sacks by-Yards	1-8	1-10
Return yards	149	38
Passes	14-28-1	21-31-0
Punts	5-44.0	3-40.3
Fumbles-Lost	1-0	3-1
Penalties-Yards	11-88	3-38
Time of possession	26:17	33:43

Attendance—63,924.

INDIVIDUAL STATISTICS

Rushing—Cleveland, M. Pruitt 17-56, White, 6-12, G. Pruitt 1-7, Hill 1-3, Sipe 1-0; Los Angeles, Bryant 19-93, Guman 13-54, Tyler 12-29, Dennard 1-21, Haden 1-16.

Passing—Cleveland, Sipe 14-28-1—250; Los Angeles, Haden 21-31-0—205.

Receiving—Cleveland, M. Pruitt 5-40, Rucker 3-65, Feacher 2-71, Newsome 2-56, G. Pruitt 1-9, Hill 1-9; Los Angeles, Dennard 7-90, Tyler 6-45, Waddy 2-33, Guman 2-15, Bryant 2-9, Miller 1-7, Childs 1-6.

Kickoff Returns—Cleveland, Montgomery 5-134, White 1-minus 1; Los Angeles, D. Hill 2-37, Moore 1-0.

Punt Returns—Cleveland, Montgomery 2-16; Los Angeles, Irvin 3-1.

Interceptions—Los Angeles, Irvin 1-0.

Punting—Cleveland, Cox 5-44.0; Los Angeles, Corral 3-40.3.

Field Goals—Cleveland, Jacobs 1-2; Los Angeles, Corral 2-3.

STEELERS 20, SAINTS 6

NEW ORLEANS—Terry Bradshaw threw for 276 yards and tossed two picture-perfect touchdown passes, but the Pittsburgh quarterback shrugged off his performance as routine.

"Just a lousy day at the office, but it turned out good," said Bradshaw after the Steelers won for the third straight week.

Bradshaw rifled a 16-yard scoring pass to Lynn Swann in the first quarter and then clinched the victory with a 47-yard bomb to John Stallworth in the final period.

New Orleans' starting quarterback, rookie Dave Wilson, would have accepted Bradshaw's 19-for-28 passing statistics. Wilson was 12-for-20, but was intercepted four times and then was replaced by Bobby Scott.

The Saints drove deep into Pittsburgh territory several times, but each time ran into trouble—the Steel Curtain. "They (the Steelers' defense) seemed to get tough when we got down there," Wilson observed.

Rookie defensive back Johnny Poe was burned on the Bradshaw-to-Stallworth play. "I saw Bradshaw was scrambling and Stallworth had two yards on me," Poe said. "It was a good throw."

Saints Coach Bum Phillips, after watching the 33-year-old Bradshaw at work, said, "He looks like he's 22 again."

OCTOBER 4
SCORE BY PERIODS

Pittsburgh	7	6	0	7—	20
New Orleans	0	3	3	0—	6

SCORING

Pittsburgh—Swann 16 pass from Bradshaw (Trout kick).
Pittsburgh—Field goal Trout 25.
New Orleans—Field goal Ricardo 26.
Pittsburgh—Field goal Trout 43.
New Orleans—Field goal Ricardo 33.
Pittsburgh—Stallworth 47 pass from Bradshaw (Trout kick).

TEAM STATISTICS

	Pittsburgh	New Orleans
First downs	19	17
Rushes-Yards	33-137	34-78
Passing yards	269	121
Sacks by-Yards	6-56	1-7
Return yards	158	122
Passes	19-29-0	16-25-4
Punts	6-41.7	5-43.2
Fumbles-Lost	5-3	3-1
Penalties-Yards	10-98	4-35
Time of possession	29:24	30:36
Attendance—64,578.		

INDIVIDUAL STATISTICS

Rushing—Pittsburgh, Harris 13-59, Pollard 12-54, Bradshaw 1-0, Davis 3-8, Thornton 2-5, Stoudt 1-10, Hawthorne 1-1; New Orleans, G. Rogers 25-77, Holmes 1-0, W. Wilson 5-9, Tyler 2- minus 2, D. Wilson 1- minus 6.

Passing—Pittsburgh, Bradshaw 19-28-0—276, Stoudt 0-1-0—0; New Orleans, D. Wilson 12-20-4—127, Scott 4-5-0—50.

Receiving—Pittsburgh, Swann 7-67, Stallworth 7-158, Pollard 2-10, Cunningham 2-37, Davis 1-4; New Orleans, W. Wilson 6-46, Hardy 2-9, Groth 4-92, Merkens 1-10, Holmes 1-0, Williams 2-20.

Kickoff Returns—Pittsburgh, Anderson 3-60; New Orleans, J. Rogers 3-97.

Punt Returns—Pittsburgh, Smith 5-23; New Orleans, Groth 2-25.

Interceptions—Pittsburgh, Thomas 1-1, Blount 2-58, Shell 1-16.

Punting—Pittsburgh, Colquitt 6-41.7; New Orleans, Erxleben 5-43.2.

Field Goals—Pittsburgh, Trout 2-2; New Orleans, Ricardo 2-2.

VIKINGS 24, BEARS 21

BLOOMINGTON—The jinx goes on. Chicago hasn't won at Metropolitan Stadium since 1971, and this time the Bears blew it when Hans Nielsen hooked a 27-yard field goal attempt on the final play of the game.

Nielsen's miss was preceded by a bizarre scene in which each team was penalized as the Bears, out of timeouts, attempted to stop the clock after Vince Evans had run to the Minnesota 9 on a quarterback draw.

The clock was ticking down the final seconds as the Bears scrambled into formation and Evans hurled a pass out of bounds, as penalty flags flew.

Both Chicago and Minnesota were whistled for having too many men on the field, stopping the clock and permitting Nielsen's kick.

"The field goal team was ready to go on short notice and then everybody got confused," said Chicago Coach Neill Armstrong. Said Minnesota's Bud Grant, "The Bears had too many men on the field. First, the officials called it that way and that would have been the end of the game, because you can't stop the clock with an offensive penalty.

"But then, they (the officials) talked it over and said we had too many men, too. That was the compromise they came up with. I did not send anybody in and we didn't have too many men on the field. Unless it was through exuberance, someone jumping up and down on the sidelines, I can't say that anybody on our side was on the field."

Back judge Banks Williams insisted there was a 12th Minnesota player on the field. In fact, he said, "There were so many (Vikings) on the field, I couldn't get the numbers."

Anyway, Nielsen missed his kick. "I just pulled it. No excuses," he said. The Vikings held on for their third straight victory.

Aside from the last-second excitement, the game was a passing duel between Evans and the Vikes' Tommy Kramer. Evans was 26-for-43 for 307 yards and two touchdowns, Kramer 20-for-38 for 223 yards and two TDs. Ahmad Rashad had four receptions, giving him 336 at Minneosta to tie the club record set by Chuck Foreman.

OCTOBER 4
SCORE BY PERIODS

Chicago	0	7	7	7—	21
Minnesota	10	7	7	0—	24

Fifth Week—Continued

SCORING
Minnesota—Brown 8 run (Danmeier kick).
Minnesota—Field goal Danmeier 43.
Minnesota—Rashad 15 pass from Kramer (Danmeier kick).
Chicago—Baschnagel 16 pass from Evans (Nielsen kick).
Chicago—Evans 4 run (Nielsen kick).
Minnesota—Senser 11 pass from Kramer (Danmeier kick).
Chicago—Baschnagel 7 pass from Evans (Nielsen kick).

TEAM STATISTICS

	Chicago	Minnesota
First downs	24	22
Rushes-Yards	31-89	34-134
Passing yards	307	211
Sacks by-Yards	1-12	0-0
Return yards	136	142
Passes	26-44-1	20-38-1
Punts	8-39.8	9-40.8
Fumbles-Lost	1-1	1-0
Penalties-Yards	8-60	7-48
Time of possession	28:00	32:00

Attendance—43,827.

INDIVIDUAL STATISTICS

Rushing—Chicago, Payton 20-49, Evans 5-23, Suhey 6-17; Minnesota, Brown 24-97, Young 7-32, Galbreath 3-5.

Passing—Chicago, Evans 26-44-1—307; Minnesota, Kramer 20-38-1—223.

Receiving—Chicago, Margerum 10-140, Baschnagel 6-69, Payton 2-33, Williams 4-21, Anderson 1-19, Earl 1-9, Suhey 1-9, Zanders 1-7; Minnesota, Rashad 4-60, Young 5-60, S. White 5-44, Senser 2-30, Brown 4-29.

Kickoff Returns—Chicago, Williams 4-114; Minnesota, Payton 2-47, Nord 1-19, McDole 1-18.

Punt Returns—Chicago, J. Fisher 4-22; Minnesota, Payton 4-30.

Interceptions—Chicago, Fencik 1-0; Minnesota, Hannon 1-28.

Punting—Chicago, Parsons 8-39.8; Minnesota, Coleman 9-40.8.

Field Goals—Chicago, Nielsen 0-1; Minnesota, Danmeier 1-1.

PATRIOTS 33, CHIEFS 17

FOXBORO—New England rediscovered its running game, avoided mistakes and came away with its first victory of the season after four losses, downing Kansas City.

"We were in a tough situation at 0-4, but you can come back from that," said Andy Johnson, who highlighted the triumph over the Chiefs with a 66-yard scoring pass to Stanley Morgan on a halfback option pass.

The Patriots rolled up 451 yards, including 240 on the ground against what had been the NFL's stingiest defense against the run. Quarterback Matt Cavanaugh passed for one touchdown, a 13-yarder to tight end Don Hasselbeck, and ran for a second TD.

"There was a big difference in our execution," said Cavanaugh, who completed 10 of 19 passes for 162 yards. "We eliminated a lot of the mistakes we had been making and we had good down and distance situations. That's a good way to get things turned around."

The Chiefs, who rushed for 219 yards (the fourth straight 200-yard effort by New Eng-

land's opponents), cut the Pats' lead to 24-17 on an 18-yard run by Joe Delaney with 14:54 left.

The Pats then faced a third-and-seven at their 26, but Cavanaugh scrambled eight yards for a first down. On the next play, Johnson took a handoff, faked a second handoff to wide receiver Harold Jackson, coming around on a reverse, and fired down the middle to Morgan. The fleet wide receiver took the ball on the K.C. 31 and went in to score.

"The trick pass play was the key to the game," said Chiefs defensive lineman Mike Bell. "They gambled and they won. Anytime you go up against an 0-4 team, you have to expect they're ready to win one."

The Patriots helped themselves with their first pass interceptions of the year—four of them. Two of the thefts set up the Pats' first two touchdowns.

Mike Hawkins intercepted a Bill Kenney pass on the third play of the game and New England coverted the break into Cavanaugh's TD pass to Hasselbeck. In the second period, linebacker Don Blackmon hit Kenney as he got off a pass and defensive end Mark Buben grabbed the ball and returned 49 yards, setting up an eight-yard bootleg by Cavanaugh for a score.

OCTOBER 4
SCORE BY PERIODS

Kansas City	7	0	3	7—17
New England	7	7	10	9—33

SCORING
New England—Hasselbeck 13 pass from Cavanaugh (Smith kick).
Kansas City—Hadnot 1 run (Lowery kick).
New England—Cavanaugh 8 run (Smith kick).
Kansas City—Field goal Lowery 35.
New England—Field goal Smith 50.
New England—Collins 13 run (Smith kick).
Kansas City—Delaney 18 run (Lowery kick).
New England—Morgan 66 pass from Johnson (kick failed).
New England—Field goal Smith 43.

TEAM STATISTICS

	Kansas City	New England
First downs	22	25
Rushes-Yards	37-219	49-240
Passing yards	91	228
Sacks by-Yards	0-0	2-17
Return yards	159	126
Passes	9-21-4	11-20-2
Punts	1-44.0	1-21.0
Fumbles-Lost	2-0	0-0
Penalties-Yards	4-32	2-20
Time of possession	26:10	33:50

Attendance—55,931.

INDIVIDUAL STATISTICS

Rushing—Kansas City, Delaney 18-101, Hadnot 14-65, McKnight 1-26, Kenney 2-25, B. Jackson 1-2, Bledsoe 1-0; New England, Collins 19-96, Ferguson 9-62, Cavanaugh 4-20, Calhoun 6-12, Cunningham 7-16, Tatupu 3-24, Morgan 1-10.

Passing—Kansas City, Kenney 9-20-3—108, Marshall 0-1-1—0; New England, Cavanaugh 10-19-2—162, Johnson 1-1-0—66.

Receiving—Kansas City, Scott 3-44, Delaney 1-7, Smith 2-23, Marshall 2-22, Hadnot 1-12; New England, Morgan 4-118, Hasselbeck 2-25, Jackson 2-27, Collins 1-5, Tatupu 1-41, Pennywell 1-12.

Kickoff Returns—Kansas City, Burruss 1-15, Bledsoe 5-99, Dombroski 1-21; New England, Sanford 1-14, Collins 3-43.

Punt Returns—New England, Haynes 1-1.

Interceptions—Kansas City, Burruss 2-24; New England, Buben 1-49, Hawkins 1-16, Haynes 1-3, Fox 1-0.

Punting—Kansas City, Grupp 1-44.0; New England, Hubach 1-21.0.

Field Goals—Kansas City, Lowery 1-2; New England, Smith 2-2.

CHARGERS 24, SEAHAWKS 10

SAN DIEGO—Although his Chargers were 4-1 after their victory over Seattle, Coach Don Coryell was predicting a tight finish in the AFC Western Division.

"I'll bet 10-6 wins the division," said Coryell.

The Chargers went into the game with several question marks. Both starting backs, Chuck Muncie and rookie James Brooks, were nursing injuries suffered the previous week in a 42-24 loss at Denver. Veterans John Cappelletti and Clarence Williams took their spots.

Newly acquired Wes Chandler lined up at wide receiver and running back, and returned punts. On defense, Pete Shaw was given his first start at safety and rookie defensive end Keith Ferguson replaced Fred Dean, who was traded to San Francisco.

The Seahawks jumped to a 7-0 lead before the Chargers came back on the passing of Dan Fouts. He completed 30 passes, a one-game Charger record, in 41 attempts for 302 yards and three TDs. Two of the scoring passes went to Charlie Joiner and the other to Kellen Winslow.

Cappelletti, effective on draw plays, galloped for 85 yards. Williams caught 10 passes and Chandler grabbed five.

Chandler practiced with the Chargers only two days after being traded from the New Orleans Saints. "It's remarkable, coming in like he did, that he didn't blow an assignment," said Fouts. "He didn't even have a question about an assignment."

The Charger defense twice stopped Seattle at the goal line in the second half.

"We had every opportunity to win," said Seattle quarterback Jim Zorn. "We had five shots at the goal line. When you can't score from six inches out, it takes the sting out of you."

Zorn produced the Seahawks' TD on a 34-yard pass to Steve Largent, who had 118 yards and five receptions for the day.

OCTOBER 4
SCORE BY PERIODS

Seattle	0	7	0	3—10
San Diego	0	10	7	7—24

SCORING

Seattle—Largent 34 pass from Zorn (Herrera kick).
San Diego—Field goal Benirschke 47.
San Diego—Winslow 9 pass from Fouts (Benirschke kick).

San Diego—Joiner 12 pass from Fouts (Benirschke kick).
Seattle—Field goal Herrera 20.
San Diego—Joiner 11 pass from Fouts (Benirschke kick).

TEAM STATISTICS

	Seattle	San Diego
First downs	15	25
Rushes-Yards	23-92	28-99
Passing yards	200	272
Sacks by-Yards	4-30	2-29
Return yards	95	66
Passes	16-34-1	30-41-0
Punts	6-44.7	5-41.4
Fumbles-Lost	4-0	6-2
Penalties-Yards	9-69	10-80
Time of possession	25:58	34:02
Attendance—51,463.		

INDIVIDUAL STATISTICS

Rushing—Seattle, Zorn 6-29, Hughes 8-26, Jodat 3-17, Lane 3-9, Smith 2-7, Doornink 1-4; San Diego, Cappelletti 14-85, C. Williams 12-6, Chandler 1-5, Bauer 1-3.

Passing—Seattle, Zorn 16-34-1—229; San Diego, Fouts 30-41-0—302.

Receiving—Seattle, Largent 5-118, Lane 4-45, Sawyer 2-27, Hughes 2-5, McGrath 1-16, McCullum 1-13, Doornink 1-5; San Diego, C. Williams 10-89, Winslow 7-82, Chandler 5-37, Joiner 3-34, Cappelletti 2-28, Sievers 2-20, Scales 1-12.

Kickoff Returns—Seattle, Lewis 3-54, Johnson 1-14, Cronan 1-21; San Diego, Chandler 2-19.

Punt Returns—Seattle, Lewis 5-6; San Diego, Chandler 3-30.

Interceptions—San Diego, Shaw 1-17.

Punting—Seattle, West 6-44.7; San Diego, Roberts 5-41.4.

Field Goals—Seattle, Herrera 1-2; San Diego, Benirschke 1-1

OILERS 17, BENGALS 10

HOUSTON—The plan to diversify the Houston offense seemed to be on a permanent hold after the Oilers let Earl Campbell do the job against Cincinnati.

All Campbell did was carry the ball 37 times, gain 182 yards and spark a victory that put Houston in a tie with Pittsburgh and Cincinnati for the lead in the AFC Central Division at 3-2.

Campbell also scored a touchdown on a two-yard run. Carl Roaches tallied the Oilers' other TD on a 96-yard dash with a kickoff. Toni Fritsch contributed the other Oiler points with a 48-yard field goal.

Houston quarterback Ken Stabler spent most of the day handing off to Campbell, running from the I-formation. Stabler attempted just six passes and completed one for minus four yards. All three figures were Oiler lows.

"I realize you can't win too many pro games throwing six passes," said new Oilers Coach Ed Biles. "But results are what count."

Meanwhile, Bengals quarterback Ken Anderson fired 52 passes and completed 30 for 290 yards. The Bengals took a 10-7 lead in the third period when Anderson tossed a 13-yard scoring pass to tight end Dan Ross, but Roaches went all the way with the ensuing kickoff.

Roaches also returned four punts for a total of 93 yards.

Fifth Week—Continued

Roaches' long kickoff return was his second of the season. He returned one 88 yards against the New York Jets in the second game of the season.

Campbell gave considerable credit for his showing to fullback Tim Wilson, his chief blocker, who was restored to the lineup after Houston dealt Rob Carpenter to the New York Giants. "Tim is invaluable to me," said Campbell. "He does a great job."

OCTOBER 4
SCORE BY PERIODS

Cincinnati	3	0	7	0—10
Houston	0	7	7	3—17

SCORING
Cincinnati—Field goal Breech 45.
Houston—Campbell 2 run (Fritsch kick).
Cincinnati—Ross 13 pass from Anderson (Breech kick).
Houston—Roaches 96 kickoff return (Fritsch kick).
Houston—Field goal Fritsch 48.

TEAM STATISTICS

	Cincinnati	Houston
First downs	20	11
Rushes-Yards	23-75	44-191
Passing yards	282	minus 4
Sacks by-Yards	1-7	1-8
Return yards	93	273
Passes	30-52-1	1-6-0
Punts	6-52.5	6-37.3
Fumbles-Lost	0-0	1-1
Penalties-Yards	9-65	3-25
Time of possession	32:13	27:47

Attendance—44,350.

INDIVIDUAL STATISTICS

Rushing—Cincinnati, Johnson 13-38, Alexander 9-29, Anderson 1-8; Houston, Campbell 37-182, T. Wilson 3-8, Armstrong 1-2, Coleman 1-3, Stabler 2-minus 4.

Passing—Cincinnati, Anderson 30-52-1—290; Houston, Stabler 1-6-0—3.

Receiving—Cincinnati, Ross 8-96, Alexander 7-54, Collinsworth 4-29, McInally 2-28, Kreider 3-35, Johnson 3-12, Verser 1-19, Griffin 2-17; Houston, Campbell 1-3.

Kickoff Returns—Cincinnati, Chapman 3-66, Griffin 1-17; Houston, Tullis 1-23, Roaches 1-96, T. Wilson 1-23.

Punt Returns—Cincinnati, Fuller 4-10; Houston, Roaches 4-93.

Interceptions—Houston, Stemrick 1-38.

Punting—Cincinnati, McInally 6-52.5; Houston, Parsley 6-37.3.

Field Goals—Cincinnati, Breech 1-3; Houston, Fritsch 1-2.

BUCCANEERS 28, LIONS 10

TAMPA—Statistically, Tampa Bay quarterback Doug Williams didn't have a good day, completing only 13 of 29 passes for 168 yards. But Coach John McKay wasn't complaining, because four of Williams' completions went for touchdowns in the victory over Detroit.

Williams took advantage of the man-to-man coverage employed by Detroit on Kevin House and threw two touchdown passes to the wide receiver, as well as one apiece to James Wilder and Jim Obradovich.

"He didn't throw particularly well?" McKay replied to a question. "I think he threw four touchdown passes. I'll take that. This 80 percent and no touchdowns is a bunch of manure. That's for people who like statistics."

Detroit, playing without injured starting quarterback Gary Danielson, jumped to a 10-0 first quarter lead on a 50-yard field goal by Eddie Murray and a five-yard touchdown pass from Jeff Komlo to Freddie Scott. But then the Williams-to-House combination took over.

Williams looped a scoring toss to House, who caught three passes for 40 yards, from 17 yards out early in the second quarter. He did it again from 13 yards out in a disputed play late in the period, giving Tampa Bay a 14-10 halftime lead. The Lions contended that House didn't get both feet in-bounds.

Tampa Bay clinched the victory early in the fourth quarter. Defensive end Bill Kollar recovered a fumble at midfield and three plays later, Williams hit Wilder, a fullback who had lined up as a flanker, for a 37-yard touchdown pass.

Williams added the final TD with a 60-yard pass to Obradovich. The score was set up on safety Cedric Brown's interception of a pass by Eric Hipple, who replaced Komlo in the second half.

Detroit quarterbacks completed only 18 of 40 passes, throwing four interceptions. Billy Sims was held to 75 yards rushing and the Lions lost two fumbles.

"I wouldn't blame the loss on the quarterbacks," said Detroit coach Monte Clark. "We just didn't play anywhere near the way we can."

OCTOBER 4
SCORE BY PERIODS

Detroit	10	0	0	0—10
Tampa Bay	0	14	0	14—28

SCORING
Detroit—Field goal Murray 50.
Detroit—Scott 5 pass from Komlo (Murray kick).
Tampa Bay—House 17 pass from Williams (Capece kick).
Tampa Bay—House 13 pass from Williams (Capece kick).
Tampa Bay—Wilder 37 pass from Williams (Capece kick).
Tampa Bay—Obradovich 6 pass from Williams (Capece kick).

TEAM STATISTICS

	Detroit	Tampa Bay
First downs	18	14
Rushes-Yards	35-93	25-49
Passing yards	239	162
Sacks by-Yards	1-6	2-16
Return yards	84	143
Passes	18-40-4	13-29-1
Punts	4-36.5	8-46.0
Fumbles-Lost	4-2	0-0
Penalties-Yards	5-50	5-4
Time of possession	34:19	25:41

Attendance—71,733.

INDIVIDUAL STATISTICS

Rushing—Detroit, Sims 24-75, Bussey 6-15, Komlo 2-minus 1, Hipple 2-4, Scott 1-0; Tampa Bay, Eckwood 16-21, Wilder 5-17, Swider 1-minus 9, Williams 1-2, Owens 2-18.

Passing—Detroit, Komlo 14-25-2—153, Hipple 4-15-2 —102; Tampa Bay, Williams 13-29-1—168.

Receiving—Detroit, L. Thompson 1-19, Bussey 2-1, King 3-7, Sims 2-11, Scott 5-97, Hill 3-46, Nichols 1-59, Kane 1-15; Tampa Bay, Wilder 4-65, T. Bell 3-34, House 3-40, Eckwood 2-23, Obradovich 1-6.

Kickoff Returns—Detroit, Martin 2-39, Harrell 1-0; Tampa Bay, Owens 3-55.

Punt Returns—Detroit, Martin 5-45; Tampa Bay, T. Bell 3-18.

Interceptions—Detroit, Cobb 1-0; Tampa Bay, Brown 2-34, Johnson 2-36.

Punting—Detroit, Skladany 4-36.5; Tampa Bay, Swider 8-46.0.

Field Goals—Detroit, Murray 1-2; Tampa Bay, None attempted.

EAGLES 16, FALCONS 13

PHILADELPHIA—In the 49-year history of the Philadelphia Eagles franchise, no team had ever won its first five games of the season. But that all changed in this Monday night encounter with Atlanta at Veterans Stadium as the Eagles beat the Falcons, 16-13, in a nationally televised contest.

The victory kept the Eagles as the only unbeaten and untied team in the NFL through the first five weeks.

The Eagles started fast. Linebackers Al Chesley and Reggie Wilkes each intercepted a Steve Bartkowski pass in the first quarter and each interception led to a Tony Franklin field goal. The Eagles led, 6-0, after one quarter.

Then, with 1:31 left in the first half, Philadelphia's Charlie Smith made a diving catch of a Ron Jaworski pass in the end zone. The play covered 30 yards and gave the Eagles a 13-0 halftime lead.

The best opportunity the Falcons had to score in the first half came when a pass interference call gave them the ball on the Eagles 6-yard line. But Atlanta rookie Mick Luckhurst's 19-yard field goal attempt bounced off an upright.

Atlanta finally did score with 4:17 left in the third quarter. Luckhurst hit on a 35-yard field goal to culminate a drive started by the Falcons on their own 8.

On the ensuing kickoff, Wally Henry, the Eagles kick returner, fumbled the ball. The Falcons' Kenny Johnson scooped up the loose ball on the 20-yard line and rambled untouched into the end zone. Within seconds, the Falcons cut a 13-0 deficit to 13-10.

But three points was as close as the Falcons could come to the Eagles all night. Franklin and Luckhurst exchanged 43-yard field goals in the final quarter as the Eagles held on to snap the Falcons' three-game winning streak against Philadelphia.

MONDAY, OCTOBER 5
SCORE BY PERIODS

Atlanta	0	0	10	3	13
Philadelphia	6	7	0	3	16

SCORING

Philadelphia—Field goal Franklin 36.
Philadelphia—Field goal Franklin 34.
Philadelphia—Smith 30 pass from Jaworski (Franklin kick).
Atlanta—Field goal Luckhurst 35.
Atlanta—Johnson 20 fumble return (Luckhurst kick).
Philadelphia—Field goal Franklin 43.
Atlanta—Field goal Luckhurst 43.

TEAM STATISTICS

	Atlanta	Philadelphia
First downs	22	14
Rushes-Yards	29-112	26-107
Passing yards	227	161
Sacks by-Yards	0-0	1-5
Return yards	76	101
Passes	23-46-2	17-26-0
Punts	4-38.3	5-39.2
Fumbles-Lost	3-1	1-1
Penalties-Yards	5-58	8-84
Time of possession	33:40	26:20

Attendance—71,488.

INDIVIDUAL STATISTICS

Rushing—Atlanta, Andrews 21-84, Cain 8-28; Philadelphia, Oliver 10-68, Montgomery 12-44, Russell 1-2, Giammona 1-minus 3, Jaworski 2-minus 4.

Passing—Atlanta, Bartkowski 23-46-2—232; Philadelphia, Jaworski 17-26-0—161.

Receiving—Atlanta, Jenkins 8-81, Andrews 5-56, Jackson 4-40, Cain 3-21, Miller 2-22, Francis 1-12; Philadelphia, Smith 5-59, Montgomery 5-14, Campfield 3-19, Carmichael 2-55, Krepfle 2-14.

Kickoff Returns—Atlanta, R. Smith 3-58, Gaison 1-10; Philadelphia, Henry 2-27, Giammona 1-19.

Punt Returns—Atlanta, R. Smith 3-8; Philadelphia, Henry 2-17.

Interceptions—Philadelphia, Chesley 1-31, Wilkes 1-7.

Punting—Atlanta, James 4-38.3; Philadelphia, Runager 5-39.2.

Field Goals—Atlanta, Luckhurst 2-3; Philadelphia, Franklin 3-3.

SIXTH WEEK

OILERS 35, SEAHAWKS 17

HOUSTON—The Houston Oilers found just the right blend of Earl Campbell's running and Ken Stabler's passing. The result was a decisive victory over the Seattle Seahawks that enabled Houston to retain a share of the AFC Central Division lead with Cincinnati and Pittsburgh at 4-2.

Campbell set a club record with 39 rushes good for 186 yards and two short touchdown runs. Stabler passed for 156 yards and three TDs.

Despite the efforts of the two, Houston trailed, 10-0, before Stabler passed on fourth-and-one at the Seattle 31. It resulted in a touchdown catch by Ken Burrough.

"We were surprised when he threw on fourth down," said Seattle Coach Jack Patera. "Campbell is their No. 1 man and we were keying on him on that play. Great as Campbell is, it was Stabler's passing that won the game for them."

Stabler had the answer for his success. "The passing game obviously depends on how well you run the ball," he declared.

Though Campbell didn't play the last seven minutes, his 39 carries were more than he'd ever achieved and two short of the NFL record set by Pittsburgh's Franco Harris in 1976.

The Oilers unleashed their strongest attack of the season. They hadn't scored more than 27 points in a game and their 21-point fourth period topped their combined fourth-quarter production in their five previous games.

OCTOBER 11
SCORE BY PERIODS

Seattle	10	0	0	7—	17
Houston	7	7	0	21—	35

SCORING

Seattle—Field goal Herrera 41.
Seattle—Hughes 17 pass from Zorn (Herrera kick).
Houston—Burrough 31 pass from Stabler (Fritsch kick).
Houston—Campbell 1 run (Fritsch kick).
Houston—Casper 32 pass from Stabler (Fritsch kick).
Houston—Burrough 24 pass from Stabler (Fritsch kick).
Houston—Campbell 4 run (Fritsch kick).
Seattle—Largent 31 pass from Adkins (Herrera kick).

TEAM STATISTICS

	Seattle	Houston
First downs	19	21
Rushes-Yards	16-75	48-216
Passing yards	214	156
Sacks by-Yards	0-0	2-18
Return yards	137	87
Passes	25-40-2	12-19-0
Punts	3-28.7	4-35.2
Fumbles-Lost	2-1	1-1
Penalties-Yards	8-50	6-55
Time of possession	22:47	37:13
Attendance—42,671.		

INDIVIDUAL STATISTICS

Rushing—Seattle, Adkins 3-28, Smith 4-19, Hughes 6-15, Zorn 1-5, Jodat 1-6, Lane 1-2; Houston, Campbell 39-186, Coleman 5-30, T. Wilson 1-0, Armstrong 1-1, Reaves 2-minus 1.

Passing—Seattle, Zorn 19-30-2—145, Adkins 6-10-0—87; Houston, Stabler 12-18-0—156, Reaves 0-1-0—0.

Receiving—Seattle, Largent 4-65, Smith 4-55, Hughes 7-44, McCullum 4-24, Tice 1-8, Sawyer 1-5, Lane 2-10, McGrath 2-21; Houston, Burrough 4-74, Casper 1-32, Coleman 2-18, Renfro 2-16, Campbell 3-16.

Kickoff Returns—Seattle, Lewis 2-55, Dufek 1-11, Johnson 3-56; Houston, Roaches 3-44.

Punt Returns—Seattle, Johns 2-15; Houston, Roaches 2-4.

Interceptions—Houston, Hartwig 1-36, Bingham 1-3.

Punting—Seattle, West 3-28.7; Houston, Parsley 4-35.2.

Field Goals—Seattle, Herrera 1-2; Houston, None attempted.

BRONCOS 27, LIONS 21

DENVER—The Lions' rushing attack rolled up 267 yards against the Broncos' defense, ranked first in the NFL in total defense, but Denver was able to shut down the Detroit offense, namely Billy Sims, when necessary in the second half.

The outcome was in doubt until 28 seconds remained, when the Denver defense stopped Detroit's final desperation drive 17 yards short of the end zone.

The victory left Denver with a 5-1 record and sole possession of first place in the AFC West.

Craig Morton threw three touchdown passes and Fred Steinfort added a pair of 24-yard field goals to account for Denver's points. Morton was 13 of 18 for 283 yards and Steve Watson caught five of those passes for 182 yards, including two for touchdowns.

Sims rushed for a career single-game high 185 yards on 28 carries and scored two touchdowns. Detroit's third score was on an interception return by Alvin Hall.

Denver led, 10-0, in the first quarter on Morton's 95-yard scoring pass to Watson and Steinfort's field goal following an interception. Detroit retaliated quickly on a six-play, 80-yard drive, with Sims zigzagging through the Denver defense 48 yards for the score.

The teams then traded touchdowns, Detroit scoring on Sims' one-yard plunge and Denver on a 40-yard strike from Morton to Watson.

The Lions' final score occurred with seconds remaining in the half when Morton tried to throw out of bounds to stop the clock and was intercepted by Hall, who dashed 60 yards for a touchdown and a 21-17 Detroit lead.

Denver ate up 11:02 on the clock, moving 74 yards in the third quarter to pull within a point on Steinfort's second field goal. Denver's winning points came on a screen pass from Morton to Rick Parros, who scored from 15 yards out.

OCTOBER 11
SCORE BY PERIODS

Detroit	7	14	0	0—	21
Denver	10	7	3	7—	27

SCORING

Denver—Watson 95 pass from Morton (Steinfort kick).
Denver—Field goal Steinfort 24.
Detroit—Sims 48 run (Murray kick).
Detroit—Sims 1 run (Murray kick).
Denver—Watson 40 pass from Morton (Steinfort kick).
Detroit—Hall 60 pass interception (Murray kick).
Denver—Field goal Steinfort 24.
Denver—Parros 15 pass from Morton (Steinfort kick).

TEAM STATISTICS

	Detroit	Denver
First downs	18	20
Rushes-Yards	48-267	37-135
Passing yards	58	266
Sacks by-Yards	2-17	2-14
Return yards	136	100
Passes	7-16-1	13-18-1
Punts	6-49.8	3-55.0
Fumbles-Lost	1-0	2-2
Penalties-Yards	8-121	4-25
Time of possession	33:08	26:52
Attendance—74,816.		

INDIVIDUAL STATISTICS

Rushing—Detroit, Sims 28-185, Bussey 12-49, Nichols 1-13, Komlo 3-9, Kane 3-6, King 1-5; Denver, Parros 20-

77, Preston 9-41, Lytle 2-20, Reed 4-minus 4, Morton 2-1.

Passing—Detroit, Komlo 7-16-1—72; Denver, Morton 13-18-1—283.

Receiving—Detroit, Nichols 2-26, Scott 2-22, King 1-12, Bussey 1-7, Kane 1-5; Denver, Watson 5-182, Moses 4-56, Parros 2-12, Odoms 1-21, Reed 1-12.

Kickoff Returns—Detroit, Martin 3-61; Denver, Manning 1-31, Harden 1-20.

Punt Returns—Detroit, Martin 2-15; Denver, Manning 3-31.

Interceptions—Detroit, Hall 1-60; Denver, Swenson 1-18.

Punting—Detroit, Skladany 6-49.8; Denver, Prestridge 3-55.0.

Field Goals—Detroit, None attempted; Denver, Steinfort 2-2.

BUCCANEERS 21, PACKERS 10

GREEN BAY—The strategy for Tampa Bay was simply to get the lead, be patient and let Green Bay make killing mistakes. It worked. The Bucs converted an interception into the clinching touchdown and then used three more pass thefts to stave off a Packer comeback.

Green Bay drove 65 yards to a TD on its first possession of the game, but the Bucs got a five-yard scoring pass from Doug Williams to tight end Jimmie Giles for a 7-7 halftime tie.

In the third period, Williams sneaked one yard for the go-ahead TD, and the Bucs' strategy took effect.

"Once we got the lead, we stayed back and let them come to us," said Coach John McKay. "Sooner or later, if you go into that zone, someone is going to pick one off."

Lynn Dickey tried to catch up in a hurry and linebacker Curtis Johnson grabbed his fourth interception in three games. He returned 29 yards, setting up James Wilder's one-yard plunge for a 21-7 Tampa Bay lead.

On the Bucs' next possession, Wilder took a 31-yard pass from Williams, but fumbled on the Green Bay 5. Packers linebacker George Cumby scooped up the ball and returned 68 yards to set up a Jan Stenerud field goal for the last points of the game. The Packers moved past midfield three times after that, but linebackers Scot Brantley and Hugh Green and safety Neal Colzie came up with interceptions.

The Packers played without starting tackle Mark Koncar, who had left the team after being criticized by Coach Bart Starr in a meeting of offensive linemen. Starr said he did not believe Koncar's absence was a factor in the game.

OCTOBER 11

SCORE BY PERIODS

Tampa Bay	0	7	14	0—21
Green Bay	7	0	0	3—10

SCORING

Green Bay—Ellis 7 run (Stenerud kick)
Tampa Bay—Giles 5 pass from Williams (Capece kick).
Tampa Bay—Williams 1 run (Capece kick).
Tampa Bay—Wilder 1 run (Capece kick).
Green Bay—Field goal Stenerud 34.

TEAM STATISTICS

	Tampa Bay	Green Bay
First downs	23	17
Rushes-Yards	45-172	22-95
Passing yards	199	203
Sacks by-Yards	2-16	1-0
Return yards	132	107
Passes	15-23-1	19-33-4
Punts	4-40.3	4-41.3
Fumbles-Lost	1-1	1-0
Penalties-Yards	5-35	3-19
Time of possession	36:13	23:47
Attendance—55,264.		

INDIVIDUAL STATISTICS

Rushing—Tampa Bay, Eckwood 22-84, Williams 5-14, Wilder 17-68, Owens 1-6; Green Bay, Ellis 8-35, Huckleby 12-57, Jensen 1-3, Dickey 1-0.

Passing—Tampa Bay, Williams 15-23-1—199; Green Bay, Dickey 19-33-4—219.

Receiving—Tampa Bay, Wilder 5-54, Giles 6-85, T. Bell 1-13, Obradovich 1-16, Carter 1-10, House 1-21; Green Bay, Lofton 4-86, Ellis 6-48, Jefferson 2-26, Coffman 2-17, Huckleby 5-42.

Kickoff Returns—Tampa Bay, Owens 3-45; Green Bay, Lee 4-78.

Punt Returns—Tampa Bay, T. Bell 1-6; Green Bay, Lee 3-26.

Interceptions—Tampa Bay, Colzie 1-0, Green 1-50, Johnson 1-29, Brantley 1-2; Green Bay, Douglass 1-13.

Punting—Tampa Bay, Swider 4-40.3; Green Bay, Stachowicz 4-41.3.

Field Goals—Tampa Bay, Capece 0-1; Green Bay, Stenerud 1-1.

RAMS 37, FALCONS 35

ATLANTA—The Los Angeles Rams thought Pat Haden was the victim of a "cheap shot." That angered them enough to turn a possible disaster into a thrilling victory over the Atlanta Falcons.

The Rams won on Frank Corral's 25-yard field goal with 24 seconds left in the game. The result left L.A. and San Francisco tied for first place in the National Football Conference Western Division, each with a 4-2 record, and dropped the Falcons to third place at 3-3.

In the second period, Atlanta ran off three touchdowns in an eight-minute span to take a 21-13 lead. Just when it seemed the Falcons were blowing the game open, the Rams found their inspiration.

Atlanta defensive end Wilson Faumuina dived into Haden's legs just as the Rams quarterback unleashed a pass from in front of the L.A. bench. Haden writhed in pain on the sideline and was removed on a cart, with his left leg in a plastic air bag. First reports indicated he had suffered a broken leg, but X-rays later showed that he had only a deep bruise.

Haden's last pass was complete for a 35-yard gain, to the Atlanta 16. Reserve quarterback Jeff Rutledge came on and converted the scoring opportunity with a one-yard touchdown pass to tight end Henry Childs. Early in the third quarter, Rutledge threw a 36-yard TD pass to Drew Hill to put the Rams ahead, 27-21.

"I felt that hit on Haden got the entire team mad," said Rams defensive back Leroy Irvin,

Sixth Week—Continued

who turned out to be the game's offensive star, returning punts 75 and 84 yards for touchdowns. "Pat's a super guy, and we hated to see him get a cheap shot. I think it was definitely a factor in the game."

Faumuina denied that his tackle was a "cheap shot." Said the 275-pounder, "I chased him and left my feet to tackle him just as he threw the ball. I hope he's not hurt seriously. I was simply trying to sack him."

The controversy over Haden's injury took some of the spotlight away from Irvin, who gained 204 yards on six punt returns. He went 75 yards to score in the first quarter and came through with his 84-yarder with 8:23 left in the game, after the Falcons had taken a 35-27 lead.

Irvin became the fourth player in pro football history to score two TDs in one game on punt returns. Jack Christiansen did it twice for the Detroit Lions, Dick Christy did it for the old New York Titans and Rick Upchurch did it for the Denver Broncos in 1976.

Irvin's total of 204 punt-return yards was one yard short of the record of 205, set by Oakland's George Atkinson against Buffalo in 1968.

The Falcons got three TD passes from Steve Bartkowski and 119 yards and two TDs from William Andrews.

OCTOBER 11
SCORE BY PERIODS

Los Angeles	13	7	7	10—37
Atlanta	0	21	7	7—35

SCORING

Los Angeles—Irvin 75 punt return (Corral kick).
Los Angeles—Field goal Corral 25.
Los Angeles—Field goal Corral 37.
Atlanta—Andrews 25 run (Luckhurst kick).
Atlanta—Miller 11 pass from Bartkowski (Luckhurst kick).
Atlanta—Jenkins 23 pass from Bartkowski (Luckhurst kick).
Los Angeles—Childs 1 pass from Rutledge (Corral kick).
Los Angeles—D. Hill 36 pass from Rutledge (Corral kick).
Atlanta—Jackson 8 pass from Bartkowski (Luckhurst kick).
Atlanta—Andrews 2 run (Luckhurst kick).
Los Angeles—Irvin 84 punt return (Corral kick).
Los Angeles—Field goal Corral 25.

TEAM STATISTICS

	Los Angeles	Atlanta
First downs	14	19
Rushes-Yards	33-87	33-152
Passing yards	165	197
Sacks by-Yards	2-17	3-23
Return yards	375	227
Passes	14-31-1	17-38-2
Punts	7-44.1	9-43.8
Fumbles-Lost	4-1	1-1
Penalties-Yards	6-36	5-35
Time of possession	32:15	27:45

Attendance—57,841.

INDIVIDUAL STATISTICS

Rushing—Los Angeles, Tyler 14-48, Bryant 10-31, Haden 2-14, Guman 1-3, Rutledge 4-minus 1, Dennard 2-minus 8; Atlanta, Andrews 21-119, Cain 12-33.

Passing—Los Angeles, Rutledge 11-20-1—130, Haden 3-10-0—58, Corral 0-1-0—0; Atlanta, Bartkowski 17-38-2—214.

Receiving—Los Angeles, Dennard 4-84, Childs 4-26, Bryant 3-30, Tyler 2-12, D. Hill 1-36; Atlanta, Jackson 4-47, Andrews 4-35, Francis 3-59, Miller 3-34, Mikeska 2-16, Jenkins 1-23.

Kickoff Returns—Los Angeles, D. Hill 5-150; Atlanta, R. Smith 7-156.

Punt Returns—Los Angeles, Irvin 6-204, D. Hill 1-12; Atlanta, Woerner 5-63.

Interceptions—Los Angeles, Perry 1-9, Cromwell 1-0; Atlanta, Butler 1-8.

Punting—Los Angeles, Corral 7-44.1; Atlanta, James 9-43.8.

Field Goals—Los Angeles, Corral 3-3; Atlanta, None attempted.

CHIEFS 27, RAIDERS 0

KANSAS CITY—Not since the Brooklyn Dodgers in 1943 had an NFL team been shut out in three consecutive games.

But the Raiders were blanked by the Chiefs in this game to run the Oakland streak to three straight games without scoring a point. The Detroit Lions (16-0) and Denver Broncos (17-0) had blanked Oakland the previous two weeks.

Oakland, which had gone 15 seasons without being shut out, was up against an injury-riddled Kansas City defense, but still could muster little offense. Kansas City was missing defensive end Art Still and linebackers Frank Manumaluega and Thomas Howard.

The Chiefs, who rank first in the NFL in defense against the run, held Oakland to 79 yards on the ground and harassed quarterbacks Jim Plunkett and Marc Wilson into a 14-of-40 passing performance. The Raiders finished the game with only 230 total yards. Ray Guy was forced to punt nine times.

"It's always a bad day when you get blown off the field," said Oakland Coach Tom Flores, whose team dropped to 2-4. "Our running game is not going at all and we're in a position where our offense is predictable. And when you get into that position, they can really tee off on you.

"We've been in that position for the last two weeks and you just can't do that against a good defensive team like Kansas City. Our backs are really up against the wall now. But we are all professionals. We have to prepare ourselves to fight back. We have to fight back."

Oakland's only real threat came in the closing minutes of the first half when Plunkett marched the Raiders 41 yards to the Kansas City 19. But Gary Barbaro intercepted a pass on the goal line on the final play of the half to preserve a 10-0 lead.

Joe Delaney, who was making his first pro start in place of the injured Ted McKnight, rushed 28 times for 106 yards and caught three passes for 104 more yards to set up three of the Kansas City scores.

Bill Kenney was 15 of 23 for 287 yards with touchdown passes of four yards to Henry

The defending Super Bowl champion Oakland Raiders and star quarterback Jim Plunkett were down in the dumps when the Raiders were shut out for the third successive week, 27-0, by the Kansas City Chiefs. It had been 38 years since an NFL team was shut out in three straight games.

Sixth Week—Continued

Marshall and nine yards to J. T. Smith. Nick Lowery kicked field goals of 52 and 25 yards and rookie Billy Jackson scored a four-yard touchdown on his only carry of the day.

OCTOBER 11
SCORE BY PERIODS

Oakland	0	0	0	0— 0
Kansas City	3	7	10	7—27

SCORING

Kansas City—Field goal Lowery 52.
Kansas City—B. Jackson 4 run (Lowery kick).
Kansas City—Field goal Lowery 25.
Kansas City—Marshall 4 pass from Kenney (Lowery kick).
Kansas City—Smith 9 pass from Kenney (Lowery kick).

TEAM STATISTICS

	Oakland	Kansas City
First downs	13	20
Rushes-Yards	22-79	48-176
Passing yards	151	278
Sacks by-Yards	1-9	0-0
Return yards	84	184
Passes	14-40-3	15-23-0
Punts	9-38.7	4-31.0
Fumbles-Lost	1-0	2-2
Penalties-Yards	2-15	5-45
Time of possession	24:22	35:38
Attendance—76,543.		

INDIVIDUAL STATISTICS

Rushing—Oakland, King 11-46, Jensen 7-21, Plunkett 3-9, Whittington 1-3; Kansas City, Delaney 28-106, Hadnot 14-57, Bledsoe 4-7, B. Jackson 1-4, Kenney 1-2.

Passing—Oakland, Plunkett 12-29-1—129, Wilson 2-11-2—22; Kansas City, Kenney 15-23-0—287.

Receiving—Oakland, Branch 4-46, Ramsey 3-23, Bradshaw 3-17, King 1-30, Whittington 1-13, Barnwell 1-13, Christensen 1-9; Kansas City, Marshall 6-110, Delaney 3-104, Smith 3-43, Rome 1-12, Hadnot 1-11, Dixon 1-7.

Kickoff Returns—Oakland, Whittington 3-48, Hawkins 1-7, Barnwell 1-24; Kansas City, Murphy 1-17.

Punt Returns—Oakland, Watts 1-5; Kansas City, Smith 5-66.

Interceptions—Kansas City, Harris 1-43, Paul 1-25, Barbaro 1-33.

Punting—Oakland, Guy 9-38.7; Kansas City, Grupp 4-31.0.

Field Goals—Oakland, None attempted; Kansas City, Lowery 2-2.

EAGLES 31, SAINTS 14

NEW ORLEANS—"We not only were playing a good football team, we were playing a hot football team," said New Orleans Coach Bum Phillips after watching Philadelphia run its record to 6-0. "We did a heck of a job not to surrender."

The Saints broke on top as George Rogers, who galloped for 134 yards on 17 carries, scored on a five-yard run. But Philadelphia came back to take a 24-7 halftime lead on Ron Jaworski's 11-yard scoring pass to Keith Krepfle, a pair of one-yard TD drives by Booker Russell, and a 22-yard field goal by Tony Franklin.

The Eagles' defense provided a third-period touchdown when linebacker Frank LeMaster scooped up Archie Manning's fumble and scampered 42 yards into the end zone.

Jaworski overcame pre-game flashbacks of the Eagles' loss to Oakland in Super Bowl XV in the Louisiana Superdome to complete 15 of 28 passes for 207 yards.

"The last time we played here, we left a little disappointed," he said. "Fortunately, there was a little retribution today and we left with our chins up. It definitely was a little eerie, though."

Jaworski said a weak Saints pass rush gave him plenty of time to throw.

"The Saints were doing a good job of disguising their pass defense, but I had a lot of time," Jaworski said.

OCTOBER 11
SCORE BY PERIODS

Philadelphia	14	10	7	0—31
New Orleans	7	0	0	7—14

SCORING

New Orleans—G. Rogers 5 run (Ricardo kick).
Philadelphia—Krepfle 11 pass from Jaworski (Franklin kick).
Philadelphia—Russell 1 run (Franklin kick).
Philadelphia—Russell 1 run (Wilkes pass from Jaworski).
Philadelphia—Field goal Franklin 22.
Philadelphia—LeMaster 47 fumble return (Franklin kick).
New Orleans—G. Rogers 3 run (Ricardo kick).

TEAM STATISTICS

	Philadelphia	New Orleans
First downs	21	18
Rushes-Yards	36-169	31-190
Passing yards	200	50
Sacks by-Yards	4-40	1-7
Return yards	146	205
Passes	15-28-2	10-24-1
Punts	1-36.0	5-36.4
Fumbles-Lost	1-0	3-3
Penalties-Yards	8-61	7-52
Time of possession	31:57	28:03
Attendance—52,728.		

INDIVIDUAL STATISTICS

Rushing—Philadelphia, Montgomery 20-83, Oliver 7-37, Russell 4-7, Jaworski 2-24, Smith 1-0, Atkins 1-21, Pisarcik 1-minus 3; New Orleans, G. Rogers 17-134, Holmes 3-12, Tyler 8-33, W. Wilson 3-11.

Passing—Philadelphia, Jaworski 15-28-2—207; New Orleans, Manning 4-15-1—43, D. Wilson 6-9-0—47.

Receiving—Philadelphia, Krepfle 3-36, Carmichael 4-88, Parker 2-30, Montgomery 3-20, Smith 1-24, Oliver 1-0, Campfield 1-9; New Orleans, Merkens 3-23, Holmes 1-16, Tyler 2-17, Martini 1-5, G. Rogers 1-4, Banks 1-12, Williams 1-13.

Kickoff Returns—Philadelphia, Henry 2-43, Atkins 1-15; New Orleans, J. Rogers 3-83, W. Wilson 3-99.

Punt Returns—Philadelphia, Henry 4-88.

Interceptions—Philadelphia, Young 1-0; New Orleans, Waymer 2-23.

Punting—Philadelphia, Runager 1-36.0; New Orleans, Erxleben 5-36.4.

Field Goals—Philadelphia, Franklin 1-3; New Orleans, None attempted.

REDSKINS 24, BEARS 7

CHICAGO—Washington turned the tables on Chicago by forcing the type of turnovers that had kept the Redskins winless in their first five games.

The Skins intercepted four Vince Evans passes, converting three into points, to post their first victory for first-year coach Joe Gibbs.

"They caught us on our best day of the year," said Gibbs. "It was time for us to get one like that."

The loss was the Bears' fifth in six games, their worst start in six years, and left them in the NFC Central Division cellar.

Washington's defense, after yielding 149 points in the five losses, recorded four sacks and shut down Chicago until the final two minutes of the game.

Evans completed only eight of 37 passes for 131 yards and Walter Payton, nursing a bruised thigh, was held to five yards in five carries.

"This is the lowest I've felt dating all the way back through college and high school," said Payton.

Washington raced out to a 17-0 halftime lead, capitalizing on the interceptions. Joe Lavender intercepted a pass in the first quarter and Washington converted it into a 38-yard field goal by Mark Moseley. Twenty-four seconds later, Neal Olkewicz scored on a 10-yard interception return. Dave Butz picked off a pass in the final minute of the second quarter and John Riggins ran one yard to score.

Riggins, who rushed for 126 yards in 23 carries, scored Washington's final touchdown in the fourth quarter on a two-yard run.

The Bears avoided their first shutout in 59 games when Mike Phipps hit Marcus Anderson on a 43-yard scoring strike with 1:37 left.

OCTOBER 11
SCORE BY PERIODS

Washington	10	7	0	7—24
Chicago	0	0	0	7— 7

SCORING
Washington—Field goal Moseley 38.
Washington—Olkewicz 10 Interception return (Moseley kick).
Washington—Riggins 1 run (Moseley kick).
Washington—Riggins 2 run (Moseley kick).
Chicago—Anderson 43 pass from Phipps (Roveto kick).

TEAM STATISTICS

	Washington	Chicago
First downs	16	13
Rushes-Yards	47-227	18-51
Passing yards	74	153
Sacks by-Yards	4-30	1-9
Return yards	211	121
Passes	12-25-1	11-41-4
Punts	8-34.4	10-40.2
Fumbles-Lost	0-0	1-0
Penalties-Yards	9-62	7-48
Time of possesion	35:18	24:42
Attendance—57,683.		

INDIVIDUAL STATISTICS
Rushing—Washington, Riggins 23-126, Washington 21-88, Wonsley 2-11, Theismann 1-2; Chicago, Suhey 9-25, Williams 1-15, Payton 5-5, McClendon 2-5, Evans 1-1.
Passing—Washington, Theismann 12-25-1—83; Chica-

go, Evans 8-37-4—137, Phipps 3-4-0—52.
Receiving—Washington, Washington 3-5, Monk 2-30, Caster 2-30, Warren 2-8, Walker 2-3, Metcalf 1-7; Chicago, Baschnagel 4-72, Margerum 3-50, Anderson 2-48, Williams 1-9, McClendon 1-4.
Kickoff Returns—Washington, Nelms 1-24, Peters 1-5; Chicago, Williams 3-49, Frazier 1-15, J. Fisher 1-23.
Punt Returns—Washington, Nelms 8-76; Chicago, J. Fisher 3-28, Walterscheid 1-6.
Interceptions—Washington, Olkewicz 1-10, Lavender 1-12, Butz 1-26, Murphy 1-29; Chicago, Fencik 1-0.
Punting—Washington, Connell 8-34.4; Chicago, Parsons 10-40.2.
Field Goals—Washington, Moseley 1-2; Chicago, None attempted.

GIANTS 34, CARDINALS 14

EAST RUTHERFORD—Rob Carpenter made his first appearance as a New York Giants running back with 3:55 left in the first half against St. Louis. Two plays later, the Giants had the lead for good.

Phil Simms tossed three touchdown passes, two of them to Johnny Perkins, and Joe Danelo kicked a pair of long field goals as the Giants evened their record at 3-3. But there was little doubt that Carpenter, recently acquired from Houston, was the catalyst.

"Rob Carpenter got the game ball and there was no question it was the best game by a Giants running back since I've been here," said third-year Coach Ray Perkins.

Carpenter, providing the Giants some sorely needed speed and moves, rambled for 103 yards on 14 carries. He ran 21 yards for the game's last touchdown and reeled off a 35-yard gain as the Giants used up the clock in the final minutes.

St. Louis handed over three fumbles and an interception, which led to a touchdown. The Cardinals took their only lead, 7-0, when Jim Hart passed 14 yards to tight end Doug Marsh in the second quarter. Then Danelo kicked a 41-yard field goal and the Giants forced a punt. They moved to the St. Louis 11 on a 22-yard pass from Simms to tight end Gary Shirk on third-and-21. Carpenter entered the lineup a few seconds later the Giants had a 10-7 lead on a five-yard Simms-to-Perkins pass.

Brian Kelley's interception led to a Simms-to-Perkins TD pass of seven yards for a 17-7 lead 26 seconds before halftime. In the third period, Danelo booted a 45-yard field goal and Earnest Gray made a one-handed catch of a 22-yard pass from Simms to boost the score to 27-7. Then it was Carpenter time.

"A lot of people are looking at us like we're the same old Giants," said defensive end Gary Jeter. "But we're a team to be reckoned with."

OCTOBER 11
SCORE BY PERIODS

St. Louis	0	7	0	7—14
New York Giants	0	17	10	7—34

SCORING
St. Louis—Marsh 14 pass from Hart (O'Donoghue kick).

— 183 —

Sixth Week—Continued

New York—Field goal Danelo 41.
New York—Perkins 5 pass from Simms (Danelo kick).
New York—Perkins 7 pass from Simms (Danelo kick).
New York—Field goal Danelo 45.
New York—Gray 22 pass from Simms (Danelo kick).
St. Louis—T. Brown 3 run (O'Donoghue kick).
New York—Carpenter 21 run (Danelo kick).

TEAM STATISTICS

	St. Louis	New York
First downs	19	27
Rushes-Yards	26-101	36-198
Passing yards	184	179
Sacks by-Yards	5-29	4-37
Return yards	101	113
Passes	19-29-1	19-33-0
Punts	4-48.5	3-47.7
Fumbles-Lost	5-3	1-1
Penalties-Yards	7-49	4-44
Time of possession	27:21	32:39

Attendance—67,128.

INDIVIDUAL STATISTICS

Rushing—St. Louis, Anderson 18-71, T. Brown 6-19, Morris 1-3, Lomax 1-8; New York, L. Jackson 10-30, Perry 5-30, Bright 5-8, Carpenter 14-103, Brunner 1-3, Simms 1-24.

Passing—St. Louis, Hart 17-26-1—195, Lomax 2-3-0—26; New York, Simms 19-33-0—208.

Receiving—St. Louis, T. Brown 3-32, Gray 3-18, La-Fleur 1-17, Marsh 4-52, Green 1-24, Anderson 5-47, Tilley 2-31; New York, Friede 2-22, Perry 1-24, Perkins 5-55, L. Jackson 1-7, Shirk 3-31, Bright 2-10, Mullady 2-14, Carpenter 2-23, Gray 1-22.

Kickoff Returns—St. Louis, Mitchell 4-68, Harrell 1-9; New York, Bright 2-43, Garrett 1-32.

Punt Returns—St. Louis, Mitchell 2-24; New York, Bright 2-19, Garrett 1-3.

Interceptions—New York, Kelley 1-16.

Punting—St. Louis, Birdsong 4-48.5; New York, Jennings 3-47.7.

Field Goals—St. Louis, O'Donoghue 0-1; New York, Danelo 2-2.

STEELERS 13, BROWNS 7

PITTSBURGH—The Steelers may be getting older, but never let it be said they aren't getting wiser.

The Browns learned the hard way in their loss to the Steelers that with age comes wisdom, and it might make them think twice before they try to fool an old dog again.

On the verge of snatching victory from Pittsburgh's grasp with time running out, Cleveland turned to the play that had worked for its only touchdown of the day a bit earlier.

But the second time, the Steelers were waiting.

Paul McDonald, playing in place of the injured Brian Sipe, called for a pass to Ozzie Newsome in the end zone on second-and-10 from the 12-yard line.

McDonald fired it perfectly. But Newsome never got it. The pass bounced off the chest of Steelers cornerback Dwayne Woodruff and into the hands of safety J.T. Thomas with 1:53 remaining, and the Steelers had their fourth straight victory.

It was the same play the Browns used in the second quarter when Sipe hit Newsome on a 29-yard strike to cut the Steelers' lead to 10-7.

Terry Bradshaw passed for 199 yards, including a nine-yard touchdown strike to John Stallworth in the first quarter, and rookie Dave Trout kicked field goals of 19 and 23 yards to account for the Steelers' scoring.

Sipe left the game three plays before the end of the third quarter after taking a shot from Jack Lambert, a play in which Lambert was called for roughing the passer.

The Browns, 2-4, had a couple of chances to put the Steelers in a hole early in the first half, but failed to make good on either of them. Dennis Winston choked off a drive by intercepting a Sipe pass at the Pittsburgh 25. Minutes later, with Cleveland on the Steelers' 33, Jack Ham stripped the ball from Charles White and Gary Dunn recovered for Pittsburgh. The Steelers turned it into Trout's first field goal.

OCTOBER 11
SCORE BY PERIODS

Cleveland	0	7	0	0— 7
Pittsburgh	7	3	0	3—13

SCORING

Pittsburgh—Stallworth 9 pass from Bradshaw (Trout kick).
Pittsburgh—Field goal Trout 19.
Cleveland—Newsome 29 pass from Sipe (Bahr kick).
Pittsburgh—Field goal Trout 23.

TEAM STATISTICS

	Cleveland	Pittsburgh
First downs	26	19
Rushes-Yards	32-166	28-166
Passing yards	279	199
Sacks by-Yards	0-0	1-10
Return yards	117	72
Passes	20-42-2	19-33-1
Punts	5-42.4	7-41.7
Fumbles-Lost	1-1	1-0
Penalties-Yards	12-97	8-95
Time of possession	31:14	28:46

Attendance—53,255.

INDIVIDUAL STATISTICS

Rushing—Cleveland, M. Pruitt 14-50, White 12-65, Sipe 3-27, G. Pruitt 2-10, Newsome 1-14; Pittsburgh, Pollard 9-53, Harris 13-80, Thornton 1-5, Bradshaw 3-20, Davis 2-28.

Passing—Cleveland, Sipe 12-26-1—183, McDonald 8-16-1—106; Pittsburgh, Bradshaw 19-33-1—199.

Receiving—Cleveland, M. Pruitt 4-44, White 5-37, Rucker 2-40, Newsome 5-120, Fulton 1-11, Hill 2-17, Logan 1-20; Pittsburgh, Harris 4-13, Cunningham 4-61, Swann 6-90, Stallworth 3-22, Pollard 2-13.

Kickoff Returns—Cleveland, White 3-78, Hall 1-22; Pittsburgh, Anderson 2-43.

Punt Returns—Cleveland, Hall 4-16; Pittsburgh, Smith 3-28.

Interceptions—Cleveland, Goode 1-1; Pittsburgh, Thomas 1-0, Winston 1-1.

Punting—Cleveland, Cox 5-42.4; Pittsburgh, Colquitt 7-41.7.

Field Goals—Cleveland, Cox 0-1, Bahr 0-1; Pittsburgh, Trout 2-2.

JETS 28, PATRIOTS 24

NEW YORK—Richard Todd threw three first-half touchdown passes for New York and the Jets' defense took over in the second half to stymie New England.

Darrol Ray, who had two of the Jets' four interceptions for the day, picked off a pass by Matt Cavanaugh in the third period and scampered 43 yards for a 28-14 lead. But the Jets had to hold off the Patriots twice inside the New York four-yard line to stay ahead.

The crushing blow for New England came on the final play of the game. The Pats had moved to the New York four with 41 seconds left, but they were pushed back to the 14 with 17 seconds left when wide receiver Ken Toller was called for pass interference.

Quarterback Steve Grogan then threw toward Harold Jackson in the left side of the end zone, but Jets cornerback Johnny Lynn intercepted at the two and then ran out the clock with a 67-yard return.

Only a few seconds earlier, Lynn had cost the Jets a 10-yard sack of Grogan when he was called for a defensive holding penalty.

"I felt bad about the penalty, but we were pulling for each other in the huddle," said Lynn. "We all wanted the big play and I'm just glad I got to make it."

The second-year player from UCLA said he slipped as he started to cover Jackson, and believes that Grogan never saw him because of that slip. "I saw the ball all the way," said Lynn. "I knew I had it as soon as it left his hand. I was hoping to take it back all the way, and I was trying to pick up my legs, but they just wouldn't go anymore."

The loss spoiled a fine performance by Grogan, who was 19-for-32 for 330 yards after replacing Cavanaugh in the third quarter.

In addition to the Jets' four interceptions, they sacked the New England quarterbacks eight times for 72 yards. That raised the Jets' season total of sacks to 25, only three fewer than the team recorded in 1980.

OCTOBER 11

SCORE BY PERIODS

New England	0	14	7	3—24
New York Jets	7	14	7	0—28

SCORING

New York—Barkum 17 pass from Todd (Leahy kick).
New England—Tatupu 2 run (Smith kick).
New York—Barkum 5 pass from Todd (Leahy kick).
New York—Walker 29 pass from Todd (Leahy kick).
New England—Collins 9 run (Smith kick).
New York—Ray 43 interception return (Leahy kick).
New England—Hasselbeck 11 pass from Grogan (Smith kick).
New England—Field goal Smith 22.

TEAM STATISTICS

	New England	New York
First downs	25	18
Rushes-Yards	27-86	24-141
Passing yards	368	156
Sacks by-Yards	3-26	8-72
Return yards	159	218
Passes	27-52-4	16-29-1
Punts	7-30.9	7-45.9
Fumbles-Lost	0-0	5-2
Penalties-Yards	6-59	5-40
Time of possession	35:29	24:31
Attendance—55,093.		

INDIVIDUAL STATISTICS

Rushing—New England, Collins 14-49, Calhoun 4-13, Ferguson 3-11, Tatupu 4-7, Cavanaugh 1-11, Jackson 1-minus 5; New York, Harper 7-70, Augustyniak 10-45, Dierking 2-7, Long 2-6, Newton 1-6, Todd 1-5, Taylor 1-2.

Passing—New England, Cavanaugh 8-20-2—110, Grogan 19-32-2—330; New York, Todd 16-29-1—182.

Receiving—New England, Hasselbeck 7-139, Jackson 6-95, Collins 3-27, Morgan 3-87, Calhoun 2-12, Johnson 4-52, Toler 1-23, Tatupu 1-5; New York, Walker 5-81, Barkum 4-47, Harper 5-40, B. Jones 1-11, Augustyniak 1-3.

Kickoff Returns—New England, Collins 5-127; New York, Harper 1-17, Sohn 2-31, L. Jones 1-6.

Punt Returns—New England, Haynes 5-11; New York, Sohn 2-0, B. Jones 1-1.

Interceptions—New England, Sanford 1-21; New York, Ray 2-77, Schroy 1-19, Lynn 1-67.

Punting—New England, Hartley 7-30.9; New York, Ramsey 7-45.9.

Field Goals—New England, Smith 1-1; New York, Leahy 0-2.

BENGALS 41, COLTS 19

BALTIMORE—Ken Anderson said he was off to the best start of his 11-year career in the National Football League. There were few doubters among the Baltimore Colts. The Cincinnati Bengals quarterback dominated the Baltimore defense, completing 21 of 27 passes for 257 yards and three touchdowns.

"Other than the first quarter of the first game (Cincinnati's 27-21 victory over Seattle), I'd have to say this has been a pretty good start for me," understated Anderson.

Anderson thought the big play came on the Bengals' second possession of the second half. With the football resting at the Baltimore two-yard line, Anderson faked play action into the middle and then looked to his right to find tight end Dan Ross for the touchdown that gave the Bengals a 24-5 lead.

"Dan isn't as big or as fast as some of the other tight ends in the league, but I'd rather have him in there than anyone else," said Anderson. Ross caught seven of Anderson's tosses for 106 yards.

Anderson completed scoring strikes of 18, 20 and two yards and Pete Johnson and Jim Hargrove scored on one-yard runs. Field goals of 20 and 24 yards by Jim Breech rounded out the Cincinnati scoring in the Bengals' fourth victory in six games.

Cincinnati Coach Forrest Gregg praised his offense, but said defense may have been the key. "Our defensive line put a lot of pressure on the Colts, and our linebackers and secondary reacted the best they have all season," said Gregg.

Sixth Week—Continued

Baltimore quarterback Bert Jones completed 22 of 30 passes for 310 yards, marking the eighth time in his NFL career he has reached 300 yards. However, the Colts gained only 56 yards on the ground.

OCTOBER 11
SCORE BY PERIODS

Cincinnati	3	14	7	17—41
Baltimore	0	5	0	14—19

SCORING

Cincinnati—Field goal Breech 38.
Baltimore—Safety, punt blocked out of end zone.
Baltimore—Field goal Wood 19.
Cincinnati—Collinsworth 18 pass from Anderson (Breech kick).
Cincinnati—Verser 20 pass from Anderson (Breech kick).
Cincinnati—Ross 2 pass from Anderson (Breech kick).
Baltimore—Franklin 1 run (Wood kick).
Cincinnati—Field goal Breech 24.
Cincinnati—Johnson 1 run (Breech kick).
Baltimore—McCall 65 pass from B. Jones (Wood kick).
Cincinnati—Hargrove 1 run (Breech kick).

TEAM STATISTICS

	Cincinnati	Baltimore
First downs	24	22
Rushes-Yards	35-121	26-56
Passing yards	257	294
Sacks by-Yards	4-42	0-0
Return yards	119	225
Passes	21-28-0	25-33-2
Punts	4-29.5	2-43.0
Fumbles-Lost	0-0	2-2
Penalties-Yards	5-54	6-51
Time of possession	30:48	29:12

Attendance—33,060.

INDIVIDUAL STATISTICS

Rushing—Cincinnati, Alexander 11-33, Johnson 20-75, Anderson 1-7, Hargrove 3-6; Baltimore, Dickey 13-19, McMillan 3-10, Dixon 6-23, B. Jones 1-3, Franklin 3-1.

Passing—Cincinnati, Anderson 21-27-0—257, Kreider 0-1-0—0, Baltimore, B. Jones 22-30-2—310, Landry 3-3-0—26.

Receiving—Cincinnati, Kreider 4-41, Ross 7-106, Collinsworth 4-48, Johnson 1-minus 4, Alexander 3-26, Verser 2-40; Baltimore, Butler 4-87, Dickey 11-88, Carr 3-35, McMillan 1-4, Franklin 1-10, McCauley 4-47, McCall 1-65.

Kickoff Returns—Cincinnati, Verser 2-43, Fuller 1-34; Baltimore, Anderson 2-38, Dixon 2-49, Williams 4-82, Glasgow 1-35.

Punt Returns—Baltimore, Shula 2-21.

Interceptions—Cincinnati, Fuller 1-31, Razzano 1-11.

Punting—Cincinnati, McInally 3-39.3; Baltimore, Garrett 2-43.0.

Field Goals—Cincinnati, Breech 2-2; Baltimore, Wood 1-2.

49ers 45, COWBOYS 14

SAN FRANCISCO—Coach Bill Walsh acknowledged that San Francisco played its best game in years, but he cautioned fans not to get too carried away by the walloping of Dallas.

"We are maturing," Walsh said, "but we're still in the developmental stage. It will take another draft or two (to make a Super Bowl team). We are competitive now, though, and that has to be a source of encouragement to our staff."

Joe Montana had his finest day as a pro, completing 19 of 29 passes for 289 yards and two touchdowns. He did not have an interception.

Meanwhile, Dallas' Danny White was sacked three times and on numerous occasions was forced to throw the ball with tacklers draped over him. Fred Dean, the All-Pro defensive end acquired from San Diego, was a particular menace, contributing all three of the 49er sacks.

The 49er defense held high-powered Dallas to 192 yards total offense. A special target was running back Tony Dorsett, limited to 21 yards in nine carries.

"We ate humble pie," Dorsett said.

The Cowboys crossed midfield on their own power only once—in the second quarter, when they went 86 yards in a 10-play TD drive. The score came on a 22-yard pass from receiver Drew Pearson to Tony Hill. The other Dallas TD came on Benny Barnes' 72-yard run with a fumble, when the Cowboys were trailing by 45-7.

The 49ers picked off two passes by White, and Ronnie Lott returned one interception 41 yards to score. Montana had scoring passes of one yard to Freddie Solomon and 78 yards to Dwight Clark.

This was Dallas' biggest margin of loss since 1970, when the Cowboys lost by 41 points to Minnesota and were shut out by St. Louis, 38-0.

OCTOBER 11
SCORE BY PERIODS

Dallas	0	7	0	7—14
San Francisco	21	3	14	7—45

SCORING

San Francisco—Solomon 1 pass from Montana (Wersching kick).
San Francisco—Hofer 4 run (Wersching kick).
San Francisco—Davis 1 run (Wersching kick).
San Francisco—Field goal Wersching 18.
Dallas—Hill 22 pass from Pearson (Septien kick).
San Francisco—Clark 78 pass from Montana (Wersching kick).
San Francisco—Lott 41 interception return (Wersching kick).
San Francisco—Lawrence 1 run (Wersching kick).
Dallas—Barnes 72 fumble return (Septien kick).

TEAM STATISTICS

	Dallas	San Fran.
First downs	10	23
Rushes-Yards	21-83	46-150
Passing yards	109	290
Sacks by-Yards	1-14	3-26
Return yards	138	110
Passes	12-29-2	20-33-0
Punts	8-39.5	6-46.2
Fumbles-Lost	3-2	4-1
Penalties-Yards	5-40	4-28
Time of possession	25:53	34:07

Attendance—57,574.

Rushing—Dallas, J. Jones 4-26, Dorsett 9-21, Cosbie 1-15, Springs 5-14, D. White 1-7, Carano 1-0; San Francisco, Hofer 11-40, Davis 8-28, Easley 8-28, Lawrence 6-27, Patton 7-16, Cooper 5-9, Montana 1-2.

Passing—Dallas, D. White 8-16-2—60, Carano 3-12-0—53, Pearson 1-1-0—22; San Francisco, Montana 19-29-0—279, Solomon 1-1-0—25, Benjamin 0-3-0—0.

Receiving—Dallas, Springs 3-9, Donley 2-26, Pearson 2-23, Hill 1-22, Newhouse 1-21, Cosbie 1-15, Dorsett 1-14, DuPree 1-5; San Francisco, Solomon 5-74, Clark 4-135, Young 3-35, Hofer 3-22, Wilson 2-22, Cooper 2-12, Patton 1-4.

Kickoff Returns—Dallas, J. Jones 2-49, Newsome 2-22, Fellows 2-46, Newhouse 2-19; San Francisco, Lawrence 2-49.

Punt Returns—Dallas, J. Jones 1-minus 1, Fellows 2-3; San Francisco, Solomon 2-5, Hicks 1-3.

Interceptions—San Francisco, Lott 2-53.

Punting—Dallas, D. White 8-39.5; San Francisco, Miller 6-46.2.

Field Goals—Dallas, None attempted; San Francisco, Wersching 1-2.

VIKINGS 33, CHARGERS 31

SAN DIEGO—Minnesota was riding a four-game winning streak, thanks to an unusual Saturday exercise involving placekicker Rick Danmeier and wide receiver Terry LeCount.

The Vikings overcame San Diego on a 38-yard field goal by Danmeier as time expired. The kick followed LeCount's recovery of an onside kickoff by Danmeier at the Chargers' 41.

In four straight attempts in regular-season games—twice in 1981 and twice in 1980—Danmeier had squirted the ball to LeCount on onside kickoffs.

"In the huddle, before I kick it, I just tell Terry that the ball is coming his way," said Danmeier. "We've been practicing the kick every Saturday for as long as I can remember."

This time, the play transformed Danmeier from goat to hero. With 1:58 remaining, Tommy Kramer had lofted a 43-yard TD pass to LeCount, but Danmeier missed the extra point after a bad snap from center and the Vikings trailed, 31-30.

Minnesota Coach Bud Grant called for the onside kick. "It was a gamble," he said. "We knew we had to get the recovery."

Danmeier dribbled the kick and the ball bounced high after traveling the required 10 yards. Defensive end Randy Holloway, who stands 6-5, was playing on the kickoff team and he leaped to catch the ball, but batted it forward—into the arms of LeCount, who then raced out of bounds. Six plays later, including a 15-yard pass from Kramer to LeCount, the Vikes were on the San Diego 20. They bled the clock down to four seconds before Danmeier came on to kick the winning points.

Kramer had a prolific day, completing 27 of 43 passes for 444 yards and four TDs. Three of his receivers gained more than 100 yards each —LeCount with 120 yards, Ted Brown with 109

and Joe Senser with 100.

"Their defensive backs weren't covering well," said Kramer. He used Senser as his prime target early in the game and then, when the Chargers went to double coverage on the tight end, the Vikings' wide receivers were open.

Dan Fouts passed for 310 yards for the Chargers, including TD bombs of 60 yards to Dwight Scales and 38 yards to Charlie Joiner. Running back Chuck Muncie, his fractured left hand bundled in a cast, ran for 102 yards and scored two TDs.

OCTOBER 11

SCORE BY PERIODS

Minnesota	0	14	10	9—33
San Diego	7	7	10	7—31

SCORING

San Diego—Muncie 2 run (Benirschke kick).
Minnesota—Young 15 pass from Kramer (Danmeier kick).
Minnesota—Brown 4 pass from Kramer (Danmeier kick).
San Diego—Scales 60 pass from Fouts (Benirschke kick).
San Diego—Field goal Benirschke 39.
Minnesota—LeCount 26 pass from Kramer (Danmeier kick).
San Diego—Joiner 38 pass from Fouts (Benirschke kick).
Minnesota—Field goal Danmeier 28.
San Diego—Muncie 1 run (Benirschke kick).
Minnesota—LeCount 43 pass from Kramer (kick failed).
Minnesota—Field goal Danmeier 38.

TEAM STATISTICS

	Minnesota	San Diego
First downs	29	18
Rushes-Yards	30-93	29-120
Passing yards	433	305
Sacks by-Yards	1-5	1-11
Return yards	114	191
Passes	27-43-2	20-38-0
Punts	3-48.7	4-41.3
Fumbles-Lost	4-1	1-1
Penalties-Yards	3-22	8-75
Time of possession	31:14	28:46

Attendance—50,708.

INDIVIDUAL STATISTICS

Rushing—Minnesota, Brown 21-68, LeCount 1-17, Young 5-9, Kramer 3 minus 1; San Diego, Muncie 21-102, Cappelletti 4-9, Fouts 4-9.

Passing—Minnesota, Kramer 27-43-2—444; San Diego, Fouts 20-38-0—310.

Receiving—Minnesota, Senser 7-100, LeCount 6-120, Brown 5-109, S. White 3-53, Rashad 3-34, Young 3-28; San Diego, Joiner 6-97, Chandler 4-61, Scales 3-80, Winslow 3-33, Muncie 1-13, Cappelletti 1-11, Sievers 2-15.

Kickoff Returns—Minnesota, McDole 5-80, Nord 1-20; San Diego, Chandler 4-81, Shaw 1-14.

Punt Returns—Minnesota, Payton 1-14, S. White 1-0; San Diego, Chandler 2-49.

Interceptions—San Diego, Buchanon 1-11, Johnson 1-36.

Punting—Minnesota, Coleman 3-48.7; San Diego, Roberts 4-41.3.

Field Goals—Minnesota, Danmeier 2-2; San Diego, Benirschke 1-2.

BILLS 31, DOLPHINS 21

BUFFALO—Things did not look rosy for the Buffalo Bills. Their opponent for this Monday

Sixth Week—Continued

night game, the Miami Dolphins, were undefeated at 4-0-1. In the previous 21 games between the two teams, the Bills had won only one. And before this game was completed, Buffalo would lose three starters—guard Reggie McKenzie, fullback Lawrence McCutcheon and strong safety Steve Freeman—to knee injuries.

So what happened? The Bills beat the Dolphins, 31-21, in a game more lopsided than the score.

Quarterback Joe Ferguson was the primary reason for the rout. He completed 20 of 27 passes for 338 yards and three touchdowns—all in the first half. It was the sixth time in his career that the nine-year pro from Arkansas threw for 300 yards in a game. The Bills were up, 31-7, at the half, and for all intents and purposes, the game was over.

The Bills grabbed a quick 10-0 lead in the first quarter. Nick Mike-Mayer hit a 37-yard field goal and Ferguson connected with Jerry Butler on a 28-yard touchdown strike. The touchdown pass to Butler came on the first play after linebacker Isiah Robertson intercepted Miami quarterback Don Strock on the Dolphins 43-yard line.

In the second period, Ferguson threw two more TD passes. He hit Joe Cribbs on a 65-yard pass play and hooked up with Butler a second time, for 25 yards. The Bills also scored on a 1-yard run by Roosevelt Leaks in the quarter. Miami was able to counter that touchdown on the ensuing kickoff when Fulton Walker sprinted 90 yards for the Dolphins' first score.

The Dolphins were able to score two second-half touchdowns, one in each quarter, but the Bills' 24-point halftime lead was too much for the men from Miami to overcome.

MONDAY, OCTOBER 12
SCORE BY PERIODS

Miami	0	7	7	7—21
Buffalo	10	21	0	0—31

SCORING

Buffalo—Field goal Mike-Mayer 37.
Buffalo—Butler 28 pass from Ferguson (Mike-Mayer kick).
Buffalo—Leaks 1 run (Mike-Mayer kick).
Miami—Walker 90 kickoff return (von Schamann kick).
Buffalo—Cribbs 65 pass from Ferguson (Mike-Mayer kick).
Buffalo—Butler 25 pass from Ferguson (Mike-Mayer kick).
Miami—Nathan 12 run (von Schamann kick).
Miami—Rose 3 pass from Strock (von Schamann kick).

TEAM STATISTICS

	Miami	Buffalo
First downs	22	22
Rushes-Yards	18-99	33-116
Passing yards	225	338
Sacks by-Yards	0-0	2-20
Return yards	202	127
Passes	26-44-4	20-29-0
Punts	4-44.0	4-35.0
Fumbles-Lost	1-0	4-1
Penalties-Yards	3-15	9-69
Time of possession	24:12	35:48
Attendance—80,020.		

INDIVIDUAL STATISTICS

Rushing—Miami, Franklin 9-31, Nathan 8-59, Strock 1-9; Buffalo, Cribbs 16-60, McCutcheon 7-21, Leaks 9-37, Ferguson 1-minus 2.

Passing—Miami, Strock 26-44-4—245; Buffalo, Ferguson 20-29-0—338.

Receiving—Miami, Nathan 2-13, Moore 6-39, Lee 2-20, Harris 6-92, Cefalo 3-34, Vigorito 1-1, Rose 5-41, Giaquinto 1-5; Buffalo, Butler 5-82, Brammer 4-46, Barnett 1-7, Cribbs 3-66, Jessie 2-31, Lewis 5-106.

Kickoff Returns—Miami, Walker 6-185; Buffalo, Franklin 3-58.

Punt Returns—Miami, Vigorito 2-17; Buffalo, Franklin 1-8, Hooks 1-0.

Interceptions—Buffalo, Robertson 1-15, Romes 1-18, Nelson 1-9, Kush 1-19.

Punting—Miami, Orosz 4-44.0; Buffalo, Cater 4-35.0.

Field Goals—Miami, None attempted; Buffalo, Mike-Mayer 1-1.

SEVENTH WEEK

DOLPHINS 13, REDSKINS 10

MIAMI—For three weeks in a row, Bert Jones of Baltimore, Richard Todd of the New York Jets and Joe Ferguson of Buffalo had plundered the Miami secondary with big passing days. So, after the Dolphins' victory over Washington, everyone wanted to know why Redskins quarterback Joe Theismann hadn't thrown more.

The Redskins ran 38 times for 162 yards, but passed only 23 times, gaining 139 yards. Did the Dolphins lure Washington into a false sense of confidence in its running game?

"We were managing to get four, five, six yards running on first downs and there was no reason to abandon that," Theismann said. "We felt we'd pound a little at them on the ground and then take our shots. We played as we planned to, but nothing much happened for us."

Joe Gibbs, the first-year Redskins coach, went down with his game plan. "We were having a tough time getting deep on them." Gibbs said. "They're a darn good defensive team, although they've taken some abuse lately."

Most of the game's big plays came from Miami quarterback David Woodley and his corps of receivers. Woodley's bombs to Duriel Harris, Joe Rose and Jimmy Cefalo set up field goals of 37 and 25 yards by Uwe von Schamann and a one-yard TD plunge by fullback Andra Franklin.

OCTOBER 18
SCORE BY PERIODS

Washington	0	3	0	7—10
Miami	0	3	7	3—13

SCORING

Washington—Field goal Moseley 20.
Miami—Field goal von Schamann 36.
Miami—Franklin 1 run (von Schamann kick).
Washington—Riggins 2 run (Moseley kick).
Miami—Field goal von Schamann 25.

— 188 —

	Washington	Miami
First downs	20	20
Rushes-Yards	38-162	31-149
Passing yards	139	296
Sacks by-Yards	0-0	1-10
Return yards	114	85
Passes	17-23-1	15-28-0
Punts	5-42.2	4-31.5
Fumbles-Lost	1-1	2-2
Penalties-Yards	3-36	3-22
Time of possession	33:02	26:58

Attendance—47,367.

INDIVIDUAL STATISTICS

Rushing—Washington, Washington 13-66, Riggins 20-77, Theismann 5-19; Miami, Nathan 13-98, Franklin 16-45, Woodley 1-5, Howell 1-1.

Passing—Washington, Theismann 17-23-1—149; Miami, Woodley 15-28-0—296.

Receiving—Washington, Caster 3-47, Monk 4-42, Warren 2-35, Washington 4-8, Thompson 2-18, Metcalf 1-5, Riggins 1-minus 6; Miami, Rose 2-67, Nathan 4-39, Moore 2-39, Giaquinto 1-minus 3, Harris 1-46, Howell 1-5, Hardy 1-6, Cefalo 2-93, Lee 1-4.

Kickoff Returns—Washington, Nelms 4-103; Miami Bessillieu 3-71.

Punt Returns—Washington, Nelms 1-11; Miami, Vigorito 2-14.

Interceptions—Miami, Walker 1-0.

Punting—Washington, Connell 5-42.2; Miami, Orosz 4-31.5.

Field Goals—Washington, Moseley 1-1; Miami, von Schamann 2-2.

JETS 33, BILLS 14

NEW YORK—Just when Buffalo had cut New York's lead to six points and forced a fumble after the kickoff, the Jets got the break they needed to stay in contention in the AFC East race.

Wide receiver Bobby Jones' 61-yard touchdown sprint with a fumble recovery highlighted a 21-point third period that enabled the Jets to avenge a 31-0 loss to the Bills in the season opener.

The Jets wiped out a 7-6 halftime deficit when Bruce Harper ran 29 yards for a score and Richard Todd fired a 19-yard touchdown pass to Jerome Barkum early in the third period.

However, Joe Ferguson threw a 67-yard TD pass to Jerry Butler to make the score 20-14. Then, on New York's next possession, fullback Mike Augustyniak fumbled and a gang of Bills headed for the ball.

Nose tackle Mike Kadish zeroed in on the ball, but accidently kicked it out of the pile—right to Jones, who had clear sailing to the goal line.

"I saw Augie get hit hard and go down, and I saw the ball loose in the pile," Jones said. "All of a sudden, it got kicked out. It bounced right to me, right into my hands. I braced myself, because I thought I was going to get hit. But once I starting going, I knew they weren't going to catch me."

Jones' touchdown gave the Jets a 27-14 lead and took the steam out of the Bills. Pat Leahy

completed the scoring in the fourth quarter with the last two of his four field goals.

Augustyniak joked that he'd never had a fumble turn out so well. "When we look at the films, I'll hear about it from the coaches," he said. "I'll just tell them it was planned."

OCTOBER 18
SCORE BY PERIODS

Buffalo	0	7	7	0—14
New York Jets	6	0	21	6—33

SCORING

New York—Field goal Leahy 24.
New York—Field goal Leahy 29.
Buffalo—Lewis 23 pass from Ferguson (Mike-Mayer kick).
New York—Harper 29 run (Leahy kick).
New York—Barkum 19 pass from Todd (Leahy kick).
Buffalo—Butler 67 pass from Ferguson (Mike-Mayer kick).
New York—B. Jones 61 fumble recovery (Leahy kick).
New York—Field goal Leahy 39.
New York—Field goal Leahy 22.

TEAM STATISTICS

	Buffalo	New York
First downs	14	21
Rushes-Yards	16-46	43-200
Passing	242	174
Sacks by-Yards	2-16	1-8
Return yards	116	123
Passes	15-36-2	17-27-0
Punts	4-42.5	1-49.0
Fumbles-Lost	3-1	3-1
Penalties-Yards	4-47	4-20
Time of possession	22:40	37:20

Attendance—54,607.

INDIVIDUAL STATISTICS

Rushing—Buffalo, Cribbs 9-44, Brown 5-5, Ferguson 1-minus 2, Leaks 1-minus 1; New York, Augustyniak 20-80, Harper 7-40, Todd 3-33, Dierking 8-26, Newton 1-13, Long 3-8, Ramsey 1-0.

Passing—Buffalo, Ferguson 15-34-2—250, Robinson 0-2-0—0; New York, Todd 17-27-0—190.

Receiving—Buffalo, Lewis 6-109, Butler 3-78, Brammer 3-36, Franklin 1-13, Cribbs 1-7, Jessie 1-7; New York, Barkum 5-66, Harper 3-33, Walker 2-17, Gaffney 1-17, Augustyniak 3-16, Dierking 1-14, B. Jones 1-14, L. Jones 1-13.

Kickoff Returns—Buffalo, Franklin 5-104, Hooks 1-12; New York, Sohn 3-72.

Punt Returns—New York, Sohn 2-20.

Interceptions—New York, Buttle 1-22, Lynn 1-9.

Punting—Buffalo, Cater 4-42.5; New York, Ramsey 1-49.0.

Field Goals—Buffalo, Mike-Mayer 0-1; New York, Leahy 4-4.

CHIEFS 28, BRONCOS 14

KANSAS CITY—The Kansas City Chiefs' defensive unit doesn't have a nickname, and its statistics hardly compare with those of the famed "Orange Crush" of the Denver Broncos.

However, when the Chiefs beat the Broncos, 28-14, to produce a three-way tie at the top of the American Football Conference Western Division, that no-name defense did the job for Kansas City.

"They played with a lot of verve," said Coach Marv Levy, praising his defense after the Chiefs improved their record to 5-2, tying Denver and the San Diego Chargers. "They kept coming up with the big plays to bail us out. They played with a looseness and with a belief. They never looked inhibited, which sometimes happens when the pendulum starts swinging the other way, as it did at times today."

The Chiefs forced five turnovers, sacked Denver quarterback Craig Morton five times, and provided one touchdown—when linebacker Whitney Paul scampered 47 yards to score with a fumble recovery in the first quarter.

Levy's reference to the pendulum was a Denver rally in the fourth quarter. Bill Kenney had thrown a 64-yard scoring pass to flanker Henry Marshall to give the Chiefs a 21-7 lead early in the period, but Denver roared back with an 82-yard touchdown drive, capped by Craig Morton's second 11-yard scoring pass of the game to Steve Watson. That made the score 21-14, and when Denver linebacker Randy Gradishar came up with his second interception of the game on Kansas City's next possession, the Broncos seemed certain to tie the score.

Gradishar gave the Broncos the ball on the Chiefs 26, and Denver moved to the 8 in two plays. But a rare illegal shift penalty set the Broncos back five yards, safety Gary Barbaro batted down a pass in the end zone, and nose guard Don Parrish sacked Morton for a seven-yard loss. That moved the ball back to the 20, and Fred Steinfort missed on a 37-yard field goal attempt with 6:08 left to play.

"In the past, all the big plays seemed to go against us," said Barbaro. "But now, we're making our share. Our defense is keeping the points down and keeping the (opponent's) offense on the defensive. They're worrying about us more than we're worrying about them."

Two plays after Steinfort's miss, rookie Joe Delaney bolted 82 yards off right tackle for the clinching TD. Delaney finished the day with 149 yards in 21 carries and became the first Chiefs back ever to run for more than 100 yards in three consecutive games.

The Chiefs, who rank first in the AFC in defense against the run, held Denver to 77 yards rushing. But Morton completed 25 of 38 passes for 342 yards, all three figures season highs for the NFL's leading passer. Watson's two TD catches gave him nine for the year.

OCTOBER 18

SCORE BY PERIODS

Denver	0	0	7	7—14
Kansas City	14	0	0	14—28

SCORING

Kansas City—B. Jackson 1 run (Lowery kick).
Kansas City—Paul 47 fumble return (Lowery kick).
Denver—Watson 11 pass from Morton (Steinfort kick).
Kansas City—Marshall 64 pass from Kenney (Lowery kick).
Denver—Watson 11 pass from Morton (Steinfort kick).
Kansas City—Delaney 82 run (Lowery kick).

TEAM STATISTICS

	Denver	Kansas City
First downs	20	13
Rushes-Yards	29-77	45-224
Passing yards	319	100
Sacks by-Yards	0-0	6-39
Return yards	103	156
Passes	28-43-3	6-12-2
Punts	7-37.7	5-38.8
Fumbles-Lost	2-2	4-3
Penalties-Yards	10-96	5-47
Time of possession	35:10	24:50

Attendance—74,672.

INDIVIDUAL STATISTICS

Rushing—Denver, Preston 13-39, Parros 10-27, Reed 4-8, Upchurch 1-3, Morton 1-0; Kansas City, Delaney 21-149, Hadnot 12-56, B. Jackson 6-12, Kenney 4-minus 8, Marshall 1-34, Grupp 1-minus 19.

Passing—Denver, Morton 25-38-1—342, DeBerg 3-5-2—16; Kansas City, Kenney 6-12-2—100.

Receiving—Denver, Upchurch 5-138, Watson 7-75, Odoms 7-74, Preston 5-47, Reed 2-13, Parros 2-11; Kansas City, Marshall 3-80, Smith 1-9, Dixon 1-6, Hadnot 1-5.

Kickoff Returns—Denver, Manning 2-45, Lytle 1-17; Kansas City, Murphy 3-64.

Punt Returns—Denver, Manning 4-32; Kansas City, Smith 5-30.

Interceptions—Denver, Gradishar 2-9; Kansas City, Burruss 1-5, Barbaro 1-32, Harris 1-25.

Punting—Denver, Prestridge 7-37.7; Kansas City, Grupp 5-38.8.

Field Goals—Denver, Steinfort 0-2; Kansas City, Lowery 0-1.

BENGALS 34, STEELERS 7

CINCINNATI—The Bengals celebrated Coach Forrest Gregg's 48th birthday with a cakewalk over Pittsburgh.

"It was the best birthday present they could have given me," said a happy Gregg. "It was the best game we've played this year."

The Bengals took sole possession of first place in the AFC Central Division with a 5-2 record. Pittsburgh and Houston shared second place at 4-3.

"It was one of those days we probably would have been better off staying in bed," moaned Steelers Coach Chuck Noll. "The Bengals were even more aggressive than we were in the introductions."

The Steelers crossed midfield only twice and didn't score until Terry Bradshaw threw a 17-yard pass to Jim Smith with 1:07 left the game.

"I'm not even tired," Bradshaw said afterward as he faced reporters. "I'm sweating more answering your questions than I did in the game."

Asked the reason for the runaway, Bradshaw said, "If you ask me, a 34-7 score shows a lack of aggressiveness. It's a lack of a lot. They knocked our tails all over the place."

Bengals quarterback Ken Anderson, off to one of the best starts in his career, passed for 346 yards and two touchdowns.

"It was one of those games where the breaks went all our way," said Anderson. "It's nice to have time to throw the ball and have guys make great catches. It makes the quarterback look good."

Anderson cited, for example, "the five-yarder that (David) Verser turned into a 73-yard touchdown." He referred to the third play of the second half when wide receiver Verser, the Bengals' No. 1 draft choice, grabbed a short pass, slipped away from a couple of would-be tacklers and sprinted to the end zone to give the Bengals a 20-0 lead.

Cincinnati rolled up 494 yards, while Pittsburgh managed 210. Said Noll, "The Bengals were just awesome. They outplayed us 1000 percent. They wanted it very badly—much more than we did."

PATRIOTS 38, OILERS 10

FOXBORO—New England eliminated its worst enemy—its own mistakes—in trouncing Houston. However, the victory was only the second of the year for the Patriots, and the question remained whether they had enough time left to get into the playoff picture.

"We seem to be back on track," said quarterback Steve Grogan, who passed for two touch-downs and ran for one, on a 24-yard bootleg with 1:53 left in the game.

The New England defense, last in the NFL against the run, held Houston's Earl Campbell to 86 yards in 27 carries. Campbell had run for more than 180 yards each of his previous two games.

"My whole body hurts," said Campbell, who carried the ball only once in the fourth quarter as Houston took to the air. "It was like a man trying, but never getting there."

Running back Andy Johnson threw a 28-yard scoring pass to Stanley Morgan in the first quarter, but Houston came back to take a 10-7 halftime lead. Then, the Pats outscored the Oilers in the second half, 31-0. Two of New England's four interceptions led to TDs.

Grogan pitched a 42-yard TD pass to Morgan to put the Patriots ahead, 14-10, and later had a 10-yard scoring pass to Johnson. Vagas Ferguson scored on a 15-yard sweep. But it was Grogan's bootleg that befuddled both teams.

Houston Coach Ed Biles was asked how he felt about Grogan's run.

"How would you feel with it already 31-10?" he said, sarcastically. "I said very little to Erhardt (Patriots Coach Ron Erhardt) after the game. Maybe he thought we'd come back."

Johnson's TD pass to Morgan made the former Georgia quarterback 5-for-5 this season, for 127 yards and three touchdowns, on the halfback option pass.

"You can't run the play all the time. You have to pick and choose," Johnson said. "It's all in when you call it."

land, Grogan 11-19-1—164, Johnson 1-1-0—28, Collins 0-1-0—0.

Receiving—Houston, Coleman 4-48, Barber 3-57, Casper 3-37, Burrough 3-22, Renfro 2-17, Armstrong 2-16, Campbell 1-4; New England, Morgan 4-98, Johnson 3-46, Jackson 3-24, Hasselbeck 2-24.

Kickoff Returns—Houston, Tullis 5-113, Roaches 1-16, Hunt 1-11; New England, Johnson 3-26, Calhoun 1-22.

Punt Returns—New England, Morgan 3-41.

Interceptions—Houston, Hartwig 1-31; New England, Fox 1-20, Zamberlin 1-11, Lee 1-0, Shoate 1-0.

Punting—Houston, Parsley 5-32.0; New England, Hartley 2-25.0.

Field Goals—Houston, Fritsch 1-1; New England, Smith 1-2.

RAIDERS 18, BUCCANEERS 16

OAKLAND—Ted Hendricks, the 6-7 Oakland linebacker, is renowned as one of the greatest kick blockers in history. He figured it was all in a day's work when he batted down a Tampa Bay extra-point attempt and then deflected Bill Capece's try for a 30-yard field goal that would have given the Bucs a last-second victory.

Hendricks was reluctant to take all the credit for blocking the chip shot at the end of the game. "We operate as four guys against three, and we try to create a mismatch," Hendricks said. "Matt Millen, John Matuszak and Howard Long put on the pressure that allowed me to penetrate."

Capece came on with eight seconds left and got off what seemed to be a cinch winning field goal from the Oakland 20. But Hendricks stretched out and tipped the ball with his right hand, causing it to fall short of the goal post.

"That Hendricks is some kind of an athlete," said Capece. "I guess that's what they pay him for, to make the big play."

Hendricks' block enabled the Raiders to snap a three-game losing streak. Oakland had broken out of its 12-quarter scoreless spell when Chris Bahr boomed a 51-yard field goal, Todd Christensen blocked a punt for a safety and Derrick Jensen ran 12 yards for a touchdown, producing a 12-0 lead in the first quarter.

A 20-yard field goal by Bahr gave Oakland a 15-0 lead in the first half, during which Tampa Bay was held to 21 net yards. But the momentum turned in the second half as the Bucs took a 16-15 lead on a 77-yard scoring pass from Doug Williams to Kevin House, a 13-yard TD pass from Williams to Jimmie Giles, and a 26-yard field goal by Capece.

Quarterback Marc Wilson, 17-for-34 passing in his role as a starter, guided the Raiders into position for a 44-yard field goal by Bahr with 2:21 left. Bahr pranced off the field, setting off an early victory celebration on the sideline, but a 40-yard pass from Williams to Giles brought the Bucs back for Capece's last-second kick.

John McKay, the Bucs' coach, was none too

happy with Hendricks' game-saving play.

"It beats the hell out of me that this team can't make a field goal," said McKay. "This is supposed to be the big time. I thought the snap was a little high."

"It wasn't the snap," corrected Capece. "It was the penetration."

OCTOBER 18
SCORE BY PERIODS

Tampa Bay	0	0	7	9—16
Oakland	12	3	0	3—18

SCORING

Oakland—Field goal Bahr 51.
Oakland—Safety, Christensen blocked punt out of end zone.
Oakland—Jensen 12 run (Bahr kick).
Oakland—Field goal Bahr 20.
Tampa Bay—House 77 pass from Williams (Capece kick).
Tampa Bay—Giles 13 pass from Williams (kick failed).
Tampa Bay—Field goal Capece 26.
Oakland—Field goal Bahr 44.

TEAM STATISTICS

	Tampa Bay	Oakland
First downs	11	22
Rushes-Yards	16-29	52-194
Passing yards	327	176
Sacks by-Yards	0-0	2-8
Return yards	138	153
Passes	16-30-0	17-34-3
Punts	7-36.6	6-45.8
Fumbles-Lost	3-3	3-0
Penalties-Yards	2-14	3-20
Time of possession	22:37	37:23

Attendance—42,288.

INDIVIDUAL STATISTICS

Rushing—Tampa Bay, Eckwood 9-14, Wilder 4-11, Owens 1-3, Williams 2-1; Oakland, King 17-87, Jensen 16-56, Whittington 9-32, Willis 4-14, Wilson 6-5.

Passing—Tampa Bay, Williams 16-30-3—335; Oakland, Wilson 17-34-3—176.

Receiving—Tampa Bay, House 4-178, Giles 4-76, Wilder 2-40, Jones 2-20, T. Bell 2-9, Eckwood 1-7, Owens 1-5; Oakland, Ramsey 6-49, King 3-32, Whittington 3-24, Bradshaw 2-31, Jensen 2-22, Branch 1-18.

Kickoff Returns—Tampa Bay, G. Davis 1-10, T. Davis 1-17, Owens 1-13; Oakland, Willis 4-102, Whittington 1-21.

Punt Returns—Tampa Bay, T. Bell 4-27; Oakland, Watts 6-30.

Interceptions—Tampa Bay, Washington 2-58, Colzie 1-13.

Punting—Tampa Bay, Swider 6-42.7; Oakland, Guy 6-45.8.

Field Goals—Tampa Bay, Capece 1-2; Oakland, Bahr 3-4.

49ers 13, PACKERS 3

MILWAUKEE—Lawrence Pillers provided the defense and Ray Wersching and Johnny Davis took care of the offense as San Francisco won its fourth straight game and took sole possession of the NFC West lead with a 5-2 record.

The 49ers' defensive line was the difference, recording four sacks and limiting Green Bay to 78 yards rushing. Pillers, a reserve lineman, led the pass rush with three sacks and four tackles.

The Packers' Lynn Dickey was sacked three times before leaving the game in the third quarter with a jammed neck, and James Lofton and John Jefferson were limited to 60 yards on four catches between them.

In the second half, the 49ers limited the Packers to just 17 offensive plays.

The Packers' only points came early in the second quarter on Jan Stenerud's 26-yard field goal. Wersching tied the game on a 26-yarder three seconds before halftime.

Joe Montana, who completed 23 of 32 passes for 210 yards, took the 49ers on two second-half scoring drives, the first of which covered 46 yards and resulted in the game's only touchdown. After a 12-yard punt return by Freddie Solomon, Montana hit Paul Hofer for a 22-yard gain to the Packers' nine-yard line. After three blasts by Earl Cooper, Davis bulled over on fourth down from the one. Wersching kicked a 32-yard field goal with 4½ minutes left in the game for the 49ers' final points.

The Packers, 2-5, have not won a home game since they beat the 49ers last November 9 and that, coupled with the cold, damp weather, resulted in 5,799 no-shows at Milwaukee County Stadium.

"We were causing a lot of our downfalls with mistakes and interceptions, but those were not there today," said Packers Coach Bart Starr. "We just couldn't get it done offensively. When we hold a team to 13 points, we should win the ball game."

OCTOBER 18
SCORE BY PERIODS

San Francisco	0	3	7	3—13
Green Bay	0	3	0	0— 3

SCORING

Green Bay—Field goal Stenerud 26.
San Francisco—Field goal Wersching 26.
San Francisco—Davis 1 run (Wersching kick).
San Francisco—Field goal Wersching 32.

TEAM STATISTICS

	San Francisco	Green Bay
First downs	21	13
Rushes-Yards	47-126	19-78
Passing yards	201	163
Sacks by-Yards	4-30	1-9
Return yards	85	101
Passes	23-32-0	14-24-1
Punts	7-35.9	7-40.0
Fumbles-Lost	2-1	1-0
Penalties-Yards	7-35	4-35
Time of possession	37:41	22:19
Attendance—50,171.		

INDIVIDUAL STATISTICS

Rushing—San Francisco, Davis 16-65, Cooper 12-38, Patton 7-15, Hofer 8-3, Montana 1-2, Easley 3-3; Green Bay, Huckleby 10-20, Ellis 7-50, Dickey 1-0, Whitehurst 1-8.

Passing—San Francisco, Montana 23-32-0—210; Green Bay, Dickey 11-18-0—156, Whitehurst 3-6-1—37.

Receiving—San Francisco, Davis 1-3, Solomon 4-49, Hofer 5-44, Patton 3-31, Cooper 2-19, Clark 6-55, Young 1-4, Lawrence 1-5; Green Bay, Ellis 5-50, Lofton 1-13, Coffman 3-67, Huckleby 1-0, Jefferson 3-47, Jensen 1-16.

Kickoff Returns—San Francisco, Lawrence 2-21; Green Bay, Lee 2-44, Coffman 1-52.

Punt Returns—San Francisco, Solomon 3-24, Hicks 1-14; Green Bay, Lee 2-5, Gray 1-0.

Interceptions—San Francisco, Hicks 1-26.

Punting—San Francisco, Miller 7-35.9; Green Bay, Stachowicz 7-40.0.

Field Goals—San Francisco, Wersching 2-2; Green Bay, Stenerud 1-2.

FALCONS 41, CARDINALS 20

ATLANTA—Two turnovers and a pass interference call brought Atlanta to life and enabled the Falcons to score 20 points in the final nine minutes of the first half in their come-from-behind victory over St. Louis.

Trailing 14-0 on a pair of one-yard plunges by St. Louis' Ottis Anderson, the Falcons recovered a fumble on their own 29-yard line to begin the turnaround. A 44-yard pass interference call on cornerback Carl Allen moved the ball to the Cardinals' 25 and, two plays later, Steve Bartkowski connected with Alfred Jenkins for a 23-yard touchdown.

The Falcons added a 24-yard Mick Luckhurst field goal, Lynn Cain's 33-yard touchdown run—following one of three interceptions of St. Louis' Jim Hart—and a 37-yard field goal by Luckhurst for a 20-14 halftime lead.

Atlanta put the game away with three touchdowns in the second half while holding the Cardinals to two Neil O'Donoghue field goals, of 26 and 22 yards. Bartkowski, who completed 18 of 32 passes for 288 yards, tossed a 35-yard touchdown strike to Jenkins midway through the third quarter and added two more, of 18 and 70 yards, to William Andrews in the fourth quarter.

Cardinals Coach Jim Hanifan was upset with a couple of officiating calls, including one pass from Hart in the third quarter which officials ruled that wide receiver Pat Tilley trapped in the end zone. The Cardinals had to settle for a field goal, which left them behind, 27-20.

With his two touchdown catches, Jenkins upped his career total to 33, breaking the Falcons' record of 32 that was held by Jim Mitchell.

Hart, who completed 24 of 49 passes for 263 yards, overtook John Brodie for third place in NFL career completions with 2,470. "Moving up in the statistics or record books is very little consolation when you lose a game like we did today," Hart said.

OCTOBER 18
SCORE BY PERIODS

St. Louis	7	7	6	0—20
Atlanta	0	20	7	14—41

SCORING

St. Louis—Anderson 1 run (O'Donoghue kick).
St. Louis—Anderson 1 run (O'Donoghue kick).
Atlanta—Jenkins 23 pass from Bartkowski (Luckhurst kick).
Atlanta—Field goal Luckhurst 24.

Atlanta—Cain 33 run (Luckhurst kick).
Atlanta—Field goal Luckhurst 37.
St. Louis—Field goal O'Donoghue 26.
Atlanta—Jenkins 45 pass from Bartkowski (Luckhurst kick).
St. Louis—Field goal O'Donoghue 22.
Atlanta—Andrews 18 pass from Bartkowski (Luckhurst kick).
Atlanta—Andrews 70 pass from Bartkowski (Luckhurst kick).

TEAM STATISTICS

	St. Louis	Atlanta
First downs	22	17
Rushes-Yards	25-120	29-114
Passing yards	263	280
Sacks by-Yards	1-8	0-0
Return yards	245	161
Passes	24-51-3	18-32-0
Punts	6-45.2	7-41.0
Fumbles-Lost	2-1	2-2
Penalties-Yards	5-68	6-43
Time of possession	31:17	28:43

Attendance—51,428.

INDIVIDUAL STATISTICS

Rushing—St. Louis, Anderson 18-59, Mitchell 3-50, Gray 1-4, Hart 1-4, Morris 1-2, Lomax 1-1; Atlanta, Cain 16-79, Andrews 9-25, Mayberry 2-7, Robinson 2-3.

Passing—St. Louis, Hart 24-49-3—263, Lomax 0-2-0—0; Atlanta, Bartkowski 18-32-0—288.

Receiving—St. Louis, Tilley 8-100, Anderson 6-47, Morris 5-35, Green 2-41, Gray 2-32, Marsh 1-8; Atlanta, Andrews 8-132, Jenkins 4-101, Jackson 3-37, Cain 2-11, Miller 1-7.

Kickoff Returns—St. Louis, Mitchell 7-178, Love 1-16; Atlanta, R. Smith 4-113.

Punt Returns—St. Louis, Mitchell 6-51; Atlanta, Woerner 2-2.

Interceptions—Atlanta, Pridemore 1-40, Glazebrook 1-3, E. Jones 1-3.

Punting—St. Louis, Birdsong 6-45.2; Atlanta, James 7-41.0.

Field Goals—St. Louis, O'Donoghue 2-4; Atlanta, Luckhurst 2-2.

CHARGERS 43, COLTS 14

BALTIMORE—San Diego's powerhouse offense rolled as expected, but the key to the Chargers' romp over Baltimore was the play of a much-maligned defensive unit.

The Chargers went into the game yielding an average of 417 yards a game. But San Diego got a strong rush from its defensive line, resulting in six sacks of Colts quarterback Bert Jones and two interceptions.

Rookie Keith Ferguson, a fifth-round draft pick, replaced Gary (Big Hands) Johnson at defensive tackle and recorded three of the San Diego sacks. Ferguson said the game signaled "a new beginning" for the Charger defense.

"We just haven't been putting it all together —until today," Ferguson said.

Coach Don Coryell also revamped the Chargers' secondary, switching Willie Buchanon from left cornerback to strong safety. Allan Ellis took Buchanon's spot at cornerback.

"The defense played by far its best game," said Coryell, who insisted he had not lost faith

in defensive coordinator Jack Pardee after the earlier games. "Jack is a great coach, and a person isn't a great coach one year and then not the next," said Coryell.

San Diego compiled 470 yards on offense, with Dan Fouts passing for 298 yards and three touchdowns. Fouts was 26-for-43 with no interceptions, giving him a string of 122 attempts without having a pass picked off.

OCTOBER 18
SCORE BY PERIODS

San Diego	7	16	7	13—43
Baltimore	7	0	7	0—14

SCORING

Baltimore—Carr 29 pass from B. Jones (Wood kick).
San Diego—Muncie 3 run (Benirschke kick).
San Diego—Cappelletti 12 pass from Fouts (kick blocked).
San Diego—Joiner 23 pass from Fouts (Benirschke kick).
San Diego—Field goal Benirschke 31.
San Diego—Muncie 3 run (Benirschke kick).
Baltimore—Dickey 5 pass from B. Jones (Wood kick).
San Diego—Cappelletti 1 run (kick failed).
San Diego—C. Williams 7 pass from Fouts (Benirschke kick).

TEAM STATISTICS

	San Diego	Baltimore
First downs	30	18
Rushes-Yards	37-172	16-68
Passing yards	298	196
Sacks by-Yards	6-59	0-0
Return yards	49	151
Passes	26-43-0	20-37-2
Punts	4-45.3	6-37.2
Fumbles-Lost	1-1	2-1
Penalties-Yards	6-30	5-45
Time of possession	32:48	27:12

Attendance—41,921.

INDIVIDUAL STATISTICS

Rushing—San Diego, J. Brooks 14-72, Muncie 14-61, Fouts 1-13, Bauer 1-4, Cappelletti 7-22; Baltimore, Dickey 6-32, McMillan 8-27, B. Jones 2-9.

Passing—San Diego, Fouts 26-43-0—298; Baltimore, B. Jones 20-37-2—255.

Receiving—San Diego, Joiner 6-82, Winslow 4-64, J. Brooks 4-23, Muncie 4-16, Chandler 2-38, Sievers 2-15, Scales 1-27, Holohan 1-14, Cappelletti 1-12, C. Williams 1-7; Baltimore, McMillan 6-60, Butler 4-42, Carr 3-63, McCall 3-52, Dickey 3-17, Burke 1-21.

Kickoff Returns—San Diego, J. Brooks 1-17; Baltimore, Anderson 2-39, Dixon 3-41, Williams 3-67.

Punt Returns—San Diego, J. Brooks 3-32; Baltimore, Shula 1-4.

Interceptions—San Diego, Lowe 1-0, M. Williams 1-0.

Punting—San Diego, Roberts 4-45.3; Baltimore, Garrett 6-37.2.

Field Goals—San Diego, Benirschke 1-1; Baltimore, None attempted.

BROWNS 20, SAINTS 17

CLEVELAND—Brian Sipe drove Cleveland 78 yards in 13 plays for the go-ahead touchdown with less than five minutes to play, and the Browns then averted overtime when New Orleans' Benny Ricardo hooked a 37-yard field goal attempt with 1:11 left.

Sipe completed 25 of 42 passes for 270 yards, but the Browns were on the short end of a 17-13 score before he got them moving in the fourth quarter. Sipe completed four passes on the march to Greg Pruitt, who had seven catches for 113 yards in the game. The touchdown came on a one-yard run by Mike Pruitt.

"Sipe does a great job moving the team when he has to," said Saints Coach Bum Phillips. "He hits his backs as well as anybody."

The Saints' TDs came on a 79-yard run by rookie George Rogers—the longest run in the club's history—and on an eight-yard shovel pass from safety Tommy Myers to running back Wayne Wilson off a fake field goal attempt. Myers, the placement holder, flipped the ball behind the line of scrimmage to Wilson, who ran a sweep instead of holding his position to block.

Rogers gained 122 yards in 18 carries, but was dejected by the Saints' sixth loss in seven games. "We had this one," he said. "I really felt we were going to win, but Cleveland had the poise to come back."

After the Browns took their lead, the Saints moved to the Cleveland 19 for Ricardo's field-goal try. "The wind was swirling around so much down there I didn't know what side to kick it toward," Ricardo said. "Before the game, everything was blowing left, so I aimed it to the right. The wind still carried it far enough left to make it wide.

"I'll tell you one thing. I've got more respect than ever for Don Cockroft (the Browns' former kicker). I don't know how he lasted 13 years here."

OCTOBER 18
SCORE BY PERIODS

New Orleans	7	7	3	0—17
Cleveland	10	0	3	7—20

SCORING

Cleveland—Field goal Bahr 34.
New Orleans—G. Rogers 79 run (Ricardo kick).
Cleveland—M. Pruitt 8 run (Bahr kick).
New Orleans—W. Wilson 8 pass from Myers (Ricardo kick).
New Orleans—Field goal Ricardo 21.
Cleveland—Field goal Bahr 19.
Cleveland—M. Pruitt 1 run (Bahr kick).

TEAM STATISTICS

	New Orleans	Cleveland
First downs	14	23
Rushes-Yards	24-142	32-94
Passing yards	192	261
Sacks by-Yards	1-9	2-15
Return yards	122	85
Passes	17-29-0	25-42-0
Punts	5-43.8	6-41.0
Fumbles-Lost	1-1	2-1
Penalties-Yards	5-35	4-33
Time of possession	27:31	32:29
Attendance—76,059.		

INDIVIDUAL STATISTICS

Rushing—New Orleans, G. Rogers 18-122, J. Rogers 3-12, Holmes 2-8, W. Wilson 1-0; Cleveland, M. Pruitt 18-83, White 11-19, Sipe 3-minus 8.

Passing—New Orleans, Manning 16-28-0—199, Myers 1-1-0—8; Cleveland, Sipe 25-42-0—270.

Receiving—New Orleans, W. Wilson 3-75, Tyler 3-11, Holmes 3-7, G. Rogers 2-36, Hardy 2-32, Merkens 2-22, Groth 1-17, Martini 1-7; Cleveland, G. Pruitt 7-113, Newsome 7-65, Feacher 3-49, M. Pruitt 3-5, White 2-13, Hill 2-10, Rucker 1-15.

Kickoff Returns—New Orleans, J. Rogers 1-25, W. Wilson 2-67, Groth 1-17; Cleveland, White 2-40, Brown 2-17.

Punt Returns—New Orleans, Groth 1-13; Cleveland, Hall 5-28.

Interceptions—None.

Punting—New Orleans, Erxleben 5-43.8; Cleveland, Cox 6-41.0.

Field Goals—New Orleans, Ricardo 1-4; Cleveland, Bahr 2-2.

VIKINGS 35, EAGLES 23

BLOOMINGTON—The Vikings avenged a loss in the 1980 National Football Conference playoffs with a 35-23 drubbing of the Philadelphia Eagles.

"We'd like to thank the Eagles for returning half the turnovers that we gave them in the playoff game last year," said Vikings Coach Bud Grant.

The Eagles (6-1), leaders in the NFC Eastern Division, fumbled twice and were intercepted twice. Tommy Kramer, who was intercepted five times in the 31-16 playoff loss last January, redeemed himself by throwing four touchdown passes against a stingy Eagles defense that had allowed only two touchdowns through the air all season. Kramer completed 24 of 46 passes for 257 yards.

Minnesota's Ted Brown, second in the NFC in total offense, caught 10 passes for 82 yards and rushed for 92 yards on 22 carries.

Although the Vikings' defense allowed 418 total yards, it still managed to shut down the Eagles when necessary. Matt Blair led the defense with 12 tackles, one fumble recovery and a blocked extra point.

The Vikings, the NFC Central leaders, won their fifth straight game after an 0-2 start. The last two victories were over San Diego and Philadelphia, considered Super Bowl contenders.

"There are none of us that are super," Grant said. "All you can do in this league is try to contend. Then you have to be good enough to take advantage of the breaks when they come your way."

The Eagles held a 9-7 lead on a 30-yard field goal by Tony Franklin and a one-yard touchdown run by Wilbert Montgomery. Franklin's missed conversion attempt ended a string of 63 consecutive successful kicks. The Vikings had scored on a 11-yard toss from Kramer to Joe Senser.

Kramer engineered two productive two-minute offense drills late in the second quarter, resulting in a 50-yard touchdown to Sammy White and a one-yard toss to Bob Bruer with four seconds left for a 21-9 halftime lead.

Kramer lofted a five-yard scoring pass to Ahmad Rashad in the third quarter for a 28-9 lead and Brown plunged in from the 1-yard line in the fourth quarter for the final Viking TD. Philadelphia Ron Jaworski, who was 30 of 45 for 345 yards, had touchdown throws of 25 and 21 yards to Montgomery and Harold Carmichael in the fourth quarter.

OCTOBER 18
SCORE BY PERIODS

Philadelphia	6	3	0	14	—23
Minnesota	0	21	7	7	—35

SCORING

Philadelphia—Montgomery 1 run (kick blocked).
Minnesota—Senser 11 pass from Kramer (Danmeier kick).
Philadelphia—Field goal Franklin 30.
Minnesota—S. White 50 pass from Kramer (Danmeier kick).
Minnesota—Bruer 1 pass from Kramer (Danmeier kick).
Minnesota—Rashad 5 pass from Kramer (Danmeier kick).
Philadelphia—Montgomery 25 pass from Jaworski (Franklin kick).
Minnesota—Brown 1 run (Danmeier kick).
Philadelphia—Carmichael 21 pass from Jaworski (Franklin kick).

TEAM STATISTICS

	Philadelphia	Minnesota
First downs	26	20
Rushes-Yards	26-105	23-94
Passing yards	313	240
Sacks by-Yards	2-17	3-32
Return yards	131	86
Passes	30-45-2	24-46-0
Punts	4-36.5	8-35.4
Fumbles-Lost	2-2	1-0
Penalties-Yards	3-25	4-25
Time of possession	31:35	28:25
Attendance—45,459.		

INDIVIDUAL STATISTICS

Rushing—Philadelphia, Montgomery 16-62, Oliver 9-43, Jaworski 1-0; Minnesota, Brown 22-92, Young 1-2.

Passing—Philadelphia, Jaworski 30-45-2—345; Minnesota, Kramer 24-46-0—257.

Receiving—Philadelphia, Montgomery 10-143, Carmichael 8-109, Smith 4-64, Krepfle 2-11, Campfield 3-8, Parker 1-10, Oliver 2-0; Minnesota, Senser 5-88, Brown 10-82, S. White 2-53, Rashad 3-20, Young 2-8, LeCount 1-5, Bruer 1-1.

Kickoff Returns—Philadelphia, Henry 4-88, Campfield 1-13; Minnesota, Payton 1-32, Nord 1-20, McDole 1-19.

Punt Returns—Philadelphia, Henry 5-30.

Interceptions—Minnesota, McNeill 1-14, Blair 1-1.

Punting—Philadelphia, Runager 3-44.3, Franklin 1-13.0; Minnesota, Coleman 8-35.4.

Field Goals—Philadelphia, Franklin 1-1; Minnesota, None attempted.

COWBOYS 29, RAMS 17

IRVING—Only one week earlier, Dallas was being buried by the local populous after a disastrous performance against the San Francisco 49ers and Los Angeles was on a four-game roll, which included a victory on the road against Atlanta. But after the Cowboys whipped the Rams in a Sunday night game at Texas Stadium, both teams had new outlooks.

The Cowboys (5-2) were a game back of Philadelphia in the NFC East while the Rams (4-3) fell behind the 49ers in the NFC West.

"We are in our toughest stretch of the season right now," said Cowboys Coach Tom Landry. "How we survive this stretch will mean a lot in whether or not we go into the playoffs. We're playing excellent football teams from here on out."

Tony Dorsett rolled up 159 yards rushing, including a 44-yard touchdown run in the second quarter, and Danny White threw a 63-yard scoring pass to Tony Hill with five minutes left in the first half to pace the Cowboys.

With the Cowboys holding a 26-17 lead late in the third quarter, the game degenerated into a sloppy show of penalties and botched plays.

"We were still in the game in the second half," said Rams Coach Ray Malavasi, "until the officials took over."

The Rams were penalized 10 times for 78 yards but the Cowboys were assessed a club-record 15 penalties for 108 yards.

The Cowboys, however, piled up 496 yards of offense. White recorded the longest touchdown pass of his career (the 63-yarder to Hill) and Rafael Septien broke the club record for consecutive field goals. He ran his streak to nine by kicking a 40-yarder in the first quarter and a 39-yarder in the fourth quarter.

The Cowboys' other points came on a one-yard run by Ron Springs and a safety when Harvey Martin sacked Pat Haden in the end zone.

The Rams fell behind, 19-0, but rallied briefly in the second quarter on a two-yard touchdown run from Wendell Tyler and a 40-yard field goal by Frank Corral. The Rams' final points came on a 43-yard throw from Haden to Drew Hill in the third quarter—the only touchdown by either team in the second half.

OCTOBER 18
SCORE BY PERIODS

Los Angeles	0	10	7	0	—17
Dallas	12	14	0	3	—29

SCORING

Dallas—Springs 1 run (Septien kick).
Dallas—Field goal Septien 40.
Dallas—Safety, Haden tackled in end zone.
Dallas—Dorsett 44 run (Septien kick).
Los Angeles—Tyler 2 run (Corral kick).
Los Angeles—Field goal Corral 40.
Dallas—Hill 63 pass from D. White (Septien kick).
Los Angeles—D. Hill 43 pass from Haden (Corral kick).
Dallas—Field goal Septien 39.

TEAM STATISTICS

	Los Angeles	Dallas
First downs	22	24
Rushes-Yards	34-171	42-221
Passing yards	203	275
Sacks by-Yards	1-2	4-34
Return yards	108	69
Passes	13-30-3	15-33-2
Punts	5-48.0	5-48.6
Fumbles-Lost	1-0	2-1
Penalties-Yards	10-78	15-108
Time of possession	27:59	32:01
Attendance—64,649.		

Rushing—Dallas, Dorsett 27-159, Springs 12-41, D. White 3-21; Los Angeles, Tyler 16-90, Bryant 14-53, Haden 2-17, Guman 2-11.

Passing—Dallas, D. White 15-33-2—277; Los Angeles, Haden 13-30-3—237.

Receiving—Dallas, Hill 4-97, Pearson 4-78, Saldi 2-17, Cosbie 1-28, Dorsett 1-22, DuPree 1-15, Johnson 1-15, Springs 1-5; Los Angeles, Miller 4-51, Moore 3-53, D. Hill 2-88, Bryant 2-13, Childs 1-19, Arnold 1-13.

Kickoff Returns—Los Angeles, D. Hill 6-95; Dallas, J. Jones 2-40, Fellows 1-14.

Punt Returns—Los Angeles, Irvin 3-13; Dallas, J. Jones 1-9, Fellows 2-6.

Interceptions—Los Angeles, Cromwell 2-0; Dallas, Walls 2-0, Thurman 1-0.

Punting—Los Angeles, Corral 5-48.0; Dallas, D. White 5-42.6.

Field Goals—Los Angeles, Corral 1-1; Dallas, Septien 2-2.

GIANTS 32, SEAHAWKS O

SEATTLE—Since the beginning of the Seattle franchise, the offense has been the team's bread and butter. But it was more like a bread and water starvation diet in the thrashing by New York.

The Giants' defense kept the Seahawks in their own territory until midway through the fourth quarter. The Seahawks gained a pitiful 127 yards in total offense and rushed for only 29 yards. It was also the first time in nearly two years that the Seahawks were held scoreless.

Seattle's Jim Zorn completed 14 of 22 passes for just 84 yards before he was lifted in the third quarter with the Seahawks trailing, 19-0.

The Giants (4-3) got a club-record six field goals in six attempts from Joe Danelo and a 116-yard rushing effort from Rob Carpenter. Danelo put on a kicking clinic with field goals of 29, 54, 21, 47, 31 and 37 yards. His total of six field goals was one short of the NFL record, set by the St. Louis Cardinals' Jim Bakken against the Pittsburgh Steelers in 1967.

Carpenter, acquired from Houston, became the first Giants back since Ron Johnson in 1972 to rush for more than 100 yards in back-to-back games.

The Giants also scored on a six-yard touchdown pass from Phil Simms to Gary Shirk and a two-yard run by Carpenter.

"It was a great victory, said Coach Ray Perkins.

OCTOBER 18
SCORE BY PERIODS

New York Giants	3	10	13	6—32
Seattle	0	0	0	0— 0

SCORING

New York—Field goal Danelo 29.
New York—Shirk 6 pass from Simms (Danelo kick).
New York—Field goal Danelo 54.
New York—Field goal Danelo 21.
New York—Field goal Danelo 47.
New York—Carpenter 2 run (Danelo kick).
New York—Field goal Danelo 31.
New York—Field goal Danelo 37.

	New York	Seattle
First downs	20	10
Rushes-Yards	44-213	14-29
Passing yards	88	98
Sacks by-Yards	5-45	2-15
Return yards	79	139
Passes	12-28-1	20-34-2
Punts	3-45.7	6-41.0
Fumbles-Lost	1-0	4-2
Penalties-Yards	2-15	5-31
Time of possession	37:20	22:40

Attendance—56,134.

INDIVIDUAL STATISTICS

Rushing—New York, Carpenter 21-116, Bright 4-39, Kotar 8-21, Perry 8-21, L. Jackson 2-10, Simms 1-6; Seattle, T. Brown 4-9, Smith 2-7, Hughes 4-7, Jodat 3-5, Doornink 1-1.

Passing—New York, Simms 12-27-1—103, Brunner 0-1-0—0; Seattle, Zorn 14-22-1—84, Krieg 5-9-0—50, Adkins 1-3-1—9.

Receiving—New York, Shirk 4-30, Mullady 2-14, Bright 1-16, Perkins 1-15, Kotar 1-9, Friede 1-8, Mistler 1-6, Perry 1-5; Seattle, Smith 6-24, Largent 4-40, T. Brown 2-24, Sawyer 2-16, McCullum 3-23, Doornink 1-9, Hughes 1-5, Jodat 1-2.

Kickoff Returns—New York, Garrett 1-32; Seattle, Lewis 3-54, Johnson 3-56.

Punt Returns—New York, Garrett 2-15, Bright 2-13; Seattle, Johns 2-29.

Interceptions—New York, Van Pelt 1-10, Flowers 1-9; Seattle, Harris 1-0.

Punting—New York, Jennings 3-45.7; Seattle, West 6-41.0.

Field Goals—New York, Danelo 6-6; Seattle, None attempted.

LIONS 48, BEARS 17

PONTIAC—It was the kind of NFL debut not even the best of story writers could have written. It may have been the greatest starting debut by a quarterback in the history of the National Football League.

Eric Hipple, a fourth-round draft choice in 1980 from Utah State, put on a spectacular show before a nationwide television audience in leading the Detroit Lions past the Chicago Bears, 48-17.

Hipple, who saw his only other NFL action in a brief stint against Tampa Bay two weeks earlier, was forced into the starting role when regular quarterback Gary Danielson was injured early in the season and his successor, Jeff Komlo, was ineffective.

The Lions were forced to play without their star running back, Billy Sims, who was sidelined with an injury. Without Sims, the Lions were going to live or die with their passing game. It didn't take Hipple very long to get it started.

He fired a 48-yard pass to split end Fred Scott on the first play from scrimmage to begin a 79-yard, nine-play drive that ended on Hipple's one-yard sneak for a touchdown.

Chicago got that touchdown right back, however, as Bears quarterback Vince Evans hit Marcus Anderson on a short pass and Anderson raced 85 yards to tie the score at 7-7.

The Lions' Eddie Murray kicked a 49-yard

field goal to put Detroit back ahead, 10-7, late in the first quarter—and the rout was on.

Hipple scored from four yards out to put the Lions up by 10 early in the second quarter; he marched his team 80 yards in 11 plays and hit running back Rick Kane from the 2-yard line later in the second; Murray hit a 53-yard field goal shortly before halftime; Hipple hit tight end David Hill on a 10-yard TD pass in the third quarter, he connected with Scott for a 45-yard touchdowns pass and with Leonard Thompson for a 94-yard bomb, both in the fourth period.

Before all was said and done, Hipple had thrown for four touchdowns and run for two more. The hapless Bears scored only two all night.

MONDAY, OCTOBER 19
SCORE BY PERIODS

Chicago	7	7	0	3—17
Detroit	10	17	7	14—48

SCORING

Detroit—Hipple 1 run (Murray kick).
Chicago—Anderson 85 pass from Evans (Roveto kick).
Detroit—Field goal Murray 49.
Detroit—Hipple 4 run (Murray kick).
Chicago—Payton 1 run (Roveto kick).
Detroit—Kane 2 pass from Hipple (Murray kick).
Detroit—Field goal Murray 53.
Detroit—Hill 10 pass from Hipple (Murray kick).
Chicago—Field goal Roveto 22.
Detroit—Scott 44 pass from Hipple (Murray kick).
Detroit—L. Thompson 94 pass from Hipple (Murray kick).

TEAM STATISTICS

	Chicago	Detroit
First downs	24	23
Rushes-Yards	37-133	32-159
Passing yards	316	326
Sacks by-Yards	1-10	1-10
Return yards	94	117
Passes	20-33-1	14-25-0
Punts	3-47.0	3-43.0
Fumbles-Lost	3-3	1-1
Penalties-Yards	12-127	7-47
Time of possession	35:35	24:25
Attendance—71,274.		

INDIVIDUAL STATISTICS

Rushing—Chicago, Payton 19-89, Suhey 14-45, Evans 2-3, Phipps 1-0, McClendon 1-minus 4; Detroit, Kane 20-101, L. Thompson 1-21, Hipple 4-13, Scott 1-9, V. Thompson 1-8, Bussey 5-7.

Passing—Chicago, Evans 18-31-1—298, Avellini 1-1-0—17, Phipps 1-1-0—11; Detroit, Hipple 14-25-0—336.

Receiving—Chicago, Anderson 6-176, Suhey 4-16, Baschnagel 3-47, Payton 3-39, Margerum 3-36, Earl 1-12; Detroit, L. Thompson 3-118, Scott 3-110, Hill 3-29, Kane 2-27, Norris 1-31, King 1-21, Bussey 1-0.

Kickoff Returns—Chicago, Williams 2-37, Frazier 2-28, J. Fisher 1-17; Detroit, Hall 1-36, Martin 2-52.

Punt Returns—Chicago, J. Fisher 2-12; Detroit, Martin 2-13.

Interceptions—Detroit, White 1-16.

Punting—Chicago, Parsons 3-47.0; Detroit, Skladany 3-43.0.

Field Goals—Chicago, Roveto 1-1; Detroit, Murray 2-2.

BEARS 20, CHARGERS 17 (Overtime)

CHICAGO—John Roveto, holding on as the Chicago kicker while Bob Thomas recovers from a leg injury, kicked a 26-yard field goal with 9:30 gone in overtime to stun San Diego.

"It was a classic upset," said Bears Coach Neill Armstrong, who had been under fire for his team's 1-6 record. "We gave Roveto enough chances and he came through."

Roveto had missed two short field-goal attempts (one of 18 yards) that he thought he should have made. "That's the worst I've ever played. I never dreamed I'd miss those short ones," said the kicker from Southwestern Louisiana, who was cut by Dallas in 1980 and by Tampa Bay before the Bears picked him up in 1981.

Roveto was able to redeem himself when safety Gary Fencik intercepted a Dan Fouts pass at the Chicago 41 and returned it to the San Diego 26. Roveto was set to try a 40-yard kick three plays later, when the Chargers were offside. That enabled the Bears to move to the nine-yard line before Roveto kicked the winner.

The Bears' secondary and a five-man pass rush did a remarkable job against Fouts, holding him to 13 completions in 43 attempts. Most of his 295 yards came in the fourth quarter, when he threw TD passes to Charlie Joiner and Wes Chandler to send the game into overtime. The 39-yarder to Chandler came with 1:40 left in regulation time.

Chicago ran 100 plays to the Chargers' 63, controlling the game with a solid ground attack. Walter Payton led the way with 107 yards in 36 carries.

OCTOBER 25
SCORE BY PERIODS

San Diego	0	3	0	14	0—17
Chicago	7	3	0	7	3—20

SCORING

Chicago—Suhey 7 run (Roveto kick).
San Diego—Field goal Benirschke 18.
Chicago—Field goal Roveto 31.
San Diego—Joiner 22 pass from Fouts (Benirschke kick).
Chicago—Payton 2 run (Roveto kick).
San Diego—Chandler 39 pass from Fouts (Benirschke kick).
Chicago—Field goal Roveto 26.

TEAM STATISTICS

	San Diego	Chicago
First downs	15	28
Rushes-Yards	20-61	61-195
Passing yards	295	219
Sacks by-Yards	0-0	0-0
Return yards	144	144
Passes	13-43-2	17-39-0
Punts	5-44.0	7-41.1
Fumbles-Lost	0-0	2-1
Penalties-Yards	10-64	9-67
Time of possession	20:40	48:50
Attendance—52,906.		

Detroit's Eric Hipple wasted no time in showing a national televison audience that he could play quarterback in the NFL. In his first career start, a Monday night game, Hipple threw four touchdown passes and ran for another two TDs as the Lions crushed the Chicago Bears, 48-17.

Eighth Week—Continued

INDIVIDUAL STATISTICS

Rushing—San Diego, J. Brooks 7-39, Muncie 12-21, Cappelletti 1-1; Chicago, Payton 36-107, Suhey 22-64, Evans 3-24.

Passing—San Diego, Fouts 13-43-2—295; Chicago, Evans 17-39-0—219.

Receiving—San Diego, Joiner 5-124, Winslow 4-78, Chandler 2-69, Scales 1-20, J. Brooks 1-4; Chicago, Baschnagel 5-80, Margerum 4-83, Payton 3-22, Suhey 3-17, Cobb 1-9, Earl 1-8.

Kickoff Returns—San Diego, J. Brooks 3-93; Chicago, J. Fisher 1-6, Moorehead 4-71.

Punt Returns—San Diego, J. Brooks 3-51; Chicago, J. Fisher 2-12.

Interceptions—Chicago, Henderson 1-23, Fencik 1-32.

Punting—San Diego, Roberts 5-44.0; Chicago, Parsons 7-41.1.

Field Goals—San Diego, Benirschke 1-2; Chicago, Roveto 2-4.

49ers 20, RAMS 17

SAN FRANCISCO—The San Francisco 49ers completed the first half of their schedule with a 6-2 record and a two-game lead in the National Football Conference Western Division after beating the Los Angeles Rams, 20-17.

San Francisco had won five in a row and had beaten the Rams for the first time in 10 games and for the first time at home since 1966. However, anyone ready to claim the NFC West title wasn't looking at the task ahead.

"This was a tremendous victory for us," said Coach Bill Walsh, "but there are an awful lot of games left. I'm willing to bet the Rams (4-4) will be in the playoff picture because they're a very fine team."

Against the Rams, Joe Montana, the NFC's leading passer, completed 18 of 32 throws for 287 yards and two first-quarter touchdowns. Ray Wersching booted two field goals and the defense did the rest.

End Fred Dean recorded 4½ of the six sacks of Rams quarterback Pat Haden and linebacker Jack Reynolds, an ex-Ram, was another defensive standout. So was end Dwaine Board, who shared a sack with Dean and blocked a 26-yard field goal attempt by the Rams' Frank Corral.

In addition to that block, Corral missed three other field-goal tries, including a 45-yarder in the final seconds that could have sent the game into overtime.

Jack Youngblood, veteran Ram defensive end, cited the play of Dean and Reynolds. "They've helped this team a lot," he said. "They're professionals, talented and an asset to any young team."

The 49ers' Walsh also praised Dean, acquired recently from San Diego, but the coach said "it would be unfair and inaccurate to say he's the whole reason for our success. Montana also played a great game."

Montana had a 41-yard scoring pass to Dwight Clark and a 14-yarder to Freddie Solo-

mon. A 50-yard completion to Earl Cooper set up Wersching's first field goal.

For the Rams, who gained 401 yards, Haden was 20-for-39 for 310 yards and was victimized by numerous dropped passes.

OCTOBER 25
SCORE BY PERIODS

Los Angeles	0	10	7	0	17
San Francisco	14	3	3	0	20

SCORING

San Francisco—Solomon 14 pass from Montana (Wersching kick).

San Francisco—Clark 41 pass from Montana (Wersching kick).

Los Angeles—Field goal Corral 25.

Los Angeles—Guman 2 run (Corral kick).

San Francisco—Field goal Wersching 42.

San Francisco—Field goal Wersching 18.

Los Angeles—Tyler 16 pass from Haden (Corral kick).

TEAM STATISTICS

	Los Angeles	San Fran.
First downs	25	14
Rushes-Yards	37-145	28-60
Passing yards	256	265
Sacks by-Yards	3-22	6-54
Return yards	267	90
Passes	20-39-1	18-32-0
Punts	5-43.0	10-43.3
Fumbles-Lost	0-0	0-0
Penalties-Yards	7-39	5-45
Time of possession	33:18	26:42
Attendance—59,190.		

INDIVIDUAL STATISTICS

Rushing—Los Angeles, Tyler 22-90, Guman 7-34, Bryant 7-13, Haden 1-8; San Francisco, Hofer 8-23, Davis 6-14, Patton 6-13, Cooper 5-7, Montana 2-3, Easley 1-0.

Passing—Los Angeles, Haden 20-39-1—310; San Francisco, Montana 18-32-0—287.

Receiving—Los Angeles, Dennard 6-119, Tyler 4-55, Waddy 4-52, Arnold 3-19, Bryant 1-39, D. Hill 1-13, Guman 1-13; San Francisco, Clark 8-109, Solomon 5-79, Cooper 2-57, Young 1-29, Patton 1-8, Wilson 1-5.

Kickoff Returns—Los Angeles, D. Hill 3-79, Sully 1-22; San Francisco, Lawrence 2-61, Ramson 1-12, Wilson 1-8.

Punt Returns—Los Angeles, Irvin 7-127, Johnson 1-39; San Francisco, Solomon 2-9.

Interceptions—San Francisco, Lott 1-0.

Punting—Los Angeles, Corral 5-43.0; San Francisco, Miller 10-43.3.

Field Goals—Los Angeles, Corral 1-5; San Francisco, Wersching 2-2.

CARDINALS 30, VIKINGS 17

ST. LOUIS—After posting five straight victories, including back-to-back shockers over San Diego and Philadelphia in the last two, Minnesota was ripe for an upset. And St. Louis was ready for one, too.

The Cardinals piled up a 13-0 lead in the first quarter and held off the explosive Vikings with their best defensive effort of the season.

"We were always in control," said Cardinals Coach Jim Hanifan. "We got the early lead and maintained it. If we play like we're capable of playing, we can beat a good team."

The Cardinals had beaten Dallas, 20-17, in the fifth week of the season, but their record had dipped to 2-5 before they burned Minnesota.

"They beat us in every aspect of the game," said Minnesota quarterback Tommy Kramer. "We expected to be able to throw on them. We had chances and just didn't execute."

Kramer completed only 25 of 55 passes, including two touchdown passes to Sammy White, and he was sacked three times. The Vikes were plagued by costly penalties in the first half, and trailed by 13-3 at the intermission. After Minnesota pulled to within 13-10 in the third period, a trick play backfired and led to the Cardinals' clinching TD.

On fourth and one from its 39, Minnesota lined up in punt formation, but the snap went to blocker Jeff Siemon, a linebacker. Siemon fumbled and punter Greg Coleman grabbed the loose ball and advanced it far enough for the first down. However, officials ruled that on a fourth-down play, only the designated ball carrier can advance his own fumble, and St. Louis took over on the Minnesota 36.

"Everybody was alert to the fact that they might try the fake," said Hanifan. "Of course, the guy fumbled the ball. That kind of helped."

Jim Hart threw a 20-yard pass to Pat Tilley and then Wayne Morris bolted 13 yards for the TD that gave the Cardinals a 20-10 lead. On the Cardinals' next possession, they put together a 16-play, 65-yard scoring drive that burned 10:36 off the clock. The payoff was an eight-yard pass from Hart to Mel Gray, making Hart the 10th player in NFL history to throw 200 career touchdown passes.

Hart threw a 37-yard scoring pass to Tilley in the first quarter and set up a Neil O'Donoghue field goal with a 48-yard bomb to Roy Green, also in the opening period. A 49-yard punt return by Stump Mitchell led to a field goal on the Cardinals' first possession.

OCTOBER 25

SCORE BY PERIODS

Minnesota	0	3	7	7—17
St. Louis	13	0	7	10—30

SCORING

St. Louis—Field goal O'Donoghue 19.
St. Louis—Tilley 37 pass from Hart (O'Donoghue kick).
St. Louis—Field goal O'Donoghue 23.
Minnesota—Field goal Danmeier 36.
Minnesota—S. White 15 pass from Kramer (Danmeier kick).
St. Louis—Morris 13 run (O'Donoghue kick).
St. Louis—Gray 8 pass from Hart (O'Donoghue kick).
Minnesota—S. White 22 pass from Kramer (Danmeier kick).
St. Louis—Field goal O'Donoghue 46.

TEAM STATISTICS

	Minnesota	St. Louis
First downs	22	18
Rushes-Yards	17-69	40-138
Passing yards	318	182
Sacks by-Yards	1-9	3-25
Return yards	116	149
Passes	25-55-2	13-26-2

	Minnesota	St. Louis
Punts	6-42.8	3-42.3
Fumbles-Lost	2-1	0-0
Penalties-Yards	11-104	7-35
Time of possession	27:36	32:24
Attendance—48,039.		

INDIVIDUAL STATISTICS

Rushing—Minnesota, Brown 13-55, Young 2-7, Kramer 1-7, Siemon 1-0; St. Louis, Anderson 23-77, Morris 16-63, Hart 1-minus 2.

Passing—Minnesota, Kramer 25-55-2—343; St. Louis, Hart 13-26-2—191.

Receiving—Minnesota, S. White 7-120, Senser 5-100, Rashad 6-71, Brown 5-41, Young 2-11; St. Louis, Tilley 5-98, Green 3-69, Gray 2-16, Anderson 2-10, Harrell 1-minus 2.

Kickoff Returns—Minnesota, Payton 5-91, McDole 1-17; St. Louis, Mitchell 3-67.

Punt Returns—Minnesota, Payton 1-4; St. Louis, Mitchell 5-82.

Interceptions—Minnesota, Teal 1-0, Knoff 1-4; St. Louis, Greene 1-0, Wehrli 1-0.

Punting—Minnesota, Coleman 6-42.8; St. Louis, Birdsong 3-42.3.

Field Goals—Minnesota, Danmeier 1-1; St. Louis, O'Donoghue 3-4.

EAGLES 20, BUCCANEERS 10

PHILADELPHIA—A pair of pass interceptions in the final period enabled Philadelphia to stave off Tampa Bay as the Eagles retained their one-game lead in the NFC East.

Tampa Bay quarterback Doug Williams had suffered only four interceptions in seven games before the Eagles picked off three in the rain at Veterans Stadium. Early in the fourth period, linebacker Al Chesley grabbed a Williams pass and returned 35 yards to set up a 44-yard field goal by Tony Franklin that gave the Eagles a 10-7 lead.

Bill Capece of the Bucs booted a 29-yarder to tie the score midway through the period. Then, a short pass from Ron Jaworski to Charlie Smith went for a 45-yard gain to set up a 32-yard Franklin field goal with 4:18 left, and Philadelphia went on top for good, 13-10.

On the pass to Smith, safety Neal Colzie slipped and fell, and Smith got away for the big gain. "It was a sure interception as far as I was concerned," said Colzie. "But I slipped and fell and that was it."

Randy Logan recovered a fumble by Jerry Eckwood on the Bucs' next possession, but the Eagles failed to score. When the Bucs got the ball back, however, nickel back Richard Blackmore intercepted a Williams pass and returned 18 yards to the Tampa Bay 5. Wilbert Montgomery, who ran for 119 yards in the game, went in for an insurance TD with 1:30 left.

"Turnovers were the difference, really," said Eagles Coach Dick Vermeil. "They were a good team that could have beaten us. I don't think they realize how good they are."

Williams passed for 238 yards, but could produce only a first-quarter TD, which he scored on a one-yard sneak. Capece missed three field-goal attempts and Bucs Coach John McKay declared he was going to reevaluate his kicking game. Capece, who was signed after the Bucs dropped Garo Yepremian, was 4-for-9 on field goal tries in his five games.

OCTOBER 25
SCORE BY PERIODS

Tampa Bay	7	0	0	3—10	
Philadelphia	0	7	0	13—20	

SCORING

Tampa Bay—Williams 1 run (Capece kick).
Philadelphia—Krepfle 6 pass from Jaworski (Franklin kick).
Philadelphia—Field goal Franklin 44.
Tampa Bay—Field goal Capece 29.
Philadelphia—Field goal Franklin 32.
Philadelphia—Montgomery 2 run (Franklin kick).

TEAM STATISTICS

	Tampa Bay	Philadelphia
First downs	24	17
Rushes-Yards	30-109	42-189
Passing yards	238	109
Sacks by-Yards	1-12	1-5
Return yards	74	98
Passes	19-45-3	9-15-1
Punts	3-33.3	4-34.3
Fumbles-Lost	2-1	4-2
Penalties-Yards	6-40	7-57
Time of possession	29:24	30:36

Attendance—70,714.

INDIVIDUAL STATISTICS

Rushing—Tampa Bay, Eckwood 13-65, Wilder 8-13, Williams 4-16, Owens 4-7, House 1-8; Philadelphia, Montgomery 22-119, Oliver 9-36, Campfield 4-12, Russell 3-12, Giammona 2-8, Jaworski 2-2.

Passing—Tampa Bay, Williams 19-45-3—243; Philadelphia, Jaworski 9-15-1—121.

Receiving—Tampa Bay, House 6-79, Giles 4-80, Wilder 4-21, Eckwood 3-20, T. Bell 1-26, Jones 1-17; Philadelphia, Smith 3-68, Montgomery 2-3, Carmichael 1-20, Oliver 1-15, Campfield 1-9, Krepfle 1-6.

Kickoff Returns—Tampa Bay, Owens 1-15, Holt 1-40; Philadelphia, Henry 1-25, Russell 1-20.

Punt Returns—Tampa Bay, T. Bell 2-7; Philadelphia, Henry 1-0.

Interceptions—Tampa Bay, Washington 1-12; Philadelphia, Young 1-0, Chesley 1-35, Blackmore 1-18.

Punting—Tampa Bay, Swider 3-33.3; Philadelphia, Runager 4-34.3.

Field Goals—Tampa Bay, Capece 1-4; Philadelphia, Franklin 2-3.

SAINTS 17, BENGALS 7

NEW ORLEANS—Cincinnati drove 82 yards on its first possession before coughing up the ball on a fumble at the New Orleans 8. From then on, the Saints' defense stuffed the Bengals and the offense came alive in the second half to bring off the upset.

"This game was settled on that first drive," said Coach Forrest Gregg, whose AFC Central Division-leading Bengals fell to 5-3. "For some reason our offense seemed to panic and from then on things didn't jell at all."

Cincinnati's starting quarterback, Ken An-derson, was knocked unconscious on a bruising tackle by defensive end Elois Grooms during a third-period pass attempt. Backup quarterback Jack Thompson was 6-for-20 passing and was sacked twice.

George Rogers, who gained 113 yards for his third straight 100-yard game and fifth of the year, broke the scoreless tie on a 19-yard run midway through the third quarter. Benny Ricardo kicked a 38-yard field goal and Archie Manning fired a 19-yard TD pass to Wayne Wilson to make it 17-0 in the final period.

"Their confidence snowballed and ours dwindled," said Thompson, who finally got the Bengals on the scoreboard with a six-yard TD pass to Dan Ross.

Coach Bum Phillips praised his young Saints, saying, "They played like wild men. They've been playing hard without reward. Today they got it."

Two bizarre plays that worked in favor of the Saints delighted the Superdome crowd. In the second quarter, Manning handed off to wide receiver Guido Merkens, who threw a 20-yard pass to Jeff Groth for a first down. In the fourth period, Russ Erxleben bobbled the snap on a punt attempt, but picked up the ball and scampered 26 yards up the middle for a first down.

OCTOBER 25
SCORE BY PERIODS

Cincinnati	0	0	0	7— 7	
New Orleans	0	0	7	10—17	

SCORING

New Orleans—G. Rogers 19 run (Ricardo kick).
New Orleans—Field goal Ricardo 38.
New Orleans—W. Wilson 19 pass from Manning (Ricardo kick).
Cincinnati—Ross 6 pass from Thompson (Breech kick).

TEAM STATISTICS

	Cincinnati	New Orleans
First downs	15	18
Rushes-Yards	19-34	37-166
Passing yards	171	170
Sacks by-Yards	2-20	3-27
Return yards	90	82
Passes	19-41-1	16-25-1
Punts	6-51.0	4-42.0
Fumbles-Lost	2-1	1-0
Penalties-Yards	7-55	6-40
Time of possession	25:59	34:01

Attendance—46,336.

INDIVIDUAL STATISTICS

Rushing—Cincinnati, Alexander 5-8, Johnson 11-51, Anderson 1-0, Verser 1-2, McInally 1-minus 27; New Orleans, G. Rogers 31-113, Holmes 2-3, Tyler 1-7, Manning 1-15, W. Wilson 1-2, Erxleben 1-26.

Passing—Cincinnati, Anderson 13-21-0—117, Thompson 6-20-1—81; New Orleans, Manning 15-24-1—170, Merkens 1-1-0—20.

Receiving—Cincinnati, Collinsworth 4-45, Alexander 3-15, Kreider 3-39, Curtis 4-50, Ross 4-39, M. Harris 1-10; New Orleans, Holmes 2-7, Groth 2-36, Merkens 4-47, W. Wilson 2-48, Thompson 1-6, G. Rogers 2-17, Hardy 2-26, Tyler 1-3.

Kickoff Returns—Cincinnati, Verser 2-59, Simmons 1-10, Griffin 1-21; New Orleans, W. Wilson 1-25.

Punt Returns—New Orleans, Groth 4-44.

Interceptions—Cincinnati, Riley 1-0; New Orleans, Kovach 1-13.

Punting—Cincinnati, McInally 6-51.0; New Orleans, Erxleben 4-42.0.

Field Goals—Cincinnati, None attempted; New Orleans, Ricardo 1-2.

REDSKINS 24, PATRIOTS 22

WASHINGTON—Joe Theismann couldn't match Steve Grogan, but Washington was satisfied.

The Redskins were outgained by New England, 409 yards to 230, and Grogan outpassed Theismann, 306 yards to 162. But the Redskins hung on to win by making fewer mistakes.

Grogan threw a pair of third-quarter interceptions that the Redskins turned into Mark Moseley's 34-yard field goal and Theismann's one-yard touchdown sprint. The Patriots also fumbled six times, losing one.

"Mistakes will kill you, no matter where or when you make them," said Theismann, who also passed 13 yards to Joe Washington for a touchdown. "This time, we made fewer mistakes and capitalized on theirs. And we got a little bit lucky at the right time, too."

Theismann's touchdown run came in the third quarter when John Riggins slipped and missed the handoff on fourth-and-goal at the one-yard line. Theismann also slipped, but regained his balance to score the winning points.

Washington's Mike Nelms returned his second punt of the season for a touchdown, this one for 75 yards.

Patriots rookie Tony Collins, who rushed for 103 yards, ran five yards for a touchdown and Sam Cunningham went four yards for the other. John Smith kicked field goals of 25, 22 and 46 yards, but missed from 53 yards with 58 seconds left.

The Patriots (2-6) were penalized nine times for 72 yards and the Redskins five times for 82 yards.

New England's Harold Jackson caught four passes for 83 yards, pushing his career total to 10,014 yards. He joined Don Maynard and Lance Alworth as the only NFL receivers to reach the 10,000 mark in reception yardage.

OCTOBER 25
SCORE BY PERIODS

New England	6	9	0	7—22
Washington	7	7	10	0—24

SCORING

New England—Field goal Smith 25.
New England—Field goal Smith 22.
Washington—Washington 13 pass from Theismann (Moseley kick).
New England—Collins 5 run (run failed).
New England—Field goal Smith 46.
Washington—Nelms 75 punt return (Moseley kick).
Washington—Field goal Moseley 34.
Washington—Theismann 1 run (Moseley kick).
New England—Cunningham 4 run (Smith kick).

TEAM STATISTICS

	New England	Washington
First downs	23	15
Rushes-Yards	39-126	32-85
Passing yards	283	145
Sacks by-Yards	2-17	3-23
Return yards	103	251
Passes	17-30-2	14-23-0
Punts	4-44.3	6-38.5
Fumbles-Lost	6-1	2-2
Penalties-Yards	9-75	5-82
Time of possession	32:02	27:58

Attendance—50,394.

INDIVIDUAL STATISTICS

Rushing—New England, Collins 22-103, Calhoun 4-1, Tatupu 3-6, Ferguson 4-3, Cunningham 1-4, Grogan 5-9; Washington, Riggins 15-40, Washington 14-47, Theismann 3-minus 2.

Passing—New England, Grogan 17-30-2—306; Washington, Theismann 14-23-0—162.

Receiving—New England, Jackson 4-83, Hasselbeck 5-112, Morgan 5-66, Johnson 3-45; Washington, Monk 2-38, Warren 2-16, Washington 9-97, Metcalf 1-11.

Kickoff Returns—New England, Collins 4-60, Lee 1-4; Washington, Nelms 4-93, Wonsley 2-37.

Punt Returns—New England, Morgan 4-39; Washington, Nelms 3-90.

Interceptions—Washington, Olkewicz 1-12, Murphy 1-19.

Punting—New England, Camarillo 4-44.3; Washington, Connell 6-38.5.

Field Goals—New England, Smith 3-4; Washington, Moseley 1-2.

GIANTS 27, FALCONS 24
(Overtime)

ATLANTA—New York gained its third straight victory and pushed its record to 5-3 when Joe Danelo booted a 40-yard field goal nine minutes, 20 seconds into overtime.

Ray Perkins, the Giants' third-year coach, described the triumph as "the best win, by far, since I've been coach because we beat a contending team after trying to give the game away."

A short kick by the Giants gave the Falcons the ball at the New York 47 early in the overtime, but Atlanta couldn't capitalize on the break.

The Giants finally broke through when Brad Van Pelt recovered a fumble by William Andrews at the Atlanta 31. Rob Carpenter pounded for eight yards in three carries before Danelo came on for his winning kick.

"It was a perfect snap and a perfect hold," said Danelo. "My job is to kick it. When everything else is right, I'm not supposed to miss."

Danelo had been 6-for-6 the previous week in the Giants' 32-0 victory at Seattle. As Falcons quarterback Steve Bartkowski said of Danelo, "I knew if there was one guy in the league who could beat you in overtime, he was the man."

The Falcons had taken a 17-7 lead in the third quarter on the passing of Bartkowski, who threw for 311 yards. But then Phil Simms fired two TD passes and Danelo booted a field goal as the Giants moved ahead, 24-17. Atlanta forged a 24-24 tie when Lynn Cain capped a

Eighth Week—Continued

66-yard drive with a three-yard TD run with 1:09 left in the fourth quarter.

Simms was brilliant as the Giants erased Atlanta's 17-7 lead. He fired a two-yard TD pass to Dave Young, set up by an 80-yard bomb to Johnny Perkins; threw a 36-yard pass to Leon Bright to set up a 27-yard Danelo field goal, and then fired a 12-yard TD strike to Perkins, set up by a 31-yard delivery to John Mistler.

The Giants' first TD came on blocked punt. Linebacker Frank Marion blocked the kick and cornerback Mike Dennis fell on it in the end zone—50 yards behind the line of scrimmage.

OCTOBER 25
SCORE BY PERIODS

New York Giants	0	7	10	7	3—27
Atlanta	7	7	3	7	0—24

SCORING

Atlanta—Miller 29 pass from Bartkowski (Luckhurst kick).
New York—Dennis recovered blocked punt in end zone (Danelo kick).
Atlanta—Francis 5 pass from Bartkowski (Luckhurst kick).
Atlanta—Field goal Luckhurst 29.
New York—Young 2 pass from Simms (Danelo kick).
New York—Field goal Danelo 27.
New York—Perkins 12 pass from Simms (Danelo kick).
Atlanta—Cain 3 run (Luckhurst kick).
New York—Field goal Danelo 40.

TEAM STATISTICS

	New York	Atlanta
First downs	12	23
Rushes-Yards	28-76	36-141
Passing yards	213	289
Sacks by-Yards	3-22	5-43
Return yards	126	127
Passes	19-32-0	24-48-1
Punts	11-43.0	9-36.4
Fumbles-Lost	3-0	3-1
Penalties-Yards	7-55	3-25
Time of possession	33:21	35:59
Attendance—48,410.		

INDIVIDUAL STATISTICS

Rushing—New York, Carpenter 17-58, Kotar 4-6, Bright 3-4, Simms 4-8; Atlanta, Andrews 21-92, Cain 13-49, Bartkowski 2-0.

Passing—New York, Simms 19-32-0—256; Atlanta, Bartkowski 24-48-1—311.

Receiving—New York, Perkins 5-126, Bright 5-58, Carpenter 3-13, Shirk 2-12, Mistler 1-31, Gray 1-12, Young 1-2, Kotar 1-2; Atlanta, Cain 10-65, Andrews 4-40, Jackson 3-92, Miller 3-53, Francis 2-33, Jenkins 2-28.

Kickoff Returns—New York, Garrett 2-31, Bright 3-46, Dennis 1-17; Atlanta, Woerner 4-80.

Punt Returns—New York, Garrett 1-4, Bright 5-26; Atlanta, Woerner 6-47.

Interceptions—New York, Currier 1-2.

Punting—New York, Jennings 11-43.0; Atlanta, James 8-41.0.

Field Goals—New York, Danelo 2-2; Atlanta, Luckhurst 1-2.

LIONS 31, PACKERS 27

PONTIAC—Eric Hipple was only half as good at producing touchdowns in his second start as he was in his pro debut—but it was good enough for Detroit to eke out a victory over stubborn Green Bay at the Silverdome.

The three touchdowns Hipple accounted for were half his output in his debut against Chicago, when he ran for two scores and passed for four.

The Lions' first touchdown was a six-yard bootleg by Hipple and the winning score, with 1:54 to play, came when Hipple went five yards on a quarterback draw.

He also passed one yard for a TD to David Hill, who caught nine passes for 98 yards, as he completed 20 of 36 passes for 271 yards.

"I know I can play. I don't have any doubts about myself," said Hipple.

David Whitehurst had an outstanding day in relief of Packers quarterback Lynn Dickey, who suffered a back injury on a late hit from Detroit defensive end Bill Gay. Gay was ejected from the game.

Whitehurst passed for 189 yards in the second half and ended 20-for-36 for 243 yards. But his effort to lead the Packers from behind in the final minute ended at midfield when Detroit's Curtis Green sacked him on third down.

Green Bay's Gerry Ellis scored on a 46-yard pass from Whitehurst with 59 seconds left in the third quarter to pull the Packers to within 24-20. Then Ellis put the Packers ahead, 27-24, on a one-yard run with 6:34 left.

However, Hipple took the Lions 76 yards in a dozen plays and finished the drive by calling his own number on the first play following the two-minute warning.

OCTOBER 25
SCORE BY PERIODS

Green Bay	7	3	10	7	—27
Detroit	7	10	7	7	—31

SCORING

Detroit—Hipple 6 run (Murray kick).
Green Bay—Lofton 75 pass from Dickey (Stenerud kick).
Green Bay—Field goal Stenerud 27.
Detroit—Field goal Murray 37.
Detroit—Hill 1 pass from Hipple (Murray kick).
Green Bay—Field goal Stenerud 39.
Detroit—Kane 2 run (Murray kick).
Green Bay—Ellis 46 pass from Whitehurst (Stenerud kick).
Green Bay—Ellis 1 run (Stenerud kick).
Detroit—Hipple 5 run (Murray kick).

TEAM STATISTICS

	Green Bay	Detroit
First downs	23	24
Rushes-Yards	21-75	38-171
Passing yards	307	238
Sacks by-Yards	4-33	3-33
Return yards	132	115
Passes	24-43-1	20-36-1
Punts	3-42.0	3-46.7
Fumbles-Lost	2-2	4-1
Penalties-Yards	5-47	9-75
Time of possession	27:44	32:16
Attendance—76,063.		

INDIVIDUAL STATISTICS

Rushing—Green Bay, Ellis 11-32, Whitehurst 2-21, Middleton 4-14, Huckleby 4-8; Detroit, Kane 21-80, V. Thompson 6-44, Hipple 5-20, Bussey 5-20, Nichols 1-7.

Passing—Green Bay, Whitehurst 20-36-1-243, Dickey

4-7-0—97; Detroit, Hipple 20-36-1—271.

Receiving—Green Bay, Ellis 7-89, Huckleby 6-41, Coffman 5-73, Lofton 2-98, Jefferson 2-26, Middleton 1-7, Cassidy 1-6; Detroit, Hill 9-98, L. Thompson 2-65, Scott 2-45, Bussey 2-18, Kane 2-16, King 2-12, V. Thompson 1-17.

Kickoff Returns—Green Bay, Lee 4-74, Gray 2-24; Detroit, Hall 4-92, Martin 2-24.

Punt Returns—Green Bay, Lee 2-4; Detroit, Martin 3-minus 2.

Interceptions—Green Bay, Harvey 1-30; Detroit, Fantetti 1-1.

Punting—Green Bay, Stachowicz 3-42.0; Detroit, Skladany 3-46.7.

Field Goals—Green Bay, Stenerud 2-2; Detroit, Murray 1-3.

SEAHAWKS 19, JETS 3

NEW YORK—Seattle had only one victory in 1981 and had won only once in its last 16 games. The Seahawks were coming off a humiliating shutout at home by the New York Giants in which they gained only 29 yards rushing.

But something happens to the Seahawks when they play the Jets. In five games since their birth in 1976, the Seahawks have never lost to the Jets.

Lined up as a running back, wide receiver Steve Largent ran 10 yards for a TD late in the first half. He caught a 27-yard touchdown pass from Jim Zorn on Seattle's first possession of the second half. Sherman Smith's four-year TD burst in the fourth quarter put the game out of reach. And Theotis Brown, playing in only his second game as a Seahawk, gained 104 yards on 14 carries.

"We're really happy to win one, finally," said Zorn. "We go into every game thinking we can win. This week, it just happened to be the Jets again. I don't think it's a jinx."

The Jets' only score came on a 34-yard field goal by Pat Leahy in the third quarter. Their four-game unbeaten streak ended and their record fell to 3-4-1.

Leading 7-0, the Seahawks nearly had another touchdown just before the half, but a blunder cost them as Largent was stopped on the two-yard line with three seconds on the clock after a reception. The Seahawks were unable to stop the clock.

"I guess if you count up all the mistakes we made today, you'd have enough for the entire 16-game season," said Walt Michaels, the New York coach.

The Jets moved to the Seahawks' 20 on their first possession and fumbled the ball away. Also, on the first play of the second half, an 80-yard touchdown pass to Wesley Walker was nullified because of a penalty.

"They talk about any given Sunday," Michaels said, "and it was our given Sunday to lose."

OCTOBER 25

SCORE BY PERIODS

Seattle	0	7	6	6—19
New York Jets	0	0	3	0— 3

SCORING

Seattle—Largent 10 run (Herrera kick).
Seattle—Largent 27 pass from Zorn (kick failed).
New York—Field goal Leahy 34.
Seattle—Smith 4 run (kick failed).

TEAM STATISTICS

	Seattle	New York
First downs	26	15
Rushes-Yards	50-217	25-118
Passing yards	163	101
Sacks by-Yards	2-20	1-9
Return yards	74	108
Passes	13-21-0	14-29-2
Punts	4-45.5	3-48.0
Fumbles-Lost	2-1	2-2
Penalties-Yards	11-65	5-50
Time of possession	33:39	26:21
Attendance—49,678.		

INDIVIDUAL STATISTICS

Rushing—Seattle, T. Brown 14-104, Doornink 11-44, Smith 16-25, Zorn 6-26, Largent 3-18; New York, Harper 8-60, Dierking 5-19, Augustyniak 6-17, Todd 2-12, L. Jones 1-5, Long 2-6, Taylor 1-minus 1.

Passing—Seattle, Zorn 13-21-0—172; New York, Todd 14-29-2—121.

Receiving—Seattle, Largent 6-80, McCullum 3-36, Sawyer 1-30, T. Brown 2-16, Smith 1-10; New York, Harper 3-23, Dierking 2-22, Gaffney 2-20, Walker 2-15, Barkum 1-14, L. Jones 1-10, Augustyniak 2-9, Newton 1-8.

Kickoff Returns—Seattle, Lewis 2-39; New York, Harper 4-108.

Punt Returns—Seattle, Johns 3-14; New York, Sohn 1-0.

Interceptions—Seattle, Simpson 1-21, Harris 1-0.

Punting—Seattle, West 4-45.5; New York, Ramsey 3-48.0.

Field Goals—Seattle, None attempted; New York, Leahy 1-1.

BROWNS 42, COLTS 28

CLEVELAND—Brian Sipe and the offense rewrote the Cleveland record book in the victory over hapless Baltimore.

Sipe completed 30 of 41 passes for four touchdowns and a team-record 444 yards. The previous record of 401 yards was set by Otto Graham against Pittsburgh in 1952.

The Browns (4-4) also broke a 30-year team record with 562 yards in total offense. Graham led the Browns to 550 yards against the Chicago Bears in 1951.

"We came out here loaded for bear and they (the Colts) just happened to get in the way," Sipe said.

Sipe entered the game with only seven scoring passes, but clicked with Ozzie Newsome, Greg Pruitt and Dave Logan in the first half and Ricky Feacher in the second. Twice in the game, Sipe threw 11 consecutive completions.

The Colts suffered their seventh straight loss since their opening-day victory against New England. The Colts had given up 126 points and more than 1,500 yards in their last three games.

Bert Jones threw for three touchdowns—one to Curtis Dickey and two to Ray Butler—and missed another when Butler was ruled out of bounds on a catch in the end zone, but it wasn't enough to make up for the shortcomings of the league's worst defense.

The Colts' other touchdown occurred at the start of the second half after the Browns' Curtis Weathers blocked a field-goal attempt by Mike Wood. The ball was picked up by Colts tight end Reese McCall, who lateralled to guard Robert Pratt, who pitched the ball to backup quarterback Greg Landry, the holder on the play, and Landry scrambled into the end zone.

Sam Rutigliano, the Cleveland head coach, was able to laugh about the bizarre play.

"I've never seen a play like that before," he said. "I defy them to do that again. It shows you the wishbone isn't dead in professional football."

OCTOBER 25
SCORE BY PERIODS

Baltimore	0	7	14	7—28
Cleveland	7	21	7	7—42

SCORING

Cleveland—Newsome 1 pass from Sipe (Bahr kick).
Cleveland—G. Pruitt 22 pass from Sipe (Bahr kick).
Cleveland—Logan 40 pass from Sipe (Bahr kick).
Baltimore—Dickey 3 pass from B. Jones (Wood kick).
Cleveland—White 2 run (Bahr kick).
Baltimore—Landry 11 fumble recovery (Wood kick).
Baltimore—Butler 36 pass from B. Jones (Wood kick).
Cleveland—Feacher 28 pass from Sipe (Bahr kick).
Baltimore—Butler 5 pass from B. Jones (Wood kick).
Cleveland—M. Pruitt 16 run (Bahr kick).

TEAM STATISTICS

	Baltimore	Cleveland
First downs	18	30
Rushes-Yards	32-118	33-131
Passing yards	239	431
Sacks by-Yards	1-13	2-10
Return yards	148	145
Passes	17-37-2	30-41-2
Punts	7-44.6	2-46.5
Fumbles-Lost	2-1	4-4
Penalties-Yards	5-33	6-56
Time of possession	29:30	30:30
Attendance—78,986.		

INDIVIDUAL STATISTICS

Rushing—Baltimore, McMillan 14-57, Dickey 14-36, B. Jones 1-17, McCauley 1-6, Dixon 2-2; Cleveland, M. Pruitt 16-87, White 6-21, C. Miller 5-20, G. Pruitt 3-11, Feacher 1-minus 1, Sipe 2-minus 7.

Passing—Baltimore, B. Jones 17-37-2—249; Cleveland, Sipe 30-41-2—444.

Receiving—Baltimore, McCauley 4-73, Carr 3-58, Butler 3-56, Dickey 3-24, Dixon 2-16, McMillan 1-17, McCall 1-5; Cleveland, G. Pruitt 9-104, Newsome 5-85, Feacher 5-55, Rucker 4-72, Logan 3-69, M. Pruitt 3-38, White 1-21.

Kickoff Returns—Baltimore, Williams 5-114, Dixon 1-26; Cleveland, White 2-36, Hall 1-32.

Punt Returns—Cleveland, Hall 7-50.

Interceptions—Baltimore, Braziel 1-8, Hatchett 1-0; Cleveland, Darden 1-1, Scott 1-26.

Punting—Baltimore, Garrett 7-44.6; Cleveland, Cox 2-46.5.

Field Goals—Baltimore, Wood 0-3; Cleveland, None attempted.

COWBOYS 28, DOLPHINS 27

IRVING—Dallas and Miami combined for nearly 1,000 net yards and a season's worth of big plays. And just when the Dolphins rallied for three touchdowns to take a 13-point lead, the Cowboys made one of their patented miracle rallies—scoring twice in a 31-second span to pull out the victory.

"This could have been one of our great games," said Miami Coach Don Shula. "Instead, it was a bitter defeat."

Dolphins quarterback David Woodley completed 21 of 37 passes for 408 yards. He hit on eight passes of 20 yards or more and repeatedly burned rookie cornerback Everson Walls.

Miami bolted to a 27-14 lead with three touchdowns in the second half—a 69-yard throw from Woodley to Jimmy Cefalo, a 10-yard run by Tony Nathan (set up by a 32-yard pass to Cefalo), and a four-yard toss to Joe Rose (following a 45-yard bomb to Duriel Harris).

But Dallas came to life after the last Miami TD, zipping 79 yards to score on a five-yard pass from Danny White to Doug Cosbie with 3:48 left. That made the score 27-21.

Two plays after the kickoff, safety Dennis Thurman intercepted a Woodley pass and returned to the Miami 32. On the first play, White threw a scoring pass to fullback Ron Springs, who had broken behind linebacker Bob Brudzinski. Rafael Septien converted and with 3:17 left, the Cowboys had their 28-27 lead.

Interceptions by Walls and by another rookie, Mike Downs, stopped Miami's comeback hopes. Although Walls had been the victim of at least four plays covering 186 yards, he came up with two interceptions in the game and led the NFL with a season total of eight.

Walls' total set a Cowboys record for a rookie, breaking the mark set in 1964 by Mel Renfro. Ironically, Renfro was at Texas Stadium being inducted into the Cowboys' Ring of Honor on the day his record fell.

"It was an up-and-down day," said Walls. "We gave up the big play, but we made the big interceptions. I guess that's all you can expect."

The defeat snapped a string of 13 straight Miami successes against NFC teams.

OCTOBER 25
SCORE BY PERIODS

Miami	0	6	7	14—27
Dallas	7	7	0	14—28

SCORING

Dallas—Springs 5 run (Septien kick).
Miami—Nathan 5 pass from Woodley (kick failed).
Dallas—Johnson 21 pass from D. White (Septien kick).
Miami—Cefalo 69 pass from Woodley (von Schamann kick).
Miami—Nathan 10 run (von Schamann kick).
Miami—Rose 4 pass from Woodley (von Schamann kick).
Dallas—Cosbie 5 pass from D. White (Septien kick).
Dallas—Springs 32 pass from D. White (Septien kick).

Dallas' Danny White drove his team to two touchdowns 31 seconds apart in the final minutes as the Cowboys edged the Miami Dolphins, 28-27.

TEAM STATISTICS

	Miami	Dallas
First downs	25	23
Rushes-Yards	35-148	36-139
Passing yards	392	327
Sacks by-Yards	2-27	2-16
Return yards	45	108
Passes	21-37-5	22-32-1
Punts	5-41.6	6-36.3
Fumbles-Lost	3-0	2-1
Penalties-Yards	2-11	3-20
Time of possession	31:34	28:26

Attendance—64,221.

INDIVIDUAL STATISTICS

Rushing—Miami, Nathan 16-76, Franklin 11-39, Woodley 5-21, Howell 1-6, Vigorito 2-6; Dallas, Dorsett 24-122, Springs 7-9, D. White 5-8.

Passing—Miami, Woodley 21-37-5—408; Dallas, D. White 22-32-1—354.

Receiving—Miami, Harris 6-165, Cefalo 5-164, Rose 4-43, Nathan 4-22, Vigorito 1-11; Dallas, Franklin 1-3; Dallas, Springs 6-93, Hill 5-106, Johnson 3-68, Dorsett 3-31, Pearson 2-31, Saldi 1-13, DuPree 1-7, Cosbie 1-5.

Kickoff Returns—Miami, Walker 2-29; Dallas, J. Jones 1-30, Fellows 1-18.

Punt Returns—Miami, Vigorito 2-13; Dallas, J. Jones 3-10.

Interceptions—Miami, Rhone 1-3; Dallas, Thurman 2-12, Walls 2-28, Fellows 1-10.

Punting—Miami, Orosz 5-41.6; Dallas, D. White 6-36.3.

Field Goals—Miami, None attempted; Dallas, Septien 0-1.

BILLS 9, BRONCOS 7

ORCHARD PARK—Somehow, the Buffalo Bills realized the seriousness of the situation.

Here they were, the defending AFC Eastern Division champions, trailing the Denver Broncos, 7-6, with three minutes left and the goal line 76 yards away.

"We knew we had to win to stay in the race and even have a chance to get to the playoffs," said Bills quarterback Joe Ferguson. So Ferguson gave Buffalo a chance, driving the Bills 58 yards in eight plays to the Denver 18. Then Nick Mike-Mayer kicked a 36-yard field goal with one second left to give Buffalo a 9-7 victory.

The kick sent the crowd of 77,757 at Rich Stadium into a frenzy. Buffalo improved its record to 5-3 and, when Miami lost to Dallas, the Bills were only a half-game out of first place in the AFC East. Denver, also 5-3, fell out of a first-place tie in the AFC West.

The game's only touchdown came in the second quarter when quarterback Craig Morton rebounded from an 11-yard sacking and fired a 36-yard scoring pass to Steve Watson.

Mike-Mayer kicked a 41-yard field goal just before halftime and booted a 46-yarder in the third period. That kick came when Buffalo got a reprieve on a punt attempt from the Denver 34. The Broncos' Larry Canada was called for encroachment and the penalty put the ball on the 29. Mike-Mayer then was sent on for a

field-goal attempt and his kick barely cleared the bar.

The game was a defensive struggle. The Broncos sacked Ferguson twice and the Bills got to Morton seven times. Denver was limited to 64 yards rushing while Buffalo gained 119, with Joe Cribbs contributing 113 on 24 carries.

"It was a tough loss," said Denver head coach Dan Reeves. "When you don't give up a touchdown and lose, it's frustrating."

OCTOBER 25
SCORE BY PERIODS

Denver	0	7	0	0—	7
Buffalo	0	3	3	3—	9

SCORING

Denver—Watson 36 pass from Morton (Steinfort kick).
Buffalo—Field goal Mike-Mayer 41.
Buffalo—Field goal Mike-Mayer 46.
Buffalo—Field goal Mike-Mayer 36.

TEAM STATISTICS

	Denver	Buffalo
First downs	10	17
Rushes-Yards	24-64	29-119
Passing yards	97	204
Sacks by-Yards	2-19	7-54
Return yards	76	62
Passes	10-25-0	21-42-1
Punts	12-44.3	9-46.9
Fumbles-Lost	0-0	1-1
Penalties-Yards	4-30	7-78
Time of possession	29:54	30:06

Attendance—80,020.

INDIVIDUAL STATISTICS

Rushing—Denver, Upchurch 1-5, Preston 11-26, Parros 10-22, Reed 2-11; Buffalo, Cribbs 24-123, Brown 2-1, Kush 1-minus 6, Butler 1-1, Leaks 1-0.

Passing—Denver, Morton 10-25-0—151; Buffalo, Ferguson 21-42-1—223.

Receiving—Denver, Watson 4-91, Parros 1-9, Preston 2-3, Odoms 2-21, Egloff 1-27; Buffalo, Brammer 4-28, Jessie 1-24, Butler 1-0, Brown 4-24, Lewis 6-90, Cribbs 2-15, Franklin 1-16, Piccone 2-26.

Kickoff Returns—Denver, Manning 2-41, Ryan 1-2.

Punt Returns—Denver, Manning 3-18; Buffalo, Hooks 1-25, Franklin 4-37.

Interceptions—Denver, Foley 1-15.

Punting—Denver, Prestridge 12-44.3; Buffalo, Cater 9-46.9.

Field Goals—Denver, Steinfort 0-1; Buffalo, Mike-Mayer 3-3.

CHIEFS 28, RAIDERS 17

OAKLAND—Little did the Raiders know as they left the field at halftime that the roof was about to fall in. Kansas City, behind reserve quarterback Steve Fuller, erased a 17-0 deficit en route to a come-from-behind victory that gave the Chiefs (6-2) sole possession of first place in the AFC West.

Using his scrambling ability, Fuller resurrected the Chiefs' offense, which gained only 14 yards on the ground in the first half when directed by Bill Kenney.

Fuller completed nine of 10 passes and rushed for 43 yards as he led the Chiefs on three drives that ended with rookie Billy Jackson, playing for the injured Joe Delaney, scoring from 29, three and three yards out, to give the Chiefs a 21-17 lead.

Marc Wilson drove the Raiders to the Chiefs' 2 but, with 40 seconds left, Wilson coughed up the ball when linebacker Charles Jackson blindsided him. Linebacker Gary Spani scooped up the fumble and raced 91 yards for the score that finished off the Raiders.

The Raiders had taken their lead on a touchdown pass from Wilson to Morris Bradshaw, a three-yard quarterback keeper by Wilson and a 51-yard field goal by Chris Bahr.

Fuller entered the game following an interception of Kenney.

"Bill was struggling and it was time for a change," said Marv Levy, the Kansas City coach.

"I thought we played well," said Oakland Coach Tom Flores. "But we just didn't score any points in the second half."

OCTOBER 25
SCORE BY PERIODS

Kansas City	0	0	7	21—28
Oakland	7	10	0	0—17

SCORING

Oakland—Bradshaw 6 pass from Wilson (Bahr kick).
Oakland—Wilson 3 run (Bahr kick).
Oakland—Field goal Bahr 55.
Kansas City—B. Jackson 29 run (Lowery kick).
Kansas City—B. Jackson 3 run (Lowery kick).
Kansas City—B. Jackson 3 run (Lowery kick).
Kansas City—Spani 91 fumble recovery (Lowery kick).

TEAM STATISTICS

	Kansas City	Oakland
First downs	22	21
Rushes-Yards	34-119	37-117
Passing yards	211	225
Sacks by-Yards	3-26	5-24
Return yards	79	158
Passes	17-35-3	19-47-4
Punts	9-34.8	9-37.0
Fumbles-Lost	1-1	2-2
Penalties-Yards	6-85	9-123
Time of possession	30:22	29:38
Attendance—38,500.		

INDIVIDUAL STATISTICS

Rushing—Kansas City, Fuller 3-43, B. Jackson 9-40, Hadnot 10-31, Delaney 11-5, Kenney 1-0; Oakland, King 11-49, Jensen 15-41, Wilson 3-24, Whittington 5-4, Willis 3-minus 1.

Passing—Kansas City, Kenney 8-25-3—132, Fuller 9-10-0—103; Oakland, Wilson 19-47-4—251.

Receiving—Kansas City, Marshall 5-85, Dixon 5-67, Smith 3-41, Rome 2-34, Hadnot 1-6, B. Jackson 1-2; Oakland, Branch 4-86, Jensen 4-42, Ramsey 3-37, Bradshaw 2-22, Whittington 2-23, Chandler 2-21, King 2-20.

Kickoff Returns—Kansas City, Murphy 2-39; Oakland, Willis 2-21, Whittington 3-91.

Punt Returns—Kansas City, Smith 3-20; Oakland, Watts 5-44.

Interceptions—Kansas City, Paul 1-5, Cherry 1-4, Green 2-11; Oakland, McKinney 1-0, O'Steen 1-2, Hayes 1-0.

Punting—Kansas City, Grupp 9-34.8; Oakland, Guy 9-37.0.

Field Goals—Kansas City, Lowery 0-1; Oakland, Bahr 1-2.

STEELERS 26, OILERS 13

PITTSBURGH—Quarterback Terry Bradshaw, one of the stalwarts of the great Steeler teams of the 1970's that won four Super Bowls, achieved a career milestone that few others have attained in Pittsburgh's 26-13 victory over Houston.

Bradshaw became only the 16th quarterback in the history of the NFL to surpass the 25,000-yard passing mark as the Steelers continued their dominance over the Oilers.

The victory put the Steelers back into a first-place tie with Cincinnati in the AFC Central Division race and dropped the Oilers into a second-place tie with Cleveland.

The Steelers did what they always seem to do when beating Houston—stop Earl Campbell. The NFL's three-time rushing champion and perennial All-Pro was held to only 56 yards on 23 carries. Campbell's career-best against Pittsburgh was just 109 yards in 1979.

"I don't have any excuses," said Campbell. "I made some mistakes and they capitalized on them." Campbell fumbled three times in the first half as the Steelers dominated play and took a 13-3 lead at the intermission.

Bradshaw, who completed 14 of 28 passes for 208 yards, threw a 46-yard TD pass to Jim Smith and David Trout hit two 19-yard field goals to account for the Steelers' points. Toni Fritsch connected on a 34-yarder to give the Oilers their only points in the half.

After a scoreless third period, the Oilers drew to within three points of the Steelers when Ken Stabler hit Dave Casper on a 52-yard pass play. They tied the score on their next possession when, on a fourth-down gamble at their own 35, Houston punter Cliff Parsley hit Adger Armstrong with a 31-yard pass. Shortly afterward, Fritsch tied it with a 44-yard field goal.

But that was as close as the Oilers could get. On their next possession following Fritsch's kick, the Steelers drove down the field to score the go-ahead touchdown. Bradshaw hit John Stallworth from six yards out.

After Stabler was intercepted when Houston got the ball back, Franco Harris bulled over from the 1-yard line for an insurance touchdown.

MONDAY, OCTOBER 26
SCORE BY PERIODS

Houston	0	3	0	10—13
Pittsburgh	10	3	0	13—26

SCORING

Pittsburgh—Field goal Trout 19.
Pittsburgh—Smith 46 pass from Bradshaw (Trout kick).
Houston—Field goal Fritsch 34.
Pittsburgh—Field goal Trout 19.
Houston—Casper 52 pass from Stabler (Fritsch kick).
Houston—Field goal Fritsch 44.
Pittsburgh—Stallworth 6 pass from Bradshaw (kick failed).
Pittsburgh—Harris 1 run (Trout kick).

Eighth Week—Continued

TEAM STATISTICS

	Houston	Pittsburgh
First downs	13	22
Rushes-Yards	28-76	37-167
Passing yards	231	196
Sacks by-Yards	1-12	3-30
Return yards	163	94
Passes	16-24-1	14-28-1
Punts	4-50.5	5-46.4
Fumbles-Lost	5-2	0-0
Penalties-Yards	6-41	5-54
Time of possession	28:10	31:50

Attendance—52,732.

INDIVIDUAL STATISTICS

Rushing—Houston, Campbell 23-56, Stabler 2-0, Coleman 3-20; Pittsburgh, Harris 17-84, Pollard 15-64, Smith 1-15, Bradshaw 4-4.

Passing—Houston, Stabler 15-23-1—230, Parsley 1-1-0—31; Pittsburgh, Bradshaw 14-28-1—208.

Receiving—Houston, Renfro 4-79, Campbell 3-minus 1, Casper 3-93, Coleman 1-5, Burrough 2-35, T. Wilson 1-11, Armstrong 2-39; Pittsburgh, Harris 2-6, Smith 5-100, Pollard 3-28, Stallworth 4-74.

Kickoff Returns—Houston, Roaches 2-65, Tullis 3-61; Pittsburgh, Anderson 2-55, Hawthorne 1-26.

Punt Returns—Houston, Roaches 1-minus 4, Tullis 2-29; Pittsburgh, Smith 3-5.

Interceptions—Houston, Perry 1-12; Pittsburgh, Johnson 1-8.

Punting—Houston, Parsley 4-50.5; Pittsburgh, Colquitt 5-46.4.

Field Goals—Houston, Fritsch 2-3; Pittsburgh, Trout 2-2.

NINTH WEEK

BENGALS 34, OILERS 21

CINCINNATI—The Cincinnati Bengals were atop the AFC Central Division, thanks to quarterback Ken Anderson. In the Bengals' romp over Houston, he completed 21 of 30 passes for 281 yards and three touchdowns.

After nine games, the 11-year veteran had completed more than 63 percent of his passes, thrown for 15 touchdowns and been intercepted only four times.

"The way Anderson's been playing, he's the difference," said Cincinnati receiver Cris Collinsworth. "If he's not in the Pro Bowl, something's wrong with the game."

"It feels really good," Anderson said of the Bengals' 6-3 record, "but we're still a long, long way from making the playoffs."

Cincinnati Coach Forrest Gregg said his team wanted the game badly. That was obvious in the second quarter, when the Bengals outscored the Oilers, 24-0, to wipe out a 7-0 first-quarter disadvantage. The Bengals led, 34-7, early in the fourth quarter, and only a couple of Houston touchdowns late in the game made the final score respectable.

Houston quarterback Kenny Stabler threw three interceptions, all of which were converted into scores—two touchdowns and a field goal. The key interception came midway through the second quarter, with the score 7-7.

Cincinnati linebacker Glenn Cameron picked off the Stabler pass at the Bengals' 33-yard line and from then on, it was all Cincinnati.

The Bengals scored 17 points in just 3:14 for a 24-7 halftime lead. Anderson threw touchdown passes of eight yards to tight end Dan Ross and 18 yards to Collinsworth. Jim Breech kicked a 51-yard field goal, the longest of his career.

In the second half, Breech kicked a 30-yarder and Anderson fired a 14-yard scoring pass to Ross.

NOVEMBER 1
SCORE BY PERIODS

Houston	7	0	0	14—21
Cincinnati	0	24	3	7—34

SCORING

Houston—Renfro 25 pass from Stabler (Fritsch kick).
Cincinnati—Johnson 4 run (Breech kick).
Cincinnati—Ross 8 pass from Anderson (Breech kick).
Cincinnati—Collinsworth 18 pass from Anderson (Breech kick).
Cincinnati—Field goal Breech 51.
Cincinnati—Field goal Breech 30.
Cincinnati—Ross 14 pass from Anderson (Breech kick).
Houston—Burrough 51 pass from Reaves (Fritsch kick).
Houston—Coleman 1 run (Fritsch kick).

TEAM STATISTICS

	Houston	Cincinnati
First downs	21	25
Rushes-Yards	26-132	36-156
Passing yards	301	266
Sacks by-Yards	2-15	0-0
Return yards	86	127
Passes	25-37-3	21-30-0
Punts	3-39.7	5-45.8
Fumbles-Lost	3-1	1-1
Penalties-Yards	7-60	4-35
Time of possession	30:14	29:46

Attendance—54,736.

INDIVIDUAL STATISTICS

Rushing—Houston, Campbell 14-74, Coleman 5-9, Armstrong 6-49, Stabler 1-0; Cincinnati, Johnson 26-114, Alexander 1-2, Anderson 4-15, A. Griffin 2-14, Hargrove 3-11.

Passing—Houston, Stabler 22-33-3—211, Reaves 3-4-0—90; Cincinnati, Anderson 21-30-0—281.

Receiving—Houston, Renfro 8-81, Casper 4-56, T. Wilson 2-9, Campbell 1-2, Holston 2-26, Burrough 2-55, Coleman 4-62, Barber 1-3, Armstrong 1-7; Cincinnati, Collinsworth 5-82, Alexander 2-5, Ross 6-83, Curtis 2-21, A. Griffin 1-9, M. Harris 2-55, Johnson 3-26.

Kickoff Returns—Houston, Tullis 2-25, Armstrong 2-33, J. C. Wilson 2-27; Cincinnati, Verser 3-53.

Punt Returns—Houston, Roaches 3-1; Cincinnati, Simmons 1-11.

Interceptions—Cincinnati, Cameron 1-0, Williams 1-14, B. Harris 1-49.

Punting—Houston, Parsley 3-39.7; Cincinnati, McInally 5-45.8.

Field Goals—Houston, Fritsch 0-1; Cincinnati, Breech 2-2.

COWBOYS 17, EAGLES 14

PHILADELPHIA—Something bad always seems to happen to Tony Dorsett whenever the Dallas Cowboy running back plays at Veterans Stadium.

The Vet was a chamber of horrors to Dorsett in the 1980 season. In the Cowboys' regular-season appearance there, Dorsett suffered cracked ribs and gained only 17 yards as the Philadelphia Eagles won, 17-10. Then, in the National Football Conference championship game, he coughed up a fumble that helped the Eagles to a 20-7 victory and a berth in Super Bowl XV.

Dorsett's jinx continued into 1981. He lost a fumble inside the Philadelphia 5-yard line in the first half and in the third quarter, with Dallas driving at the Eagles' 15, a pass slipped through his fingers and into the arms of Philadelphia linebacker Jerry Robinson at the 3.

But Dorsett's bad luck didn't last all day. The NFL's leading rusher slashed off left guard for a nine-yard touchdown run with 7 minutes, 24 seconds left, capping a 14-point fourth quarter that gave Dallas a 17-14 victory over the Eagles and a share of first place in the NFC Eastern Division.

"No, I don't feel snakebitten when I come here," said Dorsett, who gained 78 yards in 20 carries to boost his rushing total to 972 yards in nine games. "You have good days and bad days. Today wasn't a great day for me, but the touchdown made up for it."

After Dorsett's TD, the Cowboys held their breath as reserve quarterback Joe Pisarcik moved the Eagles to the Dallas 16 on a last-gasp drive, but Tony Franklin missed a 34-yard field goal attempt with 1:46 left to play.

For a while, Dorsett's errors loomed large. Just three plays after Robinson's interception in the third quarter, the Eagles took a 14-3 lead when Ron Jaworski connected with Harold Carmichael on an 85-yard pass play. Rookie cornerback Everson Walls fell as Carmichael caught the ball at midfield, and the wide receiver had clear sailing.

But the Eagles' bomb only served to spur the Cowboys.

"The character of this team shows in that we really come out fighting when our backs are against the wall," said quarterback Danny White. "It's easy to crawl into a hole and say, 'Forget it.' But we play our best football when we're behind. We get fired up."

White drove the Cowboys 75 yards and hit tight end Doug Cosbie with a 17-yard TD pass on a broken-play scramble with 12:45 left.

"That was the big play for us," said Dallas Coach Tom Landry. "The Eagles were very confident until Cosbie made that catch."

The Dallas defense then backed Philadelphia to its 3 with the help of Ed Jones' sack of Jaworski, and the Cowboys got the ball back on the Eagles' 39. Dorsett opened the scoring drive with a 15-yard run. On his TD run, he dragged an Eagles tackler the last three yards.

On Philadelphia's last drive, blitzing Dallas cornerback Dennis Thurman was called for roughing Jaworski at the Eagles' 28. Jaworski left the game with bruised ribs, but Pisarcik kept the drive going with a 24-yard pass to Carmichael and a 10-yard scramble. At the Dallas 16, a third-down pass was tipped by the Cowboys' Walls and then dropped by wide-receiver Rodney Parker at the goal line. Then Franklin's field-goal attempt went wide to the left.

NOVEMBER 1
SCORE BY PERIODS

Dallas	0	3	0	14	—17
Philadelphia	0	7	7	0	—14

SCORING

Dallas—Field goal Septien 31.
Philadelphia—Montgomery 2 run (Franklin kick).
Philadelphia—Carmichael 85 pass from Jaworski (Franklin kick).
Dallas—Cosbie 17 pass from D. White (Septien kick).
Dallas—Dorsett 9 run (Septien kick).

TEAM STATISTICS

	Dallas	Philadelphia
First downs	19	17
Rushes-Yards	37-141	24-94
Passing yards	176	197
Sacks by-Yards	4-40	4-27
Return yards	123	138
Passes	13-24-2	12-27-1
Punts	4-45.0	5-40.8
Fumbles-Lost	4-1	1-0
Penalties-Yards	4-42	10-76
Time of possession	32:47	27:13
Attendance—72,111.		

INDIVIDUAL STATISTICS

Rushing—Dallas, Dorsett 20-78, Springs 8-32, Newhouse 6-24, D. White 2-5, Cosbie 1-2; Philadelphia, Montgomery 15-67, Oliver 6-12, Pisarcik 1-10, Russell 1-4, Carmichael 1-1.

Passing—Dallas, D. White 13-24-2—203; Philadelphia, Jaworski 10-21-1—191, Pisarcik 2-6-0—46.

Receiving—Dallas, Hill 6-121, Pearson 3-30, Cosbie 2-31, Saldi 1-12, Dorsett 1-9; Philadelphia, Carmichael 5-151, Smith 3-33, Spagnola 1-28, Parker 1-16, Krepfle 1-7, Campfield 1-2.

Kickoff Returns—Dallas, Newsome 3-73; Philadelphia, Henry 4-86.

Punt Returns—Dallas, J. Jones 3-29; Philadelphia, Henry 4-25.

Interceptions—Dallas, Downs 1-21; Philadelphia, Wilson 1-24, Robinson 1-3.

Punting—Dallas, D. White 4-45.0; Philadelphia, Runager 5-40.8.

Field Goals—Dallas, Septien 1-1; Philadelphia, Franklin 0-1.

BUCS 20, BEARS 10

TAMPA—Coach John McKay was at his stinging best after Tampa Bay used two long scoring passes and a pair of field goals by Bill Capece to beat Chicago. During the build-up to the game, Bears safety Gary Fencik had been quoted as saying that the Buccaneers lacked patience on offense and that the Bears could deal with the "big plays."

So, McKay's analysis of the game was: "The Tampa Bay Buccaneers, with great patience, defeated the Chicago Bears at Tampa Stadium." He added, "The Bears should quit talking. They've got problems with their team without trying to coach our team."

Ninth Week—Continued

Doug Williams hit tight end Jimmie Giles on an 81-yard scoring play in the second quarter and threw a 51-yard touchdown pass to wide receiver Kevin House in the third quarter. On Giles' score, he caught the ball at the Tampa Bay 40 and outran safety Doug Plank for the 60 yards to the end zone.

Last year, Giles had been the victim of spearing by Plank in a Monday night game. Said Giles of his TD play, "The biggest pleasure about it is being a big part of winning the football game. It made it even better because it was against him."

The Bucs rushed for 209 yards, their first 200-plus game of the season. Jerry Eckwood gained 110 yards and James Owens, the former Olympic hurdler, picked up 68 yards on 10 carries.

The key defensive play came in the third period, with the Bucs leading by 10-3 and the Bears on the move at the Tampa Bay 23. Rookie linebacker Hugh Green intercepted a Vince Evans pass at the 20, and the Bucs went on to score on the Williams-to-House pass.

"The turning point was Green's interception," said Chicago Coach Neill Armstrong. "I felt we were going in at the time."

NOVEMBER 1
SCORE BY PERIODS

Chicago	3	0	0	7	—10
Tampa Bay	0	10	7	3	—20

SCORING

Chicago—Field goal Roveto 40.
Tampa Bay—Field goal Capece 46.
Tampa Bay—Giles 81 pass from Williams (Capece kick).
Tampa Bay—House 51 pass from Williams (Capece kick).
Chicago—Payton 1 run (Roveto kick).
Tampa Bay—Field goal Capece 30.

TEAM STATISTICS

	Chicago	Tampa Bay
First downs	18	15
Rushes-Yards	30-92	37-209
Passing yards	233	183
Sacks by-Yards	1-9	1-6
Return yards	142	68
Passes	21-36-2	9-21-1
Punts	5-36.8	4-43.8
Fumbles-Lost	3-1	2-0
Penalties-Yards	5-39	5-47
Time of possession	32:45	27:15
Attendance—63,688.		

INDIVIDUAL STATISTICS

Rushing—Chicago, Payton 22-92, Suhey 6-minus 2, McClendon 1-2, Evans 1-0; Tampa Bay, Eckwood 21-110, Wilder 3-3, Williams 3-28, Owens 10-68.

Passing—Chicago, Evans 21-36-2—239; Tampa Bay, Williams 9-21-1—192.

Receiving—Chicago, Margerum 6-78, Payton 5-28, Suhey 4-17, Baschnagel 3-40, Cobb 1-11, Watts 2-65; Tampa Bay, Wilder 1-10, T. Bell 1-5, Eckwood 3-23, House 3-73, Giles 1-81.

Kickoff Returns—Chicago, J. Fisher 1-12, Frazier 1-13, Moorehead 2-51; Tampa Bay, Owens 1-27.

Punt Returns—Chicago, J. Fisher 2-62; Tampa Bay, Holt 1-12.

Interceptions—Chicago, Schmidt 1-4; Tampa Bay, Washington 1-23, Green 1-6.

Punting—Chicago, Parsons 5-36.8; Tampa Bay, Swider 4-43.8.

Field Goals—Chicago, Roveto 1-1; Tampa Bay, Capece 2-4.

JETS 26, GIANTS 7

EAST RUTHERFORD—The game for the bragging rights of New York City turned into a public mugging of Giants quarterback Phil Simms in Giants Stadium.

The Jets defense sacked Simms nine times and limited the Giants to 166 yards total offense and 10 first downs. The win boosted the Jets record to 4-4-1.

Jets defensive ends Mark Gastineau and Joe Klecko accounted for seven of the nine sacks and are tied for the team lead with 11½ each.

"They were the better team and they certainly out-played us," said Giants Coach Ray Perkins, who saw his team's three-game winning streak snapped as the Giants' record fell to 5-4. "That was the best pass rush we've faced all year."

The Jets defense, which had been yielding 25 points per game, registered a shutout. The lone Giants score came late in the third quarter when safety Beasley Reece scooped up a fumble by Jets punter Chuck Ramsey and ran four yards for a touchdown.

That cut the Jets' lead to 16-7 and they were forced to punt four downs later. Then Gastineau sacked Simms twice for 19 yards in losses and Jets quarterback Richard Todd hooked up with receiver Wesley Walker for a 39-yard touchdown pass.

Jets safety Darrol Ray was another defensive standout. He deflected a pass late in the second quarter to prevent a touchdown on a fake field goal attempt and returned an interception 64 yards for a touchdown.

"Darrol's play really epitomizes the kind of day our defense had," said Klecko.

The Jets offense was led by Walker and placekicker Pat Leahy. Walker caught six passes for 142 yards and set up all four of Leahy's field goals. Leahy connected from 37, 33, 42 and 38 yards and has now succeeded on nine straight attempts.

"The most important thing is that we're at .500," said Jets Coach Walt Michaels. "All that talk about bragging rights gets a little exaggerated. . . . I've said over and over that you have to win the November games if you're serious about the playoffs.

"This team wanted it. They were aggressive throughout and good things happen when you play that way."

NOVEMBER 1
SCORE BY PERIODS

New York Jets	0	13	3	10	—26
New York Giants	0	0	7	0	— 7

Jets defensive end Mark Gastineau led a defense that sacked Giants quarterback Phil Simms nine times as the game for the bragging rights of New York City turned into a Giant bludgeoning. The Jets triumphed, 26-7.

SCORING

New York Jets—Field goal Leahy 37.
New York Jets—Field goal Leahy 33.
New York Jets—Walker 39 pass from Todd (Leahy kick).
New York Jets—Field goal Leahy 42.
New York Giants—Reece 4 fumble return (Danelo kick).
New York Jets—Field goal Leahy 38.
New York Jets—Ray 54 interception return (Leahy kick).

TEAM STATISTICS

	Jets	Giants
First downs	13	10
Rushes-Yards	35-114	15-55
Passing yards	185	111
Sacks by-Yards	9-71	3-22
Return yards	185	157
Passes	13-30-0	22-36-1
Punts	8-40.5	10-45.0
Fumbles-Lost	2-1	3-2
Penalties-Yards	11-91	6-61
Time of possession	31:59	28:01

Attendance—74,740.

INDIVIDUAL STATISTICS

Rushing—Jets, Harper 8-28, Dierking 7-23, Augustyniak 12-41, Long 2-8, Newton 4-8, Todd 1-6, Ramsey 1-0; Giants, Carpenter, 8-24, Bright 6-27, L. Jackson 1-4.

Passing—Jets, Todd 13-30-0—207; Giants, Simms 22-35-1—182, Brunner 0-1-0—0.

Receiving—Jets, Walker 6-142, Augustyniak 2-11, L. Jones 1-6, Harper 3-35, Barkum 1-13; Giants, Perkins 4-80, Carpenter 5-13, Bright 7-52, Shirk 2-17, Mullady 1-5, Friede 1-12, Mistler 1-4, L. Jackson 1-minus 1.

Kickoff Returns—Jets, Harper 2-60; Giants, Bright 2-51, Garrett 4-86, Dennis 1-17.

Punt Returns—Jets, Harper 6-61; Giants, Bright 1-6, Garrett 1-minus 3.

Interceptions—Jets, Ray 1-64.

Punting—Jets, Ramsey 8-40.5; Giants, Jennings 10-45.0.

Field Goals—Jets, Leahy 4-4; Giants, None attempted.

PACKERS 34, SEAHAWKS 24

GREEN BAY—David Whitehurst was given his first start in nearly two years and responded by passing for three touchdowns and running for a fourth in Green Bay's triumph over Seattle.

Whitehurst threw TD passes of eight and 38 yards to wide receiver James Lofton and seven yards to tight end Paul Coffman. He scored himself on a one-yard sneak. He overcame two first-quarter interceptions to finish the day 19-for-31 for 205 yards.

Whitehurst had not started since November 25, 1979, against Philadelphia. However, he had played most of the way in the Packers' 31-27 loss to Detroit the week prior to the Seattle game. He completed 20 of 36 passes for 243 yards in that game after Lynn Dickey went down with a back injury.

After producing Green Bay's first home victory of the season, Whitehurst was the last Packer to leave Lambeau Field. He was applauded by fans who used to boo him.

The game was tied at 21-21 at halftime, as Seattle safety John Harris returned an inter-ception 42 yards for a TD and Jim Zorn threw two scoring passes to fullback Dan Doornink. A 54-yard field goal by Efren Herrera—the longest of his career—sent the Seahawks ahead, 24-21, in the third period. Whitehurst then put Green Bay on top to stay with his 38-yarder to Lofton, and Jan Stenerud kicked two fourth-quarter field goals.

With 9:17 left in the game and Seattle trailing, 28-24, Coach Jack Patera pulled Zorn and replaced him with Dave Krieg. The second-year quarterback could not get the Seahawks on the scoreboard and threw an interception to Rich Wingo that set up Stenerud's last field goal.

NOVEMBER 1
SCORE BY PERIODS

Seattle	7	14	3	0	24
Green Bay	7	14	7	6	34

SCORING

Seattle—Harris 42 interception return (Herrera kick).
Green Bay—Coffman 7 pass from Whitehurst (Stenerud kick).
Seattle—Doornink 12 pass from Zorn (Herrera kick).
Green Bay—Whitehurst 1 run (Stenerud kick).
Green Bay—Lofton 8 pass from Whitehurst (Stenerud kick).
Seattle—Doornink 14 pass from Zorn (Herrera kick).
Seattle—Field goal Herrera 54.
Green Bay—Lofton 38 pass from Whitehurst (Stenerud kick).
Green Bay—Field goal Stenerud 19.
Green Bay—Field goal Stenerud 36.

TEAM STATISTICS

	Seattle	Green Bay
First downs	15	25
Rushes-Yards	26-119	43-182
Passing yards	102	195
Sacks by-Yards	2-10	5-31
Return yards	183	107
Passes	14-28-1	19-31-2
Punts	7-38.7	5-35.6
Fumbles-Lost	3-2	2-1
Penalties-Yards	7-65	6-39
Time of possession	26:08	33:52

Attendance—49,467.

INDIVIDUAL STATISTICS

Rushing—Seattle, Doornink 5-22, T. Brown 17-89, Jodat 2-7, Smith 1-minus 1, Zorn 1-2; Green Bay, Ellis 23-127, Huckleby 8-25, Middleton 6-16, Jensen 2-5, Whitehurst 4-9.

Passing—Seattle, Zorn 12-23-0—108, Krieg 2-5-1—25; Green Bay, Whitehurst 19-31-2—205.

Receiving—Seattle, Largent 3-45, Smith 3-18, Doornink 5-36, McCullum 2-26, T. Brown 1-8; Green Bay, Lofton 4-63, Ellis 4-11, Jensen 2-21, Huckleby 2-31, Coffman 3-30, Middleton 2-35, Jefferson 2-14.

Kickoff Returns—Seattle, Lewis 1-4, Johns 5-81, Dufek 1-17; Green Bay, Lee 1-21, Huckleby 1-19, Braggs 1-0, Middleton 1-21.

Punt Returns—Seattle, Johns 3-21; Green Bay, Cassidy 1-0, Lee 2-8.

Interceptions—Seattle, Harris 2-60; Green Bay, Wingo 1-38.

Punting—Seattle, West 7-38.7; Green Bay, Stachowicz 5-35.6.

Field Goals—Seattle, Herrera 1-1; Green Bay, Stenerud 2-2.

REDSKINS 42, CARDINALS 21

WASHINGTON—Linebacker Mel Kaufman, who made the Washington roster on a fluke, contributed two key interceptions to help the Redskins defeat St. Louis for their third victory in the last four games.

Kaufman stopped a Cardinal scoring threat with an end-zone interception in the first period. He grabbed a deflected pass in the third quarter and returned it 25 yards to the Washington 46, setting up a touchdown drive that gave the Redskins a 28-0 lead.

Kaufman, a rookie free-agent from California Poly-San Luis Obispo, had no thoughts of an NFL career until he caught the eye of Redskins General Manager Bobby Beathard, a Cal Poly product, as an extra in a workout at the school a year ago. Kaufman signed a free-agent contract, made the Redskins' roster and then got a chance to play when the team had injury problems at linebacker.

Jim Hart threw three fourth-quarter scoring passes for the Cardinals, but the Redskins countered those TDs with two of their own. Mike Nelms returned a kickoff 84 yards to set up Joe Theismann's second TD pass of the day to Art Monk.

An interception by linebacker Monte Coleman at the St. Louis 30 led to John Riggins' third scoring run of the game.

Hart was 24-for-39 for 305 yards and moved into third place in career passing yardage with 33,649 (he trails only Fran Tarkenton and Johnny Unitas). But Hart was victimized by four interceptions.

Theismann completed 14 of 19 passes for 219 yards and three touchdowns. He burned Cardinals cornerback Carl Allen on a 38-yard strike to Monk and on a 51-yarder to Virgil Seay in the first quarter. In the second period, Allen was called for interference on a pass to the end zone, giving the Redskins a first down at the 1-yard line. Riggins scored on the next play.

"I told Carl he should have been playing a different type of coverage, but I don't want to place him in the 'goat' category," said St. Louis Coach Jim Hanifan. "It's a team game and a team loss."

NOVEMBER 1
SCORE BY PERIODS

St. Louis	0	0	0	21	21
Washington	14	7	7	14	42

SCORING

Washington—Monk 38 pass from Theismann (Moseley kick).
Washington—Seay 51 pass from Theismann (Moseley kick).
Washington—Riggins 1 run (Moseley kick).
Washington—Riggins 1 run (Moseley kick).
St. Louis—Green 11 pass from Hart (O'Donoghue kick).
Washington—Monk 10 pass from Theismann (Moseley kick).
St. Louis—Tilley 14 pass from Hart (O'Donoghue kick).
St. Louis—Tilley 14 pass from Hart (O'Donoghue kick).
Washington—Riggins 4 run (Moseley kick).

TEAM STATISTICS

	St. Louis	Washington
First downs	29	25
Rushes-Yards	22-130	39-160
Passing yards	319	201
Sacks by-Yards	1-18	3-15
Return yards	166	243
Passes	27-47-4	14-19-0
Punts	2-50.0	3-39.7
Fumbles-Lost	1-0	1-1
Penalties-Yards	10-84	6-27
Time of possession	29:08	30:52

Attendance—50,643.

INDIVIDUAL STATISTICS

Rushing—St. Louis, Anderson 18-122, Morris 3-8, Mitchell 1-0; Washington, Riggins 14-53, Washington 23-93, Claitt 2-14.

Passing—St. Louis, Hart 24-39-4—305, Lomax 3-8-0—29; Washington, Theismann 14-19-0—219.

Receiving—St. Louis, Gray 4-38, Tilley 8-96, Anderson 3-30, Green 3-62, Harrell 1-17, Morris 1-3, LaFleur 3-45, Mitchell 2-3; Washington, Monk 3-77, Washington 4-22, Thompson 1-12, Warren 3-42, Seay 1-51, Metcalf 2-15.

Kickoff Returns—St. Louis, Mitchell 7-141; Washington, Nelms 3-151, Seay 1-17.

Punt Returns—St. Louis, Mitchell 3-25; Washington, Nelms 2-45.

Interceptions—Washington, Murphy 1-5, Kaufman 2-25, Coleman 1-0.

Punting—St. Louis, Birdsong 2-50.0; Washington, Connell 3-39.7.

Field Goals—St. Louis, O'Donoghue 0-2; Washington, Moseley 0-1.

CHARGERS 22, CHIEFS 20

SAN DIEGO—Rolf Benirschke, the San Diego Chargers' placekicker, could see it coming. So when his chance came to make amends for missing an extra point against the Kansas City Chiefs, he was already pumped up.

Benirschke was called on with 13 seconds left and he responded with a 22-yard field goal that gave the Chargers a 22-20 victory. The result left the Chiefs and Chargers tied for first place in the American Football Conference's Western Division, each with a 6-3 record.

"Any kicker, I think, likes it to come down to him," Benirschke said. "I just didn't want it to come down to us losing because of my missed extra point."

Benirschke said he watched the situation developing in the game's closing minutes. "I was hoping to get a chance for the field goal," he said. "We've lost two close games to field goals in the last few seconds, so this time it was our turn."

The Chiefs, overcoming a 19-7 San Diego lead at halftime, forged ahead on a 32-yard field goal by Nick Lowery with 6 minutes, 32 seconds left. Bill Kenney threw a two-yard touchdown pass to Billy Jackson in the third quarter and Lowery booted a 21-yard field goal early in the fourth quarter.

After Lowery's kick, the Chargers marched 70 yards in 16 plays to the Kansas City 4 to get in position for Benirschke's game-winning boot. The key play came on fourth down and nine from the Chiefs' 47, when quarterback Dan Fouts unleashed a 23-yard pass to wide receiver Wes Chandler.

Chuck Muncie provided the early power for the Chargers. He ran for two first-half TDs and Benrischke kicked two field goals.

Rookie Joe Delaney, just off the injured list, rushed for 117 yards in 23 carries for the Chiefs. "With two minutes to go, I thought we had the game wrapped up," Delaney said. "But as you saw, anything can happen and it did."

NOVEMBER 1
SCORE BY PERIODS

Kansas City	7	0	7	6	—20
San Diego	7	12	0	3	—22

SCORING

San Diego—Muncie 1 run (Benirschke kick).
Kansas City—Hadnot 2 run (Lowery kick).
San Diego—Muncie 4 run (kick failed).
San Diego—Field goal Benirschke 29.
San Diego—Field goal Benirschke 19.
Kansas City—B. Jackson 2 pass from Kenney (Lowery kick).
Kansas City—Field goal Lowery 21.
Kansas City—Field goal Lowery 32.
San Diego—Field goal Benirschke 22.

TEAM STATISTICS

	Kansas City	San Diego
First downs	26	21
Rushes-Yards	41-177	25-82
Passing yards	162	297
Sacks by-Yards	0-0	4-28
Return yards	100	83
Passes	13-22-0	24-39-1
Punts	5-35.2	4.48.0
Fumbles-Lost	5-3	6-3
Penalties-Yards	10-74	8-48
Time of possession	34:53	25:07
Attendance—51,307.		

INDIVIDUAL STATISTICS

Rushing—Kansas City, Delaney 23-117, Hadnot 10-47, Kenney 4-7, B. Jackson 4-6; San Diego, Muncie 16-63, J. Brooks 5-23, C. Williams 3-7, Chandler 1-minus 11.

Passing—Kansas City, Kenney 13-22-0—190; San Diego, Fouts 24-39-1—297.

Receiving—Kansas City, Smith 5-92, Dixon 3-32, Marshall 2-44, Scott 1-26, B. Jackson 1-2, Delaney 1-minus 6; San Diego, Muncie 6-71, J. Brooks 6-62, Winslow 6-38, Joiner 3-48, Chandler 2-47, Sievers 1-31.

Kickoff Returns—Kansas City, Murphy 3-45, Bledsoe 1-18; San Diego, J. Brooks 3-48, Smith 1-20, Chandler 1-14.

Punt Returns—Kansas City, Smith 4-37; San Diego, Phillips 1-0, Edwards 1-1.

Interceptions—Kansas City, Green 1-0.

Punting—Kansas City, Grupp 5-35.2; San Diego, Roberts 4-48.0.

Field Goals—Kansas City, Lowery 2-2; San Diego, Benirschke 3-3.

DOLPHINS 27, COLTS 10

MIAMI—After the bitter disappointment of a last-minute defeat at Dallas, the Miami Dolphins recovered quickly by downing the Balti-more Colts.

The victory upped Miami's record to 6-2-1 and maintained its half-game lead in the AFC East over Buffalo. The Colts suffered their eighth straight loss after an opening-game triumph over New England.

The game was particularly satisfying for Miami safety Lyle Blackwood, traded by the Colts in the preseason after nine years with the club. Because of his knowledge of the Colts system, Blackwood was able to help the Dolphins' defense contain quarterback Bert Jones. Blackwood even picked off a Jones pass.

"I'd been there so long that many times I can tell by the way he holds his head, which way he looks, what he's going to do," Blackwood said.

The Dolphins scored on David Woodley's three-yard quarterback draw and a 22-yard Woodley pass to Duriel Harris in the first half. The Colts stayed close with a three-yard touchdown throw from Jones to halfback Don McCauley and a 44-yard field goal by Mike Wood.

The Dolphins took command in the third quarter on a 41-yard field goal by Uwe von Schamann and a seven-yard scoring pass from Woodley to tight end Ronnie Lee. Von Schamann added a 32-yarder in the fourth period.

Two Colts touchdown passes were called back by penalties during a last gasp drive that ended when Miami safety Don Bessillieu intercepted a Jones pass in the end zone. The Colts were called for five holding penalties in all. Baltimore Coach Mike McCormack and Jones said the officials refused to tell them who was at fault or what they did.

"We asked the officials who and how, but they wouldn't answer us today," said McCormack. "It's frustrating for kids trying to learn."

NOVEMBER 1
SCORE BY PERIODS

Baltimore	0	10	0	0	—10
Miami	7	7	10	3	—27

SCORING

Miami—Woodley 3 run (von Schamann kick).
Baltimore—McCauley 3 pass from B. Jones (Wood kick).
Miami—Harris 22 pass from Woodley (von Schamann kick).
Baltimore—Field goal Wood 44.
Miami—Field goal von Schamann 41.
Miami—Lee 7 pass from Woodley (von Schamann kick).
Miami—Field goal von Schamann 32.

TEAM STATISTICS

	Baltimore	Miami
First downs	19	19
Rushes-Yards	21-68	33-146
Passing yards	240	164
Sacks by-Yards	0-0	1-8
Return yards	49	45
Passes	23-37-2	14-25-0
Punts	4-34.3	3-42.0
Fumbles-Lost	2-1	0-0
Penalties-Yards	7-58	6-55
Time of possession	27:58	32:02
Attendance—46,061.		

Rushing—Baltimore, Dickey 9-31, McMillan 9-30, Dixon 2-6, McCauley 1-1; Miami, Nathan 8-40, Franklin 23-101, Woodley 2-5.

Passing—Baltimore, B. Jones 23-37-2—248; Miami, Woodley 14-25-0—164.

Receiving—Baltimore, McCall 2-36, Dickey 2-25, McMillan 9-78, McCauley 6-59, Butler 2-25, Dixon 1-5, Carr 1-20; Miami, Nathan 5-36, Hardy 4-54, Harris 2-35, Cefalo 2-32, Lee 1-7.

Kickoff Returns—Baltimore, Williams 3-47; Miami, Giaquinto 1-22.

Punt Returns—Baltimore, Shula 1-2; Miami, Vigorito 2-12.

Interceptions—Miami, L. Blackwood 1-11, Bessillieu 1-0.

Punting—Baltimore, Garrett 4-34.3; Miami, Orosz 3-42.0.

Field Goals—Baltimore, Wood 1-1; Miami, von Schamann 2-2.

BILLS 22, BROWNS 13

ORCHARD PARK—After Buffalo had lost three of its first seven games, the explanation was that the defense wasn't dominating opponents as it did in 1980.

Well, Cleveland quarterback Brian Sipe was the first to admit that the Bills' defense is back on the right track. The Bills sacked Sipe six times for 59 yards and stalled a Browns passing attack that had gained 444 yards a week earlier.

"They played us about as good as can be done," Sipe said.

The Browns were limited to 14 first downs and 152 yards in total offense. Sipe completed only 14 of 37 passes for 140 yards and suffered three interceptions.

"I'm just real proud of the way our defense played," said Buffalo Coach Chuck Knox, whose team raised its record to 6-3 to stay one-half game back in the AFC East. "They just came back time and time again and really put pressure on the quarterback."

Safety Bill Simpson, who had two interceptions, credited the offense as well.

"We (the defense) spent a lot of time on the field, but came up with some big plays." Simpson said. "We had a heck of a pass rush, and I think that was the key to the game. But the offense came up with the big play when they had to."

The Browns' defense had nothing to be ashamed of except for occasional lapses in covering halfback Joe Cribbs on pass plays. Cribbs caught five throws from Joe Ferguson for 163 yards.

Ferguson completed just 14 of 30 passes, but totaled 297 yards. His three TD tosses boosted his season total to 19.

Matt Bahr's second field goal of the game pulled Cleveland within seven points in the third period. Later in the quarter, the Bills were awarded a safety when Browns backup quarterback Paul McDonald was penalized for intentionally grounding in the end zone. The Browns then pulled within 15-13 on Sipe's 12-yard scoring pass to tight end Ozzie Newsome.

The Browns had two touchdowns called back because of holding penalties.

NOVEMBER 1
SCORE BY PERIODS

Cleveland	0	3	3	7—13
Buffalo	6	7	2	7—22

SCORING

Buffalo—Cribbs 58 pass from Ferguson (bad snap).
Buffalo—Cribbs 15 pass from Ferguson (Mike-Mayer kick).
Cleveland—Field goal Bahr 36.
Cleveland—Field goal Bahr 39.
Buffalo—Safety, McDonald intentional grounding in end zone.
Cleveland—Newsome 12 pass from Sipe (Bahr kick).
Buffalo—Cribbs 60 pass from Ferguson (Mike-Mayer kick).

TEAM STATISTICS

	Cleveland	Buffalo
First downs	12	21
Rushes-Yards	20-71	44-172
Passing yards	140	297
Sacks by-Yards	0-0	6-59
Return yards	116	157
Passes	14-38-3	14-30-1
Punts	8-45.0	6-38.7
Fumbles-Lost	2-0	4-4
Penalties-Yards	5-30	8-125
Time of possession	25:27	34:33

Attendance—80,020.

INDIVIDUAL STATISTICS

Rushing—Cleveland, M. Pruitt 13-39, White 2-4, G. Pruitt 3-32, Sipe 2-6; Buffalo, Cribbs 23-85, Brown 14-58, Leaks 3-15, Hooks 2-4, Ferguson 1-minus 1, Brammer 1-11.

Passing—Cleveland, Sipe 14-37-3—199, McDonald 0-1-0—0; Buffalo, Ferguson 14-30-1—297.

Receiving—Cleveland, Newsome 3-52, G. Pruitt 2-19, Feacher 2-62, M. Pruitt 4-20, C. Miller 1-16, Rucker 1-11, Logan 1-19; Buffalo, Lewis 5-97, Cribbs 5-163, Butler 3-29, Hooks 1-8.

Kickoff Returns—Cleveland, Hall 2-42, M. Miller 1-6; Buffalo, Franklin 3-73.

Punt Returns—Cleveland, Hall 2-23; Buffalo, Hooks 2-14.

Interceptions—Cleveland, Darden 1-45; Buffalo, Simpson 2-42, Clark 1-28.

Punting—Cleveland, Cox 8-45.0; Buffalo, Cater 6-38.7.

Field Goals—Cleveland, Bahr 2-2; Buffalo, None attempted.

FALCONS 41, SAINTS 10

NEW ORLEANS—Alfred Jenkins hauled in touchdown strikes of 48, 60 and 47 yards from Steve Bartkowski in Atlanta's romp past New Orleans. The three TD receptions set a single-game Falcons record and increased Jenkins' season total to 11 touchdowns, also a club record. Jenkins caught five passes for 179 yards.

Bartkowski completed 14 of 20 passes for 258 yards. All of his scoring passes to Jenkins came after the Saints had rallied from a 10-0 deficit to tie the score in the second quarter on a Benny Ricardo field goal and a 46-yard TD pass from Archie Manning to Guido Merkens.

Jenkins beat free safety Tommy Myers on the 48-yard TD to give Atlanta a 17-10 lead.

William Andrews ran for an Atlanta score before halftime and in the second half, Jenkins burned cornerback Mike Spivey for his last two scoring plays.

Atlanta scored 10 points in 32 seconds in the first quarter. Mick Luckhurst kicked a 25-yard field goal and then, after Don Smith recovered a fumble by the Saints' George Rogers, wide receiver Wallace Francis ran eight yards to score on a double reverse.

When Atlanta beat the Saints in the season opener, Rogers had been held to 63 yards rushing and he vowed that the Falcons would "see a lot more of me this time." He was held to 20 yards in 15 carries. Asked if the Falcons had exchanged words with him on the field, he said, "I think their actions spoke for them."

NOVEMBER 1

SCORE BY PERIODS

Atlanta	10	14	10	7—41
New Orleans	0	10	0	0—10

SCORING

Atlanta—Field goal Luckhurst 25.
Atlanta—Francis 8 run (Luckhurst kick).
New Orleans—Field goal Ricardo 28.
New Orleans—Merkens 46 pass from Manning (Ricardo kick).
Atlanta—Jenkins 48 pass from Bartkowski (Luckhurst kick).
Atlanta—Andrews 1 run (Luckhurst kick).
Atlanta—Jenkins 60 pass from Bartkowski (Luckhurst kick).
Atlanta—Field goal Luckhurst 22.
Atlanta—Jenkins 47 pass from Bartkowski (Luckhurst kick).

TEAM STATISTICS

	Atlanta	New Orleans
First downs	20	14
Rushes-Yards	39-144	22-58
Passing yards	262	204
Sacks by-Yards	2-21	1-7
Return yards	172	142
Passes	15-22-1	22-38-1
Punts	4-39.0	7-45.1
Fumbles-Lost	0-0	3-2
Penalties-Yards	7-92	10-85
Time of possession	29:45	30:15

Attendance—63,637.

INDIVIDUAL STATISTICS

Rushing—Atlanta, Cain 14-29, Andrews 17-79, Francis 1-8, Mayberry 6-26, Robinson 1-2; New Orleans, G. Rogers 15-20. Holmes 1-minus 2, Groth 1-28, Merkens 1-minus 3, W. Wilson 2-5, Tyler 2-10.

Passing—Atlanta, Bartkowski 14-20-1—258, J. Jones 1-2-0—11; New Orleans, Manning 17-29-0—198, D. Wilson 9-1—27.

Receiving—Atlanta, Andrews 4-39, Jenkins 5-179, Miller 3-18, Jackson 2-26, Cain 1-7; New Orleans, Holmes 6-39, Merkens 4-85, Hardy 1-6, W. Wilson 4-16, Tyler 2-10, Brenner 3-52, G. Rogers 1-2, Martini 1-15.

Kickoff Returns—Atlanta, Woerner 3-73; New Orleans, J. Rogers 1-22, W. Wilson 4-72, Stauch 2-36.

Punt Returns—Atlanta, Woerner 4-58; New Orleans, Groth 1-10, Poe 1-2.

Interceptions—Atlanta, Butler 1-41; New Orleans, Wattelet 1-0.

Punting—Atlanta, James 4-39.0; New Orleans, Erxleben 7-45.1.

Field Goals—Atlanta, Luckhurst 2-2; New Orleans, Ricardo 1-2.

RAMS 20, LIONS 13

ANAHEIM—A quarterback controversy seems to be a constant state of affairs for Los Angeles, and a new debate was burning after Jeff Rutledge came off the bench to rally the Rams past Detroit.

Rutledge relieved starter Pat Haden midway through the third period and brought the Rams to life. He completed nine of 12 passes for 145 yards, including a 64-yard throw to Preston Dennard that set up a one-yard TD run by Wendell Tyler early in the fourth quarter, giving Los Angeles a 14-13 lead.

Frank Corral booted field goals of 42 and 31 yards to seal the Rams' victory, and then came the quarterback problem. Rutledge suffered a dislocated thumb on his passing hand when he hit the helmet of Detroit defensive end William Gay following through on a pass. Dan Pastorini, in his first appearance with the Rams, finished the game.

Rams Coach Ray Malavasi said he removed Haden from the game because he wasn't moving the team. Haden had no argument. "Sure, you're disappointed when you're not playing," he said. "But Jeff came in and led us to a win, so it must have been a good decision."

Tyler became the first back to run for more than 100 yards against the Lions this season. He picked up 136 yards in 16 carries, including a 69-yard TD run in the first quarter. He was playing with a sore right knee, which was jammed on his second carry of the day.

Eric Hipple, who had engineered victories in his first two games as Detroit's quarterback, completed just seven of 25 passes against the Rams. He was intercepted twice and sacked three times. Running back Billy Sims, playing for the first time in three weeks since suffering a toe injury, gained 66 yards in 14 carries.

NOVEMBER 1

SCORE BY PERIODS

Detroit	10	3	0	0—13
Los Angeles	7	0	0	13—20

SCORING

Los Angeles—Tyler 69 run (Corral kick).
Detroit—Hill 14 pass from Hipple (Murray kick).
Detroit—Field goal Murray 49.
Detroit—Field goal Murray 45.
Los Angeles—Tyler 1 run (Corral kick).
Los Angeles—Field goal Corral 42.
Los Angeles—Field goal Corral 31.

TEAM STATISTICS

	Detroit	Los Angeles
First downs	13	17
Rushes-Yards	33-125	37-178
Passing yards	168	143
Sacks by-Yards	5-43	3-25
Return yards	138	93
Passes	7-25-2	14-24-2
Punts	5-42.2	5-40.6
Fumbles-Lost	2-0	2-1
Penalties-Yards	5-25	6-40
Time of possession	29:55	30:05

Attendance—61,814.

Rushing—Detroit, Sims 14-66, Kane 7-40, Bussey 7-20, V. Thompson 1-7, King 1-2, Hipple 2-minus 7, L. Thompson 1-minus 3; Los Angeles, Tyler 16-136, J. Thomas 9-23, Bryant 5-11, Guman 4-14, Pastorini 2-minus 5, Dennard 1-minus 1.

Passing—Detroit, Hipple 7-25-2—193; Los Angeles, Haden 5-11-1—41, Rutledge 9-12-1—145, Pastorini 0-1-0—0.

Receiving—Detroit, Hill 3-67, King 1-41, Kane 1-40, Scott 1-26, Sims 1-19; Los Angeles, Dennard 6-119, Arnold 4-48, Tyler 2-7, Waddy 1-11, Guman 1-1.

Kickoff Returns—Detroit, Hall 2-45, Martin 2-36, Callicutt 1-12; Los Angeles, D. Hill 3-35, Meisner 1-17.

Punt Returns—Detroit, Martin 3-24; Los Angeles, Irvin 4-23.

Interceptions—Detroit, Allen 2-21; Los Angeles, Irvin 2-18.

Punting—Detroit, Skladany 4-42.2; Los Angeles, Corral 5-40.6.

Field Goals—Detroit, Murray 2-3; Los Angeles, Corral 2-2.

RAIDERS 27, PATRIOTS 17

OAKLAND—If the Oakland Raiders' victory over the New England Patriots is any indication of what quarterback Marc Wilson can do, Jim Plunkett may not regain his job very soon.

Starting for the third straight game in place of Plunkett, Wilson completed 22 of 36 passes for 275 yards and one touchdown. With the Patriots ahead, 17-13, in the third quarter, Wilson drove the Raiders 55 yards in eight plays for a touchdown. His 14-yard pass to receiver Cliff Branch put the Raiders ahead for good.

"I was pleased by the way Wilson handled himself," said Oakland Coach Tom Flores. "This easily was his best game and I would hope he could go on from here."

New England Coach Ron Erhardt said Wilson's ability to avoid sacks when he appeared to be trapped was a key factor.

"We had a chance to sack him several times," Erhardt said. "But he got away and made some first downs that kept their offense going."

The Raiders' defense sacked New England quarterback Steve Grogan five times, one of which resulted in a score. Late in the fourth quarter, defensive end Cedrick Hardman sacked Grogan, jarring the ball loose, and fellow lineman Willie Jones scooped it up and ran nine yards for an insurance touchdown.

The Raiders also scored on a three-yard run by Mark van Eeghen and field goals of 51 and 26 yards by Chris Bahr. Oakland halfback Kenny King rushed for 102 yards on 17 carries, becoming the first Raider to break 100 yards this season.

The Patriots managed only 282 yards in total offense. They scored on a one-yard run by halfback Sam Cunningham, a 19-yard Grogan pass to tight end Don Hasselbeck and a 38-yard field goal by John Smith.

NOVEMBER 1

SCORE BY PERIODS

New England	3	7	7	0—17
Oakland	3	10	0	14—27

SCORING

Oakland—Field goal Bahr 51.
New England—Field goal Smith 38.
Oakland—van Eeghen 3 run (Bahr kick).
New England—Hasselbeck 19 pass from Grogan (Smith kick).
Oakland—Field goal Bahr 26.
New England—Cunningham 1 run (Smith kick).
Oakland—Branch 14 pass from Wilson (Bahr kick).
Oakland—Jones 9 fumble return (Bahr kick).

TEAM STATISTICS

	New England	Oakland
First downs	15	25
Rushes-Yards	28-77	36-185
Passing yards	205	275
Sacks by-Yards	2-8	5-39
Return yards	83	125
Passes	18-31-1	22-36-1
Punts	9-47.4	5-37.8
Fumbles-Lost	1-1	3-2
Penalties-Yards	3-25	3-25
Time of possession	29:20	30:40
Attendance—44,246.		

INDIVIDUAL STATISTICS

Rushing—New England, Cunningham 11-28, Collins 12-28, Ferguson 5-21; Oakland, King 17-102, van Eeghen 7-34, Jensen 2-17, Willis 5-16, Wilson 3-7, Hawkins 1-5, Whittington 1-4.

Passing—New England, Grogan 17-30-1—233, Johnson 1-1-0—11; Oakland, Wilson 22-36-1—283.

Receiving—New England, Hasselbeck 4-100, Johnson 4-26, Jackson 2-43, Collins 2-16, Cunningham 2-15, Morgan 1-20, Grogan 1-11, Tatupu 1-7, Ferguson 1-6; Oakland, Ramsey 6-66, Branch 5-88, Bradshaw 3-48, van Eeghen 2-14, King 2-6, Willis 1-24, Whittington 1-22, Chandler 1-12, Jensen 1-3.

Kickoff Returns—New England, Collins 1-14, Sanford 2-41, Toler 1-20; Oakland, Willis 1-28, Whittington 2-40.

Punt Returns—Oakland, Watts 8-57.

Interceptions—New England, James 1-8; Oakland, Owens 1-0.

Punting—New England, Camarillo 9-47.4; Oakland, Guy 5-37.8.

Field Goals—New England, Smith 1-1; Oakland, Bahr 2-3.

49ers 17, STEELERS 14

PITTSBURGH—Streaking San Francisco gained its sixth straight victory and found some more believers as it took advantage of six Pittsburgh turnovers and survived two of its own at Three Rivers Stadium.

"This was our biggest physical test," said 49ers Coach Bill Walsh. "Few teams come in here and win. That's why I'm so pleased with this young team."

The 49ers pushed their record to 7-2 as they maintained their two-game lead atop the NFC Western Division. Walsh had a ready answer for the surge.

"Our young defensive backs could be the best in football; it's that simple," the coach said.

Rookie cornerback Eric Wright recovered a Franco Harris fumble and intercepted a Terry Bradshaw pass, setting up the game's first touchdown. That came on a five-yard pass from Joe Montana to tight end Charle Young with 32 seconds left in the first half.

Rookie safety Carlton Williamson recovered

Ninth Week—Continued

a Frank Pollard fumble that led to Ray Wersching's 47-yard field goal three seconds before halftime. Then, in the fourth quarter, Williamson picked off a Bradshaw pass and returned 28 yards to the Pittsburgh 43. Nine plays later, rookie Walt Easley plunged two yards for the winning TD.

Rookie cornerback Ronnie Lott also recovered a fumble and safety Dwight Hicks, a third-year man, contributed an interception.

"I wasn't surprised San Francisco played so well," said Bradshaw after the Steelers' record slipped to 5-4, "but I was surprised we played so poorly. This is a tough one to swallow. I'd like to go someplace and hide."

The Steelers' defense was on the field 13:14 of the 15 minutes in the third quarter, and the effort produced a 14-10 lead for Pittsburgh.

Cornerback Mel Blount picked off a Montana pass and raced 50 yards for a touchdown. Moments later, linebacker Jack Lambert grabbed a Montana pass and returned 31 yards to the San Francisco 22. On the next play, Bradshaw fired a TD pass to Jim Smith. And then, on the 49ers' next possession, lineman Tom Beasley blocked a 37-yard field-goal attempt by Wersching.

NOVEMBER 1
SCORE BY PERIODS

San Francisco	0	10	0	7—17
Pittsburgh	0	0	14	0—14

SCORING

San Francisco—Young 5 pass from Montana (Wersching kick).
San Francisco—Field goal Wersching 45.
Pittsburgh—Blount 50 interception return (Trout kick).
Pittsburgh—Smith 22 pass from Bradshaw (Trout kick).
San Francisco—Easley 2 run (Wersching kick).

TEAM STATISTICS

	San Francisco	Pittsburgh
First downs	25	16
Rushes-Yards	39-130	27-148
Passing yards	200	121
Sacks by-Yards	1-4	1-10
Return yards	83	192
Passes	23-38-2	12-23-3
Punts	5-45.8	2-48.5
Fumbles-Lost	0-0	3-3
Penalties-Yards	6-55	8-45
Time of possession	34:16	25:44

Attendance—52,878.

INDIVIDUAL STATISTICS

Rushing—San Francisco, Patton 13-35, Cooper 3-10, Easley 14-47, Hofer 5-26, Montana 4-12; Pittsburgh, Harris 17-104, Pollard 7-28, Bradshaw 2-11, Davis 1-5.

Passing—San Francisco, Montana 22-37-2—205, Easley 1-1-0—5; Pittsburgh, Bradshaw 12-23-3—125.

Receiving—San Francisco, Cooper 5-53, Clark 7-80, Easley 3-12, Patton 2-17, Solomon 2-33, Young 3-13, Hofer 1-2; Pittsburgh, Stallworth 3-26, Cunningham 2-9, Harris 1-8, Pollard 3-42, Smith 2-42, Grossman 1-minus 2.

Kickoff Returns—San Francisco, Wilson 2-37, Ring 1-21; Pittsburgh, Hawthorne 3-69, Thornton 1-1.

Punt Returns—Pittsburgh, Smith 4-41.

Interceptions—San Francisco, Wright 1-minus 3, Hicks 1-0, Williamson 1-28; Pittsburgh, Blount 1-50, Lambert 1-31.

Punting—San Francisco, Miller 5-45.8; Pittsburgh, Colquitt 2-48.5.

Field Goals—San Francisco, Wersching 1-2; Pittsburgh, None attempted.

BRONCOS 19, VIKINGS 17

DENVER—Rookie players in the National Football League make mistakes all the time. And if they wish to remain in the league for very long, they'd better hope their miscues don't cost their team a victory.

Rookie coaches also make mistakes. But while a coach's mistake is often less visible than a player's, it can be just as damaging. Just ask the Denver Broncos' rookie head coach, Dan Reeves.

"I may have done some stupider things in my life, but I must have been real little when I did them," said Reeves. "Thank God it didn't cost us the game."

The "stupid thing" Reeves did was order his team to go for a first down on fourth down and inches to go at the Broncos' 40-yard line with three minutes left in this Monday night game with the Minnesota Vikings. The Broncos were leading, 19-10, at the time. A punt would have been the "smart" thing to do.

"It was a rookie mistake. They (the Vikings) wanted us to gamble on fourth down," said the youngest head coach in the NFL. "But I learned from it; we'll punt next time in that situation."

Reeves' decision backfired when fullback Larry Canada was stopped for no gain by the Vikes' Randy Holloway. Only two plays later, Tony Galbreath scored his second TD of the fourth quarter from the 1-yard line. A seemingly secure Denver lead of 19-3 with eight and a half minutes left in the game suddenly turned into a 19-17 cliffhanger.

And Minnesota had one final chance to win the game. With 2:09 left to play, quarterback Tommy Kramer drove his team to the Denver 26-yard line. But just when it looked like Vikings might pull it out, Ted Brown was dumped for a 2-yard loss by Broncos cornerback Perry Smith. Minnesota was forced to try a 46-yard field goal but Rick Danmeier, who beat San Diego earlier in the year with a last-second kick, had his attempt fall well short.

MONDAY, NOVEMBER 2
SCORE BY PERIODS

Minnesota	0	3	0	14—17
Denver	0	3	3	13—19

SCORING

Denver—Field goal Steinfort 42.
Minnesota—Field goal Danmeier 32.
Denver—Field goal Steinfort 49.
Denver—Lytle 5 run (kick blocked).
Denver—Watson 15 pass from Morton (Steinfort kick).
Minnesota—Galbreath 1 run (Danmeier kick).
Minnesota—Galbreath 1 run (Danmeier kick).

TEAM STATISTICS

	Minnesota	Denver
First downs	19	17
Rushes-Yards	22-102	37-147
Passing yards	223	182
Sacks by-Yards	3-19	1-7
Return yards	77	123
Passes	22-36-1	16-30-1
Punts	7-42.7	4-40.8
Fumbles-Lost	2-1	1-1
Penalties-Yards	4-35	4-40
Time of possession	25:26	34:34

Attendance—78,834.

INDIVIDUAL STATISTICS

Rushing—Minnesota, Brown 14-47, LeCount 1-38, Galbreath 5-17, Kramer 1-1, Young 1-minus 1; Denver, Parros 12-65, Preston 10-37, Reed 5-23, Canada 6-12, Lytle 4-10.

Passing—Minnesota, Kramer 22-36-1—230; Denver, Morton 16-28-1—201, DeBerg 0-1-0—0, Reed 0-1-1—0.

Receiving—Minnesota, Senser 6-73, Rashad 4-60, LeCount 3-32, S. White 2-31, Brown 4-20, Young 2-9, Galbreath 1-5; Denver, Egloff 2-62, Reed 3-43, Upchurch 5-32, Odoms 2-31, Watson 2-21, Preston 1-7, Parros 1-5.

Kickoff Returns—Minnesota, Payton 2-59; Denver, Manning 2-45, Harden 1-14.

Punt Returns—Minnesota, Payton 2-3; Denver, Manning 4-24.

Interceptions—Minnesota, Teal 1-15; Denver, Kyle 1-40.

Punting—Minnesota, Coleman 7-42.7; Denver, Prestridge 4-40.8.

Field Goals—Minnesota, Danmeier 1-2; Denver, Steinfort 2-3.

TENTH WEEK

SEAHAWKS 24, STEELERS 21

SEATTLE—Like a prizefighter who's lost his knockout punch, Pittsburgh had Seattle on the ropes, but could not put the Seahawks away.

The Seahawks were trailing 21-3 late in the second quarter, but rallied for the victory on the passing of quarterback Jim Zorn.

The defeat dropped the Steelers to 5-5 and two games out of first place in the AFC Central Division.

Franco Harris and Sidney Thornton ran for TDs and Terry Bradshaw connected for a club-record 90-yard scoring pass to Mark Malone, a quarterback converted to wide receiver, as Pittsburgh built its 21-3 lead. But then Zorn got hot.

Zorn, benched in the fourth quarter of Seattle's loss to Green Bay the previous week, connected on 18 of 25 passes for 272 yards. He hit Dan Doornink over the middle and the fullback ran the ball in for a 44-yard TD play to cut Seattle's deficit to 21-10 at halftime.

In the fourth quarter, Zorn threw to Doornink on the same play for a 34-yard gain, setting up a one-yard TD run by Theotis Brown. Then, Zorn fired a 53-yard strike to Steve Largent that carried to the Pittsburgh nine, and Brown scored the winning TD from a yard out.

The Steelers had chances to pull the game out. An 81-yard TD pass from Bradshaw to Harris was wiped out by a holding penalty. Then

the Steelers drove from their 36 to the Seattle five, but David Trout muffed a 22-yard field-goal attempt with 13 seconds left.

"You kind of look up in the sky and say, 'Lord, why me?'" said Trout. "There's no excuse. The hold was good. The snap was good. The blocking was good. The poles didn't move. I just screwed up."

The Steelers' Harris went over the 10,000-yard mark in career rushing in the third quarter, joining Jim Brown and O. J. Simpson in the 10,000 club.

NOVEMBER 8
SCORE BY PERIODS

Pittsburgh	7	14	0	0	21
Seattle	3	7	0	14	24

SCORING

Pittsburgh—Harris 6 run (Trout kick).
Seattle—Field goal Herrera 37.
Pittsburgh—Malone 90 pass from Bradshaw (Trout kick).
Pittsburgh—Thornton 4 run (Trout kick).
Seattle—Doornink 44 pass from Zorn (Herrera kick).
Seattle—T. Brown 1 run (Herrera kick).
Seattle—T. Brown 1 run (Herrera kick).

TEAM STATISTICS

	Pittsburgh	Seattle
First downs	17	19
Rushes-Yards	38-162	33-96
Passing yards	205	260
Sacks by-Yards	2-17	1-7
Return yards	85	68
Passes	13-22-2	18-25-0
Punts	3-53.0	4-38.3
Fumbles-Lost	0-0	2-1
Penalties-Yards	10-75	4-30
Time of possession	31:23	28:37

Attendance—59,058.

INDIVIDUAL STATISTICS

Rushing—Pittsburgh, Harris 15-61, Pollard 11-58, Davis 6-25, Thornton 4-12, Bradshaw 2-6; Seattle, T. Brown 18-43, Doornink 10-28, West 1-27, Zorn 4-minus 2.

Passing—Pittsburgh, Bradshaw 13-22-2—212; Seattle, Zorn 18-25-0—277.

Receiving—Pittsburgh, Stallworth 3-32, Harris 3-23, Pollard 2-17, Davis 2-11, Malone 1-90, Thornton 1-30, Cunningham 1-9; Seattle, T. Brown 7-68, Largent 4-82, Doornink 3-82, Smith 1-21, Tice 1-11, August 1-9, McCullum 1-4.

Kickoff Returns—Pittsburgh, Anderson 4-58, Malone 1-3; Seattle, Lewis 1-21, Lane 1-27.

Punt Returns—Pittsburgh, Anderson 2-24.

Interceptions—Seattle, Jackson 1-18, D. Brown 1-2.

Punting—Pittsburgh, Colquitt 3-53.0; Seattle, West 4-38.3.

Field Goals—Pittsburgh, Trout 0-2; Seattle, Herrera 1-2.

DOLPHINS 30, PATRIOTS 27
(Overtime)

FOXBORO—Miami's overtime victory against New England, Coach Don Shula admitted, was a special one, and not just because it was his 200th as an NFL coach. Shula said the triumph was more important for maintaining the Dolphins' momentum than for his memories years from now.

"It's something I will remember," said Shula, who became the fourth coach in NFL history

Tenth Week—Continued

to reach 200 victories. "But it will be more important if it comes in a year when we get where we want to go. It's only important if it's part of a championship season."

The Dolphins improved their record to 7-2-1 and stayed on top in the AFC East with their first victory in Schaefer Stadium since 1975. The winning points came on a 30-yard field goal by Uwe von Schamann 7:01 into overtime.

Miami linebacker Bob Brudzinski intercepted a pass by Steve Grogan at the New England 45 in the overtime and returned it to the Patriots' 26. Offensive tackle Dwight Wheeler was flagged for hitting Brudzinski after he was out of bounds, and the penalty moved the ball to the 13. Shula wasted no time, sending in Von Schamann for the field goal attempt on the first play.

The Dolphins had taken a 27-24 lead with 2:11 left in regulation play after a bizarre flea-flicker play. Fullback Andra Franklin took a handoff from David Woodley, but never was in full control. The ball bounced off the backs of three Miami linemen and then back to Franklin, who flipped it to Woodley. The quarterback then uncorked a 54-yard bomb to wide receiver Duriel Harris, who made a diving catch at the Pats' three-yard line. Two plays later, Woodley rolled in for the touchdown.

The Patriots came back to tie the game, as Grogan completed six straight passes and John Smith booted a 34-yard field goal with 10 seconds left. But then New England suffered its sixth straight overtime defeat, and the second of the year.

NOVEMBER 8
SCORE BY PERIODS

Miami	0	6	14	7	3—	30
New England	7	10	0	10	0—	27

SCORING

New England—Morgan 76 pass from Grogan (Smith kick).
New England—Field goal Smith 27.
Miami—Field goal von Schamann 24.
New England—Grogan 4 run (Smith kick).
Miami—Field goal von Schamann 26.
Miami—Vigorito 30 run (von Schamann kick).
Miami—Nathan 1 run (von Schamann kick).
New England—Collins 1 run (Smith kick).
Miami—Woodley 2 run (von Schamann kick).
New England—Field goal Smith 34.
Miami—Field goal von Schamann 30.

TEAM STATISTICS

	Miami	New England
First downs	24	23
Rushes-Yards	41-203	32-141
Passing yards	216	351
Sacks by-Yards	1-4	2-26
Return yards	237	132
Passes	22-37-2	23-40-4
Punts	4-41.3	3-43.7
Fumbles-Lost	2-2	1-1
Penalties-Yards	6-51	9-77
Time of possession	37:13	29:56
Attendance—61,297.		

INDIVIDUAL STATISTICS

Rushing—Miami, Franklin 16-71, Nathan 16-79, Vigorito 1-30, Woodley 4-4, Hill 3-16, Moore 1-3; New England, Collins 17-90, Cunningham 9-26, Tatupu 1-3, Ferguson 2-6, Grogan 2-5, Morgan 1-11.

Passing—Miami, Woodley 22-37-2—242; New England, Grogan 23-40-4—355.

Receiving—Miami, Harris 8-145, Nathan 5-37, Cefalo 1-18, Lee 3-7, Hill 2-14, Giaquinto 1-5, Vigorito 1-9, Hardy 1-7; New England, Hasselbeck 3-29, Morgan 5-182, Johnson 5-69, Collins 3-21, Cunningham 5-37, Tatupu 1-11, Ferguson 1-6.

Kickoff Returns—Miami, Walker 7-166; New England, Collins 1-11, Toler 3-56.

Punt Returns—Miami, Vigorito 1-9; New England, Morgan 4-26.

Interceptions—Miami, Brudzinski 2-35, Rhone 1-16, Duhe 1-11; New England, Clayborn 2-39.

Punting—Miami, Orosz 4-41.3; New England, Camarillo 3-43.7.

Field Goals—Miami, von Schamann 3-3; New England, Smith 2-2.

EAGLES 52, CARDINALS 10

ST. LOUIS—Philadelphia quarterback Ron Jaworski said the biggest decisions he had to make in the thrashing of St. Louis was which cornerback to exploit at a particular time.

"It was a little bit tempting both ways," said Jaworski, who threw four touchdowns passes as the Eagles handed the Cardinals their worst defeat ever at Busch Stadium. "We kind of just threw the ball where we wanted."

On one side of the field, Jaworski faced rookie cornerback Jeff Griffin. On the other corner was Carl Allen.

"Allen was probably a little shellshocked," said Jaworski. "He got beat pretty badly last week (Allen gave up two TD passes in the Cardinals' 42-21 loss at Washington). But when you line up a rookie on the other side, it's kind of tough not to go at him."

Jaworski went Allen's way twice in the third quarter, and each time 6-8 wide receiver Harold Carmichael caught a touchdown pass. That increased the Eagles' 17-10 halftime lead to 31-10. Philadelphia added three TDs in the final period after giveaways by the Cardinals.

The victory enabled the Eagles (8-2) to stay at the top of the NFC East. The Cardinals fell to 3-7 and had Coach Jim Hanifan muttering.

"I'm so upset, so upset," said Hanifan. "I think the performance in the second half was the most pitiful I've ever seen. There are many factors, not one specific thing. It was a total collapse."

Carmichael caught five passes for 103 yards and Wilbert Montgomery ran for 118 yards in 20 carries and caught a 19-yard TD pass.

The game was still close when the Cardinals' Ottis Anderson fumbled after taking a pass at the start of the third quarter. Dennis Harrison recovered for the Eagles on the St. Louis 38, prying the ball away from the Cardinals' Pat Tilley. Montgomery ran 23 yards before Jaworski threw 14 yards to Carmichael, who was wide open behind Allen.

Eagles quarterback Ron Jaworski toyed with the St. Louis secondary all afternoon as the Eagles gave the Cardinals their worst beating ever at Busch Stadium, 52-10. Jaworski had a career-high four TD passes.

Tenth Week—Continued

On St. Louis' next possession, Roynell Young intercepted a Jim Hart pass and returned 33 yards to the St. Louis 47. On third and 20 from the 38, Jaworski lofted a pass to Carmichael, who used his height to make the grab and then walked over Allen into the end zone.

The 42-point loss was the worst for St. Louis since a 55-14 Thanksgiving Day massacre at the hands of Miami in 1977. Ironically, the Cardinals went into that game with 7-3 record. The same week, Philadelphia had a 3-7 record. From that 10th week of 1977 through the 10th week of '81, the Eagles' record was 42-20 and the Cardinals' was 19-43 under three coaches.

NOVEMBER 8
SCORE BY PERIODS

Philadelphia	7	10	14	21—52
St. Louis	7	3	0	0—10

SCORING

Philadelphia—Montgomery 19 pass from Jaworski (Franklin kick).
St. Louis—Gray 41 pass from Hart (O'Donoghue kick).
St. Louis—Field goal O'Donoghue 21.
Philadelphia—Parker 33 pass from Jaworski (Franklin kick).
Philadelphia—Field goal Franklin 32.
Philadelphia—Carmichael 14 pass from Jaworski (Franklin kick).
Philadelphia—Carmichael 38 pass from Jaworski (Franklin kick).
Philadelphia—Campfield 2 run (Franklin kick).
Philadelphia—Henry 20 pass from Pisarcik (Franklin kick).
Philadelphia—Russell 1 run (Franklin kick).

TEAM STATISTICS

	Philadelphia	St. Louis
First downs	30	13
Rushes-Yards	45-197	19-81
Passing yards	255	158
Sacks by-Yards	5-41	0-0
Return yards	91	217
Passes	19-35-1	14-29-2
Punts	2-44.5	3-41.7
Fumbles-Lost	1-0	3-3
Penalties-Yards	7-59	10-86
Time of possession	36:20	23:40
Attendance—48,421.		

INDIVIDUAL STATISTICS

Rushing—Philadelphia, Montgomery 20-118, Russell 8-28, Murray 6-27, Campfield 5-18, Oliver 3-7, Smith 1-5, Pisarcik 2-minus 6; St. Louis, Anderson 12-55, Morris 7-26.

Passing—Philadelphia, Jaworski 18-34-1—235, Pisarcik 1-1-0—20; St. Louis, Hart 14-26-1—199, Lomax 0-3-1—0.

Receiving—Philadelphia, Carmichael 5-103, Campfield 4-26, Smith 3-47, Montgomery 3-37, Parker 1-33, Henry 1-20, Russell 1-minus 5, Oliver 1-minus 6; St. Louis, Tilley 6-84, Gray 3-71, Anderson 3-27, Green 1-13, Morris 1-4.

Kickoff Returns—Philadelphia, Henry 2-31; St. Louis, Mitchell 6-134, Harrell 1-29.

Punt Returns—Philadelphia, Henry 3-21; St. Louis, Mitchell 1-12.

Interceptions—Philadelphia, Young 1-33, LeMaster 1-6; St. Louis, Favron 1-42.

Punting—Philadelphia, Runager 2-44.5; St. Louis, Birdsong 3-41.7.

Field Goals—Philadelphia, Franklin 1-1; St. Louis, O'Donoghue 1-2.

OILERS 17, RAIDERS 16

HOUSTON—John Reaves said he had gone from "the pits" to the "greatest thrill of my professional life" when he led Houston to victory over Oakland. The Oilers came out on top when Reaves threw a 25-yard touchdown pass to tight end Mike Barber on a fourth-down play with 7:20 left in the game.

Reaves went all the way as the Oilers' quarterback, replacing Ken Stabler, who was sidelined with a sore wrist.

Reaves completed 17 of 31 passes for 197 yards and did not throw an interception.

The performance by Reaves was all the more remarkable considering that he missed the 1980 season because he was undergoing drug and alcohol rehabilitation. The former University of Florida All-America's pro career, which included stops in Philadelphia, Cincinnati and Minnesota, had been a downer.

Reaves went to the Oilers' camp last summer as backup insurance for Gifford Nielsen, who was taking over for Stabler, who retired. And when Nielsen suffered a shoulder injury in preseason and Stabler returned from mothballs, Reaves stayed on the roster.

Reaves said the fourth-down pass to Barber was called from the bench. "Barber's my first and only choice on that play," he said. "There was a hole in there between the cornerback and safety, and I put it right between them."

The cornerback on the play was Lester Hayes, and he admitted that Reaves' pass was perfect. "There is a void area in the zone, and he found it," said Hayes.

Oakland had a chance to win in the game's last minute. Marc Wilson completed three straight passes for 47 yards to move the Raiders to the Houston 30, but Chris Bahr's 47-yard field-goal attempt was short with 10 seconds left.

NOVEMBER 8
SCORE BY PERIODS

Oakland	0	3	10	3—16
Houston	3	7	0	7—17

SCORING

Houston—Field goal Fritsch 23.
Oakland—Field goal Bahr 29.
Houston—Campbell 1 run (Fritsch kick).
Oakland—Field goal Bahr 42.
Oakland—Whittington 12 run (Bahr kick).
Oakland—Field goal Bahr 43.
Houston—Barber 25 pass from Reaves (Fritsch kick).

TEAM STATISTICS

	Oakland	Houston
First downs	16	17
Rushes-Yards	28-149	41-108
Passing yards	167	190
Sacks by-Yards	1-7	1-8
Return yards	133	170
Passes	16-32-2	17-31-0
Punts	2-32.5	5-40.4
Fumbles-Lost	1-0	3-2
Penalties-Yards	4-44	9-65
Time of possession	24:24	35:36
Attendance—45,519.		

Rushing—Oakland, King 13-79, van Eeghen 6-20, Jensen 5-19, Wilson 1-18, Whittington 3-13; Houston, Campbell 31-86, Armstrong 6-21, Reaves 3-1, Coleman 1-0.

Passing—Oakland, Wilson 16-32-2—175; Houston, Reaves 17-31-0—197.

Receiving—Oakland, Bradshaw 3-46, Ramsey 4-40, van Eeghen 3-25, Chandler 2-27, Branch 2-14, King 1-12, Whittington 1-11; Houston, Campbell 4-40, Casper 2-39, Renfro 4-38, Holston 3-29, Burrough 2-24, Barber 1-25, Armstrong 1-2.

Kickoff Returns—Oakland, Whittington 2-60, Willis 2-40; Houston, Roaches 2-56, Tullis 3-93.

Punt Returns—Oakland, Watts 4-33; Houston, Roaches 1-1.

Interceptions—Houston, Stemrick 1-18, Reinfeldt 1-2.

Punting—Oakland, Guy 2-32.5; Houston, Parsley 5-40.4.

Field Goals—Oakland, Bahr 3-5; Houston, Fritsch 1-2.

BEARS 16, CHIEFS 13
(Overtime)

KANSAS CITY—Chicago Bears Coach Neill Armstrong was suspicious of the kick-defense team of the Kansas City Chiefs after watching it block one field goal and come close on a couple of other placements.

So he sent in a message to the referees prior to John Roveto's 37-yard field-goal attempt with 2:34 left in overtime. Armstrong told the game officials to keep an eye on the Chiefs' Gary Green and Stan Rome, who he thought were illegally stepping on the backs and shoulders of linemen in their attempt to block kicks.

Roveto proceeded to miss the field-goal try, kicking the ball wide right, but the officials detected Green stepping on a Bears lineman and penalized him for unsportsmanlike conduct.

That moved the ball half the distance to the goal line and three plays later, Roveto booted his third field goal of the game, a 22-yarder with 1:53 left in overtime, to give the Bears the upset over the Chiefs.

"I've never seen that called before," said Armstrong, whose team raised its record to 3-7, "but we noticed in the films that they had been doing it all season. So we tipped off the officials and they were watching for it."

The Chiefs, with their second straight loss, fell to 6-4, one game behind Denver in the AFC West.

The Bears' defense forced six Chiefs turnovers, and the offense converted three of those into scores to build a 13-6 lead. The Bears recovered five fumbles, intercepted a pass, recorded four sacks and harassed Chiefs quarterbacks Bill Kenney and Steve Fuller into a 12-of-34 passing performance for 113 yards.

Vince Evans threw to Rickey Watts for the lone Bears touchdown before the game was 90 seconds old, following Kenney's fumble at the Chiefs' 14-yard line. A fumble by Chiefs running back Joe Delaney at his own 19 set up Roveto's 24-yarder in the second quarter, and Fuller's fumble at the Bears' 28 set up Roveto's 23-yarder in the fourth quarter.

But the Chiefs managed to send the game into overtime when Fuller passed to Henry Marshall for an 18-yard touchdown on fourth-and-two with 44 seconds left in regulation. The Chiefs also got first-half field goals of 34 and 33 yards from Nick Lowery.

NOVEMBER 8
SCORE BY PERIODS

Chicago	7	3	0	3	3—16
Kansas City	3	3	0	7	0—13

SCORING

Chicago—Watts 12 pass from Evans (Roveto kick).
Kansas City—Field goal Lowery 34.
Chicago—Field goal Roveto 24.
Kansas City—Field goal Lowery 33.
Chicago—Field goal Roveto 23.
Kansas City—Marshall 18 pass from Fuller (Lowery kick).
Chicago—Field goal Roveto 22.

TEAM STATISTICS

	Chicago	Kansas City
First downs	15	18
Rushes-Yards	61-201	39-165
Passing yards	77	84
Sacks by-Yards	4-29	0-0
Return yards	139	164
Passes	7-30-0	12-34-1
Punts	8-37.8	7-37.9
Fumbles-Lost	2-0	5-5
Penalties-Yards	9-37.0	6-38.8
Time of possession	42:22	30:45
Attendance—60,605.		

INDIVIDUAL STATISTICS

Rushing—Chicago, Payton 21-70, McClendon 17-63, Suhey 18-58, Evans 5-10; Kansas City, B. Jackson 14-56, Delaney 13-38, Hadnot 6-18, Fuller 3-minus 2, Kenney 2-24, Marshall 1-31.

Passing—Chicago, Evans 7-30-0—77; Kansas City, Kenney 5-14-0—25, Fuller 7-20-1—88.

Receiving—Chicago, Margerum 4-48, Watts 2-20, Payton 1-9; Kansas City, Marshall 4-48, Smith 3-22, Rome 2-23, Bledsoe 1-17, Hadnot 1-5, Delaney 1-minus 2.

Kickoff Returns—Chicago, Fisher 1-15, Moorehead 3-96; Kansas City, Murphy 2-67, Cherry 1-20.

Punt Returns—Chicago, Fisher 2-28; Kansas City, Smith 6-77.

Interceptions—Chicago, Schmidt 1-0.

Punting—Chicago, Parsons 9-37.0; Kansas City, Gossett 6-38.8.

Field Goals—Chicago, Roveto 3-4; Kansas City, Lowery 2-3.

SAINTS 21, RAMS 13

ANAHEIM—George Rogers, after gaining just 22 yards in 15 carries against Atlanta, made amends by shredding the Los Angeles defense for 161 yards and three touchdowns to lead New Orleans to an upset victory.

Rogers, who went over the 1,000-yard mark (1,040), came within one yard of the Saints' single-game rushing record, which he set the second week of the season against the Rams.

"What happened today was particularly nice after the horrible day I had last week," Rogers said after the Saints' third victory in 10 games and second of the season over the Rams.

"I played probably the worst game of my life against Atlanta and it really bothered me because I always take pride in playing well."

Rogers scored his first touchdown in the second quarter after Jimmy Rogers returned a kickoff to his own 41-yard line. On the first play, Rogers took a handoff from Dave Wilson, faked a reverse handoff to wide receiver Guido Merkens, and sprinted 59 yards to pull the Saints to within 10-7.

The Rams, 5-5 and three games back in the NFC West, took a 10-0 lead on a 44-yard field goal by Frank Corral and a 28-yard touchdown pass by Dan Pastorini to Preston Dennard. The Rams led by 13-7 at the half, thanks to a 24-yard field goal by Corral with 56 seconds left in the second quarter.

The Saints took a 14-13 lead with 3:55 left in the third quarter on Rogers' five-yard run, which capped an 88-yard drive. New Orleans wrapped up the scoring on Rogers' two-yard run, his eighth touchdown of the season.

Wilson, starting in place of the injured Archie Manning, completed 11 of 19 passes for 182 yards. He grew up a few blocks from Anaheim Stadium.

"I couldn't have been more excited, coming home and beating the Rams," said Wilson. "We dominated the Rams in every aspect of the game. This is the sweetest victory ever for me."

Pastorini, starting his first NFL game since being injured in the fifth game of the 1980 season with Oakland, completed 15 of 33 passes for 223 yards but was intercepted four times.

NOVEMBER 8
SCORE BY PERIODS

New Orleans	0	7	7	7—21
Los Angeles	3	10	0	0—13

SCORING

Los Angeles—Field goal Corral 44.
Los Angeles—Dennard 28 pass from Pastorini (Corral kick).
New Orleans—G. Rogers 59 run (Ricardo kick).
Los Angeles—Field goal Corral 24.
New Orleans—G. Rogers 5 run (Ricardo kick).
New Orleans—G. Rogers 2 run (Ricardo kick).

TEAM STATISTICS

	New Orleans	Los Angeles
First downs	26	16
Rushes-Yards	52-307	23-113
Passing yards	155	191
Sacks by-Yards	3-32	3-27
Return yards	112	74
Passes	11-19-0	15-33-4
Punts	4-45.3	4-43.5
Fumbles-Lost	7-2	0-0
Penalties-Yards	13-108	13-97
Time of possession	35:07	24:53
Attendance—61,068.		

INDIVIDUAL STATISTICS

Rushing—New Orleans, G. Rogers 24-161, Holmes 10-36, W. Wilson 10-34, Tyler 8-76; Los Angeles, J. Thomas 11-75, Bryant 11-36, Guman 1-2.

Passing—New Orleans, D. Wilson 11-19-0—182; Los Angeles, Pastorini 15-33-4—223.

Receiving—New Orleans, W. Wilson 3-31, Merkens 2-67, Brenner 1-28, Hardy 1-19, G. Rogers 1-14, Tyler 1-10, Groth 1-8, Holmes 1-5; Los Angeles, Dennard 4-92, J. Thomas 3-28, Bryant 3-21, Arnold 2-43, D. Hill 1-21, Miller 1-18, Guman 1-0.

Kickoff Returns—New Orleans, J. Rogers 1-31, W. Wilson 3-76; Los Angeles, D. Hill 4-74.

Punt Returns—New Orleans, Groth 1-10, Merkens 1-minus 12.

Interceptions—New Orleans, Spivey 1-0, Waymer 1-0, Redd 1-7, Gary 1-0.

Punting—New Orleans, Erxleben 4-45.3; Los Angeles, Corral 4-43.5.

Field Goals—New Orleans, Ricardo 0-2; Los Angeles, Corral 2-2.

BRONCOS 23, BROWNS 20
(Overtime)

DENVER—Fred Steinfort's 30-yard field goal 4:05 into overtime enabled patched-up Denver to escape with the victory over Cleveland and move into sole possession of first place in the AFC West with a 7-3 record. The Browns (4-6) fell into the Central Division cellar.

The Broncos were an out-of-position team. On the offensive line, guard Tom Glassic was the only regular playing in his assigned spot. In the secondary, cornerback Louie Wright was sidelined before the game and two other cornerbacks, Aaron Kyle (concussion) and Perry Smith (hamstring pull) were knocked out of action.

Steve Watson caught his 12th touchdown pass of the year, tying the club record set by Lionel Taylor in 1960, Steinfort kicked two field goals and Dave Preston ran for a score as the Broncos took a 20-14 lead into the fourth quarter.

Cleveland rallied to tie the score on two field goals by Matt Bahr, the last a 32-yarder with 29 seconds left.

In overtime, the Browns won the toss and took the ball. Brian Sipe threw a 23-yard pass to Calvin Hill, but Hill fumbled as he was tackled by rookie safety Dennis Smith, and Smith recovered the ball just before it went out of bounds on the Denver 48.

Craig Morton then fired a 33-yard pass to Rick Upchurch, setting up Steinfort's winning field goal.

"We had our chances to win the game," said Cleveland Coach Sam Rutigliano. "We moved the ball when we had to, but they're tough when you get in close. You've got to give them credit."

Denver Coach Dan Reeves said, "I have never been prouder of a football team. They (the Browns) kept threatening to blow the game open, but our defense wore them out. It was a big win."

NOVEMBER 8
SCORE BY PERIODS

Cleveland	0	7	7	6	0—20
Denver	3	7	3	7	3—23

Denver—Field goal Steinfort 45.
Cleveland—C. Miller 1 run (Bahr kick).
Denver—Watson 5 pass from Morton (Steinfort kick).
Denver—Field goal Steinfort 43.
Cleveland—Logan 23 pass from Sipe (Bahr kick).
Denver—Preston 4 run (Steinfort kick).
Cleveland—Field goal Bahr 27.
Cleveland—Field goal Bahr 32.
Denver—Field goal Steinfort 30.

TEAM STATISTICS

	Cleveland	Denver
First downs	20	22
Rushes-Yards	22-82	36-116
Passing yards	280	246
Sacks by-Yards	6-45	1-10
Return yards	152	125
Passes	20-42-2	21-33-0
Punts	6-48.3	6-39.0
Fumbles-Lost	3-2	3-2
Penalties-Yards	5-24	7-34
Time of possession	24:41	39:29
Attendance—74,859.		

INDIVIDUAL STATISTICS

Rushing—Cleveland, M. Pruitt 12-57, C. Miller 6-9, Sipe 3-10, Newsome 1-6; Denver, Parros 13-66, Preston 11-29, Reed 8-14, Morton 1-5, Upchurch 1-2, Lytle 2-0.

Passing—Cleveland, Sipe 20-42-2—290; Denver, Morton 21-33-0—291.

Receiving—Cleveland, Logan 5-86, Newsome 3-89, M. Pruitt 5-30, Hill 4-42, C. Miller 2-10, Rucker 1-33; Denver, Odoms 5-71, Preston 4-61, Watson 3-55, Upchurch 3-49, Egloff 1-18, Parros 3-22, Reed 2-15.

Kickoff Returns—Cleveland, Hall 5-114; Denver, Manning 2-49, Harden 1-22.

Punt Returns—Hall 4-38; Denver, Manning 3-38.

Interceptions—Denver, Thompson 1-0, Gradishar 1-16.

Punting—Cleveland, Cox 6-48.3; Denver, Prestridge 6-39.0.

Field Goals—Cleveland, Bahr 2-3; Denver, Steinfort 3-4.

REDSKINS 33, LIONS 31

WASHINGTON—The lead changed hands six times before Washington upended Detroit on Mark Moseley's 44-yard field goal with 43 seconds left.

The Redskins (4-6) won their third straight and fourth in five games after an 0-5 start.

The Lions, also 4-6, failed to win on the road for the sixth time.

"It looked like whoever had the ball last would win it," said Redskins Coach Joe Gibbs. "I feel very good. I think it shows a lot about our guys, the way we came back three times when we were down."

The Redskins jumped to a 10-0 lead, thanks to three first-quarter turnovers by the Lions, including Alvin Hall's fumble of the opening kickoff.

The Lions wiped out that deficit on Eric Hipple's 36-yard TD pass to Freddie Scott and Hipple's two-yard scoring run. Detroit made it 21-13 when Billy Sims went over from the 1-yard line, but Washington pulled to within 21-20 on Joe Theismann's pass to Art Monk.

Moseley put the Redskins back in front, 23-

21, midway through the third quarter with his 28-yard kick, but Sims' 13-yard dash gave the Lions a 28-23 edge in the second minute of the fourth quarter.

Joe Washington ran 12 yards for a TD and a 30-28 Redskins lead with 6:39 to play. Then, the Lions' Ed Murray kicked a 50-yarder with 1:50 remaining to set up Moseley's heroics.

Coach Monte Clark fumed over the Lions' early mistakes. "We dug a hole early," said Clark. "It was the worst start I can remember. It would be easy to make a big demonstration of how frustrated and disappointed I am, but it wouldn't do any good. We couldn't stop them."

Joe Washington rushed for 144 yards on 27 carries and scored two touchdowns, but he lost the battle of former Oklahoma running backs as Sims ran for 159 yards and scored twice.

NOVEMBER 8
SCORE BY PERIODS

Detroit	7	14	0	10	—31
Washington	10	10	3	10	—33

SCORING

Washington—Washington 7 run (Moseley kick).
Washington—Field goal Moseley 21.
Detroit—Scott 36 pass from Hipple (Murray kick).
Detroit—Hipple 2 run (Murray kick).
Washington—Field goal Moseley 33.
Detroit—Sims 1 run (Murray kick).
Washington—Monk 6 pass from Theismann (Moseley kick).
Washington—Field goal Moseley 28.
Detroit—Sims 13 run (Murray kick).
Washington—Washington 12 run (Moseley kick).
Detroit—Field goal Murray 50.
Washington—Field goal Moseley 44.

TEAM STATISTICS

	Detroit	Washington
First downs	24	25
Rushes-Yards	35-222	41-193
Passing yards	277	271
Sacks by-Yards	2-16	1-5
Return yards	155	137
Passes	14-22-3	19-32-2
Punts	2-43.5	3-36.7
Fumbles-Lost	4-3	1-1
Penalties-Yards	8-69	3-60
Time of possession	28:24	31:36
Attendance—52,096.		

INDIVIDUAL STATISTICS

Rushing—Detroit, Sims 21-159, Bussey 5-31, Kane 6-28, V. Thompson 1-2, Hipple 2-2; Washington, Riggins 12-28, Washington 27-144, Theismann 2-21.

Passing—Detroit, Hipple 14-22-3—282; Washington, Theismann 19-31-2—287, Washington 0-1-0—0.

Receiving—Detroit, Scott 8-156, Hill 1-20, L. Thompson 1-18, Sims 2-34, King 1-48, Nichols 1-48; Washington, Monk 3-45, Washington 3-20, Bostic 1-minus 4, Warren 1-14, Seay 8-145, Metcalf 3-67.

Kickoff Returns—Detroit, Hall 6-107, Martin 1-11; Washington, Nelms 3-76, Jackson 2-34, Cronan 1-18.

Punt Returns—Detroit, Martin 1-26; Washington, Nelms 1-7.

Interceptions—Detroit, Bradley 1-0, Allen 1-11; Washington, Parrish 1-1, Murphy 1-1, Peters 1-0.

Punting—Detroit, Skladany 2-43.5; Washington, Connell 3-36.7.

Field Goals—Detroit, Murray 1-1; Washington, Moseley 4-4.

Tenth Week—Continued

BENGALS 4O, CHARGERS 17

SAN DIEGO—The suddenly explosive Cincinnati Bengals left the San Diego Chargers shellshocked after a 40-17 victory.

The Bengals (7-3) took a two-game lead in the American Football Conference Central Division. San Diego (6-4) fell out of a tie for first place in the AFC West.

Cincinnati quarterback Ken Anderson, who had completed 63.3 percent of his passes this season and had thrown for 17 touchdowns while compiling a quarterback rating of 100.6 (second only to Craig Morton's 104.0 mark), passed for 288 yards against the Chargers. He threw TD passes to Isaac Curtis and Steve Kreider as Cincinnati built its early lead.

The game's defensive star was cornerback Louis Breeden, who intercepted two passes—returning one 102 yards for a score—and recovered a fumble, which set up Cincinnati's first touchdown.

Breeden's 102-yard interception return tied the NFL record, set by Bob Smith of Detroit in 1949 and tied by Erich Barnes of the New York Giants in 1961 and by Gary Barbaro of Kansas City in 1977.

"It feels good," said Breeden, whose runback came on his first interception of the season. "We had double coverage on my side and we disguised it well. After I got past Charlie Joiner, I knew I had the touchdown because I had some big guys blocking in front of me."

Breeden's play came with 34 seconds left in the first half and gave the Bengals a 31-7 lead.

Cincinnati Coach Forrest Gregg said, "We go into each game almost scared to death and feel as if we are fighting for our lives. We felt that way until the second half today. We're gaining confidence now."

Dan Fouts passed 26 yards and 51 yards to Wes Chandler for the San Diego touchdowns. But Fouts was sacked six times and gave up the two interceptions to Breeden.

Gregg disclosed that the Bengals had borrowed defensive strategy employed by the Chicago Bears when Chicago upset San Diego earlier in the season. "We took a page out of the Bears' playbook," Gregg said. "We used a five-man line and a mixed four-man line. We blitzed a great deal and, overall, we kept Fouts off-balance."

NOVEMBER 8
SCORE BY PERIODS

Cincinnati	10	21	0	9—40
San Diego	0	10	0	7—17

SCORING

Cincinnati—Curtis 4 pass from Anderson (Breech kick).
Cincinnati—Field goal Breech 43.
San Diego—Chandler 26 pass from Fouts (Benirschke kick).
Cincinnati—Kreider 10 pass from Anderson (Breech kick).
Cincinnati—Alexander 1 run (Breech kick).
Cincinnati—Breeden 102 interception return (Breech kick).
San Diego—Field goal Benirschke 47.
Cincinnati—Field goal Breech 33.
Cincinnati—Johnson 2 run (kick failed).
San Diego—Chandler 51 pass from Fouts (Benirschke kick).

TEAM STATISTICS

	Cincinnati	San Diego
First downs	29	25
Rushes-Yards	40-124	22-136
Passing yards	337	311
Sacks by-Yards	6-41	3-19
Return yards	155	161
Passes	21-33-1	20-41-2
Punts	4-42.8	5-39.2
Fumbles-Lost	3-1	4-3
Penalties-Yards	7-45	11-67
Time of possession	33:15	26:45
Attendance—51,209.		

INDIVIDUAL STATISTICS

Rushing—Cincinnati, Johnson 20-42, Anderson 3-35, Alexander 8-25, A. Griffin 6-12, Verser 1-9, Hargrove 2-1; San Diego, Muncie 17-90, J. Brooks 4-45, Fouts 1-1.

Passing—Cincinnati, Anderson 18-28-1—288, Thompson 2-4-0—32, Schonert 1-1-0—36; San Diego, Fouts 20-40-2—352, Chandler 0-1-0—0.

Receiving—Cincinnati, Curtis 8-147, Collinsworth 4-97, Kreider 3-41, Ross 2-38, A. Griffin 2-27, Alexander 1-4, M. L. Harris 1-2; San Diego, Chandler 10-194, Scales 3-102, Winslow 3-33, Joiner 2-14, Muncie 1-6, J. Brooks 1-3.

Kickoff Returns—Cincinnati, Verser 1-20, A. Griffin 2-29; San Diego, J. Brooks 6-111, Smith 1-12, Henderson 1-26.

Punt Returns—Cincinnati, Simmons 2-0, Hicks 1-4; San Diego, J. Brooks 2-12.

Interceptions—Cincinnati, Breeden 2-102; San Diego, M. Williams 1-0.

Punting—Cincinnati, McInally 4-42.8; San Diego, Roberts 5-39.2.

Field Goals—Cincinnati, Breech 2-2; San Diego, Benirschke 1-2.

PACKERS 26, GIANTS 24

MILWAUKEE—Jan Stenerud was more than happy to join the gods of kicking, but it was the field goal that followed his milestone 300th that gave him the most satisfaction.

The 15-year veteran drilled four field goals, including a 23-yarder with 2:36 left, to give the Green Bay Packers a come-from-behind victory over the New York Giants.

"I knew 300 would be a major accomplishment," Stenerud said. "Not many people have done it and I'm proud of it. But 301 was a lot more important than 300."

With 301 career field goals, Stenerud is third on the all-time list behind George Blanda (335) and Jim Turner (304).

The victory was the Packers' first in Milwaukee since November 9, 1980, and upped their record to 4-6. It also gave the Packers their first two-game winning streak in three years. The Giants, who suffered their second straight defeat and second loss of the season to the Packers, dropped to 5-5.

The Giants rallied from a 20-0 first-quarter deficit, led by reserve quarterback Scott Brunner, who started in place of the injured Phil Simms. New York took the lead, 24-23, on Joe Danelo's 33-yard field goal with 6:17 left.

But David Whitehurst, who replaced Lynn Dickey late in the third quarter, threw passes of 41 yards to John Jefferson and 17 yards to Paul Coffman to set up Stenerud's game-winning field goal.

"We have so much confidence in Jan," said Coach Bart Starr, "we let him take a shot at it. I can't think of anyone else in the National Football League I'd rather see taking it. He's been as steady as a rock."

Stenerud also kicked field goals of 32, 28 and 35 yards. The Packers' touchdowns came in the first quarter on Mark Lee's 94-yard punt return and cornerback Estes Hoods' 41-yard interception return.

Brunner threw three touchdown passes in his first start of the season, but was intercepted four times and also lost two fumbles. His 18-yarder to Jerry Shirk on a fake field goal and 24-yarder to Johnny Perkins cut the Giants' deficit to 23-14 at the half. He also tossed a seven-yard TD pass to Mike Friede in the fourth quarter.

NOVEMBER 8
SCORE BY PERIODS

New York Giants	0	14	0	10—24
Green Bay	20	3	0	3—26

SCORING
Green Bay—Hood 41 interception return (Stenerud kick).
Green Bay—Lee 94 punt return (Stenerud kick).
Green Bay—Field goal Stenerud 32.
Green Bay—Field goal Stenerud 28.
New York—Shirk 18 pass from Brunner (Danelo kick).
New York—Perkins 24 pass from Brunner (Danelo kick).
Green Bay—Field goal Stenerud 35.
New York—Friede 7 pass from Brunner (Danelo kick).
New York—Field goal Danelo 33.
Green Bay—Field goal Stenerud 23.

TEAM STATISTICS

	New York	Green Bay
First downs	17	13
Rushes-Yards	31-88	30-82
Passing yards	233	185
Sacks by-Yards	2-18	2-18
Return yards	197	227
Passes	23-46-4	14-31-2
Punts	4-45.0	6-40.8
Fumbles-Lost	4-3	1-0
Penalties-Yards	8-54	1-5
Time of possession	32:43	27:17
Attendance—54,138.		

INDIVIDUAL STATISTICS
Rushing—New York, Carpenter 15-38, Kotar 2-4, Bright 7-30, Brunner 2-minus 2, Perry 5-18; Green Bay, Ellis 20-75, Middleton 1-2, Huckleby 5-11, Jensen 1-minus 3, Whitehurst 3-minus 3.

Passing—New York, Brunner 23-46-4—251; Green Bay, Dickey 10-27-2—143, Whitehurst 4-4-0—60.

Receiving—New York, Shirk 3-27, Bright 6-78, Mullady 3-20, Friede 2-20, Carpenter 2-18, Perkins 5-82, Perry 1-9, Kotar 1-minus 3; Green Bay, Jefferson 3-71, Ellis 2-45, Lofton 2-12, Coffman 4-68, Huckleby 3-7.

Kickoff Returns—New York, Bright 3-49, Pittman 4-76; Green Bay, Lee 2-42, Coffman 2-25.

Punt Returns—New York, Bright 5-58; Green Bay, Lee 3-111.

Interceptions—New York, Reece 1-14, T. Jackson 1-0; Green Bay, Hood 2-41, Anderson 1-8, Murphy 1-0.
Punting—New York, Jennings 4-45.0; Green Bay, Stachowicz 6-40.8.
Field Goals—New York, Danelo 1-1; Green Bay, Stenerud 4-4.

JETS 41, COLTS 14

BALTIMORE—Even if Richard Todd was having his problems off the field, the New York quarterback didn't let the turmoil affect his play.

During the week before the Baltimore game, Todd was charged with assault for allegedly slamming New York sportswriter Steve Serby into a locker at the Jets' training facility. But Todd really took it out on the Colts, completing 21 of 31 passes for 277 yards and three touchdowns.

That gave Todd a season total of 18 TD passes, his career high. He went over the 2,000-yard mark in passing for the third straight year and he suffered no interceptions against the Colts. Through 10 games, he had only eight interceptions, a marked improvement over 1980, when he gave up a league-leading 30.

Todd's TD passes went for 34 yards to Wesley Walker, 25 yards to Lam Jones and one yard to Kevin Long. His passing also set up touchdown runs by Mike Augustynkiak and Bruce Harper.

The Colts, who lost for the ninth straight time, had short-lived leads of 7-3 and 14-10 before going flat.

"I feel sick," said Colts Coach Mike McCormack. "We didn't stop anybody out there."

McCormack gave the second-guessers a big day when he pulled running back Curtis Dickey from the game after Dickey fumbled on the first play from scrimmage.

"I'm really mad," said Dickey, who contended that he was removed because quarterback Bert Jones wanted him out. McCormack insisted that he was the one who decided that Dickey would not play.

Without Dickey, their leading rusher, the Colts gained 114 yards on the ground. Jones passed for 243 yards, completing 24 of 33 throws.

NOVEMBER 8
SCORE BY PERIODS

New York Jets	10	14	7	10—41
Baltimore	7	7	0	0—14

SCORING
New York—Field goal Leahy 25.
Baltimore—McMillan 2 pass from B. Jones (Wood kick).
New York—Walker 34 pass from Todd (Leahy kick).
Baltimore—McMillan 1 run (Wood kick).
New York—Augustyniak 1 run (Leahy kick).
New York—L. Jones 25 pass from Todd (Leahy kick).
New York—Long 1 pass from Todd (Leahy kick).
New York—Harper 3 run (Leahy kick).
New York—Field goal Leahy 41.

Tenth Week—Continued

TEAM STATISTICS

	New York	Baltimore
First downs	28	21
Rushes-Yards	37-122	24-114
Passing yards	271	218
Sacks by-Yards	2-25	1-6
Return yards	108	125
Passes	21-31-0	24-33-1
Punts	3-45.0	5-39.2
Fumbles-Lost	1-0	3-1
Penalties-Yards	4-25	6-74
Time of possession	34:33	25:27

Attendance—31,521.

INDIVIDUAL STATISTICS

Rushing—New York, Augustyniak 11-40, Harper 10-44, Dierking 6-15, Long 5-18, Newton 4-7, Ryan 1-minus 2; Baltimore, Dickey 2-9, B. Jones 1-3, McMillan 11-47, Dixon 9-54, Garrett 1-1.

Passing—New York, Todd 21-31-0—277; Baltimore, B. Jones 24-33-1—243.

Receiving—New York, Gaffney 3-47, Dierking 3-18, L. Jones 2-34, Walker 3-94, Augustyniak 3-33, Barkum 1-12, Harper 2-9, B. Jones 1-6, Long 1-1, Newton 2-23; Baltimore, Dixon 3-53, McMillan 11-68, McCauley 4-40, Carr 1-23, Butler 1-15, McCall 3-26, Burke 1-18.

Kickoff Returns—New York, Harper 2-49, Stephens 1-14; Baltimore, Anderson 1-21, Dixon 2-47, Williams 3-57.

Punt Returns—New York, Harper 2-1.

Interceptions—New York, Ray 1-44.

Punting—New York, Ramsey 3-45.0; Baltimore, Garrett 5-39.2.

Field Goals—New York, Leahy 2-2; Baltimore, Wood 0-1.

VIKINGS 25, BUCCANEERS 10

BLOOMINGTON—Led by Ted Brown and Tony Galbreath, the Minnesota Vikings gained 205 yards on the ground and 228 yards passing to defeat Tampa Bay and regain sole possession of first place in the NFC Central Division. The Vikings improved to 6-4 and the Bucs fell to 5-5.

Brown rushed for a career-high 129 yards on 31 carries, including one touchdown. He also caught eight passes for 48 yards.

Galbreath, who took over in the third quarter when Brown suffered a bruised hand, finished with 64 yards on 11 carries.

"We felt going into the game that we could run on them," said Vikings Coach Bud Grant. "But I'm not sure that we don't feel that way every week. We were able to run well and that encouraged us to run more."

While the Buccaneers' defense kept a close watch on quarterback Tommy Kramer, second in the NFC in passing, Brown and his cohorts ran for their first 200-yard game since the ninth week of the 1980 season against Washington.

The Buccaneers gained 193 yards overall and made only four first downs the first three quarters. Doug Williams completed 13 of 28 passes for 154 yards, including a one-yard TD toss to Jimmie Giles. But Williams was sacked in the end zone for a safety by linemen James White and Mark Mullaney.

"It was just one of those days when nothing went right for us and everything went right for them," Williams said. "Kramer didn't beat us, Minnesota beat us. Minnesota threw, ran and did everything."

The Vikings dominated the first half and took a 16-0 lead on Rick Danmeier's 33-, 38- and 41-yard field goals, plus Brown's two-yard touchdown run, which capped a 95-yard, nine-minute drive.

Running back Rickey Young caught a one-yard touchdown pass from Kramer on the Vikings' first series of the second half for a 23-0 lead.

Kevin House, who caught four passes for 73 yards, set a Tampa Bay season record for reception yardage with 733, surpassing Isaac Hagins' 692 yards in 1979.

NOVEMBER 8
SCORE BY PERIODS

Tampa Bay	0	0	3	7—10
Minnesota	3	13	7	2—25

SCORING

Minnesota—Field goal Danmeier 33.
Minnesota—Field goal Danmeier 38.
Minnesota—Brown 2 run (Danmeier kick).
Minnesota—Field goal Danmeier 41.
Minnesota—Young 1 pass from Kramer (Danmeier kick).
Tampa Bay—Field goal Capece 27.
Minnesota—Safety, Williams tackled in end zone.
Tampa Bay—Giles 1 pass from Williams (Capece kick).

TEAM STATISTICS

	Tampa Bay	Minnesota
First downs	10	26
Rushes-Yards	14-43	46-205
Passing yards	150	221
Sacks by-Yards	1-7	1-4
Return yards	123	82
Passes	13-28-1	24-41-2
Punts	6-41.7	4-38.8
Fumbles-Lost	1-1	2-2
Penalties-Yards	5-35	8-52
Time of possession	19:36	40:24

Attendance—47,038.

INDIVIDUAL STATISTICS

Rushing—Tampa Bay, Williams 2-20, Eckwood 7-16, Owens 4-4, Wilder 1-3; Minnesota, Brown 31-129, Galbreath 11-64, Young 3-11, S. White 1-1.

Passing—Tampa Bay, Williams 13-28-1—154; Minnesota, Kramer 24-41-2—228.

Receiving—Tampa Bay, House 4-73, Jones 5-59, Eckwood 2-14, Obradovich 1-7, Giles 1-1; Minnesota, Senser 8-101, Brown 8-48, LeCount 2-25, Young 3-22, S. White 1-18, Rashad 1-9, Galbreath 1-5.

Kickoff Returns—Tampa Bay, Owens 3-63, Holt 2-53; Minnesota, Payton 2-24, Nord 2-32.

Punt Returns—Tampa Bay, T. Bell 1-0, Holt 1-3; Minnesota, Payton 3-26.

Interceptions—Tampa Bay, Colzie 1-2, Lewis 1-2; Minnesota, Blair 1-0.

Punting—Tampa Bay, Swider 6-41.7; Minnesota, Coleman 4-38.8.

Field Goals—Tampa Bay, Capece 1-2; Minnesota, Danmeier 3-3.

49ers 17, FALCONS 14

SAN FRANCISCO—"Everything happened that could have happened," Coach Bill Walsh said after his San Francisco 49ers proved once again that they're for real, pulling out a 17-14 victory over the Atlanta Falcons.

"Atlanta is the most resourceful team we've seen, no question about it," said Walsh, "but we're resourceful, too. We've held our own against topflight opposition the last three weeks and we've prevailed each time. It says a lot for our young players."

Those victories over Los Angeles (20-17), Pittsburgh (17-14) and Atlanta enabled the Niners to run their winning streak to seven games and their record to 8-2.

Free safety Dwight Hicks, a third-year man who is the greybeard of the 49ers' secondary, saved the game with two interceptions. The first set up a field goal and the second prevented the Falcons from pulling out a victory in the closing seconds.

Steve Bartkowski pulled the Falcons (5-5) within three points when he threw a 25-yard touchdown pass to Alfred Jackson with one minute, 43 seconds remaining in the game. Atlanta tried an onside kickoff, and the Falcons' Kenny Johnson fell on the ball at the San Francisco 42.

Bartkowski then passed to Alfred Jenkins for 25 yards to put the ball on the 17. On the next play, Bartkowski threw to tight end Junior Miller, but Hicks made a leaping interception at the goal line and returned the ball 20 yards to kill the Falcons' last chance.

Joe Montana passed for both 49ers touchdowns, hitting Freddie Solomon for 14 yards in the second quarter and Charle Young for three yards in the fourth period. Ray Wersching drilled a 48-yard field goal with two seconds left in the first half, following Hicks' first interception.

"They did a good job on us," said Falcons Coach Leeman Bennett. "It's as simple as that."

NOVEMBER 8
SCORE BY PERIODS

Atlanta	0	0	7	7—14
San Francisco	0	10	0	7—17

SCORING

San Francisco—Solomon 14 pass from Montana (Wersching kick).
San Francisco—Field goal Wersching 48.
Atlanta—Andrews 1 run (Luckhurst kick).
San Francisco—Young 3 pass from Montana (Wersching kick).
Atlanta—Jackson 25 pass from Bartkowski (Luckhurst kick).

TEAM STATISTICS

	Atlanta	San Fran.
First downs	19	17
Rushes-Yards	26-76	34-82
Passing yards	216	205
Sacks by-Yards	2-18	3-20
Return yards	126	139
Passes	20-42-3	16-30-1
Punts	8-44.9	10-42.0
Fumbles-Lost	2-0	4-0
Penalties-Yards	8-82	10-69
Time of possession	29:29	30:31
Attendance—59,127.		

INDIVIDUAL STATISTICS

Rushing—Atlanta, Andrews 18-61, Cain 5-10, Jackson 1-5, Bartkowski 2-0; San Francisco, Easley 15-31, Patton 9-26, Solomon 3-11, Clark 1-9, Cooper 3-4, Montana 2-1, Hofer 1-0.

Passing—Atlanta, Bartkowski 20-42-3—236; San Francisco, Montana 16-30-1—223.

Receiving—Atlanta, Jenkins 7-134, Andrews 6-31, Cain 4-24, Jackson 2-35, Miller 1-12; San Francisco, Clark 7-128, Solomon 3-56, Easley 2-9, Young 2-9, Hofer 1-21, Cooper 1-0.

Kickoff Returns—Atlanta, Woerner 2-41, R. Smith 1-26; San Francisco, Ring 1-29, Hicks 1-22.

Punt Returns—Atlanta, Woerner 2-20, R. Smith 1-8, Johnson 2-8; San Francisco, Solomon 3-15, Hicks 4-36.

Interceptions—Atlanta, Johnson 1-23; San Francisco, Hicks 2-37, Martin 1-0.

Punting—Atlanta, James 8-44.9; San Francisco, Miller 10-42.0.

Field Goals—Atlanta, Luckhurst 0-1; San Francisco, Wersching 1-1.

COWBOYS 27, BILLS 14

IRVING—The Dallas Cowboys, sparked by an electrifying 73-yard touchdown pass play from Danny White to Tony Dorsett, exploded for 20 third-quarter points to defeat the Buffalo Bills, 27-14, in this Monday night game.

The Bills, who dropped to 6-4 and a game and a half behind Miami in the AFC East race, were leading 14-7 at halftime on the strength of a 17-yard TD pass from quarterback Joe Ferguson to Jerry Butler in the first quarter, and a pass from running back Joe Cribbs to Curtis Brown in the second. Dallas was able to counter those touchdowns with only one of its own—a 12-yard pass from White to tight end Doug Cosbie.

But the second half was a different story. On the first play from scrimmage, White flipped a short pass to Dorsett and the five-year pro from Pittsburgh—who went over the 1,000-yard rushing mark for the fifth consecutive year in the game—took off down the field to score the tying touchdown.

"Dorsett's play got us back in the game," said Dallas Coach Tom Landry. "If I'd been Buffalo, I would have come out in the second half pretty confident."

"The pass to Tony really got us fired up and back into the game," said White. "He made a great run on a routine play and it gave us a great lift."

If Dorsett's play gave the Cowboys a lift, the next series of plays gave them the victory. On Buffalo's next possession, rookie cornerback Everson Walls of the Cowboys intercepted a Ferguson pass at the Bills' 44-yard line. Only two plays later, the Cowboys stunned the Bills with a 37-yard White-to-Dorsett-to-White-to-Tony Hill flea flicker for a touchdown.

In less than three minutes, the Bills went from a touchdown ahead to a touchdown behind. Rafael Septien added field goals of 47 and 31 yards to close out the 20-point outburst.

The Cowboys, who improved their record to

— 231 —

8-2 with the victory and tied Philadelphia for first place in the NFC Eastern Division, won for the 15th consecutive time in a regular-season game at Texas Stadium.

MONDAY, NOVEMBER 9
SCORE BY PERIODS

Buffalo	7	7	0	0—14
Dallas	7	0	20	0—27

SCORING
Buffalo—Butler 17 pass from Ferguson (Mike-Mayer kick).
Dallas—Cosbie 12 pass from D. White (Septien kick).
Buffalo—Brown 9 pass from Cribbs (Mike-Mayer kick).
Dallas—Dorsett 73 pass from D. White (Septien kick).
Dallas—Hill 37 pass from D. White (Septien kick).
Dallas—Field goal Septien 47.
Dallas—Field goal Septien 31.

TEAM STATISTICS

	Buffalo	Dallas
First downs	18	23
Rushes-Yards	16-58	47-196
Passing yards	307	202
Sacks by-Yards	1-17	1-3
Return yards	130	117
Passes	20-43-4	9-17-1
Punts	7-35.1	4-43.3
Fumbles-Lost	3-1	3-2
Penalties-Yards	10-89	7-50
Time of possession	25:01	34:59
Attendance—62,583.		

INDIVIDUAL STATISTICS
Rushing—Buffalo, Brown 8-39, Cribbs 8-19; Dallas, Dorsett 28-117, Springs 13-65, Newsome 1-7, D. White 4-5, Newhouse 1-2.

Passing—Buffalo, Ferguson 19-42-4—301, Cribbs 1-1-0—9; Dallas, D. White 9-17-1—219.

Receiving—Buffalo, Butler 8-118, Lewis 4-72, Brammer 3-38, Cribbs 3-19, Jessie 1-44, Brown 1-9; Dallas, Cosbie 3-54, DuPree 2-36, Dorsett 1-73, Hill 1-37, Pearson 1-14, Springs 1-5.

Kickoff Returns—Buffalo, Franklin 5-96, Riddick 1-24; Dallas, J. Jones 2-49, Newsome 1-24.

Punt Returns—Buffalo, Hooks 2-10; Dallas, J. Jones 4-14.

Interceptions—Buffalo, Simpson 1-0; Dallas, Walls 2-28, Downs 1-2, Lewis 1-0.

Punting—Buffalo, Cater 7-35.1; Dallas, D. White 4-43.3.

Field Goals—Buffalo, None attempted; Dallas, Septien 2-2.

ELEVENTH WEEK

LIONS 27, COWBOYS 24

PONTIAC—Maybe the Detroit Lions thrive on confusion. They got themselves all messed up in the final seconds of their game against the Dallas Cowboys, but still managed an amazing 27-24 victory when Eddie Murray connected on a 47-yard field goal as time expired.

The defeat knocked the Cowboys (8-3) out of a first-place tie with Philadelphia in the NFC Eastern Division. Detroit (5-6), which had won all five of its games of the season in the Pontiac Silverdome but had lost all six on the road, retained a chance for a wild-card playoff berth.

The Lions' victory over Dallas was simply stunning. The Cowboys blew a 17-0 lead, but seemed to have redeemed themselves when Danny White threw a 14-yard touchdown pass to Jay Saldi for a 24-17 lead with 2 minutes, 37 seconds left.

That lead lasted until the first play after the kickoff. Eric Hipple lofted a bomb to running back Billy Sims, who sprinted the final 44 yards to complete the 81-yard play that tied the score.

Detroit forced a punt and took the ball with 1:13 remaining and no timeouts left. Hipple fired to tight end David Hill for gains of 15 and 30 yards, but then was sacked for an 11-yard loss by defensive end Harvey Martin. With the ball on the Dallas 48 and 25 seconds left, overtime seemed certain.

However, Hipple fired to backup tight end Ulysses Norris on a slant over the middle for an 18-yard gain to the Dallas 30, and Detroit's field-goal unit made a frantic dash onto the field. There were 18 seconds left when Norris made his catch, and the clock was ticking down from 15 as the kicking team started on.

"I was going to throw the ball out of bounds and stop the clock," Hipple said. "I'd already called the play in the previous huddle. Then I saw Ed coming on."

When Murray went onto the field, he didn't realize the Lions were out of timeouts.

"It could have been the biggest blunder of my life," Murray said. "I kept thinking we had a timeout left. I thought we'd be able to use it, line up clean and just kick it.

"I was at about the other 30-yard line and they should have timed me in the 40. I never ran so fast in my life to line up. I saw Eric (Hipple, the holder for the kick) point to my spot, I reminded myself to wait a second and then I just kicked it."

The Lions swarmed over Murray and Detroit Coach Monte Clark left the field saying, "It's about time we won a game like that. That's the first time the Lions have beaten the Cowboys in 21 years and I'm proud to be a part of it."

The Lions' Norris couldn't quite explain the finish. After his catch at the 30, he started to line up as a wide receiver so that Hipple could throw the ball out of bounds.

"Then I saw Ed (Murray) coming on, so I lined up in the upback position (as a blocker for the field goal attempt). I was hoping we were in the right position," Norris said. "After he kicked it, I looked at the official and he just shook his head. He couldn't believe it, either."

NOVEMBER 15
SCORE BY PERIODS

Dallas	7	10	0	7—24
Detroit	0	7	10	10—27

SCORING
Dallas—Pearson 10 pass from D. White (Septien kick).

Dallas—Field goal Septien 43.
Dallas—Pearson 12 pass from D. White (Septien kick).
Detroit—Sims 3 run (Murray kick).
Detroit—Nichols 6 pass from Hipple (Murray kick).
Detroit—Field goal Murray 37.
Dallas—Saldi 14 pass from D. White (Septien kick).
Detroit—Sims 81 pass from Hipple (Murray kick).
Detroit—Field goal Murray 47.

TEAM STATISTICS

	Dallas	Detroit
First downs	19	23
Rushes-Yards	27-98	35-198
Passing yards	225	231
Sacks by-Yards	5-52	3-19
Return yards	134	158
Passes	20-30-2	14-24-1
Punts	5-43.0	4-41.3
Fumbles-Lost	1-0	3-2
Penalties-Yards	3-20	6-51
Time of possession	31:12	28:48

Attendance—79,694.

INDIVIDUAL STATISTICS

Rushing—Dallas, Dorsett 15-55, Springs 7-22, DuPree 1-12, D. White 2-5, J. Jones 2-4; Detroit, Sims 23-119, Nichols 1-30, Hipple 5-27, Bussey 5-19, Kane 1-3.

Passing—Dallas, D. White 20-30-2—244; Detroit, Hipple 13-23-1—264, Skladany 1-1-0—19.

Receiving—Dallas, Springs 5-56, Hill 4-80, Pearson 4-45, DuPree 3-17, Dorsett 2-2, Johnson 1-30, Saldi 1-14; Detroit, Hill 4-92, L. Thompson 3-39, Scott 2-31, Sims 1-81, Cobb 1-19, Nichols 1-6, Bussey 1-minus 3, Norris 1-18.

Kickoff Returns—Dallas, J. Jones 4-91, Newsome 1-16; Detroit, Martin 3-64, Nichols 2-31.

Punt Returns—Dallas, J. Jones 2-9, Fellows 1-10; Detroit, Martin 4-37.

Interceptions—Dallas, Breunig 1-8; Detroit, Baker 1-9, Cobb 1-17.

Punting—Dallas, D. White 5-43.0; Detroit, Skladany 4-41.3.

Field Goals—Dallas, Septien 1-1; Detroit, Murray 2-2.

BRONCOS 24, BUCCANEERS 7

TAMPA—Denver remained atop the AFC West with an 8-3 record after beating Tampa Bay. But Denver quarterback Craig Morton, the league's oldest player at 38, suffered an injury to his right shoulder in the second quarter of the game. "Someone hit me and I fell on my shoulder," Morton said.

Morton had thrown a 12-yard touchdown pass to tight end Riley Odoms before leaving the game after completing 10 of 14 passes for 73 yards.

Steve DeBerg, obtained at the end of pre-season from San Francisco, led the Broncos to 17 points in the second half. DeBerg also gave the Buccaneers their only points, when safety Cedric Brown intercepted a pass and ran 40 yards for a touchdown to tie the score at 7-7 on the first series of the second half.

But the Broncos, aided by two unnecessary roughness penalties on the Bucs' Norris Thomas, charged back into the lead. Larry Canada scampered one yard for a TD in the third quarter and caught a three-yard scoring pass from DeBerg in the fourth quarter. Fred Steinfort

added a 31-yard field goal.

"You've got to prepare yourself to play," DeBerg said of having to come off the bench cold.

The Broncos' league-leading defense held the Bucs to 41 yards rushing and 186 passing. The Broncos dominated the third quarter, when the Bucs had the ball for only three offensive plays.

"We played a very, very, very poor game," said Bucs Coach John McKay. "They kicked the living hell out of us and we stood there and took it."

NOVEMBER 15
SCORE BY PERIODS

Denver	7	0	7	10—24
Tampa Bay	0	0	7	0— 7

SCORING

Denver—Odoms 12 pass from Morton (Steinfort kick).
Tampa Bay—Brown 40 interception return (Capece kick).
Denver—Canada 1 run (Steinfort kick).
Denver—Canada 3 pass from DeBerg (Steinfort kick).
Denver—Field goal Steinfort 31.

TEAM STATISTICS

	Denver	Tampa Bay
First downs	22	10
Rushes-Yards	41-153	14-41
Passing yards	128	168
Sacks by-Yards	3-21	2-15
Return yards	120	109
Passes	20-29-1	14-31-2
Punts	6-40.5	7-37.4
Fumbles-Lost	0-0	0-0
Penalties-Yards	5-40	6-59
Time of possession	37:50	22:10

Attendance—64,518.

INDIVIDUAL STATISTICS

Rushing—Denver, Preston 15-50, Reed 9-27, Parros 12-54, DeBerg 3-10, Canada 1-1, Wright 1-11; Tampa Bay, Eckwood 8-25, Wilder 4-7, Williams 1-3, R. Bell 1-6.

Passing—Denver, Morton 10-14-0—73, DeBerg 10-15-1—70; Tampa Bay, Williams 14-31-2—189.

Receiving—Denver, Preston 6-46, Parros 3-8, Odoms 2-23, Watson 3-42, Reed 4-22, Upchurch 1-minus 1, Canada 1-3; Tampa Bay, Wilder 3-21, House 4-55, Giles 4-56, Eckwood 1-8, Jones 1-44, T. Bell 1-5.

Kickoff Returns—Denver, Manning 1-30; Tampa Bay, Owens 1-23, Holt 1-29.

Punt Returns—Denver, Manning 5-56; Tampa Bay, Holt 3-17.

Interceptions—Denver, Harden 2-34; Tampa Bay, Brown 1-40.

Punting—Denver, Prestridge 6-40.5; Tampa Bay, Swider 6-43.7.

Field Goals—Denver, Steinfort 1-1; Tampa Bay, None attempted.

RAIDERS 33, DOLPHINS 17

MIAMI—Coach Tom Flores admitted it was a longshot, but he refused to count Oakland out of the playoff picture for 1981.

The Raiders (5-6) kept their chances alive with a turnover-free offense and a sturdy defense in the victory over Miami.

"If we'd lost this game, we would have been completely out of it, but now we have a chance. Even though it's a longshot, we'll fight like hell," Flores said.

Eleventh Week—Continued

"We didn't beat ourselves by turnovers—no pass interceptions, no fumbles. Instead, we got a turnover on the first play and took advantage of it. We haven't been doing that."

The Dolphins' Fulton Walker fumbled the opening kickoff and Todd Christensen recovered on the Miami 27. Three plays later, Christensen caught a 13-yard touchdown pass from Marc Wilson.

Wilson added a 37-yard touchdown pass to Bob Chandler and a one-yarder to Derrick Ramsey to make the score 21-0. The Dolphins scored in the final minute of the first half on Uwe von Schamann's 36-yard field goal.

"We dug ourselves so deep in the hole in the first half that when we did get ourselves going, it was too late," said Dolphins Coach Don Shula. "Defensively, it seemed like the ball was up for grabs in the first half, but we didn't make the play."

The Dolphins remained atop the AFC East at 7-3-1, a full game ahead of the New York Jets.

NOVEMBER 15
SCORE BY PERIODS

Oakland	7	14	3	9—33
Miami	0	3	7	7—17

SCORING

Oakland—Christensen 13 pass from Wilson (Bahr kick).
Oakland—Chandler 37 pass from Wilson (Bahr kick).
Oakland—Ramsey 1 pass from Wilson (Bahr kick).
Miami—Field goal von Schamann 36.
Oakland—Field goal Bahr 32.
Miami—Hill 5 run (von Schamann kick).
Miami—Nathan 14 pass from Strock (von Schamann kick).
Oakland—Safety, Strock forced out of end zone.
Oakland—Willis 15 run (Bahr kick).

TEAM STATISTICS

	Oakland	Miami
First downs	19	22
Rushes-Yards	32-143	20-70
Passing yards	161	236
Sacks by-Yards	6-35	2-19
Return yards	86	167
Passes	16-39-0	26-47-1
Punts	9-45.9	8-38.0
Fumbles-Lost	2-0	1-1
Penalties-Yards	9-73	7-37
Time of possession	28:09	31:51

Attendance—61,777.

INDIVIDUAL STATISTICS

Rushing—Oakland, Jensen 4-35, King 9-24, Hawkins 8-31, Wilson 3-14, Willis 4-25, Whittington 4-14; Miami, Nathan 9-14, Franklin 6-19, Woodley 1-2, Hill 4-35.

Passing—Oakland, Wilson 16-39-0—180; Miami, Woodley 10-22-0—102, Strock 16-25-1—169.

Receiving—Oakland, Ramsey 7-67, Christensen 1-13, Jensen 2-11, Hawkins 1-8, Chandler 2-45, Branch 1-9, Barnwell 1-19, Chester 1-8; Miami, Harris 3-35, Lee 1-7, Nathan 7-99, Vigorito 5-30, Hill 3-30, Cefalo 3-43, Rose 2-13, Moore 1-14, Franklin 1-0.

Kickoff Returns—Oakland, Whittington 1-25, Willis 1-18, Christensen 1-0; Miami, Walker 3-89, Bessillieu 1-20, Hill 1-11.

Punt Returns—Oakland, Watts 3-36; Miami, Vigorito 5-47.

Interceptions—Oakland, Martin 1-7.

Punting—Oakland, Guy 9-45.9; Miami, Orosz 8-38.0.
Field Goals—Oakland, Bahr 1-1; Miami, von Schamann 1-2.

CHIEFS 23, OILERS 10

KANSAS CITY—Rookie running back Joe Delaney rushed for a club-record 193 yards, scored one touchdown and set up another to help the Kansas City Chiefs snap a two-game losing streak with a 23-10 victory over the Houston Oilers.

The Chiefs raised their record to 7-4 and remained one game back of Denver in the AFC Western Division. The Oilers suffered their fourth defeat in the last five games and fell to 5-6.

Delaney, a second-round draft pick out of Northwest Louisiana, erased the Chiefs rushing record of 192 yards, set by Mike Garrett in 1967 against the New York Jets. He broke another club record with his fifth 100-yard game of the season, topping the old mark of four, also by Garrett in 1967.

"I've played against the best—O. J. Simpson, Gale Sayers, Walter Payton—and he's right up there with them," said Oilers defensive end Elvin Bethea. "He's great with a capital G. He's strong and tough and quick. We beat on him, and he took it. He kept getting up."

Delaney scored the Chiefs' first touchdown on a six-yard run in the first quarter. Cornerback Eric Harris intercepted a John Reaves pass to give the Chiefs the ball at the Oilers' 38. Delaney accounted for 34 yards on only three carries.

The Chiefs moved 46 yards for their second touchdown, a one-yard run by rookie Billy Jackson, midway through the third quarter. Delaney collected 36 of those 46 yards on four carries.

"Joe Delaney is not just another running back," said Chiefs defensive end Art Still. "He's becoming one of the very best running backs. He gets better with time. Imagine what he'll be like when he gets a little experience."

Nick Lowery contributed field goals of 37, 42 and 38 yards. His last two came in the fourth quarter and put the game away after the Oilers had drawn to within 17-10 on a 50-yard touchdown pass from Ken Stabler to Ken Burrough.

The Chiefs defense forced five turnovers, with Harris intercepting two passes and recovering a fumble. Defensive tackle Ken Kremer recorded two sacks.

NOVEMBER 15
SCORE BY PERIODS

Houston	0	3	0	7—10
Kansas City	7	3	7	6—23

SCORING

Kansas City—Delaney 6 run (Lowery kick).
Kansas City—Field goal Lowery 37.
Houston—Field goal Fritsch 21.
Kansas City—B. Jackson 1 run (Lowery kick).

Unheralded rookie running back Joe Delaney, Kansas City's second-round pick, rushed for 193 yards, a club record, as the Chiefs beat the Houston Oilers, 23-10. It was the best single-game effort in the NFL all season.

Eleventh Week—Continued

Houston—Burrough 50 pass from Stabler (Fritsch kick).
Kansas City—Field goal Lowery 42.
Kansas City—Field goal Lowery 38.

TEAM STATISTICS

	Houston	Kansas City
First downs	19	19
Rushes-Yards	28-146	47-258
Passing yards	224	25
Sacks by-Yards	2-14	2-17
Return yards	91	102
Passes	18-37-3	6-12-1
Punts	4-45.3	5-39.6
Fumbles-Lost	2-2	1-1
Penalties-Yards	6-45	4-25
Time of possession	24:46	35:14

Attendance—73,984.

INDIVIDUAL STATISTICS

Rushing—Houston, Campbell 21-99, T. Wilson 3-11, Armstrong 2-23, Reaves 1-13, Coleman 1-0; Kansas City, Delaney 29-193, Hadnot 12-47, B. Jackson 5-14, Kenney 1-4.

Passing—Houston, Reaves 6-15-1—47, Stabler 12-22-2—194; Kansas City, Kenney 6-11-0—39, Hadnot 0-1-1 —0.

Receiving—Houston, Burrough 4-80, Renfro 6-62, Holston 2-37, T. Wilson 2-20, Armstrong 1-17, Barber 1-16, Coleman 1-5, Campbell 1-4; Kansas City, Smith 1-9, Rome 1-9, Marshall 1-7, Delaney 1-7, Dixon 1-5, Hadnot 1-2.

Kickoff Returns—Houston, Tullis 3-43, Roaches 2-31; Kansas City, Murphy 1-25, Rourke 1-0, Burruss 1-22.

Punt Returns—Houston, Roaches 4-17; Kansas City, Smith 3-42.

Interceptions—Houston, Brazile 1-0; Kansas City, Harris 2-3, Green 1-10.

Punting—Houston, Parsley 4-45.3; Kansas City, Gossett 5-39.6.

Field Goals—Houston, Fritsch 1-1; Kansas City, Lowery 3-3.

CARDINALS 24, BILLS 0

ST. LOUIS—Ottis Anderson and his St. Louis teammates felt they had something to prove, and they proved it with the surprising shutout of Buffalo.

One week earlier, the Cardinals had been crushed by Philadelphia, 52-10, the worst home defeat in the team's 21-year history in St. Louis. Against the Bills, they won with a 177-yard rushing effort by Anderson, a steady quarterbacking job by rookie Neil Lomax, and an alert defense, which intercepted four passes and gobbled up two fumbles.

"We wanted to redeem ourselves," Anderson said. He scored two fourth-quarter touchdowns, on bursts of 18 and eight yards, and became the Cardinals' leading career rusher. The third-year running back had 3,867 yards, surpassing the club record of 3,863 set by Jim Otis in six seasons.

Lomax replaced veteran Jim Hart at quarterback in a move designed to give the rookie from Portland State some experience, since the Cardinals' playoff chances seemed remote after they fell to 3-7 in the loss to the Eagles. Lomax completed 13 of 23 passes, including a two-yard scoring pass to running back Stump

Mitchell. His only interception came on a deflection.

Safety Ken Greene was the Cardinals' defensive standout. He intercepted three passes and recovered one of the two fumbles coughed up by Bills fullback Curtis Brown.

Greene's first interception came at the goal line with 65 seconds left in the first half and preserved a 10-0 lead. His 47-yard interception return to the Buffalo 22 early in the fourth period set up Anderson' 18-yard TD run. His final theft came after the Bills had reached the St. Louis 27 with 1:37 left.

Anderson received a game ball, but handed it off to Bill Bidwill, the Cardinals' owner. "I wanted to give the ball to him, because of all the criticism he takes and all the people who get down on him," Anderson said. "He takes a lot of heat and keeps on ticking—just like a Timex. I have a lot of respect for him and what he's done for me."

The much-maligned St. Louis defense was the worst in the NFC going into the game, having allowed 303 points in 10 games and 24 TD passes. Buffalo's Joe Ferguson was expected to feast on the defense, but instead the Cardinals posted their first shutout since October 31, 1977, when they beat the New York Giants, 28-0.

"We were embarrassed last week (against Philadelphia)," said Greene. "We were hammered. We wanted to go out and prove something."

NOVEMBER 15
SCORE BY PERIODS

Buffalo	0	0	0	0—	0
St. Louis	3	7	0	14—	24

SCORING

St. Louis—Field goal O'Donoghue 35.
St. Louis—Mitchell 2 pass from Lomax (O'Donoghue kick).
St. Louis—Anderson 18 run (O'Donoghue kick).
St. Louis—Anderson 8 run (O'Donoghue kick).

TEAM STATISTICS

	Buffalo	St. Louis
First downs	17	22
Rushes-Yards	19-85	41-258
Passing yards	226	80
Sacks by-Yards	2-22	1-7
Return yards	109	159
Passes	21-37-4	13-23-1
Punts	3-45.0	3-33.7
Fumbles-Lost	2-2	1-0
Penalties-Yards	7-70	6-45
Time of possession	23:44	36:16

Attendance—46,214.

INDIVIDUAL STATISTICS

Rushing—Buffalo, Cribbs 14-55, Brown 3-13, Ferguson 1-13, Hooks 1-4; St. Louis, Anderson 27-177, Morris 7-25, Mitchell 3-31, Lomax 3-15, Green 1-10.

Passing—Buffalo, Ferguson 21-37-4—233; St. Louis, Lomax 13-23-1—102.

Receiving—Buffalo, Butler 6-65, Brammer 5-73, Lewis 3-51, Jessie 2-19, Cribbs 2-8, Barnett 1-10, Hooks 1-7, Leaks 1-0; St. Louis, Anderson 3-9, Gray 2-36, Tilley 2-25, Mitchell 2-11, Harrell 2-8, Green 1-9, Morris 1-4.

Kickoff Returns—Buffalo, Riddick 2-40, Hooks 3-64; St. Louis, Mitchell 1-22.

Punt Returns—Buffalo, Hooks 1-5; St. Louis, Mitchell 2-31.

Interceptions—Buffalo, Robertson 1-0; St. Louis, Greene 3-106, Green 1-0.

Punting—Buffalo, Cater 3-45.0; St. Louis, Birdsong 3-33.7

Field Goals—Buffalo, None attempted; St. Louis, O'Donoghue 1-2.

BROWNS 15, 49ers 12

SAN FRANCISCO—Are the Kardiac Kids back? Cleveland stayed alive in the AFC Central Division race and snapped San Francisco's seven-game winning streak when Matt Bahr connected on a 24-yard field goal with 43 seconds left at Candlestick Park.

The Browns (5-6) still trailed AFC Central leader Cincinnati by three games, but they were pumped up after beating the 49ers, the runaway leaders (8-3) in the NFC West.

Coach Sam Rutigliano was talking about the playoffs after the clutch victory over the 49ers.

"We've got the opportunity to control our destiny," he said. "We're not out of it by a longshot."

Ray Wersching kicked four field goals for all the 49ers' scoring. The Browns trailed, 12-5, when Brian Sipe threw a 21-yard touchdown pass to Reggie Rucker to tie the score with 6:46 left.

Sipe and Rucker combined for a 38-yard gain in the final minute to set up Bahr's winning field goal. "Just plain determination did it for us this time," said Sipe.

Bill Walsh, the 49ers' coach, shrugged off the loss. "We're not terribly dejected," he said. "Our failure to score touchdowns cost us the game. You can't be down there five times and come out with only 12 points."

NOVEMBER 15

SCORE BY PERIODS

Cleveland	2	3	0	10—15
San Francisco	0	6	6	0—12

SCORING

Cleveland—Safety, Montana intentionally grounded ball in end zone.
San Francisco—Field goal Wersching 28.
Cleveland—Field goal Bahr 28.
San Francisco—Field goal Wersching 29.
San Francisco—Field goal Wersching 28.
San Francisco—Field goal Wersching 28.
Cleveland—Rucker 21 pass from Sipe (Bahr kick).
Cleveland—Field goal Bahr 24.

* TEAM STATISTICS

	Cleveland	San Fran.
First-downs	14	21
Rushes-Yards	26-106	35-118
Passing yards	161	187
Sacks by-Yards	3-26	2-19
Return yards	165	84
Passes	16-33-1	24-42-2
Punts	5-42.4	4-36.0
Fumbles-Lost	1-1	1-0
Penalties-Yards	7-55	4-29
Time of possession	24:48	35:12
Attendance—52,445.		

INDIVIDUAL STATISTICS

Rushing—Cleveland, M. Pruitt 18-76, G. Pruitt 5-26, White 2-7, Sipe 1-minus 3; San Francisco, Easley 16-59, Hofer 10-33, Patton 4-15, Davis 2-6, Montana 2-5, Solomon 1-0.

Passing—Cleveland, Sipe 16-33-1—180; San Francisco, Montana 24-42-2—213.

Receiving—Cleveland, G. Pruitt, 4-33, Rucker 3-77, Newsome 3-36, M. Pruitt 3-11, White 2-12, Feacher 1-11; San Francisco, Hofer 7-64, Clark 6-52, Solomon 3-35, Cooper 3-21, Young 2-16, Patton 1-11, Shumann 1-8, Easley 1-6.

Kickoff Returns—Cleveland, Hall 3-82; San Francisco, Lawrence 2-52.

Punt Returns—Cleveland, Hall 3-50; San Francisco, Solomon 2-22.

Interceptions—Cleveland, Ambrose 1-0, Flint 1-33; San Francisco, Hicks 1-10.

Punting—Cleveland, Cox 5-42.4; San Francisco, Miller 4-36.0.

Field Goals—Cleveland, Bahr 2-3; San Francisco, Wersching 4-5.

REDSKINS 30, GIANTS 27 (Overtime)

EAST RUTHERFORD—Once was not enough for Washington's Mark Moseley. He drilled a 49-yard field goal through a driving rain at Giants Stadium to tie the score as time ran out in the fourth quarter. Then he connected on a 48-yarder at 3:44 of overtime to give the Redskins their fourth straight victory.

Starting quarterback Phil Simms suffered what was described as a "non-operative separated right shoulder" when he was sacked by the Redskins' Dave Butz and Dexter Manley with 1:46 left in the fourth period and Washington leading, 24-20.

Scott Brunner, the only other quarterback on the Giants' roster, took over for Simms and completed three passes, including a 27-yard TD throw to John Mistler on a fourth-down play to give New York a 27-24 lead with 45 seconds left.

However, the Giants' downfall began with the kickoff after that touchdown. Joe Danelo squibbed his kick, and Darryl Grant returned it 20 yards to the Washington 45. It took Joe Theismann five plays, including a 10-yard scramble and two short completions, to move the Redskins to the Giants' 32 before Moseley hit the tying field goal.

"I lost the game because I was talked into the squib kick," said Giants Coach Ray Perkins. "I decided to have Danelo kick it on the ground."

Before coming through on his two long-distance field goals, Moseley had missed on two shorter attempts. He failed on a 37-yarder that would have tied the score at 20-all early in the fourth quarter.

The Giants scored their first opening-quarter touchdown of the season on Simms' six-yard pass to Johnny Perkins, and they went on to build a 20-10 lead. A TD run by John Riggins cut the Redskins' deficit to 20-17 and Theis-

Eleventh Week—Continued

mann put Washington ahead for the first time on a three-yard TD pass to Don Warren with 6:35 left in the fourth quarter.

The Giants had the ball first in overtime, but were forced to punt. Mike Nelms returned the kick 26 yards to the Giants' 47. A 12-yard run by Joe Washington helped move the ball into position for Moseley's winning kick.

NOVEMBER 15
SCORE BY PERIODS

Washington	7	3	7	10	3—30
New York Giants	7	6	7	7	0—27

SCORING

New York—Perkins 6 pass from Simms (Danelo kick).
Washington—Thompson 9 pass from Theismann (Moseley kick).
New York—L. Jackson 4 run (bad snap, pass failed).
Washington—Field goal Moseley 25.
New York—Bright 1 run (Danelo kick).
Washington—Riggins 1 run (Moseley kick).
Washington—Warren 3 pass from Theismann (Moseley kick).
New York—Mistler 27 pass from Brunner (Danelo kick).
Washington—Field goal Moseley 49.
Washington—Field goal Moseley 48.

TEAM STATISTICS

	Washington	New York
First downs	29	17
Rushes-Yards	50-184	27-96
Passing yards	234	152
Sacks by-Yards	3-25	1-8
Return yards	120	143
Passes	25-38-1	9-24-1
Punts	4-39.0	6-41.3
Fumbles-Lost	0-0	1-1
Penalties-Yards	7-49	3-35
Time of possession	42:47	20:57

Attendance—63,133.

INDIVIDUAL STATISTICS

Rushing—Washington, Washington 19-53, Theismann 5-49, Riggins 26-82; New York, L. Jackson 13-22, Perry 11-67, Bright 3-7.

Passing—Washington, Theismann 25-38-1—242; New York, Simms 6-17-1—109, Brunner 3-7-0—68.

Receiving—Washington, Metcalf 5-76, Walker 1-24, Washington 7-36, Thompson 2-18, Warren 5-43, Monk 3-20, Riggins 2-25; New York, Perkins 3-47, Perry 1-12, L. Jackson 1-19, Gray 2-65, Shirk 1-7, Mistler 1-27.

Kickoff Returns—Washington, Nelms 2-41, Grant 1-20; New York, Bright 1-11, Garrett 2-50, Pittman 1-34, McLaughlin 1-4.

Punt Returns—Washington, Nelms 5-56; New York, Bright 3-17.

Interceptions—Washington, Murphy 1-3; New York, Kelley 1-27.

Punting—Washington, Connell 4-39.0; New York, Jennings 6-41.3.

Field Goals—Washington, Moseley 3-5; New York, None attempted.

BENGALS 24, RAMS 10

CINCINNATI—Thanks to a tough, clawing defense, Cincinnati hiked its record to 8-3 with a victory over faltering Los Angeles.

The Bengals' fifth victory in six games kept them two games ahead in the AFC Central. The once-powerful Rams (5-6) had lost four of their last five games.

The Bengals sacked Ram quarterbacks Dan Pastorini and Pat Haden six times for 56 yards and intercepted them four times.

"Our pass rush was great," said Coach Forrest Gregg. "We put a lot of pressure on them. The game ball went to the defensive line."

"Our pass rush is getting better every game," said Bengals defensive end Eddie Edwards, who owned three of the sacks, including one that knocked Pastorini unconscious.

Cornerback Louis Breeden intercepted two L.A. passes.

"It's the mark of a good team to take advantage of mistakes and that's what we've been doing," said Breeden. "We're playing with a lot more confidence in the defensive backfield."

Breeden returned his first interception 43 yards in the first quarter to set up Ken Anderson's three-yard TD toss to Pete Johnson.

Breeden nabbed another Pastorini pass in the fourth quarter, and that led to another Johnson touchdown, on a three-yard run.

A minute later, Reggie Williams intercepted Pastorini at the Rams' 20 and returned it to the 10 to set up Johnson's third touchdown, a one-yard run.

The Rams' lone touchdown came way too late to matter—a 10-yard pass from Haden to running back Wendell Tyler with 1:55 to go.

NOVEMBER 15
SCORE BY PERIODS

Los Angeles	0	3	0	7—10
Cincinnati	10	0	0	14—24

SCORING

Cincinnati—Field goal Breech 37.
Cincinnati—Johnson 3 pass from Anderson (Breech kick).
Los Angeles—Field goal Corral 22.
Cincinnati—Johnson 3 run (Breech kick).
Cincinnati—Johnson 1 run (Breech kick).
Los Angeles—Tyler 10 pass from Haden (Corral kick).

TEAM STATISTICS

	Los Angeles	Cincinnati
First downs	21	17
Rushes-Yards	27-107	36-146
Passing yards	189	87
Sacks by-Yards	2-10	6-56
Return yards	96	74
Passes	21-47-4	11-26-1
Punts	7-41.4	9-44.9
Fumbles-Lost	2-0	1-0
Penalties-Yards	3-16	7-55
Time of possession	27:37	32:23

Attendance—56,836.

INDIVIDUAL STATISTICS

Rushing—Los Angeles, Tyler 15-51, Cromwell 1-17, Bryant 8-37, J. Thomas 1-0, Guman 2-2; Cincinnati, Alexander 9-19, Anderson 4-58, Johnson 17-56, A. Griffin 4-5, Hargrove 2-8.

Passing—Los Angeles, Pastorini 8-24-3—78, Haden 13-23-1—167; Cincinnati, Anderson 9-21-1—76, Thompson 2-5-0—21.

Receiving—Los Angeles, Arnold 3-28, D. Hill 3-25, Waddy 6-77, Tyler 4-34, Dennard 2-47, Miller 2-34, Bryant 1-0; Cincinnati, Collinsworth 2-29, Curtis 1-2, Ross 5-47, Johnson 3-19.

Kickoff Returns—Los Angeles, D. Hill 4-63; Cincinnati, Verser 2-14.

Punt Returns—Los Angeles, Irvin 2-33; Cincinnati, Fuller 1-7.

Interceptions—Los Angeles, Thomas 1-minus 10, Perry 0-10; Cincinnati, Breeden 2-43, Williams 1-10, Riley 1-0.

Punting—Los Angeles, Corral 7-41.4; Cincinnati, McInally 9-44.9.

Field Goals—Los Angeles, Corral 1-1; Cincinnati, Breech 1-1.

VIKINGS 20, SAINTS 10

BLOOMINGTON—Tommy Kramer passed for 287 yards and one touchdown and topped 10,000 yards for his career. However, what turned out to be an incomplete pass by the Minnesota quarterback was the major topic of discussion after the Vikings' victory over New Orleans.

The Saints lost an apparent touchdown on an interception return in the fourth quarter because of an "inadvertent whistle" by line judge Boyce Smith.

Minnesota had a 20-3 lead when Kramer passed on third down from the Vikings' 20. Defensive tackle Jerry Boyarsky batted the pass into the air, and then safety Russell Gary tapped the ball into the arms of defensive end Frank Warren, who caught the ball inside the 10-yard line and raced into the end zone.

However, the official's whistle nullified the TD and the Vikings were allowed to punt from the 20. Warren and the Saints said a TD at the time "would have turned the game around for us," but the play was not reversed.

"There wasn't a reason for why the whistle was blown," said referee Dick Jorgensen. "I think inadvertent answers it." Jorgensen said the rule states that in such an instance—a pass behind the line—the ball reverts to the passer's team at the previous spot, and the play is declared an incomplete pass.

Saints Coach Bum Phillips growled, "It wasn't an inadvertent whistle. It was an incompetent whistle. Let's make that clear. You don't blow a whistle while the ball is in the air.

"They knew they blew it—the whistle and the call. Officiating is a human thing. They didn't do it on purpose, but I do believe it to be the worst call I've ever seen."

Minnesota Coach Bud Grant agreed that the call was wrong. "There was no question that it was the biggest play of the game," said Grant. "The officials were restrained after that and New Orleans felt they were cheated."

The Vikings contained the Saints' two rookie stars, quarterback David Wilson and running back George Rogers, to boost their record to 7-4. Wilson passed for 244 yards, but was sacked six times. Rogers rushed for 97 yards in 31 trips.

NOVEMBER 15
SCORE BY PERIODS

New Orleans	0	3	0	7—10
Minnesota	0	10	10	0—20

SCORING

Minnesota—Field goal Danmeier 35.
New Orleans—Field goal Ricardo 24.
Minnesota—Senser 11 pass from Kramer (Danmeier kick).
Minnesota—Field goal Danmeier 19.
Minnesota—Brown 9 run (Danmeier kick).
New Orleans—Rogers 1 run (Ricardo kick).

TEAM STATISTICS

	New Orleans	Minnesota
First downs	23	17
Rushes-Yards	38-119	23-70
Passing yards	195	287
Sacks by-Yards	0-0	6-49
Return yards	101	75
Passes	19-39-2	19-40-0
Punts	6-35.8	6-49.2
Fumbles-Lost	0-0	1-1
Penalties-Yards	12-100	8-77
Time of possession	36:54	23:06
Attendance—45,215.		

INDIVIDUAL STATISTICS

Rushing—New Orleans, G. Rogers 31-97, Holmes 4-14, Tyler 2-7, D. Wilson 1-1; Minnesota, Brown 16-54, Galbreath 5-11, Young 1-3, Senser 1-2.

Passing—New Orleans, D. Wilson 19-39-2—244; Minnesota, Kramer 19-40-0—287.

Receiving—New Orleans, W. Wilson 3-71, Groth 4-62, Hardy 2-40, Thompson 2-29, Martini 3-27, Merkens 1-7, G. Rogers 3-7, Holmes 1-1; Minnesota, Senser 7-92, S. White 2-62, Brown 5-53, LeCount 2-52, Rashad 1-16, Young 2-12.

Kickoff Returns—New Orleans, J. Rogers 3-37, W. Wilson 2-33; Minnesota, Payton 2-39, Young 1-15.

Punt Returns—New Orleans, Groth 4-31; Minnesota, Payton 1-1.

Interceptions—Minnesota, Knoff 2-20.

Punting—New Orleans, Erxleben 6-35.8; Minnesota, Coleman 6-49.2.

Field Goals—New Orleans, Ricardo 1-1; Minnesota, Danmeier 2-2.

PACKERS 21, BEARS 17

GREEN BAY—Coach Bart Starr sipped a beer and declared, "Whew! It tastes pretty good," after Green Bay held off Chicago with a stiff second-half defensive effort.

What was tasting good was a third straight victory for the Packers, who started the second half of the season with a 2-6 record, but suddenly were in the playoff picture at 5-6.

The Packers built a 21-10 halftime lead on three touchdown passes by David Whitehurst. That forced the Bears into a passing situation, and cornerback Mark Lee made two second-half interceptions to help save the game and give Green Bay a sweep of its season series with Chicago for the first time since 1972.

Whitehurst threw TD passes of one yard and 39 yards to Harlan Huckleby and two yards to Terdell Middleton. In the second half, however, he was only 2-for-10 passing, for a total of five yards.

The Bears' only touchdown of the second half came after defensive end Al Harris recovered a fumble by the Packers' Gerry Ellis. Walter Payton, who picked up 105 yards on 22 carries, ran two yards for the score.

Chicago's Vince Evans was 13-for-29 passing

Eleventh Week—Continued

and was the victim of three costly interceptions. Safety Mark Murphy's interception and 50-yard return in the second quarter set up the 39-yard TD pass from Whitehurst to Huckleby.

NOVEMBER 15

SCORE BY PERIODS

Chicago	10	0	0	7—17
Green Bay	7	14	0	0—21

SCORING

Chicago—Field goal Roveto 36.
Green Bay—Huckleby 1 pass from Whitehurst (Stenerud kick).
Chicago—Suhey 1 run (Roveto kick).
Green Bay—Huckleby 39 pass from Whitehurst (Stenerud kick).
Green Bay—Middleton 2 pass from Whitehurst (Stenerud kick).
Chicago—Payton 2 run (Roveto kick).

TEAM STATISTICS

	Chicago	Green Bay
First downs	20	18
Rushes-Yards	39-165	34-114
Passing yards	88	133
Sacks by-Yards	1-7	3-26
Return yards	106	197
Passes	13-29-3	11-32-1
Punts	7-39.7	8-41.5
Fumbles-Lost	6-0	2-1
Penalties-Yards	5-59	4-32
Time of possession	34:16	25:44

Attendance—55,338.

INDIVIDUAL STATISTICS

Rushing—Chicago, Payton 22-105, Suhey 12-18, Evans 4-31, Margerum 1-11; Green Bay, Huckleby 17-71, Ellis 13-37, Whitehurst 2-minus 2, Middleton 2-8.

Passing—Chicago, Evans 13-29-3—114; Green Bay, Whitehurst 11-31-1—140, Ellis 0-1-0—0.

Receiving—Chicago, Suhey 4-11, D. Williams 2-8, Watts 3-52, Earl 1-23, Baschnagel 1-12, Payton 2-8; Green Bay, Coffman 3-18, Lofton 5-80, Huckleby 2-40, Middleton 1-2.

Kickoff Returns—Chicago, Moorehead 2-46, Frazier 2-21; Green Bay, McCoy 2-58, Middleton 2-30.

Punt Returns—Chicago, Fisher 5-39; Green Bay, Lee 3-22, Cassidy 1-0.

Interceptions—Chicago, Fisher 1-0; Green Bay, Murphy 1-50, Lee 2-37.

Punting—Chicago, Parsons 7-39.7; Green Bay, Stachowicz 8-41.5.

Field Goals—Chicago, Roveto 1-1; Green Bay, None attempted.

JETS 17, PATRIOTS 6

FOXBORO—Three weeks into the season, Walt Michaels was a most unpopular coach.

His New York Jets, after a 4-12 mark in 1980, were 0-3 and had given up 100 points in the process. People called for his removal, but Michaels remained calm. Eight weeks later, he was having the last laugh.

During that eight-week stretch, the Jets were 6-1-1. Sparked by a defensive unit that led the NFL in sacks, the Jets ripped New England, 17-6, to boost their record to 6-4-1. They slipped into second place in the AFC East, one game behind Miami.

Bruce Harper and Tom Newton capped long drives with scoring runs, and the Jets' defense had eight sacks and forced two turnovers in sending the Patriots to their ninth loss in 11 games.

Harper dashed four yards through the driving wind and rain late in the first half and Newton added a five-yard scoring run. Pat Leahy had a 47-yard field goal for the Jets. The Patriots were held to field goals of 42 and 29 yards by John Smith.

The eight sacks, including three each by league leader Joe Klecko and runner-up Mark Gastineau, gave the Jets 46 for the season. The Jets sacked Steve Grogan three times and his replacement, Matt Cavanaugh, five times.

Linebacker Greg Buttle set up 10 points with an interception and a fumble recovery to help the Jets win at Schaefer Stadium for the first time since 1975.

"It's nice to come up here and finally beat them," said Buttle.

"We said all along that if we continued to work and play hard and be aggressive, we would start turning things around," said Michaels. "And we have. It doesn't happen overnight. It takes a lot of hard work to win in this league and our people have realized it. We look for 45 guys playing hard together and that's what we've been getting. If you get that every week, you're going to win your share of games."

NOVEMBER 15

SCORE BY PERIODS

New York Jets	0	10	7	0—17
New England	0	3	3	0— 6

SCORING

New England—Field goal Smith 42.
New York—Harper 4 run (Leahy kick).
New York—Field goal Leahy 47.
New York—Newton 5 run (Leahy kick).
New England—Field goal Smith 29.

TEAM STATISTICS

	New York	New England
First downs	17	15
Rushes-Yards	53-166	23-92
Passing yards	60	105
Sacks by-Yards	8-48	0-0
Return yards	63	103
Passes	7-17-1	14-34-1
Punts	7-37.6	7-43.0
Fumbles-Lost	1-0	3-1
Penalties-Yards	5-57	6-50
Time of possession	36:47	23:13

Attendance—45,342.

INDIVIDUAL STATISTICS

Rushing—New York, Harper 7-14, Dierking 8-35, Newton 14-45, Long 2-3, McNeil 13-50, Augustyniak 5-25, Ryan 2-minus 3, Todd 2-minus 3; New England, Collins 13-66, Tatupu 5-8, Ferguson 4-9, Grogan 1-9.

Passing—New York, Todd 6-13-0—56, Ryan 1-4-1—4; New England, Grogan 9-19-1—105, Cavanaugh 5-15-0—48.

Receiving—New York, Walker 3-25, Harper 2-19, Dierking 1-12, Augustyniak 1-4; New England, Hasselbeck 3-57, Morgan 1-4, Johnson 6-61, Collins 1-9, Tatupu 3-22.

Kickoff Returns—New York, Harper 1-14, Sohn 1-13; New England, Toler 1-26, Sanford 1-27, Johnson 1-17, Calhoun 1-16.

Punt Returns—New York, Harper 2-24; New England, Morgan 3-minus 4.

Interceptions—New York, Buttle 1-12; New England, James 1-21.

Punting—New York, Ramsey 7-37.6; New England, Camarillo 7-43.0.

Field Goals—New York, Leahy 1-2; New England, Smith 2-2.

STEELERS 34, FALCONS 20

ATLANTA—When Cliff Stoudt swung at a punching bag in a Seattle lounge and suffered a broken arm, he may have awakened Terry Bradshaw in the process.

Bradshaw, about to be replaced by Stoudt as the Pittsburgh quarterback and so upset with his recent play that he'd asked to be relieved from play-calling responsibility, responded to the loss of Stoudt by firing five touchdown passes—a personal best—in the Steelers' triumph over the Falcons.

Bradshaw connected on 14 of 22 passes for 253 yards. He had scoring throws of 19 and six yards to John Stallworth, 18 yards to Bennie Cunningham, 14 yards to Randy Grossman and 22 yards to Lynn Swann.

"It was a good feeling to win and play well, which I hadn't done in a long time," said Bradshaw.

Coach Chuck Noll said a decision on Bradshaw calling the plays in other games "depends on how he feels. He called one very big one today." On that one, Bradshaw rejected the trap play Noll sent in and threw a 53-yard bomb to Stallworth to set up Pittsburgh's last TD.

Atlanta contributed to its own downfall. Two fumbles set up Pittsburgh touchdowns. Fullback William Andrews lost a fumble at the Steelers' one-yard line as the Falcons were moving to a tying TD. And in the fourth quarter, with Atlanta trailing by 27-17, Wallace Francis dropped a pass when he was wide open in the end zone.

Steve Bartkowski set a Falcons record with 416 yards passing as he completed 33 of 50 throws. Other club records went to Andrews, who caught 15 passes coming out of the backfield, and Alfred Jenkins, who grabbed his 12th TD pass of the season.

NOVEMBER 15
SCORE BY PERIODS

Pittsburgh	7	7	13	7—34
Atlanta	0	7	3	10—20

SCORING

Pittsburgh—Cunningham 18 pass from Bradshaw (Trout kick).
Pittsburgh—Stallworth 6 pass from Bradshaw (Trout kick).
Atlanta—Jackson 35 pass from Bartkowski (Luckhurst kick).
Pittsburgh—Stallworth 19 pass from Bradshaw (Trout kick).
Atlanta—Field goal Luckhurst 43.
Pittsburgh—Grossman 14 pass from Bradshaw (kick failed).
Atlanta—Jenkins 30 pass from Bartkowski (Luckhurst kick).
Pittsburgh—Swann 22 pass from Bradshaw (Trout kick).
Atlanta—Field goal Luckhurst 22.

TEAM STATISTICS

	Pittsburgh	Atlanta
First downs	13	24
Rushes-Yards	32-72	22-61
Passing yards	221	380
Sacks by-Yards	5-36	3-32
Return yards	85	175
Passes	14-23-1	33-50-2
Punts	8-45.0	5-44.0
Fumbles-Lost	4-2	4-4
Penalties-Yards	2-25	4-45
Time of possession	31:45	28:15

Attendance—57,485.

INDIVIDUAL STATISTICS

Rushing—Pittsburgh, Harris 17-54, Pollard 7-14, Davis 3-10, Bradshaw 1-1, Hawthorne 1-minus 3, Malone 3-minus 4; Atlanta, Andrews 12-36, Cain 9-20, Bartkowski 1-5.

Passing—Pittsburgh, Bradshaw 14-22-1—253, Malone 0-1-0—0; Atlanta, Bartkowski 33-50-2—416.

Receiving—Pittsburgh, Stallworth 6-127, Cunningham 3-55, Swann 2-42, Grossman 1-14, Harris 1-9, Pollard 1-6; Atlanta, Andrews 15-124, Jackson 5-109, Jenkins 4-80, Francis 3-38, Cain 3-26, Miller 2-30, Strong 1-9.

Kickoff Returns—Pittsburgh, Anderson 1-21; Atlanta, R. Smith 5-157.

Punt Returns—Pittsburgh, Anderson 4-61; Atlanta, R. Smith 1-7, Woerner 2-7, Johnson 2-minus 2.

Interceptions—Pittsburgh, Lambert 1-3, Shell 1-0; Atlanta, Butler 1-6.

Punting—Pittsburgh, Colquitt 8-45.0; Atlanta, James 5-44.0.

Field Goals—Pittsburgh, None attempted; Atlanta, Luckhurst 2-3.

EAGLES 38, COLTS 13

PHILADELPHIA—Quarterback Ron Jaworski had a simple explanation as to why Philadelphia was able to roll up 574 yards and send Baltimore to its 10th straight defeat.

"I don't think they knew where we were coming from a lot of times," said Jaworski. "We had them groping with all the formations we showed. They were a little confused."

Jaworski, who played just three quarters, completed 19 of 29 passes for 294 yards and two touchdowns—a 15-yarder to tight end Keith Krepfle on the Eagles' first drive of the game and a 30-yard strike to Charlie Smith in the third quarter.

Wilbert Montgomery picked up 115 yards in 22 carries and scored on runs of five yards and one yard in the second quarter. He left the game midway through the third quarter with a jammed ankle.

Tony Franklin kicked a 32-yard field goal and backup quarterback Joe Pisarcik fired a 44-yard scoring pass to Wally Henry. The Eagles missed the club total offense record of 582 yards, set in 1965, by just eight yards, and

Eleventh Week—Continued

they broke a 30-year-old team record by piling up 34 first downs.

"I know a lot of people were concerned about how we would play coming off a big win (a 52-10 romp over St. Louis) and playing a team that was 1-9," said Eagles Coach Dick Vermeil. "I think our guys answered those questions today. The Colts are down and it was our job to keep them down."

Colts Coach Mike McCormack rotated Bert Jones with backup quarterback Greg Landry in the second half, but neither was effective because Baltimore could not generate a ground game. The Colts ran for just 36 yards.

NOVEMBER 15
SCORE BY PERIODS

Baltimore	6	0	0	7—13
Philadelphia	7	14	10	7—38

SCORING

Philadelphia—Krepfle 15 pass from Jaworski (Franklin kick).
Baltimore—Dickey 1 run (kick failed).
Philadelphia—Montgomery 5 run (Franklin kick).
Philadelphia—Montgomery 1 run (Franklin kick).
Philadelphia—Field goal Franklin 32.
Philadelphia—Smith 30 pass from Jaworski (Franklin kick).
Baltimore—Dixon 17 pass from B. Jones (Wood kick).
Philadelphia—Henry 44 pass from Pisarcik (Franklin kick).

TEAM STATISTICS

	Baltimore	Philadelphia
First downs	9	34
Rushes-Yards	18-36	49-235
Passing yards	172	339
Sacks by-Yards	1-13	0-0
Return yards	160	21
Passes	12-26-1	21-31-1
Punts	4-39.8	0-0.0
Fumbles-Lost	2-1	1-1
Penalties-Yards	7-53	6-45
Time of possession	18:35	41:25
Attendance—68,618.		

INDIVIDUAL STATISTICS

Rushing—Baltimore, Dickey 6-17, McMillan 6-12, Franklin 2-6, McCauley 2-6, Dixon 2-minus 5; Philadelphia, Montgomery 22-115, Murray 7-51, Oliver 7-31, Campfield 7-19, Russell 5-13, Jaworski 1-6.

Passing—Baltimore, B. Jones 8-17-1—93, Landry 4-9-0—79; Philadelphia, Jaworski 19-29-1—294, Pisarcik 2-2-0—58.

Receiving—Baltimore, Butler 3-54, Dickey 2-44, Carr 2-34, Dixon 2-23, McCall 2-18, McCauley 1-minus 1; Philadelphia, Carmichael 7-93, Krepfle 3-70, Henry 3-70, Smith 2-46, Montgomery 2-37, Campfield 2-27, Spagnola 1-15.

Kickoff Returns—Baltimore, Dixon 4-74, Williams 2-37; Philadelphia, Campfield 1-8.

Punt Returns—Philadelphia, Henry, 2-13.

Interceptions—Baltimore, Anderson 1-49; Philadelphia, Logan 1-0.

Punting—Baltimore, Garrett 4-39.8; Philadelphia, None.

Field Goals—Baltimore, None attempted; Philadelphia, Franklin 1-3.

SEAHAWKS 44, CHARGERS 23

SEATTLE—In the first Monday night game of the 1981 season, the San Diego Chargers rolled up 44 points in smashing the Cleveland Browns, 44-14. The Browns were a playoff team in 1980 and the slaughter of Cleveland confirmed the preseason predictions of many people that San Diego was a Super Bowl contender.

Exactly 10 weeks later, the Chargers gave up 44 points to the Seattle Seahawks—not the most awesome of teams—in a 44-23 Monday night beating. What a difference 10 weeks make.

"Now we're going to go out and win five. We'll make the playoffs some way, somehow," said San Diego Coach Don Coryell, whose much-maligned defense lived up to its dubious reputation in this game. The Charger defense gave up 40 points in a 23-point loss to Cincinnati the week before and, with only five games left, San Diego found itself two games behind Denver in the AFC West race.

The outcome of the game was as much the result of an excellent Seattle effort as a poor San Diego one. It was the Seahawks' third win in their last four games and raised their record to 4-7. Only the week before the Seahawks had beaten the Pittsburgh Steelers, 24-21. The win also was Seattle's first against San Diego since 1977.

Three Seattle players figured prominently in the victory. Quarterback Jim Zorn and running backs Theotis Brown and Dan Doornink each were involved in two touchdowns—Zorn passed for two, Brown ran for two and Doornink caught one and ran for another.

San Diego was led by quarterback Dan Fouts, who passed for 252 yards, and running back Chuck Muncie, who ran for 151. In fact, the Chargers led the Seahawks in nearly every offensive category—first downs, passing, rushing and return yardage. But the Chargers also led in fumbles, four, and lost three of them. That helped the Seahawks lead in the only category that really mattered—points scored.

MONDAY, NOVEMBER 16
SCORE BY PERIODS

San Diego	7	10	0	6—23
Seattle	0	24	14	6—44

SCORING

San Diego—Muncie 1 run (Benirschke kick).
Seattle—Field goal Herrera 25.
Seattle—T. Brown 2 run (Herrera kick).
Seattle—Smith 18 pass from Zorn (Herrera kick).
San Diego—Muncie 73 run (Benirschke kick).
Seattle—T. Brown 1 run (Herrera kick).
San Diego—Field goal Benirschke 32.
Seattle—Doornink 80 pass from Zorn (Herrera kick).
Seattle—Doornink 3 run (Herrera kick).
Seattle—Field goal Herrera 30.
San Diego—Chandler 22 pass from Fouts (kick failed).
Seattle—Field goal Herrera 23.

TEAM STATISTICS

	San Diego	Seattle
First downs	26	24
Rushes-Yards	30-195	37-156

	San Diego	Seattle
Passing yards	291	212
Sacks by-Yards	0-0	0-0
Return yards	178	107
Passes	24-43-1	11-22-0
Punts	1-40.0	2-41.0
Fumbles-Lost	4-3	0-0
Penalties-Yards	13-138	6-54
Time of possession	30:43	29:17
Attendance—58,628.		

INDIVIDUAL STATISTICS

Rushing—San Diego, Muncie 20-151, Brooks 6-28, Cappelletti 4-16; Seattle, T. Brown 18-83, Smith 9-43, Hughes 4-20, Doornink 4-9, Zorn 2-1.

Passing—San Diego, Fouts 20-34-1—252, Luther 4-9-0—39; Seattle, Zorn 11-22-0—212.

Receiving—San Diego, Brooks 9-90, Winslow 7-106, Chandler 2-48, Muncie 2-17, Joiner 2-13, Scales 1-9, Cappelletti 1-8; Seattle, Largent 3-44, Doornink 1-80, Sawyer 1-23, Smith 1-18, Johns 1-12, Raible 1-12, T. Brown 1-10, McCullum 1-7, Hughes 1-6.

Kickoff Returns—San Diego, Brooks 5-123, Chandler 1-11, Beaudoin 1-31, Sievers 2-4; Seattle, Ivory 2-45, Lane 1-21, Sawyer 1-8.

Punt Returns—San Diego, Brooks 2-9.

Interceptions—Seattle, Jackson 1-33.

Punting—San Diego, Roberts 1-40.0; Seattle, West 2-41.0.

Field Goals—San Diego, Benirschke 1-1; Seattle, Herrera 3-3.

TWELFTH WEEK

BUCCANEERS 37, PACKERS 3

TAMPA—The battle of the Bays was over early. Green Bay's starting quarterback, David Whitehurst, suffered a groin injury in the first quarter and was replaced by rookie Rich Campbell. The Tampa Bay defense took advantage of Campbell's inexperience by picking off four passes and converting three of the turnovers into scores.

Cornerback Cedric Brown set the pace for the Buccaneers' defense with two interceptions. He picked off a throw by Campbell on the first play of the second period and returned it 81 yards for a touchdown, giving the Bucs a 10-0 lead. Brown had a 50-yard interception return in the final period, setting up a two-yard TD pass from Chuck Fusina to Jimmie Giles.

In addition to those two scores, Neal Colzie intercepted Campbell to set up a 33-yard field goal by Bill Capece in the final seconds of the first half. Capece also kicked field goals of 47 and 51 yards (a Buc record); James Owens ran for 112 yards, including a 35-yard TD burst, and Doug Williams hit Theo Bell with a seven-yard TD pass.

Green Bay's only score came on a 53-yard field goal (a Packer record) by Jan Stenerud in the final period.

"We played our best game," said Tampa Bay Coach John McKay, whose Bucs went to 6-6 while the Packers dipped to 5-7. But McKay conceded, "Green Bay got a tough break when it lost Whitehurst. I felt sorry for Bart Starr, having to go with his third quarterback. That's difficult."

The Bucs so dominated the game that they never punted and had 211 yards to none by the Packers on interception and punt returns.

NOVEMBER 22
SCORE BY PERIODS

Green Bay	0	0	0	3—	3
Tampa Bay	3	24	0	10—	37

SCORING

Tampa Bay—Field goal Capece 47.
Tampa Bay—Brown 81 interception return (Capece kick).
Tampa Bay—Owens 35 run (Capece kick).
Tampa Bay—T. Bell 7 pass from Williams (Capece kick).
Tampa Bay—Field goal Capece 33.
Tampa Bay—Field goal Capece 51.
Green Bay—Field goal Stenerud 53.
Tampa Bay—Giles 2 pass from Fusina (Capece kick).

TEAM STATISTICS

	Green Bay	Tampa Bay
First downs	14	23
Rushes-Yards	20-70	43-210
Passing yards	212	138
Sacks by-Yards	2-12	2-11
Return yards	99	240
Passes	21-38-4	13-24-1
Punts	4-45.3	0-00.0
Fumbles-Lost	0-0	2-2
Penalties-Yards	4-37	2-15
Time of possession	26:59	33:01
Attendance—63,251.		

INDIVIDUAL STATISTICS

Rushing—Green Bay, Ellis 12-55, Huckleby 6-15, Jensen 2-0; Tampa Bay, Eckwood 6-22, Owens 16-112, Williams 3-13, Wilder 8-25, House 1-1, R. Bell 7-27, Fusina 1-7, Davis 1-3.

Passing—Green Bay, Whitehurst 6-8-0—55, Campbell 15-30-4—168; Tampa Bay, Williams 12-23-1—148, Fusina 1-1-0—2.

Receiving—Green Bay, Jefferson 2-10, Ellis 11-76, Lofton 6-102, Coffman 2-35; Tampa Bay, Owens 4-44, House 1-13, T. Bell 1-7, Giles 4-53, Wilder 2-22, R. Bell 1-11.

Kickoff Returns—Green Bay, McCoy 4-82, Huckleby 1-17; Tampa Bay, Holt 1-29.

Punt Returns—Green Bay, Holt 2-61.

Interceptions—Green Bay, Lee 1-0; Tampa Bay, Brown 2-131, Colzie 1-6, Holt 1-13.

Punting—Green Bay, Stachowicz 4-45.3; Tampa Bay, None.

Field Goals—Green Bay, Stenerud 1-1; Tampa Bay, Capece 3-3.

SAINTS 27, OILERS 24

HOUSTON—After New Orleans handed Houston its fifth loss in six games, Saints Owner John Mecom Jr. said there was only one man who could pull the Oilers out of their nosedive. And that man got on the plane and returned to New Orleans with the Saints.

Mecom is an avid Oilers fan as well as being the No. 1 booster of the Saints. He said the coach who could save Houston was Bum Phillips, who was fired by the Oilers after last season—and hired by Mecom for the Saints one day later.

Phillips, who had coached the Oilers for five seasons, came out of the Astrodome saying, "This is the biggest win I've ever had in this

Twelfth Week—Continued

building. I'm as happy as the devil that we won."

Rookie tailback George Rogers rushed for 142 yards and fullback Jack Holmes ran for two touchdowns. Archie Manning threw a 22-yard TD pass to Wayne Wilson and Benny Ricardo kicked a pair of field goals.

Mecom, who lives in Houston, said the Oilers were dispirited before the game. "I'm a fan of the Oilers and I hate to have 30 of the 45 players come over to me and ask me for advice on how they can survive the season," he said. "I told them the only way is to play with pride."

Phillips walked the sidelines wearing an Oilers blue cowboy shirt, in contrast to the black and gold of his players and assistant coaches. He received standing ovations as he entered and as he left the Astrodome, and most of the Houston players made it a point to shake his hand after the game.

"It's a hell of a note that Bum coached for both clubs," said Mecom. "The Oilers were emotionally high today to show Bum they still could play. They weren't trying to impress their own coaches."

Phillips had his Saints up for the game, too. Saints wide receiver Guido Merkins, who had played for Phillips at Houston, said, "He told us it was a matter of life and death—his life and our death."

NOVEMBER 22

SCORE BY PERIODS

New Orleans	0	10	14	3—27
Houston	0	3	7	14—24

SCORING

New Orleans—Holmes 9 run (Ricardo kick).
Houston—Field goal Fritsch 49.
New Orleans—Field goal Ricardo 46.
Houston—Campbell 1 run (Fristch kick).
New Orleans—Holmes 2 run (Ricardo kick).
New Orleans—W. Wilson 22 pass from Manning (Ricardo kick).
Houston—Holston 50 pass from Stabler (Fritsch kick).
New Orleans—Field goal Ricardo 42.
Houston—Campbell 1 run (Fritsch kick).

TEAM STATISTICS

	New Orleans	Houston
First downs	20	16
Rushes-Yards	45-181	26-99
Passing yards	140	161
Sacks by-Yards	3-29	2-7
Return yards	73	109
Passes	10-14-0	15-23-1
Punts	2-38.0	3-47.7
Fumbles-Lost	2-2	1-1
Penalties-Yards	8-67	7-112
Time of possession	36:18	23:42
Attendance—49,581.		

INDIVIDUAL STATISTICS

Rushing—New Orleans, Rogers 28-142, Tyler 5-25, Holmes 8-25, W. Wilson 3-5, Erxleben 1-minus 16; Houston, Campbell 25-96, Coleman 2-0.

Passing—New Orleans, Manning 10-14-0—147; Houston, Stabler 15-23-1—190.

Receiving—New Orleans, Holmes 5-49, Merkens 1-35, Groth 1-21, T. Wilson 1-22, Hardy 2-20; Houston, Holston 4-84, Burrough 2-42, Coleman 2-25, Casper 3-25, Campbell 3-10, Armstrong 1-4.

Kickoff Returns—New Orleans, J. Rogers 1-13, W. Wilson 3-54; Houston, Tullis 5-109.

Punt Returns—New Orleans, Groth 1-3; Houston, Roaches 2-0.

Interceptions—New Orleans, Bordelon 1-3.

Punting—New Orleans, Erxleben 2-38.0; Houston, Parsley 3-47.7.

Field Goals—New Orleans, Ricardo 2-3; Houston, Fritsch 1-1.

CHARGERS 55, RAIDERS 21

OAKLAND—James Brooks, Kellen Winslow and Dan Fouts combined their talents in leading the San Diego Chargers to their rout of the Oakland Raiders.

Winslow's and Fouts' contributions were more obvious, but Brooks' running was a factor in nearly every San Diego score as the Chargers climbed back into the AFC West race.

The victory snapped a two-game losing streak and improved the Chargers' record to 7-5, which left them a game back of Denver and Kansas City.

Winslow tied an NFL record by catching five touchdown passes while Fouts threw for six TDs to set a club mark. One of Fouts' throws went to Brooks, who set up three other scores with punt and kickoff returns.

In addition, the rookie from Auburn carried the ball 17 times for 97 yards and caught five passes for 38 yards. Brooks wound up with 292 yards overall.

"Our players showed a lot of character by coming back three times," said San Diego Coach Don Coryell. "It was quite a turnaround from our embarrassing loss to Seattle (44-23 the week before)."

The Chargers' defense played one of its best games of the season, sacking quarterbacks Marc Wilson and Jim Plunkett seven times.

Fouts completed 28 of 44 passes for 296 yards. Four of his touchdown strikes went to Winslow, one to Brooks and one to Charlie Joiner. Winslow, who caught 13 passes for 144 yards, scored his fifth touchdown on an option pass from Chuck Muncie.

No one had caught five touchdown passes in one game since Bob Shaw did it for the Chicago Cardinals against Baltimore in 1950.

NOVEMBER 22

SCORE BY PERIODS

San Diego	7	21	20	7—55
Oakland	7	14	0	0—21

SCORING

Oakland—Ramsey 66 pass from Wilson (Bahr kick).
San Diego—Muncie 1 run (Benirschke kick).
Oakland—Jensen 2 run (Bahr kick).
San Diego—Brooks 12 pass from Fouts (Benirschke kick).
Oakland—Wilson 12 run (Bahr kick).
San Diego—Winslow 15 pass from Fouts (Benirschke kick).
San Diego—Winslow 29 pass from Fouts (Benirschke kick).
San Diego—Winslow 4 pass from Fouts (Benirschke kick).

San Diego tight end Kellen Winslow tied an NFL record when he caught five touchdown passes in a 55-21 Charger victory over the Oakland Raiders.

Twelfth Week—Continued

San Diego—Winslow 5 pass from Fouts (kick failed).
San Diego—Joiner 6 pass from Fouts (Benirschke kick).
San Diego—Winslow 3 pass from Muncie (Benirschke kick).

TEAM STATISTICS

	San Diego	Oakland
First downs	31	17
Rushes-Yards	38-148	17-59
Passing yards	317	283
Sacks by-Yards	7-56	1-7
Return yards	204	189
Passes	30-47-1	20-43-3
Punts	3-43.0	5-39.2
Fumbles-Lost	1-1	2-0
Penalties-Yards	5-30	10-72
Time of possession	36:28	23:32
Attendance—50,199.		

INDIVIDUAL STATISTICS

Rushing—San Diego, Brooks 17-97, Muncie 17-45, Cappelletti 4-6; Oakland, King 8-21, Jensen 5-19, Wilson 2-16, Hawkins 1-5, Whittington 1-minus 2.

Passing—San Diego, Fouts 28-44-1—296, Muncie 1-1-0—3, Luther 1-1-0—25, Winslow 0-1-0—0; Oakland, Wilson 12-24-2—203, Plunkett 8-19-1—136.

Receiving—San Diego, Winslow 13-144, Brooks 5-38, Chandler 4-32, Joiner 3-38, Scales 2-39, Muncie 2-8, Cappelletti 1-25; Oakland, Ramsey 4-122, Jensen 4-34, Chandler 3-56, Branch 3-31, Hawkins 2-44, King 2-14, Christensen 1-30, Chester 1-8.

Kickoff Returns—San Diego, Brooks 2-68, Gregor 1-12; Oakland, Whittington 5-105, Barnwell 3-48, Christensen 1-17.

Punt Returns—San Diego, Brooks 2-79; Oakland, Watts 1-11.

Interceptions—San Diego, Shaw 2-33, Horn 1-12; Oakland, Browning 1-8.

Punting—San Diego, Roberts 3-43.0; Oakland, Guy 5-39.2.

Field Goals—San Diego, None attempted; Oakland, None attempted.

BENGALS 38, BRONCOS 21

CINCINNATI—The Denver Broncos brought the NFL's No. 1 defense to Riverfront Stadium and the Cincinnati Bengals made mincemeat of it in winning, 38-21.

The Bengals rolled up 571 yards in total offense, with Ken Anderson doing the most damage, passing for 396 yards and three touchdowns.

The Bengals' fourth straight victory upped their record to 9-3, good for a two-game lead in the AFC Central Division. Denver (8-4) fell into a tie with Kansas City atop the AFC West.

When Anderson wasn't passing, Pete Johnson was running. And the 250-pound running back rumbled for 99 yards in 19 carries and scored two touchdowns, one on a 39-yard run.

The Cincinnati defense gave Broncos quarterback Steve DeBerg fits. The Bengals sacked DeBerg four times and pressured him all game long.

"They just did to us what they've been doing to San Diego and Los Angeles," said DeBerg. "They were all over Dan Fouts and Dan Pastorini."

DeBerg played the entire game in place of Craig Morton, who rested a bruised right shoul-

der. "If I'd played today," Morton said, "I wouldn't be playing the rest of the season."

The Bengals grabbed a 14-0 first-quarter lead before Denver even had a first down. Johnson's 39-yard run and a two-yard pass from Anderson to Johnson accounted for the points.

After Rob Lytle ran five yards for a Denver touchdown, Cincinnati scored twice in the final two minutes of the first half—on a two-yard run by Anderson and a seven-yard pass from Anderson to Cris Collinsworth. That put the Bengals up 28-7 at the half.

NOVEMBER 22
SCORE BY PERIODS

Denver	0	7	0	14—21
Cincinnati	14	14	0	10—38

SCORING

Cincinnati—Johnson 39 run (Breech kick).
Cincinnati—Johnson 2 pass from Anderson (Breech kick).
Denver—Lytle 5 run (Steinfort kick).
Cincinnati—Anderson 2 run (Breech kick).
Cincinnati—Collinsworth 7 pass from Anderson (Breech kick).
Cincinnati—Field goal Breech 38.
Denver—Watson 14 pass from DeBerg (Steinfort kick).
Cincinnati—Alexander 65 pass from Anderson (Breech kick).
Denver—Lytle 14 pass from DeBerg (Steinfort kick).

TEAM STATISTICS

	Denver	Cincinnati
First downs	17	25
Rushes-Yards	19-68	33-184
Passing yards	269	387
Sacks by-Yards	2-9	4-36
Return yards	94	59
Passes	21-34-2	25-38-0
Punts	5-38.8	2-32.0
Fumbles-Lost	2-2	2-1
Penalties-Yards	2-18	6-45
Time of possession	26:57	33:03
Attendance—57,207.		

INDIVIDUAL STATISTICS

Rushing—Denver, Preston 5-17, DeBerg 6-30, Parros 2-5, Reed 5-11, Lytle 1-5; Cincinnati, Johnson 19-99, Alexander 4-10, Anderson 3-11, Kreider 1-21, Hargrove 5-42, A. Griffin 1-1.

Passing—Denver, DeBerg 21-34-2—305; Cincinnati, Anderson 25-37-0—396, Kreider 0-1-0—0.

Receiving—Denver, Preston 5-60, Parros 5-50, Watson 5-102, Lytle 2-17, Reed 4-76; Cincinnati, M.L. Harris 4-57, Ross 7-123, Johnson 6-46, Collinsworth 2-25, Alexander 3-82, Kreider 3-63.

Kickoff Returns—Denver, Manning 4-81, Lytle 1-0, Egloff 1-7, Canada 1-6; Cincinnati, Verser 2-37.

Punt Returns—Cincinnati—Fuller 2-16.

Interceptions—Cincinnati—Riley 2-6.

Punting—Denver, Prestridge 5-38.8; Cincinnati, McInally 2-32.0.

Field Goals—Denver, None attempted; Cincinnati, Breech 1-3.

STEELERS 32, BROWNS 10

CLEVELAND—Pittsburgh recorded its first "easy" victory over Cleveland since 1978 by shutting down Brian Sipe.

The Steelers limited Sipe to 18 completions in 39 attempts and made six interceptions, three by safety Donnie Shell.

The Steelers hiked their record to 7-5 and were the only team with a realistic chance of catching Cincinnati for the AFC Central title. The Browns dropped to 5-7.

"The story of the game was that our defense gave us the ball so many times," said Pittsburgh Coach Chuck Noll. "Six interceptions and one fumble recovery can make up for a lot of mistakes."

Cleveland took a 3-0 lead after the opening kickoff on a 33-yard field goal by Matt Bahr. The Steelers came back with two touchdowns on short runs by Greg Hawthorne and Sidney Thornton later in the first quarter, but both conversions were missed.

The Browns pulled within two points, 12-10, on a 13-yard pass from Sipe to Dave Logan late in the second quarter.

The turning point came on Pittsburgh's opening drive in the second half. With a fourth-and-four on Cleveland's 18-yard line, Noll sent in his field goal unit—with one important exception.

The holder was backup quarterback Mark Malone instead of punter Craig Colquitt. Malone took the snap and ran around left end for five yards and the first down. Four plays later, the Steelers scored to make it 18-10 after another missed conversion.

The Browns, hampered by Sipe's interceptions and nearly three times as many penalties as the Steelers, failed to get on the board in the second half.

Terry Bradshaw threw fourth-quarter scoring passes to Ray Pinney on a tackle-eligible play and to reserve running back Rick Moser.

"Today was the first time in a long time we've had control of the game in the fourth quarter (against Cleveland)," said Bradshaw. "It feels like we're playing at home when things go so well."

NOVEMBER 22

SCORE BY PERIODS

Pittsburgh	12	0	6	14—32
Cleveland	3	7	0	0—10

SCORING

Cleveland—Field goal Bahr 33.
Pittsburgh—Hawthorne 1 run (kick failed).
Pittsburgh—Thornton 3 run (kick failed).
Cleveland—Logan 13 pass from Sipe (Bahr kick).
Pittsburgh—Harris 2 run (kick failed).
Pittsburgh—Pinney 1 pass from Bradshaw (Trout kick).
Pittsburgh—Moser 1 pass from Bradshaw (Trout kick).

TEAM STATISTICS

	Pittsburgh	Cleveland
First downs	25	22
Rushes-Yards	43-139	28-146
Passing yards	223	219
Sacks by-Yards	1-8	0-0
Return yards	91	101
Passes	17-32-2	18-39-6
Punts	2-35.0	1-37.0
Fumbles-Lost	3-3	1-1
Penalties-Yards	4-35	11-94
Time of possession	32:04	27:56
Attendance—77,958.		

Rushing—Pittsburgh, Harris 20-75, Thornton 15-52, Malone 1-5, Bradshaw 2-4, Hawthorne 4-3, Davis 1-0; Cleveland, M. Pruitt 16-96, Sipe 4-27, G. Pruitt 7-17, White 1-6.

Passing—Pittsburgh, Bradshaw 17-32-2—223; Cleveland, Sipe 18-39-6—227.

Receiving—Pittsburgh, Thornton 4-31, Smith 3-72, Harris 3-36, Stallworth 2-40, Swann 1-19, Hawthorne 1-12, Grossman 1-7, Moser 1-5, Pinney 1-1; Cleveland, Newsome 5-61; Feacher 4-79, M. Pruitt 3-31, G. Pruitt 3-19, Rucker 1-18, Logan 1-13, Oden 1-6.

Kickoff Returns—Pittsburgh, Anderson 2-44; Cleveland, Hall 4-60, G. Pruitt 1-26.

Punt Returns—Cleveland, Hall 1-0.

Interceptions—Pittsburgh, Shell 3-36, Washington 2-11, Johnson 1-0; Cleveland, Bolton 1-3, Scott 1-12.

Punting—Pittsburgh, Colquitt 2-35.0; Cleveland, Cox 1-37.0.

Field Goals—Pittsburgh, None attempted; Cleveland, Bahr 1-3.

CARDINALS 35, COLTS 24

BALTIMORE—During the week leading up to St. Louis' game at Baltimore, Cardinals Coach Jim Hanifan had lectured rookie quarterback Neil Lomax about staying in the pocket when he went back to pass.

So what happened? Lomax directed the Cardinals to victory over the Colts by pulling off three key plays in which he strayed from the pocket.

Lomax completed 12 of 21 passes for 219 yards. He did all right as a rusher, too, scrambling for 24 yards in four carries, including a 10-yard touchdown run. The victory was the Cardinals' second in succession since Lomax replaced Jim Hart at quarterback. The loss was the 11th straight for the Colts.

One of Lomax' key scrambles came in the closing minutes after the Colts had cut St. Louis' lead to 28-24 with 5:21 left. On third-and-4 at the Baltimore 44, the Cardinals' brain trust sent in a play designed for Lomax to roll out of the pocket. Lomax faked a handoff to the left, and sprinted to the right. He spotted tight end Greg LaFleur all alone and fired to him for a 27-yard gain. That moved the ball to the Baltimore 17, and two plays later Ottis Anderson scooted 11 yards for the clinching touchdown.

"The thing that scared me to death about Lomax was his scrambling out of the pocket and throwing on the run," said Colts Coach Mike McCormack.

McCormack got an early look. On the third play of the game, with the Cardinals facing third-and-12 at their 18, Lomax was trapped behind the line. He twisted away from two tacklers and lobbed a pass to Pat Tilley. The play was good for 75 yards and set up Anderson's first of two TD runs.

Tilley had five receptions for 158 yards and Anderson rushed for 130 yards, giving him 1,040 for the year—his third straight 1,000-yard season. Rookie linebacker Dave Ahrens returned an interception for another Cardinal TD.

Curtis Dickey raced 36 yards for Baltimore's first TD and Bert Jones threw scoring passes to Roger Carr and Ray Butler.

NOVEMBER 22
SCORE BY PERIODS

St. Louis	14	7	7	7—35
Baltimore	10	0	7	7—24

SCORING

St. Louis—Anderson 4 run (O'Donoghue kick).
Baltimore—Dickey 36 run (Wood kick).
St. Louis—Ahrens 14 interception return (O'Donoghue kick).
Baltimore—Field goal Wood 40.
St. Louis—Lomax 10 run (O'Donoghue kick).
Baltimore—Carr 5 pass from B. Jones (Wood kick).
St. Louis—Morris 3 run (O'Donoghue kick).
Baltimore—Butler 8 pass from B. Jones (Wood kick).
St. Louis—Anderson 11 run (O'Donoghue kick).

TEAM STATISTICS

	St. Louis	Baltimore
First downs	24	22
Rushes-Yards	48-241	28-155
Passing yards	211	230
Sacks by-Yards	0-0	1-8
Return yards	128	86
Passes	12-21-0	23-45-2
Punts	4-36.3	5-33.8
Penalties-Yards	7-60	6-54
Time of possession	34:22	25:38

Attendance—24,784.

INDIVIDUAL STATISTICS

Rushing—St. Louis, Anderson 29-130, Morris 12-64, Lomax 4-24, Mitchell 3-23; Baltimore, Dixon 12-64, Dickey 2-48, McMillan 7-19, B. Jones 2-12, McCauley 2-5, Franklin 1-3.

Passing—St. Louis, Lomax 12-21-0—219; Baltimore, B. Jones 23-45-2—230.

Receiving—St. Louis, Tilley 5-158, Green 2-19, Lafleur 1-27, Anderson 1-7, Morris 1-4, Gray 1-4, Harrell 1-0; Baltimore, Butler 7-56, Carr 4-28, McMillan 4-59, McCall 2-28, McCauley 2-25, Dixon 2-19, Franklin 2-15.

Kickoff Returns—St. Louis, Mitchell, 3-56, Harrell 2-45; Baltimore, Anderson 1-15, Dixon 2-56, Shula 1-9.

Punt Returns—St. Louis, Mitchell 3-8; Baltimore, Anderson 1-6.

Interceptions—St. Louis, Ahrens 1-14, Junior 1-15.

Punting—St. Louis, Birdsong 4-36.3; Baltimore, Garrett 5-33.8.

Field Goals—St. Louis, O'Donoghue 0-2; Baltimore, Wood 1-2.

JETS 16, DOLPHINS 15

NEW YORK—Richard Todd, playing despite a broken rib, threw an 11-yard touchdown pass to Jerome Barkum with just 16 seconds left, and Pat Leahy added the tie-breaking conversion as the Jets edged the Miami Dolphins, 16-15, at Shea Stadium.

The victory continued the Jets' four-year domination of the Dolphins (7-0-1). More important, it enabled New York to tie Miami for the AFC Eastern Division lead at 7-4-1. The Jets had not led the division at this stage of the season since 1969.

"I stood on the sidelines crying after we scored. It was like a dream," said Todd, who wore a flak jacket to protect his injured rib.

"It's a good feeling to be in first place. Now that we're here, we can't let it go."

The Jets took over on their 23-yard line with three minutes left after Uwe von Schamann's 23-yard field goal had given Miami a 15-9 lead. Todd hit Wesley Walker for 18 yards to the Miami 37-yard line, Bobby Jones for 12 yards and Lam Jones for 14 yards to Miami's 11 to set up the game-winning throw to Barkum.

"To become a good football team, you have to learn to play those last two minutes," said Jets Coach Walt Michaels.

Miami Coach Don Shula said the key moment came when his Dolphins had to kick a field goal with just over three minutes left. Miami, leading 12-9, had moved to the Jets' five, but on third down tackle Abdul Salaam broke through to bring down Tony Nathan for a loss and force a field goal.

"We were trying for the TD at the end," said Shula. "We wanted it bad. Salaam made a big play.

"On their march, they made two long curlins where we retreated too far. One of our guys was too cautious. It cost us. But give them all the credit in the world. They made the plays when they had to."

The Jets took a 6-0 lead in the second quarter on Leahy field goals of 29 and 49 yards. Miami then scored 12 points in the final 4:56 of the half to go ahead. Nathan ran four yards for a touchdown to give Miami a 7-6 lead. Larry Gordon dumped Todd in the end zone for a safety with 2:04 to go to make the score 9-6, and won Schamann's 46-yard field goal with 27 seconds left in the half made it 12-6.

NOVEMBER 22
SCORE BY PERIODS

Miami	0	12	0	3—15
New York Jets	3	3	0	10—16

SCORING

New York—Field goal Leahy 29.
New York—Field goal Leahy 49.
Miami—Nathan 4 run (von Schamann kick).
Miami—Safety, Todd tackled by Gordon in end zone.
Miami—Field goal von Schamann 46.
New York—Field goal Leahy 45.
Miami—Field goal von Schamann 23.
New York—Barkum 11 pass from Todd (Leahy kick).

TEAM STATISTICS

	Miami	New York
First downs	13	21
Rushes-Yards	31-146	29-120
Passing yards	41	165
Sacks by-Yards	4-38	3-22
Return yards	56	104
Passes	10-22-2	21-38-0
Punts	7-43.9	4-41.0
Fumbles-Lost	3-0	3-2
Penalties-Yards	2-30	5-53
Time of possession	28:43	31:17

Attendance—59,962.

Rushing—Miami, Nathan 15-56, Franklin 7-45, Woodley 4-41, Hill 5-4; New York, McNeil 19-75, Harper 3-12, Dierking 2-16, Newton 4-7, Todd 1-10.

Passing—Miami, Woodley 10-22-2—63; New York, Todd 21-38-0—203.

Receiving—Miami, Harris 2-30, Nathan 3-26, Lee 2-minus 3, Hardy 1-3, Hill 1-4, Cefalo 1-3; New York, Barkum 4-43, Walker 3-36, L. Jones 3-37, McNeil 3-30, Dierking 2-17, Harper 4-26, B. Jones 1-12, Newton 1-2.

Kickoff Returns—Miami, Bessillieu 2-16, Vigorito 2-36; New York, Harper 3-50, Sohn 1-22.

Punt Returns—Miami, Vigorito 1-4; New York, Harper 4-17.

Interceptions—New York, Blinka 1-15, Springs 1-0.

Punting—Miami, Orosz 7-43.9; New York, Ramsey 4-41.0.

Field Goals—Miami, von Schamann 2-2; New York, Leahy 3-3.

BILLS 20, PATRIOTS 17

ORCHARD PARK—Reserve running back Roland Hooks' touchdown catch of a desperation 36-yard pass with five seconds left lifted Buffalo to victory over New England.

Hooks came off the bench in the first quarter when Joe Cribbs suffered a rib injury. He rushed for 45 yards, returned three kickoffs for 55 yards and caught six passes for 111 yards, including both Buffalo touchdowns.

His efforts kept the Bills in the thick of the AFC East race with a 7-5 record, one-half game behind the New York Jets and Miami.

Buffalo was down, 17-13, with 1:56 left, when Matt Cavanaugh connected with Don Hasselbeck on a five-yard scoring pass. The Bills, their playoff hopes going down the drain, started their final possession at their 27-yard line with 35 seconds left.

Joe Ferguson fired a 37-yard pass to Hooks to the New England 36, then threw incomplete.

With 12 seconds left, Ferguson dropped back and threw into a 20-mph wind against New England's present defense. A crowd of Bills and Patriots waited in the end zone.

New England linebacker Mike Hawkins got his fingertips on the ball and deflected it into the waiting hands of Hooks.

"We all went up for it and that was it," said New England linebacker Steve Nelson. "Nothing's going to surprise me now. I guess fate is just taking its course."

The Bills held a 13-10 lead until the final two minutes of the game. They built the lead on field goals of 28 and 23 yards by Nick Mike-Mayer and an 11-yard Ferguson-to-Hooks pass.

New England countered with a 56-yard option pass from running back Andy Johnson to Stanley Morgan and a 43-yard field goal by John Smith. Johnson's TD pass on the option play was his fourth of the season.

NOVEMBER 22
SCORE BY PERIODS

New England	7	0	3	7—17
Buffalo	3	10	0	7—20

SCORING

Buffalo—Field goal Mike-Mayer 28.

New England—Morgan 66 pass from Johnson (Smith kick).

Buffalo—Field goal Mike-Mayer 23.

Buffalo—Hooks 11 pass from Ferguson (Mike-Mayer kick).

New England—Field goal Smith 43.

New England—Hasselbeck 5 pass from Cavanaugh (Smith kick).

Buffalo—Hooks 36 pass from Ferguson (Mike-Mayer kick).

TEAM STATISTICS

	New England	Buffalo
First downs	11	19
Rushes-Yards	39-116	43-185
Passing yards	181	249
Sacks by-Yards	1-9	1-8
Return yards	64	79
Passes	7-13-0	15-34-1
Punts	5-50.4	5-34.6
Fumbles-Lost	3-2	2-1
Penalties-Yards	4-33	2-20
Time of possession	24:49	35:11
Attendance—76,374.		

INDIVIDUAL STATISTICS

Rushing—New England, Collins 4-5, Cunningham 18-57, Tatupu 1-minus 1, Johnson 1-minus 4, Ferguson 14-59, Cavanaugh 1-0; Buffalo, Cribbs 10-32, Leaks 19-92, Hooks 13-45, Ferguson 1-16.

Passing—New England, Cavanaugh 6-12-0—133, Johnson 1-1-0—56; Buffalo, Ferguson 15-34-1—258.

Receiving—New England, Morgan 3-141, Cunningham 1-7, Hasselbeck 3-41; Buffalo, Hooks 6-111, Lewis 4-84, Brammer 1-19, Butler 3-39, Leaks 1-5.

Kickoff Returns—New England, Collins 1-28, Toler 2-15, Dombroski 1-21, Hamilton 1-0; Buffalo, Hooks 3-55, Riddick 1-24.

Punt Returns—None.

Interceptions—New England, Sanford 1-0.

Punting—New England, Camarillo 5-50.4; Buffalo, Cater 5-34.6.

Field Goals—New England, Smith 1-2; Buffalo, Mike-Mayer 2-4.

CHIEFS 40, SEAHAWKS 13

KANSAS CITY—Kansas City turned in a near-perfect performance in the wipeout of Seattle.

The Chiefs scored the first six times they touched the football, did not commit a turnover and did not punt until only 12 seconds remained in the game. The defense, which held the opposition under 17 points for the eighth time in the season, chipped in a touchdown on a 46-yard interception return by rookie safety Lloyd Burruss.

The victory left Kansas City with an 8-4 mark and a share of first place with Denver in the AFC West.

Bill Kenney completed 17 of 22 passes for 181 yards, with touchdown passes of 14 yards to J. T. Smith and two yards to Willie Scott. James Hadnot rushed for his first 100-yard day as a pro with 106 yards in 10 carries, as the Chiefs ran up their highest point since 1975.

"The Chiefs did not do anything today that they had done previously," said Seattle Coach Jack Patera, whose Seahawks fell to 4-8. "We were more fearful of what they would do with Joe Delaney and that's not to say Hadnot is not

Twelfth Week—Continued

a quality player. Look at his stats. They're just a good, solid football team."

Kansas City drove 54 and 62 yards on its first two possessions for field goals of 37 and 24 yards by Nick Lowery. The Chiefs marched 73 yards for Smith's touchdown and, 36 seconds later, scored on Burruss' interception return for a 20-6 halftime lead.

Kansas City moved 75 yards at the start of the second half, with Billy Jackson going one yard for the score. Scott's touchdown capped a 70-yard Kansas City drive. The Chiefs went 56 yards for their final points, with Jackson getting his second TD on a two-yard run.

Seattle scored on first-half field goals of 26 and 30 yards by Efren Herrera and a second-half touchdown pass of 30 yards from Jim Zorn to Steve Largent.

NOVEMBER 22
SCORE BY PERIODS

Seattle	3	3	7	0—13
Kansas City	3	17	7	13—40

SCORING

Seattle—Field goal Herrera 26.
Kansas City—Field goal Lowery 37.
Kansas City—Field goal Lowery 24.
Seattle—Field goal Herrera 30.
Kansas City—Smith 14 pass from Kenney (Lowery kick).
Kansas City—Burruss 46 interception return (Lowery kick).
Kansas City—B. Jackson 1 run (Lowery kick).
Seattle—Largent 30 pass from Zorn (Herrera kick).
Kansas City—Scott 2 pass from Kenney (kick failed).
Kansas City—B. Jackson 2 run (Lowery kick).

TEAM STATISTICS

	Seattle	Kansas City
First downs	21	29
Rushes-Yards	23-83	43-269
Passing yards	256	181
Sacks by-Yards	0-0	1-2
Return yards	159	99
Passes	19-30-1	17-22-0
Punts	2-37.0	1-49.0
Fumbles-Lost	2-1	1-0
Penalties-Yards	2-20	7-60
Time of possession	25:32	34:28
Attendance—49,002.		

INDIVIDUAL STATISTICS

Rushing—Seattle, T. Brown 16-63, Doornink 3-13, Smith 2-6, Hughes 2-1; Kansas City, Hadnot 10-106, B. Jackson 17-70, Delaney 11-65, Bledsoe 4-19, Kenney 1-9.

Passing—Seattle, Zorn 19-30-1—258; Kansas City, Kennedy 17-22-0—181.

Receiving—Seattle, Largent 4-63, T. Brown 4-38, Smith 3-45, Doornink 3-32, Sawyer 3-26, Johns 1-34, McCullum 1-20; Kansas City, Smith 7-70, Marshall 4-51, Delaney 3-31, Hadnot 2-27, Scott 1-2.

Kickoff Returns—Seattle, Ivory 5-88, Lane 3-53; Kansas City, Murphy 1-21, Burruss 2-32, Rourke 1-0.

Punt Returns—Seattle, Johns 1-18.

Interceptions—Kansas City, Burruss 1-46.

Punting—Seattle, West 2-37.0; Kansas City, Gossett 1-49.0.

Field Goals—Seattle, Herrera 2-2; Kansas City, Lowery 2-2.

49ers 33, RAMS 31

ANAHEIM—Ray Wersching kicked his fourth field goal of the game, a 37-yarder as the final gun sounded, to give San Francisco the victory over Los Angeles and a sweep of its season series with the Rams for the first time since 1972.

"I've had a lot of game-winning kicks, but this was easily the biggest because I grew up here," said Wersching, who was born in Austria but went to high school and attended junior college in Downey, Calif., about 10 miles from Anaheim Stadium.

The victory gave the NFC West-leading 49ers a 9-3 record. Meanwhile, the Rams dropped to 5-7.

San Francisco moved from its 20 to the L.A. 19 before calling time out with two seconds left and sending in Wersching. Joe Montana completed six passes for 54 yards on the drive, including a 16-yarder to Dwight Clark on a third-down situation and a 15-yarder to Clark that carried to the Rams' 20.

The 49ers' rally wiped out a clutch relief effort by Rams quarterback Pat Haden, who directed two touchdown drives to put L.A. into the lead. Haden replaced Dan Pastorini in the third quarter after the 49ers had surged to a 27-17 lead.

The Rams had a 17-10 lead at halftime, but Amos Lawrence tied the score by returning the second-half kickoff 92 yards for a touchdown. Then, after Wersching put the Niners ahead with a 34-yard field goal, rookie cornerback Ronnie Lott picked off a Pastorini pass and sprinted 25 yards to score. The interception return for a TD was Lott's third of the season, a 49er record.

Haden guided the Rams 80 yards and then 90 yards for touchdowns. He threw a two-yard pass to Walt Arnold on the first drive. On the second, he hit Mike Guman for 14 yards on fourth-and-10 at the San Francisco 16. And on the next play 49ers linebacker Willie Harper was called for pass interference in the end zone, giving the Rams a first down at the one. Wendell Tyler dived over for the TD and Frank Corral's extra point gave L.A. a 31-30 lead with 1:51 left.

But the 49ers had one more chance, and they had Wersching. After the last-second kick, Coach Bill Walsh said of Wersching, "He's the greatest kicker in the history of the 49ers. The number of clutch field goals he's kicked is just tremendous."

NOVEMBER 22
SCORE BY PERIODS

San Francisco	3	7	17	6—33
Los Angeles	0	17	7	7—31

SCORING

San Francisco—Field goal Wersching 47.
Los Angeles—Field goal Corral 44.
Los Angeles—Tyler 22 pass from Pastorini (Corral kick).
San Francisco—Davis 1 run (Wersching kick).

Los Angeles—Dennard 7 pass from Guman (Corral kick).
San Francisco—Lawrence 92 kickoff return (Wersching kick).
San Francisco—Field goal Wersching 34.
San Francisco—Lott 25 interception return (Wersching kick).
Los Angeles—Arnold 2 pass from Haden (Corral kick).
San Francisco—Field goal Wersching 32.
Los Angeles—Tyler 1 run (Corral kick).
San Francisco—Field goal Wersching 37.

TEAM STATISTICS

	San Francisco	Los Angeles
First downs	19	27
Rushes-Yards	28-71	47-203
Passing yards	259	208
Sacks by-Yards	1-0	3-24
Return yards	220	91
Passes	19-30-1	18-32-1
Punts	2-44.0	4-44.8
Fumbles-Lost	1-1	4-1
Penalties-Yards	5-51	7-71
Time of possession	25:00	35:00

Attendance—63,456.

INDIVIDUAL STATISTICS

Rushing—San Francisco, Davis 8-23, Patton 8-20, Hofer 5-16, Cooper 4-4, Lawrence 2-9, Montana 1-minus 1; Los Angeles, Tyler 23-97, Guman 17-64, Pastorini 2-13, Bryant 2-4, Dennard 1-14, Haden 1-9, J. Thomas 1-2.

Passing—San Francisco, Montana 19-30-1—283; Los Angeles, Pastorini 8-18-1—79, Haden 9-13-0—122, Guman 1-1-0—7.

Receiving—San Francisco, Solomon 5-124, Cooper 5-55, Clark 4-59, Hofer 2-20, Young 2-18, Shumann 1-7; Los Angeles, Tyler 4-39, Arnold 2-22, D. Hill 1-43, Waddy 1-8, Bryant 1-7, J. Thomas 1-5.

Kickoff Returns—San Francisco, Lawrence 3-138, Ring 2-45; Los Angeles, D. Hill 5-86.

Punt Returns—San Francisco, Hicks 2-12; Los Angeles, Irvin 1-5.

Interceptions—San Francisco, Lott 1-25; Los Angeles, Cromwell 1-0.

Punting—San Francisco, Miller 2-44.0; Los Angeles, Corral 4-44.8.

Field Goals—San Francisco, Wersching 4-4; Los Angeles, Corral 1-1.

GIANTS 2O, EAGLES 1O

PHILADELPHIA—Even Ray Perkins, the usually stoic coach of the New York Giants, was excited. His team had just upset the Philadelphia Eagles, 20-10, and Perkins blurted, "We shocked the country."

It was quite a shock, all right. The Giants had lost 12 straight times to the Eagles, the last New York victory coming in the opening game of the 1975 season. Philadelphia went into the game with the best record (9-2) in the National Football League, while the Giants were coming off two tough defeats and had lost their starting quarterback.

"After those two losses (the Giants had been beaten by Green Bay, 26-24, and by Washington, 30-27 in overtime, in their two previous games), other teams would have bitten the dust and gotten down," Perkins said. "We could have played our last five games and gone home for Christmas. But as this (game) indicated, we did not."

The victory boosted the Giants' record to 6-6 and kept alive their hopes for a wild-card play-off berth. The Eagles, meanwhile, slipped into a first-place tie with Dallas in the NFC Eastern Division.

Joe Danelo kicked a 30-yard field goal in the fourth quarter to break a 10-10 tie. Less than three minutes later, cornerback Terry Jackson returned an interception 32 yards for a clinching touchdown.

The New York defense played a ferocious game, holding the Eagles to 97 yards total offense in the second half. Philadelphia went scoreless in the second half for the first time in 1981. The Eagles were forced to start second half drives on their 6, 12, 4 and 15-yard lines.

"We had lousy field position, and all kinds of penalties," said Eagles Coach Dick Vermeil. "And that one big turnover (Jackson's interception) was probably a lousy call on my part."

The interception came after two penalties and a 17-yard sack of quarterback Ron Jaworski by Giants linebacker Brad Van Pelt had set the Eagles back to their own 16, where they faced third-and-33. Jaworski tried to hit Charlie Smith on a deep sideline route, but Jackson picked off the ball and had clear sailing to a TD with 6:56 left in the game.

"He (Jaworski) was looking at me all the way," Jackson said. "When I jumped in front of Smith, I knew I had it and as soon as I started running, I knew it was six."

Jaworski threw a six-yard scoring pass to Keith Krepfle in the first quarter for a 7-3 lead. But Scott Brunner engineered a TD drive for the Giants and the Eagles never led again.

NOVEMBER 22
SCORE BY PERIODS

New York Giants	3	7	0	10—20
Philadelphia	7	3	0	0—10

SCORING

New York—Field goal Danelo 39.
Philadelphia—Krepfle 6 pass frm Jaworski (Franklin kick).
New York—Bright 1 run (Danelo kick).
Philadelphia—Field goal Franklin 27.
New York—Field goal Danelo 30.
New York—T. Jackson 32 interception return (Danelo kick).

TEAM STATISTICS

	New York	Philadelphia
First downs	14	20
Rushes-Yards	29-120	35-139
Passing yards	172	154
Sacks by-Yards	3-33	1-9
Return yards	76	61
Passes	10-27-2	20-45-1
Punts	5-41.8	8-33.6
Fumbles-Lost	1-1	4-0
Penalties-Yards	6-59	10-83
Time of possession	23:59	36:01

Attendance—66,872.

INDIVIDUAL STATISTICS

Rushing—New York, Carpenter 24-111, L. Jackson 2-2, Forte 2-6, Bright 1-1; Philadelphia, Montgomery 25-102, Oliver 5-18, Campfield 2-11, Jaworski 2-6, Russell 1-2.

Passing—New York, Brunner 10-27-2—181; Philadelphia, Jaworski 20-45-1—187.

Twelfth Week—Continued

Receiving—New York, Perkins 4-43, Gray 3-56, Shirk 2-39, Friede 1-43; Philadelphia, Campfield 6-69, Smith 3-38, Henry 3-36, Montgomery 3-8, Krepfle 2-16, Carmichael 2-14, Oliver 1-6.

Kickoff Returns—New York, Bright 1-12, Pittman 1-16; Philadelphia, Campfield 2-36.

Punt Returns—New York, Bright 3-3, Pittman 1-13; Philadelphia, Henry 1-0, Sciarra 3-26.

Interceptions—New York, T. Jackson, 1-32; Philadelphia, Phillips 1-0, Logan 1-minus 1.

Punting—New York, Jennings 5-41.8; Philadelphia, Runager 8-33.6.

Field Goals—New York, Danelo 2-3; Philadelphia, Franklin 1-3.

LIONS 23, BEARS 7

CHICAGO—Neill Armstrong, the Chicago coach, sounded as if he was reciting the opening lines to "Love Story." At least, he was talking about a team that had died early in the loss to Detroit.

"What can you say about an offense when it makes 24 yards? How can it get any worse?" said Armstrong. "We looked bad getting in and out of the huddle, and it went downhill from there."

The Lions gained their first road victory of 1981 by holding Chicago to 24 yards, the worst output ever by a Bears team. The previous low was 66 yards against Denver in 1971.

Chicago managed only four first downs and had a minus 20 yards passing when its quarterbacks were sacked seven times for 61 yards lost. The Bears completed only seven of 30 passes and had three intercepted.

Walter Payton, held to 37 yards rushing, said the collapse wasn't Armstrong's fault. "This is beyond rock bottom. It's like a cancer. You think you've cut it out, but there it is, springing back again," Payton said. "You could get Tom Landry or Bear Bryant in here, and it wouldn't change."

"We actually got a shutout," said cornerback James Hunter, speaking for the Detroit defense. The Bears' TD came on a 92-yard interception return by rookie cornerback Todd Bell with 16 seconds left in the first half.

Eric Hipple, who threw the interception, atoned for the mistake by throwing a 46-yard bomb to Freddie Scott in the third quarter. That play put the ball on the Chicago 5, and Hipple scored on a rollout on the next play.

Billy Sims rushed for 117 yards for the Lions and his backup, Rick Kane, ran two yards for a score in the final period.

Lions defensive end Bubba Baker was ejected after he flattened Chicago quarterback Vince Evans in the third quarter. Evans had to leave the game.

"I respect what is said about violence in this game, but I didn't deserve to be ejected," Baker said. "I didn't drop my helmet and it wasn't a late hit. I was shocked when the ref-

eree told me, 'No. 60, you're out of the game.' I think Vince knows it wasn't anything deliberate."

NOVEMBER 22

SCORE BY PERIODS

Detroit	3	6	7	7—23
Chicago	0	7	0	0— 7

SCORING

Detroit—Field goal Murray 24.
Detroit—Field goal Murray 23.
Detroit—Field goal Murray 49.
Chicago—Bell 92 interception return (Roveto kick).
Detroit—Hipple 5 run (Murray kick).
Detroit—Kane 2 run (Murray kick).

TEAM STATISTICS

	Detroit	Chicago
First downs	20	4
Rushes-Yards	59-229	17-44
Passing yards	127	minus 20
Sacks by-Yards	7-61	2-18
Return yards	133	176
Passes	10-29-1	7-30-3
Punts	6-44.2	11-38.0
Fumbles-Lost	3-2	3-0
Penalties-yards	11-104	9-83
Time of possession	37:55	22:05
Attendance—50,820.		

INDIVIDUAL STATISTICS

Rushing—Detroit, Sims 32-117, Bussey 7-31, Hipple 9-32, Kane, 5-21, V. Thompson 4-16, Scott 2-12; Chicago, Payton 13-37, Suhey 4-7.

Passing—Detroit, Hipple 10-29-1—145; Chicago, Evans 4-19-2—21, Avellini 3-10-1—20, Parsons 0-1-0—0.

Receiving—Detroit, Scott 3-68, Norris 2-32, Nichols 2-19, Kane 1-19, L. Thompson 1-7, King 1-0; Chicago, Suhey 3-10, Watts 2-24, Payton 2-7.

Kickoff Returns—Detroit, Hall 2-52; Chicago, Moorehead 4-65, Fisher 1-8, Anderson 1-minus 5.

Punt Returns—Detroit, Martin 6-42; Chicago, Fisher 2-16.

Interceptions—Detroit, Hunter 1-10, White 1-14, Cobb 1-15; Chicago, Bell 1-92.

Punting—Detroit, Skladany 6-44.2; Chicago, Parsons, 11-38.0.

Field Goals—Detroit, Murray 3-4; Chicago, None attempted.

COWBOYS 24, REDSKINS 10

IRVING—Dallas finally came to life and held off Washington at Texas Stadium to grab a share of the NFC East lead.

The Redskins had tied the score at 10-10 on a 26-yard field goal by Mark Moseley in the third period, after Mike Nelms returned the second-half kickoff 51 yards. But the Cowboys then drove 80 yards for the go-ahead touchdown. They clinched the victory with a stout fourth-quarter defense and a trick play that set up a TD in the final minute.

Danny White threw a 10-yard scoring pass to Doug Cosbie to give Dallas a 17-10 lead. The Cowboys' drive was kept alive by a 34-yard pass from White to Drew Pearson on third-and-18 from the Dallas 36.

In the fourth period, the Dallas defense held Washington to minus two yards over three possessions, and the Cowboys put the game away on a one-yard TD run by Ron Springs with 52 seconds left. That score was set up by Pearson's 25-yard gain on a wide-receiver-around play. All 11 Redskins started the wrong way on the play and had to put on the brakes to chase Pearson, who reached the 1-yard line before he was dragged down.

The Redskins were handicapped by the loss of running back Joe Washington, who left the game late in the second quarter with a torn rib cartilage. Washington had rushed for 84 yards and caught three passes for 47 yards.

The Redskins' only touchdown came on a seven-yard pass from Joe Theismann to Nick Giaquinto, who replaced Washington.

NOVEMBER 22
SCORE BY PERIODS

Washington	0	7	3	0—10
Dallas	7	3	7	7—24

SCORING

Dallas—Johnson 28 pass from D. White (Septien kick).
Dallas—Field goal Septien 25.
Washington—Giaquinto 7 pass from Theismann (Moseley kick).
Washington—Field goal Moseley 26.
Dallas—Cosbie 10 pass from D. White (Septien kick).
Dallas—Springs 1 run (Septien kick).

TEAM STATISTICS

	Washington	Dallas
First downs	17	27
Rushes-Yards	25-125	47-258
Passing yards	131	212
Sacks by-Yards	1-10	4-27
Return yards	178	66
Passes	14-34-1	13-27-0
Punts	5-41.4	3-39.0
Fumbles-Lost	2-0	3-2
Penalties-Yards	3-22	12-94
Time of possession	27:03	32:57
Attendance—64,583.		

INDIVIDUAL STATISTICS

Rushing—Washington, Washington 12-84, Giaquinto 2-18, Riggins 9-12, Theismann 2-11; Dallas, Dorsett 23-115, Springs 17-85, Pearson 1-25, J. Jones 4-19, D. White 2-14.

Passing—Washington, Theismann 14-34-1—158; Dallas, D. White 13-27-0—222.

Receiving—Washington, Thompson 4-56, Washington 3-47, Giaquinto 3-26, Metcalf 2-11, Monk 1-13, Walker 1-5; Dallas, Pearson 6-111, Hill 3-48, Johnson 1-28, Springs 1-22, Cosbie 1-10, Saldi 1-3.

Kickoff Returns—Washington, Nelms 4-163; Dallas, J. Jones 1-0, Newsome 1-25, Newhouse 1-15.

Punt Returns—Washington, Nelms 2-15; Dallas, J. Jones 4-23, Donley 1-3.

Interceptions—Dallas, Waters 1-0.

Punting—Washington, Connell 5-41.4; Dallas, D. White 3-39.0.

Field Goals—Washington, Moseley 1-3; Dallas, Septien 1-2.

FALCONS 31, VIKINGS 30

ATLANTA—Few people would blame the Minnesota Vikings if they asked the National Football League not to schedule them for any Monday night games during the 1982 season.

The Vikings lost their third Monday night game in as many appearances in 1981 as the Atlanta Falcons beat them, 31-30. Previously, the Vikes took it on the chin from the Oakland Raiders and Denver Broncos.

The defeat dropped the Vikings to 7-5 for the season and cut their lead in the NFC Central Division to one game over Tampa Bay and Detroit. Atlanta's record improved to 6-6 and kept the Falcons in the hunt for the final NFC wild-card spot.

The Vikings led at halftime, 21-7, on the strength of three Tommy Kramer touchdown passes. The Minnesota quarterback threw two scoring passes to Ahmad Rashad, covering six and 42 yards, and one to Bob Bruer for three yards. The Falcons could counter only with an 8-yard TD pass from Steve Bartkowski to Alfred Jackson.

The Vikings were able to move on the ground as well as in the air in the first half. Running back Ted Brown rushed for 101 yards in nine carries before intermission. The Falcons' first-half running game was less than awesome as fullback William Andrews fumbled three times.

But the second half was a different story. Atlanta scored the first 24 points of the half as Bartkowski, who completed 21 of 32 passes in the contest, threw two scoring passes, one to Junior Miller from three yards out and another to Wallace Francis from 29 yards away. Mick Luckhurst hit a 32-yard field goal to put the Falcons ahead, 24-21, and then linebacker Buddy Curry intercepted a Kramer pass and returned it 35 yards for a touchdown. Curry's TD gave the Falcons a 31-21 lead with only 4:06 remaining in the game.

However, the game was far from over. After the Falcons gave up a safety rather than punt out of their own end zone to cut their lead to eight points, Kramer, who finished the game with 24 completions in 47 attempts, drove Minnesota 58 yards in two plays. He hit Leo Lewis on a 42-yard pass to the Falcons 16 and then connected with Joe Senser on the following play for the touchdown.

With the Atlanta lead cut to one point, the Vikes tried on onside kick—a play they had used earlier in the season to upset San Diego. But it didn't work this time. Atlanta recovered and ran out the clock for the victory.

MONDAY, NOVEMBER 23
SCORE BY PERIODS

Minnesota	7	14	0	9—30
Atlanta	7	0	14	10—31

SCORING

Minnesota—Rashad 6 pass from Kramer (Danmeier kick).
Atlanta—Jackson 8 pass from Bartkowski (Luckhurst kick).
Minnesota—Rashad 42 pass from Kramer (Danmeier kick).
Minnesota—Bruer 3 pass from Kramer (Danmeier kick).
Atlanta—Miller 3 pass from Bartkowski (Luckhurst kick).
Atlanta—Francis 29 pass from Bartkowski (Luckhurst kick).

Twelfth Week—Continued

Atlanta—Field goal Luckhurst 32.
Atlanta—Curry 35 interception return (Luckhurst kick).
Minnesota—Safety, James runs out of end zone.
Minnesota—Senser 16 pass from Kramer (Danmeier kick).

TEAM STATISTICS

	Minnesota	Atlanta
First downs	25	19
Rushes-Yards	22-130	37-149
Passing yards	330	193
Sacks by-Yards	2-20	0-0
Return yards	122	109
Passes	24-47-4	21-32-0
Punts	6-40.8	6-40.7
Fumbles-Lost	2-1	4-3
Penalties-Yards	7-55	7-69
Time of possession	27:24	32:36

Attendance—54,086.

INDIVIDUAL STATISTICS

Rushing—Minnesota, Brown 16-108, Lewis 1-16, Galbreath 1-5, Young 2-3, Kramer 1-0, White 1-minus 2; Atlanta, Andrews 22-91, Cain 11-67, Jackson 1-0, Bartkowski 2-minus 2, James 1-minus 7.

Passing—Minnesota, Kramer 24-47-4—330; Atlanta, Bartkowski 21-32-0—213.

Receiving—Minnesota, Rashad 9-151, Brown 5-35, Senser 4-56, Lewis 2-58, S. White 2-18, Galbreath 1-9, Bruer 1-3; Atlanta, Cain 6-52, Jenkins 5-65, Francis 4-58, Jackson 3-23, Andrews 2-12, Miller 1-3.

Kickoff Returns—Minnesota, Payton 5-106; Atlanta, Woerner 1-16, R. Smith 3-54.

Punt Returns—Minnesota, Payton 2-16; Atlanta, Woerner 1-0.

Interceptions—Atlanta, Johnson 1-4, Pridemore 2-0, Curry 1-35.

Punting—Minnesota, Coleman 6-40.8; Atlanta, James 6-40.7.

Field Goals—Minnesota, Danmeier 0-1; Atlanta, Luckhurst 1-1.

THIRTEENTH WEEK

LIONS 27, CHIEFS 10

PONTIAC—Eric Hipple threw two first-half touchdown passes and Detroit's defense came up with the big plays in the second half in the Thanksgiving Day Victory over Kansas City. The triumph boosted the Lions' record to 6-0 in the Silverdome for 1981.

"We seem to have the big play in us," said Hipple, who fired a 10-yard scoring pass to tight end David Hill and a 40-yarder to wide receiver Freddie Scott. "We're now able to sustain a drive, and we're winning. Maybe down the road we have a chance at the playoffs."

Billy Sims clinched the Detroit victory when he capped a 70-yard drive with a four-yard scoring run with 2:46 left, dragging linebacker Cal Peterson the last three yards to the goal line. Eddie Murray booted two field goals.

"If you ask me," said Chiefs Coach Marv Levy, "their defense is what makes the team go. In the second half, their defense really dug in and went after our quarterback."

That was Steve Fuller, who had replaced starter Bill Kenney at the intermission. Fuller was sacked three times, after the Silver Rush—ends Bubba Baker and Dave Pureifory and tackles Doug English and William Gay—got to Kenney twice in the first half.

Kansas City scored a touchdown (on a four-yard run by Billy Jackson) on its first possession of the game and got a field goal on its first drive of the second half.

Joe Delaney, the Chiefs' standout rookie running back, gained 77 yards to top the 1,000-yard mark. That left him 25 yards short of Mike Garrett's club record of 1,087 yards, set in 1967, and he was inches short of a critical first down in the first quarter.

Delaney needed three yards on a fourth-down play from the Detroit 33, with the Lions leading, 20-10, and 7:30 to play. Delaney skidded to a stop with his waist clearly past the 30, but the official spotted the ball short of a first down. The Lions then went 70 yards, all on the ground, for Sims' TD.

The Chiefs had not permitted a back to rush for 100 yards against them in 1981, and they limited Sims to 64 yards on 20 trips. He was bothered much of the game with hyperextended left toes.

THURSDAY, NOVEMBER 26
SCORE BY PERIODS

Kansas City	7	0	3	0—10
Detroit	7	10	3	7—27

SCORING

Detroit—Hill 10 pass from Hipple (Murray kick).
Kansas City—B. Jackson 4 run (Lowery kick).
Detroit—Field goal Murray 34.
Detroit—Scott 40 pass from Hipple (Murray kick).
Kansas City—Field goal Lowery 33.
Detroit—Field goal Murray 46.
Detroit—Sims 4 run (Murray kick).

TEAM STATISTICS

	Kansas City	Detroit
First downs	14	21
Rushes-Yards	28-116	41-171
Passing yards	129	114
Sacks by-Yards	3-18	5-40
Return yards	141	120
Passes	14-25-2	10-22-0
Punts	5-37.4	4-42.5
Fumbles-Lost	1-1	3-1
Penalties-Yards	5-78	4-42
Time of possession	30:35	29:25

Attendance—76,735.

INDIVIDUAL STATISTICS

Rushing—Kansas City, Delaney 17-77, Fuller 2-19, Hadnot 5-16, B. Jackson 4-4; Detroit, Sims 20-64, V. Thompson 8-40, Bussey 5-31, Hipple 3-22, L. Thompson 1-9, Kane 2-5, King 1-1, Scott 1-minus 1.

Passing—Kansas City, Kenney 4-8-2—38, Fuller 10-17-0—131; Detroit, Hipple 10-22-0—132.

Receiving—Kansas City, Smith 5-61, Rome 3-32, Hadnot 2-24, Delaney 2-12, Murphy 1-22, Dixon 1-18; Detroit, Scott 3-71, Nichols 2-19, Sims 1-11, Hill 1-10, Bussey 1-9, King 1-6, L. Thompson 1-6.

Kickoff Returns—Kansas City, Murphy 4-97, Cherry 1-22; Detroit, Martin 1-21, Nichols 2-43.

Punt Returns—Kansas City, Smith 3-22; Detroit, Martin 4-20.

Interceptions—Detroit, Allen 1-34, White 1-2.

Punting—Kansas City, Gossett 5-37.4; Detroit, Skladany 4-42.5.

Field Goals—Kansas City, Lowery 1-1; Detroit, Murray 2-3.

COWBOYS 10, BEARS 9

IRVING—Quarterback Glenn Carano, forced into his first meaningful action in five years because of a injury to Danny White, guided Dallas to a fourth-quarter touchdown. The Cowboys (10-3) held on to win and grab the NFC East lead when a Chicago field-goal attempt went wide in the final seconds Thanksgiving Day at Texas Stadium.

White was knocked out of the game with a cracked rib, suffered when he was tackled after a scramble late in the second quarter. Though doctors said x-rays showed no fracture, White said, "My shoulder was cramping and I just couldn't go back in there."

Carano, who has spent his entire pro career as a third-stringer behind Roger Staubach and White or as a backup to White, completed only six of 15 passes and didn't exactly steal the show. But he came through when the game was on the line in the fourth period.

After Chicago had broken a 3-3 tie on an 80-yard drive, capped by quarterback Vince Evans' two-yard run, Too Tall Jones blocked John Roveto's extra-point attempt.

After the kickoff, Carano fired a 55-yard pass to Tony Hill and the Cowboys moved to the Bears' 2-yard line, where a fourth-down pass was batted down by Mike Hartenstine.

But Chicago was forced to punt and James Jones returned the kick 17 yards to the Bears' 37. Carano scrambled for 11 yards and then threw a screen pass to Ron Springs for a 15-yard gain to the 11. Tony Dorsett ran for six yards and then Springs skirted left end on a five-yard TD run with 5:09 left. Rafael Septien's extra point gave the Cowboys the lead.

The Bears had one last chance, but Roveto was wide to the right on a 49-yard field goal attempt with 31 seconds left.

Cowboys Coach Tom Landry said of Carano, "Glenn was very nervous when he went into the game, but he settled down in the second half and executed well. We've got some good backup quarterbacks on this club. The only problem is that they don't get to play much."

Neither Landry nor his players figured the Cowboys would score much with Carano in the game, but they expressed confidence in his play. "We just had to assure him that we had confidence in him," said Springs.

Dallas' victory dulled a brilliant rushing performance by the Bears' Walter Payton, who gained 179 yards in 38 carries. "We didn't win, so it doesn't matter how many yards I gained," Payton said. "I just think we should have won it."

THURSDAY, NOVEMBER 26
SCORE BY PERIODS

Chicago	0	3	0	6— 9
Dallas	3	0	0	7—10

SCORING

Dallas—Field goal Septien 41.

Chicago—Field goal Roveto 43.
Chicago—Evans 2 run (kick blocked).
Dallas—Springs 5 run (Septien kick).

TEAM STATISTICS

	Chicago	Dallas
First downs	15	11
Rushes-Yards	50-229	31-95
Passing yards	43	178
Sacks by-Yards	2-19	2-17
Return yards	51	81
Passes	6-19-1	9-23-1
Punts	7-37.7	6-42.7
Fumbles-Lost	4-2	3-2
Penalties-Yards	5-29	4-45
Time of possession	34:48	25:12
Attendance—63,499.		

INDIVIDUAL STATISTICS

Rushing—Chicago, Payton 38-179, Suhey 8-41, Evans 4-9; Dallas, Dorsett 19-72, Springs 4-9, Carano 6-9, D. White 1-8, Hill 1-minus 3.

Passing—Chicago, Evans 6-18-1—60, Payton 0-1-0—0; Dallas, Carano 6-15-0—131, D. White 3-7-0—66, Springs 0-1-1—0.

Receiving—Chicago, Watts 2-28, B. Williams 2-28, Payton 2-4; Dallas, Hill 4-117, Pearson 2-16, Johnson 1-27, DuPree 1-22, Springs 1-15.

Kickoff Returns—Chicago, Moorehead 2-41; Dallas, J. Jones 2-43.

Punt Returns—Chicago, Fisher 1-10; Dallas, J. Jones 3-38.

Interceptions—Chicago, Henderson 1-0; Dallas, Wilson 1-0.

Punting—Chicago, Parsons 7-37.7; Dallas, D. White 4-48.5, Septien 2-31.0.

Field Goals—Chicago, Roveto 1-3; Dallas, Septien 1-3.

BUCCANEERS 31, SAINTS 14

NEW ORLEANS—Quarterback Doug Williams had a great homecoming as he threw two touchdown passes and ran for a third score in Tampa Bay's comeback victory over New Orleans in the Superdome.

With his mother looking on in a crowd of supporters from his hometown of Zachary, La., Williams completed 16 of 24 passes for 218 yards as the Buccaneers shrugged off an early 14-0 Saints lead.

"I love the Superdome," said Williams. "I have never lost here." As a collegian at Grambling State, he directed three victories over arch-rival Southern University in the Superdome. He's played in two exhibitions and two regular-season victories for the Bucs in the building. The first was in 1977, when the Bucs snapped a 26-game losing streaking by beating the Saints, 33-14, for their first NFL victory.

"It's great to be at home. It's great to see my people and give everybody in Zachary an opportunity to see me play," said Williams. "I had a lot of people in the stands—including my mom. My father couldn't come because he was sick, but I know he was watching on the tube."

Williams zeroed in on Kevin House with a 16-yard TD pass in the second period and fired a four-yard scoring pass to Gordon Jones in the fourth quarter. Williams' two-yard rollout for a score put the Bucs ahead for good, 17-14, in the third quarter.

Thirteenth Week—Continued

Archie Manning threw a two-yard pass to tight end Larry Hardy and rookie running back George Rogers zipped eight yards for a TD as the Saints built their early lead. Rogers ran for 120 yards in 23 carries and had 1,399 yards after 13 games.

NOVEMBER 29
SCORE BY PERIODS

Tampa Bay	0	10	7	14—31
New Orleans	7	7	0	0—14

SCORING

New Orleans—Hardy 2 pass from Manning (Ricardo kick).
New Orleans—G. Rogers 8 run (Ricardo kick).
Tampa Bay—Field goal Capece 51.
Tampa Bay—House 16 pass from Williams (Capece kick).
Tampa Bay—Williams 2 run (Capece kick).
Tampa Bay—Jones 4 pass from Williams (Capece kick).
Tampa Bay—Owens 6 run (Capece kick).

TEAM STATISTICS

	Tampa Bay	New Orleans
First downs	21	20
Rushes-Yards	38-127	27-137
Passing yards	218	204
Sacks by-Yards	2-11	0-0
Return yards	113	203
Passes	16-24-1	19-31-2
Punts	3-46.7	2-35.0
Fumbles-Lost	2-1	2-1
Penalties-Yards	8-96	3-30
Time of possession	30:52	29:08
Attendance—62,209.		

INDIVIDUAL STATISTICS

Rushing—Tampa Bay, Eckwood 7-15, Wilder 7-47, Owens 17-50, Williams 5-19, Fusina 2-minus 4; New Orleans, G. Rogers 23-120, Holmes 3-16, Stauch 1-1.

Passing—Tampa Bay, Williams 16-24-1—218; New Orleans, Manning 16-23-2—162, D. Wilson 3-8-0—53.

Receiving—Tampa Bay, House 6-107, Giles 2-46, Eckwood 4-36, Wilder 2-14, Owens 1-11, Jones 1-4; New Orleans, Merkens 4-57, Groth 1-54, Holmes 7-35, Thompson 1-25, Brenner 1-17, Martini 1-11, Hardy 2-11, Tyler 2-5

Kickoff Returns—Tampa Bay, Owens 3-63; New Orleans, J. Rogers 3-60, W. Wilson 2-51, Stauch 1-29.

Punt Returns—New Orleans, Groth 2-47.

Interceptions—Tampa Bay, Washington 1-34, Johnson 1-16; New Orleans, Myers 1-16.

Punting—Tampa Bay, Swider 3-46.7; New Orleans, Erxleben 2-35.0

Field Goals—Tampa Bay, Capece 1-1; New Orleans, Ricardo 0-1.

STEELERS 24, RAMS O

PITTSBURGH—Several Steelers set individual records during Pittsburgh's shutout of Los Angeles, but those players could not have cared less about personal honors.

"The most important thing is playing on a championship team," said Franco Harris, who set a couple of records while rushing for 118 yards and a touchdown.

His performance helped push the Steelers' record to 8-5, keeping alive their hopes for a playoff berth. The Rams, shut out for the first time since 1976, dropped to 5-8.

"What's more important is to play as a team and make the contributions expected of the position," said cornerback Mel Blount, who set a record with his two interceptions.

Terry Bradshaw, who also made history with his 204-yard, one-touchdown passing performance, thinks the Steelers have their act together.

"We're a much better football team," Bradshaw said. "We've worked out our problems. We're playing as good as anybody. The attitude is here now. We know we're going to win. And that's the big difference."

The Rams looked as bad as the Steelers looked good, particularly after starting quarterback Pat Haden left the game with a bruised shoulder early in the second quarter. He was hurt trying to make the tackle after throwing an interception to Jack Ham, who returned the ball to the Rams' 2-yard line, setting up the Steelers' third touchdown.

The Steelers intercepted Dan Pastorini three times and sacked him three times for 32 yards and allowed him to complete just 14 of 33 passes for 125 yards. The Rams gained only 71 yards on the ground.

"We couldn't get anything going offensively," said Rams Coach Ray Malavasi. "We had a lot of things we wanted to do, but when Pat got hurt we stuck with the basic stuff."

Blount's interceptions raised his career total to 51—the most of any active defender in the NFL. Ham raised his interception total to 31, making him the leader among active linebackers.

Harris became the NFL's all-time leader in rushing attempts with 2,420 and his one-yard touchdown run was his 84th rushing TD, putting him in second place on the all-time list.

Bradshaw's nine-yard scoring pass to Lynn Swann was the 192nd touchdown throw of his career, tying him with Bob Griese for 18th on the all-time list. Bradshaw also moved into 16th place for career completions with 1,907.

NOVEMBER 29
SCORE BY PERIODS

Los Angeles	0	0	0	0— 0
Pittsburgh	7	14	3	0—24

SCORING

Pittsburgh—Harris 1 run (Trout kick).
Pittsburgh—Swann 9 pass from Bradshaw (Trout kick).
Pittsburgh—Bradshaw 1 run (Trout kick).
Pittsburgh—Field goal Trout 21.

TEAM STATISTICS

	Los Angeles	Pittsburgh
First downs	12	18
Rushes-Yards	21-71	44-211
Passing yards	103	170
Sacks by-Yards	4-34	3-32
Return yards	68	68
Passes	15-37-4	10-19-0
Punts	9-43.8	6-44.8
Fumbles-Lost	1-0	6-3
Penalties-Yards	5-51	2-15
Time of possession	26:19	33:41
Attendance—51,854.		

Pittsburgh's Franco Harris became the NFL's all-time leader in rushing attempts with 2,420 as the Steelers blanked the Los Angeles Rams, 24-0.

Thirteenth Week—Continued

Rushing—Los Angeles, Tyler 7-19, Guman 11-33, Haden 2-16, Bryant 1-3; Pittsburgh, Harris 18-114, Thornton 9-21, Bradshaw 5-16, Pollard 4-28, Davis 4-10, Hawthorne 3-18, Moser 1-4.

Passing—Los Angeles, Haden 1-4-1—9, Pastorini 14-33-3—126; Pittsburgh, Bradshaw 10-19-0—204.

Receiving—Los Angeles, Guman 5-41, Tyler 6-59, Arnold 2-9, Waddy 2-26; Pittsburgh, Cunningham 1-28, Swann 1-9, Stallworth 1-55, Harris 2-30, Hawthorne 1-3, Sweeney 2-53, Smith 1-7, Davis 1-19.

Kickoff Returns—Los Angeles, D. Hill 3-65, Sully 1-minus 3.

Punt Returns—Los Angeles, Irvin 1-6; Pittsburgh, Anderson 6-47.

Interceptions—Pittsburgh, Blount 2-minus 4, Lambert 1-2, Ham 1-23.

Punting—Los Angeles, Corral 9-43.8; Pittsburgh, Colquitt 6-44.8.

Field Goals—Los Angeles, Corral 0-1; Pittsburgh, Trout 1-1.

49ers 17, GIANTS 10

SAN FRANCISCO—Back in August of 1981, before the National Football League regular season got under way, the Nevada oddsmakers were listing the San Francisco 49ers as 40-to-1 longshots to win a division title and 60-to-1 to land in the Super Bowl.

Well, the longshot came through. With three games left in the regular season, the 49ers clinched the NFC Western Division championship. They were the first team to clinch a playoff berth.

The 49ers boosted their record to 10-3 and wrapped up the NFC West title with a 17-10 victory over the New York Giants at Candlestick Park.

San Francisco's offense didn't overwhelm the Giants, but the 49ers' defense recovered two New York fumbles and picked off three Scott Brunner passes to keep the Giants bottled up most of the game.

Coach Bill Walsh called it a typical 49er victory. Except for a 45-14 romp over Dallas, the 49ers have played every game close, capitalizing on their opponents' mistakes. That was the case against New York, as an interception and a fumble recovery set up both San Francisco touchdowns.

Safety Dwight Hicks grabbed a deflected pass and returned 54 yards to the New York 16 to set up a one-yard TD run by Johnny Davis in the first quarter. Linebacker Keena Turner's fumble recovery at the Giants' 40 in the second period led to a 20-yard scramble for a score by quarterback Joe Montana. Ray Wersching's 23-yard field goal in the fourth quarter concluded the 49ers' scoring.

"It's a great tribute to this team to win the division," said Walsh, in his third year as the Niners' coach. "Who knows what will happen in the next five or six weeks? We can't make any promises about the Super Bowl, but who knows?

"Winning the division early gives us a chance to rest some of our players who are hurt," said Walsh. "It also gives us a chance to use some players who have not been in a whole lot, especially (quarterback) Guy Benjamin. But we want to win as many more games as possible because of the playoff advantages."

NOVEMBER 29
SCORE BY PERIODS

New York Giants	0	3	0	7—10
San Francisco	7	7	0	3—17

SCORING

San Francisco—Davis 1 run (Wersching kick).
San Francisco—Montana 20 run (Wersching kick).
New York—Field goal Danelo 52.
New York—Carpenter 3 run (Danelo kick).
San Francisco—Field goal Wersching 23.

TEAM STATISTICS

	New York	San Fran.
First downs	12	19
Rushes-Yards	22-80	39-123
Passing yards	143	214
Sacks by-Yards	3-20	2-19
Return yards	119	136
Passes	13-34-3	27-40-0
Punts	6-42.8	8-37.5
Fumbles-Lost	3-2	1-0
Penalties-Yards	9-65	5-48
Time of possession	21:44	38:16
Attendance—57,186.		

INDIVIDUAL STATISTICS

Rushing—New York, Carpenter 13-40, Forte 7-31, Perkins 1-10, Brunner 1-minus 1; San Francisco, Davis 11-21, Hofer 8-33, Patton 7-20, Ring 4-9, Cooper 3-12, Montana 2-24, Solomon 1-6, Clark 1-5, Lawrence 2-minus 7.

Passing—New York, Brunner 13-34-3—162; San Francisco, Montana 27-39-0—234, Clark 0-1-0—0.

Receiving—New York, Carpenter 5-55, Gray 2-40, Perkins 2-28, Friede 2-21, Mullady 1-13, Forte 1-5; San Francisco, Clark 7-87, Patton 5-23, Cooper 4-37, Hofer 4-31, Young 3-33, Solomon 1-25, Davis 2-minus 4, Lawrence 1-2.

Kickoff Returns—New York, Pittman 2-45, Dennis 1-17, Reece 1-24; San Francisco, Lawrence 1-25, Ring 1-23.

Punt Returns—New York, Bright 5-32, T. Jackson 1-1; San Francisco, Hicks 3-19, Solomon 1-8.

Interceptions—San Francisco, Hicks 1-54, Williamson 2-7.

Punting—New York, Jennings 6-42.8; San Francisco, Miller 8-37.5.

Field Goals—New York, Danelo 1-1; San Francisco, Wersching 1-3.

CHARGERS 34, BRONCOS 17

SAN DIEGO—Heavy overnight rains had left nearly two inches of water on the tarpaulin covering San Diego Jack Murphy Stadium before the troops from San Diego and Denver did battle.

Then, when groundkeepers pulled back the tarp, they forgot to remove the water first, and it sloshed back into the turf, creating a quagmire. Helicopters were called out, but even with the action of the rotating blades, puddles remained on the field as the Chargers and Broncos squared off.

San Diego won easily, 34-17, as the Chargers' human tank—Chuck Muncie, a 233-pound running back—plowed for four touchdowns in the first half and quarterback Dan Fouts provided adequate air support.

The result left the Chargers, Broncos and Kansas City Chiefs in a three-way tie atop the AFC West, each with a record of 8-5 and three games remaining.

Muncie lifted his season total of touchdowns by rushing to 18—one short of the National Football League record shared by Jim Taylor and Earl Campbell. He scored from 14 yards, one yard, four yards and three yards as the Chargers ran up a 27-10 halftime lead.

While Muncie was bowling over the Broncos on the ground, Fouts completed 19 of 29 passes for 256 yards. He threw a one-yard TD pass to reserve tight end Eric Sievers in the third quarter, faking a rollout on a fourth-and-goal play.

San Diego's defense held Denver to 67 yards rushing, intercepted three passes and recovered two fumbles. Two of the turnovers led to touchdowns.

"The last couple of weeks we have been pushed into a corner where we had to win," said Chargers safety Glen Edwards. "All week I was saying this would be a battle of hitting. And we won the battle."

Craig Morton, who had missed a game and a half with a sprained shoulder, returned as Denver's quarterback. He was 19-for-31, passing for 270 yards, before he was replaced by Steve DeBerg, who produced a 10-yard scoring pass to Haven Moses with 10 seconds left in the game.

NOVEMBER 29
SCORE BY PERIODS

Denver	0	10	0	7—	17
San Diego	14	13	7	0—	34

SCORING

San Diego—Muncie 14 run (Benirschke kick).
San Diego—Muncie 1 run (Benirschke kick).
Denver—Canada 5 run (Steinfort kick).
San Diego—Muncie 4 run (kick failed).
Denver—Field goal Steinfort 21.
San Diego—Muncie 3 run (Benirschke kick).
San Diego—Sievers 1 pass from Fouts (Benirschke kick).
Denver—Moses 10 pass from DeBerg (Steinfort kick).

TEAM STATISTICS

	Denver	San Diego
First downs	19	20
Rushes-Yards	17-67	38-148
Passing yards	322	260
Sacks by-Yards	0-0	4-31
Return yards	117	105
Passes	26-46-3	21-34-1
Punts	4-40.5	6-38.5
Fumbles-Lost	3-2	2-1
Penalties-Yards	3-20	11-84
Time of possession	27:35	32:25
Attendance—51,533.		

INDIVIDUAL STATISTICS

Rushing—Denver, Parros 5-36, Preston 5-25, Canada 1-4, Reed 4-2, Lytle 2-0; San Diego, Muncie 18-75, Brooks 11-44, C. Williams 4-12, Chandler 1-9, Cappelletti 3-9, Luther 1-minus 1.

Passing—Denver, Morton 19-31-2—270, DeBerg 7-15-1—83; San Diego, Fouts 19-29-0—256, Luther 2-5-1—4.

Receiving—Denver, Reed 6-30, Watson 4-95, Upchurch 4-86, Preston 4-43, Moses 3-32, Egloff 2-30, Parros 2-16, Odoms 1-21; San Diego, Chandler 4-111, Sievers 4-36, Muncie 4-30, Winslow 3-18, Brooks 3-15, Joiner 2-27, Scales 1-23.

Kickoff Returns—Denver, Manning 4-59, Harden 1-1, Lytle 1-24; San Diego, Brooks 3-51, Shaw 1-24.

Punt Returns—Denver, Manning 2-9; San Diego, Brooks 2-17, Bauer 1-7.

Interceptions—Denver, Foley 1-24; San Diego, Buchanon 1-0, Lowe 1-0, Edwards 1-6.

Punting—Denver, Prestridge 4-40.5; San Diego, Roberts 6-38.5.

Field Goals—Denver, Steinfort 1-1; San Diego, Benirschke 0-2.

RAIDERS 32, SEAHAWKS 31

SEATTLE—Marc Wilson fired three touchdown passes to bring Oakland back from a 24-3 third-quarter deficit to a victory over Seattle.

Wilson threw touchdown passes of five yards to Derrick Ramsey, eight yards to Bob Chandler and 16 yards to running back Arthur Whittington to help raise the Raiders' record to 6-7.

"I thought Marc did very well," said Raiders Coach Tom Flores. "He held his poise tremendously. It would have been easy to lose his poise early in the second half, but he hung in there."

After Seattle built its 24-3 lead, the Oakland comeback began with a safety when Seahawks punter Jeff West inadvertently stepped on the back line of the end zone before kicking the ball. That made the score 24-5. The Raiders took a 25-24 lead on Wilson's third touchdown pass and then added another score on a three-yard run by Derrick Jensen with 1:51 left.

Seattle, with Dave Krieg replacing injured Jim Zorn at quarterback, came back to score on an 11-yard pass to Steve Largent with only eight seconds remaining, but the Seahawks' onside kick was recovered by Oakland and the Raiders ran out the clock.

After the Raiders narrowed the lead to 24-18, the Seahawks tried a trick play out of punt formation. West connected with Eric Lane on a 59-yard pass play, but it was nullified and the Seahawks were penalized for unsportsmanlike conduct when the officials ruled that Lane attempted to deceive Oakland by running onto the field just before the center snap.

Seattle scored on rookie Wilson Alvarez' 22-yard field goal, Zorn's three-yard run, Sherman Smith's three-yarder and rookie Rodell Thomas' five-yard return of a fumbled kickoff.

Zorn was carried off the field after suffering a broken left ankle when he was tackled by defensive lineman Johnny Robinson after releasing a pass with 3:20 left in the game.

NOVEMBER 29
SCORE BY PERIODS

Oakland	0	3	8	21—	32
Seattle	0	10	14	7—	31

Thirteenth Week—Continued

SCORING

Seattle—Field goal Alvarez 22.
Oakland—Field goal Bahr 20.
Seattle—Zorn 3 run (Alvarez kick).
Seattle—Smith 3 run (Alvarez kick).
Seattle—Thomas 5 fumble return (Alvarez kick).
Oakland—Safety, West stepped out of end zone.
Oakland—Ramsey 5 pass from Wilson (kick blocked).
Oakland—Chandler 8 pass from Wilson (Bahr kick).
Oakland—Whittington 16 pass from Wilson (Bahr kick).
Oakland—Jensen 3 run (Bahr kick).
Seattle—Largent 11 pass from Krieg (Alvarez kick).

TEAM STATISTICS

	Oakland	Seattle
First downs	28	18
Rushes-Yards	36-181	32-69
Passing yards	156	314
Sacks by-Yards	1-4	6-62
Return yards	111	119
Passes	20-33-1	19-36-0
Punts	5-44.8	4-36.8
Fumbles-Lost	4-3	1-1
Penalties-Yards	4-20	8-71
Time of possession	32:30	27:30

Attendance—57,147.

INDIVIDUAL STATISTICS

Rushing—Oakland, King 13-75, Hawkins 12-68, Jensen 6-21, Wilson 4-10, Whittington 1-7; Seattle, T. Brown 18-34, Doornink 8-23, Smith 3-8, Zorn 2-6, West 1-minus 2.

Passing—Oakland, Wilson 20-33-1—218; Seattle, Zorn 14-25-0—239, Krieg 5-11-0—79.

Receiving—Oakland, Ramsey 5-82, Branch 3-38, Hawkins 3-18, King 3-16, Jensen 2-11, Whittington 1-16, Christensen 1-15, Bradshaw 1-14, Chandler 1-8; Seattle, McCullum 4-91, Doornink 4-36, T. Brown 3-67, Largent 3-63, Smith 3-39, Johns 1-13, Tice 1-9.

Kickoff Returns—Oakland, Whittington 4-72, Hill 1-21, Christensen 1-18; Seattle, Ivory 4-59, Lane 1-16.

Punt Returns—Seattle, Johns 2-44.

Interceptions—Seattle, Harris 1-0.

Punting—Oakland, Guy 5-44.8; Seattle, West 4-36.8.

Field Goals—Oakland, Bahr 1-1; Seattle, Alvarez 1-3.

BENGALS 41, BROWNS 21

CLEVELAND—The reason for Cincinnati's turnaround was perfectly clear to the Cleveland players following the Bengals' trouncing of the Browns: Ken Anderson.

The Bengals' quarterback riddled the Cleveland defense, completing 26 of 32 passes for 235 yards and four touchdowns. That gave Anderson 250 completions and 25 touchdowns this season, the best figures of his 11-year career.

The victory was the Bengals' fifth in a row and their 10th against three losses. Cincinnati maintained its two-game lead over Pittsburgh in the AFC Central Division. Cleveland, the defending division champion, fell to 5-8 and was out of the playoffs.

"The whole difference is Kenny," said Cleveland's Dave Logan. "He's just throwing BB's all over the place."

"I think they finally designed an offense to keep him healthy," said Browns safety Thom Darden. "Now he's just getting the ball 10 to 15 yards downfield. They used to throw deep a lot more and he used to take a lot of hits because of it."

"I think part of (Anderson's) problems in the past must have been a lack of protection," said Bengals rookie receiver Cris Collinsworth. "Now, he's just standing back there like the Rock of Gibraltar and throwing."

Collinsworth caught two of Anderson's scoring strikes and the others went to M.L. Harris and running back Pete Johnson. Johnson also scored a pair of touchdowns on the ground and rolled up 105 yards in 21 carries.

Despite the score, the statistics were close. The Bengals had only one more first down, five more yards rushing and two more yards passing than the Browns. But Cleveland lost three fumbles, all in its own territory and two in the first quarter.

The Browns moved the ball well on the ground early, but turnovers forced Brian Sipe to the air, leaving him vulnerable to the fierce Cincinnati rush. The Bengals sacked him five times for 53 yards in losses. Sipe was lifted late in the game after a blind-side hit by linebacker Reggie Williams forced him to fumble.

NOVEMBER 29
SCORE BY PERIODS

Cincinnati	14	14	0	13—41
Cleveland	0	7	0	14—21

SCORING

Cincinnati—Johnson 5 pass from Anderson (Breech kick).
Cincinnati—Collinsworth 39 pass from Anderson (Breech kick).
Cincinnati—Collinsworth 7 pass from Anderson (Breech kick).
Cleveland—Feacher 30 pass from Sipe (Bahr kick).
Cincinnati—M.L. Harris 2 pass from Anderson (Breech kick).
Cleveland—M. Pruitt 1 run (Bahr kick).
Cincinnati—Johnson 11 run (kick blocked).
Cincinnati—Johnson 1 run (Breech kick).
Cleveland—G. Pruitt 7 pass from McDonald (Bahr kick).

TEAM STATISTICS

	Cincinnati	Cleveland
First downs	24	23
Rushes-Yards	29-130	29-125
Passing yards	226	224
Sacks by-Yards	5-53	3-28
Return yards	91	198
Passes	27-34-0	22-34-0
Punts	6-39.7	5-37.4
Fumbles-Lost	0-0	3-3
Penalties-Yards	4-24	7-45
Time of possession	30:02	29:58

Attendance—75,186.

INDIVIDUAL STATISTICS

Rushing—Cincinnati, Johnson 21-105, Alexander 4-11, Bass 1-9, Anderson 2-7, Hargrove 1-minus 2; Cleveland, M. Pruitt 21-83, Sipe 4-43, G. Pruitt 1-1, C. Miller 1-0, White 2-minus 2.

Passing—Cincinnati, Anderson 26-32-0—235, Thompson 1-2-0—19; Cleveland, Sipe 19-28-0—217, McDonald 3-6-0—60.

Receiving—Cincinnati, Johnson 7-37, Ross 6-66, Collinsworth 5-76, Curtis 3-39, M.L. Harris 3-25, Alexander 2-8, Kreider 1-3; Cleveland, M. Pruitt 8-57, Newsome 4-58, G. Pruitt 4-30, Feacher 3-98, Logan 2-13, Rucker 1-21.

Kickoff Returns—Cincinnati, Verser 2-52, A. Griffin 1-24, Dinkel 1-0; Cleveland, Hall 7-169.

Punt Returns—Cincinnati, Fuller 2-15; Cleveland, Hall 4-29.

Interceptions—None.

Punting—Cincinnati, McInally 6-39.7; Cleveland, Cox 5-37.4.

Field Goals—Cincinnati, None attempted; Cleveland, None attempted.

BILLS 21, REDSKINS 14

ORCHARD PARK—Subbing for injured running back Joe Cribbs, Roland Hooks was fast shedding his image as an unknown by scoring the winning touchdowns in Buffalo's last two games.

Hooks grabbed a desperation touchdown pass in the Bills' victory over New England and ran 18 yards for a third-quarter score in the triumph over Washington.

The Bills improved their record to 8-5 and remained in the AFC playoff hunt. The Redskins dropped to 5-8.

Hooks rushed for 109 yards on 19 carries and scored two touchdowns. His first was from four yards in the second quarter.

"To be able to come in and contribute gives me a lot of satisfaction," said Hooks.

Hooks' winning touchdown came with three minutes gone in the third quarter, breaking a 14-14 tie.

"It was a very good win for us," said Buffalo Coach Chuck Knox. "We broke on top 14-0 and they came back and put pressure on us, but I was real happy the way our team came back in the third quarter and the way we played in the second half."

The Bills scored first on a 21-yard pass from Joe Ferguson to Jerry Butler. Hooks' four-yard run made it 14-0.

The Redskins scored twice in the final 2:08 of the first half to tie the game. John Riggins went in on a two-yard run and Joe Theismann fired a 25-yard strike to Art Monk with 11 seconds left.

The Redskins self-destructed, however, with nine penalties for 80 yards and four lost fumbles.

"We just had too many things for us to overcome and win the game," Washington Coach Joe Gibbs said. "I thought we played real hard, but we had the penalties and we turned the ball over."

NOVEMBER 29
SCORE BY PERIODS

Washington	0	14	0	0—14
Buffalo	7	7	7	0—21

SCORING

Buffalo—Butler 21 pass from Ferguson (Mike-Mayer kick).
Buffalo—Hooks 4 run (Mike-Mayer kick).
Washington—Riggins 2 run (Moseley kick).
Washington—Monk 25 pass from Theismann (Moseley kick).
Buffalo—Hooks 18 run (Mike-Mayer kick).

TEAM STATISTICS

	Washington	Buffalo
First downs	19	18
Rushes-Yards	27-91	39-188
Passing yards	202	41
Sacks by-Yards	3-35	3-18
Return yards	117	74
Passes	22-34-1	6-18-0
Punts	3-41.0	5-35.4
Fumbles-Lost	5-4	3-2
Penalties-Yards	9-80	5-40
Time of possession	28:21	31:39

Attendance—61,452.

INDIVIDUAL STATISTICS

Rushing—Washington, Washington 16-69, Riggins 7-6, Theismann 4-16; Buffalo, Leaks 13-50, Hooks 19-109, Riddick 3-29, Ferguson 4-0.

Passing—Washington, Theismann 22-34-1—220; Buffalo, Ferguson 6-18-0—76.

Receiving—Washington, Warren 4-38, Seay 4-55, Monk 6-60, Washington 7-64, Metcalf 1-3; Buffalo, Lewis 1-13, Butler 3-38, Jessie 1-15, Brammer 1-10.

Kickoff Returns—Washington, Nelms 2-50, Wonsley 1-27, Garrett 1-19; Buffalo, Hooks 1-16, Riddick 2-30.

Punt Returns—Washington, Nelms 3-21; Buffalo, Piccone 1-7, Riddick 1-7.

Interceptions—Buffalo, Clark 1-14.

Punting—Washington, Connell 3-41.0; Buffalo, Cater 5-35.4.

Field Goals—Washington, None attempted; Buffalo, Mike-Mayer 0-1.

JETS 25, COLTS O

NEW YORK—The New York defense throttled Baltimore as the Jets gained their fifth victory in a row and raised their record to 8-4-1, which kept them in first place in the AFC East.

Their first shutout in five years assured the Jets of their first winning season since 1969.

The Jets' defense dropped Colts quarterback Bert Jones five times and held the Baltimore offense to just 49 yards rushing and 113 yards total offense. The Jets allowed only 33 points during their five-game November winning streak.

"The biggest thing about this game was that the defense played under adverse conditions and did the job," said Jets Coach Walt Michaels. "The defense did it when it had to do it."

Rookie Freeman McNeil scored his first two NFL touchdowns and Pat Leahy kicked four field goals. McNeil, the Jets' No. 1 draft choice who spent five weeks on the injured reserve list, gave the Jets a 7-0 lead with a 30-yard dash in the first quarter and put the game out of reach with a one-yard burst in the third quarter.

"The more I work the more I'll get into the flow," said McNeil. "I still feel I have a long way to go. I'm grateful to the coaches for giving me the work. I'm still a rookie and I have a lot to learn. I made a lot of mistakes out there."

While there was unbridled optimism surrounding the Jets, there was little cause for joy on the part of the Colts, whose club-record losing streak was extended to 12 games.

Thirteenth Week—Continued

"Our offense didn't do a thing," said Colts Coach Mike McCormack. "We're killing ourselves. We blew the audibles—that makes us look ridiculous. There was no blocking. Bert didn't even get time to plant his foot.

"It was perhaps our defense's best game but, on offense, we looked confused. That's what's discouraging. If it was just the young guys. . . but it's everybody. In the second half, the Jets smelled blood and just started going after us."

NOVEMBER 29
SCORE BY PERIODS

Baltimore	0	0	0	0— 0
New York Jets	7	6	9	3—25

SCORING

New York—McNeil 30 run (Leahy kick).
New York—Field goal Leahy 37.
New York—Field goal Leahy 22.
New York—McNeil 1 run (bad snap).
New York—Field goal Leahy 27.
New York—Field goal Leahy 27.

TEAM STATISTICS

	Baltimore	New York
First downs	11	22
Rushes-Yards	24-49	41-161
Passing yards	103	139
Sacks by-Yards	1-4	5-39
Return yards	87	98
Passes	10-24-1	16-29-0
Punts	8-35.3	2-32.5
Fumbles-Lost	0-0	3-0
Penalties-Yards	9-82	6-40
Time of possession	24:30	35:30

Attendance—53,595.

INDIVIDUAL STATISTICS

Rushing—Baltimore, Dixon 12-22, McCauley 2-8, McMillan 8-12, B. Jones 2-7; New York, McNeil 24-93, Newton 7-34, Long 7-21, Dierking 2-12, Harper 1-1.

Passing—Baltimore, B. Jones 10-24-1—142; New York, Todd 16-28-0—143, Ryan 0-1-0—0.

Receiving—Baltimore, Butler 5-88, McCall 2-31, Dixon 2-14, McCauley 1-9; New York, B. Jones 4-46, Harper 3-29, Newton 3-1, Barkum 2-33, Dierking 2-18, McNeil 2-16.

Kickoff Returns—Baltimore, Anderson 3-68, Dixon 1-19.

Punt Returns—New York, Harper 4-59.

Interceptions—New York, Schroy 1-39.

Punting—Baltimore, Garrett 8-35.3; New York, Ramsey 2-32.5.

Field Goals—Baltimore, None attempted; New York, Leahy 4-6.

FALCONS 31, OILERS 27

HOUSTON—The Houston game plan was to shore up its leaky defense against the run. Unfortunately for the Oilers, Steve Bartkowski burned them with two touchdown bombs and Atlanta stayed in the chase for an NFC wild-card playoff berth.

Bartkowski completed 18 of 25 passes for 372 yards, an average gain of nearly 21 yards per completion. He stunned the Oilers with a 43-yard scoring pass to Alfred Jackson and a 42-yard TD throw to Alfred Jenkins just 22 seconds apart in the final two minutes of the first half.

Those two plays gave the Falcons a 24-6 lead, and they gave Bartkowski a season total of 29 touchdown passes. He would have had his 30th if running back William Andrews hadn't fumbled at the 1-yard line after carrying a pass 23 yards in the third period. On that play, the ball rolled into the end zone and Jackson recovered the fumble for a score that gave Atlanta a 31-13 lead.

"We came in with the idea of trying to rush the football," said Bartkowski. "People had been rushing on them. But they shut us off and forced us to pass."

The Oilers rallied for two touchdowns in the last 10 minutes with Gifford Nielsen at quarterback in his first action of the season. Nielsen suffered a torn shoulder muscle in preseason, and Ken Stabler came out of retirement to guide the Oilers.

Nielsen completed eight of 15 passes for 116 yards. On Nielsen's first drive, Earl Campbell ran 18 yards to score. On the second, Nielsen pitched a three-yard TD pass to Adger Armstrong, cutting Atlanta's lead to 31-27 with 1:45 left.

However, the Falcons' Lynn Cain recovered an onside kickoff by the Oilers and then cornerback Bobby Butler intercepted a Nielsen pass in the final seconds after Houston got the ball back.

NOVEMBER 29
SCORE BY PERIODS

Atlanta	10	14	7	0—31
Houston	0	13	0	14—27

SCORING

Atlanta—Andrews 3 run (Luckhurst kick).
Atlanta—Field goal Luckhurst 36.
Houston—Holston 15 pass from Stabler (kick failed).
Atlanta—Jackson 43 pass from Bartkowski (Luckhurst kick).
Atlanta—Jenkins 42 pass from Bartkowski (Luckhurst kick).
Houston—Casper 15 pass from Stabler (Fritsch kick).
Atlanta—Jackson recovered fumble in end zone (Luckhurst kick).
Houston—Campbell 18 run (Fritsch kick).
Houston—Armstrong 3 pass from Nielsen (Fritsch kick).

TEAM STATISTICS

	Atlanta	Houston
First downs	18	23
Rushes-Yards	33-111	20-83
Passing yards	349	235
Sacks by-Yards	1-10	3-23
Return yards	160	67
Passes	18-25-1	25-48-3
Punts	3-42.3	6-37.3
Fumbles-Lost	2-1	1-0
Penalties-Yards	5-35	1-10
Time of possession	32:44	27:16

Attendance—40,201.

INDIVIDUAL STATISTICS

Rushing—Atlanta, Andrews 25-101, Cain 7-12, Bartkowski 1-minus 2; Houston, Campbell 19-81, Coleman 1-2.

Passing—Atlanta, Bartkowski 18-25-1—372; Houston,

Stabler 17-33-2—139, Nielsen 8-15-1—106.

Receiving—Atlanta, Jenkins 6-122, Miller 3-69, Jackson 2-54, Andrews 3-48, Francis 2-44, Cain 2-35; Houston, Holston 8-101, Smith 2-37, Casper 4-39, Barber 2-32, Campbell 6-25, Burrough 1-3, Armstrong 2-8.

Kickoff Returns—Atlanta, R. Smith 3-68, Gaison 1-9; Houston, Roaches 1-2, Tullis 2-21, Hunt 1-6, Armstrong 1-3, T. Wilson 1-2.

Punt Returns—Atlanta, Woerner 3-4; Houston, Roaches 2-3.

Interceptions—Atlanta, Pridemore 1-48, Gaison 1-0, Butler 1-31; Houston, Kay 1-30.

Punting—Atlanta, James 3-42.3; Houston, Parsley 6-37.3.

Field Goals—Atlanta, Luckhurst 1-3; Houston, None attempted.

PACKERS 35, VIKINGS 23

BLOOMINGTON—"We're still tied for first place and we can control what happens. This is just going to make it a little more interesting," said Minnesota quarterback Tommy Kramer after Green Bay's victory over the Vikings threw the NFC Central race into a three-way tie.

Lynn Dickey, in his first start since suffering a back injury in October, completed 18 of 33 passes for 294 yards and three touchdowns to lead the Packers from behind. Kramer threw a pair of TD passes in the game's first four minutes to give the Vikings a 14-0 lead.

Kramer, who completed 38 of 55 passes for 384 yards, was intercepted five times. "When you throw five interceptions, it's tough to win," he said.

The Packers got their first TD on a 56-yard drive in the second quarter. Dickey completed four of five passes and Harlan Huckleby scored after a pass interference call against Vikings safety Kurt Knoff put the ball on the 1-yard line. Then, Packers safety Estus Hood intercepted Kramer to set up a 30-yard scoring pass from Dickey to John Jefferson that tied the game at halftime.

An interception by Green Bay's other safety, Maurice Harvey, put the Pack on the Minnesota 38 in the third quarter. Dickey fired a nine-yard TD strike to Huckleby and Green Bay took a 21-14 lead. Minnesota countered on a TD run by Ted Brown, but Rick Danmeier's extra-point attempt was wide.

A 42-yard pass from Dickey to James Lofton on third-and-12 keyed a 64-yard drive that made the score 28-20, with Huckleby diving over from a yard out. And then came Green Bay's biggest break.

In the fourth period, Minnesota's Dennis Johnson was penalized for running into punter Ray Stachowicz and Green Bay retained possession. Dickey then connected with Lofton on a 47-yard scoring play.

"They had some easy points early and realizing they didn't really earn them, we knew we could come back," said Lofton, who caught seven passes for 159 yards and became the

first Packer receiver ever to top 1,000 yards for two consecutive seasons.

Gerry Ellis had six receptions, giving him a Green Bay record for catches by a running back. Ellis' total of 53 topped the mark of 50, set in 1980 by Eddie Lee Ivery.

NOVEMBER 29
SCORE BY PERIODS

Green Bay	0	14	14	7—35
Minnesota	14	0	6	3—23

SCORING

Minnesota—Rashad 50 pass from Kramer (Danmeier kick).
Minnesota—Senser 13 pass from Kramer (Danmeier kick)
Green Bay—Huckleby 1 run (Stenerud kick).
Green Bay—Jefferson 30 pass from Dickey (Stenerud kick).
Green Bay—Huckleby 9 pass from Dickey (Stenerud kick).
Minnesota—Brown 6 run (kick failed).
Green Bay—Huckleby 1 run (Stenerud kick).
Green Bay—Lofton 47 pass from Dickey (Stenerud kick).
Minnesota—Field goal Danmeier 22.

TEAM STATISTICS

	Green Bay	Minnesota
First downs	24	23
Rushes-Yards	41-115	11-28
Passing yards	294	376
Sacks by-Yards	1-8	0-0
Return yards	151	143
Passes	18-33-2	38-55-5
Punts	5-34.6	6-36.3
Fumbles-Lost	2-2	0-0
Penalties-Yards	7-61	8-56
Time of possession	35:08	24:52
Attendance— 46,025.		

INDIVIDUAL STATISTICS

Rushing—Green Bay, Ellis 19-77, Huckleby 14-25, Middleton 2-13, Jensen 1-2, Dickey 5-minus 2; Minnesota, Brown 11-28.

Passing—Green Bay, Dickey 18-33-2-294; Minnesota, Kramer 38-55-5-384.

Receiving—Green Bay, Lofton 7-159, Ellis 6-62, Jefferson 2-43, Huckleby 2-20, Coffman 1-10; Minnesota, Senser 11-98, Rashad 4-87, S. White 6-77, Brown 7-42, Galbreath 4-35, LeCount 3-33, Young 3-12.

Kickoff Returns—Green Bay, Nixon 2-37, McCoy 2-46, Middleton 1-14; Minnesota, Payton 4-87, Nord 2-28.

Punt Returns—Green Bay, Whitaker 2-1; Minnesota, Payton 3-28.

Interceptions—Green Bay, Hood 1-18, Lee 1-0, Harvey 1-32, Anderson 1-2, Douglass 1-1; Minnesota, Hannon 1-0, Swain 1-0.

Punting—Green Bay, Stachowicz 5-34.6; Minnesota, Coleman 6-36.3.

Field Goals—Green Bay, None attempted; Minnesota, Danmeier 1-1.

CARDINALS 27, PATRIOTS 20

FOXBORO—For the second straight week, New England lost a game in the final minute on a touchdown pass. This time, St. Louis won on a 33-yard pass from rookie Neil Lomax to Roy Green with only 33 seconds left. In their previous game, Buffalo beat the Patriots on a deflected pass in the last five seconds.

The victory upped the Cardinals' record to 6-7 and the Pats fell to 2-11 with their sixth straight loss.

The Cardinals might not have had such good

Thirteenth Week—Continued

fortune without a critical non-call by referee Fred Silva.

St. Louis' first play on its winning drive was a 15-yard pass from Lomax to running back Ottis Anderson. But before the pass, Patriots defensive end Julius Adams had Lomax in his grasp, actually tearing the quarterback's jersey before Lomax slipped away.

New England Coach Ron Erhardt protested so vigorously that Lomax should have been ruled down that he was penalized 15 yards for his barnyard comments.

"If they're going to have the rule (calling a sack when the quarterback is in the grasp of a lineman) they should enforce it," said Erhardt.

The Cardinals still faced third-and-eight on the Patriots' 33 after the penalty, but Lomax found Green wide open over the middle at the 25, and he raced down the left sideline for the score.

"I started outside, but the defensive back (Rick Sanford) overreacted, so I cut back the other way and no one was in the zone," said Green.

St. Louis got field goals of 45 and 44 yards from Neil O'Donoghue in the first half and touchdown runs of one yard from Wayne Morris and 14 yards from Anderson in the second half before Green's game winner.

New England's scoring came on a one-yard run by Sam Cunningham, a six-yarder by Tony Collins and a three-yarder by Vagas Ferguson. Cunningham became the Patriots' all-time rushing leader with 5,330 yards, surpassing Jim Nance's 5,323.

NOVEMBER 29
SCORE BY PERIODS

St. Louis	3	3	7	14	27
New England	7	0	6	7	20

SCORING

St Louis—Field goal O'Donoghue 44.
New England—Cunningham 1 run (Smith kick).
St. Louis—Field goal O'Donoghue 45.
New England—Collins 6 run (kick failed).
St. Louis—Morris 1 run (O'Donoghue kick).
St. Louis—Anderson 14 run (O'Donoghue kick).
New England—Ferguson 3 run (Smith kick).
St. Louis—Green 33 pass from Lomax (O'Donoghue kick).

TEAM STATISTICS

	St. Louis	New England
First downs	25	19
Rushes-Yards	41-157	27-127
Passing yards	255	226
Sacks by-Yards	3-19	3-25
Return yards	87	54
Passes	20-28-0	17-25-2
Punts	2-35.0	5-33.2
Fumbles-Lost	3-2	3-0
Penalties-Yards	3-20	6-46
Time of possession	34:43	25:17
Attendance— 39,946.		

INDIVIDUAL STATISTICS

Rushing—St. Louis, Anderson 25-95, Mitchell 3-21, Morris 11-41, Lomax 1-2, Birdsong 1-minus 2; New Eng-

land, Collins 9-49, Cunningham 9-35, Ferguson 7-32, Cavanaugh 2-11.

Passing—St. Louis, Lomax 20-28-0-280; New England, Cavanaugh 17-24-2-245, Johnson 0-1-0-0.

Receiving—St. Louis, Anderson 4-25, Gray 2-46, Tilley 5-76, Green 3-79, LaFleur 2-18, Harrell 1-6, Morris 3-30; New England, Hasselbeck 3-38, Morgan 4-94, Jackson 4-71, Johnson 3-19, Collins 1-10, Cunningham 2-13.

Kickoff Returns—St. Louis, Mitchell 3-81, Harrell 1-1; New England, Collins 1-9, Toler 2-31.

Punt Returns—New England, Morgan 1-14.

Interceptions—St. Louis, Greene 2-5.

Punting—St. Louis, Birdsong 2-35.0; New England, Camarillo 5-33.2.

Field Goals—St. Louis, O'Donoghue 2-2; New England, Smith 0-1.

DOLPHINS 13, EAGLES 10

MIAMI—Duriel Harris had just hooked up with reserve quarterback Don Strock on a 17-yard pass play to pull the Miami Dolphins into a 10-10 tie with the Philadelphia Eagles with only 5:21 left in this Monday night game. Coming before 67,797 screaming fans in the Orange Bowl, Harris was the envy of the crowd.

But he soon became an embarrassment to himself. In his exuberance over the touchdown, he leaped into the air and spiked the ball. When he came back down, he twisted his left knee. He had to be carried from the field—as a national television audience watched.

"I've seen it happen before but never thought it would happen to me. My first thought when I went to the ground was 'Man, I sure don't want to be embarrassed like this on national television,'" said the fleet-footed receiver.

Embarrassed or not, Harris' catch was the key play in a key game for both the Dolphins and Eagles. Miami went on to win, 13-10, when Uwe von Schamann kicked a 27-yard field goal with only 1:04 left to play.

The victory kept the Dolphins (8-4-1) in a tie in the AFC Eastern Division race with the New York Jets and dropped the Eagles (9-4) one game behind Dallas in the NFC East.

The game started out looking like a Philadelphia romp. The Eagles took the opening kickoff on their own 20 and marched 80 yards for a touchdown. Wilbert Montgomery went over from the 1-yard line for the score. But that was the only Philadelphia touchdown scored in this game.

The Dolphins scored their only points of the first half on a 42-yard field goal by von Schamann in the second period. The Eagles led, 7-3, at the intermission.

The Eagles got their 7-point lead back in the third period on a 42-yard field goal by Tony Franklin, but the fourth period was all Miami's.

Strock replaced starter David Woodley with 12:13 remaining in the game and Miami trailing, 10-3. He connected on three of five passes for 20 yards before the TD pass to Harris.

"A lot of times we have settled for three points and come up short," said Harris, who criticized Coach Don Shula's play-calling the previous week. "This time we went for six, came up with the big play, and went on to win." '

MONDAY, NOVEMBER 30

SCORE BY PERIODS

Philadelphia	7	0	3	0—10
Miami	0	3	0	10—13

SCORING

Philadelphia—Montgomery 1 run (Franklin kick).
Miami—Field goal von Schamann 42.
Philadelphia—Field goal Franklin 42.
Miami—Harris 17 pass from Strock (von Schamann kick).
Miami—Field goal von Schamann 27.

TEAM STATISTICS

	Philadelphia	Miami
First downs	11	14
Rushes-Yards	31-136	34-73
Passing yards	80	132
Sacks by-Yards	3-22	2-11
Return yards	65	134
Passes	12-24-1	15-30-0
Punts	8-44.1	7-42.4
Fumbles-Lost	1-1	3-1
Penalties-Yards	8-59	1-5
Time of possession	32:00	28:00
Attendance—67,797.		

INDIVIDUAL STATISTICS

Rushing—Philadelphia, Montgomery 16-55, Oliver 6-27, Jaworski 4-39, Russell 4-8, Campfield 1-7; Miami, Nathan 13-41, Franklin 8-13, Woodley 5-18, Hill 3-10, Strock 5-minus 9.

Passing—Philadelphia, Jaworski 12-24-1—91; Miami, Woodley 11-23-0—117, Strock 4-6-0—37, Nathan 0-1-0—0.

Receiving—Philadelphia, Montgomery 4-33, Campfield 1-7, Henry 1-minus 3, Carmichael 4-61, Oliver 2-minus 7; Miami, Harris 9-114, Lee 2-14, Nathan 2-16, Hill 1-minus 7, Rose 1-17.

Kickoff Returns—Philadelphia, Henry 2-41; Miami, Walker 3-61.

Punt Returns—Philadelphia, Henry 5-24; Miami, Vigorito 6-73.

Interceptions—Miami, L. Blackwood 1-0.

Punting—Philadelphia, Runager 8-44.1; Miami, Orosz 7-42.4.

Field Goals—Philadelphia, Franklin 1-1; Miami, von Schamann 2-2.

FOURTEENTH WEEK

OILERS 17, BROWNS 13

HOUSTON—With 1:10 left in the Thursday night TV attraction in the Astrodome, Cleveland drove to a first down on the Houston 3-yard line. There seemed no doubt the Browns would score and wipe out the Oilers' 17-13 lead. After all, the Browns had dominated the statistics, piling up 28 first downs to the Oilers' seven.

However, three plays produced a minus one yard. Then, quarterback Brian Sipe called a draw play and Cleo Walker was stopped for no gain. Immediately, Sipe signaled for a timeout, even though the Browns had lost the ball with eight seconds left in the game.

Although players on the sideline believed that Sipe had lost track of the downs and thought the draw play was run on third down instead of fourth down, the quarterback took responsibility for the call.

"I called the play and I thought it would score," he said. "For some reason, the execution wasn't right."

Although the Oilers produced only 154 yards to 367 for Cleveland, two third-quarter touchdowns were enough to produce a victory. Gifford Nielsen replaced Ken Stabler at quarterback at the start of the third period and promptly marched Houston 80 yards for a touchdown. Nielsen hit on five of six passes for 68 yards in the drive, including his 30-yard scoring pass to tight end Dave Casper. That gave Houston a 10-6 lead.

On the Browns' next possession, the Oilers forced a punt and Houston's Avon Riley broke through to block Steve Cox' punt. Adger Armstrong then picked up the rolling ball and carried it eight yards to the 3, setting up a one-yard TD plunge by Earl Campbell.

Campbell was held to 31 yards rushing on 15 carries, but Coach Ed Biles said there was no reason to run Campbell more. "Statistically, it was not the way you want it," he said of the game, "but it was a win."

THURSDAY, DECEMBER 3

SCORE BY PERIODS

Cleveland	3	3	0	7—13
Houston	3	0	14	0—17

SCORING

Cleveland—Field goal Bahr 18.
Houston—Field goal Fritsch 32.
Cleveland—Field goal Bahr 19.
Houston—Casper 30 pass from Nielsen (Fritsch kick).
Houston—Campbell 1 run (Fritsch kick).
Cleveland—C. Miller 1 run (Bahr kick).

TEAM STATISTICS

	Cleveland	Houston
First downs	28	7
Rushes-Yards	43-190	20-34
Passing yards	177	120
Sacks by-Yards	2-14	4-29
Return yards	92	98
Passes	21-31-2	12-20-1
Punts	2-17.0	4-41.0
Fumbles-Lost	0-0	0-0
Penalties-Yards	4-35	7-74
Time of possession	40:12	19:48
Attendance—44,502.		

INDIVIDUAL STATISTICS

Rushing—Cleveland, M. Pruitt 32-155, C. Miller 8-17, Sipe 1-12, G. Pruitt 1-3, White 1-3; Houston, Campbell 15-31, Coleman 1-3, T. Wilson 2-2, Nielsen 2-minus 2.

Passing—Cleveland, Sipe 21-31-2—206; Houston, Nielsen 7-11-0—86, Stabler 5-9-1—48.

Receiving—Cleveland, M. Pruitt 7-58, Logan 4-38, G. Pruitt 4-37, Newsome 3-26, Rucker 1-24, C. Miller 2-23; Houston, Casper 2-39, Barber 1-35, Armstrong 1-19, Brooks 2-16, Coleman 1-10, Burrough 2-9, T. Wilson 1-3, Campbell 2-3.

Kickoff Returns—Cleveland, Hall 4-84; Houston, Roaches 1-24, Tullis 1-28.

Punt Returns— Houston, Roaches 1-13.

Fourteenth Week—Continued

Interceptions—Cleveland, Scott 1-8; Houston, Kay 1-17, Reinfeldt 1-16.

Punting—Cleveland, Cox 1-34.0; Houston, Parsley 4-41.0.

Field Goals—Cleveland, Bahr 2-3; Houston, Fritsch 1-2.

SCORING

Denver—Lytle 3 run (Steinfort kick).
Denver—Field goal Steinfort 23.
Denver—Canada 2 run (bad snap).
Kansas City—Field goal Lowery 43.
Kansas City—Field goal Lowery 45.
Kansas City—Hadnot 1 run (Lowery kick).

TEAM STATISTICS

	Kansas City	Denver
First downs	18	16
Rushes-Yards	24-74	29-77
Passing yards	233	265
Sacks by-Yards	4-16	4-28
Return yards	53	90
Passes	18-34-1	16-24-0
Punts	4-44.0	4-42.8
Fumbles-Lost	0-0	3-1
Penalties-Yards	2-29	7-68
Time of possession	28:42	31:18
Attendance—74,744.		

INDIVIDUAL STATISTICS

Rushing—Kansas City, Delaney 11-36, Fuller 2-17, Hadnot 7-15, B. Jackson 4-6; Denver, Preston 13-38, Parros 7-26, Upchurch 1-9, Lytle 3-7, Canada 1-2, Reed 4-minus 5.

Passing—Kansas City, Fuller 18-34-1—261; Denver, Morton 16-24-0—281.

Receiving—Kansas City, Dixon 6-86, Smith 4-61, Hadnot 3-40, Rome 2-40, Delaney 2-20, Murphy 1-14; Denver, Watson 2-103, Upchurch 4-70, Egloff 2-27, Preston 2-33, Parros 2-24, Studdard 1-10, Reed 2-8, Wright 1-6.

Kickoff Returns—Kansas City, Murphy 1-19; Denver, Harden 2-41.

Punt Returns—Kansas City, Smith 3-34; Denver, Upchurch 3-17.

Interceptions—Denver, Swenson 1-32.

Punting—Kansas City, Gossett 4-44.0; Denver, Prestridge 4-42.8.

Field Goals—Kansas City, Lowery 2-4; Denver, Steinfort 1-2.

BRONCOS 16, CHIEFS 13

DENVER—Dan Reeves' insides were probably doing somersaults in the last two minutes of Denver's victory over Kansas City.

The Broncos' coach stood grimly on the sideline as the Chiefs marched downfield, eating up yardage. The Broncos were unable to stop the Chiefs on a fourth-and-one gamble at the Denver 48-yard line.

A half-dozen plays later, behind by only three points, the Chiefs had advanced to the Broncos' 22. With a kicker like Nick Lowery, who had entered the game second in the AFC in scoring, their chances of sending the game into overtime seemed excellent.

But quarterback Steve Fuller's pass was picked off by Broncos linebacker Bob Swenson, who returned it to the Chiefs' 48.

"I don't know how he caught it," said Reeves. "The ball had zip on it, and I don't know if I've ever seen someone intercept a ball like that so near the quarterback." The line of scrimmage had been the 22. Swenson caught the ball at the 20.

"I'd do it again if I had to," said Fuller of the ill-fated throw. "He just made a great defensive play. I never saw him; I didn't expect him to be there, but their defense was like that."

Although the Chiefs had one more possession before the final gun, their chances of victory fizzled when Lowery's desperation 57-yard field goal went wide left.

The three-way tie in the AFC West was shattered and the Broncos found themselves in sole possession of first place with a 9-5 mark. The Chiefs were tied with the Chargers at 8-6.

The Chiefs trailed at one point in the second quarter, 16-0, but collected a quick pair of field goals by Lowery before the end of the half. They scored on a one-yard touchdown run by James Hadnot in the third quarter.

Besides Swenson's interception, another key play was a second-quarter interference call on Chiefs cornerback Eric Harris. That gave the Broncos the ball on the Chiefs' 3. Two plays later, Larry Canada scored the Broncos' second touchdown. The interference call nullified Harris' goal-line interception. Denver also scored on Rob Lytle's three-yard run and Fred Steinfort's 23-yard field goal.

DECEMBER 6
SCORE BY PERIODS

Kansas City	0	6	7	0—	13
Denver	7	9	0	0—	16

49ers 21, BENGALS 3

CINCINNATI—One week after San Francisco clinched the championship in the NFC West, the 49ers went into Cincinnati and many observers figured they'd be flat. Those observers were flat-out wrong.

"We didn't spend a lot of time talking about Cincinnati," said Bill Walsh, coach and general manager of the 49ers. "We talked about maintaining our hard-hitting standard of play. Our players made a pact that they would continue to hit just as hard as always."

Although the Bengals had a 10-3 record going into the game, the same mark as the 49ers, they'd been "psyched" a bit when Walsh called them the "best team in the NFL" and "the Super Bowl favorite."

Rookie cornerback Ronnie Lott said, "We felt Cincinnati really hadn't been hit since New Orleans (the only team to beat the Bengals in six weeks). We hoped to hit hard and get a few turnovers."

The Bengals coughed up four fumbles and San Francisco recovered three. The 49ers also intercepted three passes.

While Cincinnati failed to score a touchdown for the first time this year, the Niners' Joe

San Francisco quarterback Joe Montana accounted for all of his team's touchdowns in a 24-3 triumph over Cincinnati. Montana passed for two and ran for a third as the 49ers improved their league-leading record to 11-3.

Fourteenth Week—Continued

Montana fired TD passes of four yards to Bill Ring and 15 yards to Dwight Clark and then sneaked in from one yard out.

The Bengals were forced to play most of the second half without Ken Anderson, who had been the NFL's most effective quarterback. He suffered a sprained right big toe with 10:38 left in the third quarter and sat out the rest of the way.

Anderson completed 11 of 20 passes, but was intercepted twice. The only points for the Bengals came on a 30-yard field goal by Jim Breech.

DECEMBER 6
SCORE BY PERIODS

San Francisco	7	7	0	7—21
Cincinnati	0	3	0	0— 3

SCORING

San Francisco—Ring 4 pass from Montana (Wersching kick).
Cincinnati—Field goal Breech 30.
San Francisco—Clark 15 pass from Montana (Wersching kick).
San Francisco—Montana 1 run (Wersching kick).

TEAM STATISTICS

	San Francisco	Cincinnati
First downs	24	24
Rushes-Yards	35-146	20-155
Passing yards	179	190
Sacks by-Yards	3-21	1-8
Return yards	40	102
Passes	23-37-1	21-38-3
Punts	6-36.8	3-45.7
Fumbles-Lost	0-0	4-3
Penalties-Yards	7-55	9-70
Time of possession	26:48	33:12
Attendance—56,796.		

INDIVIDUAL STATISTICS

Rushing—San Francisco, Cooper 12-62, Patton 10-36, Davis 8-21, Lawrence 1-5, Ring 2-8, Montana 2-14; Cincinnati, Alexander 4-24, Johnson 12-86, Anderson 4-45.

Passing—San Francisco, Montana 23-37-1—187; Cincinnati, Anderson 11-20-2—97, Thompson 10-18-1—114.

Receiving—San Francisco, Young 3-22, Shumann 1-6, Clark 6-78, Ring 1-4, Cooper 6-34, Wilson 2-28, Patton 3-11, Ramson 1-4; Cincinnati, Ross 7-69, Collinsworth 3-32, Curtis 1-10, Johnson 4-26, Alexander 1-6, Kreider 4-57, M. L. Harris 1-11.

Kickoff Returns—San Francisco, Ring 1-17; Cincinnati, Verser 3-90, Kemp 1-0.

Punt Returns—San Francisco, Hicks 1-10; Cincinnati, Fuller 2-12.

Interceptions—San Francisco, Lott 1-13, Wright 1-0, Turner 1-0; Cincinnati, Riley 1-0.

Punting—San Francisco, Miller 6-36.8; Cincinnati, McInally 3-45.7.

Field Goals—San Francisco, None attempted; Cincinnati, Breech 1-1.

BUCCANEERS 24, FALCONS 23

TAMPA—Doug Williams sat clutching the game ball and savoring both his personal performance and the Tampa Bay Buccaneers' 24-23 victory over the Atlanta Falcons.

Williams had one of the best days of his ca-

reer, completing 19 of 29 passes for 336 yards and two touchdowns as the Bucs gained their third straight triumph and vaulted into first place in the NFC Central Division. Tampa Bay was 8-6, one notch ahead of Minnesota, Green Bay and Detroit.

The significance of the standings wasn't lost on the Bucs, who had games left with San Diego and Detroit.

"Once again we are in the driver's seat," said wide receiver Kevin House. "I hope we don't let down now."

Tight end Jimmie Giles added, "If we continue to play like this, we'll go all the way. We can control our destiny."

House and Giles were on the receiving end of Williams' two TD passes against Atlanta. Giles grabbed a 38-yard pass in the second quarter and House scored on a 71-yard bomb with 9:39 left in the game, wiping out a 23-17 lead for the Falcons.

That Williams-to-House TD and Bill Capece's extra point marked the sixth time that the lead changed hands. And there was nearly a seventh—when the Falcons' Nick Luckhurst was wide to the right on a 45-yard field-goal attempt with eight seconds left.

Steve Bartkowski, who completed 24 of 34 passes for 237 yards, moved the Falcons from their 20 to the Tampa Bay 28 in six plays before the field-goal try.

The defeat left the Falcons gasping in their bid to capture a wild-card playoff berth. Atlanta was one of six NFC teams at 7-7.

DECEMBER 6
SCORE BY PERIODS

Atlanta	3	6	7	7—23
Tampa Bay	7	7	3	7—24

SCORING

Atlanta—Field goal Luckhurst 38.
Tampa Bay—Eckwood 1 run (Capece kick).
Atlanta—Field goal Luckhurst 44.
Tampa Bay—Giles 38 pass from Williams (Capece kick).
Atlanta—Field goal Luckhurst 32.
Atlanta—Andrews 8 run (Luckhurst kick).
Tampa Bay—Field goal Capece 42.
Atlanta—Andrews 2 run (Luckhurst kick).
Tampa Bay—House 71 pass from Williams (Capece kick).

TEAM STATISTICS

	Atlanta	Tampa Bay
First downs	23	22
Rushes-Yards	27-137	28-93
Passing yards	236	327
Sacks by-Yards	1-9	1-1
Return yards	116	86
Passes	24-34-1	19-29-0
Punts	3-44.7	3-39.0
Fumbles-Lost	0-0	1-1
Penalties-Yards	6-50	4-49
Time of possession	29:02	30:58
Attendance—69,221.		

INDIVIDUAL STATISTICS

Rushing—Atlanta, Andrews 17-80, Cain 10-57; Tampa Bay, Wilder 7-16, Eckwood 11-54, Owens 7-15, T. Bell 1-7, Williams 2-1.

Passing—Atlanta, Bartkowski 24-34-1—237; Tampa Bay, Williams 19-29-0—336.

Receiving—Atlanta, Andrews 13-98, Jenkins 6-96, Mayberry 1-6, Jackson 1-13, Cain 1-4, Miller 1-10, Francis 1-10; Tampa Bay, House 5-126, Eckwood 2-19, T. Bell 3-33, Wilder 6-96, Giles 3-62.

Kickoff Returns—Atlanta, R. Smith 5-116; Tampa Bay, Holt 4-78.

Punt Returns—Atlanta, Pridemore 1-0, Woerner 1-0; Tampa Bay, Holt 2-7.

Interceptions—Tampa Bay, Brown 1-1.

Punting—Atlanta, James 3-44.7; Tampa Bay, Swider 3-39.0.

Field Goals—Atlanta, Luckhurst 3-4; Tampa Bay, Capece 1-2.

COWBOYS 37, COLTS 13

BALTIMORE—Dallas was playing without its regular quarterback in a stadium whipped by a stiff December gale. So Coach Tom Landry told the Cowboys to keep the ball on the ground and play good defense against Baltimore.

The Cowboys (11-3) rolled up 354 yards rushing, with Tony Dorsett contributing 175 yards in 30 carries. James Jones ran for 86 yards in five carries and Ron Springs ran for three touchdowns.

"Because of the wind (24 miles per hour at kickoff), we decided to try to control the ball on the ground," Landry said.

Regular quarterback Danny White, who suffered a cracked rib Thanksgiving Day, was used only as a punter. Glenn Carano quarterbacked the Cowboys, making his first start. He was 7-for-18 passing for 51 yards.

In one of the few razzle-dazzle plays, wide receiver Drew Pearson took a lateral and threw a 59-yard pass to Tony Hill.

There was one more fancy play, and it didn't sit well with Landry. That was when White ran for a first down from punt formation in the fourth quarter.

"I could have shot him," Landry said, well aware that White might have aggravated his rib injury had he been tackled as he tried to get out of bounds.

Baltimore's loss was its 13th in a row since an opening-day triumph. The worst previous Colts team was the 2-12 squad of 1974.

The Colts used David Humm at quarterback in place of injured Bert Jones. Humm missed his first nine passes and finished the day 7-for-24. "I think Dave proved he's a tough son of a gun. He hung in there, but the wind affected his passes," said Colts Coach Mike McCormack.

Curtis Dickey scored for the Colts on runs of 67 and 20 yards, and gained 130 yards for the day in 15 carries.

DECEMBER 6

SCORE BY PERIODS

Dallas	17	10	0	10	37
Baltimore	6	0	7	0	13

SCORING

Dallas—Springs 1 run (Septien kick).
Dallas—Field goal Septien 42.
Dallas—Springs 2 run (Septien kick).
Baltimore—Dickey 67 run (kick failed).
Dallas—Springs 2 pass from Carano (Septien kick).
Dallas—Field goal Septien 35.
Baltimore—Dickey 20 run (Wood kick).
Dallas—Field goal Septien 31.
Dallas—J. Jones 59 run (Septien kick).

TEAM STATISTICS

	Dallas	Baltimore
First downs	29	9
Rushes-Yards	66-354	20-156
Passing yards	110	82
Sacks by-Yards	1-8	0-0
Return yards	78	76
Passes	8-19-1	7-24-2
Punts	2-30.0	7-39.1
Fumbles-Lost	3-1	2-1
Penalties-Yards	6-33	11-87
Time of possession	41:26	18:34

Attendance—54,871.

INDIVIDUAL STATISTICS

Rushing—Dallas, Dorsett 30-175, Springs 16-40, Newsome 12-31, Carano 1-0, J. Jones 5-86, D. White 1-13, Cosbie 1-9; Baltimore, Dickey 15-130, McMillan 4-22, Franklin 1-4.

Passing—Dallas, Carano 7-18-1—51, Pearson 1-1-0—59; Baltimore, Humm 7-24-2—90.

Receiving—Dallas, Pearson 1-12, Springs 3-13, Hill 2-69, J. Jones 1-6, Dorsett 1-10; Baltimore, Sherwin 1-11, Butler 3-40, Burke 1-17, Dickey 1-2, Carr 1-20.

Kickoff Returns—Dallas, J. Jones 2-30, Wilson 1-15; Baltimore, Anderson 2-19, Dixon 2-38, Shula 1-15.

Punt Returns—Dallas, J. Jones 2-9; Baltimore, Anderson 1-0.

Interceptions—Dallas, Breunig 1-0, Barnes 1-24; Baltimore, Glasgow 1-4.

Punting—Dallas, D. White 2-30.0; Baltimore, Garrett 7-39.1.

Field Goals—Dallas, Septien 3-3; Baltimore, None attempted.

GIANTS 10, RAMS 7

EAST RUTHERFORD—New York used a 55-yard punt return by Leon Bright and Joe Danelo's subsequent 19-yard field goal in the fourth quarter to register the triumph over Los Angeles in wind-swept Giants Stadium, eliminating the Rams from playoff competition.

In a defensive struggle played in winds gusting to 45 mph and a wind-chill factor of five degrees, the Giants evened their record at 7-7 by blanking the Rams in the second half.

"I was scared to death the entire fourth quarter until Bill Neill fell on that ball," said Giants safety Beasley Reece, referring to the rookie nose tackle's fumble recovery with 21 seconds left that snuffed out the Rams' final threat.

"I'm very, very disappointed," said Rams quarterback Pat Haden, who hit only eight of 21 passes for 81 yards. "I had high hopes of winning three straight games, but the weather was more of a factor than we thought."

Wendell Tyler's 15th touchdown of the year, a two-yard run off right tackle on the Rams' first possession, helped L.A. to a 7-0 haltime lead as the Giants were limited to four first downs.

Fourteenth Week—Continued

A 49-yard punt by the Giants' Dave Jennings pinned the Rams at their own 4-yard-line midway through the third quarter and helped engineer the Giants' touchdown drive. The Rams were forced to punt and Bright returned 16 yards to the L.A. 34. Five plays later, aided by a 15-yard personal foul against linebacker Carl Ekern, Rob Carpenter plunged over from one yard out.

The Rams were bottled up on their next possession and Bright made the biggest play of the game, taking Frank Corral's punt at his own 37 and weaving 55 yards to the Rams' 8. Danelo then snapped the tie on the first play of the fourth quarter.

The Rams' defense limited the Giants to 147 yards, but the Rams couldn't score over the last 54 minutes.

DECEMBER 6
SCORE BY PERIODS

Los Angeles	7	0	0	0— 7
New York Giants	0	0	7	3—10

SCORING

Los Angeles—Tyler 2 run (Corral kick).
New York—Carpenter 1 run (Danelo kick).
New York—Field goal Danelo 19.

TEAM STATISTICS

	Los Angeles	New York
First downs	16	10
Rushes-Yards	47-172	39-87
Passing yards	68	60
Sacks by-Yards	2-7	3-13
Return yards	57	125
Passes	8-21-1	5-22-0
Punts	7-34.4	9-35.9
Fumbles-Lost	3-2	2-0
Penalties-Yards	9-69	7-60
Time of possession	31:26	28:34
Attendance—59,659.		

INDIVIDUAL STATISTICS

Rushing—Los Angeles, Tyler 24-94, Guman 19-71, Haden 3-8, J. Thomas 1-minus 1; New York, Carpenter 23-58, Brunner 5-minus 5, Forte 3-19, Bright 5-12, Perry 3-3.

Passing—Los Angeles, Haden 8-21-1—81; New York, Brunner 5-22-0—67.

Receiving—Los Angeles, J. Thomas 1-4, Tyler 1-4, Arnold 1-7, Dennard 5-66; New York, Young 1-11, Carpenter 2-38, Shirk 1-13, Bright 1-5.

Kickoff Returns—Los Angeles, D. Hill 1-40, Penaranda 1-1; New York, Pittman 1-23.

Punt Returns—Los Angeles, Irvin 4-16; New York, Bright 4-101.

Interceptions—New York, Taylor 1-1.

Punting—Los Angeles, Corral 7-34.4; New York, Jennings 9-35.9.

Field Goals—Los Angeles, Corral 0-1; New York, Danelo 1-3.

DOLPHINS 24, PATRIOTS 14

MIAMI—The Dolphins improved to 9-4-1 and regained sole possession of first place in the AFC East, one-half game ahead of Buffalo and a full game ahead of the Jets, by beating New England in the Orange Bowl. The Patriots dropped to 2-12 with their seventh straight defeat. It marked the first time since 1970 that the Patriots had lost a dozen games in a season.

David Woodley led the Dolphins by sneaking for one touchdown and throwing to running back Eddie Hill for another, but it wasn't all smooth sailing for the second-year quarterback.

"Woodley had his ups and downs," said Miami Coach Don Shula. "But when they tied the score (at 14-14 in the third quarter), he came up with two big throws after we got bogged down and got us going again."

Woodley put the Dolphins ahead for good, 21-14, on a four-yard pass to Hill, who staggered past three Patriots into the end zone.

The Patriots had opened the scoring with a one-yard touchdown pass from Matt Cavanaugh to Don Hasselbeck, but the Dolphins tied it on Woodley's one-yard sneak and went ahead on a 25-yard fumble return by reserve safety Mike Kozlowski.

The Patriots came back with a one-yard touchdown sneak of their own by Cavanaugh in the fourth quarter to tie the game at 14, but then came Hill's score and an insurance field goal by Uwe von Schamann from 32 yards.

Miami's Tony Nathan logged the first 100-yard day in his NFL career with 119 yards in 17 carries.

DECEMBER 6
SCORE BY PERIODS

New England	7	0	7	0—14
Miami	0	14	7	3—24

SCORING

New England—Hasselbeck 6 pass from Cavanaugh (Smith kick).
Miami—Woodley 1 run (von Schamann kick).
Miami—Kozlowski 25 fumble return (von Schamann kick).
New England—Cavanaugh 1 run (Smith kick).
Miami—Hill 4 pass from Woodley (von Schamann kick).
Miami—Field goal von Schamann 32.

TEAM STATISTICS

	New England	Miami
First downs	17	19
Rushes-Yards	30-134	42-212
Passing yards	122	128
Sacks by-Yards	0-0	2-16
Return yards	114	71
Passes	12-20-0	11-24-1
Punts	5-38.4	3-43.7
Fumbles-Lost	2-2	2-1
Penalties-Yards	4-33	5-45
Time of possession	25:56	34:04
Attendance—50,421.		

INDIVIDUAL STATISTICS

Rushing—New England, Ferguson 8-43, Cunningham 9-22, Collins 8-46, Cavanaugh 4-17, Calhoun 1-6; Miami, Nathan 17-119, Franklin 16-52, Woodley 9-41.

Passing—New England, Cavanaugh 12-20-0—138; Miami, Woodley 11-24-1—128.

Receiving—New England, Hasselbeck 3-18, Cunningham 1-11, Morgan 4-55, Dawson 3-48, Collins 1-6; Miami, Nathan 3-23, Cefalo 2-53, Moore 3-20, Vigorito 1-9, Rose 1-19, Hill 1-4.

Kickoff Returns—New England, Collins 5-107; Miami, Walker 3-67.

Punt Returns—Miami, Vigorito 3-4.

Interceptions—New England, Sanford 1-7.

Punting—New England, Camarillo 5-38.4; Miami, Orosz 3-43.7.

Field Goals—New England, Smith 0-2; Miami, von Schamann 1-2.

CARDINALS 30, SAINTS 3

ST. LOUIS—Roy Green, who had done almost everything for St. Louis in 1981, had one more wish he would have liked to fulfill in the last two games.

"I want to throw a pass," Green said.

Green had done virtually everything but attempt a pass.

Against New Orleans, he ran 44 yards with a fake punt for a touchdown and intercepted a pass.

The victory was the fourth in a row by the Cardinals, their longest winning streak since they won four straight in 1978. It also evened their record at 7-7, the first time they've won that many games since 1977.

"After the Philadelphia game (a 52-10 loss), everybody was just embarrassed," said cornerback Roger Wehrli. "We kind of regrouped. We've been playing together instead of going in different directions."

Part of the reason for the Cardinals' success is Green, a third-year pro from Henderson State who, until this year, had been limited to playing in the secondary and returning kicks.

Coach Jim Hanifan converted Green to a wide receiver in the second game this season, and he has responded with 29 receptions for 632 yards and four touchdowns, and provided the Cardinals much-needed spark.

The spark against the Saints came four plays into the fourth quarter, as the Cardinals tried to protect a 17-3 lead and faced fourth and eight from the Saints 44-yard line.

Green had been waiting for that situation all week after spotting what he thought was a flaw in the Saints' punt return team.

Instead of snapping the ball to punter Carl Birdsong the Cardinals gave the ball to Green, the short man in punt formation.

Green only had to beat one defender on his way to the end zone.

"We felt if the occasion presented itself to us we were definitely going to go with it," said Hanifan. "It was clean. Nobody even knew he had the thing for about 30 yards."

Saints Coach Bum Phillips said the fake punt decided the game, even though St. Louis had already scored on a 22-yard scramble by Neil Lomax, a one-yard dive by Wayne Morris and the first of three Neil O'Donoghue's field goals.

"We just got slickered by a better slickerer than us," said Phillips, who had called runs off a fake field goal and a fake punt himself.

SCORE BY PERIODS

New Orleans	3	0	0	0— 3
St. Louis	7	10	0	13—30

SCORING

New Orleans—Field goal Ricardo 44.
St. Louis—Lomax 22 run (O'Donoghue kick).
St. Louis—Morris 1 run (O'Donoghue kick).
St. Louis—Field goal O'Donoghue 41.
St. Louis—Green 44 run (O'Donoghue kick).
St. Louis—Field goal O'Donoghue 31.
St. Louis—Field goal O'Donoghue 24.

TEAM STATISTICS

	New Orleans	St. Louis
First downs	11	19
Rushes-Yards	30-117	41-155
Passing yards	59	140
Sacks by-Yards	4-33	5-46
Return yards	186	115
Passes	7-18-3	13-19-1
Punts	1-43.0	2-44.0
Fumbles-Lost	1-0	2-0
Penalties-Yards	5-44	4-25
Time of possession	25:28	34:32
Attendance— 46,923.		

INDIVIDUAL STATISTICS

Rushing—New Orleans, G. Rogers 23-98, Holmes 2-4, Myers 1-6, J. Rogers 1-5, W. Wilson 1-2, Merkens 1-2, Manning 1-0; St. Louis, Anderson 26-64, Morris 8-18, Lomax 2-19, Love 2-8, Mitchell 2-2, Green 1-44.

Passing—New Orleans, Manning 7-17-2-105, D. Wilson 0-1-1-0; St. Louis, Lomax 13-19-1-173.

Receiving—New Orleans, Hardy 2-37, Merkens 2-22, G. Rogers 1-25, Groth 1-18, Holmes 1-3; St. Louis, Tilley 4-75, LaFleur 2-23, Combs 2-19, Anderson 2-16, Green 1-28, Morris 1-9, Gray 1-3.

Kickoff Returns—New Orleans, J. Rogers 4-98, W. Wilson 1-25; St. Louis, Mitchell 2-33, Love 0-25.

Punt Returns—New Orleans, Groth 1-9; St. Louis, Mitchell 1-7.

Interceptions—New Orleans, Myers 1-54; St. Louis, Wehrli 1-2, Green 1-29, Johnson 1-19.

Punting—New Orleans, Erxleben 1-43.0; St. Louis, Birdsong 2-44.0.

Field Goals—New Orleans, Ricardo 1-3; St. Louis, O'Donoghue 3-3.

SEAHAWKS 27, JETS 23

SEATTLE—With Jim Zorn sidelined for the rest of the season with a fractured ankle, reserve quarterback Dave Krieg, in his first National Football League start, stepped in without missing a beat and propelled the Seattle Seahawks to a 27-23 upset of the New York Jets in the Kingdome.

The loss dropped the Jets to 8-5-1 and out of a first-place tie in the AFC Eastern Division. With their five-game winning streak ended, the Jets fell to third place behind Miami and Buffalo. The Seahawks lifted their record to 5-8 and now are 6-0 lifetime against the Jets.

Krieg, from little-known Milton College in Wisconsin, connected on 20 of 26 passes for 264 yards and two touchdowns, including a 57-yard game-winner to Steve Largent in the fourth quarter.

Krieg threw three interceptions but made up for them with some timely running, scoring a

Fourteenth Week—Continued

touchdown in the third quarter on a one-yard plunge and rambling 29 yards on a bootleg midway through the fourth quarter when the Seahawks were pinned deep in their own territory.

"He performed like a real veteran," said Jerry Rhome, the Seahawks' offensive coordinator. "For him to play against a defense like the Jets', well, you couldn't ask for more."

One of the keys to Krieg's success was the Seahawks' ability to keep the Jets' pass rush under control. The Jets led the NFL in sacks entering the game but were able to nail Krieg just once.

The Seahawks led 13-9 at halftime on Krieg's seven-yard scoring toss to Sam McCullum and Theotis Brown's 21-yard touchdown run.

The Jets took advantage of a pair of Seahawk turnovers to take leads in the third quarter and again in the fourth. Each time, Krieg was able to rally the Seahawks for a go-ahead score.

The Jets scored on Richard Todd's touchdown passes of 11 yards to running back Scott Dierking and one yard to running back Kevin Long, a 15-yard run by Dierking and a 26-yard field goal by Pat Leahy.

Largent caught seven passes for a career-high 169 yards, which pushed him over the 1,000-yard mark in reception yardage for the fourth straight year.

DECEMBER 6
SCORE BY PERIODS

New York Jets	0	9	7	7—23
Seattle	6	7	7	7—27

SCORING

Seattle—McCullum 7 pass from Krieg (kick failed).
New York—Dierking 11 pass from Todd (kick blocked).
Seattle—T. Brown 21 run (Alvarez kick).
New York—Field goal Leahy 26.
New York—Dierking 15 run (Leahy kick).
Seattle—Krieg 1 run (Alvarez kick).
New York—Long 1 pass from Todd (Leahy kick).
Seattle—Largent 57 pass from Krieg (Alvarez kick).

TEAM STATISTICS

	New York	Seattle
First downs	23	18
Rushes-Yards	28-119	35-127
Passing yards	276	256
Sacks by-Yards	1-8	1-10
Return yards	84	89
Passes	27-51-2	20-27-3
Punts	4-40.5	4-41.5
Fumbles-Lost	1-1	1-1
Penalties-Yards	6-40	6-50
Time of possession	27:46	32:14
Attendance—53,105.		

INDIVIDUAL STATISTICS

Rushing—New York, Long 11-51, Dierking 4-33, McNeil 7-28, Newton 4-5, Harper 1-2, Ramsey 1-0; Seattle, T. Brown 18-73, Krieg 5-30, Smith 6-20, Doornink 6-4.

Passing—New York, Todd 27-51-2—286; Seattle, Krieg 20-26-3—264, West 0-1-0—0.

Receiving—New York, Harper 8-67, Dierking 7-60, J. Jones 3-59, Long 3-25, McNeil 3-23, Barkum 2-43, B. Jones 1-9; Seattle, Largent 7-169, McCullum 3-37, Doornink 3-23, T. Brown 3-minus 6, Hughes 2-18, Sawyer 1-18, Tice 1-5.

Kickoff Returns—New York, Harper 5-80; Seattle, Ivory 1-17, Lane 2-47.

Punt Returns—New York, Harper 1-minus 1; Seattle, Johns 1-11.

Interceptions—New York, Holmes 1-0, Mehl 1-0, Springs 1-5; Seattle, Harris 1-14, D. Brown 1-0.

Punting—New York, Ramsey 4-40.5; Seattle, West 4-41.5.

Field Goals—New York, Leahy 1-2; Seattle, Alvarez 0-1.

PACKERS 31, LIONS 17

GREEN BAY—The victory over Detroit was Green Bay's fifth in its last six games and threw the NFC Central Division race into further disarray. The Packers joined the crowd at 7-7, but still needed help to make it to the playoffs.

"We have to win our games and as far as we're concerned, nothing else matters," Packers Coach Bart Starr said.

Detroit grabbed a 10-0 lead before the Packers rallied on the passing of Lynn Dickey and the receiving of John Jefferson. The cheer-leading of Jefferson also gave the Packers a lift.

"A lot of people call it hotdogging. I call it John Jefferson," said the All-Pro receiver who came to Green Bay from San Diego early in the season. Jefferson caught eight passes for 113 yards against Detroit. Green Bay's other All-Pro receiver, James Lofton, had four catches for 90 yards, and one touchdown.

Jefferson had caught only 18 passes in his first nine games with Green Bay. "Now, they're just working in some plays for J. J.," he said.

After Billy Sims pulled Detroit within 21-17, Jefferson keyed a scoring drive for the clinching touchdown. He accounted for 36 yards on two receptions and an end-around.

Detroit Coach Monte Clark thought the game's turning point was in the final minute of the first half. Detroit led, 10-7, and Eddie Murray's 31-yard field-goal attempt died in the wind. Dickey then took the Packers 80 yards to score on five plays in 36 seconds. He heaved a 46-yarder to Lofton and a 15-yard scoring pass to Paul Coffman that gave Green Bay a 14-10 halftime lead.

"It's the offensive line," said Dickey, who was 20-for-31 for 279 yards. "When I get that kind of time, I feel I can really produce."

DECEMBER 6
SCORE BY PERIODS

Detroit	3	7	7	0—17
Green Bay	0	14	7	10—31

SCORING

Detroit—Field goal Murray 38.
Detroit—V. Thompson 9 run (Murray kick).

— 272 —

Green Bay—Huckleby 1 run (Stenerud kick).
Green Bay—Coffman 5 pass from Dickey (Stenerud kick).
Green Bay—Lofton 15 pass from Dickey (Stenerud kick).
Detroit—Sims 3 run (Murray kick).
Green Bay—Huckleby 1 run (Stenerud kick).
Green Bay—Field goal Stenerud 36.

TEAM STATISTICS

	Detroit	Green Bay
First downs	20	24
Rushes-Yards	31-143	34-68
Passing yards	217	265
Sacks by-Yards	2-14	4-23
Return yards	48	30
Passes	17-33-2	20-31-0
Punts	3-36.7	5-35.8
Fumbles-Lost	1-0	0-0
Penalties-Yards	6-39	2-31
Time of possession	27:52	32:08

Attendance—54,481.

INDIVIDUAL STATISTICS

Rushing—Detroit, Sims 20-64, V. Thompson 5-34, Bussey 2-18, Hipple 4-27; Green Bay, Ellis 13-46, Huckleby 17-18, Jefferson 1-7, Dickey 3-minus 3.

Passing—Detroit, Hipple 17-33-2—240; Green Bay, Dickey 20-31-0—279.

Receiving—Detroit, L. Thompson 3-60, Hill 1-15, Sims 4-72, Scott 5-89, Bussey 2-minus 3, Kane 1-2, King 1-5; Green Bay, Jefferson 8-113, Ellis 3-9, Coffman 5-67, Lofton 4-90.

Kickoff Returns—Detroit, Martin 1-16, Hall 1-16, Lee 1-0; Green Bay, Jensen 1-15.

Punt Returns—Detroit, Martin 2-16; Green Bay, Nixon 1-10.

Interceptions—Green Bay, Anderson 1-2, Cumby 1-3.

Punting—Detroit, Skladany 3-36.7; Green Bay, Stachowicz 5-35.8.

Field Goals—Detroit, Murray 1-2; Green Bay, Stenerud 1-1.

BEARS 10, VIKINGS 9

CHICAGO—Bob Avellini's first touchdown pass in more than two years brought Chicago from behind and threw a bombshell on Minnesota's playoff plans.

Minnesota had taken a 7-3 lead on Tommy Kramer's three-yard pass to Ahmad Rashad early in the fourth quarter. Chicago returned the kickoff to the 28, and on the first play Avellini connected with wide receiver Brian Baschnagel on a 72-yard scoring pass. That came with 13:06 left.

Avellini had gone into the game in the second quarter when Vince Evans couldn't move the team. Avellini completed only three of seven passes, but one was enough.

The TD pass was suggested by Baschnagel, who had spotted a weakness in the Vikings' secondary.

"It was a stop-and-go," said Baschnagel. "Bob gave a great fake. We had this play in our book all season and hadn't used it."

The Vikings had opportunities to win the game after the Avellini TD pass. With about two minutes left, Rashad caught a long pass from Kramer, but fumbled the ball away on the Chicago 5-yard line.

"We didn't lose on Rashad's fumble," said Minnesota Coach Bud Grant. "As long as you

have a play left and trail by less than a touchdown, you still have a chance to win."

But the Vikes never got that chance. The Bears elected to take a safety when punter Bob Parsons ran out of the end zone. On the free kick, returner Eddie Payton fumbled the ball and the Bears recovered and ran out the clock.

DECEMBER 6
SCORE BY PERIODS

Minnesota	0	0	0	9— 9
Chicago	0	3	0	7—10

SCORING

Chicago—Field goal Roveto 28.
Minnesota—Rashad 3 pass from Kramer (Danmeier kick).
Chicago—Baschnagel 72 pass from Avellini (Roveto kick).
Minnesota—Safety, Parsons ran out of end zone.

TEAM STATISTICS

	Minnesota	Chicago
First downs	16	13
Rushes-Yards	19-38	51-175
Passing yards	254	69
Sacks by-Yards	4-33	2-14
Return yards	43	133
Passes	21-36-2	4-11-2
Punts	7-40.3	6-39.7
Fumbles-Lost	5-3	0-0
Penalties-Yards	9-45	7-59
Time of possession	24:15	35:45

Attendance—50,766.

INDIVIDUAL STATISTICS

Rushing—Minnesota, Brown 16-38, Young 1-1, Kramer 2-minus 1; Chicago, Payton 33-112, Suhey 14-70, Avellini 3-minus 1, Parsons 1-minus 6.

Passing—Minnesota, Kramer 21-36-2—268; Chicago, Evans 0-3-1—0, Avellini 3-7-1—84, Baschnagel 1-1-0—18.

Receiving—Minnesota, S. White 8-112, Rashad 5-84, LeCount 2-51, Bruer 3-25, Brown 2-minus 2, Young 1-minus 2; Chicago, Baschnagel 1-72, Harris 1-18, Suhey 2-12.

Kickoff Returns—Minnesota, Payton 1-0; Chicago, Moorehead 2-42.

Punt Returns—Minnesota, Payton 4-43; Chicago, Fisher 5-49.

Interceptions—Minnesota, Teal 1-0, Hannon 1-0; Chicago, Henderson 1-39, Fisher 1-3.

Punting—Minnesota, Coleman 7-40.3; Chicago, Parsons 6-39.7.

Field Goals—Minnesota, None attempted; Chicago, Roveto 1-2.

BILLS 28, CHARGERS 27

SAN DIEGO—Buffalo kept its playoff hopes alive and surged into second place in the AFC East after a narrow one-point victory over San Diego.

The Bills upped their record to 9-5, while the Chargers slipped to 8-6 and into a second-place tie in the AFC West with Kansas City, a game behind Denver.

"I think we can hold this intensity for two more games and make the playoffs," said the Bills' Joe Cribbs, who scored the go-ahead touchdown on a one-yard run late in the third quarter to give his team the lead for good, 28-24. "We've been up and down all year long and now we've got it together."

Fourteenth Week—Continued

The Bills had allowed only six points in their last two second halves of football. After shutting out Washington in the final 30 minutes of a 21-14 victory the previous week, the Bills only gave up a pair of field goals to the Chargers, who boast the NFL's most potent offense.

Trailing 28-27 and driving deep into Bills territory with only two minutes to play, the Chargers were in a position to pull the game out. But Chuck Muncie fumbled on the 26-yard line and Bills cornerback Rufus Bess recovered.

It was a day of records for the Chargers in the losing cause. Dan Fouts, who threw touchdown passes of 17 yards to Wes Chandler and 67 yards to Kellen Winslow in the second quarter, went over the 4,000-yard passing mark for the third straight season.

Muncie, who scored the game's first touchdown on a nine-yard run in the first quarter, gained 119 yards on 22 carries to bring his season total to 1,023 yards. His 19 touchdowns rushing tied the NFL record held by former Green Bay running back Jim Taylor and Houston's Earl Campbell.

The Bills, who trailed at halftime 21-14, got their other scores on a three-yard run by Ferguson in the first quarter and Roosevelt Leaks' touchdown runs of nine yards in the second quarter and one yard in the third.

The Chargers' second-half points came on field goals of 29 and 27 yards by Rolf Benirschke.

DECEMBER 6
SCORE BY PERIODS

Buffalo	7	7	14	0—28
San Diego	7	14	3	3—27

SCORING

San Diego—Muncie 9 run (Benirschke kick).
Buffalo—Ferguson 3 run (Mike-Mayer kick).
San Diego—Chandler 17 pass from Fouts (Benirschke kick).
Buffalo—Leaks 9 run (Mike-Mayer kick).
San Diego—Winslow 67 pass from Fouts (Benirschke kick).
Buffalo—Leaks 1 run (Mike-Mayer kick).
San Diego—Field goal Benirschke 29.
Buffalo—Cribbs 1 run (Mike-Mayer kick).
San Diego—Field goal Benirschke 27.

TEAM STATISTICS

	Buffalo	San Diego
First downs	19	28
Rushes-Yards	34-84	32-145
Passing yards	234	337
Sacks by-Yards	1-6	2-14
Return yards	158	124
Passes	13-29-0	28-42-1
Punts	7-37.0	4-33.3
Fumbles-Lost	0-0	3-1
Penalties-Yards	9-88	8-78
Time of possession	28:26	31:34
Attendance—51,488.		

INDIVIDUAL STATISTICS

Rushing—Buffalo, Cribbs 14-35, Brown 8-28, Brown 5-20, Hooks 1-8, Ferguson 5-4, Franklin 1-minus 11; San Diego, Muncie 22-119, Cappelletti 3-21, Chandler 1-4, Brooks 3-3, Fouts 3-minus 2.

Passing—Buffalo, Ferguson 13-29-0—248; San Diego, Fouts 28-42-1—343.

Receiving—Buffalo, Lewis 5-113, Cribbs 2-67, Piccone 2-24, Butler 2-19, Barnett 1-16, Leaks 1-9; San Diego, Joiner 7-106, Chandler 7-60, Winslow 6-126, Muncie 4-36, Brooks 3-9, Scales 1-6.

Kickoff Returns—Buffalo, Riddick 4-70, Brown 2-26; San Diego, Brooks 3-88, Shaw 1-9, Gregor 1-20.

Punt Returns—Buffalo, Hooks 1-9; San Diego, Brooks 2-7.

Interceptions—Buffalo, Clark 1-53.

Punting—Buffalo, Cater 7-37.0; San Diego, Roberts 4-33.3.

Field Goals—Buffalo, Mike-Mayer 0-1; San Diego, Benirschke 2-2.

REDSKINS 15, EAGLES 13

WASHINGTON—"Maybe we're just snake-bit," said Philadelphia Coach Dick Vermeil after the Eagles missed clinching a playoff berth when they messed up on a field-goal attempt in the final minute and lost to Washington.

Philadelphia (9-5) had driven to the Washington 7-yard line, and Tony Franklin lined up for a 25-yard field goal attempt with 54 seconds left. However, holder John Sciarra bobbled the snap from center and then, after retrieving the ball, was tackled for a 16-yard loss.

In the second quarter, Sciarra had dropped the snap on an extra-point attempt after the second of Ron Jaworski's two touchdown passes to Billy Campfield had put the Eagles ahead, 13-6.

"There's nothing to make excuses about," said Sciarra. "I just muffed the hold. I feel bad that I let my teammates down. That's my job and I didn't get it done."

Said Vermeil, "John is the most sure-handed player we have, but he dropped the ball." That's when the coach wondered if the Eagles were snakebit, but there was another prime example.

The Eagles were leading 13-9 and had the ball at their 40 with seven minutes to play. A screen pass was ordered when Vermeil realized he wanted different players in the lineup and frantically tried to call time out. Booker Russell was a running back at the time, and the coach wanted to send in Wilbert Montgomery or Campfield.

"Vermeil was in a frenzy over there trying to get different personnel in the game," said Jaworski. "Calvin Murray was at wide receiver and normally he wouldn't be there. I saw Dick yelling from the sideline. I was tempted to call time, but I didn't feel like it was necessary. I just felt the people in there knew what they were doing and we could execute the play."

However, defensive end Dexter Manley pressured Jaworski and he overthrew the pass. The throw was picked off by linebacker Monte Coleman, who scooted 52 yards to score.

Coleman had to elude only Jaworski to reach the end zone, and he cut back to the middle of the field to leave the quarterback sprawling.

DECEMBER 6
SCORE BY PERIODS

Philadelphia	0	13	0	0—13
Washington	6	0	0	9—15

SCORING

Washington—Washington 6 run (kick failed).
Philadelphia—Campfield 25 pass from Jaworski (Franklin kick).
Philadelphia—Campfield 5 pass from Jaworski (kick blocked).
Washington—Field goal Moseley 45.
Washington—Coleman 52 interception return (kick failed).

TEAM STATISTICS

	Philadelphia	Washington
First downs	25	11
Rushes-Yards	37-161	32-108
Passing yards	255	68
Sacks by-Yards	1-19	1-11
Return yards	128	144
Passes	16-35-3	13-22-2
Punts	4-41.8	5-44.2
Fumbles-Lost	3-1	0-0
Penalties-Yards	3-20	2-15
Time of possession	31:28	28:32
Attendance— 52,206.		

INDIVIDUAL STATISTICS

Rushing—Philadelphia, Russell 5-28, Montgomery 27-116, Jaworski 1-5, Campfield 3-12, Sciarra 1-0; Washington, Riggins 11-61, Washington 17-54, Theismann 4-minus 7.

Passing—Philadelphia, Jaworski 16-35-3-266; Washington Theismann 13-22-2-87.

Receiving—Philadelphia, C. Smith 4-66, R. Smith 1-15, Carmichael 2-47, Montgomery 3-53, Campfield 4-54, Krepfle 1-14, Spagnola 1-17; Washington, Monk 1-8, Washington 3-6, Thompson 2-25, Warren 1-5, Seay 2-22, Metcalf 4-21.

Kickoff Returns—Philadelphia, Campfield 2-31, Russell 1-8, Murray 1-14; Washington, Nelms 2-62, Garrett 1-21.

Punt Returns—Philadelphia, Henry 5-29; Washington, Nelms 2-9.

Interceptions—Philadelphia, Wilson 1-21, Blackmore 1-25; Washington, Lavender 1-0, Murphy 1-0, Coleman 1-52.

Punting—Philadelphia, Runager 4-41.8; Washington, Connell 5-44.2.

Field Goals—Philadelphia, None attempted; Washington, Moseley 1-1.

RAIDERS 30, STEELERS 27

OAKLAND—Ever since the National Football League began playing one of its regular-season games each week on Monday night, the undisputed kings of such encounters have been the Oakland Raiders. In more than a decade of Monday night football, the Raiders' record in such games stood at 18-1-1.

"I wish we could play all our games on Monday night," said Oakland Coach Tom Flores after his Raiders edged Pittsburgh, 30-27. "We really played good football."

The Raiders used a 16-point fourth period to beat the Steelers. Quarterback Marc Wilson, who succeeded Super Bowl XV hero Jim Plunkett as the Oakland signal-caller, hit Bob Chandler on a 38-yard TD pass—Wilson's third touchdown pass of the night. Rookie Ted Watts, the Raiders' first-round draft choice, returned a punt 53 yards for another touchdown and Chris Bahr's 29-yard field goal accounted for the other scoring in the period.

Wilson had earlier connected with Derrick Ramsey and Arthur Whittington on touchdown passes. He completed 18 of 29 passes for 275 yards in the game.

The Steelers were forced to play most of the game without their star quarterback, Terry Bradshaw. Bradshaw suffered a broken right hand after completing four of nine passes for 29 yards, including a TD pass to Bennie Cunningham. His replacement, second-year pro Mark Malone, threw two touchdown passes to wide receiver Jim Smith. Malone also ran for another touchdown from 11 yards out. But each time Malone gave Pittsburgh the lead, Wilson got it back for the Raiders.

The Raiders, who improved to 7-7 for the year, were able to survive five turnovers, four of them fumbles. The Steelers, who fell to 8-6, were not so lucky. Malone was intercepted twice in the final period to kill Pittsburgh drives.

MONDAY, DECEMBER 7
SCORE BY PERIODS

Pittsburgh	7	7	6	7—27
Oakland	7	0	7	16—30

SCORING

Pittsburgh—Cunningham 5 pass from Bradshaw (Trout kick).
Oakland—Ramsey 25 pass from Wilson (Bahr kick).
Pittsburgh—Smith 19 pass from Malone (Trout kick).
Oakland—Whittington 17 pass from Wilson (Bahr kick).
Pittsburgh—Malone 11 run (kick blocked).
Oakland—Chandler 38 pass from Wilson (kick failed).
Oakland—Watts 53 punt return (Bahr kick).
Oakland—Field goal Bahr 29.
Pittsburgh—Smith 17 pass from Malone (Trout kick).

TEAM STATISTICS

	Pittsburgh	Oakland
First downs	24	22
Rushes-Yards	30-96	38-213
Passing yards	235	257
Sacks by-Yards	4-38	3-18
Return yards	15	94
Passes	21-36-2	18-29-1
Punts	9-46.6	5-39.0
Fumbles-Lost	1-0	5-4
Penalties-Yards	5-45	5-33
Time of possession	31:21	28:39
Attendance—51,769.		

INDIVIDUAL STATISTICS

Rushing—Pittsburgh, Malone 3-29, Hawthorne 9-19, Thornton 6-31, Harris 11-15, Davis 1-2; Oakland, King 11-102, Jensen 6-42, Hawkins 8-25, Wilson 5-21, Whittington 8-23.

Passing—Pittsburgh, Bradshaw 4-9-0—29, Malone 17-27-2—244; Oakland, Wilson 18-29-1—275.

Receiving—Pittsburgh, Cunningham 5-97, Swann 4-65, Harris 5-24, Stallworth 3-42, Smith 2-36, Thornton 1-13, Hawthorne 1-minus 4; Oakland, Whittington 6-64, Ramsey 5-68, Chandler 4-83, Branch 3-60.

Kickoff Returns—Pittsburgh, Anderson 3-64, Moser 1-21; Oakland, Whittington 3-70, Willis 1-19.

Punt Returns—Pittsburgh, Anderson 2-13; Oakland, Whittington 2-4, Watts 2-56.

Fourteenth Week—Continued

Interceptions—Pittsburgh, Blount 1-2; Oakland, Hayes 1-0, McKinney 1-34.

Punting—Pittsburgh, Colquitt 9-46.6; Oakland, Guy 5-39.0.

Field Goals—Pittsburgh, None attempted; Oakland, Bahr 1-1.

FIFTEENTH WEEK

LIONS 45, VIKINGS 7

PONTIAC—Eric Hipple threw two touchdown passes in the last 1:54 of a 31-point first half as Detroit destroyed Minnesota, keeping the Lions in contention for their first playoff berth since 1970.

The Lions improved to 8-7 with their fourth victory in five games while the Vikings dropped to 7-8, losing their fourth straight game.

Detroit was tied for the NFC Central lead with Tampa Bay and Green Bay.

"We were at home, our backs were to the wall and we were on national television," Lions Coach Monte Clark said. "Those seem to be three external factors that are integral to our playing well."

Billy Sims' 14-yard scoring run and rookie Robbie Martin's 45-yard punt return for a touchdown gave the Lions a 14-0 lead with 1:39 left in the first quarter.

The Lions then intercepted Tommy Kramer, but lost the ball when cornerback James Hunter fumbled safety Jimmy Allen's lateral. The Vikings took advantage of the break to produce their only touchdown.

Kramer hit Joe Senser with a three-yard scoring pass to pull the Vikings within 14-7 just 1:29 into the second quarter.

Vikings Coach Bud Grant ordered an onside kick and the Lions recovered, leading to Ed Murray's 26-yard field goal that made the score 17-7.

Before the half was over, linebacker Ken Fantetti's interception led to a seven-yard touchdown pass from Hipple to Fred Scott, and Hipple tossed a 10-yard scoring pass to Leonard Thompson.

The Lions put the game away with a 69-yard drive at the start of the second half, with Thompson scoring on an end-around from one yard out on fourth down.

Their final touchdown came on Gary Danielson's 27-yard pass to rookie Tracy Porter in the fourth quarter.

SATURDAY, DECEMBER 12
SCORE BY PERIODS

Minnesota	0	7	0	0— 7
Detroit	14	17	7	7—45

SCORING

Detroit—Sims 14 run (Murray kick).
Detroit—Martin 45 punt return (Murray kick).
Minnesota—Senser 3 pass from Kramer (Danmeier kick).
Detroit—Field goal Murray 26.
Detroit—Scott 7 pass from Hipple (Murray kick).
Detroit—L. Thompson 10 pass from Hipple (Murray kick).
Detroit—L. Thompson 1 run (Murray kick).
Detroit—Porter 27 pass from Danielson (Murray kick).

TEAM STATISTICS

	Minnesota	Detroit
First downs	16	29
Rushes-Yards	22-72	35-205
Passing yards	144	271
Sacks by-Yards	3-24	3-11
Return yards	175	74
Passes	17-44-4	18-29-1
Punts	4-42.5	1-36.0
Fumbles-Lost	0-0	3-3
Penalties-Yards	7-55	10-87
Time of possession	25:56	34:04

Attendance—79,428.

INDIVIDUAL STATISTICS

Rushing—Minnesota, Brown 15-55, Young 6-21, LeCount 1-minus 4; Detroit, Sims 13-110, Kane 8-36, Bussey 6-30, V. Thompson 4-19, Hipple 1-9, Scott 1-2, L. Thompson 1-1, Danielson 1-minus 1.

Passing—Minnesota, Kramer 17-42-2-155, Wilson 0-2-2-0; Detroit, Hipple 13-21-1-188, Danielson 5-7-0-107, Scott 0-1-0-0.

Receiving—Minnesota, White 5-66, Senser 5-41, Rashad 3-52, Brown 3-minus 3, Young 1-minus 1; Detroit, L. Thompson 4-69, Porter 3-63, King 3-59, Sims 3-37, V. Thompson 2-18, Norris 1-34, Kane 1-8, Scott 1-7.

Kickoff Returns—Minnesota, Payton 4-108, Nord 1-27, Galbreath 1-16, Blair 1-0; Detroit, Hall 1-23.

Punt Returns—Minnesota, Payton 1-6; Detroit, Martin 3-47.

Interceptions—Minnesota, Swain 1-18; Detroit, Fantetti 1-17, Oldham 1-0, Gray 1-0, Allen 1-0, Hunter 0-minus 13.

Punting—Minnesota, Coleman 4-42.5; Detroit, Skladany 1-36.0.

Field Goals—Minnesota, Danmeier 0-1; Detroit, Murray 1-1.

JETS 14, BROWNS 13

CLEVELAND—New York last played in a postseason game in 1969, and no one thought this year would be any different from the last 11 after the Jets started with three straight losses.

But after narrowly defeating Cleveland, the Jets were in position to clinch a playoff spot with a victory against Green Bay in Shea Stadium, despite trailing Miami by one game and Buffalo by one-half game in the AFC East.

"We're close—but still a long way off," said tight end Jerome Barkum.

After a scoreless first quarter, the Jets went ahead on Richard Todd's 28-yard touchdown pass to Lam Jones. A seven-yard pass to running back Bruce Harper kept the drive alive on fourth and three from the Browns' 35-yard line.

The Browns cut the lead to 7-3 on their next possession. Dino Hall returned the kickoff 48 yards and Brian Sipe passed the Browns to the Jets' 8 before Cleveland settled for Matt Bahr's 26-yard field goal.

The Jets increased the lead to 14-3 with 24

seconds left in the half as Todd's seven-yard pass to Harper capped a nine-play, 87-yard drive.

Sipe cut the margin to 14-10 with 7:20 left in the third quarter on a eight-yard pass to running back Calvin Hill. Bahr's 21-yard field goal with 8:23 to go cut the lead to one, but the Browns only had one more possession and failed to gain a first down.

The Browns, defending AFC Central champions, dropped to 5-10.

"It's been a frustrating 15 games and we're terribly disappointed about it, but we're certainly not despairing," said Browns Coach Sam Rutigliano.

SATURDAY, DECEMBER 12
SCORE BY PERIODS

New York Jets	0	14	0	0—14
Cleveland	0	3	7	3—13

SCORING

New York—L. Jones 8 pass from Todd (Leahy kick).
Cleveland—Field goal Bahr 26.
New York—Harper 7 pass from Todd (Leahy kick).
Cleveland—Hill 8 pass from Sipe (Bahr kick).
Cleveland—Field goal Bahr 20.

TEAM STATISTICS

	New York	Cleveland
First downs	18	17
Rushes-Yards	34-164	24-74
Passing yards	150	260
Sacks by-Yards	2-20	1-9
Return yards	100	106
Passes	15-28-2	20-35-0
Punts	7-32.3	5-36.4
Fumbles-Lost	2-0	2-2
Penalties-Yards	7-55	6-50
Time of possession	29:40	30:20
Attendance—56,866.		

INDIVIDUAL STATISTICS

Rushing—New York, Dierking 13-76, Long 5-27, McNeil 4-21, Newton 7-20, Harper 2-13, Todd 3-7; Cleveland, M. Pruitt 15-41, Sipe 3-19, White 4-15, G. Pruitt 1-1, C. Miller 1-minus 2.

Passing—New York, Todd 15-28-2-159; Cleveland, Sipe 20-35-0-280.

Receiving—New York, J. Jones 5-83, Harper 4-42, Barkum 2-9, Gaffney 1-10, B. Jones 1-9, Dierking 1-5, McNeil 1-1; Cleveland, Newsome 5-79, G. Pruitt 5-44, C. Miller 3-32, Feacher 2-75, Rucker 1-17, Logan 1-15, Hill 1-8, M. Pruitt 1-6, White 1-4.

Kickoff Returns—New York, Harper 2-62, Sohn 1-15; Cleveland, Hall 3-94.

Punt Returns—New York, Harper 3-23; Cleveland, Hall 1-6.

Interceptions—Cleveland, Matthews 1-6, Scott 1-0.

Punting—New York, Ramsey 7-32.3; Cleveland, Cox 5-36.4

Field Goals—New York, None attempted; Cleveland, Bahr 2-3.

COWBOYS 21, EAGLES 10

IRVING—The Dallas Cowboys were filled with the yuletide spirit, even if there was no champagne, after they clinched the NFC Eastern Division championship with a 21-10 victory over the Philadelphia Eagles.

"You will never see champagne in our locker room," said Dallas Coach Tom Landry, who prefers iced tea. The Cowboys' subdued title celebration was in contrast to the Eagles' when they won the NFC East championship in 1980 despite a final-game loss at Texas Stadium.

The Cowboys improved their record to 12-3 and saddled the Eagles (9-6) with their fourth straight loss, largely because of the Eagles' generosity in giving up the ball.

Philadelphia quarterback Ron Jaworski suffered four pass interceptions, three of them by cornerback Dennis Thurman, and a fumble by the Eagles' John Sciarra on a Dallas punt gave the Cowboys a touchdown in the final minute of the first half and swung the momentum in the game.

Holding a 10-0 lead, Philadelphia stopped Dallas at the Eagles' 45 with less than two minutes to play in the half. Rather than risk losing the ball on a fourth-and-one gamble, Landry chose to have Danny White punt the ball away. But Sciarra fumbled as he tried to catch the punt and Anthony Dickerson recovered for Dallas on the Philadelphia 20. Seconds later, White threw a nine-yard touchdown pass to Tony Hill to make the score 10-7 at halftime.

Dallas dominated the second half, scoring on a 36-yard pass from White to Butch Johnson and on a 12-yard run by Ron Springs after a 47-yard pass from White to Johnson had moved the ball out of Dallas territory.

"The fumbled punt was the key play for us," said Landry. "Getting points on the scoreboard in the first half made a lot of difference. The Eagles are a good team, but they haven't been getting the breaks and after a while that tends to build on your mind."

On the fumbled punt, Sciarra said, "I got caught in a moment of indecision. I didn't know whether to catch it or not. There were white jerseys (Dallas) all around me."

Dickerson admitted, "We were screaming and yelling at him, 'Hey, hey, miss it.' I think it broke his concentration. Suddenly, the ball rolled out and right into my hands."

Dallas got two good breaks in the second half when fumbles by Tony Dorsett wound up in the hands of teammates. Guard Kurt Peterson picked one fumble out of the air and gained three yards, while the other bobble was picked up by Springs, who proceeded to gain 10 yards.

DECEMBER 13
SCORE BY PERIODS

Philadelphia	3	7	0	0—10
Dallas	0	7	7	7—21

SCORING

Philadelphia—Field goal Franklin 50.
Philadelphia—Russell 1 run (Franklin kick).
Dallas—Hill 8 pass from D. White (Septien kick).
Dallas—Johnson 36 pass from D. White (Septien kick).
Dallas—Springs 12 run (Septien kick).

Fifteenth Week—Continued

TEAM STATISTICS

	Philadelphia	Dallas
First downs	14	23
Rushes-Yards	23-90	43-148
Passing yards	135	264
Sacks by-Yards	0-0	1-5
Return yards	81	103
Passes	11-32-4	17-30-0
Punts	2-44.5	3-36.0
Fumbles-Lost	2-1	4-2
Penalties-Yards	3-20	5-50
Time of possession	25:20	34:40

Attendance—64,955.

INDIVIDUAL STATISTICS

Rushing—Philadelphia, Montgomery 17-67, Oliver 2-8, Jaworski 1-7, R. Smith 1-7, Russell 1-1, Campfield 1-0; Dallas, Dorsett 28-101, Springs 8-44, J. Jones 1-3, Newhouse 2-3, D. White 3-2, Pearson 1-minus 5.

Passing—Philadelphia, Jaworski 11-32-4—140; Dallas, D. White 17-30-0—264.

Receiving—Philadelphia, R. Smith 3-69, Montgomery 2-21, Carmichael 2-21, Spagnola 2-17, C. Smith 1-10, Oliver 1-2; Dallas, Hill 7-95, Johnson 3-90, Springs 2-19, Saldi 1-18, Pearson 1-14, DuPree 1-13, Dorsett 1-9, Cosbie 1-6.

Kickoff Returns—Philadelphia, Campfield 3-67; Dallas, Newsome 3-57.

Punt Returns—Philadelphia, Henry 1-14, Sciarra 1-0; Dallas, J. Jones 1-8.

Interceptions—Dallas, Walls 1-1, Thurman 3-37.

Punting—Philadelphia, Runager 2-44.5; Dallas, D. White 3-36.0.

Field Goals—Philadelphia, Franklin 1-2; Dallas, Septien 0-2.

BENGALS 17, STEELERS 10

PITTSBURGH—The Pittsburgh Steelers scared the Cincinnati Bengals half to death before finally conceding the game and the AFC Central Division championship in Three Rivers Stadium—and the Bengals wouldn't have had it any other way.

"They made it tough for us, and that's good. They really made us earn it," Bengals Coach Forrest Gregg said after the Bengals (11-4) finally put away a 17-10 victory, which gave them their first division title since 1973.

The victory also eliminated the four-time Super Bowl champion Steelers (8-7) from the playoffs for the second consecutive season.

"It just wasn't in the cards for us to get where we had to go," said Steelers Coach Chuck Noll. "The Bengals are a great football team, and I hope they go all the way."

Until the final minutes of the fourth quarter, it appeared the Bengals would breeze to an easy victory. The Bengals had a 17-3 lead and were marching for another score when linebacker Jack Lambert intercepted a Ken Anderson pass on the Steelers' 17-yard line and returned it to the 30.

Suddenly, it was a new game.

Quarterback Mark Malone, struggling in his first NFL start as a replacement for injured Terry Bradshaw, promptly moved the Steelers 70 yards in nine plays, completing a two-yard touchdown pass to running back Franco Harris to cut the deficit to 17-10 with 2:52 to play.

The Steelers' defense forced the Bengals to punt 53 seconds later, and Malone coolly moved the Steelers to the Bengals' 3 in three plays.

But the Steelers' luck ran out as Malone threw four straight incompletions.

Anderson threw touchdown passes of two yards to Isaac Curtis and 22 yards to Steve Kreider.

"I can't describe the feeling that winning it in Pittsburgh gives me," said Anderson, who played despite a toe injury that had sidelined him the previous week. "They've been rivals of mine for a long, long time."

The Steelers took a 3-0 lead in the second quarter on Dave Trout's 48-yard field goal, but the Bengals quickly tied it on Jim Breech's 38-yarder, and went ahead for good before halftime on Curtis' touchdown catch.

DECEMBER 13

SCORE BY PERIODS

Cincinnati	0	10	7	0—17
Pittsburgh	0	3	0	7—10

SCORING

Pittsburgh—Field goal Trout 48.
Cincinnati—Field goal Breech 38.
Cincinnati—Curtis 2 pass from Anderson (Breech kick).
Cincinnati—Kreider 22 pass from Anderson (Breech kick).
Pittsburgh—Harris 2 pass from Malone (Trout kick).

TEAM STATISTICS

	Cincinnati	Pittsburgh
First downs	19	14
Rushes-Yards	33-103	25-87
Passing yards	215	120
Sacks by-Yards	3-17	0-0
Return yards	64	123
Passes	21-35-1	15-30-2
Punts	4-42.3	5-38.2
Fumbles-Lost	2-1	1-0
Penalties-Yards	8-66	3-19
Time of possession	33:40	26:20

Attendance—50,623.

INDIVIDUAL STATISTICS

Rushing—Cincinnati, Johnson 18-49, Alexander 7-17, Anderson 8-37; Pittsburgh, Harris 14-42, Pollard 7-24, Malone 3-19, Thornton 1-2.

Passing—Cincinnati, Anderson 21-35-1—215; Pittsburgh, Malone 15-30-2—137.

Receiving—Cincinnati, Curtis 3-50, Ross 2-20, Johnson 6-27, Alexander 1-6, Collinsworth 8-90, Kreider 1-22; Pittsburgh, Harris 7-33, Thornton 1-3, Swann 4-69, Cunningham 1-1, Stallworth 2-31.

Kickoff Returns—Cincinnati, Verser 1-17, A. Griffin 1-28; Pittsburgh, Anderson 3-79, Davis 1-8.

Punt Returns—Cincinnati, Fuller 1-19; Pittsburgh, Anderson 3-23.

Interceptions—Cincinnati, LeClair 1-0, Williams 1-0; Pittsburgh, Lambert 1-13.

Punting—Cincinnati, McInally 4-42.3; Pittsburgh, Colquitt 5-38.2.

Field Goals—Cincinnati, Breech 1-2; Pittsburgh, Trout 1-1.

BILLS 19, PATRIOTS 10

FOXBORO—Buffalo set its sights on a second consecutive AFC East title after clinching

Cincinnati quarterback Ken Anderson directed the Bengals to a 17-10 victory over the Steelers in Pittsburgh. The win clinched Cincinnati's first American Football Conference Central Division title since 1973.

Fifteenth Week—Continued

a playoff berth with a Joe Cribbs-led triumph over woeful New England.

The Bills upped their record to 10-5 with their fourth straight victory.

"It feels good to go back to the playoffs, but we'd all like to go back as division champions," Cribbs said after rushing for 153 yards to total 1,003 for the year and catching a 39-yard touchdown pass from Joe Ferguson. "This was one of the most satisfying games of my career."

The Patriots suffered their eighth straight loss and fell to 2-13, a club record for losses. Attention was on Patriots Owner Billy Sullivan after the game as he pondered a decision on Coach Ron Erhardt's future.

"If you have any sense at all, the time to make the decision isn't at the end of a frustrating series of losses. It takes time to sit back and look at the entire picture," said Sullivan. "But there is considerable sentiment to keep the guy."

The Bills jumped out to a 14-0 first-quarter lead on Roosevelt Leaks' five-yard touchdown run and Cribbs' scoring catch.

The Patriots managed only a 19-yard touchdown run by Vagas Ferguson and a 42-yard field goal by John Smith. Ferguson's run came 3:35 into the second quarter and cut the Bills' lead to 14-7. The Pats came within inches of tying the game when Matt Cavanaugh overthrew fullback Mosi Tatupu in the end zone on a flea flicker. The Bills came right back, and Nick Mike-Mayer kicked a 29-yard field goal with 49 seconds left in the half.

The Patriots also yielded a safety when defensive end Ben Williams sacked Cavanaugh in the end zone.

"You know, this is kind of typical of the season we've had," said Patriots linebacker Steve Nelson. "We won three-quarters of the game and still lost."

DECEMBER 13

SCORE BY PERIODS

Buffalo	14	3	2	0—19
New England	0	7	0	3—10

SCORING

Buffalo—Leaks 5 run (Mike-Mayer kick).
Buffalo—Cribbs 39 pass from Ferguson (Mike-Mayer kick).
New England—Ferguson 19 run (Smith kick).
Buffalo—Field goal Mike-Mayer 29.
Buffalo—Safety, Cavanaugh tackled in end zone.
New England—Field goal Smith 42.

TEAM STATISTICS

	Buffalo	New England
First downs	20	16
Rushes-Yards	47-192	27-97
Passing yards	137	107
Sacks by-Yards	3-26	2-14
Return yards	110	83
Passes	10-18-0	12-28-2
Punts	6-31.2	3-44.0
Fumbles-Lost	1-0	1-0
Penalties-Yards	6-48	3-15
Time of possession	33:58	26:02
Attendance—42,549.		

Rushing—Buffalo, Cribbs 33-153, Leaks 5-24, Brown 7-18, Ferguson 2-minus 3; New England, Collins 9-13, Cunningham 11-42, Ferguson 7-42.

Passing—Buffalo, Ferguson 10-18-0—151; New England, Cavanaugh 6-13-0—51, Owen 6-14-1—82, Johnson 0-1-1—0.

Receiving—Buffalo, Lewis 1-25, Butler 4-50, Cribbs 3-48, Jessie 1-17, Leaks 1-11; New England, Morgan 1-9, Jackson 5-47, Dawson 2-22, Collins 1-8, Ferguson 1-20, Westbrook 2-27.

Kickoff Returns—Buffalo, Riddick 1-9, Brown 2-41, Piccone 1-15; New England, Collins 3-63, Matthews 1-5.

Punt Returns—Buffalo, Hooks 1-6, Piccone 1-12; New England, Collins 3-15.

Interceptions—Buffalo, Romes 1-25, Clark 1-2.

Punting—Buffalo, Cater 6-31.2; New England, Camarillo 3-44.0.

Field Goals—Buffalo, Mike-Mayer 1-1; New England, Smith 1-1.

DOLPHINS 17, CHIEFS 7

KANSAS CITY—Andra Franklin plunged one yard for a fourth-quarter touchdown following a botched Kansas City field-goal attempt to clinch the Dolphins a postseason appearance after a year's absence and eliminate the slumping Chiefs from the playoff chase.

Tony Nathan had a five-yard touchdown run and Uwe von Schamann kicked a 39-yard field goal as the Dolphins raised their record to 10-4-1, giving them a half-game lead over Buffalo and a one-game lead over the New York Jets in the AFC East.

The Dolphins sewed up at least a wild-card playoff berth.

"This is the first step," said Dolphins Coach Don Shula. "We set out a long time ago to do things in stages. We wanted to have a good preseason, then a fast (regular season) start and then be there at the end. This puts us there at the end. We knew we had to win one of our last two to get in the playoffs and we wanted to do it in Kansas City."

The turning point occurred with the Dolphins leading 10-7 late in the third quarter. Nick Lowery lined up to attempt a 45-yard field goal which would have tied the game. But center Jack Rudnay's snap bounced past both Lowery and holder Steve Fuller 28 yards downfield before Lowery finally fell on it at the Kansas City 44-yard line. The Chiefs' regular deep snapper, rookie Todd Thomas, suffered a dislocated right shoulder during coverage of a third-quarter punt by Jeff Gossett, leaving Rudnay to handle the long snaps.

It took the Dolphins nine plays to cover those 44 yards for the touchdown that stopped the Chiefs' bid for their first playoff berth since 1971.

"I had several frustrating moments today," Rudnay said. "I had a bad snap . . . and we lost the game. Both are frustrating. I have no excuses."

The Chiefs (8-7) scored on a two-yard pass from Fuller to Al Dixon in the second quarter.

DECEMBER 13
SCORE BY PERIODS

Miami	7	3	0	7—	17
Kansas City	0	7	0	0—	7

SCORING

Miami—Nathan 5 run (von Schamann kick).
Kansas City—Dixon 2 pass from Fuller (Lowery kick).
Miami—Field goal von Schamann 39.
Miami—Franklin 1 run (von Schamann kick).

TEAM STATISTICS

	Miami	Kansas City
First downs	16	16
Rushes-Yards	40-93	28-91
Passing yards	160	185
Sacks by-Yards	3-21	1-5
Return yards	68	110
Passes	14-28-3	21-37-1
Punts	5-38.6	5-41.2
Fumbles-Lost	0-0	4-1
Penalties-Yards	4-32	5-55
Time of possession	32:08	27:52

Attendance—57,407.

INDIVIDUAL STATISTICS

Rushing—Miami, Franklin 17-40, Nathan 11-33, Hill 4-13, Orosz 1-13, Woodley 2-10, Vigorito 2-0, Strock 3-minus 16; Kansas City, Delaney 6-23, Fuller 8-42, B. Jackson 10-25, Hadnot 4-1.

Passing—Miami, Woodley 6-12-1—56, Strock 8-16-2—109; Kansas City, Fuller 21-37-1—206.

Receiving—Miami, Vigorito 3-42, Nathan 3-23, Rose 3-21, Hill 2-22, Moore 1-39, Harris 1-10, Hardy 1-8; Kansas City, Smith 5-99, Dixon 5-42, Hadnot 4-24, B. Jackson 3-24, Rome 3-12, Delaney 1-5.

Kickoff Returns—Miami, Walker 2-49; Kansas City, Carson 1-21, Cherry 1-10.

Punt Returns—Miami, Vigorito 4-18; Kansas City, Smith 3-31.

Interceptions—Miami, L. Blackwood 1-1; Kansas City, Harris 2-14, Barbaro 1-34.

Punting—Miami, Orosz 5-38.6; Kansas City, Gossett 5-41.2.

Field Goals—Miami, von Schamann 1-1; Kansas City, None attempted.

CHARGERS 24, BUCS 23

TAMPA—Rolf Benirschke kicked a 29-yard field goal with 45 seconds to play to lift San Diego to victory over Tampa Bay, preventing the Buccaneers from clinching the NFC Central Division title.

Tampa Bay fell to 8-7 and needed a season-ending victory at Detroit to claim the division title. San Diego's record went to 9-6, keeping the Chargers alive for a possible AFC West championship or a wild-card playoff berth.

San Diego's Dan Fouts and Tampa Bay's Doug Williams both passed for more than 300 yards, and both teams went over 400 yards in total offense. The game was decided on two short kicks—Benirschke's field goal that was good and Bill Capece's extra-point attempt that missed in the fourth quarter.

The Chargers seemed to have put the game away when James Brooks scooted one yard for a touchdown to make the score 21-10 in the final period. But the Bucs rallied to take a 23-21 lead as rookie running back James

Wilder ran for two touchdowns 27 seconds apart.

Wilder's first TD, on a eight-yard run, made the score 21-16 and Capece missed the extra point. After the kickoff, linebacker David Lewis intercepted a Fouts pass and Wilder raced 23 yards to score on the Bucs' first play. Capece converted that time and Tampa Bay had its 23-21 lead.

On San Diego's next series, John Cappelletti fumbled and Lewis recovered at the Chargers' 36. But Williams fired a pass to tight end Jimmie Giles and the ball bounced into the air, with Chargers linebacker Woodrow Lowe intercepting at the 29. San Diego then drove into position for its field goal.

When the Chargers got into field-goal range, Benirschke said, "I felt the weight of the kick, because the season would have been over if we'd lost. I thought about it on the sideline, but then I put it out of my mind."

Fouts threw a 27-yard pass to Eric Sievers in the first quarter for his 32nd TD pass of the year, tops in the NFL. The Chargers set a league record by piling up more than 400 yards in total offense for the sixth game in a row.

DECEMBER 13
SCORE BY PERIODS

San Diego	7	7	0	10—	24
Tampa Bay	7	0	3	13—	23

SCORING

San Diego—Sievers 27 pass from Fouts (Benirschke kick).
Tampa Bay—T. Bell 58 pass from Williams (Capece kick).
San Diego—Cappelletti 7 run (Benirschke kick).
Tampa Bay—Field goal Capece 49.
San Diego—Brooks 1 run (Benirschke kick).
Tampa Bay—Wilder 7 run (kick failed).
Tampa Bay—Wilder 23 run (Capece kick).
San Diego—Field goal Benirschke 29.

TEAM STATISTICS

	San Diego	Tampa Bay
First downs	26	18
Rushes-Yards	31-94	19-114
Passing yards	351	290
Sacks by-Yards	3-31	0-0
Return yards	181	94
Passes	33-51-2	22-36-2
Punts	4-47.3	5-41.0
Fumbles-Lost	2-2	2-1
Penalties-Yards	5-30	3-30
Time of possession	33:45	26:15

Attendance—67,388.

INDIVIDUAL STATISTICS

Rushing—San Diego, Chandler 1-minus 8, Muncie 3-17, Cappelletti 9-32, Brooks 17-50, Fouts 1-3; Tampa Bay, R. Bell 2-0, Owens 11-61, Williams 1-17, Wilder 4-34, Eckwood 1-2.

Passing—San Diego, Fouts 33-49-2—351, Winslow 0-1-0—0, Chandler 0-1-0—0; Tampa Bay, Williams 22-35-2—321, House 0-1-0—0.

Receiving—San Diego, Chandler 8-112, Joiner 7-99, Winslow 8-55, Sievers 1-27, Brooks 7-31, Cappelletti 1-5, Scales 1-22; Tampa Bay, T. Bell 3-96, Owens 4-36, Wilder 6-78, Eckwood 2-12, Giles 4-38, House 3-61.

Kickoff Returns—San Diego, Brooks 4-99, Bauer 1-14; Tampa Bay, Owens 2-52, Davis 1-13, Wilder 1-19.

Punt Returns—San Diego, Brooks 2-29; Tampa Bay, Colzie 1-0.

Fifteenth Week—Continued

Interceptions—San Diego, Lowe 1-0, Edwards 1-39; Tampa Bay, Brown 1-0, Lewis 1-10.

Punting—San Diego, Roberts 4-47.3; Tampa Bay, Swider 5-41.0.

Field Goals—San Diego, Benirschke 1-1; Tampa Bay, Capece 1-1.

GIANTS 20, CARDINALS 10

ST. LOUIS—The New York defense battered Neil Lomax, St. Louis' rookie quarterback, and the Giants (8-7) stayed alive in the race for a wild-card playoff berth while the Cardinals were eliminated at 7-8.

Lomax had guided the Cardinals to four straight victories before being mugged by the Giants. He was sacked three times, intercepted once, hurried into some bad passes and was knocked out of the game briefly in the first quarter when a late hit by defensive end Gary Jeter left him dizzy.

"I've never been hit like that," Lomax said of his long afternoon. "They drilled my head into the ground (Jeter's hit) one time and I felt it the rest of the way."

The Cardinals took the opening kickoff and went 70 yards for a field goal, but then Lomax got his rude awakening. On St. Louis' second possession, Lomax went back to pass and was blindsided by rookie linebacker Lawrence Taylor, knocking the ball loose. Defensive end George Martin picked up the fumble and went 20 yards for a touchdown, dragging St. Louis tight end Greg LaFleur the last 10 yards.

"I saw Lawrence out of the corner of my eye," Martin said. "No one even blocked him. When I saw the ball, I just hurdled my blocker, recovered the ball and started thinking goal line."

Just three plays later, after the Giants' kickoff, Lomax was slammed down by Jeter after completing a pass and was knocked out of the game. Jim Hart went in for Lomax and his third-down pass was intercepted.

Any doubt that the Giants' defense was controlling the game was wiped out in the third quarter, when Lomax was sacked by rookie linebacker Byron Hunt and then by Taylor for 23 yards in losses in a span of three plays. Hunt, who replaced injured Brad Van Pelt, led the Giants with six tackles plus his sack.

The Giants got a bit of offense in the second half, with running back Rob Carpenter contributing 72 of his 117 yards rushing. Carpenter dived one yard for a third-quarter touchdown that made the score 17-3 and Joe Danelo hit a 33-yard field goal in the fourth period to boost the Giants' lead to 20-3. The Cardinals' only touchdown came on a three-yard pass from Lomax to LaFleur with 20 seconds left.

The Giants went into the game with a defensive yield of 4.30 yards per play, best in the NFL. The Cardinals netted 222 yards against them in 56 plays, less than four yards a crack.

"We knew they were going to be good," Lomax said.

DECEMBER 13

SCORE BY PERIODS

New York Giants	7	3	7	3—20
St. Louis	3	0	0	7—10

SCORING

St. Louis—Field goal O'Donoghue 30.
New York—Martin 20 fumble return (Danelo kick).
New York—Field goal Danelo 27.
New York—Carpenter 1 run (Danelo kick).
New York—Field goal Danelo 33.
St. Louis—LaFleur 3 pass from Lomax (O'Donoghue kick).

TEAM STATISTICS

	New York	St. Louis
First downs	16	12
Rushes-Yards	39-175	24-92
Passing yards	77	130
Sacks by-Yards	3-33	1-9
Return yards	109	153
Passes	12-24-1	16-32-2
Punts	6-46.3	8-40.3
Fumbles-Lost	2-1	1-1
Penalties-Yards	7-70	4-30
Time of possession	33:08	26:52
Attendance—47,358.		

INDIVIDUAL STATISTICS

Rushing—New York, Carpenter 26-117, Forte 5-10, Perry 4-21, Brunner 3-2, Bright 1-25; St. Louis, Anderson 18-75, Lomax 2-6, Morris 2-4, Green 1-6, Mitchell 1-1.

Passing—New York, Brunner 12-24-1—86; St. Louis, Lomax 16-31-1—163, Hart 0-1-1—0.

Receiving—New York, Carpenter 3-30, Shirk 3-25, Perkins 2-16, Forte 2-6, Gray 1-11, Bright 1-minus 2; St. Louis, Anderson 6-32, Tilley 3-44, Gray 2-19, Morris 2-16, Green 1-39, Combs 1-10, LaFleur 1-3.

Kickoff Returns—New York, Bright 1-25; St. Louis, Mitchell 4-94, Harrell 1-24.

Punt Returns—New York, Bright 5-22, T. Jackson 1-21; St. Louis, Mitchell 3-18.

Interceptions—New York, Reece 1-32, Haynes 1-9; St. Louis, E. Williams 1-17.

Punting—New York, Jennings 6-46.3; St. Louis, Birdsong 8-40.3.

Field Goals—New York, Danelo 2-3; St. Louis, O'Donoghue 1-1.

BEARS 23, RAIDERS 6

OAKLAND—The cheers he heard in the 1980 season returned for Jim Plunkett in the fourth quarter of Oakland's game with Chicago. But it was a fleeting moment, and Plunkett was unable to pull off a miracle finish in relief of Marc Wilson.

The Bears had a 23-6 lead, thanks to three touchdown passes by Vince Evans and a safety, when the "We want Plunkett" chant began.

Midway through the final period, Wilson was forced out with a thumb injury and Plunkett trotted onto the field. But there was no fairy tale ending this time by the man who had rescued the Raiders and led them to the Super Bowl championship after the 1980 season.

The Bears treated Plunkett the same as they'd treated Wilson—they blitzed him. Plunkett was able to complete only three of eight passes and the Raiders' record fell to 7-8.

Evans threw TD passes of 42 yards and three yards to Rickey Watts and launched a 22-yarder to rookie Ken Margerum, for his first NFL score. The Raiders' TD came on a 27-yard pass from Wilson to Bob Chandler, but the extra-point attempt was blocked by veteran defensive tackle Alan Page. Page set up the TD pass to Margerum with a fumble recovery.

"I just wish we could have played like this all season," Evans said. "This was one of those enjoyable games where the offense and defense put things together."

DECEMBER 13
SCORE BY PERIODS

Chicago	7	0	14	2—23
Oakland	6	0	0	0— 6

SCORING

Chicago—Watts 42 from Evans (Roveto kick).
Oakland—Chandler 27 pass from Wilson (kick blocked).
Chicago—Watts 3 pass from Evans (Roveto kick).
Chicago—Margerum 22 pass from Evans (Roveto kick).
Chicago—Safety, Wilson tackled in end zone.

TEAM STATISTICS

	Chicago	Oakland
First downs	19	15
Rushes-Yards	38-150	17-46
Passing yards	228	217
Sacks by-Yards	6-54	2-12
Return yards	52	86
Passes	15-32-1	20-46-1
Punts	7-41.3	7-40.9
Fumbles-Lost	1-1	3-1
Penalties-Yards	7-60	8-75
Time of possession	34:32	25:28
Attendance—40,834.		

INDIVIDUAL STATISTICS

Rushing—Chicago, Harper 15-49, Evans 5-47, Payton 7-28, Suhey 2-18, McClendon 9-8; Oakland, Whittington 9-32, Jensen 4-10, Hawkins 3-4, Plunkett 1-0.

Passing—Chicago, Evans 15-32-1—240; Oakland, Wilson 17-38-1—240, Plunkett 3-8-0—31.

Receiving—Chicago, Watts 5-90, Margerum 3-73, Baschnagel 3-45, Payton 3-32, McClendon 1-0; Oakland, Chandler 4-73, Ramsey 4-70, Barnwell 4-54, Hawkins 3-29, Whittington 3-9, Jensen 1-21, Branch 1-15.

Kickoff Returns—Chicago, Moorehead 1-13, J. Fisher 1-21, Baschnagel 1-11; Oakland, Barnwell 2-44, Whittington 1-31.

Punt Returns—Chicago, J. Fisher 1-7; Oakland, Watts 4-11.

Interceptions—Chicago, Fencik 1-0; Oakland, M. Davis 1-0.

Punting—Chicago, Parsons 7-41.3; Oakland, Guy 7-40.9.

Field Goals—Chicago, Roveto 0-1; Oakland, Bahr 0-1.

PACKERS 35, SAINTS 7

NEW ORLEANS—Lynn Dickey threw five touchdown passes, tying a Green Bay club record, as the Packers overwhelmed New Orleans. Dickey completed 19 of 21 passes, a 90.5 percentage.

"It's been a long time coming for me to have one of these kind of days," Dickey said. "You know what it's like. It's a great feeling to see a guy running wide open and being able to just step up and drill it to him."

Dickey threw for 218 yards. His scoring passes went for 24 and 30 yards to John Jefferson, nine yards to Gerry Ellis, 25 yards to James Lofton and two yards to Paul Coffman. Dickey's 90.5 percentage is the second best mark in NFL history, topped only by Ken Anderson's 90.9 (20-for-22) for Cincinnati against Pittsburgh in 1974.

Dickey went into the Green Bay record book with Cecil Isbell and Don Horn when he threw his fifth TD pass. Isbell threw for five against the Cleveland Rams in 1942 and Horn did it against the St. Louis Cardinals in 1969.

The last TD came with 9:37 left in the game, and Dickey did not play the rest of the way. He said the thought of going for a record sixth TD pass against his old Houston coach, Bum Phillips, did not enter his mind.

"If the shoe were on the other foot, I think Bum would have done the same thing," Dickey said. "I had no itch to get in there and score again. I don't think it (a possible record) proves anything."

Lofton had three receptions for 52 yards and set a Green Bay record for season yardage. His total of 1,267 topped the old mark of 1,231 set by Bill Howton in 1952.

DECEMBER 13
SCORE BY PERIODS

Green Bay	14	7	7	7—35
New Orleans	0	0	7	0— 7

SCORING

Green Bay—Ellis 9 pass from Dickey (Stenerud kick).
Green Bay—Jefferson 24 pass from Dickey (Stenerud kick).
Green Bay—Lofton 25 pass from Dickey (Stenerud kick).
New Orleans—G. Rogers 1 run (Ricardo kick).
Green Bay—Coffman 2 pass from Dickey (Stenerud kick).
Green Bay—Jefferson 30 pass from Dickey (Stenerud kick).

TEAM STATISTICS

	Green Bay	New Orleans
First downs	17	16
Rushes-Yards	29-116	34-87
Passing yards	202	165
Sacks by-Yards	0-0	2-16
Return yards	139	164
Passes	19-21-0	14-21-4
Punts	4-43.5	3-41.3
Fumbles-Lost	1-1	2-2
Penalties-Yards	4-30	1-12
Time of possession	28:53	31:07
Attendance—45,518.		

INDIVIDUAL STATISTICS

Rushing—Green Bay, Ellis 11-64, Huckleby 10-29, Middleton 4-13, Jensen 4-10; New Orleans, G. Rogers 26-70, Tyler 2-9, Stauch 1-5, J. Rogers 3-2, Holmes 1-2, Groth 1-minus 1.

Passing—Green Bay, Dickey 19-21-0—218; New Orleans, Manning 10-15-3—121, D. Wilson 4-6-1—44.

Receiving—Green Bay, Jefferson 4-91, Lofton 3-52, Coffman 4-30, Ellis 5-26, Lewis 1-7, Huckleby 1-6, Middleton 1-6; New Orleans, Merkens 3-67, Brenner 1-26, Tyler 1-18, Hardy 1-16, Groth 2-15, J. Rogers 1-9, Stauch 1-7, G. Rogers 2-4, Holmes 2-3.

Kickoff Returns—Green Bay, Huckleby 2-21; New Orleans, J. Rogers 2-43, W. Wilson 4-79.

Fifteenth Week—Continued

Punt Returns—Green Bay, Lee 1-3, Nixon 2-10; New Orleans, Groth 4-42.

Interceptions—Green Bay, Harvey 2-99, McCoy 1-4, Cumby 1-2.

Punting—Green Bay, Stachowicz 4-43.5; New Orleans, Erxleben 3-41.3.

Field Goals—Green Bay, None attempted; New Orleans, None attempted.

REDSKINS 38, COLTS 14

WASHINGTON—Coach Joe Gibbs breathed a sigh of relief and said, "I'm glad that's over. It was a hard game to prepare for, very hard."

Baltimore carried a 13-game losing streak into the game against Washington, and Gibbs was worried. "We had to be aggressive and go after them making sure we were trying to win, not avoiding a loss," said Gibbs. "We couldn't sit back and wait."

Gibbs need not have worried so much. The Redskins piled up 486 yards, with Joe Theismann passing for 339 yards. He had touchdown passes of 38 yards to Virgil Seay and 13 yards to Art Monk, and ran eight yards to score on a quarterback draw. John Riggins had TD runs of eight and 14 yards and Mark Moseley kicked a 32-yard field goal.

Bert Jones passed 10 yards to Ray Butler and six yards to Reese McCall for the Colts' TDs.

Coach Mike McCormack was joined on the sideline by Colts owner Robert Irsay for most of the game. Irsay confined himself to a cheerleading role and did not call any plays, as he had done from the press box in an earlier game.

DECEMBER 13

SCORE BY PERIODS

Baltimore	7	0	7	0—14
Washington	7	21	10	0—38

SCORING

Washington—Seay 38 pass from Theismann (Moseley kick).

Baltimore—Butler 10 pass from B. Jones (Wood kick).

Washington—Riggins 8 run (Moseley kick).

Washington—Riggins 14 run (Moseley kick).

Washington—Theismann 8 run (Moseley kick).

Washington—Monk 13 pass from Theismann (Moseley kick).

Baltimore—McCall 6 pass from B. Jones (Wood kick).

Washington—Field goal Moseley 32.

TEAM STATISTICS

	Baltimore	Washington
First downs	21	27
Rushes-Yards	33-120	34-147
Passing yards	217	339
Sacks by-Yards	0-0	1-0
Return yards	125	95
Passes	14-25-2	23-36-1
Punts	3-34.7	2-33.5
Fumbles-Lost	0-0	0-0
Penalties-Yards	3-73	6-60
Time of possession	26:27	33:33
Attendance—46,706.		

INDIVIDUAL STATISTICS

Rushing—Baltimore, Dickey 17-56, McMillan 12-47, B. Jones 2-5, Dixon 2-12; Washington, Riggins 7-50, Washington 20-73, Giaquinto 5-12, Theismann 2-12.

Passing—Baltimore, B. Jones 14-25-2—217; Washington, Theismann 23-36-1—339.

Receiving—Baltimore, Carr 6-114, McMillan 2-21, McCall 3-43, Butler 3-39; Washington, Monk 7-148, Washington 5-61, Warren 1-7, Seay 7-104, Metcalf 2-9, Walker 1-10.

Kickoff Returns—Baltimore, Dixon 6-96, Shula 1-15; Washington, Nelms 2-41, Claitt 1-14.

Punt Returns—Baltimore, Shula 1-2; Washington, Nelms 2-29.

Interceptions—Baltimore, Laird 1-12; Washington, Murphy 1-11, Peters 1-0.

Punting—Baltimore, Garrett 3-34.7; Washington, Connell 2-33.5.

Field Goals—Baltimore, Wood 0-1; Washington, Moseley 1-1.

BRONCOS 23, SEAHAWKS 13

DENVER—Five Seattle fumbles plus the inability of the Seahawks to score a touchdown were the key factors in the game played in an on-again, off-again snowstorm in Denver. The victory put Denver one step closer to its third AFC West championship.

The Broncos hiked their record to 10-5 and remained one game ahead of San Diego in the division race. The Broncos needed a victory at Chicago in their final regular-season game to clinch the title.

Two of the Seahawks' fumbles stopped drives deep in Broncos' territory. In addition, the Seahawks marched to the Denver 1-yard line in the third quarter, but couldn't score a touchdown as Theotis Brown was nailed for a loss on third-and-goal.

Dave Krieg, quarterbacking his second game in place of injured Jim Zorn, wasn't as sharp as when he led the Seahawks to an upset of the Jets the previous week. Krieg completed 18 of 40 passes for 219 yards and one touchdown.

Craig Morton threw for 144 yards, including a 22-yard touchdown strike to Riley Odoms, bringing his season passing yardage to 3,107. That broke the previous club record of 3,038 set by Frank Tripucka in 1960.

The Broncos' other points came on an eight-yard run by Rick Parros and field goals of 33, 43 and 24 yards by Fred Steinfort.

The Seahawks' lone touchdown was a five-yard pass from Krieg to fullback David Hughes with only three seconds left. Wilson Alvarez added field goals of 28 and 20 yards.

"Coming in, I thought Denver was the best club in the division, and I have no reason to change my mind now," said Seahawks Coach Jack Patera, whose team fell to 5-10. "They've been playing exceptionally well. They're alone at the top and that's where they should be."

DECEMBER 13

SCORE BY PERIODS

Seattle	0	3	3	7—13
Denver	7	3	6	7—23

Denver—Odoms 22 pass from Morton (Steinfort kick).
Seattle—Field goal Alvarez 28.
Denver—Field goal Steinfort 33.
Denver—Field goal Steinfort 43.
Denver—Field goal Steinfort 24.
Seattle—Field goal Alvarez 20.
Denver—Parros 8 run (Steinfort kick).
Seattle—Hughes 5 pass from Krieg (Alvarez kick).

TEAM STATISTICS

	Seattle	Denver
First downs	18	23
Rushes-Yards	27-86	41-237
Passing yards	199	136
Sacks by-Yards	1-8	2-20
Return yards	129	60
Passes	18-40-0	15-30-2
Punts	4-34.8	4-37.5
Fumbles-Lost	6-5	1-1
Penalties-Yards	8-70	11-99
Time of possession	25:22	34:38

Attendance—74,527.

INDIVIDUAL STATISTICS

Rushing—Seattle, Doornink 6-22, Krieg 4-21, Largent 2-21, T. Brown 11-12, Smith 2-6, Hughes 1-4, West 1-0; Denver, Parros 16-82, Preston 13-59, Lytle 8-41, Upchurch 1-37, Canada 3-18.

Passing—Seattle, Krieg 18-40-0—219; Denver, Morton 15-30-2—144.

Receiving—Seattle, Largent 3-72, Smith 5-46, McCullum 3-39, Sawyer 1-26, Doornink 4-23, T. Brown 1-8, Hughes 1-5; Denver, Odoms 2-38, Lytle 4-30, Parros 1-19, Egloff 3-17, Preston 2-16, Canada 1-14, Upchurch 2-10.

Kickoff Returns—Seattle, Ivory 1-22, Dufek 1-17; Denver, Harden 1-11, Lytle 2-39.

Punt Returns—Seattle, Johns 1-22, Johnson 1-16; Denver, Upchurch 2-10.

Interceptions—Seattle, Harris 1-22, Easley 1-30.

Punting—Seattle, West 4-34.8; Denver, Prestridge 4-37.5.

Field Goals—Seattle, Alvarez 2-2; Denver, Steinfort 3-3.

49ers 28, OILERS 6

SAN FRANCISCO—This was supposed to be a playoffs tuneup for San Francisco, but Coach Bill Walsh wasn't able to pull his regulars until the final quarter. That's because the Houston defense shut out the 49ers until collapsing in a 21-point explosion in the third period.

"We wanted to use this game as a learning experience," said Walsh, "and, in some ways, it was. Our backup players showed well, especially Guy Benjamin, and that has to help us later on (in the playoffs)."

Joe Montana completed 18 of 26 passes for 204 yards and one touchdown in his three quarters. Benjamin quarterbacked the fourth period and was 7-for-9 for 82 yards and one TD.

Ricky Patton and Earl Cooper each scored on a three-yard run for the 49ers in the third quarter and Montana threw a two-yard TD pass to wide receiver Dwight Clark. Benjamin's scoring pass was a 27-yarder to Mike Wilson.

Clark caught five passes, giving him a 49ers

season record with 84 receptions. The old one-year mark was 83, set in 1980 by Cooper.

The San Francisco defense held Houston to 186 yards and limited Earl Campbell to 45 yards rushing. Campbell ran for the Oilers' TD in the game's final minute.

DECEMBER 13
SCORE BY PERIODS

Houston	0	0	0	6—	6
San Francisco	0	0	21	7—	28

SCORING

San Francisco—Patton 3 run (Wersching kick).
San Francisco—Cooper 3 run (Wersching kick).
San Francisco—Clark 2 pass from Montana (Wersching kick).
San Francisco—Wilson 27 pass from Benjamin (Wersching kick).
Houston—Campbell 1 run (kick blocked).

TEAM STATISTICS

	Houston	San Fran.
First downs	11	22
Rushes-Yards	22-56	29-148
Passing yards	130	266
Sacks by-Yards	2-20	1-10
Return yards	163	34
Passes	21-30-0	25-35-0
Punts	7-36.4	6-42.3
Fumbles-Lost	2-2	3-0
Penalties-Yards	8-47	8-77
Time of possession	27:40	32:20

Attendance—55,707.

INDIVIDUAL STATISTICS

Rushing—Houston, Campbell 18-45, Armstrong 3-11, Nielsen 1-0; San Francisco, Patton 9-57, Cooper 7-38, Ring 5-18, Clark 1-18, Davis 5-15, Montana 2-2.

Passing—Houston, Nielsen 21-30-0—140; San Francisco, Montana 18-26-0—204, Benjamin 7-9-0—82.

Receiving—Houston, Armstrong 9-62, Burrough 4-14, Casper 3-44, Coleman 2-11, Holston 2-7, Campbell 1-2; San Francisco, Cooper 6-77, Clark 5-35, Young 4-36, Solomon 3-56, Wilson 2-36, Ring 2-24, Ramson 1-14, Hofer 1-11, Patton 1-minus 3.

Kickoff Returns—Houston, Roaches 2-32, Tullis 1-17, Hunt 1-2, Riley 1-51; San Francisco, Ring 1-18.

Punt Returns—Houston, Roaches 5-61; San Francisco, Hicks 3-14, Solomon 2-2.

Interceptions—None.

Punting—Houston, Parsley 7-36.4; San Francisco, Miller 6-42.3.

Field Goals—Houston, None attempted; San Francisco, None attempted.

RAMS 21, FALCONS 16

ANAHEIM—It was a game the Atlanta Falcons desperately needed to win. They entered this Monday night encounter with the Los Angeles Rams with a 7-7 record and needed victories in their last two games to have a shot at the remaining wild-card playoff berth in the NFC. But for Falcon fans, they'll just have to wait until 1982—the Rams won this pivotal game, 21-16.

"It looks like we finally ran out of chances," said Atlanta quarterback Steve Bartkowski. "We were simply outplayed in this game."

It was a game the much-maligned Rams wanted just as bad as the favored Falcons. Entering the contest with a 5-9 record and out of the playoff picture, the Los Angeles players had something to prove. "We all wanted this one just for us," said linebacker Jim Youngblood. "This meant a lot."

It was a see-saw game from start to finish. The Falcons took the early lead when running back Lynn Cain bolted over from the 2-yard line in the opening period. The Rams countered that score with a touchdown of their own in the second quarter. Wendell Tyler, who later in the game would go over the 1,000-yard mark for the season, scored from six yards out to tie the score at 7-7.

Atlanta rebounded to take the lead again when Mick Luckhurst hit on a 45-yard field goal. But the play of the game came shortly thereafter.

With Atlanta leading, 10-7, late in the first half, the Falcons had the ball on the Ram 11-yard line and appeared on the verge of scoring another touchdown. Los Angeles safety Nolan Cromwell, however, had different ideas. He intercepted a Bartkowski pass three yards deep in the end zone and brought it back 94 yards. Mike Guman carried it over from the 2-yard line to give the Rams the lead. A probable 17-7 Atlanta lead was quickly turned into a 14-10 Ram advantage.

"I felt the key (to the game) was the interception by Nolan Cromwell when it looked like we were going to score," said Falcons Coach Leeman Bennett. "That was a swing of 10 or 14 points."

The Falcons were able to rebound on the strength of two second-half Luckhurst field goals to regain the lead at 16-14. But their defense couldn't stop the Rams when they had to. The Rams traveled 80 yards with the help of two critical pass-interference calls against the Falcons' Bobby Butler and Kenny Johnson.

Tyler then took it over from the 7 for his second TD of the night to clinch the Rams' victory.

MONDAY, DECEMBER 14

SCORE BY PERIODS

Atlanta	7	3	3	3—16
Los Angeles	0	14	0	7—21

SCORING

Atlanta—Cain 2 run (Luckhurst kick).
Los Angeles—Tyler 6 run (Corral kick).
Atlanta—Field goal Luckhurst 45.
Los Angeles—Guman 2 run (Corral kick).
Atlanta—Field goal Luckhurst 25.
Atlanta—Field goal Luckhurst 22.
Los Angeles—Tyler 7 run (Corral kick).

TEAM STATISTICS

	Atlanta	Los Angeles
First downs	16	19
Rushes-Yards	30-122	45-162
Passing yards	130	111
Sacks by-Yards	0-0	3-30
Return yards	177	222
Passes	14-36-2	11-22-2

	Atlanta	Los Angeles
Punts	8-30.6	5-38.6
Fumbles-Lost	0-0	5-3
Penalties-Yards	5-89	7-55
Time of possession	30:11	29:49

Attendance—57,054.

INDIVIDUAL STATISTICS

Rushing—Atlanta, Cain 7-7, Andrews 23-115; Los Angeles, Tyler 22-79, Guman 18-70, J. Thomas 1-2, D. Hill 1-14, Pastorini 3-minus 3.

Passing—Atlanta, Bartkowski 14-36-2—160; Los Angeles, Pastorini 11-22-2—111.

Receiving—Atlanta, Cain 1-5, Andrews 2-3, Miller 3-48, Jenkins 4-67, Francis 2-18, Jackson 2-19; Los Angeles, Waddy 5-94, Guman 2-8, Arnold 1-4, Tyler 3-5.

Kickoff Returns—Atlanta, R. Smith 2-68, Gaison 1-24; Los Angeles, D. Hill 4-78, Guman 1-10.

Punt Returns—Atlanta, Woerner 2-37; Los Angeles, Irvin 5-41.

Interceptions—Atlanta, E. Jones 1-39, Richardson 1-9; Los Angeles, Cromwell 1-94, Perry 1-minus 1.

Punting—Atlanta, James 8-30.6; Los Angeles, Corral 5-38.6.

Field Goals—Atlanta, Luckhurst 3-3; Los Angeles, Corral 0-1.

SIXTEENTH WEEK

GIANTS 13, COWBOYS 10 (Overtime)

EAST RUTHERFORD—All things considered, the New York Giants would rather be in Philadelphia.

And that's exactly where the Giants were headed as they qualified to face the Eagles in the NFC wild-card playoff game. The trip to the playoffs was the Giants' first since 1963, when they lost to the Chicago Bears, 14-10, in the National Football League championship game.

The Giants raised their 1981 record to 9-7 with a dramatic 13-10 victory in overtime against the Dallas Cowboys at Giants Stadium. Then they had to wait until the next day—the last Sunday of the regular season—to find out whether they were a wild-card entry or just another also-ran.

"This means I can hold my head up at league meetings," Giants President Wellington Mara said after the New York Jets routed the Green Bay Packers, 28-3, to put both New York teams in the playoffs. "It's been a long time for me without a playoff game. It was strange rooting for the Jets, but I had to do it."

The entire Giants family watched the playoff berth become a reality as they viewed the Jets-Packers game on television in the press lounge at Giants Stadium.

"We got into the playoffs approaching a peak, which is exactly what you aim for," said Giants Coach Ray Perkins.

Placekicker Joe Danelo delivered a 35-yard field goal 6:19 into overtime to beat the Cowboys (he missed a 33-yarder earlier in the extra session when his kick hit the upright).

As usual, the Giants' stout defense was the

key factor in the victory. Tony Dorsett, seeking to become the first Cowboy to win the NFL rushing title, was held to 39 yards in 21 carries and wound up the season at 1,646 yards. New Orleans rookie George Rogers passed him on the final day and won the title with 1,674 yards.

Dorsett had two costly fumbles against the Giants. The first was recovered by George Martin at the Dallas 45 with 2:08 left in regulation time. Scott Brunner's 22-yard pass to John Mistler on fourth-and-13 set up a game-tying 40-yard field goal by Danelo.

Dorsett fumbled again in overtime, with Lawrence Taylor recovering, just after Dallas appeared to have taken good field position near midfield after forcing a Giants punt. Brunner rambled 23 yards on a bootleg to set up Danelo's 33-yard field-goal try that hit the upright. But then rookie linebacker Byron Hunt intercepted a Danny White pass at the Dallas 31, leading to the winning field goal.

"We knew that the only way the Giants could beat us was to make mistakes and give them the ball in good field position—and that's exactly what we did," said White.

Dallas	0	0	0	10	0—10
New York Giants	0	0	7	3	3—13

SCORING

New York—Mullady 20 pass from Brunner (Danelo kick).
Dallas—Cosbie 3 pass from D. White (Septien kick).
Dallas—Field goal Septien 36.
New York—Field goal Danelo 40.
New York—Field goal Danelo 35.

TEAM STATISTICS

	Dallas	New York
First downs	16	15
Rushes-Yards	34-90	40-139
Passing yards	164	158
Sacks by-Yards	1-5	4-36
Return yards	40	79
Passes	17-33-1	13-27-1
Punts	7-39.7	5-40.0
Fumbles-Lost	5-2	4-1
Penalties-Yards	8-70	5-42
Time of possession	34:07	32:12

Attendance—73,009.

INDIVIDUAL STATISTICS

Rushing—Dallas, Dorsett 21-39, Springs 11-43, D. White 2-8; New York, Carpenter 29-83, Perry 6-22, Brunner 2-23, Bright 1-3, Forte 2-8.

Passing—Dallas, D. White 17-33-1—200; New York, Brunner 13-27-1—163.

Receiving—Dallas, Springs 3-16, Dorsett 2-16, Cosbie 3-27, DuPree 3-44, J. Jones 3-13, Hill 2-61, Pearson 1-23; New York, Young 3-36, Gray 2-35, Pittman 1-8, Carpenter 2-11, Perry 1-16, Mullady 1-20, Mistler 3-37.

Kickoff Returns—Dallas, J. Jones 2-33; New York, Bright 2-48, Pittman 1-0.

Punt Returns—Dallas, J. Jones 2-7; New York, Bright 3-24, Reece 1-0.

Interceptions—Dallas, Downs 1-0; New York, Hunt 1-7.

Punting—Dallas, D. White 7-39.7; New York, Jennings 5-40.0.

Field Goals—Dallas, Septien 1-2; New York, Danelo 2-5.

DOLPHINS 16, BILLS 6

MIAMI—It took all season, but Miami finally gained the respect it was fighting for with the victory over Buffalo for the AFC East title.

The Dolphins finished the regular season 11-4-1 and were to get a week off before being host to their first playoff game.

"For a bunch of guys who were a lot of question marks, they've been able to answer a lot of those questions," said Dolphins Coach Don Shula.

The Dolphins drove 58 yards in 13 plays for running back Tommy Vigorito's seven-yard touchdown catch of a David Woodley pass on their first possession. The march consumed 5:20 of the first quarter as the Dolphins, with running back Eddie Hill subbing for injured Tony Nathan, stayed mostly on the ground.

The Dolphins drove again midway in the second quarter, starting from their 20-yard line and moving to the Bills' 4 before stalling. Woodley sparked the drive with completions of 16 and 33 yards to Joe Rose and scrambles of 18 and six yards to set up Uwe von Schamann's 22-yard field goal.

At the end of the second quarter, the Bills moved 66 yards in 11 plays, but couldn't punch the ball over the goal line, settling for Nick Mike-Mayer's 31-yard field goal.

In the third quarter, von Schamann connected from 30 yards to give the Dolphins a 13-3 cushion.

The Bills, who haven't won in the Orange Bowl since 1966, crept within a touchdown when Mike-Mayer hit from 36 yards with 9:09 left. But von Schamann put the game out of reach with 2:15 left by kicking a 34-yard field goal—his 17th in his last 19 tries.

"The only good part about the loss is that a lot of teams are going home after tomorrow and we aren't," said Bills Coach Chuck Knox.

"This game was no mystery, it was just a tough, tight game. We had plenty of chances to get it in the end zone, but we couldn't get it in when it counted."

Buffalo	0	3	0	3— 6
Miami	7	3	3	3—16

SCORING

Miami—Vigorito 7 pass from Woodley (von Schamann kick).
Miami—Field goal von Schamann 22.
Buffalo—Field goal Mike-Mayer 31.
Miami—Field goal von Schamann 30.
Buffalo—Field goal Mike-Mayer 36.
Miami—Field goal von Schamann 34.

TEAM STATISTICS

	Buffalo	Miami
First downs	15	18
Rushes-Yards	23-111	47-157
Passing yards	129	125
Sacks by-Yards	4-26	1-11
Return yards	105	96

	Buffalo	Miami
Passes	14-30-2	11-22-0
Punts	5-37.4	5-39.0
Fumbles-Lost	1-1	1-1
Penalties-Yards	6-39	4-20
Time of possession	23:52	36:08
Attendance—72,956.		

INDIVIDUAL STATISTICS

Rushing—Buffalo, Leaks 6-17, Cribbs 17-94; Miami, Franklin 15-49, Hill 13-27, Woodley 15-52, Vigorito 4-29.

Passing—Buffalo, Ferguson 14-29-2—140, Leaks 0-1-0—0; Miami, Woodley 10-21-0—137, Hill 1-1-0—14.

Receiving—Buffalo, Cribbs 4-26, Lewis 4-59, Leaks 3-26, Piccone 1-15, Hooks 2-14; Miami, Moore 1-5, Cefalo 1-7, Vigorito 1-7, Rose 3-69, Hardy 3-55, Hill 1-2, Harris 1-6.

Kickoff Returns—Buffalo, Riddick 3-60; Miami, Bessillieu 1-7, Vigorito 2-48.

Punt Returns—Buffalo, Piccone 1-4, Riddick 3-41; Miami, Vigorito 1-12.

Interceptions—Miami, Kozlowski 2-29.

Punting—Buffalo, Cater 5-37.4; Miami, Orosz 5-39.0.

Field Goals—Buffalo, Mike-Mayer 2-3; Miami, von Schamann 3-3.

JETS 28, PACKERS 3

NEW YORK—Christmas came five days early in New York as the Jets crushed the Green Bay Packers, 28-3, in Shea Stadium to earn an AFC wild-card playoff berth.

The Jets captured their first playoff berth in 12 years by finishing the regular season 10-5-1 and in second place in the AFC East, one game back of Miami.

Kevin Long and Bruce Harper scored on short runs and Richard Todd threw touchdown passes of 47 yards to Lam Jones and 38 yards to Wesley Walker for the Jets.

Meanwhile, the Jets' defense overwhelmed the Packers. The Jets bottled up the Packers' explosive receivers, James Lofton and John Jefferson, and sacked Lynn Dickey nine times to finish the season with a league-leading 66 sacks.

"A lot of people talk about a good defensive team in this area," Jets Coach Walt Michaels said, referring to the New York Giants. "Well, I saw another one today. I feel good; it's always great when you make the playoffs. I also feel good for management. When we were 0-3 early this year and things looked darkest, they were the brightest."

The Jets' front four—Joe Klecko, Marty Lyons, Abdul Salaam and Mark Gastineau—hounded Dickey throughout the game. Even when Klecko missed much of the second quarter with a foot injury, rookie Kenny Neil came in and kept the pressure on.

"We were conscious of the (sacks) record and it's too bad we missed," said Klecko. "But the playoffs are the most important thing. I thought our defense was simply superb. When you allow a professional team less than 100 yards total offense (84 yards), it's got to give

you quite a bit of gratification."

Packers Coach Bart Starr admitted his team was outclassed. "Except for a few plays defensively and a few offensively, we didn't do anything," said Starr. The Packers finished 8-8 and tied for second in the NFC Central Division.

The Jets needed just 2:18 to go ahead, then scored two more touchdowns in the second quarter to take a 21-3 halftime lead.

After the Packers were stopped on their first possession, rookie punter Ray Stachowicz had trouble with a low snap from center, was forced to run and his desperation punt was blocked by Al Washington.

The Jets took over at the Packers' 11-yard line, and three plays later, Long ran one yard for a TD.

The Jets chewed up the next 9:43 of the second quarter, after a Green Bay field goal, by moving 80 yards in 20 plays for a 14-3 lead. The Jets converted five third-down situations as Todd hit passes of 16 yards to Walker, 13 to Harper, eight to Jones and seven to running back Scott Dierking to set up third-and-goal at the Packers' 3. Harper ran for the score with 1:57 left in the half.

The Jets got the ball back with 55 seconds left and Todd hit Jones streaking down the right sideline for a third TD 42 seconds before halftime.

DECEMBER 20

SCORE BY PERIODS

Green Bay	0	3	0	0—	3
New York Jets	7	14	0	7—	28

SCORING

New York—Long 1 run (Leahy kick).
Green Bay—Field goal Stenerud 31.
New York—Harper 3 run (Leahy kick).
New York—L. Jones 47 pass from Todd (Leahy kick).
New York—Walker 38 pass from Todd (Leahy kick).

TEAM STATISTICS

	Green Bay	New York
First downs	8	22
Rushes-Yards	15-45	49-153
Passing yards	39	240
Sacks by-Yards	1-7	9-57
Return yards	77	59
Passes	12-33-1	15-33-1
Punts	9-34.2	4-32.5
Fumbles-Lost	6-2	3-3
Penalties-Yards	3-16	5-53
Time of possession	20:03	39:57
Attendance—56,340.		

INDIVIDUAL STATISTICS

Rushing—Green Bay, Ellis 11-44, Huckleby 2-1, Dickey 2-0; New York, McNeil 18-70, Long 15-57, Dierking 7-20, Newton 2-7, Harper 4-1, Todd 3-minus 2.

Passing—Green Bay, Dickey 12-33-1—96; New York, Todd 15-33-1—247.

Receiving—Green Bay, Jefferson 2-39, Lofton 2-27, Huckleby 2-14, Ellis 4-14, Coffman 2-2; New York, L. Jones 3-68, Dierking 3-38, Harper 3-30, Barkum 2-29, Walker 2-54, B. Jones 1-19, McNeil 1-9.

Kickoff Returns—Green Bay, McCoy 3-35, Middleton 2-35; New York, Harper 2-27.

Punt Returns—Green Bay, Lee 1-0, Nixon 1-0; New York, Harper 4-22.

Interceptions—Green Bay, Murphy 1-7; New York, Mehl 1-10.

Punting—Green Bay, Stachowicz 8-38.5; New York, Ramsey 4-32.5.

Field Goals—Green Bay, Stenerud 1-1; New York, Leahy 0-2.

BUCS 20, LIONS 17

PONTIAC—"In a championship game," said Detroit Coach Monte Clark, "you have to make championship plays. They made those plays, and we were a little bit short."

That was the story of Tampa Bay's triumph in the Silverdome before a crowd of 80,444—largest turnout ever for a regular-season game. Detroit hadn't lost in its first seven home games and could have made it an 8-0 home season except for the Bucs' championship plays.

Three times, the Lions were inside the Tampa Bay 15-yard line and failed to score. Two of those thrusts were stopped on interceptions by safety Cedric Brown and on the other drive, Eddie Murray missed on a 34-yard field-goal attempt.

Detroit had a 7-3 lead and was moving toward a second score in the second period when Brown intercepted an Eric Hipple pass at the Tampa Bay 3-yard line and made a nine-yard return before fumbling out of bounds at the 16.

On the first play, quarterback Doug Williams cranked up and fired a bomb to wide receiver Kevin House, who caught the ball on the Detroit 46 and raced into the end zone. That made the score 10-7 at the half.

Detroit tied the score on a 47-yard field goal by Murray before the Bucs wrapped up their victory by scoring 10 points in a span of 70 seconds early in the final period. A 35-yard pass from Williams to James Owens, who caught the ball while flat on his back, set up a 30-yard field goal by Bill Capece that put the Bucs ahead, 13-10.

On Detroit's next possession, Hipple faded back to pass and was hit by defensive end Lee Roy Selmon, forcing a fumble. Nose tackle David Logan scooped up the ball at the Detroit 21 and ran untouched into the end zone. That made the score 20-10.

Detroit quickly marched to the Tampa Bay 13, but Hipple's pass bounced off the shoulder pads of wide receiver Fred Scott and Brown plucked off his second interception in the end zone.

Hipple managed an eight-yard TD pass to Leonard Thompson with 1:21 left, but the Bucs' Theo Bell then recovered an onside kickoff and Tampa Bay ran out the clock.

DECEMBER 20

SCORE BY PERIODS

Tampa Bay	3	7	0	10—20
Detroit	0	7	3	7—17

SCORING

Tampa Bay—Field goal Capece 40.
Detroit—Hipple 9 run (Murray kick).
Tampa Bay—House 84 pass from Williams (Capece kick).
Detroit—Field goal Murray 47.
Tampa Bay—Field goal Capece 30.
Tampa Bay—Logan 21 fumble return (Capece kick).
Detroit—L. Thompson 8 pass from Hipple (Murray kick).

TEAM STATISTICS

	Tampa Bay	Detroit
First downs	11	21
Rushes-Yards	23-104	35-159
Passing yards	172	181
Sacks by-Yards	4-24	0-0
Return yards	90	182
Passes	8-19-0	18-28-2
Punts	5-42.2	4-39.5
Fumbles-Lost	1-0	4-1
Penalties-Yards	5-33	6-40
Time of possession	25:51	34:09
Attendance—80,444.		

INDIVIDUAL STATISTICS

Rushing—Tampa Bay, Owens 7-61, Wilder 8-28, Williams 6-8, Eckwood 2-7; Detroit, Sims 19-76, V. Thompson 4-29, Bussey 4-24, Hipple 4-19, Kane 2-7, L. Thompson 2-4.

Passing—Tampa Bay, Williams 8-19-0-172; Detroit, Hipple 18-28-2-205.

Receiving—Tampa Bay, Owens 2-49, Giles 2-19, House 1-84, T. Bell 1-9, Wilder 1-8, Eckwood 1-3; Detroit, Bussey 4-32, Scott 3-56, Sims 3-39, L. Thompson 3-34, Hill 3-33, Kane 1-6, V. Thompson 1-5.

Kickoff Returns—Tampa Bay, Holt 2-45; Detroit, Hall 1-21, Martin 4-105.

Punt Returns—Tampa Bay, T. Bell 3-24, Colzie 1-12; Detroit, Martin 5-56.

Interceptions—Tampa Bay, Brown 2-9.

Punting—Tampa Bay, Swider 5-42.2; Detroit, Skladany 4-39.5.

Field Goals—Tampa Bay, Capece 2-2; Detroit, Murray 1-2.

EAGLES 38, CARDINALS 0

PHILADELPHIA—As Philadelphia struggled through a four-game losing streak that took the Eagles out of the chase for the NFC East title, quarterback Ron Jaworski took the heat. He was the target of boo-birds at Veterans Stadium.

Before the Eagles ended their skid with the easy victory over St. Louis, backup quarterback Joe Pisarcik had leaned into the trainers' room and called to Jaworski, "Hey, Jaws, they're out there waiting for you."

Sure enough. As Jaworski stepped onto the field, he was greeted with a chorus of boos. But by the time Jaworski had stepped off the field in the third period, he had won over most of the fans and the Eagles had clinched the home field for the NFC wild-card playoff game.

Jaworski threw three touchdown passes against the patchwork St. Louis secondary and finished his day's work with 13 completions in 19 attempts for 172 yards. Wilbert Montgomery added 108 yards in rushing on 13 carries and went over the 5,000-yard mark in career rushing.

Sixteenth Week—Continued

The Eagles rolled up 444 yards in total offense. Philadelphia's defense was solid, too, holding the Cardinals to just 67 yards the first three quarters. The Eagles fought off two scoring threats in the final period to preserve their first 1981 shutout and finish the season as the NFL's best defense against scoring (221 points allowed).

"No doubt about it, they definitely were fired up," said St. Louis quarterback Neil Lomax, who was sacked seven times, intercepted three times and lost one fumble. "They put a lot of pressure on me. We didn't execute and they did."

Jaworski's three TD passes went to Charlie Smith, Harold Carmichael and Billy Campfield.

DECEMBER 20
SCORE BY PERIODS

St. Louis	0	0	0	0— 0
Philadelphia	7	21	10	0—38

SCORING

Philadelphia—C. Smith 4 pass from Jaworski (Franklin kick).
Philadelphia—Montgomery 9 run (Franklin kick).
Philadelphia—Oliver 18 run (Franklin kick).
Philadelphia—Carmichael 6 pass from Jaworski (Franklin kick).
Philadelphia—Campfield 29 pass from Jaworski (Franklin kick).
Philadelphia—Field goal Franklin 44.

TEAM STATISTICS

	St. Louis	Philadelphia
First downs	11	25
Rushes-Yards	32-139	39-259
Passing yards	72	185
Sacks by-Yards	0-0	7-57
Return yards	133	43
Passes	11-26-3	15-24-2
Punts	6-42.0	2-37.0
Fumbles-Lost	4-3	4-3
Penalties-Yards	8-80	4-20
Time of possession	28:29	31:31
Attendance—56,656.		

INDIVIDUAL STATISTICS

Rushing—St. Louis, Anderson 19-102, Lomax 2-13, Morris 6-9, Mitchell 3-8, Love 1-3, Harrell 1-4; Philadelphia Montgomery 13-108, Murray 10-56, Jaworski 2-34, Oliver 3-26, Russell 5-18, Campfield 3-17, Pisarcik 2-2, Henry 1-minus 2.

Passing—St. Louis, Lomax 11-26-31—29; Philadelphia, Jaworski 13-19-0—172, Pisarcik 2-5-2—13.

Receiving—St. Louis, Tilley 5-61, Green 3-37, Gray 2-11, LaFleur 1-20; Philadelphia, Carmichael 6-67, Campfield 2-32, C. Smith 2-16, Oliver 1-27, Henry 1-22, Krepfle 1-6, Montgomery 1-8, Murray 1-7.

Kickoff Returns—St. Louis, Mitchell 4-98, Griffin 1-8.

Punt Returns—St. Louis, Mitchell 2-21; Philadelphia, Henry 6-42.

Interceptions—St. Louis, Wehrli 2-6; Philadelphia, Edwards 2-1, Sciarra 1-0.

Punting—St. Louis, Birdsong 6-42.0; Philadelphia, Runager 2-37.0.

Field Goals—St. Louis, O'Donoghue 0-1; Philadelphia, Franklin 1-1.

BENGALS 30, FALCONS 28

ATLANTA—Cincinnati's 30-28 victory at Atlanta came down to a 33-yard field-goal attempt that missed as the final gun sounded, but Bengals quarterback Ken Anderson said the victory should have been wrapped up long before.

The Bengals (12-4), AFC Central champs, secured the home-field advantage in the playoffs when Mick Luckhurst hooked the last-second attempt.

Anderson, who passed for 299 yards and two touchdowns, thought the Bengals should have applied the clincher when they were on top, 24-7, in the second quarter.

"We had opportunities to put the game away time and again but didn't," he said. "We knew we were playing for the home-field advantage, but we still didn't play like I thought we should have."

The Falcons, trailing 30-21, drove 97 yards for a touchdown with 1:19 left, then recovered an onside kickoff to set up Luckhurst's final attempt.

"The films will show the pass from center was low and to the left, which affected me but shouldn't have," said Luckhurst. "John James (the holder) took it and made a perfect hold, but I hurried the kick and hooked it."

The Falcons' William Andrews gained 63 yards rushing and had another 49 in pass receptions to become the fifth back in NFL history to go over the 2,000-yard mark in combined yardage. His total was 2,037.

DECEMBER 20
SCORE BY PERIODS

Cincinnati	10	17	0	3—30
Atlanta	0	21	0	7—28

SCORING

Cincinnati—M.L. Harris 21 pass from Anderson (Breech kick).
Cincinnati—Field goal Breech 25.
Atlanta—Cain 10 pass from Bartkowski (Luckhurst kick).
Cincinnati—Collinsworth 74 pass from Anderson (Breech kick).
Cincinnati—Griffin 18 run (Breech kick).
Atlanta—Andrews 1 run (Luckhurst kick).
Atlanta—Andrews 1 run (Luckhurst kick).
Cincinnati—Field goal Breech 29.
Cincinnati—Field goal Breech 20.
Atlanta—Cain 3 run (Luckhurst kick).

TEAM STATISTICS

	Cincinnati	Atlanta
First downs	23	26
Rushes-Yards	27-133	28-91
Passing yards	300	237
Sacks by-Yards	2-15	2-12
Return yards	101	151
Passes	19-35-1	25-47-1
Punts	4-38.5	5-39.2
Fumbles-Lost	0-0	2-0
Penalties-Yards	11-100	6-35
Time of possession	30:29	29:31
Attendance—35,972.		

INDIVIDUAL STATISTICS

Rushing—Cincinnati, Johnson 14-66, Alexander

8-33, Griffin 3-27, Anderson 2-7; Atlanta, Andrews 18-63, Cain 6-22, Mayberry 1-2, Moroski 2-3, Bartkowski 1-1.

Passing—Cincinnati, Anderson 18-34-1—299, Kreider 1-1-0—13; Atlanta, Bartkowski 14-23-1—122, Moroski 11-23-0—130, James 0-1-0—0.

Receiving—Cincinnati, Collinsworth 5-128, Ross 4-54, Johnson 2-26, Alexander 2-25, Kreider 2-22, M.L. Harris 1-21, Griffin 1-15, Curtis 1-15, Verser 1-6; Atlanta, Cain 7-61, Andrews 6-49, Jackson 3-57, Francis 3-38, Jenkins, 2-26, Miller 2-23, Mayberry 2-minus 2.

Kickoff Returns—Cincinnati, Verser 4-75; Atlanta, R. Smith 6-132.

Punt Returns—Cincinnati, Fuller 2-17; Atlanta, Woerner 2-11.

Interceptions—Cincinnati, Williams 1-9; Atlanta, Johnson 1-8.

Punting—Cincinnati, McInally 4-38.5; Atlanta, James 5-39.2.

Field Goals—Cincinnati, Breech 3-4; Atlanta, Luckhurst 0-2.

49ers 21, SAINTS 17

NEW ORLEANS—"It all turned out well for us, other than losing the game," a smiling George Rogers said after the Saints lost to San Francisco, 21-17, in New Orleans.

The new NFL rushing king shattered Ottis Anderson's record of most yards by a rookie —1,605, set in 1979—and he tied Anderson's record of most 100-yard games by a rookie (nine) when he ran for 107 in 30 carries against the 49ers.

San Francisco finished 13-3 while New Orleans wound up 4-12, but 49ers Coach Bill Walsh praised the Saints, saying they were a team on the rise.

Rogers ran for both New Orleans TDs. Joe Montana threw TD passes to Charle Young and Freddie Solomon, and Johnny Davis plunged for the winning score in the fourth period.

DECEMBER 20
SCORE BY PERIODS

San Francisco	7	7	0	7—21
New Orleans	14	0	3	0—17

SCORING

San Francisco—Young 13 pass from Montana (Wersching kick).
New Orleans—G. Rogers 6 run (Ricardo kick).
New Orleans—G. Rogers 5 run (Ricardo kick).
San Francisco—Solomon 2 pass from Montana (Wersching kick).
New Orleans—Field goal Ricardo 27.
San Francisco—Davis 3 run (Wersching kick).

TEAM STATISTICS

	San Francisco	New Orleans
First downs	19	15
Rushes-Yards	31-154	36-133
Passing yards	195	89
Sacks by-Yards	2-21	0-0
Return yards	74	111
Passes	17-25-1	14-23-1
Punts	4-46.0	4-34.8
Fumbles-Lost	3-2	1-0
Penalties-Yards	6-55	2-10
Time of possession	26:03	33:57
Attendance—43,639.		

Rushing—San Francisco, Patton 8-36, Cooper 1-minus 3, Ring 11-71, Davis 6-19, Montana 1-10, Easley 2-4, Benjamin 1-1, Solomon 1-16; New Orleans, G. Rogers 30-107, Holmes 2-5, J. Rogers 2-18, Tyler 2-3.

Passing—San Francisco, Montana 9-11-0—106, Benjamin 8-14-1—89; New Orleans, Manning 14-21-1—110, D. Wilson 0-2-0—0.

Receiving—San Francisco, Patton 4-25, Solomon 5-38, Young 1-13, Cooper 1-36, Easley 3-35, Clark 1-21, Ramson 2-27; New Orleans, Holmes 1-8, Martini 1-7, Tyler 5-21, Merkens 1-12, Groth 1-10, Hardy 1-8, Thompson 2-21, J. Rogers 1-3, Brenner 1-20.

Kickoff Returns—San Francisco, Ring 2-41, Lawrence 2-24; New Orleans, J. Rogers 1-23, W. Wilson 2-39, Brock 1-6.

Punt Returns—San Francisco, Solomon 1-0; New Orleans, Groth 4-43.

Interceptions—San Francisco, Williamson 1-9; New Orleans, Wattelet 1-0.

Punting—San Francisco, Miller 4-46.0; New Orleans, Erxleben 4-34.8.

Field Goals—San Francisco, None attempted; New Orleans, Ricardo 1-1.

BEARS 35, BRONCOS 24

CHICAGO—Denver could have wrapped up both the AFC West title and a playoff bid with a victory over Chicago, but the Bears, long since out of playoff contention, turned the tables on the Broncos.

"We just have to hope for a miracle from Oakland, and I'd say our chances are slim," said Broncos Coach Dan Reeves, whose club ended the regular season 10-6. "Your stomach feels very empty when you have it in your grasp and don't get it."

Two critical mistakes in the third quarter turned the game around for the Bears, who completed the season with three straight victories and a 6-10 record. Safety Gary Fencik intercepted a Craig Morton pass and returned it 69 yards for a touchdown and defensive end Al Harris added a 44-yard touchdown off an interception to doom the Broncos.

"There's no excuse for throwing two touchdowns to the other team, said Morton. "I'll have to take the blow for this loss."

But it just wasn't the interceptions that allowed the Bears to pull off the upset. The Bears' defense recorded six sacks and held the Broncos to 76 yards on the ground.

Defensive tackle Alan Page got 3½ sacks in the final game of his 15-year NFL career.

Running back Walter Payton caught two touchdown passes from Vince Evans—a 19-yarder with 14:07 left in the first half and a seven-yarder with 6:05 left in the game.

Roland Harper added a four-yard touchdown in the first half to help build the Bears' lead to 14-3 at intermission. Fencik's interception on the Broncos' second play of the second half increased the margin to 21-3 before Morton hit Riley Odoms on a six-yard scoring pass to close the gap to 21-10.

Harris' interception rebuilt the lead to 18 points before Steve DeBerg, replacing Morton, threw the first of two touchdown passes to

Sixteenth Week—Continued

Rick Upchurch, a 25-yarder with 2:45 left in the third quarter. The second was a 39-yard pass after Chicago had restored its 18-point lead at 35-17.

DECEMBER 20
SCORE BY PERIODS

Denver	3	0	14	7—24
Chicago	0	14	14	7—35

SCORING

Denver—Field goal Steinfort 46.
Chicago—Payton 19 pass from Evans (Roveto kick).
Chicago—Harper 4 run (Roveto kick).
Chicago—Fencik 69 interception return (Roveto kick).
Denver—Odoms 6 pass from Morton (Steinfort kick).
Chicago—Harris 44 interception return (Roveto kick).
Denver—Upchurch 25 pass from DeBerg (Steinfort kick).
Chicago—Payton 7 pass from Evans (Roveto kick).
Denver—Upchurch 39 pass from DeBerg (Steinfort kick).

TEAM STATISTICS

	Denver	Chicago
First downs	19	15
Rushes-Yards	19-76	41-170
Passing yards	222	111
Sacks by-Yards	1-7	6-56
Return yards	161	217
Passes	22-49-3	10-20-2
Punts	7-37.6	6-35.0
Fumbles-Lost	1-0	1-0
Penalties-Yards	9-74	11-101
Time of possession	28:00	32:00
Attendance—40,125.		

INDIVIDUAL STATISTICS

Rushing—Denver, Preston 6-25, Parros 3-20, Canada 5-17, Lytle 4-14, Reed 1-0; Chicago, Payton 19-62, Harper 15-48, Evans 6-50, Baschnagel 1-10.

Passing—Denver, Morton 8-23-3—88, DeBerg 14-26-0—190; Chicago, Evans 10-20-2—118.

Receiving—Denver, Upchurch 6-102, Watson 6-82, Preston 5-55, Egloff 3-21, Odoms 1-6, Moses 1-12; Chicago, Payton 3-42, Margerum 3-28, Watts 2-42, Williams 1-4, Harper 1-2.

Kickoff Returns—Denver, Harden 4-69, Canada 1-13; Chicago, Moorehead 3-51, Williams 1-35.

Punt Returns—Denver, Upchurch 2-14, Kyle 1-0; Chicago, J. Fisher 3-21.

Interceptions—Denver, Kyle 1-0, Smith 1-65; Chicago, Fencik 1-69, Singletary 1-minus 3, Harris 1-44.

Punting—Denver, Prestridge 7-37.6; Chicago, Parsons 6-35.0.

Field Goals—Denver, Steinfort 1-1; Chicago, Roveto 0-1.

SEAHAWKS 42, BROWNS 21

SEATTLE—Cleveland (5-11) lost seven fumbles and had three passes intercepted, leaving the Browns just two turnovers short of the NFL record for a single game in a 42-21 loss at Seattle.

Seattle (6-10) converted six of the Browns' turnovers into touchdowns, including an 82-yard pass interception return by safety Kenny Easley and a 31-yard return following a fumble recovery by safety Gregory Johnson.

In addition, the Seahawks scored touchdowns on passes of four and 14 yards from Dave Krieg to Steve Largent, a 10-yard strike from Krieg to rookie Paul Johns, and a three-yard run by Theotis Brown.

"We've self-destructed all year," said Cleveland Coach Sam Rutigliano. After winning the AFC Central Division in 1980 with an 11-5 record, the Browns finished last in the division in '81.

DECEMBER 20
SCORE BY PERIODS

Cleveland	0	7	7	7—21
Seattle	14	14	14	0—42

SCORING

Seattle—Easley 82 interception return (Alvarez kick).
Seattle—T. Brown 3 run (Alvarez kick).
Seattle—Largent 4 pass from Krieg (Alvarez kick).
Seattle—Johnson 31 fumble return (Alvarez kick).
Cleveland—G. Pruitt 5 pass from McDonald (Bahr kick).
Seattle—Johns 10 pass from Krieg (Alvarez kick).
Seattle—Largent 14 pass from Krieg (Alvarez kick).
Cleveland—Logan 16 pass from McDonald (Bahr kick).
Cleveland—Hill 8 pass from McDonald (Bahr kick).

TEAM STATISTICS

	Cleveland	Seattle
First downs	27	16
Rushes-Yards	32-151	37-110
Passing yards	301	182
Sacks by-Yards	3-24	6-43
Return yards	162	205
Passes	27-40-3	14-22-1
Punts	1-37.0	2-37.0
Fumbles-Lost	9-7	4-3
Penalties-Yards	5-88	9-66
Time of possession	32:50	27:10
Attendance—51,435.		

INDIVIDUAL STATISTICS

Rushing—Cleveland, White 18-68, M. Pruitt 9-51, Hill 2-18, Sipe 1-14, McDonald 2-0; Seattle, Ivory 9-38, T. Brown 7-21, Hughes 8-18, Doornink 5-16, Largent 1-8, Lane 3-6, Krieg 2-5, Smith 2-minus 2.

Passing—Cleveland, McDonald 24-34-1—297, Sipe 3-6-2—47; Seattle, Krieg 14-21-1—206, Largent 0-1-0—0.

Receiving—Cleveland, Logan 5-101, Hill 5-49, G. Pruitt 5-44, White 4-35, Feacher 3-65, M. Pruitt 3-12, Fulton 1-27, Newsome 1-11; Seattle, Largent 6-80, Sawyer 2-40, T. Brown 1-35, Smith 1-15, Tice 1-14, Johns 1-10, McCullum 1-6, Hughes 1-6.

Kickoff Returns—Cleveland, Hall 5-98, G. Pruitt 2-56; Seattle, Ivory 2-50, Lane 1-27.

Punt Returns—Cleveland, Hall 1-0; Seattle, Johns 1-3.

Interceptions—Cleveland, Matthews 1-8; Seattle, Easley 2-125, Butler 1-0.

Punting—Cleveland, Cox 1-37.0; Seattle, Garcia 2-37.0.

Field Goals—Cleveland, None attempted; Seattle, Alvarez 0-1.

OILERS 21, STEELERS 20

HOUSTON—Gifford Nielsen gave the Oilers' fans something to think about over the winter as he riddled Pittsburgh for 376 yards passing in a 21-20 thriller at Houston.

Nielsen threw three touchdown passes to Dave Casper—the last with 1:51 remaining—and Tony Fritsch's extra point ended the Steelers' nine-year streak of winning seasons. They wound up 8-8.

The game was a disappointment for Steeler running back Franco Harris. His fumble with 69 seconds left ended his team's final chance and his hope for a record eighth straight 1,000-yard season.

Steelers quarterback Mark Malone ran two yards for a touchdown and Sidney Thornton went 17 yards for another.

"The Blue will be back in '82," said Houston Coach Ed Biles after the victory. In their first season under the direction of Biles, the Oilers finished 7-9 and out of the playoffs. In 1980, they were 11-5 and made the playoffs under former coach Bum Phillips.

Pittsburgh	3	3	14	0—20
Houston	7	7	0	7—21

SCORING

Pittsburgh—Field goal Trout 40.
Houston—Casper 15 pass from Nielsen (Fritsch kick).
Houston—Casper 23 pass from Nielsen (Fritsch kick).
Pittsburgh—Field goal Trout 37.
Pittsburgh—Thornton 17 run (Trout kick).
Pittsburgh—Malone 2 run (Trout kick).
Houston—Casper 16 pass from Nielsen (Fritsch kick).

TEAM STATISTICS

	Pittsburgh	Houston
First downs	17	18
Rushes-Yards	36-126	19-41
Passing yards	151	335
Sacks by-Yards	6-42	3-21
Return yards	177	193
Passes	13-30-1	24-37-2
Punts	6-47.7	7-37.7
Fumbles-Lost	1-1	2-0
Penalties-Yards	7-65	7-81
Time of possession	30:30	29:30
Attendance—41,056.		

INDIVIDUAL STATISTICS

Rushing—Pittsburgh, Thornton 4-39, Harris 17-36, Pollard 8-28, Malone 6-19, Davis 1-4; Houston, Campbell 13-24, Armstrong 3-13, Nielsen 3-4.

Passing—Pittsburgh, Malone 13-30-1—172; Houston, Nielsen 24-37-2—377.

Receiving—Pittsburgh, Stallworth 6-90, Smith 3-50, Swann 1-12, Harris 2-12, Pollard 1-8; Houston, Casper 6-139, Holston 5-128, Burrough 3-48, Armstrong 5-30, Campbell 4-18, Coleman 1-14.

Kickoff Returns—Pittsburgh, Anderson 2-43, Moser 2-55; Houston, Roaches 2-77, Tullis 2-43.

Punt Returns—Pittsburgh, Anderson 2-34; Houston, Roaches 5-62.

Interceptions—Pittsburgh, Thomas 1-16, Cole 1-29; Houston, Hartwig 1-11.

Punting—Pittsburgh, Colquitt 6-47.7; Houston, Parsley 7-37.7.

Field Goals—Pittsburgh, Trout 2-2; Houston, Fritsch 0-1.

CHIEFS 10, VIKINGS 6

BLOOMINGTON—Steve Fuller threw a 15-yard touchdown pass to Stan Rome and Kansas City foiled Minnesota's last-second pass in the end zone for a 10-6 victory in the last game ever played in 25-year-old Metropolitan Stadium at Bloomington, Minn.

Tommy Kramer guided the Vikings from their own 29-yard line to the Chiefs 3, hitting five of six passes. On fourth-and-goal with 19 seconds left, Kramer fired a pass intended for

Joe Senser in the end zone, but it was broken up by two defenders.

The game was tied 3-3 at halftime after a 43-yard field goal by the Vikings' Rick Danmeier and a 30-yarder by the Chiefs' Nick Lowery. Fuller hit Rome with 10:03 left in the third quarter for a 10-3 lead. The Vikings added a 33-yard field goal by Danmeier.

"Maybe things are catching up with us," said Vikings Coach Bud Grant after the Vikes finished the season 7-9 and out of the playoffs. "Maybe we ran out of miracles."

Kansas City	3	0	7	0—10
Minnesota	3	0	3	0— 6

SCORING

Minnesota—Field goal Danmeier 43.
Kansas City—Field goal Lowery 30.
Kansas City—Rome 15 pass from Fuller (Lowery kick).
Minnesota—Field goal Danmeier 33.

TEAM STATISTICS

	Kansas City	Minnesota
First downs	13	16
Rushes-Yards	37-140	23-84
Passing yards	133	161
Sacks by-Yards	2-16	1-12
Return yards	105	78
Passes	12-16-1	17-38-1
Punts	3-30.7	3-34.7
Fumbles-Lost	1-1	3-3
Penalties-Yards	5-45	2-20
Time of possession	33:39	26:21
Attendance—41,110.		

INDIVIDUAL STATISTICS

Rushing—Kansas City, B. Jackson 25-102, Bledsoe 11-39, Fuller 1-minus 1; Minnesota, Galbreath 11-55, Brown 6-16, Kramer 2-7, Young 4-6.

Passing—Kansas City, Fuller 12-16-1—145; Minnesota, Kramer 17-38-1—177.

Receiving—Kansas City, Carson 3-78, Smith 5-39, Rome 1-15, Bledsoe 2-10, B. Jackson 1-3; Minnesota, Galbreath 7-60, Rashad 2-37, Senser 3-32, S. White 3-27, Brown 1-16, LeCount 1-5.

Kickoff Returns—Kansas City, Murphy 2-63; Minnesota, Payton 2-35, Nord 1-21.

Punt Returns—Kansas City, Smith 2-26; Minnesota, Payton 2-10.

Interceptions—Kansas City, Green 1-16; Minnesota, McNeill 1-12.

Punting—Kansas City, Gossett 3-30.7; Minnesota, Coleman 3-34.7.

Field Goals—Kansas City, Lowery 1-2; Minnesota, Danmeier 2-2.

REDSKINS 30, RAMS 7

ANAHEIM—Joe Theismann set a team record for completions in a season with his 14-for-22 day for 247 yards and a pair of touchdowns as the Washington Redskins beat the Los Angeles Rams, 30-7, in Anaheim, Calif.

Theismann finished the year with 293 completions, breaking the Redskins mark of 288 set by Sonny Jurgensen in 1967. His scoring passes went for four yards to Joe Washington and 37 yards to Virgil Seay.

The Redskins finished the year 8-8, but an

Sixteenth Week—Continued

0-5 start knocked them out of the NFC East championship race. The Rams' 6-10 season was their worst since 1965.

Washington rolled up 502 yards to just 165 by the Rams. Said Theismann, "Who knows what we might have done in the playoffs?"

The game marked the end of an 11-year NFL career for Rams center Rich Saul, who is retiring.

DECEMBER 20
SCORE BY PERIODS

Washington	6	10	14	0—30
Los Angeles	0	7	0	0— 7

SCORING

Washington—Washington 4 pass from Theismann (kick blocked).
Los Angeles—Guman 1 run (Corral kick).
Washington—Riggins 1 run (Moseley kick).
Washington—Field goal Moseley 35.
Washington—Riggins 1 run (Moseley kick).
Washington—Seay 37 pass from Theismann (Moseley kick).

TEAM STATISTICS

	Washington	Los Angeles
First downs	25	14
Rushes-Yards	44-241	28-78
Passing yards	261	87
Sacks by-Yards	4-40	2-11
Return yards	98	78
Passes	15-25-1	10-27-2
Punts	2-35.5	6-45.3
Fumbles-Lost	1-0	2-0
Penalties-Yards	4-46	3-25
Time of possession	32:01	27:59

Attendance—52,224.

INDIVIDUAL STATISTICS

Rushing—Washington, Washington 14-96, Theismann 4-40, Riggins 15-57, Giaquinto 10-43, Claitt 1-5; Los Angeles, J. Thomas 3-12, Tyler 11-16, Guman 12-41, Kemp 2-9.

Passing—Washington, Theismann 14-22-1-247, Flick 1-3-0-25; Los Angeles, Pastorini 8-21-1-102, Kemp 2-6-1-25.

Receiving—Washington, Monk 2-98, Metcalf 4-60, Seay 1-37, Giaquinto 2-29, Washington 4-19, Warren 1-15, Thompson 1-14; Los Angeles, D. Hill 2-45, Dennard 1-26, Moore 2-25, Tyler 2-13, Guman 2-12, Waddy 1-6.

Kickoff Returns—Washington, Nelms 2-60; Los Angeles, D. Hill 5-72.

Punt Returns—Washington, Nelms 5-28; Los Angeles, Irvin 1-6.

Interceptions—Washington, Coleman 1-0, Lavender 1-10; Los Angeles, P. Thomas 1-0.

Punting—Washington, Connell 2-35.5; Los Angeles, Corral 6-45.3.

Field Goals—Washington, Moseley 1-1; Los Angeles, None attempted.

COLTS 23, PATRIOTS 21

BALTIMORE—Bert Jones fired three touchdown passes, two to Ray Butler, and the Colts snapped a 14-game losing streak with a 23-21 victory over New England. The Patriots wound up 2-14, same as the Colts, but were guaranteed the first pick in the 1982 college draft. Baltimore beat the Patriots, 29-28, in the season opener but hadn't won since.

Jones hit Butler for scoring strikes of 53 and 37 yards and added a five-yard TD toss to Don McCauley. Mike Wood kicked a 30-yard field goal to complete the Colts' scoring.

The Patriots, who were handed their ninth straight loss, held leads of 7-3 and 14-10 in the first half on a four-yard run by Sam Cunningham and a 15-yard pass from Tom Owen to Don Westbrook. Matt Cavanaugh came off the bench to lead the Pats to a fourth-quarter score, on his two-yard pass to Westbrook with 1:58 left.

A dismal crowd of 17,073—just 19 more than the number of no-shows—turned out to watch the two worst teams in the NFL.

The victory helped the Colts avoid setting a new league record for consecutive losses in one season (15). They tied the 1976 Tampa Bay Buccaneers and 1980 New Orleans Saints at 14 straight.

DECEMBER 20
SCORE BY PERIODS

New England	7	7	0	7—21
Baltimore	10	7	6	0—23

SCORING

Baltimore—Field goal Wood 30.
New England—Cunningham 4 run (Smith kick).
Baltimore—McCauley 5 pass from B. Jones (Wood kick).
New England—Westbrook 15 pass from Owen (Smith kick).
Baltimore—Butler 53 pass from B. Jones (Wood kick).
Baltimore—Butler 37 pass from B. Jones (kick failed).
New England—Westbrook 2 pass from Cavanaugh (Smith kick).

TEAM STATISTICS

	New England	Baltimore
First downs	20	19
Rushes-Yards	23-77	41-128
Passing yards	273	255
Sacks by-Yards	1-12	1-8
Return yards	137	42
Passes	20-38-3	17-28-1
Punts	6-30.2	4-38.0
Fumbles-Lost	3-1	1-1
Penalties-Yards	6-20	9-53
Time of possession	25:02	34:58

Attendance—17,073.

INDIVIDUAL STATISTICS

Rushing—New England, Ferguson 6-15, Cunningham 5-15, Calhoun 9-34, Collins 3-13; Baltimore, Dickey 9-16, B. Jones 3-11, McMillan 15-48, Dixon 13-52, Franklin 1-1.

Passing—New England, Owen 9-22-3—136, Cavanaugh 11-16-0—145; Baltimore, B. Jones 17-28-1—267.

Receiving—New England, Westbrook 3-42, Jackson 4-71, Cunningham 1-9, Toler 4-47, Calhoun 1-16, Ferguson 1-7, Dawson 2-56, Johnson 2-18, Tatupu 2-15; Baltimore, Burke 5-69, McCauley 5-35, Butler 2-90, DeRoo 1-38, McMillan 2-31, Dixon 1-5, Huff 1-minus 1.

Kickoff Returns—New England, Collins 4-82, Dombroski 1-24; Baltimore, Dixon 2-19.

Punt Returns—New England, James 2-31; Baltimore, Shula 1-7.

Interceptions—New England, Fox 1-0; Baltimore, Pinckney 1-0, Smith 1-8, Hatchett 1-8.

Punting—New England, Camarillo 6-30.2; Baltimore, Garrett 4-38.0.

Field Goals—New England, None attempted, Baltimore, Wood 1-2.

CHARGERS 23, RAIDERS 10

SAN DIEGO—The odds did not look good for the San Diego Chargers. Entering the final weekend of play in the National Football League, the Chargers trailed the Denver Broncos by one game in the AFC Western Division race. And the Broncos had the good fortune of playing the lowly Chicago Bears (5-10) in their last game. The Chargers, on the other hand, had to play the Oakland Raiders—the defending Super Bowl champions—on Monday night. And the Raiders hadn't lost on a Monday night in seven years—or 15 games ago.

But miracles do happen, even in the NFL. The Bears crushed Denver, 35-24, on Sunday afternoon, and the Chargers crushed Oakland, 23-10, on the last Monday night game of 1981. Although they finished the season with identical 10-6 records, San Diego won the division for the third successive year by virtue of a better intradivisional record.

The Chargers did not win this game in typical San Diego fashion—pass, pass and pass some more. Instead, Coach Don Coryell's team used an effective combination of Chuck Muncie's running and Dan Fouts' throwing to beat the Raiders. Muncie gained 94 yards on the ground and Fouts passed for 222 more—one of his lowest totals of the year. But it was enough to win the game and help Fouts establish three new NFL single-season records: passing yardage (4,802), most passes (609) and most completions (360). All three totals bettered records set by Fouts in 1980.

The Chargers never trailed in the game. Rookie running back James Brooks put them ahead, 7-0, with a 28-yard tackle-busting run in the first quarter. After both teams swapped second-quarter field goals, Fouts connected with wide receiver Charley Joiner for a 29-yard touchdown play. It was Fouts' only TD pass of the night and put the Chargers up, 17-3, at the half. An interception by veteran cornerback Willie Buchanon of Oakland's Marc Wilson with less than two minutes remaining in the half set up the touchdown.

Oakland opened the second half with a 15-play, 71-yard drive that ended with Mark van Eeghen carrying it over from the 1, cutting the San Diego lead to 17-10.

But that was as close as the Raiders could get. Two more Rolf Benirschke field goals, from 27 and 39 yards out, gave the Chargers their margin of victory.

MONDAY, DECEMBER 21

SCORE BY PERIODS

Oakland	0	3	7	0—10
San Diego	7	10	3	3—23

SCORING

San Diego—Brooks 28 run (Benirschke kick).
Oakland—Field goal Bahr 34.
San Diego—Field goal Benirschke 24.
San Diego—Joiner 29 pass from Fouts (Benirschke kick).
Oakland—van Eeghen 1 run (Bahr kick).
San Diego—Field goal Benirschke 27.
San Diego—Field goal Benirschke 39.

TEAM STATISTICS

	Oakland	San Diego
First downs	20	21
Rushes-Yards	28-107	39-147
Passing yards	229	214
Sacks by-Yards	1-8	3-26
Return yards	92	56
Passes	14-38-1	14-27-0
Punts	4-43.8	5-25.4
Fumbles-Lost	1-1	0-0
Penalties-Yards	8-52	6-29
Time of possession	25:46	34:14
Attendance—52,279.		

INDIVIDUAL STATISTICS

Rushing—Oakland, Hawkins 7-27, van Eeghen 8-18, Wilson 4-31, Whittington 4-17, Jensen 5-14; San Diego, Muncie 28-94, Brooks 8-48, Cappelletti 3-5.

Passing—Oakland, Plunkett 2-4-0—36, Wilson 12-34-1—219; San Diego, Fouts 14-27-0—222.

Receiving—Oakland, Whittington 1-10, Barnwell 2-43, Chandler 6-128, Ramsey 1-21, Christensen 1-5, Branch 2-38, Hawkins 1-10; San Diego, Chandler 2-48, Cappelletti 1-11, Sievers 1-32, Joiner 6-94, Winslow 3-38, Muncie 1-minus 1.

Kickoff Returns—Oakland, Montgomery 3-48, Barnwell 3-43; San Diego, Brooks 1-15, Gregor 1-15, Shaw 1-17.

Punt Returns—Oakland, Watts 1-1; San Diego, Brooks 1-9.

Interceptions—San Diego, Buchanon 1-0.

Punting—Oakland, Guy 4-43.8; San Diego, Roberts 4-31.8.

Field Goals—Oakland, Bahr 1-1; San Diego, Benirschke 3-3.

DIVISIONAL PLAYOFFS AND
CONFERENCE CHAMPIONSHIP GAMES

FIRST ROUND GAMES

BILLS 31, JETS 27

NEW YORK—For 51 weeks, the scene had been rerun so many times on television that it was burned almost indelibly into the psyche of the Buffalo Bills.

Ron Smith, then a San Diego Charger wide receiver, would run a post pattern, break clear and Dan Fouts would pass to him for the winning 50-yard touchdown, with Buffalo safety Bill Simpson in futile pursuit.

The film clip would end with John Jefferson, also then a Charger receiver, vaulting into Smith's arms and the two of them tumbling to the turf in San Diego Jack Murphy Stadium, exulting over a 20-14 playoff victory, while Simpson was far back upfield in dejection.

That scene set up one of the ironies of the 1981 season as the Bills beat the New York Jets, 31-27, in the American Football Conference wild-card playoff game.

With 10 seconds to play in a game which put emotions into a shredder with its explosive beginning, stirring comeback, controversial penalties, dropped touchdown passes (two by the Jets' Wesley Walker), great catches, questionable strategies and shifts in momentum, there was time for one more big play.

The question was, who would make it?

The ball was on the Buffalo 11-yard line. Richard Todd set up to pass for the Jets.

Simpson, admitting that "things were happening so fast out on the field that there wasn't enough time to digest it all," made a quick decision. He left his coverage, running back Scott Dierking, and drifted between Todd and wide receiver Derrick Gaffney, who had tormented Buffalo all afternoon.

Todd threw the ball just as Simpson reached his desired position. He intercepted at the 1-yard line and returned the ball to the 10.

Buffalo had survived in a game in which it nearly blew a 24-0 lead. The victory was the Bills' first in the playoffs since the 1965 team defeated San Diego, 23-0, in the American Football League championship game.

Buffalo's victory marked the first time a team from the AFC Eastern Division had won a playoff game since the Miami Dolphins defeated the Minnesota Vikings, 24-7, in Super Bowl VIII. Of course, that streak was bound to end, since both the Bills and Jets are in the AFC East and one of them had to win.

"I guess we started out the game bad and ended it bad, with turnovers," said New York Coach Walt Michaels.

The first turnover came on the game's opening kickoff, when Bruce Harper fumbled on the return and Bills cornerback Charles Romes scooped up the loose ball and raced 26 yards into the end zone.

The Bills had scored with the game only 16 seconds old, stunning the Shea Stadium crowd of 57,050. (That wasn't the fastest touchdown in an NFL playoff game. In 1974, Nat Moore of Miami returned the opening kickoff for a TD against Oakland. That play took 15 seconds).

Buffalo took a 17-0 lead in the first quarter and built the spread to 24-0 by midway in the second quarter as Joe Ferguson picked apart the New York secondary with passes to Frank Lewis. The 34-year-old wide receiver who set a Buffalo pass receiving record this season with 70 catches, then was named to the Pro Bowl for the first time in 1981.

Lewis turned a short square-in pass into a 50-yard touchdown play in the first quarter by outracing Donald Dykes and Ken Schroy of the Jets the last 33 yards to the end zone. That touchdown made the score 14-0 and Nick Mike-Mayer's 29-yard field goal, following an interception and 49-yard return by cornerback Rufus Bess, boosted the Bills' lead to 17-0.

In the second period, Lewis took a 26-yard TD pass from Ferguson on a post pattern to make the score 24-0. With 12:35 left in the first half, Ferguson had completed 12 of 15 passes for 211 yards. Then he went stone cold.

Buffalo Coach Chuck Knox, who has a reputation for conservatism, became almost too bold as the Bills gained possession with less than two minutes to play in the half, after the Jets had put their first points on the scoreboard on a 30-yard pass from Todd to tight end Mickey Shuler.

Knox ordered Ferguson into the shotgun formation, intent on adding to Buffalo's 24-7 lead. But Jets linebacker Greg Buttle intercepted a pass, which led to a 26-yard field goal by Pat Leahy that cut the Bills' lead to 24-10.

After his hot start, Ferguson completed only five of 19 passes and was intercepted four times. He finished the game 17-for-34 for 268 yards. Todd, meanwhile, wound up 28-for-50 for 377 yards and also threw four interceptions.

Two elements kept the Jets' comeback from turning into an outright disaster for Ferguson. One was the play of his offensive tackles, Joe Devlin and Ken Jones. They neutralized the heart of the New York Sack Exchange, the defensive line that had led the NFL in sacks with a total of 66 in 1981. Ferguson was sacked only twice, and never faced any of the intense pressure from the New York pass rush that had blown away Green Bay's playoff chances a week earlier in a 28-3 New York victory.

Jets safety Darrol Ray pushes Buffalo's star running back, Joe Cribbs, out of the end zone after Cribbs' game-winning touchdown helped push the Jets out of the NFL playoffs, 31-27.

The other key factor was the gritty play of the Bills' defense, which was helped only once by the offense in the second half. That came on Joe Cribbs' 45-yard touchdown run that made the score 31-13 with 10:16 left in the game.

But the Jets roared back after that on Todd's 30-yard scoring pass to Bobby Jones and Kevin Long's one-yard run with 3:44 left. Two Todd-to-Shuler passes good for 33 yards had been the key plays in that scoring drive.

The Jets held on Buffalo's next possession and took the ball on their 20 with 2:36 remaining. Todd passed for 29 yards to Shuler, 13 to Jones and 26 yards to Gaffney to put the Jets on the Buffalo 11 with 14 seconds left.

Todd threw an incomplete pass on first down and then Simpson's big play took the pressure off Buffalo for good.

Simpson, reminded after the game of the play that cost the Bills a year ago in San Diego, said, "People made more out of that play than I ever did. And I made mistakes today (against the Jets) that a lot of people don't know about. All they will remember is the big play I made at the end."

DECEMBER 27
SCORE BY PERIODS

Buffalo	17	7	0	7—31
New York Jets	0	10	3	14—27

SCORING

Buffalo—Romes 26 fumble return (Mike-Mayer kick).
Buffalo—Lewis 50 pass from Ferguson (Mike-Mayer kick).
Buffalo—Field goal Mike-Mayer 29.
Buffalo—Lewis 26 pass from Ferguson (Mike-Mayer kick).
New York—Shuler 30 pass from Todd (Leahy kick).
New York—Field goal Leahy 26.
New York—Field goal Leahy 19.
Buffalo—Cribbs 45 run (Mike-Mayer kick).
New York—B. Jones 30 pass from Todd (Leahy kick).
New York—Long 1 run (Leahy kick).

TEAM STATISTICS

	Buffalo	New York
TOTAL FIRST DOWNS	15	23
By Rushing	4	3
By Passing	11	17
By Penalty	0	3
THIRD DOWN EFFICIENCY	4-13	9-17
TOTAL NET YARDS	321	419
Total Offensive Plays	58	77
Average Gain Per Play	5.5	5.4
NET YARDS RUSHING	91	71
Total Rushing Plays	22	22
Avg. Gain Per Rush	4.1	3.2
NET YARDS PASSING	230	348
Yards Lost Attempting to Pass	2-38	5-29
Gross Yards Passing	268	377
PASSES	17-34-4	28-50-4
Avg. Gain Per Pass	6.4	6.3
PUNTS	4-43.8	4-33.0
Had Blocked	0	0
TOTAL RET. YARDS	191	203
Punt Returns	11	31
Kickoff Returns	101	110
Interception Returns	79	62
PENALTIES/YARDS	8-62	6-55
FUMBLES/LOST	1-0	3-1
TIME OF POSSESSION	29:56	30:04
Attendance—57,050.		

INDIVIDUAL STATISTICS

Rushing—Buffalo, Cribbs 14-83, Leaks 6-12, Ferguson 2-minus 4; New York, McNeil 12-32, Long 8-28, Todd 2-11.

Passing—Buffalo, Ferguson 17-34-4—268; New York, Todd 28-50-4—377.

Receiving—Buffalo, Lewis 7-158, Cribbs 4-64, Leaks 3-23, Brammer 2-17, Butler 1-6; New York, Shuler 6-116, B. Jones 4-64, Barkum 2-41, Gaffney 4-64, Dierking 7-52, Harper 1-4, Newton 1-12, Walker 3-24.

Kickoff Returns—Buffalo, Brown 1-27, Riddick 4-73, Villapiano 1-1; New York, Harper 4-82, Sohn 1-28.

Punt Returns—Buffalo, Riddick 1-6, Piccone 1-5; New York, Harper 3-31.

Interceptions—Buffalo, Bess 1-49, Villapiano 1-18, Simpson 2-12; New York, Buttle 2-40, Dykes 1-22, Holmes 1-0.

Punting—Buffalo, Cater 4-43.8; New York, Ramsey 4-33.0.

Field Goals—Buffalo, Mike-Mayer 1-2; New York, Leahy 2-3.

Fumbles—Buffalo, Ferguson; New York, Harper, Todd 2.

Fumble Recoveries—Buffalo, Romes 1-26, Jones; New York, Todd, Fields.

GIANTS 27, EAGLES 21

PHILADELPHIA—Jim Clack is the leader of the New York Giants' offensive line. He's the veteran center, an 11-year man in the National Football League. He knows what it takes to win.

He started for the Pittsburgh Steelers in their first two Super Bowl triumphs, following the 1974 and '75 seasons. Now he's in the NFL playoffs again, and he says he sees encouraging similarities between this Giants team and his old Steelers bunch.

"This team has the Pittsburgh syndrome," Clack said. "If we need an offensive drive, we seem to get it. If we need a turnover, we seem to get it. We never get discouraged; we just keep on fighting.

"The Steelers went a long way with that kind of football. The way we're going now . . . who knows how far we can go?"

The Giants pulled off a dramatic 27-21 upset of the Philadelphia Eagles in the NFC wild-card game at Veterans Stadium.

The Giants, appearing in their first postseason game since the Y. A. Tittle-Frank Gifford era (1963), stunned the defending NFC champions, jumping off to a 20-0 lead in the first quarter. The Eagles contributed to that with some shoddy special teams play.

The pattern for the game was established on only the fourth play, when Eagles return specialist Wally Henry fumbled a punt when hit by New York rookie linebacker Lawrence Taylor. Beasley Reece recovered for the Giants at the Eagles' 25.

They scored in seven plays, the payoff coming on Scott Brunner's nine-yard pass to running back Leon Bright, who was wide open at the flag. Brunner mishandled the snap, causing Joe Danelo to miss the extra point, but the Giants led 6-0 just 4:42 into the game.

The second time the Giants touched the ball,

— 298 —

they drove 62 yards in 11 plays, fullback Rob Carpenter doing most of the heavy work. On third and goal from the 10, Brunner hit wide receiver John Mistler for the touchdown.

This time Danelo's conversion was good and the Giants led, 13-0, with 13:54 gone. The Eagles were already reeling at this point, but the worst was still to come.

Danelo's kickoff was a low knuckleball that squirted toward the goal line. Henry bobbled it, slipped, then tried to pick it up and lost it altogether when he was hit by Mike Dennis.

The ball spun into the end zone, where it was recovered by Mike Haynes for a touchdown. Danelo's conversion gave the Giants 14 points in just 12 seconds and put the Eagles in a hole they never could escape.

"Those things seem like they've been happening to us the whole year," Eagles Coach Dick Vermeil said. "That's why we didn't win more football games than we did before. When those things happened early today, it shook us in a way. We lost our concentration and poise a little bit. And it gave them real impetus and confidence.

"It's just hard to give a team 13 points, especially a team with that kind of defense, and go ahead and win. We just got our butts whipped."

"I feel terrible," said Henry, who played for Vermeil at UCLA and was the NFC's return specialist in the Pro Bowl two years ago. "I guess somebody's gotta be blamed for every defeat, so I'll take the blame for this one."

While the special teams' breakdowns put the Eagles in an unenviable position, it didn't totally knock them out of the game. They had their chances to get back in it, but their proud defensive unit kept collapsing at the most inopportune times.

For example, Herm Edwards intercepted a pass at the Giants' 26 and Ron Jaworski hit Harold Carmichael on a 15-yard touchdown pass with 2:26 left in the second quarter. Tony Franklin's conversion pulled the Eagles within 20-7 and the 71,611 Vet Stadium fans came roaring to life.

The momentum had swung to the Eagles' side for the first time in the gloomy afternoon.

However, the Giants took the ensuing kickoff and swept 62 yards in five plays, Carpenter carrying four times, then Brunner passing to tight end Tom Mullady on a 22-yard touchdown play. That put New York up 27-7 with just 34 seconds left in the half.

In the second half, the Eagles put together drives of 80 and 82 yards and scored 14 points —both on short Wilbert Montgomery runs— and they were just six points down with 2:51 left.

There was a chance for the Giants to crack under the pressure, but they didn't. Carpenter hammered up the middle for two consecutive first downs, exhausting the Eagles' supply of both timeouts and miracles.

The game ended with Brunner, the kid quarterback who played his college football at the University of Delaware—just down the interstate highway from Philadelphia—flopping on

DECEMBER 27
SCORE BY PERIODS

New York Giants	20	7	0	0—27
Philadelphia	0	7	7	7—21

SCORING

New York—Bright 9 pass from Brunner (kick blocked).
New York—Mistler 10 pass from Brunner (Danelo kick).
New York—Haynes recovered fumbled kickoff in end zone (Danelo kick).
Philadelphia—Carmichael 15 pass from Jaworski (Franklin kick).
New York—Mullady 22 pass from Brunner (Danelo kick).
Philadelphia—Montgomery 6 run (Franklin kick).
Philadelphia—Montgomery 1 run (Franklin kick).

TEAM STATISTICS

	New York	Phila.
TOTAL FIRST DOWNS	16	19
By Rushing	10	8
By Passing	6	8
By Penalty	0	3
THIRD DOWN EFFICIENCY	7-13	2-11
TOTAL NET YARDS	275	226
Total Offensive Plays	57	56
Avg. Gain Per Play	4.8	4.0
NET YARDS RUSHING	183	93
Total Rushing Plays	42	29
Avg. Gain Per Rush	4.4	3.2
NET YARDS PASSING	92	133
Yards lost attempting to pass	1-4	3-21
Gross Yards Passing	96	154
PASSES	9-14-1	13-24-0
Avg. Gain Per Pass	6.1	4.9
PUNTS	4-44.8	7-42.4
Had blocked	0	0
TOTAL RET. YARDS	128	76
Punt Returns	41	16
Kickoff Returns	87	59
Interception Returns	0	1
PENALTIES/YARDS	5-54	4-23
FUMBLES/LOST	1-0	5-2
TIME OF POSSESSION	31:09	28:51

Attendance—71,611.

INDIVIDUAL STATISTICS

Rushing—New York, Carpenter 33-161, Brunner 6-11, Perry 3-11; Philadelphia, Montgomery 18-65, Campfield 1-10, Jaworski 5-6, Oliver 5-12.

Passing—New York, Brunner 9-14-1—96; Philadelphia, Jaworski 13-24-0—154.

Receiving—New York, Carpenter 4-32, Gray 1-12, Bright 1-9, Mistler 1-10, Perkins 1-11, Mullady 1-22; Philadelphia, Carmichael 2-43, C. Smith 2-19, Oliver 1-7, Montgomery 3-32, Krepfle 1-18, R. Smith 3-31, Russell 1-4.

Kickoff Returns—New York, Reece 3-64, L. Jackson 1-23; Philadelphia, Campfield 1-19, Henry 2-16, Russell 2-24.

Punt Returns—New York, Bright 4-32, Reece 1-9; Philadelphia, Henry 1-0, Sciarra 2-16.

Interceptions—Philadelphia, Edwards 1-1.

Punting—New York, Jennings 4-44.8; Philadelphia, Runager 7-42.4.

Field Goals—New York, Danelo 0-1; Philadelphia, None attempted.

Fumbles—New York, Carpenter; Philadelphia, Henry 2, Jaworski 2, Morriss.

Fumble Recoveries—New York, Reece 1-0, Carpenter 1-0, Haynes 1-0; Philadelphia, Jaworski 3-0.

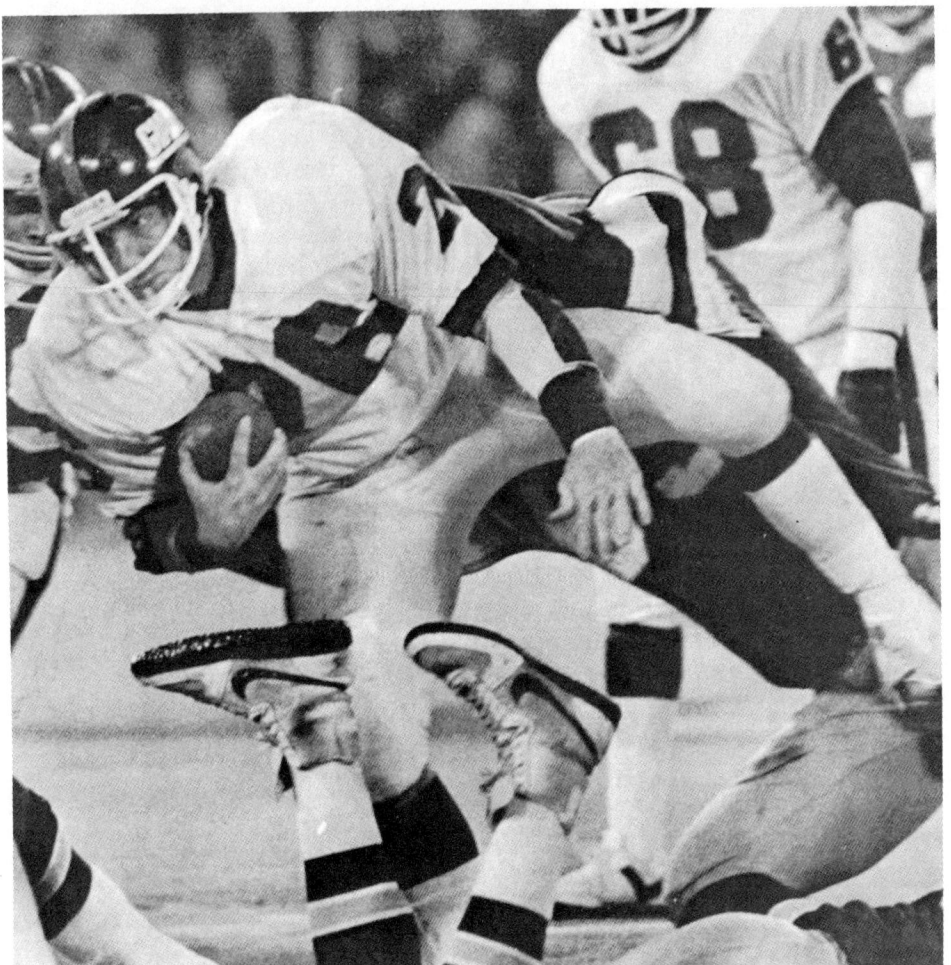

Rob Carpenter's 161 yards helped the Giants beat the Eagles, 27-21.

the ball twice and watching the clock run out.

Carpenter was probably the biggest hero in the Giants' upset victory. He finished with 161 yards on 33 carries and he had four of the Giants' nine pass receptions for 32 yards. Not bad for a guy who couldn't touch the ball in Houston.

"I'm really happy to be here," said Carpenter, who came to the Giants in a trade from the Oilers early in the season. Carpenter played in 11 games with the Giants and gave them a rushing attack that had been nonexistent.

"It's nice to be in a pressure game, where what I do will have an effect on whether my team wins or loses," said Carpenter. "In Houston, Rob Carpenter might have made a few yards, or he might have picked up a first down, but he didn't determine the outcome of a game. Here, I have that kind of role, and I enjoy it."

Brunner admitted he was mildly concerned about Carpenter wearing out during the second half. On the Giants' first 16 plays in the second half, Carpenter handled the ball on all but one.

"Before every play, I checked with Rob to make sure he was okay," said Brunner, who completed nine of 14 passes for 96 yards and three scores. "He kept saying he was fine, so I kept handing him the ball."

In the victorious Giants locker room, there was much celebrating and some gloating over people who had counted the Giants out during the week.

"All week, we heard we didn't deserve to be here," said offensive tackle Gordon King. "People said Philly deserved to be here and they were gonna wipe up the field with us . . ."

King didn't finish his thought, but then he didn't have to.

CHARGERS 41, DOLPHINS 38
(Overtime)

MIAMI—For most of those who played in it and most of those who witnessed it, it was perhaps the greatest professional football game ever played. Certainly, it was among the most exciting, incredible back-and-forth, up-and-down, heart-stopping spectacles the National Football League has produced.

And when it was over the San Diego Chargers proved that they were a field goal better than the Miami Dolphins in a game that shattered 11 NFL playoff records and the nerves of 73,735 spectators in the Orange Bowl and millions of television viewers across the nation.

There was elation and there was despair and there was every emotion in between, but when San Diego's Rolf Benirschke kicked a 29-yard field goal with 13:52 played in overtime to give the Chargers a 41-38 victory over the Dolphins in this American Football Conference playoff game, there was little argument about the classic nature of the contest.

"Without a doubt, this was the most exciting game I've ever been involved with," said Chargers quarterback Dan Fouts, a man who should know all about excitement. Fouts, who set NFL records during the regular season for attempts, completions and yardage, did the same thing against the Dolphins in the playoff game.

He completed a record 33 of 53 attempts for 433 yards and three TDs, also records, overshadowing the heroics of Don Strock's 28 completions in 42 attempts for 397 yards and four touchdowns. It also thwarted the Dolphins' team effort that featured a climb back from a 24-0 first-quarter deficit to a 38-31 fourth-quarter lead.

"This may have been the best-played game ever between two football teams in a playoff," Fouts said.

From the San Diego point of view, that might well be true. The Chargers all but buried Miami in the first quarter only to wake up just in time to keep from being strangled by a corpse. The Chargers scored 24 points before the Dolphins had run seven plays.

Benirschke opened the scoring with a 32-yard field goal to cap a 64-yard drive on the Chargers' first possession. Wes Chandler ran back a Tom Orosz punt 56 yards for a touchdown moments later. The Chargers recovered the ensuing kickoff when it bounced around behind the front wall of blockers at the Miami 29, and Chuck Muncie ran in from one yard out seven plays later. Next, a David Woodley pass was intercepted by Glen Edwards at the Dolphins' 46 and returned to the 11. Three plays later, Fouts hit James Brooks on an eight-yard touchdown pass.

Boom, boom, boom, boom. Turn out the lights. But all the early scoring really did was set the stage for the unbelievable heroics that were to follow in the final three quarters of regulation and the overtime period, all of which left Dolphins Coach Don Shula shaken at the end of the game.

"This is going to be a tough one to live with," Shula said. "But these guys are men, as they proved out there today. They'll be able to handle it."

The Dolphins very nearly were able to handle the Chargers. Shula pulled Woodley in the second quarter and inserted Strock—"I just thought it had become the kind of game that Strock could do more in than Woodley," Shula said—and Miami came alive. The Dolphins scored on a 34-yard Uwe von Schamann field goal to cap Strock's first drive of 63 yards in 11 plays; they scored on a one-yard TD pass to Joe Rose and, incredibly, they scored on a 40-yard flea-flicker just as time ran out in the half when Strock hit Duriel Harris, who lateraled to Tony Nathan at the San Diego 25.

All of a sudden, Miami was back in it, and when Strock hit Rose on a 15-yard TD pass to tie the game at 24 in the third quarter, the unthinkable suddenly became very thinkable indeed.

"They caught us napping with the flea-flicker," said the Chargers' Edwards. "If it hadn't been for that flea-flicker, we would have won in regulation. They really caught us with our pants down and then everything went from there."

After the tie at 24, the Chargers countered with a 25-yard TD pass from Fouts to Kellen Winslow. Miami came back with a 50-yard TD pass from Strock to Bruce Hardy, and the third quarter ended with the teams tied at 31. The Dolphins took the lead back on the first play of the fourth quarter on a 12-yard run by Nathan that was set up by Lyle Blackwood's interception.

Then came the errors Miami had avoided since the first quarter. Andra Franklin, the rookie fullback, fumbled as the Dolphins were driving late in the period for a score that might have put the game away. The Chargers recovered at their 18, and drove down the field in 10 plays. Fouts hit Brooks on a nine-yard TD pass to tie the game, 38-38, with 58 seconds remaining.

Miami had a chance to put it away in regulation, but von Schamann's 43-yard attempt with time running out was tipped by Winslow after a high snap threw off the kicker's timing.

That miss was a harbinger of kicking failure. Von Schamann later hit the ground before the ball on a 34-yarder in overtime—"It was a good snap, a good hold, I just kicked the ground before the ball," von Schamann said—and Ben-

San Diego tight end Kellen Winslow carries the ball after one of his 13 receptions during the overtime win against Miami. Dan Fouts (right) completed 33 of 53 passes for 433 yards in one of the most exciting games in NFL history.

irschke pulled a 27-yarder wide left earlier in overtime, before he got the chance to redeem himself.

"I've never been so proud in my life," San Diego Coach Don Coryell said. "I've coached for 31 or 32 years, and this is tremendous. There has never been a game like this. It was probably the most exciting game in pro football history."

For the 45 players on the Miami roster, it also was the most excruciating game in pro football history. One of the 45 who felt it most acutely was Franklin. He was as composed as a 22-year-old rookie could be expected to be under the circumstances. In fact, he was more composed than anyone had a right to expect.

"I got hit at the line and I was struggling to pick up more yards," Franklin said of the fumble at the San Diego 21, recovered by strong safety Pete Shaw at the 18. "Someone hit me from the side (Gary Johnson) and somebody pulled my arm back (Linden King) and the ball came loose."

Franklin was asked if this one event in this monumental game would be difficult to live with. "Yes," he said. "But it goes along with playing the game. You can't drive a car without risking an accident. But it will be with me for a while. It will toss and turn in my mind."

It was a game that will toss and turn in the minds of everyone who played in it or watched it.

SATURDAY, JANUARY 2
SCORE BY PERIODS

San Diego	24	0	7	7	3	41
Miami	0	17	14	7	0	38

SCORING

San Diego—Field goal Benirschke 32.
San Diego—Chandler 56 punt return (Benirschke kick).
San Diego—Muncie 1 run (Benirschke kick).
San Diego—Brooks 8 pass from Fouts (Benirschke kick).
Miami—Field goal von Schamann 34.
Miami—Rose 1 pass from Strock (von Schamann kick).
Miami—Nathan 40 pass from Strock (von Schamann kick).
Miami—Rose 15 pass from Strock (von Schamann kick).
San Diego—Winslow 25 pass from Fouts (Benirschke kick).
Miami—Hardy 50 pass from Strock (von Schamann kick).
Miami—Nathan 12 run (von Schamann kick).
San Diego—Brooks 9 pass from Fouts (Benirschke kick).
San Diego—Field goal Benirschke 29.

TEAM STATISTICS

	San Diego	Miami
TOTAL FIRST DOWNS	34	25
By Rushing	10	3
By Passing	21	21
By Penalty	3	1
THIRD DOWN EFFICIENCY	8-15	8-16
TOTAL NET YARDS	564	472
Total Offensive Plays	85	79
Average Gain Per Play	6.6	6.0
NET YARDS RUSHING	149	78
Total Rushing Plays	29	28
Avg. Gain Per Rush	5.1	2.8
NET YARDS PASSING	415	394
Yards Lost Attempting to Pass	2-18	3-29
Gross Yards Passing	433	423

	San Diego	Miami
PASSES	33-54-1	31-48-2
Avg. Gain Per Pass	7.4	7.8
PUNTS	4-40.3	5-42.0
Had Blocked	0	0
TOTAL RET. YARDS	189	140
Punt Returns	64	12
Kickoff Returns	100	98
Interception Returns	35	30
PENALTIES/YARDS	9-55	7-50
FUMBLES/LOST	3-3	2-1
TIME OF POSSESSION	28:06	31:54
Overtime	9:38	4:14
Attendance—73,735.		

INDIVIDUAL STATISTICS

Rushing—San Diego, Muncie 24-120, Brooks 3-19, Fouts 2-10; Miami, Nathan 14-48, Franklin 9-6, Woodley 1-10, Hill 3-8, Vigorito 1-6.

Passing—San Diego, Fouts 33-53-1—433, Muncie 0-1-0—0; Miami, Woodley 2-5-1—20, Strock 29-43-1—403.

Receiving—San Diego, Muncie 2-5, Chandler 6-106, Winslow 13-166, Joiner 7-108, Brooks 4-31, Scales 1-17; Miami, Rose 4-37, Harris 6-106, Nathan 9-114, Cefalo 3-62, Hill 2-3, Hardy 5-89, Vigorito 2-12.

Kickoff Returns—San Diego, Brooks 5-85, Beaudoin 1-15; Miami, Walker 1-18, Vigorito 4-67, Hill 1-13.

Punt Returns—San Diego, Chandler 1-56, Brooks 1-8; Miami, Vigorito 1-12.

Interceptions—San Diego, Edwards 1-35, Buchanon 1-0; Miami, L. Blackwood 1-8, Small 0-22.

Punting—San Diego, Roberts 4-40.3; Miami, Orosz 5-42.0.

Field Goals—San Diego, Benirschke 2-4; Miami, von Schamann 1-3.

Fumbles—San Diego, Fouts, Buchanon, Muncie; Miami, Woodley, Franklin.

Fumble Recoveries—San Diego, Shaw; Miami, Laakso, Baumhower, Vigorito, Betters.

BENGALS 28, BILLS 21

CINCINNATI—The Buffalo Bills were one second late. And now it's the Cincinnati Bengals who have a very important date.

The Bengals advanced to the AFC championship game by defeating the Bills, 28-21, in Riverfront Stadium, thanks in part to a Buffalo time out that looked like it was orchestrated by the Mad Hatter.

The Bills were driving for the potential tying touchdown with three minutes to go in the game when quarterback Joe Ferguson called a timeout before a fourth-down-and-three play at the Bengal 20. The Bills thus had 1 minute and 30 seconds to talk it over and get the next play off. They took 1:31.

The delay of game penalty—whistled after the play on which Lou Piccone caught a five-yard pass for an apparent first down—presented Buffalo with a fourth-and-eight situation instead. Ferguson then threw incomplete to Roland Hooks in the end zone and the Bills' postseason party was over.

"It was a mistake that shouldn't have happened," Ferguson understated. "I thought right there we had a first down and four more chances to score."

The confusion came as a result of a pair of late Buffalo substitutions on the play. With about 20 seconds remaining on the 30-second clock (after the time out), the Bills sent receivers Piccone and Ron Jessie in for fullback Curtis Brown and tight end Mark Brammer. The same play from the shotgun was called, but the Bills wanted Piccone running the pattern instead of Brown.

"When we broke the huddle, we had 11 seconds left on the clock. That's normally enough time," Ferguson said. But the crowd noise caused Ferguson to slow the count and he didn't get the snap off in time. Even though the play was run, the Bills didn't argue with the call itself.

The Bengals figured it was a maneuver on Buffalo's part to keep them in their 3-4 defense instead of going to six defensive backs. "I think they were trying to confuse us," said Cincinnati cornerback Ken Riley, about the only guy who heard the refs' whistle before the snap.

"That play didn't cost us the game," Buffalo Coach Chuck Knox said. "We just had a heck of a time stopping them (the Bengals)."

Buffalo anticipated some problems checking the Cincinnati offense, but the Bills encountered trouble from a most unlikely source—running back Charles Alexander.

Relegated to a bit role in the offense most of the season, Alexander seized the opportunity provided when the Bills started keying on Pete Johnson. Alexander rushed 13 times for 72 yards and two touchdowns.

"Charles unleashed himself," said guard Dave Lapham. "He was like a caged lion. You could tell after Charles' first run that he was ready to play. He came back to the huddle and he had, you know, beady eyes, like he was ready to kill people."

Alexander got the first score of the game on a four-yard run, capping a 42-yard drive set up by Mike Fuller's 27-yard punt return. The Bengals went up by 14-0 on Johnson's one-yard plunge after a drive that started with a Ken Riley interception at the Buffalo 48.

Ferguson, Joe Cribbs and Jerry Butler got the Bills back in the game. The quarterback hit Butler with a 54-yard pass to set up Cribbs' one-yard TD plunge just before the half. The Pro Bowl running back scampered 44 yards for a second TD early in the third quarter.

Alexander made it 21-14 on a 20-yard run and Buffalo responded with Ferguson's 21-yard TD pass to Butler. Midway through the final quarter, Cris Collinsworth caught a 16-yard scoring strike from Ken Anderson for the winning TD.

Anderson, who threw only 21 passes (the low for Cincinnati this year), said the Bengals hadn't planned on running as much as they did (33 for 136 yards) but "we're not fussy. If the running game is going, we'll try to work on it." He ended up completing 14 of 21 for 192 yards and lived up to his rating as the NFL's No. 1 quarterback.

Collinsworth said the winning TD play was "complicated and hard to explain," but added that he had three or four options on where to go. "There's not really a primary receiver," he added. "Kenny just picks out the guy who's open."

The Bengals received a scare in the first period when Anderson was helped from the field on Cincinnati's third offensive play. Anderson merely had the wind knocked out of him, however, and missed only one play.

Buffalo was less fortunate, losing Cribbs, its outstanding running back, early in the third period with a bruised knee. Cribbs did not return after gaining 90 yards in 15 plays.

"It obviously hurts to lose a player like Cribbs," said Knox, "but we thought we could still move the ball. The Bengals didn't have a turnover, and when you can do that in a critical game, it really means a lot."

Gregg and his players were quick to cite Anderson as the key ingredient in their remarkable season. Said Gregg:

"I want to say up front that I appreciate that Paul Brown (general manager) gave me a chance to coach this team. But a lot of the reason we are here today is standing right here (pointing to Anderson)."

Gregg also lauded Alexander for his clutch showing. "Alexander had a great day," said Gregg. "They were keying on Johnson. Charlie had a great year, but not like he might have had. We did what we had to do. They were well prepared for us and we had to use something we hadn't used before—like running Charlie. Pete did a good job of blocking for Charlie, just like Charlie had done before for Pete."

Said Collinsworth of Anderson: "He means so much to us in the huddle. He's not a cheerleader out there. It's like he almost gets bored. I get more nervous watching games on TV than I do out on the field with Kenny."

Said Anderson: "All of us believed all year we could do it, so we're not really surprised that we're here."

SUNDAY, JANUARY 3
SCORE BY PERIODS

Buffalo	0	7	7	7—21
Cincinnati	14	0	7	7—28

SCORING

Cincinnati—Alexander 4 run (Breech kick).
Cincinnati—Johnson 1 run (Breech kick).
Buffalo—Cribbs 1 run (Mike-Mayer kick).
Buffalo—Cribbs 44 run (Mike-Mayer kick).
Cincinnati—Alexander 20 run (Breech kick).
Buffalo—Butler 21 pass from Ferguson (Mike-Mayer kick).
Cincinnati—Collinsworth 16 pass from Anderson (Breech kick).

TEAM STATISTICS

	Buffalo	Cincinnati
TOTAL FIRST DOWNS	21	22
By Rushing	11	11
By Passing	8	9
By Penalty	2	2
THIRD DOWN EFFICIENCY	3-9	6-11

TOTAL NET YARDS	336	305
Total Offensive Plays	59	58
Average Gain Per Play	5.7	5.3
NET YARDS RUSHING	134	136
Total Rushing Plays	28	33
Avg. Gain Per Rush	4.8	4.1
NET YARDS PASSING	202	169
Yards Lost Attempting to Pass	0-0	4-23
Gross Yards Passing	202	192
PASSES	15-31-2	14-21-0
Avg. Gain Per Pass	6.5	6.7
PUNTS	3-42.0	4-44.5
Had Blocked	0	0
TOTAL RET. YARDS	90	137
Punt Returns	8	27
Kickoff Returns	82	94
Interception Returns	0	16
PENALTIES/YARDS	6-56	5-44
FUMBLES/LOST	0-0	0-0
TIME OF POSSESSION	28:19	31:41
Attendance—55,420.		

INDIVIDUAL STATISTICS

Rushing—Buffalo, Cribbs 15-90, Leaks 3-12, Hooks 9-30, Brown 1-2; Cincinnati, Alexander 13-72, Johnson 17-45, Anderson 2-15, Griffin 1-4.

Passing—Buffalo, Ferguson 15-31-2—202; Cincinnati, Anderson 14-21-0—192.

Receiving—Buffalo, Brammer 3-23, Lewis 3-38, Leaks 2-16, Butler 4-98, Jessie 1-12, Hooks 2-15; Cincinnati, Johnson 3-23, Ross 6-71, Curtis 1-22, Alexander 1-10, Collinsworth 2-24, Kreider 1-42.

Kickoff Returns—Buffalo, Riddick 4-68, C. Brown 1-14; Cincinnati, Verser 4-94.

Punt Returns—Buffalo, Riddick 2-8; Cincinnati, Fuller 1-2.

Interceptions—Buffalo, None; Cincinnati, Riley 1-0, Harris 1-16.

Punting—Buffalo, Cater 3-42.0; Cincinnati, McInally 4-44.5.

Field Goals—Buffalo, None attempted; Cincinnati, Breech 0-1.

Fumbles—None.

NFC DIVISIONAL PLAYOFFS

COWBOYS 38, BUCCANEERS O

DALLAS—Expressions of bewilderment were frozen on the faces of several Tampa Bay Buccaneers. It appeared as if a hypnotist had wandered through their locker room after their playoff shame and placed them in a trance.

The widespread catatonia after the 38-0 mugging by the Dallas Cowboys was understandable. Tampa Bay has prided itself, even in woeful times, of avoiding the blowout. The Bucs couldn't always bring joy to their fans after a game, but the record showed they could keep their followers' attention all the way through it.

Not so this time. The Cowboys didn't turn complacent, despite an attitude of their fans that was depicted in a newspaper advertisement. It showed Dallas Coach Tom Landry asking Tampa Bay Coach John McKay, "John, they say we're favored by 8 . . . is that points or touchdowns?"

That defensive ends Dave Stalls and Lee Roy Selmon were the most dazed of all was no coincidence. Stalls had seen for himself why he became expendable and was traded by Dallas to Tampa Bay last season. Selmon had seen a mastery of the position that even he so rarely attains. Ed Jones and Harvey Martin simply were awesome.

"I was talking to Dennis Thurman after the game, and he said he hasn't seen them rush like that before," said tight end Jimmie Giles. "It was almost like they were possessed."

Wide receiver Theo Bell grew weary of running useless pass patterns. "It's a little frustrating," he said, "when you think you are running a good route, get open and look back to see the man fighting for his life."

The man, quarterback Doug Williams, was lucky to survive. He was sacked four times, belted across the helmet twice, forced into two intentional grounding penalties and hurried into four interceptions.

"I didn't expect the Cowboys to have such an effective pass rush against us," said Williams, aching from a sore back. "Our offensive line didn't have its best day, but let's not forget they're the guys who got us here."

The transformation of the line from leaky to airtight coincided with the Bucs' turnaround this year. The line protected Williams well and punctured holes for Buc running backs in the last five regular-season games. Tampa Bay won four and lost one by a point.

In Texas Stadium, the line backtracked to its status as the Bucs' most glaring weakness. "They just mauled us on the line," said McKay. "The name of the game is the block. We didn't block them."

Tony Dorsett didn't gain his 100 rushing yards, as he normally does in Dallas victories, but he broke three hefty gainers (one on a screen pass) to pop the game open. The Bucs' defense held tight for one half before the seams burst in the third quarter. It also didn't force one turnover, which is the trademark of Tampa Bay's tattooing tacklers.

"Some people will think, 'A 38-0 loss—the Bucs are nothing,' said wide receiver Kevin House. "They can say what they want. We will make the playoffs again next year."

The majority of Bucs were too shell-shocked to speak coherently. Things were so bad that placekicker Bill Capece was required for only one play, the second-half kickoff; that two center snaps on punt attempts were fumbled; that one of their few assertive drives began with three seconds left in the first half and was aided by penalties, and that one ball launched by a Buc split the uprights—except it was a Williams pass.

Only one Buc, ex-Pittsburgh Steeler Bell, had previously experienced the devastation that Dallas can wreak in the playoffs.

The Dallas defense made life rough for quarterback Doug Williams all day.

"They are loaded with players with playoff experience, and you can't kid yourself. That's what it is all about. It makes a difference," Bell said. "We came in here very confident and got our bubble busted. No one dreamed it could have gone the way it did."

SATURDAY, JANUARY 2
SCORE BY PERIODS

Tampa Bay	0	0	0	0—	0
Dallas	0	10	21	7—	38

SCORING

Dallas—Hill 9 pass from D. White (Septien kick).
Dallas—Field goal Septien 32.
Dallas—Springs 1 run (Septien kick).
Dallas—Dorsett 5 run (Septien kick).
Dallas—J. Jones 5 run (Septien kick).
Dallas—Newsome 1 run (Septien kick).

TEAM STATISTICS

	Tampa Bay	Dallas
TOTAL FIRST DOWNS	12	26
By Rushing	3	15
By Passing	7	10
By Penalty	2	1
THIRD DOWN EFFICIENCY	4-12	5-12
TOTAL NET YARDS	222	345
Total Offensive Plays	55	73
Average Gain Per Play	4.0	4.7
NET YARDS RUSHING	74	212
Total Rushing Plays	22	46
Avg. Gain Per Rush	3.3	4.6
NET YARDS PASSING	148	133
Yards Lost Attempting to Pass	4-39	1-10
Gross Yards Passing	187	143
PASSES	10-29-4	15-26-0
Avg. Gain Per Pass	4.5	5.1
PUNTS	5-38.4	4-30.0
Had Blocked	0	0
TOTAL RET. YARDS	148	124
Punt Returns	1	53
Kickoff Returns	147	0
Interception Returns	0	71
PENALTIES/YARDS	10-105	8-40
FUMBLES/LOST	2-0	0-0
TIME OF POSSESSION	26:35	33:25

Attendance—64,848.

INDIVIDUAL STATISTICS

Rushing—Tampa Bay, Owens 12-40, Wilder 4-23, Williams 2-9, Eckwood 4-2; Dallas, Dorsett 16-86, Springs 15-70, J. Jones 9-32, Newhouse 4-23, Newsome 1-1, Cosbie 1-0.

Passing—Tampa Bay, Williams 10-29-4—187; Dallas, D. White 15-26-0—143, Carano 0-0-0—0.

Receiving—Tampa Bay, T. Bell 3-36, Owens 3-32, Giles 2-98, Wilder 1-11, House 1-10; Dallas, Dorsett 4-48, DuPree 3-22, Pearson 2-21, Hill 2-18, J. Jones 2-15, Donley 1-14, Cosbie 1-5.

Kickoff Returns—Tampa Bay, Owens 3-92, Holt 2-55; Dallas, None.

Punt Returns—Tampa Bay, T. Bell 1-1; Dallas, J. Jones 3-53.

Interceptions—Tampa Bay, None; Dallas, Downs 1-21, Thurman 2-50, E. Jones 1-0.

Punting—Tampa Bay, Swider 5-38.4; Dallas, D. White 4-30.0.

Field Goals—Tampa Bay, Capece 0-0; Dallas, Septien 1-1.

Fumbles—Tampa Bay, Wilson 2; Dallas, None.

Fumble Recoveries—Tampa Bay, Williams, Swider; Dallas, None.

49ers 38, GIANTS 24

SAN FRANCISCO—Is San Francisco's dream ready for America's team, or just another rude awakening?

The way the 49ers defeated the New York Giants, 38-24, in this divisional playoff game at Candlestick Park, there remained questions aplenty whether they were ready for the National Football Conference championship game against the Dallas Cowboys.

The offense certainly seemed ready as quarterback Joe Montana opened up his attack to pass for a career-high 304 yards and two touchdowns against the NFL's No. 2-ranked defense.

It was a timely explosion because the 49ers had to overcome 145 yards in penalties, and defensive lapses which allowed the Giants to come back from a 24-7 deficit to be within four yards of tying the score in the third quarter.

It was a day of big plays and big mistakes, but the 49ers managed more of the former and the Giants more of the latter, including an extracurricular punch which KO'd their last chance for a comeback.

"We wanted to get respect or get points and we got both," said Montana, who connected on 20 of 31 passes and two touchdowns, an eight-yarder to tight end Charle Young and a 58-yarder to wide receiver Freddie Solomon.

"Our offensive execution was as good as I've seen with the 49ers," Coach Bill Walsh said.

In fact, the 49ers' 423 yards in total offense was the most they amassed since trouncing the Cowboys, 45-14, in the sixth game of the season.

And everybody seemed to get into the act.

Solomon, who committed several errors himself in the early going, compensated by catching six passes for 107 yards. Pro Bowl wide receiver Dwight Clark added five grabs for 104 yards, which are pretty big numbers for an offense which had been accused of being conservative.

That helped open the way for the 49ers' much-maligned rushing attack to gain 135 yards, its highest total since traveling 150 yards against the Cowboys. Fullback Earl Cooper led the infantry with 52 yards in seven carries and halfback Ricky Patton added a 25-yard touchdown run, San Francisco's longest of the season.

All these statistics were made possible by great play along the offensive line, especially at left guard, where John Ayers spent most of the day neutralizing New York's great rookie linebacker, Lawrence Taylor.

Meanwhile, the 49ers' defense contributed big plays both ways. All-Pro rookie cornerback Ronnie Lott intercepted two passes, one which set up a touchdown and one which he returned 20 yards for his fourth TD of the season. And the 49ers also recovered two fumbles, one which set up another touchdown.

"But we made the kind of elementary mistakes that we haven't made since we were in Rocklin," Lott said, naming the team's summer training site.

And those "mistakes" resulted in quick touchdown passes from Scott Brunner to Earnest Gray for 72 yards and 59 yards to Johnny Perkins. The Perkins score was only the second touchdown pass over Lott this season.

"I was supposed to have him man-to-man all the way, but I had a lapse in thinking," Lott said. "I was lucky to even get close enough to touch the ball."

That TD by Perkins made the score 24-17 with 11:13 left in the third quarter and put the Giants very much back into the game. It was a one-play drive that was set up when Montana tried to force a pass under pressure and it was intercepted by safety Bill Currier.

After Perkins' touchdown, the Giants drove to the San Francisco 4-yard line the next time they had the ball. But on third-and-four, 49ers rookie cornerback Eric Wright stripped the ball from Gray on a pass to the goal line. Then kicker Joe Danelo watched in disbelief as his 21-yard field goal attempt hit the left upright.

But there was another big hit to come that would help the 49ers even more. Only this one was by a Giant, defensive end Gary Jeter. He made it after the 49ers had gained only six yards on a third-and-24 play. With 12:59 left the 49ers, ahead by only seven, would have been punting from the Giants' 41-yard line. But . . .

"Jeter punched me right in the stomach and yelled a bunch of obscenities at me," 49ers left tackle Dan Audick said. "Then the official threw the flag and he yelled a bunch of obscenities at him. . . . Nothing I would say in front of my mother."

That gave the 49ers a first down and allowed them to move in and score an insurance touchdown on a three-yard run by Bill Ring, making it 31-17 with 10:37 left.

"He was holding all day," Jeter complained of Audick. "It was obvious, so damn obvious. I just hope he sleeps well at night."

Lott's first interception early in the second quarter set up the key offensive play of the day.

"That touchdown to Solomon was big because it made them really respect our deep pass," tight end Eason Ramson said.

Ironically, the play was called after the 49ers had to take time out because of confusion over how to line up when they sent a two tight end alignment into the game on first-and-10.

"We had called for a 'wham,' which is a run," explained Walsh, "but after the confusion and the time out, I told Joe to just go for the long one on play action."

"We lined up with two tight ends and did all we could to make it look like a run, with a fake to Patton," Montana said.

The fake was so good, in fact, it fooled linebacker Harry Carson, who followed Patton; safety Larry Flowers, who ran in before seeing the ball flying overhead; and, most important, cornerback Terry Jackson, who was frozen for just a second.

"One second, one false step, is all Freddie needs to get behind anybody," Montana said.

Then the 49ers turned their thoughts to Dallas, the team that stopped them the last three times they made the playoffs. The Cowboys turned back the 49ers in the 1970 and 1971 NFC title games, and stopped them again in a 1972 divisional playoff.

SUNDAY, JANUARY 3
SCORE BY PERIODS

New York Giants	7	3	7	7—24
San Francisco	7	17	0	14—38

SCORING

San Francisco—Young 8 pass from Montana (Wersching kick).
New York—Gray 72 pass from Brunner (Danelo kick).
San Francisco—Field goal Wersching 22.
San Francisco—Solomon 58 pass from Montana (Wersching kick).
San Francisco—Patton 25 run (Wersching kick).
New York—Field goal Danelo 48.
New York—Perkins 59 pass from Brunner (Danelo kick).
San Francisco—Ring 3 run (Wersching kick).
San Francisco—Lott 20 interception return (Wersching kick).
New York—Perkins 17 pass from Brunner (Danelo kick).

TEAM STATISTICS

	New York	San Fran.
TOTAL FIRST DOWNS	13	24
By Rushing	3	8
By Passing	9	13
By Penalty	1	3
THIRD DOWN EFFICIENCY	6-16	5-14
TOTAL NET YARDS	346	423
Total Offensive Plays	61	68
Average Gain Per Play	5.7	6.2

NET YARDS RUSHING	65	135
Total Rushing Plays	22	34
Avg. Gain Per Play	3.0	4.0
NET YARDS PASSING	281	288
Yards Lost Attempting to Pass	2-9	3-16
Gross Yards Passing	290	304
PASSES	16-37-2	20-31-1
Avg. Gain Per Pass	7.2	8.5
PUNTS	4-43.8	5-41.2
Had Blocked	0	0
TOTAL RET. YARDS	162	147
Punt Returns	3-18	1-22
Kickoff Returns	7-142	5-93
Interception Returns	1-2	2-32
PENALTIES/YARDS	9-61	14-145
FUMBLES/LOST	4-2	2-0
TIME OF POSSESSION	25:42	34:18
Attendance—58,360.		

INDIVIDUAL STATISTICS

Rushing—New York, Carpenter 17-61, Bright 1-5, Perry 2-1, Brunner 2-minus 2; San Francisco, Cooper 7-52, Patton 7-32, Ring 10-29, Solomon 1-12, Easley 4-9, Clark 1-6, Davis 1-4, Montana 3-minus 9.

Passing—New York, Brunner 16-37-2—290; San Francisco, Montana 20-31-1—304.

Receiving—New York, Perkins 7-121, Gray 3-118, Carpenter 3-18, Young 2-15, Mistler 1-18; San Francisco, Solomon 6-107, Clark 5-104, Patton 2-38, Young 2-22, Wilson 2-21, Ramson 1-11, Elliott 1-5, Ring 1-minus 4.

Kickoff Returns—New York, Bright 5-113, McLaughlin 1-15, Dennis 1-14; San Francisco, Lawrence 3-88, Ring 1-5, Lott 1-0.

Punt Returns—New York, Bright 3-18; San Francisco, Solomon 1-22.

Interceptions—New York, Currier 1-2; San Francisco, Lott 2-32.

Punting—New York, Jennings 4-43.8; San Francisco, Miller 5-41.2.

Field Goals—New York, Danelo 1-2; San Francisco, Wersching 1-2.

Fumbles—New York, Brunner 2, Carpenter, Bright; San Francisco, Ring, Patton.

Fumble Recoveries—New York, Brunner, Weston; San Francisco, Ring, Patton, Leopold, Turner.

AFC CHAMPIONSHIP GAME

BENGALS 27, CHARGERS 7

CINCINNATI—It will be the cold, the breath-stealing, frostbiting, awful cold that will be remembered long after the score is forgotten in the American Football Conference championship game.

The numbers on the scoreboard—Cincinnati 27, San Diego 7—were impressive, especially to fans of the Cincinnati Bengals. But those scoreboard numbers were not nearly so impressive as the following numbers:

Temperature: 9 degrees below zero.

Wind: Gusting up to 35 miles an hour out of the northwest.

Wind-chill factor: 59 degrees below zero.

Brutally cold. Miserably cold.

"The cold brought something extra out of me," said Cincinnati fullback Pete Johnson, who ripped through the Chargers' defense for 80 yards. "You wanted to get out there and score a touchdown in a hurry so you could get back to the bench and get warm."

The cold, a cold that nearly matched the National Football League's infamous Ice Bowl—the 1967 championship game between the Dallas Cowboys and the Green Bay Packers—a game played when the wind-chill index showed minus 60.

"It was as cold a day as I've ever seen as a player or coach," said Bengals Coach Forrest Gregg, who played in the 1967 game at Green Bay as a offensive tackle for the Packers.

The cold.

NFL Commissioner Pete Rozelle, recuperating from a virus ailment at his home in New York, briefly considered postponing the game. But the NFL consulted with an expert in environmental medicine from the U.S. Army Research Institute and declared, "The show must go on."

And it did.

After the players had rubbed mountain-climbing lubricants on their feet and all exposed skin, and after they had climbed into their thermal underwear and panty hose and pulled on their rubber scuba gloves, and after heated benches were imported from Philadelphia and both teams had made sure they were well-stocked with insulated boots and mittens, the show went on surprisingly well.

And when it was over, the Chargers had to admit they had been beaten by themselves and by the Bengals, not the elements.

For the most part, the Chargers were willing to confess to that, except for a hint from Coach Don Coryell that maybe Cincinnati had thrown a little bit of a dirty trick into the game.

The alleged dirty trick involved a huge sliding door at the west end of the stadium. Certainly, Coryell had a good hunk of circumstancial evidence to support his questions about the door.

The door, you see, is directly behind the goal posts and when it is open, wind pours into the stadium.

The Bengals won the game's opening toss and elected to take the wind. The door was wide open and the Chargers, for the first quarter, were forced to march toward that open door.

"The conditions for passing were very poor," said Coryell, "especially in the first quarter when that door was open."

But, miracle of miracles, the door was closed in the second quarter when the Bengals were forced to march toward it. And, miracle of miracles, Bengals quarterback Ken Anderson was able to complete passes that San Diego's Dan Fouts had been unable to complete.

There were still more miracles to open the third quarter. The Chargers again were to march toward the door, which again was open.

"I'm not accusing anybody of anything," said Coryell, "but we had to request that the door be shut. I guess it was opened for the band."

As it turned out, the band—from Zanesville (O.) High School—never had a chance, either. Its scheduled appearance on the field was scrubbed when the bitter cold silenced the brass section.

Anyhow, the door was shut and it remained shut for the remainder of a long afternoon. The Chargers, too, were shut out the rest of the way.

Who had been responsible for the opening and closing of the door?

Gregg seemed insulted that he would even be suspected of such a deed.

"I don't control those doors," he said. "I don't operate the button."

And who can doubt the word of a Super Bowl coach?

And who can doubt the Bengals would have won this game with or without a door, with or without wind, with or without that miserable cold?

The Bengals, who didn't commit a turnover in defeating Buffalo, 28-21, in the playoffs a week earlier, committed just one turnover against the Chargers. Meanwhile, San Diego lost three fumbles (two by Chuck Muncie, one by James Brooks) and two of Fouts' passes were intercepted.

Ultimately, this game came down to a showdown between Fouts and Anderson as much as it did between humans and inhuman weather.

Anderson was the winner. His advantage on this day showed in his ability to run, as well as his ability to throw. In addition to completing 14 of 22 passes for 161 yards and two touchdowns, Anderson ran five times for 39 yards.

Fouts completed 15 of 28 passes for 185 yards and a touchdown and he ran once, for six yards. He needed to run twice.

The Chargers were trailing, 17-7, with slightly more than a minute to play in the first half. They had driven to the Bengals' 21-yard line.

Fouts dropped back to pass, and then the field to his right was wide open. Fouts tentatively took a few steps toward the line of scrimmage. He could have run—easily—for 10 yards. Instead, he tried for six points, throwing to tight end Kellen Winslow, who was double-covered in the end zone. The pass was intercepted by Bobby Kemp and it suddenly got a whole lot colder for San Diego.

San Diego's only touchdown came on a 33-yard screen pass from Fouts to Winslow in the second quarter. That cut Cincinnati's lead to 10-7, but David Verser then returned the San Diego kickoff 40 yards, and the Bengals went 55 yards in seven plays to score, with fullback Pete Johnson plowing over from one yard out.

Cincinnati had jumped to a 10-0 lead in the first quarter on a 31-yard field goal by Jim Breech and an eight-yard touchdown pass from Anderson to backup tight end M.L. Harris two plays after Brooks fumbled on a kickoff return and Don Bass recovered for the Bengals on the San Diego 12.

Breech drilled a 38-yard field goal and Bass caught a three-yard scoring pass from Anderson in the second half. The reception was the first of the season for Bass, who had been injured.

Again, how cold was it?

"It really wasn't all that bad," said Anderson. "I've been colder at other times."

For on a miserably cold day in Cincinnati, Anderson was the only player to suffer from frostbite—he got it on the right ear—and yet he said he felt warm all over.

SUNDAY, JANUARY 10
SCORE BY PERIODS

San Diego	0	7	0	0— 7
Cincinnati	10	7	3	7—27

SCORING

Cincinnati—Field goal Breech 31.
Cincinnati—M. L. Harris 8 pass from Anderson (Breech kick).
San Diego—Winslow 33 pass from Fouts (Benirschke kick).

Cincinnati—Johnson 1 run (Breech kick).
Cincinnati—Field goal Breech 38.
Cincinnati—Bass 3 pass from Anderson (Breech kick).

TEAM STATISTICS

	San Diego	Cincinnati
TOTAL FIRST DOWNS	18	19
By Rushing	11	8
By Passing	7	11
By Penalty	0	0
THIRD DOWN EFFICIENCY	5-12	5-11
TOTAL NET YARDS	301	318
Total Offensive Plays	61	59
Avg. Gain Per Play	4.9	5.4
NET YARDS RUSHING	128	143
Total Rushing Plays	31	36
Avg. Gain Per Play	4.1	3.9
NET YARDS PASSING	173	175
Yards Lost Attempting to Pass	2-12	0-0
Gross Yards Passing	185	175
PASSES	15-28-2	13-25-0
Avg. Gain Per Play	5.8	7.6
PUNTS	2-29.5	3-30.6
Had Blocked	0	0
TOTAL RET. YARDS	139	64
Punt Returns	1-7	0-0
Kickoff Returns	7-132	1-40
Interception Returns	0-0	2-24
PENALTIES/YARDS	2-15	3-25
FUMBLES/LOST	4-2	3-1
TIME OF POSSESSION	29:42	30:18
Attendance—46,302.		

INDIVIDUAL STATISTICS

Rushing—San Diego, Muncie 23-94, Brooks 6-23, Cappelletti 1-5, Fouts 1-6; Cincinnati, Johnson 21-80, Alexander 9-22, Anderson 5-39, Collinsworth 1-2.

Passing—San Diego, Fouts 15-28-2—185; Cincinnati, Anderson 14-22-0—161, Thompson 1-1-0—14.

Receiving—San Diego, Winslow 3-47, Chandler 6-79, Joiner 3-41, Brooks 2-5, Sievers 1-13; Cincinnati, Alexander 3-25, Ross 5-69, M.L. Harris 1-8, Collinsworth 2-28, Curtis 2-28, Johnson 1-14, Bass 1-3.

Kickoff Returns—San Diego, Brooks 4-87, Shaw 1-7, Beaudoin 2-38; Cincinnati, Verser 1-40.

Punt Returns—San Diego, Chandler 1-7; Cincinnati, None.

Interceptions—San Diego, None; Cincinnati, Breeden 1-0, Kemp 1-24.

Punting—San Diego, Roberts 2-29.5; Cincinnati, McInally 3-30.6.

Field Goals—San Diego, Benirschke 0-2; Cincinnati, Breech 2-2.

Fumbles—San Diego, Brooks, Muncie 3; Cincinnati, Ross, Collinsworth, Johnson.

Fumble Recoveries—San Diego, Macek, Wilkerson, Buchanon 1-8; Cincinnati, Collinsworth, Johnson, Bass, Browner.

NFC CHAMPIONSHIP GAME

49ers 28, COWBOYS 27

SAN FRANCISCO—The comeback encompassed more than the 89 yards on a magnificent final drive. If the truth be known, it spanned three years, from the moment a long-time assistant coach named Bill Walsh finally was given a team of his own and selected, in his very first college draft, a quarterback named Joe Montana and a receiver named Dwight Clark.

In the end, it took a breathtaking six-yard pass play, designed by Walsh and executed spectacularly by Montana and Clark, to make the San Francisco 49ers what they are.

And what they are, of course, is a Super Bowl team. Not any old Super Bowl team, either, but the second Super Bowl team to have risen from a losing record the previous season (the Cincinnati Bengals beat them to the honor by about four hours).

The 49ers were a sorry sight when Walsh

assembled them at Santa Clara for training camp in 1979. They were 2-14 that first year. They were 6-10 in 1980 as Montana and Clark established themselves as two of the best young players in the National Football League. In 1981, they hoped to reach .500.

"I would have been happy to be 8-8," said Ed DeBartolo Jr., the club president, on the eve of the National Football Conference championship game against the Dallas Cowboys.

So this was a team that bypassed mediocrity, a team which overhauled the Dallas Cowboys, 28-27, in the final minute of play. And despite their youth, despite their lack of experience in the playoffs, the 49ers made that final, amazing drive to the first league championship game in the 36-year history of the franchise.

It all came down to Montana and Clark and a 13-play march to the end zone because the 49ers, who had the fewest turnovers in the league during the regular season, played giveaway much of the day. Montana threw three interceptions and the backs contributed three fumbles to the Dallas cause.

"Some people might call it a mistake-filled game," Walsh said. "I'm sure the Dallas defense is saying, 'We forced six errors.' And they'd be right. This is championship football. It's like a championship fight, like (Renaldo) Snipes knocking down (Larry) Holmes."

Not only did the 49ers have to climb off Candlestick's sticky canvas after those setbacks, they also had to contend with a suspect call by an official. Side judge Dean Look nullifed an interception by star cornerback Ronnie Lott midway through the second period with a strange interference call. That gave the Cowboys a first down at the San Francisco 12-yard line. Dallas scored three plays later on a Tony Dorsett sweep for a 17-14 halftime lead.

There was another pass interference call on Lott near the end of the third quarter, this one apparent to just about everyone in the record Candlestick crowd of 60,525. It positioned the Cowboys for the second of Rafael Septien's two field goals.

"There wasn't much doubt (about the second pass interference call)," said Lott. "Those two calls added up to 10 points. The offense certainly took some pressure off my back."

But first the offense placed some additional pressure on itself. Walt Easley fumbled on the next series, Everson Walls recovered for Dallas and Danny White passed 21 yards to Doug Cosbie four plays later for a 27-21 Cowboy lead.

Then Montana threw his second interception to Walls, the rookie free agent who led the NFL in thefts. The 49ers' uphill journey, like the cable cars which climb the city's picturesque streets, apparently had ended halfway to the stars.

When the 49ers finally got the ball back, four minutes and 54 seconds remained and the goal line was 89 yards away. The first play, an incomplete pass to Lenvil Elliott, gained nothing.

Then Elliott ran six yards on a trap play designed to offset the lethal pass rush of Harvey Martin. Montana threw a six-yard pass to wide receiver Freddie Solomon on the first of three critical third-down plays and, suddenly, the resourceful San Francisco offense was rolling again.

Down the field swept the 49ers, Elliott running for two first downs, Solomon making another on a reverse, Montana passing to Clark along the right sidelines for 10 yards and to Solomon for 12 on the left. Montana knows about comebacks. He once brought Notre Dame back from a 34-12 deficit to win a Cotton Bowl game, 35-34, as time expired. And he sparked th 49ers from a 28-point deficit as they overcame New Orleans in overtime, 38-35, in 1980.

But on the first play from the Dallas 13, Montana overthrew an open Solomon in the end zone. "Usually, Bill doesn't get very excited," Montana said. "But when I missed Freddie in the end zone, he was pretty upset. So was I."

"The real surge of emotion came when the ball just went over Fred Solomon's fingertips," Walsh confessed. "I jumped as high as I could trying to catch it myself. We had set up that play perfectly. That was the National Conference championship right there."

So much for what might have been. The 49ers still had three cracks and more than a minute to work with. Elliott swept seven yards on second down and San Francisco called the second of its three time outs. Montana huddled with Walsh. Third and three. Fifty eight seconds left.

Montana rolled to his right, away from Martin's side, stringing out the pass rush. Solomon broke for the flag but was covered. Clark curled into the end zone, braked at the end line and looked for his quarterback. Walls and free safety Michael Downs were nearby. Montana was sprinting toward the sideline.

"I thought of throwing it away," Montana said. "I cocked my arm to do that when I saw Dwight covered. I didn't want to take a loss in that situation. But just then I saw Dwight getting away from the coverage."

Clark's responsibility was to freeze the defenders, then slide down the end line parallel to Montana. He doesn't have much speed, one reason for his low standing in the 1979 draft (10th round), but his moves and routes are picture perfect. Already this day, they'd been responsible for seven catches, one for a touchdown. Now Montana was throwing the most significant pass in 49er annals toward him. And high, as the play was intended.

"I thought it was too high," said the 6-3 Clark, "because I don't jump that well. And I was real tired. I had the flu last week and I had trouble getting my breath on that last drive. I don't know how I caught the ball. How does a lady pick up a car when it's on top of her baby? You get it from somewhere."

Dwight Clark's miraculous TD catch against Dallas in the waning moments of the NFC title game propelled the 49ers into their first-ever Super Bowl.

Clark came down with the ball. And the 49er defense snuffed out a potential miracle Dallas finish when Lawrence Pillers, waived by the New York Jets during the 1980 season, sacked White. It caused a fumble recovered by Jim Stuckey.

The 49ers, who had lost their three most recent playoff opportunities, all to Dallas, in 1970, 1971 and 1972, had come back to beat America's Team.

"Well," Clark said, "I think we deserved it." He was not alone in that feeling.

SUNDAY, JANUARY 10

SCORE BY PERIODS

Dallas	10	7	0	10—27
San Francisco	7	7	7	7—28

SCORING

San Francisco—Solomon 8 pass from Montana (Wersching kick).

Dallas—Field goal Septien 44.

Dallas—Hill 26 pass from D. White (Septien kick).

San Francisco—Clark 20 pass from Montana (Wersching kick).

Dallas—Dorsett 5 run (Septien kick).

San Francisco—Davis 2 run (Wersching kick).

Dallas—Field goal Septien 22.

Dallas—Cosbie 21 pass from D. White (Septien kick).

San Francisco—Clark 6 pass from Montana (Wersching kick).

TEAM STATISTICS

	Dallas	San Fran.
TOTAL FIRST DOWNS	16	26
By Rushing	5	6
By Passing	9	17
By Penalty	2	3
THIRD DOWN EFFICIENCY	5-13	4-10
TOTAL NET YARDS	250	393
Total Offensive Plays	60	69
Avg. Gain Per Play	4.2	5.7

	Dallas	San Fran.
NET YARDS RUSHING	115	127
Total Rushing Plays	32	31
Avg. Gain Per Play	3.6	4.1
NET YARDS PASSING	135	266
Yards Lost Attempting to Pass	4-38	3-20
Gross Yards Passing	173	286
PASSES	16-24-1	22-35-3
Avg. Gain Per Play	4.8	7.0
PUNTS	6-39.3	3-35.7
Had Blocked	0	0
TOTAL RET. YARDAGE	102	136
Punt Returns	3-13	3-24
Kickoff Returns	5-89	6-107
Interception Returns	3-0	1-5
PENALTIES/YARDS	5-39	7-106
FUMBLES/LOST	4-2	3-3
TIME OF POSSESSION	32:57	27:03
Attendance—60,525.		

INDIVIDUAL STATISTICS

Rushing—Dallas, Dorsett 22-91, J. Jones 4-14, Springs 5-10, D. White 1-0; San Francisco, Elliott 10-48, Cooper 8-35, Ring 6-27, Solomon 1-14, Easley 2-6, Davis 1-2, Montana 3-minus 5.

Passing—Dallas, D. White 16-24-1—173; San Francisco, Montana 22-35-2—286.

Receiving—Dallas, J. Jones 3-17, DuPree 3-15, Springs 3-13, Hill 2-43, Pearson 1-31, Cosbie 1-21, Johnson 1-20, Saldi 1-9, Donley 1-4; San Francisco, Clark 8-120, Solomon 6-75, Young 4-45, Cooper 2-11, Elliott 1-24, Shumann 1-11.

Kickoff Returns—Dallas, J. Jones 3-56, Newsome 2-33; San Francisco, Lawrence 3-60, Ring 3-47.

Punt Returns—Dallas, J. Jones 3-13; San Francisco, Hicks 2-21, Solomon 1-3.

Interceptions—Dallas, Walls 2-0, R. White 1-0; San Francisco, Leopold 1-5.

Punting—Dallas, D. White 6-39.3; San Francisco, Miller 3-35.7.

Field Goals—Dallas, Septien 2-2; San Francisco, None attempted.

Fumbles—Dallas, J. Jones 2, D. White 2; San Francisco, Ring, Montana, Easley.

Fumble Recoveries—Dallas, J. Jones, D. White, Hegman, Bethea, Walls; San Francisco, Lawrence, Stuckey.

Rags To Riches For 49ers

By LOWELL REIDENBAUGH
Senior Editor

PONTIAC, Mich.—On the sidelines the bespectacled, white-haired gentleman doffed the electronic gadgetry he had worn for more than three hours and permitted himself to be hoisted onto the shoulders of white-shirted behemoths.

Fourteen seconds remained on the Silverdome clock, but Dwight Clark had just recovered an onside kickoff and the football was securely in the San Francisco 49ers' possession.

Super Bowl XVI was virtually over and the 49ers were champions of professional football, winners by 26-21 over the Cincinnati Bengals. As 81,270 filed out of the enclosed stadium and the Niners strolled into their locker room, one of the National Football League's unlikeliest sagas took its place among other improbable tales.

Two years after the 49ers had gone 2-14 in Bill Walsh's first season as coach, there he was, coach of the world champions.

Never before had a team climbed so far so quickly. From their 2-14 mark in 1979, the 49ers rose to 6-10 in 1980 and then to world-title class. Their 16-3 record included a 13-3 regular-season log, the best in the NFL. Defensively, they had ranked 18th among 28 teams in 1980. In 1981, with three rookies in their secondary, they ranked second in the league in fewest points allowed.

The 49ers' offense was supervised by Joe Montana, in only his second full season. At 25, Montana was the same age as Joe Namath when Broadway Joe led the New York Jets to a staggering upset of the Baltimore Colts in Super Bowl III.

Walsh's route to supreme command of an NFL club also was strewn with stardust. A one-time assistant coach of the Bengals, he had been instrumental in the emergence of Kenny Anderson as one of the NFL's premier quarterbacks. When legendary Paul Brown retired as head coach, however, Walsh was passed over as a successor.

He took a position as assistant coach with the San Diego Chargers and then moved on to Stanford University as head coach. From Palo Alto, Calif., it was only a backyard jump to Candlestick Park when 49ers Owner Edward DeBartolo Jr. offered him the reins after the 1978 season.

In less than 30 months after he assembled his first San Francisco squad, Walsh was standing in the glare of television floodlights in the winners' clubhouse.

A telephone was thrust into his hands and, plastering one hand over his ear to muffle the shouts of the jubilant world champions, he said:

"I thought it might be you."

"Tell Joe Montana and the fellas that they really won one for the Gipper," said the caller. President Ronald Reagan was well acquainted with the story of the legendary George Gipp and his deathbed wish that some future Notre Dame team, facing imminent defeat, would "win one for the Gipper."

More than 40 years earlier, the Chief Executive had portrayed George Gipp in a Hollywood production of Knute Rockne and Notre Dame, the alma mater of Montana.

"I'll tell Joe about the Gipper. Thank you very, very much," concluded Walsh, who had been a White House visitor after the 49ers won the National Conference crown with a last-minute victory over the Dallas Cowboys.

The 49ers' conquest of the Bengals was not from the world of make-believe, although there were moments when Walsh wished for storybook assistance. The 49ers piled up a 20-0 halftime lead, the largest margin for two quarters in Super Bowl history. An electrifying Cincinnati attack in the third quarter, however, cast a different complexion on the contest and threatened to wreck the Niners' dreams.

The team that yielded 15 first downs in the opening half while posting only seven itself registered eight in the third quarter while holding the 49ers to none. Three times during the period, the NFC champions ran off three plays and were forced to punt.

In nine plays opening the third quarter, the American Conference champion Bengals, aided by two penalties, marched 83 yards for their first touchdown.

With third-and-four at the San Francisco 5-yard line, Kenny Anderson, the second best rusher on the Cincinnati team, faded as though to pass, then bolted up the middle and into the end zone.

With 6:53 of the period remaining, the Bengals gained possession of the football at midfield and promptly went into reverse. A holding penalty, a personal foul and a Fred Dean sack of Anderson placed the Bengals in a third-and-23 situation on their own 37. But the entire deficit was expunged on a 49-yard pass, Anderson to wide receiver Cris Collinsworth, and shortly the Bengals were knocking again, with first down and goal to go at the San Francisco three.

Pete Johnson, the running back of undetermined weight (estimates start at 250 pounds), gained two yards at center, then hit left guard, where he was met by rookie defensive tackle John Harty for no gain.

Anderson passed to Charles Alexander, but

Cornerback Eric Wright stripped the ball from Cincinnati's Cris Collinsworth deep in 49er territory (above), and San Francisco's stubborn defense stopped the Bengals' big Pete Johnson just short of the goal line in two of the most pivotal plays in Super Bowl XVI.

linebacker Dan Bunz nailed the running back 18 inches from the goal line.

Once more, Johnson hammered the center and was met by the entire defensive line.

The decision to attempt the touchdown, rather than accept an almost certain field goal with an entire quarter remaining, was "a staff decision," explained Lindy Infante, who directs the Bengals' offense.

"We had run twice to the left and David Verser (wide receiver) missed a block on the second call because of the crowd noise and he failed to pick up an audible blocking change.

"Rather than run to the same place three times, we felt we could go to the right. We had great success with that play all season, but this time their defense got good penetration."

The goal line stand was not surprising to Walsh. "It is something we have done before," said the coach, whose team defeated the Bengals, 21-3, during the regular season.

"That is where we showed our character. Dan Bunz and Jack Reynolds (linebackers) were tremendous. That might have been the difference in the game."

Reynolds, the 12-year pro who was signed as a free agent after servering his ties with the Los Angeles Rams, considered the goal-line stand the key series in the game.

"We had one in an earlier loss to Atlanta, but we haven't made one like that in a long while," Reynolds said. "We were good, possibly great today, and nobody can take that away from us."

The AFC champions did make a concerted effort to take the game away from the 49ers in the fourth period, unleashing a seven-play drive that consumed 53 yards in the first five minutes.

Anderson's four-yard pass to tight end Dan Ross climaxed the drive and when Jim Breech kicked his second extra point, the Bengals trailed only 20-14.

At this point, 10:06 remained. The 49ers had not made a first down since late in the second period. Now, however, they were ready to shed their lethargy. Nine plays, five of them rushes by Ricky Patton, took them to the Cincinnati 23, and Ray Wersching kicked a 40-yard field goal.

On the succeeding kickoff, Verser returned the ball to the Cincinnati 22. The clock showed 5:14 to play, but Anderson's first-down pass, intended for Collinsworth, was picked off by rookie cornerback Eric Wright, who made a 25-yard return.

Six plays, all on the ground, consumed three minutes and 16 yards and carried to the Bengals' 6. Wersching came on to boot a 23-yard field goal. It was his fourth field goal of the game, tying a Super Bowl record set by Don Chandler of the Green Bay Packers in Super Bowl II.

Less than two minutes remained for the Bengals to erase a 12-point handicap and it was insufficient, although Anderson completed six consecutive passes, the last to Ross for a pride-saving TD with 16 seconds left.

When Breech attempted an onside kick, Clark scooped up the football. The clock headed for the zero mark, and Walsh watched from his shoulder-top seat as Montana took the snap, retreated a few steps and knelt on the synthetic turf. The 49ers' rise from the dungeon to the penthouse suite was complete.

For the first 30 minutes of this engagement of first-time Super Bowl participants, all indications were that the gold-helmeted Californians would make a mockery of Forrest Gregg's Midwesterners.

In the first quarter, after Amos Lawrence fumbled the opening kickoff and John Simmons recovered at the San Francisco 26, the Bengals advanced to the San Francisco 11 before an Anderson pass intended for Isaac Curtis was picked off by free safety Dwight Hicks at the 5 and returned to the 32. In 11 plays, the 49ers drove 68 yards and took a 7-0 lead when Montana, the games Most Valuable Player sneaked one yard and Wersching added the extra point.

On their next possession, early in the second period, the Bengals, in four plays, moved from their 49 to a first-and-10 on the San Francisco 27. The drive came to a shattering halt when Collinsworth, after catching one of his five passes during the day, was stripped of the football by Wright and Lynn Thomas recovered on the 49ers' 8.

No previous Super Bowl team had marched more than 89 yards for a touchdown, but the 49ers went 92 yards in 12 plays. Montana's 11-yard pass to Earl Cooper concluded the drive and San Francisco enjoyed a 14-0 lead.

On their next possesssion, the 49ers drove 61 yards in 13 plays, Wersching kicking a 22-yard field goal with only 15 seconds left in the first half.

But the charitable Bengals had one more turnover remaining. On the kickoff, Archie Griffin fumbled and Milt McColl recovered for the 49ers. There was enough time for Wersching to split the posts from 26 yards away.

The four first-half turnovers three of which produced 17 San Francisco points, were too great an obstacle for the Bengals to surmount, observed Gregg, the first Super Bowl player (Green Bay and Dallas) ever to coach in the NFL's grand finale. "You don't help a team like San Francisco with four turnovers and expect to win. You can't spot them 20 points."

"Too many mistakes against a good team," added Paul Brown, founder of the Cincinnati franchise and now its general manager.

Those mistakes more than outweighed the Bengals' superiority in yardage. The Bengals became the first Super Bowl team to outgain its rival and still lose.

Except for those Cincinnati blunders, the 49ers very likely would not have joined the Green Bay Packers (Super Bowls I and II) and the Dallas Cowboys (Super Bowls VI and XI) as the only National Conference teams to win world championships.

SCORE BY PERIODS

San Francisco	7	13	0	6—26
Cincinnati	0	0	7	14—21

SCORING

San Francisco—Montana 1 run (Wersching kick)
San Francisco—Cooper 11 pass from Montana (Wersching kick)
San Francisco—Field goal Wersching 22
San Francisco—Field goal Wersching 26
Cincinnati—Anderson 5 run (Breech kick)
Cincinnati—Ross 4 pass from Anderson (Breech kick)
San Francisco—Field goal Wersching 40
San Francisco—Field goal Wersching 23
Cincinnati—Ross 3 pass from Anderson (Breech kick)

TEAM STATISTICS

	San Fran.	Cincinnati
TOTAL FIRST DOWNS	20	24
By Rushing	9	7
By Passing	9	13
By Penalty	2	4
THIRD-DOWN EFFICIENCY	8-15	6-12
TOTAL NETS YARDS	275	356
Total Offensive Plays	63	63
Avg. Gain Per Carry	4.4	5.7

	San Fran.	Cincinnati
NET YARDS RUSHING	127	72
Total Rushing Plays	40	24
Avg. Gain Per Rush	3.2	3.0
NET YARDS PASSING	148	284
Sacks-Yards Lost	1-9	5-16
Gross Yards Passing	157	300
PASSES	14-22-0	25-34-2
Avg. Gain Per Pass	6.4	7.3
PUNTS	4-46.3	3-43.7
Had Blocked	0	0
TOTAL RET. YARDS	98	87
Punt Returns	1-6	4-35
Kickoff Returns	3-40	7-52
Interceptions Returns	2-52	0-0
PENALTIES-YARDS	8-65	8-57
FUMBLES-LOST	2-1	2-2
TIME OF POSSESSION	32:13	27:47
Attendance—81,270.		

INDIVIDUAL STATISTICS

Rushing—San Francisco, Cooper 9-34, Ring 5-17, Montana 6-18, Patton 17-55, J. Davis 2-5, Clark 1-minus 2; Cincinnati, Johnson 14-36, Alexander 5-17, Anderson 4-15, A. Griffin 1-4.

Passing—San Francisco, Montana 14-22-0—157; Cincinnati, Anderson 25-34-2—300.

Receiving—San Francisco, Patton 1-6, Clark 4-45, Solomon 4-52, Young 1-14, Cooper 2-15, Ring 1-3, Wilson 1-22; Cincinnati, Curtis 3-42, Ross 11-104, Johnson 2-8, Collinsworth 5-107, Alexander 2-3, Kreider 2-36.

Interceptions—San Francisco, Hicks, 1-27, Wright 1-25.

Punt Returns—San Francisco, Hicks 1-6; Cincinnati, Fuller 4-35.

Kickoff Returns—San Francisco, Lawrence 1-17, Hicks 1-23, Clark 1-0; Cincinnati, Verser 5-52, A. Griffin 1-0, Frazier 1-0.

Punting—San Francisco, Miller 4-46.3; Cincinnati, McInally 3-43.7.

PRO BOWL

HONOLULU—Whether or not the Pro Bowl, the National Football League's season farewell, has a home in Hawaii remains to be seen.

One thing is certain, though. Kellen Winslow, the San Diego Chargers' tight end, has found a home in the Pro Bowl.

Winslow was voted co-Most Valuable Player of the 1982 Pro Bowl at Aloha Stadium, sharing the honor with defensive end Lee Roy Selmon of the Tampa Bay Buccaneers as experts in the press box split their votes the way Winslow splits defenders.

Winslow's performance on the final Sunday of the season helped the American Football Conference end a four-game losing streak and defeat the National Football Conference, 16-13.

Winslow had six catches—which was more than any other two receivers combined—for 86 yards. One of those receptions, an over-the-middle catch for 23 yards, came in a last-minute drive that concluded with a 23-yard field goal by Kansas City's Nick Lowery with six seconds left to play.

It should be duly noted for posterity that at 2:24 p.m., Hawaiian Standard Time (7:24 p.m. EST), the season was finished.

Even though the fans had to get up early for the 11 a.m. start, support remained enthusiastic for the NFL All-Star game in the Pacific, and some NFL executives would like to make the site permanent. But the Japanese have made a bid to play the 1983 game in Tokyo, and anything's possible.

Maybe they can even have a little more offense, though John McKay of Tampa Bay, the NFC coach, pointed to the difficulties of installing a workable offense in a game such as the Pro Bowl.

"I figured it would be a low-scoring game," he said. "There was just too much defense. It takes longer to get an offense coordinated."

The San Francisco 49ers' Joe Montana, the Super Bowl XVI hero, said he found the adjustment confusing at times.

"There's a lot of pressure on the quarterbacks in a game like this," he said. "New plays and formations to learn, new people to get to know.

"I know I started to call plays from our (49ers) formations a few times."

On the winning side, Miami's Don Shula, who coached the AFC, had better luck in meshing his offense, even though Selmon got through to record four quarterback sacks.

"We were moving the ball well and I felt we could get going in the second half," he said. "With four pass rushers like we had (Joe Klecko and Mark Gastineau of the New York Jets, Gary Johnson of San Diego, and Miami's Bob Baumhower), their quarterbacks did not have a lot of time to throw."

San Diego's Dan Fouts, a master at last-minute heroics, guided the AFC to its winning field goal, moving the team 69 yards in 2:29.

He passed for 46 yards on completions to Denver's Steve Watson, Cleveland's Ozzie Newsome and Winslow, moving the ball to the NFC 5.

"We knew we didn't need a touchdown because Lowery has such a strong leg. We were just trying to get the ball to the 30-yard line and Lowery into position for the field goal," Fouts said. "The pass to Winslow broke their backs."

The drive followed a 74-yard scoring march by the NFC, after Dallas' Everson Walls made his second interception of the game. A five-yard TD run by Tony Dorsett of the Cowboys tied the score with 2:43 left.

Walls' first interception of a Fouts pass set up the game's first score in the second period, a four-yard pass from Montana to Tampa Bay's Jimmie Giles.

The AFC moved ahead in the third quarter with Chuck Muncie of San Diego capping an 80-yard drive with a two-yard sweep and Houston's Earl Campbell plunging over from one yard out.

Campbell's score was set up by the Klecko-Gastineau combination. Klecko stripped Montana of the ball and Gastineau scooped it up at the NFC 22 and ran it back to the 1.

SUNDAY, JANUARY 31
SCORE BY PERIODS

NFC	0	6	0	7—13
AFC	0	0	13	3—16

SCORING

NFC—Giles 4 pass from Montana (kick blocked).
AFC—Muncie 2 run (kick failed).
AFC—Campbell 1 run (Lowery kick).
NFC—Dorsett 4 run (Septien kick).
AFC—Field goal Lowery 23.

TEAM STATISTICS

	NFC	AFC
First downs	12	25
Rushes-Yards	28-16	45-154
Passing yards	42	195
Sacks by-Yards	3-30	7-54
Return yards	91	57
Passes	7-29-2	16-30-3
Punts	9-45.3	5-45.0
Fumbles-Lost	4-2	4-1
Penalties-Yards	6-35	1-5
Time of possession	26:55	33:05

Attendance—50,402.

INDIVIDUAL STATISTICS

RUSHING—NFC, Dorsett 13-39, Sims 6-23, Montana 2-19, Andrews, 4-12, Rogers 2-12, Bartkowski 1-11. AFC, Campbell 11-52, Johnson 9-32, Delaney 11-28, Muncie 8-28, Anderson 3-18, Largent 1-0, Fouts 1-0, Lewis 1-(minus-4).

PASSING—NFC, Montana 4-14-1—23, Bartkowski 3-15-1—49. AFC, Anderson 8-14-1—106, Fouts 8-16-2—143.

RECEIVING—NFC, Jenkins 2-33, Giles 2-20, Clark 1-23, Andrews 1-4, Rogers 1-(minus-8). AFC, Winslow 6-86, Watson 3-51, Newsome 2-28, Johnson 2-16, Largent 1-35, Lewis 1-19, Collinsworth 1-14.

SUPER BOWL SUMMARIES

SUPER BOWL I

January 15, 1967 at Los Angeles

Attendance—61,946

Kansas City (AFL)	0	10	0	0 —	10
Green Bay (NFL)	7	7	14	7 —	35

Winning coach—Vince Lombardi.
Most Valuable Player—Bart Starr.

SUPER BOWL II

January 14, 1968 at Miami

Attendance—75,546

Green Bay (NFL)	3	13	10	7 —	33
Oakland (AFL)	0	7	0	7 —	14

Winning coach—Vince Lombardi.
Most Valuable Player—Bart Starr.

SUPER BOWL III

January 12, 1969 at Miami

Attendance—75,389

New York (AFL)	0	7	6	3 —	16
Baltimore (NFL)	0	0	0	7 —	7

Winning coach—Weeb Ewbank.
Most Valuable Player—Joe Namath.

SUPER BOWL IV

January 11, 1970 at New Orleans

Attendance—80,562

Minnesota (NFL)	0	0	7	0 —	7
Kansas City (AFL)	3	13	7	0 —	23

Winning coach—Hank Stram.
Most Valuable Player—Len Dawson.

SUPER BOWL V

January 17, 1971 at Miami

Attendance—79,204

Baltimore (AFC)	0	6	0	10 —	16
Dallas (NFC)	3	10	0	0 —	13

Winning coach—Don McCafferty.
Most Valuable Player—Chuck Howley.

SUPER BOWL VI

January 16, 1972 at New Orleans

Attendance—81,023

Dallas (NFC)	3	7	7	7 —	24
Miami (AFC)	0	3	0	0 —	3

Winning coach—Tom Landry.
Most Valuable Player—Roger Staubach.

SUPER BOWL VII

January 14, 1973 at Los Angeles

Attendance—90,182

Miami (AFC)	7	7	0	0 —	14
Washington (NFC)	0	0	0	7 —	7

Winning coach—Don Shula.
Most Valuable Player—Jake Scott.

SUPER BOWL VIII

January 13, 1974 at Houston

Attendance—71,882

Minnesota (NFC)	0	0	0	7 —	7
Miami (AFC)	14	3	7	0 —	24

Winning coach—Don Shula.
Most Valuable Player—Larry Csonka.

SUPER BOWL IX

January 12, 1975 at New Orleans

Attendance—80,997

Pittsburgh (AFC)	0	2	7	7 —	16
Minnesota (NFC)	0	0	0	6 —	6

Winning coach—Chuck Noll.
Most Valuable Player—Franco Harris.

SUPER BOWL X

January 18, 1976 at Miami

Attendance—80,187

Dallas (NFC)	7	3	0	7 —	17
Pittsburgh (AFC)	7	0	0	14 —	21

Winning coach—Chuck Noll.
Most Valuable Player—Lynn Swann.

SUPER BOWL XI

January 9, 1977 at Pasadena

Attendance—103,428

Oakland (AFC)	0	16	3	13 —	32
Minnesota (NFC)	0	0	7	7 —	14

Winning coach—John Madden.
Most Valuable Player—Fred Biletnikoff.

SUPER BOWL XII

January 15, 1978 at New Orleans

Attendance—75,804

Dallas (NFC)	10	3	7	7 —	27
Denver (AFC)	0	0	10	0 —	10

Winning coach—Tom Landry.
Most Valuable Players—Harvey Martin and Randy White.

Pasadena's Rose Bowl will be the site of Super Bowl XVII.

SUPER BOWL XIII

January 21, 1979 at Miami

Attendance—78,656

Pittsburgh (AFC)	7	14	0	14 —	35
Dallas (NFC)	7	7	3	14 —	31

Winning coach—Chuck Noll.
Most Valuable Player—Terry Bradshaw.

SUPER BOWL XIV

January 20, 1980 at Los Angeles

Attendance—103,985

Los Angeles (NFC)	7	6	6	0 —	19
Pittsburgh (AFC)	3	7	7	14 —	31

Winning coach—Chuck Noll.
Most Valuable Player—Terry Bradshaw.

SUPER BOWL XV

January 25, 1981 at New Orleans

Attendance—75,500

Oakland (AFC)	14	0	10	3 —	27
Philadelphia (NFC)	0	3	0	7 —	10

Winning coach—Tom Flores.
Most Valuable Player—Jim Plunkett.

SUPER BOWL XVI

January 24, 1982 at Pontiac

Attendance—81,270

San Francisco (NFC)	7	13	0	6 —	26
Cincinnati (AFC)	0	0	7	14 —	21

Winning coach—Bill Walsh.
Most Valuable Player—Joe Montana.

1981 NFL Statistics
1981 RUSHING

YARDS
>NFC: 1674—George Rogers, New Orleans.
>AFC: 1376—Earl Campbell, Houston.

YARDS PER ATTEMPT
>AFC: 5.3—Tony Nathan, Miami (147 attempts, 782 yards).
>NFC: 4.9—Wilbert Montgomery, Philadelphia (286 attempts, 1402 yards).

TOUCHDOWNS
>AFC: 19—Chuck Muncie, San Diego.
>NFC: 13—John Riggins, Washington.
>   13—George Rogers, New Orleans.
>   13—Billy Sims, Detroit.

ATTEMPTS
>NFC: 378—George Rogers, New Orleans.
>AFC: 361—Earl Campbell, Houston.

LONGEST
>AFC: 82 yards—Joe Delaney, Kansas City vs. Houston, November 15 (TD).
>NFC: 79 yards—George Rogers, New Orleans vs. Cleveland, October 18 (TD).

MOST YARDS, GAME
>AFC: 193 (29 attempts)—Joe Delaney, Kansas City vs. Houston, November 15.
>NFC: 185 (28 attempts)—Billy Sims, Detroit vs. Denver, October 11.

TEAM LEADERS
>AFC: BALTIMORE: 779, Curtis Dickey; BUFFALO: 1097, Joe Cribbs; CIN-
>CINNATI: 1077, Pete Johnson; CLEVELAND: 1103, Mike Pruitt;
>DENVER: 749, Rick Parros; HOUSTON: 1376, Earl Campbell;
>KANSAS CITY: 1121, Joe Delaney; MIAMI: 782, Tony Nathan;
>NEW ENGLAND: 873, Anthony Collins; NEW YORK: 623, Free-
>man McNeil; OAKLAND: 828, Kenny King; PITTSBURGH: 987,
>Franco Harris; SAN DIEGO: 1144, Chuck Muncie; SEATTLE: 583,
>Theotis Brown.
>NFC: ATLANTA: 1301, William Andrews; CHICAGO: 1222, Walter Payton;
>DALLAS: 1646, Tony Dorsett; DETROIT: 1437, Billy Sims; GREEN
>BAY: 860, Gerry Ellis; LOS ANGELES: 1074, Wendell Tyler; MIN-
>NESOTA: 1063, Ted Brown; NEW ORLEANS: 1674, George Rogers;
>NEW YORK: 822, Rob Carpenter; PHILADELPHIA: 1402, Wilbert
>Montgomery; ST. LOUIS: 1376, Ottis Anderson; SAN FRANCISCO:
>543, Rickey Patton; TAMPA BAY: 651, Jerry Eckwood; WASH-
>INGTON: 916, Joe Washington.

TEAM CHAMPION
>NFC: 2795—Detroit
>AFC: 2633—Kansas City

RUSHING—TEAM
AMERICAN FOOTBALL CONFERENCE

	Att.	Yards	Avg.	Long	TDs.
Kansas City	610	2,633	4.3	t82	22
Pittsburgh	554	2,372	4.3	50	21
New York Jets	571	2,341	4.1	43	11
Miami	535	2,173	4.1	46	18
Buffalo	524	2,125	4.1	35	13
Oakland	493	2,058	4.2	60	11
New England	499	2,040	4.1	43	23
San Diego	481	2,005	4.2	t73	26
Cincinnati	493	1,973	4.0	t39	19
Cleveland	474	1,929	4.1	26	11
Denver	515	1,895	3.7	37	12
Baltimore	441	1,850	4.2	t67	11
Houston	466	1,734	3.7	43	11
Seattle	440	1,594	3.6	43	14
Conference Total	7,096	28,722	.....	t82	223
Conference Average	506.9	2,051.6	4.0	.....	15.9

NATIONAL FOOTBALL CONFERENCE

	Att.	Yards	Avg.	Long	TDs.
Detroit	596	2,795	4.7	51	26
Dallas	630	2,711	4.3	t75	15
Philadelphia	559	2,509	4.5	41	17
New Orleans	546	2,286	4.2	t79	16
Los Angeles	559	2,236	4.0	t69	17
St. Louis	519	2,213	4.3	t44	20
Chicago	608	2,171	3.6	39	13
Washington	532	2,157	4.1	32	19
Atlanta	495	1,965	4.0	35	15
San Francisco	560	1,941	3.5	28	17
Tampa Bay	458	1,731	3.8	59	13
New York Giants	481	1,685	3.5	35	11
Green Bay	478	1,670	3.5	34	11
Minnesota	391	1,512	3.9	38	8
Conference Total	7,412	29,582	.....	t79	218
Conference Average	529.4	2,113.0	4.0	....	15.6
League Total	14,508	58,304	.....	t82	441
League Average	518.1	2,082.3	4.0	.....	15.8

TOP TEN RUSHERS

	Att.	Yards	Avg.	Long	TDs.
ROGERS, GEORGE, New Orleans	378	1674	4.4	t79	13
Dorsett, Tony, Dallas	342	1646	4.8	t75	4
Sims, Billy, Detroit	296	1437	4.9	51	13
Montgomery, Wilbert, Philadelphia	286	1402	4.9	41	8
Anderson, Ottis, St. Louis	328	1376	4.2	28	9
Campbell, Earl, Houston	361	1376	3.8	43	10
Andrews, William, Atlanta	289	1301	4.5	29	10
Payton, Walter, Chicago	339	1222	3.6	39	6
Muncie, Chuck, San Diego	251	1144	4.6	t73	19
Delaney, Joe, Kansas City	234	1121	4.8	t82	3

AFC—INDIVIDUALS

Player—Team	Att.	Yds.	Avg.	Lng.	TD	Player—Team	Att.	Yds.	Avg.	Lng.	TD
CAMPBELL, Hou.	361	1376	3.8	43	10	Cunningham, N.E.	86	269	3.1	12	4
Muncie, S.D.	251	1144	4.6	t73	19	Cappelletti, S.D.	68	254	3.7	30	4
Delaney, K.C.	234	1121	4.8	t82	3	S. Smith, Sea.	83	253	3.0	21	3
M. Pruitt, Clev.	247	1103	4.5	21	7	Hooks, Buff.	51	250	4.9	19	3
Cribbs, Buff.	257	1097	4.3	35	3	Newton, N.Y.J.	73	244	3.3	13	1
Johnson, Cin.	274	1077	3.9	t39	12	Brown, Buff.	62	226	3.6	13	0
Harris, Pitt.	242	987	4.1	50	8	Whittington, Oak.	69	220	3.2	13	1
Collins, N.E.	204	873	4.3	29	7	Calhoun, N.E.	57	205	3.6	33	2
King, Oak.	170	828	4.9	60	0	Thornton, Pitt.	56	202	3.6	t17	4
Nathan, Mia.	147	782	5.3	46	5	Tatupu, N.E.	38	201	5.3	43	2
Dickey, Balt.	164	779	4.8	t67	7	McKnight, K.C.	54	195	3.6	26	5
Parros, Den.	176	749	4.3	25	2	Doornink, Sea.	65	194	3.0	11	1
Franklin, Mia.	201	711	3.5	29	7	Hawkins, Oak.	40	165	4.1	19	0
Preston, Den.	183	640	3.5	23	3	C. Miller, Clev.	52	165	3.2	13	2
McNeil, N.Y.J.	137	623	4.5	43	2	A. Griffin, Cin.	47	163	3.5	23	3
Hadnot, K.C.	140	603	4.3	30	3	Bradshaw, Pitt.	38	162	4.3	16	2
McMillan, Balt.	149	597	4.0	42	3	Reed, Den.	68	156	2.3	10	0
T. Brown, St.L.-Sea.	156	583	3.7	43	8	Sipe, Clev.	38	153	4.0	22	1
Pollard, Pitt.	123	570	4.6	29	2	van Eeghen, Oak.	39	150	3.8	11	2
J. Brooks, S.D.	109	525	4.8	t28	3	Wilson, Oak.	30	147	4.9	18	2
Jensen, Oak.	117	456	3.9	33	4	Armstrong, Hou.	31	146	4.7	18	0
B. Jackson, K.C.	111	398	3.6	31	10	Hill, Mia.	37	146	3.9	24	1
Harper, N.Y.J.	81	393	4.9	t29	4	Zorn, Sea.	30	140	4.7	20	1
Leaks, Buff.	91	357	3.9	31	6	McCutcheon, Buff.	34	138	4.1	12	0
White, Clev.	97	342	3.5	26	1	Hughes, Sea.	47	135	2.9	15	0
Ferguson, N.E.	78	340	4.4	t19	3	Todd, N.Y.J.	32	131	4.1	19	0
Augustyniak, N.Y.J.	85	339	4.0	12	1	G. Pruitt, Clev.	31	124	4.0	15	0
Dierking, N.Y.J.	74	328	4.4	t15	1	Fuller, K.C.	19	118	6.2	27	0
Anderson, Cin.	46	320	7.0	25	1	Vigorito, Mia.	35	116	3.3	t30	1
Alexander, Cin.	98	292	3.0	16	2	Canada, Den.	33	113	3.4	11	3
Dixon, Balt.	73	285	3.9	41	0	B. Taylor, NYG-NYJ	38	111	2.9	14	2
Woodley, Mia.	63	272	4.3	26	4	Lytle, Den.	30	106	3.5	18	4
Davis, Pitt.	47	270	5.7	28	1	Jodat, Sea.	31	106	3.4	15	1
Long, N.Y.J.	73	269	3.7	19	2	Bennett, Mia.	28	104	3.7	12	0

Player—Team	Att.	Yds.	Avg.	Lng.	TD	Player—Team	Att.	Yds.	Avg.	Lng.	TD
Cavanaugh, N.E.	17	92	5.4	11	3	Orosz, Mia.	1	13	13.0	13	0
Coleman, Hou.	21	91	4.3	30	1	Reaves, Hou.	6	13	2.2	13	0
Kenney, K.C.	24	89	3.7	21	1	Landry, Balt.	1	11	11.0	11	0
B. Jones, Balt.	20	85	4.3	17	0	J. Wright, Den.	1	11	11.0	11	0
Marshall, K.C.	3	69	23.0	34	0	Verser, Cin.	2	11	5.5	9	0
Malone, Pitt.	16	68	4.3	19	2	Stoudt, Pitt.	3	11	3.7	10	0
Hargrove, Cin.	16	66	4.1	27	1	Bass, Cin.	1	9	9.0	9	0
Bledsoe, K.C.	20	65	3.3	13	0	Colquitt, Pitt.	1	8	8.0	8	0
Hawthorne, Pitt.	25	58	2.3	16	2	Bauer, S.D.	2	7	3.5	4	0
Upchurch, Den.	5	56	11.2	37	0	Watson, Den.	2	6	3.0	6	0
Krieg, Sea.	11	56	5.1	29	1	Moser, Pitt.	1	4	4.0	4	0
Fouts, S.D.	22	56	2.5	13	0	Garrett, Balt.	2	4	2.0	3	0
Willis, Oak.	16	54	3.4	t15	1	Miller, Sea.	2	4	2.0	2	0
Franklin, Balt.	21	52	2.5	8	1	Moore, Hou.	1	3	3.0	3	0
Grogan, N.E.	12	49	4.1	t24	2	Pennywell, N.E.	1	3	3.0	3	0
Largent, Sea.	6	47	7.8	15	1	Roberts, S.D.	1	2	2.0	2	0
Schonert, Cin.	7	41	5.9	19	0	Nielsen, Hou.	6	2	0.3	4	0
DeBerg, Den.	9	40	4.4	11	0	Butler, Buff.	1	1	1.0	1	0
Ivory, Sea.	9	38	4.2	7	0	Johnson, N.E.	2	1	0.5	5	0
Plunkett, Oak.	12	38	3.2	t13	1	Anderson, Balt.	1	0	0.0	0	0
McCauley, Balt.	10	37	3.7	8	0	L. Jones, N.Y.J.	2	0	0.0	5	0
T. Wilson, Hou.	13	35	2.7	7	0	McDonald, Clev.	2	0	0.0	2	0
Riddick, Buff.	3	29	9.7	12	0	Williams, K.C.	2	0	0.0	3	0
Ferguson, Buff.	20	29	1.5	16	1	Ramsey, N.Y.J.	3	0	0.0	0	0
Adkins, Sea.	3	28	9.3	13	0	Chandler, S.D.	5	−1	−0.2	9	0
C. Williams, S.D.	20	26	1.3	6	0	Carson, K.C.	1	−1	−1.0	−1	0
West, Sea.	3	25	8.3	27	0	Feacher, Clev.	1	−1	−1.0	−1	0
Hill, Clev.	4	23	5.8	9	0	Robinson, Buff.	1	−2	−2.0	−2	0
Lane, Sea.	8	22	2.8	5	0	Stabler, Hou.	10	−3	−0.3	4	0
Kreider, Cin.	1	21	21.0	21	0	Ryan, N.Y.J.	3	−5	−1.7	−1	0
Morgan, N.E.	2	21	10.5	11	0	Dixon, K.C.	1	−5	−5.0	−5	0
Howell, Mia.	5	21	4.2	9	0	Kush, Buff.	1	−6	−6.0	−6	0
Newsome, Clev.	2	20	10.0	14	0	Luther, S.D.	3	−8	−2.7	−1	0
Lewis, N.Y.J.	6	18	3.0	7	0	Franklin, Buff.	1	−11	−11.0	−11	0
Morton, Den.	8	18	2.3	5	0	Jackson, N.E.	2	−14	−7.0	−5	0
Stallworth, Pitt.	1	17	17.0	17	0	Grupp, K.C.	1	−19	−19.0	−19	0
Brammer, Buff.	2	17	8.5	11	0	Strock, Mia.	14	−26	−1.9	9	0
Moore, Sea.	1	15	15.0	15	0	McInally, Cin.	1	−27	−27.0	−27	0
Smith, Pitt.	1	15	15.0	15	0						

NFC—INDIVIDUALS

Player—Team	Att.	Yds.	Avg.	Lng.	TD	Player—Team	Att.	Yds.	Avg.	Lng.	TD
G. ROGERS, N.O.	378	1674	4.4	t79	13	Hofer, S.F.	60	193	3.2	12	1
Dorsett, Dall.	342	1646	4.8	t75	4	J. Jones, Dall.	34	183	5.4	t59	1
Sims, Det.	296	1437	4.9	51	13	Tyler, N.O.	36	183	5.1	42	0
Montgomery, Phila.	286	1402	4.9	41	8	Jackson, Wash.	46	183	4.0	14	0
Anderson, St.L.	328	1376	4.2	28	9	Middleton, G.B.	53	181	3.4	34	0
Andrews, Atl.	289	1301	4.5	29	10	Theismann, Wash.	36	177	4.9	24	2
Payton, Chi.	339	1222	3.6	39	6	Mitchell, St.L.	31	175	5.6	43	0
Tyler, L.A.	260	1074	4.1	t69	12	Hipple, Det.	41	168	4.1	18	7
Brown, Minn.	274	1063	3.9	34	6	Kotar, N.Y.G.	46	154	3.3	18	1
Washington, Wash.	210	916	4.4	32	4	Harrington, Phila.	34	140	4.1	16	2
Ellis, G.B.	196	860	4.4	29	4	W. Wilson, N.O.	44	137	3.1	13	1
Carpenter, Hou.-NYG.	208	822	4.0	35	5	Murray, Phila.	23	134	5.8	20	0
Riggins, Wash.	195	714	3.7	24	13	Young, Minn.	47	129	2.7	13	0
Eckwood, T.B.	172	651	3.8	59	2	Jaworski, Phila.	22	128	5.8	26	0
Springs, Dall.	172	625	3.6	16	10	Russell, Phila.	38	123	3.2	17	4
Patton, S.F.	152	543	3.6	28	4	J. Thomas, L.A.	34	118	3.5	40	0
Cain, Atl.	156	542	3.5	35	4	Campfield, Phila.	31	115	3.7	13	1
Suhey, Chi.	150	521	3.5	26	3	Ring, S.F.	22	106	4.8	16	0
Bussey, Det.	105	446	4.2	23	0	Harper, Chi.	34	106	3.1	11	1
Bryant, L.A.	109	436	4.0	20	1	Haden, L.A.	18	104	5.8	16	0
Guman, L.A.	115	433	3.8	18	4	Lomax, St.L.	19	104	5.5	t22	2
Morris, St.L.	109	417	3.8	14	5	Giaquinto, Mia-Wash.	20	104	5.2	20	0
Owens, T.B.	91	406	4.5	t35	3	D. White, Dall.	38	104	2.7	17	0
Huckleby, G.B.	139	381	2.7	22	5	Giammona, Phila.	35	98	2.8	9	1
Wilder, T.B.	107	370	3.5	t23	4	Montana, S.F.	25	95	3.8	t20	2
Kane, Det.	77	332	4.3	20	2	R. Bell, T.B.	30	80	2.7	8	0
Cooper, S.F.	98	330	3.4	23	1	Jensen, G.B.	27	79	2.9	15	0
Oliver, Phila.	75	329	4.4	39	1	L. Thompson, Det.	10	75	7.5	21	1
Davis, S.F.	94	297	3.2	14	7	Forte, N.Y.G.	19	74	3.9	15	0
Perry, N.Y.G.	72	257	3.6	23	0	McClendon, Chi.	30	74	2.5	17	0
Easley, S.F.	76	224	2.9	9	1	Ivery, G.B.	14	72	5.1	28	1
Evans, Chi.	43	218	5.1	25	3	L. Jackson, N.Y.G.	27	68	2.5	9	1
V. Thompson, Det.	35	211	6.0	30	1	Mayberry, Atl.	18	66	3.7	11	0
Williams, St.L.	48	209	4.4	29	4	Green, St.L.	3	60	20.0	t44	1
Galbreath, Minn.	42	198	4.7	21	2	Metcalf, Wash.	18	60	3.3	12	0
Bright, N.Y.G.	51	197	3.9	25	2	LeCount, Minn.	3	51	17.0	38	0
Holmes, N.O.	58	194	3.3	11	2	Whitehurst, G.B.	15	51	3.4	15	1

Billy Sims was the main reason Detroit led the NFL in team rushing.

Player—Team	Att.	Yds.	Avg.	Lng.	TD	Player—Team	Att.	Yds.	Avg.	Lng.	TD
Nichols, Det.	3	50	16.7	30	0	Strong, Atl.	3	6	2.0	3	0
Lawrence, S.F.	13	48	3.7	14	1	Harrell, St.L.	5	6	1.2	4	1
Solomon, S.F.	9	43	4.8	16	0	Dickey, G.B.	19	6	0.3	13	0
Simms, N.Y.G.	19	42	2.2	24	0	Walker, Wash.	1	5	5.0	5	0
Newsome, Dall.	13	38	2.9	7	0	Davis, T.B.	2	5	2.5	3	0
J. Rogers, N.O.	9	37	4.1	15	0	Jackson, Atl.	2	5	2.5	5	0
Cosbie, Dall.	4	33	8.3	15	0	C. Smith, Phila.	2	5	2.5	5	0
Atkins, G.B.-Phila.	12	33	2.8	21	0	Pastorini, L.A.	7	5	0.7	13	0
Newhouse, Dall.	14	33	2.4	6	0	Gray, St.L.	1	4	4.0	4	0
Clark, S.F.	3	32	10.7	18	0	Harmon, Wash.	1	4	4.0	4	0
Pearson, Dall.	3	31	10.3	25	0	Torkelson, G.B.	1	4	4.0	4	0
Dennard, L.A.	6	29	4.8	21	0	Fusina, T.B.	3	3	1.0	7	0
Elliott, S.F.	7	29	4.1	9	0	Komlo, Det.	6	3	0.5	5	0
Manning, N.O.	2	28	14.0	15	0	Daykin, Atl.	1	2	2.0	2	0
Groth, N.O.	2	27	13.5	28	0	Garrett, N.Y.G.	1	2	2.0	2	0
King, Det.	7	25	3.6	7	0	Senser, Minn.	1	2	2.0	2	0
Scott, Det.	7	25	3.6	10	0	Thompson, G.B.	1	2	2.0	2	0
Robinson, Atl.	9	24	2.7	5	0	Hart, St.L.	3	2	0.7	4	0
Danielson, Det.	9	23	2.6	t11	2	Avellini, Chi.	5	2	0.4	2	0
Jefferson, G.B.	2	22	11.0	15	0	Bartkowski, Atl.	11	2	0.2	5	0
Redwine, Minn.	5	20	4.0	8	0	Benjamin, S.F.	1	1	1.0	1	0
Brunner, N.Y.G.	14	20	1.4	23	0	Carmichael, Phila.	1	1	1.0	1	0
D. Williams, Chi.	2	19	9.5	15	0	D. Wilson, N.O.	5	1	0.2	9	0
Claitt, Wash.	3	19	6.3	11	0	Pisarcik, Phila.	7	1	0.1	10	0
Cromwell, L.A.	1	17	17.0	17	0	Blanchard, T.B.	1	0	0.0	0	0
Moroski, Atl.	3	17	5.7	14	0	Childs, L.A.	1	0	0.0	0	0
Lewis, Minn.	1	16	16.0	16	0	Connell, Wash.	1	0	0.0	0	0
D. Hill, L.A.	1	14	14.0	14	0	Phipps, Chi.	1	0	0.0	0	0
Dils, Minn.	4	14	3.5	7	0	Sciarra, Phila.	1	0	0.0	0	0
Matthews, N.Y.G.	4	14	3.5	6	0	Siemon, Minn.	1	0	0.0	0	0
Kramer, Minn.	10	13	1.3	8	0	Merkens, N.O.	2	−1	−0.5	2	0
DuPree, Dall.	1	12	12.0	12	0	Perkins, N.Y.G.	2	−1	−0.5	10	0
Margerum, Chi.	1	11	11.0	11	0	S. White, Minn.	2	−1	−0.5	1	0
Love, St.L.	3	11	3.7	4	0	J. Jones, Atl.	1	−1	−1.0	−1	0
Wonsley, Wash.	3	11	3.7	7	0	Birdsong, St.L.	1	−2	−2.0	−2	0
Baschnagel, Chi.	1	10	10.0	10	0	Henry, Phila.	1	−2	−2.0	−2	0
Erxleben, N.O.	2	10	5.0	26	0	Rutledge, L.A.	5	−3	−0.6	4	0
House, T.B.	2	9	4.5	8	0	Myers, N.O.	2	−3	−1.5	6	0
Kemp, L.A.	2	9	4.5	7	0	Caster, N.O.	1	−3	−3.0	−3	0
Carano, Dall.	8	9	1.1	11	0	Hill, Dall.	1	−3	−3.0	−3	0
Francis, Atl.	1	8	8.0	t8	1	Scott, N.O.	3	−4	−1.3	−1	0
Stief, St.L.	1	8	8.0	8	0	Monk, Wash.	1	−5	−5.0	−5	0
T. Bell, T.B.	1	7	7.0	7	0	Neal, Chi.	1	−6	−6.0	−6	0
Harrell, Minn.	1	7	7.0	7	0	Parsons, Chi.	1	−6	−6.0	−6	0
LeMaster, Phila.	1	7	7.0	7	0	James, Atl.	1	−7	−7.0	−7	0
R. Smith, Phila.	1	7	7.0	7	0	Swider, T.B.	1	−9	−9.0	−9	0
Stauch, N.O.	2	6	3.0	5	0						

1981 PASSING

HIGHEST RATING
> AFC: 98.5—Ken Anderson, Cincinnati.
> NFC: 88.2—Joe Montana, San Francisco.

ATTEMPTS
> AFC: 609—Dan Fouts, San Diego.
> NFC: 593—Tommy Kramer, Minnesota.

COMPLETIONS
> AFC: 360—Dan Fouts, San Diego.
> NFC: 322—Tommy Kramer, Minnesota.

COMPLETION PERCENTAGE
> NFC: 63.7—Joe Montana, San Francisco (488 attempts, 311 completions).
> AFC: 62.6—Ken Anderson, Cincinnati (479 attempts, 300 completions).

YARDS
> AFC: 4802—Dan Fouts, San Diego.
> NFC: 3912—Tommy Kramer, Minnesota.

YARDS PER ATTEMPT
> AFC: 8.61—Steve Grogan, New England (216 attempts, 1859 yards).
> NFC: 8.45—Eric Hipple, Detroit (279 attempts, 2358 yards).

TOUCHDOWN PASSES
> AFC: 33—Dan Fouts, San Diego.
> NFC: 30—Steve Bartkowski, Atlanta.

TOUCHDOWN PERCENTAGE
> AFC: 6.1—Ken Anderson, Cincinnati (479 attempts, 29 touchdowns).
> NFC: 5.6—Steve Bartkowski, Atlanta (533 attempts, 30 touchdowns).

INTERCEPTIONS
> AFC: 25—Brian Sipe, Cleveland.
> NFC: 24—Tommy Kramer, Minnesota.

LOWEST PERCENTAGE INTERCEPTED
> AFC: 2.1—Ken Anderson, Cincinnati (479 attempts, 10 intercepted).
> NFC: 2.5—Joe Montana, San Francisco (488 attempts, 12 intercepted).

LONGEST
> AFC: 95 yards—Craig Morton, Denver vs. Detroit, October 11 (to Steve Watson)—TD.
> NFC: 94 yards—Eric Hipple, Detroit vs. Chicago, October 19 (to Leonard Thompson)—TD.

TEAM CHAMPION
> AFC: 93.4—Cincinnati.
> NFC: 87.8—San Francisco.

PASSING—TEAM

AMERICAN FOOTBALL CONFERENCE

	Atts.	Com.	Pct. Com.	Gross Yards	Tkd.- Yds. Lost	Avg. Yds. Att.	Avg. Yds. Com.	TD	Lng.	Had Int.	Pct. Int.	Rating Pts.
Cincinnati	550	332	60.4	4,200	35-205	7.64	12.65	30	t74	12	2.2	93.4
San Diego	629	368	58.5	4,873	19-134	7.75	13.24	34	t67	18	2.9	89.1
Denver	485	289	59.6	3,992	61-461	8.23	13.81	27	t95	21	4.3	86.8
Seattle	524	307	58.6	3,727	37-300	7.11	12.14	21	t80	15	2.9	81.8
New York Jets	507	283	55.8	3,279	30-224	6.47	11.59	26	49	14	2.8	80.9
Pittsburgh	461	247	53.6	3,457	27-231	7.50	14.00	25	t90	19	4.1	78.9
Houston	441	258	58.5	3,119	40-342	7.07	12.09	21	t71	23	5.2	74.6
Buffalo	503	253	50.3	3,661	16-146	7.28	14.47	25	t67	20	4.0	74.3
Baltimore	479	265	55.3	3,379	37-321	7.05	12.75	21	t67	23	4.8	72.2
Cleveland	624	348	55.8	4,339	40-353	6.95	12.47	21	62	27	4.3	71.0
Miami	498	271	54.4	3,385	30-236	6.80	12.49	18	t69	21	4.2	70.3
Kansas City	410	224	54.6	2,917	37-277	7.11	13.02	12	t64	22	5.4	64.4
New England	482	254	52.7	3,904	45-321	8.10	15.37	17	t76	34	7.1	61.8
Oakland	545	267	49.0	3,356	53-437	6.16	12.57	18	t66	28	5.1	58.3
Conf. Totals	7,138	3,966	....	51,588	507-3,988	....	....	316	t95	297	.....	....
Conf. Average	509.9	283.3	55.6	3,684.9	36.2-284.9	7.23	13.01	22.6	....	21.2	4.2	75.7

NATIONAL FOOTBALL CONFERENCE

	Atts.	Com.	Pct. Com.	Gross Yards	Tkd.- Yds. Lost	Avg. Yds. Att.	Avg. Yds. Com.	TD	Lng.	Had Int.	Pct. Int.	Rating Pts.
San Francisco	517	328	63.4	3,766	29-223	7.28	11.48	20	t78	13	2.5	87.8
Dallas	439	241	54.9	3,414	31-245	7.78	14.17	24	t73	15	3.4	84.4
Atlanta	563	311	55.2	3,986	37-287	7.08	12.82	30	t70	24	4.3	77.3
Tampa Bay	473	239	50.5	3,565	19-136	7.54	14.92	20	t84	14	3.0	77.1
Washington	525	307	58.5	3,743	30-277	7.13	12.19	19	t79	22	4.2	75.1
Philadelphia	476	258	54.2	3,249	22-205	6.83	12.59	25	t85	22	4.6	74.2
Green Bay	514	286	55.6	3,576	52-387	6.96	12.50	24	t75	24	4.7	73.5
Detroit	436	228	52.3	3,475	44-337	7.97	15.24	18	t94	23	5.3	70.5
Minnesota	709	382	53.9	4,567	29-234	6.44	11.96	27	63	29	4.1	69.4
St. Louis	477	253	53.0	3,269	48-405	6.85	12.92	15	75	24	5.0	64.3
N.Y. Giants	506	251	49.6	3,009	47-368	5.95	11.99	16	80	20	4.0	62.2
New Orleans	441	238	54.0	2,778	41-359	6.30	11.67	8	55	27	6.1	53.9
Chicago	489	222	45.4	2,728	35-266	5.58	12.29	14	t85	23	4.7	53.3
Los Angeles	477	235	49.3	3,008	50-451	6.31	12.80	15	t67	32	6.7	51.9
Conf. Totals	7,042	3,779	......	48,133	514-4,180	......	....	275	t94	312	....	....
Conf. Average	503.0	269.9	53.7	3,438.1	36.7-298.6	6.84	12.74	19.6		22.3	4.4	70.0
League Totals	14,180	7,745	......	99,721	1,021-8,168	......	....	591	t95	609	....	....
League Avg.	506.4	276.6	54.6	3,561.5	36.5-291.7	7.03	12.88	21.1		21.8	4.3	73.0

TOP TEN INDIVIDUAL QUALIFIERS

Player—Team	Att.	Cmp.	Pct. Cmp.	Yds.	Avg. Gain	TD	Pct. TD	Lg.	Int.	Pct. Int.	Rating Pts.
ANDERSON, KEN, Cin.	479	300	62.6	3754	7.84	29	6.1	t74	10	2.1	98.5
Morton, Craig, Den................	376	225	59.8	3195	8.50	21	5.6	t95	14	3.7	90.6
Fouts, Dan, S.D.	609	360	59.1	4802	7.89	33	5.4	t67	17	2.8	90.6
Montana, Joe, S.F...................	488	311	63.7	3565	7.31	19	3.9	t78	12	2.5	88.2
White, Danny, Dall................	391	223	57.0	3098	7.92	22	5.6	t73	13	3.3	87.5
Bradshaw, Terry, Pitt..........	370	201	54.3	2887	7.80	22	5.9	t90	14	3.8	83.7
Zorn, Jim, Sea.	397	236	59.4	2788	7.02	13	3.3	t80	9	2.3	82.3
Todd, Richard, N.Y.J.	497	279	56.1	3231	6.50	25	5.0	49	13	2.6	81.8
Bartkowski, Steve, Atl.	533	297	55.7	3829	7.18	30	5.6	t70	23	4.3	79.2
Dickey, Lynn, G.B.	354	204	57.6	2593	7.32	17	4.8	t75	15	4.2	79.1

AFC INDIVIDUAL QUALIFIERS

Player—Team	Att.	Cmp.	Pct. Cmp.	Yds.	Avg. Gain	TD	Pct. TD	Lg.	Int.	Pct. Int.	Rating Pts.
ANDERSON, KEN, Cin	479	300	62.6	3754	7.84	29	6.1	t74	10	2.1	98.5
Morton, Craig, Den................	376	225	59.8	3195	8.50	21	5.6	t95	14	3.7	90.6
Fouts, Dan, S.D.	609	360	59.1	4802	7.89	33	5.4	t67	17	2.8	90.6
Bradshaw, Terry, Pitt..........	370	201	54.3	2887	7.80	22	5.9	t90	14	3.8	83.7
Zorn, Jim, Sea	397	236	59.4	2788	7.02	13	3.3	t80	9	2.3	82.3
Todd, Richard, N.Y.J.	497	279	56.1	3231	6.50	25	5.0	49	13	2.6	81.8
Jones, Bert, Balt...................	426	244	57.3	3094	7.26	21	4.9	67	20	4.7	76.8
Ferguson, Joe, Buff..............	498	252	50.6	3652	7.33	24	4.8	t67	20	4.0	74.1
Woodley, David, Mia............	366	191	52.2	2470	6.75	12	3.3	t69	13	3.6	69.7
Stabler, Ken, Hou.................	285	165	57.9	1988	6.98	14	4.9	t71	18	6.3	69.5
Sipe, Brian, Clev...................	567	313	55.2	3876	6.84	17	3.0	62	25	4.4	68.3
Kenney, Bill, K.C.	274	147	53.6	1983	7.24	9	3.3	t64	16	5.8	63.8
Grogan, Steve, N.E...............	216	117	54.2	1859	8.61	7	3.2	t76	16	7.4	63.0
Cavanaugh, Matt, N.E.	219	115	52.5	1633	7.46	5	2.3	65	13	5.9	60.0
Wilson, Marc, Oak	366	173	47.3	2311	6.31	14	3.8	t66	19	5.2	58.8

AFC NON-QUALIFIERS

Player—Team	Att.	Cmp.	Pct. Cmp.	Yds.	Avg. Gain	TD	Pct. TD	Lg.	Int.	Pct. Int.	Rating Pts.
McDonald, Paul, Clev..........	57	35	61.4	463	8.12	4	7.0	46	2	3.5	95.8
Nielsen, Gifford, Hou............	93	60	64.5	709	7.62	5	5.4	44	3	3.2	92.3
Krieg, Dave, Sea	112	64	57.1	843	7.53	7	6.3	t57	5	4.5	83.3
Schonert, Turk, Cin	19	10	52.6	166	8.74	0	0.0	36	0	0.0	82.3
DeBerg, Steve, Den...............	108	64	59.3	797	7.38	6	5.6	44	6	5.6	77.6
Fuller, Steve, K.C.	134	77	57.5	934	6.97	3	2.2	53	4	3.0	73.9
Adkins, Sam, Sea	13	7	53.8	96	7.38	1	7.7	t31	1	7.7	71.3
Strock, Don, Mia	130	79	60.8	901	6.93	6	4.6	52	8	6.2	71.1
Reaves, John, Hou	61	31	50.8	379	6.21	2	3.3	t51	2	3.3	67.6
Malone, Mark, Pitt...............	88	45	51.1	553	6.28	3	3.4	30	5	5.7	58.4
Plunkett, Jim, Oak...............	179	94	52.5	1045	5.84	4	2.2	42	9	5.0	56.7
Landry, Greg, Balt	29	14	48.3	195	6.72	0	0.0	34	1	3.4	56.2
Thompson, Jack, Cin............	49	21	42.9	267	5.45	1	2.0	21	2	4.1	50.1
Ryan, Pat, N.Y.J.	10	4	40.0	48	4.80	1	10.0	18	1	10.0	49.2
Luther, Ed, S.D.	15	7	46.7	68	4.53	0	0.0	25	1	6.7	32.0
Owen, Tom, N.E....................	36	15	41.7	218	6.06	1	2.8	28	4	11.1	31.8
Humm, David, Balt...............	24	7	29.2	90	3.75	0	0.0	20	2	8.3	8.1

Ken Anderson was the league's highest-rated (98.5) quarterback in 1981.

	Att	Comp	Pct	Yds	Avg	TD	TD%	Long	Int	Int%
(Less than 10 attempts)										
Chandler, Wes, S.D.	2	0	0.0	0	0.00	0	0.0	0	0	0.0
Collins, Anthony, N.E...........	1	0	0.0	0	0.00	0	0.0	0	0	0.0
Cribbs, Joe, Buff....................	1	1	100.0	9	9.00	1	100.0	t9	0	0.0
Hadnot, James, K.C.	1	0	0.0	0	0.00	0	0.0	0	1	100.0
Hill, Eddie, Mia	1	1	100.0	14	14.00	0	0.0	14	0	0.0
Jackson, Harold, N.E.	1	0	0.0	0	0.00	0	0.0	0	0	0.0
Johnson, Andy, N.E.	9	7	77.8	194	21.56	4	44.4	t66	1	11.1
Kreider, Steve, Cin	3	1	33.3	13	4.33	0	0.0	13	0	0.0
Largent, Steve, Sea................	1	0	0.0	0	0.00	0	0.0	0	0	0.0
Leaks, Roosevelt, Buff..........	1	0	0.0	0	0.00	0	0.0	0	0	0.0
Marshall, Henry, K.C............	1	0	0.0	0	0.00	0	0.0	0	1	100.0
Mike-Mayer, Nick, Buff.......	1	0	0.0	0	0.00	0	0.0	0	0	0.0
Muncie, Chuck, S.D.	1	1	100.0	3	3.00	1	100.0	t3	0	0.0
Nathan, Tony, Mia	1	0	0.0	0	0.00	0	0.0	0	0	0.0
Parsley, Cliff, Hou	2	2	100.0	43	21.50	0	0.0	31	0	0.0
Reed, Tony, Den.....................	1	0	0.0	0	0.00	0	0.0	0	1	100.0
Robinson, Matt, Buff.............	2	0	0.0	0	0.00	0	0.0	0	0	0.0
Stoudt, Cliff, Pitt....................	3	1	33.3	17	5.67	0	0.0	17	0	0.0
West, Jeff, Sea	1	0	0.0	0	0.00	0	0.0	0	0	0.0
Winslow, Kellen, S.D.	2	0	0.0	0	0.00	0	0.0	0	0	0.0

t—Touchdown

NFC INDIVIDUAL QUALIFIERS

Player—Team	Att.	Cmp.	Pct. Cmp.	Yds.	Avg. Gain	TD	Pct. TD	Lg.	Int.	Pct. Int.	Rating Pts.
MONTANA, JOE, S.F.	488	311	63.7	3565	7.31	19	3.9	t78	12	2.5	88.2
White, Danny, Dallas	391	223	57.0	3098	7.92	22	5.6	t73	13	3.3	87.5
Bartkowski, Steve, Atl	533	297	55.7	3829	7.18	30	5.6	t70	23	4.3	79.2
Dickey, Lynn, G.B.	354	204	57.6	2593	7.32	17	4.8	t75	15	4.2	79.1
Theismann, Joe, Wash	496	293	59.1	3568	7.19	19	3.8	t79	20	4.0	77.3
Williams, Doug, T.B.	471	238	50.5	3563	7.56	19	4.0	t84	14	3.0	76.5
Simms, Phil, N.Y.G.	316	172	54.4	2031	6.43	11	3.5	80	9	2.8	74.2
Jaworski, Ron, Phila	461	250	54.2	3095	6.71	23	5.0	t85	20	4.3	74.0
Hipple, Eric, Det	279	140	50.2	2358	8.45	14	5.0	t94	15	5.4	73.3
Kramer, Tommy, Minn	593	322	54.3	3912	6.60	26	4.4	63	24	4.0	72.8
Hart, Jim, St.L	241	134	55.6	1694	7.03	11	4.6	t58	14	5.8	68.9
Haden, Pat, L.A.	267	138	51.7	1815	6.80	9	3.4	t67	13	4.9	64.4
Manning, Archie, N.O.	232	134	57.8	1447	6.24	5	2.2	55	11	4.7	64.0
Lomax, Neil, St.L	236	119	50.4	1575	6.67	4	1.7	75	10	4.2	60.1
Evans, Vince, Chi	436	195	44.7	2354	5.40	11	2.5	t85	20	4.6	51.0

NFC NON-QUALIFIERS

Player—Team	Att.	Cmp.	Pct. Cmp.	Yds.	Avg. Gain	TD	Pct. TD	Lg.	Int.	Pct. Int.	Rating Pts.
Phipps, Mike, Chi.	17	11	64.7	171	10.06	2	11.8	t43	0	0.0	137.3
Pisarcik, Joe, Phila	15	8	53.3	154	10.27	2	13.3	t44	2	13.3	89.3
Rutledge, Jeff, L.A.	50	30	60.0	442	8.84	3	6.0	64	4	8.0	75.6
Benjamin, Guy, S.F.	26	15	57.7	171	6.58	1	3.8	t27	1	3.8	74.4
Danielson, Gary, Det	96	56	58.3	784	8.17	3	3.1	45	5	5.2	73.4
Whitehurst, David, G.B.	128	66	51.6	792	6.19	7	5.5	t46	5	3.9	73.0
Dils, Steve, Minn	102	54	52.9	607	5.95	1	1.0	44	2	2.0	66.0
Carano, Glenn, Dall	45	16	35.6	235	5.22	1	2.2	55	1	2.2	51.7
Komlo, Jeff, Det	57	29	50.9	290	5.09	1	1.8	46	3	5.3	49.6
Wilson, Dave, N.O.	159	82	51.6	1058	6.65	1	0.6	50	11	6.9	46.1
Moroski, Mike, Atl	26	12	46.2	132	5.08	0	0.0	22	1	3.8	45.9
Brunner, Scott, N.Y.G.	190	79	41.6	978	5.15	5	2.6	43	11	5.8	42.7
Avellini, Bob, Chi	32	15	46.9	185	5.78	1	3.1	t72	3	9.4	36.4
Flick, Tom, Wash	27	13	48.1	143	5.30	0	0.0	33	2	7.4	33.4
Scott, Bobby, N.O.	46	20	43.5	245	5.33	1	2.2	31	5	10.9	28.3
Campbell, Rich, G.B.	30	15	50.0	168	5.60	0	0.0	27	4	13.3	27.5
Pastorini, Dan, L.A.	152	64	42.1	719	4.73	2	1.3	46	14	9.2	22.9
Wilson, Wade, Minn	13	6	46.2	48	3.69	0	0.0	22	2	15.4	16.4

(Less than 10 attempts)

Player—Team	Att.	Cmp.	Pct. Cmp.	Yds.	Avg. Gain	TD	Pct. TD	Lg.	Int.	Pct. Int.
Baschnagel, Brian, Chi	1	1	100.0	18	18.00	0	0.0	18	0	0.0
Brown, Ted, Minn	1	0	0.0	0	0.00	0	0.0	0	1	100.0
Clark, Dwight, S.F.	1	0	0.0	0	0.00	0	0.0	0	0	0.0
Corral, Frank, L.A.	1	0	0.0	0	0.00	0	0.0	0	0	0.0
Easley, Walt, S.F.	1	1	100.0	5	5.00	0	0.0	5	0	0.0
Ellis, Gerry, G.B.	2	1	50.0	23	11.50	0	0.0	23	0	0.0
Fusina, Chuck, T.B.	1	1	100.0	2	2.00	1	100.0	t2	0	0.0
Guman, Mike, L.A.	1	1	100.0	7	7.00	1	100.0	t7	0	0.0
House, Kevin, T.B.	1	0	0.0	0	0.00	0	0.0	0	0	0.0
James, John, Atl	1	0	0.0	0	0.00	0	0.0	0	0	0.0
Jones, June, Atl	3	2	66.7	25	8.33	0	0.0	14	0	0.0
Kemp, Jeff, L.A.	6	2	33.3	25	4.17	0	0.0	19	1	16.7
Merkens, Guido, N.O.	2	1	50.0	20	10.00	0	0.0	20	0	0.0
Myers, Tommy, N.O.	2	1	50.0	8	4.00	1	50.0	t8	0	0.0
Parsons, Bob, Chi	1	0	0.0	0	0.00	0	0.0	0	0	0.0
Payton, Walter, Chi	2	0	0.0	0	0.00	0	0.0	0	0	0.0
Pearson, Drew, Dall	2	2	100.0	81	40.50	1	50.0	59	0	0.0
Scott, Freddie, Det	1	0	0.0	0	0.00	0	0.0	0	0	0.0
Skladany, Tom, Det	3	3	100.0	43	14.33	0	0.0	19	0	0.0
Solomon, Freddie, S.F.	1	1	100.0	25	25.00	0	0.0	25	0	0.0
Springs, Ron, Dall	1	0	0.0	0	0.00	0	0.0	0	1	100.0
Washington, Joe, Wash	2	1	50.0	32	16.00	0	0.0	32	0	0.0

t—Touchdown

1981 PASS RECEIVING

RECEPTIONS
AFC: 88—Kellen Winslow, San Diego.
NFC: 85—Dwight Clark, San Francisco.

YARDS
NFC: 1358—Alfred Jenkins, Atlanta.
AFC: 1244—Frank Lewis, Buffalo.
1244—Steve Watson, Denver.

YARDS PER RECEPTION
AFC: 23.4—Stanley Morgan, New England (44 receptions, 1029 yards).
NFC: 21.0—Kevin House, Tampa Bay (56 receptions, 1176 yards).

TOUCHDOWNS
AFC: 13—Steve Watson, Denver.
NFC: 13—Alfred Jenkins, Atlanta.

LONGEST
AFC: 95 yards—Steve Watson, Denver vs Detroit, October 11 (from Craig Morton)—TD.
NFC: 94 yards—Leonard Thompson, Detroit vs Chicago, October 19 (from Eric Hipple)—TD.

MOST RECEPTIONS, GAME
NFC: 15 (124 yards)—William Andrews, Atlanta vs Pittsburgh, November 15.
AFC: 13 (144 yards)—Kellen Winslow, San Diego vs Oakland, November 22.

MOST YARDS, GAME
AFC: 210 (7 receptions)—Nat Moore, Miami vs New York Jets, October 4.
NFC: 179 (8 receptions)—James Lofton, Green Bay vs Atlanta, September 13.
179 (5 receptions)—Alfred Jenkins, Atlanta vs New Orleans, November 1.

TEAM LEADERS
AFC: BALTIMORE: 50, Randy McMillan; BUFFALO: 70, Frank Lewis; CINCINNATI: 71, Dan Ross; CLEVELAND: 69, Ozzie Newsome; DENVER: 60, Steve Watson; HOUSTON: 40, Ken Burrough; KANSAS CITY: 63, J. T. Smith; MIAMI: 53, Duriel Harris; NEW ENGLAND: 46, Don Hasselbeck; NEW YORK: 52, Bruce Harper; OAKLAND: 52, Derrick Ramsey; PITTSBURGH: 63, John Stallworth; SAN DIEGO: 88, Kellen Winslow; SEATTLE: 75, Steve Largent.

NFC: ATLANTA: 81, William Andrews; CHICAGO: 41, Walter Payton; DALLAS: 46, Tony Hill; DETROIT: 53, Freddie Scott; GREEN BAY: 71, James Lofton; LOS ANGELES: 49, Preston Dennard; MINNESOTA: 83, Ted Brown; NEW ORLEANS: 38, Jack Holmes; NEW YORK: 51, Johnny Perkins; PHILADELPHIA: 61, Harold Carmichael; ST. LOUIS: 66, Pat Tilley; SAN FRANCISCO: 85, Dwight Clark; TAMPA BAY: 56, Kevin House; WASHINGTON: 70, Joe Washington.

TOP TEN PASS RECEIVERS

Player—Team	No.	Yards	Avg.	Long	TDs.
WINSLOW, KELLEN, S.D.	88	1075	12.2	t67	10
Clark, Dwight, S.F.	85	1105	13.0	t78	4
Brown, Ted, Minn.	83	694	8.4	63	2
Andrews, William, Atl.	81	735	9.1	t70	2
Senser, Joe, Minn.	79	1004	12.7	53	8
Largent, Steve, Sea.	75	1224	16.3	t57	9
Lofton, James, G.B.	71	1294	18.2	t75	8
Ross, Dan, Cin.	71	910	12.8	37	5
Jenkins, Alfred, Atl.	70	1358	19.4	67	13
Lewis, Frank, Buff.	70	1244	17.8	33	4
Joiner, Charlie, S.D.	70	1188	17.0	57	7
Washington, Joe, Wash.	70	558	8.0	32	3

TOP TEN PASS RECEIVERS BY YARDS

Player—Team	Yards	No.	Avg.	Long	TDs.
JENKINS, ALFRED, Atl.	1358	70	19.4	67	13
Lofton, James, G.B.	1294	71	18.2	t75	8
Lewis, Frank, Buff.	1244	70	17.8	33	4
Watson, Steve, Den.	1244	60	20.7	t95	13
Largent, Steve, Sea.	1224	75	16.3	t57	9
Joiner, Charlie, S.D.	1188	70	17.0	57	7
House, Kevin, T.B.	1176	56	21.0	t84	9
Chandler, Wes, N.O.-S.D.	1142	69	16.6	t51	6
Clark, Dwight, S.F.	1105	85	13.0	t78	4
Stallworth, John, Pitt.	1098	63	17.4	55	5

AFC—INDIVIDUALS

Player—Team	No.	Yds.	Avg.	Lng.	TD
WINSLOW, S.D.	88	1075	12.2	t67	10
Largent, Sea.	75	1224	16.3	t57	9
Ross, Cin.	71	910	12.8	37	5
Lewis, Buff.	70	1244	17.8	33	4
Joiner, S.D.	70	1188	17.0	57	7
Chandler, N.O.-S.D.	69	1142	16.6	t51	6
Newsome, Clev.	69	1002	14.5	62	6
Collinsworth, Cin.	67	1009	15.1	t74	8
G. Pruitt, Clev.	65	636	9.8	33	4
Stallworth, Pitt.	63	1098	17.4	55	5
Smith, K.C.	63	852	13.5	42	2
M. Pruitt, Clev.	63	442	7.0	21	1
Watson, Den.	60	1244	20.7	t95	13
Butler, Buff.	55	842	15.3	t67	8
Harris, Miami	53	911	17.2	55	2
Ramsey, Oak.	52	674	13.0	t66	4
Preston, Den.	52	507	9.8	37	0
Harper, N.Y.J.	52	459	8.8	24	1
McMillan, Balt.	50	466	9.3	31	1
Nathan, Miami	50	452	9.0	31	3
Walker, N.Y.J.	47	770	16.4	49	9
Butler, Balt.	46	832	18.1	t67	9
Hasselbeck, N.E.	46	808	17.6	51	6
McCullum, Sea.	46	567	12.3	t36	3
J. Brooks, S.D.	46	329	7.2	t29	3
Johnson, Cin.	46	320	7.0	33	4
Morgan, N.E.	44	1029	23.4	t76	6
S. Smith, Sea.	44	406	9.2	28	1
Muncie, S.D.	43	362	8.4	32	0
Branch, Oak.	41	635	15.5	53	1
Cunningham, Pitt.	41	574	14.0	30	3
Burrough, Hou.	40	668	16.7	t71	7
Cribbs, Buff.	40	603	15.1	t65	7
Jackson, N.E.	39	669	17.2	45	0
Barkum, N.Y.J.	39	495	12.7	t40	7
Renfro, Hou.	39	451	11.6	43	1
Johnson, N.E.	39	429	11.0	36	1
Marshall, K.C.	38	620	16.3	t64	4
Carr, Balt.	38	584	15.4	43	3
Odoms, Den.	38	516	13.6	28	5
Curtis, Cin.	37	609	16.5	68	2
Kreider, Cin.	37	520	14.1	46	5
Dickey, Balt.	37	419	11.3	50	3
Harris, Pitt.	37	250	6.8	26	1
McCauley, Balt.	36	347	9.6	31	2
Campbell, Hou.	36	156	4.3	17	0
Hughes, Sea.	35	263	7.5	22	2
Swann, Pitt.	34	505	14.9	44	5
Reed, Den.	34	317	9.3	33	0
Casper, Hou.	33	572	17.3	t52	8
Brammer, Buff.	33	365	11.1	24	2
Vigorito, Mia.	33	237	7.2	t31	2
Upchurch, Den.	32	550	17.2	63	3
Logan, Clev.	31	497	16.0	t40	4
Feacher, Clev.	29	654	22.6	48	3
Cefalo, Mia.	29	631	21.8	t69	3
Smith, Pitt.	29	571	19.7	t46	7
Dixon, K.C.	29	356	12.3	48	2
T. Brown, St.L.-Sea.	29	328	11.3	51	0
Armstrong, Hou.	29	278	9.6	48	1
Jensen, Oak.	28	271	9.7	21	0
Alexander, Cin.	28	262	9.4	t65	1
Rucker, Clev.	27	532	19.7	49	1
Holston, Hou.	27	427	15.8	t50	2
Doornink, Sea.	27	350	13.0	t80	4
White, Clev.	27	219	8.1	21	0
King, Oak.	27	216	8.0	30	0
Chandler, Oak.	26	458	17.6	45	4
Moore, Mia.	26	452	17.4	52	2
Collins, N.E.	26	232	8.9	22	0
Dierking, N.Y.J.	26	228	8.8	23	1
Parros, Den.	25	216	8.6	26	1
Rose, Mia.	23	316	13.7	50	2
Hadnot, K.C.	23	215	9.3	20	0
Whittington, Oak.	23	213	9.3	22	2
Bradshaw, Oak.	22	298	13.5	t29	3
Sievers, S.D.	22	276	12.5	32	3
Delaney, K.C.	22	246	11.2	61	0
McCall, Balt.	21	314	15.0	t65	2
Sawyer, Sea.	21	272	13.0	30	0
L. Jones, N.Y.J.	20	342	17.1	t47	3
A. Griffin, Cin.	20	160	8.0	17	1
Scales, S.D.	19	429	22.6	t60	1
Coleman, Hou.	19	211	11.1	24	0
Pollard, Pitt.	19	156	8.2	26	0
McNeil, N.Y.J.	18	171	9.5	18	1
Augustyniak, N.Y.J.	18	144	8.0	15	0
Egloff, Den.	17	231	13.6	40	1
Rome, K.C.	17	203	11.9	23	1
Dixon, Balt.	17	169	9.9	41	1
Hill, Clev.	17	150	8.8	23	2
Newton, N.Y.J.	17	104	6.1	13	0
B. Jones, N.Y.J.	16	239	14.9	t36	1
C. Miller, Clev.	16	139	8.7	17	0
Moses, Den.	15	246	16.4	30	1
Jessie, Buff.	15	200	13.3	44	0
Hardy, Mia.	15	174	11.6	21	0
Gaffney, N.Y.J.	14	246	17.6	39	0
Lee, Mia.	14	64	4.6	11	1
Barber, Hou.	13	190	14.6	35	1
M. L. Harris, Cin.	13	181	13.9	42	2
Chester, Oak.	13	93	7.2	15	1
Long, N.Y.J.	13	66	5.1	18	3
Tatupu, N.E.	12	132	11.0	41	1
C. Williams, S.D.	12	108	9.0	15	1
Cunningham, N.E.	12	92	7.7	12	0
Hill, Mia.	12	73	6.1	16	1
Burke, Balt.	10	153	15.3	24	0
Hooks, Buff.	10	140	14.0	37	2
Cappelletti. S.D.	10	126	12.6	25	1
Hawkins, Oak.	10	109	10.9	35	0
Barnwell, Oak.	9	190	21.1	t61	1
Johns, Sea.	8	131	16.4	34	1
Christensen, Oak.	8	115	14.4	30	2
Thornton, Pitt.	8	78	9.8	30	0
McKnight, K.C.	8	77	9.6	23	0
Carson, K.C.	7	179	25.6	t53	1
Dawson, N.E.	7	126	18.0	42	0
Westbrook, N.E.	7	122	17.4	32	2
Calhoun, N.E.	7	71	10.1	20	0
van Eeghen, Oak.	7	60	8.6	13	0
Lane, Sea.	7	58	8.3	22	0
Leaks, Buff.	7	51	7.3	13	0
Brown, Buff.	7	46	6.6	10	1
Verser, Cin.	6	161	26.8	t73	2
McInally, Cin.	6	68	11.3	20	0
Lytle, Den.	6	47	7.8	t14	1
Franklin, Balt.	6	39	6.5	10	0
B. Jackson, K.C.	6	31	5.2	10	1
Scott, K.C.	5	72	14.4	26	1
Toler, N.E.	5	70	14.0	23	0
Piccone, Buff.	5	65	13.0	16	0
Tice, Sea.	5	47	9.4	14	0
McCutcheon, Buff.	5	40	8.0	17	0
T. Wilson, Hou.	5	33	6.6	11	0
Jodat, Sea.	4	52	13.0	26	0
McGrath, Sea.	4	47	11.8	16	0
Ferguson, N.E.	4	39	9.8	20	0
Barnett, Buff.	4	36	9.0	16	1
Davis, Pitt.	4	34	8.5	19	0
Hawthorne, Pitt.	4	23	5.8	12	0
Bennett, Mia.	4	22	5.5	10	0
Manning, Den.	3	49	16.3	34	0
Pennywell, N.E.	3	49	16.3	t22	1
B. Brooks, S.D.-Hou.	3	37	12.3	21	0
Canada, Den.	3	37	12.3	20	1
Bledsoe, K.C.	3	27	9.0	17	0
J. Wright, Den.	3	22	7.3	14	1
Grossman, Pitt.	3	19	6.3	t14	1
Moore, Sea.	3	18	6.0	10	0
Franklin, Mia.	3	6	2.0	t3	1
Sweeney, Pitt.	2	53	26.5	32	0
Fulton, Clev.	2	38	19.0	27	0
Smith, Hou.	2	37	18.5	25	0
Murphy, K.C.	2	36	18.0	22	0
Franklin, Buff.	2	29	14.5	16	0
Grogan, N.E.	2	27	13.5	16	0
Sherwin, Balt.	2	19	9.5	11	0

Player—Team	No.	Yds.	Avg.	Lng.	TD	Player—Team	No.	Yds.	Avg.	Lng.	TD
Lewis, N.Y.J.	2	14	7.0	8	0	Cavanaugh, N.E.	1	9	9.0	9	0
Howell, Mia.	2	9	4.5	5	0	Oden, Clev.	1	6	6.0	6	0
Malone, Pitt.	1	90	90.0	t90	1	Moser, Pitt.	1	5	5.0	t5	1
DeRoo, Balt.	1	38	38.0	38	0	Bauer, S.D.	1	4	4.0	t4	1
Adams, Clev.	1	24	24.0	24	0	Boyd, Sea.	1	3	3.0	t3	1
Willis, Oak.	1	24	24.0	24	0	Williams, K.C.	1	3	3.0	3	0
Holohan, S.D.	1	14	14.0	14	0	Pinney, Pitt.	1	1	1.0	t1	1
Raible, Sea.	1	12	12.0	12	0	Todd, N.Y.J.	1	1	1.0	1	0
Studdard, Den.	1	10	10.0	10	0	Hargrove, Cin.	1	0	0.0	0	0
August, Sea.	1	9	9.0	9	0	Huff, Balt.	1	−1	−1.0	−1	0

AFC—TOP 25 PASS RECEIVERS BY YARDS

Player—Team	Yds.	No.	Avg.	Lng.	TD	Player—Team	Yds.	No.	Avg.	Lng.	TD
LEWIS, Buff.	1244	70	17.8	33	4	Butler, Balt.	832	46	18.1	t67	9
Watson, Den.	1244	60	20.7	t95	13	Hasselbeck, N.E.	808	46	17.6	51	6
Largent, Sea.	1224	75	16.3	t57	9	Walker, N.Y.J.	770	47	16.4	49	9
Joiner, S.D.	1188	70	17.0	57	7	Ramsey, Oak.	674	52	13.0	t66	4
Chandler, N.O.-S.D.	1142	69	16.6	t51	6	Jackson, N.E.	669	39	17.2	45	0
Stallworth, Pitt.	1098	63	17.4	55	5	Burrough, Hou.	668	40	16.7	t71	7
Winslow, S.D.	1075	88	12.2	t67	10	Feacher, Clev.	654	29	22.6	48	3
Morgan, N.E.	1029	44	23.4	t76	6	G. Pruitt, Clev.	636	65	9.8	33	4
Collinsworth, Cin.	1009	67	15.1	t74	8	Branch, Oak.	635	41	15.5	53	1
Newsome, Clev.	1002	69	14.5	62	6	Cefalo, Mia.	631	29	21.8	t69	3
Harris, Mia.	911	53	17.2	55	2	Marshall, K.C.	620	38	16.3	t64	4
Smith, K.C.	852	63	13.5	42	2	Curtis, Cin.	609	37	16.5	68	2
Butler, Buff.	842	55	15.3	t67	8						

NFC—INDIVIDUALS

Player—Team	No.	Yds.	Avg.	Lng.	TD	Player—Team	No.	Yds.	Avg.	Lng.	TD
CLARK, S.F.	85	1105	13.0	t78	4	L. Thompson, Det.	30	550	18.3	t94	3
Brown, Minn.	83	694	8.4	63	2	Francis, Atl.	30	441	14.7	36	4
Andrews, Atl.	81	735	9.1	t70	2	Merkens, N.O.	29	458	15.8	50	1
Senser, Minn.	79	1004	12.7	53	8	Warren, Wash.	29	335	11.6	32	1
Lofton, G.B.	71	1294	18.2	t75	8	Sims, Det.	28	451	16.1	t81	2
Jenkins, Atl.	70	1358	19.4	67	13	Thompson, Wash.	28	423	15.1	57	4
Washington, Wash.	70	558	8.0	32	3	Bright, N.Y.G.	28	291	10.4	36	0
Tilley, St.L.	66	1040	15.8	75	3	Watts, Chi.	27	465	17.2	t42	3
S. White, Minn.	66	1001	15.2	53	3	Gray, St.L.	27	310	11.5	t41	2
Ellis, G.B.	65	499	7.7	t46	3	Hofer, S.F.	27	244	9.0	22	0
Carmichael, Phil.	61	1028	16.9	t85	6	Huckleby, G.B.	27	221	8.2	t39	3
Solomon, S.F.	59	969	16.4	t60	8	Patton, S.F.	27	195	7.2	t31	1
Rashad, Minn.	58	884	15.2	53	7	Seay, Wash.	26	472	18.2	60	3
House, T.B.	56	1176	21.0	t84	9	Johnson, Dall.	25	552	22.1	55	5
Monk, Wash.	56	894	16.0	t79	6	LeCount, Minn.	24	425	17.7	t43	2
Coffman, G.B.	55	687	12.5	29	4	Eckwood, T.B.	24	213	8.9	33	0
Cain, Atl.	55	421	7.7	28	2	Hardy, N.O.	23	275	12.0	27	1
Scott, Det.	53	1022	19.3	48	5	Tyler, N.O.	23	135	5.9	18	0
Perkins, N.Y.G.	51	858	16.8	80	6	Gray, N.Y.G.	22	360	16.4	45	2
Cooper, S.F.	51	477	9.4	50	0	Bryant, L.A.	22	160	7.3	39	0
Anderson, St.L.	51	387	7.6	27	0	T. Bell, T.B.	21	318	15.1	t58	2
Dennard, L.A.	49	821	16.8	64	4	Groth, N.O.	20	380	19.0	54	1
Montgomery, Phil.	49	521	10.6	35	2	Jones, N.O.	20	276	13.8	44	1
Metcalf, Wash.	48	595	12.4	52	0	Arnold, L.A.	20	212	10.6	24	2
Wilder, T.B.	48	507	10.6	38	1	King, Det.	20	211	10.6	41	1
Hill, Dall.	46	953	20.7	t63	4	Krepfle, Phil.	20	210	10.5	26	5
Springs, Dall.	46	359	7.8	t32	2	DuPree, Dall.	19	214	11.3	t33	2
Giles, T.B.	45	786	17.5	t81	6	Morris, St.L.	19	165	8.7	21	0
Tyler, L.A.	45	436	9.7	t67	5	Friede, N.Y.G.	18	250	13.9	43	1
Young, Minn.	43	296	6.9	22	2	Kane, Det.	18	187	10.4	40	1
Shirk, N.Y.G.	42	445	10.6	46	3	Galbreath, Minn.	18	144	8.0	23	0
Payton, Chi.	41	379	9.2	30	2	Guman, L.A.	18	130	7.2	14	0
Jefferson, G.B.	39	632	16.2	41	4	D. Williams, Chi.	18	126	7.0	t18	2
Margerum, Chi.	39	584	15.0	41	1	Bussey, Det.	18	92	5.1	16	0
Pearson, Dall.	38	614	16.2	t42	3	Cosbie, Dall.	17	225	13.2	28	5
C. Smith, Phil.	38	564	14.8	45	4	D. Hill, L.A.	16	355	22.2	45	3
Holmes, N.O.	38	206	5.4	19	0	G. Rogers, N.O.	16	126	7.9	25	0
Jackson, Atl.	37	604	16.3	49	6	LaFleur, St.L.	14	190	13.6	t27	2
Young, S.F.	37	400	10.8	29	5	Mullady, N.Y.G.	14	136	9.7	21	1
Carpenter, Hou-NYG	37	281	7.6	37	1	Harrell, St.L.	14	131	9.4	t62	1
Campfield, Phil.	36	326	9.1	t29	3	Perry, N.Y.G.	13	140	10.8	24	1
Baschnagel, Chi.	34	554	16.3	t72	5	Caster, N.O.-Wash.	12	185	15.4	31	0
Green, St.L.	33	708	21.5	60	4	Childs, L.A.	12	145	12.1	39	1
Hill, Det.	33	462	14.0	34	4	Owens, T.B.	12	145	12.1	35	0
Suhey, Chi.	33	168	5.1	15	0	Giaquinto, Mia.-Wash.	12	93	7.8	25	2
Miller, Atl.	32	398	12.4	37	3	Middleton, G.B.	12	86	7.2	27	1
Dorsett, Dall.	32	325	10.2	t73	2	Walker, Wash.	11	112	10.2	24	1
Waddy, L.A.	31	460	14.8	46	0	Harmon, Wash.	11	98	8.9	23	0
W. Wilson, N.O.	31	384	12.4	55	4	Nichols, Det.	10	222	22.2	59	1

Player—Team	No.	Yds.	Avg.	Lng.	TD	Player—Team	No.	Yds.	Avg.	Lng.	TD
Miller, L.A.	10	147	14.7	20	0	Floyd, St.L.	3	32	10.7	16	0
Earl, Chi.	10	118	11.8	24	1	G. Lewis, G.B.	3	31	10.3	15	0
Oliver, Phil.	10	37	3.7	27	0	Ring S.F.	3	28	9.3	21	1
Anderson, Chi.	9	243	27.0	t85	2	L. Jackson, N.Y.G.	3	25	8.3	19	0
Henry, Phil.	9	145	16.1	t44	2	Shumann, S.F.	3	21	7.0	8	0
Wilson, N.Y.G.	9	125	13.9	t27	1	McCrary, Wash.	3	13	4.3	12	0
Easley, S.F.	9	62	6.9	21	0	Forte, N.Y.G.	3	11	3.7	6	0
Kotar, N.Y.G.	9	32	3.6	11	0	Lawrence, S.F.	3	10	3.3	5	0
Harrington, Phil.	9	27	3.0	12	0	Mayberry, Atl.	3	4	1.3	6	0
Parker, Phil.	8	168	21.0	t55	2	Davis, S.F.	3	−1	−0.3	3	0
Norris, Det.	8	132	16.5	34	0	Lewis, Minn.	2	58	29.0	52	0
Mistler, N.Y.G.	8	119	14.9	31	1	Harris, N.O.	2	33	16.5	20	0
Thompson, G.B.-N.O.	8	111	13.9	25	0	Nixon, G.B.	2	27	13.5	19	0
R. Bell, T.B.	8	92	11.5	22	0	Callicutt, Det.	2	24	12.0	16	0
Saldi, Dall.	8	82	10.3	18	1	Harrell, Minn.	2	23	11.5	17	0
B. Williams, N.O.-Chi.	8	82	10.3	16	0	Cobb, Chi.	2	20	10.0	11	0
Martini, N.O.	8	72	9.0	15	0	Banks, N.O.	2	18	9.0	12	0
B. Taylor, N.Y.G.	8	71	8.9	39	0	Mikeska, Atl.	2	16	8.0	11	0
R. Smith, S.D.-Phil.	7	168	24.0	42	2	Matthews, N.Y.G.	2	13	6.5	11	0
Brenner, N.O.	7	143	20.4	34	0	J. Rogers, N.O.	2	12	6.0	9	0
Moore, L.A.	7	105	15.0	35	0	Harper, Chi.	2	10	5.0	8	0
Elliott, S.F.	7	81	11.6	19	0	Ivery, G.B.	2	10	5.0	8	0
Jackson, Wash.	7	51	7.3	16	0	McClendon, Chi.	2	4	2.0	4	0
Bruer, Minn.	7	38	5.4	10	3	Newhouse, Dall.	1	21	21.0	21	0
Spagnola, Phil.	6	83	13.8	28	0	Cobb, Det.	1	19	19.0	19	0
Marsh, St.L.	6	80	13.3	20	1	Harris, Chi.	1	18	18.0	18	0
Riggins, Wash.	6	59	9.8	22	0	Carter, T.B.	1	10	10.0	10	0
Giammona, Phil.	6	54	9.0	19	1	Strong, Atl.	1	9	9.0	9	0
J. Jones, Dall.	6	37	6.2	16	0	Pittman, N.Y.G.	1	8	8.0	8	0
Mitchell, St.L.	6	35	5.8	16	1	Murray, Phil.	1	7	7.0	7	0
Stief, St.L.	5	77	15.4	29	1	Stauch, N.O.	1	7	7.0	7	0
Combs, St.L.	5	54	10.8	13	0	Zanders, Chi.	1	7	7.0	7	0
Jensen, G.B.	5	49	9.8	16	0	Cassidy, G.B.	1	6	6.0	6	0
Young, N.Y.G.	5	49	9.8	15	1	Lafary, N.O.	1	5	5.0	5	0
J. Thomas, L.A.	5	37	7.4	13	0	Peets, S.F.	1	5	5.0	5	0
Ramson, S.F.	4	45	11.3	16	0	Wonsley, Wash.	1	5	5.0	5	0
Obradovich, T.B.	4	42	10.5	16	1	Atkins, G.B.	1	2	2.0	2	0
V. Thompson, Det.	4	40	10.0	17	0	Swanke, G.B.	1	2	2.0	t2	1
Porter, Det.	3	63	21.0	t27	1	Bostic, Wash.	1	−4	−4.0	−4	0
Donley, Dall.	3	32	10.7	17	0	Russell, Phil.	1	−5	−5.0	−5	0

NFC—TOP 25 PASS RECEIVERS BY YARDS

Player—Team	Yds.	No.	Avg.	Lng.	TD	Player—Team	Yds.	No.	Avg.	Lng.	TD
Jenkins, Atl.	1358	70	19.4	67	13	Perkins, N.Y.G.	858	51	16.8	80	6
Lofton, G.B.	1294	71	18.2	t75	8	Dennard, L.A.	821	49	16.8	64	4
House, T.B.	1176	56	21.0	t84	9	Giles, T.B.	786	45	17.5	t81	6
Clark, S.F.	1105	85	13.0	t78	4	Andrews, Atl.	735	81	9.1	t70	2
Tilley, St.L.	1040	66	15.8	75	3	Green, St.L.	708	33	21.5	60	4
Carmichael, Phil.	1028	61	16.9	t85	6	Brown, Minn.	694	83	8.4	63	2
Scott, Det.	1022	53	19.3	48	5	Coffman, G.B.	687	55	12.5	29	4
Senser, Minn.	1004	79	12.7	53	8	Jefferson, G.B.	632	39	16.2	41	4
White, Minn.	1001	66	15.2	53	3	Pearson, Dall.	614	38	16.2	t42	3
Solomon, S.F.	969	59	16.4	t60	8	Jackson, Atl.	604	37	16.3	49	6
Hill, Dall.	953	46	20.7	t63	4	Metcalf, Wash.	595	48	12.4	52	0
Monk, Wash.	894	56	16.0	t79	6	Smith, Phil.	564	38	14.8	45	4
Rashad, Minn.	884	58	15.2	53	7						

t-Touchdown
Leader based on most passes caught

1981 INTERCEPTIONS

INTERCEPTIONS
NFC: 11—Everson Walls, Dallas.
AFC: 10—John Harris, Seattle.

YARDS
NFC: 239—Dwight Hicks, San Francisco.
AFC: 227—Darrol Ray, New York.

TOUCHDOWNS
NFC: 3—Ronnie Lott, San Francisco.
AFC: 2—John Harris, Seattle.
2—Darrol Ray, New York.

LONGEST

AFC: 102 yards—Louis Breeden, Cincinnati vs. San Diego, November 8 (TD).

NFC: 101 yards—Tom Pridemore, Atlanta vs. San Francisco, September 20 (TD).

TEAM LEADERS

AFC: BALTIMORE: 3, Larry Braziel & Bruce Laird; BUFFALO: 5, Mario Clark; CINCINNATI: 5, Ken Riley; CLEVELAND: 4, Clarence Scott; DENVER: 5, Steve Foley; HOUSTON: 3, Carter Hartwig & Greg Stemrick; KANSAS CITY: 7, Eric Harris; MIAMI: 4, Glenn Blackwood; NEW ENGLAND: 3, Tim Fox & Rick Sanford; NEW YORK: 7, Darrol Ray; OAKLAND: 3, Lester Hayes & Odis McKinney; PITTSBURGH: 6, Mel Blount & Jack Lambert; SAN DIEGO: 5, Willie Buchanon; SEATTLE: 10, John Harris.

NFC: ATLANTA: 7, Tom Pridemore; CHICAGO: 6, Gary Fencik; DALLAS: 11, Everson Walls; DETROIT: 9, Jim Allen; GREEN BAY: 6, Maurice Harvey & Mark Lee; LOS ANGELES: 5, Nolan Cromwell; MINNESOTA: 4, Tom Hannon & Willie Teal; NEW ORLEANS: 4, Dave Waymer; NEW YORK: 4, Beasley Reece; PHILADELPHIA: 5, Brenard Wilson; ST, LOUIS: 7, Ken Greene; SAN FRANCISCO: 9, Dwight Hicks; TAMPA BAY: 9, Cedric Brown; WASHINGTON: 7, Mark Murphy.

TEAM CHAMPION

NFC: 37—Dallas.

AFC: 30—Pittsburgh.

INTERCEPTIONS—TEAM

AMERICAN FOOTBALL CONFERENCE

Player—Team	No.	Yards	Avg.	Long	TDs.
Pittsburgh	30	376	12.5	t50	1
Kansas City	26	406	15.6	t46	1
Denver	23	342	10.5	65	0
San Diego	23	224	9.7	39	1
New York Jets	21	432	20.6	67	2
Seattle	21	397	18.9	t82	3
Buffalo	19	352	18.5	53	0
Cincinnati	19	318	16.7	t102	1
Houston	18	330	18.3	38	0
Miami	18	254	14.1	39	0
Baltimore	16	210	13.1	49	0
New England	16	195	12.2	49	0
Cleveland	15	165	11.0	45	0
Oakland	13	97	7.5	34	1
Conference Total	278	4,098	....	t102	10
Conference Average	19.9	292.7	14.7	......	0.7

NATIONAL FOOTBALL CONFERENCE

Player—Team	No.	Yards	Avg.	Long	TDs.
Dallas	37	482	13.0	96	0
Tampa Bay	32	648	20.3	t82	4
Green Bay	30	495	16.5	53	1
San Francisco	27	448	16.6	72	4
Philadelphia	26	266	10.2	35	0
Atlanta	25	494	19.8	t101	3
Detroit	24	286	11.9	t60	1
Washington	24	249	10.4	t52	2
St. Louis	21	281	13.4	47	1
Chicago	18	345	19.2	t92	3
Los Angeles	17	237	13.9	94	0
New York Giants	17	222	13.1	t32	1
New Orleans	17	214	12.6	54	0
Minnesota	16	120	7.5	28	0
Conference Total	331	4,787	....	t101	20
Conference Average	23.6	341.9	14.5	......	1.4
League Total	609	8,885	....	t102	30
League Average	21.8	317.3	14.6	......	1.1

TOP TEN INTERCEPTORS

Player—Team	No.	Yards	Avg.	Long	TDs.
WALLS, EVERSON, Dallas	11	133	12.1	33	0
Harris, John, Seattle	10	155	15.5	t42	2
Hicks, Dwight, San Francisco	9	239	26.6	72	1
Brown, Cedric, Tampa Bay	9	215	23.9	t81	2
Thurman, Dennis, Dallas	9	187	20.8	96	0
Allen, Jim, Detroit	9	123	13.7	34	0
Ray, Darrol, New York Jets	7	227	32.4	t64	2
Pridemore, Tom, Atlanta	7	221	31.6	t101	1
Lott, Ronnie, San Francisco	7	117	16.7	t41	3
Greene, Ken, St. Louis	7	111	15.9	47	0
Harris, Eric, Kansas City	7	109	15.6	43	0
Downs, Michael, Dallas	7	81	11.6	25	0
Murphy, Mark, Washington	7	68	9.7	29	0

AFC—INDIVIDUALS

Player—Team	No.	Yds.	Avg.	Lng.	TD
HARRIS, Sea	10	155	15.5	t42	2
Ray, N.Y.J.	7	227	32.4	t64	2
Harris, K.C.	7	109	15.6	43	0
Blount, Pitt	6	106	17.7	t50	1
Lambert, Pitt	6	76	12.7	31	0
Clark, Buffalo	5	142	28.4	53	0
Barbaro, K.C.	5	134	26.8	34	0
Foley, Den	5	81	16.2	24	0
Shell, Pitt	5	52	10.4	25	0
Green, K.C.	5	37	7.4	16	0
Buchanon, S.D.	5	31	6.2	18	0
Riley, Cin	5	6	1.2	6	0
Breeden, Cin	4	145	36.3	t102	1
G. Blackwood, Mia	4	124	31.0	39	0
Romes, Buff	4	113	28.3	35	0
Burruss, K.C.	4	75	18.8	t46	1
Scott, Clev	4	46	11.5	26	0
Simpson, Buff	4	42	10.5	42	0
Gradishar, Den	4	38	9.5	16	0
Williams, Cin	4	33	8.3	14	0
Thomas, Pitt	4	18	4.5	16	0
Thompson, Den	4	14	3.5	14	0
Easley, Sea	3	155	51.7	t82	1
Stemrick, Hou	3	94	31.3	38	0
Hartwig, Hou	3	78	26.0	36	0
Lynn, N.Y.J.	3	76	25.3	67	0
Darden, Clev	3	68	22.7	45	0
Laird, Balt	3	59	19.7	24	0
Swenson, Den	3	53	17.7	32	0
Shaw, S.D.	3	50	16.7	23	0
Washington, Pitt	3	46	15.3	35	0
McKinney, Oak	3	38	12.7	34	0
Kozlowski, Mia	3	37	12.3	29	0
Braziel, Balt	3	35	11.7	27	0
Rhone, Mia	3	35	11.7	16	0
Sanford, N.E.	3	28	9.3	21	0
Fox, N.E.	3	20	6.7	20	0
Mehl, N.Y.J.	3	17	5.7	10	0
L. Blackwood, Mia	3	12	4.0	11	0
Hayes, Oak	3	0	0.0	0	0
Lowe, S.D.	3	0	0.0	0	0
M. Williams, S.D.	3	0	0.0	0	0
B. Harris, Cin	2	92	46.0	49	0
Schroy, N.Y.J.	2	58	29.0	39	0
Jackson, Sea	2	51	25.5	33	0
Kay, Hou	2	47	23.5	30	0
Perry, Hou	2	46	23.0	34	0
Edwards, S.D.	2	45	22.5	39	0
Kyle, Den	2	40	20.0	40	0
Clayborn, N.E.	2	39	19.5	39	0
Brudzinski, Mia	2	35	17.5	19	0
Glasgow, Balt	2	35	17.5	31	0
Buttle, N.Y.J.	2	34	17.0	22	0
Harden, Den	2	34	17.0	38	0
Simpson, Sea	2	34	17.0	21	0
Flint, Clev	2	33	16.5	33	0
Owens, Oak	2	30	15.0	t30	1
Paul, K.C.	2	30	15.0	25	0
James, N.E.	2	29	14.5	21	0
Bingham, Hou	2	20	10.0	17	0
Reinfeldt, Hou	2	18	9.0	16	0
Manumaleuga, K.C.	2	17	8.5	12	0
Robertson, Buff	2	15	7.5	15	0
Matthews, Clev	2	14	7.0	8	0
Gregor, S.D.	2	11	5.5	11	0
Smith, Balt	2	11	5.5	8	0
Hatchett, Balt	2	8	4.0	8	0
Johnson, Pitt	2	8	4.0	8	0
Brazile, Hou	2	7	3.5	7	0
Springs, N.Y.J.	2	5	2.5	5	0
D. Brown, Sea	2	2	1.0	2	0
Butler, Sea	2	0	0.0	0	0
Smith, Den	1	65	65.0	65	0
Anderson, Balt	1	49	49.0	49	0
Buben, N.E.	1	49	49.0	49	0
Johnson, S.D.	1	41	41.0	36	1
Fuller, Cin	1	31	31.0	31	0
Cole, Pitt	1	29	29.0	29	0
King, S.D.	1	28	28.0	28	0
Ham, Pitt	1	23	23.0	23	0
Kush, Buff	1	19	19.0	19	0
Washington, Hou	1	19	19.0	19	0
Woodruff, Pitt	1	17	17.0	17	0
Hawkins, N.E.	1	16	16.0	16	0
Manor, Den	1	16	16.0	16	0
Blinka, N.Y.J.	1	15	15.0	15	0
Bess, Buff	1	12	12.0	12	0
Horn, S.D.	1	12	12.0	12	0
Watts, Oak	1	12	12.0	12	0
Duhe, Mia	1	11	11.0	11	0
Razzano, Cin	1	11	11.0	11	0
Zamberlin, N.E.	1	11	11.0	11	0
Krauss, Balt	1	10	10.0	10	0
Nelson, Buff	1	9	9.0	9	0
Browning, Oak	1	8	8.0	8	0
Martin, Oak	1	7	7.0	7	0
Jones, S.D.	1	6	6.0	6	0
Cherry, K.C.	1	4	4.0	4	0
Bolton, Clev	1	3	3.0	3	0
Green, Balt	1	3	3.0	3	0
Haynes, N.E.	1	3	3.0	3	0
O'Steen, Oak	1	2	2.0	2	0
Evans, Den	1	1	1.0	1	0
Goode, Clev	1	1	1.0	1	0
J. C. Wilson, Hou	1	1	1.0	1	0
Winston, Pitt	1	1	1.0	1	0
Ambrose, Clev	1	0	0.0	0	0
Bessillieu, Mia	1	0	0.0	0	0
Cameron, Cin	1	0	0.0	0	0
Davis, Oak	1	0	0.0	0	0
Duncan, S.D.	1	0	0.0	0	0
Holmes, N.Y.J.	1	0	0.0	0	0
LeClair, Cin	1	0	0.0	0	0
Lee, N.E.	1	0	0.0	0	0
Logan, Clev	1	0	0.0	0	0
Pinkney, Balt	1	0	0.0	0	0
Shoate, N.E.	1	0	0.0	0	0
Walker, Mia	1	0	0.0	0	0
Williams, Buff	1	0	0.0	0	0

NFC—INDIVIDUALS

Player—Team	No.	Yds.	Avg.	Lng.	TD
WALLS, Dall.	11	133	12.1	33	0
Hicks, S.F.	9	239	26.6	72	1
Brown, T.B.	9	215	23.9	t81	2
Thurman, Dall.	9	187	20.8	96	0
Allen, Det.	9	123	13.7	34	0
Pridemore, Atl.	7	221	31.6	t101	1
Lott, S.F.	7	117	16.7	t41	3
Greene, St.L.	7	111	15.9	47	0
Downs, Dall.	7	81	11.6	25	0
Murphy, Wash.	7	68	9.7	29	0
Harvey, G.B.	6	217	36.2	53	0
Washington, T.B.	6	156	26.0	34	1
Fencik, Chi.	6	121	20.2	t69	1
Colzie, T.B.	6	110	18.3	t82	1
Lee, G.B.	6	50	8.3	25	0
Cromwell, L.A.	5	94	18.8	94	0
Butler, Atl.	5	86	17.2	41	0
Johnson, T.B.	5	84	16.8	36	0
Wilson, Phila.	5	73	14.6	26	0
Henderson, Chi.	4	84	21.0	39	0
Reece, N.Y.G.	4	84	21.0	32	0
P. Thomas, L.A.	4	80	20.0	64	0
Waymer, N.O.	4	54	13.5	31	0
Lavender, Wash.	4	52	13.0	30	0
Williamson, S.F.	4	44	11.0	28	0
White, Det.	4	37	9.3	16	0
Young, Phila.	4	35	8.8	33	0
Hannon, Minn.	4	28	7.0	28	0
Teal, Minn.	4	23	5.8	15	0
Wehrli, St.L.	4	8	2.0	6	0
Hood, G.B.	3	59	19.7	t41	1
T. Jackson, N.Y.G.	3	57	19.0	t32	1
Murphy, G.B.	3	57	19.0	50	0
Coleman, Wash.	3	52	17.3	t52	1
Green, St.L.	3	44	14.7	29	0
Johnson, Atl.	3	35	11.7	23	0
Cobb, Det.	3	32	10.7	17	0
Wright, S.F.	3	26	8.7	26	0
Knoff, Minn.	3	24	8.0	20	0
Cumby, G.B.	3	22	7.3	17	0
Waters, Dall.	3	21	7.0	21	0
Douglass, G.B.	3	20	6.7	13	0
Irvin, L.A.	3	18	6.0	18	0
Perry, L.A.	3	18	6.0	10	0
Wattelet, N.O.	3	16	5.3	16	0
Anderson, G.B.	3	12	4.0	8	0
Currier, N.Y.G.	3	2	0.7	2	0
Edwards, Phila.	3	1	0.3	1	0
Peters, Wash.	3	0	0.0	0	0
Myers, N.O.	2	70	35.0	54	0
Chesley, Phila.	2	66	33.0	35	0
Green, T.B.	2	56	28.0	50	0
Blackmore, Phila.	2	43	21.5	25	0
Kelley, N.Y.G.	2	43	21.5	27	0
E. Jones, Atl.	2	42	21.0	39	0
LeMaster, Phila.	2	28	14.0	22	0
McNeill, Minn.	2	26	13.0	14	0
Kaufman, Was.	2	25	12.5	25	0
Olkewicz, Wash.	2	22	11.0	12	1
Glazebrook, Atl.	2	21	10.5	18	0
McCoy, G.B.	2	20	10.0	16	0
Fantetti, Det.	2	18	9.0	17	0
Swain, Minn.	2	18	9.0	18	0
Wilkes, Phila.	2	18	9.0	11	0
Lewis, T.B.	2	12	6.0	10	0
Breunig, Dall.	2	8	4.0	8	0
Schmidt, Chi.	2	4	2.0	4	0
J. Fisher, Chi.	2	3	1.5	3	0
Wilson, Dall.	2	0	0.0	0	0
Logan, Phila.	2	−1	−0.5	0	0
Bell, Chi.	1	92	92.0	t92	1
Hall, Det.	1	60	60.0	t60	1
Harris, Chi.	1	44	44.0	t44	1
Favron, St.L.	1	42	42.0	42	0
Wingo, G.B.	1	38	38.0	38	0
Curry, Atl.	1	35	35.0	t35	1
Ray, N.O.	1	33	33.0	33	0
Brown, Dall.	1	28	28.0	28	0
Butz, Wash.	1	26	26.0	26	0
Williams, Atl.	1	25	25.0	25	0
Barnes, Dall.	1	24	24.0	24	0
McColl, S.F.	1	22	22.0	22	0
Kuykendall, Atl.	1	20	20.0	t20	1
Jim Youngblood, L.A.	1	20	20.0	20	0
Johnson, St.L.	1	19	19.0	19	0
Nairne, St.L.	1	18	18.0	18	0
Collier, St.L.	1	17	17.0	17	0
Williams, St.L.	1	17	17.0	17	0
Ahrens, St.L.	1	14	14.0	t14	1
Holt, T.B.	1	13	13.0	13	0
Kovach, N.O.	1	13	13.0	13	0
Oldham, Det.	1	10	10.0	10	0
Van Pelt, N.Y.G.	1	10	10.0	10	0
Baker, Det.	1	9	9.0	9	0
Flowers, N.Y.G.	1	9	9.0	9	0
Haynes, N.Y.G.	1	9	9.0	9	0
Richardson, Atl.	1	9	9.0	9	0
Harris, L.A.	1	7	7.0	7	0
Hunt, N.Y.G.	1	7	7.0	7	0
Redd, N.O.	1	7	7.0	7	0
Junior, St.L.	1	5	5.0	5	0
Griffin, St.L.	1	4	4.0	4	0
Bordelon, N.O.	1	3	3.0	3	0
Nelms, Wash.	1	3	3.0	3	0
Robinson, Phila.	1	3	3.0	3	0
Brantley, T.B.	1	2	2.0	2	0
Blair, Minn.	1	1	1.0	1	0
Parrish, Wash.	1	1	1.0	1	0
L. Taylor, N.Y.G.	1	1	1.0	1	0
Bradley, Det.	1	0	0.0	0	0
Gaison, Atl.	1	0	0.0	0	0
Gary, N.O.	1	0	0.0	0	0
Gray, Det.	1	0	0.0	0	0
Johnson, Phila.	1	0	0.0	0	0
Lewis, Dall.	1	0	0.0	0	0
Martin, S.F.	1	0	0.0	0	0
Musser, Atl.	1	0	0.0	0	0
Phillips, Phila.	1	0	0.0	0	0
Poe, N.O.	1	0	0.0	0	0
Reynolds, S.F.	1	0	0.0	0	0
Sciarra, Phila.	1	0	0.0	0	0
Spivey, N.O.	1	0	0.0	0	0
Turner, S.F.	1	0	0.0	0	0
Walterscheid, Chi.	1	0	0.0	0	0
Hunter, Det.	1	−3	−3.0	−3	0
Singletary, Chi.	1	−3	−3.0	−3	0

t—Touchdown
Leader based on most interceptions

1981 SCORING

POINTS

Kickers

NFC: 121—Ed Murray, Detroit.
     121—Rafael Septien, Dallas.
AFC: 115—Jim Breech, Cincinnati.
     115—Nick Lowery, Kansas City.

Non-Kickers

AFC: 114—Chuck Muncie, San Diego.
NFC: 102—Wendell Tyler, Los Angeles.

TOUCHDOWNS
AFC: 19—Chuck Muncie, San Diego (19 rushing).
NFC: 17—Wendell Tyler, Los Angeles (12 rushing, 5 passing).

EXTRA POINTS
AFC: 55—Rolf Benirschke, San Diego (61 attempts).
NFC: 51—Mick Luckhurst, Atlanta (51 attempts).

FIELD GOALS
NFC: 27—Rafael Septien, Dallas (35 attempts).
AFC: 26—Nick Lowery, Kansas City (36 attempts).

MOST POINTS, GAME
AFC: 30—Kellen Winslow, San Diego vs. Oakland, November 22 (5-TD).
NFC: 20—Joe Danelo, New York vs. Seattle, October 18 (2-XP, 6-FG).

TEAM LEADERS
AFC: BALTIMORE: 60, Curtis Dickey; BUFFALO: 79, Nick Mike-Mayer; CINCINNATI: 115, Jim Breech; CLEVELAND: *79, Matt Bahr; DENVER: 87, Fred Steinfort; HOUSTON: 77, Toni Fritsch; KANSAS CITY: 115, Nick Lowery; MIAMI: 109, Uwe von Schamann; NEW ENGLAND: 82, John Smith; NEW YORK: 113, Pat Leahy; OAKLAND: 69, Chris Bahr; PITTSBURGH: 74, David Trout; SAN DIEGO: 114, Chuck Muncie; SEATTLE: 60, Steve Largent.

NFC: ATLANTA: 114, Mick Luckhurst; CHICAGO: 49, John Roveto; DALLAS: 121, Rafael Septien; DETROIT: 121, Ed Murray; GREEN BAY: 101, Jan Stenerud; LOS ANGELES: 102, Wendell Tyler; MINNESOTA: 97, Rick Danmeier; NEW ORLEANS: 78, George Rogers; NEW YORK: 103, Joe Danelo; PHILADELPHIA: 101, Tony Franklin; ST. LOUIS: 93, Neil O'Donoghue; SAN FRANCISCO: 81, Ray Wersching; TAMPA BAY: 75, Bill Capece; WASHINGTON: 95, Mark Moseley.

*Includes 18 points with S.F.

TEAM CHAMPION
AFC: 478—San Diego.
NFC: 426—Atlanta.

SCORING—TEAM

AMERICAN FOOTBALL CONFERENCE

	Tot. Tds.	Tds. R.	Tds. P.	Tds. Misc.	XP	XPA	FG	FGA	Saf.	Tot. Pts.
San Diego	61	26	34	1	55	61	19	26	0	478
Cincinnati	51	19	30	2	49	51	22	32	0	421
Pittsburgh	47	21	25	1	38	46	12	17	0	356
New York Jets	40	11	26	3	38	40	25	36	1	355
Miami	39	18	18	3	37	39	24	31	1	345
Kansas City	38	22	12	4	37	38	26	36	0	343
New England	40	23	17	0	37	40	15	24	0	322
Seattle	40	14	21	5	37	40	15	24	0	322
Denver	39	12	27	0	36	39	17	30	0	321
Buffalo	38	13	25	0	37	38	14	24	2	311
Houston	34	11	21	2	32	34	15	22	0	281
Cleveland	32	11	21	0	31	32	17	33	1	276
Oakland	33	11	18	4	27	33	14	24	3	273
Baltimore	33	11	21	1	29	33	10	18	1	259
Conference Total	565	223	316	26	520	564	245	377	9	4,663
Conference Average	40.4	15.9	22.6	1.9	37.1	40.3	17.5	26.9	0.6	333.1

NATIONAL FOOTBALL CONFERENCE

	Tot. Tds.	Tds. R.	Tds. P.	Tds. Misc.	XP	XPA	FG	FGA	Saf.	Tot. Pts.
Atlanta	52	15	30	7	51	52	21	33	0	426
Detroit	46	26	18	2	46	46	25	35	0	397
Philadelphia	44	17	25	2	42	44	20	31	1	368
Dallas	40	15	24	1	40	40	27	35	3	367
San Francisco	43	17	20	6	42	43	19	29	0	357
Washington	42	19	19	4	38	42	19	30	0	347
Minnesota	37	8	27	2	34	37	21	25	3	325
Green Bay	37	11	24	2	36	37	22	24	0	324

	Tot. Tds.	Tds. R.	Tds. P.	Tds. Misc.	XP	XPA	FG	FGA	Saf.	Tot. Pts.
St. Louis	37	20	15	2	36	37	19	32	0	315
Tampa Bay	38	13	20	5	36	38	17	28	0	315
Los Angeles	36	17	15	4	36	36	17	26	0	303
New York Giants	32	11	16	5	31	32	24	38	0	295
Chicago	31	13	14	4	29	31	12	23	1	253
New Orleans	24	16	8	0	24	24	13	25	0	207
Conference Total	539	218	275	46	521	539	276	414	8	4,599
Conference Average	38.5	15.6	19.6	3.3	37.2	38.5	19.7	29.6	0.6	328.5
League Total	1,104	441	591	72	1,041	1,103	521	791	17	9,262
League Average	39.4	15.8	21.1	2.6	37.2	39.4	18.6	28.3	0.6	330.8

TOP TEN SCORERS

NON-KICKERS

Player—Team	Total TDs.	Rush TDs.	Pass TDs.	Misc. TDs.	Tot. Pts.
MUNCIE, San Diego	19	19	0	0	114
Tyler, Los Angeles	17	12	5	0	102
Johnson, Cincinnati	16	12	4	0	96
Sims, Detroit	15	13	2	0	90
Jenkins, Atlanta	13	0	13	0	78
Riggins, Washington	13	13	0	0	78
Rogers, New Orleans	13	13	0	0	78
Watson, Denver	13	0	13	0	78
Andrews, Atlanta	12	10	2	0	72
Springs, Dallas	12	10	2	0	72

KICKERS

Player—Team	XP Made	XP Att.	FG. Made	FG. Att.	Tot. Pts.
MURRAY, Detroit	46	46	25	35	121
Septien, Dallas	40	40	27	35	121
Breech, Cincinnati	49	51	22	32	115
Lowery, Kansas City	37	38	26	36	115
Luckhurst, Atlanta	51	51	21	33	114
Leahy, New York Jets	38	39	25	36	113
Benirschke, San Diego	55	61	19	26	112
von Schamann, Miami	37	38	24	31	109
Danelo, N.Y. Giants	31	31	24	38	103
Franklin, Philadelphia	41	43	20	31	101
Stenerud, Green Bay	35	36	22	24	101

AFC—INDIVIDUALS

KICKERS

Player—Team	XP Made	XP Att.	FG. Made	FG. Att.	Tot. Pts.
BREECH, Cincinnati	49	51	22	32	115
Lowery, Kansas City	37	38	26	36	115
Leahy, New York Jets	38	39	25	36	113
Benirschke, San Diego	55	61	19	26	112
von Schamann, Miami	37	38	24	31	109
Steinfort, Denver	36	37	17	30	87
Smith, New England	37	39	15	24	82
Bahr, S.F.-Clev	34	34	15	26	79
Mike-Mayer, Buffalo	37	37	14	24	79
Fritsch, Houston	32	34	15	22	77
Trout, Pittsburgh	38	46	12	17	74
Bahr, Oakland	27	33	14	24	69
Herrera, Seattle	23	25	12	17	59
Wood, Baltimore	29	33	10	18	59
Alvarez, Seattle	14	15	3	7	23
Jacobs, Cleveland	9	10	4	12	21
Cox, Cleveland	0	0	0	1	0

NON-KICKERS

Player—Team	Total TDs.	Rush TDs.	Pass TDs.	Misc. TDs.	Tot. Pts.
MUNCIE, San Diego	19	19	0	0	114
Johnson, Cincinnati	16	12	4	0	96
Watson, Denver	13	0	13	0	78
B. Jackson, Kan. City	11	10	1	0	66
Campbell, Houston	10	10	0	0	60
Cribbs, Buffalo	10	3	7	0	60
Dickey, Baltimore	10	7	3	0	60
Largent, Seattle	10	1	9	0	60
Winslow, San Diego	10	0	10	0	60
Butler, Baltimore	9	0	9	0	54
Harris, Pittsburgh	9	8	1	0	54
Walker, New York Jets	9	0	9	0	54
T. Brown, St.L.-Sea	8	8	0	0	48
Butler, Buffalo	8	0	8	0	48
Casper, Houston	8	0	8	0	48
Collinsworth, Cinn	8	0	8	0	48
Franklin, Miami	8	7	1	0	48
Nathan, Miami	8	5	3	0	48
M. Pruitt, Cleveland	8	7	1	0	48
Barkum, N.Y. Jets	7	0	7	0	42
Burrough, Houston	7	0	7	0	42

Player—Team	Total TDs.	Rush TDs.	Pass TDs.	Misc. TDs.	Tot. Pts.
Collins, New England	7	7	0	0	42
Joiner, San Diego	7	0	7	0	42
Smith, Pittsburgh	7	0	7	0	42
J. Brooks, San Diego	6	3	3	0	36
Chandler, N.O-S.D.	6	0	6	0	36
Hasselbeck, New Eng	6	0	6	0	36
Leaks, Buffalo	6	6	0	0	36
Morgan, New England	6	0	6	0	36
Newsome, Cleveland	6	0	6	0	36
Cappelletti, San Diego	5	4	1	0	30
Doornink, Seattle	5	1	4	0	30
Harper, New York Jets	5	4	1	0	30
Hooks, Buffalo	5	3	2	0	30
Kreider, Cincinnati	5	0	5	0	30
Long, New York Jets	5	2	3	0	30
Lytle, Denver	5	4	1	0	30
McKnight, Kansas City	5	5	0	0	30
Odoms, Denver	5	0	5	0	30
Ross, Cincinnati	5	0	5	0	30
Stallworth, Pittsburgh	5	0	5	0	30
Swann, Pittsburgh	5	0	5	0	30
Canada, Denver	4	3	1	0	24
Chandler, Oakland	4	0	4	0	24
Cunningham, New Eng	4	4	0	0	24
A. Griffin, Cincinnati	4	3	1	0	24
Jensen, Oakland	4	4	0	0	24
Lewis, Buffalo	4	0	4	0	24
Logan, Cleveland	4	0	4	0	24
Marshall, Kansas City	4	0	4	0	24
McMillan, Baltimore	4	3	1	0	24
G. Pruitt, Cleveland	4	0	4	0	24
Ramsey, Oakland	4	0	4	0	24
S. Smith, Seattle	4	3	1	0	24
Thornton, Pittsburgh	4	4	0	0	24
Vigorito, Miami	4	1	2	1	24
Woodley, Miami	4	4	0	0	24
Alexander, Cincinnati	3	2	1	0	18
Bradshaw, Oakland	3	0	3	0	18
Carr, Baltimore	3	0	3	0	18
Cavanaugh, New Eng	3	3	0	0	18
Cefalo, Miami	3	0	3	0	18
Cunningham, Pitt	3	0	3	0	18
Delaney, Kansas City	3	3	0	0	18

Player—Team	Total TDs.	Rush TDs.	Pass TDs.	Misc. TDs.	Tot. Pts.	Player—Team	Total TDs.	Rush TDs.	Pass TDs.	Misc. TDs.	Tot. Pts.
Feacher, Cleveland	3	0	3	0	18	Carson, Kansas City	1	0	1	0	6
Ferguson, New Eng.	3	3	0	0	18	Chester, Oakland	1	0	1	0	6
Hadnot, Kansas City	3	3	0	0	18	Coleman, Houston	1	1	0	0	6
L. Jones, N.Y. Jets	3	0	3	0	18	Davis, Pittsburgh	1	1	0	0	6
Malone, Pittsburgh	3	2	1	0	18	Dixon, Baltimore	1	0	1	0	6
McCullum, Seattle	3	0	3	0	18	Easley, Seattle	1	0	0	1	6
McNeil, New York Jets	3	2	1	0	18	Egloff, Denver	1	0	1	0	6
Parros, Denver	3	2	1	0	18	Ferguson, Buffalo	1	1	0	0	6
Preston, Denver	3	3	0	0	18	Franklin, Baltimore	1	1	0	0	6
Sievers, San Diego	3	0	3	0	18	Grossman, Pittsburgh	1	0	1	0	6
Tatupu, New England	3	2	1	0	18	Hardman, Oakland	1	0	0	1	6
Upchurch, Denver	3	0	3	0	18	Hargrove, Cincinnati	1	1	0	0	6
Whittington, Oakland	3	1	2	0	18	Howard, Kansas City	1	0	0	1	6
Christensen, Oakland	2	0	2	0	*14	Jodat, Seattle	1	1	0	0	6
Bradshaw, Pittsburgh	2	2	0	0	12	Johns, Seattle	1	0	1	0	6
Brammer, Buffalo	2	0	2	0	12	Johnson, New England	1	0	1	0	6
Calhoun, New England	2	2	0	0	12	Johnson, San Diego	1	0	0	1	6
Curtis, Cincinnati	2	0	2	0	12	Johnson, Seattle	1	0	0	1	6
Dierking, N.Y. Jets	2	1	1	0	12	Jones, Oakland	1	0	0	1	6
Dixon, Kansas City	2	0	2	0	12	Kenney, Kansas City	1	1	0	0	6
Grogan, New England	2	2	0	0	12	Kozlowski, Miami	1	0	0	1	6
Harris, Miami	2	0	2	0	12	Krieg, Seattle	1	1	0	0	6
Harris, Seattle	2	0	0	2	12	Landry, Baltimore	1	0	0	1	6
M. L. Harris, Cinn.	2	0	2	0	12	Lee, Miami	1	0	1	0	6
Hawthorne, Pittsburgh	2	2	0	0	12	Moser, Pittsburgh	1	0	1	0	6
Hill, Cleveland	2	0	2	0	12	Moses, Denver	1	0	1	0	6
Hill, Miami	2	1	1	0	12	Newton, New York Jets	1	1	0	0	6
Holston, Houston	2	0	2	0	121	Owens, Oakland	1	0	0	1	6
Hughes, Seattle	2	0	2	0	12	Paul, Kansas City	1	0	0	1	6
B. Jones, N.Y. Jets	2	0	1	1	12	Pennywell, New Eng	1	0	1	0	6
McCall, Baltimore	2	0	2	0	12	Pinney, Pittsburgh	1	0	1	0	6
McCauley, Baltimore	2	0	2	0	101	Plunkett, Oakland	1	1	0	0	6
C. Miller, Cleveland	2	2	0	0	12	Renfro, Houston	1	0	1	0	6
Moore, Miami	2	0	2	0	12	Roaches, Houston	1	0	0	1	6
Pollard, Pittsburgh	2	2	0	0	12	Rome, Kansas City	1	0	1	0	6
Ray, New York Jets	2	0	0	2	12	Rucker, Cleveland	1	0	1	0	6
Rose, Miami	2	0	2	0	12	St. Clair, Cincinnati	1	0	0	1	6
Smith, Kansas City	2	0	2	0	12	Scales, San Diego	1	0	1	0	6
Smith, San Diego	2	0	2	0	12	Scott, Kansas City	1	0	1	0	6
van Eeghen, Oakland	2	2	0	0	12	Sipe, Cleveland	1	1	0	0	6
Verser, Cincinnati	2	0	2	0	12	Spani, Kansas City	1	0	0	1	6
Westbrook, New Eng	2	0	2	0	12	Thomas, Seattle	1	0	0	1	6
Wilson, Oakland	2	2	0	0	12	Tullis, Houston	1	0	0	1	6
Anderson, Cincinnati	1	1	0	0	6	Watts, Oakland	1	0	0	1	6
Armstrong, Houston	1	0	1	0	6	Walker, Miami	1	0	0	1	6
Augustyniak, N.Y. Jets.	1	1	0	0	6	White, Cleveland	1	1	0	0	6
Barber, Houston	1	0	1	0	6	C. Williams, San Diego .	1	0	1	0	6
Barnett, Buffalo	1	0	1	0	6	Willis, Oakland	1	1	0	0	6
Barnwell, Oakland	1	0	1	0	6	Wright, Denver	1	0	1	0	6
Bauer, San Diego	1	0	1	0	6	Zorn, Seattle	1	1	0	0	6
Blount, Pittsburgh	1	0	0	1	6	Buttle, New York Jets ..	0	0	0	0	*2
Boyd, Seattle	1	0	1	0	6	Gordon, Miami	0	0	0	0	*2
Branch, Oakland	1	0	1	0	6	Robinson, Oakland	0	0	0	0	*2
Breeden, Cincinnati	1	0	0	1	6	Taylor, Baltimore	0	0	0	0	*2
Brown, Buffalo	1	0	1	0	6	Williams, Buffalo	0	0	0	0	*2
Burruss, Kansas City	1	0	0	1	6						

*Safety (also 1 each: Buffalo, Cleveland, Oakland.)

NFC—INDIVIDUALS

KICKERS

Player—Team	XP Made	XP Att.	FG Made	FG Att.	Tot. Pts.
MURRAY, Detroit	46	46	25	35	121
Septien, Dallas	40	40	27	33	121
Luckhurst, Atlanta	51	51	21	33	114
Danelo, N.Y. Giants	31	31	24	38	103
Franklin, Philadelphia	41	43	20	31	101
Stenerud, Green Bay	35	36	22	24	101
Danmeier, Minnesota	34	37	21	25	97
Moseley, Washington	38	42	19	30	95
O'Donoghue, St. Louis	36	37	19	32	93
Corral, Los Angeles	36	36	17	26	87
Wersching, San Fran.	30	30	17	23	81
Capece, Tampa Bay	30	32	15	24	75
Ricardo, New Orleans	24	24	13	25	63
Roveto, Chicago	19	20	10	18	49
Yepremian, Tampa B.	6	6	2	4	12
Nielsen, Chicago	8	8	0	2	8
Thomas, Chicago	2	3	2	3	8

NON-KICKERS

Player—Team	Total TDs.	Rush TDs.	Pass TDs.	Misc. TDs.	Tot. Pts.
Tyler, Los Angeles	17	12	5	0	102
Sims, Detroit	15	13	2	0	90
Jenkins, Atlanta	13	0	13	0	78
Riggins, Washington	13	13	0	0	78
G. Rogers, New Orleans	13	13	0	0	78
Andrews, Atlanta	12	10	2	0	72
Springs, Dallas	12	10	2	0	72
Montgomery, Phila.	10	8	2	0	60
Anderson, St. Louis	9	9	0	0	54
House, Tampa Bay	9	0	9	0	54
Brown, Minnesota	8	6	2	0	48
Huckleby, Green Bay	8	5	3	0	48
Lofton, Green Bay	8	0	8	0	48
Payton, Chicago	8	6	2	0	48
Senser, Minnesota	8	0	8	0	48
Solomon, San Fran.	8	0	8	0	48
Davis, San Francisco	7	7	0	0	42

Player—Team	Total TDs.	Rush TDs.	Pass TDs.	Misc. TDs.	Tot. Pts.
Ellis, Green Bay	7	4	3	0	42
Hipple, Detroit	7	7	0	0	42
Jackson, Atlanta	7	0	6	1	42
Rashad, Minnesota	7	0	7	0	42
Washington, Wash.	7	4	3	0	42
Cain, Atlanta	6	4	2	0	36
Carmichael, Phila.	6	0	6	0	36
Carpenter, Hou.-N.Y.G.	6	5	1	0	36
Dorsett, Dallas	6	4	2	0	36
Giles, Tampa Bay	6	0	6	0	36
Monk, Washington	6	0	6	0	36
Perkins, N.Y. Giants	6	0	6	0	36
Cosbie, Dallas	5	0	5	0	30
Francis, Atlanta	5	1	4	0	30
Green, St. Louis	5	1	4	0	30
Johnson, Dallas	5	0	5	0	30
Krepfle, Philadelphia	5	0	5	0	30
Morris, St. Louis	5	5	0	0	30
Patton, San Francisco	5	4	1	0	30
Scott, Detroit	5	0	5	0	30
Wilder, Tampa Bay	5	4	1	0	30
W. Wilson, N. Orleans	5	1	4	0	30
Young, San Francisco	5	0	5	0	30
Campfield, Phila.	4	1	3	0	24
Clark, San Francisco	4	0	4	0	24
Coffman, Green Bay	4	0	4	0	24
Dennard, Los Angeles	4	0	4	0	24
Guman, Los Angeles	4	4	0	0	24
Hill, Detroit	4	0	4	0	24
Hill, Dallas	4	0	4	0	24
Jefferson, Green Bay	4	0	4	0	24
Russell, Philadelphia	4	4	0	0	24
C. Smith, Philadelphia	4	0	4	0	24
L. Thompson, Detroit	4	1	3	0	24
Thompson, Washington	4	0	4	0	24
Williams, Tampa Bay	4	4	0	0	24
Baschnagel, Chicago	3	0	3	0	18
Bruer, Minnesota	3	0	3	0	18
Evans, Chicago	3	3	0	0	18
D. Hill, Los Angeles	3	0	3	0	18
Irvin, Los Angeles	3	0	0	3	18
Kane, Detroit	3	2	1	0	18
Lott, San Francisco	3	0	0	3	18
Miller, Atlanta	3	0	3	0	18
Owens, Tampa Bay	3	3	0	0	18
Pearson, Dallas	3	0	3	0	18
Seay, Washington	3	0	3	0	18
Shirk, N.Y. Giants	3	0	3	0	18
Suhey, Chicago	3	3	0	0	18
Tilley, St. Louis	3	0	3	0	18
Watts, Chicago	3	0	3	0	18
S. White, Minnesota	3	0	3	0	18
Anderson, Chicago	2	0	2	0	12
Arnold, Los Angeles	2	0	2	0	12
T. Bell, Tampa Bay	2	0	2	0	12
Bright, N.Y. Giants	2	2	0	0	12
Brown, Tampa Bay	2	0	0	2	12
Danielson, Detroit	2	2	0	0	12
DuPree, Dallas	2	0	2	0	12
Eckwood, Tampa Bay	2	2	0	0	12
Galbreath, Minnesota	2	2	0	0	12
Giammona, Phila.	2	1	1	0	12
Giaquinto, Mia.-Wash.	2	0	2	0	12
Gray, New York Giants	2	0	2	0	12
Gray, St. Louis	2	0	2	0	12
Harrell, St. Louis	2	1	1	0	12
Harrington, Phila.	2	2	0	0	12
Henry, Philadelphia	2	0	2	0	12
Hicks, San Francisco	2	0	0	2	12
Holmes, New Orleans	2	2	0	0	12
Johnson, Atlanta	2	0	0	2	12
LaFleur, St. Louis	2	0	2	0	12
Lawrence, San Fran.	2	1	0	1	12
LeCount, Minnesota	2	0	2	0	12
Lomax, St. Louis	2	2	0	0	12
Martin, N.Y. Giants	2	0	0	2	12
Mitchell, St. Louis	2	0	1	1	12
Montana, San Fran.	2	2	0	0	12
Nelms, Washington	2	0	0	2	12
Parker, Philadelphia	2	0	2	0	12
B. Taylor, N.Y. Giants	2	2	0	0	12
Theismann, Wash.	2	2	0	0	12
D. Williams, Chicago	2	0	2	0	12
Young, Minnesota	2	0	2	0	12
Ahrens, St. Louis	1	0	0	1	6
Barnes, Dallas	1	0	0	1	6
Bell, Chicago	1	0	0	1	6
Brown, Philadelphia	1	0	0	1	6
Bryant, Los Angeles	1	1	0	0	6
Childs, Los Angeles	1	0	1	0	6
Coleman, Washington	1	0	0	1	6
Colzie, Tampa Bay	1	0	0	1	6
Cooper, San Francisco	1	1	0	0	6
Curry, Atlanta	1	0	0	1	6
Dennis, N.Y. Giants	1	0	0	1	6
Earl, Chicago	1	0	1	0	6
Easley, San Francisco	1	1	0	0	6
Fencik, Chicago	1	0	0	1	6
J. Fisher, Chicago	1	0	0	1	6
Friede, N.Y. Giants	1	0	1	0	6
Groth, New Orleans	1	0	1	0	6
Hall, Detroit	1	0	0	1	6
Hardy, New Orleans	1	0	1	0	6
Harper, Chicago	1	1	0	0	6
Harris, Chicago	1	0	0	1	6
Harris, Los Angeles	1	0	0	1	6
Hofer, San Francisco	1	1	0	0	6
Holloway, Minnesota	1	0	0	1	6
Hood, Green Bay	1	0	0	1	6
Ivery, Green Bay	1	1	0	0	6
L. Jackson, N.Y. Giants	1	1	0	0	6
T. Jackson, N.Y. Giants	1	0	0	1	6
Jones, Tampa Bay	1	0	1	0	6
J. Jones, Dallas	1	1	0	0	6
King, Detroit	1	0	1	0	6
Kotar, N.Y. Giants	1	1	0	0	6
Kuykendall, Atlanta	1	0	0	1	6
Lee, Green Bay	1	0	0	1	6
LeMaster, Philadelphia	1	0	0	1	6
Logan, Tampa Bay	1	0	0	1	6
Margerum, Chicago	1	0	1	0	6
Marsh, St. Louis	1	0	1	0	6
Martin, Detroit	1	0	0	1	6
Merkens, New Orleans	1	0	1	0	6
Middleton, Green Bay	1	0	1	0	6
Mistler, N.Y. Giants	1	0	1	0	6
Mullady, N.Y. Giants	1	0	1	0	6
Nichols, Detroit	1	0	1	0	6
Obradovich, Tampa B.	1	0	1	0	6
Oliver, Philadelphia	1	1	0	0	6
Olkewicz, Washington	1	0	0	1	6
Payton, Minnesota	1	0	0	1	6
Perry, N.Y. Giants	1	0	1	0	6
Porter, Detroit	1	0	1	0	6
Pridemore, Atlanta	1	0	0	1	6
Reece, N.Y. Giants	1	0	0	1	6
Ring, San Francisco	1	0	1	0	6
Saldi, Dallas	1	0	1	0	6
Stief, St. Louis	1	0	1	0	6
Swanke, Green Bay	1	0	1	0	6
V. Thompson, Detroit	1	1	0	0	6
Walker, Washington	1	0	1	0	6
Warren, Washington	1	0	1	0	6
Washington, Tampa B.	1	0	0	1	6
Whitehurst, Green Bay	1	1	0	0	6
Williams, Atlanta	1	0	0	1	6
Wilson, San Francisco	1	0	1	0	6
Young, N.Y. Giants	1	0	1	0	6
Hannon, Minnesota	0	0	0	0	**4
Clarke, Philadelphia	0	0	0	0	*2
Dutton, Dallas	0	0	0	0	*2
Martin, Dallas	0	0	0	0	*2
Plank, Chicago	0	0	0	0	*2
Williams, Minnesota	0	0	0	0	*2
Wilkes, Philadelphia	0	0	0	0	†1
Wingo, Green Bay	0	0	0	0	†1

*—Safety (also 1 team: Dallas)
†—Scored extra point on pass reception

1981 PUNTING

YARDS PER PUNT
AFC: 45.4—Pat McInally, Cincinnati (72 punts, 3272 yards).
NFC: 43.5—Tom Skladany, Detroit (64 punts, 2784 yards).

NET AVERAGE
NFC: 37.3—Tom Skladany, Detroit (64 total punts, 2385 net yards).
AFC: 36.1—Jeff West, Seattle (66 total punts, 2385 net yards).
    36.1—Pat McInally, Cincinnati (73 total punts, 2636 net yards).

LONGEST
AFC: 75 yards—Rich Camarillo, New England vs. Oakland, November 1.
NFC: 75 yards—Carl Birdsong, St. Louis vs. Philadelphia, December 20.

PUNTS
NFC: 114—Bob Parsons, Chicago (4531 yards).
AFC: 96—Ray Guy, Oakland (4195 yards).

TEAM CHAMPION
AFC: 44.8—Cincinnati.
NFC: 43.5—Detroit.

PUNTING—TEAM

AMERICAN FOOTBALL CONFERENCE

	Total Punts	Yards	Long	Avg.	TB.	Blk.	Opp. Ret.	Ret. Yds.	In 20	Net Avg.
Cincinnati	73	3,272	62	44.8	11	1	42	416	17	35.6
Pittsburgh	84	3,641	74	43.3	16	0	34	358	25	35.3
Oakland	98	4,238	69	43.2	16	0	45	514	23	34.7
Cleveland	70	2,884	66	41.2	12	2	30	253	11	33.2
Miami	83	3,386	61	40.8	11	0	45	286	21	34.7
New York Jets	81	3,290	65	40.6	13	0	31	149	27	35.6
Denver	86	3,478	67	40.4	5	0	46	388	20	34.8
San Diego	63	2,540	61	40.3	7	1	31	168	16	34.9
Buffalo	80	3,175	71	39.7	12	0	34	220	16	33.9
Houston	79	3,137	62	39.7	3	0	47	360	17	34.4
Baltimore	78	3,071	57	39.4	2	0	44	402	11	33.7
New England	75	2,951	75	39.3	13	0	35	305	14	31.8
Seattle	68	2,652	56	39.0	2	0	33	153	16	36.2
Kansas City	70	2,697	57	38.5	4	0	46	293	9	33.2
Conference Total	1,088	44,412	75	....	127	4	543	4,265	243	....
Conference Average	77.7	3,172.3	....	40.8	9.1	0.3	38.8	304.6	17.4	34.4

NATIONAL FOOTBALL CONFERENCE

	Total Punts	Yards	Long	Avg.	TB.	Blk.	Opp. Ret.	Ret. Yds.	In 20	Net Avg.
Detroit	64	2,784	74	43.5	5	0	39	299	21	37.3
New York Giants	97	4,198	62	43.3	12	0	61	561	19	35.0
Los Angeles	89	3,735	67	42.0	3	0	52	481	19	35.9
St. Louis	69	2,883	75	41.8	8	0	37	276	18	35.5
San Francisco	93	3,858	65	41.5	15	0	57	664	14	31.1
Minnesota	88	3,646	73	41.4	11	0	46	399	17	34.4
Tampa Bay	82	3,375	62	41.2	6	2	52	668	17	30.8
Dallas	81	3,284	56	40.5	7	0	38	231	19	36.0
New Orleans	66	2,672	60	40.5	6	0	36	282	11	34.4
Philadelphia	64	2,580	64	40.3	6	0	34	246	18	34.6
Atlanta	88	3,543	62	40.3	5	1	59	577	13	32.2
Washington	73	2,923	57	40.0	5	0	50	388	13	33.4
Chicago	114	4,531	55	39.7	7	0	66	594	31	33.3
Green Bay	84	3,330	72	39.6	9	2	50	511	16	30.7
Conference Total	1,152	47,342	75	....	105	5	677	6,177	246	....
Conference Average	82.3	3,381.6	....	41.1	7.5	0.4	48.4	441.2	17.6	33.8
League Total	2,240	91,754	75	....	232	9	1,220	10,442	489	....
League Average	80.0	3,276.9	....	41.0	8.3	0.3	43.6	372.9	17.5	34.1

TOP TEN PUNTERS

Player—Team	Net Punts	Yards	Long	Avg.	Total Punts	TB	Blk.	Opp. Ret.	Ret. Yds.	In 20	Net Avg.
McInally, Pat, Cin	72	3272	62	45.4	73	11	1	42	416	17	36.1
Guy, Ray, Oak	96	4195	69	43.7	96	15	0	45	514	23	35.2
Skladany, Tom, Det	64	2784	74	43.5	64	5	0	39	299	21	37.3
Colquitt, Craig, Pitt	84	3641	74	43.3	84	16	0	34	358	25	35.3
Jennings, Dave, N.Y.G.	97	4198	62	43.3	97	12	0	61	561	19	35.0
Swider, Larry, T.B.	58	2476	62	42.7	60	4	2	39	409	13	33.1
Cox, Steve, Clev	68	2884	66	42.4	70	12	2	30	253	11	34.2
Corral, Frank, L.A.	89	3735	67	42.0	89	3	0	52	481	19	35.9
Birdsong, Carl, St.L.	69	2883	75	41.8	69	8	0	37	276	18	35.5
Camarillo, Rich, N.E.	47	1959	75	41.7	47	9	0	20	209	12	33.4

AFC—INDIVIDUALS

Player—Team	Net Punts	Yards	Long	Avg.	Total Punts	TB	Blk.	Opp. Ret.	Ret. Yds.	In 20	Net Avg.
McINALLY, PAT, Cin.	72	3272	62	45.4	73	11	1	42	416	17	36.1
Guy, Ray, Oak.	96	4195	69	43.7	96	15	0	45	514	23	35.2
Colquitt, Craig, Pitt.	84	3641	74	43.3	84	16	0	34	358	25	35.3
Cox, Steve, Clev.	68	2884	66	42.4	70	12	2	30	253	11	34.2
Camarillo, Rich, N.E.	47	1959	75	41.7	47	9	0	20	209	12	33.4
Roberts, George, S.D.	62	2540	61	41.0	63	7	1	31	168	16	35.4
Orosz, Tom, Mia.	83	3386	61	40.8	83	11	0	45	286	21	34.7
Ramsey, Chuck, N.Y.J.	81	3290	65	40.6	81	13	0	31	149	27	35.6
Prestridge, Luke, Den.	86	3478	67	40.4	86	5	0	46	388	20	34.8
Parsley, Cliff, Hou.	79	3137	62	39.7	79	3	0	47	360	17	34.4
Cater, Greg, Buff.	80	3175	71	39.7	80	12	0	34	220	16	33.9
Garrett, Mike, Balt.	78	3071	57	39.4	78	2	0	44	402	11	33.7
West, Jeff, Sea.	66	2578	56	39.1	66	2	0	32	153	16	36.1
Grupp, Bob, K.C.	41	1556	57	38.0	41	1	0	26	165	5	33.4
(Non-Qualifiers)											
Gossett, Jeff, K.C.	29	1141	55	39.3	29	3	0	20	128	4	32.9
Hubach, Mike, N.E.	19	726	56	38.2	19	2	0	12	95	2	31.1
Hartley, Ken, N.E.	9	266	41	29.6	9	2	0	3	1	0	25.0
Bahr, Chris, Oak.	2	43	32	21.5	2	1	0	0	0	0	11.5
Garcia, Frank, Sea.	2	74	41	37.0	2	0	0	1	0	0	37.0

NFC—INDIVIDUALS

Player—Team	Net Punts	Yards	Long	Avg.	Total Punts	TB	Blk.	Opp. Ret.	Ret. Yds.	In 20	Net Avg.
SKLADANY, TOM, Det.	64	2784	74	43.5	64	5	0	39	299	21	37.3
Jennings, Dave, N.Y.G.	97	4198	62	43.3	97	12	0	61	561	19	35.0
Swider, Larry, T.B.	58	2476	62	42.7	60	4	2	39	409	13	33.1
Corral, Frank, L.A.	89	3735	67	42.0	89	3	0	52	481	19	35.9
Birdsong, Carl, St.L.	69	2883	75	41.8	69	8	0	37	276	18	35.5
Miller, Jim, S.F.	93	3858	65	41.5	93	15	0	57	664	14	31.1
Coleman, Greg, Minn.	88	3646	73	41.4	88	11	0	46	399	17	34.4
White, Danny, Dall.	79	3222	60	40.8	79	7	0	38	231	19	36.1
Runager, Max, Phil.	63	2567	64	40.7	63	6	0	34	246	18	34.9
James, John, Atl.	87	3543	62	40.7	88	5	1	59	577	13	32.6
Stachowicz, Ray, G.B.	82	3330	72	40.6	84	9	2	50	511	16	31.4
Erxleben, Russell, N.O.	66	2672	60	40.5	66	6	0	36	282	11	34.4
Connell, Mike, Wash.	73	2923	57	40.0	73	5	0	50	388	13	33.4
Parsons, Bob, Chi.	114	4531	55	39.7	114	7	0	66	594	31	33.3
(Non-Qualifiers)											
Blanchard, Tom, T.B.	22	899	58	40.9	22	2	0	13	259	4	27.3
Septien, Rafael, Dall.	2	62	33	31.0	2	0	0	0	0	0	31.0
Franklin, Tony, Phil.	1	13	13	13.0	1	0	0	0	0	0	13.0

Leader based on gross average, minimum 40 punts.

1981 PUNT RETURNS

YARDS PER RETURN
NFC: 13.4—LeRoy Irvin, Los Angeles (46 returns, 615 yards).
AFC: 13.2—James Brooks, San Diego (22 returns, 290 yards).

YARDS
NFC: 615—LeRoy Irvin, Los Angeles (46 returns).
AFC: 528—J. T. Smith, Kansas City (50 returns).

RETURNS
NFC: 54—Wally Henry, Philadelphia (396 yards).
AFC: 50—J. T. Smith, Kansas City (528 yards).

FAIR CATCHES

NFC: 20—Jeff Fisher, Chicago (63 chances).
AFC: 13—Ted Watts, Oakland (48 chances).
13—Mike Fuller, Cincinnati (36 chances).

LONGEST

NFC: 94 yards—Mark Lee, Green Bay vs. New York Giants, November 11 (TD).
AFC: 87 yards—Tommy Vigorito, Miami vs. Pittsburgh, September 10 (TD).

TOUCHDOWNS

AFC: Tommy Vigorito, Miami vs. Pittsburgh, September 10 (87 yards).
Ted Watts, Oakland vs. Pittsburgh, December 7 (52 yards).
NFC: LeRoy Irvin, Los Angeles vs. Chicago, September 28 (55 yards); vs. Atlanta, October 11 (75 yards); vs. Atlanta, October 11 (84 yards).
Mike Nelms, Washington vs. San Francisco, October 4 (58 yards); vs. New England, October 25 (75 yards).
Jeff Fisher, Chicago vs. Tampa Bay, September 20 (88 yards).
Mark Lee, Green Bay vs. New York Giants, November 11 (94 yards).
Robby Martin, Detroit vs. Minnesota, December 12 (45 yards).
Stump Mitchell, St. Louis vs. Washington, September 20 (50 yards).

TEAM CHAMPION

NFC: 13.8—Los Angeles (49 returns, 676 yards).
AFC: 12.2—San Diego (31 returns, 378 yards).

PUNT RETURNS—TEAM

AMERICAN FOOTBALL CONFERENCE

	No.	FC	Yards	Avg.	Long	TDs
San Diego	31	10	378	12.2	42	0
Kansas City	50	7	528	10.6	62	0
Miami	45	17	458	10.2	t87	1
Seattle	32	6	293	9.2	34	0
Denver	51	5	441	8.6	39	0
Buffalo	35	7	292	8.3	25	0
Pittsburgh	50	9	412	8.2	33	0
Houston	41	4	325	7.9	40	0
Cleveland	50	6	369	7.4	40	0
Oakland	52	16	380	7.3	t52	1
Cincinnati	29	19	205	7.1	34	0
New York Jets	50	13	337	6.7	46	0
New England	31	7	199	6.4	26	0
Baltimore	12	7	56	4.7	11	0
Conference Total	559	133	4,673	.....	t87	2
Conference Average	39.9	9.5	333.8	8.4	....	0.1

NATIONAL FOOTBALL CONFERENCE

	No.	FC	Yards	Avg.	Long	TDs
Los Angeles	49	8	676	13.8	t84	3
Chicago	45	24	518	11.5	t88	1
St. Louis	43	2	453	10.5	t50	1
New Orleans	41	7	426	10.4	36	0
Washington	49	4	507	10.3	t75	2
Detroit	52	9	450	8.7	t45	1
New York Giants	64	5	502	7.8	55	0
Minnesota	39	10	303	7.8	18	0
Atlanta	50	19	383	7.7	53	0
Green Bay	40	10	306	7.7	t94	1
Philadelphia	58	8	422	7.3	52	0
San Francisco	48	10	344	7.2	39	0
Tampa Bay	38	3	244	6.4	56	0
Dallas	45	5	235	5.2	17	0
Conference Total	661	124	5,769	.....	t94	9
Conference Average	47.2	8.9	412.1	8.7	....	0.6
League Total	1,220	257	10,442	.....	t94	11
League Average	43.6	9.2	372.9	8.6	....	0.4

TOP TEN PUNT RETURNERS

	No.	FC	Yards	Avg.	Long	TDs
IRVIN, LeROY, L.A.	46	6	615	13.4	t84	3
Brooks, James, S.D.	22	6	290	13.2	42	0
Fisher, Jeff, Chi.	43	20	509	11.8	t88	1
Groth, Jeff, N.O.	37	6	436	11.8	36	0
Johns, Paul, Sea.	16	4	177	11.1	34	0
Nelms, Mike, Wash.	45	1	492	10.9	t75	2
Mitchell, Stump, St.L.	42	0	445	10.6	t50	1
Smith, J.T., K.C.	50	7	528	10.6	62	0
Vigorito, Tommy, Mia.	36	12	379	10.5	t87	1
Anderson, Larry, Pitt.	20	8	208	10.4	33	0

AFC—INDIVIDUALS

Player—Team	No.	FC.	Yds.	Avg.	Lng.	TD	Player—Team	No.	FC.	Yds.	Avg.	Lng.	TD
J. BROOKS, S.D.	22	6	290	13.2	42	0	Haynes, N.E.	6	1	12	2.0	6	0
Johns, Sea.	16	4	177	11.1	34	0	Chandler, S.D.	5	3	79	15.8	30	0
Smith, K.C.	50	7	528	10.6	62	0	Walker, Mia.	5	1	50	10.0	17	0
Vigorito, Mia.	36	12	379	10.5	t87	1	Franklin, Buff.	5	3	45	9.0	15	0
Anderson, Pitt.	20	8	208	10.4	33	0	Simmons, Cin.	5	6	24	4.8	11	0
Manning, Den.	41	4	378	9.2	39	0	Riddick, Buff.	4	0	48	12.0	22	0
Hooks, Buff.	17	2	142	8.4	25	0	Collins, N.E.	3	0	15	5.0	15	0
Watts, Oak.	35	13	284	8.1	t52	1	Tullis, Hou.	2	0	29	14.5	16	0
Fuller, Cin.	23	13	177	7.7	34	0	G. Blackwood, Mia.	2	2	8	4.0	6	0
Roaches, Hou.	39	4	296	7.6	40	0	Anderson, Balt.	2	0	6	3.0	6	0
Harper, N.Y.J.	35	9	265	7.6	46	0	Whittington, Oak...	2	1	4	2.0	4	0
Hall, Clev.	33	6	248	7.5	40	0	Johnson, Sea.	1	0	16	16.0	16	0
Montgomery, Clev.	17	0	121	7.1	17	0	Bessillieu, Mia.	1	1	12	12.0	12	0
Smith, Pitt.	30	1	204	6.8	28	0	Kozlowski, Mia.	1	1	9	9.0	9	0
(Non-Qualifiers)							Bauer, S.D.	1	0	7	7.0	7	0
Morgan, N.E.	15	4	116	7.7	26	0	Schroy, N.Y.J.	1	1	5	5.0	5	0
Lewis, Sea.	15	2	100	6.7	23	0	Hicks, Cin.	1	0	4	4.0	4	0
Matthews, Oak.	15	2	92	6.1	26	0	Edwards, S.D.	1	0	1	1.0	1	0
Sohn, N.Y.J.	13	3	66	5.1	14	0	B. Jones, N.Y.J.	1	0	1	1.0	1	0
Shula, Balt.	10	7	50	5.0	11	0	Shaw, S.D.	1	0	1	1.0	1	0
Upchurch, Den.	9	1	63	7.0	15	0	Kyle, Den.	1	0	0	0.0	0	0
Piccone, Buff.	9	2	57	6.3	13	0	Phillips, S.D.	1	0	0	0.0	0	0
James, N.E.	7	2	56	8.0	18	0	M. Williams, S.D. ...	0	1	0	.....	0	0

NFC—INDIVIDUALS

Player—Team	No.	FC.	Yds.	Avg.	Lng.	TD	Player—Team	No.	FC.	Yds.	Avg.	Lng.	TD
IRVIN, L.A.	46	6	615	13.4	t84	3	T. Jackson, N.Y.G.	2	0	22	11.0	21	0
J. Fisher, Chi.	43	20	509	11.8	t88	1	Colzie, T.B.	2	0	12	6.0	12	0
Groth, N.O.	37	6	436	11.8	36	0	Whitaker, G.B.	2	0	1	0.5	1	0
Nelms, Wash.	45	1	492	10.9	t75	2	Banks, N.O.	2	0	0	0.0	0	0
Mitchell, St.L.	42	0	445	10.6	t50	1	Cassidy, G.B.	2	4	0	0.0	0	0
Lee, G.B.	20	1	187	9.4	t94	1	Johnson, L.A.	1	2	39	39.0	39	0
Hicks, S.F.	19	4	171	9.0	39	0	Pittman, N.Y.G.	1	1	13	13.0	13	0
Martin, Det.	52	8	450	8.7	t45	1	Harrell, St.L.	1	1	8	8.0	8	0
Woerner, Atl.	33	16	278	8.4	38	0	Walterscheid, Chi...	1	0	6	6.0	6	0
Payton, Minn.	38	8	303	8.0	18	0	Donley, Dall.	1	0	3	3.0	3	0
Bright, N.Y.G.	52	0	410	7.9	55	0	Plank, Chi.	1	1	3	3.0	3	0
Henry, Phil.	54	8	396	7.3	52	0	Poe, N.O.	1	0	2	2.0	2	0
Solomon, S.F.	29	6	173	6.0	19	0	Gray, G.B.	1	1	0	0.0	0	0
J. Jones, Dallas	33	2	188	5.7	17	0	Pridemore. Atl.	1	0	0	0.0	0	0
T. Bell, T.B.	27	0	132	4.9	13	0	Reece, N.Y.G.	1	2	0	0.0	0	0
(Non-Qualifiers)							S. White, Minn.	1	0	0	0.0	0	0
Nixon, G.B.	15	4	118	7.9	17	0	Merkens, N.O.	1	1	—12	—12.0	—12	0
Smith, Atl.	12	3	99	8.3	53	0	Greene, St.L.	0	1	0	.....	0	0
Fellows, Dall.	11	1	44	4.0	10	0	Hannon, Minn.	0	1	0	.....	0	0
Holt, T.B.	9	3	100	11.1	56	0	Nord, Minn.	0	1	0	.....	0	0
Garrett, N.Y.G.	8	2	57	7.1	18	0	Porter, Det.	0	1	0	.....	0	0
Sciarra, Phil.	4	0	26	6.5	10	0	Thurman, Dall.	0	1	0	.....	0	0
Metcalf, Wash.	4	0	15	3.8	13	0	Wilson, Dall.	0	1	0	.....	0	0
Johnson, Atl.	4	0	6	1.5	4	0	Baschnagel, Chi.	0	3	0	.....	0	0
D. Hill, L.A.	2	0	22	11.0	12	0	Seay, Wash.	0	3	0	.....	0	0

t—Touchdown
Leader based on average return, minimum 16 returns

1981 KICKOFF RETURNS

YARDS PER RETURN
  NFC: 29.7—Mike Nelms, Washington (37 returns, 1099 yards).
  AFC: 27.5—Carl Roaches, Houston (28 returns, 769 yards).

YARDS
  NFC: 1292—Stump Mitchell, St. Louis (55 returns).
  AFC: 949—James Brooks, San Diego (40 returns).

RETURNS
  NFC: 60—Drew Hill, Los Angeles (1170 yards).
  AFC: 40—James Brooks, San Diego (949 yards).

LONGEST
  NFC: 99 yards—Eddie Payton, Minnesota vs. Oakland, September 14 (TD).
  AFC: 96 yards—Carl Roaches, Houston vs. Cincinnati, October 4 (TD).

TOUCHDOWNS
  AFC: Carl Roaches, Houston vs. Cincinnati, October 14 (96 yards).
       Willie Tullis, Houston vs. Los Angeles, September 6 (95 yards).
       Fulton Walker, Miami vs. Buffalo, October 12 (90 yards).
  NFC: Amos Lawrence, San Francisco vs. Los Angeles, November 22 (92 yards).
       Eddie Payton, Minnesota vs. Oakland, September 14 (99 yards).

TEAM CHAMPION
  NFC: 25.0—Washington (67 returns, 1673 yards).
  AFC: 23.9—Houston (72 returns, 1722 yards).

KICKOFF RETURNS—TEAM

AMERICAN FOOTBALL CONFERENCE

Player—Team	No.	Yards	Avg.	Long	TDs.
Houston	72	1,722	23.9	t96	2
Miami	54	1,228	22.7	t90	1
Cincinnati	49	1,056	21.6	78	0
Cleveland	72	1,537	21.3	48	0
Pittsburgh	53	1,096	20.7	35	0
San Diego	70	1,422	20.3	47	0
Kansas City	52	1,043	20.1	48	0
Oakland	71	1,411	19.9	47	0
New York Jets	58	1,151	19.8	42	0
Baltimore	84	1,651	19.7	46	0
Buffalo	57	1,085	19.0	36	0
Seattle	69	1,278	18.5	36	0
New England	65	1,190	18.3	32	0
Denver	47	801	17.0	31	0
Conference Total	873	17,671	....	t96	3
Conference Average	62.4	1,262.2	20.2	....	0.2

NATIONAL FOOTBALL CONFERENCE

Player—Team	No.	Yards	Avg.	Long	TDs.
Washington	67	1,673	25.0	84	0
Atlanta	62	1,419	22.9	52	0
New Orleans	70	1,523	21.8	57	0
St. Louis	75	1,625	21.7	67	0
San Francisco	45	909	20.2	t92	1
Tampa Bay	46	912	19.8	40	0
Minnesota	67	1,328	19.8	t99	1
New York Giants	57	1,120	19.6	41	0
Philadelphia	43	832	19.3	43	0
Detroit	61	1,164	19.1	36	0
Chicago	64	1,214	19.0	56	0
Dallas	53	981	18.5	33	0
Green Bay	58	1,066	18.4	52	0
Los Angeles	68	1,244	18.3	50	0
Conference Total	836	17,010	....	t99	2
Conference Average	59.7	1,215.0	20.3	....	0.1
League Total	1,709	34,681	....	t99	5
League Average	61.0	1,238.6	20.3	....	0.2

TOP TEN KICKOFF RETURNERS

Player—Team	No.	Yards	Avg.	Long	TDs.
NELMS, MIKE, Washington	37	1099	29.7	84	0
Roaches, Carl, Houston	28	769	27.5	t96	1
Lawrence, Amos, San Francisco	17	437	25.7	t92	1
Walker, Fulton, Miami	38	932	24.5	t90	1
Tullis, Willie, Houston	32	779	24.3	t95	1
Smith, Reggie, Atlanta	47	1143	24.3	52	0
Verser, David, Cincinnati	29	691	23.8	78	0
Brooks, James, San Diego	40	949	23.7	47	0
Mitchell, Stump, St. Louis	55	1292	23.5	67	0
Wilson, Wayne, New Orleans	31	722	23.3	57	0

Player—Team	No.	Yds.	Avg.	Lng.	TD
ROACHES, Hou	28	769	27.5	t96	1
Walker, Mia	38	932	24.5	t90	1
Tullis, Hou	32	779	24.3	t95	1
Verser, Cin	29	691	23.8	78	0
J. Brooks, S.D.	40	949	23.7	47	0
Murphy, K.C.	20	457	22.9	46	0
Hall, Clev	36	813	22.6	48	0
Whittington, Oak	25	563	22.5	47	0
Montgomery, Clev-Oak	17	382	22.5	38	0
Anderson, Pitt	37	825	22.3	35	0
Harper, N.Y.J.	23	480	20.9	42	0
Franklin, Buff	21	436	20.8	33	0
Dixon, Balt	36	737	20.5	46	0
Sohn, N.Y.J.	26	528	20.3	31	0
K. Williams, Balt	20	399	20.0	35	0
Collins, N.E.	39	773	19.8	30	0
Manning, Den	26	514	19.8	31	0
Anderson, Balt	20	393	19.7	30	0
Lewis, Sea	20	378	18.9	30	0
Ivory, N.E.-Sea	16	300	18.8	32	0

(Non-Qualifiers)					
Player—Team	No.	Yds.	Avg.	Lng.	TD
Willis, Oak	15	309	20.6	43	0
Barnwell, Oak	15	265	17.7	26	0
Riddick, Buff	14	257	18.4	25	0
Johnson, Sea	13	235	18.1	25	0
White, Clev	12	243	20.3	32	0
Hooks, Buff	11	215	19.5	36	0
Harden, Den	11	178	16.2	23	0
Carson, K.C.	10	227	22.7	48	0
Lane, Sea	10	208	20.8	27	0
Toler, N.E.	9	148	16.4	32	0
Chapman, Cin	8	171	21.4	29	0
Chandler, S.D.	8	125	15.6	30	0
Matthews, Oak	7	144	20.6	39	0
Brown, Buff	7	140	20.0	30	0
Hawthorne, Pitt	7	138	19.7	30	0
Bessillieu, Mia	7	114	16.3	30	0
A. Griffin, Cin	6	119	19.8	28	0
Bledsoe, K.C.	6	117	19.5	26	0
Shaw, S.D.	6	103	17.2	24	0
Lewis, N.Y.J.	5	108	21.6	30	0
Burruss, K.C.	5	91	18.2	22	0
Johns, Sea	5	81	16.2	20	0
Lytle, Den	5	80	16.0	24	0
Shula, Balt	5	65	13.0	16	0
Vigorito, Mia	4	84	21.0	25	0
Sanford, N.E.	4	82	20.5	27	0
Christensen, Oak	4	54	13.5	19	0
C. Williams, S.D.	4	47	11.8	23	0
G. Pruitt, Clev	3	82	27.3	30	0
Moser, Pitt	3	76	25.3	29	0
Dombroski, K.C.-N.E.	3	66	22.0	24	0
Jackson, K.C.	3	60	20.0	23	0
Johnson, N.E.	3	53	17.7	19	0
Cherry, K.C.	3	52	17.3	22	0
Gregor, S.D.	3	47	15.7	20	0

Player—Team	No.	Yds.	Avg.	Lng.	TD
Dirden, Pitt	3	45	15.0	22	0
Dufek, Sea	3	45	15.0	17	0
T. Wilson, Hou	3	41	13.7	23	0
Armstrong, Hou	3	36	12.0	18	0
C. Miller, Clev	3	35	11.7	22	0
Hunt, Hou	3	19	6.3	11	0
Thompson, S.D.	2	44	22.0	25	0
Calhoun, N.E.	2	38	19.0	22	0
Smith, S.D.	2	32	16.0	20	0
R. Griffin, Cin.	2	31	15.5	17	0
Piccone, Buff	2	31	15.5	16	0
J. C. Wilson, Hou	2	27	13.5	14	0
Stephens, N.Y.J.	2	21	10.5	14	0
Lee, N.E.	2	20	10.0	16	0
Canada, Den	2	19	9.5	13	0
Brown, Clev	2	17	8.5	10	0
Sievers, S.D.	2	4	2.0	4	0
Rourke, K.C.	2	0	0.0	0	0
Riley, Hou	1	51	51.0	51	0
Kozlowski, Mia	1	40	40.0	40	0
Glasgow, Balt	1	35	35.0	35	0
Fuller, Cin	1	34	34.0	34	0
Beaudoin, S.D.	1	31	31.0	31	0
Henderson, S.D.	1	26	26.0	26	0
Giaquinto, Mia	1	22	22.0	22	0
Sims, Balt	1	22	22.0	22	0
Hill, Oak	1	21	21.0	21	0
Harris, Mia	1	20	20.0	20	0
Bauer, S.D.	1	14	14.0	14	0
Delaney, K.C.	1	11	11.0	11	0
Hill, Mia	1	11	11.0	11	0
Simmons, Cin	1	10	10.0	10	0
Davis, Pitt	1	8	8.0	8	0
Rudolph, N.Y.J.	1	8	8.0	8	0
Sawyer, Sea	1	8	8.0	8	0
Egloff, Den	1	7	7.0	7	0
Hasselbeck, N.E.	1	7	7.0	7	0
Hawkins, Oak	1	7	7.0	7	0
Johnson, Clev	1	7	7.0	7	0
Williams, K.C.	1	7	7.0	7	0
Bess, Buff	1	6	6.0	6	0
L. Jones, N.Y.J.	1	6	6.0	6	0
M. Miller, Clev	1	6	6.0	6	0
Matthews, N.E.	1	5	5.0	5	0
Rose, Mia	1	5	5.0	5	0
Malone, Pitt	1	3	3.0	3	0
Ryan, Den	1	2	2.0	2	0
Preston, Den	1	1	1.0	1	0
Thornton, Pitt	1	1	1.0	1	0
Dinkel, Cin	1	0	0.0	0	0
Foote, Balt	1	0	0.0	0	0
Freeman, Buff	1	0	0.0	0	0
Hamilton, N.E.	1	0	0.0	0	0
Kemp, Cin	1	0	0.0	0	0

FAIR CATCH: Rick, Cin.

NFC—INDIVIDUALS

Player—Team	No.	Yds.	Avg.	Lng.	TD
NELMS, Wash.	37	1099	29.7	84	0
Lawrence, S.F.	17	437	25.7	t92	1
R. Smith, Atl.	47	1143	24.3	52	0
Mitchell, St.L.	55	1292	23.5	67	0
W. Wilson, N.O.	31	722	23.3	57	0
Payton, Minn.	39	898	23.0	t99	1
Garrett, N.Y.G.-Wash.	18	401	22.3	35	0
J. Rogers, N.O.	28	621	22.2	44	0
Henry, Phila.	25	533	21.3	43	0
D. Williams, Chi.	23	486	21.1	42	0

Player—Team	No.	Yds.	Avg.	Lng.	TD
Hall, Det.	25	525	21.0	36	0
Moorehead, Chi.	23	476	20.7	56	0
Martin, Det.	25	509	20.4	34	0
Owens, T.B.	24	473	19.7	34	0
D. Hill, L.A.	60	1170	19.5	50	0
Bright, N.Y.G.	25	481	19.2	41	0
J. Jones, Dall.	27	517	19.1	33	0

(Non-Qualifiers)

Player—Team	No.	Yds.	Avg.	Lng.	TD
Metcalf, Wash.	14	283	20.2	36	0
Lee, G.B.	14	270	19.3	31	0
Nord, Minn.	14	229	16.4	27	0
Newsome, Dall.	12	228	19.0	27	0
Campfield, Phila.	12	223	18.6	32	0
Nixon, G.B.	12	222	18.5	25	0
Holt, T.B.	11	274	24.9	40	0
McCoy, G.B.	11	221	20.1	36	0
McDole, Minn.	11	170	15.5	22	0
Ring, S.F.	10	217	21.7	29	0
Woerner, Atl.	10	210	21.0	27	0
Pittman, N.Y.G.	10	194	19.4	34	0
Fellows, Dall.	8	170	21.3	31	0
Green, St.L.	8	135	16.9	28	0
Huckleby, G.B.	7	134	19.1	27	0
Harrell, St.L.	7	118	16.9	29	0
Lott, S.F.	7	111	15.9	20	0
J. Fisher, Chi.	7	102	14.6	23	0
Wonsley, Wash.	6	124	20.7	27	0
Middleton, G.B.	6	100	16.7	30	0
Frazier, Chi.	6	77	12.8	15	0
Davis, T.B.	5	81	16.2	21	0
Nichols, Det.	4	74	18.5	26	0
Wilson, S.F.	4	67	16.8	22	0
Coffman, G.B.	3	77	25.7	52	0
Stauch, N.O.	3	65	21.7	29	0
Cronan, Sea.-Wash.	3	60	20.0	21	0
Davis, T.B.	3	51	17.0	21	0
Dennis, N.Y.G.	3	51	17.0	17	0
Groth, N.O.	3	50	16.7	21	0
Love, St.L.	3	46	15.3	25	0
Gaison, Atl.	3	43	14.3	24	0
Jones, S.F.	3	43	14.3	22	0
Newhouse, Dall.	3	34	11.3	15	0
King, Det.	3	33	11.0	14	0
Sully, L.A.	3	31	10.3	22	0
Merkens, N.O.	2	38	19.0	20	0
Seay, Wash.	2	36	18.0	19	0
Baschnagel, Chi.	2	34	17.0	23	0
Griffin, St.L.	2	34	17.0	26	0
Jackson, Wash.	2	34	17.0	17	0
Wilson, Dall.	2	32	16.0	17	0
Russell, Phila.	2	28	14.0	20	0
Gray, G.B.	2	24	12.0	19	0
Callicutt, Det.	2	23	11.5	12	0
Mayberry, Atl.	2	23	11.5	15	0
Brock, N.O.	2	18	9.0	12	0
McLaughlin, N.Y.G.	2	9	4.5	5	0
B. Williams, Chi.	1	35	35.0	35	0
Reece, N.Y.G.	1	24	24.0	24	0
Hicks, S.F.	1	22	22.0	22	0
Grant, Wash.	1	20	20.0	20	0
Giammona, Phila.	1	19	19.0	19	0
Wilder, T.B.	1	19	19.0	19	0
Meisner, L.A.	1	17	17.0	17	0
Galbreath, Minn.	1	16	16.0	16	0
Atkins, Phila.	1	15	15.0	15	0
Jensen, G.B.	1	15	15.0	15	0
Thomas, L.A.	1	15	15.0	15	0
Young, Minn.	1	15	15.0	15	0
Claitt, Wash.	1	14	14.0	14	0
Murray, Phila.	1	14	14.0	14	0
Obradovich, T.B.	1	14	14.0	14	0
Ramson, S.F.	1	12	12.0	12	0
Guman, L.A.	1	10	10.0	10	0
Banks, N.O.	1	9	9.0	9	0
B. Fisher, Chi.	1	9	9.0	9	0
Peters, Wash.	1	5	5.0	5	0
Jefferson, G.B.	1	3	3.0	3	0
Penaranda, L.A.	1	1	1.0	1	0
Blair, Minn.	1	0	0.0	0	0
Braggs, G.B.	1	0	0.0	0	0
Brantley, T.B.	1	0	0.0	0	0
Clarke, Phila.	1	0	0.0	0	0
Cosbie, Dal.	1	0	0.0	0	0
Davis, S.F.	1	0	0.0	0	0
Harrell, Det.	1	0	0.0	0	0
Lee, Det.	1	0	0.0	0	0
Pankey, L.A.	1	0	0.0	0	0
Patton, S.F.	1	0	0.0	0	0
Anderson, Chi.	1	−5	−5.0	−5	0

t—Touchdown
Leader based on average return, minimum 16 returns

1981 AFC FIELD GOALS—INDIVIDUAL

Kicker and Club	1-19	20-29	30-39	40-49	50 & over	Totals	Avg. Yds. Att.	Avg. Yds. Made	Avg. Yds. Miss	Lg.
von Schamann, Uwe, ... Miami	0-0	9-9 1.000	11-12 .917	4-10 .400	0-0	24-31 .774	34.5	32.0	43.3	46
Benirschke, Rolf,........... San Diego	2-2 1.000	7-7 1.000	5-8 .625	3-4 .750	2-5 .400	19-26 .731	35.6	33.4	41.6	52
Lowrey, Nick,................. Kansas City	0-0	5-5 1.000	13-15 .867	7-9 .778	1-7 .143	26-36 .722	38.3	34.8	47.2	52
Herrera, Efren, ... Seattle	0-0	6-7 .857	3-3 1.000	2-5 .400	1-2 .500	12-17 .706	34.8	31.4	42.8	54
Trout, David,.................. Pittsburgh	3-3 1.000	5-6 .833	1-2 .500	3-5 .600	0-1 .000	12-17 .706	32.9	28.5	43.4	48
Leahy, Pat, ... N.Y. Jets	0-0	11-13 .846	6-8 .750	8-12 .667	0-3 .000	25-36 .694	36.4	34.4	37.7	49
Breech, Jim,................... Cincinnati	0-0	9-11 .818	7-9 .778	5-11 .455	1-1 1.000	22-32 .688	35.3	33.3	39.7	51
Fritsch, Toni,................. Houston	0-0	3-4 .750	4-4 1.000	7-13 .538	1-1 1.000	15-22 .682	38.9	31.5	41.3	50
Smith, John,................... New England	0-0	7-7 1.000	2-6 .333	5-7 .714	1-4 .250	15-24 .625	37.3	33.7	43.3	50
Bahr, Chris,................... Oakland	0-0	6-8 .750	2-4 .500	3-7 .429	3-5 .600	14-24 .583	37.6	35.2	41.0	51
Mike-Mayer, Nick,........ Buffalo	0-0	4-6 .667	5-7 .714	5-10 .500	0-1 .000	14-24 .583	37.0	35.1	39.6	46
Bahr, Matt, ... S.F.-Clev.	3-3 1.000	5-7 .714	5-10 .500	2-5 .400	0-1 .000	15-26 .577	33.3	29.7	38.2	47
Steinfort, Fred,............. Denver	0-0	6-9 .667	5-11 .455	6-8 .750	0-2 .000	17-30 .567	35.0	33.4	37.1	49
Wood, Mike, ... Baltimore	2-2 1.000	2-3 .667	3-5 .600	3-7 .429	0-1 .000	10-18 .556	35.4	31.0	40.9	48
Alvarez, Wilson, ... Seattle	0-0	3-3 1.000	0-0	0-4 .000	0-0	3-7 .429	34.3	23.3	42.5	28
Jacobs, Dave,................. Cleveland	0-0	2-3 .667	2-6 .333	0-1 .000	0-2 .000	4-12 .333	36.3	30.5	39.1	35
Cox, Steve,...................... Cleveland	0-0	0-0	0-0	0-0	0-1 .000	0-1 .000	53.0	0.0	53.0	0
AFC Totals.....................	10-10 1.000	90-106 .849	74-109 .679	61-115 .530	10-37 .270	245-377 .650	36.0	33.1	41.4	54
League Totals................	22-24 .917	182-213 .854	162-231 .701	134-256 .523	21-67 .313	521-791 .659	36.1	33.5	41.1	55

1981 NFC FIELD GOALS—INDIVIDUAL

Kicker and Club	1-19	20-29	30-39	40-49	50 & over	Totals	Avg. Yds. Att.	Avg. Yds. Made	Avg. Yds. Miss	Lg.
Stenerud, Jan,	2-2	7-8	9-9	2-3	2-2	22-24	33.0	32.6	37.0	53
Green Bay	1.000	.875	1.000	.667	1.000	.917				
Danmeier, Rick,	1-1	5-6	11-12	4-6	0-0	21-25	33.7	33.1	36.8	45
Minnesota	1.000	.833	.917	.667	......	.840				
Septien, Rafael,	1-1	11-11	8-9	7-12	0-2	27-35	35.1	32.0	45.8	47
Dallas	1.000	1.000	.889	.583	.000	.771				
Wersching, Ray,	2-2	7-7	4-7	4-7	0-0	17-23	33.3	31.8	37.5	48
San Francisco	1.000	1.000	.571	.571	......	.739				
Murray, Ed,	1-1	5-5	9-14	7-11	3-4	25-35	38.5	38.3	39.1	53
Detroit	1.000	1.000	.643	.636	.750	.714				
Thomas, Bob,	0-0	1-2	1-1	0-0	0-0	2-3	28.7	31.0	24.0	37
Chicago	......	.500	1.000	......	......	.667				
Corral, Frank,	0-0	6-9	5-6	6-11	0-0	17-26	35.1	33.7	37.7	44
Los Angeles	......	.667	.833	.545	......	.654				
Franklin, Tony,	0-0	5-5	7-9	7-13	1-4	20-31	39.5	36.1	45.8	50
Philadelphia	......	1.000	.778	.538	.250	.645				
Luckhurst, Mick,	1-2	7-7	8-12	5-11	0-1	21-33	35.2	32.7	39.7	47
Atlanta	.500	1.000	.667	.455	.000	.636				
Moseley, Mark,	1-1	7-8	6-8	5-12	0-1	19-30	36.1	32.4	42.4	49
Washington	1.000	.875	.750	.417	.000	.633				
Danelo, Joe,	1-1	7-9	7-9	6-11	3-8	24-38	38.8	35.4	44.7	55
N.Y. Giants	1.000	.778	.778	.545	.375	.632				
Capece, Bill,	0-0	5-7	3-5	5-10	2-2	15-24	37.1	36.9	37.4	51
Tampa Bay	......	.714	.600	.500	1.000	.625				
O'Donoghue, Neil,	2-2	8-8	4-6	5-11	0-5	19-32	37.0	30.4	46.5	47
St. Louis	1.000	1.000	.667	.455	.000	.594				
Roveto, John,	0-1	6-7	2-3	2-7	0-0	10-18	33.0	29.5	33.4	43
Chicago	.000	.857	.667	.286	......	.556				
Ricardo, Benny,	0-0	5-5	3-9	5-10	0-1	13-25	37.8	34.9	40.8	46
New Orleans	......	1.000	.333	.500	.000	.520				
Yepremian, Garo,	0-0	0-0	1-1	1-3	0-0	2-4	41.0	38.0	44.0	44
Tampa Bay	......	......	1.000	.333	......	.500				
Nielsen, Hans,	0-0	0-1	0-1	0-0	0-0	0-2	28.0	0.0	28.0	0
Chicago	......	.000	.000	......	......	.000				
NFC Totals	12-14	92-107	88-122	73-141	11-30	276-414	36.2	33.8	40.9	55
	.857	.860	.721	.518	.367	.667				
League Totals	22-24	182-213	162-231	134-256	21-67	521-791	36.1	33.5	41.1	55
	.917	.854	.701	.523	.313	.659				

1981 FUMBLES—TEAM

AMERICAN FOOTBALL CONFERENCE

	Fum.	Own Rec.	Fum. *O.B.	Yds.	TDs.	Opp. Rec.	Yds.	TDs.	Tot. Rec.
Cincinnati	25	10	3	−5	0	18	28	1	28
Denver	26	6	2	1	0	23	5	0	29
Miami	26	13	3	−21	0	15	40	1	28
Baltimore	27	11	2	10	1	14	3	0	25
New England	32	14	2	−8	0	17	44	0	31
Buffalo	33	13	2	0	0	17	42	0	30
Houston	33	10	2	−18	0	13	6	0	23
Kansas City	36	10	2	−4	0	21	260	3	31
Cleveland	38	11	1	−39	0	20	21	0	31
New York Jets	38	19	2	7	1	15	4	0	34
Pittsburgh	39	14	3	−35	0	16	39	0	30
San Diego	39	13	4	−22	0	18	40	0	31
Seattle	41	14	4	8	0	27	94	2	41
Oakland	42	20	2	14	0	19	83	2	39
Conference Totals	475	178	34	−112	2	253	709	9	431
Conference Average	33.9	12.7	2.4	−8.0	0.1	18.1	50.6	0.6	30.8

*Fumbled out of bounds.

NATIONAL FOOTBALL CONFERENCE

	Fum.	Own Rec.	Fum. *O.B.	Yds.	TDs.	Opp. Rec.	Yds.	TDs.	Tot. Rec.
San Francisco	26	11	3	0	0	21	83	1	32
Tampa Bay	27	10	3	−37	0	14	29	1	24
Atlanta	31	13	1	−21	1	21	160	3	34
Green Bay	31	14	0	−28	0	24	92	0	38
Washington	32	11	2	−8	0	15	23	0	26
Philadelphia	33	14	2	−25	0	21	85	2	35
St. Louis	33	10	3	−7	0	17	7	0	27
Los Angeles	34	16	3	−6	0	16	44	1	32
Chicago	37	19	1	−14	0	22	56	0	41
New York Giants	38	21	1	−13	0	17	41	3	38
Minnesota	39	15	3	−3	0	19	87	1	34
New Orleans	40	18	2	57	0	17	30	0	35
Detroit	41	19	2	−20	0	15	24	0	34
Dallas	45	22	3	−58	0	16	72	1	38
Conference Totals	487	213	29	−183	1	255	833	13	468
Conference Average	34.8	15.2	2.1	−13.1	0.1	18.2	59.5	0.9	33.4
League Totals	962	391	63	−295	3	508	1542	22	899
League Average	34.4	14.0	2.3	−10.5	0.1	18.1	55.1	0.8	32.1

*Fumbled out of bounds.

AFC FUMBLES—INDIVIDUAL

Player—Team	Fum.	Own Rec.	Yds.	Opp. Rec.	Yds.	Player—Team	Fum.	Own Rec.	Yds.	Opp. Rec.	Yds.
Alexander, Cin	0	1	0	0	0	Braziel, Balt	1	0	0	1	0
Alzado, Clev	0	0	0	1	0	Breeden, Cin	0	0	0	1	10
Ambrose, Clev	0	0	0	2	0	Brock, N.E.	0	1	0	0	0
Anderson, Cin	5	2	−20	0	0	J. Brooks, S.D.	7	2	0	0	0
Anderson, Balt	2	3	−1	0	0	Brown, Buff	4	0	0	0	0
Anderson, Pitts	1	0	0	0	0	D. Brown, Sea	0	0	0	1	8
Armstrong, Hou	2	0	0	0	0	T. Brown, St.L.-Sea	8	3	0	0	0
Augustyniak, N.Y.J.	3	0	0	0	0	Brown, Clev	0	0	0	1	0
Baker, Hou	0	0	0	1	0	Browner, Cin	0	0	0	1	0
Banaszak, Pitts	0	0	0	1	0	Browning, Oak	0	0	0	1	0
Barbaro, K.C.	0	0	0	1	0	Bryan, Den	1	0	0	0	0
Barkum, N.Y.J.	0	3	0	0	0	Buben, N.E.	0	0	0	1	31
Barnwell, Oak	2	0	0	0	0	Buchanon, S.D.	0	0	0	4	0
Bass, Cin	0	0	0	1	0	Burrough, Hou	1	2	0	0	0
Baumhower, Mia	0	0	0	3	10	Burruss, K.C.	1	0	0	1	4
Beamon, Clev	0	0	0	1	5	Bush, Cin	0	1	12	0	0
Bell, K.C.	0	0	0	1	0	Busick, Den	0	0	0	2	3
Bennett, Mia	1	1	0	0	0	Butler, Buff	2	0	0	0	0
Bess, Buff	0	1	0	1	4	Butler, Sea	1	0	0	0	0
Bessillieu, Mia	1	1	0	1	0	Buttle, N.Y.J.	0	0	0	2	0
Bingham, Hou	0	0	0	1	0	Calhoun, N.E.	1	0	0	0	0
G. Blackwood, Mia	0	0	0	1	5	Camarillo, N.E.	1	1	0	0	0
Bledsoe, K.C.	4	1	0	0	0	Campbell, Hou	10	2	0	0	0
Bolton, Clev	0	0	0	2	0	Canada, Den	1	1	0	0	0
Borchardt, Buff	0	1	0	0	0	Cancik, K.C.	0	0	0	1	0
Bradley, Clev	0	0	0	1	0	Cappelletti, S.D.	3	0	0	0	0
Bradshaw, Pitts	7	3	−23	0	0	Carson, K.C.	1	1	0	0	0
Brammer, Buff	3	1	0	0	0	Carter, Hou	0	1	0	0	0

Player—Team	Fum.	Own Rec.	Yds.	Opp. Rec.	Yds.
Carter, Den	0	0	0	1	0
Cavanaugh, N.E.	2	0	0	0	0
Chandler, Oak	2	1	22	0	0
Chandler, N.O.-S.D.	1	1	51	0	0
Chavous, Den	0	0	0	1	0
Christensen, Oak	0	0	0	1	0
Christopher, K.C.	0	0	0	1	0
Clark, Buff	0	0	0	2	5
Clayborn, N.E.	0	0	0	2	4
Cole, Pitts	0	0	0	1	0
Coleman, Hou	2	0	0	0	0
Collins, N.E.	8	2	0	0	0
Collinsworth, Cin	3	1	0	0	0
Condon, K.C.	0	1	0	0	0
Courson, Pitts	0	2	0	0	0
Cribbs, Buffalo	12	1	0	0	0
Cronan, Sea	0	1	0	0	0
Cunningham, Pitts	0	1	0	0	0
Cunningham, N.E.	2	0	0	0	0
Curtis, Cin	1	1	0	0	0
Darden, Clev	0	0	0	2	0
Davis, Pitts	3	2	0	0	0
DeBerg, Den	2	0	0	0	0
Delaney, K.C.	9	0	0	0	0
Dickey, Balt	8	0	0	0	0
Dierking, N.Y.J.	2	1	0	0	0
Dixon, Balt	1	0	0	0	0
Dobler, Buffalo	0	1	0	0	0
Donaldson, Balt	0	1	0	0	0
Doornink, Sea	3	1	0	0	0
Dorris, Hou	0	0	0	1	0
Duhe, Mia	0	0	0	1	0
Dunn, Pitts	0	0	0	1	1
Dykes, N.Y.J.	0	1	0	0	0
Easley, Sea	0	1	21	3	4
Edwards, Cin	0	0	0	1	0
Edwards, S.D.	1	1	0	2	−3
Egloff, Den	2	0	0	1	6
Evans, Den	0	0	0	1	0
Ferguson, Buff	2	0	0	0	0
Ferguson, N.E.	1	1	0	0	0
Fields, N.Y.J.	1	0	−15	0	0
Foley, Den	0	0	0	1	0
Fouts, S.D.	9	2	−22	0	0
Franklin, Mia	5	1	0	0	0
Franklin, Buff	2	0	0	0	0
Franklin, Balt	2	0	0	0	0
Fuller, Cin	1	0	0	1	0
Fuller, K.C.	4	1	−6	0	0
Gaines, Sea	0	0	0	1	0
Gastineau, N.Y.J.	0	0	0	2	0
Giesler, Mia	0	1	0	0	0
Glasgow, Balt	0	0	0	2	0
Glassic, Den	0	1	0	0	0
Golic, N.E.	0	0	0	1	0
Gordon, Mia	0	0	0	1	0
Grant, Buff	0	1	0	0	0
Green, Balt	0	0	0	1	0
Green, K.C.	0	0	0	1	0
Green, Sea	0	0	0	1	0
R. Griffin, Cin	0	0	0	1	0
Grogan, N.E	5	2	−8	0	0
Guy, Oak	1	0	0	0	0
Hadnot, K.C.	4	1	0	0	0
Hall, Clev	5	0	0	0	0
Ham, Pitts	0	0	0	3	0
Hamilton, N.E.	1	0	0	0	0
Hannah, N.E.	0	2	0	0	0
Harden, Den	0	0	0	1	0
Hardman, Oak	0	0	0	1	52
Hardy, Mia	1	0	0	0	0
Hardy, Sea	0	0	0	2	3
Hargrove, Cin	1	0	0	0	0
Harper, N.Y.J.	7	2	0	0	0
Harris, K.C.	0	0	0	2	20
Harris, Pitts	6	0	0	0	0
Harris, Sea	1	0	0	3	0
M. L. Harris, Cin	1	0	0	2	3
Hartwig, Hou	0	0	0	1	0
Hasselbeck, N.E.	2	0	0	0	0
Haslett, Buff	0	0	0	1	0
Hawkins, Oak	1	1	0	0	0
Hawkins, N.E.	0	0	0	2	0
Hawthorne, Pitts	1	0	0	0	0
Hendricks, Oak	0	0	0	1	0
Henderson, S.D.	0	0	0	3	0
Herkenhoff, K.C.	0	1	0	0	0
Hicks, Cin	0	0	0	2	3
Hill, Clev	1	0	0	0	0
Hill, Mia	2	0	0	0	0
Holloway, N.E.	0	1	0	0	0
Holmes, N.Y.J.	0	0	0	1	0
Hooks, Buff	1	0	0	0	0
Horn, Cin	0	0	0	1	0
Howard, K.C.	0	1	0	1	65
Howell, Mia	0	1	0	0	0
Hughes, Sea	4	1	0	0	0
Humiston, Buff	0	1	0	0	0
Ilkin, Pitts	0	1	0	0	0
Ivory, Sea	1	0	0	0	0
B. Jackson, K.C.	1	0	0	0	0
C. Jackson, K.C.	0	0	0	3	33
Jackson, N.E.	1	0	0	0	0
Jackson, Sea	0	1	0	1	0
Jackson, Oak	0	1	0	0	0
Robt. L. Jackson, Clev	0	0	0	2	0
Jackson, Den	0	0	0	1	0
James, N.E.	1	0	0	1	0
Jensen, Oak	0	1	0	0	0
Jodat, Sea	4	0	0	1	0
Johns, Sea	1	0	0	0	0
Johnson, N.E.	1	0	0	0	0
Johnson, Clev	0	0	0	1	0
Johnson, S.D.	0	0	0	1	0
Johnson, Sea	2	1	0	3	31
Johnson, N.Y.J.	0	0	0	1	0
Johnson, Buff	0	1	0	1	0
Johnson, Cin	4	1	0	0	0
Joiner, S.D.	2	0	0	0	0
B. Jones, Balt	3	1	0	0	0
B. Jones, N.Y.J.	0	1	61	0	0
L. Jones, N.Y.J.	2	2	0	0	0
Jones, Buffalo	0	2	0	0	0
Jones, S.D.	0	0	0	1	5
R. Jones, Balt	0	1	0	0	0
Jones, Den	0	0	0	1	0
Jones, Oak	0	0	0	1	9
Justin, Sea	0	0	0	1	43
Kelcher, S.D.	0	0	0	1	0
Kennard, Hou	0	0	0	1	0
Kenney, K.C.	4	0	−2	0	0
King, Oak	10	2	0	0	0
Klecko, N.Y.J.	0	0	0	2	0
Kohrs, Pitts	0	0	0	1	0
Kozlowski, Mia	0	0	0	1	25
Krauss, Balt	0	0	0	2	0
Kreider, Cin	2	0	0	0	0
Kremer, K.C.	0	0	0	2	0
Krieg, Sea	4	0	0	0	0
Kush, Buff	1	0	0	3	5
Kyle, Den	0	0	0	4	1
Laakso, Mia	0	1	0	0	0
Laird, Balt	0	0	0	1	3
Lambert, Pitts	0	0	0	2	38
Landry, Balt	2	1	11	0	0
Lane, Sea	0	1	0	0	0
Largent, Sea	2	0	0	0	0
Laslavic, S.D.	0	0	0	1	38
Latimer, Den	0	0	0	1	0
Lawrence, Oak	0	2	0	0	0
Leaks, Buff	1	0	0	0	0
LeClair, Cin	0	0	0	1	0
Lewis, Buff	1	1	0	0	0
Lewis, Sea	5	1	0	0	0
Little, Pitts	0	0	0	1	0
Long, N.Y.J.	2	1	0	0	0
Lowery, K.C.	0	1	0	0	0
Lyons, N.Y.J.	0	0	0	1	0
Lytle, Den	1	0	0	0	0
Macek, S.D.	0	1	0	0	0
Malone, Pitts	2	0	0	0	0
Manning, Den	3	0	0	0	0

Player—Team	Fum.	Own Rec.	Yds.	Opp. Rec.	Yds.
Manumaleuga, K.C.	1	0	0	0	0
Marsh, Oak	0	0	0	1	0
Marshall, K.C.	2	0	0	0	0
Martin, Oak	0	1	0	2	0
Marvin, Oak	0	1	0	0	0
Matthews, N.E.	0	0	0	1	0
Matthews, Clev	0	0	0	2	16
Matthews, Oak	5	2	0	0	0
Matuszak, Oak	0	0	0	1	0
McClanahan, Oak	0	0	0	3	0
McCullum, Sea	1	0	0	0	0
McCutcheon, Buf	1	0	0	0	0
McDonald, Clev	4	0	0	0	0
McGee, N.E.	0	0	0	1	0
McKinney, Oak	0	0	0	1	0
McKnight, K.C.	2	0	0	0	0
McMillan, Balt	1	0	0	0	0
McNeal, Mia	0	0	0	1	0
McNeil, N.Y.J.	5	0	0	0	0
Mehl, N.Y.J.	0	0	0	1	0
Mike-Mayer, Buf	0	1	0	0	0
Millen, Oak	0	0	0	1	0
Minor, Sea	0	1	0	0	0
Montgomery, Clev	2	1	0	0	0
Montoya, Cin	0	1	0	0	0
Morgan, N.E.	2	2	0	0	0
Morton, Den	2	0	0	0	0
Moses, Den	1	0	0	0	0
Muncie, S.D.	9	4	0	0	0
Nathan, Mia	2	2	0	0	0
Neil, N.Y.J.	0	1	0	0	0
Newton, N.Y.J.	2	0	0	0	0
Nielsen, Hou	3	1	−15	0	0
Norman, Sea	0	0	0	2	0
Odoms, Den	1	0	0	0	0
Orosz, Mia	0	1	0	0	0
Orvis, Balt	0	0	0	2	0
O'Steen, Oak	0	1	0	2	0
Owen, N.E.	1	0	0	0	0
Owens, Oak	0	0	0	2	22
Parker, Buf	0	0	0	1	0
Parrish, K.C.	0	0	0	3	0
Parros, Den	6	1	0	0	0
Paul, K.C.	0	0	0	1	47
Perry, Hou	0	0	0	1	0
Phillips, S.D.	1	0	0	1	0
Piccone, Buf	0	1	0	0	0
Plunkett, Oak	3	1	−6	0	0
Pollard, Pitts	5	1	−12	0	0
Pratt, Balt	1	1	0	0	0
Preston, Den	4	0	0	0	0
Prestridge, Den	1	0	0	0	0
G. Pruitt, Clev	3	0	0	0	0
M. Pruitt, Clev	5	2	0	0	0
Ramsey, N.Y.J.	2	1	−39	0	0
Ramsey, Oak	2	1	0	0	0
Ray, N.Y.J.	1	0	0	2	4
Reaves, Hou	2	0	−2	0	0
Reed, Den	1	0	0	0	0
Reinfeldt, Hou	0	0	0	2	0
Renfro, Hou	2	1	12	1	0
Rhone, Mia	0	0	0	1	0
Riddick, Buf	1	0	0	0	0
Riley, Hou	0	0	0	1	6
Riley, Cin	0	0	0	1	0
Robinson, Oak	0	0	0	1	0
Robinson, Buf	1	0	0	0	0
Robinson, Clev	0	0	0	1	0
Rome, K.C.	0	1	13	0	0
Romes, Buf	1	0	0	2	11
Rose, Mia	0	0	0	1	0
Ross, Cin	3	1	3	0	0
Rudnay, K.C.	1	0	−28	0	0
St. Clair, Cin	0	0	0	1	12
Salaam, N.Y.J.	0	0	0	1	0
Sanford, Buf	0	0	0	1	0
Sanford, N.E.	0	0	0	3	2
Scales, S.D.	1	0	0	0	0
Schonert, Cin	1	0	0	0	0
Schuh, Cin	0	0	0	1	0
Schuhmacher, Hou	0	1	0	0	0
Scott, Clev	0	0	0	3	0
Shaw, S.D.	0	0	0	1	0
Shell, Pitts	0	0	0	2	0
Shiver, Bal	0	0	0	1	0
Shoate, N.E.	1	0	0	2	7
Shula, Balt	2	2	0	0	0
Shull, Mia	0	0	0	2	0
Sievers, S.D.	1	0	0	1	0
Simmons, Cin	1	1	0	0	0
Simonini, Balt	0	0	0	1	0
Simpson, Buf	0	0	0	1	0
Simpson, Sea	0	0	0	1	0
Sipe, Clev	10	4	−39	0	0
Skaugstad, Hou	0	0	0	2	0
Small, Mia	0	0	0	2	0
Smerlas, Buf	0	0	0	1	17
Smith, Den	0	0	0	2	0
Smith, Pitts	1	1	0	0	0
Smith, K.C.	2	1	19	0	0
Smith, Sea	3	2	0	0	0
Sohn, N.Y.J.	5	2	0	0	0
Spani, K.C.	0	0	0	2	91
Springs, N.Y.J.	1	1	0	1	0
Stabler, Hou	7	2	−13	0	0
Stallworth, Pitts	4	0	0	0	0
Stensrud, Hou	0	0	0	1	0
Still, K.C.	0	0	0	1	0
Sullivan, Clev	0	1	0	1	0
Sutherland, Sea	0	0	0	1	0
Swann, Pitts	1	1	0	0	0
Sweeney, Pitts	1	0	0	0	0
Swenson, Den	0	0	0	3	0
Tatupu, N.E.	2	1	0	2	0
Taylor, Balt	0	0	0	1	0
Thomas, Pitts	0	0	0	1	0
Thomas, Sea	0	0	0	2	5
Thompson, Den	0	0	0	2	0
Thompson, Balt	0	0	0	1	0
Thornton, Pitts	6	1	0	0	0
Todd, N.Y.J.	5	2	0	0	0
Toews, Pitts	0	1	0	0	0
Toler, N.E.	0	1	0	0	0
Trout, Pitts	0	0	0	1	0
Tuiasosopo, Sea	0	0	0	3	0
Valentine, Pitts	0	1	0	1	0
Verser, Cin	2	0	0	0	0
Vigorito, Mia	1	0	0	0	0
Villapiano, Buf	0	0	0	1	0
Walker, Mia	4	2	0	0	0
Watson, Den	0	2	0	0	0
Watts, Oak	3	2	1	0	0
West, Sea	1	0	−13	0	0
White, Clev	8	3	0	0	0
White, Sea	0	0	0	1	0
White, Buf	0	0	0	1	0
Whittington, Oak	4	0	0	0	0
Wilkerson, S.D.	0	1	0	0	0
Williams, Buf	0	0	0	1	0
C. Williams, S.D.	2	0	0	0	0
Williams, Balt	4	1	0	0	0
Williams, Cin	0	0	0	3	0
Willis, Oak	1	1	0	0	0
J. C. Wilson, Hou	1	0	0	0	0
Wilson, Oak	8	2	−3	0	0
T. Wilson, Hou	2	0	0	0	0
Winslow, S.D.	2	2	0	0	0
Woodcock, S.D.	0	0	0	2	0
Woodley, Mia	9	2	−21	0	0
Woodring, N.Y.J.	0	1	0	1	0
Woodruff, Pitts	1	0	0	1	0
Woods, Balt	0	0	0	1	0
J. Wright, Den	0	1	1	0	0
L. Wright, Den	0	0	0	1	−5
Yarno, Sea	0	1	0	0	0
Zamberlin, N.E.	0	0	0	1	0
Zorn, Sea	2	0	0	0	0

Touchdowns: Landry, Baltimore; St. Clair, Cincinnati; Howard, Paul and Spani, Kansas City; Kozlowski, Miami; B. Jones, New York Jets; Hardman and Jones, Oakland; Johnson and Thomas, Seattle 1 each.

NFC FUMBLES—INDIVIDUAL

Player—Team	Fum.	Own Rec.	Yds.	Opp. Rec.	Yds.
Allen, Det.	0	0	0	1	0
Allerman, G.B.	0	0	0	1	0
Anderson, G.B.	0	0	0	4	22
Anderson, Chi	1	0	0	0	0
Anderson, St.L.	13	3	0	0	0
Andrews, Atl	12	0	0	0	0
Ane, G.B.	0	1	0	1	0
Ard, N.Y.G.	0	1	0	0	0
Atkins, G.B.	1	0	0	0	0
Audick, S.F.	0	2	0	0	0
Baker, St.L.	0	1	0	0	0
Banks, N.O.	2	1	0	0	0
Barnes, Dal	1	0	0	2	72
Bartkowski, Atl	4	3	−1	0	0
Baschnagel, Chi	2	2	0	0	0
R. Bell, T.B.	1	1	0	0	0
T. Bell, T.B.	1	0	0	0	0
Bell, Chi	0	1	0	0	0
Blackmore, Phila	0	0	0	1	0
Blair, Minn	1	0	0	2	0
Blanchard, T.B.	1	2	0	0	0
Bolinger, Det	0	2	0	0	0
Bostic, Wash	0	1	0	0	0
Bradley, Det	0	0	0	1	0
Brahaney, St.L.	0	1	0	0	0
Brenner, N.O.	1	0	0	0	0
Bright, N.Y.G.	3	4	0	0	0
Brock, N.O.	0	2	0	0	0
Brooks, Wash	0	0	0	2	0
Brown, T.B.	1	0	0	1	0
Brown, Phila	0	0	0	2	7
Brown, Minn	3	2	0	1	0
Bruer, Minn	1	0	0	0	0
Brunner, N.Y.G.	6	2	−3	0	0
Bryant, L.A.	1	0	0	0	0
Bunting, Phila	0	0	0	1	16
Bunz, S.F.	0	0	0	2	0
Bussey, Det	3	0	0	0	0
Cain, Atl	3	2	0	0	0
Callicutt, Det	0	0	0	1	0
Campbell, Chi	0	0	0	1	0
Campfield, Phila	3	2	1	0	0
Carano, Dal	3	0	−6	0	0
Carmichael, Phila	3	1	0	0	0
Carpenter, Hou-N.Y.G.	3	0	0	0	0
Carson, N.Y.G.	0	0	0	1	2
Cassidy, G.B.	1	0	0	0	0
Caster, N.O.	2	0	0	0	0
Chesley, Phila	0	0	0	2	11
Childs, L.A.	1	0	0	0	0
Cobb, Det	0	0	0	3	0
Cobb, Chi	0	1	0	0	0
Coffman, G.B.	1	0	0	1	0
Coleman, Wash	0	0	0	1	2
Coleman, Minn	0	1	0	0	0
Collins, St.L.	0	1	0	0	0
Colzie, T.B.	1	0	0	1	0
Connell, Wash	2	2	−8	0	0
Cooper, S.F.	3	1	0	0	0
Cosbie, Dal	1	0	0	0	0
Cromwell, L.A.	0	1	0	2	4
Cumby, G.B.	0	0	0	2	70
Curcio, Phila	0	0	0	1	0
Currier, N.Y.G.	0	0	0	1	0
Danielson, Det	2	0	0	0	0
Davis, T.B.	1	0	0	0	0
Davis, S.F.	1	0	0	0	0
Dawson, St.L.	0	0	0	2	0
Dennard, L.A.	1	1	0	0	0
Dickerson, Dal	0	0	0	2	0
Dickey, G.B.	8	3	−26	0	0
Dierdorf, St.L.	0	1	0	0	0
Dils, Minn	3	2	0	0	0
Donovan, Dal	0	1	0	0	0
Dorney, Det	0	1	0	0	0
Dorsett, Dal	10	2	0	0	0
Doss, L.A.	0	0	0	1	0
Douglass, G.B.	0	0	0	3	0
Downs, Dal	0	0	0	1	0
Dusek, Wash	0	0	0	1	0
Easley, S.F.	2	2	0	0	0
Eckwood, T.B.	3	2	0	0	0
Edwards, Phila	0	0	0	1	4
Elias, Det	0	2	0	0	0
Elliott, S.F.	2	0	0	0	0
Ellis, G.B.	5	1	0	0	0
Ellis, Phila	0	0	0	1	0
English, Det	0	0	0	3	20
Erxleben, N.O.	1	0	0	0	0
Evans, Chi	13	2	−10	0	0
Fahnhorst, S.F.	0	2	0	0	0
Fanning, L.A.	0	0	0	1	0
Fantetti, Det	0	0	0	1	0
Faumuina, Atl	0	0	0	1	0
Favron, St.L.	0	0	0	1	5
Fencik, Chi	0	0	0	1	0
J. Fisher, Chi	3	0	0	1	0
Flick, Wash	2	1	0	0	0
Flowers, N.Y.G.	0	0	0	1	0
Forte, N.Y.G.	1	0	0	0	0
Fowler, Det	0	2	−10	0	0
Francis, Atl	1	1	0	1	0
Gaison, Atl	0	0	0	1	0
Galbreath, Minn	2	0	0	0	0
Garrett, N.Y.G.	1	0	0	0	0
Gay, Det	0	0	0	1	0
Giammona, Phila	2	0	0	0	0
Glazebrook, Atl	0	0	0	1	22
Gofourth, G.B.	0	1	0	0	0
Gray, N.Y.G.	1	0	0	0	0
Gray, G.B.	0	0	0	1	0
Green, Det	0	0	0	1	0
Green, T.B.	0	0	0	1	0
Green, St.L.	2	0	0	0	0
Greene, St.L.	0	0	0	1	0
Greer, St.L.	0	0	0	4	2
Grimm, Wash	0	1	0	0	0
Grooms, N.O.	0	0	0	1	20
Guman, L.A.	2	0	0	0	0
Haden, L.A.	5	1	−5	0	0
Hairston, Phila	0	0	0	1	0
Hall, Det	1	0	0	0	0
Hannon, Minn	0	0	0	1	31
Hardy, N.O.	2	2	0	0	0
Harper, Chi	1	0	0	0	0
Harper, S.F.	0	0	0	1	0
Harrell, St.L.	0	1	2	0	0
Harrington, Phila	1	0	0	0	0
Harris, Chi	0	0	0	3	5
Harris, L.A.	0	0	0	2	21
Harris, G.B.	0	1	0	0	0
Harrison, Phila	0	0	0	3	0
Hart, St.L.	4	0	−9	0	0
Hartenstine, Chi	0	0	0	1	4
Harvey, G.B.	1	1	0	2	0
Hawkins, T.B.	0	0	0	1	3
Haynes, N.Y.G.	0	0	0	1	0
Heath, Phila	0	0	0	1	0
Henderson, Chi	0	0	0	1	0
Henry, Phila	4	1	0	0	0
Herron, Chi	0	0	0	1	0
Hicks, S.F.	1	1	0	3	80
Hill, Det	1	0	0	0	0
D. Hill, L.A.	1	1	0	0	0
Hill, Dal	1	0	0	0	0
Hipple, Det	14	4	−10	0	0
Hofer, S.F.	1	0	0	0	0
Holloway, Minn	0	0	0	1	45
Holt, T.B.	1	0	0	0	0
House, T.B.	2	0	0	0	0
Huckleby, G.B.	3	0	0	0	0
Hudson, N.O.	0	1	14	0	0
Hughes, N.Y.G.	2	2	0	0	0
Hunter, Det	1	0	0	1	0
Irvin, L.A.	3	2	0	1	14
Jackson, Atl	0	1	0	0	0
L. Jackson, N.Y.G.	1	0	0	0	0
Jackson, N.O.	0	0	0	1	0

Player—Team	Fum.	Own Rec.	Yds.	Opp. Rec.	Yds.
T. Jackson, N.Y.G.	0	0	0	1	0
Jackson, Wash	2	0	0	0	0
Jacoby, Wash	0	1	0	0	0
Jaworski, Phila	3	3	-2	0	0
Jenkins, Atl	3	0	0	0	0
Jensen, G.B.	1	0	0	0	0
Johnson, T.B.	1	0	0	0	0
Johnson, St.L.	1	0	0	0	0
Johnson, Phila	0	0	0	2	0
Johnson, L.A.	0	0	0	5	5
Johnson, Atl	1	0	0	2	55
Jones, S.F.	1	0	0	0	0
Jones, L.A.	0	0	0	1	0
E. Jones, Dal	0	0	0	3	0
J. Jones, Dal	4	2	0	0	0
Jones, Wash	0	1	0	0	0
Jones, G.B.	0	0	0	2	0
Kane, Det	2	0	0	0	0
Kelley, N.Y.G.	0	0	0	2	0
Kenn, Atl	0	1	0	0	0
Kenney, Phila	0	2	0	0	0
King, Dal	0	1	0	1	0
King, N.Y.G.	0	1	0	0	0
Knoff, Minn	0	0	0	1	0
Kollar, T.B.	0	0	0	3	0
Komlo, Det	2	2	0	0	0
Koncar, G.B.	0	1	0	0	0
Kovach, N.O.	0	0	0	1	0
Kramer, Minn	8	3	0	0	0
Kuykendall, Atl	0	0	0	1	0
Lafary, N.O.	0	1	0	0	0
Laughlin, Atl	0	0	0	1	0
Lawrence, S.F.	3	0	0	0	0
LeCount, Minn	0	0	0	1	0
Lee, G.B.	0	0	0	1	0
LeMaster, Phila	0	0	0	2	47
Leonard, T.B.	1	0	-6	0	0
Leopold, S.F.	0	0	0	2	0
Lewis, T.B.	0	0	0	1	0
Lewis, Dal	1	0	-2	0	0
Lofton, G.B.	0	1	0	0	0
Logan, T.B.	0	0	0	1	21
Logan, Phila	0	0	0	1	0
Lomax, St.L.	6	0	0	0	0
Lorch, Wash	0	0	0	2	0
Lott, S.F.	1	0	0	2	0
Love, St.L.	0	1	0	1	0
Manning, N.O.	3	0	0	0	0
Margerum, Chi	0	1	0	0	0
Marion, N.Y.G.	0	0	0	1	3
Marsh, St.L.	1	0	0	0	0
Martin, Minn	0	0	0	1	0
Martin, N.Y.G.	0	0	0	3	28
Martin, Dal	0	0	0	1	0
Martin, Det	3	2	0	0	0
Mayberry, Atl	1	0	0	0	0
Mays, St.L.	0	0	0	1	0
McCarren, G.B.	1	0	0	0	0
McCoy, G.B.	1	1	0	0	0
McDole, Minn	1	1	0	0	0
McMichael, Chi	0	1	0	0	0
McNeill, Minn	0	0	0	1	11
Mendenhall, Wash	0	0	0	2	0
Merkens, N.O.	1	1	0	2	0
Merrill, G.B.	0	0	0	3	0
Metcalf, Wash	6	1	0	0	0
Middleton, G.B.	2	1	0	0	0
Milot, Wash	1	0	0	1	18
Mitchell, St.L	3	0	0	0	0
Montana, S.F.	2	0	0	0	0
Montgomery, Phila	6	2	0	0	0
Moore, N.O.	0	0	0	1	0
Moriarty, Atl	0	0	0	1	0
Morriss, Phila	2	0	-8	0	0
Mullady, N.Y.G.	1	0	0	0	0
Mullaney, Minn	0	0	0	1	0
Murphy, G.B.	0	0	0	2	0
Murphy, Wash	0	0	0	3	0
Murphy, L.A.	0	0	0	1	0
Myers, N.O.	1	1	0	0	0
Nafziger, T.B.	0	0	0	1	0
Nairne, N.O.	0	0	0	2	0
Neal, Chi	2	0	-4	0	0
Neill, N.Y.G.	0	0	0	1	0
Nelms, Wash	2	0	0	0	0
Nelson, St.L.	0	0	0	2	0
Newsome, Dal	1	0	0	0	0
Nichols, Det.	1	0	0	0	0
Nixon, G.B.	2	0	0	0	0
Nord, Minn	2	1	0	0	0
O'Donoghue, St.L	0	0	0	1	0
Oliver, Phila	1	0	0	0	0
Osborne, Chi	0	0	0	2	7
Owens, T.B.	1	1	0	0	0
Page, Chi	0	0	0	1	0
Pankey, L.A.	0	2	0	0	0
Parrish, Wash	0	0	0	1	0
Pastorini, L.A.	4	1	-2	0	0
Patton, S.F.	3	0	0	0	0
Payton, Minn	5	1	0	0	0
Payton, Chi	9	3	0	0	0
Pearson, Dal	4	0	0	0	0
Pelluer, N.O.	0	0	0	1	0
Perkins, N.Y.G.	2	0	0	0	0
Perry, N.Y.G.	4	2	2	0	0
Peters, Wash	0	1	0	0	0
Petersen, Dal	0	2	3	0	0
Pittman, N.Y.G.	2	1	0	0	0
Plank, Chi	0	0	0	4	6
Poe, N.O.	0	0	0	1	10
Pollard, St.L.	0	0	0	1	0
Pridemore, Atl	0	0	0	3	24
Puki, S.F.	0	0	0	2	0
Quillan, S.F.	1	0	0	0	0
Radford, St.L	0	0	0	1	0
Rafferty, Dal	2	1	-30	0	0
Rashad, Minn	1	1	0	0	0
Redwine, Minn	1	0	0	0	0
Reece, N.Y.G.	1	3	3	2	4
Riggins, Wash	1	0	0	0	0
Ring, S.F.	1	0	0	1	0
Robinson, Phila	0	0	0	2	0
G. Rogers, N.O.	13	1	0	0	0
J. Rogers, N.O.	3	1	0	0	0
Russell, Phila	3	0	0	0	0
Saldi, Dal	0	1	0	1	0
Saul, L.A.	0	1	0	0	0
Schmidt, Chi	0	0	0	1	0
Sciarra, Phila	3	2	-16	0	0
Scott, N.O.	1	1	0	0	0
Sendlein, Minn	0	0	0	1	0
Senser, Minn	3	2	0	0	0
Shirk, N.Y.G.	1	0	0	0	0
Shumann, S.F.	1	0	0	0	0
Siemon, Minn	1	0	-3	1	0
Simmons, N.Y.G.	0	2	0	0	0
Simms, N.Y.G.	7	2	-15	0	0
Sims, Det	9	3	0	0	0
C. Smith, Phila	2	0	0	0	0
D. Smith, Atl	0	0	0	3	2
D. Smith, L.A.	1	0	0	0	0
L. Smith, L.A.	0	0	0	1	0
R. Smith, Atl	4	1	0	0	0
Smith, Det	0	0	0	1	4
Solomon, S.F.	3	2	0	0	0
Sorey, Chi	0	1	0	0	0
Spagnola, Phila	0	1	0	0	0
Springs, Dal	3	3	11	1	0
Stalls, T.B.	0	0	0	1	0
Stauch, N.O.	1	1	0	0	0
Stokes, N.Y.G.	0	1	0	0	0
Strong, Atl	1	1	0	2	0
Stuckey, S.F.	0	0	0	1	0
Studwell, Minn	0	0	0	3	0
Suhey, Chi	3	3	0	0	0
Sully, L.A.	1	1	0	1	0
Swain, Minn	0	0	0	1	0
B. Taylor, N.Y.G.	2	0	0	0	0
Taylor, N.O.	0	1	0	0	0
L. Taylor, N.Y.G.	1	0	0	1	4

Player—Team	Fum.	Own Rec.	Yds.	Opp. Rec.	Yds.
Theismann, Wash	7	1	0	0	0
Thielemann, Atl	0	2	0	0	0
Thomas, L.A.	1	1	0	0	0
Thomas, T.B.	0	0	0	2	5
Thompson, G.B.	0	1	0	0	0
L. Thompson, Det	1	1	0	0	0
V. Thompson, Det	1	0	0	0	0
Thurman, Dal	0	0	0	1	0
Tilley, St.L	1	0	0	0	0
Titensor, Dal	0	0	0	1	0
Turner, S.F.	0	0	0	3	0
Tyler, N.O.	4	0	0	0	0
Tyler, L.A.	11	4	1	0	0
Van Horne, Chi	0	1	0	0	0
Van Note, Atl	1	1	−20	0	0
Van Pelt, N.Y.G.	0	0	0	2	0
Waddy, L.A.	2	0	0	0	0
Walker, Wash	0	1	0	0	0
Walls, Dal	0	0	0	1	0
Walterscheid, Chi	0	0	0	2	3
Warren, N.O.	0	0	0	1	0
Washington, Wash	8	0	0	0	0
Washington, T.B.	0	0	0	1	0
Waters, Dal	0	1	0	0	0
Wattelet, N.O.	0	0	0	1	0
Watts, Chi	3	2	0	0	0
Waymer, N.O.	0	0	0	2	0
Whitaker, G.B.	0	0	0	1	0
D. White, Dal	14	8	−34	0	0
J. White, Minn	0	0	0	2	0
White, Wash	0	0	0	2	3
S. White, Minn	1	0	0	0	0
White, Detroit	0	0	0	1	0
Whitehurst, G.B.	4	1	−2	0	0
Wilder, T.B.	3	1	0	0	0
Wilks, N.O.	0	0	0	2	0
Williams, T.B.	9	3	−31	0	0
Williams, St.L	0	0	0	2	0
Williams, Atl	0	0	0	2	57
Williamson, S.F.	0	0	0	2	3
D. Wilson, N.O.	4	3	−8	0	0
Wilson, S.F.	0	1	0	0	0
Wilson, Chi	0	0	0	3	31
Wilson, Dal	0	0	0	1	0
Wilson, Minn	2	1	0	0	0
W. Wilson, N.O.	1	0	0	1	0
Woerner, Atl	0	0	0	1	0
Wonsley, Wash	1	0	0	0	0
Wright, S.F.	0	0	0	2	0
Yakavonis, Minn	0	0	0	1	0
Yeates, Atl	0	0	0	1	0
Young, Minn	4	0	0	0	0
Zanders, Chi	0	1	0	0	0

Touchdowns: Johnson, Atlanta and Martin, N.Y. Giants 2 each. Jackson and Williams, Atlanta; Barnes, Dallas; Harris, Los Angeles; Holloway, Minnesota; Reece, N.Y. Giants; Brown and LeMaster, Philadelphia; Hicks, San Francisco; Logan, Tampa Bay 1 each.

CLUB RANKINGS BY YARDS

	OFFENSE				DEFENSE		
	Total	Rush	Pass		Total	Rush	Pass
Atlanta	7	18	5		14	2	25
Baltimore	22	22	18		28	26	27
Buffalo	8	13	9		7	17	4
Chicago	26	11	27		19	20	14
Cincinnati	2	17	3		12	9	22
Cleveland	4	20	4		16	18	15
Dallas	5	2	15		20	16	21
Denver	14	21	8		6	13	5
Detroit	3	1	17		4	1	13
Green Bay	23	26	14		9	19	10
Houston	27	23	23		24	24	17
Kansas City	17	3	25		t17	3	23
Los Angeles	24	8	26		8	23	2
Miami	16	10	16		15	14	19
Minnesota	6	28	2		t17	15	18
New England	t9	15	6		25	28	6
New Orleans	25	7	28		11	11	20
New York Giants	28	25	24		3	10	7
New York Jets	15	6	19		5	7	8
Oakland	21	14	21		21	6	24
Philadelphia	12	4	20		1	4	1
Pittsburgh	11	5	13		22	8	26
St. Louis	19	9	22		23	25	16
San Diego	1	16	1		27	5	28
San Francisco	13	19	7		2	12	3
Seattle	20	27	12		26	27	11
Tampa Bay	18	24	11		13	22	12
Washington	t9	12	10		10	21	9

t—Tie for position

1981 NFL TEAM-BY-TEAM STATISTICAL SUMMARY

AMERICAN FOOTBALL CONFERENCE

OFFENSE

	Balt.	Buff.	Cin.	Clev.	Den.	Hou.	K.C.	Mia.	N.E.	N.Y.J.	Oak.	Pitt.	S.D.	Sea.
First Downs	274	315	361	364	306	241	315	306	306	318	296	318	379	295
Rushing	95	127	124	131	91	103	160	123	124	122	108	137	127	103
Passing	158	163	210	196	181	124	132	157	166	170	166	156	224	166
Penalty	21	25	27	37	34	14	23	26	16	26	22	25	28	26
Rushes	441	524	493	474	515	466	610	535	499	571	493	554	481	440
Net Yards Gained	1850	2125	1973	1929	1895	1734	2633	2173	2040	2341	2058	2372	2005	1594
Avg. Gain	4.2	4.1	4.0	4.1	3.7	3.7	4.3	4.1	4.1	4.1	4.2	4.3	4.2	3.6
Avg. Yards per Game	115.6	132.8	123.3	120.6	118.4	108.4	164.6	135.8	127.5	146.3	128.6	148.3	125.3	99.6
Passes Attempted	479	503	550	624	485	441	410	498	482	507	545	461	629	524
Completed	265	253	332	348	289	258	224	271	254	283	267	247	368	307
Pct. Completed	55.3	50.3	60.4	55.8	59.6	58.5	54.6	54.4	52.7	55.8	49.0	53.6	58.5	58.6
Total Yards Gained	3379	3661	4200	4339	3992	3119	2917	3385	3904	3279	3356	3457	4873	3727
Passer Tackled	37	16	35	40	61	40	37	30	45	30	53	27	19	37
Yards Lost	321	146	205	353	461	342	277	236	321	224	437	231	134	300
Net Yards Gained	3058	3515	3995	3986	3531	2777	2640	3149	3583	3055	2919	3226	4739	3427
Avg. Yards per Game	191.1	219.7	249.7	249.1	220.7	173.6	165.0	196.8	223.9	190.9	182.4	201.6	296.2	214.2
Net Yards per Pass Play	5.93	6.77	6.83	6.00	6.47	5.77	5.91	5.96	6.80	5.69	4.88	6.61	7.31	6.11
Yards Gained per Completion	12.75	14.47	12.65	12.47	13.81	12.09	13.02	12.49	15.37	11.59	12.57	14.00	13.24	12.14
Combined Net Yards Gained	4908	5640	5968	5915	5426	4511	5273	5322	5623	5396	4977	5598	6744	5021
Pct. Total Yards Rushing	37.69	37.68	33.06	32.61	34.92	38.44	49.93	40.83	36.28	43.36	41.35	42.37	29.73	31.75
Pct. Total Yards Passing	62.31	62.32	66.94	67.39	65.08	61.56	50.07	59.17	63.72	56.62	58.65	57.63	70.27	68.25
Avg. Yards per Game	306.8	352.5	373.0	369.7	339.1	281.9	329.6	332.6	351.4	337.3	311.1	349.9	421.5	313.8
Ball Control Plays	957	1043	1078	1138	1061	947	1057	1063	1026	1108	1091	1042	1129	1001
Avg. Yards per Play	5.1	5.4	5.5	5.2	5.1	4.8	5.0	5.0	5.5	4.9	4.6	5.4	6.0	5.0
Avg. Time of Possession	26:28	30:24	30:52	30:59	32:27	27:56	31:01	30:14	27:51	31:21	28:20	30:17	29:17	26:59
Third Down Efficiency	33.3	43.3	45.2	40.9	37.0	32.5	40.5	38.2	37.0	41.4	37.9	41.1	48.9	37.3

AFC OFFENSE—Continued

	Balt.	Buff.	Cin.	Clev.	Den.	Hou.	K.C.	Mia.	N.E.	N.Y.J.	Oak.	Pitt.	S.D.	Sea.
Had Intercepted	23	20	12	27	21	23	22	21	34	14	28	19	18	15
Yards Opponents Returned	281	333	143	347	405	289	247	288	570	212	339	226	377	257
Returned by Opposition for TD	1	0	1	1	4	0	1	0	1	0	0	0	1	1
Punts	78	80	73	70	86	79	70	83	75	81	98	84	63	68
Yards Punted	3071	3175	3272	2884	3478	3137	2697	3386	2951	3290	4238	3641	2540	2652
Avg. Yards per Punt	39.4	39.7	44.8	41.2	40.4	39.7	38.5	40.8	39.3	40.6	43.2	43.3	40.3	39.0
Punt Returns	12	35	29	50	51	41	50	45	31	50	52	50	31	32
Yards Returned	56	292	205	369	441	325	528	458	199	337	380	412	378	293
Avg. Yards per Return	4.7	8.3	7.1	7.4	8.6	7.9	10.6	10.2	6.4	6.7	7.3	8.2	12.2	9.2
Returned for TD	0	0	0	0	0	0	0	1	0	0	1	0	0	0
Kickoff Returns	84	57	49	72	47	72	52	54	65	58	71	53	70	69
Yards Returned	1651	1085	1056	1537	801	1722	1043	1228	1190	1151	1411	1096	1422	1278
Avg. Yards per Return	19.7	19.0	21.6	21.3	17.0	23.9	20.1	22.7	18.3	19.8	19.9	20.7	20.3	18.5
Returned for TD	0	0	0	0	0	2	0	1	0	0	0	0	0	0
Penalties	106	114	109	109	99	93	97	71	89	112	101	97	128	106
Yards Penalized	913	1001	896	971	833	825	924	541	742	936	867	840	947	823
Fumbles	27	33	25	38	26	33	36	26	32	38	42	39	39	41
Lost	14	18	12	26	18	21	24	10	16	17	20	22	22	23
Out of Bounds	2	2	3	1	2	2	2	3	2	2	2	3	4	4
Own Recovered for TD	1	0	0	0	0	0	0	0	0	1	0	0	0	0
Opposition Recovered by	14	17	18	20	23	13	21	15	17	15	19	16	18	27
Opposition Recovered for TD	0	0	1	0	0	0	3	1	0	0	2	0	0	2
Total Points Scored	259	311	421	276	321	281	343	345	322	355	273	356	478	322
Total TDs	33	38	51	32	39	34	38	39	40	40	33	47	61	40
TDs Rushing	11	13	19	11	12	11	22	18	23	11	11	21	26	14
TDs Passing	21	25	30	21	27	21	12	18	17	26	18	25	34	21
TDs on Return and Recovery	1	0	2	0	0	2	4	3	0	3	4	1	1	5
Extra Points	29	37	49	31	36	32	37	37	37	38	27	38	55	37
Safeties	1	2	0	1	1	0	0	1	0	1	3	0	0	0
Field Goals Made	10	14	22	17	17	15	26	24	15	25	14	12	19	15
Field Goals Attempted	18	24	32	33	30	22	36	31	24	36	24	17	26	24
Pct. Successful	55.6	58.3	68.8	51.5	56.7	68.2	72.2	77.4	62.5	69.4	58.3	70.6	73.1	62.5

AMERICAN FOOTBALL CONFERENCE

DEFENSE

	Balt.	Buff.	Cin.	Clev.	Den.	Hou.	K.C.	Mia.	N.E.	N.Y.J.	Oak.	Pitt.	S.D.	Sea.
First Downs	406	298	324	299	268	325	316	296	328	291	316	323	365	371
Rushing	162	113	126	119	103	138	112	124	160	112	104	114	114	175
Passing	214	154	167	157	142	162	177	160	148	155	178	181	216	173
Penalty	30	31	31	23	23	25	27	12	20	24	34	28	35	23
Rushes	607	516	465	516	467	549	507	492	644	465	524	500	491	588
Net Yards Gained	2665	2075	1881	2078	2005	2411	1747	2032	2950	1867	1832	1869	1825	2806
Avg. Gain	4.4	4.0	4.0	4.0	4.3	4.4	3.4	4.1	4.6	4.0	3.5	3.7	3.7	4.8
Avg. Yards per Game	166.6	129.7	117.6	129.9	125.3	150.7	109.2	127.0	184.4	116.7	114.5	116.8	114.1	175.4
Passes Attempted	491	474	548	469	497	502	567	509	439	505	537	544	571	502
Completed	301	267	316	275	267	295	291	297	243	275	289	302	313	294
Pct. Completed	61.3	56.3	57.7	58.6	53.7	58.8	51.3	58.3	55.4	54.5	53.8	55.5	54.8	58.6
Total Yards Gained	4228	3243	3757	3512	3168	3554	3821	3645	3052	3522	4011	4108	4695	3394
Passer Tackled	13	47	42	29	36	33	27	38	20	66	52	40	47	36
Yards Lost	100	373	349	223	295	239	195	314	175	518	370	325	384	260
Net Yards Gained	4128	2870	3408	3289	2873	3315	3626	3331	2877	3004	3641	3783	4311	3134
Avg. Yards per Game	258.0	179.4	213.0	205.6	179.6	207.2	226.6	208.2	179.8	187.8	227.6	236.4	269.4	195.9
Net Yards per Pass Play	8.19	5.51	5.78	6.60	5.39	6.20	6.10	6.09	6.27	5.26	6.18	6.48	6.98	5.83
Yards Gained per Completion	14.05	12.15	11.89	12.77	11.87	12.05	13.13	12.27	12.56	12.81	13.88	13.60	15.00	11.54
Combined Net Yds. Gained	6793	4945	5289	5367	4878	5726	5373	5363	5827	4871	5473	5652	6136	5940
Pct. Total Yds. Rushing	39.23	41.96	35.56	38.72	41.10	42.11	32.51	37.89	50.63	38.33	33.47	33.07	29.74	47.24
Pct. Total Yds. Passing	60.77	58.04	64.44	61.28	58.90	57.89	67.49	62.11	49.37	61.67	66.53	66.93	70.26	52.76
Avg. Yds. per Game	424.6	309.1	330.6	335.4	304.9	357.9	335.8	335.2	364.2	304.4	342.1	353.3	383.5	371.3
Ball Control Plays	1111	1037	1055	1014	1000	1084	1101	1039	1103	1036	1113	1084	1109	1126
Avg. Yds. per Play	6.1	4.8	5.0	5.3	4.9	5.3	4.9	5.2	5.3	4.7	4.9	5.2	5.5	5.3
Third Down Efficiency	51.4	33.0	42.5	36.8	33.8	43.4	36.5	37.9	43.5	34.7	36.4	39.1	42.3	48.6
Intercepted by	16	19	19	15	23	18	26	18	16	21	13	30	23	21
Yds. Returned by	210	352	318	165	342	330	406	254	195	432	97	376	224	397
Returned for TD	0	0	1	0	0	0	1	0	0	2	1	1	1	3

	Balt.	Buff.	Cin.	Clev.	Den.	Hou.	K.C.	Mia.	N.E.	N.Y.J.	Oak.	Pitt.	S.D.	Sea.
Punts	48	77	81	78	88	70	80	87	74	94	101	78	72	55
Yds. Punted	1817	3237	3266	3173	3789	2935	3109	3565	2872	3802	3928	3286	2900	2337
Avg. Yds. per Punt	37.9	42.0	40.3	40.7	43.1	41.9	38.9	41.0	38.8	40.4	38.9	42.1	40.3	42.5
Punt Returns	44	34	42	30	46	47	46	45	35	31	45	34	31	33
Yds. Returned	402	220	416	253	388	360	293	286	305	149	514	358	168	153
Avg. Yds. per Return	9.1	6.5	9.9	8.4	8.4	7.7	6.4	6.4	8.7	4.8	11.4	10.5	5.4	4.6
Returned for TD	0	0	0	0	0	0	0	0	1	0	0	2	0	0
Kickoff Returns	43	61	80	45	47	59	68	60	68	63	49	52	88	67
Yds. Returned	864	1268	1612	1156	1007	1201	1296	1218	1326	1415	1068	1253	1528	1177
Avg. Yds. per Return	20.1	20.8	20.2	25.7	21.4	20.4	19.1	20.3	19.5	22.5	21.8	24.1	17.4	17.6
Returned for TD	0	1	1	0	0	0	0	0	0	0	1	0	0	0
Penalties	101	93	104	100	104	102	89	104	83	106	102	112	108	104
Yds. Penalized	776	690	787	870	949	838	740	886	763	935	826	960	877	944
Fumbles	28	38	32	31	36	20	42	30	34	35	28	31	38	43
Lost	14	17	18	20	23	13	21	15	17	15	19	16	18	27
Out of Bounds	2	6	2	1	2	1	4	1	1	0	0	2	3	3
Own Recovered for TD	0	1	0	1	0	1	0	1	1	0	0	0	0	0
Opponent Recovered	14	18	12	26	18	21	24	10	16	17	20	22	22	23
Opponent Recovered for TD	0	0	0	1	1	0	0	0	2	2	2	1	0	0
Total Points scored	533	276	304	375	289	355	290	275	370	287	343	297	390	388
Total TDs	68	30	38	45	35	39	34	33	42	36	42	35	48	46
TDs Rushing	30	7	12	14	17	16	17	10	20	19	15	10	25	20
TDs Passing	37	21	24	28	13	22	16	23	18	15	24	22	22	25
TDs on Ret. and Recovery	1	2	2	3	5	1	1	0	4	2	3	3	1	1
Extra Points	65	30	38	40	34	38	29	33	39	33	38	33	45	41
Safeties	0	0	1	1	0	1	0	1	2	1	1	0	0	0
Field Goals Made	20	22	12	21	15	27	19	14	25	12	17	18	19	23
Field Goals Attempted	31	26	21	34	27	42	27	21	39	20	30	33	26	29
Pct. Successful	64.5	84.6	57.1	61.8	55.6	64.3	70.4	66.7	64.1	60.0	56.7	54.5	73.1	79.3

	Atl.	Chi.	Dall.	Det.	G.B.	L.A.	Minn.	N.O.	N.Y.G.	Phil.	St.L.	S.F.	T.B.	Wash.
First Downs	318	278	321	340	308	305	343	280	253	332	300	317	269	334
Rushing	116	126	137	167	104	142	91	126	92	157	135	110	95	136
Passing	176	126	158	150	174	134	217	124	140	150	141	183	159	173
Penalty	26	26	26	23	30	29	35	30	21	25	24	24	15	25
Rushes	495	608	630	596	478	559	391	546	481	559	519	560	458	532
Net Yards Gained	1965	2171	2711	2795	1670	2236	1512	2286	1685	2509	2213	1941	1731	2157
Avg. Gain	4.0	3.6	4.3	4.7	3.5	4.0	3.9	4.2	3.5	4.5	4.3	3.5	3.8	4.1
Avg. Yds. per Game	122.8	135.7	169.4	174.7	104.4	139.8	94.5	142.9	105.3	156.8	138.3	121.3	108.2	134.8
Passes Attempted	563	489	439	436	514	477	709	441	506	476	477	517	473	525
Completed	311	222	241	228	286	235	382	238	251	258	253	328	239	307
Pct. Completed	55.2	45.4	54.9	52.3	55.6	49.3	53.9	54.0	49.6	54.2	53.0	63.4	50.5	58.5
Total Yds. Gained	3986	2728	3414	3475	3576	3008	4567	2778	3009	3249	3269	3766	3565	3743
Passer Tackled	37	35	31	44	52	50	29	41	47	22	48	39	19	30
Yds. Lost	287	266	245	337	387	451	234	359	368	205	405	223	136	277
Net Yds. Gained	3699	2462	3169	3138	3189	2557	4333	2419	2641	3044	2864	3543	3429	3466
Avg. Yds. per Game	231.2	153.9	198.1	196.1	199.3	159.8	270.8	151.2	165.1	190.3	179.0	221.4	214.3	216.6
Net Yds. per Pass Play	6.17	4.70	6.74	6.54	5.63	4.85	5.87	5.02	4.78	6.11	5.46	6.49	6.97	6.25
Yds. Gained per Completions	12.82	12.29	14.17	15.24	12.50	12.80	11.96	11.67	11.99	12.59	12.92	11.48	14.92	12.19
Combined Net Yds. Gained	5664	4633	5880	5933	4859	4793	5845	4705	4326	5553	5077	5484	5160	5623
Pct. Total Yds., Rushing	34.69	46.86	46.11	47.11	34.37	46.65	25.87	48.59	38.95	45.18	43.59	35.39	33.55	38.36
Pct. Total Yds., Passing	65.31	53.14	53.89	52.89	65.63	53.35	74.13	51.41	61.05	54.82	56.41	64.61	66.45	61.64
Avg. Yds. per Game	354.0	289.6	367.5	370.8	303.7	299.6	365.3	294.1	270.4	347.1	317.3	342.8	322.5	351.4
Ball Control Plays	1095	1132	1100	1076	1044	1086	1129	1028	1034	1057	1044	1106	950	1087
Avg. Yds. per Play	5.2	4.1	5.3	5.5	4.7	4.4	5.2	4.6	4.2	5.3	4.9	5.0	5.4	5.2
Avg. Time of Possession	29:34	31:55	32:08	31:35	29:23	29:26	28:54	31:19	28:09	31:42	30:39	31:38	27:33	31:23
Third Down Efficiency	41.0	35.5	40.6	39.3	34.3	34.5	36.7	40.4	34.3	44.4	38.5	44.0	32.3	43.3
Had Intercepted	24	23	15	23	24	32	29	27	20	22	24	13	14	22
Yds. Opp. Returned	301	385	124	274	475	361	384	479	252	357	312	297	179	391
Ret. by Opp. for TD	0	2	1	1	3	1	3	1	2	2	0	2	0	1

NFC OFFENSE—Continued

	Atl.	Chi.	Dall.	Det.	G.B.	L.A.	Minn.	N.O.	N.Y.G.	Phil.	St.L.	S.F.	T.B.	Wash.
Punts	88	114	81	64	84	89	88	66	97	64	69	93	82	73
Yds. Punted	3543	4531	3284	2784	3330	3735	3646	2672	4198	2580	2883	3858	3375	2923
Avg. Yds. per Punt	40.3	39.7	40.5	43.5	39.6	42.0	41.4	40.5	43.3	40.3	41.8	41.5	41.2	40.0
Punt Returns	50	45	45	52	40	49	39	41	64	58	43	48	38	49
Yds. Returned	383	518	235	450	306	676	303	426	502	422	453	344	244	507
Avg. Yds. per Return	7.7	11.5	5.2	8.7	7.7	13.8	7.8	10.4	7.8	7.3	10.5	7.2	6.4	10.3
Returned for TD	0	1	0	1	1	3	0	0	0	0	1	0	0	2
Kickoff Returns	62	64	53	61	58	68	67	70	57	43	75	45	46	67
Yds. Returned	1419	1214	981	1164	1066	1244	1328	1523	1120	832	1625	909	912	1673
Avg. Yds. per Return	22.9	19.0	18.5	19.1	18.4	18.3	19.8	21.8	19.6	19.3	21.7	20.2	19.8	25.0
Returned for TD	0	0	0	0	0	0	1	0	0	0	0	1	0	0
Penalties	90	121	103	111	84	117	109	109	108	113	106	92	89	98
Yds. Penalized	940	996	839	990	687	916	865	899	897	855	877	752	779	940
Fumbles	31	37	45	41	31	34	39	40	38	33	33	26	27	32
Lost	17	17	20	20	17	15	21	20	16	17	20	12	14	19
Out of Bounds	1	1	3	2	0	3	3	2	1	2	3	3	3	2
Own Rec. for TD	1	0	0	0	0	0	0	0	0	0	0	0	0	0
Opp. Rec. by	21	22	16	15	24	16	19	17	17	21	17	21	14	15
Opp. Rec. for TD	3	0	1	0	0	1	1	0	3	2	0	1	1	0
Total Points Scored	426	253	367	397	324	303	325	207	295	368	315	357	315	347
Total TDs	52	31	40	46	37	36	37	24	32	44	37	43	38	42
TDs Rushing	15	13	15	26	11	17	8	16	11	17	20	17	13	19
TDs Passing	30	14	24	18	24	15	27	8	16	25	15	20	20	19
TDs on Returns and Recoveries	7	4	1	2	2	4	2	0	5	2	2	6	5	4
Extra Points	51	29	40	46	36	36	34	24	31	42	36	42	36	38
Safeties	0	1	3	0	0	0	3	0	0	1	0	0	0	0
Field Goals Made	21	12	27	25	22	17	21	13	24	20	19	19	17	19
Field Goals Attempted	33	23	35	35	24	26	25	25	38	31	32	29	28	30
Pct. Successful	63.6	52.2	77.1	71.4	91.7	65.4	84.0	52.0	63.2	64.5	59.4	65.5	60.7	63.3

NATIONAL FOOTBALL CONFERENCE

DEFENSE

	Atl.	Chi.	Dall.	Det.	G.B.	L.A.	Minn.	N.O.	N.Y.G.	Phil.	St.L.	S.F.	T.B.	Wash.
First Downs	303	290	286	279	326	285	299	303	291	266	328	280	320	310
Rushing	94	120	106	93	140	125	117	127	106	102	134	113	123	133
Passing	172	144	162	158	168	128	163	161	156	137	171	144	174	152
Penalty	37	26	18	28	18	32	19	15	29	27	23	23	23	25
Rushes	459	521	468	469	546	585	540	504	553	476	509	464	551	532
Net Yards Gained	1666	2146	2049	1623	2098	2397	2045	1916	1891	1751	2428	1918	2172	2161
Avg. Gain	3.6	4.1	4.4	3.5	3.8	4.1	3.8	3.8	3.4	3.7	4.8	4.1	3.9	4.1
Avg. Yards per Game	104.1	134.1	128.1	101.4	131.1	149.8	127.8	119.8	118.2	109.4	151.8	119.9	135.8	135.1
Passes Attempted	565	525	511	475	505	439	481	471	544	507	495	514	541	452
Completed	322	233	236	261	284	204	265	287	294	248	282	273	317	214
Pct. Completed	57.0	44.4	46.2	54.9	56.2	46.5	55.1	60.9	54.0	48.9	57.0	53.1	58.6	47.3
Total Yards Gained	3927	3527	3717	3596	3353	3057	3599	3578	3318	3050	3547	3135	3297	3310
Passer Tackled	29	31	42	47	36	43	33	27	35	40	32	36	23	32
Yards Lost	239	279	347	373	266	330	271	241	384	354	252	290	157	265
Net Yards Gained	3688	3248	3370	3223	3087	2727	3328	3337	2934	2696	3295	2845	3140	3045
Avg. Yards per Game	230.5	203.0	210.6	201.4	192.9	170.4	208.0	208.6	183.4	168.5	205.9	177.8	196.3	190.3
Net Yards per Pass Play	6.21	5.84	6.09	6.17	5.71	5.66	6.47	6.70	4.99	4.93	6.25	5.17	5.57	6.29
Yards Gained per Completion	12.20	15.14	15.75	13.78	11.81	14.99	13.58	12.47	11.29	12.30	12.58	11.48	10.40	15.47
Combined Net Yards Gained	5354	5394	5419	4846	5185	5124	5373	5253	4825	4447	5723	4763	5312	5206
Pct. Total Yards, Rushing	31.12	39.78	37.81	33.49	40.46	46.78	38.06	36.47	39.19	39.37	42.43	40.27	40.89	41.51
Pct. Total Yards, Passing	68.88	60.22	62.19	66.51	59.54	53.22	61.94	63.53	60.81	60.63	57.57	59.73	59.11	58.49
Avg. Yards per Game	334.6	337.1	338.7	302.9	324.1	320.3	335.8	328.3	301.6	277.9	357.7	297.7	332.0	325.4
Ball Control Plays	1053	1077	1021	991	1087	1067	1054	1002	1141	1023	1036	1014	1115	1016
Avg. Yards per Play	5.1	5.0	5.3	4.9	4.8	4.8	5.1	5.2	4.2	4.3	5.5	4.7	4.8	5.1
Third Down Efficiency	33.5	29.6	35.5	36.7	44.8	33.3	38.1	45.0	37.7	42.8	39.8	38.8	39.1	41.3
Intercepted by	25	18	37	24	30	17	16	17	17	26	21	27	32	24
Yards Returned by	494	345	482	286	495	237	120	214	222	266	281	448	648	249
Returned for TD	3	3	0	1	1	0	0	0	1	0	1	4	4	2

NFC DEFENSE—Continued

	Atl.	Chi.	Dall.	Det.	G.B.	L.A.	Minn.	N.O.	N.Y.G.	Phil.	St.L.	S.F.	T.B.	Wash.
Punts	96	98	80	81	69	94	84	69	105	76	69	83	73	80
Yards Punted	4050	3985	3293	3471	2738	3856	3415	3045	4160	3096	2852	3433	3006	3338
Avg. Yards per Punt	42.2	40.7	41.2	42.9	39.7	41.0	40.7	44.1	39.6	40.7	41.3	41.4	41.2	41.7
Punt Returns	59	66	38	39	50	52	46	36	61	34	37	57	52	50
Yards Returned	577	594	231	299	511	481	399	282	561	246	276	664	668	388
Avg. Yards per Return	9.8	9.0	6.1	7.7	10.2	9.3	8.7	7.8	9.2	7.2	7.5	11.6	12.8	7.8
Returned for TD	2	1	0	0	0	0	1	0	1	0	0	1	1	1
Kickoff Returns	67	44	71	70	70	60	62	50	50	60	55	67	64	69
Yards Returned	1286	937	1508	1257	1183	1443	1260	966	959	1334	1163	1389	1332	1275
Avg. Yards per Return	19.2	21.3	21.2	18.0	16.9	24.1	20.3	19.3	19.2	22.2	21.1	20.7	20.8	18.5
Returned for TD	0	0	0	0	0	2	0	0	0	1	0	0	0	0
Penalties	97	119	104	95	108	118	115	118	111	91	98	108	79	108
Yards Penalized	804	961	837	872	907	1018	991	1089	876	813	845	866	650	921
Fumbles	43	33	43	29	42	37	27	31	38	38	35	36	32	32
Lost	21	22	16	15	24	16	19	17	17	21	17	21	14	15
Out of Bounds	4	3	3	2	2	2	1	5	2	3	3	2	2	1
Own Recovered for TD	0	0	0	0	0	0	0	0	0	0	0	0	0	0
Opponent Recovered	17	17	20	20	17	15	21	20	16	17	20	12	14	19
Opponent Recovered for TD	0	0	0	1	3	0	1	2	0	1	1	1	0	3
Total Points Scored	355	324	277	322	361	351	369	378	257	221	408	250	268	349
Total TDs	43	39	34	38	45	39	46	46	27	26	50	30	27	43
TDs Rushing	10	13	16	14	21	19	15	17	10	11	20	10	16	17
TDs Passing	30	23	17	22	18	17	26	26	14	12	29	16	10	21
TDs on Returns and Recoveries	3	3	1	2	6	3	5	3	3	3	1	4	1	5
Extra Points	41	37	31	37	43	37	42	45	27	23	48	29	27	38
Safeties	1	1	0	0	0	1	0	0	1	0	0	1	2	1
Field Goals Made	18	17	14	19	16	26	17	19	22	14	20	13	25	17
Field Goals Attempted	29	29	29	22	24	33	27	25	33	28	26	23	33	24
Pct. Successful	62.1	58.6	48.3	86.4	66.7	78.8	63.0	76.0	66.7	50.0	76.9	56.5	75.8	70.8

1981 AFC, NFC, AND NFL SUMMARY

	AFC Offense Total	AFC Offense Average	AFC Defense Total	AFC Defense Average	NFC Offense Total	NFC Offense Average	NFC Defense Total	NFC Defense Average	NFL Total	NFL Average
First Downs	4394	313.9	4526	323.3	4298	307.0	4166	297.6	8692	310.4
Rushing	1675	119.6	1776	126.9	1734	123.9	1633	116.6	3409	121.8
Passing	2369	169.2	2384	170.3	2205	157.5	2190	156.4	4574	163.4
Penalty	350	25.0	366	26.1	359	25.6	343	24.5	709	25.3
Rushes	7096	506.9	7331	523.6	7412	529.4	7177	512.6	14,508	518.1
Net Yards Gained	28,722	2051.6	30,043	2145.9	29,582	2113.0	28,261	2018.6	58,304	2082.3
Avg. Gain	......	4.0	......	4.1	......	4.0	......	3.9	......	4.0
Avg. Yards per Game	......	128.2	......	134.1	......	132.1	......	126.2	......	130.1
Passes Attempted	7138	509.9	7155	511.1	7042	503.0	7025	501.8	14,180	506.4
Completed	3966	283.3	4025	287.5	3779	269.9	3720	265.7	7745	276.6
Pct. Completed	......	55.6	......	56.3	......	53.7	......	53.0	......	54.6
Total Yards Gained	51,588	3684.9	51,710	3693.6	48,133	3438.1	48,011	3429.4	99,721	3561.5
Passer Tackled	507	36.2	526	37.6	514	36.7	495	35.4	1021	36.5
Yards Lost	3988	284.9	4120	294.3	4180	298.6	4048	289.1	8168	291.7
Net Yards Gained	47,600	3400.0	47,590	3399.3	43,953	3139.5	43,963	3140.2	91,553	3269.8
Avg. Yards per Game	......	212.5	......	212.5	......	196.2	......	196.3	......	204.4
Net Yards per Pass Play	......	6.23	......	6.20	......	5.82	......	5.85	......	6.02
Yards Gained per Completion	......	13.01	......	12.85	......	12.74	......	12.91	......	12.88
Combined Net Yards Gained	76,322	5451.6	77,633	5545.2	73,535	5252.5	72,224	5158.9	149,857	5352.0
Pct. Total Yards Rushing	......	37.63	......	38.70	......	40.23	......	39.13	......	38.91
Pct. Total Yards Passing	......	62.37	......	61.30	......	59.77	......	60.87	......	61.09
Avg. Yards per Game	......	340.7	......	346.6	......	328.3	......	322.4	......	334.5
Ball Control Plays	14,741	1052.9	15,012	1072.3	14,968	1069.1	14,697	1049.8	29,709	1061.0
Avg. Yards per Play	......	5.2	......	5.2	......	4.9	......	4.9	......	5.0
Third Down Efficiency	......	39.7	......	40.0	......	38.6	......	38.2	......	39.1
Interceptions	278	19.9	297	21.2	331	23.6	312	22.3	609	21.8
Yards Returned	4098	292.7	4314	308.1	4787	341.9	4571	326.5	8885	317.3
Returned for TD	10	0.7	11	0.8	20	1.4	19	1.4	30	1.1

1981 AFC, NFC AND NFL SUMMARY—Continued

	AFC Offense Total	AFC Offense Average	AFC Defense Total	AFC Defense Average	NFC Offense Total	NFC Offense Average	NFC Defense Total	NFC Defense Average	NFL Total	NFL Average
Punts	1088	.....	1083	.....	1152	.....	1157	.....	2240	80.0
Yards Punted	44,412	3172.3	44,016	3144.0	47,342	3381.6	47,738	3409.9	91,754	3276.9
Avg. Yards per Punt	.....	40.8	.....	40.6	.....	41.1	.....	41.3	.....	41.0
Punt Returns	559	.....	543	.....	661	.....	677	.....	1220	43.6
Yards Returned	4673	333.8	4265	304.6	5769	412.1	6177	441.2	10,442	372.9
Avg. Yards per Return	.....	8.4	.....	7.9	.....	8.7	.....	9.1	.....	8.6
Returned for TD	2	0.1	3	0.2	9	0.6	8	0.6	11	0.4
Kickoff Returns	873	.....	850	.....	836	.....	859	.....	1709	61.0
Yards Returned	17,671	1262.2	17,389	1242.1	17,010	1215.0	17,292	1235.1	34,681	1238.6
Avg. Yards per Return	.....	20.2	.....	20.5	.....	20.3	.....	20.1	.....	20.3
Penalties	1431	.....	1412	.....	1450	.....	1469	.....	2881	102.9
Yards Penalized	12,059	861.4	11,841	845.8	12,232	873.7	12,450	889.3	24,291	867.5
Fumbles	475	33.9	466	33.3	487	34.8	496	35.4	962	34.4
Lost	263	18.8	253	18.1	245	17.5	255	18.2	508	18.1
Out of Bounds	34	2.4	28	2.0	29	2.1	35	2.5	63	2.3
Own Recovered for TD	2	0.1	3	0.2	1	0.1	0	0.0	3	0.1
Opp. Recovered	253	18.1	263	18.8	255	18.2	245	17.5	508	18.1
Opp. Recovered for TD	9	0.6	9	0.6	13	0.9	13	0.9	22	0.8
Total Points Scored	4663	333.1	4772	340.9	4599	328.5	4490	320.7	9262	330.8
Total TDs	565	40.4	571	40.8	539	38.5	533	38.1	1104	39.4
TDs Rushing	223	15.9	232	16.6	218	15.6	209	14.9	441	15.8
TDs Passing	316	22.6	310	22.1	275	19.6	281	20.1	591	21.1
TDs on Returns and Recoveries	26	1.9	29	2.1	46	3.3	43	3.1	72	2.6
Extra Points	520	37.1	536	38.3	521	37.2	505	36.1	1041	37.2
Safeties	9	0.6	9	0.6	8	0.6	8	0.6	17	0.6
Field Goals Made	245	17.5	264	18.9	276	19.7	257	18.4	521	18.6
Field Goals Attempted	377	26.9	406	29.0	414	29.6	385	27.5	791	28.3
Pct. Successful	.....	65.0	.....	65.0	.....	66.7	.....	66.8	.....	65.9

CLUB LEADERS

	Offense	Defense
First Downs	San Diego 379	Philadelphia 266
Rushing	Detroit 167	Detroit 93
Passing	San Diego 224	Los Angeles 128
Penalty	Cleveland 37	Miami 12
Rushes	Dallas 630	Atlanta 459
Net Yards Gained	Detroit 2795	Detroit 1623
Avg. Gain	Detroit 4.7	New York Giants 3.4
Passes Attempted	Minnesota 709	Los Angeles & New Eng. 439
Completed	Minnesota 382	Los Angeles 204
Pct. Completed	San Francisco 63.4	Chicago 44.4
Total Yards Gained	San Diego 4873	Philadelphia 3050
Passer Tackled	Buffalo 16	New York Jets 66
Yards Lost	San Diego 134	New York Jets 518
Net Yards Gained	San Diego 4739	Philadelphia 2696
Net Yards per Pass Play	San Diego 7.31	Philadelphia 4.93
Yards Gained per Completion	New England 15.37	Tampa Bay 10.40
Combined Net Yards Gained	San Diego 6744	Philadelphia 4447
Pct. Total Yards, Rushing	Kansas City 49.93	San Diego 29.74
Pct. Total Yards, Passing	Minnesota 74.13	New England 49.37
Ball Control Plays	Cleveland 1138	Detroit 991
Avg. Yards per Play	San Diego 6.0	New York Giants 4.2
Avg. Time of Possession	Denver 32:27	
Third Down Efficiency	San Diego 48.9	Chicago 29.6
Interceptions		Dallas 37
Yards Returned		Tampa Bay 648
Returned for TD		San Fran. & Tampa Bay 4
Punts	Chicago 114	
Yards Punted	Chicago 4531	
Avg. Yards per Punt	Cincinnati 44.8	
Punt Returns	New York Giants 64	Cleveland 30
Yards Returned	Los Angeles 676	New York Jets 149
Avg. Yards per Return	Los Angeles 13.8	Seattle 4.6
Returned for TD	Los Angeles 3	
Kickoff Returns	Baltimore 84	Baltimore 43
Yards Returned	Houston 1722	Baltimore 864
Avg. Yards per Return	Washington 25.0	Green Bay 16.9
Returned for TD	Houston 2	
Total Points Scored	San Diego 478	Philadelphia 221
Total TDs	San Diego 61	Philadelphia 26
TDs Rushing	Detroit & San Diego 26	Buffalo 7
TDs Passing	San Diego 34	Tampa Bay 10
TDs on Returns and Recoveries	Atlanta 7	Miami 0
Extra Points	San Diego 55	Philadelphia 23
Safeties	Three with 3	
Field Goals Made	Dallas 27	Cincinnati & N.Y. Jets 12
Field Goals Attempted	New York Giants 38	New York Jets 20
Pct. Successful	Green Bay 91.7	Dallas 48.3

COACHES WITH 100 CAREER VICTORIES

		REGULAR SEASON				POST-SEASON			CAREER			
	Yrs.	Won	Lost	Tied	Pct.	Won	Lost	Pct.	Won	Lost	Tied	Pct.
George Halas	40	320	148	30	.673	6	3	.667	326	151	30	.673
Curley Lambeau	33	231	133	23	.627	3	2	.600	234	135	43	.626
Tom Landry	22	196	112	6	.634	19	15	.559	215	127	6	.626
Don Shula	19	194	74	6	.719	12	9	.571	206	83	6	.708
Paul Brown	21	166	100	6	.621	4	9	.308	170	109	6	.607
Steve Owen	23	151	100	17	.595	3	8	.273	154	108	17	.582
Bud Grant	15	138	75	5	.644	9	12	.429	147	87	5	.626
Hank Stram	17	131	97	10	.571	5	3	.625	136	100	10	.573
Weeb Ewbank	20	130	129	7	.502	4	1	.800	134	130	7	.507
Chuck Noll	13	117	72	1	.618	14	4	.778	131	76	1	.632
Sid Gillman	18	122	99	7	.550	1	5	.167	123	104	7	.541
George Allen	12	116	47	5	.705	4	7	.364	120	54	5	.684
John Madden	10	103	32	7	.750	9	7	.563	112	39	7	.731
Buddy Parker	15	104	75	9	.577	3	2	.600	107	77	9	.578
Vince Lombardi	10	96	34	6	.728	8	2	.800	104	36	6	.733

ACTIVE COACHES CAREER RECORDS

(Ranked according to career percentage)

		REGULAR SEASON				POST-SEASON			CAREER			
	Yrs.	Won	Lost	Tied	Pct.	Won	Lost	Pct.	Won	Lost	Tied	Pct.
Don Shula	19	194	74	6	.719	12	9	.571	206	83	6	.708
Chuck Noll	13	117	72	1	.618	14	4	.778	131	76	1	.632
Chuck Knox	9	87	46	1	.653	4	7	.364	91	53	1	.631
Tom Landry	22	196	112	6	.634	19	15	.559	215	127	6	.626
Bud Grant	15	138	75	5	.644	9	12	.429	147	87	5	.626
CFL Total	10	102	56	2	.644	20	10	.667	122	66	2	.647
Dan Reeves	1	10	6	0	.625	0	0	.000	10	6	0	.625
Don Coryell	9	83	46	1	.642	2	5	.286	85	51	1	.624
Tom Flores	3	27	21	0	.563	4	0	1.000	31	21	0	.596
Bum Phillips	7	59	47	0	.557	4	3	.571	63	50	0	.558
Ray Malavasi	5	42	34	0	.553	3	3	.500	45	37	0	.549
Dick Vermeil	6	51	41	0	.554	3	4	.429	54	45	0	.545
Leeman Bennett	5	41	37	0	.526	1	2	.333	42	39	0	.519
Sam Rutigliano	4	33	31	0	.516	0	1	.000	33	32	0	.508
Forrest Gregg	5	36	37	0	.493	2	1	.667	38	38	0	.500
CFL Total	1	5	11	0	.313	0	0	.000	5	11	0	.313
Joe Gibbs	1	8	8	0	.500	0	0	.000	8	8	0	.500
Bill Walsh	3	21	27	0	.438	3	0	1.000	24	27	0	.471
Marv Levy	4	28	36	0	.438	0	0	.000	28	36	0	.438
CFL Total	5	43	31	4	.577	7	3	.700	50	34	4	.591
Ed Biles	1	7	9	0	.438	0	0	.000	7	9	0	.438
Monte Clark	5	34	44	0	.436	0	0	.000	34	44	0	.436
Walt Michaels	5	33	44	1	.429	0	1	.000	33	45	1	.424
Ray Perkins	3	19	29	0	.396	1	1	.500	20	30	0	.400
Jack Patera	6	35	57	0	.380	0	0	.000	35	57	0	.380
Bart Starr	7	39	65	1	.376	0	0	.000	39	65	1	.376
Jim Hanifan	2	12	20	0	.375	0	0	.000	12	20	0	.375
John McKay	6	31	60	1	.342	1	2	.333	32	62	1	.342
Mike Ditka	0	0	0	0	.000	0	0	.000	0	0	0	.000
Frank Kush	0	0	0	0	.000	0	0	.000	0	0	0	.000
CFL Total	1	11	4	1	.719	0	1	.000	11	5	1	.676
Ron Meyer	0	0	0	0	.000	0	0	.000	0	0	0	.000

LEADING AFC ACTIVE PASSERS

(Based on 1,000 or more attempts)

	Yrs.	Att.	Comp.	Pct.	Yds.	Avg. Gain	TD	Pct. TD	Int.	Pct. Int.	Pts.
Ken Anderson, Cin.	11	3539	2036	57.5	25562	7.22	160	4.5	124	3.5	80.5
Dan Fouts, S.D.	9	3203	1849	57.7	24256	7.57	145	4.5	142	4.4	78.4
Ken Stabler, Hous.	12	3223	1944	60.3	24268	7.53	177	5.5	189	5.9	77.5
Brian Sipe, Cleve.	8	2758	1552	56.3	19083	6.92	124	4.5	118	4.3	74.9
Craig Morton, Den.	17	3760	2035	54.1	27715	7.37	183	4.9	184	4.9	73.8
Greg Landry, Balt.	14	2280	1265	55.5	15853	6.95	97	4.3	100	4.4	73.3
Joe Ferguson, Buff.	9	3050	1572	51.5	21007	6.89	136	4.5	132	4.3	70.8
Terry Bradshaw, Pitt.	12	3653	1893	51.8	26144	7.16	193	5.3	199	5.4	70.3
Jim Zorn, Sea.	6	2523	1357	53.8	17336	6.87	93	3.7	113	4.5	69.1
James Harris, S.D.	12	1149	607	52.8	8136	7.08	45	3.9	59	5.1	67.3
Steve Grogan, N.E.	7	2187	1123	51.3	16485	7.54	114	5.2	140	6.4	66.9
Richard Todd, N.Y.	6	1844	972	52.7	12802	6.94	78	4.2	104	5.6	65.6
Steve DeBerg, Den.	4	1309	734	56.1	8017	6.12	43	3.3	66	5.0	64.5
Jim Plunkett, Oak.	11	2508	1249	49.8	16650	6.64	107	4.3	143	5.7	61.8

LEADING NFC ACTIVE PASSERS

(Based on 1,000 or more attempts)

	Yrs.	Att.	Comp.	Pct.	Yds.	Avg. Gain	TD	Pct. TD	Int.	Pct. Int.	Pts.
Bert Jones, L.A.	9	2464	1382	56.1	17663	7.17	122	5.0	97	3.9	79.1
Ron Jaworski, Phila.	8	2154	1123	52.1	14682	6.82	103	4.8	89	4.1	72.8
Joe Theismann, Wash.	8	2113	1157	54.8	14294	6.76	86	4.1	89	4.2	72.3
Tommy Kramer, Minn.	5	1754	971	55.4	11366	6.48	73	4.2	76	4.3	71.3
Steve Bartkowski, Atl.	7	2256	1181	52.3	15502	6.87	108	4.8	114	5.1	69.1
Archie Manning, N.O.	11	3328	1848	55.5	21731	6.53	115	3.5	154	4.6	68.1
Jim Hart, St.L.	16	4945	2521	51.0	33848	6.84	204	4.1	239	4.8	66.8
Doug Williams, T.B.	4	1583	731	46.2	10577	6.68	64	4.0	62	3.9	65.5
Lynn Dickey, G.B.	9	1708	925	54.2	11673	6.83	57	3.3	100	5.9	62.1
Bob Avellini, Chi.	7	1037	522	50.3	6739	6.50	33	3.2	66	6.4	55.1

LEADING AFC ACTIVE SCORERS

	Yrs.	TDs.	FGs.	XPs.	Pts.
Toni Fritsch, Houston	10	0	153	279	738
John Smith, New England	8	0	120	290	650
Efren Herrera, Seattle	7	0	108	245	569
Nick Mike-Mayer, Buffalo	9	0	114	222	564
Pat Leahy, New York	8	0	114	206	548
Franco Harris, Pittsburgh	10	91	0	0	546
Chris Bahr, Oakland	6	0	95	198	483
Rolf Benirschke, San Diego	5	0	82	171	417
Cliff Branch, Oakland	10	58	0	0	348
Don McCauley, Baltimore	11	58	0	0	348
Earl Campbell, Houston	4	55	0	0	330
Lynn Swann, Pittsburgh	8	53	0	0	318
Chuck Muncie, San Diego	6	52	0	0	312
Ken Burrough, Houston	12	50	0	0	300
Isaac Curtis, Cincinnati	9	50	0	0	300
Sam Cunningham, New England	8	49	0	0	294
Pete Johnson, Cincinnati	5	49	0	0	294
Bob Chandler, Oakland	11	48	0	1	289
Raymond Chester, Oakland	12	48	0	0	288
Nat Moore, Miami	8	48	0	0	288
Charlie Joiner, San Diego	13	47	0	0	282
Steve Largent, Seattle	6	47	0	0	282
Uwe von Schamann, Miami	3	0	59	105	282

LEADING NFC ACTIVE SCORERS

	Yrs.	TDs.	FGs.	XPs.	Pts.
Jan Stenerud, Green Bay	15	0	304	432	1344
Mark Moseley, Washington	12	0	189	300	867
Ray Wersching, San Francisco	9	0	109	189	516
Rafael Septien, Dallas	5	0	91	217	490
Joe Danelo, New York	7	0	103	162	481
Walter Payton, Chicago	7	78	0	0	468
Harold Carmichael, Philadelphia	11	72	0	0	432
Bob Thomas, Chicago	7	0	87	169	430
John Riggins, Washington	10	67	0	0	402
Frank Corral, Los Angeles	4	0	75	154	379
Benny Ricardo, New Orleans	5	0	64	133	325
Rick Danmeier, Minnesota	4	0	62	131	317
Tony Franklin, Philadelphia	3	0	59	125	302
Tony Dorsett, Dallas	5	47	0	0	282
Wilbert Montgomery, Philadelphia	5	47	0	0	282
Neil O'Donoghue, St. Louis	5	0	56	113	282

NOTE: Harold Jackson, with 14 years, 75 touchdowns and 450 points was not with any team at press time.

LEADING AFC ACTIVE RUSHERS

	Yrs.	Att.	Yds.	TDs.		Yrs.	Att.	Yds.	TDs.
Franco Harris, Pitt.	10	2462	10339	84	Archie Griffin, Cin.	6	679	2769	6
L. McCutcheon, Buf.	10	1521	6578	26	Ronnie Coleman, Hou.	8	700	2769	16
Earl Campbell, Hou.	4	1404	6457	55	Scott Dierking, N.Y.	5	665	2658	14
Mark van Eeghen, Oak.	8	1475	5907	35	Greg Landry, Balt.	14	428	2654	20
Greg Pruitt, Oak.	9	1158	5496	25	Don McCauley, Balt.	11	770	2627	40
Sam Cunningham, N.E.	8	1376	5432	43	Clark Gaines, K.C.	5	581	2552	8
Chuck Muncie, S.D.	6	1174	5196	51	Cleo Miller, Clev.	8	577	2430	16
Mike Pruitt, Clev.	6	996	4334	28	Ted McKnight, K.C.	5	528	2344	22
Pete Johnson, Cin.	5	1036	4036	43	Tony Reed, Den.	5	581	2340	8
Don Calhoun, N.E.	8	860	3559	23	Joe Cribbs, Buf.	2	563	2282	14
Sherman Smith, Sea.	6	747	3227	28	Terry Bradshaw, Pitt.	12	435	2244	32
Ricky Bell, S.D.	5	820	3057	15	Kevin Long, N.Y.	5	574	2190	25
John Cappelletti, S.D.	7	801	2864	24	Andy Johnson, N.E.	7	491	2017	13

LEADING NFC ACTIVE RUSHERS

	Yrs.	Att.	Yds.	TDs.		Yrs.	Att.	Yds.	TDs.
Walter Payton, Chi.	7	2204	9608	71	Doug Kotar, N.Y.	7	900	3380	20
John Riggins, Wash.	10	1861	7536	55	Cullen Bryant, L.A.	9	801	3117	20
Tony Dorsett, Dal.	5	1368	6270	40	Tony Galbreath, Minn.	6	802	3063	29
W. Montgomery, Phil.	5	1121	5095	36	Roland Harper, Chi.	6	754	3037	15
Robert Newhouse, Dal.	10	1137	4671	30	Wayne Morris, St. L.	6	735	2844	31
Dexter Bussey, Det.	8	1066	4629	18	Billy Sims, Det.	2	609	2740	26
Ottis Anderson, St. L.	3	960	4333	26	Wendell Tyler, L.A.	5	583	2702	24
Wilbur Jackson, Wash.	7	967	3846	13	Rob Carpenter, N.Y.	5	623	2536	17
William Andrews, Atl.	3	793	3632	17	Ted Brown, Minn.	3	623	2526	15
Rickey Young, Minn.	7	956	3527	20	Archie Manning, N.O.	11	357	2058	18
Terry Metcalf, Wash.	6	766	3498	24	Terdell Middleton, G.B.	5	559	2044	15
Joe Washington, Wash.	5	898	3475	9	Horace King, Det.	7	528	2008	9

LEADING AFC ACTIVE RECEIVERS

	Yrs.	No.	Yds.	TDs.		Yrs.	No.	Yds.	TDs.
Charlie Joiner, S.D.	13	495	8476	47	Lynn Swann, Pitt.	8	318	5197	51
Reggie Rucker, Clev.	12	447	7065	44	Dave Casper, Hou.	8	318	4363	44
Ken Burrough, Hou.	12	421	7102	49	Jerome Barkum, N.Y.	10	275	4222	38
Cliff Branch, Oak.	10	405	7013	58	John Stallworth, Pitt.	8	272	4863	37
Riley Odoms, Den.	10	384	5611	41	Roger Carr, Balt.	8	254	4770	29
Bob Chandler, Oak.	11	370	5243	48	Sam McCullum, Sea.	8	241	3572	24
Steve Largent, Sea.	6	365	6041	46	Franco Harris, Pitt.	10	241	1757	7
Raymond Chester, Oak.	12	364	5013	48	Wes Chandler, S.D.	4	234	3658	20
Isaac Curtis, Cin.	9	340	6080	50	Duriel Harris, Miami	6	229	3919	16
Frank Lewis, Buf.	11	333	5795	35	Dave Logan, Clev.	6	202	3274	20
Don McCauley, Balt.	11	333	3026	17	Kellen Winslow, S.D.	3	202	2620	21
Nat Moore, Miami	8	331	5201	47	Rick Upchurch, Den.	7	201	3323	19
Greg Pruitt, Oak.	9	323	3022	17					

LEADING NFC ACTIVE RECEIVERS

	Yrs.	No.	Yds.	TDs.		Yrs.	No.	Yds.	TDs.
Harold Carmichael, Phil.	11	516	7923	72	Freddie Solomon, S.F.	7	256	3865	30
Ahmad Rashad, Minn.	9	472	6598	44	Billy Joe DuPree, Dal.	9	248	3382	38
Drew Pearson, Dal.	9	416	6895	40	Terry Metcalf, Wash.	6	245	2457	9
Rickey Young, Minn.	7	383	3048	15	Fred Scott, Det.	8	244	3968	18
Mel Gray, St. L.	11	347	6610	45	Wallace Francis, Atl.	9	244	3695	27
Richard Caster, Wash.	12	322	5515	45	Walter Payton, Chi.	7	243	2170	7
Sammy White, Minn.	6	306	5010	40	James Lofton, G.B.	4	242	4306	22
Tony Galbreath, Minn.	6	302	2365	6	James Jefferson, G.B.	4	238	4063	40
Charle Young, S.F.	9	299	3700	22	David Hill, Det.	6	223	2802	19
Alfred Jenkins, Atl.	7	297	5424	38	John Riggins, Wash.	10	222	1950	12
Pat Tilley, St. L.	6	284	4315	19	Henry Childs, L.A.	8	219	3369	28
Joe Washington, Wash.	5	279	2423	10	Ike Harris, N.O.	7	211	3305	16

NOTE: Harold Jackson, with 14 years, 571 receptions, 10,246 yards and 75 touchdowns and Charles Smith, with 8 years, 218 receptions, 3,349 yards and 24 touchdowns, were not active at press time.

LEADING AFC ACTIVE INTERCEPTORS

	Yrs.	No.	Yds.	TDs.		Yrs.	No.	Yds.	TDs.
Mel Blount, Pitt.	12	52	702	2	Burgess Owens, Oak.	9	26	402	3
Ken Riley, Cin.	13	52	419	2	Ted Hendricks, Oak.	13	26	332	1
Lemar Parrish, Buf.	12	46	454	4	Donnie Shell, Pitt.	8	26	265	0
Billy Thompson, Den.	13	40	784	3	Mario Clark, Buf.	6	25	438	0
Glen Edwards, S.D.	8	39	961	3	Dick Jauron, Cin.	8	25	432	2
Gary Barbaro, K.C.	6	36	723	2	Mike Reinfeldt, Hou.	6	25	356	0
Clarence Scott, Clev.	11	34	378	2	Jack Lambert, Pitt.	8	25	238	0
Ron Bolton, Clev.	10	34	327	1	Lyle Blackwood, Miami	9	24	428	2
Jack Ham, Pitt.	11	31	216	1	Mike Haynes, N.E.	6	24	367	1
Bill Simpson, Buf.	7	30	469	0	Isiah Robertson, Buf.	11	24	349	3
Lester Hayes, Oak.	5	28	486	3	Dave Brown, Sea.	7	24	262	1
Steve Foley, Den.	6	28	411	0	Monte Jackson, Oak.	7	22	289	3
Willie Buchanon, S.D.	10	28	278	2	John Harris, Sea.	4	22	278	2

LEADING NFC ACTIVE INTERCEPTORS

	Yrs.	No.	Yds.	TDs.		Yrs.	No.	Yds.	TDs.
Roger Wehrli, St. L.	13	40	309	2	James Hunter, Det.	6	25	243	1
Rolland Lawrence, Atl.	8	39	658	1	Mike Washington, T.B.	6	23	364	3
Tom Myers, N.O.	10	36	621	2	Pat Thomas, L.A.	6	23	292	1
Joe Lavender, Wash.	9	33	434	3	Randy Logan, Phil.	9	22	293	0
Stan White, Det.	10	31	407	2	Herman Edwards, Phil.	5	22	87	0
Jimmy Allen, Det.	8	31	307	0	Cedric Brown, T.B.	6	21	470	2
Rod Perry, L.A.	7	25	329	4	Gary Fencik, Chi.	6	21	270	1

NATIONAL FOOTBALL CONFERENCE
INDIVIDUAL LEADERS, 1960-81
(National Football League, 1960-69)

RUSHING

	Net Yds.	Att.	TD		Net Yds.	Att.	TD
1981—George Rogers, NO	1,674	378	13	1970—Larry Brown, Washington	1,125	237	5
1980—Walter Payton, Chicago	1,460	317	6	1969—Gale Sayers, Chicago	1,032	236	8
1979—Walter Payton, Chicago	1,610	369	14	1968—Leroy Kelly, Cleveland	1,239	248	16
1978—Walter Payton, Chicago	1,395	333	11	1967—Leroy Kelly, Cleveland	1,205	235	11
1977—Walter Payton, Chicago	1,852	339	14	1966—Gale Sayers, Chicago	1,231	229	8
1976—Walter Payton, Chicago	1,390	311	13	1965—Jim Brown, Cleveland	1,544	289	17
1975—Jim Otis, St. Louis	1,076	269	5	1964—Jim Brown, Cleveland	1,446	280	7
1974—Lawrence McCutcheon, LA	1,109	236	3	1963—Jim Brown, Cleveland	1,863	291	12
1973—John Brockington, GB	1,144	265	3	1962—Jim Taylor, Green Bay	1,474	272	19
1972—Larry Brown, Washington	1,216	285	8	1961—Jim Brown, Cleveland	1,408	305	8
1971—John Brockington, GB	1,105	216	4	1960—Jim Brown, Cleveland	1,257	215	9

PASSING

	Passes	Com.	Yds.	TD	Int.
1981—Joe Montana, San Francisco	488	311	3,565	19	12
1980—Ron Jaworski, Philadelphia	451	257	3,529	27	12
1979—Roger Staubach, Dallas	461	267	3,586	27	11
1978—Roger Staubach, Dallas	413	231	3,190	25	16
1977—Roger Staubach, Dallas	361	210	2,620	18	9
1976—James Harris, Los Angeles	158	91	1,460	8	6
1975—Fran Tarkenton, Minnesota	425	273	2,994	25	13
1974—Sonny Jurgensen, Washington	167	107	1,185	11	5
1973—Roger Staubach, Dallas	286	179	2,428	23	15
1972—Norm Snead, New York Giants	325	196	2,307	17	12
1971—Roger Staubach, Dallas	211	126	1,882	15	4
1970—John Brodie, San Francisco	378	223	2,941	24	10
1969—Sonny Jurgensen, Washington	442	274	3,102	22	15
1968—Earl Morrall, Baltimore	317	182	2,909	26	17
1967—Sonny Jurgensen, Washington	508	288	3,747	31	16
1966—Bart Starr, Green Bay	251	156	2,257	14	3
1965—Rudy Bukich, Chicago Bears	312	176	2,641	20	9
1964—Bart Starr, Green Bay	272	163	2,144	15	4
1963—Y. A. Tittle, New York	367	221	3,145	36	14
1962—Bart Starr, Green Bay	285	178	2,438	12	9
1961—Milt Plum, Cleveland	302	177	2,416	18	10
1960—Milt Plum, Cleveland	250	151	2,297	21	5

PASS RECEIVING

	No.	Yds.	TD		No.	Yds.	TD
1981—Dwight Clark, SF	85	1,105	4	1970—Dick Gordon, Chicago	71	1,026	13
1980—Earl Cooper, San Francisco	83	567	4	1969—Dan Abramowicz, NO	73	1,015	7
1979—Ahmad Rashad, Minnesota	80	1,156	9	1968—Clifton McNeil, San Fran.	71	994	7
1978—Rickey Young, Minnesota	88	704	5	1967—Charley Taylor, Wash.	70	990	9
1977—Ahmad Rashad, Minnesota	51	681	2	1966—Charley Taylor, Wash.	72	1,119	12
1976—Drew Pearson, Dallas	58	806	6	1965—Dave Parks, San Francisco	80	1,344	12
1975—Chuck Foreman, Minnesota	73	691	9	1964—Johnny Morris, Chicago	93	1,200	10
1974—Charles Young, Phila.	63	696	3	1963—Bobby Joe Conrad, St. Louis	73	967	10
1973—Harold Carmichael, Phila.	67	1,116	9	1962—Bobby Mitchell, Wash.	72	1,384	11
1972—Harold Jackson, Phila.	62	1,048	4	1961—Jim Phillips, Los Angeles	78	1,092	5
1971—Bob Tucker, NY Giants	59	791	4	1960—Raymond Berry, Baltimore	74	1,298	10

SCORING

	TD	PAT	FG	Tot.		TD	PAT	FG	Tot.
1981—Ed Murray, Detroit	0	46	25	121	1970—Fred Cox, Minnesota	0	35	30	125
Rafael Septien, Dallas	0	40	27	121	1969—Fred Cox, Minnesota	0	43	26	121
1980—Ed Murray, Detroit	0	35	27	116	1968—Leroy Kelly, Cleveland	20	0	0	120
1979—Mark Moseley, Wash.	0	39	25	114	1967—Jim Bakken, St. Louis	0	36	27	117
1978—Frank Corral, Los Angeles	0	31	29	118	1966—Bruce Gossett, LA	0	29	28	113
1977—Walter Payton, Chicago	16	0	0	96	1965—Gale Sayers, Chicago	22	0	0	132
1976—Mark Moseley, Wash.	0	31	22	97	1964—Lenny Moore, Baltimore	20	0	0	120
1975—Chuck Foreman, Minn.	22	0	0	132	1963—Don Chandler, New York	0	52	18	106
1974—Chester Marcol, GB	0	19	25	94	1962—Jim Taylor, Green Bay	19	0	0	114
1973—David Ray, Los Angeles	0	40	30	130	1961—Paul Hornung, GB	10	41	15	146
1972—Chester Marcol, GB	0	29	33	128	1960—Paul Hornung, GB	15	41	15	176
1971—Curt Knight, Washington	0	27	29	114					

FIELD GOALS

1981—Rafael Septien, Dallas 27	1970—Fred Cox, Minnesota..................................30
1980—Ed Murray, Detroit............................27	1969—Fred Cox, Minnesota...............................26
1979—Mark Moseley, Washington..............25	1968—Mac Percival, Chicago.........................25
1978—Frank Corral, Los Angeles 29	1967—Jim Bakken, St. Louis............................27
1977—Mark Moseley, Washington 21	1966—Bruce Gossett, Los Angeles 28
1976—Mark Moseley, Washington 22	1965—Fred Cox, Minnesota...........................23
1975—Toni Fritsch, Dallas 22	1964—Jim Bakken, St. Louis...........................25
1974—Chester Marcol, Green Bay.............25	1963—Jim Martin, Baltimore 24
1973—David Ray, Los Angeles 30	1962—Lou Michaels, Pittsburgh...................26
1972—Chester Marcol, Green Bay..............33	1961—Steve Myhra, Baltimore.......................21
1971—Curt Knight, Washington..................29	1960—Tommy Davis, San Francisco.............19

PASS INTERCEPTIONS

	No.	Yds.		No.	Yds.
1981—Everson Walls, Dallas	11	133	1969—Mel Renfro, Dallas.......................	10	118
1980—Nolan Cromwell, Los Angeles	8	140	1968—Willie Williams, New York..........	10	103
1979—Lemar Parrish, Washington........	9	65	1967—Lem Barney, Detroit	10	232
1978—Ken Stone, St. Louis	9	139	Dave Whitsell, New Orleans.......	10	178
Willie Buchanon, Green Bay	9	93	1966—Larry Wilson, St. Louis	10	180
1977—Rolland Lawrence, Atlanta..........	7	138	1965—Bobby Boyd, Baltimore................	9	78
1976—Monte Jackson, Los Angeles	10	173	1964—Paul Krause, Washington	12	140
1975—Paul Krause, Minnesota	10	201	1963—Dick Lynch, New York Giants	9	251
1974—Ray Brown, Atlanta	8	164	Rosie Taylor, Chicago	9	172
1973—Bob Bryant, Minnesota	7	105	1962—Willie Wood, Green Bay..............	9	132
1972—Bill Bradley, Philadelphia	9	73	1961—Dick Lynch, New York Giants	9	60
1971—Bill Bradley, Philadelphia	11	248	1960—Dave Baker, San Francisco.........	10	96
1970—Dick Le Beau, Detroit...................	9	96	Jerry Norton, St. Louis.................	10	96

PUNTING

	No.	Avg.		No.	Avg.
1981—Tom Skladany, Detroit.................	64	43.5	1970—Julian Fagan, New Orleans	77	42.5
1980—Dave Jennings, NY Giants	94	44.8	1969—David Lee, Baltimore	50	45.3
1979—Dave Jennings, New York	104	42.7	1968—Billy Lothridge, Atlanta..............	75	44.3
1978—Tom Skladany, Detroit.................	86	42.5	1967—Billy Lothridge, Atlanta...............	87	43.7
1977—Tom Blanchard, New Orleans	82	42.4	1966—David Lee, Baltimore	49	45.6
1976—John James, Atlanta.....................	101	42.1	1965—Gary Collins, Cleveland	65	46.7
1975—Herman Weaver, Detroit..............	80	42.0	1964—Bobby Walden, Minnesota...........	72	46.4
1974—Tom Blanchard, New Orleans	88	42.1	1963—Yale Lary, Detroit	35	48.9
1973—Tom Wittum, San Francisco	79	43.7	1962—Tommy Davis, San Francisco	48	45.8
1972—Dave Chapple, Los Angeles	53	44.2	1961—Yale Lary, Detroit	52	48.4
1971—Tom McNeill, Philadelphia	73	42.0	1960—Jerry Norton, St. Louis.................	39	45.6

PUNT RETURNS

	No.	Yds.	Avg.		No.	Yds.	Avg.
1981—LeRoy Irvin, Los Angeles.......	46	615	13.4	1970—Bruce Taylor, San Francisco.	43	516	12.0
1980—Kenny Johnson, Atlanta.........	23	281	12.2	1969—Alvin Haymond, Los Angeles.	33	435	13.2
1979—John Sciarra, Philadelphia....	16	182	11.4	1968—Bob Hayes, Dallas..................	15	312	20.8
1978—Jackie Wallace, Los Angeles .	52	618	11.9	1967—Ben Davis, Cleveland	18	229	12.7
1977—Larry Marshall, Philadelphia	46	489	10.6	1966—Johnny Roland, St. Louis........	20	221	11.1
1976—Eddie Brown, Washington......	48	646	13.5	1965—Leroy Kelly, Cleveland	17	265	15.6
1975—Terry Metcalf, St. Louis..........	23	285	12.4	1964—Tommy Watkins, Detroit.........	16	238	14.9
1974—Dick Jauron, Detroit	17	286	16.8	1963—Dick James, Washington........	16	214	13.4
1973—Bruce Taylor, San Francisco.	15	207	13.8	1962—Pat Studstill, Detroit..............	29	457	15.8
1972—Ken Ellis, Green Bay.............	14	215	15.4	1961—Willie Wood, Green Bay..........	14	225	16.1
1971—Les Duncan, Washington........	22	233	10.6	1960—Abe Woodson, San Francisco .	13	174	13.4

KICKOFF RETURNS

	No.	Yds.	Avg.		No.	Yds.	Avg.
1981—Mike Nelms, Washington.......	37	1099	29.7	1970—Cecil Turner, Chicago	23	752	32.7
1980—Rich Mauti, New Orleans.......	31	798	27.6	1969—Bobby Williams, Detroit	17	563	33.1
1979—Jimmy Edwards, Minnesota..	44	1103	25.1	1968—Preston Pearson, Baltimore...	15	527	35.1
1978—Steve Odom, Green Bay	25	677	27.1	1967—Travis Williams, Green Bay...	18	739	41.1
1977—Wilbert Montgomery, Phila...	23	619	26.9	1966—Gale Sayers, Chicago..............	23	718	31.2
1976—Cullen Bryant, Los Angeles....	16	459	28.7	1965—Tommy Watkins, Detroit	17	584	34.4
1975—Walter Payton, Chicago..........	14	444	31.7	1964—Clarence Childs, NYG	34	987	29.0
1974—Terry Metcalf, St. Louis..........	20	623	31.2	1963—Abe Woodson, San Francisco.	29	935	32.3
1973—Carl Garrett, Chicago.............	16	486	30.4	1962—Abe Woodson, San Francisco .	37	1157	31.3
1972—Ron Smith, Chicago.................	30	924	30.8	1961—Dick Bass, Los Angeles...........	23	698	30.3
1971—Travis Williams, Los Angeles	25	743	29.7	1960—Tom Moore, Green Bay..........	12	397	33.1

AMERICAN FOOTBALL CONFERENCE
INDIVIDUAL LEADERS, 1960-81
(American Football League, 1960-69)

RUSHING

Year	Player	Net Yds.	Att.	TD		Year	Player	Net Yds.	Att.	TD
1981	Earl Campbell, Houston	1,376	361	10		1970	Floyd Little, Denver	901	209	3
1980	Earl Campbell, Houston	1,460	373	13		1969	Dick Post, San Diego	873	182	6
1979	Earl Campbell, Houston	1,697	368	19		1968	Paul Robinson, Cincinnati	1,023	238	8
1978	Earl Campbell, Houston	1,450	302	13		1967	Jim Nance, Boston	1,216	269	7
1977	Mark van Eeghen, Oakland	1,273	324	7		1966	Jim Nance, Boston	1,458	299	11
1976	O. J. Simpson, Buffalo	1,503	290	8		1965	Paul Lowe, San Diego	1,121	222	7
1975	O. J. Simpson, Buffalo	1,817	329	16		1964	Cookie Gilchrist, Buffalo	981	230	6
1974	Otis Armstrong, Denver	1,407	263	9		1963	Clem Daniels, Oakland	1,099	215	3
1973	O. J. Simpson, Buffalo	2,003	332	12		1962	Cookie Gilchrist, Buffalo	1,096	214	13
1972	O. J. Simpson, Buffalo	1,251	292	6		1961	Billy Cannon, Houston	948	200	6
1971	Floyd Little, Denver	1,133	284	6		1960	Abner Haynes, Dallas	875	156	9

PASSING

Year	Player	Passes	Com.	Yds.	TD	Int.
1981	Ken Anderson, Cincinnati	479	300	3,754	29	10
1980	Brian Sipe, Cleveland	554	337	4,132	30	14
1979	Dan Fouts, San Diego	530	332	4,082	24	24
1978	Terry Bradshaw, Pittsburgh	368	207	2,915	28	20
1977	Bob Griese, Miami	307	180	2,252	22	13
1976	Ken Stabler, Oakland	291	194	2,737	27	17
1975	Ken Anderson, Cincinnati	377	228	3,169	21	11
1974	Ken Anderson, Cincinnati	328	213	2,667	18	10
1973	Ken Stabler, Oakland	260	163	1,997	14	10
1972	Earl Morrall, Miami	150	83	1,360	11	7
1971	Bob Griese, Miami	263	145	2,089	19	9
1970	Daryle Lamonica, Oakland	356	179	2,516	22	15
1969	Greg Cook, Cincinnati	197	106	1,854	15	11
1968	Len Dawson, Kansas City	224	131	2,109	17	9
1967	Daryle Lamonica, Oakland	425	220	3,228	30	20
1966	Len Dawson, Kansas City	284	159	2,527	26	10
1965	John Hadl, San Diego	348	174	2,798	20	21
1964	Len Dawson, Kansas City	354	199	2,879	30	18
1963	Tobin Rote, San Diego	286	170	2,510	20	17
1962	Len Dawson, Dallas	310	189	2,759	29	17
1961	George Blanda, Houston	362	187	3,330	36	22
1960	Jack Kemp, Los Angeles	406	211	3,018	20	25

PASS RECEIVING

Year	Player	No.	Yds.	TD		Year	Player	No.	Yds.	TD
1981	Kellen Winslow, San Diego	88	1,075	10		1970	Marlin Briscoe, Buffalo	57	1,036	8
1980	Kellen Winslow, San Diego	89	1,290	9		1969	Lance Alworth, San Diego	64	1,003	4
1979	Joe Washington, Baltimore	82	750	3		1968	Lance Alworth, San Diego	68	1,312	10
1978	Steve Largent, Seattle	71	1,168	8		1967	George Sauer, New York	75	1,189	6
1977	Lydell Mitchell, Baltimore	71	620	4		1966	Lance Alworth, San Diego	73	1,383	13
1976	MacArthur Lane, KC	66	686	1		1965	Lionel Taylor, Denver	85	1,131	6
1975	Reggie Jackson, Cleveland	60	770	3		1964	Charley Hennigan, Houston	101	1,546	8
1974	Lydell Mitchell, Baltimore	72	544	2		1963	Lionel Taylor, Denver	78	1,101	10
1973	Fred Willis, Houston	57	371	1		1962	Lionel Taylor, Denver	77	908	4
1972	Fred Biletnikoff, Oakland	58	802	7		1961	Lionel Taylor, Denver	100	1,176	4
1971	Fred Biletnikoff, Oakland	61	929	9		1960	Lionel Taylor, Denver	92	1,235	12

SCORING

Year	Player	TD	PAT	FG	Tot.		Year	Player	TD	PAT	FG	Tot.
1981	Jim Breech, Cincinnati	0	49	22	115		1970	Jan Stenerud, Kansas City	0	26	30	116
	Nick Lowery, Kansas City	0	37	26	115		1969	Jim Turner, New York	0	33	32	129
1980	John Smith, New England	0	51	26	129		1968	Jim Turner, New York	0	43	34	145
1979	John Smith, New England	0	46	23	115		1967	George Blanda, Oakland	0	56	20	116
1978	Pat Leahy, New York	0	41	22	107		1966	Gino Cappelletti, Boston	6	35	16	119
1977	Errol Mann, Oakland	0	39	20	99		1965	Gino Cappelletti, Boston	9	27	17	132
1975	O. J. Simpson, Buffalo	23	0	0	138		1964	Gino Cappelletti, Boston	7	36	25	155
1974	Roy Gerela, Pittsburgh	0	33	20	93		1963	Gino Cappelletti, Boston	2	35	22	113
1973	Roy Gerela, Pittsburgh	0	36	29	123		1962	Gene Mingo, Denver	4	32	27	137
1972	Bobby Howfield, NY Jets	0	40	27	121		1961	Gino Cappelletti, Boston	8	48	17	147
1971	Garo Yepremian, Miami	0	33	28	117		1960	Gene Mingo, Denver	6	33	18	123

FIELD GOALS

1981—Nick Lowery, Kansas City............................26	1970—Jan Stenerud, Kansas City.........................30
1980—John Smith, New England........................26	1969—Jim Turner, New York................................32
Fred Steinfort, Denver.........................26	1968—Jim Turner, New York................................34
1979—John Smith, New England........................23	1967—Jan Stenerud, Kansas City.........................21
1978—Pat Leahy, New York................................22	1966—Mike Mercer, Oakland-Kansas City.........21
1977—Errol Mann, Oakland.............................20	1965—Pete Gogolak, Buffalo..............................28
1975—Jan Stenerud, Kansas City...................22	1964—Gino Cappelletti, Boston...........................25
1974—Roy Gerela, Pittsburgh.............................20	1963—Gino Cappelletti, Boston...........................22
1973—Roy Gerela, Pittsburgh.............................29	1962—Gene Mingo, Denver.................................27
1972—Roy Gerela, Pittsburgh.............................28	1961—Gino Cappelletti, Boston...........................17
1971—Garo Yepremian, Miami..........................28	1960—Gene Mingo, Denver.................................18

PASS INTERCEPTIONS

	No.	Yds.		No.	Yds.
1981—John Harris, Seattle......................	10	155	1969—Emmitt Thomas, Kansas City.....	9	146
1980—Lester Hayes, Oakland................	13	273	1968—Dave Grayson, Oakland..............	10	195
1979—Mike Reinfeldt, Houston.............	12	205	1967—Miller Farr, Houston......................	10	264
1978—Thom Darden, Cleveland.............	10	200	Tom Janik, Buffalo......................	10	222
1977—Lyle Blackwood, Baltimore..........	10	163	Dick Westmoreland, Miami........	10	127
1976—Ken Riley, Cincinnati....................	9	141	1966—Johnny Robinson, Kansas City....	10	136
1975—Mel Blount, Pittsburgh................	11	121	Bobby Hunt, Kansas City	10	113
1974—Emmitt Thomas, Kansas City.....	12	214	1965—W. K. Hicks, Houston..................	9	156
1973—Dick Anderson, Miami	8	136	1964—Dainard Paulson, New York.......	12	157
Mike Wagner, Pittsburgh............	8	134	1963—Fred Glick, Houston	12	180
1972—Mike Sensibaugh, Kansas City	8	65	1962—Lee Riley, New York	11	122
1971—Ken Houston, Houston..................	9	220	1961—Bill Atkins, Buffalo	10	158
1970—Johnny Robinson, Kansas City....	10	155	1960—Austin Gonsoulin, Denver.............	11	98

PUNTING

	No.	Avg.		No.	Avg.
1981—Pat McInally, Cincinnati.............	72	45.4	1970—Dave Lewis, Cincinnati................	79	46.2
1980—Luke Prestridge, Denver	70	43.9	1969—Dennis Partee, San Diego	71	44.6
1979—Bob Grupp, Kansas City..............	89	43.6	1968—Jerrel Wilson, Kansas City	63	45.1
1978—Pat McInally, Cincinnati.............	91	43.1	1967—Bob Scarpitto, Denver	105	44.9
1977—Ray Guy, Oakland	59	43.4	1966—Bob Scarpitto, Denver..................	76	45.8
1976—Marv Bateman, Buffalo................	86	42.8	1965—Jerrel Wilson, Kansas City	69	45.4
1975—Ray Guy, Oakland	68	43.8	1964—Jim Fraser, Denver	73	44.2
1974—Ray Guy, Oakland	74	42.2	1963—Jim Fraser, Denver	81	44.4
1973—Jerrel Wilson, Kansas City	80	45.5	1962—Jim Fraser, Denver	55	43.6
1972—Jerrel Wilson, Kansas City	66	44.8	1961—Bill Atkins, Buffalo	85	44.5
1971—Dave Lewis, Cincinnati................	72	44.8	1960—Paul Maguire, Los Angeles..........	43	40.5

PUNT RETURNS

	No.	Yds.	Avg.		No.	Yds.	Avg.
1981—James Brooks, San Diego	22	290	13.2	1970—Ed Podolak, Kansas City........	23	311	13.5
1980—J. T. Smith, Kansas City	40	581	14.5	1969—Bill Thompson, Denver	25	288	11.5
1979—Tony Nathan, Miami..............	28	306	10.9	1968—Noland Smith, Kansas City....	18	270	15.0
1978—Rick Upchurch, Denver	36	493	13.7	1967—Floyd Little, Denver..............	16	270	16.9
1977—Billy Johnson, Houston..........	30	539	15.4	1966—Leslie Duncan, San Diego	18	238	13.2
1976—Rick Upchurch, Denver..........	39	536	13.7	1965—Leslie Duncan, San Diego.......	30	464	15.5
1975—Billy Johnson, Houston..........	40	612	18.8	1964—Bobby Jancik, Houston..........	12	220	18.3
1974—Lemar Parrish, Cincinnati......	18	338	18.8	1963—Claude Gibson, Oakland........	26	307	11.8
1973—Ron Smith, San Diego	27	352	15.0	1962—Dick Christy, New York	15	250	16.7
1972—Chris Farasopolous, NYJ	17	179	10.5	1961—Dick Christy, New York	18	383	21.3
1971—Leroy Kelly, Cleveland	30	292	9.7	1960—Abner Haynes, Dallas..............	14	215	15.4

KICKOFF RETURNS

	No.	Yds.	Avg.		No.	Yds.	Avg.
1981—Carl Roaches, Houston	28	769	27.5	1970—Jim Duncan, Baltimore	20	707	35.4
1980—Horace Ivory, New England .	36	992	27.6	1969—Bill Thompson, Denver	19	594	31.3
1979—Larry Brunson, Oakland........	17	441	25.9	1968—George Atkinson, Oakland	32	802	25.1
1978—Keith Wright, Cleveland	30	789	26.3	1967—Zeke Moore, Houston..............	14	405	28.9
1977—Raymond Clayborn, NE	20	869	31.0	1966—Goldie Sellers, Denver	19	541	28.5
1976—Duriel Harris, Miami	17	559	32.9	1965—Abner Haynes, Denver............	34	901	26.5
1975—Harold Hart, Oakland	17	518	30.5	1964—Bo Roberson, Oakland............	36	975	27.1
1974—Greg Pruitt, Cleveland............	22	606	27.5	1963—Bobby Jancik, Houston..........	45	1,317	29.3
1973—Wallace Francis, Buffalo	23	687	29.9	1962—Bobby Jancik, Houston..........	24	726	30.3
1972—Bruce Laird, Baltimore..........	29	843	29.1	1961—Dave Grayson, Dallas	16	453	28.3
1971—Mercury Morris, Miami..........	15	423	28.2	1960—Ken Hall, Houston....................	19	594	31.3

ALL-TIME PRO FOOTBALL RECORDS

RUSHING

LEADING LIFETIME RUSHERS

(Courtesy of Pro Football's Hall of Fame, Canton, Ohio)

Player	League	Yrs.	Att.	Yards	Avg.	TD
JIM BROWN	NFL	9	2359	12312	5.2	106
O. J. SIMPSON	AFL-NFL	11	2404	11236	4.7	61
FRANCO HARRIS	NFL	10	2462	10339	4.2	84
JOE PERRY	AAFC-NFL	16	1929	9723	5.0	71
WALTER PAYTON	NFL	7	2204	9608	4.4	71
JIM TAYLOR	NFL	10	1941	8597	4.4	83
LARRY CSONKA	AFL-NFL	11	1891	8081	4.3	64
JOHN RIGGINS	NFL	10	1861	7536	4.0	55
LEROY KELLY	NFL	10	1727	7274	4.2	74
JOHN HENRY JOHNSON	NFL-AFL	13	1571	6803	4.3	48
LAWRENCE McCUTCHEON	NFL	10	1521	6578	4.3	26
LYDELL MITCHELL	NFL	9	1675	6534	3.9	30
EARL CAMPBELL	NFL	4	1404	6457	4.6	55
FLOYD LITTLE	AFL-NFL	9	1641	6323	3.8	43
TONY DORSETT	NFL	5	1368	6270	4.6	40
DON PERKINS	NFL	8	1500	6217	4.1	42
KEN WILLARD	NFL	10	1622	6105	3.8	45
CALVIN HILL	NFL	12	1452	6083	4.2	42
CHUCK FOREMAN	NFL	8	1556	5950	3.8	53
MARK VAN EEGHEN	NFL	8	1475	5907	4.0	35

NOTE—Earl Campbell, Tony Dorsett and Mark van Eeghen were added to the Top Twenty rushing rankings during the 1981 season. As a result, Larry Brown (5875 yards), Steve Van Buren (5860) and Bill Brown (5838) were dropped from the list. Of those players active in 1981, Greg Pruitt (5496 yards), Chuck Muncie (5196) and Wilbert Montgomery (5095) stand next in line for the Top Twenty rankings.

AAFC—All-America Football Conference

AFL—American Football League

NFL—National Football League

Most Yards Gained, Season

2,003—O. J. Simpson, Buffalo Bills, 1973
1,934—Earl Campbell, Houston Oilers, 1980
1,863—Jim Brown, Cleveland Browns, 1963
1,852—Walter Payton, Chicago Bears, 1977

1,000-Yard Rushing Seasons by First-Year Players

Beattie Feathers, Chicago Bears, 1934, 1,004 yards
Cookie Gilchrist, Buffalo Bills, 1962, 1,096 yards
Paul Robinson, Cincinnati Bengals, 1968, 1,023 yards
John Brockington, Green Bay Packers, 1971, 1,105 yards
Franco Harris, Pittsburgh Steelers, 1972, 1,055 yards
Larry McCutcheon, Los Angeles Rams, 1973, 1,097 yards. (McCutcheon considered a 1973 rookie as he played only 3 games in 1972 and did not carry the ball, playing only on special teams.)
Don Woods, San Diego Chargers, 1974, 1,162 yards
Tony Dorsett, Dallas Cowboys, 1977, 1,007 yards
Earl Campbell, Houston Oilers, 1978, 1,450 yards
Terry Miller, Buffalo Bills, 1978, 1,060 yards
Ottis Anderson, St. Louis Cardinals, 1979, 1,605 yards
William Andrews, Atlanta Falcons, 1979, 1,023 yards
Billy Sims, Detroit Lions, 1980, 1,303 yards
Joe Cribbs, Buffalo Bills, 1980, 1,185 yards
George Rogers, New Orleans Saints, 1981, 1,674 yards
Joe Delaney, Kansas City Chiefs, 1981, 1,121 yards

Most Yards Gained Rushing by a Quarterback

968—Bobby Douglass, Chicago Bears, 1972

Most Yards Gained, Game

275—Walter Payton, Chicago Bears vs. Minnesota Vikings, November 20, 1977.

Longest Run From Scrimmage

97—Andy Uram, Green Bay Packers vs. Chicago Cardinals, October 8, 1939 (scored touchdown)
Bob Gage, Pittsburgh Steelers vs. Chicago Bears, December 4, 1949 (scored touchdown)

Most Games, 100 Yards or More, Season

11—O. J. Simpson, Buffalo Bills, 1973

Most Games, 100 Yards or More, Career

58—Jim Brown, Cleveland Browns, 1957-1965

Most Games, 200 Yards or More, Career

6—O. J. Simpson, Buffalo Bills, 1969-1976

Most Games, 200 Yards or More, Season

3—O.J. Simpson, Buffalo Bills, 1973
Earl Campbell, Houston Oilers, 1980

Most Touchdowns Rushing, Career

106—Jim Brown, Cleveland Browns, 1957-1965

Most Touchdowns Rushing, Season

19—Jim Taylor, Green Bay Packers, 1962
Earl Campbell, Houston Oilers, 1979.
Chuck Muncie, San Diego Chargers, 1981

Most Touchdowns Rushing, Game

6—Ernie Nevers, Chicago Cardinals vs. Chicago Bears, November 8, 1929

Most Rushing Attempts, Season

378—George Rogers, New Orleans Saints, 1981

Most Rushing Attempts, Game

41—Franco Harris, Pittsburgh Steelers vs. Cincinnati Bengals, October 17, 1976

PASSING

LEADING LIFETIME PASSERS
Minimum 1500 attempts
(Courtesy of Pro Football's Hall of Fame, Canton, Ohio)

Player	League	Yrs.	Att.	Comp.	Yds.	TD	Int.	Pts.
OTTO GRAHAM	AAFC-NFL	10	2626	1464	23,584	174	135	86.8
ROGER STAUBACH	NFL	11	2958	1685	22,700	153	109	83.5
SONNY JURGENSEN	NFL	18	4262	2433	32,224	255	189	82.8
LEN DAWSON	NFL-AFL	19	3741	2136	28,711	239	183	82.6
KEN ANDERSON	NFL	11	3539	2036	25,562	160	124	80.5
FRAN TARKENTON	NFL	18	6467	3686	47,003	342	266	80.5
BART STARR	NFL	16	3149	1808	24,718	152	138	80.3
BERT JONES	NFL	9	2464	1382	17,663	122	97	79.1
DAN FOUTS	NFL	9	3203	1849	24,256	145	142	78.4
JOHNNY UNITAS	NFL	18	5186	2830	40,239	290	253	78.2
FRANK RYAN	NFL	13	2133	1090	16,042	149	111	77.7
KEN STABLER	AFL-NFL	12	3223	1944	24,268	177	189	77.5
BOB GRIESE	AFL-NFL	14	3429	1926	25,092	192	172	77.3
NORM VAN BROCKLIN	NFL	12	2895	1553	23,611	173	178	75.3
SID LUCKMAN	NFL	12	1744	904	14,686	137	132	75.0
BRIAN SIPE	NFL	8	2758	1552	19,083	124	118	74.9
DON MEREDITH	NFL	9	2308	1170	17,199	135	111	74.7
ROMAN GABRIEL	NFL	16	4498	2366	29,444	201	149	74.5
Y. A. TITTLE	AAFC-NFL	17	4395	2427	33,070	242	248	74.4
EARL MORRALL	NFL	21	2689	1379	20,809	161	148	74.2

NOTE—No new players were added to the Top Twenty passing rankings during the 1981 season. Of those players active in 1981 with more than 1500 career attempts, Craig Morton (73.8), Greg Landry (73.3), Ron Jaworski (72.8) and Joe Theismann (72.1) rank highest among those not on the Top Twenty list.

Rating points based on a combination of performances in the following four categories: percentage of completions, percentage of touchdown passes, percentage of interceptions and average gain per pass attempt.

AAFC—All-America Football Conference
AFL—American Football League
NFL—National Football League

Most Yards Gained, Season

4,802—Dan Fouts, San Diego Chargers, 1981.

Most Yards Gained, Game

554—Norm Van Brocklin, Los Angeles Rams vs. New York Yankees, September 28, 1951 (27 completions in 41 attempts)

Longest Pass Completion (99 Yards; All Touchdowns)

Frank Filchock to Andy Farkas, Washington Redskins vs. Pittsburgh Steelers, October 15, 1939
Otto Graham to Mac Speedie, Cleveland Browns vs. Buffalo Bills, November 2, 1947
George Izo to Bobby Mitchell, Washington Redskins vs. Cleveland Browns, September 15, 1963
Karl Sweetan to Pat Studstill, Detroit Lions vs. Baltimore Colts, October 16, 1966
Sonny Jurgensen to Gerry Allen, Washington Redskins vs. Chicago Bears, September 15, 1968

Most Touchdowns Passing, Career

342—Fran Tarkenton, Minnesota Vikings, 1961-65; New York Giants 1967-71; Minnesota Vikings, 1972-78.

Most Touchdowns Passing, Season

36—George Blanda, Houston Oilers, 1961
Y. A. Tittle, New York Giants, 1963

Most Touchdowns Passing, Game

7—Sid Luckman, Chicago Bears vs. New York Giants, November 14, 1943
Adrian Burk, Philadelphia Eagles vs. Washington Redskins, October 17, 1954
George Blanda, Houston Oilers vs. New York Titans, November 19, 1961
Y. A. Tittle, New York Giants vs. Washington Redskins, October 28, 1962
Joe Kapp, Minnesota Vikings vs. Baltimore Colts, September 28, 1969

Most Consecutive Games, Touchdown Passes

47—Johnny Unitas, Baltimore, 1956-60

Most Passing Attempts, Season

609—Dan Fouts, San Diego Chargers, 1981

Most Passing Attempts, Game

68—George Blanda, Houston Oilers vs. Buffalo Bills, November 1, 1964 (37 com pletions)

Most Passes Completed, Season

360—Dan Fouts, San Diego Chargers, 1981

Most Passes Completed, Game

37—George Blanda, Houston Oilers vs. Buffalo Bills, November 1, 1964 (68 at tempts)

Most Consecutive Passes Completed

17—Bert Jones, Baltimore Colts vs. New York Jets, December 15, 1974

Most Passes Had Intercepted, Game

8—Jim Hardy, Chicago Cardinals vs. Philadelphia Eagles, September 24, 1950 (39 attempts)

Most Passes Had Intercepted, Season

42—George Blanda, Houston Oilers, 1962 (418 attempts)

Most Passes Had Intercepted, Career

277—George Blanda, Chicago Bears, 1949-1958; Houston Oilers, 1960-1966; Oak land Raiders, 1967-75 (4,007 attempts)

Most Consecutive Passes Attempted Without Interception

294—Bart Starr, Green Bay Packers, 1964-1965

PASS RECEIVING
LEADING LIFETIME RECEIVERS
(Courtesy of Pro Football's Hall of Fame, Canton, Ohio)

Player	League	Yrs.	No.	Yards	Avg.	TD
CHARLEY TAYLOR	NFL	13	649	9110	14.0	79
DON MAYNARD	NFL-AFL	15	633	11834	18.7	88
RAYMOND BERRY	NFL	13	631	9275	14.7	68
FRED BILETNIKOFF	AFL-NFL	14	589	8974	15.2	76
HAROLD JACKSON	NFL	14	571	10246	17.9	75
LIONEL TAYLOR	NFL-AFL	10	567	7195	12.7	45
LANCE ALWORTH	AFL-NFL	11	542	10266	18.9	85
BOBBY MITCHELL	NFL	11	521	7954	15.3	65
HAROLD CARMICHAEL	NFL	11	516	7923	15.4	72
BILLY HOWTON	NFL	12	503	8459	16.8	61
CHARLIE JOINER	AFL-NFL	13	495	8476	17.1	47
TOMMY McDONALD	NFL	12	495	8410	17.0	84
DON HUTSON	NFL	11	488	7991	16.4	99
JACKIE SMITH	NFL	16	480	7918	16.5	40
ART POWELL	AFL-NFL	10	479	8046	16.8	81
BOYD DOWLER	NFL	12	474	7270	15.4	40
AHMAD RASHAD	NFL	9	472	6598	14.0	44
PETE RETZLAFF	NFL	11	452	7412	16.4	47
ROY JEFFERSON	NFL	12	451	7539	16.7	52
HAVEN MOSES	AFL-NFL	13	448	8091	18.1	56

NOTE—Charlie Joiner and Ahmad Rashad were added to the Top Twenty receiving rankings during the 1981 season. Inasmuch as a tie existed for 20th
place at the start of the season, Carroll Dale (438 receptions), Paul Warfield and Mike Ditka (427 each) were removed from the list. Of those
players active in 1981, Reggie Rucker (447 receptions), Ken Burrough
(421), Drew Pearson (416) and Cliff Branch (405) stand next in line for
the Top Twenty rankings.

AFL—American Football League
NFL—National Football League

Most Yards Gained, Season

1,746—Charley Hennigan, Houston Oilers, 1961

Most Yards Gained, Game

303—Jim Benton, Cleveland Rams vs. Detroit Lions, November 22, 1945 (10 receptions)

Longest Pass Reception

(See receivers mentioned under Longest Pass Completion)

Most Pass Receptions, Season
  101—Charley Hennigan, Houston Oilers, 1964

Most Pass Receptions, Game
  18—Tom Fears, Los Angeles Rams vs. Green Bay Packers, December 3, 1950 (189 yards)

Most Consecutive Games, Pass Receptions
  127—Harold Carmichael, Philadelphia Eagles, 1971-1980 (streak ended December 21, 1980)
  117—Mel Gray, St. Louis Cardinals, 1971-1981 (active streak)

Most Touchdown Passes, Career
  99—Don Hutson, Green Bay Packers, 1935-1945

Most Touchdown Passes, Season
  17—Don Hutson, Green Bay Packers, 1942
    Elroy Hirsch, Los Angeles Rams, 1951
    Bill Groman, Houston Oilers, 1961

Most Touchdowns Passes, Game
  5—Bob Shaw, Chicago Cardinals vs. Baltimore Colts, October 2, 1950

Most Consecutive Games, Touchdown Passes
  11—Elroy Hirsch, Los Angeles Rams, 1950-1951
    Buddy Dial, Pittsburgh Steelers, 1957-1960

PASS INTERCEPTIONS

Most Interceptions, Game
  4—Sam Baugh, Washington Redskins vs. Detroit Lions, November 14, 1943
    Dan Sandifer, Washington Redskins vs. Boston Yanks, October 31, 1948
    Don Doll, Detroit Lions vs. Chicago Cardinals, October 23, 1949
    Bob Nussbaumer, Chicago Cardinals vs. New York Bulldogs, November 13, 1949
    Russ Craft, Philadelphia Eagles vs. Chicago Cardinals, September 24, 1950
    Bob Dillon, Green Bay Packers vs. Detroit Lions, November 26, 1953
    Jack Butler, Pittsburgh Steelers vs. Washington Redskins, December 13, 1953
    Jerry Norton, St. Louis Cardinals vs. Washington Redskins, November 20, 1960; vs. Pittsburgh
      Steelers, November 26, 1961
    Goose Gonsoulin, Denver Broncos vs. Buffalo Bills, September 18, 1960
    Dave Baker, San Francisco 49ers vs. Los Angeles Rams, December 4, 1960
    Bobby Ply, Dallas Texans vs. San Diego Chargers, December 16, 1962
    Bobby Hunt, Kansas City Chiefs vs. Houston Oilers, October 4, 1964
    Willie Brown, Denver Broncos vs. New York Jets, November 15, 1964
    Dick Anderson, Miami Dolphins vs. Pittsburgh Steelers, December 3, 1973
    Willie Buchanon, Green Bay Packers vs. San Diego Chargers, September 24, 1978.

Most Interceptions, Season
  14—Dick Lane, Los Angeles Rams, 1952

Most Interceptions, Career
  81—Paul Krause, Washington Redskins, 1964-1967; Minnesota Vikings, 1968- 1979

Most Consecutive Games, Passes Intercepted By
  8—Tom Morrow, Oakland Raiders, 1962 (4), 1963 (4)

Most Yardage Gained via Pass Interceptions, Career
  1,282—Emlen Tunnell, New York Giants, 1948-1958; Green Bay Packers, 1959- 1961

Most Yardage Gained via Pass Interceptions, Season
  349—Charles McNeil, San Diego Chargers, 1961

Most Yardage Gained via Pass Interceptions, Game
  177—Charles McNeil, San Diego Chargers vs. Houston Oilers, September 24, 1961

Longest Run With Intercepted Pass
  102—Bob Smith, Detroit Lions vs. Chicago Bears, November 24, 1949
    Erich Barnes, New York Giants vs. Dallas Cowboys, October 22, 1961
    Gary Barbaro, Kansas City Chiefs vs. Seattle Seahawks, December 11, 1977
    Louis Breeden, Cincinnati Bengals vs. San Diego Chargers, November 8, 1981

Most Touchdowns Scored via Pass Interceptions, Lifetime
  9—Ken Houston, Houston Oilers, 1967 (2), 1968 (2), 1969, 1971 (4)

Most Touchdowns Scored via Pass Interceptions, Season
  4—Ken Houston, Houston Oilers, 1971
    Jim Kearney, Kansas City Chiefs, 1972

Most Touchdowns Scored via Pass Interceptions, Game
  2—Bill Blackburn, Chicago Cardinals vs. Boston Yanks, October 24, 1948
    Dan Sandifer, Washington Redskins vs. Boston Yanks, October 31, 1948
    Bob Franklin, Cleveland Browns vs. Chicago Bears, December 11, 1960
    Bill Stacy, St. Louis Cardinals vs. Dallas Cowboys, November 5, 1961
    Jerry Norton, St. Louis Cardinals vs. Pittsburgh Steelers, November 26, 1961

Most Touchdowns Scored in Pass Interceptions, Game—Continued

Miller Farr, Houston Oilers vs. Buffalo Bills, December 7, 1968
Ken Houston, Houston Oilers vs. San Diego Chargers, December 19, 1971
Jim Kearney, Kansas City Chiefs vs. Denver Broncos, October 1, 1972
Lemar Parrish, Cincinnati Bengals vs. Houston Oilers, December 17, 1972
Dick Anderson, Miami Dolphins vs. Pittsburgh Steelers, December 3, 1973
Prentice McCray, New England Patriots vs. New York Jets, November 21, 1976.

SCORING
LEADING LIFETIME SCORERS
(Courtesy of Pro Football's Hall of Fame, Canton, Ohio)

Player	League	Yrs.	TD	PAT	FG	Tot.
GEORGE BLANDA	NFL-AFL	26	9	943	335	2002
LOU GROZA	AAFC-NFL	21	1	810	264	1608
JIM TURNER	AFL-NFL	16	1	521	304	1439
JIM BAKKEN	NFL	17	0	534	282	1380
FRED COX	NFL	15	0	519	282	1365
JAN STENERUD	AFL-NFL	15	0	432	304	1344
GINO CAPPELLETTI	AFL	11	42	350	176	1130
DON COCKROFT	NFL	13	0	432	216	1080
GARO YEPREMIAN	NFL-AFL	14	0	444	210	1074
BRUCE GOSSETT	NFL	11	0	374	219	1031
SAM BAKER	NFL	15	2	428	179	977
LOU MICHAELS	NFL	13	1	386	187	*955
ROY GERELA	AFL-NFL	11	0	351	184	903
BOBBY WALSTON	NFL	12	46	365	80	881
MARK MOSELEY	NFL	11	0	300	189	867
PETE GOGOLAK	AFL-NFL	10	0	344	173	863
ERROL MANN	NFL	11	0	315	177	846
DON HUTSON	NFL	11	105	172	7	823
PAUL HORNUNG	NFL	9	62	190	66	760
JIM BROWN	NFL	9	126	0	0	756

*Includes safety.
  AAFC—All-America Football Conference
  AFL—American Football League
  NFL—National Football League

Note—There were no players added to the Top Twenty scoring list in 1981. Of those players not in the Top Twenty who were active in 1981, only Tony Fritsch (738 points) and John Smith (650 points) have a chance to enter the Top Twenty in 1982.

Most Points, Season

176—Paul Hornung, Green Bay Packers, 1960 (15 TD's, 41 PAT's, 15 FG's)

Most Points, Game

40—Ernie Nevers, Chicago Cardinals vs. Chicago Bears, November 28, 1929 (6 TD's, 4 PAT's)

Most Touchdowns, Season

23—O. J. Simpson, Buffalo Bills, 1975 (16 rushing, 9 pass receptions)

Most Touchdowns, Game

6—Ernie Nevers, Chicago Cardinals vs. Chicago Bears, November 28, 1929 (6 rushing)
Dub Jones, Cleveland Browns vs. Chicago Bears, November 25, 1951 (4 rushing, 2 pass receptions)
Gale Sayers, Chicago Bears vs. San Francisco 49ers, December 12, 1965 (4 rushing, 1 pass reception, 1 punt return)

Most Points After Touchdown, Game

9—Pat Harder, Chicago Cardinals vs. New York Giants, October 17, 1948
Joe Vetrano, San Francisco 49ers vs. Brooklyn Dodgers, November 21, 1948
Bob Waterfield, Los Angeles Rams vs. Baltimore Colts, October 22, 1950
Charlie Gogolak, Washington Redskins vs. New York Giants, November 27, 1966

Most Points After Touchdown, Season

64—George Blanda, Houston Oilers, 1961 (65 attempts)

Most Consecutive Points After Touchdown

234—Tommy Davis, San Francisco 49ers, 1959-1965

Most Points After Touchdown (no misses), Season

56—Danny Villanueva, Dallas Cowboys, 1966

Most Points After Touchdown (no misses), Game

9—Pat Harder, Chicago Cardinals vs. New York Giants, October 17, 1948
Joe Vetrano, San Francisco 49ers vs. Brooklyn Dodgers, November 21, 1948
Bob Waterfield, Los Angeles Rams vs. Baltimore Colts, October 22, 1950

Most Points After Touchdown Attempted, Season

66—Joe Vetrano, San Francisco 49ers, 1948 (62 successful)

Most Points After Touchdown Attempted, Game
    10—Charlie Gogolak, Washington Redskins vs. New York Giants, November 27, 1966 (9 successful)

Most Field Goals, Game
    7—Jim Bakken, St. Louis Cardinals vs. Pittsburgh Steelers, September 24, 1967

Most Field Goals, Season
    34—Jim Turner, New York Jets, 1968 and 1969

Most Field Goals Attempted, Season
    49—Bruce Gossett, Los Angeles Rams, 1966
       Curt Knight, Washington Redskins, 1971

Most Field Goals Attempted, Game
    9—Jim Bakken, St. Louis Cardinals vs. Pittsburgh Steelers, September 24, 1967 (7 successful)

Most Consecutive Field Goals
    20—Garo Yepremian, Miami Dolphis, 1978; New Orleans Saints, 1979.

Most Consecutive Games, Field Goal
    31—Fred Cox, Minnesota, 1968-1970

Longest Field Goal
    63—Tom Dempsey, New Orleans Saints vs. Detroit Lions, November 8, 1970

Highest Field Goal Completion Percentage, Season (20 attempts)
    91.7—Jan Stenerud, Green Bay Packers, 1981 (22 FG's in 24 attempts)

Highest Field Goal Percentage, Game (6 attempts)
    100—Gino Cappelletti, Boston Patriots vs. Denver Broncos, October 4, 1964 (6 FG's in 6 attempts)

Most Safeties, Career
    3—Bill McPeak, Pittsburgh Steelers, 1954, 1956, 1957
       Charlie Krueger, San Francisco 49ers, 1959, 1960, 1961
       Ernie Stautner, Pittsburgh Steelers, 1950, 1958, 1962
       Jim Katcavage, New York Giants, 1958, 1961, 1965
       Roger Brown, Detroit Lions, 1962 (2), 1965
       Bruce Maher, Detroit Lions, 1960, 1963, 1967
       Ron McDole, Buffalo Bills, 1964 (2); Washington Redskins, 1976
       Ted Hendricks, Green Bay Packers, 1974; Oakland Raiders, 1975, 1976.

Most Safeties, Season
    2—Tom Nash, Green Bay Packers, 1932
       Roger Brown, Detroit Lions, 1962
       Ron McDole, Buffalo Bills, 1964
       Alan Page, Minnesota Vikings, 1971
       Benny Barnes, Dallas Cowboys, 1973
       Fred Dryer, Los Angeles Rams, 1973

Most Safeties, Game
    2—Fred Dryer, Los Angeles vs. Green Bay Packers, October 21, 1973

PUNT RETURNS

Most Yardage Returning Punts, Career
    2,714—Rick Upchurch, Denver Broncos, 1975-1981

Most Yardage Returning Punts, Season
    655—Neal Colzie, Oakland Raiders, 1975

Most Yardage Returning Punts, Game
    207—LeRoy Irvin, Los Angeles Rams vs. Atlanta Falcons, October 11, 1981

Most Touchdowns Scored via Punt Returns, Career
    8—Jack Christiansen, Detroit Lions, 1951 (4), 1952 (2), 1954, 1956

Most Touchdowns Scored via Punt Returns, Season
    4—Jack Christiansen, Detroit Lions, 1951
       Rick Upchurch, Denver Broncos, 1976

Most Touchdowns Scored via Punt Returns, Game
    2—Jack Christiansen, Detroit Lions vs. Los Angeles Rams, October 14, 1951; vs. Green Bay Packers, November 22, 1951
       Dick Christy, New York Titans vs. Denver Broncos, September 24, 1961
       Rick Upchurch, Denver Broncos vs. Cleveland Browns, September 26, 1976
       LeRoy Irvin, Los Angeles Rams vs. Atlanta Falcons, October 11, 1981.

Most Punt Returns, Career
    258—Emlen Tunnell, New York Giants, 1948-1958; Green Bay Packers, 1959-1961

Most Punt Returns, Season
    70—Danny Reece, Tampa Bay Buccaneers, 1979

Most Punt Returns, Game

    11—Eddie Brown, Washington Redskins vs. Tampa Bay Buccaneers, October 9, 1977

Longest Punt Return

    98—Gil LeFebvre, Cincinnati Reds vs. Brooklyn Dodgers, December 3, 1933 (scored touchdown)
        Charlie West, Minnesota Vikings vs. Washington Redskins, November 3, 1968 (scored touchdown)

KICKOFF RETURNS

Most Yardage Returning Kickoffs, Career

    6,922—Ron Smith, Chicago Bears, 1965; Atlanta Falcons, 1966-67; Los Angeles Rams, 1968-1969; Chicago Bears, 1970-1972; San Diego Chargers, 1973;Oakland Raiders, 1974

Most Yardage Returning Kickoffs, Season

    1,317—Bobby Jancik, Houston Oilers, 1963

Most Yardage Returning Kickoffs, Game

    294—Wally Triplett, Detroit Lions vs. Los Angeles Rams, October 29,1950 (4 re turns)

Most Touchdowns Scored via Kickoff Returns, Career

    6—Ollie Matson, Chicago Cardinals, 1952 (2), 1954, 1956, 1958 (2)
      Gale Sayers, Chicago Bears, 1965, 1966 (2), 1967 (3)
      Travis Williams, Green Bay Packers, 1967 (4), 1969; Los Angeles Rams, 1971

Most Touchdowns Scored via Kickoff Returns, Season

    4—Travis Williams, Green Bay Packers, 1967
      Cecil Turner, Chicago Bears, 1970

Most Touchdowns Scored via Kickoff Returns, Game

    2—Tim Brown, Philadelphia Eagles vs. Dallas Cowboys, November 6, 1966
      Travis Williams, Green Bay Packers vs. Cleveland Browns, November 12, 1967

Most Kickoff Returns, Career

    275—Ron Smith, Chicago Bears, 1965; Atlanta Falcons, 1966-67; Los Angeles Rams, 1968-1969; Chicago Bears, 1970-1972; San Diego Chargers, 1973;Oakland Raiders, 1974

Most Kickoff Returns, Season

    60—Drew Hill, Los Angeles Rams, 1981

Most Kickoff Returns, Game

    9—Noland Smith, Kansas City Chiefs vs. Denver Broncos, December 17, 1967
      Dino Hall, Cleveland Browns vs. Pittsburgh Steelers, October 7, 1979

Longest Kickoff Return

    106—Al Carmichael, Green Bay Packers vs. Chicago Bears, October 7, 1956
      Noland Smith, Kansas City Chiefs vs. Denver Broncos, December 17, 1967
      Roy Green, St. Louis Cardinals vs. Dallas Cowboys, October 21, 1979

PUNTING

Highest Punting Average, Career (300 Punts)

    45.10—Sam Baugh, Washington Redskins, 1937-1952 (338 punts)

Highest Punting Average, Season (20 Punts)

    51.3—Sam Baugh, Washington Redskins, 1940 (35 punts)

Highest Punting Average, Game (4 Punts)

    61.6—Bob Cifers, Detroit Lions vs. Chicago Bears, November 24, 1946.

Highest Punting Average, Game (5 Punts)

    59.4—Sam Baugh, Washington Redskins vs. Detroit Lions, October 27, 1940 (5 punts)

Longest Punt

    98—Steve O'Neal, New York Jets vs. Denver Broncos, September 21, 1969

Most Punts, Career

    1,072—Jerrel Wilson, Kansas City Chiefs, 1963-1977; New England Patriots, 1978

Most Punts, Season

    114—Bob Parsons, Chicago Bears, 1981

Most Punts, Game

    14—Sam Baugh, Washington Redskins vs. Philadelphia Eagles, November 5, 1939
      John Kinscherf, New York Giants vs. Detroit Lions, November 7, 1943
      George Taliaferro, New York Yankees vs. Los Angeles Rams, September 28, 1951

MISCELLANEOUS RECORDS

Most Fumbles, Season
17—Dan Pastorini, Houston Oilers, 1973

Most Fumbles, Game
7—Len Dawson, Kansas City Chiefs vs. San Diego Chargers, November 15, 1964

Longest Run With Recovered Fumble
104—Jack Tatum, Oakland Raiders vs. Green Bay Packers, September 24, 1972

Longest Winning Streak (Includes Post-Season Play)
18—games, Chicago Bears 1933-34 and 1941-42; Cleveland Browns, 1947-48; Miami Dolphins, 1972-73.

Longest Winning Streak (Regular Season)
17—games, Chicago Bears, 1933-1934

Longest Undefeated Streak (Includes Tie Games)
29—games, Cleveland Browns, 1947-1949 (Won 27, Tied 2)

Most Seasons, Active Player
26—George Blanda, Chicago Bears, 1949-1958; Houston Oilers, 1960-1966; Oak land Raiders, 1967-1975 (340 games)

The Sporting News AWARDS

NFL Coach of the Year (since 1970)

1970—Don Shula, Miami
1971—George Allen, Washington
1972—Don Shula, Miami
1973—Chuck Knox, Los Angeles
1974—Don Coryell, St. Louis
1975—Ted Marchibroda, Baltimore
1976—Chuck Fairbanks, New England
1977—Red Miller, Denver
1978—Jack Patera, Seattle
1979—Dick Vermeil, Philadelphia
1980—Chuck Knox, Buffalo
1981—Bill Walsh, San Francisco

Player of the Year (since 1970)

1970—NFC: John Brodie, QB, San Francisco   AFC: George Blanda, QB-PK, Oakland
1971—NFC: Roger Staubach, QB, Dallas   AFC: Bob Griese, QB, Miami
1972—NFC: Larry Brown, RB, Washington   AFC: Earl Morrall, QB, Miami
1973—NFC: John Hadl, QB, Los Angeles   AFC: O.J. Simpson, RB, Buffalo
1974—NFC: Chuck Foreman, RB, Minnesota   AFC: Ken Stabler, QB, Oakland
1975—NFC: Fran Tarkenton, QB, Minnesota   AFC: O.J. Simpson, RB, Buffalo
1976—NFC: Walter Payton, RB, Chicago   AFC: Ken Stabler, QB, Oakland
1977—NFC: Walter Payton, RB, Chicago   AFC: Craig Morton, QB, Denver
1978—NFC: Archie Manning, QB, New Orleans   AFC: Earl Campbell, RB, Houston
1979—NFC: Ottis Anderson, RB, St. Louis   AFC: Dan Fouts, QB, San Diego
1980—*Brian Sipe, QB, Cleveland
1981—Ken Anderson, QB, Cincinnati

*In 1980, The Sporting News began selecting one player as Player of the Year for the entire NFL.

Rookie of the Year (since 1970)

1970—NFC: Bruce Taylor, CB, San Francisco   AFC: Dennis Shaw, QB, Buffalo
1971—NFC: John Brockington, RB, Green Bay   AFC: Jim Plunkett, QB, New England
1972—NFC: Chester Marcol, PK, Green Bay   AFC: Franco Harris, RB, Pittsburgh
1973—NFC: Chuck Foreman, RB, Minnesota   AFC: Boobie Clark, RB, Cincinnati
1974—NFC: Wilbur Jackson, RB, San Francisco   AFC: Don Woods, RB, San Diego
1975—NFC: Steve Bartkowski, QB, Atlanta   AFC: Robert Brazile, LB, Houston
1976—NFC: Sammy White, WR, Minnesota   AFC: Mike Haynes, CB, New England
1977—NFC: Tony Dorsett, RB, Dallas   AFC: A.J. Duhe, DT, Miami
1978—NFC: Al Baker, DE, Detroit   AFC: Earl Campbell, RB, Houston
1979—NFC: Ottis Anderson, RB, St. Louis   AFC: Jerry Butler, WR, Buffalo
1980—*Billy Sims, RB, Detroit
1981—George Rogers, RB, New Orleans

*In 1980, The Sporting News began selecting one player as Rookie of the Year for the entire NFL.

College Player of the Year (since 1970)

1970—Jim Plunkett, QB, Stanford
1971—Ed Marinaro, RB, Cornell
      Pat Sullivan, QB, Auburn
1972—Bert Jones, QB, Louisiana State
1973—John Hicks, T, Ohio State
1974—Archie Griffin, RB, Ohio State
1975—Archie Griffin, RB, Ohio State
1976—Tony Dorsett, RB, Pittsburgh
1977—Earl Campbell, RB, Texas
1978—Billy Sims, RB, Oklahoma
1979—Charles White, RB, Southern California
1980—Hugh Green, DE, Pittsburgh
1981—Marcus Allen, RB, Southern California

College Coach of the Year (since 1970)

1970—John Ralston, Stanford
1971—Chuck Fairbanks, Oklahoma
1972—John McKay, Southern California
1973—Barry Switzer, Oklahoma
1974—Jerry Claiborne, Maryland
1975—Emory Bellard, Texas A & M
1976—Johnny Majors, Pittsburgh
1977—Lou Holtz, Arkansas
1978—Darryl Rogers, Michigan State
1979—John Mackovic, Wake Forest
1980—Vince Dooley, Georgia
1981—Hayden Fry, Iowa

1981 NATIONAL FOOTBALL LEAGUE
ALL-STAR TEAM
OFFENSE

Pos.	Player and Club	Hgt.	Wgt.	Pro Yrs.
WR—**James Lofton**, Green Bay		6:03	187	4
WR—**Alfred Jenkins**, Atlanta		5:10	172	7
TE—**Kellen Winslow**, San Diego		6:05	252	3
OT—**Anthony Munoz**, Cincinnati		6:06	278	2
OT—**Marvin Powell**, New York Jets		6:05	268	5
G—**John Hannah**, New England		6:03	265	9
G—**Herbert Scott**, Dallas		6:02	252	7
C—**Mike Webster**, Pittsburgh		6:01	250	8
QB—**Ken Anderson**, Cincinnati		6:03	208	11
RB—**Tony Dorsett**, Dallas		5:11	190	5
RB—**George Rogers**, New Orleans		6:02	220	R

DEFENSE

Pos.	Player and Club	Hgt.	Wgt.	Pro Yrs.
DE—**Joe Klecko**, New York Jets		6:03	265	5
DE—**Fred Dean**, San Francisco		6:02	230	7
DT—**Randy White**, Dallas		6:04	250	7
DT—**Bob Baumhower**, Miami		6:05	260	5
ILB—**Randy Gradishar**, Denver		6:03	231	8
ILB—**Jack Lambert**, Pittsburgh		6:04	220	8
OLB—**Lawrence Taylor**, New York Giants		6:03	237	R
OLB—**Bob Swenson**, Denver		6:03	225	5
CB—**Ronnie Lott**, San Francisco		6:00	199	R
CB—**Lester Hayes**, Oakland		6:00	200	5
SS—**Gary Fencik**, Chicago		6:01	197	6
FS—**Nolan Cromwell**, Los Angeles		6:01	199	5

SPECIALISTS

Pos.	Player and Club	Hgt.	Wgt.	Pro Yrs.
P—**Pat McInally**, Cincinnati		6:06	213	6
PK—**Rafael Septien**, Dallas		5:09	174	5
PR—**LeRoy Irvin**, Los Angeles		5:11	183	2
KOR—**Mike Nelms**, Washington		6:00	185	2

NFL Player of the Year—**Ken Anderson**, Cincinnati
NFL Rookie of the Year—**George Rogers**, New Orleans

NFL ANNUAL SELECTION MEETING

April 27, 1982

Start of Round:
10:00 a.m.

FIRST ROUND

1.	New England	SIMS, Ken (1)	DT	Texas
2.	Baltimore	COOKS, Johnie (2)	LB	Mississippi State
	New Orleans	Surrendered choice in 1981 Supplemental Draft (Dave Wilson, QB, Illinois)		
3.	Cleveland	BANKS, Chip (3)	LB	Southern Cal
4.	Baltimore from Los Angeles	SCHLICHTER, Art (4)	QB	Ohio State
5.	Chicago	McMAHON, Jim (5)	QB	Brigham Young
6.	Seattle	BRYANT, Jeff (6)	DE	Clemson
7.	Minnesota	NELSON, Darrin (7)	RB	Stanford
8.	Houston	MUNCHAK, Mike (8)	G	Penn State
9.	Atlanta	RIGGS, Gerald (9)	RB	Arizona State
10.	Oakland	ALLEN, Marcus (10)	RB	Southern Cal
11.	Kansas City from St. Louis	HANCOCK, Anthony (11)	WR	Tennessee
12.	Pittsburgh	ABERCROMBIE, Walter (12)	RB	Baylor
13.	New Orleans from Green Bay through San Diego	SCOTT, Lindsay (13)	WR	Georgia
14.	Los Angeles from Washington	REDDEN, Barry (14)	RB	Richmond
15.	Detroit	WILLIAMS, Jimmy (15)	LB	Nebraska
16.	St. Louis from Kansas City	SHARPE, Luis (16)	T	UCLA
17.	Tampa Bay	FARRELL, Sean (17)	G	Penn State
18.	New York Giants	WOOLFOLK, Butch (18)	RB	Michigan
19.	Buffalo from Denver	TUTTLE, Perry (19)	WR	Clemson
20.	Philadelphia	QUICK, Mike (20)	WR	North Carolina St.
21.	Denver from Buffalo	WILLHITE, Gerald (21)	RB	San Jose State
22.	Green Bay from San Diego	HALLSTROM, Ron (22)	G	Iowa
23.	New York Jets	CRABLE, Bob (23)	LB	Notre Dame
24.	Miami	FOSTER, Roy (24)	G	Southern Cal
25.	Dallas	HILL, Rod (25)	DB	Kentucky State
26.	Cincinnati	COLLINS, Glen (26)	DE	Mississippi State
27.	New England from San Francisco	WILLIAMS, Lester (27)	DT	Miami

End of Round:	**Time of Round:**	**Elapsed Time:**
1:30 p.m.	3 hours, 30 minutes	3 hours, 30 minutes

NFL ANNUAL SELECTION MEETING

April 27, 1982

SECOND ROUND

1. Baltimore	WISNIEWSKI, Leo (28)	DT	Penn State
2. San Francisco from New England	PARIS, Bubba (29)	T	Michigan
3. New Orleans	EDELMAN, Brad (30)	C	Missouri
4. Cleveland	BALDWIN, Keith (31)	DE	Texas A & M
5. Tampa Bay from Chicago	REESE, Booker (32)	DE	Bethune-Cookman
6. Seattle	SCHOLTZ, Bruce (33)	LB	Texas
7. Baltimore from Los Angeles	STARK, Rohn (34)	P	Florida State
8. Oakland from Houston	SQUIREK, Jack (35)	LB	Illinois
9. Atlanta	ROGERS, Doug (36)	DE	Stanford
10. Oakland	ROMANO, Jim (37)	C	Penn State
11. St. Louis	GALLOWAY, David (38)	DT	Florida
12. Minnesota	TAUSCH, Terry (39)	T	Texas
13. New England from Green Bay through San Diego	WEATHERS, Robert (40)	RB	Arizona State
14. New England from Washington through San Francisco	TIPPETT, Andre (41)	LB	Iowa
15. Detroit	WATKINS, Bobby (42)	DB	S.W. Texas State
16. Pittsburgh	MEYER, John (43)	T	Arizona State
17. Houston from Tampa Bay through Miami and Los Angeles	LUCK, Oliver (44)	QB	West Virginia
18. New York Giants	MORRIS, Joe (45)	RB	Syracuse
19. Kansas City	DANIELS, Calvin (46)	LB	North Carolina
20. Philadelphia	SAMPLETON, Lawrence (47)	TE	Texas
21. Buffalo	KOFLER, Matt (48)	QB	San Diego State
22. Washington from San Diego through Los Angeles	DEAN, Vernon (49)	DB	San Diego State
23. Denver	McDANIEL, Orlando (50)	WR	Louisiana State
24. New York Jets	McELROY, Reggie (51)	T	West Texas State
25. Miami	DUPER, Mark (52)	WR	N.W. Louisiana
26. Dallas	ROHRER, Jeff (53)	LB	Yale
27. Cincinnati	WEAVER, Emanuel (54)	DT	South Carolina
28. New England from San Francisco	HALEY, Darryl (55)	T	Utah

End of Round:
4:20 p.m.

Time of Round:
2 hours, 50 minutes

Elapsed Time:
6 hours, 20 minutes

NFL ANNUAL SELECTION MEETING

April 27, 1982

Start of Round:
4:20 p.m.

THIRD ROUND

1. New England	JONES, Cedric (56)		WR	Duke
2. Baltimore	BURROUGHS, James (57)		DB	Michigan State
3. New Orleans	LEWIS, Rodney (58)		DB	Nebraska
4. Buffalo from Cleveland	MARVE, Eugene (59)		LB	Saginaw Valley
5. New England from Seattle	WEISHUHN, Clayton (60)		LB	Angelo State
6. Washington from Los Angeles	POWELL, Carl (61)		WR	Jackson State
7. Chicago	WRIGHTMAN, Tim (62)		TE	UCLA
8. Atlanta	BAILEY, Stacey (63)		WR	San Jose State
9. Oakland	McELROY, Vann (64)		DB	Baylor
10. St. Louis	PERRIN, Benny (65)		DB	Alabama
11. New Orleans from Minnesota	GOODLOW, Eugene (66)		WR	Kansas State/ Winnipeg CFL
12. Los Angeles from Houston	BECHTOLD, Bill (67)		C	Oklahoma
13. New Orleans from Washington	DUCKETT, Ken (68)		WR	Wake Forest
14. Detroit	DOIG, Steve (69)		LB	New Hampshire
15. Pittsburgh	MERRIWEATHER, Mike (70)		LB	Pacific
16. Green Bay	RODGERS, Del (71)		RB	Utah
17. Houston from N.Y. Giants	EDWARDS, Stanley (72)		RB	Michigan
18. St. Louis from Kansas City	GUILBEAU, Rusty (73)		DE	McNeese State
19. Tampa Bay	BELL, Jerry (74)		TE	Arizona State
20. Seattle from Buffalo	METZELAARS, Pete (75)		TE	Wabash
21. New Orleans from San Diego	KRIMM, John (76)		DB	Notre Dame
22. Houston from Denver through Los Angeles	ABRAHAM, Robert (77)		LB	North Carolina St.
23. Philadelphia	KAB, Vyto (78)		TE	Penn State
24. New York Jets	CRUTCHFIELD, Dwayne (79)		RB	Iowa State
25. Miami	LANKFORD, Paul (80)		DB	Penn State
26. Dallas	ELIOPULOS, Jim (81)		LB	Wyoming
27. Cincinnati	HOLMAN, Rodney (82)		TE	Tulane
28. Tampa Bay from San Francisco through San Diego	CANNON, John (83)		DE	William & Mary

End of Round:
5:27 p.m.

Time of Round:
1 hour, 7 minutes

Elapsed Time:
7 hours, 27 minutes

NFL ANNUAL SELECTION MEETING

April 27, 1982

FOURTH ROUND

1. Baltimore	PAGEL, Mike (84)	QB	Arizona State
2. New England	CRUMP, George (85)	DE	East Carolina
3. New Orleans	ANDERSEN, Morten (86)	K	Michigan State
4. Cleveland	WALKER, Dwight (87)	WR	Nicholls State
5. Los Angeles	GAYLORD, Jeff (88)	LB	Missouri
6. Chicago	GENTRY, Dennis (89)	RB	Baylor
7. St. Louis from Seattle	ROBBINS, Tootie (90)	T	East Carolina
8. Oakland	MURANSKY, Ed (91)	T	Michigan
9. *Minnesota	FAHNHORST, Jim (92)	LB	Minnesota
10. Buffalo from St. Louis	WILLIAMS, Van (93)	RB	Carson Newman
11. Houston	BRYANT, Steve (94)	WR	Purdue
12. Atlanta	BROWN, Reggie (95)	RB	Oregon
13. Detroit	McNORTON, Bruce (96)	DB	Georgetown, Ky.
14. Pittsburgh	WOODS, Rick (97)	DB	Boise State
15. Green Bay	BROWN, Robert (98)	LB	Virginia Tech
16. Washington	LIEBENSTEIN, Todd (99)	DE	Nevada-Las Vegas
17. Kansas City	HAYNES, Louis (100)	LB	North Texas State
18. Dallas from Tampa Bay	CARPENTER, Brian (101)	DB	Michigan
19. New York Giants	RAYMOND, Gerry (102)	G	Boston College
20. Tampa Bay from San Diego	BARRETT, Dave (103)	RB	Houston
21. Kansas City from Denver	ANDERSON, Stuart (104)	LB	Virginia
22. Philadelphia	GRIGGS, Anthony (105)	LB	Ohio State
23. Denver from Buffalo	PLATER, Dan (106)	WR	Brigham Young
24. New York Jets	FLOYD, George (107)	DB	Eastern Kentucky
25. Miami	BOWSER, Charles (108)	LB	Duke
26. Dallas	HUNTER, Monty (109)	DB	Salem, W.Va.
27. Cincinnati	TATE, Rodney (110)	RB	Texas
28. New England from San Francisco	INGRAM, Brian (111)	LB	Tennessee

*Minnesota selected ahead of St. Louis which passed and traded its choice to Buffalo.

End of Round:	Time of Round:	Elapsed Time:
6:42 p.m.	1 hour, 15 minutes	8 hours, 42 minutes

NFL ANNUAL SELECTION MEETING

April 27, 1982

FIFTH ROUND

1.	New England	MARION, Fred (112)	DB	Miami
2.	Baltimore	CROUCH, Terry (113)	G	Oklahoma
3.	New Orleans	ELLIOTT, Tony (114)	DE	North Texas State
4.	Cleveland	BAAB, Mike (115)	C	Texas
5.	Chicago	HARTNETT, Perry (116)	T	SMU
6.	Los Angeles from Seattle	KERSTEN, Wally (117)	T	Minnesota
7.	Los Angeles	BARNETT, Doug (118)	DE	Azusa Pacific
8.	St. Louis	BEDFORD, Vance (119)	DB	Texas
9.	Miami from Minnesota	NELSON, Bob (120)	DT	Miami, Fla.
10.	Houston	TAYLOR, Malcolm (121)	DE	Tennessee State
11.	Atlanta	MANSFIELD, Von (122)	DB	Wisconsin
12.	Oakland	JACKSON, Ed (123)	LB	Louisiana Tech
13.	Pittsburgh	DALLAFIOR, Ken (124)	T	Minnesota
14.	*St. Louis from Washington	FERRELL, Earl (125)	RB	East Tennessee St.
15.	Green Bay	MEADE, Mike (126)	RB	Penn State
16.	Detroit	GRAHAM, William (127)	DB	Texas
17.	Tampa Bay	DAVIS, Jeff (128)	LB	Clemson
18.	New York Giants	UMPHREY, Rich (129)	C	Colorado
19.	Kansas City	THOMPSON, Delbert (130)	RB	Texas-El Paso
20.	Denver	WINDER, Sammy (131)	RB	Southern Miss.
21.	Philadelphia	DeVAUGHN, Dennis (132)	DB	Bishop
22.	Washington from Buffalo	WILLIAMS, Michael (133)	TE	Alabama A&M
23.	Chicago from San Diego	TABRON, Dennis (134)	DB	Duke
24.	New York Jets	JERUE, Mark (135)	LB	Washington
25.	Miami	DIANA, Rich (136)	RB	Yale
26.	Dallas	POZDERAC, Phil (137)	T	Notre Dame
27.	Cincinnati	SORENSEN, Paul (138)	DB	Washington State
28.	San Francisco	WILLIAMS, Newton (139)	RB	Arizona State

*St. Louis selected ahead of Green Bay which passed.

End of Round:	Time of Round:	Elapsed Time:
7:49 p.m.	1 hour, 7 minutes	9 hours, 49 minutes

NFL ANNUAL SELECTION MEETING

April 27, 1982

SIXTH ROUND

1. Baltimore	BEACH, Pat (140)	TE	Washington State
2. New England	SMITH, Ricky (141)	DB	Alabama State
3. New Orleans	LEWIS, Marvin (142)	RB	Tulane
4. Dallas from Cleveland	HAMMOND, Ken (143)	G	Vanderbilt
5. Seattle	CAMPBELL, Jack (144)	T	Utah
6. Los Angeles	LOCKLIN, Kerry (145)	TE	New Mexico State
7. Chicago	BECKER, Kurt (146)	G	Michigan
8. Minnesota	STORR, Greg (147)	LB	Boston College
9. Houston	ALLEN, Gary (148)	RB	Hawaii
10. Atlanta	KELLEY, Mike (149)	QB	Georgia Tech
11. *St. Louis	SHAFFER, Craig (150)	LB	Indiana State
12. San Francisco from Oakland	WILLIAMS, Vince (151)	RB	Oregon
13. Green Bay	PARLAVECCHIO, Chet (152)	LB	Penn State
14. Washington	JEFFERS, Lemont Holt (153)	LB	Tennessee
15. Detroit	MACHUREK, Mike (154)	QB	Idaho State
16. Pittsburgh	PERKO, Mike (155)	DT	Utah State
17. New York Giants	NICHOLSON, Darrell (156)	LB	North Carolina
18. Kansas City	ROQUEMORE, Durwood (157)	DB	Texas A & I
19. Tampa Bay	TYLER, Andre (158)	WR	Stanford
20. Philadelphia	GRIEVE, Curt (159)	WR	Yale
21. Buffalo	CHIVERS, De Wayne (160)	TE	South Carolina
22. Miami from San Diego	TUTSON, Tom (161)	DB	South Carolina St.
23. Cleveland from Denver	WHITWELL, Mike (162)	WR	Texas A & M
24. New York Jets	PHEA, Lonell (163)	WR	Houston
25. Miami	HESTER, Ron (164)	LB	Florida State
26. Dallas	DAUM, Charles (165)	DT	Cal Poly-Obispo
27. Cincinnati	KING, Arthur (166)	DE	Grambling
28. Pittsburgh	BINGHAM, Craig (167)	LB	Syracuse

from San Francisco thru New Orleans

*St. Louis selected ahead of San Francisco which passed.

End of Round: 8:54 p.m.	**Time of Round:** 1 hour, 5 minutes	**Elapsed Time:** 10 hours, 54 minutes

NFL ANNUAL SELECTION MEETING

April 28, 1982

Start of Round:
10:00 a.m.

SEVENTH ROUND

1. New England	ROBERTS, Jeff (168)	LB	Tulane
2. Baltimore	JENKINS, Fletcher (169)	DT	Washington
3. Miami	JOHNSON, Dan (170)	TE	Iowa State
from New Orleans			
4. Buffalo	ANDERSON, Gary (171)	K	Syracuse
from Cleveland			
5. Pittsburgh	NELSON, Edmund (172)	DT	Auburn
from Los Angeles			
6. Chicago	WAECHTER, Henry (173)	DT	Nebraska
7. Seattle	WILLIAMS, Eugene (174)	LB	Tulsa
8. Detroit	BATES, Phil (175)	RB	Nebraska
from Houston			
9. Atlanta	TOLOUMU, David (176)	RB	Hawaii
10. Oakland	JACKSON, Jeff (177)	DE	Toledo
11. St. Louis	SEBRO, Bob (178)	C	Colorado
12. Minnesota	JORDAN, Steve (179)	TE	Brown
13. Washington	SCHACHTNER, John (180)	LB	Northern Arizona
14. Los Angeles	SHEARIN, Joe (181)	G	Texas
from Detroit			
15. Pittsburgh	BOURES, Emil (182)	C	Pittsburgh
16. Green Bay	WHITLEY, Joey (183)	DB	Texas-El Paso
17. Kansas City	SMITH, Greg (184)	DT	Kansas
18. Tampa Bay	MORRIS, Thomas (185)	DB	Michigan State
19. New York Giants	WISKA, Jeff (186)	G	Michigan State
20. Detroit	SIMMONS, Victor (187)	WR	Oregon State
from Buffalo through Los Angeles			
21. San Diego	HALL, Hollis (188)	DB	Clemson
22. Denver	RUBEN, Alvin (189)	DE	Houston
23. Philadelphia	ARMSTRONG, Harvey (190)	DT	SMU
24. New York Jets	COOMBS, Tom (191)	TE	Idaho
25. Miami	COWAN, Larry (192)	RB	Jackson State
26. Dallas	PURIFOY, Bill (193)	DE	Tulsa
27. Cincinnati	NEEDHAM, Ben (194)	LB	Michigan
28. San Francisco	FERRARI, Ron (195)	LB	Illinois

End of Round: **Time of Round:** **Elapsed Time:**
11:00 a.m. **1 hour** **11 hours, 54 minutes**

NFL ANNUAL SELECTION MEETING
April 28, 1982

EIGHTH ROUND

#	Team	Player	Pos	College
1.	Baltimore	LOIA, Tony (196)	T	Arizona State
2.	New England	COLLINS, Ken (197)	DT/LB	Washington State
3.	New Orleans	SLAUGHTER, Chuck (198)	T	South Carolina
4.	Cleveland	KAFENTZIS, Mark (199)	DB	Hawaii
5.	Chicago	DOERGER, Jerry (200)	T	Wisconsin
6.	Seattle	COOPER, Chester (201)	WR	Minnesota
7.	Los Angeles	JONES, A. J. (202)	RB	Texas
8.	Atlanta	EBERHART, Ricky (203)	DB	Morris Brown
9.	Cleveland from Oakland	HEFLIN, Van (204)	TE	Vanderbilt
10.	St. Louis	LINDSTROM, Chris (205)	DT	Boston U.
11.	Minnesota	HARMON, Kirk (206)	LB	Pacific
12.	Los Angeles from Houston	REILLY, Mike (207)	LB	Oklahoma
13.	Detroit	MOSS, Martin (208)	DE	UCLA
14.	Pittsburgh	GOODSON, John (209)	P	Texas
15.	Green Bay	BOYD, Thomas (210)	LB	Alabama
16.	Cleveland from Washington	JACKSON, Bill (211)	DB	North Carolina
17.	Tampa Bay	ATKINS, Kelvin (212)	LB	Illinois
18.	New York Giants	HUBBLE, Robert (213)	TE	Rice
19.	Kansas City	DE BRUIJN, Case (214)	P-K	Idaho State
20.	San Diego	BUFORD, Maury (215)	P	Texas Tech
21.	Dallas from Denver through Buffalo	PEOPLES, George (216)	RB	Auburn
22.	Philadelphia	FRITZSCHE, Jim (217)	T	Purdue
23.	Buffalo	TOUSIGNANT, Luc (218)	QB	Fairmont State
24.	New York Jets	TEXADA, Lawrence (219)	RB	Henderson, Ark.
25.	Miami	RANDLE, Tate (220)	DB	Texas Tech
26.	Dallas	SULLIVAN, Dwight (221)	RB	North Carolina St.
27.	Cincinnati	YLI-RENKO, Kari (222)	T	Cincinnati
28.	Washington from San Francisco through New Orleans	WARTHEN, Ralph (223)	DT	Gardner-Webb

End of Round:
12:01 p.m.

Time of Round:
1 hour, 1 minute

Elapsed Time:
12 hours, 55 minutes

NFL ANNUAL SELECTION MEETING

April 28, 1982

NINTH ROUND

1. New England — MURDOCK, Kelvin (224) — WR — Troy State
2. Baltimore — BERRYHILL, Tony (225) — C — Clemson
3. Washington — COFFEY, Ken (226) — DB — S.W. Texas State
   from New Orleans
4. Cleveland — BAKER, Milton (227) — TE — West Texas State
5. Seattle — JEFFERSON, David (228) — LB — Miami, Fla.
6. Los Angeles — SPEIGHT, Bob (229) — T — Boston U.
7. Chicago — HATCHETT, Mike (230) — DB — Texas
8. Detroit — WAGONER, Dan (231) — DB — Kansas
   from Oakland through Los Angeles
9. St. Louis — DAILEY, Darnell (232) — LB — Maryland
10. Minnesota — HOWARD, Bryan (233) — DB — Tennessee State
11. Houston — BRADLEY, Matt (234) — DB — Penn State
12. Atlanta — HORAN, Mike (235) — P — Cal St.-Long Beach
13. Pittsburgh — HIRN, Mike (236) — TE — Central Michigan
14. Green Bay — RIGGINS, Charles (237) — DE — Bethune-Cookman
15. Washington — TRAUTMAN, Randy (238) — DT — Boise State
16. Miami — CLARK, Steve (239) — DT — Utah
    from Detroit
17. New York Giants — HIGGINS, John (240) — DB — Nevada-Las Vegas
18. Kansas City — BYFORD, Lyndle (241) — T — Oklahoma
19. Tampa Bay — LANE, Bob (242) — QB — N.E. Louisiana
20. Denver — UECKER, Keith (243) — T — Auburn
21. Philadelphia — WOODRUFF, Tony (244) — WR — Fresno State
22. Buffalo — EDWARDS, Dennis (245) — DT — Southern Cal
23. San Diego — LYLES, Warren (246) — DT — Alabama
24. New York Jets — KLEVER, Rocky (247) — RB — Montana
25. Miami — BOATNER, Mack (248) — RB — S.E. Louisiana
26. Dallas — GARY, Joe (249) — DT — UCLA
27. Cincinnati — BENNETT, James (250) — WR — N.W. Louisiana
28. San Francisco — CLARK, Bryan (251) — QB — Michigan State

End of Round:	Time of Round:	Elapsed Time:
1:04 p.m.	1 hour, 3 minutes	13 hours, 58 minutes

NFL ANNUAL SELECTION MEETING

April 28, 1982

TENTH ROUND

1. Baltimore	DEERY, Tom (252)	DB	Widener
2. New England	CLARK, Brian (253)	K	Florida
3. Washington from New Orleans	SMITH, Harold (254)	DE	Kentucky State
4. Cleveland	FLOYD, Ricky (255)	RB	Southern Miss.
5. Los Angeles	McPHERSON, Miles (256)	DB	New Haven
6. Chicago	TURNER, Joe (257)	DB	Southern Cal
7. Seattle	AUSTIN, Craig (258)	LB	South Dakota
8. St. Louis	McGILL, Eddie (259)	TE	Western Carolina
9. Minnesota	LUCEAR, Gerald (260)	WR	Temple
10. Houston	REEVES, Ron (261)	QB	Texas Tech
11. Atlanta	STOWERS, Curtis (262)	LB	Mississippi State
12. Oakland	D'AMICO, Rich (263)	LB	Penn State
13. Green Bay	GARCIA, Eddie (264)	K	SMU
14. Washington	DANIELS, Terry (265)	DB	Tennessee
15. Detroit	BARNES, Roosevelt (266)	LB	Purdue
16. Pittsburgh	SUNSERI, Sal (267)	LB	Pittsburgh
17. Kansas City	BRODSKY, Larry (268)	WR	Miami, Fla.
18. San Francisco from Tampa Bay	McLEMORE, Dana (269)	DB/KR	Hawaii
19. New York Giants	BALDINGER, Richard (270)	T	Wake Forest
20. Miami from Philadelphia	FISHER, Robin (271)	LB	Florida
21. Buffalo	JAMES, Vic (272)	DB	Colorado
22. San Diego	YOUNG, Andre (273)	DB	Louisiana Tech
23. Denver	WOODARD, Ken (274)	LB	Tuskegee
24. New York Jets	HEMPHILL, Darryl (275)	DB	West Texas State
25. Miami	JONES, Wayne (276)	T	Utah
26. Dallas	ECKERSON, Todd (277)	T	North Carolina St.
27. Cincinnati	HOGUE, Larry (278)	DB	Utah State
28. San Francisco	BARBIAN, Tim (279)	DT	Western Illinois

End of Round:	Time of Round:	Elapsed Time:
2:04 p.m.	1 hour	14 hours, 58 minutes

NFL ANNUAL SELECTION MEETING

April 28, 1982

ELEVENTH ROUND

New England	Surrendered choice in 1981 Supplemental Draft (Chy Davidson, WR, Rhode Island)		
1. Baltimore	MEACHAM, Lamont (280)	DB	Western Kentucky
2. Washington from New Orleans	MILLER, Dan (281)	K	Miami, Fla.
3. Cleveland	MICHUTA, Steve (282)	QB	Grand Valley State
4. Chicago	BOLIAUX, Guy (283)	LB	Wisconsin
5. Seattle	CLANCY, Sam (284)	DT	Pittsburgh
6. Los Angeles	COFFMAN, Ricky (285)	WR	UCLA
7. Minnesota	ROUSE, Curtis (286)	G	Tennessee-Chatt.
8. Houston	CAMPBELL, Jim (287)	TE	Kentucky
9. Atlanta	KELLER, Jeff (288)	WR	Washington State
10. Oakland	TURNER, Willie (289)	WR	Louisiana State
11. St. Louis	WILLIAMS, James (290)	DE	North Carol. A&T
12. Washington	HOLLY, Bob (291)	QB	Princeton
13. Detroit	LEE, Edward (292)	WR	South Carolina St.
14. Pittsburgh	ABDUL-SABOOR, Mikal (293)	G	Morgan State
15. Green Bay	MACAULAY, John (294)	C	Stanford
16. Dallas from Tampa Bay	THOMPSON, George (295)	WR	Albany State, Ga.
17. New England from N. Y. Giants	SANDON, Steve (296)	QB	Northern Iowa
18. Kansas City	CARTER, Bob (297)	WR	Arizona
19. Buffalo	KALIL, Frank (298)	G	Arizona
20. San Diego	WATSON, Anthony (299)	DB	New Mexico State
21. Denver	YATSKO, Stuart (300)	G	Oregon
22. Philadelphia	INGRAM, Ron (301)	WR	Oklahoma State
23. New York Jets	PARMELEE, Perry (302)	WR	Santa Clara
24. Miami	CRUM, Gary (303)	T	Wyoming
25. Dallas	WHITING, Mike (304)	RB	Florida State
26. Cincinnati	DAVIS, Russell (305)	RB	Idaho
27. San Francisco	GIBSON, Gary (306)	LB	Arizona

End of Round:	**Time of Round:**	**Elapsed Time:**
3:10 p.m.	1 hour, 6 minutes	16 hours, 4 minutes

NFL ANNUAL SELECTION MEETING

April 28, 1982

Start of Round:
3:10 p.m.

TWELFTH ROUND

1. Baltimore	WRIGHT, Johnnie (307)	RB	South Carolina
2. New England	TAYLOR, Greg (308)	WR	Virginia
3. Washington from New Orleans	LASTER, Donald (309)	T	Tennessee State
4. Cleveland	NICOLAS, Scott (310)	LB	Miami, Fla.
5. Seattle	NAYLOR, Frank (311)	C	Rutgers
6. Los Angeles	COLEY, Raymond (312)	DT	Alabama A & M
7. Chicago	YOUNG, Ricky (313)	LB	Oklahoma State
8. Houston	CRAFT, Donald (314)	RB	Louisville
9. Atlanta	LEVENICK, Dave (315)	LB	Wisconsin
10. Oakland	SMITH, Randy (316)	WR	East Texas State
11. St. Louis	ATHA, Bob (317)	K	Ohio State
12. Minnesota	MILNER, Hobson (318)	RB	Cincinnati
13. Detroit	PORTER, Ricky (319)	RB	Slippery Rock
14. Pittsburgh	HUGHES, Al (320)	DE	Western Michigan
15. Green Bay	EPPS, Phillip (321)	WR	Texas Christian
16. Washington	GOFF, Jeff (322)	LB	Arkansas
17. New York Giants	SEALE, Mark (323)	DT	Richmond
18. Kansas City	MILLER, Mike (324)	DB	S.W. Texas State
19. Tampa Bay	MORTON, Michael (325)	WR/KR	Nevada-Las Vegas
20. Detroit from San Diego	RUBICK, Rob (326)	TE	Grand Valley State
21. Denver	CLARK, Brian (327)	G	Clemson
22. Philadelphia	TAYLOR, Rob (328)	T	Northwestern
23. Buffalo	SUBER, Tony (329)	DT	Gardner-Webb
24. New York Jets	CARLSTROM, Tom (330)	G	Nebraska
25. Miami	RODRIGUE, Mike (331)	WR	Miami, Fla.
26. Dallas	BURTNESS, Rich (332)	G	Montana
27. Cincinnati	FERADAY, Dan (333)	QB	Toronto
28. San Francisco	WASHINGTON, Tim (334)	DB	Fresno State

End of Round:
4:04 p.m.

Time of Round:
54 minutes

Elapsed Time:
16 hours, 58 minutes

1982 INTERCONFERENCE TRADES

Linebacker DAVID LEWIS from Tampa Bay to San Diego for third-round selection in 1982 draft and fourth-round selection in 1984. Tampa Bay subsequently selected defensive end JOHN CANNON (William & Mary) (2/1).

Running back RICKY BELL from Tampa Bay to San Diego for fourth-round selection in 1982. Tampa Bay subsequently selected running back DAVE BARRETT (Houston) (3/10).

Linebacker DEWEY SELMON from Tampa Bay to San Diego for fourth-round selection (previously acquired from San Francisco) in 1984 (3/29).

Quarterback BERT JONES from Baltimore to Los Angeles for the Rams' first and second round choices in the 1982 draft. Baltimore subsequently selected quarterback ART SCHLICHTER (Ohio State) and punter ROHN STARK (Florida State) (4/27).

Tight end MIKE BARBER and third and eighth round choices in 1982 from Houston to Los Angeles for tight end LEWIS GILBERT and second and third round choices in 1982. Houston subsequently selected quarterback OLIVER LUCK (West Virginia) and linebacker ROBERT ABRAHAM (North Carolina State). Los Angeles subsequently selected center BILL BECHTOLD (Oklahoma) and defensive end MIKE REILLY (Oklahoma) (4/27).

St. Louis' first choice in 1982 to Kansas City for the Chiefs' first and third round choices in 1982. Kansas City subsequently selected wide receiver ANTHONY HANCOCK (Tennessee). St. Louis subsequently selected tackle LUIS SHARPE (UCLA) and defensive end RUSTY GUILBEAU (McNeese State) (4/27).

Tight end RUSS FRANCIS from New England to San Francisco for the 49ers' first and fourth round choices in the 1982 draft. New England subsequently selected defensive tackle LESTER WILLIAMS (Miami, Fla.) and linebacker BRIAN INGRAM (Tennessee) (4/27).

San Francisco's two second round choices (one acquired earlier from Washington) to New England for the Patriots' second round choice in 1982. San Francisco subsequently selected tackle BUBBA PARIS (Michigan). New England subsequently selected linebacker ANDRE TIPPETT (Iowa) and tackle DARRYL HALEY (Utah) (4/27).

St. Louis' fourth round choice in 1982 to Buffalo for the Bills' third round choice in 1983. Buffalo subsequently selected running back VAN WILLIAMS (Carson-Newman) (4/27).

Washington cornerback LAMAR PARRISH to Buffalo for fourth round choice in 1982. Washington subsequently selected defensive back MICHAEL WILLIAMS (Alabama A&M) (4/27).

Pittsburgh linebacker DENNIS WINSTON to New Orleans for sixth round choice in the 1982 draft. Pittsburgh subsequently selected linebacker CRAIG BINGHAM (Syracuse) (4/27).

Detroit safety LUTHER BRADLEY to Houston for seventh round choice in 1982. Detroit subsequently selected running back PHIL BATES (Nebraska) (4/28).

New England linebacker ROD SHOATE to Chicago for fifth round choice in 1983 (4/28).

Linebacker TERRY BEESON from Seattle to Atlanta for a draft choice (4/30).

New England defensive end JOHN LEE to Chicago for future draft choice (5/25).

Minnesota linebacker JEFF SIEMON to San Diego for future draft choice (5/28).

San Diego linebacker BOB HORN to San Francisco for future draft choice (6/9).

1982 AMERICAN FOOTBALL CONFERENCE TRADES

Linebacker TOM COUSINEAU from Buffalo to Cleveland for first round selection in 1983 and future draft choices (4/26).

Denver's first round choice in 1982 to Buffalo for the Bills' first and fourth round choices in 1982. Buffalo subsequently selected wide receiver PERRY TUTTLE (Clemson). Denver subsequently selected running back GERALD WILLHITE (San Jose State) and wide receiver DAN PLATER (Brigham Young) (4/27).

Defensive back TIM FOX from New England to San Diego for second round choice in 1982 and third round choice in 1983. New England subsequently selected running back ROBERT WEATHERS (Arizona State) (4/27).

Linebacker ROBERT L. JACKSON from Cleveland to Denver for sixth round choice in 1982. Cleveland subsequently selected wide receiver MIKE WHITWELL (Texas A&M) (4/27).

Defensive tackle LYLE ALZADO from Cleveland to Oakland for eighth round choice in the 1982 draft. Cleveland subsequently selected tight end VAN HEFLIN (Vanderbilt) (4/28).

Running back GREG PRUITT from Cleveland to Oakland for a 1983 draft choice (4/29).

Baltimore safety BRUCE LAIRD to San Diego for future draft choice (5/26).

Cleveland linebacker DON GOODE to Oakland for past considerations (5/27).

1982 NATIONAL FOOTBALL CONFERENCE TRADES

Tampa Bay's first round choice in 1983 to Chicago for the Bears' second round choice in 1982. Tampa Bay subsequently selected defensive end BOOKER REESE (Bethune-Cookman) (4/27).

Detroit's seventh round choice in 1982 to Los Angeles for seventh and ninth round choices in the 1982 draft. Los Angeles subsequently selected guard JOE SHEARIN (Texas). Detroit subsequently selected wide receivers VICTOR SIMMONS (Oregon State) and defensive back DANNY WAGONER (Kansas) (4/28).

Washington's fourth round choice in 1983 to New Orleans for the Saints' eighth, ninth, 10th, 11th and 12th round choices in 1982. Washington subsequently selected defensive tackle RALPH WARTHEN (Gardner-Webb), defensive back KEN COFFEY (Southwest Texas), defensive end HAROLD SMITH (Kentucky State), kicker DAN MILLER (Miami, Fla.), and tackle DON LASTER (Tennessee State) (4/28).

Green Bay defensive tackle BRUCE CLARK to New Orleans for the Saints' first round choice in 1983 (6/10).

1982 NFL DRAFT SUMMARY

AMERICAN FOOTBALL CONFERENCE

	—OFFENSE—								—DEFENSE—					SPEC.
---	QB	RB	WR	TE	C	G	T	Tot.	DE	DT	LB	DB	Tot.	K-P-KR
Baltimore (14)	*2	1	0	1	1	2	0	7	0	2	*1	3	6	1
Buffalo (11)	2	1	*1	1	0	1	0	6	0	2	1	1	4	1
Cincinnati (12)	1	2	1	1	0	0	1	6	*1	2	1	2	6	0
Cleveland (12)	1	1	2	2	1	0	0	7	1	0	*2	2	5	0
Denver (9)	0	*2	2	0	0	2	1	7	1	0	1	0	2	0
Houston (11)	2	3	1	1	0	*1	0	8	1	0	1	1	3	0
Kansas City (12)	0	1	*3	0	0	0	1	5	0	1	3	2	6	1
Miami (17)	0	3	2	1	0	*1	2	9	1	1	3	3	8	0
New England (17)	1	1	3	0	0	1	0	6	1	**2	5	2	10	1
New York Jets (12)	0	3	2	1	0	1	1	8	0	0	*2	2	4	0
Oakland (10)	0	*1	2	0	1	0	1	5	1	0	3	1	5	0
Pittsburgh (14)	0	*1	0	1	1	1	2	6	1	2	3	1	7	1
San Diego (5)	0	0	0	0	0	0	0	0	0	1	0	3	4	1
Seattle (10)	0	0	1	1	1	0	1	4	*2	0	4	0	6	0
Totals (166)	9	20	20	10	5	10	10	84	10	13	30	23	76	6

NATIONAL FOOTBALL CONFERENCE

	—OFFENSE—								—DEFENSE—					SPEC.
---	QB	RB	WR	TE	C	G	T	Tot.	DE	DT	LB	DB	Tot.	K-P-KR
Atlanta (12)	1	*3	2	0	0	0	0	6	1	0	2	2	5	1
Chicago (12)	*1	1	0	1	0	2	1	6	0	1	2	3	6	0
Dallas (16)	0	3	1	0	0	2	2	8	1	2	2	*3	8	0
Detroit (14)	1	2	2	1	0	0	0	6	1	0	*3	4	8	0
Green Bay (11)	0	2	1	0	1	*1	0	5	1	0	3	1	5	1
Los Angeles (13)	0	*2	1	1	1	1	2	8	2	1	1	1	5	0
Minnesota (10)	0	*2	1	1	0	1	1	6	0	0	3	1	4	0
New Orleans (10)	0	1	*3	0	1	0	1	6	1	0	0	2	3	1
N.Y. Giants (10)	0	*2	0	1	1	2	1	7	0	1	1	1	3	0
Philadelphia (11)	0	0	*4	2	0	0	2	8	0	1	1	1	3	0
St. Louis (14)	0	1	0	1	1	0	*2	5	1	3	2	2	8	1
San Francisco (9)	1	2	0	0	0	0	1	4	0	1	2	1	4	1
Tampa Bay (11)	1	1	1	1	0	*1	0	5	2	0	2	1	5	1
Washington (15)	1	0	1	1	0	0	1	4	2	2	3	3	10	1
Totals (168)	6	22	17	10	5	10	14	84	12	12	27	26	77	7
28-Team Totals (334)	15	42	37	20	10	20	24	168	22	25	57	49	153	13

*Denotes first round choice by clubs (18 offense, 9 defense).
Figures in parentheses denote team's total draft choices.

1982 NATIONAL FOOTBALL LEAGUE SCHEDULE

(All times local)

FIRST WEEK

SUNDAY, SEPTEMBER 12

1. Atlanta at New York Giants 1:00
2. Chicago at Detroit 1:00
3. Cleveland at Seattle 1:00
4. Houston at Cincinnati 1:00
5. Kansas City at Buffalo 1:00
6. Los Angeles vs. Green Bay at Milw. 12:00
7. Miami at New York Jets 4:00
8. New England at Baltimore 2:00
9. Oakland at San Francisco 1:00
10. St. Louis at New Orleans 12:00
11. San Diego at Denver 2:00
12. Tampa Bay at Minnesota 12:00
13. Washington at Philadelphia 1:00

MONDAY, SEPTEMBER 13

14. Pittsburgh at Dallas 8:00

SECOND WEEK

THURSDAY, SEPTEMBER 16

15. Minnesota at Buffalo 8:30

SUNDAY, SEPTEMBER 19

16. Baltimore at Miami 4:00
17. Cincinnati at Pittsburgh 1:00
18. Dallas at St. Louis 12:00
19. Detroit at Los Angeles 1:00
20. New Orleans at Chicago 12:00
21. New York Jets at New England 1:00
22. Oakland at Atlanta 1:00
23. Philadelphia at Cleveland 1:00
24. San Diego at Kansas City 12:00
25. San Francisco at Denver 2:00
26. Seattle at Houston 3:00
27. Washington at Tampa Bay 4:00

MONDAY, SEPTEMBER 20

28. Green Bay at New York Giants 9:00

THIRD WEEK

THURSDAY, SEPTEMBER 23

29. Atlanta at Kansas City 7:30

SUNDAY, SEPTEMBER 26

30. Buffalo at Houston 12:00
31. Chicago at San Francisco 1:00
32. Dallas at Minnesota 12:00
33. Denver at New Orleans 12:00
34. Los Angeles at Philadelphia 1:00
35. Miami at Green Bay 12:00
36. New York Giants at Pittsburgh 1:00
37. New York Jets at Baltimore 4:00
38. Oakland at San Diego 1:00
39. St. Louis at Washington 1:00
40. Seattle at New England 1:00
41. Tampa Bay at Detroit 1:00

MONDAY, SEPTEMBER 27

42. Cincinnati at Cleveland 9:00

FOURTH WEEK

SUNDAY, OCTOBER 3

43. Baltimore at Detroit 1:00
44. Cleveland at Washington 1:00
45. Houston at New York Jets 1:00
46. Kansas City at Seattle 1:00
47. Los Angeles at St. Louis 12:00
48. Miami at Cincinnati 1:00
49. Minnesota at Chicago 12:00

50. New England at Buffalo 1:00
51. New Orleans at Oakland 1:00
52. New York Giants at Dallas 3:00
53. Philadelphia vs. Green Bay at Milw. 12:00
54. Pittsburgh at Denver 2:00
55. San Diego at Atlanta 1:00

MONDAY, OCTOBER 4

56. San Francisco at Tampa Bay 9:00

FIFTH WEEK

SUNDAY, OCTOBER 10

57. Atlanta at Los Angeles 1:00
58. Buffalo at Baltimore 2:00
59. Cincinnati at New England 1:00
60. Cleveland at Oakland 1:00
61. Denver at New York Jets 4:00
62. Detroit at Miami 4:00
63. Green Bay at Chicago 12:00
64. Houston at Kansas City 12:00
65. Minnesota at Tampa Bay 1:00
66. St. Louis at New York Giants 1:00
67. San Francisco at New Orleans 12:00
68. Seattle at San Diego 1:00
69. Washington at Dallas 12:00

MONDAY, OCTOBER 11

70. Philadelphia at Pittsburgh 9:00

SIXTH WEEK

SUNDAY, OCTOBER 17

71. Atlanta at Detroit 1:00
72. Baltimore at Cleveland 1:00
73. Chicago at St. Louis 12:00
74. Cincinnati at New York Giants 1:00
75. Dallas at Philadelphia 4:00
76. Denver at Houston 12:00
77. Kansas City at San Diego 1:00
78. Los Angeles at San Francisco 1:00
79. New England at Miami 1:00
80. New Orleans at Minnesota 12:00
81. Oakland at Seattle 1:00
82. Pittsburgh at Washington 1:00
83. Tampa Bay at Green Bay 12:00

MONDAY, OCTOBER 18

84. Buffalo at New York Jets 9:00

SEVENTH WEEK

SUNDAY, OCTOBER 24

85. Cleveland at Pittsburgh 1:00
86. Dallas at Cincinnati 9:00
87. Detroit at Buffalo 1:00
88. Green Bay at Minnesota 12:00
89. Miami at Baltimore 2:00
90. New Orleans at Los Angeles 1:00
91. New York Jets at Kansas City 12:00
92. Oakland at Denver 2:00
93. St. Louis at New England 1:00
94. San Diego at Seattle 1:00
95. San Francisco at Atlanta 1:00
96. Tampa Bay at Chicago 12:00
97. Washington at Houston 12:00

MONDAY, OCTOBER 25

98. New York Giants at Philadelphia 9:00

EIGHTH WEEK

SUNDAY, OCTOBER 31

99. Atlanta at New Orleans 12:00

100.	Buffalo at Denver	2:00
101.	Chicago at Green Bay	12:00
102.	Dallas at New York Giants	4:00
103.	Houston at Cleveland	1:00
104.	Los Angeles at San Diego	1:00
105.	Miami at Oakland	1:00
106.	New England at New York Jets	1:00
107.	Philadelphia at St. Louis	12:00
108.	Pittsburgh at Cincinnati	1:00
109.	San Francisco at Washington	1:00
110.	Seattle at Kansas City	12:00
111.	Tampa Bay at Baltimore	2:00

MONDAY, NOVEMBER 1
112.	Detroit at Minnesota	8:00

NINTH WEEK
SUNDAY, NOVEMBER 7
113.	Atlanta at Chicago	12:00
114.	Baltimore at New England	1:00
115.	Denver at Seattle	1:00
116.	Detroit at Philadelphia	1:00
117.	Green Bay at Tampa Bay	1:00
118.	Houston at Pittsburgh	1:00
119.	Kansas City at Oakland	1:00
120.	Los Angeles at New Orleans	12:00
121.	Minnesota at San Francisco	1:00
122.	New York Giants at Cleveland	1:00
123.	New York Jets at Buffalo	4:00
124.	St. Louis at Dallas	12:00
125.	Washington at Cincinnati	1:00

MONDAY, NOVEMBER 8
126.	San Diego at Miami	9:00

TENTH WEEK
SUNDAY, NOVEMBER 14
127.	Buffalo at New England	1:00
128.	Chicago at Tampa Bay	1:00
129.	Cincinnati at Houston	12:00
130.	Cleveland at Miami	4:00
131.	Dallas at San Francisco	1:00
132.	Denver at Kansas City	12:00
133.	Green Bay at Detroit	1:00
134.	Minnesota at Washington	1:00
135.	New Orleans at San Diego	1:00
136.	New York Giants at Los Angeles	1:00
137.	New York Jets at Pittsburgh	1:00
138.	Oakland at Baltimore	2:00
139.	Seattle at St. Louis	12:00

MONDAY, NOVEMBER 15
140.	Philadelphia at Atlanta	9:00

ELEVENTH WEEK
SUNDAY, NOVEMBER 21
141.	Baltimore at New York Jets	1:00
142.	Cincinnati at Philadelphia	1:00
143.	Detroit at Chicago	12:00
144.	Kansas City at New Orleans	12:00
145.	Los Angeles at Atlanta	1:00
146.	Miami at Buffalo	1:00
147.	Minnesota vs. Green Bay at Milw.	12:00
148.	New England at Cleveland	1:00
149.	Pittsburgh at Houston	12:00
150.	San Francisco at St. Louis	3:00
151.	Seattle at Denver	2:00
152.	Tampa Bay at Dallas	12:00
153.	Washington at New York Giants	4:00

MONDAY, NOVEMBER 22
154.	San Diego at Oakland	6:00

TWELFTH WEEK
THURSDAY, NOVEMBER 25
155.	Cleveland at Dallas	3:00
156.	New York Giants at Detroit	12:00

SUNDAY, NOVEMBER 28
157.	Baltimore at Buffalo	1:00
158.	Chicago at Minnesota	12:00
159.	Denver at San Diego	1:00
160.	Green Bay at New York Jets	1:00
161.	Houston at New England	1:00
162.	Kansas City at Los Angeles	1:00
163.	New Orleans at San Francisco	1:00
164.	Oakland at Cincinnati	1:00
165.	Philadelphia at Washington	1:00
166.	Pittsburgh at Seattle	1:00
167.	St. Louis at Atlanta	1:00

MONDAY, NOVEMBER 29
168.	Miami at Tampa Bay	9:00

THIRTEENTH WEEK
THURSDAY, DECEMBER 2
169.	San Francisco at Los Angeles	6:00

SUNDAY, DECEMBER 5
170.	Atlanta at Denver	2:00
171.	Buffalo vs. Green Bay at Milw.	12:00
172.	Cincinnati at Baltimore	2:00
173.	Dallas at Washington	4:00
174.	Houston at New York Giants	1:00
175.	Kansas City at Pittsburgh	1:00
176.	Minnesota at Miami	1:00
177.	New England at Chicago	12:00
178.	St. Louis at Philadelphia	1:00
179.	San Diego at Cleveland	1:00
180.	Seattle at Oakland	1:00
181.	Tampa Bay at New Orleans	12:00

MONDAY, DECEMBER 6
182.	New York Jets at Detroit	9:00

FOURTEENTH WEEK
SATURDAY, DECEMBER 11
183.	Philadelphia at New York Giants	12:30
184.	San Diego at San Francisco	1:00

SUNDAY, DECEMBER 12
185.	Baltimore at Minnesota	12:00
186.	Chicago at Seattle	1:00
187.	Cleveland at Cincinnati	1:00
188.	Denver at Los Angeles	1:00
189.	Detroit at Green Bay	12:00
190.	Miami at New England	1:00
191.	New Orleans at Atlanta	4:00
192.	Oakland at Kansas City	3:00
193.	Pittsburgh at Buffalo	12:00
194.	Tampa Bay at New York Jets	1:00
195.	Washington at St. Louis	12:00

MONDAY, DECEMBER 13
196.	Dallas at Houston	8:00

FIFTEENTH WEEK
SATURDAY, DECEMBER 18
197.	Los Angeles at Oakland	1:00
198.	New York Jets at Miami	12:30

SUNDAY, DECEMBER 19
199.	Atlanta at San Francisco	6:00
200.	Buffalo at Tampa Bay	1:00
201.	Green Bay at Baltimore	2:00
202.	Houston at Philadelphia	1:00
203.	Kansas City at Denver	2:00
204.	Minnesota at Detroit	1:00
205.	New England at Seattle	1:00

206.	New Orleans at Dallas	3:00
207.	New York Giants at Washington	1:00
208.	Pittsburgh at Cleveland	1:00
209.	St. Louis at Chicago	12:00

MONDAY, DECEMBER 20

210.	Cincinnati at San Diego	6:00

SIXTEENTH WEEK
SUNDAY, DECEMBER 26

211.	Baltimore at San Diego	1:00
212.	Chicago at Los Angeles	1:00
213.	Cleveland at Houston	12:00

214.	Denver at Oakland	1:00
215.	Detroit at Tampa Bay	1:00
216.	Green Bay at Atlanta	1:00
217.	New England at Pittsburgh	1:00
218.	New York Giants at St. Louis	12:00
219.	New York Jets at Minnesota	12:00
220.	Philadelphia at Dallas	3:00
221.	San Francisco at Kansas City	12:00
222.	Seattle at Cincinnati	1:00
223.	Washington at New Orleans	12:00

MONDAY, DECEMBER 27

224.	Buffalo at Miami	9:00

NFL POSTSEASON GAMES

SUNDAY, JANUARY 2
NFL First Round Playoffs

SATURDAY, JANUARY 8
AFC & NFC Divisional Playoffs

SUNDAY, JANUARY 9
AFC & NFC Divisional Playoffs

SUNDAY, JANUARY 16
AFC Championship Game
NFC Championship Game

SUNDAY, JANUARY 30
NFL Championship Game
at the Rose Bowl, Pasadena, California

SUNDAY, FEBRUARY 6
AFC-NFC Pro Bowl at Honolulu (day)

NFL PRESEASON GAMES

HALL OF FAME GAME
SATURDAY, AUGUST 7

Baltimore vs. Minnesota at Canton, O.	3:30

FIRST WEEK
THURSDAY, AUGUST 12

New Orleans at Houston	7:00

FRIDAY, AUGUST 13

St. Louis at Seattle	7:30

SATURDAY, AUGUST 14

New York Giants at Baltimore	8:00
New York Jets at Green Bay	7:00
Buffalo at Dallas	8:00
Cleveland at Detroit	7:00
Pittsburgh vs. New England at Knoxville	7:30
Cincinnati at Kansas City	7:35
Denver at Los Angeles	7:00
Oakland at San Francisco	6:00
Philadelphia at Tampa Bay	7:00
Washington at Miami	8:00
Minnesota at Atlanta	8:00

MONDAY, AUGUST 16

Chicago at San Diego	7:00

SECOND WEEK
THURSDAY, AUGUST 19

Los Angeles at Cleveland	7:30

SATURDAY, AUGUST 21

Atlanta vs. Baltimore at Tempe, Ariz.	7:00
Cincinnati vs. Green Bay at Milwaukee	7:00
Chicago at Buffalo	6:00
Pittsburgh at New York Giants	8:00
Dallas at San Diego	6:00
Miami at Denver	7:00
Oakland at Detroit	7:00
Kansas City at New Orleans	7:05
New England at Philadelphia	6:00
St. Louis at San Francisco	6:00

Seattle at Minnesota	7:30
Washington at Tampa Bay	7:00

SUNDAY, AUGUST 22

New York Jets at Houston	12:00

THIRD WEEK
FRIDAY, AUGUST 27

Buffalo at Washington	7:30
Philadelphia at Atlanta	8:30

SATURDAY, AUGUST 28

Baltimore at Pittsburgh	6:00
Green Bay at Oakland	6:00
Cleveland at New Orleans	7:00
St. Louis at Chicago	6:00
Detroit at Cincinnati	7:00
New England at Dallas	8:00
Minnesota at Denver	7:00
Miami at Kansas City	7:35
Seattle at Los Angeles	7:00
New York Jets at New York Giants	8:00
San Francisco at San Diego	6:00
Tampa Bay at Houston	8:00

FOURTH WEEK
FRIDAY, SEPTEMBER 3

Washington at Cincinnati	7:00
New York Giants at Miami	8:00
San Francisco at Seattle	7:30

SATURDAY, SEPTEMBER 4

Baltimore at Chicago	6:00
Green Bay at New England	1:00
Detroit at Buffalo	6:00
Cleveland at Oakland	3:00
Philadelphia at Pittsburgh	6:00
New Orleans at Minnesota	7:30
Houston at Dallas	8:00
Denver at New York Jets (Meadowlands)	8:00
Kansas City at St. Louis	6:05
San Diego at Los Angeles	7:00
Atlanta at Tampa Bay	7:00

1982 NATIONALLY TELEVISED GAMES
(All games also carried on CBS Radio Network)

REGULAR SEASON

Monday,   Sept. 13—Pittsburgh at Dallas (night, ABC)
Thursday, Sept. 16—Minnesota at Buffalo (night, ABC)
Monday,   Sept. 20—Green Bay at New York Giants (night, ABC)
Thursday, Sept. 23—Atlanta at Kansas City (night, ABC)
Monday,   Sept. 27—Cincinnati at Cleveland (night, ABC)
Monday,   Oct. 4—San Francisco at Tampa Bay (night, ABC)
Monday,   Oct. 11—Philadelphia at Pittsburgh (night, ABC)
Monday,   Oct. 18—Buffalo at New York Jets (night, ABC)
Sunday,   Oct. 24—Dallas at Cincinnati (night, ABC)
Monday,   Oct. 25—New York Giants at Philadelphia (night, ABC)
Monday,   Nov. 1—Detroit at Minnesota (night, ABC)
Monday,   Nov. 8—San Diego at Miami (night, ABC)
Monday,   Nov. 15—Philadelphia at Atlanta (night, ABC)
Monday,   Nov. 22—San Diego at Oakland (night, ABC)
Thursday, Nov. 25—(Thanksgiving) Cleveland at Dallas (day, NBC)
                       New York Giants at Detroit (day, CBS)
Monday,   Nov. 29—Miami at Tampa Bay (night, ABC)
Thursday, Dec. 2—San Francisco at Los Angeles (night, ABC)
Monday,   Dec. 6—New York Jets at Detroit (night, ABC)
Saturday, Dec. 11—Philadelphia at New York Giants (day, CBS)
                       San Diego at San Francisco (day, NBC)
Monday,   Dec. 13—Dallas at Houston (night, ABC)
Saturday, Dec. 18—Los Angeles at Oakland (day, CBS)
                       New York Jets at Miami (day, NBC)
Sunday,   Dec. 19—Atlanta at San Francisco (night, ABC)
Monday,   Dec. 20—Cincinnati at San Diego (night, ABC)
Monday,   Dec. 27—Buffalo at Miami (night, ABC)

NOTE: CBS and NBC also will televise a national doubleheader game each Sunday
      during the regular season.

POSTSEASON

Sunday,   Jan. 2—NFL First Round Playoffs (CBS and NBC)
Saturday, Jan. 8—AFC and NFC Divisional Playoffs (NBC and CBS)
Sunday,   Jan. 9—AFC and NFC Divisional Playoffs (NBC and CBS)
Sunday,   Jan. 16—AFC Championship Game (NBC)
                       NFC Championship Game (CBS)
Sunday,   Jan. 30—Super Bowl XVII at Rose Bowl, Pasadena, Calif. (NBC)
Sunday,   Feb. 6—AFC-NFC Pro Bowl at Honolulu, Hawaii (ABC)

MONDAY NIGHT GAMES AT A GLANCE
(All times local; televised by ABC and broadcast by CBS Radio)

Sept. 13—Pittsburgh at Dallas	8:00
Sept. 20—Green Bay at New York Giants	9:00
Sept. 27—Cincinnati at Cleveland	9:00
Oct. 4—San Francisco at Tampa Bay	9:00
Oct. 11—Philadelphia at Pittsburgh	9:00
Oct. 18—Buffalo at New York Jets	9:00
Oct. 25—New York Giants at Philadelphia	9:00
Nov. 1—Detroit at Minnesota	8:00
Nov. 8—San Diego at Miami	9:00
Nov. 15—Philadelphia at Atlanta	9:00
Nov. 22—San Diego at Oakland	6:00
Nov. 29—Miami at Tampa Bay	9:00
Dec. 6—New York Jets at Detroit	9:00
Dec. 13—Dallas at Houston	8:00
Dec. 20—Cincinnati at San Diego	6:00
Dec. 27—Buffalo at Miami	9:00

SUNDAY-THURSDAY NIGHT GAMES AT A GLANCE

(All times local; televised by ABC and broadcast by CBS Radio)

Thursday, Sept. 16—Minnesota at Buffalo 8:30
Thursday, Sept. 23—Atlanta at Kansas City 7:30
Sunday,   Oct. 24—Dallas at Cincinnati 9:00
Thursday, Dec. 2—San Francisco at Los Angeles 6:00
Sunday,   Dec. 19—Atlanta at San Francisco... 6:00

Heisman Trophy winner Marcus Allen of Southern California, the Oakland Raiders' No. 1 choice in the NFL draft, will be expected to add spark to a team that finished 7-9 in 1981 after winning the Super Bowl the year before.

1982 AFC-NFC INTERCONFERENCE GAMES

(All times local. All games Sunday unless noted otherwise.)

Sept.	12—Oakland at San Francisco	1:00
Sept.	13—Pittsburgh at Dallas (Monday night)	8:00
Sept.	16—Minnesota at Buffalo (Thursday night)	8:30
Sept.	19—Oakland at Atlanta	1:00
	—Philadelphia at Cleveland	1:00
	—San Francisco at Denver	2:00
Sept	23—Atlanta at Kansas City (Thursday night)	7:30
Sept.	26—Denver at New Orleans	12:00
	—Miami at Green Bay	12:00
	—New York Giants at Pittsburgh	1:00
Oct.	3—Baltimore at Detroit	1:00
	—Cleveland at Washington	1:00
	—New Orleans at Oakland	1:00
	—San Diego at Atlanta	1:00
Oct.	10—Detroit at Miami	4:00
Oct.	11—Philadelphia at Pittsburgh (Monday night)	9:00
Oct.	17—Cincinnati at New York Giants	1:00
	—Pittsburgh at Washington	1:00
Oct.	24—Dallas at Cincinnati	9:00
	—Detroit at Buffalo	1:00
	—St. Louis at New England	1:00
	—Washington at Houston	12:00
Oct.	31—Los Angeles at San Diego	1:00
	—Tampa Bay at Baltimore	2:00
Nov.	7—New York Giants at Cleveland	1:00
	—Washington at Cincinnati	1:00
Nov.	14—New Orleans at San Diego	1:00
	—Seattle at St. Louis	12:00
Nov.	21—Cincinnati at Philadelphia	1:00
	—Kansas City at New Orleans	12:00
Nov.	25—Cleveland at Dallas (Thursday)	3:00
Nov.	28—Green Bay at New York Jets	1:00
	—Kansas City at Los Angeles	1:00
Nov.	29—Miami at Tampa Bay (Monday night)	9:00
Dec.	5—Atlanta at Denver	2:00
	—Buffalo vs. Green Bay at Milwaukee	12:00
	—Houston at New York Giants	1:00
	—Minnesota at Miami	1:00
	—New England at Chicago	12:00
Dec.	6—New York Jets at Detroit (Monday night)	9:00
Dec.	11—San Diego at San Francisco (Saturday)	1:00
Dec.	12—Baltimore at Minnesota	12:00
	—Chicago at Seattle	1:00
	—Denver at Los Angeles	1:00
	—Tampa Bay at New York Jets	1:00
Dec.	13—Dallas at Houston (Monday night)	8:00
Dec.	18—Los Angeles at Oakland (Saturday)	1:00
Dec.	19—Buffalo at Tampa Bay	1:00
	—Green Bay at Baltimore	2:00
	—Houston at Philadelphia	1:00
Dec.	26—New York Jets at Minnesota	12:00
	—San Francisco at Kansas City	12:00

NFL POST-SEASON PLAN,
1982 DIVISION TIES

DIVISION TIES

Two Clubs

1. Head-to-Head (best won-lost-tied percentage in games between the clubs.)
2. Best won-lost-tied percentage in games played within the division.
3. Best won-lost-tied percentage in games played within the conference.
4. Best won-lost-tied percentage in common games, if applicable.
5. Best net points in division games.
6. Best net points in all games.
7. Strength of schedule.
8. Best net touchdowns in all games.
9. Coin toss.

Three or More Clubs

(Note: If two clubs remain tied after other clubs are eliminated during any step, tie-breaker reverts to Step One of two-club format.)

1. Head-to-Head (best won-lost-tied percentage in games among the clubs.)
2. Best won-lost-tied percentage in games played within the division.
3. Best won-lost-tied percentage in games played within the conference.
4. Best won-lost-tied percentage in common games.
5. Best net points in division games.
6. Best net points in all games.
7. Strength of schedule.
8. Best net touchdowns in all games.
9. Coin toss.

WILD CARD TIES

If necessary to break ties to determine the two Wild Card clubs from each conference, the following steps will be taken:

1. If all the tied clubs are from the same division, apply division tie-breaker.
2. If the tied clubs are from different divisions, apply the following steps:

Two Clubs

1. Head-to-Head, if applicable.
2. Best won-lost-tied percentage in games played within the conference.
3. Best won-lost-tied percentage in common games, minimum of four.
4. Best net points in conference games.
5. Best net points in all games.
6. Strength of schedule.
7. Best net touchdowns in all games.
8. Coin toss.

Three or More Clubs

(Note: If two clubs remain tied after other clubs are eliminated, tie-breaker reverts to Step One of applicable two-club format.)

1. Head-to-Head Sweep (Applicable only if one club has defeated each of the others or one club has lost to each of the others.)
2. Best won-lost-tied percentage in games within the conference.
3. Best won-lost-tied percentage in common games, minimum of four.
4. Best net points in conference games.
5. Best net points in all games.
6. Strength of schedule.
7. Best net touchdowns in all games.
8. Coin toss.

1981 NFL PAID ATTENDANCE IS RECORD 13,606,990 FOR HIGHEST AVERAGE EVER OF 60,745 FOR 224 GAMES

Official National Football League figures reveal that the NFL set a paid attendance record during the 1981 season.

Total paid attendance for 224 regular season games was 13,606,990 for an average of 60,745, the highest in the league's 62-year history. It also was the first time the average has exceeded 60,000 in any season. This total bettered the previous record of 13,392,230 set in 1980. The 1981 record total represents 93.8 percent of stadia capacity.

Paid attendance at all NFL games—including exhibitions, regular and postseason—surpassed 17 million for the first time. The total for 291 games was a record 17,223,212 for an average of 59,186.

Paid attendance for 10 postseason games was 637,763. The largest postseason crowd was the 81,270 that attended Super Bowl XVI at the Pontiac Silverdome. They saw NFC champion San Francisco defeat AFC champion Cincinnati 26-21 for the NFL Championship and the Vince Lombardi Trophy.

The Detroit Lions led the NFL in home paid attendance with 612,635, followed closely by Buffalo with 612,276. Also over 600,000 were Cleveland at 611,884 and the New York Giants at 604,294. Nine other teams exceeded 500,000, including Denver 596,344; Philadelphia 566,289; Tampa Bay 558,678; Los Angeles 538,407; Miami 512,645; Kansas City 512,505; Seattle 510,616; Dallas 508,352, and Chicago 507,163.

In the ninth season during which NFL games were made available to local television after selling out 72 hours in advance of kickoff, 160 of 224 regular season games were televised in the home team area. No-shows totaled 943,767 (7 percent).

1981 ATTENDANCE BREAKDOWN

	G.	Attendance	Avg.
AFC Exhibition Games	10	478,920	47,892
NFC Exhibition Games	10	529,701	52,970
AFC-NFC Exhibitions, Interconference	37	1,969,838	53,239
NFL Exhibition Total	57	2,978,459	52,254
AFC Regular Season	86	5,127,069	
NFC Regular Season	86	5,333,046	
AFC-NFC Regular Season, Interconference	52	3,146,875	
NFL Regular Season Total	224	13,606,990	60,745
AFC First Round Playoff	1		
(Buffalo-New York Jets)		59,067	
AFC Divisional Playoffs	2		
(San Diego-Miami)		74,233	
(Buffalo-Cincinnati)		59,032	
AFC Championship	1		
(San Diego-Cincinnati)		59,579	
NFC First Round Playoff	1		
(New York Giants-Philadelphia)		70,952	
NFC Divisional Playoffs	2		
(Tampa Bay-Dallas)		63,510	
(New York Giants-San Francisco)		58,657	
NFC Championship	1		
(Dallas-San Francisco)		61,061	
NFL Championship Game at Pontiac, Mich.	1		
(San Francisco-Cincinnati)		81,270	
AFC-NFC Pro Bowl at Honolulu, Hawaii	1		50,402	
Postseason Total	10	637,763	63,776
NFL All Games	291	17,223,212	59,186

PAID ATTENDANCE
NATIONAL FOOTBALL LEAGUE

	Regular Season		Average	*Post-Season	
1981	13,606,990	(224 games)	60,745	587,361	(9)
1980	13,392,230	(224 games)	59,787	577,186	(9)
1979	13,182,039	(224 games)	58,848	582,266	(9)
1978	12,771,800	(224 games)	57,017	578,107	(9)
1977	11,018,632	(196 games)	56,218	483,588	(7)
1976	11,070,543	(196 games)	56,482	428,733	(7)
1975	10,213,193	(182 games)	56,116	443,811	(7)
1974	10,236,322	(182 games)	56,224	412,180	(7)
1973	10,730,933	(182 games)	58,961	458,515	(7)
1972	10,445,827	(182 games)	57,395	435,466	(7)
1971	10,076,035	(182 games)	55,363	430,244	(7)
1970	9,533,333	(182 games)	52,381	410,371	(7)
1969	6,096,127	(112 games)	54,430	242,841	(4)
1968	5,882,313	(112 games)	52,521	291,279	(4)
1967	5,938,924	(112 games)	53,026	241,754	(4)
1966	5,337,044	(105 games)	50,829	135,098	(2)
1965	4,634,021	(98 games)	47,296	100,304	(2)
1964	4,563,049	(98 games)	46,562	79,544	(1)
1963	4,163,643	(98 games)	42,486	45,801	(1)
1962	4,003,421	(98 games)	40,851	64,892	(1)
1961	3,986,159	(98 games)	40,675	39,029	(1)
1960	3,128,296	(78 games)	40,106	67,325	(1)
1959	3,140,409	(72 games)	43,617	57,545	(1)
1958	3,006,124	(72 games)	41,752	123,659	(2)
1957	2,836,318	(72 games)	39,393	119,579	(2)
1956	2,551,263	(72 games)	35,434	56,836	(1)
1955	2,521,736	(72 games)	35,026	85,693	(1)
1954	2,190,571	(72 games)	30,425	43,827	(1)
1953	2,164,585	(72 games)	30,064	54,577	(1)
1952	2,052,126	(72 games)	28,502	97,507	(2)
1951	1,913,019	(72 games)	26,570	57,522	(1)
1950	1,977,753	(78 games)	25,356	136,647	(3)
1949	1,391,735	(60 games)	23,196	27,980	(1)
1948	1,525,243	(60 games)	25,421	36,309	(1)
1947	1,837,437	(60 games)	30,624	66,268	(2)
1946	1,732,135	(55 games)	31,493	58,346	(1)
1945	1,270,401	(50 games)	25,408	32,178	(1)
1944	1,019,649	(50 games)	20,393	46,016	(1)
1943	969,128	(50 games)	19,383	71,315	(2)
1942	887,920	(55 games)	16,144	36,006	(1)
1941	1,108,615	(55 games)	20,157	55,870	(2)
1940	1,063,025	(55 games)	19,328	36,034	(1)
1939	1,071,200	(55 games)	19,476	32,279	(1)
1938	937,197	(55 games)	17,040	48,120	(1)
1937	963,039	(55 games)	17,510	15,878	(1)
1936	816,007	(54 games)	15,111	29,545	(1)
1935	638,178	(53 games)	12,041	15,000	(1)
1934	492,684	(60 games)	8,211	35,059	(1)

*Includes conference and league championship and AFL-NFL championship games; number of post-season games in parentheses. Pro Bowl not included.

AMERICAN FOOTBALL LEAGUE

Season	Attendance	Teams-Games	Avg. per Game	AFL-NFL Championship	AFL Championship
1969***	2,843,373	10 teams—70 games	40,619	80,562	53,564
1968**	2,635,004	10 teams—70 games	37,643	75,377	62,627
1967	2,295,697	9 teams—63 games	36,439	75,546	53,330
1966	2,160,369	9 teams—63 games	34,291	61,946	42,080
1965	1,782,384	8 teams—56 games	31,899		30,361
1964	1,447,875	8 teams—56 games	25,855		40,242
1963*	1,241,741	8 teams—56 games	22,174		30,127
1962	1,147,302	8 teams—56 games	20,487		37,981
1961	1,002,657	8 teams—56 games	17,904		29,556
1960	926,156	8 teams—56 games	16,538		32,183

***Inter-Divisional Playoffs: Kansas City-New York, 61,832; Houston-Oakland, 51,692.
**Kansas City-Oakland Playoff, 51,811.
*Boston-Buffalo Playoff, 33,044.

NATIONAL PROFESSIONAL FOOTBALL
HALL OF FAME

The Pro Football Hall of Fame in Canton, Ohio.

FOUR NEW INDUCTEES IN 1982

Doug Atkins, Sam Huff, George Musso and Merlin Olsen were inducted into Pro Football's Hall of Fame in 1982, expanding the list of former stars honored at Canton, Ohio, to 114.

PRO FOOTBALL HALL OF FAME
MEMBERSHIP REACHES 114

The National Professional Football Hall of Fame is located in Canton, Ohio, site of the organizational meeting in 1920 from which the National Football League grew.

The League recognized Canton as the Hall of Fame site on April 27, 1961, and ground was broken for the Hall on August 11, 1962. Dedication ceremonies were held September 7, 1963.

The National Board of Selectors, consisting of representatives from professional football cities, elected 17 charter members to the Hall. The selections were announced on January 29, 1963.

Subsequent selections were announced on February 28, 1964, January 19, 1965, March 23, 1966, February 8, 1967, February 19, 1968, February 6, 1969, February 2, 1970, February 4, 1971, February 8, 1972, February 6, 1973, February 5, 1974, January 20, 1975, January 26, 1976, January 17, 1977, January 23, 1978, January 30, 1979, January 26, 1980, January 31, 1981, and January 28, 1982.

ROSTER OF MEMBERS (114)

*Deceased member.

HERB ADDERLY (Michigan State), 1980, cornerback, Green Bay Packers (1961-69), Dallas Cowboys (1970-72).

LANCE ALWORTH (Arkansas), 1978, wide receiver, San Diego Chargers (1962-70), Dallas Cowboys (1971-72)

DOUG ATKINS (Tennessee), 1982, defensive end, Cleveland Browns (1953-54), Chicago Bears (1955-66), New Orleans Saints (1967-69).

MORRIS (RED) BADGRO (Southern California), 1981, end, New York Yankees (1926), New York Giants (1930-35).

CLIFF BATTLES (West Virginia Wesleyan), 1968, halfback-quarterback, Boston Braves, Boston Redskins, Washington Redskins (1932-37); coach, Brooklyn Dodgers (1946-47).

SAMMY BAUGH (Texas Christian), Charter 1963, quarterback, Washington Redskins (1937-52); coach, New York Titans (1960-61); Houston Oilers (1964).

CHUCK BEDNARIK (Pennsylvania), 1967, center and linebacker, Philadelphia Eagles (1949-62).

*BERT BELL (Pennsylvania), Charter 1963, NFL Commissioner (1946-59).

RAYMOND BERRY (Southern Methodist), 1973, offensive end, Baltimore Colts (1955-67).

*CHARLES W. BIDWILL (Loyola), 1967, owner, Chicago Cardinals (1933-47).

GEORGE BLANDA (Kentucky), 1981, quarterback-placekicker, Chicago Bears (1949-58), Houston Oilers (1960-66), Oakland Raiders (1967-73).

JIM BROWN (Syracuse), 1971, fullback, Cleveland Browns (1957-65).

PAUL BROWN (Miami, Ohio), 1967, coach, Cleveland Browns (1946-62), Cincinnati Bengals (1968-75).

ROOSEVELT BROWN (Morgan State), 1975, tackle, New York Giants (1953-66).

DICK BUTKUS (Illinois), 1979, linebacker, Chicago Bears (1965-73).

TONY CANADEO (Gonzaga), 1974, halfback, Green Bay Packers (1941-44, 1946-52).

*JOE CARR, Charter 1963, NFL President (1921-39).

*GUY CHAMBERLIN (Nebraska), 1965, player-coach, Canton Bulldogs, Cleveland, Frankford Yellowjackets, Chicago Bears, and Chicago Cardinals (1919-28).

JACK CHRISTIANSEN (Colorado A&M), 1970, defensive back, Detroit Lions (1951-58), coach, San Francisco 49ers (1963-67).

*DUTCH CLARK (Colorado College), Charter 1963, quarterback, Portsmouth Spartans and Detroit Lions (1931-38).

GEORGE CONNOR (Notre Dame), 1975, tackle and linebacker, Chicago Bears (1948-55).

*JIMMY CONZELMAN (Washington, Mo.), 1964, halfback, coach, executive, Decatur, Rock Island, Milwaukee, Detroit, Providence, Chicago Cardinals (1920-48).

Hall of Fame defensive end Doug Atkins.

WILLIE DAVIS (Grambling), 1981, defensive end, Cleveland Browns (1958-59), Green Bay Packers (1960-69).

ART DONOVAN (Boston College), 1968, defensive tackle, Baltimore Colts, New York Yanks, Dallas Texans, Baltimore Colts (1950-61).

*PADDY DRISCOLL (Northwestern), 1965, player-coach, Chicago Cardinals and Chicago Bears (1919-31, 1941-68).

BILL DUDLEY (Virginia), 1966, halfback, Pittsburgh Steelers, Detroit Lions and Washington Redskins (1942-53).

*TURK EDWARDS (Washington State), 1969, tackle, Boston Braves, Boston Redskins, Washington Redskins (1932-40).

WEEB EWBANK (Miami, O.), 1978, coach, Baltimore Colts (1954-1962) and New York Jets (1963-1973).

TOM FEARS (Santa Clara, UCLA), 1970, end, Los Angeles Rams (1948-56), coach, New Orleans Saints (1967-70).

RAY FLAHERTY (Gonzaga), 1976, player-coach, Los Angeles Wildcats, New York Yankees (AFL), New York Giants, Boston Redskins, Washington Redskins, New York Yankees (AAFC), Chicago Hornets (1926-1949).

*LEN FORD (Michigan), 1976, end, Los Angeles Dons and Cleveland Browns (1948-1958).

DANNY FORTMANN (Colgate), 1965, guard, Chicago Bears (1936-43).

BILL GEORGE (Wake Forest), 1974, linebacker, Chicago Bears, and Los Angeles Rams (1952-66).

FRANK GIFFORD (Southern California), 1977, halfback and end, New York Giants (1952-60 and 1962-64).

OTTO GRAHAM (Northwestern), 1965, quarterback, Cleveland Browns (1946-55), coach, Washington Redskins (1966-68).

RED GRANGE (Illinois), Charter 1963, halfback, Chicago Bears (1925; 1929-34), New York Yankees (1926-27).

FORREST GREGG (Southern Methodist), 1977, tackle, Green Bay Packers and Dallas Cowboys (1956; 1958-71).

LOU GROZA (Ohio State), 1974, offensive tackle and placekicker, Cleveland Browns (1946-59, 1961-67).

*JOE GUYON (Carlisle, Georgia Tech), 1966, halfback, Canton Bulldogs, Cleveland Indians, Oorang Indians, Rock Island Inde Gpendents, Kansas City Cowboys and New York Giants (1918-27).

GEORGE HALAS (Illinois), Charter 1963, player, coach, founder, Chicago Bears (1920-77).

*ED HEALEY (Dartmouth), 1964, tackle, Rock Island and Chicago Bears (1920-27).

MEL HEIN (Washington State), Charter 1963, center, New York Giants (1931-45).

*WILBUR HENRY (Washington & Jefferson), Charter 1963, tackle, Canton Bulldogs, Akron Indians, New York Giants, Pottsville Ma Groons, Pittsburgh Steelers (1920-30).

*ARNIE HERBER (Regis), 1966, halfback, Green Bay Packers and New York Giants (1930-45).

*BILL HEWITT (Michigan), 1971, end, Chicago Bears (1932-36), Philadelphia Eagles (1937-39), Philadelphia-Pittsburgh (1943).

CLARKE HINKLE (Bucknell), 1964, fullback, Green Bay Packers (1932-41).

ELROY (CRAZYLEGS) HIRSCH (Wisconsin), 1968, end-halfback, Chicago Rockets, Los Angeles Rams (1946-57).

*CAL HUBBARD (Centenary, Geneva), Charter 1963, tackle and end, New York Giants, Green Bay Packers and Pittsburgh Steelers (1927-36).

SAM HUFF (West Virginia), 1982, linebacker, New York Giants (1956-63), Washington Redskins (1964-67, 69).

LAMAR HUNT (Southern Methodist), 1972, founder, American Football League, 1959; president, Dallas Texans (1960-62), Kansas City Chiefs (1963-81).

DON HUTSON (Alabama), Charter 1963, end, Green Bay Packers (1935-45).

DEACON JONES (South Carolina State), 1980, defensive end, Los Angeles Rams (1961-71), San Diego Chargers (1972-73), Washington Redskins (1974).

Hall of Fame linebacker Sam Huff.

*WALTER KIESLING (St. Thomas), 1966, player-coach, Duluth Eskimos, Pottsville Maroons, Boston Braves, Chicago Cardinals, Chicago Bears, Green Bay Packers and Pittsburgh Steelers (1926-56).

FRANK (BRUISER) KINARD (Mississippi), 1971, tackle, Brooklyn Dodgers (1938-45) New York Yankees (1946-47).

*CURLY LAMBEAU (Notre Dame), Charter 1963, founder, player, coach, Green Bay Packers (1919-49).

DICK (NIGHT TRAIN) LANE (Scottsbluff Jr. Coll.), 1974, defensive back, Los Angeles Rams, Chicago Cardinals, Detroit Lions (1952-65).

YALE LARY (Texas A&M), 1979, defensive back, Detroit Lions (1952-53, 1956-64).

DANTE LAVELLI (Ohio State), 1975, end, Cleveland Browns (1946-56).

BOBBY LAYNE (Texas), 1967, quarterback, Chicago Bears, New York Bulldogs, Detroit Lions, Pittsburgh Steelers (1948-62).

*TUFFY LEEMANS (George Washington), 1978, fullback, New York Giants (1936-1943).

BOB LILLY (Texas Christian), 1980, defensive tackle, Dallas Cowboys (1961-1974).

*VINCE LOMBARDI (Fordham), 1971, coach, Green Bay Packers (1959-67), Washington Redskins (1969).

SID LUCKMAN (Columbia), 1965, quarterback, Chicago Bears (1939-50).

*ROY (LINK) LYMAN, 1964, tackle, Canton Bulldogs, Cleveland, Chicago Bears (1922-34).

*TIM MARA, Charter 1963, founder, New York Giants (1925-65).

GINO MARCHETTI (San Francisco), 1972, defensive end, Dallas Cowboys (1952), Baltimore Colts (1953-66).

*GEORGE PRESTON MARSHALL, Charter 1963, founder, Washington Redskins (1932-1965).

OLLIE MATSON (San Francisco), 1972, halfback, Chicago Cardinals (1952, 1954-58), Los Angeles Rams (1959-62), Detroit Lions (1963), Philadelphia Eagles (1964-66).

GEORGE McAFEE (Duke), 1966, halfback, Chicago Bears (1940-41, 1945-50).

HUGH McELHENNY (Washington), 1970, halfback, San Francisco 49ers, Minnesota Vikings, New York Giants and Detroit Lions (1952-64).

JOHN "BLOOD" McNALLY (St. John's, Minn.), Charter 1963, halfback, Milwaukee Badgers, Duluth Eskimos, Pottsville Maroons, Green Bay Packers, Pittsburgh Steelers (1925-39).

AUGUST (MIKE) MICHALSKE (Penn State), 1964, guard, New York Yankees and Green Bay Packers (1927-37).

*WAYNE MILLNER (Notre Dame), 1968, end, Boston Redskins, Washington Redskins (1936-41, 1945).

RON MIX (Southern California), 1979, offensive tackle, Los Angeles Chargers (1960), San Diego Chargers (1961-69), Oakland Raiders (1971).

LENNY MOORE (Penn State), 1975, halfback, Baltimore Colts (1956-67).

MARION MOTLEY (Nevada), 1968, fullback-linebacker, Cleveland Browns, Pittsburgh Steelers (1946-1955).

GEORGE MUSSO (Millikin), 1982, offensive guard and defensive tackle, Chicago Bears (1933-44).

BRONKO NAGURSKI (Minnesota), Charter 1963, fullback and tackle, Chicago Bears (1930-37, 1943).

*EARLE (GREASY) NEALE (West Virginia Wesleyan), 1969, coach, Philadelphia Eagles (1941-50).

*ERNIE NEVERS (Stanford), Charter 1963, fullback, Duluth Eskimos and Chicago Cardinals (1926-37).

RAY NITSCHKE (Illinois), 1978, linebacker, Green Bay Packers (1958-72).

LEO NOMELLINI (Minnesota), 1969, defensive tackle, San Francisco 49ers (1953-63).

MERLIN OLSEN (Utah State), 1982, defensive tackle, Los Angeles Rams (1962-76).

JIM OTTO (Miami, Fla.), 1980, center, Oakland Raiders (1960-1974).

*STEVE OWEN (Phillips), 1966, player-coach, Kansas City Cowboys and New York

Hall of Fame guard and tackle George Musso.

Giants (1924-53).

CLARENCE (ACE) PARKER (Duke), 1972, halfback, Brooklyn Dodgers (1937-41), Boston Yanks (1945), New York Yankees (1946).

JIM PARKER (Ohio State), 1973, guard, Baltimore Colts (1957-67).

JOE PERRY (Compton J. C.), 1969, fullback, San Francisco 49ers, Baltimore Colts (1948-62).

PETE PIHOS (Indiana), 1970, end, Philadelphia Eagles (1947-55).

*HUGH (SHORTY) RAY (Illinois), 1966, NFL technical advisor and supervisor of officials (1938-56).

*DANIEL F. REEVES (Georgetown), 1967, founder, Los Angeles Rams (1941-71).

JIM RINGO (Syracuse), 1981, center, Green Bay Packers (1953-63), Philadelphia Eagles (1964-67).

ANDY ROBUSTELLI (Arnold), 1971, defensive end, Los Angeles Rams (1951-55), New York Giants (1956-64).

ARTHUR J. ROONEY (Georgetown), 1964, founder, Pittsburgh Steelers (1933-81).

GALE SAYERS (Kansas), 1977, running back, Chicago Bears (1965-72).

JOE SCHMIDT (Pittsburgh), 1973, linebacker, Detroit Lions (1953-65); coach, Detroit Lions (1967-72).

BART STARR (Alabama), 1977, quarterback, Green Bay Packers (1956-71); coach, Green Bay Packers (1975-81).

ERNIE STAUTNER (West Virginia), 1969, defensive tackle, Pittsburgh Steelers (1950-63).

*KEN STRONG (New York U.), 1967, halfback-placekicker, Staten Island Stapletons, New York Yankees and New York Giants (1929-39, 1944-47).

*JOE STYDAHAR (West Virginia), 1967, tackle, Chicago Bears (1936-42, 1945-46).

JIM TAYLOR (Louisiana State), 1976, fullback, Green Bay Packers (1958-1966), New Orleans Saints (1967).

*JIM THORPE (Carlisle), Charter 1963, halfback, Canton Bulldogs, Oorang Indians, Cleveland Indians, Toledo Maroons, Rock Island Independents, New York Giants (1915-26, 1929).

Y. A. TITTLE (Louisiana State), 1971, quarterback, Baltimore Colts (1948-50), San Francisco 49ers (1951-60), New York Giants (1961-64).

*GEORGE TRAFTON (Notre Dame), 1964, center, Chicago Bears (1920-32).

CHARLIE TRIPPI (Georgia), 1968, halfback, Chicago Cardinals (1947-55).

*EMLEN TUNNELL (Iowa), 1967, defensive back, New York Giants and Green Bay Packers (1948-61).

CLYDE (BULLDOG) TURNER (Hardin-Simmons), 1966, center-linebacker, Chicago Bears (1940-52); coach, New York Titans (1962).

JOHN UNITAS (Louisville), 1979, quarterback, Baltimore Colts (1956-72), San Diego Chargers (1973).

NORM VAN BROCKLIN (Oregon), 1971, quarterback, Los Angeles Rams (1949-57), Philadelphia Eagles (1958-60), coach, Minnesota Vikings (1961-66), Atlanta Falcons (1968-74).

STEVE VAN BUREN (Louisiana State), 1965, halfback, Philadelphia Eagles (1944-52).

BOB WATERFIELD (UCLA), 1965, quarterback, Cleveland Rams and Los Angeles Rams (1945-52); coach, Los Angeles Rams (1960-62).

LARRY WILSON (Utah), 1978, defensive back, St. Louis Cardinals (1960-72).

BILL WILLIS (Ohio State), 1977, guard, Cleveland Browns (1946-53).

ALEX WOJCIECHOWICZ (Fordham), 1968, center-linebacker Detroit Lions, Philadelphia Eagles (1938-50).

Hall of Fame defensive tackle Merlin Olsen.

1982 ROSTER OF OFFICIALS

REFEREES

No.	Name	College	Yrs.
14	Gene Barth	St. Louis	12
43	Red Cashion	Texas A & M	11
6	Tom Dooley	VMI	5
12	Ben Dreith	Colorado State	23
71	Bob Frederic	Colorado	15
40	Pat Haggerty	Colorado State	18
46	Chuck Heberling	Wash. & Jefferson	18
60	Dick Jorgensen	Wisconsin	15
9	Jerry Markbreit	Illinois	7
48	Gordon McCarter	Western Reserve	16
95	Bob McElwee	U.S. Naval Academy	7
70	Jerry Seeman	Winona State	8
7	Fred Silva	San Jose State	16
32	Jim Tunney	Occidental	23
75	Fred Wyant	West Virginia	17

UMPIRES

No.	Name	College	Yrs.
110	Ron Botchan	Occidental	3
101	Bob Boylston	Alabama	5
27	Al Conway	Army	14
78	Art Demmas	Vanderbilt	15
57	Ed Fiffick	Marquette	4
50	Neil Gereb	Calif.-Berkeley	2
42	Dave Hamilton	Utah	8
88	Pat Harder	Wisconsin	17
19	Tommy Hensley	Tennessee	16
67	John Keck	Cornell	11
68	John Leimbach	Missouri	2
81	Dave Moss	Dartmouth	3
10	Tom Myers	San Jose State	4
20	Frank Sinkovitz	Duke	25
89	Gordon Wells	Occidental	11

HEAD LINESMEN

No.	Name	College	Yrs.
17	Jerry Bergman	Duquesne	17
74	Ray Dodez	Wooster	15
111	Earnie Frantz	No College	2
72	Terry Gierke	Portland State	2
85	Frank Glover	Morris Brown	11
63	Ligouri Hagerty	Syracuse	7
104	Dale Hamer	California State	5
114	Tom Johnson	Miami-Ohio	1
65	Norm Kragseth	Northwestern	9
26	Ed Marion	Pennsylvania	23
108	Bob McLaughlin	Xavier	5
35	Leo Miles	Virginia State	14
109	Sid Semon	Southern California	5
37	Burl Toler	San Francisco	18
36	Tony Veteri	No College	22
8	Dale Williams	California State	3

LINE JUDGES

No.	Name	College	Yrs.
115	Hendi Ancich	Harbor	1
59	Bob Beeks	Lincoln	15
45	Ron DeSouza	Morgan State	3
33	John Everett	Illinois	4
39	Jack Fette	No College	18
15	Bama Glass	Colorado	4
4	Wilson Gosier	Fort Valley State	3
54	Jack Johnson	Pacific Lutheran	7
94	Vern Marshall	Linfield College	7
41	Dick McKenzie	Ashland	5
117	Ben Montgomery	Xavier	1
51	Dale Orem	Louisville	3
44	Walt Peters	Indiana State	15
53	Bill Reynolds	West Chester State	8
3	Boyce Smith	Vanderbilt	2

BACK JUDGES

No.	Name	College	Yrs.
22	Paul Baetz	Heidelberg	5
24	Roy Clymer	New Mexico State	3
5	Ray Douglas	Baltimore	15
105	Dick Hantak	Southeast Missouri	5
106	Al Jury	S. Bernardino Valley	5
107	Jim Kearney	Pennsylvania	5
25	Tom Kelleher	Holy Cross	23
73	Pat Knight	Southern Methodist	10
92	Jim Poole	San Diego State	8
98	Jimmy Rosser	Auburn	6
29	J.W. Sanders	Southern Illinois	3
38	Bill Swanson	Lake Forest	19
52	Ben Tompkins	Texas	12
28	Don Wedge	Ohio Wesleyan	11
99	Banks Williams	Houston	5

SIDE JUDGES

No.	Name	College	Yrs.
112	Gerald Austin	Western Carolina	1
16	Royal Cathcart	Calif.-Santa Barb.	12
61	Richard Creed	Louisville	5
102	Merrill Douglas	Utah	2
87	Dick Ferguson	West Virginia	9
62	Duwayne Gandy	Tulsa	2
66	Dave Hawk	Southern Methodist	11
11	Vince Jacob	No College	8
97	Nate Jones	Lewis and Clark	6
120	Gary Lane	Missouri	1
49	Dean Look	Michigan State	11
90	Gil Mace	Westminister	9
64	Dave Parry	Wabash	8
58	William Quinby	Iowa State	5
80	Bob Rice	Denison	14
79	Ed Ward	Southern Methodist	5

FIELD JUDGES

No.	Name	College	Yrs.
31	Dick Dolack	Ferris State	17
34	Fritz Graf	Western Reserve	23
23	Johnny Grier	D.C. Teachers	2
96	Don Hakes	Bradley	6
18	Bob Lewis	No College	7
82	Pat Mallette	Nebraska	14
116	Chuck McCallum	Michigan State	1
76	Ed Merrifield	Missouri	8
55	Charley Musser	North Carolina St.	18
83	Bill O'Brien	Indiana	16
77	Don Orr	Vanderbilt	12
119	Ron Spitler	Panhandle State	1
91	Bill Stanley	Redlands	9
93	Jack Vaughn	Mississippi State	7
84	Bob Wortman	Findlay	17